WESTERN CIVILIZATION

A Social and Cultural History

VOLUME II: 1500–THE PRESENT

MARGARET L. KING

Brooklyn College and the Graduate Center
City University of New York

Prentice Hall, Upper Saddle River, NJ. 07458

Prentice Hall
A Division of Pearson Education
Upper Saddle River, New Jersey 07458

10 9 8 7 6 5 4 3 2 1

ISBN 0-13-978644-9

This book was designed and produced by
Calmann & King Ltd., London
www.calmann-king.com

Development Editors: Melanie White and Barbara Muller
Editor: Nell Webb
Senior Managing Editor: Richard Mason
Copy Editor: Michael Bird
Designer: Ian Hunt Design
Cover Designer: Design Deluxe
Photo Researcher: Callie Kendall
Maps: Liz Wyse and Andrea Fairbrass
Line Art: Fred van Deelen and Hardlines
Compositor: Fakenham Phototypesetting
Repro House: Articolor, Italy
Printer: R. R. Donnelley and Sons Company, U.S.A.

Cover: Edouard Manet, *Music in the Tuileries Gardens*, 1862 (detail). Oil on canvas, 30 x 46½ in (76.2 x 118.1 cm) (National Gallery, London)

Acknowledgments

The author and publisher would like to thank the many scholars and teachers whose thoughtful and often detailed comments helped shape this book:

John F. Battick, University of Maine
Wood Bouldin, Villanova University
Blaine T. Browne, Broward Community College
Amy Burnett, University of Nebraska-Lincoln
Jack Cargill, Rutgers University
Anna Clark, University of North Carolina at Charlotte
Cyndia Susan Clegg, Pepperdine University
Jessica A. Coope, University of Nebraska Lincoln
Gerald Danzer, University of Illinois at Chicago
Steven Fanning, University of Illinois at Chicago
Allan Fletcher, Boise State University
Neal Galpern, University of Pittsburgh
Richard Gerberding, University of Alabama
Gay Gullickson, University of Maryland
Jeff Horn, Stetson University
Patrick Kelly, Adelphi University
Mavis Mate, University of Oregon
John Mauer, Tri-County Technical College
Eleanor McCluskey, Broward Community College
Marion S. Miller, University of Illinois at Chicago
Joseph R. Mitchell, Howard Community College
Jim Murray, University of Cincinnati
Jasonne Grabher O'Brien, University of Kansas
William Percy, University of Massachusetts, Boston
John Powell, Penn State University at Erie
Thomas Preisser, Sinclair Community College
Carole A. Putko, San Diego State University
Timothy A. Ross, Arkansas State University
Roger Schlesinger, Washington State University
Hugo B. Schwyzer, Pasadena City College
James Smither, Grand Valley State University
Francis Stackenwalt, East Central University
Emily Sohmer Tai, Queensborough Community College
Robert W. Thurston, Miami University
Michael Weiss, Linn-Benton Community College
Norman J. Wilson, Methodist College
Michael Zirinsky, Boise State University.

CONTENTS

CHAPTER 18

TOWN, COURT, AND COUNTRY

Privilege and Poverty in Early Modern Europe

(1500–1780)

CHAPTER 19

INALIENABLE RIGHTS

Revolution and its Promises in Anglo- and Latin America

(1500–1880)

CHAPTER 20

REVOLT AND REORGANIZATION IN EUROPE

From Absolute Monarchy to the Paris Commune

(1750–1871)

PART SIX

THE WEST BECOMES MODERN

Industrialization, Imperialism, Ideologies

(1750–1914)

CHAPTER 21

MACHINES IN THE GARDEN

The Industrialization of the West

(1750–1914)

CHAPTER 22

LIVES OF THE OTHER HALF

Western Society in an Industrial Age

(1750–1914)

CHAPTER 23

THE WESTERN IMPERIUM

European Migration, Settlement, and Domination around the Globe

(1750–1914)

CHAPTER 24

Storm, Stress, and Doubt

European Culture from Classicism to Modernism

(1780–1914)

PART SEVEN

Toward a New West

Post-War, Post-Modern, Post-Industrial

(1914–2000)

CHAPTER 25

The Mighty are Fallen

The Trauma of World War I

(1914–1920)

CHAPTER 26

THE TRIUMPH OF UNCERTAINTY

Cultural Innovation, Social Disruption, and Economic Collapse

(1915–1945)

CHAPTER 27

STATES IN CONFLICT

Communism, Fascism, Democracy, and the Crisis of World War II

(1917–1945)

CHAPTER 28

THE END OF IMPERIALISM

Decolonization and Statebuilding around the Globe

(1914–1990s)

CHAPTER 29

BACK FROM ARMAGEDDON

From the Bomb to the Internet

(1945–1990)

CHAPTER 30

EPILOGUE

The Last Decade: Where We've Been and What May Be

(THE 1990S)

WITNESSES BOXES

TIMELINES

MAPS

Preface

When I teach the introductory history course at Brooklyn College of the City University of New York, I start each semester by asking my students, "Where is the West?" I send an unfortunate individual to the global map mounted on the back wall of the room. A finger roams around the continents of the globe. The class suggests many possibilities: Western Europe? the Western Hemisphere? the Wild West? The search goes on all semester—a search of special complexity for the many students who, together speaking tens of languages, professing all the world's major religions, and hailing from all its inhabited continents, have no association by birth with Western civilization.

This book must begin with the same question. To embark upon the study of "Western Civilization," we must first ask where, or what, is the West.

WHERE OR WHAT IS THE WEST?

The West should not be understood to be the Western Hemisphere, the North American West, or Western Europe. It is not, in fact, a place. Nor is it a specific people, race, or set of nations. It is, rather, a body of ideas, values, customs, and beliefs forged over centuries on the continent of Europe, which lay to the west of the then more advanced civilizations of the East. In the centuries of European expansion—from approximately 1000 to 1900 of the Common Era (C.E.)—these Western values flourished, following Western merchants, travellers, armies, and governors into every corner of the inhabited globe. They are what the West means, and they are the meaning of the West.

Here are a few of the many concepts that have made the West what it is today and that constitute its soul and core meaning:

human dignity: the principle that all human beings are equal in worth (if not in talents, beauty, shape, or size); that they possess fundamental rights which cannot be taken away; and that to the greatest possible degree they are free
justice: the idea that no person should be unfairly privileged above another
democracy: the belief that the power to shape the future of a community belongs to its people as a whole and not to arbitrarily selected leaders
rationalism: the assumption that all phenomena (even those pertaining to God, essence, or spirit) may be subject to the critical scrutiny of the human mind
progress: the inclination to work toward goals to be achieved in the future
self-examination: the encouragement of human beings to examine themselves seriously and often in order to test whether they have fulfilled their promise and their responsibilities.

THE WEST AND THE REST OF THE WORLD

We learn more about the Western world when we also examine the rest of the world. Some features of Western civilization are not unique to the West. They appear also in the cultural systems of other people around the globe, although not all of them appear in the same way in any other civilization. In many cases, particularly in the era of its origins, the West borrowed customs and ideas from the civilizations of Asia and Africa. More recently, a fully developed Western culture has lent, shared, or imposed its values on those civilizations and the newer ones of the Western Hemisphere.

This book frequently pauses in its narration of Western development to consider key aspects of non-Western civilizations, both past and present. It makes no sense to isolate the West from other regions that have helped shape it, and upon which it has impacted, especially in an age that is now no longer dominated by the West but is truly global.

A global perspective transcends any claims for the superiority of one civilization to another. The civilization of the West is the focus of this book not because it is better (which is arguable) or because it is ours (it is not "ours" to many Americans by virtue of birth), but because it embodies principles of permanent value that will survive as long as there are those who learn them, reflect on them, and teach them to future generations, both in the West and elsewhere in the world.

ORGANIZATION OF THE TEXT

If the West is not a place but a collection of ideas, values, customs, and beliefs, we still need to understand its development. How did it arise? Who were its main architects? Where did it begin its journey, and where did it travel? When did it begin, when did it crystallize, and when was it most challenged? Why did

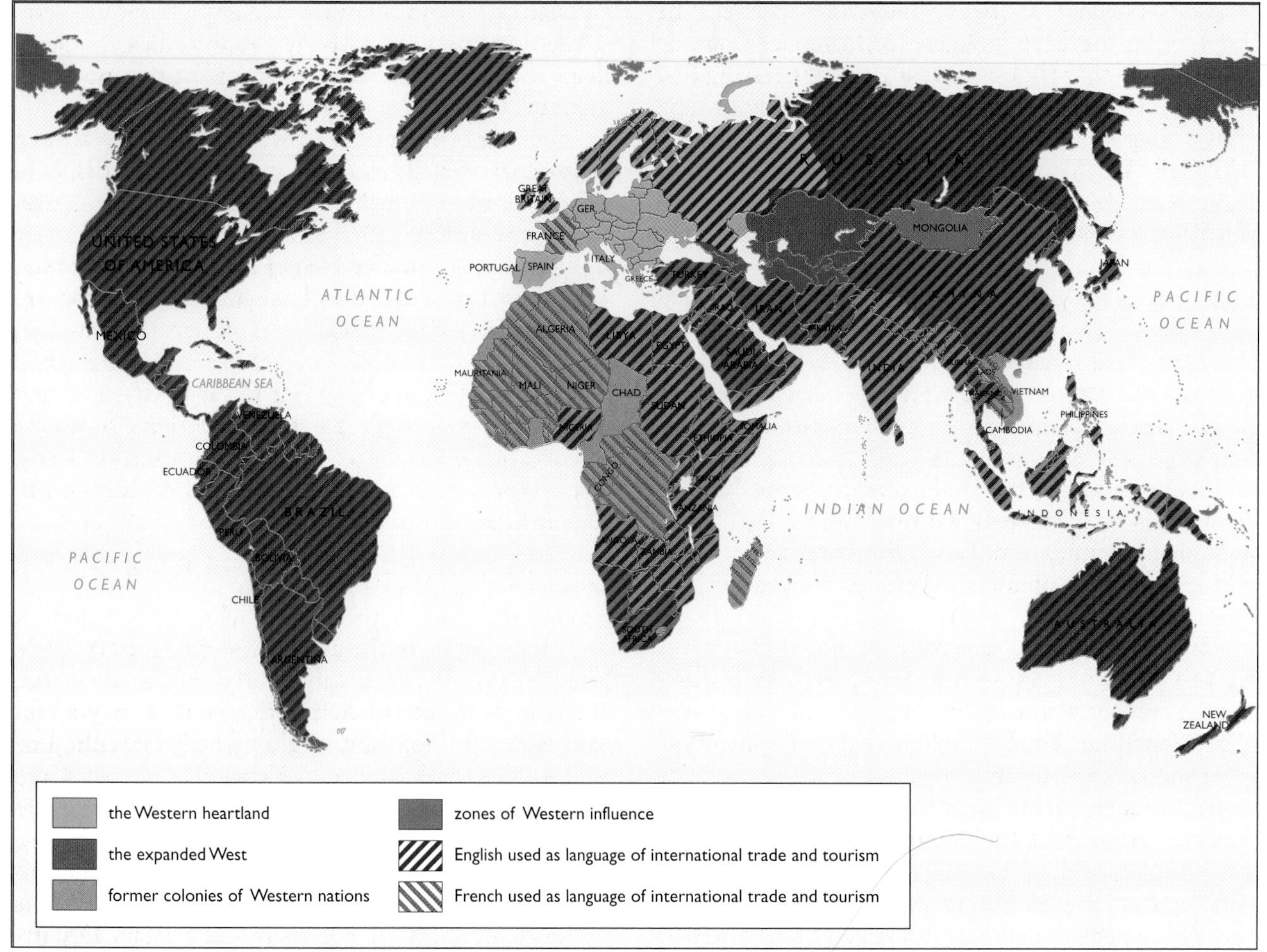

***Where is the West:** Shown here is one way of thinking about the West geographically. Its heartland is Europe, where the cultural, social, and political traditions of the West developed their modern form after about 1000 c.e. 'The expanded West' includes regions of European settlement, where Western civilization was transplanted from Europe after 1500 but where it has since developed in modified form because of contacts with other peoples. 'Former colonies of Western nations' include those regions where Western civilization was imposed upon other nations, nations now largely liberated from colonial rule but still retaining some features of that civilization. Finally, areas designated as 'zones of Western influence' have been largely free of any period of direct domination by Western nations, but have to a greater or lesser extent adopted selected Western political and economic institutions.*

it emerge as it did, and why is it important for us to know these things? These are the kinds of large questions posed by history that lie behind the smaller ones: Why did this king follow that one? Who opened up this pass or invented that tool? How did that army triumph or that book win notice? Where did those people live? When did disease or starvation claim the most lives?

This book explores these questions, in a way perhaps different from that of history books which students have used before. It looks at the story of nations, rulers, and wars, as histories have always done. But it looks more than most at the story of religion and ideas and the arts, those areas of human thought and imagination in which the ideas and values that distinguish the West have taken form.

It also looks closely at societies and households, the daily lives of parents and children, men and women. In these settings Western values were born and nurtured. Yet in these contexts, the principles defined above as Western—especially those of human dignity and justice—were often violated. Such contradictions are a central part of the story of the West.

Because this book gives special attention to the history of culture and society, its organization is topical. Some chapters focus on politics, others on society, others on religion or ideas. Often two or three chapters in succession will deal with the same historical period, but from different topical vantage points. The chapters on the Middle Ages, for instance, examine the whole of that thousand-year period, stressing first politics and society (Chapter 9), then religion and ideas (Chapter 10), then commerce and urbanization (Chapter 11). A topical division has the virtue that students are introduced systematically to the variety of ways in which historians study the past.

FEATURES OF THE TEXT

Since the focus of this book is on society and culture, it is important to orient the reader to the framework of time and space. Each chapter opens with a **timeline** charting the major events and processes that are discussed in the pages that follow, and a **map** defining the borders and principal features of the geographical area under examination. **Key Topics** are also outlined at the beginning of each chapter as preparation for what lies ahead.

The aim of this book is to tell a story—an engaging and important one—not only from the author's perspective but also through images and voices, witnesses, from the past. Examples from the visual arts—many in color—appear not only because they are beautiful, but because they illumine the past. They are arranged so that they converse with each other: this portrait with that building, this tool with that painting of men and women bringing in the harvest. Selected images in each chapter are gathered together in **Windows** boxes to highlight and expand on specific issues. The main object is not to follow the history of artistic style (an interesting venture for another textbook) but to illumine this history of Western culture and society.

In the same way, historical voices have their place in this narrative because they can convey more authentically than any modern author the perceptions that people had long ago of the world about them. These **Witnesses** boxes are arranged to converse with one another throughout the text: poets and scientists, historians and merchants, warriors and saints. Readers are invited to pause a moment—even though it may be late, a paper is due, or an examination looms—and listen to these faithful witnesses to the evolution of the West.

Numbers and statistics are important in contemporary civilization. We use such data to measure health (rates of mortality), education (years of study or test scores), and welfare (standard of living), as well as population and wealth. This book frequently draws attention to such measures of human prosperity in the past, sometimes within the narrative but mostly through the **How Many?** boxes and charts that present information in a lively, graphic format. **Color maps** throughout the book supplement this graphical material and provide a geographical context.

The names and contributions of those who lived a century or twenty centuries ago are often difficult to remember when they are mentioned rapidly in a narrative stream. For this reason, especially important figures are identified and listed in **Who's Who** boxes, with their principal contributions noted. So too are book titles of exceptional importance presented in **Must Reads** boxes. At the end of each chapter, a **Conclusion** box condenses the major themes and issues discussed, while **Review Questions** stimulate critical thought and understanding. For further study, readers are directed to the **Suggested Readings** section at the end of each chapter.

WITH GRATITUDE

The single name of the author appearing on the title page disguises the reality that I have had many guides and helpers in the creation of this book. I am grateful to the staff at Calmann & King (Nell Graville, Lee Ripley Greenfield, Peter Kent, Laurence King, Richard Mason, Judy Rasmussen, and Melanie White) and former staff member Rosemary Bradley, who have had confidence in the project, assisted it in every way, and alternately soothed and bullied its restive author. My colleagues in the History Department at Brooklyn College—Bonnie S. Anderson, David Berger, Philip Dawson, Paula S. Fichtner, Philip Gallagher, Leonard Gordon, Stuart Schaar—have contributed ideas and criticisms for which I am immensely grateful; as has former colleague Michael Mendle, now in the History Department at the University of Alabama (Tuscaloosa), and former student and associate Michael Sappol, now at the National Library of Medicine (Bethesda, Maryland). Special thanks go to Brian Bonhomme, also on the Brooklyn staff, a young scholar whose insight and imagination have contributed greatly to all the chapters of the second volume.

My severest critics and most valiant sustainers have been my sons and my husband—David, Jeremy, and Robert Kessler—who look forward to the day when the stacks of books on the floor of my study return to their home on library shelves, and normalcy returns to our household.

Margaret L. King
Brooklyn College and the Graduate Center
City University of New York
June 1999

Supplementary Materials

The *Instructor's Manual with Test Item File* by Dolores Davison Peterson combines teaching resources with testing material. The *Instructor's Manual* includes chapter outlines, overviews, key concepts, discussion questions, and audiovisual resources. The *Test Item File* offers a menu of multiple choice, true-false, essay, and map questions for each chapter. A collection of blank maps can be photocopied and used for map testing or other class exercises.

Prentice Hall Custom Test, a commercial-quality computerized, test management program is available for Windows and Macintosh environments. This allows instructors to select items from the *Test Item File* in the *Instructor's Manual* and design their own exams.

The *Study Guide* (Volumes I and II) by Paul Teverow provides, for each chapter, a brief overview, a list of chapter objectives, study exercises, and multiple-choice, short-answer, and essay questions. In addition, each chapter includes a number of specific map questions and exercises.

The *Documents Set* (Volumes I and II) by Arlene Sindelar and Mary Chalmers is a collection of additional primary and secondary source documents that underscore the themes in the text. Organized by chapter, this set for each volume includes review questions for each document.

The Companion Website (www.prenhall.com/king) works in tandem with the text to help students use the World Wide Web to enrich their understanding of Western civilization. Featuring chapter objectives, study questions, web links, and new updates, it also links the text with related material available on the Internet.

Understanding and Answering Essay Questions suggests analytical tools for understanding different types of essay questions, and provides precise guidelines for preparing well-crafted essay answers. This brief guide is available free to students when packaged with *Western Civilization: A Social and Cultural History*.

A *Transparency Pack* provides instructors with full-color transparency acetates of the maps, charts, and graphs in the text for classroom use.

Themes of the Times is a newspaper supplement prepared jointly for students by Prentice Hall and the premier news publication, *The New York Times*. Issued twice a year, it contains recent articles pertinent to historical study. These articles connect the classroom to the world. For information about a reduced-rate subscription to *The New York Times*, call toll-free: 1-800-631-1222.

History on the Internet is a brief guide to the Internet that provides students with strategies for navigating the Internet and World Wide Web. Exercises within and at the ends of the chapters allow students to practice searching for the myriad resources available to the student of history. This supplementary book is free to students when packaged with *Western Civilization: A Social and Cultural History*.

Reading Critically about History is a brief guide to reading effectively that provides students with helpful strategies for reading a history textbook. It is available free to students when packaged with *Western Civilization: A Social and Cultural History*.

The Hammond Historical Atlas of the World is a collection of maps illustrating the most significant periods and events in the history of civilization. This atlas is available at a discounted price to students when packaged with *Western Civilization: A Social and Cultural History*.

Digital Art Library: Western Civilization is a collection of the maps, charts, graphs, and other lecture material from the text on disk for use with Microsoft Powerpoint™. The material can be used in a lecture or as a slide show.

World History: An Atlas and Study Guide is a four-color map workbook that includes over 100 maps with exercises, activities, and questions that help students learn both geography and history.

Literary Credits

Beacon press, Boston: from *Broken Spears: Aztec Account of the Conquest of Mexico* by Miguel Leon Portilla, © 1992 Miguel Leon Portilla; **Blackwell Publishers**: from *Venice: A Documentary History, 1450–1630*, eds. David Chambers and Brian Pullan (1992); **Georges Borchardt Inc**: from *The Kingdom of Memory* by Elie Wiesel (Elirion, 1990); **Columbia University Press**: from *The Imperial Rescript Declaring War on the United States and British Empire* by Tokutomi Iichir, adapted from version in *Sources of the Japanese Tradition*, ed. William Theodore de Bary (Columbia University Press, 1958), © 1958 Columbia University Press; **Commentary**: from "Eurocentrism Revisited, 1994" by Bernard Lewis from *Commentary* (Dec. 1994). All rights reserved; **Condé Nast Publications**: from "After Communism" by Robert Heilbroner. Originally in *The New Yorker* (Sept. 10, 1990); **The Continuum Publishing Company**: from *The Devastation of the Indies: A Brief Account*, trs. Herma Briffault (Seabury Press/Continuum, 1974), © 1974 The Seabury Press; **Dutton, a division of Penguin Putnam Inc.**: from *Notes from the Underground and the Grand Inquisitor* by Fyodor Dostoevsky, trs. Ralph E. Matlaw, translation © 1960, 1988 E. P. Dutton; **G. S. P. Freeman-Grenville**: from *The East African Coast: Selected Documents* (Oxford University Press, 1962); **HMSO**: from *Documents on British Foreign Policy, 1919-1939*, eds. E. L. Woodward and Rohan Butler. 3rd Series (1954). Crown copyright is reproduced with the permission of the Controller of Her Majesty's Stationery Office; **Houghton Mifflin Company**: from *The Human Record*, Volume II, Second Edition, by A. J. Andrea and James H. Overfield (Houghton Mifflin, 1994), © 1994 Houghton Mifflin Company; from *Mein Kampf* by Adolf Hitler, trs. Ralph Manheim (Houghton Mifflin, 1943), © 1943, renewed 1971 by Houghton Mifflin Company. All rights reserved; **Nikki Keddie**: "On the Importance of Science" by Al-Afghani from *Islamic Response to Imperialism: Political and Religious Writings of Sayyid Jam I al-Din n al-Afgh n*, ed. and trs. Nikki R. Keddie (University of California Press, 1983); **Barbara Levy Literary Agency**: from "Suicide in the Trenches" by Siegfried Sassoon from *Collected Poems 1908–1956* (Faber & Faber, 1984), © Siegfried Sassoon by kind permission of George Sassoon; **Los Angeles Times Syndicate**: for "Joel Barr Interview" by Elizabeth Shogren of *Los Angeles Times*, reported by Irvin Molotsky in *New York Times* (August 16, 1998); **The New York Times**: from "The Short Century–It's Over" by John Lukacs from *The New York Times* (Feb. 17, 1991); **The Orion Publishing Group**: from *The Condition of the Working Class in England* by Friedrich Engels (1844), from *Engels, Manchester and the Working Class* by S. Marcus (Weidenfeld & Nicolson, 1974); **Prentice-Hall Inc**: "The Attack of King Industry," trs. Chimanbhai Trivedi and Howard Spodek, from *The World's History* by Howard Spodek (1998); and from *A Documentary Survey of the French Revolution*, trs. J. H. Stewart (Macmillan, 1951), © 1951; **Random House Inc**: from *Preparing for the Twenty-First Century* by Paul Kennedy (Random House, 1993), © 1993 Paul Kennedy; from *Restless Days* by Lilo Linke (1935), © 1935 Alfred A. Knopf Inc and renewed 1963 by Lilo Linke; **Scribner, a division of Simon & Schuster Inc.**: from *Hope Against Hope: A Memoir by Nadezhda Mandelstam*, trs. Max Hayward (Macmillan, 1970), English translation © 1970 Atheneum Publishers; **University of California Press**: from *History of a Voyage to the Land of Brazil Otherwise Called America*, ed. and trs. Janet Whatley, © 1990 The Regents of the University of California; **University of Oklahoma Press**: from *Diario of Christopher Columbus's First Voyage to America, 1492–1493*, eds. and trs. Oliver C. Dunn and James E. Kelley, Jr. (1969); **A. P. Watt Ltd** on behalf of The National Trust for Places of Historic Interest or Natural Beauty: from "The White Man's Burden" by Rudyard Kipling from *Selected Poems* (Penguin Twentieth Century Classics, 1993)

Every effort has been made to trace or contact all copyright holders. The publishers would be pleased to rectify any omissions brought to their notice at the earliest opportunity.

PICTURE CREDITS

All numbers refer to page numbers (*t* = top; *b* = bottom; *l* = left; *r* = right; *c* = center)

Chapter 15 353, 449 *The Battle of Pavia* (detail), 1525. Museo di Capodimonte/ Scala/Art Resource NY; 451*t* AKG London/Erich Lessing; 451*b* Mary Evans Picture Library, London; 452 Collections/Yuri Lewinski UK; 456 Sonia Halliday, Weston Turville, UK; 464*bl* Cameraphoto Arte, Venice; 475*t* RMN-Gérard Blot; 475*b* Institut Amatller D'Art Hispànic, Barcelona

Chapter 16 353, 479, 482 Städelisches Kunstinstitut, Frankfurt/ Artothek, Peissenberg; 483 © Patrimonio Nacional, Madrid. Photo: Institut Amatller D'Art Hispànic, Barcelona; 484*tl* E.T. Archive, London; 484*tr* Mary Evans Picture Library, London; 484*b*, 500, 501*b* Hulton Getty, London; 494*t* AKG London; 494*b* MicroFoto srl. Florence; 495*b* AKG London; 501*t* Bridgeman Art Library, London

Chapter 17 513*t*, 515 Rembrandt, sketch of woman reading, 1634, Library of Congress; 518 Science Museum/Science & Society Picture Library, London; 523*l* from C. Singer, *The Discovery of the Circulation of the Blood*, 1956, courtesy Mr A.W. Singer; 523*r*, 540*tl* Wellcome Institute Library, London; 530*t* AKG London; 530*b* Photo: © Metropolitan Museum of Art, Harris Brisbane Dick Fund, 1930 (30.67.2); 536 RMN-Hervé Lewandowski; 538 RMN-Arnaudet; 539 RMN-Gérard Blot; 540*bl* Mary Evans Picture Library, London; 540*r* from Hevelius, *Machinae Coelestis*

Chapter 18 513*ct*, 545 Velásquez, *Old Woman Cooking Eggs* (detail), 1618, National Gallery of Scotland; 549*t* RMN; 549*b* RMN-Gérard Blot; 554*t* RMN-R.G. Ojeda; 554*b* Scala, Florence; 557 Giraudon, Paris; 564*tl* © Studio Fotografico Quattrone, Florence; 564*tr* Bibliothèque Nationale, Paris; 566*t* Photo: Ursula Seitz-Gray; 570*l* AKG London; 570*r* Bulloz, Paris; 571 Artothek, Peissenberg

Chapter 19 513*cb*, 575 (detail), 583*tr* Gift of Ms. Gwendolyn O.L. Conkling (40.59.A); 583*l* American Antiquarian Society, Worcester, MA; 583*br* Schomburg Center for Research in Black Culture, New York Public Library; 586*r* Photo: John Lee; 589 National Archives & Records Administration, Washington, D.C.; 593 South American Pictures, Woodbridge, UK; 597*l* Bob Schalkwijk/© DACS 1999; 597*r* Mary Evans Picture Library; 601*l*, 602 Library of Congress; 601*r* Art Resource, NY

Chapter 20 513*b*, 609 (detail), 627 Museo del Prado, Madrid; 612 Photothèque des Musées de la Ville de Paris/I. Andreani; 616 Photothèque des Musées de la Ville de Paris/Toumazet/P. H. Ladet; 619*t* Photothèque des Musées de la Ville de Paris/Berthier; 619*cl* Photothèque des Musées de la Ville de Paris/Jean-Yve Trocaz; 622 RMN; 637*b* Photothèque des Musées de la Ville de Paris/Joffre

Chapter 21 641*t* , 643 (detail), 653*bl* Hulton Getty, London; 650*t*, 662 Ann Ronan Picture Library/Image Select, London; 650*c*, 650*b*, 653*br*, 665 Mary Evans Picture Library, London; 651 Derby Museums and Art Gallery, UK; 653*tl* Science Museum/Science & Society Picture Library, London; 653*tr* Encyclopædia Britannica, Inc./Cambridge University Library; 657*t* The Illustrated London News Picture Library, London; 657*b* Mansell Collection/Time Inc./Katz Pictures, London; 658 Paul M.R. Maeyaert, Mont de l'Enclus (Orroir), Belgium; 659 Deutsches Museum, Munich; 671 United Nations/DPI, New York

Chapter 22 641*ct*, 675 (detail), 696 Museum of the City of New York, Jacob A. Riis Collection; 679*t* AKG London; 679*c* National Museum of Wales; 679*b* © Fried. Krupp GmbH/Historisches Archiv Krupp, Essen, Germany; 685*tl* Mary Evans Picture Library, London; 685*tr*, 698 Hulton Getty, London; 685*br* Lauros-Giraudon, Paris; 690 Giraudon, Paris; 691 Bibliothèque Nationale, Paris; 697 Ann Ronan Picture Library/Image Select, London; 699 RMN-Hervé Lewandowski; 700 Mansell Collection/Time Inc./Katz Pictures, London; 701 Photo © 1989 Metropolitan Museum of Art, purchased with special contributions and purchase funds given or bequeathed by friends of the Museum, 1967 (67.241)

Chapter 23 641*cb*, 705 (detail), 719*t* Mariners' Museum, Virginia; 712*t* Roy Miles, Esq./Bridgeman Art Library, London; 712*b* Public Record Office Image Library, Kew; 725*t* © M&E Bernheim /Woodfin Camp & Associates, New York; 725*c* Mary Evans Picture Library, London; 725*b* Corbis/Hulton Getty, London; 729*tl* Art Resource, NY; 729*tr* Harper's Weekly/Weidenfeld & Nicolson Archives; 729*b* Wiener Library, London

Chapter 24 641*b*, 739 (detail), 764*c*, Museum of Modern Art. Acquired through the Lillie P. Bliss Bequest, photo © 1999 Museum of Modern Art, New York; 741*tl* RMN-Hervé Lewandowski; 741*br* © 1999 Museum of Fine Arts, Boston. Gift of Edward Southworth Hawes in memory of his father, Josiah Johnson Hawes; 748*l* © Punch Ltd; 748*r* The Curie and Joliot-Curie Association, Paris; 757 Mary Evans Picture Library, London; 759 Hulton Getty, London; 764*t* Giraudon, Paris

Chapter 25 767*t*, 769 (detail), 782*t* Photo © 1999 Museum of Modern Art, New York. Gift of Abby Aldrich Rockefeller; 773 Topham Picture-Point, Kent, UK; 776*t*, 777, 782*b* Imperial War Museum, London; 776*b* Bibliothèque Nationale, Paris; 778*t* David King Collection, London; 778*b* Roger Viollet/Frank Spooner Pictures, London; 787*t*, 787*bl* Crown copyright (Imperial War Museum, London); 787*br* Paul M. R. Maeyaert, Mont de l'Enclus (Orroir) Belgium; 791 © Novosti, London; 795 Illustrated London News Picture Library, London

Chapter 26 767*ct*, 801 (detail), 805*b* Photo: INDEX, Florence/Pizzi; 802 Illustrated London News Picture Library, London; 803 Culver Pictures, New York; 805*t* Bridgeman Art Library, London/© ADAGP, Paris and DACS, London, 1999; 806 Bill Spilka/Archive Photos, New York; 814 Bettmann/Corbis, London; 815 Mary Evans Picture Library, London; 816 © Good Housekeeping Magazine/The National Magazine Company; 821*tl* AKG London; 821*tr* Corbis, London; 821*b* Hulton Getty, London; 825*t* Associated Press, London; 825*b* Photo: San Francisco Art Commission

Chapter 27 767*c*, 831 (detail), 849, 862*tl* AKG, London; 839, 860*l* © Novosti (London); 840 David King Collection, London; 843*t* Index, Florence; 843*b* Canadian War Museum, Ottawa; 855*t* Hulton Getty, London; 855*b* David Low/Evening Standard/Solo Syndication Ltd, London/Photo: University of Kent, UK; 860*r* Corbis-Bettmann, London; 862*bl* Camera Press, London; 862*tr* Yad Vashem Photo Archives, courtesy USHMM Photo Archives, Washington, D.C.; 862*b* Topham PicturePoint, Kent, UK © 1999; 865 TRH Pictures, London/DOD/USAF

Chapter 28 767*cb*, 869 (detail), 899*t* Nick Ut/Associated Press, London; 872 Hulton Getty, London; 873, 883 Topham PicturePoint, Kent, UK; 878*t*, 903*br* Associated Press, London; 878*b* Ulli Michel-Reuters/Archive Photos, NY; 886 ©1999 Olivier Rebbot/Contact Press Images; 888*t* David King Collection, London; 888*b* Camera Press, London; 890 Stuart Franklin/Magnum, London; 895*t* Bob Schalkwijk/Art Resource, NY/ © DACS 1999; 895*b* Burt Glinn/Magnum, London; 899*b* David Burnett/Contact Press Images; 903*tl* Popperfoto, Northampton, UK; 903*bl* UPI/Corbis, London

Chapter 29 767*b*, 907, 910*r* Archive Photos, NY; 910*l* Topham Picture-Point, Kent, UK; 912*t* Corbis-Bettmann/Corbis, London; 912*b* Corbis-Bettmann/UPI/Corbis, London; 917*t*, 917*b* Popperfoto, Northampton, UK; 920 Associated Press, London; 921 © Novosti, London; 926*t* Paul Conklin/© Time Inc/Katz Pictures, London; 926*b* Ans Westra, Lower Hutt, NZ; 932*tl* Sayyid Azim/Associated Press, London; 932*tr* John Ward Anderson/The Washington Post; 932*b* A. Chin/NYT Pictures, NY; 944 Epix/Sygma, London

Chapter 30 946*t* (detail), 959 *The Independent*, London/Brian Harris; 946*b* Peter Kent, London; 948 Popperfoto, Northampton, UK/Reuters; 952 EPA/PA News, London; 954 NASA/Science Photo Library, London; 956 Popperfoto, Northampton, UK/Reuters

ABSOLUTE POWER

1500 | 1550 | 1600 | 1650 | 1700 | 1750 | 1800

Rulers, Nations, and War

French religious wars, 1562-94

Thirty Years' War, 1618-48

Anglo-Dutch Wars, 1652-74

Seven Years' War, 1756-63

Independence struggle in Netherlands, 1579-1648

War of Spanish Succession, 1701-14

Polish partitions, 1772, 1793, 1795

Elizabeth I in England, 1558-1603

English Civil War, 1642-51

Peter the Great in Russia. 1682-1725

Frederick the Great in Prussia, 1740-86

Philip II in Spain, 1556-98

Louis XIV in France, 1643-1715

Maria Theresa in Austria, 1740-80

- Fall of Granada, 1492
- Peace of Augsburg, 1555
- Treaty of Câteau-Cambrésis, 1559
- Defeat of Spanish Armada, 1588
- Henry IV assumes throne of France, 1589
- Peace of Westphalia, 1648
- Execution of King Charles I, 1649
- English Restoration, King Charles II, 1660
- Glorious Revolution, 1688
- Peace of Utrecht, 1713
- Treaty of Paris, 1763
- U.S. Constitution ratified, 1788
- French Revolution begins, 1789

Society and Economy

Plague endemic in Europe, 1347-1720

Atlantic slave trade, c. 1500-1888

- Expulsion of Jews from Spain, 1492
- Peasants' Revolt suppressed, 1525
- Spanish "New Laws" prohibit Amerindian slavery, 1542
- Approx. 10% of Europeans live in cities, 1600
- Bank of Amsterdam founded, 1609
- Stock Exchange completed, Amsterdam, 1611
- London's population tops 500,000, 1700
- Southern U.S. slave population tops 700,000, 1790
- London's population 1,000,000

Religion and Ideas

First century of printing, 1460-1560

The Enlightenment, 1685-1795

The Scientific Revolution, 1543-1687

- Erasmus' *Praise of Folly*, 1511
- Luther's *Ninety-Five Theses*, 1517
- Loyola's *Spiritual Exercises*, 1541
- St. Bartholomew's Day Massacre, 1572
- Jean Bodin's *Six Books of the Commonwealth*, 1576
- Edict of Nantes, 1598
- Thomas Hobbes' *Leviathan*, 1651
- Newton's *Mathematical Principles of Natural Philosophy*, 1687
- John Locke's *Letter on Toleration, Essay Concerning Human Understanding*, and *Second Treatise on Civil Government*, 1689-90
- Rousseau's *Social Contract*, 1762

Beyond the West

Mughal Empire, India, 1526-1857

Ming dynasty, 1368-1644

Qin dynasty, 1644-1912

- Columbus' first voyage, 1492
- Magellan sails the world, 1519-22
- Cortés conquers Mexico, 1521–2
- Chinese officials allow Portuguese trading, Macao, 1557
- Drake circumnavigates globe, 1577-80
- Jamestown founded, 1607
- Dutch East India Company, Batavia (Jakarta, Java), 1619
- Plymouth Bay Colony founded, 1620
- Dutch acquire Malacca from Portuguese, 1641
- East India Company founds port, Calcutta, India, 1690
- British control Dutch Cape colony, 1795
- Ireland incorporated into the U.K., 1800

CHAPTER

15

ABSOLUTE POWER

War and Politics in Early Modern Europe

1500–1750

KEY TOPICS

- **Power and Gunpowder:** The emerging nations of Europe gain new strength—and face mounting costs—as guns outpace swords, infantry displaces cavalry, and demand grows for drillmasters and engineers.
- **War Games:** Wars fought increasingly for plain political advantage culminate in a struggle between France and Great Britain in the global struggle of the Seven Years' War.
- **An Age of Kings:** Kings aim to rule absolutely in Spain, France, England, Prussia, Austria, and Russia; in England, Parliament imposes limits on monarchy.
- **Mirrors for Princes:** Artists and intellectuals celebrate kings; some thinkers propose a social contract and the rights of citizens, which will in time undo the absolutist pretensions of kings.

The Perfect Prince *Around the beginning of the sixteenth century, the Italian duke Cesare Borgia (1475–1507) was engaged in acquiring for himself a large chunk of central Italy. To bolster his authority in the city of Cesena, he decided to rid himself of the agent he had placed in charge of it. He waited for the right moment; "Then, one morning, Remirro's body was found cut in two pieces on the piazza . . ., with a block of wood and a bloody knife beside it." The brutal message had its intended effect, keeping the citizens, at least for a while, "appeased and stupefied."*

This incident was narrated by Niccolò Machiavelli (1469–1527) in his handbook for the perfect prince (see Chapter 13). For Machiavelli, the concern of a prince is to gain and hold power—by any means necessary. He should crush enemies, rather than forgive them; inflict cruelties as necessary, swiftly and all at once. His subjects need not love him; better that they fear him, since "fear is strengthened by a dread of punishment which is always effective." Such a prince might possibly, Machiavelli thought, save Italy.

Machiavelli's prince never came. Hopelessly fragmented, Italy fell to nations beyond the Alps. Those nations embodied new dimensions of power, not seen since the days of the Roman Empire—enough to consume each other and to dominate much of the rest of the world. Their ascension owed much to their ambitious kings, who exemplified the principles that Machiavelli proposed.

The period from 1500 to 1750—often called the "early modern" era—saw a great concentration of power in Europe: the power of armies, the power of states, and, above all, the power of kings. Changes in military organization and funding, as well as terrible new weapons, made their progress possible and their ambitions urgent. Those ambitions erupted into a series of wars, fought at first in the name of religious principle and later for ***raison d'état***, "reason of state." The kings and princes who profited from these wars—who taxed their subjects, reined in their fractious nobles, and compelled hundreds of thousands of ordinary men to fight—not only expanded their states but maximized their power. In several states, they reached for absolute power, power that would allow them to decree and execute law without the restraint of parliament or peerage. As monarchs gathered power, abetted by prime ministers, advisers, and **courtiers**, intellectuals developed theories of monarchy that justified the power of kings to the people who had none.

POWER AND GUNPOWDER

Machiavelli's hypothetical prince was armed with acute intelligence and supreme force of will. The states of Europe armed themselves with new weapons and new military methods. By 1500, armies that depended on the force of their **infantry** had supplanted armies of mounted knights. Lance and sword gave way to **arquebus** and **pike**, then to **musket** and **bayonet**; the cavalry charge, to rows and columns of uniformed soldiers; the simple medieval wall, punctuated by gates and towers, to elaborate systems of fortification, designed to foil the force of cannon fire. Military leaders—now required to be management experts as much as battle chiefs—forged armies that performed on the battlefield with the precision they learned on the drill field.

Knights and Guns

On late medieval battlefields, ordinary foot soldiers had already proved themselves a match for mounted knights. In Flanders, in 1302, a mob of urban workers smashed an army of French cavalry. Afterwards, the fragments of the noble warriors' expensive arms and armor littered the "Field of Golden Spurs," as the disaster was expressively named. In 1346, at Crécy, and 1415, at Agincourt, two battlefields of the Hundred Years' War, English peasants armed with longbows, made from the flexible wood of their native yew trees, mowed down heavily armed knights.

Within a century, the advent of guns clinched the triumph of infantry over cavalry. Basically, the gun is an iron tube in which gunpowder—a mixture of potassium nitrate, sulfur, and charcoal—is exploded to fire a missile. The Chinese and the Arabs had used gunpowder since the eighth century C.E., mainly for fireworks. The Mongols who attacked Sung Chinese fortifications early in the thirteenth century exploded gunpowder-packed bamboo stalks, the ancestor of the first guns. When Mongol armies swung westward to Poland and Hungary in 1240, Europeans first experienced the deadly might of gunfire. Soon European ironworkers—who honed their skills making swords and horseshoes, metal plowshares and great church bells—learned to manufacture guns.

Around 1400, the Ottoman Turks employed German and Hungarian metalworkers to construct the cannon they fired in their advance through the Middle East and the Balkans. Cannon fire figured in the Ottoman victory at Constantinople in 1453. Europeans soon surpassed the Turks, however, developing gun technology to an extraordinary degree.

The Tools of War

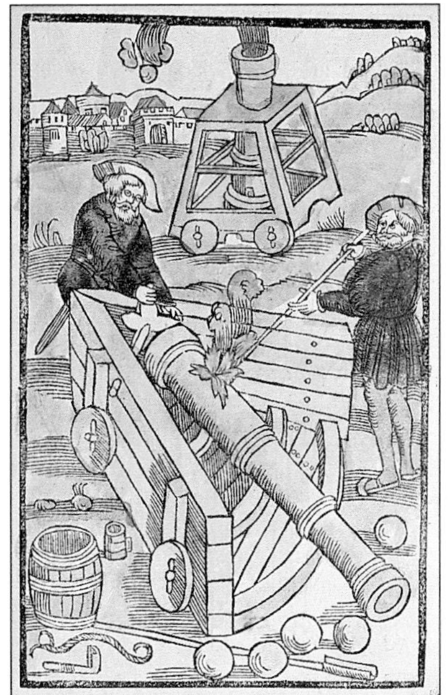

The cannon: *From the mid-fifteenth century, innovations in weapons changed the nature, costs, and social implications of warfare. The most dramatic changes affected the cannon, as shown here in* Four Books of Knighthood, *1528.*

Guns would be the premier tool of European explorers, conquerors, and merchants as they penetrated other continents of the globe.

In the short run, guns prompted the creation of tougher suits of armor for mounted knights. In the long run, they spelled the death of knighthood. No cavalry force could withstand the direct assault of a battery of guns, although as late as the twentieth century some were still trying to. Ordinary foot soldiers armed with better and better guns formed the heart of the modern army, replacing mounted warriors as these had once replaced the ancient legion and phalanx. In the sixteenth and seventeenth centuries, ranks of arquebusiers surrounded a core of pikemen (soldiers armed with long spears). In the eighteenth, lines or columns of musketeers—their more accurate weapons fitted with bayonets which made the pike obsolete—fired in unison, in precise rhythm on command, to halt an enemy charge.

At first, guns could not fire straight or very far. The main use of the new weaponry was in big guns, used to batter down gates and walls. Huge cannon, finely adorned by the talents of engravers and sculptors, were dragged by beasts or before the besieged town or castle. Firing ball after ball, they eventually breached the defenses. The greedy horde of soldiers then swarmed in to sack, rape, and burn. Among the first to use these tactics was the French king Charles VII (r. 1422–1461), who, in 1450, drove the English from their strongholds in France at the close of the Hundred Years' War.

Siege warfare had long figured in human conflict—as testified by the protective circuit of walls that ringed some of the most ancient communities. But now the siege became newly destructive. Innocent populations, trapped within their walls, hearing the cannon fire, awaited in fear the ending that must come as walls gave way to explosive force.

Responding to the challenge of cannon fire, military engineers designed a new type of fortification. The long, exposed **curtain walls** of medieval castles and towns were vulnerable to bombardment. The squat walls of the new-style fortifications, equipped with projecting **bastions** and thickened by earthworks, withstood cannon fire painlessly. The triangular bastions distanced the battle from the town within, and enabled crossbowmen, **musketeers**, and riflemen to rain missiles upon attackers from two sides at once. These fortifications required fat purses and master designers—among the first of whom were the Renaissance artists Leonardo da Vinci and Michelangelo. The craft of military engineering developed sophistication as the demand for fortifications increased, and was advanced by the experience of battle.

Although the development of land warfare was crucial, much of the fighting took place at sea. Europe's expanding dominion in the world, linked together by oceans and rivers, owed much to its naval power. Here, too, firepower proved its value, giving European navies an incontestable advantage over those of other civilizations precisely when the stakes of shipborne commerce peaked. Cannon mounted on shipboard or below deck could defend merchant convoys or fight all-out naval battles.

The gun: *The gun, which later developed to become a musket with bayonet, was also an important innovation (shown here in a 1508 drawing).*

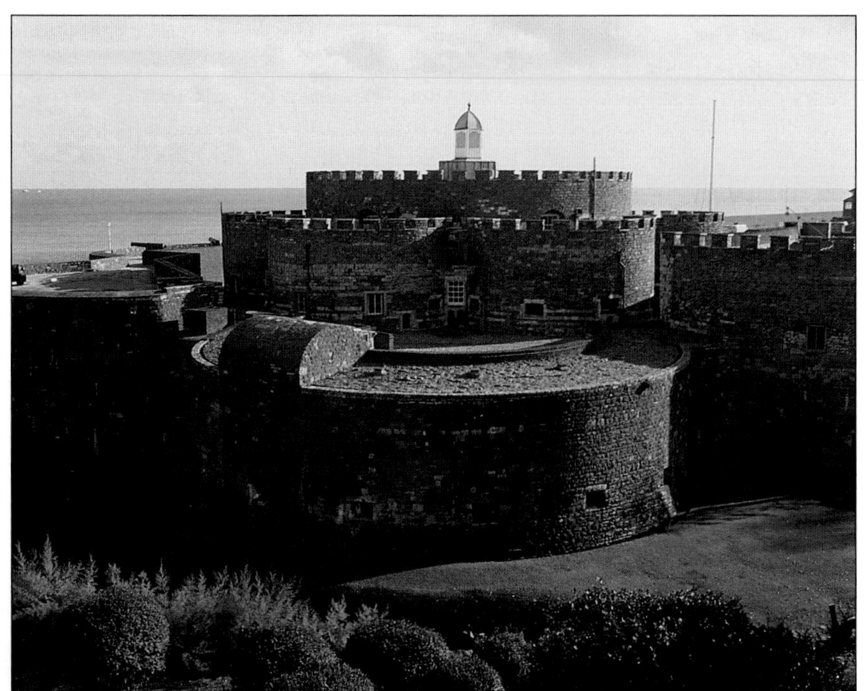

***The castle:** The curtain walls of medieval castles, which were incapable of withstanding cannon fire, were replaced by massive fortifications like at Deal Castle in the sixteenth century, specially designed to face artillery attack from all angles.*

Guns and fortifications were expensive, as were the accoutrements of the new mode of warfare. Soldiers and sailors required not only weapons, but helmets and armor, ammunition and cannonballs, powder flasks and water canteens. Armies traveled with baggage wagons and construction gear, bringing in their wake servants, wives, mistresses, children, and spare horses. In the Greek *polis* or ancient Rome or medieval Europe, the soldier came to fight bearing his own equipment. Now the principality or nation supplied that equipment. The machinery of revenue collection strained to meet the cost of outfitting forces that numbered, by 1600, tens of thousands of men.

Military Organization

The use of guns and the greater reliance on infantry constitute major changes in methods of warfare. But these were only part of what some scholars have called the "military revolution" of the early modern period. Military organization also developed, as gifted leaders forged the modern, professional army.

Italy Modern warfare first unfolded on the Italian stage, where war was a paid profession. Unlike the armies of the north, which consisted of native noblemen and their peasant auxiliaries, those of the Italian cities consisted of hired warriors, paid with liquid cash. Managing these hired, or mercenary, armies were generals called *condottieri* ("contractors"). The *condottieri* were first-rate strategists, economists, and engineers, as well as soldiers. They were experts at recruiting troops, keeping them paid, pitching camp, and retreating, if necessary, in the face of danger. They fought to fulfill the terms of their contract with their paymaster state. They aimed to spill as little blood, and to face as few battles, as possible. Thus organized, Italian warfare was an efficient tool of statecraft, but it was not especially deadly.

It was on the shrewdest of such *condottieri* that Machiavelli modeled his prince (although he deplored the use of mercenary soldiers, who he thought would fight less well than natives). Such men as Cesare Borgia (the son and agent of Pope Alexander VI) and Francesco Sforza (1401–1466, who in 1450 became Duke of Milan) battled their way to eminence and, in the case of the latter, to sovereign power. Their skills of military organization lifted them above the ranks of ordinary men and close to the thrones of hereditary monarchs.

Switzerland Among the mercenaries hired by the combative Italian states were soldiers from Switzerland. In that mountainous southwestern zone of the Holy Roman Empire, local regions called **cantons** had been engaged, since the late thirteenth century, in a struggle for independence. This struggle encouraged the development of native military skills. Swiss soldiers, like the hoplites of ancient Greece, fought on foot and side by side, mutually supporting each other. Armed with pikes and arrayed in tight squares from which their weapons bristled, they could withstand the cavalry charges led by the Empire's noblemen. The ordinary male citizen of a Swiss canton was of necessity a soldier. When the Swiss finally won their independence in 1499, these disciplined infantrymen sold their skills abroad.

Sweden Far to the north, Sweden's King Gustavus II Adolphus (r. 1611–1632) led the way in creating a national standing army, rather than a knightly or mercenary one. Sweden was then a small and rather poor country whose role in European affairs before the seventeenth century was minimal. That role was changed with the outbreak of the Thirty Years' War. Gustavus Adolphus intervened in that conflict in 1630 to protect Protestant interests and to secure a footing on the south shore of the Baltic Sea. The supreme performance of his disciplined troops and mobile cannon won fame for Sweden, whose hymn-singing soldiers were forbidden by their pious king to pillage or rape—a unique prohibition in that era.

England A generation later, the Englishman Oliver Cromwell (1599–1658), a leader of Parliamentary opposition to the king, organized the New Model Army, which defeated the Royalist forces in 1645. He personally led the military unit known as the Ironsides, men who as he said, "had the fear of God before them." Forming tight squares, their unflinching pikes projecting at set angles like a deadly, mechanical porcupine, his soldiers set a new standard for disciplined warfare.

France Also contributing to the military revolution was France. In the mid-1400s King Charles VII reorganized the French army, building up a strong artillery and de-emphasizing the role of knights (who had once been so shamefully vanquished by England's bowmen). As knights became less important, the power of the nobility (which often challenged that of the monarch) could be curtailed. Charles ordered the castle towers of feudal strongholds cut down and extended his mandate into every pocket of regional power, seeking to create a national spirit and a national military organization.

Despite Charles's efforts, the French military remained a motley combination of individual units recruited by semi-independent generals. Then, in the later 1600s, King Louis XIV (r. 1643–1715) thoroughly reconstituted the army as an instrument of state policy. Its captains and generals became part of a hierarchy arrayed under the king's personal authority. Its soldiers wore standard uniforms, drilled and marched, and were provisioned by a central office. By the early 1700s, intensive recruiting had resulted in an increase from 100,000 to 400,000 men, making the French army the largest in Europe.

Prussia It was in Prussia, however, that the professionalization of the early modern army reached its zenith. Prussia was a new state, formed by the Great Elector Frederick William (1640–1688) from two non-adjacent territories—the imperial electorate of Brandenburg and the Polish duchy of Prussia. Geographically fragmented (it included several other small territories) Prussia required a powerful army for its defense. Its first ruler, the Great Elector Frederick William, made military values and needs the linchpin of his political strategy. Prudently providing for all other state expenses from the modest resources of his private purse, he dedicated all tax revenues to the maintenance of the army, while recruiting nearly the whole of the Prussian aristocracy—called the *Junkers*—to lead it. By these methods, he built the army up to 40,000 men, enormous for its time and for the size of the principality, which then numbered 1.5 million inhabitants. His successors in the next century raised that total to 200,000, one-half that of the army of France, with a population more than ten times that of Prussia.

By the eighteenth century, the miscellaneous cavalry contingents of the Middle Ages had been replaced by the modern army.

War and Diplomacy The eighteenth-century army centered on an infantry force armed with smoothbore muskets, descendants of the earlier arquebus, which were transformed into spears by affixing a sharp dagger or bayonet. The infantry faced an enemy who had already been ravaged by artillery teams with mobile, increasingly accurate cannon. Salaried soldiers wore centrally-issued uniforms, slept in barracks, and drilled regularly the maneuvers that they would be called upon to perform in battle. Officers of noble origin learned the art of command at military academies such as those in Paris, Saint Petersburg, or Turin (modern Italy). Conducting a siege, according to King Frederick II, the Great, of Prussia (r. 1740–1786), was a craft "like that of carpenter or clock-maker." Battle itself—unlike the whirling charges of mounted warriors or the relentless pressure of a siege—was a formal, choreographed event in which two bodies of men faced each other across an open field and fired precisely on command.

Why did they fire? Because they were drilled to load, aim, and shoot in unison, and paid to do so—however meagerly and irregularly. Certainly, they did not fight for glory or territory, or for their faith; in the eighteenth century, religious differences did not spark wars. Nor did they fight from patriotism, a sentiment not yet invented. But if patriotism was not yet born, national and dynastic interests were very much alive. European wars were fought in the service of those interests, as rulers jostled for prestige, for land, and for power. To win those ends, they tolerated devastating losses of life and property, and incurred huge expenses borne by the citizenry.

Then, as now, talk was the main alternative to war. By the fourteenth century, especially in Flanders and Italy, the role of the medieval herald, who conveyed messages from one leader to another, was beginning to develop into that of the modern **ambassador**. Like the herald, the ambassador represented a state or ruler at the courts or assemblies of another. He brought information; conveyed messages of sympathy or congratulations for deaths, births, and weddings; and presented terms for the settlement of disputes.

Even in the midst of hostilities, the ambassador enjoyed promises of personal security from all parties. By the sixteenth century, ambassadors were often permanently based in the main European centers and regularly accomplished negotiations between states. Those negotiations, constituting what is called **diplomacy**, prepared the bases of the treaties of peace that followed major conflicts. In many cases, they prevented conflicts altogether. In 1619, an experienced Spanish diplomat advised that wars were no longer a test of strength, like a bullfight, to be decided by "mere battles"; "rather they depend on losing or gaining friends and allies, and it is to this end that good statesmen must turn all their attention and energy."

The citizens of *Utopia*, the ideal "nowhereland" envisioned by the sixteenth-century English writer Thomas More, did not go to war. If necessary, mercenaries were dispatched to do so. Utopian ambassadors arranged for a settlement of differences even at great financial cost. When diplomacy failed, Utopian policy called for the assassination of the enemy leader—an atrocity resorted to only to prevent the worse one of war. Europe was not yet so civilized.

WAR GAMES

Three centuries of war trace the shifts in the political configuration of Europe after 1500. Cities and principalities lost out to nations, as nations competed for dominance. Each sought security, territory, commercial advantages, and a share in the balance of power that national leaders attempted to maintain. Equipped with the latest military technology, rulers and statesmen employed the official violence of war to reconfigure the map of Europe, playing a game that dealt its winners status, wealth, and power.

In the first phase of early modern warfare from 1500 to 1648, the enmity between two great players—France (successively under Valois and Bourbon rulers) and the House of Habsburg (Holy Roman Emperors, whose domains included Austria, part of the Netherlands, and Spain) stoked the fires of religious conflict. By the end of the Thirty Years' War, religious issues had waned, outpaced by political objectives. In the second phase, from 1648 to 1763, France again played a central role. Having emerged from the Thirty Years' War the most powerful nation in Europe, France ceded that title, in 1763, to the new dynamo on the world stage, Great Britain.

Wars over Faith and Turf, 1500–1648

From 1500 to 1648, religious controversies and territorial disputes between rival dynasties saw Europe in a nearly constant state of warfare. By 1500, Italy was overrun with Spanish, German, and French soldiers—"barbarians," they were called, but barbarians in such numbers as to overwhelm the once-proud Italian city-states. At the same time, the Protestant Reformation created the issues that precipitated warfare between Protestants and Catholics, especially in the Holy Roman Empire and in France. Religious differences also figured in a war for independence in the Netherlands and in a civil war in England, although these conflicts also had political dimensions. From 1618 to 1648, much of Europe became involved in the Thirty Years' War, fought largely on German soil. At its outset, religious issues were prominent. By its close, religious factors had been overshadowed by the contest between the dynasties of France and the German lands: the Bourbons and the Habsburgs.

The trends in international politics characteristic of the early modern era first emerged in Italy, where the experience of city-states prefigures that of the nations beyond the Alps. Intermittently at war, some of the principal Italian states, including Milan, Naples, Rome, Venice, and Florence, had arrived at an agreement by the Peace of Lodi in 1454. This truce aimed at maintaining a balance of power among contending nations. Within a generation, however, the five participants were at war again. Soon they looked for assistance to the nations on the far side of the Alps. Beginning in 1494, France, the Empire, and Spain sent their armies. Where the Italians had sought helpers, instead they stirred up conquerors.

The process of conquest rolled on for fifty years more on the slippery battlefronts of the Italian Wars (1494–1559). At the end, by the Treaty of Câteau-Cambrésis in 1559, the Spanish and allied imperial forces had bested the French and seized control of the peninsula. Of the major Italian states, only four remained independent: the two republics of Venice and Genoa, and the two principalities of Savoy and Tuscany (the region of which Florence was capital), now under the Grand Dukes of Tuscany, descendants of the Medici family of Renaissance days. Italy was mortally wounded, but the political system of balanced competitive states which it pioneered set the pattern for relations between European nations until World War I in the twentieth century.

As cities and nations contended on Italian soil, north of the Alps a series of conflicts arose as a consequence of the Protestant Reformation (see Chapter 14). Within the Empire, Protestant and Catholic princes and states maneuvered against and fought each other, as did Huguenot, Catholic, and *politique* nobles in France. In the German lands these wars lasted until 1555, when they ended with the Peace of Augsburg. War in France continued until the reign of Henry IV (1589–1610), drawing to a close with his conversion to Catholicism in 1593 and his issuing, in 1598, of the Edict of Nantes. These conflicts, ending in territorial settlements for Protestants and Catholics and some hope of reconciliation, belong to the history of the Reformation.

Although religion figured in other conflicts in the Netherlands, the Empire, and England, these were essentially struggles between competing nations and interests. The first was the Dutch war of independence against Spain, begun officially in 1579 (though fighting dated from 1568). The second was the Thirty Years' War (1618–1648), which began as a struggle between Protestant and Catholic rulers in the Empire, and ended as a European-wide conflict in which religious identification had lost political significance. The third was the English Civil War (1642–1651).

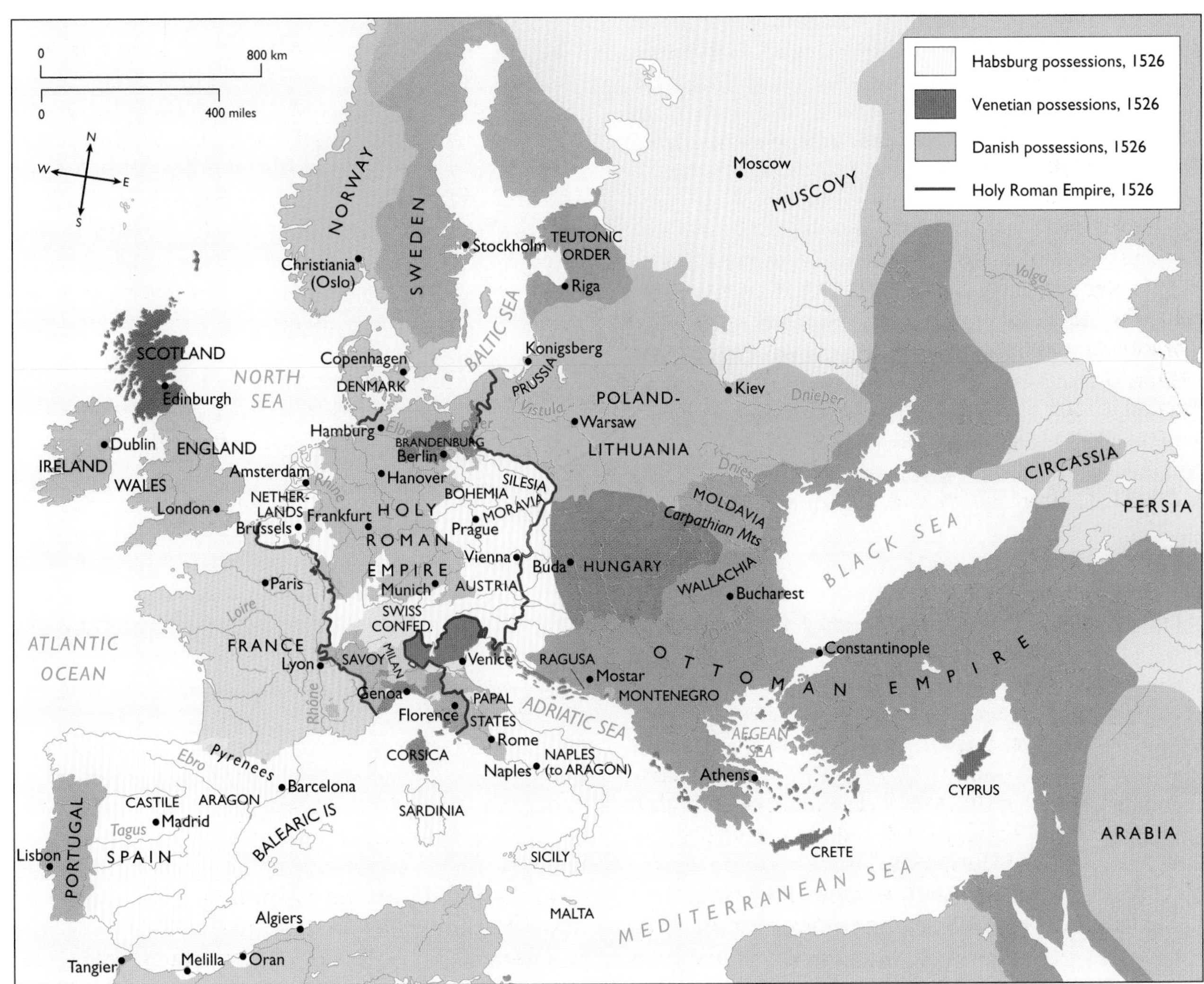

***Map 15.1* The European States in 1526:** *The map of Europe in the early 1500s was dominated by the House of Habsburg, with possessions in Spain, the Netherlands, southern Italy, and central Europe. Northern Italy and the German-speaking center of Europe were fragmented into hundreds of cities and principalities. To the east, the duchy of Muscovy was being transformed into Russia, bordering on the great expanses of Poland and Lithuania. To the southeast, the Ottoman Empire expanded ominously.*

In the seventeen provinces of the Netherlands, in 1566, discontent with Spanish rule, especially among Protestants, gave way to full-scale protests and to riots. The Spanish responded by sending the Duke of Alba at the head of an army, to subdue these unruly subjects and administer the Inquisition. "Everyone must be made to live in constant fear of the roof breaking down over his head," ordained the Duke. His Council of Troubles, set up to track down heretics, sentenced thousands of Protestants to death, and ordered the confiscation of many noble estates. In the face of this tyranny, Catholics and Protestants of all classes united in armed revolt.

In 1578, the more moderate Duke of Parma, sent by the Spanish to reestablish obedience, rallied the support of the largely Catholic southern provinces. These ten provinces returned to Spanish dominion calmly, and after 1713 to the Austrian Habsburgs. The seven largely Protestant northern provinces, led by Holland and Zeeland, formed the Union of Utrecht in 1579 and declared independence from Spain in 1581. Their leader was Prince William I, called "the Silent," of the House of Orange (1533–1584). Previously appointed *stadholder*, or lieutenant-governor in Holland, by the emperor Charles V, he had already begun, in the 1570s, to direct military and naval operations against Spanish rule.

The United Provinces, as they were called after 1579, were supported by England, which sent several thousand troops to assist in the struggle. It was partly to stop this support that Spain launched, in 1588, its fearsome Armada. Although the Armada boasted formidable guns, its ships were cumbersome. The sleeker, swifter English vessels, fitted with excellent guns, chased the Spanish fleet from the English Channel into the North Sea—and into oblivion. As England stood poised to enter into Continental power struggles, it perceived its success in this incident as providential.

Dutch and Spanish armies struggled until 1609, when the Twelve Years' Truce provided for a division between Catholic south and Protestant north. Dutch independence was officially recognized in 1648, and the new federal Dutch Republic took its place in the political arena. The Dutch had already greatly expanded their maritime ventures (see Chapter 16), which flourished as the English became involved in their Civil War. Emerging from that struggle, the English Parliament responded to Dutch competition by issuing the Navigation Act of 1651. This act (subsequently reissued several times) limited the shipment of goods to England to English-owned ships or the ships of the region of origin. The Navigation Acts challenged the Dutch carrying trade, the source of that Republic's wealth, and provoked war between these two Protestant powers—the First Anglo-Dutch War of 1652–54, followed by two others before 1674—who not long before had cooperated in resisting the Spanish.

War in Action

The Turkish army outside Vienna: *This miniature painting shows a depiction of the "Battle of Mohacs" outside Vienna in 1526. In it Suleiman I, "the Magnificent," is shown directing his Turkish army from behind a row of cannon.* (Topkapi Museum, Istanbul)

The Thirty Years' War Sparked by rebellious Protestant nobles, the Thirty Years' War developed into a general European melee involving at least seventeen sovereign powers. The war was fought largely on German soil between, on the one hand, the Habsburg dynasty (both its Austrian and Spanish branches) and, on the other, the German Protestant princes and their allies, both Protestant (Denmark, Sweden, the United Provinces) and Catholic (France). The Habsburgs stood for a strong central European empire, backed by the Roman Catholic Church. Their opponents, both Protestant and

Catholic, wished for political and religious reasons to preserve the autonomy of the states composing the Holy Roman Empire—now a nearly vaporous entity.

Coursing through several phases—Bohemian, Rhineland, Dutch, Swedish, and French—as different generals and interests came to the fore, the conflict was finally settled in 1648 by the Peace of Westphalia. That treaty provided for a balance of power between the main contenders (the Habsburg and French Bourbon powers) and associates. Granting virtual sovereignty to the component German states, it dictated the effective death of the Holy Roman Empire (although the Empire lingered in name until 1806) and created a power vacuum in central Europe, threatening danger to come. Finally, the treaty recognized existing religious differences, thereby signaling the end of religious warfare in Europe.

What was indisputably accomplished by thirty years of battle was the devastation of Germany: its people, of whom perhaps 20 percent died; and its towns, its commerce, its blighted economy, its ruined fields. From the German perspective alone, this may have been the most catastrophic war in modern European history.

States in Competition, 1648–1763

One consequence of the Thirty Years' War was to bring France to the front rank of European power. As she attempted to pursue that advantage, she collided with England, which had emerged from relative insignificance in the late Middle Ages to become a major commercial and political presence in Europe. As the duel between those nations proceeded, other rivalries were pursued by the new nations of eastern Europe (the term denoting during this era the lands of modern Poland, the Czech Republic, Slovakia, Hungary, the eastern German region, and Austria), Prussia and Austria, the most successful remnants of the Holy Roman Empire, and a reinvigorated Russia.

By the 1660s, France possessed the largest army in Europe and nurtured vast ambitions. It sought to limit Habsburg power on its borders, and to annex nearby lands, especially Alsace-Lorraine and the southern, or Spanish, Netherlands. The French strategy was checked in 1688 by a coalition of alarmed nations. It was contained again in the War of the Spanish Succession (1701–1714), when again most of the other major European powers united to combat it.

This war was precipitated when the last Habsburg king of Spain, Charles II, died in 1700, having willed all of his possessions, to be kept intact, to the grandson of Louis XIV of France. Had the terms of the will been observed without protest, France would have dominated Europe (and much of the Western Hemisphere as well). An enormous alliance rose up against this possibility. The Peace of Utrecht of 1713 between England and France settled the conflict (although fighting continued between some parties for another year), and, together with the Peace of Rastatt (1714) drew new lines of authority in Europe. A French king of the Bourbon dynasty would rule in Spain and in Spanish America, but other Spanish dominions—principally the southern Netherlands and Spanish domains in Italy—were conveyed to Habsburg Austria. The rulers of the small states of Savoy and Prussia obtained territorial gains and the status of king, and the Dutch Republic received small concessions.

All contenders won something, but Great Britain (created by joining the crowns of England and Scotland in 1707) emerged the winner. She won the fortress of Gibraltar on the Spanish Mediterranean shore and parts of French Canada, which enabled her to pursue her maritime ambitions. Even more precious was the grant of the *asiento* ("contract") from Spain, giving Britain the right to carry African slaves to Spanish America (see Chapter 16). As a bonus, she won a promise that France would not attempt to place a Catholic king on the British throne, now Protestant by law.

After some twenty-five years of relative peace, the European nations began fighting again in the 1740s,

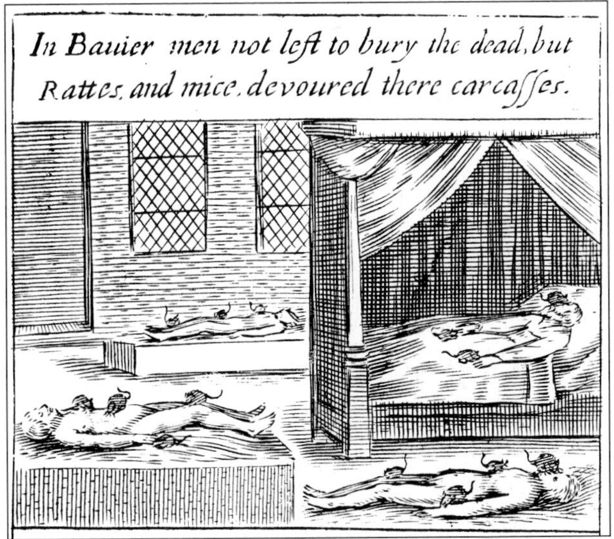

Carcasses devoured by rats and mice: *There were many tragic consequences of war. Casualties from the Thirty Years' War, 1618–48, where bodies, left unburied, were devoured by rats and mice, are shown in this woodcut from* The Lamentations of Germany, *1638.* (British Library, London)

intent on gaining slips of territory and small advantages. An eight-year interlude between 1748 and 1756 was followed by the Seven Years' War (1756–1763), fought on three continents— not only in Europe but also in India and in North America, where it was known as the French and Indian War. Overarching all other issues was the continuing duel between Britain and France.

This time, the duel was fought largely overseas, as colonial possessions and foreign trade increasingly became the measure of national preeminence. By 1761, Britain had seized French possessions in India, and was poised for further ventures in the domination of that subcontinent. In 1759 a British force launched a surprise attack on the key French fortress at Quebec. After a ten-minute battle on the Plains of Abraham, outside the fortress, which the British won with disciplined musket volleys at close range, French prospects in North America were doomed. The Treaty of Paris of 1763 secured Britain's triumph over her main rival in India, in North America, and in Europe.

Eastern Europe By 1700, three states dominated eastern Europe: Austria, Prussia, and Russia. The homeland of the Habsburg family, Austria had a strong monarchy and an expansive agenda. It absorbed Hungary, Bohemia, Transylvania, and parts of the northern Balkans, knitting its empire together through the figure of the king, who ruled as monarch in each kingdom. It held the southeast frontier of Europe against the Ottoman Turks, whose vigor had waned since the siege of Vienna in 1529, though it resurged in 1683 to threaten that outpost once again.

The kingdom of Prussia developed from the ancestral lands of the Hohenzollern family: Brandenburg, some tiny states in the Empire, and the duchy of Prussia itself. These lands were patiently acquired over generations and combined to form an independent state; it was granted the status of kingdom by the Peace of Utrecht of 1713. Farther east, Tsar Peter I (r. 1682–1725), called "the Great," who had toured the successful nations of western Europe, learned what he could, and imported trained experts, now built a new capital city on the Baltic Sea and reoriented his political goals. For the first time, Russia looked westward, ready to engage as a great power in European struggles for sovereignty.

In 1713, Prussia, along with most other European nations, had agreed to the Pragmatic Sanction. Issued by the Holy Roman Emperor Charles VI (r. 1711–1740), this provided that his daughter and heir, Maria Theresa (r. 1740–1780), would inherit all the Habsburg lands intact (although, as a woman, she was ineligible to become Holy Roman Emperor). In 1740, on the basis of no other principle than *raison d'état*, the young king of Prussia, Frederick II (r. 1740–1786) broke this agreement. Frederick needed Silesia—a prosperous province under Austrian domination. And so he took it. Other nations entered into the fray, nibbling at the Habsburg lands. By the 1748 Peace of Aix-la-Chapelle, which settled the War of the Austrian Succession, Silesia was his. A few years later, in the Seven Years' War, Austria allied itself with France and Russia, to block Prussia's further expansion. Bankrolled by Britain but left to fight on its own, Prussia stayed firm and retained its position.

In 1772, Prussia was still hungry for territory to round out the boundaries of its domain. Along with Austria and Russia, it annexed small bits of Poland, an ailing republic dominated by a fractious nobility under an elected king, fatally resistant to centralization. In 1793 and 1795, Poland's neighbors completed her dismemberment. In the final "partition," it disappeared from the map, not to be reconstituted until after World War I. Prussia, Austria, and Russia, fat with new territory, now held unrivaled domination of eastern Europe. As recently as 1500, they had been overshadowed by the Holy Roman Empire, now in tatters; by the Ottoman Empire, in retreat through the Balkans; and by Poland, devoured whole.

During the early modern era, the violence that had characterized medieval Europe in an era of invasion became the official tool of the state. As a result, the map of Europe was radically altered as winners took their prizes and losers shrank behind their borders. Soon after 1500, the Italian cities yielded their primacy, as Machiavelli had feared, to more powerful nations beyond the Alps. By 1600, the most potent states in Europe were monarchies poised on the Atlantic coast: Spain, France, and England. Emerging as major players soon thereafter were the kingdom of Sweden, the newly constituted Dutch Republic, and the German electorate of Brandenburg, subsequently the kingdom of Prussia. Meanwhile, the Holy Roman Empire withered, while the Habsburg dynasty, which had long held the imperial title, raised its hereditary domain of Austria to international importance. Portugal, the rising star of the early 1500s, languished, and Poland was obliterated. Led by a series of tsars, who considered themselves the successors of Roman Caesars, Russia moved into the European arena.

AN AGE OF KINGS

As the nations of Europe competed, they also developed forms of government that endured into the modern era. This process usually involved the refinement of monarchy, as the ability to make laws and exercise force was concentrated in the figure of the king—or, in a few cases, the queen. Such kings were "absolute" monarchs, because they tried to rule "absolutely" (believing in complete, unrestricted powers due to their divine right), unchecked by councils, legislatures, guilds, or representatives of the people. By the end of the eighteenth century, that newly evolved monarchy would be challenged and, in some places, limited by those institutions. In diverse ways, monarchy developed in the direction of **absolutism** in several European countries: in Spain, France, and England in the western zone; and in Prussia, Austria, and Russia in the eastern one.

Spain: Religious Zeal and Royal Absolutism

The autonomous kingdoms that formed on the Iberian peninsula in the Middle Ages were united by a common dedication to the centuries-long crusade called the *Reconquista* (see Chapter 9). After the fall of the last Moorish fortress at Granada in 1492, the Inquisition fostered the crusading spirit by pursuing lapsed converts to Christianity, as well as heretics.

WITNESSES

The Experience of War in Works of Shakespeare and Voltaire

King Henry V threatens the French city of Harfleur with battery, capture, rape, and sack:

How yet resolves the Governor of the town?
This is the latest parle we will admit:
Therefore to our best mercy give yourselves,
Or, like to men proud of destruction,
Defy us to our worst; for, as I am a soldier,
A name that in my thoughts becomes me best,
If I begin the batt'ry once again,
I will not leave the half-achieved Harfleur
Till in her ashes she lie buried.
The gates of mercy shall be all shut up,
And the fleshed soldier, rough and hard of heart,
In liberty of bloody hand shall range
With conscience wide as hell, mowing like grass
Your fresh fair virgins and your flow'ring infants. . . .
. . . Therefore, you men of Harfleur,
Take pity of your town and of your people
Whiles yet my soldiers are in my command,
Whiles yet the cool and temperate wind of grace
O'erblows the filthy and contagious clouds
Of heady murder, spoil, and villainy.
If not—why, in a moment look to see
The blind and bloody soldier with foul hand
Defile the locks of your shrill-shrieking daughters;
Your fathers taken by the silver beards,
And their most reverend heads dashed to the walls;
Your naked infants spitted upon pikes,
While the mad mothers with their howls confused
Do break the clouds, as did the wives of Jewry
At Herod's bloody-hunting slaughtermen.
What say you? Will you yield, and this avoid?
Or, guilty in defense, be thus destroyed?

(Shakespeare, *Henry V*, 1600, III. iii. 1–14, 27–43; ed. J. R. Brown, 1998)

Candide is impressed into the Bulgarian army: Nothing could be smarter, more splendid, more brilliant, better drawn up than the two armies. Trumpets, fifes, hautboys, drums, cannons, formed a harmony such as has never been heard even in hell. The cannons first of all laid flat about six thousand men on each side; then the musketry removed from the best of worlds* some nine or ten thousand blackguards who infested its surface. The bayonet also was the sufficient reason* for the death of some thousands of men. The whole might amount to thirty thousand souls. Candide, who trembled like a philosopher, hid himself as well as he could during this heroic butchery.

At last, while the two Kings each commanded a *Te Deum* [a hymn of thanksgiving to God] in his camp, Candide decided to go elsewhere to reason about effects and causes. He clambered over heaps of dead and dying men and reached a neighboring village, which was in ashes; it was an Abare village which the Burgundians had burned in accordance with international law. Here, old men dazed with blows watched the dying agonies of their murdered wives who clutched their children to their bleeding breasts; there, disembowelled girls who had been made to satisfy the natural appetites of heroes gasped their last sighs; others, half-burned, begged to be put to death. Brains were scattered on the ground among dismembered arms and legs.

(Voltaire, *Candide*, 1759, Ch. 3; ed. N. L. Torrey, 1946)

*With the phrases "best of worlds" and "sufficient reason," Voltaire is mocking a foolishly optimistic school of contemporary philosophy.

The same crusading spirit inspired Spanish missionaries to the Americas, to convert the native population. Before it became a nation, Spain was a culture united by its dedication to Roman Catholic orthodoxy. On this basis, kings from the fifteenth and sixteenth centuries built a strong, centralized state.

Crucial developments in this unifying process were achieved in the reigns of Ferdinand II of Aragon (r. 1479–1516) and Isabella of Castile (r. 1474–1504), whose marriage in 1479 linked their two kingdoms. (Portugal had already taken a separate path to nationhood before the events about to be described.) Although the component states of Castile and Aragon retained their separate judicial, political, and adminis-

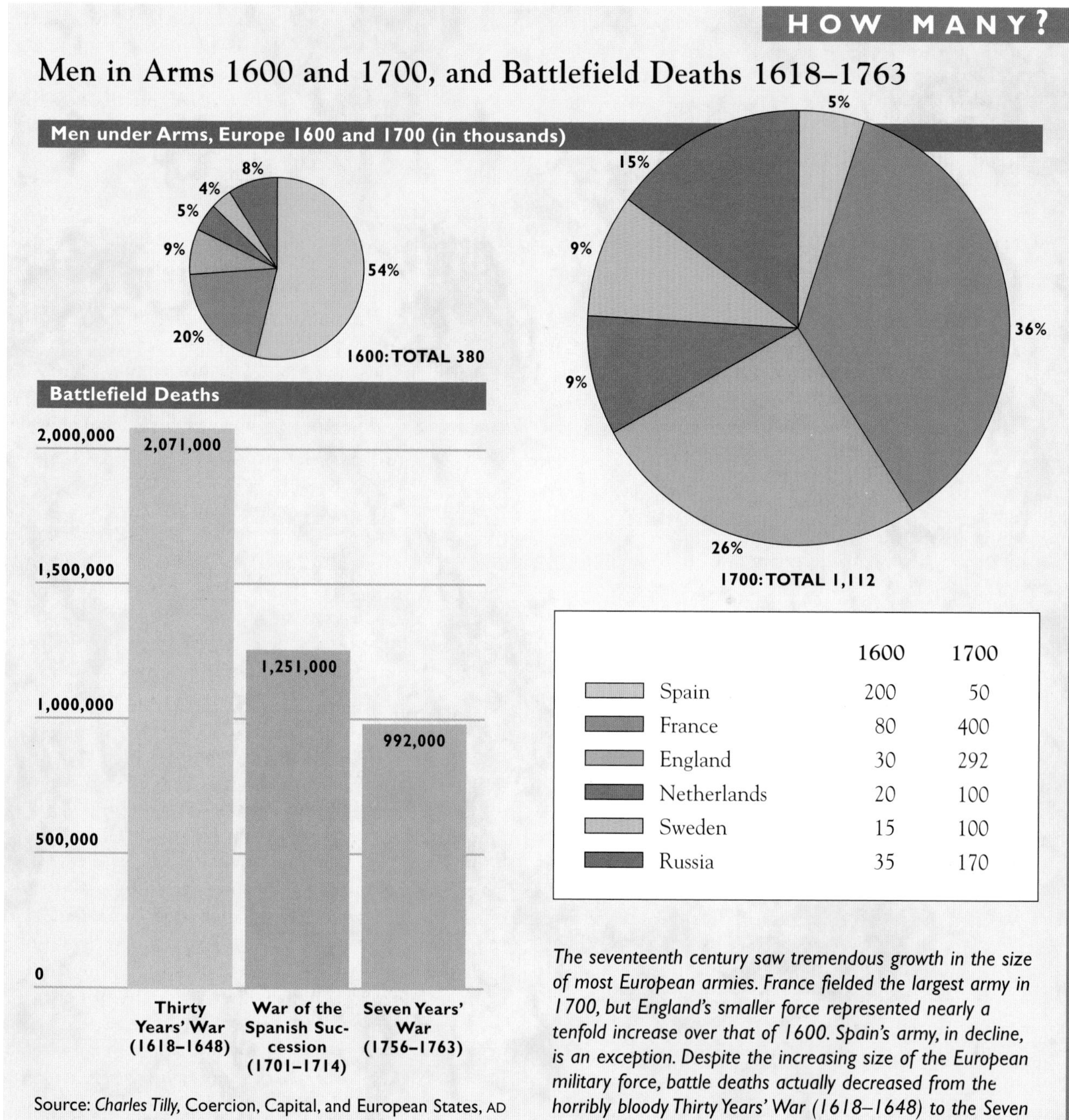

	1600	1700
Spain	200	50
France	80	400
England	30	292
Netherlands	20	100
Sweden	15	100
Russia	35	170

Source: *Charles Tilly,* Coercion, Capital, and European States, AD 990–1990 *(Cambridge, MA: Basil Blackwell, 1990), pp. 79, 165–166.*

The seventeenth century saw tremendous growth in the size of most European armies. France fielded the largest army in 1700, but England's smaller force represented nearly a tenfold increase over that of 1600. Spain's army, in decline, is an exception. Despite the increasing size of the European military force, battle deaths actually decreased from the horribly bloody Thirty Years' War (1618–1648) to the Seven Years' War (1756–1763), a crucial conflict that was not grossly wasteful of human life.

trative laws and institutions, a strong commonality of purpose marked the reigns of their respective sovereigns—displayed most dramatically by their conquest of Granada.

In 1516, on the death of Ferdinand, a now-united Spain passed to his and Isabella's grandson, Charles I. The grandson also of the Holy Roman Emperor Maximilian I and Mary of Burgundy, Charles inherited the Habsburg lands on Maximilian's death in 1519 and, as Charles V (r. 1519–1556), became Holy Roman Emperor. Ruler of several states, and required by circumstances to manage the Italian Wars, the consequences of the Protestant Reformation, the rivalry of France, and the threat of Turkish invasion, Charles could not concentrate exclusively on Spain. When he abdicated in 1556, the Spanish inheritance (along with title to the Netherlands and parts of Italy) passed to his son Philip, and the Habsburg lands of central Europe to his brother Ferdinand I.

Under Philip II (r. 1556–1598) the Spanish state rose to an apex of wealth and influence. Outside the capital of Madrid, Philip constructed the Escorial, a combined palace and monastery, vast and austere. There he attended mass daily and ruled his far-flung possessions. Aided by a staff of diplomats and spies, he worked diligently to extend Spanish rule and to reassert Catholic orthodoxy in Europe. Those goals were not implausibly grandiose, given that the great wealth then pouring into Spain from its American possessions (see Chapter 16) could fund a formidable military organization. Philip succeeded in acquiring Portugal in 1580. With his marriage in 1554 to the queen of England, Mary Tudor (r. 1553–1558), came the opportunity, never realized, to add that kingdom to his other possessions and to restore it to the roster of Catholic nations.

The great success of sixteenth-century Spain faded during the seventeenth, as its silver imports from the Americas failed to enrich the nation. After 1665, the deterioration was rapid. Charles II, who ascended the throne in that year as a child, was sickly, stupid, and impotent. It was his death in 1700 that precipitated the War of the Spanish Succession, resulting in the importation to Spain of a French Bourbon dynasty. Spanish fortunes revived in the 1700s as Bourbon monarchs and ministers created administrative systems on the French model, but Spain no longer played its earlier role of foremost European monarchy.

France: The Apogee of Absolutism

That role fell to France, which had lain in Spain's shadow in the sixteenth century, but towered above it in the next. Thanks to a larger and more productive population, the kings of France were able to build an impressive administrative machine, field an enormous army, and claim cultural leadership in Europe.

The French kings had already traveled far along the road toward sovereignty during the medieval centuries. They had gained recognition from the feudal nobility of their preeminence in the realm, and from the pope of their rights over the French clergy—the "Gallican liberties" won by the Pragmatic Sanction of Bourges in 1438 and the Concordat of Bologna in 1516. They had defended French territorial rights against other claimants, particularly the English, against whom they ultimately prevailed in the Hundred Years' War. The ascension to the throne of Henry IV (r. 1589–1610), the first of the Bourbon line, brought an end to the chaotic era of religious warfare. It also marked the opening of an especially fruitful era in the building of the French monarchy.

If Henry IV had done nothing else he would be remarkable for his promulgation in 1598 of the Edict of Nantes guaranteeing generous freedoms to his former coreligionists, the Huguenots. But Henry did much more. He saw to France's recovery from the civil wars, collected forgotten taxes and paid forgotten salaries, repaired roads and bridges and the mechanisms of government, administered justice, and promoted commerce. In the twenty-one years of his reign, he never summoned the Estates-General (an assembly of representatives of France's three **estates**, clergy, nobility, and commoners, comparable to the English Parliament). He signaled the capacity of the monarch to rule without consulting a representative assembly. An unusually effective ruler, he laid the foundations for absolute monarchy in France.

After the death of Henry IV, the true ruler of France was neither his son Louis XIII (r. 1610–1643) nor his widow, Marie de' Medici (1573–1642), regent for Louis, then only nine years old. It was the nobleman and cardinal Armand Jean du Plessis, the Duke de Richelieu (1585–1642). This prudent cleric, who became secretary of state in 1616 and Louis's chief minister in 1624, devoted himself to the secular interests of the French monarchy. In the last phase of the Thirty Years' War he intervened on the Protestant side against the Catholic Habsburgs.

Cardinal Richelieu promoted commerce in France and in its overseas possessions, encouraging poor nobles to enrich themselves in business ventures and wealthy merchants to gain titles of nobility by funneling cash to the royal treasury. He reined in aristocratic pretensions, prohibited private dueling, and destroyed fortified castles not in royal service. He also stripped the Huguenot community of its right to bear arms and live in fortified towns, although he reaffirmed the freedom of worship guaranteed by Henry IV.

Cardinal Richelieu's protégé, the Italian-born Jules Mazarin (1602–1661), followed his mentor's model. Made Cardinal in 1641, Mazarin effectively ruled France from 1643 to 1661 as chief adviser to Anne of Austria, widow of Louis XIII and regent for Louis XIV. Like Cardinal Richelieu, Mazarin managed domestic and international affairs in the interests of the French monarchy, deftly surviving a rebellion of restive nobles and peasants called the Fronde.

The Bourbon dynasty benefited from the service of yet a third royal servant: Jean-Baptiste Colbert (1619–1683). The son of a merchant, Colbert began his career by monitoring Mazarin's investments. In 1665, recommended by his mentor, Colbert was employed by Louis XIV (r. 1643–1715) as France's chief financial minister, a position he held until his death in 1683. Colbert reduced France's debt, systematized its accounting methods, and attempted (unsuccessfully) to equalize tax burdens. Aiming at economic self-sufficiency, he encouraged commerce and discouraged misuse of natural resources, built roads and canals, set standards of quality for manufactured goods and agricultural products, increased foreign tariffs and reduced internal ones—all features of the strategy of **mercantilism**.

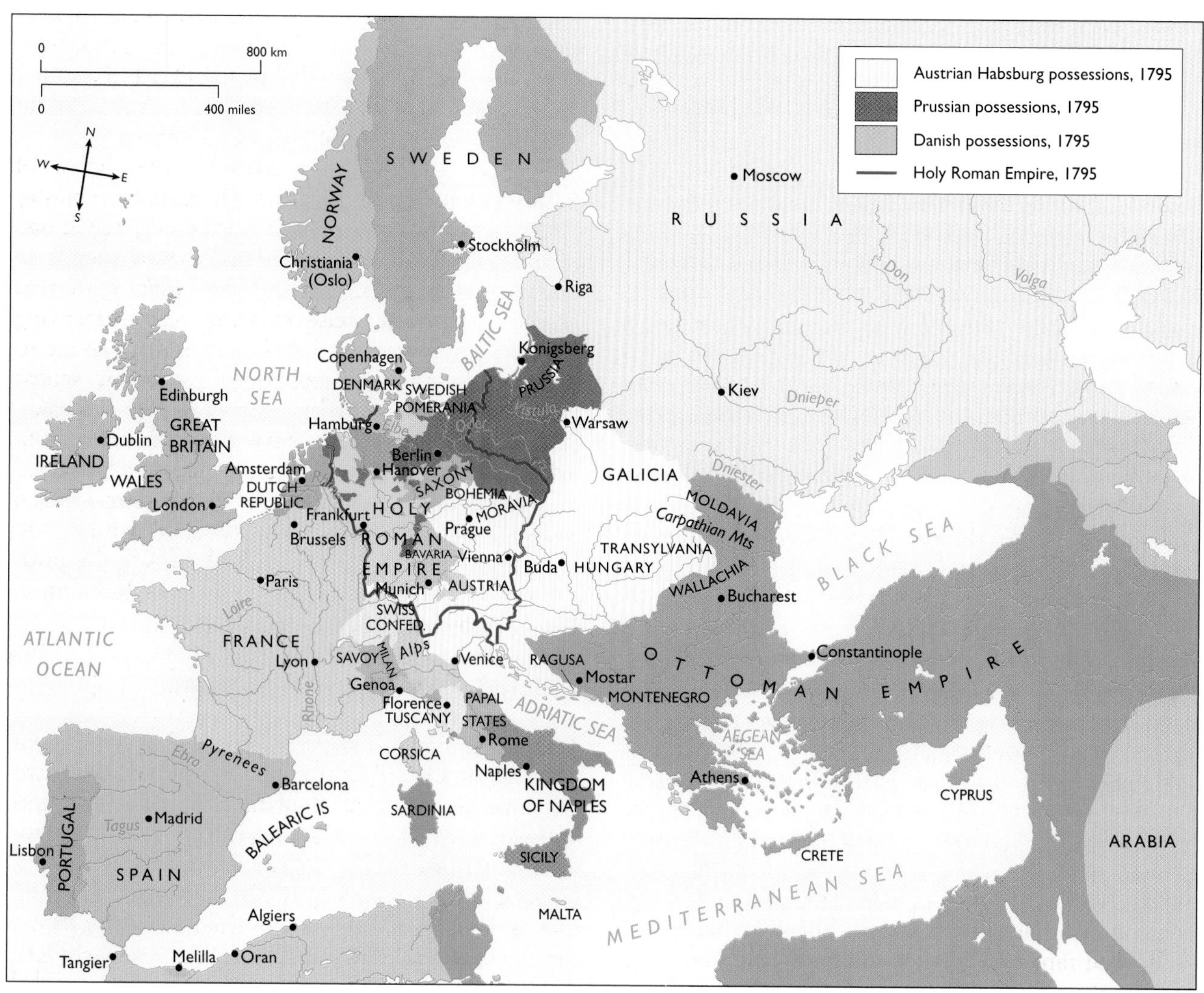

Map 15.2 The European States in 1795: *By 1795, France and England had fought their battles for supremacy, with France the loser in the global conflict that ended in 1763. Yet France remained a contender under its revolutionary leadership, and would soon strike out under Napoleon's leadership for hegemony in Europe. To the east the Ottoman Empire had weakened; Russia, Austria, and Prussia dominated the region, and by 1795 had partitioned and obliterated the enormous Polish state.*

The French kings were brilliantly served by their ministers Richelieu, Mazarin, and Colbert. It was the genius of the third Bourbon ruler, Louis XIV, himself to raise the monarchy to a new zenith of power. Already under Henry IV, the Estates-General had ceased to function. After 1614, when a fruitless meeting of the Estates-General was dismissed, it was not summoned again until 1789. Those 175 years mark the span of royal absolutism in France—its achievement due principally to Louis XIV.

The Sun King Louis was four years old when his father died. His mother, assisted by Mazarin, ruled in his stead. He was ten when the Peace of Westphalia was signed, preparing the ground for France's assumption of European leadership. In 1661, Mazarin died and Louis, aged twenty-two, undertook personal rule. He guided France until 1715, when he was succeeded by his great-grandson. At that point he had reigned for seventy-two years and outlived two generations, his sheer endurance unmatched by other monarchs. Heir to the achievements of Richelieu and Mazarin, Louis labored for the supremacy of France in Europe, and of the king within France.

Louis may have said, as it is reported, "I am the state." If so, it would have been an accurate statement of the role of the absolute monarch, in whom were centered all the capacities of the political realm. Louis's central role in the French state and culture was expressed visually as well as politically: in the architecture, gardens, and rituals of the royal complex he built at Versailles, twelve miles outside the ancient capital of Paris.

Beginning in the 1660s, Louis converted the small royal hunting lodge at Versailles into the most splendid palace in Europe. According to the statesman Montesquieu, there were "more statues in [the king's] palace gardens than there are citizens in a large town." Palace and gardens, 1400 fountains (fed by a river diverted from its natural course), a panoply of nobles, administrators, and servants (more than 10,000 in all) and nearly as many well-stabled horses—all served to furnish an image of royal grandiloquence. Ranks of courtiers and servants attended the king's daily acts, from waking up to eating dinner to strolling through the gardens or meeting with important officials. Their attendance in itself, their rank and privilege indicated by their dress and proximity to the king, was the business of the court, where all of life was a ceremony underscoring the importance of the king—*le Roi Soleil*, as he was called, "the Sun King." As the prestige of the king rose, the status of the aristocracy sank and the patterns of French culture—costume, behavior, and diet, as well as music, literature, drama, and dance—became the standard in the West.

As Louis gathered the tamed nobles of France at Versailles to dance and play, he centralized in his court the administration of justice and the determination of law, eroding the authority of regional courts and assemblies (the ***parlements*** and "estates"). To supervise affairs in the provinces, he dispatched bureaucrats called ***intendants***, directly responsible to the crown. Royal appointees were often men from the middle classes who had purchased both their office and a title of nobility. These were members of the "nobility of the robe," to distinguish them from the ancient "nobility of the sword." In a further assertion of royal authority, Louis repealed the Edict of Nantes. French Huguenots who wished to continue to worship as Protestants—among them many productive merchants and artisans—fled to the Dutch Republic, to England and to the Americas. An absolute monarch could not abide religious diversity.

In 1715, a child again ascended the throne of France—Louis XV (r. 1715–1774); again the country was governed by a regent. The aristocracy, which had been brought to heel by Louis XIV, now sought to recover their prestige and to curtail royal authority. The local *parlements* reasserted themselves, insisting on the right to register legislation and to assent to taxation. In this atmosphere of resurgent feudal claims, Louis XV and his grandson and successor, Louis XVI (r. 1774–1793), never enjoyed the absolute authority of their great ancestor. Louis XVI enlisted the aid of a series of capable and reform-minded finance ministers but never succeeded in winning the cooperation of the nobility. Indeed, he saw the principle of absolutism utterly defeated by the Revolution of 1789, which even cost him his life.

England: The Sharing of Power

The career of absolutism in England was different from the one it followed in Spain or France, for two principal reasons. First, England had a long tradition of the political rights of groups represented in its representative assembly, called Parliament. Second, England was, by the early 1600s, a Protestant nation; thus its kings could not bolster their authority, as did the Bourbon and Habsburg monarchs, by alignment with the Catholic Church. These realities tended against the accumulation of royal authority. Nevertheless, England achieved a strong, centralized monarchy; and, thereafter, a strong, centralized state, of which a limited monarch was titular head.

Gentile Bellini, **Muhammad II,** *c. 1480*

Warriors and Peacemakers

Hans Holbein, **The Ambassadors,** *1533*

Gentile Bellini's portrait (above left) from the life of Muhammad II, the Ottoman Turkish ruler who conquered Constantinople and destroyed the Byzantine Empire, depicts its subject as poised and statesmanlike, in retirement from battle.

The two splendidly attired ambassadors painted by Holbein (above right), experts in the avoidance of war, are surrounded by astronomical and musical instruments, appropriately remote from the field of battle.

In contrast, the bronze statue by Verrocchio of the Italian mercenary captain Bartolommeo Colleoni (below) epitomizes the early modern warrior possessed of power and determination.

(top left: National Gallery, London; top right: National Gallery, London)

Andrea del Verrocchio, **Bartolommeo Colleoni,** *Venice, c. 1481–1496*

In 1485, the first king of the Tudor line, Henry VII (r. 1485–1509), acquired not only a throne, but the job of patching together a nation torn by the Wars of the Roses, fought between claimants from the York and Lancaster families. He succeeded in this task, organizing national finances, promoting trade and exploration, avoiding foreign entanglements, subduing rebellious nobles, and establishing the court of Star Chamber as a central judicial authority.

In 1509, his son Henry VIII (r. 1509–1547) succeeded him. Supported by shrewd ministers, Henry VIII pursued his father's centralizing strategies (but not his fiscal prudence). His concerns about the succession led him into a controversial series of marriages—six in all. Four of his unlucky wives were dismissed or beheaded; one died, and one survived him. The surviving progeny of these marriages were two daughters and, the youngest, a son—all of whom would accede to the throne, in 1547, 1553, and 1558 respectively: Edward (d. 1553), son of Henry's third wife, Jane Seymour; Mary (d. 1558), daughter of his first wife, Catherine of Aragon; and Elizabeth (d. 1603), daughter of his second wife, Anne Boleyn.

Great controversy surrounded the dissolution by annulment of Henry's first marriage. To effect it, Henry repudiated the pope and had himself declared the "supreme governor" of the Church in England, precipitating the Reformation in that country. His role as head of the Church enhanced Henry's authority. Later, religious controversy would flare up several times under his successors.

A child during most of his six-year reign (he died at fifteen), Edward VI was unable himself to act to shape the English monarchy. His advisers tended to the business of foreign affairs and the establishment of Protestant Christianity in England. On Edward's premature death, their labors on behalf of a Protestant Church were rendered futile. The young king's elder half sister Mary succeeded, having been passed over earlier in favor of the male heir. Granddaughter of Ferdinand and Isabella, raised by her mother an earnest Catholic, and married the year after her succession to the zealous Philip II of Spain, Mary sought to reestablish Catholicism in England. This attempt was thwarted by her death and the accession of Henry VIII's middle child, Elizabeth, whom Catholics considered illegitimate.

Elizabeth overcame this liability and that of her sex in a forty-five year reign that is among the most remarkable in all of European history. A moderate Protestant, a classical scholar, and an extraordinarily intelligent leader, Elizabeth completed the task of forging an absolute monarchy begun by her Tudor forebears. Guided but not overshadowed by her very effective covey of ministers—notably Sir William Cecil (1520–1598), Sir Francis Walsingham (c. 1532–1590), and Robert Cecil (1563–1612)—she clarified the nature of English Protestantism, rallied popular support in foreign affairs, and guided financial and judicial institutions. Refusing to marry, she was able even as a woman to maintain authority in her own person and to command the respect of people and Parliament alike. Meanwhile, England's naval successes and deft diplomacy brought it recognition as a major nation.

In 1587, Elizabeth reluctantly authorized the execution—after eighteen years of imprisonment—of her cousin Mary Stuart (r. 1542–1567), the exiled queen of Scotland. (A Catholic with French ties, Mary was implicated in plots against Elizabeth just at the moment when Spain was planning to launch its Armada against England.) On her deathbed, in 1603, Elizabeth named as her successor the son of the woman she had executed, James VI, the reigning king of Scotland. As James I (r. 1603–1625), he assumed the thrones of England and Ireland as well, becoming the first of England's Stuart dynasty.

Twice a king, James was an advocate of absolutism in theory and reached for it in practice. As king in Scotland, he established royal authority over warring Protestant lords, his mother's Catholic friends and kin, and leaders of the Calvinist (called Presbyterian in Scotland) church. An author and scholar, he wrote in defense of royal absolutism: *The True Law of Free Monarchy*. In England, he chose to challenge or evade the authority of Parliament, acquiring the funds to manage the state and his lavish court from unpopular customs taxes or grants of monopoly.

The Parliament James antagonized included a growing number of Puritan representatives who were critical of the practices of the established Anglican Church. He also antagonized Catholics, who sought an amelioration of the civil disabilities under which they suffered. And the flagrant immorality of his court aroused general disapproval. Serious tensions persisted when James died in 1625 and his son Charles I (r. 1625–1649) succeeded.

Civil War and Commonwealth Married to a French Catholic Bourbon Charles soon revealed a tendency toward absolutism and was suspected of favoring his wife's religion. Whether or not that was so, he certainly did his best to impose the Anglican faith upon all of his subjects. His ministers took repressive measures against nonconforming Protestants, and angered the Presbyterian Scots to the point of armed rebellion. Charles followed his father's lead in relations with Parliament, ignoring it when it did not vote him funds and, not long after the French king's dissolution of the Estates-General, dismissing it altogether in 1629. Eleven years later, desperate for funds, he recalled Parliament. In 1642, Parliament demanded greater powers, including approval of the king's ministers. Charles raised his military standard against Parliament.

At least some of the members of the Parliament that assembled in 1640—called the Long Parliament—continued to meet until 1653 (after 1649, consisting of a remnant of some 100 members, it was called the "Rump" Parliament). They presided over a war between royalists and parliamentarians, and between Anglicans and other Protestants, which permanently changed the course of government in England. In 1649, the victorious parliamentarians created a High Court of Justice, which tried Charles for treason and condemned him to death. His execution followed. At the very moment of the triumph of royal absolutism on the Continent, the English had demonstrated the superiority of assemblies to kings. Although Charles I's sons would later reach for absolute power, the possibility of establishing such power in England had been gravely wounded.

In 1653, the leader of the parliamentary army, Oliver Cromwell (1599–1658), engineered his own elevation to "Lord Protector" of the new Commonwealth of England under a written constitution called the Instrument of Government. Cromwell enforced Puritan policies that suppressed, among other activities, theatrical performances and Sunday games on the village green. He repressed political dissent, such as that offered by the sectarian Ranters and Quakers, and harshly persecuted the Irish, whose religion and culture he attempted to crush. He did, however, favor religious tolerance within a Protestant community. Generally hated, Cromwell was a curious amalgam of religious zeal and military skill, a dictator who had destroyed a monarch. At his death in 1658, Englishmen from all sectors turned from his path and looked forward to the Restoration of the monarchy, which was accomplished in 1660.

Kings and Queens

Anonymous, Elizabeth I: *The kings and queens of Europe were the subjects of celebratory art. This sixteenth-century "Rainbow Portrait" of Elizabeth I shows her possessing the authority of a ruler, youthful despite increasing age.* (Hatfield House, Hertfordshire; Courtesy, Marquess of Salisbury)

Restoration and "Glorious Revolution" The Stuart line returned in the person of Charles II (r. 1660–1685), son of the executed Charles I. Mindful of the need to conciliate parliamentary opponents, Charles agreed to all the demands made by those groups—including a general amnesty to nearly all of those who had opposed and killed his father. He further conciliated both elites and people by setting a new cultural tone. During the Restoration, as the years of his reign are called, Puritan repression ended and the quest for pleasure was back in fashion.

Nevertheless, in the course of his reign Charles repeated the patterns that had led to friction before. He tended to Roman Catholicism, to a pro-French foreign policy, to noncooperation with Parliament, and to absolutism. Worse, as Charles had no legitimate children, his successor was his brother James, an avowed Catholic. One parliamentary faction, called "Whig," called for the exclusion of James from that inheritance, while another, called "Tory," supported the king. James in fact succeeded on Charles' death in 1685, with little opposition.

But Tories and Whigs joined in opposition to James II when, in 1688, his wife gave birth to a son, assuring the continuance of a Roman Catholic monarchy. Parliamentary leaders offered the throne jointly to Mary II (r. 1689–1694), James's elder and

Francisco de Goya, Family of Charles IV: *A more critical portrayal of a king and queen is seen in Goya's depiction of the Spanish royal family in 1800. The opulence of attire of Charles IV and his family does not disguise a weakness of intellect and will.* (Prado, Madrid)

Protestant daughter, and her husband William III, the Prince of Orange (r. 1689–1702), zealous opponent of French expansionism in the Netherlands. William arrived with his army, the king's commanders disbanded, and James took refuge in France. These events constitute the "Glorious Revolution," a bloodless rechanneling of authority in perfect contrast to the Civil War which had resulted in the execution of a king and the elevation of a dictator.

By accepting Parliament's Declaration of Right of 1689, William and Mary accepted, as a condition of their joint rule, limits on monarchical power articulated in the Bill of Rights (also 1689). The Bill of Rights reaffirmed constitutional principles that had developed over the previous few stormy decades, providing that the king would not be able to suspend a law of Parliament nor raise taxes nor maintain an army without parliamentary consent; nor could any subject be arrested without full due legal process. Furthermore, the throne would pass to the descendants in turn of Mary and her younger sister Anne; but no Roman Catholic could ever succeed to the English monarchy. The Act of Settlement of 1701 reaffirmed these principles and extended the provisions for the succession. The Toleration Act in the same year protected the rights of non-Anglican Protestants to worship, though it continued to exclude them from political office—as Catholics had been so excluded since the Test Act of 1673. The guarantees in these key documents were added to the traditional rights of Englishmen inherited from medieval custom.

By the complicated events of the 1600s, the government of England achieved a delicate but fruitful balance between the king and Parliament, and of both with the established Anglican Church. The king could not hold absolute power, but would yield to decisions of Parliament. Kings and public officials could be neither Catholics nor non-Anglican Protestant dissenters, although private worship was tolerated (not, however, in Ireland, where Catholicism was illegal and vital). Even Jews, expelled from England in 1290, had been permitted by Cromwell to return without conversion.

Over the next century, the struggle between kings and Parliament gave way to a government dominated by political parties, prominent ministers, and the policies of the Bank of England. Great Britain in the eighteenth century, under the last Stuart monarch, Anne, and the first three kings of the House of Hanover, all Georges, was a different world from that ruled by Stuart kings before 1688.

Three New Empires: The Reshaping of Eastern Europe

The Thirty Years' War left central and eastern Europe in fragments. The Holy Roman Empire was a mere shell. Its more than 300 component cities and principalities, populated largely by German speakers, proceeded to develop independently. To the east of a line formed by the Elbe River and the mountains of Bohemia, largely Slavic and Hungarian peoples lived under Polish, Russian, or Ottoman overlordship.

After 1648, three strong monarchies expanded to fill the vacuum of authority in central and eastern Europe—Austria, Prussia, and Russia.

Austria The Habsburg family had long ruled the principality of Austria and had held the title of Holy Roman Emperor since 1438. By 1714, these Austrian rulers had added to their title sovereignty over Bohemia, Hungary, and parts of the Balkans (wrested from the Ottoman Turks by 1699), as well as, in the west, the southern Netherlands, parts of Italy, and some Mediterranean possessions (taken from Spain). They were emperors over many different peoples who spoke different languages, practiced different religions, and possessed very different historical traditions.

Although Habsburg rulers managed this disparate empire with skill, it continually threatened to disintegrate. Ethnic rivalries among Magyars, Germans, Czechs, Poles, Croatians, and Italians were inevitable. Religious tensions were severe. Austria had been re-Catholicized during the Thirty Years' War, and now imposed strict Catholic uniformity in all of its possessions. Yet the Polish and Czech nobility had strong Protestant leanings, and Eastern Orthodox (and later Muslim) subjects in the Balkans resisted Catholic preeminence. Partly to win over the landowning classes, Habsburg rulers permitted the enserfment or reenserfment of the peasantry, now an oppressed group perpetually liable to restlessness and revolt.

With the Pragmatic Sanction of 1713, Charles VI attempted to guarantee the inheritance of his daughter and only heir, Maria Theresa (r. 1740–1780). Yet on her succession in 1740, she faced the aggressions of other European states which little respected a female ruler when there was so much land to be had. Nevertheless, Maria Theresa managed to hold the bulk of her lands and even acquired additional territory by the first partition of Poland in 1772.

By that date Maria Theresa was ruling jointly with her son Joseph II (r. 1765–1790). After her death in 1780, Joseph ruled alone. He continued his mother's policy of centralizing authority, attempting agrarian reforms, and making the capital, Vienna, a center for the arts and learning. But he attempted more fundamental reforms than his mother would have countenanced. These included, notably, the abolition of serfdom in 1781; the creation of a civil service based on the principle of merit; and the reform of the justice system, including the abolition of torture and capital punishment. These and other of Joseph's projects aroused opposition and were suspended after his death in 1790.

Prussia By the time of Joseph's death, Prussia was overtaking Austria as the major power of the fading Holy Roman Empire. Piecing together the small states of Brandenburg, Prussia, and Pomerania, lands scattered across the southern coast of the Baltic Sea, the "Great Elector" Frederick William (r. 1640–1688) had assembled a small nation. He had also built up a mighty army to defend it. His successor was granted the title "King in Prussia" in 1701 and reigned as Frederick I (r. 1688–1713). Frederick's son Frederick William I (r. 1713–1740) continued in his grandfather's path, hoarding his wealth, promoting the landowning class, from which he drew his officers, and modernizing and expanding the army.

These achievements were the inheritance of his son, the capable Frederick II, the Great (r. 1740–1786). The edifice of Prussian power rested on the army. Civil servants, the middle class, the serfs, were all subordinate to its needs and to the will of the aristocracy, who led an enormous military force consisting of 200,000 soldiers out of a population of only 6 million. The prince who ruled this successful state was also a flute-player and author of note, who corresponded easily with the finest minds of the age and shared their skeptical spirit. An absolute monarch himself, Frederick thought little of the theory of the divine right of kings (see below).

Russia By the time of Frederick the Great, Russia had developed from the medieval duchy of Muscovy to become a modern state, governed by an absolute ruler. Having won independence from their Mongol overlords after 1480, the grand princes of Muscovy continued a policy of annexing adjacent territories. Under Ivan III, called "the Great" (r. 1462–1505), and Ivan IV, called "the Terrible" (r. 1533–1584), the new state of Russia became a powerful kingdom. The "Terrible" Ivan earned his designation by crushing the traditional landowner caste, the boyars, installing his own supporters as territorial lords, and supplying them with serfs. He further inspired fear when he established a corps of state spies, the *oprichniki*, the ancestor of the much-hated tsarist political police of the nineteenth century; and when, in 1581, he killed his own son in a fit of rage. Viewing himself as the heir to the Roman and Byzantine empires, Ivan had himself proclaimed "tsar" ("caesar") at his coronation in 1547. Anarchy followed his death in 1584, but in 1613, the establishment of the Romanov dynasty, destined to rule until 1917, restored stability.

Traditionally eastward-looking because of its history and because of its Orthodox Christianity, Russia turned westward under Peter I, "the Great" (r. 1682–

WHO'S WHO

Europe's Rulers in an Era of Concentrating Power, I

Charles V (r. 1519–1556, d. 1558) Habsburg emperor who briefly ruled much of Europe from the Iberian peninsula to the Ottoman border, including Italian possessions and Mediterranean islands, and much of the New World in addition.

Philip II (r. 1556–1598) Habsburg king of Spain, who from his monastic fortress (the Escorial) reigned over a Spanish Empire reaching to the New World and Italy, and defended Spanish naval supremacy and Atlantic monopoly.

Elizabeth I, "the Great" (r. 1558–1603) Queen of England who presided over the Anglican religious settlement, victory over the Spanish Armada, and the New World exploration.

Gustavus Adolphus (r. 1611–1632) King of Sweden who led reorganized Swedish army in Thirty Years' War.

Louis XIV (r. 1643–1715) King of France and patron of the court of Versailles, who best illustrates the concept of "absolute monarch," reportedly claiming: "I am the State."

Oliver Cromwell (r. 1653–1658) Parliamentary leader in English Civil War; subsequently, as Lord Protector, uncrowned ruler of England.

1725). From 1689, when he ended the regency of his mother, Peter guided Russia to participation in the European cultural realm. He promoted the commercial and intellectual innovations of the West in order to develop the skills Russia needed to become a modern, sovereign state. The Church, too, was put under his control. He suppressed the old landed nobility and created a new aristocratic elite, subservient to the tsar but granted extraordinary powers over their serfs, who, since 1675, were reduced to the condition of slaves; that is, they could be bought and sold separately from the land. He required the sons of the nobles to gain a Western education, and directed the printing presses to publish newspapers and books like those read in such cities as Paris and London. He created a Baltic fleet, completely rebuilt the army, and encouraged industry (while punishing financial failure). Totally ruthless, he had his own son and heir condemned to death when that young man balked at the Tsar's cultural revolution.

By the time of Peter the Great, Russia had swollen far beyond the limits of old Muscovy. It extended eastward to the region of the Volga River, dominating the Asian descendants of the once-victorious Mongols, called Tatars. Passing the Ural Mountains, Russia reached still father across the arc of northern Asia into Siberia and to the Pacific shore. Pushing northward into the region of the Baltic Sea, it faced Sweden, which it stripped of vital territory in the Great Northern War (1700–1721). Here Peter constructed a new capital, facing west across the Gulf of Finland, named after himself: Saint Petersburg.

Pushing southward to the Black Sea, gateway to the Mediterranean, Russia faced Tatar chiefs who paid tribute to Ottoman Turkish rulers. To the west, it bordered the regions of Belarus and Ukraine, then under Polish domination. Much of this territory it acquired by the three eighteenth-century partitions of Poland accomplished under the most capable of Peter's successors, Catherine II, called "the Great" (r. 1762–1796).

A German princess by birth, Catherine came to the throne by the assassination of her husband, the grandson of Peter the Great. Although at first a committed reformer, seriously educated in political thought, she nevertheless worked to enhance the nobility's power over their serfs, at the same time insisting upon their obedience to herself. In foreign affairs she succeeded in expanding Russia's presence in the Middle East, and she acquired land from both Poland and the Ottoman Empire, including a precious outlet on the Black Sea. Considered an "enlightened" monarch, like her contemporaries in Austria and Prussia, Catherine, too, retained absolute power.

By the late eighteenth century, Europe was unique in being largely organized into nation-states (sovereign states containing a population linked by language, ethnicity, or history), and most Europeans were the subjects of monarchs who ruled, or wished to rule, absolutely. Of the continent's major political units, only Venice, the Swiss cantons, and the Dutch republic were not monarchies. Britain, though a monarchy, was a limited one, its king hedged around with constitutional restrictions. Yet although this was an age of kings, the forces that would someday dethrone them were already gathering strength.

MIRRORS FOR PRINCES

In the thirteenth century, the saintly French King Louis IX (r. 1226–1270) had administered justice in a grove of trees, reclining against a great oak to hear the petitions of his subjects. In the seventeenth, his successor the "Sun King" Louis XIV was surrounded by circles of advisers and bureaucrats, laws and institutions, rituals and splendor. The four centuries that lie between saw the development of the notion of monarchy and the apparatus of the court—and, concurrently, the arguments for resistance to unjust power, and the theories of natural law and inborn rights that would in time dismantle both.

The Idea of the Prince

Almost as soon as kings appeared in Europe, writers began telling them how to rule. The same university-trained clerics who wrote on philosophy and theology wrote works on the ideal king. These "mirrors for princes," as they were called, urged moral values on the ruler: he should be kind, just, generous. The prince or king was to look into such books and see a perfected image of himself, which he was to emulate.

The idealized model of kingship projected by these works was remote from kingship in the flesh. Medieval monarchy had rested largely on force—military, judicial, personal. A theoretical understanding of the role of the sovereign, the figure in whom all authority resided, had not yet crystallized. Still less had the idea of the state as an abstract entity served by the king for the benefit of the people. From the fourteenth through seventeenth centuries, these concepts developed, culminating in the theoretical model of absolute monarchy.

The struggle between popes and emperors, originating in the eleventh century, stimulated in the fourteenth works challenging the notion of papal supremacy. Political theorists such as John of Jandun, Marsilius of Padua, and William of Ockham, as well as the poet Dante Alighieri aimed to free politics from papal ambitions and proposed the model of a universal monarchy. They observed that rulers operated in a realm of necessity separate from the realm of spirit, and made the decisions most beneficial to the state. These theories helped dismantle the secular authority of the papacy, which had peaked in the previous two centuries, and paved the way for the development of discrete secular monarchies in the two that followed.

Machiavelli's lawless prince, with whom this chapter opened, enters into consideration here. Italy, the arena where the struggle between pope and emperor took place, had no national monarchy until the nineteenth century. It was a patchwork of autonomous city republics and principalities. This region of fragmented authority and endemic violence was the context for Machiavelli's prince, a figure representing an abrupt departure from medieval tradition. He was to act unburdened by piety, compassion, or ideals of any sort. He was calculating, opportunistic, and ambitious for power. His aim was only to secure his state; the purpose of the state merely to exist, to avert conquest by another prince.

Machiavelli's contemporary Erasmus developed his own conception of the ideal monarch, in his *Education of the Christian Prince*, as well as in other treatises and letters. Like the subject of the medieval mirrors for princes, that figure was to be just, well-advised, and all-provident. But he had particularly Erasmian features, in addition: he would have a classical education, he would avoid war at all costs, and he would support with special diligence the productive middling and poorer citizens of his state. Erasmus's prince resembles not at all his Machiavellian counterpart.

Although Erasmus and Machiavelli differed in their view of the ideal monarch, they agreed that the modern world required a modern type of monarch. For Machiavelli, that new monarch, the "prince," would need to be ruthlessly focused on the problem of maintaining his power. For Erasmus, he would need to assume increased cultural, social, and economic responsibilities, and his ability to perform these primary duties would be jeopardized by the enormous costs of warfare.

Both were right. The ideal of the monarch developed by later sixteenth- and seventeenth-century theorists had both Machiavellian and Erasmian dimensions. The monarch would be truly sovereign,

HOW MANY?

European Wars, 1500–1763

The Italian Wars: 1494–1559 (Italian states, Papacy, Habsburg armies, France)

Dutch wars of independence: 1579–1648 (Provinces of Northern Netherlands, Spain)

Thirty Years' War: 1618–1648 (States of Holy Roman Empire [Bohemia, Palatinate], France, Austrian Habsburg Empire, Sweden)

English Civil War: 1642–1651 (England [Parliamentary and Royalist forces], Scotland)

War of the Spanish Succession: 1701–1714 (Spain, France, England, Netherlands)

Seven Years' War: 1756–1763 (Spain, France, England, Netherlands)

concentrating in himself all authority and pursuing all means necessary to further the interests of the state. At the same time, he would set standards in the cultural realm, promote the economic welfare of his subjects, secure peace and administer justice, and serve in his person as the symbol of national unity. He was an absolute monarch, who ruled by divine right.

The notion of the "divine right of kings" is implicit in the medieval worldview, with its hierarchies of perfection culminating in God. It was but a step more to declare that the king in his kingdom was comparable to God in the universe. Answering only to God, an absolute monarch might free himself of the laws passed by parliaments or urged by the Church or embodied in traditional customs. The king himself, deriving his powers from God, was the embodiment of law.

The French philosopher Jean Bodin (1530–1596) presented a classic statement of the theory of absolute monarchy in his *Six Books of the Commonwealth* of 1576. Just as families fell naturally under the authority of the father (a definition of patriarchy), so communities of families fell under the authority of the state and its prince. The sovereign power could maintain peace, make laws, ensure justice, promote well-being. He was not all-powerful, but was limited, like his subjects, by natural law. Those subjects, too, had their rights, which the monarch was to respect. Bodin's theory implies the notion of an abstract state, a sovereign power embodied in the monarch but conceivable without him as an independent entity.

In his *Politics Drawn from the Very Words of Scripture* published posthumously in 1709, another Frenchman, Bishop Jacques-Bénigne Bossuet (1627–1704), allowed kings more authority than did Bodin. As God's representatives on earth, kings naturally produced judgments that were reasonable and just, like the will of God. So long as the king conformed to the divine law that reigned over all, what he willed, in the secular state, was the law itself. Bossuet put into words the assumptions of power made by his own prince, Louis XIV.

Across the English Channel, too, the monarch's claims for absolute power were voiced—as in the *True Law of Free Monarchy* written in 1598 by James VI of Scotland, the future James I of England. James argued for the elevation of the king's will over Parliament, law, and custom. It was precisely such a claim that caused English absolutism to fail in the next generation, when Parliament dispatched monarchy for eleven years and absolute monarchy forever.

Yet in 1651, amid the throes of that revolution, the *Leviathan* (a reference to the Biblical monster appearing in the Book of Job, chapter 41) of Thomas Hobbes (1588–1679) promoted a different kind of absolutism: that of the state itself. Viewing human nature in an infamously negative light, Hobbes argued that people allowed their freedom would descend to anarchy, corruption, and violence—a "state of war." They must be reined in by a "Leviathan," a stern and vigilant government (not necessarily a king), to which they voluntarily conferred their obedience in an implicit contract. Thenceforth, the state would order the lives of those made desperate because their existence was, in Hobbes' memorably succinct and sad expression, "solitary, poor, nasty, brutish, and short."

WHO'S WHO

Europe's Rulers in an Era of Concentrating Power, II

Peter I, "the Great" (r. 1682–1725) Tsar of Russia who labored on political, commercial, and cultural fronts to bring Russia into the world of western European nations.

Frederick II, "the Great" (r. 1740–1786) King of Prussia who continued to build his nation's military strength and who struck aggressively to annex further European territory.

Maria Theresa (r. 1740–1780) Habsburg Queen of the Austrian Empire, who struggled to secure and expand the multinational state left her by her father.

Catherine II, "the Great" (r. 1762–1796) German-born Tsar of Russia who extended her nation's boundaries, invited *philosophes* to St. Petersburg, and established a school for girls (see Chapter 17).

The "Monstrous Regiment of Women" As theoreticians elevated the status of the king, the question of female monarchy was reexamined. What if the heir to the throne were a woman? A woman, it was believed, was unfit to rule. She would be fickle, deceitful, incapable of leading an army, obsessed with male relationships. In France, women were legally barred from ascending the throne.

Yet the early modern era boasts many female rulers. Isabella of Castile presided jointly with her husband, Ferdinand, over the *Reconquista* and the Spanish expansion into the New World. The British Isles saw three women rulers in the sixteenth century alone: Mary I, Elizabeth I, and their cousin Mary, Queen of Scots. In seventeenth-century Sweden, Christina (r. 1632–1654; d. 1689) succeeded her father Gustavus Adolphus. In the eighteenth century, Russia had four reigning empresses: Catherine I, Anna, Elizabeth, and Catherine II. The empress Maria Theresa (r. 1740–1780) ruled the disparate German, Hungarian, and Balkan areas of the Habsburg empire. In France, where a woman could not reign, Catherine de' Medici, Marie de' Medici, and Anne of Austria all ruled France as regents for their sons, its future kings.

WITNESSES

A King's Right to Rule

Jean Bodin argues the king's right to impose laws without consent (1576): On the other hand it is the distinguishing mark of the sovereign that he cannot in any way be subject to the commands of another, for it is he who makes law for the subject, abrogates law already made, and amends obsolete law. No one who is subject either to the law or to some other person can do this. That is why it is laid down in the civil law [Roman law] that the prince is above the law, for the word *law* in Latin implies the command of him who is invested with sovereign power. . . . From all of this it is clear that the principal mark of sovereign majesty and absolute power is the right to impose laws generally on all subjects regardless of their consent. . . .

(Jean Bodin, *Six Books of the Commonwealth*, 1576, 1:8, 10; ed. R. Brown, 1990)

Jacques-Bénigne Bossuet claims that kings are God's ministers on earth (1678): It is God who establishes kings. . . . Princes thus act as ministers of God and His lieutenants on earth. It is through them that he rules. . . . This is why we have seen that the royal throne is not the throne of a man, but the throne of God himself. . . . It appears from this that the person of kings is sacred, and to move against them is sacrilege. . . . Since their power comes from on high, kings should not believe that they are its masters and may use it as they wish; they should exercise it with fear and restraint as a thing which has come to them from God, and for which God will demand an account. . . .

Therefore let them respect their power, since is not theirs but the power of God, and must be used holily and religiously.

(Jacques-Bénigne Bossuet, *Politiques tirées des propres paroles de L'Ecriture sainte*, 1678; ed. W. F. Church, 1984)

Facing the imminent ascension of Elizabeth I to the throne of England (in the wake of Queen Mary I) and with his native Scotland under the titular rule of Mary Stuart, the Protestant reformer John Knox (c. 1514–1572) wrote, in 1558, his *First Blast of the Trumpet against the Monstrous Regiment of Women*. For Knox, women were defects in nature, and rule by women was a hideous contradiction in terms. Assembling the misogynist views of ancient philosophers, pagan poets, the Bible, and Church Fathers, he thundered that the English and Scottish nobility were worse than "brute beasts" for tolerating female sovereignty: "for that they do to women which no male amongst the common sort of beasts can be proved to do to their female, that is, they reverence them, and quake at their presence; they obey their commandments, and that against God."

In order to withstand such criticism, women who ruled often adopted the guise of androgyny. Queen Elizabeth I of England played with such male/female images—positive ones, of course—in representing herself to her subjects. She was a prince, and manly, she asserted, even though she was female. She was also (she claimed) a virgin, a condition absolutely essential if she were to avoid the attacks of her opponents, for whom female nature always inclined to lust. In her last years, she defied the limits of female sexual identification. "My sex," she said, a few weeks before her death, "cannot diminish my prestige."

Catherine de' Medici skirted the boundaries of male and female identifications in the imagery she adopted to define her position. She chose as one symbol the figure of Artemisia, an androgynous ancient warrior-heroine, who combined a female persona with masculine powers. Thus clothed in androgynous imagery, these women rulers could, like their male counterparts, claim to be princes and absolute sovereigns.

Some later female rulers readily acknowledged and even exploited their gender. Maria Theresa, devoted to her wayward husband and to her thirteen children, was the embodiment of the motherly queen, while at the same time being an outstanding monarch. Catherine the Great indulged her own sexual appetites with the same freedom shown by male monarchs, taking numerous lovers—but never allowing them to distract her from affairs of state.

Halls of Mirrors

Just as political philosophers developed the theory of absolute monarchy, architects designed spaces in which those monarchs might display their power.

On grand staircases and in splendid reception rooms, such as the huge Hall of Mirrors built for Louis XIV at Versailles (and imitated in other royal courts) the king shone in glory; and those gathered around him, like glass, reflected his brilliant image. In addition to the crowds of courtiers pressing forward to catch a glimpse of majesty, the monarch was attended by poets and playwrights, composers and painters, all competing for the honor (and financial rewards) of royal patronage.

During the Middle Ages, as before, events of importance to the community had been celebrated with processions—solemn ritual marches, featuring a display of special objects. In the early modern era, kings adapted the ritual device of the procession to their purposes. When a ruler was scheduled to enter a city, a team of artists, architects, and mechanics constructed props and scenery to make the arrival more imposing. Costume, music, and the careful choreography of the prince's retinue also enhanced the effect.

In the prince's private dwelling, too, sound, imagery, and movement were designed to reflect the sovereign's power. The paintings on the wall, the carving of the furniture, the patterns of the glass in the window, or the carpet on the floor—all could be designed to label the space inhabited by the prince. Throughout the Middle Ages, works of art and literature had been mainly religious, whether commissioned by the Church or by a private individual. In the early modern age, in the precincts of royal power, to communicate the authority and prestige of the prince was itself the business of the arts.

To convey their grandeur, kings built palaces increasingly distinct, in size and magnificence, from the homes of the subjects they ruled. Both the Escorial, near Madrid, and Versailles, near Paris, were not mere palaces, but immense complexes engineered to express the raw fact of royal power. The Austrian princes built palaces of commensurate grandeur and Peter the Great, of Russia, built a whole city, Saint Petersburg, in his image. Even the dukes and despots of Italy and the petty German princes of the Holy Roman Empire surrounded themselves with splendor.

The arrogance of royal power is nowhere expressed so eloquently as in these palaces, whose purpose was frankly not to live or to rule but to overawe. The claim to absolute power made by the kings of Europe and portrayed in stone, glass, and gilding would be challenged by other currents of early modern culture. In time these new ideas would variously reshape monarchy or abolish it, and would make of those palaces what most of them are today: museums, displaying the customs and values of a remote past.

WITNESSES

A Queen's Right to Rule

John Knox blasts his trumpet against rule by women (1558): The empire of a Woman is a thing repugnant to Nature. . . . For who can deny but it is repugnant to nature, that the blind shall be appointed to lead and conduct such as do see? That the weak, the sick, and impotent persons shall nourish and keep the whole and strong? And finally, that the foolish, mad, and frenetic shall govern the discrete, and give counsel to such as be sober of mind? And such be all women, compared unto man in bearing of authority. For their sight in civil regiment is but blindness; their strength, weakness; their counsel, foolishness; and judgment, frenzy, if it be rightly considered.

(John Knox, *The First Blast of the Trumpet against the Monstrous Regiment of Women*, 1558; ed. D. Laing, 1864, modernized)

Queen Elizabeth addresses the troops encamped at Tilbury (9 August 1588), asserting her sovereignty even in a military situation—the naval battle against the Spanish Armada had commenced–where her enemies might hope she would weaken: I know I have the body but of a weak and feeble woman; but I have the heart and stomach of a king, and of a king of England too, and think foul scorn that Parma or Spain or any prince of Europe should dare to invade the borders of my realm; to which, rather than any dishonor should grow by me, I myself will take up arms; I myself will be your general, judge, and rewarder of every one of your virtues in the field. . . not doubting but by your obedience to my general, by your concord in the camp, and your valor in the field, we shall shortly have a famous victory over those enemies of my God, of my kingdoms, and of my people.

(Elizabeth I, "To the Troops at Tilbury, 1588"; ed. G. P. Rice, Jr., 1951)

Roman Law and Natural Right

As European monarchs accumulated power and as writers and artists celebrated it, traditions of law evolved that variously supported or undermined royal claims to authority. Concepts of natural right, based on both legal and philosophical traditions, also emerged to pose a challenge to political absolutism.

When Roman authority evaporated in the fifth century C.E., the peoples of Europe outside the old Empire—Celtic, Germanic, and Slavic—continued to follow the customs of their ancestors: tribal law. These customs satisfactorily regulated community life and disciplined criminal behavior so long as those communities remained simple. As tribes and villages became incorporated into nations, the increased complexity of life required the development of more complex systems of law. In many parts of western Europe, the sophisticated apparatus of Roman law, which had served the needs of the largest empire of the ancient Mediterranean world, was drawn upon to alter and even replace customary law.

While medieval philosophers fitted the concepts of Christian theology into the framework of Aristotelian metaphysics, medieval jurists studied the *Code* of Justinian. Centered at Bologna from the twelfth century, a series of jurists wrote commentaries showing how Roman law could be applied to the patterns of Christian society and medieval communities. Soon Roman legal concepts were employed by the advisers to the kings of Europe. Roman law had been developed for a state in which power was centered in a ruler, the emperor. Its concepts were now useful to kings seeking tools by which to discipline their nobility, administer their states, and become "emperors" in their own lands. Indeed, the very concept of a "state" was made available in the language of Roman law. It was the precondition of the further development of the nations of Europe.

WITNESSES

The Origins of Government in the Consent of the Citizens

Thomas Hobbes shows how all citizens consent to the sovereign power (1651): II.17. The only way to erect such a common power, as may be able to defend [men] from the invasion of foreigners, and the injuries of one another, and thereby to secure them in such sort, as that by their own industry, and by the fruits of the earth, they may nourish themselves and live contentedly, is, to confer all their power and strength upon one man, or upon one assembly of men, that may reduce all their wills, by plurality of voices, unto one will. . . . This is more than consent, or concord; it is a real unity of them all, in one and the same person, made by covenant of every man, in such manner, as if every man should say to every man, "I authorize and give up my right of governing myself, to this man, or to this assembly of men, on this condition, that thou give up thy right to him, and authorize all his actions in like manner." This done, the multitude so united in one person is called a "commonwealth," in Latin *civitas*. This is the generation of that great LEVIATHAN, or rather, to speak more reverently, of that "mortal god," to which we owe under the "immortal God," our peace and defence. For by this authority, given him by every particular man in the commonwealth, he has the use of so much power and strength conferred on him, that by terror thereof, he is enabled to perform the wills of them all, to peace at home, and mutual aid against their enemies abroad. And in him consists the essence of the commonwealth . . . .

And he that carries this person is called "sovereign," and is said to have "sovereign power"; and every one besides, his "subject."

(Thomas Hobbes, *Leviathan*, 1651, 2:17; ed. E. Weber, 1990)

John Locke explains why people will surrender their freedom to form civil government (1690): Men, being, as has been said, by nature all free, equal, and independent, no one can be put out of this estate and subjected to the political power of another without his own consent. The only way whereby anyone divests himself of his own natural liberty and puts on the bonds of civil society, is by agreeing with other men, to join and unite into a community for their comfortable, safe and peaceable living one among another, in a secure enjoyment of their properties, and a greater security against any that are not of it. . . . When any number of men have so consented to make one community or government, they are thereby presently incorporated, and make one body politic, wherein the majority have a right to act and conclude the rest. . . .

If man in the state of nature be so free as has been said. . . why will he part with his freedom? Why will he give up this empire, and subject himself to the dominion and control of any other power? To which it is obvious to answer, that though in the state of nature he has such a right, yet the enjoyment of it is very uncertain. . . . This makes him willing to quit this condition which, however free, is full of fears and continual dangers; and it is not without reason that he seeks out and is willing to join in society with others who. . . unite for the mutual preservation of their lives, liberties and estates, which I call by the general name—property.

The great and chief end, therefore, of men uniting into commonwealths, and putting themselves under government, is the preservation of their property. . . .

(John Locke, *The Second Treatise on Government*, 1690; ed. E. Weber, 1990)

In England, newly revived concepts of Roman law encountered an independent tradition of common law, developed during the Middle Ages and rooted in Anglo-Saxon and Norman practice. English common law was based on the principle that previous judicial decisions, rather than codes or statutes, established right. The jury system and the system of criminal procedure based on "grand" and "petty" inquests are components of English common law. The kings of England promoted common law, which was the law administered in the kings' courts, and shaped its procedures to the benefit of royal authority. In time, they also incorporated elements of Roman law into the tradition, especially those that tended to exalt the authority of the monarch. As elsewhere in Europe, the law of the Roman Church, or "canon law," modeled on Roman principles, also helped shape common law.

If Roman law served to bolster the authority of the state and its ruler, it also conveyed another concept important in the development of modern politics: that of natural law. Roman jurists distinguished between the positive law by which Roman citizens were bound—the "law of nations" which regulated interactions between peoples—and natural law, which mirrored eternal principles of good and evil that were intrinsic in nature. Those concepts were transmitted in Christian Europe through the work of medieval jurists, and flourished anew in the early modern era. "The law of nature is a dictate of right reason," wrote the seventeenth-century Dutch theorist Hugo Grotius (1583–1645); an act is judged morally worthy if in accord with rational nature, or base if it is not. Human law, God's law, nature's law were all different, he maintained, but they could exist in congruence.

If medieval and Reformation thinkers wished to bring human activity into accord with divine mandates, some political thinkers of the early modern era wished to limit the state by the principles of natural law. Whereas Roman law favored state-building, the theory of natural law encouraged the building of states according to principles of right and justice unattached to any specific nation or people or system of belief.

The Royal Palace

Pierre Patel the elder, View of Versailles: *In the sixteenth and seventeenth centuries, Europe's rulers built palaces to match their claims for glory. Greatest of these was Louis XIV's palace at Versailles, built between 1669 and 1686, whose vast extent is barely grasped by this contemporary painting.*

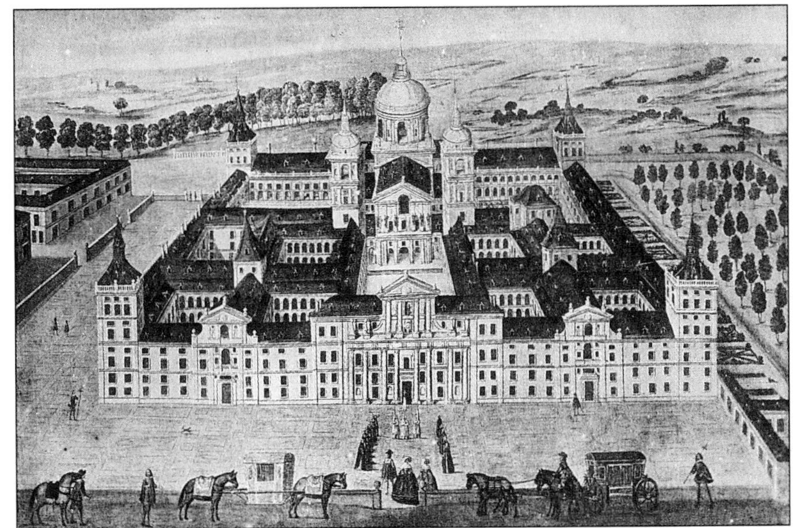

View of the Escorial: *The Spanish king Philip II's gloomier palace, the Escorial, was built outside Madrid between 1563 and 1584 more for labor and penitence than for the leisured elegance of Versailles.*

Another school of political theory developed to justify resistance to states perceived as unjust. Some religious communities fostered an ethic of skepticism toward those in power, and even sanctioned disobedience to governments that violated independent standards of justice. These attitudes often prospered in radical Protestant groups, and in many cases they were extinguished as the adherents of such groups were suppressed. But similar attitudes also characterized the reformed churches radiating from Calvin's Geneva, born of a man who had himself fled a persecuting regime. "Obedience to man must not become disobedience to God," wrote that sober reformer. Next to God, Calvin acknowledged, we are subject to kings—but only so long as their command is godly. "If they command anything against Him, let it go unesteemed."

The right to resist unjust governors, cautiously but clearly stated here, is the proto-democratic germ of Calvinist political theory. The theme was not so prominent in Geneva (where Protestants were in power) as in the further reaches of the Calvinist network, where the reformers were opposed to the majority: in England, Scotland (until the late 1600s), Huguenot France, and Hungary, Poland and Bohemia before their re-conversion to Catholicism in the Thirty Years' War. Later Calvinist theorists went so far as to propose the notion that sovereignty lies in the people, who have the authority to make laws, appoint magistrates, and create kings.

It was but a step further to propose that government was based on a contract between the ruler and the ruled. Sovereignty resided in the people, who, by a kind of contract, agreed to surrender their independence in order to gain the benefits of a well-regulated state. These views form part of the famous analysis of civil government forged in the late seventeenth century by the English liberal John Locke.

A university-trained philosopher who witnessed in his youth the struggles of the English Civil War, John Locke (1632–1704) worked as secretary to a nobleman of the Whig party, which engineered the 1688 Revolution. By that time, Locke himself was living in the Dutch Republic, a center for the circulation of the latest and most daring ideas. From there in 1689–1690 he published four fundamental works: the *Letter on Toleration*, the *Essay Concerning Human Understanding*, and *Two Treatises on Civil Government*. Each was a groundbreaking work of momentous significance. The second of the two *Treatises* is specifically relevant here.

According to Locke, human beings were born absolutely free to pursue their own welfare as best they might amid the natural abundance that God provided at the Creation. All were born with fundamental rights: to life, to liberty, and to the pursuit of property. Some chose to labor diligently and acquire private property. When the others, propertyless, sought to seize what they had not labored to accumulate, the property-owners joined together to create civil government—which was, in effect, the result of a contract. That contract was reminiscent of that called for by Hobbes, but unlike his, it was reversible.

The participants chose representatives to a legislature, which reported to a king. If the government failed to perform the functions for which it was created, it could be dismantled and refounded on the original principles. If the king abused his position and interfered with the proper function of a just government, he could be removed. Locke's treatise is a roadmap at once for the creation of a society based on capitalist notions of the accumulation of property and for the founding of a government rooted in the consent and will of the people. These views passed directly to the authors of the American Declaration of Independence and inform its core principles.

Conclusion

POWER, RESISTANCE, AND THE MEANING OF THE WEST

Although Machiavelli's prince never appeared and Italy was lost, elsewhere the European monarchs of the early modern era adopted the objective that Machiavelli defined: the pursuit of power. By the mid-eighteenth century, the states of Europe were the most powerful in the world, and the rulers who governed them were, in most cases, absolute. Yet the possibility of resistance to unjust monarchy had also become apparent—in the example of the English Revolution on the one hand, and, on the other, in the philosophical vision of the proponents of natural law and social contracts. The tendencies to the concentration of power and, at the same time, to its limitation would both continue to characterize the civilization of the West, as Westerners set out to explore and to dominate the rest of the globe.

REVIEW QUESTIONS

1. Name major developments that changed the nature of power in the "early modern" era. How did gunpowder change warfare? Why did the foot soldier achieve dominance on the battlefield?

2. Explain how the following changed warfare: Italy, mercenary soldiers; Sweden, Gustavus Adolphus; England, Oliver Cromwell; France, Louis XIV; Prussia, Frederick the "Great Elector."

3. Explain the importance of the following wars: wars of Reformation; Dutch revolt in Spain; wars of Louis XIV; colonial conflicts in the New World; War of Austrian Succession; Seven Years' War.

4. What was the importance of Philip II's reign? Why did Spain decline as a great power? Why did France emerge as the strongest power in Europe? What were the contributions of Louis XIV?

5. How did England's development differ from Spain, France, and Austria? What were the issues that divided the English Parliament and the king? What was most significant about the Restoration and the Glorious Revolution?

6. How did the Thirty Years' War affect the development of emerging states in central and eastern Europe? Why did Prussia emerge as a major power? Explain the importance of Ivan the Terrible; Peter the Great; Catherine the Great.

SUGGESTED READINGS

Power and Gunpowder

Black, Jeremy, *European Warfare, 1660–1815* (New Haven: Yale University Press, 1994). Taking issue with the formulation of a "military revolution" by Parker (see below) and others, this innovation places the period of greatest creativity in military in the eighteenth century.

Brewer, John, *The Sinews of Power: War, Money, and the English State, 1688–1783* (New York: Knopf, 1989). A methodical analysis of the fiscal-military complex that powered the English state through a period of nearly continuous warfare.

McNeill, William H., *The Pursuit of Power: Technology, Armed Force, and Society since* A.D. *1000* (Chicago: University of Chicago Press, 1982). Argues that the emergence of free enterprise in Europe allowed wealth, technology, and political power to reinforce each other.

Parker, Geoffrey, *The Military Revolution: Military Innovation and the Rise of the West, 1500–1800*, 2nd ed. (Cambridge: Cambridge University Press, 1996). A classic description of a "military revolution" that was a major factor in Europe's achievement of global power during the early modern era.

Phillips, Carla Rahn, *Six Galleons for the King of Spain: Imperial Defense in the Early Seventeenth Century* (Baltimore: Johns Hopkins University Press, 1991). A vivid study of shipbuilding, the logistics of naval defense, and the problems of the effort to defend the Spanish Atlantic Empire.

War Games

DuPlessis, Robert S., *Lille and the Dutch Revolt: Urban Stability in an Era of Revolution, 1500–1582* (Cambridge–New York: Cambridge University Press, 1991). Shows that Lille remained loyal to Philip II during the Dutch revolt because of the political response of its ruling class.

Kamen, Henry, *The War of Succession in Spain, 1700–1715* (Bloomington: Indiana University Press, 1969). The best study of the War of Spanish Succession and Philip V's early years.

Parker, Geoffrey, *The Thirty Years' War* (London–Boston: Routledge, Kegan Paul, 1984). A masterful account of this most devastating conflict of the early modern era.

An Age of Kings

Bonney, Richard, *The European Dynastic States, 1494–1660* (Oxford: Oxford University Press, 1991). An excellent overview of the political development of Europe's nation states in the early modern era.

Burns, J. H., *Lordship, Kingship and Empire: The Idea of Monarchy 1400–1525* (Oxford: Clarendon Press of Oxford University Press, 1988). An examination of lordship in late medieval and early modern France, England, Spain, the papacy, and the Holy Roman Empire.

De Madariaga, Isabel, *Russia in the Age of Catherine the Great* (New Haven: Yale University Press, 1981). An influential account of Catherine the Great as enlightened despot.

Major, J. Russell, *From Renaissance Monarchy to Absolute Monarchy: French Kings, Nobles, and Estates* (Baltimore: Johns Hopkins University Press, 1994). Considers kings, aristocrats, and assemblies in the struggle for power, with the monarchy edging ahead in the end.

Mirrors for Princes

Ballon, Hillary, *The Paris of Henri IV: Architecture and Urbanism* (Cambridge, MA–London: MIT Press, 1991). A study of how the first Bourbon monarch used city planning to enhance royal prestige.

Brown, Jonathan and J. H. Elliott, *A Palace for the King: The Buen Retiro and the Court of Philip IV* (New Haven: Yale University Press, 1980). Analyzes the 1630s construction of the Buen Retiro palace, showing how the palace was a contrived presentation of kingship, intended to awe spectators and subjects.

Burke, Peter, *The Fabrication of Louis XIV* (New Haven–London: Yale University Press, 1992). An imaginative analysis of the staging of the French kingship during the high point of absolutism.

Muir, Edward, *Civic Ritual in Renaissance Venice* (Princeton: Princeton University Press, 1981). A study of the civic myths and pageants that worked to legitimize the Venetian state as a sacred political institution.

EUROPE REACHES OUT

1500 | 1550 | 1600 | 1650 | 1700 | 1750 | 1800

Conquest and Discovery

Diseases ravage Amerindian populations, 1500s-1600s

Thirty Years' War, 1618-48

Anglo-Dutch Wars, 1652-74

Seven Years' War, 1756-63

English Civil War, 1642-51

- Voyages of Columbus, 1492-1504
- Cabot in Newfoundland, 1497
- Da Gama in Calicut, Goa, 1498
- De León in Florida, 1513
- Cortés conquers Mexico, 1519-21
- Magellan sails the world, 1519-22
- Verrazano in New York harbor, 1524
- Pizarro conquers Peru, 1531-39
- Cartier explores Canada, 1534-42
- De Soto in Mississippi, Texas, 1539-42
- Coronado in Arizona, New Mexico, 1539-42
- Cabrillo in California, 1542
- Drake circumnavigates globe, 1577-80
- Raleigh in Virginia, 1585-87
- Champlain explores Canada, 1603
- Foundation of Jamestown, 1607
- Completion of Stock Exchange, Amsterdam, 1613
- Dutch East India Company, Batavia (Jakarta, Java), 1619
- Pilgrims found Plymouth Bay Colony, 1620
- Dutch acquire Malacca from Portuguese, 1641
- English Navigation Acts, 1651-96
- Marquette, Jolliet explore Mississippi valley, 1673
- De la Salle explores Mississippi region, 1682
- Treaty of Paris, 1763
- Stamp Act repealed, 1766
- U.S. Declaration of Independence, 1776
- U.S. Constitution, Bill of Rights ratified, 1788, 1791

Slavery and Abolition

Atlantic slave trade, 1500-1888

Plantation cultivation in Americas of sugar and tobacco, then cotton and rice

- Spanish "New Laws" prohibit Amerindian slavery, 1542
- Abolition Society founded, 1787
- Haiti independent, 1804
- Britain abolishes slave trade, 1807
- U.S. abolishes slave trade, 1808

Religion and Ideas

First century of printing, 1460-1560

The Enlightenment, 1685-1795

The Scientific Revolution, 1543-1687

- Martin Waldseemüller's, world map 1507
- Erasmus' *Praise of Folly*, 1511
- Luther's *Ninety-five Theses*, 1517
- Copernicus's *On the Revolutions of the Heavenly Spheres*, 1543
- Galileo's *Dialogue Concerning the two Chief World Systems*, 1632
- Hobbes' *Leviathan*, 1651
- Newton's *Mathematical Principles of Natural Philosophy*, 1687
- Locke's *Second Treatise on Civil Government*, 1690
- Rousseau's *Social Contract*, 1762
- Adam Smith's *Wealth of Nations*, 1776

Beyond the West

Ming dynasty, 1368-1644

Qin dynasty, 1644-1912

Mughal Empire, India, 1526-1857

CHAPTER 16

EUROPE REACHES OUT

Global Voyages and Cultural Encounters

1500–1750

KEY TOPICS

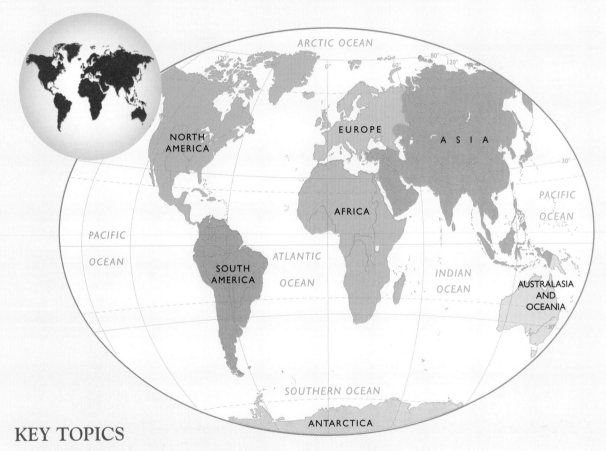

- **The Open Seas:** Led by skilled Portuguese navigators, European merchants establish footholds in Africa, India, the East Indies, and East Asia.
- **Brave New World:** With Christopher Columbus in the vanguard, Spanish and Portuguese conquerors settle much of South and North America; the English, Dutch, and French follow, as native Amerindians are displaced, and African slaves are imported to work the mines and the fields.
- **The Wealth of Nations:** New world commodities flood Europe, which exports its manufactures to the new colonies of the Western Hemisphere and the ancient markets of the east; "mercantilist" strategies are challenged by the proposition that free trade is an even better tool for building the wealth of nations.

*W**ho is the Cannibal?** The Tupinambá, wrote the sixteenth-century French essayist Michel de Montaigne (1533–1592) of the* **Amerindian** *inhabitants of Brazil, roasted and then ate their war captives. As the victims awaited their fate, they suffered without flinching the winners' abuse and mockery. A well-bred European of the ruling noble class, Montaigne did not quite admire this behavior, but neither did he condemn it. Did not Europeans perpetrate worse cruelties? "I think there is more barbarity in eating a man alive than in eating him dead," wrote Montaigne referring to then current judicial punishments, "and in tearing by torture and the rack a body still full of feeling, in roasting a man bit by bit, and mangled by dogs and swine . . ., than in roasting and eating him after he is dead."*

Montaigne's attitude—at once curious, skeptical, and tolerant—could have crystallized only after Europeans began their great expansion into the other inhabited continents of the globe. During that 500-year venture, European peoples encountered the diverse peoples of Asia, Africa, Australia, and the Western Hemisphere. Non-Europeans and Europeans were transformed by the interactions that followed.

From the mid-fifteenth to the mid-seventeenth century, Europeans ranged over the globe, buying and selling, measuring and mapping, conquering and settling. First tiny Portugal ranged beyond the Mediterranean, and around the African coast to India and east Asia. Portugal's competitors quickly joined the race and extended the European presence in Asia. In the Western Hemisphere, meanwhile, European nations explored and settled the Americas, the setting for wholly unanticipated encounters among diverse Amerindian, African, and European peoples. Stimulated by European colonization, a global commercial system of unprecedented complexity developed, while conflicts flared up among competing nations which had committed their wealth and their people, and other peoples and their wealth too, in the quest for greater profits.

THE OPEN SEAS

In the late 1400s, European ships which had rarely ventured beyond the Mediterranean Sea launched out into the open ocean: the Indian, the Pacific, and the Atlantic, called the "Ocean Sea." These waters were the key to Europe's powerful leap forward in the early modern era. They were conquered by sturdy ships, refined navigational tools, cast-iron cannon, and better maps. The tiny Iberian state of Portugal took the lead, establishing footholds in Africa, India, China, Japan, and the famed "Spice Islands" or Moluccas (in modern Indonesia). Immense profits flowed into the port of Lisbon and the Portuguese royal treasury. Dutch, French, and English merchants followed their lure. By 1700, these nations had footholds of their own on the African coasts and in south and east Asia and the Pacific islands.

Portugal Takes the Lead

Since the earliest days of civilization, world trade had centered on the Mediterranean. In the Middle Ages, Byzantine, Arab, and Italian merchants carried across the Mediterranean goods hauled overland and over water from the three continents that surrounded it. Driving this commerce was the demand for luxury products from India and China, the islands of southeast Asia, and the African interior. These were, above all, spices—pepper, cloves, nutmeg—craved as preservatives and flavorings; also silks and cottons, exotic woods, ivory, and gems. Much as Europeans craved these luxury commodities, European merchants craved even more the gold with which to buy them.

It was in order to find both gold and spices that, in the fifteenth century, the captains of Portuguese ships set out on unprecedentedly long journeys. The little kingdom of Portugal bordered the Atlantic Ocean on the western edge of the Iberian peninsula. Under Moorish domination until the twelfth century, it was isolated both from the main currents of European life and from Mediterranean commerce. But Portuguese merchants had knowledge of Arab science and navigational tools, and enjoyed royal patronage, assets enabling them to win the prize they sought: direct access to the trading depots of the Old World.

Navigation Aids Previously, the impediment to exploring the open ocean had been the difficulty of knowing where you were, where you were going, and where the winds might blow you. Late in the Middle Ages, several technical advances came together to solve the problem. The **astrolabe**, invented by the Greek scientist Hipparchus in the second century B.C.E. and later refined by Arab scientists, permitted the navigator to measure the apparent height of a star and thus determine his latitude. Meanwhile, astronomers worked out detailed tables of the positions of the stars. These tables allowed the technician with an astrolabe to determine a ship's position.

The **quadrant** and, later, the more advanced **sextant**, also measured the altitude of heavenly bodies and thus determined position. Mechanical clocks could check the bearing of the sun—although longitude could not be measured until precision chronometers in the eighteenth century. The **compass**, used by Chinese navigators from around 1100, was adopted by Europeans, who designated as its four cardinal points the fixed directions North, South, East, and West. The device pointed to a magnetic, and therefore variable, north, rather than a true north, which limited its usefulness.

As nautical tools improved, so too did maps. **Portolan** charts gave sailing distances in clear quantities and bearings in straight lines. Lacking parallels and **meridians**, or any indication of the curvature of the earth, they could be used for enclosed seas, such as the Mediterranean and Black seas, but not on the open oceans. Better charts became available as geographical knowledge improved.

Early in the fifteenth century, a copy of the *Geography* by the Greek scientist Ptolemy (c. 90–168 C.E.), began to circulate in western Europe, spurring the creation of a new generation of world maps. These

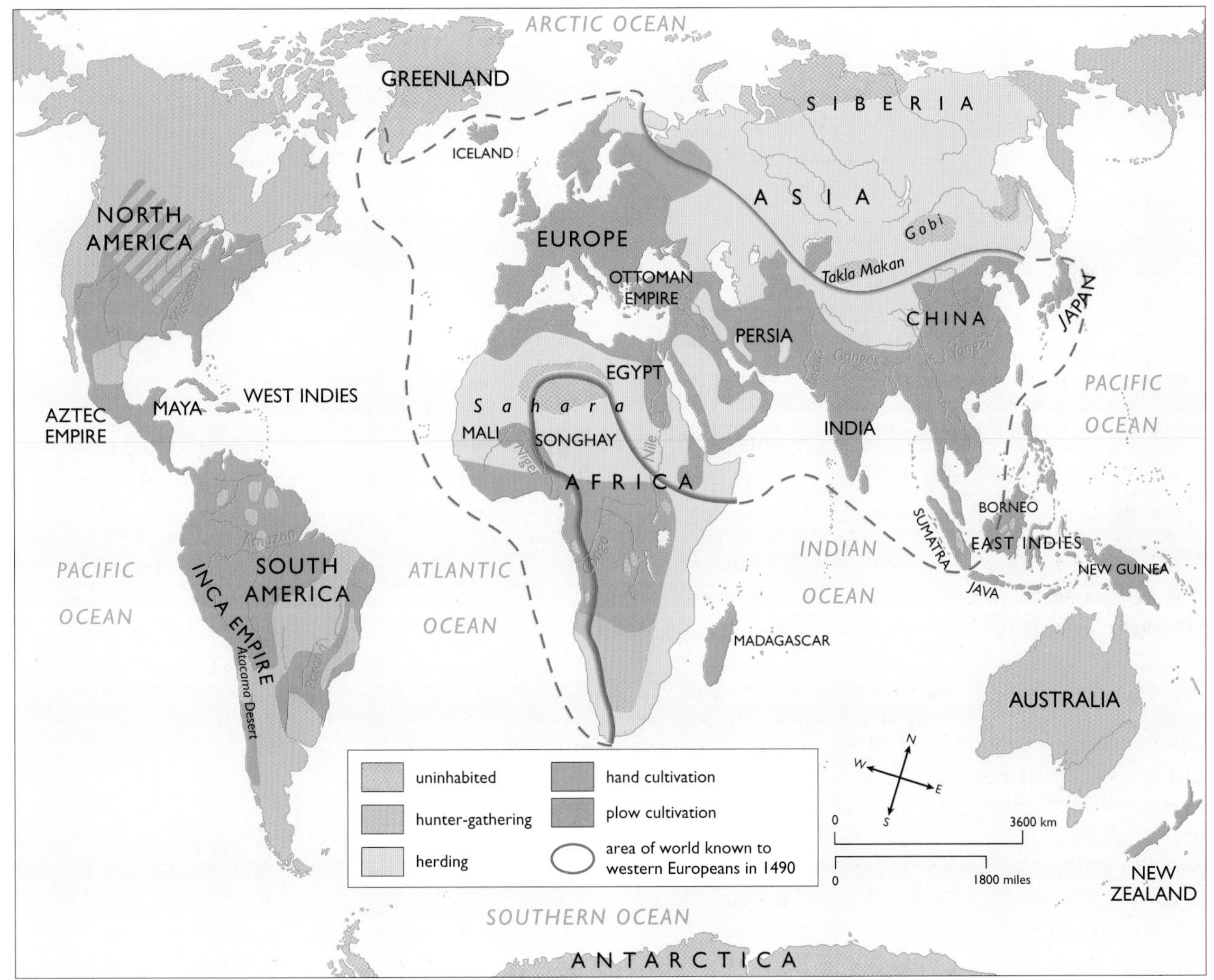

Map 16.1 World Economies and Movements of Peoples around 1500: *On the eve of European expansion, advanced economies based on cultivation with the plow were found in Europe, Asia Minor and the Near East, South and East Asia and some of the Pacific islands, and a small fraction of mostly Mediterranean Africa—the areas of the original Eurasian civilizations and those regions that developed from contact with them. Here the production of food surplus had also made possible the intensive development of urban centers. Food gatherers, hand cultivators, and pastoralists occupied the rest of the inhabited globe, the major part of its surface. Beginning in the late fifteenth century, peoples from the more advanced areas and especially Europeans began the settlement, expansion, and transformation of those unvisited areas.*

first ventures of modern **cartography** (the science of mapmaking) sadly preserved Ptolemy's errors. He underestimated the circumference of the earth by one-sixth and imagined a huge "unknown land" covering much of the Southern Hemisphere. Portuguese expeditions enabled cartographers to partially correct the maps and charts and called for the drawing of at least one meridian and lines of latitude. By the mid-sixteenth century, map projections regularly described the earth as a sphere. Thereafter maps were more accurate than Ptolemy's, as science and experience improved on the knowledge inherited from antiquity.

As shipbuilding also improved, so too did ships. The ships of medieval Europe were square-masted and depended on oars for maneuverability and speed. Arab ships called **dhows**, designed for the deep waters of the Indian Ocean, were rigged with triangular, or **lateen**, sails. From these two types of vessel, Spanish and Portuguese shipbuilders developed the small, fast **caravel**. The key to the caravel's speed was its enlarged sail area, achieved by increasing the number of masts and rigging the middle mast with a square sail or sails, the fore and aft with lateen sails. The stern rudder, a recent innovation, allowed for quick, precise steering. Navigators learned to overcome the westerly winds of the Atlantic and to make use of wind patterns on the Indian Ocean. Because oarsmen were unnecessary, their places could be taken by sailors, cargo, or soldiers.

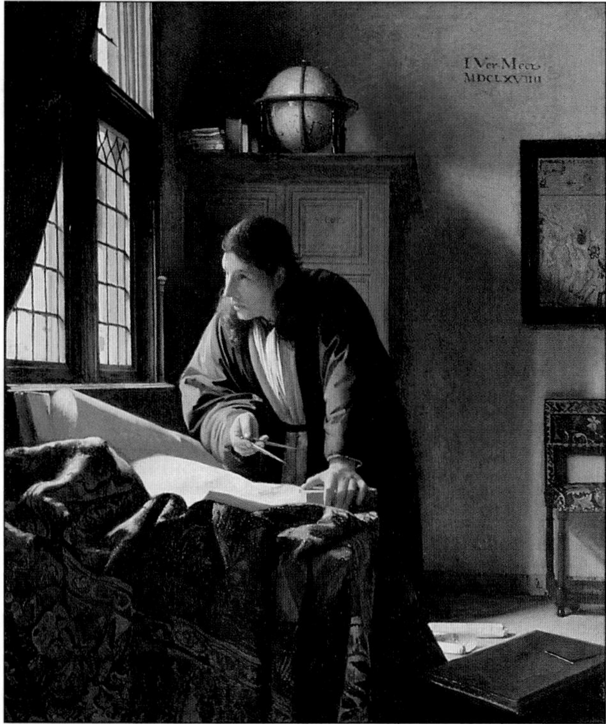

Jan Vermeer, The Geographer: *In this 1669 painting by the Dutch artist Vermeer can be seen articles of navigation: a compass, maps, and a globe.* (Städelsches Kunstinstitut, Frankfurt)

These superior sailing ships also developed fighting capacity. In the 1400s, they carried cannon on deck, as well as soldiers armed with crossbows and arquebuses. By the early 1500s, guns were permanently mounted between the decks so as to fire broadside through special gunports. Hulls were strengthened, and the whole structure braced by multiple decks, so that the ship could withstand enemy bombardment and cannon recoil. Wherever they went, the new men-of-war (as these warships were called) out-powered other ships and even coastal defences. "At the rumor of our coming," a Portuguese general wrote his king in 1513, "the native ships all vanished, and even the birds ceased to skim over the water." This armed, oceangoing craft made possible the European domination of the seas.

Safe, fast, and formidable, well-steered and powered entirely by sails, manned by a smaller crew but equipped to sustain long journeys, these ships constituted an improvement over the Mediterranean carriers used by the Genoese and Venetians. They brought explorers to the New World, and escorted convoys of heavy merchant vessels across the oceans. (The "New World," designating the lands of the Western Hemisphere, was isolated from the Old World civilizations of Afro-Eurasia until Columbus' arrival in 1492.) By 1600, European ships, once inferior, were the best in the world.

The African Route The first nation to benefit from this improved technology was Portugal. Emerging from the wars of the *Reconquista*, Portugal entered upon its most glorious age around 1400, during the long reign of King John I (r. 1385–1433). John was not only a state-builder but the founder of Portugal's maritime success, even more brilliantly patronized by his brother Prince Henry the Navigator (1394–1460). In 1415, Henry participated in the Portuguese capture of Ceuta, a Moorish depot on the North African coast opposite Gibraltar. The next year he summoned cartographers and seamen to form an institute for navigation. Under Henry's patronage, dozens of vessels sailed straight from the shore into unknown waters, to Africa and beyond.

Plucking up the Atlantic archipelagoes of the Azores and Madeiras Islands on the way (while Spain took the Canaries), Portuguese sea captains turned south to plant garrisons along the west African shore. By the 1470s, they had founded permanent trading stations, where they loaded the gold, spices, ivory, and exotic woods of the interior on ships bound for home. Although their original objectives were gold and spices, they quickly developed an appetite for slaves. As early as 1433, Prince Henry approved the traffic in human cargoes. Soon the crown was taxing the revenues of this trade at 20 percent. The slave trade funded the Portuguese state.

Late in the fifteenth century, Portuguese exploration reached beyond the west coast of Africa. In 1488, Bartolomeu Dias (1430–1500) looped around Africa's southern tip (later named the Cape of Good Hope) and continued northeast along the further coast. Repelled by Arab merchants, and daunted by unfamiliar winds, Dias returned to Portugal.

Ten years later, and under Dias' tutelage, Vasco da Gama (c. 1460–1524) completed the mission his predecessor had launched. With four ships, he sailed past the Cape of Good Hope and into the Indian Ocean, previously the preserve of Arab merchants. In 1498, he anchored off Calicut, on the west (Malabar) coast of India, one of the main depots for the Asian spice trade. Although hostilities erupted between the Portuguese and the ruler of Calicut, Da Gama managed to return to Portugal with a quantity of pepper. That pepper signaled the accomplishment of a route to the east that started from the western coast of Europe.

Soon the Portuguese established a firm base at the city of Goa, farther north on the west coast of India. This would serve as the Asian capital of their commercial empire of "the Indies" (meaning at the time all of Asia) which embraced merchant depots in the spice-rich Molucca islands, China, and Japan. Governor-general Afonso de Albuquerque (1453–1515) wrested the depot from Arab merchants and military forces who had long-established colonies there, committing terrible atrocities in the process. Portuguese merchants sent the precious commodities of the east directly back to Lisbon on an average of twelve ships per year. There they sold cheaply (the prices uninflated by the middlemen costs that Venice had had to pay), but at profits sufficient to make the tiny country rich. The kings of Portugal took 20 percent of the profit.

The Portuguese achievement was unprecedented. With a population of only 2 million, Portugal quickly acquired an empire vastly greater than itself. Its ships pierced the zone of Arab mercantile supremacy, crossed the Indian Ocean, and opened a European sea route to India, Indonesia, and China. The port at Lisbon now rivaled once-mighty Venice. After 1600, her mastery of the Mediterranean devalued by Portuguese competition, Venice was reduced to enjoying the small profits of Middle Eastern commerce. The future of merchant ventures lay on the open ocean.

Old World Ventures

In the early 1500s, the Dutch, English, and French followed the Portuguese into the commercial heart of the Old World, and had usurped their position by 1700. They did so by developing merchant empires, consisting of far-flung networks of garrisoned depots, often managed by **joint-stock** merchant companies which acted like nations in themselves.

Joint-stock companies were corporations more complex than the partnerships created by medieval Italian merchants. Now hundreds or thousands of individuals contributed funding for an ongoing commercial enterprise, and awaited, passively, a share of profits in return. The company itself had an identity independent of its participating partners, or shareholders. It sold its shares where merchants gathered—

Alejo Fernandez, Our Lady of the Navigators: *This 1535 painting of the Virgin Mary as protectress of several known explorers (Columbus may be the figure at the left), and depicting some of the kinds of ships in which they would have sailed, was painted for the Casa de Contratación, or Trade House, in Seville, the center for New World shipping in Spain.*

WINDOWS ON

Mapping the World

Grazioso Benincasa, Portolan chart of the east coast of Africa, 1468

Anonymous, Amerigo Vespucci, 1673

Perhaps the most important navigational device was the map. But advances in map creation had consequences beyond just practical considerations. Improved, realistic world maps based on data collected by acute explorers provided Europeans with an entirely new concept of the globe on which they lived. Shown here (above) is an example of a Portolan chart (showing the east coast of Africa), which guided navigators before the development of modern maps. The intersecting lines connect known locations, and the coastline is drawn freehand based on the careful observation of experienced sailors.

Amerigo Vespucci, Italian navigator, is shown (above right) complete with a compass, a map, and a globe.

Hondius' sophisticated map (below) shows the route of Sir Francis Drake's circumnavigation of the globe in 1580.

(top left: British Library)

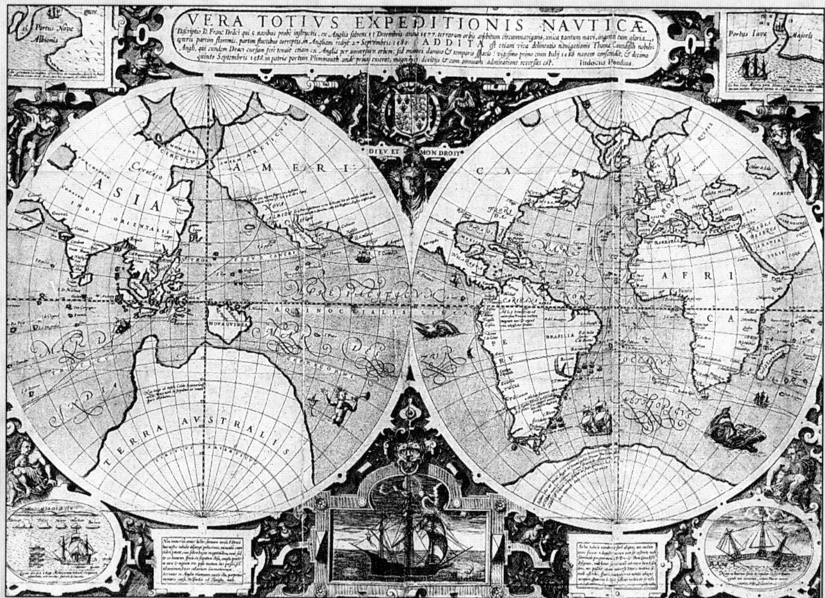

Hondius, World map showing Drake's voyage (1580), seventeenth century

at the *bourse* (French for "purse"), or stock market, such as the one in Antwerp (Europe's first), founded in 1531, or the more important one in Amsterdam, completed in 1613. The company developed its own bureaucracy and hierarchy of officers and agents, and even its own security force, which looked much like a small army. A joint-stock company had the power not merely to buy and sell, but also to settle, manage, and defend a merchant **colony**.

The European agents of merchant companies pressed for trade privileges everywhere along the coasts of southern and eastern Asia. They succeeded especially well in establishing themselves in India, where most of the local rulers, possessing no naval capacity and at odds among themselves, were accustomed to commercial interaction with foreign merchants. Portuguese merchants maintained the base at Goa until it was reclaimed by an independent India in 1961. By 1700, English and Dutch competitors had taken over Indian trade with Europe. Their enterprises in India were organized by the English East India Company, established in 1600, and the Dutch East India Company, established in 1602.

India As the Portuguese, English, and Dutch planted their commercial colonies on the coasts of India, great changes occurred in the interior. Since the Gupta kings died out on the Indian subcontinent in the mid-sixth century CE, India had split into a multitude of states and kingdoms, but it still sustained a lively commercial life. By 1192, Islamic invaders from the frontier Sind region had conquered much of northern India and established a sultanate at Delhi which gained sovereignty in the northern part of the subcontinent. Meanwhile, Arab Muslim traders established commercial depots along the coasts. The Delhi sultanate fell in 1398 to the Mongol-Turkic conqueror Tamerlane (c. 1336–1405), to be succeeded by small Muslim kingdoms. After 1526, Tamerlane's descendant Babur (1483–1530) swept in, defeated the petty states of the north, and established the Mughal Empire. The Great Mughals, as the emperors were called, gained dominion over much of the region, creating a united empire, and presided over a blossoming of culture.

In the late 1600s, the Hindu kingdoms of the center and south reasserted themselves, however, and by the mid-1700s, the Mughal Empire had weakened, leaving India in a disarray the British then exploited. By 1757, the English East India Company, with bases at Bombay, Madras, and Calcutta, and employing its own army and diplomats, had become the principal power in the subcontinent (see Chapter 23). Over the next century it would defeat one regional power after another until it came to rule all of India—about two-thirds directly, and one-third indirectly.

China In China, European merchants never controlled local rulers as they did in India. Prosperous China was uninterested in the goods and services proffered by Europeans. Under the Ming dynasty (which had replaced the Mongol Yuan dynasty in 1368), the Chinese people were better fed, clothed, and educated, and perhaps better ruled than peoples anywhere else on the globe. Even a poor boy from one of the remote farming villages could aspire to pass the difficult examinations that permitted entrance to the ruling bureaucracy. Steeped in the ancient Confucian tradition, these mandarins advocated enlightened self-sufficiency and disdained both commercial enterprises and projects of territorial expansion.

Such attitudes had not always prevailed in China. Between 1405 and 1433 (two generations before Columbus' voyages), the emperor's Muslim eunuch Zheng He had made a remarkable series of expeditions through the Indian Ocean to the east African coast. On the first occasion, Zheng had sailed with a fleet of sixty-two vessels, carrying 28,000 men. Under the influence of mandarin officials, Chinese rulers later halted these expeditions, and even banned the building of ships. Commerce had low priority for the ruling Chinese. But Europeans yearned to sell Chinese goods to the west—especially since the decline of the ancient caravan link between the Middle East and China, through which had flowed Chinese silks and luxury products. Chinese rulers stood firm. They might grant Europeans a trading base, such as that gained by the Portuguese at Macao in 1557, but they insulated Chinese society from Europeans.

Japan Japanese rulers felt much the same way. From the twelfth century, Japan had been dominated by a class of warrior landowners—the **samurai**, roughly similar to the knights of medieval Europe—who owed obedience to an overlord, or shogun. Shoguns and samurai overshadowed the emperor, isolated in his court but protected from challenges by his divine descent. This Japanese elite opposed European influence. In 1636, the Japanese abandoned all seafaring activity and sealed themselves within their borders. In the 1630s, they expelled all Europeans except the Dutch, who were allowed to dock one ship each year and remain, segregated, on an island near Nagasaki. But the Dutch were to have no contact with Japanese, nor even learn that language; and the Japanese, similarly, were

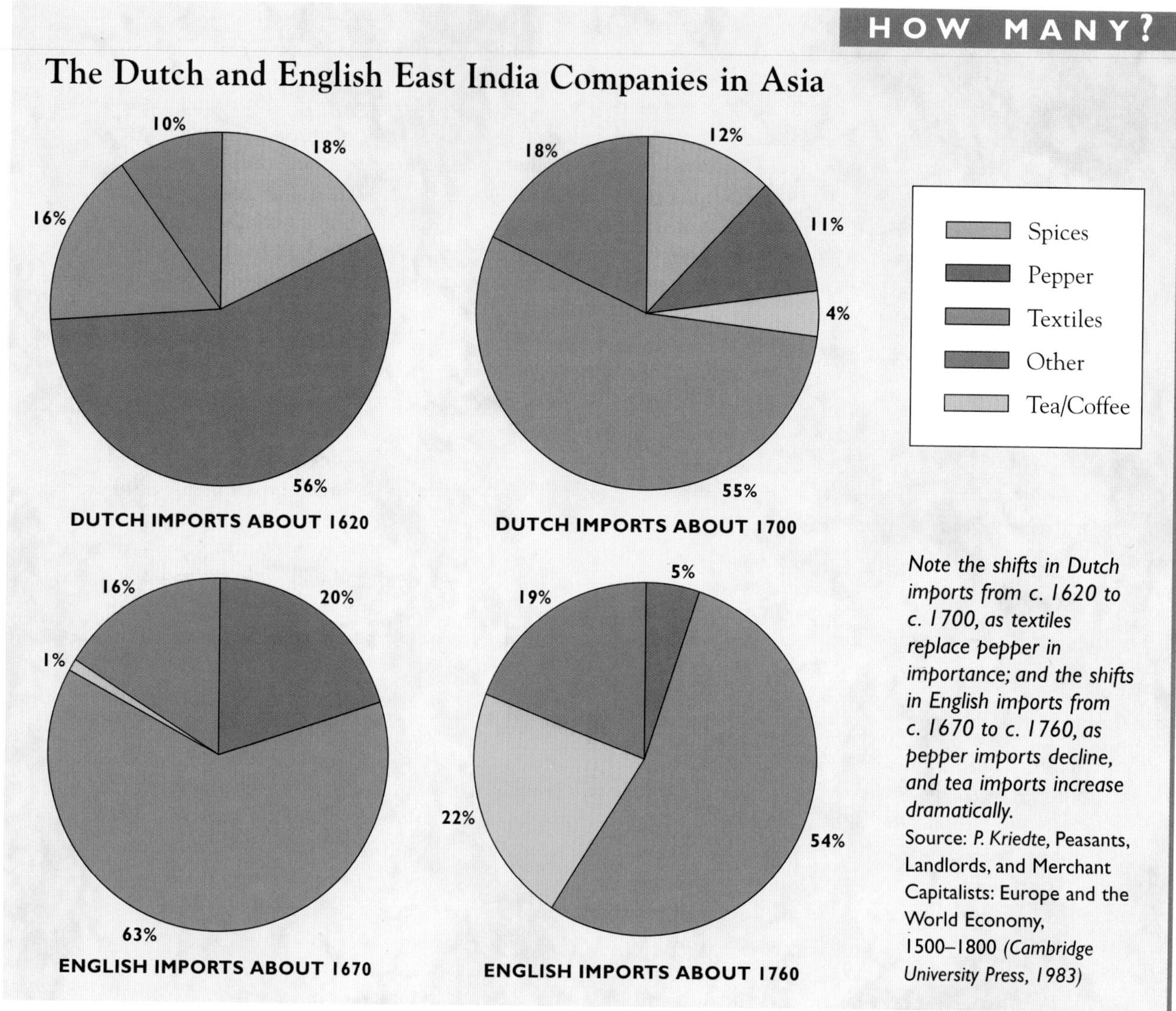

Note the shifts in Dutch imports from c. 1620 to c. 1700, as textiles replace pepper in importance; and the shifts in English imports from c. 1670 to c. 1760, as pepper imports decline, and tea imports increase dramatically.
Source: *P.* Kriedte, Peasants, Landlords, and Merchant Capitalists: Europe and the World Economy, 1500–1800 *(Cambridge University Press, 1983)*

prohibited from learning Dutch, with the result that the two merchant communities were forced to converse in the language of the now-absent Portuguese. The Dutch merchant colony was the main link between Japan and the West until the nineteenth century.

The Dutch Initiative The Malay Peninsula (part of modern Malaysia), the islands of the South Pacific (including modern Indonesia and the Philippines), and other Pacific islands, including New Zealand and the continent of Australia, all became known to European merchant fleets between 1500 and 1800. The prime commercial target was the Moluccas, or Spice Islands, producers of cloves and nutmeg. In this vast Pacific region, as in India, the Portuguese were the first venturers, establishing a base at Malacca (in modern Malaysia) by 1511. But farther east the Dutch outpaced the Portuguese to win the prize. They gained title to the Moluccas by 1613, and in 1619 established an administrative center at Batavia (now Jakarta, in modern Indonesia). Dutch merchants became the main exploiters of the spice trade, and they were the first Europeans to sight New Zealand and Australia. The Dutch explorer Willem Schouten discovered the southern tip of South America in 1616 and named it Cape Hoorn (or Horn) after his birth place. In 1652 the Dutch settled the African Cape of Good Hope, indicating their leadership in world trade by their presence at these two southernmost outcroppings.

In the seventeenth century, the immense Pacific looked like a Dutch sea. How could such a tiny nation command so far-flung and efficient an empire, if only a merchant empire? The answer lay in its familiarity with the sea—a constant threat to the low-lying

Dutch terrain but also a stimulus to shipbuilding. By 1600, the Dutch had 10,000 ships, which sailed the Baltic and Northern seas, as well as the Atlantic and Pacific oceans. The ***fluyt*** or "flyboat," a Dutch innovation, was an efficient vessel designed for inexpensive, utilitarian hauling. The Dutch became the common carriers of Europe, transporting both utilitarian and luxury goods and linking ports all over the globe. Of these entrepreneurs, the English writer Daniel Defoe (1660–1731) wrote with some awe: "They buy to sell again, take in to send out, and the greatest part of their vast commerce consists in being supplied from all parts of the world that they may supply all the world again."

From the coasts of Africa, across the Indian Ocean and on into the Pacific, merchant vessels probed the ports of the Old World. The next frontier lay on the far side of the Atlantic.

BRAVE NEW WORLD

In the Old World, while the human species evolved and developed communities, the New World of the Western Hemisphere remained uninhabited. It acquired its first human immigrants only during the last Ice Age (which ended about 10,000 years ago). These peoples developed their own varied cultures and civilization in isolation from Old World influences. After 1492, explorers, conquerors, and settlers came in turn to the Western Hemisphere, overwhelming the New World's tens of millions of Amerindian natives, importing more than 10 million African strangers, and planting the seeds of new cultures descended from those of Europe. The New World became part of Western civilization; but its Amerindian and African inhabitants, whose labor enriched merchant and professional elites on both sides of the Atlantic, remained, to varying degrees, alienated from it.

Exploration and Conquest

The first explorers to visit the Western Hemisphere entered a world inhabited by defenseless peoples, rich in resources, and ripe for exploitation. They learned the extent and nature of the land and claimed it for the European nations that had sent them. Conquest followed exploration, resulting in the destruction of two advanced New World civilizations.

During the last Ice Age (from about 30,000 to 10,000 years before the present), Asian hunters wandered over the land bridge that stretched some 50 miles (80 km.) from Siberia (modern Russia) to Alaska—a region Europeans later called "Beringia," after the straits named for the Danish explorer Vitus Bering (1681–1741). These Asian migrants were the true discoverers of the lands of the Western Hemisphere. Material remains of their culture testify to their residence at various sites of North and South America from between 20,000 and 10,000 years ago.

Over thousands of years, the Amerindians migrated across the land mass to its southernmost tip, developing into numerous tribes and nations, speaking hundreds of languages. Most had not progressed beyond a Neolithic condition before the arrival of Europeans. Some remained hunters and gatherers, while others, beginning about 7000 years ago, learned to farm. More than half of them lived in Mexico and the Andes regions, where they developed, respectively, the Aztec and Inca civilizations. Perhaps 4 to 6 million lived in what is now the continental United States, and as many more in the Caribbean. In all, perhaps as many as 75 million Amerindians inhabited the Western Hemisphere before Europeans "discovered" that world and proclaimed it "new."

As early as the late tenth century, Viking sailors were exploring the waters of the north Atlantic near the coast of modern Canada. In 982 Erik the Red founded a settlement on the island of Greenland (so named by him to make it more attractive to colonists). A few years later some Viking sailors are believed to have accidentally discovered the Atlantic coast of North America; they reported their discovery to their compatriots in Greenland. Erik's son Leif Eriksson repeated the journey in 1003, naming the site of his landing as that of Vinland (possibly in Newfoundland). Two subsequent expeditions failed to establish a lasting settlement, and the Viking adventure was forgotten except in Greenland sagas. Nearly 500 years later, as Vasco da Gama and Dias were skirting Africa, a European expedition again arrived on the fringes of the Western Hemisphere. This time the newcomers stayed, and were followed by many others.

Columbus and the Spanish In 1492 the Genoese sea captain Christopher Columbus (1451–1506), funded by the Spanish monarchs Ferdinand and Isabella, set out with three ships on a daring expedition on the open ocean. His goal was to sail to the rich markets of the Indies, claiming for Spain any islands or mainlands he discovered en route. Assuming that Japan and China lay only 3000 miles (4380 km.) to the west, Columbus planned to reach Asia by traversing the Atlantic. This "Admiral of the Ocean Sea" died in 1506 still thinking he had reached Asia, called the "Indies."

In fact, Japan lay more than 13,000 miles (20,900 km.) to the west—more than half the circumference of the globe. Just under 4000 miles (6440 km.) away were the continents of the Western Hemisphere. Columbus first landed on the island he named San Salvador in the Bahamas, then visited other Caribbean islands. On a second journey, he established a base on the island he named Hispaniola (now shared by Haiti and the Dominican Republic). In two subsequent voyages he reached what is now Venezuela (1498) and the shores of Central America (1502)—by which time he realized that his expedition had encountered not just some islands, but at least one huge land mass.

Columbus wanted to find gold, as he wrote in his notebook soon after the discovery: "I do not wish to delay but to discover and go to many islands to find gold." In Hispaniola, he established a trading depot. This was the first of a circuit of fortified mercantile settlements which, within a generation, ringed the Caribbean Sea along the coasts of Mexico, Central America, northern South America, and Florida, and on various islands including Cuba.

Within weeks of his arrival in the New World, Columbus had formed an opinion of its aboriginal residents, whom he named *Indios*, or Indians, thinking he had reached the Indies, or Asia. He concluded that the native Amerindians "would make good and industrious servants" and were "fit to be ruled." Columbus's men put the Taino natives to work hauling the goods to be sent back to Spain. Appointed viceroy of the island, Columbus sparked a native revolt by his authoritarian rule. He was sent back to Spain in disgrace, but allowed to return again. In 1503, Queen Isabella granted his request for permission to enslave the Taino tribespeople. "Being as they are hardened in their bad habits of idolatry and cannibalism, I hereby give license and permission . . . to capture them . . . and to sell them and utilize their services. . . ." Thus used, the Tainos were extinct within a century.

Meanwhile, Portugal laid claim to Spain's new possessions, announcing that they were an extension of the Atlantic islands of the Azores. Spain appealed to the reigning pope, Alexander VI (r. 1492–1503), who was Spanish by birth. In 1493, Alexander issued a series of papal bulls confirming Spanish possession of the new lands, and drawing an imaginary boundary between Spanish and Portuguese zones: a north-south line about 300 miles west of the Portuguese Azores. By the 1494 Treaty of Tordesillas between Spain and Portugal, the north-south line was redrawn farther west. The effect of the Treaty was that Portugal retained title to what is now Brazil, and Spain to the remaining lands of North and South America claimed by her explorers.

Papal intervention into the realm of geopolitics had a sound foundation. According to medieval theology, all property came from God. Who better to determine its allocation than the pope—according to Roman Catholic thought, God's representative on earth? Later Protestant participants in the race for New World properties were naturally unpersuaded by this line of reasoning.

Spurred by Columbus's example and his promotion of New World opportunities, a stream of explorers now journeyed across the Atlantic. Most were Italians or Portuguese in the employ of other nations. Soon after Columbus's first voyage, the Italian explorer Amerigo Vespucci (1454–1512), scion of an important commercial family of Florence, set out in the employ of Spain and (later) Portugal. Probing the coast of South America, he found and explored some of the vast expanse of the Amazon River. He was the first to conclude that the new lands were not part of Asia but part of a previously unknown continent. He called it the "New World." The New World, ironically, was later named after him. In 1507, the German cartographer Martin Waldseemüller published an updated world map in which the New World lands were designated, in honor of the pioneering Florentine, "America."

Over the next fifty years, Spanish explorers crossed Panama to the Pacific Ocean (Vasco Nuñez de Balboa, 1475–1517), and claimed the lands of Florida (Juan Ponce de León, c. 1460–1521), Mississippi and Texas (Hernando de Soto, c. 1496–1542), Arizona and New Mexico (Francisco Vásquez de Coronado, c. 1510–1554), and California (Juan Rodríguez Cabrillo, d. 1543). Their expeditions in search of gold and of a miraculous "fountain of youth" were largely fruitless, but they acquired for their Spanish overlords the lands of western North America stretching as far north as Utah.

The venture of the Portuguese navigator Ferdinand Magellan (c. 1480–1521) was of another sort. In Spain's employ, Magellan set out in 1519 to reach Asia. He sailed from Atlantic to Pacific through the narrow strait near the tip of South America later named after him, the Strait of Magellan, and then across the Pacific, with a starving crew for sixty-eight days, before reaching land (on the island of Guam). Touching on some islands which were later named the Philippines (after the future King Philip II of Spain), Magellan died in a battle with hostile natives. The expedition continued under the second in command. Of the five ships and 270 men who began the

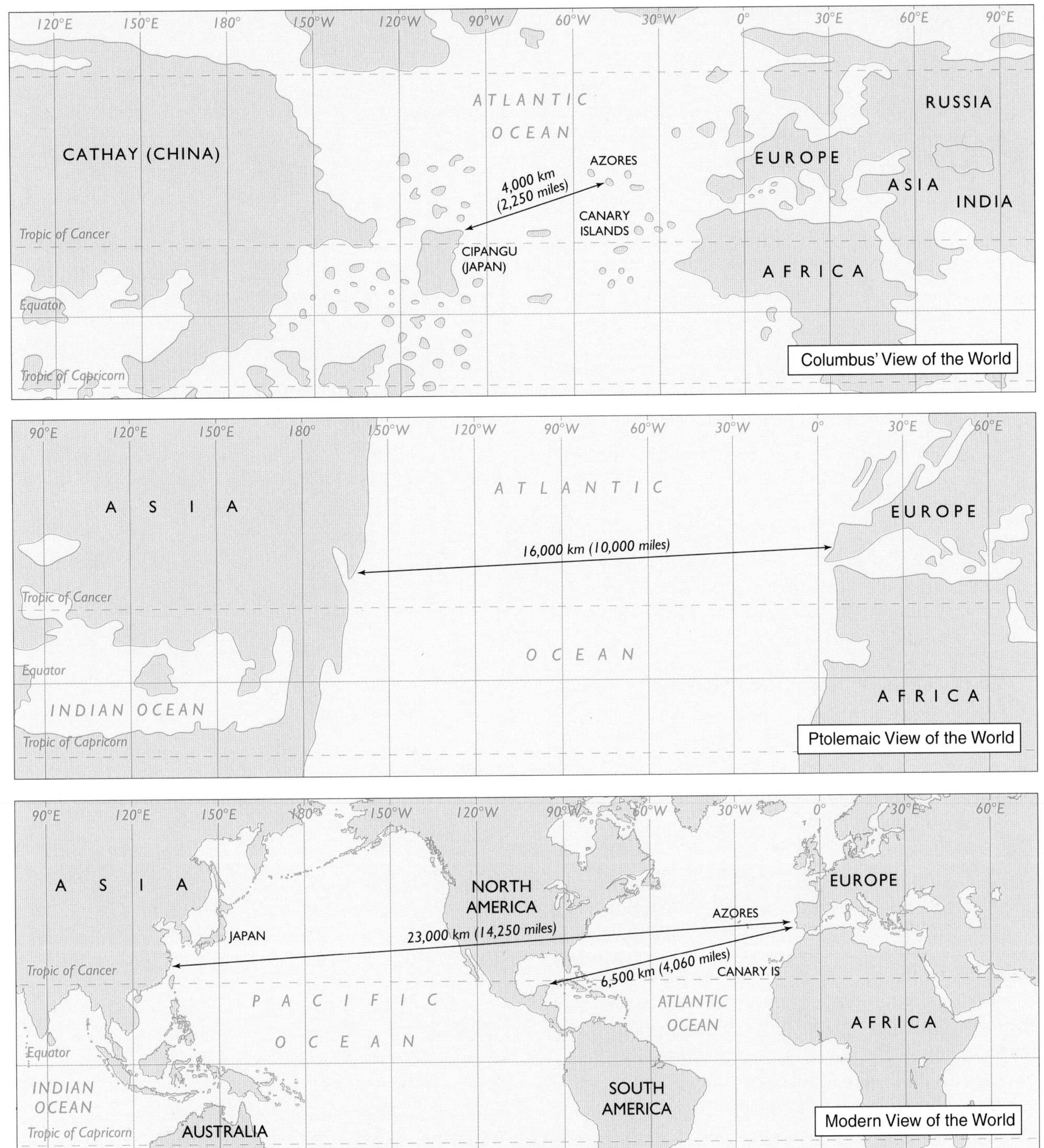

***Map 16.2* Columbus' World:** *Columbus fully intended to reach Japan after a westward journey across some 3000 miles of the Atlantic—"correcting" the prevailing Ptolemaic (ancient Greek) model that placed Asia at a distance nearly three times that. Both theories were wrong, as the unknown continents of North and South America and the unknown Pacific Ocean lay between the coast of Spain and the coast of Asia.*

journey in 1519, one ship and a mere eighteen men returned to Spain in 1522. Accomplishing for the first time in history the feat of circumnavigating the globe, they had learned how vast was the Pacific, and how distant Asia was from Europe.

Opening up North America The other Atlantic nations now entered the race for American lands, focusing their efforts on the coast of North America. The English sent the Italian Giovanni Caboto (John Cabot, 1450–1499) with one small ship and eighteen sailors to explore in 1497. Cabot reached Newfoundland (in modern Canada), establishing a foothold on the basis of which England would later claim rights to much of North America.

Years later, the English adventurer Sir Walter Raleigh (c. 1552–1618) journeyed three times to the coast of what is now the southeastern United States—a land he named Virginia, in honor of the "Virgin Queen," Elizabeth I. On Roanoke Island (in modern North Carolina) he formed a colony, which failed. Francis Drake (c. 1540–1596), famed for his persistent raids on Spanish Atlantic commerce, repeated in 1577–1580 the feat of circumnavigation achieved first by Magellan's crew. Henry Hudson (d. 1611) explored for England Canada's immense northern bay, later named after him. For the Netherlands, Hudson explored the New York river also named after him, along which the Dutch established trading depots.

Hoping to find a "northwest passage"—an alternative northern route through the American land mass to the Pacific—the French sent the Italian navigator Giovanni da Verrazano (c. 1485–1528) in 1524 to explore the North American coast. Venturing south from Newfoundland, he entered what is now New York harbor. For over 200 years, French captains explored the Canadian coast and the Saint Lawrence, Great Lake, and Mississippi waterways as far as the Gulf of Mexico. Among the most notable were Jacques Cartier (1491–1557), Samuel de Champlain (1567–1635), Louis Jolliet (1645–1700), along with the priest Jacques Marquette (1637–1675), and Robert de la Salle (1643–1687).

The Aztecs Even before the English, French, and Dutch embarked on North American ventures, Spain had completed its conquest of much of the Americas. Most Amerindian communities succumbed quickly to

WITNESSES

Exploration and Conquest

João de Barros describes the sack of Mombasa, eastern Africa, by the forces of Portuguese grand-captain Dom Francisco d'Almeida (15–16 August 1505): The Portuguese attack and burn the town; the fire raged all night long, and many houses collapsed.... [The next morning.] The Grand-Captain ordered that the town should be sacked.... Then everyone started to plunder the town and to search the houses, forcing open the doors with axes and iron bars.... A large quantity of rich silk and gold embroidered clothes was seized.... [The next day] they also carried away provisions, rice, honey, butter, maize, countless camels and a large number of cattle, and even two elephants.... There were many prisoners, and white women among them and children, and also some merchants....
(From G. S. P. Freeman-Grenville, *The East African Coast*, 1962)

Vasco da Gama arrives in Calicut, India (20–29 May 1498), according to an eyewitness: The king was in a small court, reclining upon a couch covered with a cloth of green velvet... and upon this again a sheet of cotton stuff, very white and fine, more so than any linen.... On the right side of the king stood a basin of gold, so large that a man might just encircle it with his arms.... The canopy above the couch was all gilt....

On Tuesday the captain got ready the following things to be sent to the king, viz., twelve pieces of *lambel* [a striped cloth], four scarlet hoods, six hats, four strings of coral... a case of sugar, two casks of oil, and two of honey.... [The king's officials came] and when they saw the present they laughed at it, saying that it was not a thing to offer to a king, that the poorest merchant from Mecca, or any other part of India, gave more, and that if he wanted to make a present it should be in gold, as the king would not accept such things. When the captain heard this he grew sad, and said that he had brought no gold, that, moreover, he was no merchant, but an ambassador; that he gave of that which he had.... Upon this they declared that they would not forward his presents, nor consent to his forwarding them himself.
(*A Journal of the First Voyage of Vasco da Gama, 1497–1499*; trs., ed. E. J. Ravenstein, 1848)

Eyewitness Antonio Pigafetta describes Magellan's Pacific crossing (1521): We were three months and twenty days without getting any kind of fresh food. We ate biscuit, which was no longer biscuit, but powder of biscuits swarming with worms, for they had eaten the good. It stank strongly of the urine of rats. We drank yellow water that had been putrid for many days. Rats for sold for one-half ducado apiece, and even then we could not get them.... Had not God and His blessed mother given us so good weather we would all have died of hunger in that exceeding vast sea....
(From L. Wright, *Gold, Glory, and the Gospel*, 1970)

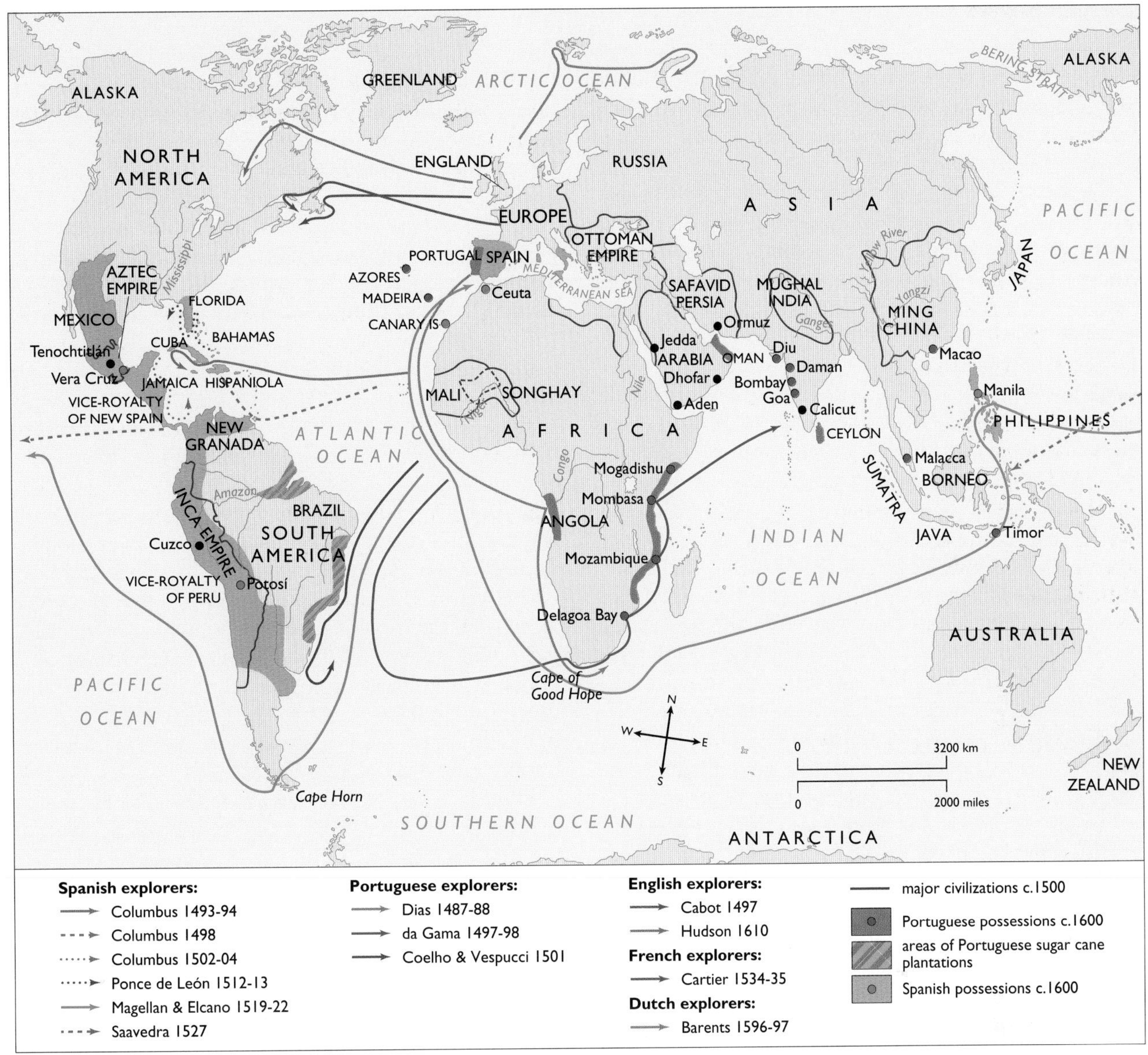

Map 16.3 European Exploration, 1450–1600: *By 1600, Spanish and Portuguese explorers and traders established settlements in South America and the Caribbean, and commercial depots on the coasts of Africa, India, the Pacific islands, China, and Japan—at a time when English, Dutch, and French explorations of North America had just begun.*

European force. The Aztec and Inca empires, centered respectively in modern Mexico and Peru, promised serious resistance. In 1521 and 1533, two ***conquistadores***, conquerors from a nation with a long history of conquest, destroyed these civilizations within a brief time and with only a handful of men.

Spain had only just completed the reconquest of the Iberian peninsula from the Moors when it set out to conquer the lands of the New World. Behind it was a centuries-old military tradition, fueled by a religious zeal tinged deeply with intolerance. Ahead was a project that also invited the use of arms and the missionary muscle of the Roman Catholic Church. The goal of the medieval *Reconquista* was the recovery of Iberian land from foreign domination. That of the American conquest was gold. The extraction of gold from the earth—and later silver, in much greater abundance—was the major economic activity of the Spanish in the New World.

The Amerindian people who constructed the civilization that Europeans called "Aztec" (they called themselves the Mexicas) had moved into central Mexico in the middle of the thirteenth century, establishing a harsh dominion over existing tribal groups. There they claimed inheritance of the culture of the Olmecs and Maya, creators of successive Mesoamerican civilizations (see Chapter 8). On an island in the middle of Lake Texcoco, the Aztecs built their capital of Tenochtitlán (incorporated in modern Mexico City), the preeminent metropolis of pre-Conquest culture.

Tenochititlán bristled with temples, sculptures, and shrines, with palaces and schools, workshops and markets, interspersed with floating gardens and equipped with roads and movable bridges to the mainland. It had a population of about 100,000; few cities in contemporary Europe were larger or more splendid. A Spanish chronicler described the reaction of the soldiers—some of whom had seen Constantinople and the cities of Italy—who reported that "so large a market place and so full of people, and so well regulated and arranged, they had never beheld before."

The Aztecs worshiped many gods, especially a sun god having male and female attributes, the dual deity represented by an eagle on a cactus. Guided by remembered Mayan traditions recorded in sacred picture books (for they had no written language), Aztec priests supervised religious life according to calendar cycles of worship, sacrifice, and feasting. Rite and sacrifice shaped the civilization—including human sacrifice, a celebration of the spilling of blood, in which the victim's still-beating heart was ripped from their chest and offered up to the divinity. The need to secure sacrificial victims to appease the sun god provided the stimulus for wars of conquest. From childhood, young warriors were trained to capture rather than slay enemies, so that prisoners might be brought back for ceremonial deaths—"the flowered death by the obsidian knife"—on temple stones.

This was the civilization that fell to the conquistador Hernán Cortés (1485–1547). Arriving in 1519 with about 600 men and 11 vessels, in defiance of an order of recall from the Spanish governor of Cuba, Cortés and his troops made their way to Tenochtitlán. Having been received cordially, they proceeded to take prisoner the Aztec emperor, the oddly compliant Montezuma II (the familiar form of the name; more properly Moctezuma, r. 1502–1520). Cortés had burned his own ships, closing off any escape route for his men. He sallied from Tenochtitlán to meet a force of his own compatriots come to put an end to his mission. Defeating the leaders, he persuaded the men to return with him and pursue the conquest of Mexico.

In Cortés's absence, warfare broke out in Tenochtitlán, triggered by a Spanish massacre of a group of natives during a religious festival. Cortés returned; Montezuma died (possibly as a result of stoning by his angered people, possibly at the hands of the Spanish); and Cortés withdrew again during a "Sad Night" in which half his men were killed. Regrouping, the Spanish forces returned in 1521 to besiege the city, having constructed a fleet of twelve small oar- and sail-powered boats to do so. A few months later, after firing cannon from the decks of their ships, they seized and razed Tenochtitlán. A few Spanish soldiers armed with arquebuses and cannon achieved this military conquest (assisted by epidemic, caused by microbes for which the Aztecs had no immunity) over thousands of Mexicans armed merely with arrows and swords carved from obsidian, a volcanic glass. A cultural conquest followed. In an attempt to extinguish Aztec religion, the conquerors burned the sacred books and erected Christian churches, often on the sites of native temples.

The Incas The other great indigenous civilization was the Inca Empire, centered at Cuzco (in modern Peru), in the Andes Mountains. The Inca domain, extending 2000 miles (3200 km.) north to south along the Pacific coast of South America, included parts of modern Bolivia, Chile, Argentina, and Ecuador, as well as Peru. The empire had reached its greatest extent just prior to the arrival in 1531 of the Spaniard Francisco Pizarro (1475–1541), whose forces conquered and destroyed it.

The Inca emperor was an absolute monarch, whose legitimacy was marked by ceremonies of veneration for the mummies of his deceased ancestors. The emperor commanded the obedience of his subjects and was considered responsible for their welfare. The state owned virtually all property, which was sustained by the labor of the inhabitants. The agricultural wealth thus generated, and stored in an elaborate warehousing system, supported an elite of priests, government workers, and merchants, as well as the elderly, the ill, and widows. The priests managed the feasts, ceremonies, and sacrifices (including human ones) necessary to gain the favor of a roster of deities, among whom the sun god held sway.

The Incas used advanced engineering to terrace, drain, and irrigate the mountainous terrain and maximize productivity on plots as high as 9000 feet (2745 m.) above sea level. They were also expert builders, working from models rather than plans (as they had no system of writing) to create large cities. A network of roads and bridges extended more than 12,000 miles (19,000 km.), negotiating chasms, rivers, and solid rock. Metals buried in the earth, especially silver and gold, were reserved for the use of the emperor—until the arrival of Pizarro and his followers.

Pizarro arrived in Peru in 1531 with a mere 168 men, 67 horses, and 3 cannon, to assail an empire with a population of several millions and a military force of some 100,000. He captured, deceived, tortured, and executed the uncomprehending ruler Atahuallpa. Moving briskly to the capital at Cuzco, he began a conquest in which European guns and European steel swords overcame the force of wooden spears and clubs of the Incas. Pizarro's men accomplished the victory by unparalleled brutality, of which one participant has left this testimony: "I can bear witness that this is the most dreadful and cruel war in the world," in which both sides "give each other the cruelest deaths they can imagine." By 1539, the Spanish victors had quelled native resistance and established their colonial regime, subordinating almost as slaves a people who had administered one of the world's great empires. The Spanish soon opened the mines of Potosí (in modern Bolivia), an immense reservoir of silver, rich enough to supply the Spanish **bullion** fleets for decades.

Patterns of Settlement

After the first phase of New World exploration and conquest, settlers built European communities in what seemed like an endlessly fertile expanse. The pattern of settlement varied from region to region. Two main colonial zones emerged: the southern zone, or "Latin" America (including those regions of South America, the Caribbean, and Mexico where Spanish, Portuguese, or French—all derived from Latin—are spoken); and the northern zone, including much of North America, predominantly English- and French-speaking. The southern zone was settled earlier, and its main characteristics established by 1600. The northern zone was settled after 1600. The administrative blocs in both areas were called colonies, each related to its own European "mother" country, or metropolis.

Latin America By the mid-1500s, Spanish settlers had organized the main population centers of Peru and Mexico. Spanish administrators and landowners, drawn primarily from the lesser nobility of the metropolis, recreated so far as they could the culture of their homeland. Their native Spanish language soon developed into a **creole**—a colloquial language containing elements of local Amerindian and African dialects. Their cities, modeled on European cities, boasted cathedrals, palaces, theaters, printing houses, and universities (five by 1636, when the first university of Anglo-America, Harvard, was founded). The new American culture was a mixture of imported Spanish and native Amerindian customs.

The Amerindian inhabitants worked for the proprietors of the *encomiendas* (royal land grants to the conquistadors), or as domestic and agricultural laborers on *haciendas*, the large ranches or plantations owned by the Spanish-speaking elite. The natives who lived on the land granted in *encomienda* owed labor services to the proprietor—who in turn owed the laborers protection, security, religious training, and even education. Haciendas drew on the labor services both of permanent residents—often **peons**, or debt slaves—and of seasonal workers from nearby Indian villages. These arrangements seemed to promise advantage to both laborer and contractor or landowner. In practice, the laborers were abused while the proprietors got richer.

The kingdom of Castile directly ruled the Spanish colonies and closely supervised their governance. Two governors—called viceroys ("vice-kings"), respectively, of "New Spain" (modern Mexico) and Peru—administered the whole of Spanish territory (the number of viceroys increased after 1700). Each viceroy presided over a regional advisory council established in the principal cities, and sent out inspectors to report on local administrations. The position of viceroy conferred high status and attracted ambitious noblemen from Spain. There, a Council of the Indies, based in Madrid, scrutinized the records of each viceroy's service upon completion, and intervened to direct the course of colonial events.

In contrast, Portuguese settlement in the New World followed the pattern of Portuguese expansion in Africa and Asia. Garrisoned merchant colonies were planted at key locations on the coast of Brazil, as fueling stations for fleets bound for the Caribbean. Later, Portuguese governors and landowners took over the settled areas of the interior, intending to control the native population more than to establish European communities.

By the late 1500s, settlers had brought to Brazil the **plantation system** (with lands worked by slave labor under supervision) for sugar cultivation developed in the Portuguese Atlantic islands, especially the island of São Tomé, just off the African coast. English, French, and Spanish landowners later adopted this system in the Caribbean (where tobacco, generally farmed on a smaller scale and yielding lower profits, had previously been the main cash crop).

The Dutch, although possessing small colonial bases in the West Indies and on the north Brazilian coast, were more interested in trade than in settlement. Their Dutch West India Company, established in 1621, organized a profitable trade in Brazil and the Caribbean. From the West Indies ports of Havana (Cuba) and San Juan (Puerto Rico), the Spanish bullion fleets took off twice each year, an irresistible lure for Dutch, English, and French raiders.

New World Encounters

Columbus' first voyage: *This woodcut by Giuliano Dati, 1493, depicts the imminent arrival of Columbus' ship in the Bahamas, with idealized representations of natives on the shore.*

North American Colonies After 1600, a northern zone of European settlement in the Americas established itself from Savannah (in modern Georgia) to Quebec (in modern Canada). Most of the settlers were English-speakers; some were French, German, or Dutch; there were even a few hundred Swedes. English settlement was at first organized by joint-stock companies. These obtained from the crown a charter enabling the creation of single agricultural communities, centered in Virginia and New England. Jamestown (in modern Virginia), settled by English emigrants, was founded on this pattern in 1607. The Virginia colony thrived, based as it was on the cultivation of tobacco as a cash crop.

In 1620, Plymouth (in modern Massachusetts) was the second English-speaking community to be established. The aim of the Plymouth **Separatists** (Puritans who had separated from the Church of England—later dubbed "Pilgrims") was not simply to gain farmland but also to secure the right to practice their own form of Protestant worship. Other Puritans settled the Massachusetts Bay Colony (1630), while other New England and mid-Atlantic settlements were also motivated by the quest for religious freedom.

By 1700, twelve colonies had been established (the thirteenth, Georgia, was founded in 1732), and about one-half million English-speakers dwelled in North America, equivalent to one-eighth to one-tenth of the population of England itself. Without initially planning to do so, the English had created a sizable empire abroad. Ruled theoretically by King and Parliament (although they had no representatives in Parliament), the colonies developed effective regional, representative governments.

The Dutch and French settlements more closely resembled the Portuguese pattern of coastal enclaves, and contained fewer colonists. These nationals established merchant colonies respectively in New Netherland (modern New York State) and New France (modern Canada, especially the province of Quebec). The Dutch merchants dealt in a variety of commodities, but the French (who competed with the Portuguese for fish in these northern waters) were particularly interested in the valuable furs that their hunters and traders obtained from the forested interior. French settlement was sparse. By the mid-1600s, there were only about 3000 Europeans in all of New

Human sacrifice: *The Aztec practice of human sacrifice by excising the heart of a living victim, pictured in this sixteenth-century* Florentine Codex, *was condemned as barbaric by the conquerors.* (Biblioteca Medicea Laurenziana, Ms. Laur. Med. Palat. 218, c. 175v, Florence)

France, many fewer than in the single English colony of Virginia. The French crown ruled its colony directly, sending military governors and financial supervisors responsible to officials in Paris.

In 1664 the Dutch lost their North American mainland possessions to their English challengers on the seas. The French would intermittently fight the British for theirs until an eventual British victory in 1763. By the time that the American War of Independence broke out in 1775 (see Chapter 19), the Atlantic region of North America was largely English by language and tradition. Although the Spanish and the Portuguese had opened up the New World, the British eventually dominated in North America.

Religion played a major role in shaping the post-conquest civilizations of the New World. A main objective of many of the settlements, especially of the Spanish, was the conversion of Amerindian natives. In the English colonies of North America, as has been seen, a main motive for colonization was religious freedom—or freedom, in effect, from other Europeans. That impulse for liberation would express itself again, years later, when an ideology of political liberty took root in the same region. Meanwhile, the freedom sought by some colonists was steadily denied by all of them to the two "other" peoples with whom they interacted in the New World—the native Amerindians and the newcomer Africans.

Encountering Others

The "discovery" of the New World was more than the discovery by Europeans of lands previously unknown to them. It was a mutual discovery of different peoples, as European strangers, Amerindian natives, and, in time, African captives interacted. For the Amerindians, the encounter was deadly.

Silver mines: *Once conquered, Amerindians were pressed into service as laborers. At the "Silver Mountain" mines in Potosí (modern Bolivia), as in this engraving, c. 1584, 40,000 poorly paid laborers were employed to mine the silver which was then shipped back to Spain and made into coinage.* (Hispanic Society, New York)

The Amerindians When Columbus and his sailors landed on San Salvador, native Amerindian Tainos greeted them with gifts. Impressed by the Europeans' unusual appearance, the Tainos concluded that they

Committed atrocities: *The conquerors performed savageries of their own against the native populations, as in this engraving by Théodore de Bry (from* Brevissima Relación, *1598, by Bartolomé de Las Casas) of Spaniards hanging and burning the inhabitants of a village.* (Bibliothèque Nationale, Paris)

were gods. The European newcomers were equally startled by the appearance and customs of a people they had never seen before: largely naked, with painted bodies and long hair, smoking tobacco. The Tainos lived in stable communities, in well-constructed houses equipped with hammocks—an object the Europeans had never seen. Their enemies on nearby islands, the Caribs (after whom we name the Caribbean Sea), had a reputation for ferocity—specifically for cannibalism (possibly undeserved). With such stories Columbus and later visitors impressed readers back in Europe.

The millions of natives inhabiting the Western Hemisphere before the European advent consisted of hundreds of nations and tribes and peoples too diverse to be considered as a single Amerindian culture. However, they did have some things in common. Their hundreds of languages ultimately descended from a common pool of Asian languages. None of these was a written language. Only the Mayan peoples acquired the ability to record spoken language in symbols. Although this skill vanished with their decline, the Maya transmitted to successor Mesoamerican peoples—who composed sacred texts using pictographs—a memory of writing and a respect for books.

Based on collectives of family, tribe, and clan, Amerindian societies could be highly stratified, with extended lineages generally traced in the male line. Some formed federations, while others developed representative assemblies. Respected priests, or shamans, were in charge of religious rites, medicine, and magic, all of which might overlap considerably. Some groups practiced human sacrifice, often of war captives. In many, women performed agricultural work.

Amerindians wielded as weapons spears, bows, and clubs of wood, stone, and, more rarely, copper or bronze; they had no iron and no sharp-edged swords, a key factor in their military defeat. They had no horses and no pack animals for hauling heavy loads long distances (the Andean llama could bear only a light burden) or for pulling plows—and perhaps for that reason never developed the wheeled vehicles such beasts might haul. They ate corn rather than wheat as a cereal staple. Where the climate permitted, they wore little or no clothing. They wore adornments crafted from stone and metal, shells, teeth, and feathers, and often painted their faces or bodies. Their skin was tawny.

The Amerindians worshiped many gods, among whom were gods of sun and sky like those the ancestors of the European newcomers had once worshiped. Their forests were alive with indwelling spirits—of the trees, of the eagles, of the jaguars. The land, like the air, was free for the use of all, and sacred in its generative power. To these communities, the European languages and their artifacts—treaties, contracts, documents, treatises of theology—must have seemed inexpressibly strange. The tools and weapons and clothing and armor and horses of the newcomers were awesome. Their guns were "iron which has a spirit." Their white skin seemed luminous. At Roanoke Island (modern North Carolina) in 1584, an eyewitness reported, the natives "wondered marvelously . . . at the whiteness of our skins, ever coveting to touch our breasts, and to view the same." The religious rites, institutions, and personnel—the robed priests and friars with their crucifixes and sacred vessels—must have seemed odd and overwhelming.

The customs of Amerindian communities both shocked and surprised the European newcomers. They were impressed by the nakedness of the natives, and the brilliant hues of their adornments; their unfamiliar sexual customs, their generally meager technology and (in the European sense) their illiteracy; the ferocity and (from the European viewpoint) barbarous customs of a few—the cannibalism of the Caribs and the human sacrifices of the Aztecs and Incas. These permitted the invaders to label the inhabitants of the new land "primitive"; and because primitive, inherently suited to serve the new arrivals. Even if they were not to serve, they were at least expected not to impede Europeans as they settled new lands that they considered to be empty wilderness.

Nevertheless, each group learned from the other. Europeans learned to eat corn and potatoes, to smoke or sniff tobacco, to equip their ships with hammocks (an improvement over the deck in terms of comfort and hygiene), and to employ some Amerindian methods of coping with the climate and cultivating crops. Amerindians learned to use horses and guns—to such an extent that some of them fundamentally changed their way of life. They craved European goods. One native hunter who delivered cherished beaver pelts to European fur traders observed contentedly that "the beaver does everything perfectly well"; and indeed, the beaver had netted him a fortune in "kettles, hatchets, swords, knives, bread."

Some Amerindians, often those kidnapped by settlers, learned to speak Spanish, Portuguese, English, or French, and served as translators and interpreters. The need to teach the natives the language of the conquerors encouraged the creation of language-teaching tools. The author of the first Castilian (Spanish) grammar, published in 1492, observed correctly that "language has always been the companion of empire."

WITNESSES

New World Peoples and Customs

From Columbus' Diary: The arrival in the New World (1492): In order that they would be friendly to us . . . to some of them I gave red caps, and glass beads which they put on their chests, and many other things of small value, in which they took so much pleasure and became so much our friends that it was a marvel. . . .

But it seemed to me that they were a people very poor in everything. All of them go around as naked as their mothers bore them. . . . They are very well formed, with handsome bodies and good faces. Their hair [is] coarse—almost like the tail of a horse—and short. . . . And some of them paint their faces, and some of them the whole body, and some of them only the eyes, and some of them only the nose. . . . They should be good and intelligent servants. . . and I believe that they would become Christians easily, for it seemed to me that they had no religion.

(Christopher Columbus, *The Diario of Christopher Columbus' First Voyage to America, 1492–1493*; ed. trs. O. Dunn, J. E. Kelley Jr., 1969)

Aztec King Motecuhzoma (Montezuma) hears his messengers' report of Cortés' men (who they think are gods), according to an Aztec account (1521): Motecuhzoma was also terrified to learn how the cannon roared, how its noise resounded, how it caused one to faint and grow deaf. The messengers told him: "A thing like a ball of stone comes out of its entrails; it comes out shooting sparks and raining fire. The smoke that comes out with it has a pestilent odor, like that of rotten mud. . . . If the cannon is aimed against a mountain, the mountain splits and cracks open. If it is aimed against a tree, it shatters the tree into splinters. . . ."

The messengers also said: "Their trappings and arms are all made of iron. They dress in iron and wear iron casques on their heads. Their swords are iron; their bows are iron; their shields are iron; their spears are iron. Their deer [horses] carry them on their backs wherever they wish to go. These deer, our lord, are as tall as the roof of a house. . . . Their skin is white, as if it were made of lime. They have yellow hair, though some of them have black. . . . Their dogs are enormous, with flat ears and long, dangling tongues. The color of their eyes is a burning yellow; their eyes flash fire and shoot off sparks. . . . They bound here and there, panting, with their tongues hanging out. And they are spotted like an ocelot."

When Motecuhzoma heard this report, he was filled with terror. It was as if his heart had fainted, as if it had shriveled. It was as if he were conquered by despair.

(From M. L. Portilla, *The Broken Spears*, 1992)

Huguenot explorer Jean de Léry describes how the Tupinambá treat their war captives (1556): Now when the captive has hurled everything he could pick up near him on the ground—stones, even clods of earth—he who is to strike the blow . . . approaches the prisoner with, for instance, "Are you not of the nation called Margaia, which is our enemy? And have you not yourself killed and eaten of our kinsmen and our friends?" The prisoner, more fearless than before, replies in his language . . . "Yes, I am very strong, and have slain and eaten a great many." ". . . And for that reason," says he who is standing there ready to slaughter him, "since you are now in our power, you will presently be killed by men, and then roasted on the *boucan* and eaten by all the rest of us." "Very well," replies the prisoner . . ., "my kinsmen will avenge me in turn." . . . [He] who is there ready to perform this slaughter lifts his wooden club with both hands and brings down the rounded end of it with such force on the head of the poor prisoner that . . . I have seen some who fell stonedead on the first blow. . . .

(Jean de Léry, *History of a Voyage to the Land of Brazil, Otherwise called America*, 1556; trs., ed. J. Whatley, 1990)

So also was religion. Dominican, Franciscan, Augustinian, and, after 1540, Jesuit missionaries accompanied the Spanish expeditions. The Jesuits were especially active in Brazil. (Suspected of pursuing an agenda hostile to the monarchy, the Jesuits were expelled from several European nations in this period, and from the Portuguese colonies in 1759, the Spanish in 1767.) Missions constituted some of the first permanent European settlements in the Spanish American periphery, beyond the main regions of settlement in Mexico and the Andes. Missions were establishments modeled on European monastery communities; they offered medical assistance and skills training to Amerindian communities while urging conversion to Christianity. On a smaller scale, Protestant missionaries also attempted the conversion of native populations. Christian beliefs, institutions, and rituals were deeply alien to Amerindian belief systems. Conversions remained largely unsuccessful in the case of the Protestants, or incomplete in the case of the Roman Catholics, where native attitudes heavily colored alien doctrines. Each Amerindian group thought of itself as "the people," or "the true people," and were not disposed to adopt the spiritual habits of alien folk they considered inferior to themselves.

Over the same centuries, as Christian clergy attempted the conversion of the Amerindians, European farmers and landowners claimed their land. The original inhabitants were sometimes, initially, tolerated. More often, they were pushed away to more remote regions of the interior, or pressed into labor service. In the latter case, they worked as virtual serfs—dependent on a European owner and paid meager wages to work the land that had once been theirs. Others were set to labor under hideous conditions in the gold and silver mines that fed the Spanish Empire for nearly a century.

Amerindian workers proved an unsatisfactory labor force—resistant to regimentation, prone to disease. The debased condition of the enslaved Amerindians prompted attempts at reform. The "Laws of Burgos" of 1512–1513 limited to 150 the number of forced laborers one person could maintain in Spanish America, but tacitly sanctioned the *encomienda* system. The "New Laws" of 1542 prohibited Amerindian slavery, even of war captives, and banned the *encomiendas*. The laws were not enforced.

During these years, the problem of Amerindian servitude aroused the attention of, among others, one of the West's most original and profound moralists: the priest Bartolomé de las Casas (1474–1566). As a young man and an owner of enslaved natives, de las Casas observed the settlement of Spanish America and the harsh treatment of the Amerindians. In 1512 or 1513, he became a priest. In 1514, he gave up his slaves and committed himself to exposing the atrocities against American natives. His opposition was based on the view that natural laws and rights were common to all peoples, Christian and non-Christian. Moreover, the Amerindians were inherently a gentle, teachable, amenable people. He felt that if priests, and not armed conquerors, were sent to the New World, the Amerindians could be guided peacefully to live as Christians in a society based on European standards. Thus de las Casas did not propose to abandon plans to settle the New World and subordinate the Amerindians—but only to accomplish those projects without brutalizing them.

De las Casas described Spanish atrocities and his proposals for ideal Amerindian communities in works written over a long lifetime: in direct appeals to the Spanish monarchs, in a history of the new territories, in memoranda to the council that administered New World affairs, in a scathing *Brief Relation of the Destruction of the Indies*. After the composition of this work, but before its publication in 1552, he held a public debate with the theologian Juan Ginés de Sepúlveda. Sepúlveda argued that slavery was natural, that the Amerindians were inherently suited to be slaves, and that the evils that accompanied the conquest were outweighed by the greater good achieved for civilization. In response, de las Casas swayed his audience by reporting vividly the tortures of innocent natives that he had witnessed.

In the end, he convinced King Philip II of Spain. In 1573, Philip approved new regulations decreeing that the occupation of the New World was not to be considered a "conquest," and that the natives were to be treated with love. "The Indians," read the ordinance, "[are] to be pacified and indoctrinated, but in no way are they to be harmed, for all we seek is their welfare and conversion." Such decrees ruled out the actual enslavement of the Amerindian population, but could not reverse (nor was that the intention) the destruction of its pre-conquest way of life.

The brutal conquest, the hideous conditions of labor, the disruption of Amerindian communities, the dispossession of the natives from their lands were terrible events. But these are responsible for only a small fraction of the Amerindian death toll that resulted from the European arrival in the New World. The rest were victims of "microbe shock."

Before the arrival of Columbus, the approximately 75 million Amerindian inhabitants of the Western Hemisphere constituted nearly one-fifth of the world population. A little more than 50 years later, only about 10 million remained. In Mexico, a pre-conquest native population of as many as 25 million inhabitants had, by 1600, sunk to about 1 million. The number of Caribs sank almost to zero. Most of the natives of the Western Hemisphere vanished in the first century after the arrival of the Europeans. They died from disease: smallpox, diphtheria, influenza, measles, mumps, and other illnesses. The inhabitants of the Old World had been exposed to the microbes causing these diseases, and had developed some immunity against them. New World populations, isolated from Eurasia for many millennia, had none. (Perhaps the New World retaliated; some scholars believe that syphilis, which infected Europe about the time of Columbus, originated in the Americas.) More than guns, more than abuse and dislocation, the common illnesses of Europe battered and nearly consumed the flourishing societies of the Americas. The continent became, it appeared, what the first European visitors proclaimed it to be: a wilderness.

The African Solution

Amerindians became less available as a labor force because they were deemed not subject to enslavement, because they resisted the regimentation of the mines and plantations, and because they were ravaged by disease (imported from Europe) and declining in numbers. Europeans then turned to another labor source: that of African slaves. African slavery would have enormous consequences for the later development of American culture.

Two circumstances combined to trigger the exploitation of Africans in the New World by European landowners and entrepreneurs. The first was that the Portuguese had settled the west African coast at about the same time as the opening and exploitation of the Western Hemisphere. The second was that these same Portuguese had already experimented successfully, on their recently acquired Atlantic islands, with the plantation farming of sugar using African slave labor. Once the Portuguese inaugurated sugar planting in the Western Hemisphere, the importation there of the necessary slaves was inevitable. This happened in the 1530s, in Portuguese Brazil. Soon Dutch entrepreneurs had carried the system to the West Indies, where Spanish, French, and English landowners developed into a slakeless market for slaves.

Continuing a pattern begun in the first millennium C.E., the east African coastal cities, dominated by Arab traders, looked toward the mercantile zones of the Persian Gulf and Indian Ocean. Christian Ethiopia, facing the Red Sea, was also related to those trading centers. The states of North Africa were culturally Arab; their merchants traded south across the Sahara and on the Mediterranean, where they were trade rivals of Italian, Spanish, and Portuguese merchants. Egypt, in the northeast, previously part of the Arab network, and for nearly three centuries (1250–1517) governed by the Mamluk sultans, became part of the Ottoman Empire in 1517.

In contrast to northern and eastern Africa, central and south Africa was characterized by village-based societies and small states. Though geographically more remote, these communities had been involved in local and even continental trade for centuries. West Africa was the zone of the great medieval kingdoms of Ghana, Mali, and Songhay, centers for commerce in gold and salt, and was still dominated by Songhay. Other, smaller states continued to form in west Africa. From these, and from the Kongo region to the south, flowed the stream of men and (in lesser numbers) women who were involuntarily removed to labor across the Atlantic Ocean.

Slaves were the major commodity that Portuguese merchants traded from their African depots. During the Middle Ages, most of the slaves exchanged in Mediterranean markets were of Asian or Slavic origin—whence the word "slave" and its equivalents in European languages. The supply of these victims diminished in Europe after the conquest of Constantinople by the Ottoman Turks in 1453. Black African slaves took their place, and soon were exchanged in greater numbers than Eurasian captives had been earlier. Like the ancient Romans, Arab purchasers enslaved white and black workers indiscriminately.

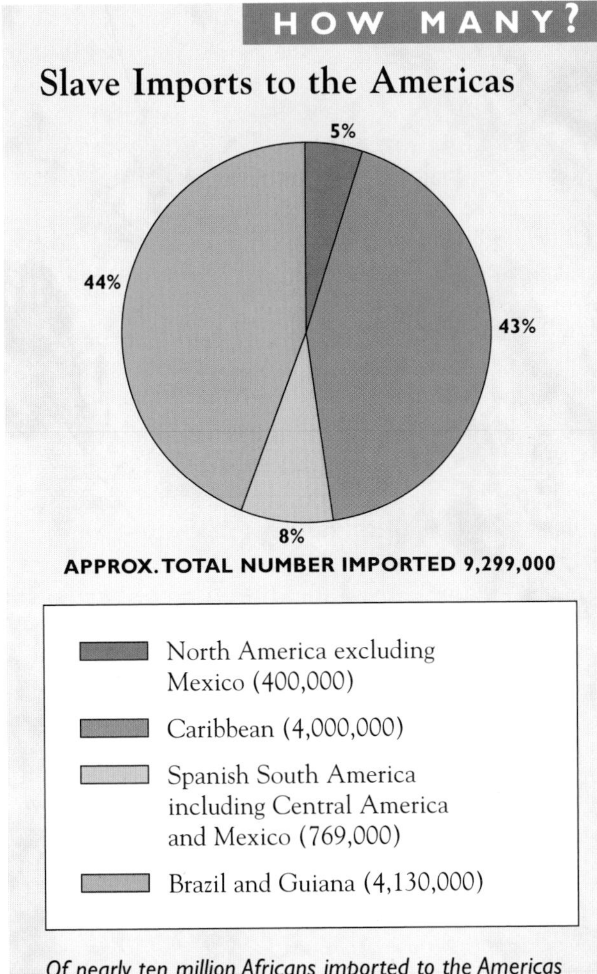

Of nearly ten million Africans imported to the Americas and enslaved, the greatest numbers remained in Brazil (and nearby Guiana) and the Caribbean (totalling 87% of the whole), with lesser numbers dispersed over the great areas of Spanish America and North or Anglo-America (totalling 13% of the whole).
Source: *H. Spodek,* The World's History *(Upper Saddle River, NJ: Prentice Hall, 1998), p. 448*

North African Arab dealers supplied African slaves from the continent's interior to Mediterranean markets and to the courts and cities of Islamic Africa. After the Portuguese settlement on the west coast, mainly near modern Ghana, these dealers brought slaves also to the western coastal markets, where European traders waited to purchase them. European traders also recruited slaves directly from the nations and tribes of the interior, who willingly surrendered their war captives to the care of the new entrepreneurs. In exchange, African suppliers received textiles and hardware, especially guns. The guns permitted more war, and war produced more slaves.

From the 1440s, Portuguese ships brought African slaves to Europe. After 1503, slaves were transported across the Atlantic. Their numbers rose into the nineteenth century, to constitute the largest instance ever of the mass-transplantation of captive peoples. This trade enriched the Atlantic nations of Europe.

Different estimates are given for the numbers of slaves transported across the Atlantic, but recent research indicates the magnitude of that transshipment. Some 9 to 12 million African slaves arrived in the Western Hemisphere (in addition to one to 2 million others who died during the voyage) between the first shipment in 1503 and the last in the 1880s. The numbers were low at first (a few thousand per year in the 1500s), but mounted rapidly in the 1600s (20,000 per year) to peak in the late 1700s (nearly 100,000 per year). Before 1800, more Africans than Europeans crossed the Atlantic, carried first by the Portuguese, and then the Dutch and the British. Realizing annual profits of close to 10 percent, after 1730 the British became the chief traffickers in slaves.

Of the 9 to 12 million transported, men outnumbered women by a ratio of two to one. Most were put to work in the Caribbean and South America, where the lives of laborers were short—slaves being, as one Portuguese official commented, "a commodity that died with such ease." They were swiftly replaced with new arrivals. The impact on African society of the steady removal, over three centuries, of mostly young men can well be surmised. Only about 400,000 slaves came to North America, where they were able to reproduce themselves, so that plantation owners did not depend so heavily on new importation.

The journey itself was punishing. Slavers brought the bands of new slaves to the ship, stripped them naked, and examined them—only the strong and healthy were valuable. For a passage of eight to twelve weeks, the slaves lived below deck, chained together and lying on specially constructed shelves where they could neither sit up straight nor move about. They were exercised on the deck, in which sessions female slaves were vulnerable to rape. The food was scarce and shared from common buckets. Contagious disease ran rampant. Vomit, mucus, excreta, and blood pooled in the slave quarters, breeding new waves of illness. Despair drove many to suicide. The dead were thrown overboard. On the other side of the Atlantic, the survivors faced the degradation of the slave markets. Here, many were wrenched from family members and compatriots before being dispatched to a life of forced, unremunerated labor.

The system of African slavery developed to provide a labor force in places where Amerindians could not or would not constitute one, and where European workers were unavailable. Those circumstances differed in the northern and southern zones of settlement. In the south, especially in the Caribbean, African laborers were immediately impressed into labor on the sugar plantations—indeed, the numbers of slaves shipped rose directly in proportion to the establishment and increase of sugar farming. In the north, where sugar was not a key crop, slavery was slower to develop. In Brazil in later years, coffee plantations, displacing sugar as the main form of agriculture, eventually absorbed great numbers of slaves.

Captives awaiting transportation: *From around 1500, human slaves were the most important commodity that European traders exported from Africa. Often African chieftains acted as intermediaries. Depicted here is a group of captives under native guard awaiting transportation in a European carrier.*

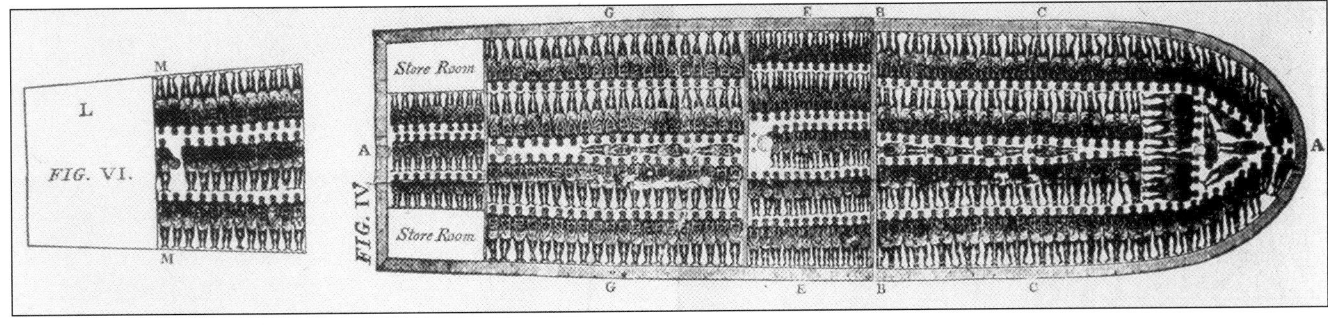

Commerce in Human Flesh

A slave ship: *In this drawing, 1789, of the slave ship* Brookes, *a slave cargo is arranged below decks for the horrific "Middle Journey" across the Atlantic. The slaves were squashed so tightly that they hardly had room to move. Contagious diseases spread quickly, leading to significant loss of life.* (Wilberforce House Museum, Hull, England)

In the early years of North American settlement, European immigrants farmed the lands themselves. For additional labor services, they could employ convicted felons who had been transported to the colonies in lieu of punishment at home (a phenomenon also found in the West Indies). Or they could employ **indentured servants**, who worked without wages for a contractually defined period of years in exchange for the price of passage to the colonies and clothing, room, and board while in service. From the employment of these workers—tantamount to temporary slaves—it was not a long distance to the use of imported African slaves.

The first African laborers in the English colonies were brought to Virginia by Dutch traders in 1619, twelve years after the colony's founding. They worked as indentured servants, however. So long as tobacco—the first cash crop—was farmed on a small scale, there was little reason to resort to slaves. As late as 1660, there were only 1700 black workers in Virginia, when slaves in West Indian Barbados numbered 20,000. As tobacco plantations grew, slavery was established in Virginia. In the Carolinas, the cultivation of rice—requiring intense labor under unpleasant and dangerous conditions—also encouraged the adoption of slavery. The introduction of cotton in the warmer colonies in the early 1700s gave a further impetus to the use of slave labor. By 1700, there were 20,000 African slaves in the Chesapeake Bay region of Virginia and Maryland; by 1775, some 331,000 African slaves in the North American British colonies, outstripping the number of those on the islands of Barbados and Jamaica together. These slaves, generally better treated than in the West Indies, enjoyed a higher birth rate and lower mortality rate and were able to reproduce themselves.

New World Women Women of all races and peoples, such as Amerindian natives and African slaves, were another kind of "other" in the New World: they did not number among the explorers, conquerors, settlers, and governors, but instead were subordinate to them. They had the main responsibility for domestic labor, and they were sexually exploited by the men of the ruling elite. Although all women shared this subordinate position, European women were by far the most privileged. The wives and daughters of upper-class men lived comfortable and protected lives. Even those who began their lives in the Americas as servants or laborers might improve their status by marrying rich planters or professional men—for women were in high demand in the largely male communities of European settlers, and found unusual opportunity for social mobility through employment or marriage.

Quite the opposite was true of Amerindian and African women. In their own cultures, they were already subordinated, and very often assigned responsibility (in addition to domestic service) for agricultural work held in low esteem. Additionally, they were vulnerable to the sexual demands of European males. Often they were coerced into such sexual

A slave auction: *A slave family is sold on the auction block in Virginia, 1861. The placard reads "Negroes for sale at Auction this day at 1 o'clock."*

WITNESSES

Voices of Protest

The Spanish Priest Bartolomé de las Casas describes the native Amerindians and condemns Spanish atrocities (1552): And of all the infinite universe of humanity, these people are the most guileless, the most devoid of wickedness and duplicity, the most obedient and faithful to their native masters and to the Spanish Christians whom they serve. . . . And because they are so weak and complaisant, they are less able to endure heavy labor and soon die of no matter what malady. . . They are very clean in their persons, with alert, intelligent minds, docile and open to doctrine, very apt to receive our holy Catholic faith, to be endowed with virtuous customs, and to behave in a godly fashion. . . .

[Towards these gentle people, for the last forty years, the Spaniards have been] . . . acting like ravening beasts, killing, terrorizing, afflicting, torturing, and destroying the native peoples, doing all this with the strangest and most varied new methods of cruelty, never seen or heard of before, and to such a degree that this Island of Hispaniola, once so populous (having a population that I estimated to be more than three millions), has now a population of barely two hundred persons. . . .

(Bartolomé de las Casas, *The Devastation of the Indies: A Brief Account*, 1552; ed. H. Briffault, 1974)

Former slave Olaudah Equiano describes the sale of his fellow slaves at auction (1789): We. . . were sold after their usual manner, which is this: On a signal given . . ., the buyers rush at once into the yard where the slaves are confined, and make choice of that parcel they like best. . . . . In this manner, without scruple, are relations and friends separated, most of them never to see each other again. . . . O, ye nominal Christians! Might not an African ask you—Learned you this from your God, who says unto you, Do unto all men as you would men should do unto you? Is it not enough that we are torn from our country and friends, to toil for your luxury and lust of gain? Must every tender feeling be likewise sacrificed to your avarice? . . . Why are parents to lose their children, brothers their sisters, or husbands their wives? Surely, this is a new refinement in cruelty, which. . . adds fresh horrors even to the wretchedness of slavery.

("The Life of Olaudah Equiano, or Gustavus Vassa, the African," 1789; ed. A. Bontemps, 1969)

A British physician inspects slaves on a ship bound for Brazil (1843): After the first paroxysm of horror and disgust had subsided, I remarked on the poop another wretched group, composed entirely of females. Some were mothers with infants who vainly endeavoring to suck a few drops of moisture from the lank, withered, and skinny breasts of their wretched mothers. . . most of them destitute even of the decency of a rag. . . .

While employed in examining the negroes individually . . . I obtained a closer insight into their actual condition. Many I found afflicted with a confluent smallpox, still more with purulent ophthalmia, and the majority of what remained, with dysentery, ulcers, emaciation, and exhaustion. . . . Not the least distressing sight on that pest-laden deck was the negroes whom the ophthalmia had struck blind, and who cowered in seeming apathy to all that was going around. This was indeed the ultimatum of wretchedness. . . . Deprived of liberty, and torn from their native country, there was nothing more of human misery but to make them the victims of a physical darkness as deep as they had already been made a moral one.

(Thomas Nelson, "Remarks on the Slavery and Slave Trade of the Brazils," 1843; from eds. P. Riley et al., 1998)

relationships, ranging from rape to concubinage or marriage, from fleeting to long-term. From these sexual relationships was born a whole new population of persons of mixed ancestry. In Spanish America, where intermixture of races was common, persons with mixed Amerindian and European ancestries were called ***mestizos***, meaning simply "mixed." Men and women with mixed African and European ancestries were called ***mulattoes***, an insulting term derived from the Spanish word for "mule." In the West Indies, light-skinned mulattoes, often slaves, in some circumstances obtained higher status than their fully black peers and kin.

In addition to sexual services, African slave women labored hard as field hands or domestics, often, in the latter case, bearing full responsibility for the functioning of the slave-owner's household. They served as nurses for the infants and the elderly members of the slave-owner's family, and their young children were the companions of the slave-owner's heirs, until separated in adolescence.

In time, slavery received the detestation it deserved. The French theoretician Montesquieu concluded as early as 1721 that the institution of slavery was opposed to natural law (see Chapter 17). In Britain, Quakers proclaimed an ardent anti-slavery message. Later in the century, the former slave Olaudah Equiano (c. 1750–1797) raised his voice for the abolition of slavery. Using the name Gustavus Vassa given him by his English purchaser, he published his compelling autobiography in 1789. In it he described his capture in Nigeria at age eleven and the cruelties of his passage across the Atlantic, the slave market where he was sold, and the different masters for whom he labored. Eventually he bought his freedom, taught himself to read and write, settled in England, and publicized his story. In this case, one man was instrumental in changing public opinion.

The system of African slavery gradually ceased over a period of nearly a hundred years. The London-based Abolition Society, founded in 1787, and the French Declaration of the Rights of Man of 1789 spelled out the principle of the fundamental evil of slavery—which was also implicit, but without immediate fruit, in the "all men are created equal" clause of the Declaration of Independence (1776) of the new United States. In 1794, the French decreed the abolition of slavery at home and in its colonies; but the system was later reinstated in the colonies by Napoleon and lasted until 1848. In 1804, nevertheless, the Caribbean nation of Haiti, populated almost entirely by slaves, won independence from France. In 1807 and 1808 respectively, Britain and the United States banned the slave trade. The former abolished slavery throughout the British Empire in 1838; the latter abolished it only in 1865.

In 1813, the independent government of Buenos Aires (Argentina) decreed that all children born of slaves would be deemed free, thus launching the process of emancipation in Latin America. New World slavery ended only in 1886 and 1888, when the Spanish colony of Cuba and the nation of Brazil, respectively, decreed abolition. The scar left by the institution of slavery on the societies of the new nations of the Americas was indelible. Like the metropolitan nations of Europe, the nations of the Americas are heirs of the civilization of the West—in all aspects, good and bad. We are all the descendants of societies that profited from slavery; and that fact has had persistent and inescapable consequences.

In the same way, these nations are the children of societies that dispossessed the Amerindian inhabitants of the Western Hemisphere. That heritage, too, conditions the civilization that American nations, north and south, have inherited.

MEANWHILE

Towards Abolition

1776: American "Declaration of Independence" asserts that "all men are created equal."

1787: Abolition Society (London) founded.

1794: French National Convention decrees the abolition of slavery at home and in the colonies; but it was reinstituted by Napoleon, and not finally abolished until 1848 in the colonies.

1804: Haiti, populated almost entirely by freed slaves, achieves independence.

1807: Britain abolishes the international trade slave trade in its possessions.

1808: The United States outlaws the international slave trade.

1813: Government of Buenos Aires (Argentina) decrees that children born to slaves shall be deemed free; other Latin American governments gradually follow suit.

1838: Britain abolishes slavery in all its colonies.

1865: The United States abolishes slavery.

1880–1886: Cuba abolishes slavery.

1883–1888: Brazil is the last Western slaveowning nation to abolish slavery.

THE WEALTH OF NATIONS

Just as the encounter among European, African, and Amerindian peoples shaped the cultural systems that developed in the New World, so did the economic dynamics that developed during the first hundred years of European presence in this vast region. The commercial energies of Europeans, which in previous centuries had built mercantile cities and trading empires, now produced modern capitalism. The origins of today's global economy lie in the Atlantic age that Columbus, it might be said, "discovered."

Bringing Home the Bacon

Before about 1500, Europe's foreign trade was fundamentally unbalanced. Wealthy nobles, prelates, and patricians craved the spices and gems, exquisite porcelains and finished silks found in the East. Having little of value to offer in exchange, Europe paid mostly in **specie,** with gold or silver coin. That pattern shifted after the opening of the New World.

The Americas provided new sources of silver and gold, but also beneficial new commodities and raw materials for Europe's manufacturing enterprises. By the 1700s the products of these enterprises had found markets in Asia. Eastern luxuries still satisfied the appetites of the rich, but other imports fed the European economy in more productive ways. By 1750, instead of draining Europe of coin, trade with other regions of the globe contributed to Europe's wealth.

The conquistadors, it was said, set out from Spain for "God, gold, and glory." They found gold and silver in abundance, although not as much of the former as they would have liked. From the mid-1500s, annual shipments of bullion loaded on twenty to sixty ships escorted in convoy by two to six men-of-war left American ports for Spain (mostly) and Portugal. One-fifth of the wealth went directly to the royal treasury. From Columbus's first voyage until 1800, the New World supplied 85 percent of the world's silver and 70 percent of its gold; Spanish coins (the **reales**, each one-eighth of a **peso**, or "piece of eight") circulated worldwide.

Profitable New Crops Meanwhile, some people saw that a potentially greater treasure was present in a plant for which Europeans developed an enormous appetite—the sugar cane. In medieval Europe, honey was the principal sweetener, and sugar was rare. It was sold only in small pellets as a pharmaceutical, the ancestor of the modern candy bar. Sugar cane grew in Arab lands, including Sicily. From there, Portuguese entrepreneurs transplanted it to their newly settled Atlantic islands in the late fifteenth century, and to Brazil early in the sixteenth. From Brazil, sugar cultivation spread to the West Indies, where it grew on plantations owned by nationals of several different countries, with the labor of African slaves.

By itself, sugar constituted a whole economy, and its cultivation was a preeminent agricultural pursuit. It became doubly profitable when merchants learned to derive molasses and rum from it. In the eighteenth century, sugar and sugar products accounted for more imports to Britain (where their consumption reached huge proportions) than all the goods of the North American mainland, or all of those from Asia.

Of greater benefit to the European diet were some native American crops that proved cultivable in the Old World. None was more basic than the potato. Rich in vitamins, easily grown, capable of being prepared in innumerable ways, this root vegetable which was already a prime source of nutrition (unlike sugar) for the Amerindian soon became a staple of the European (and African) diet. Its consumption in some places came to rival that of bread, which in Eurasia had held pride of place since antiquity.

Corn, tomatoes, yams, beans, squash, and cacao beans (for chocolate) and cashews also traveled to Europe, and even the ungainly turkey found some consumers on the eastern side of the Atlantic. Other North American animals were valuable not as food, but for the products they yielded. The beaver's fur (for warmth and fashion), the whale's blubber (for heat and light) were readily available in the huge forests and waters of the new continent. From a Mexican insect came the valuable dyestuff cochineal, which produced a rich red hue.

Some crops and beasts made the journey the other way. European pigs, sheep, horses, cattle, and chickens; honey bees; apple, peach, and pear trees; and, of course, wheat came with European farmers and thrived on new soil. Europeans also transplanted from Asia white rice (the Amerindian cereals were corn and wild rice), coffee and bananas, indigo (another dye), and cotton.

One other American crop added much to European culture, though nothing of benefit to its health: tobacco leaves, grown in southeastern North America. Europeans learned from Amerindian users to dry, age, and pulverize it into a powder called **snuff**, to be inhaled, or shred it into a coarse mix to be smoked in pipes, cigars, or in cigarettes, invented as early as the sixteenth century but refined in the later 1700s. This new luxury product complemented the spices, silks, porcelains, and other luxuries already imported from Asia.

European planters in warmer regions of North America experimented with crops grown in tropical regions of the Old World. Rice, the staple grain of much of Asia, thrived in the marshy lands of the Carolinas, whose economy it boosted from the 1690s. Slaves first undertook its cultivation, using their experience of growing rice in Africa. The cotton plant, the source of the principal textile of the Indian subcontinent, could grow throughout the North American southeast. Cotton cultivation was already established in the 1600s, but took off after 1800 to become the "king" of American agriculture (see Chapter 19). Both of these were plantation crops, grown by methods first developed for sugar cultivation in the West Indies, and absorbed the labor of African slaves. Coffee grown in Brazil also used forced labor.

New World products greatly invigorated the European economy and made the Atlantic a theater of world trade as great as, and soon greater than, those

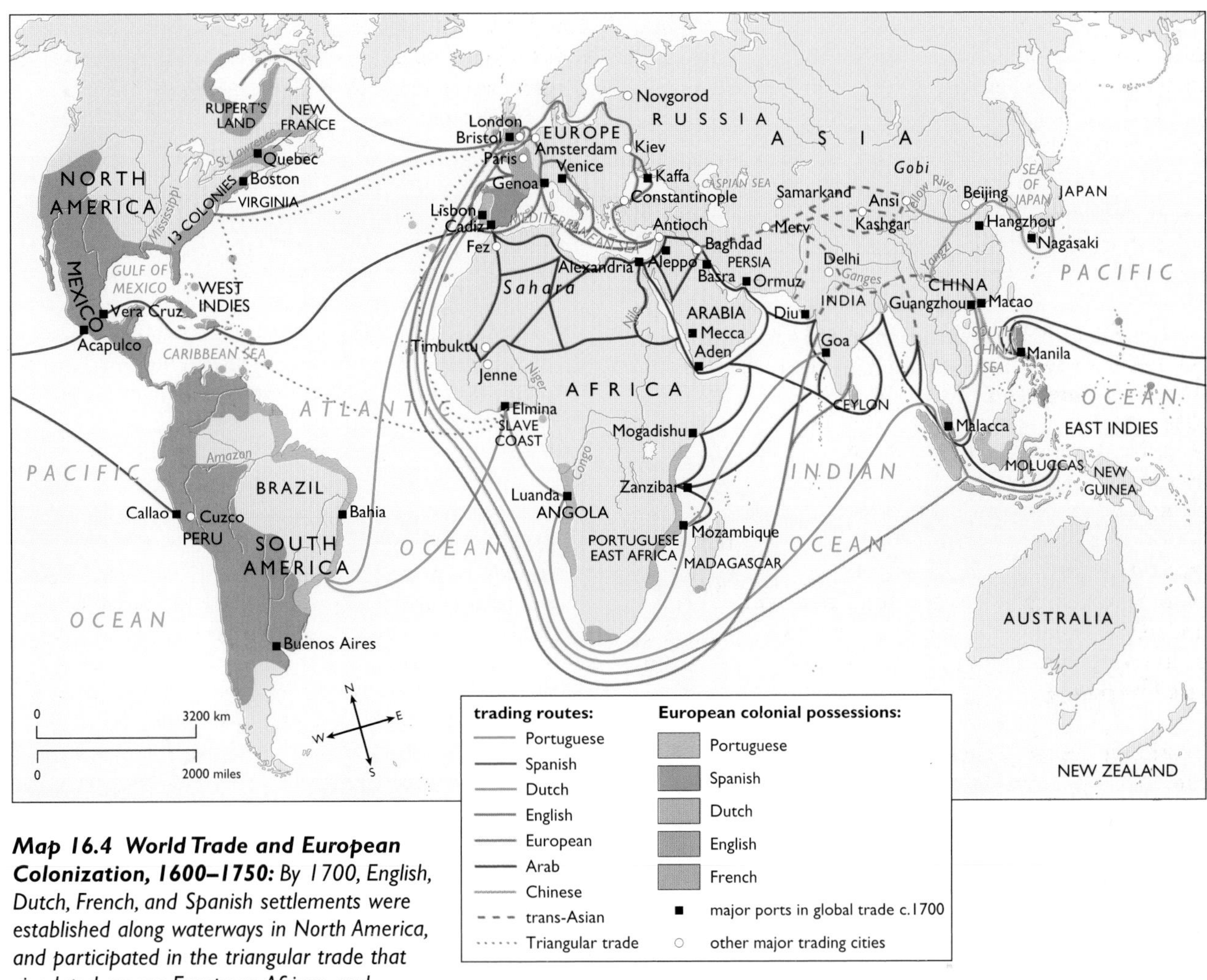

Map 16.4 World Trade and European Colonization, 1600–1750: *By 1700, English, Dutch, French, and Spanish settlements were established along waterways in North America, and participated in the triangular trade that circulated among European, African, and American ports. Meanwhile, French, Dutch, and English ships joined Portuguese and Spanish ones on the trade routes across the Indian and Pacific Oceans. Europeans had not yet fully explored the interiors of the Americas, Africa, and parts of Asia. They came to know of the existence of Australia and New Zealand only late in the eighteenth century.*

of the Old World. But the old trade routes still functioned. At the height of Dutch sea trade in the 1600s, one-third of this trade was committed to the Baltic Sea, where Dutch ships had supplanted those of the medieval Hanseatic League after the late 1400s. The Baltic route, which extended from London in the west to Novgorod in the east, carried tar and timber, flax and hemp, honey, wax, and, most important, grain from the plains of eastern Europe. That ready supply of grain permitted some western European laborers to leave the soil and tend to manufacturing tasks—a precondition of subsequent industrialization.

European-made products and those transshipped from Asia—textiles above all, plus tools, furniture, nails, and tea—won ready markets on the western side of the Atlantic. The American colonists required these high-cost goods for survival and comfort and paid for them with low-cost raw materials in bulk. In the Atlantic trading system, trade was again unbalanced, but now in Europe's favor.

Trade Wars

With the creation of the Atlantic trade system, Europe's role in the global economy changed dramatically. Now she became the pivot of world trade (the nations of east Asia remaining aloof from the West for three more centuries). Her manufactures diversified, her appetite grew, her need for markets expanded, her merchant fleets swelled, and her treasuries fattened. The quest for profit, which had once driven Italian entrepreneurs to scour the Mediterranean, now drove the capitalists of Spain and Portugal, Britain and France, the Netherlands and Germany to expand their business empires to the farthest possible limits. By 1750, Europe was the wealthiest region on the globe. On the wave of this expansion, prices increased, populations soared, cities grew; and the ancient rivalries between European states gave way to a new generation of commercial competition and trade wars.

In the race for wealth, the European nation states took the lead in a departure from the medieval trade pattern, in which Italian merchants won the first fortunes of the modern West. But as navigation and commerce shifted to the Atlantic, these states developed under the aegis of newly powerful monarchies, whose rulers and chief ministers understood wealth to be the wealth of the nation.

This outlook was the outlook of mercantilism. Mercantilist strategies involved both economic and political measures, which sought to increase the nation's wealth in various ways: by encouraging domestic industries (often by grants of monopoly right), by limiting foreign imports, by assuring a favorable balance of trade, by securing ample quantities of gold and silver bullion, and by outpacing rival nations, whose increased wealth meant a relative decrease of their own. In mercantilist logic, these objectives were to be won, if necessary, by force. "Trade cannot be maintained without war, nor war without trade," pronounced an official of the Dutch East India Company, stating a commonplace of mercantilist thought.

Thus mercantilism pitted nation against nation in the race for wealth. The Portuguese were at first in the forefront, then were displaced by the Spaniards, who had meanwhile acquired the gold and silver resources of the Americas. Spanish ships laden with gold and silver attracted pirates and privateers, the semi-official raiding ships of the northern Atlantic nations which were ready to steal from Spain, but not yet to compete with her. The Spanish bullion hoards did not enrich the nation as planned (most of the money went to foreign bankers), and by the early seventeenth century Spain had fallen behind the Dutch.

For nearly a century, the Dutch were the masters of European trade, with England and France nipping at their heels. In those years, approximately three times as many Dutch ships as English ones set off for Asia. England's several Navigation Acts, passed between 1651 and 1696, aimed at undercutting Dutch competition. In the three Anglo-Dutch wars fought between 1652 and 1674, the English navy edged ahead of the Dutch. In the next century, with France as a primary rival, the British struggled for economic supremacy, which it achieved at the close of the Seven Years' War in 1763.

From 1500 to 1800, foreign trade grew steadily, as more raw materials from the New World were used for European manufacture, and as more European products found markets in the west or in Asia. By 1700, almost half of England's merchant fleet was trading with America or India—the cargoes of many guaranteed by Lloyd's, a new company which set the pattern for the modern insurance industry. In the following century, British exports to other parts of the world rose from a trickle to more than a third of the whole,

WITNESSES

The Profits of Trade

French Minister Jean-Baptiste Colbert instructs King Louis XIV about finances (1670): The palpable reward . . . will be that by attracting a great quantity of wealth into the kingdom by trade, not only will you soon re-establish that due proportion between the money circulating in trade and the taxes paid by the people, but both will be increased proportionately, so that revenue will rise and the people will be in a condition to assist more effectively in the event of war or other emergency.
(Jean-Baptiste Colbert, "Mémoire au Roi sur les Finances," 1670; from ed. A. Lossky, trs. G. Symcox, 1967)

Scots economist Adam Smith criticizes mercantilist theories and argues for Free Trade and the regulation of an "Invisible Hand" (1776): The annual revenue of every society is always precisely equal to the exchangeable value of the whole annual produce of its industry.... As every individual, therefore, endeavours as much as he can both to employ his capital in the support of domestic industry, and so to direct that industry that its produce may be of the greatest value; every individual necessarily labours to render the annual revenue of the society as great as he can. He generally, indeed, neither intends to promote the public interest, nor knows how much he is promoting it.... [H]e intends only his own gain, and he is in this... led by an invisible hand to promote an end which was no part of his intention. Nor is it always the worse for the society that it was not part of it. By pursuing his own interest he frequently promotes that of the society more effectually than when he really intends to promote it.
(Adam Smith, *The Wealth of Nations*, 1776; ed. E. Cannan, 1987)

while imports from those lands rose to over one-half of all imports. At the same time, France's foreign trade trailed Britain's and the Dutch share fell behind, while Spain and Portugal were no longer serious competitors.

The profits from this commerce went to merchant capitalists, but also to small investors, who sometimes greedily participated in unwise ventures: notoriously the "Louisiana bubble" (in France) and the "South Sea bubble" (in Britain). In these early-eighteenth-century episodes, private investors, sometimes pledging family estates and life savings, purchased stock in investment ventures that promised huge profits. Speculation proceeded unchecked, the stock values collapsed, and the investors were left with nothing from the exploded "bubble."

While western Europe's large nation-states seized the leadership of European trade, other areas were quiescent, and still mainly agrarian in character. Eastern Europe turned deliberately to more intensive agricultural production. Italy lost its preeminence, although some Italian cities continued to produce profitable luxury goods, such as Venetian glass and lace.

Proto-industrialization Another way to enhance the wealth of the nation was to build up its manufacturing base. The old merchant and craft guilds that had generated economic growth during the Middle Ages had become restrictive, discouraging innovation or the circulation of personnel. Mercantilist projects tended to enliven the manufacturing sector, stimulating certain crafts or inviting joint-stock companies to undertake new endeavors. For example, Colbert (1619–1683), finance minister to Louis XIV, encouraged a variety of manufacturing enterprises (including the famous Gobelins tapestry workshop). To promote commerce, Colbert also oversaw the construction of new roads and canals, harbors and shipyards, and built up the French navy. The failure of Spain to support its industries, especially as silver imports dwindled, helps to explain its economic decline.

The devices that promoted the wealth of nations also enriched individuals, who accumulated enough wealth to fund extensive investments. Still, the wealthy merchants of the early modern era must be distinguished from later industrial capitalists, whose great factories won them previously extraordinary profits. These earlier merchants took commodities made by others and shipped them to distant markets. Or they supervised manufacturing enterprises, especially textiles, which worked on the domestic or "putting-out" system. In this system, the merchant acquired raw materials, distributed them to country workers who labored in their own cottages, and collected the finished goods for sale. Employing men, women, and children, this system flourished into the eighteenth century. It constituted a "proto-industrial" phase of European manufacturing, featuring rural production and city-directed exchange.

Technological innovations also contributed to the growth of the European economy. By 1500, Europe already had put machines to work in productive ways.

HOW MANY?

A Mountain of Spanish Treasure

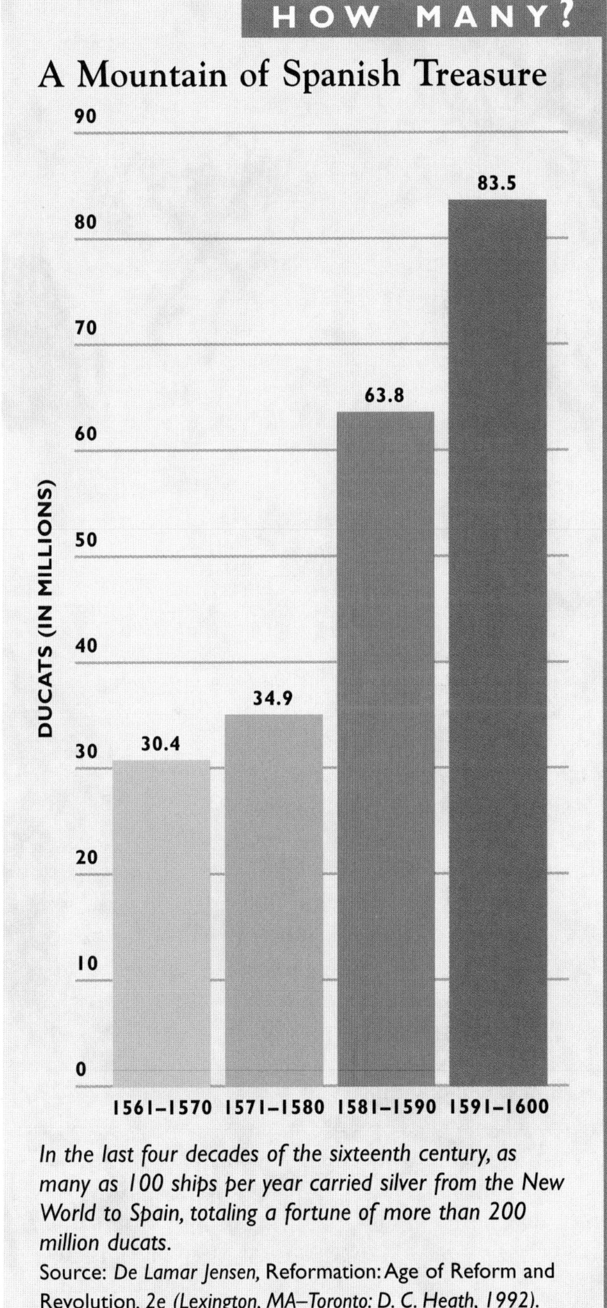

In the last four decades of the sixteenth century, as many as 100 ships per year carried silver from the New World to Spain, totaling a fortune of more than 200 million ducats.

Source: *De Lamar Jensen,* Reformation: Age of Reform and Revolution, 2e *(Lexington, MA–Toronto: D. C. Heath, 1992).*

Engines of Commerce

The great crane at Bruges: *Machines in early modern Europe speeded up enterprise but were powered by the energy of human beings or beasts, as shown in the operation by human beings of a treadmill in this sixteenth-century manuscript illumination.* (Bayerisches Staatsbibliothek, Munich)

Waterwheels and windmills helped grind grain, brew ale, pump water, make paper, saw wood, and treat textiles. The circulation of goods was facilitated by the building of canal networks which in turn was made possible by the invention of locks. Changes in ship design and gun manufacture have already been noted. Over the next centuries, other new machines and industrial processes improved textile and glass manufacturing, coal mining, and iron production.

All this growth, however, had a disadvantage: rapid inflation. The injection of new quantities of bullion into the European economy, the deliberate devaluation of existing currencies, and the steady climb of the European population caused an explosion of values and prices. Prices rose for goods, while wages and rents lagged, with regional variations: in Spain, prices more than tripled in the century before 1600; in England, the prices of basic goods rose nearly sixfold during the same period. The pattern of steep price increases affected different groups differently—it allowed merchants to accumulate capital for investment in more manufacture and trade, while it mercilessly pinched peasants and urban workers.

The forward wave of the commercial economy favored population increase, which in turn undergirded the economic boom. European population generally increased until about 1600, when it surpassed for the first time the pre-Black Death level of 73 million. During the seventeenth century, population growth slowed again, owing in part to the disastrous effect of the Thirty Years' War, which reduced the population of central Europe by 30–40 percent. The marriage age increased in many regions, showing that people were adopting a familiar strategy to reduce the birth rate. Spain and Italy fell behind the north Atlantic nations, and France's rate of growth fell behind England's. In the eighteenth century, the population began again to increase as mortality rates declined. After a last outbreak of bubonic plague in Marseilles in 1720, the plague left Europe (perhaps because of unfavorable shifts in the ecology of the black rat, the critical carrier of the deadly infectious flea). The cycle of famine receded too, and the proto-industrial cottage industries, which allowed young persons to make a profit from their labor without delaying marriage, drove the numbers upward.

Emanuel de Witte, The Amsterdam Stock Exchange: *At the Amsterdam stock exchange, completed in 1613, merchants might purchase shares in the commercial and industrial enterprises that fueled the prosperity of the age.* (Willem van der Vorm Foundation, Museum Boijmans van Beuningen, Rotterdam)

Despite economic growth, the steady upward pressure on prices and the increasing population brought hardship, especially to the rural poor. Grain prices rose by factors of three, four, even six, while the average price of manufactured goods merely doubled. Bread was expensive or scarce, while landowners strove to extract more labor from their workers. The real wages of agricultural workers fell catastrophically, and the force of hunger, briefly subdued in the aftermath of the Black Death, returned. The numbers of the landless increased, and beggars proliferated.

The high price of grain resulted not only from general inflationary trends but also from a shortage of good soil due to over-plowing and too little fertilization. In response, in England and the Netherlands, farmers opened up new land for cultivation of more grain. They drained low-lying lands, fenced off fields to raise stock, and systematized crop rotation to increase the yield of already-plowed soil. These practices were only slowly diffused to the other countries of Europe.

Urbanization With economic growth came urbanization. Merchants concentrated in cities, where goods changed hands, where banks held funds, where artisans labored, and where consumers purchased. In the early modern centuries, towns became cities, cities expanded. For the first time, many European cities grew to exceed the largest cities previously known in the Western world (London, Paris, Naples, and Milan). Not only did large cities grow larger, but a greater proportion of Europeans lived in cities and towns; even country workers often migrated to the city for part of their lives before returning to their villages, their mental outlook forever changed. No longer islands in a world of fields, the cities were open to the countryside and linked to each other in large regional networks of economic activity.

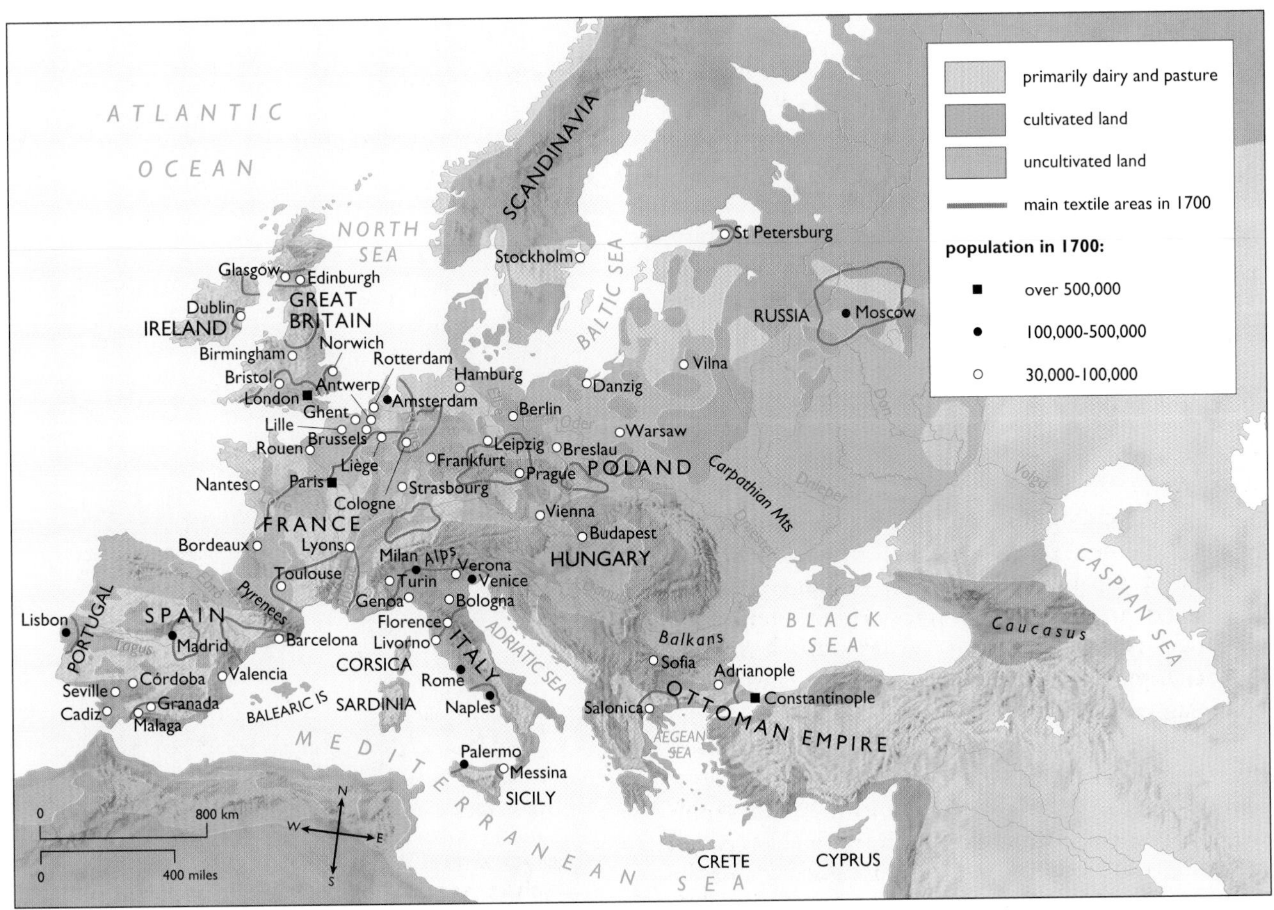

Map 16.5 European Commerce, Industry, and Urbanization, 1550–1750: *The medieval centers of commerce in Italy and Flanders expanded from the fifteenth through the eighteenth centuries, while new areas of textile production and zones of intensive mining enriched the European economic scene. Population increased overall, and especially in towns, many of which grew to be cities, two approaching the million mark in population, while others, like Amsterdam and Madrid, surpassed 100,000.*

Before 1500, few people lived in concentrations greater than 10,000. Between 1500 and 1800, the number of western European cities larger than 10,000 more than doubled (from 154 to 364). At the same time, the number of people living in those cities more than tripled (from 3,441,000 to 12,218,000). From 1500 to 1750, the percentage of Europeans living in cities of more than 10,000 inhabitants increased from 6.1 to 9.9 percent. The growth was heaviest in areas of new urbanization—western and northern Europe—rather than in Italy, whose cities had been the power centers of medieval commerce. Farther east—in Russia, for example—urbanization was minimal, and only a few towns held populations as large as 30,000.

Some individual cities mushroomed. By 1600 the populations of Seville (Spain), Lisbon (Portugal), and Antwerp (modern Belgium), all involved in transatlantic trade, had jumped to 100,000—the size previously reached only by the largest Italian cities. By the same year, the populations of London and Paris approached 200,000; by the end of the eighteenth century, they reached 800,000 and 670,000 respectively. Lyons, France's second commercial city, had nearly 100,000 inhabitants. Smaller cities, with populations hovering around 20,000, were nevertheless important centers of regional trade. The major German cities (Augsburg, Nuremberg, Cologne), subject to the political fragmentation of the Empire, never exceeded this range in the early modern period.

Medieval cities, concentrated in Italy and Flanders, had flourished in the absence of strong national governments. In contrast, the largest early modern cities were the centers of powerful nations, often the capitals. They looked the part. Their streets were straightened, for displays of military and state power and for the carriages of the wealthy. Their secular buildings—palaces, banks, **stock exchanges** and theaters—began to rival cathedrals in grandeur, both secular and sacred buildings being designed in styles that raised classical forms to new levels of opulence.

Amsterdam The city of Amsterdam is a noteworthy example of early modern urbanization. In the Middle Ages, Amsterdam had been a town of little importance, but the political developments of the sixteenth century boosted it to eminence. Nearby Antwerp, a port city with access to the Atlantic, had preceded Amsterdam as the major port (and thus the commercial and banking center) of northern Europe. It reigned supreme in the sixteenth century, when it handled much of Portuguese trade as well as the commerce of the textile manufactures of the region. But Antwerp's career suddenly declined around 1650,

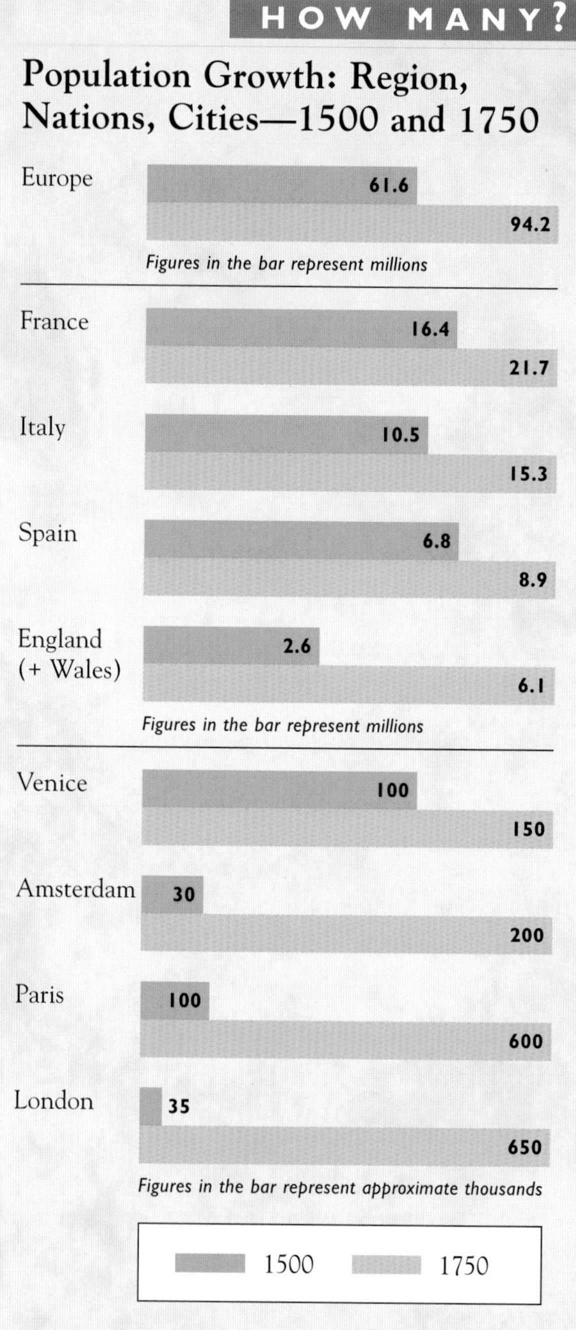

The population of Europe increased more than 50% (from a base of about 60 million) from 1500–1750. But nations and cities increased at different rates. While the population of France increased only about 32%, the population of England increased 135%, to reach by 1750 more than twice its 1500 figure. Meanwhile Venice, the front-ranking city of 1500, fell to a poor fourth place by 1750, when London, having increased more than twentyfold, reached preeminence with a population of 650,000.

Source: *J. de Vries,* European Urbanization, 1500–1800 *(Cambridge, MA: Harvard University Press, 1984)*

when the newly independent United Provinces were allowed (by the Treaty of Münster, 1648) to close the Scheldt River, the city's route to the sea. Located not far to the north of Antwerp and in closer proximity to the sea, Amsterdam took its place.

In the seventeenth and eighteenth centuries, Amsterdam was the banking center of Europe, the fulcrum of world trade. Its population grew from a mere 30,000 in 1567 to more than 200,000 by the early 1780s. Its bank, founded in 1609 on the model of the Venetian Rialto banks, issued its own gold florin. By 1700, the bank provided safety for more than 2000 depositors and the lowest interest rates in Europe (4 percent or less) on investment loans. At its stock exchange (completed 1611), merchants could participate in ventures around the globe, trading in as many as 491 commodities by 1674 (when London, its rising competitor, dealt in 305). A weekly bulletin listed options and gave updated prices.

Even after the 1713 Peace of Utrecht, when the Netherlands fell behind the British and French as a European power, Amsterdam remained the center of European financial life. During the eighteenth century, the city lived on the capital it had accumulated over the previous 200 years, which now helped fund, at profitable rates of interest, nearly every major commercial venture in Europe.

The growing mercantilist commercial system of the sixteenth, seventeenth, and eighteenth centuries enriched European nations, swelled their towns and cities, and lavishly rewarded the merchant investors. It seemed a great success. And yet it also had many defects. The intervention of government into the business of business, while often protective, also retarded the pace of commerce. Tariffs set to shelter domestic manufactures and monopolies created by royal edict interfered with the free flow of trade and the mechanisms which, as later experts argued, allowed the market to regulate itself.

Such problems of mercantilist organization encouraged the Scottish professor Adam Smith (1723–1790) to argue for an alternative organization of manufacture and commerce. In his *Inquiry into the Nature and Causes of the Wealth of Nations* (published in 1776, the same year as the Declaration of Independence), he argued that the absence of intervention would enhance production within the nation, as myriad individuals all pursuing their own self-interest would both yield high profits and benefit the public. Similarly, he claimed, free trade policies would allow the entrepreneurs competing for foreign trade to realize the greatest possible wealth, and thus enrich the nation. Directed only by merchant interest and buyer need, "as though by an invisible hand," free trade would more greatly increase the "wealth of nations" than would a trade system controlled by jealous states and governors. The nation states that had just matured in the political life of Europe were now instructed to limit their functions to those of defense and security. They did not easily retreat.

Conclusion

THE EXPANSION OF EUROPE AND THE MEANING OF THE WEST

From 1500 to 1750, Europe expanded beyond its earlier borders physically, economically, and psychologically. The expansion had begun even earlier, with the commercial revolution achieved by Italian merchants and the foreign adventures of the Crusades. The cultural and religious movements of the Renaissance and the Reformation, although contained within the geographical boundaries of Europe, entailed an enormous broadening of Europeans' mental horizons. Now, however, the expansion was fundamental and taking place on all fronts: it sent people of many nations around the world on new ships driven by new technology; it stimulated Europeans to reconsider their view of themselves upon contact with human communities previously unknown; it changed what ordinary people ate and wore, their work and their homes; it impacted on the lives of nearly every European, from the Dutch ship hand to the Polish peasant.

The same expansion made Europe the master of the globe. Europeans were involved in the rout of Amerindian culture, in the mass enslavement of Africans, and in the enlistment of Indian and Indonesian (if not yet east Asian) producers into the economy of the West. At the beginning of the episode of European expansion, Montaigne wrote about the Amerindian Caribs who ate their war captives. But he had already detected that, much as his fellow Europeans feared and deplored the cannibal, the cannibal had much to dread in the advent to his world of European civilization.

REVIEW QUESTIONS

1. Why was Portugal a leader in African and Asian explorations? Who were the shoguns and samurai of Japan? What advantages contributed to the rise of Dutch power?

2. What were the strengths and weaknesses of Columbus' accomplishments? How were other avenues to North America discovered? Who were the Aztecs and Incas and why were Cortés and Pizarro able to defeat them?

3. Describe the culture of Amerindians before European colonization. What role did missions play in colonial development?

4. What led to the emergence of the African slave trade? What was the final destination of most African slaves and why? What role did women of African and Amerindian descent play in colonial development?

5. How did the New World contribute to Europe's wealth? Explain the European colonial trade routes. Why did Spain and the Netherlands decline as colonial powers?

6. What was proto-industrialization? What were the positive and negative economic and social effects of colonial trade for Europe? Why was the burgeoning city of Amsterdam a good example of early modern urbanization?

SUGGESTED READINGS

The Open Seas

Braudel, Fernand, *The Mediterranean and the Mediterranean World in the Age of Philip II*, 2 vols. (New York: Harper & Row, 1972). A classic portrait of the Mediterranean, detailing material practices, beliefs and customs.

Chaudhuri, K. N., *Asia before Europe: Economy and Civilisation of the Indian Ocean from the Rise of Islam to 1750* (New York: Cambridge University Press, 1990). A study of cultural practices and beliefs: food and drink, architecture, clothing, symbolism, land, nomadism, urbanism.

Fernández-Armesto, Felipe, *Before Columbus: Exploration and Colonization from the Mediterranean to the Atlantic, 1229–1492* (Philadelphia: University of Pennsylvania Press, 1991). A collection of essays on the pre-Columbian European expansion in northwest Africa and the Atlantic islands.

Tracy, James D., ed., *The Rise of Merchant Empires: Long-Distance Trade in the Early Modern World, 1350–1750* (Cambridge: Cambridge University Press, 1990). Thirteen essays by leading scholars on merchant networks, the transatlantic slave trade, trans-Saharan trade, and Central Asian trade.

Brave New World

Anderson, Karen, *Chain Her by One Foot: The Subjugation of Women in Seventeenth-Century New France* (London: Routledge, 1991). An imaginative analysis of gender relations among the Huron and Montaignais Amerindians.

Axtell, James, *Beyond 1492: Encounters in Colonial North America* (Oxford: Oxford University Press, 1992). Essays on themes relating to interactions between Amerindians and Europeans.

Blackburn, Robin, *The Making of New World Slavery: From the Baroque to the Modern, 1492–1800* (New York: Verso, 1998). A discussion of New World slavery in a comparative and historical perspective.

Crosby, Alfred W., *Ecological Imperialism: The Biological Expansion of Europe 900–1900* (Cambridge: Cambridge University Press, 1993). A survey of the biological impact of European contact on the Americas, Africa, Asia, Australia, and the Pacific islands.

Curtin, Philip D., *The Rise and Fall of the Plantation Complex: Essays in Atlantic History* (Cambridge: Cambridge University Press, 1990). A study of plantation agriculture from the medieval Mediterranean to the Atlantic islands and the American tropics.

Hemming, John, *The Conquest of the Incas* (New York: Harcourt Brace Jovanovich, 1970). A narrative of the Spanish conquest of Peru, from its beginnings to the execution of Tupac Amaru in 1572.

Josephy, Alvin M., Jr., ed., *America in 1492: The World of the Indian Peoples before the Arrival of Columbus*. 2nd ed. (New York: Knopf, 1993). A collection of essays surveying the Indian peoples by region and by theme—language, religion, trade, technology, etc.

Pagden, Anthony, *Lords of All the World: Ideologies of Empire in Spain, Britain and France, c. 1500–c. 1800* (New Haven: Yale University Press, 1995). A brilliant reconstruction of the ideological traditions that authorized European conquerors to dominate other peoples.

Wolf, Eric R., *Europe and the People Without History* (Berkeley–Los Angeles: University of California Press, 1982). A history of the interaction between European commercial development and the settlement and exploitation of Amerindians, Africans, and Asians.

The Wealth of Nations

Hirschman, Albert O., *The Passions and the Interests: The Argument for Capitalism before its Triumph* (Princeton: Princeton University Press, 1981). A study of changes in moral and political perceptions of profit-making from 1500 to 1800.

Israel, Jonathan I., *Dutch Primacy in World Trade, 1585–1740* (Oxford: Clarendon Press of Oxford University Press, 1989). An ambitious attempt to classify and explain the phases of Dutch economic activity.

Mintz, Sidney, W., *Sweetness and Power* (New York: Penguin, 1985). A study of sugar in the rise of plantations and the world economy.

PART FIVE

THE WEST EXPANDS

Science, Enlightenment, and Revolution (1500–1900)

The social and cultural changes of the sixteenth through eighteenth centuries formed a prelude to the great political upheavals of the eighteenth and nineteenth centuries, together bringing the West to the threshold of modernity. The first scientists constructed a new model of the cosmos, discovered by observation and described with mathematics, while philosophers refined the logical and theoretical methods needed to explore both cosmic and human realms. In the intellectual movement known as the Enlightenment, critics questioned the bases of prevailing political and social systems, while an increasingly literate public joined in the conversation.

These new ideas challenged the system of social orders inherited from the Middle Ages—the Old Regime—prompting nobles to cling to the signs of their status and bourgeois hopefuls to try to "live nobly"; the peasantry, meanwhile, suffered the effects of economic change and political ambition. Across the ocean in the Americas North and South, the civilization of the West was reinvented in a new land and among new peoples, where opportunity beckoned to those who sought refuge from the cruelties of Europe. Along the Atlantic seaboard, the first Americans to cast off the rule of kings created a new nation, while in Europe the accumulated weaknesses of the French polity led to the French Revolution, which destroyed the Old Regime without establishing a society free of its defects.

The French Revolution bred sporadic later revolutions in France and elsewhere through 1871, when the Paris Commune was violently suppressed. The other major nations of Europe mobilized to suppress such revolutionary activity, while Britain, a unique case, gradually opened its political process to widening circles of ordinary citizens. Nationalist aspirations, meanwhile, another product of the French Revolution, culminated by 1871 in the unification of Italy and Germany, which for the first time took their place among the nation states of Europe.

THE AGE OF REASON

1450 | 1500 | 1550 | 1600 | 1650 | 1700 | 1750 | 1800

Society and Politics

- "Glorious Revolution" in England, 1688
- Peter the Great of Russia creates "ciphering schools," 1714
- Frederick II of Prussia decrees obligatory elementary education, 1763
- American Declaration of Independence, 1776
- French Revolution begins, 1789

Scientific Developments

Scientific Revolution, 1543–1687

- Nicholas Copernicus' *On the Revolutions of the Celestial Spheres*, 1543
- Andreas Vesalius' *On the Structure of the Human Body*, 1543
- Tycho Brahe observes a comet, 1577
- Galileo makes first astronomical observations with telescope, 1609
- Johannes Kepler's *New Astronomy*, 1609
- Johannes Kepler's *Harmonies of the World*, 1619
- William Harvey's *Circulation of the Blood*, 1628
- Galileo's *Dialogue Concerning the Two Chief World Systems*, 1632
- English Royal Society founded in London, 1662
- Academy of Sciences founded in Paris, 1666
- Isaac Newton's *Mathematical Principles of Natural Philosophy (Principia)*, 1687
- Bernard de Fontenelle's *A Plurality of Worlds*, 1688
- Lady Mary Wortley Montagu champions smallpox innoculation in Britain, 1721

Art, Religion, and Ideas

First century of printing, c. 1460–1560

The Enlightenment, c. 1685–1789

- Peter Martyr's *Chronicles of the New World*, 1530
- Richard Hakluyt's *Principal Navigations, Voyages, Traffics and Discoveries of the English Nation*, 1589
- Francis Bacon's *The Advancement of Learning*, 1605
- Francis Bacon's *Novum Organum (New Method)*, 1620
- Galileo condemned by Roman Catholic Church, 1633
- René Descartes' *Discourse on Method*, 1637
- Poulain de la Barre's *On the Equality of the Two Sexes*, 1673
- Louis XIV of France revokes Edict of Nantes, 1685
- Aphra Behn's *Oroonoko*, 1688
- Locke's *Essay Concerning Human Understanding* and *Two Treatises of Government*, 1690
- Daniel Defoe's *Robinson Crusoe*, 1710
- Montesquieu's *Spirit of Laws*, 1748
- Denis Diderot and Jean d'Alembert's *Encyclopedia*, 1751–80
- British Museum established in London, 1753
- Jean-Jacques Rousseau's *The Social Contract*, 1762
- Voltaire's *Philosophical Dictionary*, 1764
- Immanuel Kant's "What is Enlightenment?", 1784
- Louvre Museum opens in Paris, 1793
- Condorcet's *Sketch for a Historical Account of the Progress of the Human Mind*, 1795

Beyond the West

Mughal Empire, India, 1526–1857

Ming Dynasty, China, 1368–1644

Qing Dynasty, China, 1644–1912

- Portuguese capture Malacca (Malaysia) and the Moluccas, 1511–13
- Ferdinand Magellan claims Philippines for Spanish crown, 1521
- Japanese expel Christian missionaries, 1614
- Dutch wrest Malacca from Portuguese, 1641
- Viceroyalty of New Granada created, 1717
- Viceroyalty of Rio de la Plata created, 1776

CHAPTER 17

THE AGE OF REASON

Science, Schooling, and Thought in Early Modern Europe

1500–1780

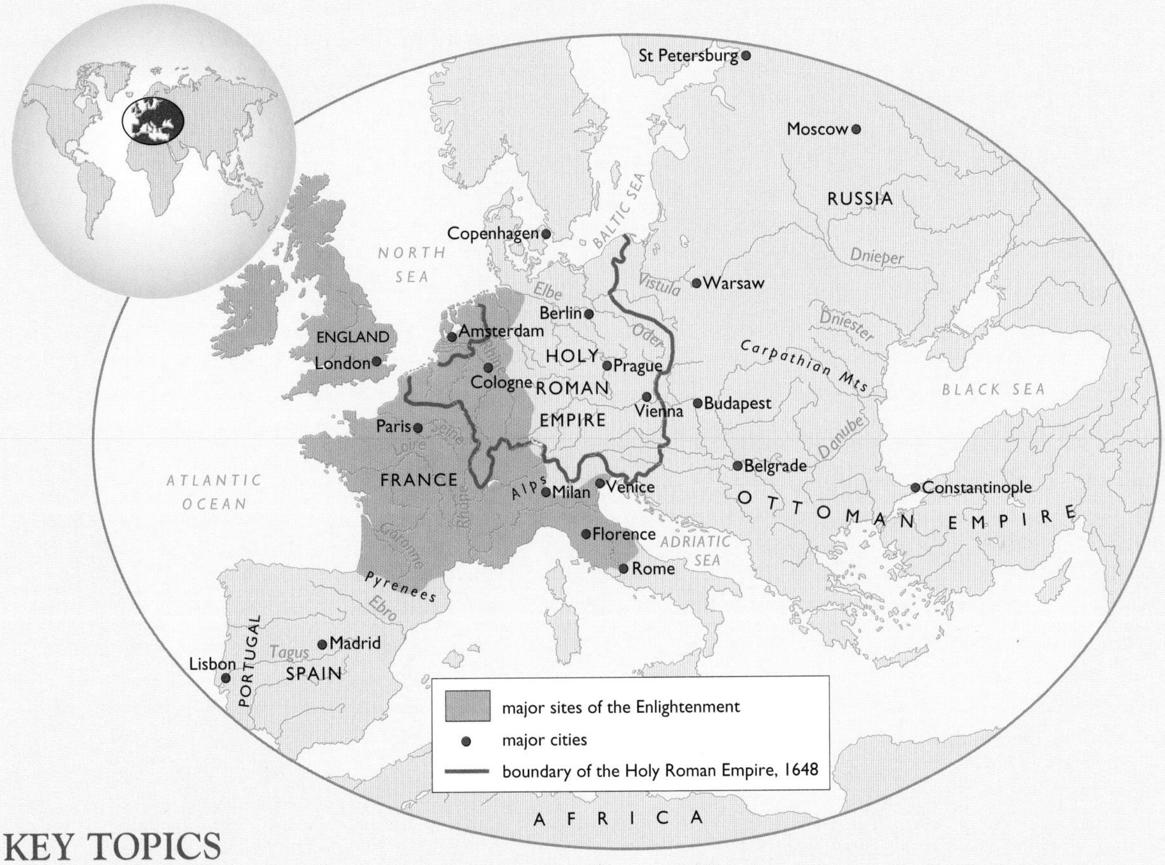

major sites of the Enlightenment

major cities

boundary of the Holy Roman Empire, 1648

KEY TOPICS

- **New Heaven, New Earth:** Scientists from Copernicus to Newton transform Western models of the cosmos (now it would be infinite, governed by universal laws, defined by mathematics); they explore the workings of the human body, search for clear, distinct truths, and discard magic and superstition.
- **The Lights Go On:** Demanding hard facts, and guided by clear reason, the *philosophes* question the norms of politics and society, and create the culture of the Enlightenment.
- **A Little Learning:** In an era of greater educational opportunities, as printing presses produce pamphlets, newspapers, and books, ideas are more rapidly disseminated than ever and the rate of literacy rises.

Descartes' Dilemma *During a pause in the Thirty Years' War (1618–1648), the French nobleman René Descartes (1596–1650) turned his mind to a basic but important question: did he in fact exist? His senses of vision and touch told him that he was alive—but could he rely upon their evidence? In an anxious mental exercise, he stripped away from his consciousness everything he knew by means of his senses. Only one clear, distinct idea remained: his doubting, thinking mind. And if he was thinking, he concluded, he must exist. He announced his conclusion: "I think, therefore I am."*

This statement in Descartes' *Discourse on Method* (1637) marks the beginning of modern **rationalism**, the principle that human reason is the source of knowledge. Where medieval rationalism had used logical arguments to prove the existence of God, Descartes would deduce God's existence from his own—the first step in a new way of thinking that would shift the attention of European thinkers from the divine to the physical world.

Descartes' thought epitomizes the intellectual culture of the early modern era. From 1500 to 1750, European thinkers remapped the universe and unveiled the workings of the human body. They created the scientific method, reformulated the rules of logic, and distinguished verifiable truth from magic and superstition. Applying the test of reason to social institutions and assumptions, they opened the door to fundamental change in the way Europeans lived. Making their ideas available to an ever-growing public, they even included in their number some women, who employed the tools of reason to advance the condition of their peers.

NEW HEAVEN, NEW EARTH: THE SCIENTIFIC REVOLUTION

During the early modern period, a series of thinkers including Descartes transformed the way Europeans viewed the universe and laid the foundations of modern scientific thought. In the Middle Ages, the universe had been seen as a closed system, controlled by God, centered on the earth and its human inhabitants. Now it became an infinite system that governed itself by immutable, natural laws.

While these scientists taught Europeans to see "a new heaven, and a new earth" (in the prophetic words of the Biblical writer of *Revelations*), others investigated the structure of the human body and the human mind—all became aspects of nature to be explored and known in their own right, not simply celebrated as evidence of God's creative powers. This expansion of the field of human inquiry, and the new methods used to pursue it, constitute what some historians term the **Scientific Revolution**.

The Advent of Infinity

The creation of a new world system entailed an entirely changed conceptualization of the place of the human and the divine in an immeasurable cosmos. The old model of the universe had prevailed for some 1400 years, since it was first formulated by the ancient Greek mathematician, geographer, and philosopher Ptolemy (second century C.E.; see Chapter 5). It was geocentric, meaning that the earth stood at its center, circled by the planets and stars, including the sun. In this traditional scheme, complex patterns of the planetary paths were devised to make the geocentric model plausible. European philosophers of the Middle Ages added a Christian dimension to the **Ptolemaic** cosmos: they imagined the movements of the planets and stars to describe a series of spheres within spheres, contained in a vast outer sphere on which were fixed the most remote stars. Outside the outermost sphere lay the realm of God and his angels, who guided the motion of the spheres.

Nicholas Copernicus Nicholas Copernicus (1473–1543), a Polish cleric who had studied Greek, astronomy, and medicine in Cracow and Italian universities, was the first to challenge the Ptolemaic model. He rejected the accepted patterns of planetary motion as unwieldy and implausible. In his reading of Greek scientific texts, he encountered the alternative theory of a sun-centered system first proposed by Aristarchus of Samos in the third century B.C.E. (see Chapter 5). If the earth were understood to move around the sun, Copernicus argued, everything else fell into place: "if the motions of the other planets are connected with the orbiting of the earth . . . not only do their phenomena [movements] follow therefrom but also the order and size of all the planets and spheres, and heaven itself is so linked together that in no portion of it can anything be shifted without disrupting the remaining parts and the universe as a whole." Although he had formed his theory by around 1530, Copernicus did not publish his epochal work *On the Revolutions of the Celestial Spheres* until 1543, when he was on his deathbed and therefore safely beyond the reach of critics. Against Copernicus' ideas were

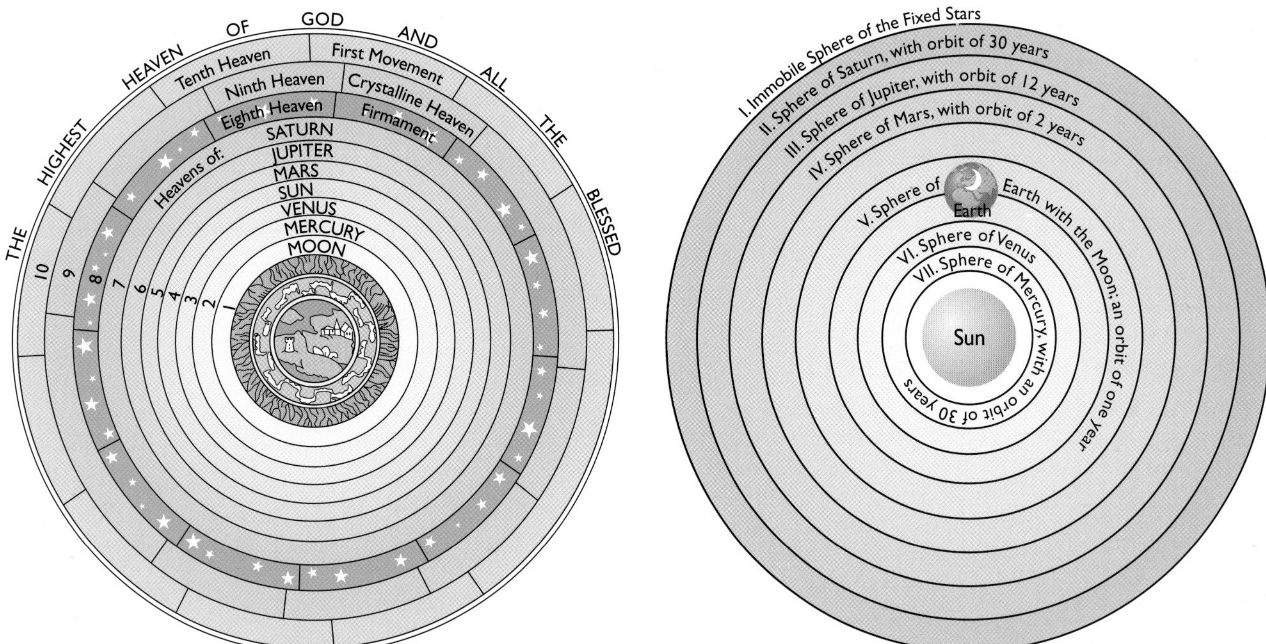

Mapping the heavens: *The Scientific Revolution saw the creation of a new cosmology (an understanding of the shape and structure of the universe). The medieval view had placed the stationary earth in the center of a finite universe composed of concentric crystalline spheres (left). Each sphere rotated about the earth, carrying with it one or more of the heavenly bodies. God himself moved the outermost sphere, thereby causing all motion in the universe. This model was shattered by Nicholas Copernicus who in 1543 proposed that the sun was central and that the earth was the third planet from the center (right). Copernicus retained other elements of the medieval view, however, in that his universe was still finite and composed of crystalline spheres.*

ranged centuries of tradition and the overwhelming weight of orthodox Christian thought. The validation of his theory by later scientists over the following 150 years firmly established the new world order of the Scientific Revolution.

Brahe, Kepler, and Bruno Born three years after Copernicus' death, the Danish nobleman Tycho Brahe (1546–1601) gathered meticulous astronomical records from a well-equipped observatory built to his own design. Situated in Brahe's castle on his private island—both gifts from his royal patron, Frederic II of Denmark, it contained a model of the globe 5 feet (1.5m) in diameter. While Brahe's astronomical observations, including sensational sightings of a supernova (a super-bright, exploding star) in 1572 and a new comet in 1577, led him to reject the Ptolemaic model, he never fully accepted the Copernican system. He maintained that the sun revolved around the earth, while the other planets revolved around the sun. Brahe nevertheless provided the data from which later scientists could pursue the implications of Copernicus' theory.

Some of the materials Brahe left unpublished on his death were edited by his assistant at the imperial court at Prague (where Brahe had settled in his last years), the German mathematician and mystic Johannes Kepler (1571–1630). Kepler employed Brahe's data of celestial motion to test the Copernican theory, concluding that nature operated in regular patterns that could be described mathematically. By 1619, Kepler had developed three principles or "laws" of planetary motion around the sun, still accepted today. The first demonstrated that the planets moved in ellipses, not circles around the sun. The second demonstrated that planets moved at varying speeds in their elliptical orbits, so that the area of the ellipse defined by their path and their radii drawn to the sun were equal in any period of time. The third revealed a mathematical harmony in cosmic relationships that was doubtless most gratifying to a mystic such as Kepler—namely that the square of the period of each planet's revolution is proportional to the cube of its mean distance from the sun. The planets danced like ballerinas according to a common script, written in numbers.

When Kepler was still a young man, the Italian philosopher and Dominican friar Giordano Bruno (?1548–1600) was burned at the stake, charged with pantheism (the concept that the universe and Go

WITNESSES

Pioneers of a New Cosmology

Copernicus claims that the earth rotates (1543): [Copernicus criticizes earlier thinkers whose calculations did not explain planetary motion correctly and whose methods were inconsistent.] I pondered long upon this uncertainty of mathematical tradition in establishing the motion of the system of the spheres. . . . I therefore took pains to read again the works of all the philosophers on whom I could lay hand to seek out whether any of them had ever supposed that the motions of the spheres were other than those demanded by the mathematical schools. . . . [Copernicus soon finds that certain antique authors had suggested the earth itself moves.] Taking advantage of this I too began to think of the mobility of the Earth . . . [and] . . . by long and frequent observations I have at last discovered that, if the motions of the rest of the planets be brought into relation with the circulation of the Earth and be reckoned in proportion to the orbit of each planet, not only do their phenomena presently ensue, but the order and magnitudes of all stars and spheres, nay the heavens themselves, become so bound together that nothing in any part thereof could be moved from its place without producing confusion of all the other parts and the Universe as a whole. [Having established the motion of the earth, Copernicus carries on to describe other aspects of his cosmology including the order of the planets, with the sun at the center.]
(Copernicus, *On the Revolutions of the Celestial Spheres*, 1543; ed. M. Munitz, 1957)

Newton defines the whole burden of philosophy—to explain the universal system (1687): I offer this work as the mathematical principles of philosophy, for the whole burden of philosophy seems to consist in this: from the phenomena of motions to investigate the forces of nature, and then from these forces to demonstrate the other phenomena; and to this end the general propositions in the first and second Books are directed. In the third Book I give an example of this in the explication of the System of the World; for by the propositions mathematically demonstrated in the former Books, in the third I derive from the celestial phenomena the forces of gravity with which bodies tend to the sun and the several planets. Then from these forces, . . . I deduce the motions of the planets, the comets, the moon, and the sea. I wish we could derive the rest of the phenomena of Nature by the same kind of reasoning from mechanical principles, for I am induced by many reasons to suspect that they may all depend upon certain forces by which the particles of bodies . . . are either mutually impelled towards one another . . . or are repelled and recede from one another. These forces being unknown, philosophers have hitherto attempted the search of Nature in vain; but I hope the principles here laid down will afford some light either to this or some truer method of philosophy.
(Isaac Newton, *Mathematical Principles of Natural Philosophy*, Vol. I, 1687; ed. Cajori, 1974)

An island of knowledge: *Sixteenth- and early seventeenth-century astronomers worked with relatively simple equipment. Tycho Brahe's observatory at Stjerneborg in Denmark was state-of-the-art in around 1600.*

are ultimately identical). Bruno's theories included the claim that the universe was infinite, and composed of innumerable irreducible elements. Bruno's theory of infinity was not based either on observations such as Brahe's or on the scholarly examination of ancient theories undertaken by Copernicus: he was an original thinker who believed that the perceptions of the human mind were conditioned by a person's spatial, chronological, and even psychological position. The universe might roll on for ever, and anything conceivable by the mind might be true, in some universe or other. Bruno's concept of an infinite universe contributed to the definitive revision of European ideas of the shape and extent of the cosmos, inaugurating the modern conception of the world.

Galileo Galilei The new spirit of inquiry put increasing emphasis on the need to support theories about the material world with careful observation—the basis of modern scientific method. To make possible more accurate observation of the heavens, the mathematician, musician, and philosopher Galileo Galilei (1564–1642) employed techniques learned from a Dutch lens-grinder to construct the first astronomical telescope. From 1609, he used this new instrument to verify Copernican theory and record many other observations. He saw the spots on the sun and the mountainous surface of the moon; he found that Jupiter had satellites and Saturn rings, and that the Milky Way was made up of innumerable stars.

Galileo announced his discoveries in his *Starry Messenger* (1610), winning public applause and offers of patronage. He also gained enemies as the forces of intellectual and religious orthodoxy turned against him, in particular church leaders who, still engaged in the mission of Catholic Reformation (see Chapter 14), maintained that the Copernican theory was contrary to faith. In 1632, a generation after his observations had finally consigned the Ptolemaic cosmos to the realms of fiction, Galileo published his *Dialogue Concerning the Two Chief World Systems*. Constructed as a dialogue between proponents of the Ptolemaic and Copernican cosmic models, it unequivocally supported the latter. Galileo chose to write in Italian, rather than in Latin, the language still used for scholarly publications throughout Europe, which meant that his work could reach a wider audience in his own country. In 1633, a church court examined Galileo and ordered him to repudiate his views. Threatened with torture, he acceded—an act that one modern philosopher termed "the crime of Galileo." (In 1992, more than six centuries later, the Church at last reversed Galileo's conviction.) Still, church condemnation did not halt the circulation of his ideas. He had shattered existing frontiers to formulate the possibility of a universe that was wholly without center or boundary: an infinitude of bodies unthinkably remote.

Galileo was also a pioneer physicist. He used new equipment and experimentation to reveal flaws in prevailing beliefs about the nature and behavior of matter, which were largely derived from the writings of the Greek philosopher Aristotle (384–322 B.C.E.). Galileo described the law of falling bodies (that they fall at the same rate of acceleration regardless of their weight) and discovered the law of pendular motion (that any pendulum takes the same time to traverse its maximum and minimum arcs). He contested Aristotle's view that the natural condition of material bodies was to be at rest: according to Galileo (and modern physics since that time), matter was naturally in motion.

Isaac Newton It was the English scientist Isaac Newton (1642–1727) who went on to discover the principles that governed the limitless universe imagined by Bruno and investigated by Galileo, thus completing the early modern reconceptualization of the world system. In his *Mathematical Principles of Natural Philosophy* (1687), published in the Latin of university scholars, Newton defined the principle of universal

MUST READS

Books that Made the Scientific Revolution

Nicholas Copernicus	*On the Revolutions of the Celestial Spheres* (1543)
Andreas Vesalius	*On the Structure of the Human Body* (1543)
Francis Bacon	*The Advancement of Learning* (1605)
William Harvey	*Circulation of the Blood* (1628)
Johannes Kepler	*New Astronomy* (1609)
Galileo Galilei	*The Starry Messenger* (1610)
Isaac Newton	*Mathematical Principles of Natural Philosophy* (1687)

gravitation. Gravity explained the movements of both earthly and celestial bodies, providing the new world system with a unity and coherence that seemed to have been lost when Copernicus had removed the earth from the center of the cosmos a century and a half before. Newton further elaborated three laws of motion that have served as a framework for physical mechanics ever since. He also developed the branch of mathematics known as calculus and demonstrated using a glass prism that white light could be split into the sequence of colors that make up the spectrum.

Despite the breakthrough concepts they developed, early modern scientists worked squarely within the framework of the medieval intellectual tradition they transcended. They were considered "natural philosophers," whose range of inquiry embraced the whole material universe. This lack of more closely defined specialization helps explain the versatility of a Galileo or a Newton, who ranged easily from mathematics to physics to astronomy. Moreover, these early scientists used Latin, the universal language of learning in Europe, to communicate their findings across languages (Polish, Danish, German, Italian, English) and religious divides—Copernicus and Galileo were Roman Catholic; Brahe, Kepler, and Newton Protestant—while also permitting them to speak to the generalists among their educated public.

WITNESSES

Science and Religion in Conflict

Cardinal Bellarmine finds no compromise between Copernicanism and Catholic doctrine (April 12, 1615): To want to affirm that in reality the sun is at the center of the world and only turns on itself without moving from east to west, and the earth . . . revolves with great speed around the sun . . . is a very dangerous thing. . . . [If you read] not only the Holy Fathers, but also the modern commentaries on Genesis, the Psalms, Ecclesiastes, and Joshua, you will find all agreeing in the literal interpretation that the sun is in heaven and turns around earth with great speed, and that the earth is very far from heaven and sits motionless at the center of the world. Consider now, with your sense of prudence, whether the Church can tolerate giving Scripture a meaning contrary to the Holy Fathers and to all the Greek and Latin commentators.
(From M. A. Finnochiaro ed., *Galileo Affair: A Documentary History*, 1989)

Writing to Grand Duchess Christina, Galileo distinguishes scientific from theological inquiry (1615): I am inclined to think that Holy Scripture is intended to convince men of those truths which are necessary for their salvation, and which being far above man's understanding cannot be made credible by any learning, or by any other means than revelation. But that the same God who has endowed us with senses, reason, and understanding, does not permit us to use them, and desires to acquaint us in another way with such knowledge as we are in a position to acquire for ourselves by means of those faculties—that, it seems to me I am not bound to believe, especially concerning those sciences about which the Holy Scriptures contain only small fragments and varying explanations; and this is precisely the case with astronomy, of which there is so little that the planets are not [even] all enumerated. . . . I think that in discussing natural phenomena we ought not to begin with texts from Scripture but with experiment and demonstration, for from the Divine Word Scripture and nature do alike proceed.
(From J. J. Fahie ed., *Galileo: His Life and Work*, 1903)

Writing to Reverend Bentley, Newton explains God's indispensable role in the Newtonian universe (December 10, 1692): When I wrote my treatise about our system [*Mathematical Principles of Natural Philosophy*, published in 1687], I had an eye upon such principles as might work with considering men for the belief of a Deity; and nothing can rejoice me more than to find it useful for that purpose. . . . The motions which the planets now have . . . could not spring from any natural cause alone, but were impressed by an intelligent Agent. . . . Nor is there any natural cause which could give the planets those just degrees of velocity, in proportion to their distances from the sun and other central bodies, which were requisite to make them move in such concentric orbs about those bodies. . . . To make this system, therefore, with all its motions, required a cause which understood and compared together the quantities of matter in the several bodies of the sun and planets and the gravitating powers resulting from thence. . . . [A]nd to compare and adjust all these things together, in so great a variety of bodies, argues that cause to be, not blind and fortuitous, but very well skilled in mechanics and geometry.
(From M. Munitz ed., *Theories of the Universe*, 1957)

"Man the Machine": Exploration of the Human Body

Before about 1500 in Europe, the human body was unknown terrain. Ancient physicians had made extensive clinical observations and acquired some practical surgical experience, but they could not explain what they observed. In the sixteenth and seventeenth centuries, however, anatomists and physicians learned that the human being was an autonomous mechanism governed by natural laws. Exploration of the fabric of the body yielded a new model of the human being: in the words of one French writer, "man the machine." This breakthrough in medical thought was comparable to the breakthroughs in the realm of astronomy.

Ancient physicians had proposed the theory of **humors** to explain the functioning of the body. It was based on early Greek speculations, codified in the works of Galen (second century C.E.; see Chapter 6), and repeated by Arab and Christian followers. It held that each healthy body possessed a balance of four bodily fluids: blood, black and yellow bile, and phlegm. These governed in turn four temperamental tendencies or humors—sanguine ("bloody," connoting optimism or good spirits); the black bilious (melancholic, depressed); the yellow bilious (choleric, hostile); the phlegmatic (slow and complaisant). Physicians examined their patients' bodily fluids and drained their blood, confident in their theory although dubious about the prospects of a cure. But they did not understand how or why the blood circulated, or even how a baby was conceived.

The course of medicine changed with direct exploration of the body. Renaissance artists seeking accuracy in the representation of the human form (notably Leonardo da Vinci) began to draw careful studies of its visible parts. Physicians, meanwhile, began to dissect cadavers. Progress was rapid, resulting in a new understanding of the body as a complex natural machine made up of interacting systems.

Among the first to practice the dissection of human cadavers was the Flemish anatomist Andreas Vesalius (1514–1564). He demonstrated his art before crowds of students and curious noblemen at the university of Padua in Italy. In 1543, the same year as the publication of the Copernican theory, Vesalius published his *On the Structure of the Human Body*, which provided direct evidence about human anatomical structures and helped dismantle the Galenic system.

The ancient humoral theory, meanwhile, had already been challenged by the Swiss physician Theophrastus von Hohenheim, known by his Latin nickname Paracelsus (1493–1541). A systematic observer, Paracelsus experimented with various chemicals as therapies which, inspired though it was by the false science of **alchemy**, led to the development of some effective new treatments, such as opiates to kill pain. An experienced surgeon, Paracelsus also compiled in the German of ordinary readers the first practical surgical manual.

Vesalius' approach was pursued by the English physician William Harvey (1578–1657), who proclaimed: "I profess to learn and teach anatomy not from books but from dissections, not from the tenets of philosophers but from the fabric of nature." Having acquired his medical degree in Padua, he returned to London to practice and teach, serving eventually as court physician to James I and Charles I. His most important discovery, fundamental to all later progress in the field, was that the blood circulated through the body via arteries and veins, propelled by the heart functioning as a pump. The implications of Vesalius' observations, Paracelsus' experiments, and Harvey's hypothesis were not to be fully realized until the nineteenth century. In the mean time, however, some patients began to benefit from their proposals. On the battlefields of sixteenth- and seventeenth-century Europe, surgeons learned to close wounds without cautery (sealing with a hot iron), to improve amputation techniques on limbs that could not be restored to function, and to apply prosthetic devices. And in the domestic realm, doctors, shouldering midwives aside, began to deliver babies.

For the first time, anatomists began to understand how the female body functioned differently from the male. Ancient tradition on this issue was divided: according to the Aristotelians, the female body was that of a "defective male," and the male sperm was the sole cause of the creation of new life. The woman's uterus merely housed the growing fetus until the moment of birth. The Galenists took a more positive view of the female role in conception and gestation, hypothesizing that the fetus was formed by the conjunction of the male sperm and "female seed." This theory accorded women's bodies greater respect than in the Aristotelian formulation, and was at least one step closer to what modern biology knows to be the case. In the seventeenth century, physicians began to develop the fields of gynecology and obstetrics (the study of the female body and of childbearing respectively). First among them was William Harvey, who made important observations of embryonic growth in animals, which resulted in a better understanding both of the female role in conception and gestation, and of general female dysfunctions and diseases.

At this point, the male medical establishment collided with the traditional midwives. These were women who, over the generations, often from mother to daughter, transmitted what knowledge there was of the process of giving birth. Midwives guided women in their pregnancy and prepared them for labor; they knew when the fetus was well-positioned, and when its position needed to be adjusted by a skilled woman's hand, and they knew when there was no hope, but that mother and child would perish. Midwives directed a team of female relatives and friends throughout the whole birth process. After the birth, they instructed the mother in the care of her child, and the personal care she needed to recover from the frightening, painful experience of giving birth.

Over the early modern centuries, male physicians took over the power to manage birth. By the eighteenth century, the forceps had been developed to aid in the extraction of an infant in a difficult birth. Their use was limited to trained physicians, all male, who warned future mothers of the dangers they faced from "untrained" midwives.

Discovering the Human Body

Dissecting the body: *The sixteenth and seventeenth centuries saw a revolution in notions about human biology. An increasing reliance on experiment and empiricism began to replace subservience to the texts of the great anatomists of antiquity such as Aristotle and Galen. This illustration from the title page of Andreas Vesalius'* On the Structure of the Human Body, *1543, shows Vesalius breaking with tradition by doing his own dissections.*

ANDREAE VESALII
BRVXELLENSIS, SCHOLAE
medicorum Patauinæ professoris, de
Humani corporis fabrica
Libri septem.
CVM CAESAREAE
Maiest. Galliarum Regis, ac Senatus Veneti gratia & priuilegio, ut in diplomatis eorundem continetur.
BASILEAE.

Progress in medicine also made an impact in the treatment of disease. Although physicians did not yet know that microbes or viruses caused disease, they understood that disease had objective causes, and that it required strenuous treatment. In the early eighteenth century, during a stay in the Ottoman Empire, Lady Mary Wortley Montagu (1689–1762), wife of the English ambassador to Constantinople (modern Istanbul), observed the practice of smallpox inoculation, in effect the deliberate infection of the patient with a mild case of the disease. She had her own children vaccinated, and championed smallpox prevention in England on her return in 1721. Later in the century, Edward Jenner (1749–1823) refined the vaccine, and smallpox became the first disease to be conquered by medical science—both advances saving millions of lives.

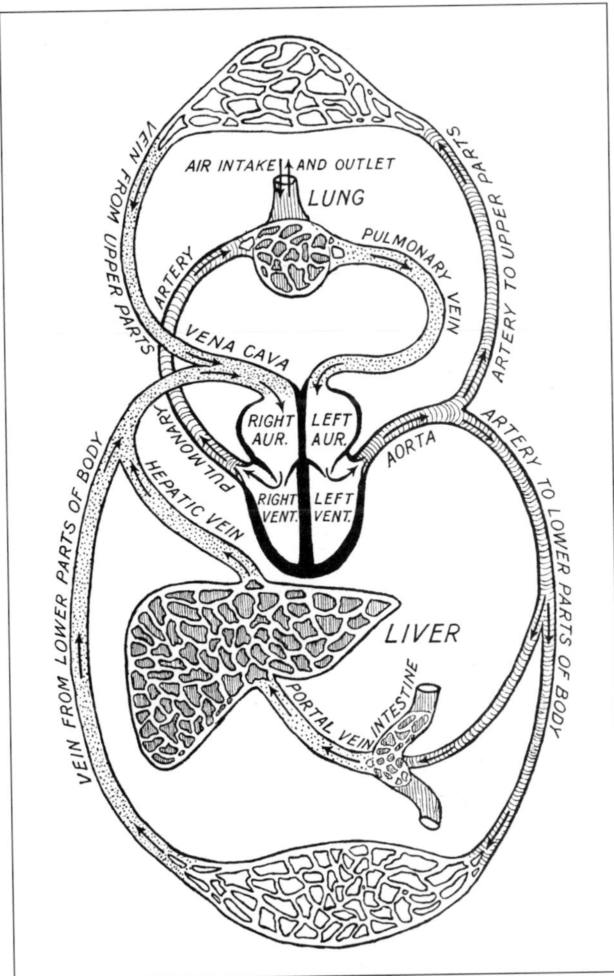

Circulation of the blood: *William Harvey's theories about the circulation of blood through veins and arteries, explained here in his diagram, were backed up by simple, yet highly effective empirical proofs.*

Midwifery and childbirth: *Trained in the new culture of science, the male-dominated medical establishment frequently discredited earlier practices. In some cases, women were pushed out of fields they had traditionally dominated. Such is the case with midwifery, which had once been almost exclusively a female occupation, as shown here in this 1554 woodcut.*

Hard Facts and Pure Reason: New Modes of Thinking

Advances in science in the early modern period owed much to the development of new modes of thinking. Trained in critical methods (and the Greek language) by Renaissance humanists (see Chapter 13), philosophers began to develop original systems of metaphysics. They created methods of reasoning that, unlike the propositions and syllogisms of medieval disputation, enabled scientific inquiry. They doubted everything, including the authority, once supreme, of Aristotle; and the assumptions, once self-evident, of Christianity. They studied nature more than reports of nature, and saw that its framework could be described in the language of mathematics. They accepted the evidence of indisputable facts, often gathered through experimentation. They trusted in, and could often demonstrate, the fundamental rationality of the world.

Map 17.1 The Major Scientific Thinkers and Philosophes: *Both the Scientific Revolution and Enlightenment were transnational movements, whose major exponents hailed from a variety of national, cultural, and religious backgrounds. Though it is true that the culture of science flourished best in Protestant countries, many of the most important thinkers came from, lived in, and wrote in Catholic countries.*

Aristotle continued to reign for 200 years after the humanist Lorenzo Valla (1405–1457) challenged his monopoly (see Chapter 13). While Aristotelianism stood for the old world order, it could also become a weapon against traditional ideas, as when the Italian Pietro Pomponazzi (1462–1524) challenged the central Christian doctrine of the immortality of the soul: how could the soul be immortal, when it was so thoroughly enmeshed with the material body?

Such explorations of the possibilities of Aristotelianism during the sixteenth century paved the way for the development in the seventeenth century of philosophies spun out of pure reason. For the French nobleman René Descartes, the Dutch-Jewish lens-grinder Benedict Baruch de Spinoza (1632–1677), and the German nobleman and politician Gottfried Wilhelm von Leibniz (1646–1716), the universe, or nature itself, was perfectly rational.

According to Descartes, everything in the universe was either mind (a "thinking substance") or body (an "extended substance"), and the universe itself a vortex of matter directed by a thinking mind. Descartes' followers, who made up the Cartesian school, sustained this clean separation of matter from mind, substance from spirit.

For Spinoza, the universe was one single substance, alternately Nature or God himself, a perfect amalgam of matter and reason. In a significant break with Judeo-Christian thought, Spinoza saw God as enmeshed in nature, no longer a purely spiritual being capable of judging and directing the cosmos. His heterodoxy caused him to be expelled from the Jewish community of Amsterdam in 1656.

Leibniz, in contrast, won wide acclaim, and was courted by the princes of central Europe. He acknowledged the existence of a wholly immaterial God, the creator of the universe, and, like his own creation, infinite in space and time. But that universe was self-sufficient in its operations—consisting of a divinely ordained, perfectly ordered infinitude of immaterial particles, called "monads," each constituting a mirror of the whole, harmonious universe.

Other early modern thinkers, inspired by ancient texts, adopted the philosophical outlook of **skepticism**: an attitude of universal doubt. Whereas in the eleventh century the medieval philosopher Saint Anselm stated "I believe in order to understand," these men doubted in order to know. Descartes doubted the evidence of sense experience but proposed instead a logical method of **deducing** further principles from essential first principles—the **deductive** method, based ironically on a faith in the capacity of pure reason.

French mathematician Blaise Pascal (1623–1662) doubted the capacity of reason to know anything: the only source of certainty for human beings, he argued, was a faith based not on tradition but on probability. For the Scots philosopher David Hume (1711–1776), even hard facts offered no dependable knowledge, let alone the vapors of mysticism. It may *appear* that the hammer strikes the nail, Hume argued, but the relationship can never be proved, as the natural world is only a sequence of impressions.

Other early modern philosophers continued to believe in the reliability of sense perception, and in the evidence of hard facts. In late Renaissance Italy, the Dominican friar Bernardino Telesio (1509–1588) argued for a systematic understanding of nature based on experience and observation in his giant work *On Nature According to Its Own Principles* (1565). Circulating widely at the end of the sixteenth century, it encouraged a preference for experienced-based, or **empirical** knowledge of the kind essential to scientific inquiry.

Bacon, Galileo, and Locke The English philosopher, essayist, and statesman Francis Bacon (1561–1626) took up Telesio's mission. He declared war on traditional Aristotelian philosophy, constructed from mere tissues of words, which could neither harness nature nor benefit humanity. Bacon aimed to reshape philosophy, planning to publish a *Great Instauration*, or "re-establishment," of knowledge. Parts of that project, never quite finished, appeared in such works as *The Advancement of Learning* (1605) and the *New Method* (*Novum Organum*) (1620). For Bacon, the new knowledge would have to be established on the observation of hard facts, without which the human being "neither knows anything nor can do anything."

First of all, the human mind must be freed of its prejudices and presuppositions, the glittering but false "idols" that people continued to worship. Bacon defined four classes of idols: the "idols of the tribe," those inherent in the human condition because of its essential nature and cultural heritage; the "idols of the cave," or the particular prejudices of individuals; the "idols of the marketplace," those shared commonplaces that arise from inaccurate understanding of words; and the "idols of the theater," the mistaken beliefs learned from unworthy others, including "the various dogmas of philosophers."

According to Bacon, the mind was to be cleared of these prejudices and presuppositions, so that it could apprehend hard facts with pure reason. Then, it would proceed by **inductive** reasoning: from observed data to more generalized statements "rising by a gradual and unbroken ascent, so that it arrives at the most general axioms last of all." The observer would systematically gather information about a phenomenon until a regular pattern emerged. From that pattern, he would form a theory, or **hypothesis**, about the phenomenon, which could be tested, verified, and expressed as a general statement. The accumulation of those general statements would amount to knowledge—or "science"—itself.

In Italy, Galileo developed the method of reasoning that would come to be called "the scientific method." Like Bacon, he held that the observation of clear facts led to universal statements. From data gathered about the movement of bodies in space, for example, theories might be devised to explain them. Impatient of waiting for sufficient data, however, and

WITNESSES

Pioneers of New Scientific Methodologies

From the senses to judgment—Francis Bacon advocates the Inductive Method (1620): There are and can be only two ways of searching into and discovering truth. The one flies from the senses and particulars to the most general axioms, and from these principles, the truth of which it takes for settled and immoveable, proceeds to judgment and to the discovery of middle axioms. And this way is now in fashion. The other derives axioms from the senses and particulars, rising by a gradual and unbroken assent, so that it arrives at the most general axioms last of all. This is the true way, but as yet untried.
(From H. G. Dick ed., *Selected Writings of Francis Bacon*, 1955)

Dissections not books—William Harvey defends the Empirical Method (1628): True philosophers, who are only eager for truth and knowledge, never regard themselves as already so thoroughly informed, but that they welcome further information from whomsoever and from whencesoever it may come; . . . very many, on the contrary, maintain that all we know is still infinitely less than all that still remains unknown. . . . Neither do they think it unworthy of them to change their opinion if truth and undoubted demonstration require them so to do. . . . I profess both to learn and to teach anatomy, not from books but from dissections; not from the positions of philosophers but from the fabric of nature. . . . I avow myself the partisan of truth alone; and I can indeed say that I have used all my endeavors, bestowed all my pains on an attempt to produce something that should be agreeable to the good, profitable to the learned, and useful to letters.
(William Harvey, *Circulation of the Blood*, 1628; ed. C. D. Leake, 1931)

Truth firm and assured—the rationalism of René Descartes (1637): Inasmuch as I desired to devote myself wholly to the search for truth, I thought that I should . . . reject as absolutely false anything of which I could have the least doubt, in order to see whether anything would be left after this procedure which could be called wholly certain. Thus, as our senses deceive us at times, I was ready to suppose that nothing was at all the way our senses represented them to be. As there are men who make mistakes in reasoning even on the simplest topics in geometry, I judged that I was as liable to error as any other, and rejected as false all the reasoning which I had previously accepted as valid demonstration. Finally, as the same percepts [i.e., perceptions] we have when awake may come to us when asleep without their being true, I decided to suppose that nothing that had ever entered my mind was more real than the illusions of my dreams. But I soon noticed that while I thus wished to think everything false, it was necessarily true that I who thought so was something. Since this truth, I think, therefore I am, was so firm and assured that all the most extravagant suppositions of the sceptics were unable to shake it, I judged that I could safely accept it as the first principle of the philosophy I was seeking.
(Descartes, *Philosophical Essays*, 1637; ed. J. Lafleur, 1964)

dissatisfied with their quality in the imperfect world around him, Galileo developed the method of **experiment**: the staged and repeated "experiencing" of phenomena, controlled so that the factors of greatest interest are isolated and made visible. This method of inductive reasoning based on data gathered from the controlled observation of nature or from experiment remains the method of modern science.

It was Bacon the theorist rather than Galileo the experimenter who provided the inspiration for the English philosopher John Locke (1632–1704) in his advancement of the cause of inductive logic. His *Essay Concerning Human Understanding* is as important for philosophy, pedagogy, and psychology as his *Two Treatises on Civil Government* (both published 1690) (see Chapter 15) is for the development of political thought. In the former he argued against Descartes' contention that the mind contained true ideas of reality even at birth. Instead, Locke proposed that the mind at birth contained no ideas at all—it was a "blank slate," a *tabula rasa* as empty of thought as a teacher's empty blackboard. It is written on by experience. As the mind experiences things through the five senses, it forms ideas about the material world. The things come first; the mind fits thought to them, and after that, words. Everything in the mind arrives first through experience.

Consequently, evil thoughts and actions derived not from an innate evil in the soul, but from unfortunate experience in the world of things. Such moral deficiencies could be repaired, Locke implied, by a new round of more positive experience. The implications of Locke's theory of learning for social change were immense: immorality was not rooted in the soul, the blood, or the social order. It resulted simply from exposure to a poor environment. A correction of the environment would necessarily result in an improvement in mental condition.

While Bacon, Galileo, and Locke grappled with theories aimed at explaining the hard facts of material reality, others rushed to collect the facts themselves. Historians amassed documents chronicling their city's, country's, or religion's past. Others, following but surpassing Classical and Renaissance models, catalogued famous men or famous women. Surveys of topography, botany, geography, and mineralogy poured off the presses. How-to books described methods of zinc-smelting, fishing, or housekeeping; the biology of bees, birds, and silkworms; drainage and irrigation systems; the making of glass.

Other "moderns" (those who hunted for new truths in the present, in contrast to admirers of the "ancients," who studied them in the past) not only described things but also invented them. New pieces of equipment, specially devised for investigating the world with greater detail and accuracy, included the telescope, microscope, thermometer, and barometer. Measuring and calculating devices included the pendulum clock and adding machine (the last by Pascal), the mechanical pump, the flexible hose for fighting fires and lightning rod for preventing them (by the American philosopher and statesman Benjamin Franklin, see Chapter 20), new uses for windmills, and early versions of the typewriter, the sock knitter, and the sewing machine.

The new curiosity about, and desire to master, material reality is evidenced in the rush of discovery, invention, and data-collection that characterized the seventeenth and eighteenth centuries. That absorption in the concrete, the manipulable, the massive, and the movable contrasted both with the passive contemplation of the Middle Ages and the intellectual and aesthetic values of the Renaissance, with its passion for the past and its idealizing quest for truth, beauty, and perfection. The new age was more concerned with how things worked than whether they had reached the highest pitch of perfection—more interested in science, in sum, than in art.

The End of Magic

In a new world where facts were hard and reason prevailed, magical explanations of events were doomed. During the Renaissance, the possibilities of magic had expanded, boosted by learned humanists for whom ancient magical beliefs were as intriguing as ancient knowledge. Two centuries later, however, confidence in magical constructs withered among the learned, and took a last refuge in peasant huts and villages. Reason was the solvent that put an end to magic.

The most widely accepted form of secular magical thought was **astrology**, the study of the ways in which heavenly bodies supposedly affected human life. Until well into the seventeenth century, astrology remained a respectable branch of knowledge. Physicians, especially, were likely to boast secondary expertise as astrologers, and rulers routinely consulted astrologers about the best place to build a palace or the best time for a military expedition. The citizens of the republic of Venice included a horoscope of their city in public chronicles, knowing that it promised Venice a long and prosperous future, while an English astrologer accurately predicted the critical but unlikely 1645 Parliamentary victory in England's Civil War and the later, unprecedented execution of the king.

By the time Newton published his *Mathematical Principles* (1687), however, it was no longer possible for the educated elites to accept the principles of astrology. In a universe systematically ordered and governed by laws expressed in mathematical relationships, there was no room for mysterious communications between the heavens and the earth. Astrology retreated to the margins, to become a lure to the untutored and a pastime for the privileged.

Meanwhile, science made other inroads on the domain of the occult. Occult or "hidden" knowledge at the beginning of the early modern period included much of what later became modern physics, chemistry, and biology. Occultists were mainstream thinkers who strove to learn much about many things: among them were Paracelsus, Brahe, and Kepler. Newton, proponent of a grandly rational view of the cosmos, was an alchemist who believed in the possibility of transforming elements into each other and creating more valuable substances from baser ones. The experiments conducted by alchemists, which involved heating, mixing, dissolving, and generally observing the behavior of many different substances, contributed directly to the development of the modern science of chemistry.

As astrology became distinct from astronomy, and chemistry from alchemy, the field of magic was shrinking. "White" magic, in other words those practices, including astrology and alchemy, by which the course of nature could be understood and altered, was yielding to science. "Black" magic, namely practices intended to cause harm, was already in deep disrepute—the "witches" condemned of such practices were hounded into obedience or tried and executed (see Chapter 14). By the mid-seventeenth century in much of Europe, however, the prosecution of witches had ceased. Rational thought could no longer entertain the possibility of nocturnal black sabbaths or aerial broomstick escapades.

As witches disappeared from towns and villages, so monsters disappeared from maps. **Cartography**, the science of mapmaking, which had been immensely stimulated by the discoveries and voyages of the fifteenth and sixteenth century (see Chapter 16), now became rationalized and, like astronomy, mathematicized. Legendary monsters vanished from their positions at the previously uncharted ocean peripheries of the maps of the world to be replaced with the parallels and meridians that quantified and codified space and dealt magic another blow.

Magic did not entirely die. Uneducated people continued to believe in what the learned called superstitions. Among the educated, the figure of the learned practitioner of magic—so much more than what modern people think of as a "magician"—had an afterlife in literature and drama as the passion-stirred individualist, ceaselessly but fatally curious and creative. That figure, epitomizing heroic modern humanity in its desire to stretch the boundaries of what can be known or achieved, was immortalized in the play *Doctor Faustus* by the English author Christopher Marlowe (1564–1593). Three centuries later, Faust returned in German drama and French opera.

By 1750, for intellectuals and their audience, magic had largely died and credence in traditional authority had faded. Replacing them were faith in pure reason and a commitment to hard empirical facts, in an infinite world perceived through the senses of the body, which was in essence a machine. The "disenchantment" of the world, in the words of the twentieth-century German sociologist Max Weber, had been accomplished.

THE LIGHTS GO ON: THE ENLIGHTENMENT

Science and philosophy cleared away the magical beliefs and stale orthodoxies of an intellectual tradition dating back to antiquity. In the clean air and bright light of a new mental age, intellectuals in late seventeenth- and eighteenth-century Europe turned their attention from science and metaphysics to society. Now they inquired into how people lived and prospered, and how they were governed. These thinkers are known by the French term *philosophes*. They created the era known as the "**Enlightenment**."

The Enlightenment was the predominant intellectual movement of the century extending from England's Glorious Revolution of 1688 (see Chapter 15) and the greatest works of Locke and Newton to the outbreak of the French Revolution in 1789 (see Chapter 20). Centered in France and England, it was also a powerful trend in Scotland, Italy, and the Netherlands, in some of the German courts and cities, and in the North American colonies. The *philosophes* redefined the terms of Western thought and experience, discovered new foundations for political life, looked afresh at non-European places, customs, and beliefs, and drafted new blueprints for the future of humanity. At the core of the Enlightenment was the relentless deployment of reason to confront reality and to challenge traditional authority. In his 1784 essay "What is Enlightenment?," the philosopher Immanuel Kant (1724–1804) summarized the movement's mission as well as anyone can in the ringing imperative: "Dare to know!"

MUST READS

Books that Made the Enlightenment

Isaac Newton	*Mathematical Principles of Natural Philosophy* (1687)
John Locke	*Essay Concerning Human Understanding* (1690)
John Locke	*Two Treatises of Civil Government* (1690)
Voltaire	*Philosophical Letters* (1734)
Montesquieu	*The Spirit of Laws* (1748)
Jean-Jacques Rousseau	*The Social Contract* (1762)
Jean-Jacques Rousseau	*Émile: or On Education* (1762)
Denis Diderot and Jean d'Alembert	*Encyclopedia* (1751–81)
Condorcet	*Sketch for a Historical Picture of the Progress of the Human Mind* (1795)

Common Sense

"I offer nothing but plain facts and *common sense*," wrote the English journalist and professional revolutionary Thomas Paine (1737–1809), explaining the purpose of his incendiary pamphlet (1776) of that name. Just as Descartes had sought "clear and distinct" ideas about universal reality, Enlightenment thinkers sought truths so plain and simple that they could be understood by everyone. Mere common sense would suffice.

"Common sense" was a deceptively innocent concept, as Paine well knew. It could be used as a weapon to slash through the obfuscations and pretensions of traditional culture, as by the French Huguenot refugee Pierre Bayle (1647–1706) in his *Historical and Critical Dictionary* (1695–1697). Bayle wielded common sense to demolish traditional concepts of society and thought as he redefined the very words that Europeans used. Reprinted frequently, translated, abridged, and extracted, Bayle's *Dictionary* was, as one modern historian has called it, "a great engine of skepticism," and a "ponderous machine of war." With a copy propped on a shelf in every major library, it detached a generation of European intellectuals from traditional pieties and prejudices alike.

Some fifty years later, the French essayist, playwright, and literary critic Denis Diderot (1713–1784) masterminded the creation of a huge *Encyclopedia* (subtitled *A Classified Dictionary of the Sciences, Arts, and Trades*) that, like Bayle's *Dictionary*, redefined the outlook of the European public. The largest publishing venture of the age, it contained 60,000 brilliantly illustrated articles written by a team of authors. Publication of its thirty-five volumes took more than thirty years, beginning in 1751. The *Encyclopedia* aimed to encapsulate the whole of human knowledge. Its effect was to alter the way people thought. It provided up-to-date and rational information about such diverse subjects as farming and the soul, with pungent entries on "history," "humanity," and the "slave trade." With a novel emphasis on science, crafts, and technology, the *Encyclopedia* told a spellbound public that dikes and waterwheels were as important as the symbols of heraldry or the calendar of saints. It sold widely, mostly in France, but also reached Madrid, Naples, and St. Petersburg at the fringes of Enlightenment Europe. In North America, both Thomas Jefferson (1743–1826) and Benjamin Franklin (1706–1790) subscribed. The *Encyclopedia* won profits for the publisher and notoriety for the editors as it made the Enlightenment message the common property of the learned.

In his *Philosophical Letters*, Voltaire (1694–1778)—the most important *philosophe*—also sought to reinvent the universe of knowledge, urging his readers to

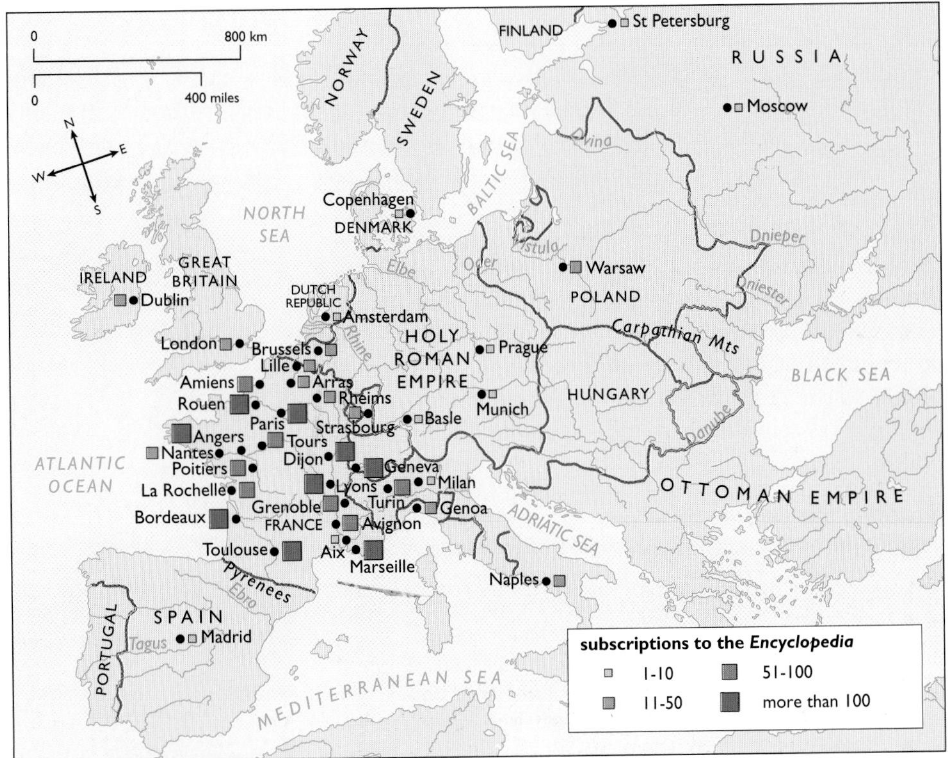

***Map 17.2 Subscriptions to Diderot and d'Alembert's* Encyclopedia**
Source: *Based on J. Merriman,* A History of Europe, Vol. I: From the Renaissance to the Age of Napoleon *(New York: W.W. Norton, 1996), p. 411.*

Work and Leisure

Diderot and d'Alembert's Encyclopedia: *Printed books and journals allowed a widespread diffusion of scientific ideas. The* Encyclopedia, *published in France beginning in 1751, gathered together in one easily accessible source virtually all the key ideas of the Scientific Revolution and Enlightenment. Practical subjects, such as coin stamping, illustrated here, were especially well represented.*

cast off their inherited misconceptions. Its famous entry on "Religion," for example, blasted the injustices wrought in the name of God by Jews, Muslims, and especially Christians. Voltaire's savage criticism of traditional customs and beliefs is also the mainspring of his novellas *Candide*, *Zadig*, and *Micromégas*.

Voltaire's younger contemporary, the Swiss-born author Jean-Jacques Rousseau (1712–1778), saw in the human being an endless possibility for good that was stifled by the paraphernalia of schools, books, and teachers. In *Émile* (1762), a book now considered to be one of the foundations of modern pedagogy, Rousseau argued that the young child should learn from nature, not books, until the age of twelve. He should learn science by doing it, and history from his exploration of current issues: "It is not a question of knowing what is, but only what is useful." Tutored in this way, the child would gain self-confidence, as well as the good sense to learn whatever was necessary for success.

Learning from nature: *An aristocratic family puts into practice the new educational philosophies of Jean-Jacques Rousseau in this 1778 print by J. B. Simonet entitled "Here is the Law of Nature....". Rousseau criticized the earlier stress on strict discipline and book learning from an early age and stressed instead the importance of allowing young children the freedom to interact with nature, learn by experience, and develop their own innate personalities.* (Metropolitan Museum of Art, New York)

The war on tradition waged by Enlightenment thinkers necessarily involved a war on the Christian churches, whose whole history, they believed, was stained by indefensible notions and cruel practices. The whole Christian enterprise was snarlingly dubbed by Voltaire, "*l'infâme*,"—an infamous, or detestable thing. To the apostles of common sense, the acceptance of rigid dogmas, and the act of faith itself, went directly against the imperatives of reason. The churches, in turn, had generally been either slow to accept or downright hostile to the discoveries of science, as in Galileo's case. Even the instigator of the Protestant Reformation (see Chapter 14), Martin Luther (1483–1546), cried out on first hearing of Copernicus' theory: "This fool wants to turn the whole of astronomy upside down!" Newton, however, found no contradiction between physics and faith, declaring that "the most beautiful system of the sun, planets and comets could only proceed from the . . . dominion of an intelligent and powerful Being . . . [who] endures forever and is everywhere present."

Even so, few Enlightenment thinkers were ready to do without religion altogether, and many adopted the stance of **deism**. Deists believed in "nature and nature's God," in the words of the American author of the Declaration of Independence, Thomas Jefferson, a "supreme being" and benevolent creator, who permitted the universe to operate according to natural law. They rejected wholesale the doctrines, rituals, and hierarchies of the churches—"truth has no sect," pronounced Voltaire. Others were agnostics or atheists who viewed Christianity as wholly irrelevant to the pursuit of truth; a religion full of miracles, grumbled Hume, which required a miracle for a rational man to believe in it. In such a climate of opinion, the cause of religious toleration, already championed by some Reformation figures (see Chapter 14), acquired new support: John Locke's *Letter Concerning Toleration* (1689) urged openness to all religious expressions—except those of Roman Catholics and atheists, whom this early liberal Protestant thinker considered outside the margins of what could be tolerated!

One alternative to Christianity was provided in eighteenth-century Europe by Freemasonry. Blending beliefs supposedly from ancient Egyptian polytheism with the mysteries of medieval guild organization, it retained a belief in divine power and propounded an ethic of brotherly love. Opposed alike to the ceremonies of the old Church and the tyranny of traditional monarchy, it nevertheless involved the performance of complex and secret initiation rituals. Its members, who ranged from artisans and sailors to the great Voltaire, were undismayed, and Masonic lodges proliferated throughout Europe—numbering 800 in France alone on the eve of the 1789 Revolution. Freemasonry seemed to offer a secular religion to those who craved common sense.

Social Contracts

Common sense provided a corrective not only to traditional beliefs and prejudices, but also to overabstract theory and bookish rationality. It persuaded men and women to think and act in new ways and to question the established framework of society and government. Enlightenment thinkers used it to undermine political authority in their development of the concept of a "social contract" (see Chapter 15).

In his *Second Treatise of Civil Government*, John Locke saw government as a contract created by male property-owners, powered by their consent, and responsible to their interests. If government was a practical arrangement of this kind, its pressing object was not to extract obedience from the subject but to avoid tyranny by the ruler. Locke's eighteenth-century followers included Montesquieu, Rousseau, and Thomas Jefferson.

In his *Spirit of Laws* (1748) the nobleman and professional *philosophe* Montesquieu (Charles-Louis de Secondat, 1689–1755) argued that laws determined the spirit of a nation, having evolved over time according to local conditions and historical accident. Public assemblies should act, in the preferred system he called "constitutionalism," to safeguard the freedom of citizens both from the arbitrariness of kings and the chaos of too free a democracy: "the government [must] be so constituted," he advised, "that one man need not be afraid of another." He also formulated the principle of the "separation of powers," in which each of the government's three functions—executive, legislative, and judicial—acts as a check and balance to the others. This distinction that Montesquieu saw as essential to good government and the preservation of liberty later became central to the world's first written national constitution, that of the United States (see Chapter 19).

Rousseau's *Social Contract* (1762) was concerned with the relation between the individual and the whole of society, whose intentions were expressed as a "general will." Each person willingly surrendered some of his natural liberty to the community of the whole in order to gain protection and security. He could do so with confidence, because the state was guided not by a monarch but by "a moral and collective body" of citizens. The individual, "in giving himself to all, gives himself to nobody." Nevertheless, the

WITNESSES

Visions of a Just Society

Voltaire calls for toleration (1763): I no longer address myself to man, but to You, eternal God of all beings and of all worlds. . . . You have not given us a heart to hate each other, nor hands to strangle one another. . . . May You prevent our different clothes, insufficient languages, ridiculous customs, imperfect laws and foolish opinions from becoming causes for hatred and persecution. Let those who light candles in broad daylight in Your honor cherish those who content themselves with the light of the sun. . . . And may the poor look upon the rich without envy, for You know that wealth and titles are unworthy reasons for vanity and pride. Have all men remember that they are brothers! . . . If the plague of war is inevitable, let us not hate one another and torture each other in times of peace. And let us employ the short period of our existence in thanking You, wherever we may reside, be it in Siam or Califomia, and in whatever language we command, for the life You have granted us.
(From V. W. Topazio ed., *Voltaire: A Critical Study of his Major Works*, 1967)

Locke sees government as a revocable social contract between ruler and ruled (1690): The reason men enter into society [create governments and laws] is for the preservation of their property; and the reason they choose and authorize a legislature is that laws may be made . . . as guards and fences for the properties of all the members of the society, to limit the power . . . of every part and member of the society. . . . Whenever the legislators endeavor to . . . destroy the property of the people, or to reduce them to slavery under arbitrary power, they put themselves into a state of war with the people, who are thereupon absolved from any farther obedience, and are left to the common refuge, which God has provided for all men, against force and violence. Whensoever therefore the legislature . . . endeavors to grasp themselves, or put into the hands of any other, an absolute power over the lives, liberties, and property of the people; by that breach of trust they forfeit the power the people had put into their hands for quite contrary ends, and it devolves to the people, who have a right to resume their original liberty, and, by the establishment of a new legislature . . . provide for their own safety and security, which is the end for which they are in society.
(John Locke, *Two Treatises of Government*, 1690; ed. C. B. Macpherson, 1980)

Condorcet envisions reason as the basis for unlimited human progress (1794): The aim of the work that I have undertaken . . . will be to show by appeal to reason and fact that nature has set no term to the perfection of human faculties; that the perfectibility of man is truly indefinite; and that the progress of this perfectibility, from now onwards independent of any power that might wish to halt it, has no other limit than the duration of the globe upon which nature has cast us. This progress will doubtless vary in speed, but it will never be reversed. . . . The time will . . . come when the sun will shine only on free men who know no other master but their reason; when tyrants and slaves, priests and their stupid or hypocritical instruments will exist only in works of history and on the stage; and when we shall . . . learn how to recognize and destroy, by force of reason, the first seeds of tyranny and superstition, should they ever dare to reappear amongst us.
(Condorcet, *Sketch for a Historical Picture of the Progress of the Human Mind*, 1795; ed. J. Barraclough, 1955, reissued 1979)

effect of Rousseau's reasoning was to elevate the "state" in relation to the individual. Freed from the constraints of royal or divine authority, it defined itself and decreed its own laws.

While Rousseau's theory of social contract allowed the state more power than did Locke, the English philosopher's more libertarian view was adopted by his eloquent follower across the Atlantic, the Virginian lawyer Thomas Jefferson. The core attitudes of the Enlightenment toward government are succinctly expressed in the American Declaration of Independence, which Jefferson authored (although his original language was modified by a cautious committee). In a few sentences, he recapitulated Locke's notions of government by consent and the right to dissolve a government usurped by tyranny. To secure their natural rights of life, liberty, and happiness, he wrote, "governments are instituted among men, deriving their just powers from the consent of the governed." When the government no longer serves those ends, "it is the right of the people to alter or abolish it," and to start anew to design a government as "shall seem to them most likely to effect their safety and happiness."

The social contract theories of Enlightenment thinkers did not create, nor did they even recommend, democracy, in which all the governed participate in the machinery of government. It was still to be a long time before women, or men who did not own land or property, were to have any voice in the processes of government. Nevertheless, these theories formed a first step in the development of genuinely democratic political systems.

Other Places, Other Customs

As Enlightenment authors hammered out new frameworks for political life, they sometimes looked to the experience of other peoples in other places, who acted according to very different customs and beliefs. Travel literature is an ancient genre, in which a distinctly new phase began with the opening of the New World to European explorers (see Chapter 16). Inevitably, eye-witness reports of the pre-Columbian civilizations of the Americas, which had evolved quite separately from those in Europe and the East, prompted Europeans to reflect on the meaning for their own society of the other cultures of humankind. Such works as the Italian Peter Martyr's *Chronicles of the New World* (1530), the French Jean de Léry's *History of a Voyage to the Land of Brazil* (1578), and the English Richard Hakluyt's *The Principal Navigations, Voyages, Traffics and Discoveries of the English Nation* (1589) forced Europeans to revise their notion of the heroic, now played out in various forms in distant wildernesses. In her 1688 novel *Oroonoko*, the English novelist and playwright Aphra Behn (1640–89) depicted the courageous martyrdom of a noble African king caught in the violent trap of South American slavery. A generation or so later Daniel Defoe celebrated the conquest of nature and "savage" alike by his hero Robinson Crusoe (1719), who survived abandonment in the wilderness because of his superior mental and practical skills. In his novella *Candide*, Voltaire empathized with the Amerindians of Peru, in his view victims of the extraordinary cruelty of European Jesuits. Montaigne, Diderot, and Rousseau respected, even celebrated, the "savages" of the other hemisphere—in contrast to the English lexicographer Samuel Johnson (1696–1772), who grumbled that "savages" made up four-fifths of the inhabitants of the globe.

Asian and Islamic cultures also found European interpreters. China's Confucian traditions, which resembled those of the contemporary West in their lucid rationality, impressed Enlightenment *philosophes*, and Hindu and Buddhist mysticism won sympathetic students. The East, especially the Ottoman Empire—still a formidable political presence in eastern Europe although languishing—provided an exotic contrast to prosaic European customs. Voltaire situated his comic hero Zadig in ancient Babylon, and Montesquieu's satirical *Persian Letters*, supposedly written by Asian observers of contemporary France, drew on the differences between Eastern and Western perspectives in its disguised attack on French royal absolutism (see Chapter 15).

The geographical explorations of the early modern era opened up realms of previously inconceivable possibility—to one commentator, a "horizon that recedes without end." Not surprisingly, the encounter with other real worlds encouraged the creation of fictitious ones. An early example is the English author and statesman Thomas More's *Utopia* (see Chapter 14), which certainly drew on New World themes: the work's narrator is a survivor of a shipwreck in unknown seas, so that a seemingly real journey introduces a plausible but imaginary one. The Dominican friar Tommaso Campanella (1568–1639), a prisoner of the Inquisition for twenty-seven years and possibly insane, described a more extensive utopia in his *City of the Sun*. The people inhabiting a world based on the astronomy of Copernicus, Bruno, and Galileo are transformed into what they know, a condition that is defined as the only form of eternal life. Campanella's contemporary, the English philosopher Francis Bacon constructed a utopian "New Atlantis" described in a book of the same title, whose citizens utilized scientific principles as they worked to improve their daily lives. And in the Enlightenment period, the Anglo-Irish author Jonathan Swift's satire *Gulliver's Travels* (1726) criticized contemporaries and explored the indeterminacy of moral values while depicting wholly imaginary foreign realms.

These authors shared an awareness of other worlds beyond the limits of Western civilization—known, imaginary, and possible—which allowed them to reexamine their own. In the wider arena of the unfolded globe, the old European boundaries of identity faded: "Once past the equator," wrote Denis Diderot, "a man is neither English, nor Dutch, nor French, nor Spanish, nor Portuguese"; he has become "nothing." In these shifting realities, European assumptions could be shown for what they were—intrinsically no better, sometimes more deceptive or more shallow, than those of other cultures.

Encounters with other realities stimulated European reflection on the future of humankind. One popularizer of science announced fantastically (as it then seemed) that someday human beings might walk on the moon, while the French *philosophe*, the Marquis de Condorcet (Marie-Jean-Antoine Caritat,

1743–1794) predicted phenomenal advancements for the human race. He foresaw the elimination of poverty, the extension of human life, the establishment of mass education, and the equality of the sexes in his *Sketch for a Historical Account of the Progress of the Human Mind* (1795)—written, ironically, while evading the grip of the revolutionary Terror (see Chapter 20), which perhaps prompted his suicide.

Optimism like Condorcet's, based on secular faith in reason, suffuses the products of the Enlightenment. Fundamentally, all things in heaven and on earth were orderly, splendid, and benign. "Whatever is," as the English poet Alexander Pope (1688–1744) declared, "is right."

A LITTLE LEARNING: LITERACY AND EDUCATION

The order of the world might be essentially right, according to Pope, but understanding it was still a matter for the select few: "A little learning is a dangerous thing," he warned. Enlightenment, in his view, was for the well-educated only—it was not enough to be able to read; one needed to be widely read and intellectually well-equipped. This exclusive view did not reflect the enormous broadening of the audience for science, literature, and ideas that occurred in the early modern centuries. While the ruling classes retained their privileged access to education (for their male offspring, at least) schools in general took on a broader mission, printshops poured out books, more people read, and many wrote. Teachers and bureaucrats, women and amateurs possessing what Pope dismissed as a "little learning" now participated in the intellectual world, which extended beyond the study and university to include learned and artistic academies, fashionable salons, and public as well as private museums.

Pleasure Reading

The creation of a broader audience for the intellectual products of the early modern era can be ascribed to two institutions: the school and the printshop. Where medieval schools had trained priests and monks, and Renaissance schools the sons of wealthy merchants, despots, and noblemen, from the sixteenth through eighteenth centuries, more people in general had the chance to go to school and learn to read. They became the reading public of the Enlightenment era, avid consumers of many types of literature and new ideas propounded in cheap, easily available printed books.

The seventeenth and eighteenth centuries saw many, varied educational initiatives as the ability to read became an increasingly essential skill. In both England and France, private endowments established hundreds of different schools for the children of certain cities, craft professions, or religious denominations. In 1698, King Louis XIV of France (r. 1643–1715) ordered the establishment of a school in each rural district. In 1714, Peter the Great of Russia (r. 1682–1725) ordered the creation of "ciphering schools" throughout the realm, to train future technicians in arithmetic and geometry. In 1763, Frederick the Great of Prussia (r. 1740–1786) decreed that elementary education was obligatory, and the Austrian emperor Joseph II (r. 1765–1790) created state schools in which students destined for bureaucratic positions were trained to read and write their native languages (including the Magyar, Croatian, Slovak, Romanian, and Ruthenian of the empire's ethnic minorities, in addition to German).

Some privately endowed schools were created specifically for girls, including two of the most famous schools of the era, at Port-Royal and Saint-Cyr, both in France. A century later, in Russia, Empress Catherine the Great (r. 1763–1796) founded the Smolny Institute, a school for 500 daughters of noblemen, modeled on Saint-Cyr. All of these girls' schools aimed to prepare their students for marriage and polite society, rather than for scholarship or public life, since the future leaders of society were overwhelmingly male. Wealthy boys were often tutored at home by professionals, while their sisters sometimes listened in.

At the advanced level, the European universities continued to train physicians, lawyers, clergymen, and philosophers. Their enrollments grew, however, as more laymen and students from the lesser nobility and the middle classes attended. A university education was a prerequisite for entry to the professions. Hence women, barred from universities into modern times, failed to enter professional careers. While the older universities in Italy and France experienced some stagnation, others flourished, especially in the Dutch Republic and in Scotland. New universities continued to be founded notably in the German lands, Spain, Spanish America, and British North America.

Elementary schools succeeded in raising rates of literacy in the vernacular languages in western Europe. Overall, more than fifty percent of city dwellers gained basic literacy, and not all peasants (as was once the case) were illiterate. While men attained higher literacy rates, women too experienced rising literacy. Women became an important component of the reading audience, and tended to support women authors, to read novels about women's experience, and to subscribe to periodical publications pertaining to women's lives.

While the sons of elite groups learned Latin and perhaps Greek, for most people literacy meant the ability to read the vernacular language of their state. In the early modern centuries, these vernacular languages were just becoming standardized, as one form or regional dialect took precedence over others. This process can often be linked to the emergence of a preeminent literary figure and the adoption of his works as national "classics." Dante (1265–1321) performed this service for Italian, and Luther, in his translation of the Bible, for German. The dramatist William Shakespeare (1564–1616) was a key figure in the creation of modern English, and the French language reached a similar peak in the mock-heroic works of François Rabelais (c. 1494–c. 1553). For Spanish, the novel *Don Quixote* by Miguel de Cervantes (1547–1616) is central. Some of the major scientific and philosophical works of the early modern period were also written in vernacular languages, for example those by Galileo in Italian and Descartes in French.

By the seventeenth century, standardization of the grammar and spelling of European languages followed. Vernacular dictionaries became available in some languages, and boards of experts such as the French Academy, established in 1634, met to regularize and safeguard the newly formed modern languages. Latin remained into the nineteenth century (into the twentieth in parts of east-central Europe) a useful language for communicating philosophy, science, medicine, theology, law, and sometimes history. But from the seventeenth century most literature, political theory, and other ideas were expressed in the vernacular whose readership formed the widest possible circle.

The development of vernacular languages was aided by the printing press, while printing establishments benefited from larger audiences. The scope of printed material expanded as vernacular readers bought more books.

In the sixteenth century—the first full century of printing—religious and classical works dominated. The Bible, saints' lives, prayerbooks and other devotional works, were initially the works most favoured by presses and sought by readers. The war between the Protestant Reformation and Roman Catholicism from the early sixteenth century was waged in print. With regard to Classical works, the first aim was to produce clear, legible, and accurate versions of ancient Latin and Greek texts. By 1500, however, vernacular translations were being produced, making such authors as Cicero, Plutarch, and Tacitus available to a wider public.

The vernacular readership was interested in a diverse range of subjects. They bought almanacs and books on etiquette and history, animal husbandry, beermaking or viniculture, and collections of choral hymns. They read fairy tales and novels, kept abreast of things with newspapers (published daily in the big cities of the later eighteenth century) and laughed at satirical cartoons. They studied the explorers' narratives of their journeys to the New World, and sought

Literacy Rates: France and the German States

Literacy in Urban France	
1683	51%
1770	60%

Source: *E. Le Roy Ladurie,* The Ancien Regime: A History of France 1610–1774 *(Cambridge, MA: Basil Blackwell, 1996), p. 309.*

Literacy in Rural Normandy	Males	Females
Late 17th Century	37%	7%
Late 18th Century	73%	46%

Source: *F. Furet and M. Ozouf,* Reading and Writing Literacy in France from Calvin to Jules Ferry *(New York: Cambridge University Press, 1982), p. 160.*

Literacy in the German States	
c. 1500	3–4%
c. 1800	50% (Males 50–66%; Females 33–50%)

Source: *J. Merriman,* A History of Modern Europe: From the Renaissance to the Age of Napoleon *(New York: W.W. Norton, 1996), pp. 38, 417.*

The eighteenth century was a time when great numbers of Europeans learned to read and write for the first time. Though measures of literacy are notoriously inaccurate (partly because of problems defining specifically what level of ability constitutes literacy), the figures above provide a good guide to overall trends.

advice about marriage, childrearing, and childbirth. These books opened a world of knowledge to audiences beyond the university and the monastery: with the Enlightenment, for the first time in Europe, the lights turned on in the homes of ordinary folk.

Major printing centers included Venice, Rome, Basel (Switzerland), Strasbourg, Antwerp, Amsterdam, London, and Paris. These cities were magnets for editors, translators, and authors from many countries, who joined intellectuals and artists in a process that stimulated new understandings.

Such a lively intellectual milieu led to the expression of unconventional ideas that often provoked official censorship, which in turn broached the issue of free speech. Many of the *philosophes*' books were censored but continued to be distributed via a covert trade in prohibited books. Bayle and Locke published their work in the safe haven of the Dutch Republic, where dissent was tolerated, but Voltaire and Diderot found some of their works condemned. Rousseau learned from a bookseller friend of the fate of his book on educational proposals: "I saw your *Emile* . . . publicly consigned to the flames in Madrid," he wrote, in front of a Dominican church one Sunday "in the presence of a whole crowd of gaping imbeciles." Demand for the book soared.

The English Puritan poet John Milton (1608–1674) addressed the problem of the regulation of ideas, hurling against a recent act of Parliament to censor "scandalous, seditious and libellous works" an elegant and impassioned defense of free speech and free thought. "For books are not absolutely dead things, but do contain a potency of life in them to be as active as the soul was whose progeny they are," Milton argued in his *Areopagitica*. "Who kills a man kills a reasonable creature, . . . but he who destroys a good book, kills reason itself." It is no accident that, in this environment of intellectual debate women thinkers began actively to assert the worth of the female sex and the capacity of the female mind.

A Cat and a Catte: Women and Learning

Marie de Gournay (1565–1645), close associate of the French essayist Michel de Montaigne, observed of the graceful creature adorning her room that there was no difference between *un chat* ("a cat") and *une chatte* ("a catte," or female cat): "the human animal is neither male nor female." That conclusion was reached—and even then, accepted by few—only after a struggle over the nature of female identity known as the *querelle des femmes* ("the debate on women").

The *querelle* had its origins in the deep misogyny of medieval literature, which presented women as vain, self-centered, deceitful, corrupting, and lecherous. Beginning with Christine de Pisan (1364–c. 1430) (see Chapter 12), a series of authors in most of the European languages—some male but mostly female—wrote in defense of women. Their defenses elicited a correspondingly large group of responses. Through the course of this *querelle* may be traced an increasingly sophisticated justification for the spiritual and intellectual equality of the female to the male.

The first stage of the debate included many catalogues of "women worthies"—powerful and important women in history and legend. More serious issues pertaining to women's spiritual and intellectual equality were developed by Italian humanists, especially among women humanists (see "Nogarola" in Chapter 13), whose arguments were elaborated in the six-

Women and Learning

Louis Michel Dumesnil,* Queen Christina of Sweden with Descartes*: *Only a minority of major scientific and philosophical figures during the seventeenth and eighteenth centuries considered women intellectually equal to men. One such was René Descartes, seen here tutoring Queen Christina of Sweden.* (Palace of Versailles, France) teenth century by Erasmus (c. 1466–1536) and Vives (1492–1540), and especially by Henry Cornelius Agrippa von Nettesheim (1486–1535), a philosopher and physician who also dabbled in alchemy. Agrippa not merely defended women but proposed their supremacy. His work *On the Nobility and Preeminence of the Female Sex* was widely translated and imitated, influencing two notable seventeenth-century works: Marie de Gournay's *The Equality of Men and Women* (1622) and Lucrezia Marinella's (1571–1653) *The Nobility and Excellence of Women.* With Mary Wollstonecraft's *A Vindication of the Rights of Woman* (1792), this tradition reaches its culmination.

A closely related issue was women's capacity for education. Their defenders include the influential Dutch scholar Anna Maria van Schurman (1607–1678), whose Latin treatise *On the Capacity of the Female Mind for Learning* was widely read in translation, and her contemporary, the Englishwoman Margaret Cavendish, Duchess of Newcastle (c. 1623–1673) who grumpily complained about the limitations of her own training: "As for learning, that I am not versed in it, no body, I hope, will blame me for it, since it is sufficiently known, that our sex is not brought up to it, as being not suffered to be instructed in schools and universities." Around 1700, Cavendish's compatriot Mary Astell (1666–1731) urged the higher education of women in a kind of Protestant nunnery, set apart from male-dominated society, in her *Serious Proposal to the Ladies*. In France, meanwhile, François Poulain de la Barre (1647–1723) presented a comprehensive defense of female capacity for advanced education in his book *On the Equality of the Two Sexes*, while Bernard de Fontenelle (1657–1757) designed his work on scientific popularization, *Conversations on the Plurality of Worlds*, as a dialogue between a philosopher and a woman. Finally, the Marquis de Condorcet advocated not only women's equal capacity for advanced education, but, additionally and unprecedentedly, their participation as citizens in public affairs.

Women Writers Even as the debate about women's nature and rationality reached a higher pitch, women had begun to write (see Chapters 10, 12, 13). Prior to the Renaissance, nearly all women's public writing was religious. Saints and nuns, writing themselves or through dictation to confessors or mentors, had contributed to the Western mystical tradition as well as to a female tradition of self-exploration. In the Renaissance, women humanists, while not departing from a Christian framework, used Classical models in their letters, orations, and dialogues, which often gave expression to strong feminist themes.

***Attributed to Jan van Belcamp,* The Clifford "Great Picture":** *The Englishwoman Lady Clifford, seen in the panel at left with her books in a painting from around 1646, was a contemporary of Queen Christina of Sweden and profited from a similar sort of tutoring (see illustration opposite). Contrast the portrait of Margaret Cavendish on p. 540, depicted in her library but without books!* (Collection of Abbot Hall Art Gallery, England)

The next three centuries saw an explosion of female creativity, as the grip of a traditional intellectual culture, dominated by the university, Latin, and the priesthood, weakened. The humanist dethroning of medieval Scholasticism (see Chapter 13), the use of the vernacular, the proliferation of the printshop, the views of Locke and Descartes, which located the ability to think in a mind unformed by class, profession, or gender, and the new worlds opened by explorers or discovered by scientists, all combined to create a milieu in which women felt free to write and impelled to express themselves.

In Italy, the number of published women writers soared to around 250 for the period from 1500 to 1700. Of these, about a third continued to write on religious themes but others composed love poems (mostly courtesans), occasional letters, and moral treatises which were sought by publishers and purchased by the public in great quantity. In England and France, works by, for, and about women increased markedly in the seventeenth century.

What did women write about? Some wrote devotional works, but the proportion of these to the whole of women's production diminished sharply after 1600. Some wrote about the family, others wrote about themselves. Some joined in discussions of philosophy, science, language, and love; they wrote histories or biographies, or translated the works of famous men; they wrote poetry or **novels**, a genre which originated in the seventeenth century and was influenced by the need to address a female readership. One scholar counts 106 women authors of 568 novels writing in English before Jane Austen (1775–1817) became, as used to be thought, the "first" woman novelist.

Works about the family predominate. Women wrote diaries about their experience as mothers and wives, and guidebooks to life and manners for their children. The Jewish woman Glückel (1656–1724) of Hameln, a widow who had survived two husbands and raised twelve children, described in her memoirs the resourcefulness, diligence, and faith that allowed the family to survive in the world of seventeenth-century mid-European ghettoes. Arcangela Tarabotti (1604–1652) wrote in protest of "paternal tyranny" in Catholic Italy, where fathers disposed of superfluous daughters in convents. Women wrote against the constraints of marriage, as did Mary Astell in her *Reflections on Marriage* and the Italian Moderata

Discourse in Salons and Academies

A. Lemonnier, The Salon of Madame Geoffrin: *Educated women played a key role in spreading Enlightenment culture through the many salons they ran. In this painting from 1812 an actor reads from Voltaire at the salon of Madame Geoffrin. Some of the most famous* philosophes *found a congenial atmosphere for debate and philosophy.* (Châteaux de Malmaison et Bois-Préau, France)

Members of the French Royal Academy of Sciences: *During the eighteenth century, learning became an important cultural accomplishment among the well-to-do. New ideas and philosophies were spread via various media. Of great importance were the growing number of scientific academies established from the seventeenth century on. In this 1666 tapestry by Henri Testelin, members of the French Royal Academy of Sciences gather for their inaugural meeting.* (Palace of Versailles, France)

Fonte (1555–1592) in her dialogue on *Women's Worth*. The chief speaker in the latter work proclaims: "I would rather die than subordinate myself to any man."

Women also participated in the discussion of pedagogy, defending the educability of women. They debated the theories of Descartes in France and Italy, and studied Platonism in England. In Italy, Lucrezia Marinella demonstrated an encyclopedic command of contemporary philosophical debates in the seventeenth century, and Laura Bassi pursued a professional scientific career in the eighteenth. The French noblewoman Emilie du Châtelet (1706–1749), Voltaire's patron and lover, worked daily on the latest problems raised by science and philosophy. In England, Lady Mary Wortley Montagu published a newspaper that discussed current philosophical and political issues.

In France, meanwhile, women acted as literary critics and promoted an elaborate, stylized manner of speaking and writing that earned them the name *les précieuses* (the precious ones). Brilliant women hosted **salons**, sessions in their homes attended by the leading men of letters of the day in which new ideas were debated and criticized. Although not themselves *philosophes* or authors, Madame Geoffrin (1699–1777), Madame du Deffand (1697–1780), and the latter's former protegée Julie de Lespinasses (1732–1776), were leaders of intellectual conversation in Paris at a time when to think was to converse, and when Paris led Europe in the generation of ideas.

The English playwright and novelist Aphra Behn presents an outstanding case of the woman author who recognized the predicament she faced as an educated woman in a society dominated by men. During her adventurous youth she lived in the Dutch colony of Surinam in South America, served as a spy in the Netherlands, and married a Dutch businessman, whose death in 1666 when she was twenty-five freed her for a writer's career. Behn's distinctively feminist plays (successfully staged in London in the 1670s and 1680s) explored the realms of marriage and adultery, featuring plucky heroines who defied male power and greed. Her plays were among the first on the English stage to employ female actresses. Her thirteen novels may perhaps establish her, 150 years before Austen, as the first woman novelist in English. Among these is the extraordinary *Oroonoko*, set in the New World, with its uncompromising repudiation of slavery. In her own words, she faulted the prejudices that kept women from receiving a serious education:

Women and Science

Anna Morandi Manzolini

Margaret Cavendish, Duchess of Newcastle

Elisabetha and Johannes Hevelius, 1673

Among Western nations, Italy offered perhaps the best environment for women scientists. Anna Morandi Manzolini (top), for example, made several original discoveries in anatomy and held a professorship at the University of Bologna from 1760 until her death in 1774. In many cases, women accepted and repeated arguments about their intellectual inferiority to men. Margaret Cavendish, Duchess of Newcastle (left), herself an active participant in the important scientific debates of her time, nonetheless stated that women's brains were "cold" and "soft" compared to men's. Women often worked alongside their more celebrated husbands as scientific assistants or, occasionally, as full partners. In a print from 1673 (above) Elisabetha and Johannes Hevelius take astronomical readings together using a sextant.

WITNESSES

Women, Men, and Learning

François Poulain de la Barre declares that the mind has no sex (1673): It is easy to see that sexual differences apply only to the body since . . . it is only the body which is used for human reproduction; the mind is involved in reproduction only in giving its assent and, since it does this in the same way in everyone, one may conclude that it has no sex.

If one considers the mind in itself, one finds that it is equal and has the same nature in all human beings, and that it is capable of all kinds of thoughts. . . . The difference between the sexes does not result from their minds. . . .

This is even more obvious if we consider the head, which is the unique organ of the sciences and the place where the mind exercises all its functions. Our most accurate anatomical investigations do not uncover any difference between men and women in this part of the body. The brain of women is exactly like ours.

(François Poulain de la Barre, *On the Equality of the Two Sexes*, 1673; ed. D. M. Clarke, 1990)

Mary Astell explains why men seem to know more than women (c. 1700): There are strong and prevalent reasons which demonstrate the superiority and preeminence of the men. For in the first place, boys have much time and pains, care and cost bestowed on their education, girls have little or none. The former are early initiated in the sciences, are made acquainted with ancient and modern discoveries, they study books and men, have all imaginable encouragement. . . . The latter are restrained, frowned upon, and beaten . . .; laughter and ridicule, that never-failing scarecrow, is set up to drive them from the tree of knowledge. But if in spite of all difficulties nature prevails, and they can't be kept so ignorant as their masters would have them, they are stared upon as monsters, censured, envied, and every way discouraged.

(Mary Astell, *The First English Feminist: Reflections on Marriage and Other Writings*; ed. B. Hill, 1986)

Permitting not the female sex to tread,
The mighty paths of learned heroes dead . . .

Conscious of her talents and ambitious to win the fame due to her, she sought above all the freedom that male writers enjoyed: "If I must not because of my sex, have this freedom, I lay down my quill and you shall hear no more of me . . . I value fame as much as if I had been born a hero." Seeing no difference between a catte and a cat, Behn claimed her due place in the world of letters.

In the early modern centuries, women began to emerge from the subordinate position in which they had previously been placed by custom and belief. Women thinkers and writers, who first confronted on the level of language the assumptions that had kept them imprisoned, were the pioneers of that advance. Wider social change would follow later; at the end of the twentieth century, that process was not yet everywhere completed.

Halls of Reason: The Social Context

If the disputation was characteristic of the intellectual life of the Middle Ages, the collection was characteristic of the early modern period: collections of books, natural objects, and scientific instruments; and collections of people interested in intellectual pursuits.

In the early modern era, the passion for collecting (previously confined to kings) spread to members of the nobility, bourgeoisie, and learned elite. Objects that were precious or unusual because of their antiquity, craftsmanship, or materials; items brought from across the wide oceans now navigated by European ships; and exotic plants and animals found their way into famous collections. The apartments of the Habsburg emperor Rudolph II (1576–1612) were littered with clocks and machinery, books and statues, while paintings lined the walls. Remnants of antiquity, contemporary art works, and scientific and musical instruments were heaped together as a kind of summation of all that was known and valued. More specialized collections developed in the hands of scholars, scientists, or wealthy amateurs. The sixteenth-century Italian Ulisse Aldrovandi (1522–1605) gathered specimens of rare and exotic creatures, which were visited by at least the 1579 persons who signed his guest book (at least ten percent were members of the nobility). By the eighteenth century the gentleman-collector's study and the dilettante prince's palace crammed with curios had given rise to the first modern museums: the Ashmolean in Oxford, the British Museum in London, the Brera in Milan, the Louvre in Paris.

The society of the learned gathered together in a range of associations. In Renaissance Italy, humanists met in the gardens of their patrons for polite conversations; later, during the sixteenth century, they moved into academies. These were associations in which both noble and commoner, and male and

Official Scientific Academies in Europe During the Eighteenth Century

	Official Scientific Societies in all Europe (excluding colonies)	Official Scientific Societies in France
1700	5	2
1789	65	29

Much more than universities, scientific academies were the vital institutions of scientific discourse during the Scientific Revolution and Enlightenment. The great increase in their number during the eighteenth century testifies to the growing interest in science among the governments, crowns, and other elites who funded them. The table above shows only official societies (ones formally recognized or funded by their respective governments).

Source: *Based on J. E. McClellan III,* Science Reorganized: Scientific Societies in the Eighteenth Century *(New York: Columbia University Press, 1985), pp. 261–280.*

female participants mingled to discuss ideas, the arts, or the news of the day. In the informal and vivid setting of the academy, ideas and styles originated that could not have been heard in the hierarchical setting of the university or court.

In the seventeenth century, north of the Alps, academies took a different direction. More official and formal, they served as laboratories for the creation of new knowledge. The French Royal Academy of Sciences, established by King Louis XIV in 1666, was expected both to explore technologies useful to the state and to reflect glory upon the monarch. Provincial academies encouraged both literary and scientific activities, frequently sponsoring essay competitions or rewarding exceptional achievement. Private academies and literary societies on the Italian model also flourished, in France closely resembling private salons. The English Royal Society, founded like the French by royal initiative in 1662, left its members free to pursue their own interests. By 1670 its membership numbered 200 and included, alongside amateur merchants and artisans, the most prominent scientists, mathematicians, and philosophers in the nation.

Outside these gatherings of professional thinkers, people gathered informally in the hundreds of coffeehouses and clubs that sprang up in the cities of western Europe. The English insurance company Lloyds grew up in one London coffeehouse visited by businessmen engaged in international shipping; in another, courses on Newtonian mechanics and optics were available. Members of private clubs or Masonic lodges formed reading groups and developed lending libraries. The salons over which gifted women presided in the major European capitals brought together the wealthy, the learned, and the famous to discuss the latest literary or philosophical works.

Informal associations of the learned and talented, at first in Italy, subsequently in the Netherlands, France, and England, were the matrix of the new ideas and visions that fueled the Enlightenment. Superseding the monastery, the cathedral, and the court, more lively than the contemporary university, located in homes and shops that were magnets alike for those with a little or a great deal of learning, they were the halls of reason that characterize the age as much as the monarchs' halls of mirrors. Here the age of reason took form, guided by the transcendent discoveries of intellectual leaders and extended by the buzzing conversation of their readers, followers, and admirers.

Conclusion

DESCARTES' DILEMMA AND THE MEANING OF THE WEST

Because he thought, Descartes concluded, he must exist. And because he existed, he could know. It was confidence in the knowability of things that knit the intellectual world of the West into one system and that gave the Enlightenment its momentum. In the early modern centuries, the rationalism of Western culture that was already apparent in medieval thought was reaffirmed. But now reason reigned alone and triumphant, sharing no space with the Christian faith that had unified the West in the Middle Ages. Loosed from its moorings in faith, expanding around the globe, certain of the knowledge it garnered from the operations of reason, the civilization of the West approached the threshold of the modern age fired with confidence and titanic ambition.

REVIEW QUESTIONS

1. What did Descartes mean when he said, "I think, therefore I am"? How was the rationalism of the early modern era different from that of the Middle Ages? Why did the new rationalism clash with Christian beliefs?

2. What was the Scientific Revolution? How did the new discoveries in astronomy change the way Europeans thought about the cosmos? What was the significance of Newton's theory of gravity?

3. Why did the study of anatomy advance so rapidly in the sixteenth and seventeenth centuries? How did new knowledge about the human body affect the practice of medicine? Why did male physicians take over the power to manage births from midwives?

4. What is the scientific method? How was it different from Aristotelian philosophy? Why did belief in magic and the occult decline in the early modern era?

5. What was the Enlightenment? Why did the *philosophes* attack the Church? Why were the "social contract" theories a step toward democracy?

6. Why did the number of literate Europeans increase in the early modern era? Why did more women writers appear at this time? What was the debate on women?

SUGGESTED READINGS

New Heaven, New Earth

Butterfield, Herbert, *The Origins of Modern Science* (New York: Free Press, 1957). Classic introduction to the revolutions in physics, astronomy, physiology, and chemistry.

Debus, Allen G., *Man and Nature in the Renaissance* (Cambridge: Cambridge University Press, 1978). Impact of Renaissance humanism on scientific thought.

Kuhn, Thomas S., *The Copernican Revolution* (Cambridge, MA: Harvard University Press, 1957). Definitive study of the Aristotelian and Ptolemaic background to Copernicus' achievement.

Porter, Roy, and Mikulás Teich, eds., *The Scientific Revolution in National Context* (Cambridge: Cambridge University Press, 1992). Examines the interaction between science and scientists, and social, political, and cultural forces. Argues that the nature and fate of science in the 16th and 17th centuries varied significantly in different national contexts.

Schiebinger, Londa L., *The Mind Has No Sex? Women in the Origins of Modern Science* (Cambridge, MA: Harvard University Press, 1989). Argues that women, too, played a role in pioneering the new sciences of the 17th and 18th centuries.

Shapin, Steven, *The Scientific Revolution* (Chicago: University of Chicago Press, 1996). Updated introduction, emphasizing social and cultural factors.

Thomas, Keith, *Religion and the Decline of Magic* (New York: Scribner, 1971). Examines the nature, context, and social meaning of a variety of mystical practices in the early modern period, the decline of which was a necessary prerequisite for the rise of science and modernity.

The Lights Go On

Crosby, Alfred W., *The Measure of Reality: Quantification and Western Society, 1250–1600* (Cambridge: Cambridge University Press, 1997). Traces the shift to quantitative and visual thinking.

Gay, Peter, *The Enlightenment: An Interpretation*, 2 Vols. (New York: Knopf, 1966–69). Probably the best synthesis of the Enlightenment.

Goodman, Dena, *The Republic of Letters: A Cultural History of the French Enlightenment* (Ithaca: Cornell University Press, 1994). Focusing largely on salons, argues that women provided sociability, discussion, and civility to the overall culture of the Enlightenment.

Porter, Roy, and Mikulás Teich, eds., *The Enlightenment in National Context* (Cambridge: Cambridge University Press, 1981). Essays highlighting the varying character of the Enlightenment in twelve European regions and in North America.

A Little Learning

Eisenstein, Elizabeth L., *The Printing Press as an Agent of Change: Communications and Cultural Transformations in Early Modern Europe*, 2 Vols. (Cambridge: Cambridge University Press, 1979). Examines the revolutionary consequences of the change from script to print culture.

Febvre, Lucien, and Henri-Jean Martin, *The Coming of the Book: The Impact of Printing 1450–1800*, New ed. (London: N.L.B., 1976). Cultural transformations wrought by the transition from manuscript to print culture.

Houston, Robert Allen A., *Literacy in Early Modern Europe: Culture and Education, 1500–1800* (London: Longman, 1988). Investigates the nature and significance of literacy across Europe.

Kelly, Gary, *Revolutionary Feminism: The Mind and Career of Mary Wollstonecraft* (New York: St. Martin's Press, 1992). Biography of this pioneering feminist, which also introduces wider currents in feminist and literary scholarship.

Lewalski, Barbara K., *Writing Women in Jacobean England* (Cambridge, MA: Harvard University Press, 1993). Focuses on educated, typically aristocratic, women and their relationship—either as patrons or writers—with print culture during the early 17th century.

Melton, James Van Horn, *Absolutism and the Eighteenth Century Origins of Compulsory Schooling in Prussia and Austria* (Cambridge: Cambridge University Press, 1988). Argues that public education was undertaken largely in order to maintain public order and social hierarchy at a time when profound social changes were threatening to upset these.

TOWN, COURT, AND COUNTRY

1450 | 1500 | 1550 | 1600 | 1650 | 1700 | 1750 | 1800

Society and Politics

- Jews expelled from Spain, 1492
- Columbus reaches the Americas, 1492
- Around 9% of Europeans live in cities, 1500
- Peasant Revolt in Germany, 1525
- Around 10% of Europeans live in cities, 1600
- Paris rules that beggars should be whipped, branded, and driven out of town, 1606
- Irish revolt, 1641
- The Fronde in France, 1648–53
- Climax of English Civil War, 1649
- "Glorious Revolution" in England, 1688
- Population of London tops 500,000, 1700
- Jews make up 4% of population of Amsterdam, 1700
- Some three-fourths of all Jews in world live in Poland, 1700
- Last major outbreak of Plague in Western Europe, 1720
- Peter the Great of Russia introduces Table of Ranks, 1722
- Around 11% of Europeans live in cities, 1750
- Emilian Pugachev leads peasant uprising in Russia, 1773–75
- Catherine the Great of Russia's "Charter of the Nobility," 1785
- Final partition of Poland, 1795
- Population of London exceeds 1 million, 1800

Art and Ideas

Scientific Revolution, 1543–1687

The Enlightenment, c. 1685–1789

- Peter Bruegel the Elder's *The Peasants' Wedding*, 1568
- Margaret Cavendish, Duchess of Newcastle's *Sociable Letters*, 1664
- Mary Astell's *Some Reflections on Marriage*, 1700
- Daniel Defoe's *Conjugal Lewdness, or Matrimonial Whoredom*, 1727
- John Gay's *The Beggar's Opera*, 1728
- Cesare Beccaria's *Essay on Crimes and Punishments*, 1764

Beyond the West

Mughal Empire, India, 1526–1857

Ming Dynasty, China, 1368–1644

Qing Dynasty, China, 1644–1912

- Portuguese capture Malacca (Malaysia) and the Moluccas, 1511–13
- Ferdinand Magellan claims Philippines for Spanish crown, 1521
- Japanese expel Christian missionaries, 1614
- Dutch wrest Malacca from Portuguese, 1641
- Viceroyalty of New Granada created, 1717
- Viceroyalty of Rio de la Plata created, 1776

CHAPTER 18

TOWN, COURT, AND COUNTRY

Privilege and Poverty in Early Modern Europe

1500–1780

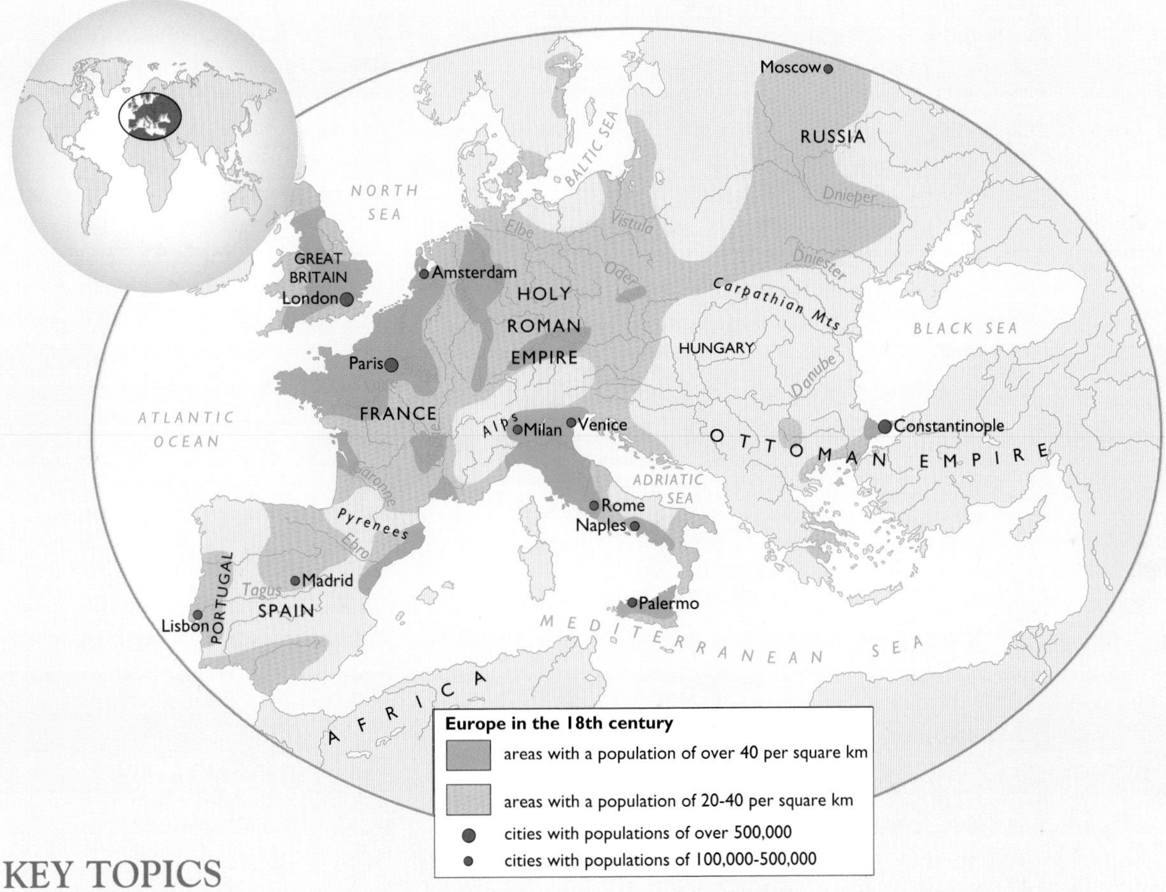

Europe in the 18th century

- areas with a population of over 40 per square km
- areas with a population of 20-40 per square km
- cities with populations of over 500,000
- cities with populations of 100,000-500,000

KEY TOPICS

◆ **Honorable Pursuits:** In the courts of early modern Europe, monarchs fashion exalted images of themselves, while nobles compete at court and consume art, music, and literature as indices of refinement and gentility.

◆ **New Ways with New Wealth:** Wealthier than ever before, bourgeois city-dwellers fill their townhouses with copious items of luxury; the urban poor, meanwhile, are dogged by hunger, disease, homelessness, and crime.

◆ **Field and Village:** In the countryside, some peasants gain new freedoms while others are newly enserfed, as agricultural improvements lead to increased grain yields, more diversified crops, and fatter, healthier livestock.

The Would-Be Gentleman *The French playwright Molière (1622–1673) amused King Louis XIV (r. 1643–1715) with sprightly comedies lampooning hypocrites, pretentious ladies, hypochondriacs, and social-climbing members of the bourgeoisie—such as Monsieur Jourdain, the main character in* The Would-Be Gentleman. *In his desperate effort to turn himself into a nobleman, Jourdain hires a music master, a dancing master, and a philosopher—but fails hilariously. Molière's play, first performed in 1670, highlights the key social issue of the age: the exclusive hold on status and privilege retained by the nobility, and the subordination of all other social groups.*

The early modern age (approximately the period from 1500 to 1750) was still one of social orders, or estates, entered at birth. As previous chapters have shown, this was an era of enormous cultural, economic, and political change. It saw the succession of Renaissance, Reformation, Scientific Revolution, and Enlightenment movements, all heightened by the development of printing and the spread of literacy; the Atlantic "encounter" with new continents and new peoples; the expansion of European mercantile networks worldwide; and the development of **absolute monarchy** and parliamentary resistance to absolutism. Early modern society also experienced turbulence during the transition from medieval to modern times, as individuals strove to better or maintain their social status.

The would-be gentleman was laughable to his audience because he yearned to acquire a status to which he was not born. As Molière's bourgeois gentleman strove to be like the nobility, nobles strove to be like kings, and kings raised themselves above humanity. Beneath the ranks of the bourgeoisie, artisans and shopkeepers also craved the marks of social prestige, lest they fall further down the ladder of social rank. There, toward the bottom, the quest for prestige dimmed in importance. Workers, migrants, and servants fought to survive, along with deserted women and abandoned children and the bands of the utterly destitute. The struggle of the poor for subsistence and the aspirations of the propertied for status in town, court, and country mark the social relations of the early modern era. They foreshadow the boundaries of social class that still prevail in the Western world today, drawn in the colors of honor, wealth, and desperation.

HONORABLE PURSUITS: THE EUROPEAN NOBILITY OF THE EARLY MODERN AGE

Comprising between one and ten percent of the population in most parts of Europe, the nobility was the traditional landowning and military class. Noble status was defended by the idea of honor, which expressed pride in ancient heritage and moral code. Its status increased in the early modern era because of its monopoly of cultural refinement and its closeness to those who held real power: the kings.

Lines and Houses

Europe's most powerful noblemen came from ancient "**lines**" that held title to ancient "**houses**." The line was the series of family connections leading back through male ancestors to the earliest possessors of the land that gave the family its noble status. The "house" was the place or even the building with which the family was associated and from which it took its aristocratic title. For example, the Marquis de Lafayette (1757–1834), a participant in both the American and French revolutions (see Chapters 19, 20), was a member of the house of Lafayette; his family name, seldom used, was "du Motier."

The preeminence of the house in defining noble status stemmed from the nobility's original role in European society in the Middle Ages (see Chapter 9). Because land was originally the reward bestowed by a monarch for military service, it was the nobleman's identity as warrior that established his right as householder. It also provided the emblems of his high social status, the shield and the sword. The symbols decorating a nobleman's shield—his coat of arms—would once have served to identify fully-armed knights on the battlefield.

Shield and sword represented the value of **honor** that noblemen believed was uniquely theirs. To maintain noble status, it was not sufficient or even necessary to be wealthy; it was only necessary to preserve one's honor. In this cause, European aristocrats were willing to kill or be killed, often resorting to dueling as a ritualized form of private warfare. At the same time, the European nobleman could still win honor in the manner of his medieval forebears in the frequent real wars that engulfed Europe in the early modern era. The mounted knight became an army officer, in a transformation that helped the aristocracy to keep its hold into the twentieth century on senior military positions. Away from the battlefield, meanwhile, the nobleman was a hunter, intent on fine

Social Inequalities

Percentage of Population Formed by the Nobility in Five Countries, c. 1750

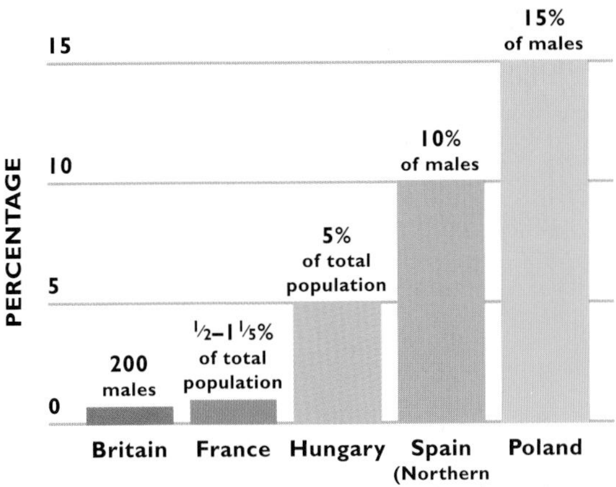

Source: *Based on J. Merriman,* A History of Modern Europe: From the Renaissance to the Age of Napoleon *(New York: W. W. Norton, 1996) p. 356.*

Distribution of Population and Wealth in Lyon, France, 1545

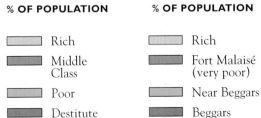

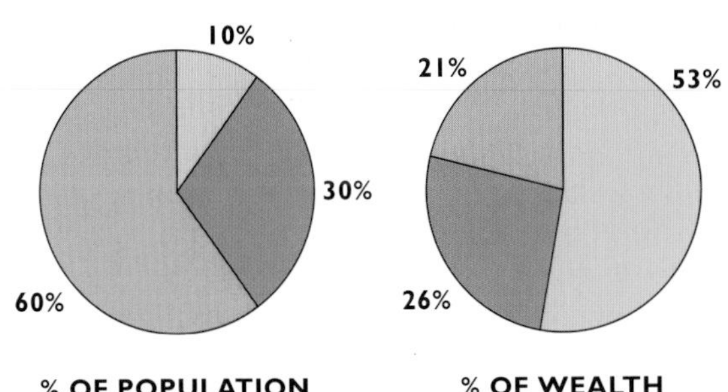

Note that 10% of the population controls 53% of the wealth, and 90% of the population the remaining 47%—less than half.

In the early modern period, social inequalities were a source of great tension. These graphs show four different patterns of social inequality. The percentage of the population formed by the nobility in five countries is seen in the first graph (top left). The other graphs show breakdowns of the population into groups designed by status or wealth: the city of Lyon in France in 1545 (above); England in 1688 (top right); Florence in 1457 (right); and France in 1698 (far right).

Source: *Based on C. M. Cipolla,* Before the Industrial Revolution: European Society and Economy, 1000-1700 *(New York: W. W. Norton, 1976), pp. 10, 11, 12, 13.*

Distribution of Income in England in 1688 According to the Calculations of Gregory King

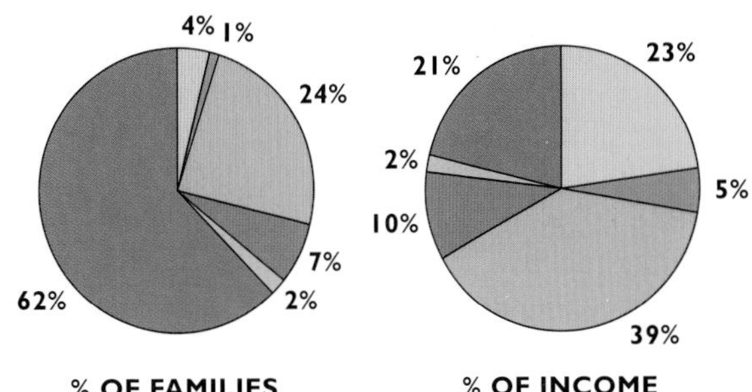

Socioeconomic Class

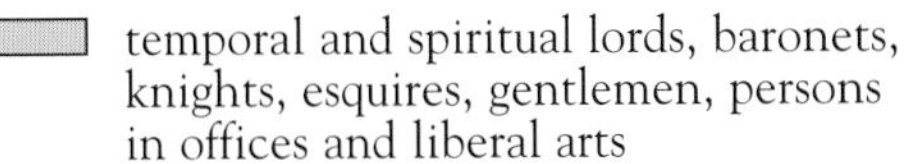

- temporal and spiritual lords, baronets, knights, esquires, gentlemen, persons in offices and liberal arts
- merchants and traders by sea

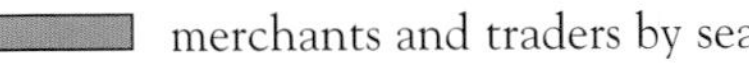

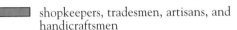

- freeholders and farmers
- shopkeepers, tradesmen, artisans, and handicraftsmen
- naval and military officers and clergymen
- common seamen, laboring people and outservants, cottagers and paupers, common soldiers

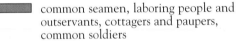

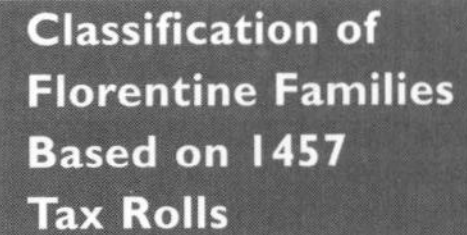

Classification of Florentine Families Based on 1457 Tax Rolls

Vauban's Classification of French Population in 1698

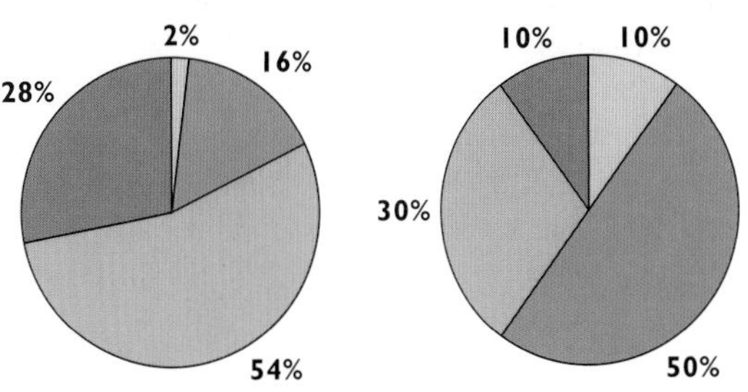

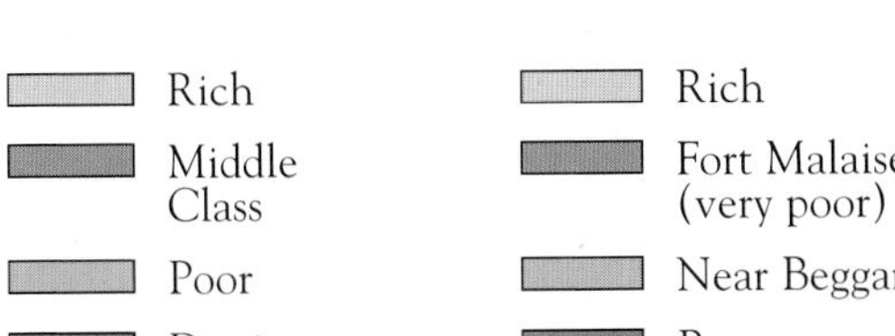

sport, good exercise, and dominion over the forest. When nobles entered their treed reserves, accompanied by their wives and servants, they were demonstrating their power over nature itself. Poor men might have the right to gather chestnuts or firewood there, or to let their pigs run through the brush, but they were barred from stalking the deer, boar, or hares that provided the well-fed nobility with an even richer diet of meat.

Men and women of other social groups were expected to show the nobility deference, by bowing or curtseying, making way for them in the street, or yielding to them the front pew in church. Such privileges of nobility were legally enforceable. The nobleman, in turn, was accustomed to wielding authority over those of lesser social status. The French writer Voltaire (see Chapter 17) had little recourse against a lofty nobleman who took revenge on him for insults in print by having him beaten and left in the street.

During the early modern era the intrusion into the old nobility of men possessed of wealth or professional skills changed the nature of the class. New nobles, called *noblesse de robe* ("of the robe") in France after the robes worn by judges, assimilated quickly to the old nobility "of the sword." They purchased land and acquired coats of arms and army commissions. At the same time, they brought a new dynamism to a class whose political importance was fading.

Some commoners were ennobled because of service to the crown through their exceptional administrative talents. Trained lawyers often rose to become royal ministers and advisers. These new nobles swelled the bureaucracies of the nation states which increased in pace with royal budgets. Overall, the cost of government, the number of officials, and the size of the nobility, all tripled or quadrupled in the early modern centuries.

Townsmen who had grown by commerce—an activity that was considered dishonorable for noblemen and in some places actually forbidden them—yearned to join the aristocracy. The cash-starved monarchs of Europe, with armies to supply and palaces to build, granted their wish through the sale of titles. This practice led to a numerical increase in the nobility, which grew by one-half in seventeenth-century Spain and doubled in France between 1715 and 1789. In the republic of Venice, nobility admitted 127 new families to their ranks between 1646 and 1718 for the enormous sum of 100,000 ducats apiece.

In England, a unique case, it was virtually impossible for a commoner to buy or insinuate his way into the restricted noble elite called the peerage. There were only about 200 peers in a nation of several million. But wealthy commoners regularly purchased country estates and so became members of the gentry. This non-noble landowning elite had access to power and privilege in England comparable to that of the nobilities of continental European countries.

By the eighteenth century, the presence among the nobility of many people who had been born commoners gave strong cause for reflection on what nobility was: was it determined by birth, wealth, virtue, or education? Such discussions led to a profound criticism of noble privilege in the Enlightenment (see Chapter 17), and ultimately to the revolutionary rejection of all that it stood for.

In the mean time, Europeans generally accepted the nobility as a hereditary ruling class. The aim of new nobles was to become assimilated as quickly as possible to the old elite: they acquired estates and coats of arms; they enjoyed exemption from some taxes in a number of countries; and they sought to marry their children to the children of the old nobles. As newcomers gained high status, however, some members of the traditional nobility were experiencing difficulties. Where income from land declined, nobles could fall into poverty, possessing little but their sword and their coat of arms and the threadbare costume of a magistrate.

Some noblemen met the challenges of the early modern period by engaging in commerce, by vigorously managing their estates, or by marrying a wealthy commoner's daughter. Their willingness to accept a redefinition of what it was to be an aristocrat permitted them to survive into a new age in the position of dominance to which they were accustomed. Not all noblemen were free to adapt in this way, however. In France and Spain, a nobleman who engaged in trade was liable to "derogation"—to be struck from the rolls of nobility. In some localities, marriages between nobles and commoners were illegal. Those noblemen who survived best the transition from medieval to early modern society did so by playing an active part in the more sophisticated royal administration and growing bureaucracy required by modern states, and by adapting to the needs of the marketplace, both in their land management and in their cash investments.

Though the nobility was an ancient class, it was a dynamic one in the early modern centuries. New members entered the nobility, while poor nobles struggled to maintain their hereditary status. The wealthiest nobles, of the old sword families, continued to dominate the choicest positions and access to power and privilege.

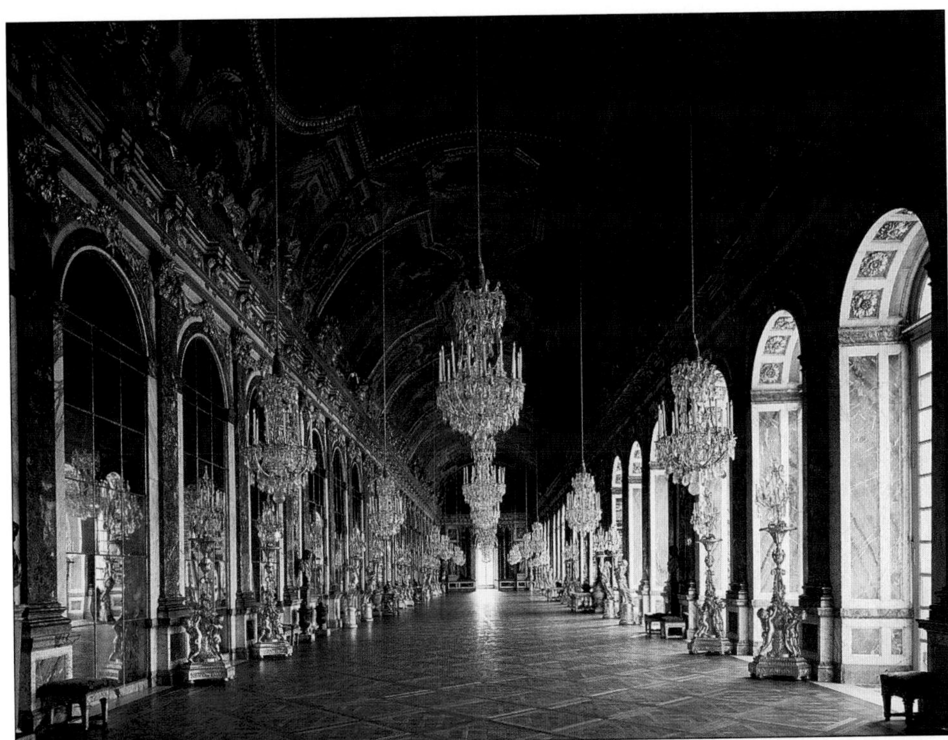

Images of Power

Hall of Mirrors, Versailles: *In the Hall of Mirrors at Louis XIV's palace at Versailles, the king could see his sovereignty reflected as he proceeded from one formal appointment to the next. Versailles served to attract and distract nobles, who arrived from their country estates to vie with each other in elaborate rituals to win the king's favor.*

***François Marot,* Louis XIV Instituting the Order of Saint Louis:** *In this 1710 painting, Louis XIV exercises his function as royal patron and rewards the efforts of his nobles at Versailles by conferring the Order of Saint Louis.* (Palace of Versailles, France)

Patterns of Nobility

The nature of the European nobility varied from region to region. Each community had its own particular set of relationships between nobleman and peasant, nobleman and king.

In Russia, an autocratic tsar distributed privileges to a nobility defined entirely by its service to the crown, and rewarded those servants with the right to dominate a nearly enslaved peasantry (**serfs**). Here the nobility originated not from the earlier landowning or military elite, known as the boyars, which had been suppressed, but from the decrees of the tsars. Ivan the Terrible (r. 1533–1584) and Peter the Great (r. 1682–1725) (see Chapter 15) transformed the Russian elite into a service nobility, a process culminating under Peter in the 1722 "Table of Ranks." The Table of Ranks set out the military and bureaucratic services in fourteen ascending categories. It was intended to replace promotion according to birth and ancestry by promotion according to ability, and to open up the highest ranks of the nobility to commoners who gave distinguished service as administrators or officers.

To compensate nobles for their lifelong commitment to government the tsars gave them total authority over their serfs, who became virtual slaves, bound not only to the land but also to their lords. Catherine the Great (r. 1762–1796), in her "Charter of the Nobility" of 1785, reaffirmed the privileges held by lords over serfs, and attempted to mold the Russian nobility into a cultural as well as political elite (constituting two to three percent of the population).

In central Europe, a large noble class both suppressed the peasantry and kept kings in check. In Prussia the ruler granted economic and judicial privileges to the nobles, called Junkers, in exchange for military service. Here, as in Russia, the near-total mobilization of the nation brought the interests of the nobility into line with national aims, at the expense of the peasant population. In the aristocratic republic of Poland, a nobility comprising some ten to fifteen percent of the population tyrannized its peasantry while also having a say in the election of its king. Enriched by grain exports to the more urbanized areas of western Europe, the Polish nobility jealously guarded its medieval rights to assemble and vote on national issues. It possessed, in addition, the liberum veto ("free veto"), enabling any individual nobleman to thwart the intentions, for good or ill, of any monarch. This constitutional situation invited anarchy and contributed to the series of international maneuvers that culminated in the partition and final disappearance of the Polish nation in 1795. Much of the rest of eastern Europe (excluding the Balkans, still largely under Ottoman rule) fell under the domination of the **Habsburg** dynasty. As in Poland, the Czech and Hungarian nobility constituted a large percentage of the population, and profited from commerce in grain. While they resented their subordination to the German-speaking Habsburg emperors, they often filled posts in the royal administration. In the northern countries of Denmark and Sweden, as in Russia and Prussia, nobles received their privileges from the king in proportion to their service to the crown.

The principalities that made up the many German-speaking states of central Europe, as well as Sweden and Habsburg Austria, modeled themselves on the western absolute monarchies, and their nobility also resembled those in the west. In northern Italy, Switzerland, and the Netherlands, the nobility were not a preeminent political class, but shared authority in various ways with the wealthy urban bourgeoisie who controlled civic affairs, and frequently engaged in commerce themselves. As landowners, they were concerned with agricultural productivity, but did not necessarily supervise the work of tenant farmers. Nobles of once-great mercantile centers such as Venice, whose ancestors had scoured the Mediterranean for profit, lived in the countryside in leisured detachment.

In England, the nobility consisted of some 200 peers with long medieval traditions who played an important role in Parliament. Despite owning fifteen to forty percent of the land, they had little direct authority over a largely free peasantry. Both this nobility and the gentry often took great interest in the productivity of their landholdings, which were farmed largely by tenant farmers employing landless day laborers. An exception to the general European pattern, the English nobility had surrendered its tax privileges, but voted in Parliament to tax itself as required to supplement the monarch's own funds. With the gentry, it was deeply involved in government and unafraid of the power of the crown, limited decisively by the two revolutions of 1649 and 1688 (see Chapter 15).

In France and Spain, nobles maintained traditional roles at the apex of a steep social hierarchy, overseen by monarchs jealous of their autonomy. In Spain, the nobility (totaling some 500,000 adult males) ranged from powerful grandees to simple *hidalgos*. Taking particular interest in maintaining the purity and distinctiveness of noble lines, the crown supported the *hidalgos* with modest state pensions, and until 1773 barred noble participation in trade or manual labor. That prohibition was a disability for the *hidalgos*, many of whom were impoverished and unable to keep themselves as befitted their status.

The French nobility also considered commercial activity incompatible with high status. Poor nobles suffered as land values fell, while the "grand" nobility managed well on its vast estates, advantageous marriages, financial investments, and royal patronage. Altogether, from 25,000 to 55,000 families claimed noble status, and owned a quarter to a third of all cultivated land. Of these, up to sixty percent were poor.

In the 1630s, Cardinal Richelieu (1585–1642) tried to strengthen the power of the crown in relation to these grand nobles. He restricted their role as generals of private armies, ordered their fortified castles and towers destroyed, and prohibited their duels of honor, labeling them crimes against the state. Aristocrats chafed at these restrictions, and seized the opportunity to recover their lost autonomy shortly after the deaths of the Cardinal and of his master Louis XIII (r. 1610–1643). The young king Louis XIV was still a minor, and France was ruled by the queen mother, the regent Anne of Austria (1601–1666) and her lover, the Italian-born Cardinal Jules Mazarin (1602–1661). In 1648 a protest against royal financial policies grew into a full-scale insurrection that

The Italian Court

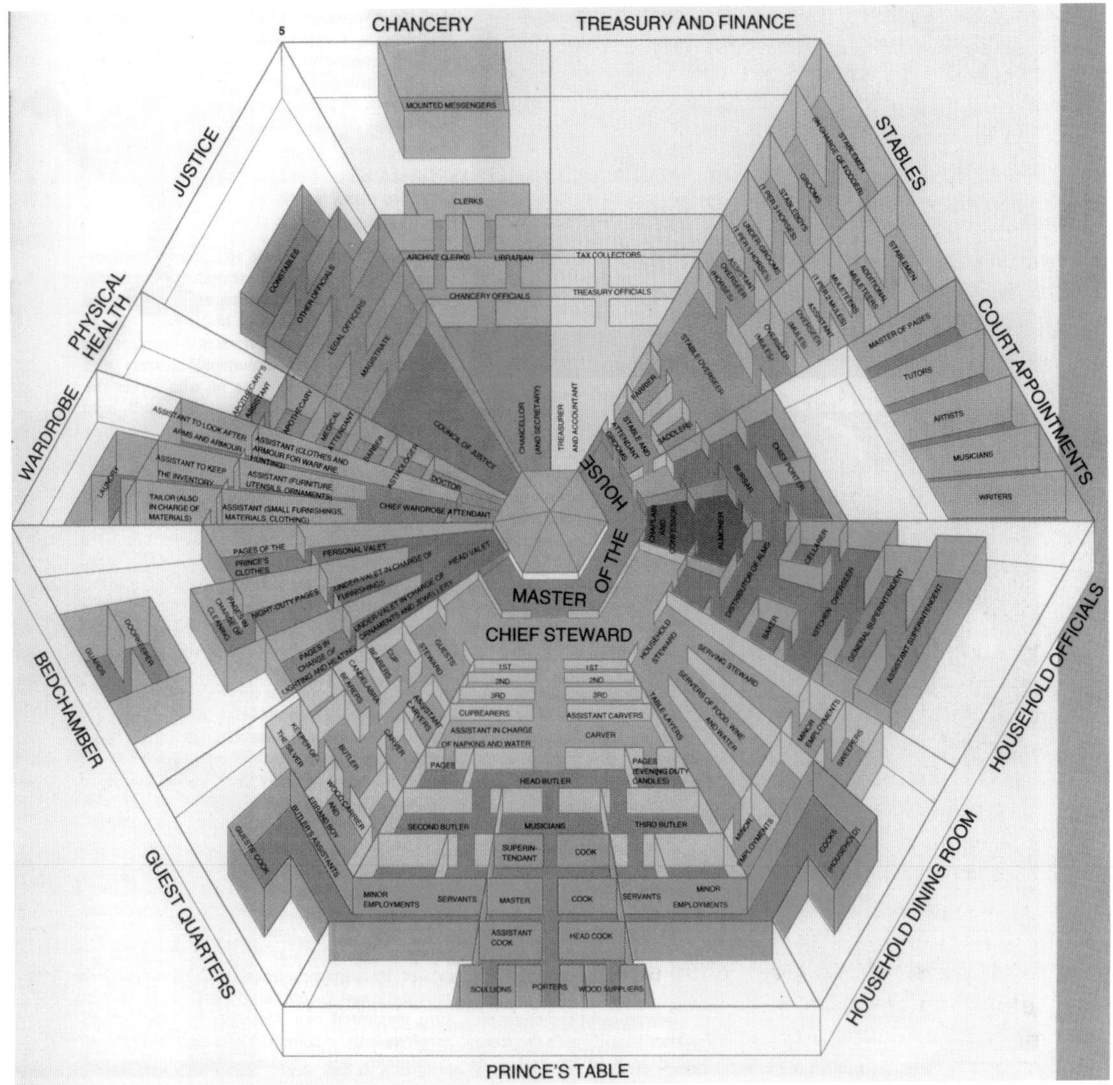

Just as Italy produced the classic manual (by Castiglione) instructing aristocrats of Europe how to behave at court, it also first elaborated the organization of the princely court. The courts of tiny Mantua, Ferrara, and Urbino (see Chapter 13) then served as models for the monarchical courts of France, England, Spain, and wealthier German states. Shown here is a structural representation of an Italian court.

Source: *S. Bertelli et al,* The Courts of the Italian Renaissance *(New York–Oxford: Facts on File Publications, 1986).*

engaged not only the nobility but also townspeople and peasants. The Fronde, named after the slingshot used by Parisian children to shoot pebbles at rich folk in carriages, was suppressed in 1653, resulting in the humiliation of the aristocracy and the triumph of the crown. Traumatized by his experience at age twelve of rebellious Frondeurs, Louis XIV later distracted his potentially troublesome grand nobles in the salons and gardens of his huge palace of Versailles outside Paris. Meanwhile, robe nobles wielded regional power in their judicial assemblies, or *parlements*, or transacted with quiet efficiency the business of government.

Courtiers and Kings

Some members of the aristocratic elite were not only nobles but courtiers too. They attended Europe's kings, princes, and prelates in palatial settings that expressed the ruler's glory. These courts had a dual

WITNESSES

Aristocratic Culture and Values

Castiglione tells the would-be gentlemen of Europe how to live at the courts of princes (1528): Now your request is that I should describe what, in my view, is the form of courtiership most appropriate for a gentleman living at the Courts of princes . . . in short, . . . what kind of man must be one who deserves the name of a perfect courtier. . . . I would have our courtier of noble birth and good family, since it matters far less to a common man if he fails to perform virtuously and well than to a nobleman. For if a gentleman strays from the path of his forebears, he dishonours his family name and not only fails to achieve anything but loses what has already been achieved. . . . The first and true profession of the courtier must be that of arms; and this above everything else I wish him to pursue vigorously. Let him also stand out from the rest as enterprising, bold and loyal to whomever he serves. . . . So I wish our courtier . . . demonstrate strength and lightness and suppleness and be good at all the physical exercises befitting a warrior. Here, I believe, his first duty is to know how to handle expertly every kind of weapon, either on foot or mounted. . . . [One must always] steer away from affectation at all costs, as if it were a rough and dangerous reef, and . . . practice in all things a certain nonchalance which conceals all artistry and makes whatever one says or does seem uncontrived and effortless. I am sure that grace springs especially from this, since everyone knows how difficult it is to accomplish some unusual feat perfectly, and so facility in such things excites the greatest wonder; whereas, in contrast, to labour at what one is doing and, as we say, to make bones over it, shows an extreme lack of grace.
(Baldassare Castiglione, *The Book of the Courtier*, 1528; ed. G. Bull, 1967)

Catherine the Great commands the nobility to show selfless service to the imperial Russian state (April 21, 1785): The name and dignity of well-born nobility are acquired by service and labors useful to the Empire and to the throne in the past, the present, and in the future, and as the actual station of the Russian nobility is dependent upon the security of the fatherland and the throne; so therefore at any such time as needed by the Russian autocracy, when the service of the nobility is needed and necessary for the common good, then every well-born nobleman is obliged, at the first summons from the sovereign authority, not to spare either labor or life itself for the state service.
(From J. T. Alexander ed., *Catherine the Great: Life and Legend*, 1989)

function: they served to subordinate the nobility to the greater power of the monarch, and—increasingly in the early modern period—they were places where elite arts and social graces were nurtured, setting a new standard for European culture. Those monarchs who still aimed to possess absolute power needed to win the cooperation of their nobles, to reward loyalty, and to discipline resistance. To this end, they drew their nobles to court, where the monarch stood at the center controlling the courtier nobility who, like planets, circled around their sun. This court system had its roots less in the rough, itinerant councils of medieval monarchs than in the lavish ritual systems of the local despots of the Italian Renaissance (see Chapter 13). The jewelbox courts of Ferrara and Mantua, Milan and Urbino, spawned imitations on the grand scale in Madrid, Prague and Vienna, St. Petersburg, and London, but above all at Versailles.

The sparkle of aristocratic activity heightened the grandeur of the monarch. A throng of courtiers and servants busily engaged in little of importance formed a kind of collective human prop for the symbolic authority of the prince. Courts also attracted artists and intellectuals with the promise of royal patronage: their brilliant productions added further luster to princely authority. Architecture and the arts were designed to reflect the monarch's grandeur—literally in the case of Louis XIV's Hall of Mirrors at Versailles. Conspicuous expressions of wealth and high culture ranged from the gems sewn on courtiers' clothes or hung about the necks of their wives, to the silver forks that, for the first time in the history of the West, were used for the delicate science of proper dining; in an older and cruder age, the elite ate with their fingers, just like their peasant subjects.

The early modern court system evolved through the need of monarchs to engage the cooperation of their nobles in their determination to retain absolute power. At the same time, bureaucrats, accountants, and secretaries began to carry on more of the business of government. Guided in that direction by the Italian city states and the papal curia, Europe's monarchs made great progress by 1750 in developing centralized and efficient methods of government, staffed by administrators, like the *intendants* instituted by Richelieu. Even so, monarchs still relied on nobles to recruit armies, keep order, and deal out justice.

A great weakness of the court system was that it was precisely those nobles who resided at court, closest to the monarch, who often turned out to be most likely to disobey him. This made court society rife with suspicion, aspiration, and deception, the perfect breeding ground for intrigue and rebellion. Both women and men joined in this intrigue and deception involved in playing for power. In this setting, women's general exclusion from warfare or government was irrelevant: they, like their menfolk, became easy experts in such methods as innuendo and gossip. The aim of intrigue was to gain power and privilege in a system of patronage in which monarchs bestowed rewards on loyal nobles. While lesser offices were filled by members of the lower nobility, gentry, or bourgeoisie, high positions were generally reserved for the high nobility. Salaries dispensed in this way took on the nature of bribes, and the whole system was, to modern eyes, thoroughly corrupt. While official state payments often lined the pockets of those entrusted with distributing them, nobles who depended on royal handouts often waited for months or years for their promised rewards.

Court life also served as a school, in which the self-willed nobles of Europe learned the new arts of civility. Civility entailed far more than showing reverence to a monarch: it involved a code of manners and attitudes that would become the standard of proper behavior for the next few centuries. Nobles at court needed to know how to behave at table, in the bedroom, in the garden, and in the great halls; in what way and where to bow, speak, or attend to bodily functions; how to address people of different ranks; how to dress for each occasion. To advise the aspiring courtier there were etiquette manuals, supplemented by letters from parents and advice from patrons. The classic manual, a Europe-wide bestseller, was *The Book of the Courtier* by the Italian diplomat Baldassare Castiglione (1478–1529). Translated into five languages, and circulating in 115 editions before 1600, it provided a model for the ideal courtier, who should combine the qualities of a sportsman and a warrior, a musician and a poet, a conversationalist and a counsellor to the prince. He should possess all these virtues lightly, with a quality Castiglione called *sprezzatura*, translatable as lively nonchalance, an effortless display of the most refined and developed abilities.

The great chasm that divided the early modern courtier from the warrior knight of the Middle Ages can now be understood. The nobleman who wished to succeed in the new game played in the corridors of power must learn cultural skills unknown in the earlier era. The modern courtier went to school, watched his manners, and participated in music, dance, and theatrical events as both performer and spectator.

Noblewomen Noblewomen too became expert courtiers. Except for female monarchs, women of the highest social class had been warriors only as surrogates for their husbands and held no public office. A woman's manners and artistry were her sole means of announcing high status, to which she claimed right through her father's line or the wealth of her husband. Woman's role as a civilizing force had roots in the courtly games of the Middle Ages (see Chapter 9), in which a noblewoman might hold sway through the yearning love and admiration she inspired in young aristocrats and troubadours. Women's role as social arbiter persisted in the early modern era: in the model court described by Castiglione, women presided as moderators and judges of the conversation and behavior of men. "Society depends on women," Voltaire noted, however much men were the agents in realms outside the court. No wonder that the salon—a lady's sitting room—became in the Enlightenment the principal setting for the exchange of ideas (see Chapter 17).

Nevertheless, even noblewomen remained subject to their husbands, just as in the Middle Ages. Marriage choices were made by fathers, with an eye to family honor and prosperity. Women often were dispatched at young ages to older husbands. Bearing children in quick succession, who were quickly dispatched to wet nurses, they might find relief in early widowhood, or perhaps a discreet love affair—the latter a risky choice, since adultery on a wife's part was punishable in many places by death (although openly tolerated in high aristocratic circles). Or they might find amusement in court intrigue, salon conversations, or the world of fashion.

Fashion and Culture Fashion—the idea that we can choose what we wear and that this choice is meaningful—had arrived at the end of the Middle Ages, in courts and cities that had access to luxury fabrics, often obtained by foreign trade. First aristocratic, and then burgher dress became distinguished from that of peasants, the clergy, and lawyers and other professionals (the latter two groups continued to wear the long robe of the previous era, while peasants still dressed in their customary homespun tunics and cloaks). The elites, meanwhile, clothed themselves in silks, brocades, velvets, laces, luxury wools, and furs, adorned

Aristocratic Leisure

Giovanni Pannini, Gallery of Scenes from Ancient Rome: *During the seventeenth and eighteenth centuries, the European nobility enjoyed power, indulged in luxury, and consumed culture. Here, in a painting dated 1759, fashionably dressed aristocrats examine the accumulated artifacts of Classical civilization, displayed floor to ceiling in the vast halls of an imaginary palace.* (Louvre, Paris)

Oliviero Domenico, Teatro Regio, Turin: *Aristocratic culture found clear expression in opera. Lavish, flamboyant, and highly formalized—as demonstrated by this contemporary painting of an opera house in Turin—this art form saw its basic development in the eighteenth century.* (Museo Civico, Turin)

with jewels, ribbons, buttons, clasps, and colors. Outlandish styles came and faded: shoes with long toes; detachable sleeves slashed to show the silk beneath; headdresses stacked high on wire frames and wide skirts supported by wire basketwork; deep decolletés that revealed women's bosoms and stiff codpieces that accentuated, while covering, male genitals; stockings that ended below or over the knee, and breeches that closed over or above the stockings.

Amid this panoply, a few clear trends can be distinguished in upper-class fashion. First, at the beginning of the early modern era, men's clothing diverged from women's (they had both previously worn gowns, cassocks, robes, and cloaks). The main garment became the short doublet (a close-fitting jacket), while women's robes remained long. Then, toward the end of the seventeenth century, the doublet gave way to two garments, an inner sleeveless waistcoat and an outer coat, that are the forerunners of the modern vest and jacket. Finally, in the eighteenth century, women's dress for the first time became more elaborate and luxurious than men's.

In the realm of culture, the court replaced the church as the primary institution. It was initially through royal and noble patronage that modern European music, theater, dance, and the visual arts developed. During the early modern period, many of the great composers were still hired primarily to produce religious music, but the patronage of music was being assumed by the kings, princes, and prelates whose courts also supported the first orchestras of string, brass, and wind instruments. By the eighteenth century, most formal music was secular and performed in the courts. Elaborate festivals, ballets, and masques were organized for such occasions as weddings and victories, diplomatic visits and sacred events.

Art was also essential to the culture of the high nobility. Royal and aristocratic patrons competed with each other in amassing collections of works of art. These collections announced the good taste, learning, and wealth of the patron. Many works were created in styles that evoked or imitated the art of ancient Greece and Rome. A renewed interest in and admiration for this art, which survived most obviously in the ruins of ancient Rome itself, gave birth to Renaissance Classicism. Classical features, such as balanced proportions, colonnades, and grand entrance porticos with columns, became the mark of high-prestige buildings, from the country houses of the nobility to churches and palaces. In the seventeenth and eighteenth centuries the Baroque style was also important, especially in Italy, Spain, Germany, and Austria. This was characterized by bold, dramatic rhythms, with strongly curving, often disrupted forms. A highly decorative variation of Baroque called Rococo won favor in France and eastern Europe in the early eighteenth century. Meanwhile, as the nobility and their favored architects and artists began to travel more widely, visiting ancient sites on the so-called Grand Tour, a more precise and scholarly form of Classicism, termed Neoclassicism, evolved. The Baroque style of architecture was especially suited for displaying the grandiose ambitions of the European royalty and nobility who commissioned the great building projects of the age. In Russia, Peter the Great constructed a whole new city, St. Petersburg, much of which was designed in the Baroque style by architects brought from western Europe. This gigantic enterprise was at once a display of the despotic power of an absolute monarch and an expression of civilized good taste on a grand scale.

Princes and nobles commissioned portraits of themselves and their families, which record the importance of the noble line and the luxury of the age. In England, Sir Anthony van Dyck (1599–1641) painted numerous portraits of Charles I (r. 1625–1649) and his family, while his contemporary in France, Pierre Mignard (1612–1695), immortalized the "Sun King" Louis XIV and his court. In Spain Diego Velázquez (1599–1660) painted forty portraits of King Philip IV. Family portraits carefully emphasize the role of the patriarch, and illustrate the fecundity and respectability of his wife. Despite the changes forced on it during this period, the early modern nobility was a successful class. In many cases, it maintained its honor, its social and economic privileges, while ceding some political power to the monarch. At the same time, it had been transformed by the experience of the high noblemen and women who attended the kings of Europe at court. They created an ideal of behavior that set a new standard in European culture, at precisely that point in history when European culture took precedence on a global stage. Into the twentieth century, to belong to the European elite was to possess as the accompaniments of power a superior education, refined manners, and cultivated taste.

NEW WAYS WITH NEW WEALTH: THE EARLY MODERN BOURGEOISIE

As the European nobility was transformed during the early modern era, so the bourgeoisie developed in size, complexity, wealth, and in the range of its aspirations. Europe's leading cities became cultural centers rivaling the kingly courts, as its once-modest private homes became showplaces of domestic virtues and lavish material consumption. Some members of the bourgeoisie, such as Molière's would-be gentleman, practiced the social and cultural skills that were now the earmarks of high status and sought to enter the ranks of the aristocracy. As they yearned to climb the social ladder, those beneath them sold their crafts in the shops and on the streets, labored in burgher homes as servants, or acquired their daily bread by theft or prostitution. Those who were idle and unpaid sought charity from the institutions that guarded well the wealth of riches commanded by urban patriciates.

The Ranks of the Bourgeoisie

The bourgeoisie derived from the merchants who lived as exceptions in a society that comprised clergy, nobles, and peasants—the three medieval social orders, or estates. They were called, in French, *bourgeois* (in English, German, and Italian: burgher, *Bürger*, *borghese*) because they lived in *bourgs* (borough, *Burg*, *borgo*), or towns. As towns multiplied, the bourgeoisie also grew, early becoming an exceptionally prosperous and dynamic class in Italy and Flanders (see Chapter 11). By the seventeenth century, the bourgeoisie were the dominant social group in Europe's urban centers: in London and Amsterdam, for example, they rivaled the aristocracy in power and influence.

WITNESSES

Bourgeois and Commercial Culture

The merchant and the country gentleman—Adam Smith and the wealth of nations (1776): A merchant is accustomed to employ his money chiefly in profitable projects; whereas a mere country gentleman is accustomed to employ it chiefly in expense. The one often sees his money go from him and return to him again with a profit; the other, when he parts with it, very seldom expects to see any more of it. Those different habits naturally affect their temper and disposition in every sort of business. A merchant is commonly a bold, a country gentleman, a timid undertaker. . . . The habits, beside, of order, economy and attention, to which mercantile business naturally forms a merchant, render him much fitter to execute, with profit and success, any project of improvement.
(Adam Smith, *The Wealth of Nations*, 1776; ed. E. Cannan, 1976)

The global outlook of the bourgeoisie—Daniel Defoe celebrates England's overseas trade (1730): Our Manufacture, like a flowing Tide, if 'tis bank't out in one Place, it spreads by other Channels at the same Time into so many different Parts of the World, and finds every Day so many new Outlets, that . . . like the Land to the Sea, what it loses in one Place, it gains in another. . . . If our Trade is the Envy of the World, and they [other nations] are conspiring to break in upon it . . . we are the more engaged to look out for its Support; and we have Room enough: The World is wide: There are new Countries, and new Nations, who may be so planted, so improv'd, and the People so manag'd, as to create a new Commerce; and Millions of People shall call for our Manufacture, who never call'd for it before.
(Daniel Defoe, *A Plan of the English Commerce*, 2nd ed., 1730)

Benjamin Franklin recommends self-discipline and hard work (1771): Reading was the only amusement I allow'd myself. I spent no time in taverns, games or frolicks of any kind; and my industry in my business continu'd as indefatigable as it was necessary. . . . My circumstances, however, grew daily easier. My original habits of frugality continuing, and my father having, among his instructions to me when a boy, frequently repeated a proverb of Solomon, "Seest thou a man diligent in his calling, he shall stand before kings, he shall not stand before mean men," I from thence considered industry as a means of obtaining wealth and distinction, which encourag'd me, tho' I did not think that I should ever literally *stand before kings*, which, however, has since happened; for I have stood before *five*, and even had the honor of sitting down with one, the King of Denmark, to dinner.
(Benjamin Franklin, *The Autobiography of Benjamin Franklin*; ed. J. Bigelow, 1867)

The early modern bourgeoisie developed great social complexity. Constituting as much as ten percent of the population in England, France, and the Netherlands, although only a tiny percentage of the regions of eastern Europe, it included merchants, bankers, and entrepreneurs as well as patricians, professionals, guildsmen, and prosperous artisans. Among these were the dynamic leaders of Europe's economic expansion. Some were conservators of outmoded and restrictive mercantile traditions. And some, having amassed their wealth in commerce, invested it in land and lived like nobles. There was no longer a single but many bourgeois orders uncomfortably ranked among the commoners, mostly peasant, of the Third Estate.

The entrepreneurs and bankers, descendants of the great medieval merchant princes, were engaged in those activities that yielded the greatest profits: long-distance trade and the financial back-up that made it possible to fit out oceangoing ships and undertake other costly ventures. Resident mainly in the most populous cities of western Europe, these men invested in the joint stock companies that trade with Asia and the Americas, in the ships that carried African slaves across the Atlantic or wheat cargoes in the Baltic, and in the mines providing iron for guns and machinery. Bankers lent cash to monarchs and startup funds to other merchants. Energetic, creative, and risk-taking, these entrepreneurs opened up world markets and mapped out the commercial system that made Europe the foremost economic power in the world (see Chapter 16).

The patricians were the traditional elites of the European cities. These more conservative "city fathers" were outpaced in Amsterdam and London by dynamic entrepreneurs, but continued to flourish in smaller independent cities such as Strasbourg or Hamburg. Their merchant ancestors had accumulated the wealth that enabled later generations to live on rents and investments while maintaining control of town councils. Where the entrepreneurs drove forward the European economic engine, the patricians' outlook was often local and limited. Other members of the bourgeoisie whose prosperity was not primarily based on mercantile activity included bureaucrats and public officials, who were often trained lawyers.

In the frequent civic and religious processions that wound through streets and market squares, the patricians marched first, followed by guildsmen and artisans, costumed and accoutred according to their ranks. The guildsmen were artisans who were masters of their craft, as certified by the guild organization. Unlike entrepreneurs, whose mercantile activities had burst the bounds of guild-organized commerce, the guildsmen of the early modern period were a conservative force: they tended to resist change in production methods, trade patterns, and the social organization of industries. Below guildsmen in status were journeymen ("day-laborers," from the French *journée*, a day) or craftspersons not admitted to guilds, or practicing crafts that had no guild structure. Very rarely, women workers, especially in such specialized textile crafts as gold embroidery or pursemaking, might belong to guilds in their own right, rather than as the widow or daughter of a master.

In Protestant regions, members of the clergy were considered as professionals with bourgeois or gentry status. In Catholic regions, they remained a class apart: privileged like most nobles, with freedom from taxation, they were accorded the highest social honors. In the nations of Catholic Europe, the clergy constituted the highest ranking social group, or "First Estate," technically followed by the nobility as second, although many high-ranking clergy were nobles.

The sons of the bourgeoisie—entrepreneurial, patrician, or artisan—often joined their fathers in commercial partnerships. But increasingly, following a pattern already seen in the towns of late medieval Italy, these young men proceeded from the elementary schooling that equipped them to be merchants to the secondary and advanced education that permitted them to be lawyers, clergymen, or physicians. From this professional order came not only most of Europe's administrators and bureaucrats, but nearly all its theorists and intellectuals. Other young men from wealthy bourgeois families sought to acquire the land that made it possible for a burgher to live like a nobleman, even without the official title of nobility. In the Dutch Republic, the distinction between wealthy landowner and nobleman was fine. In England, landownership of itself conferred social status, making it possible for a man rich from trade to become a member of the gentry: "Trade in England makes gentlemen and has peopled this nation with gentlemen," commented the novelist Daniel Defoe (1660–1731). The defection of successful bourgeois to the countryside, and worse, to the ranks of the nobility, tended to retard the development of the commercial classes and their most energetic members, the entrepreneurs.

Going to market: *Trade and commerce (later industry) were the lifeblood and culture of Europe's urban bourgeoisie. In this anonymous contemporary painting buyers and sellers fill the cheese market in the busy Dutch merchant city of Alkmaar.* (Stedelijk Museum, Alkmaar)

At Home

Those wealthy bourgeois who did not emigrate to the countryside aimed, in town, to "live nobly"—which meant to have servants to do the menial work, and to spend lavishly on beautiful or useful things made by others' hands. In the intimacy of their well-furnished homes, however, townspeople seem to have experienced domestic lives more infused with sentiments of love and devotion than was typical of the aristocracy, or available to most of the laboring poor.

The interior spaces of burgher households began to shine with the kinds of luxuries—carved furniture, tiled or sculpted fireplaces, elegantly decorated chests, painted and glazed dishware, silver implements, and glass vessels—that had previously been the possessions of only wealthy nobles or the most successful of Italy's merchant princes. Less conspicuously lavish items were still expensive, including window glass, candles, and fine soap, and such foodstuffs as meat, fish, and cheeses in abundance, and imported wines, tea, and coffee. In a world where simply having enough to eat amounted to prosperity, bourgeois magnates reveled in material goods and consumables. In costume as in diet, they imitated aristocratic opulence, as far as their budgets and their mercantile prudence would allow.

Particularly in the Netherlands, where the bourgeoisie achieved a maximum of success in the seventeenth century, the contents of households and laden tables were enshrined in art. While painters elsewhere celebrated royalty and nobility, here such artists as Jan Vermeer (1632–1675) depicted the clean, ample, and tranquil space of the bourgeois household.

Already in the Middle Ages, the wealthier towndwellers protected household wealth by adopting the system of giving daughters a "marriage portion," or dowry, and limiting inheritance either to the eldest son (primogeniture) or all males. Like noblemen (see Chapter 9), burgher patriarchs traced their descent in the male line, and carefully chose their children's marriage partners to enhance family status and prevent the drain of capital. Emotional ties between family members, including sentiments of affection for children, were often subordinated in these circumstances to the needs of household maintenance.

The prominent role of the father in this household system was further reinforced by the advent of the Reformation in some parts of Europe (see Chapter 14), and of absolutism in many (see Chapter 15). In Protestant families, the patriarch summoned the family to daily prayer and enforced discipline not just as the eldest male, but also as the minister of divine authority. The father was understood to be monarch in his family, as the ruler was in the state: to obey him was to learn to obey the king. "A family is . . . a little Commonwealth," wrote one English preacher, "a school wherein the first principles and grounds of government and subjection are learned."

In a family system dominated in this way by the husband and father, a wife's duty was to be subordinate—not a new obligation in the early modern era (see Chapter 12). Among the bourgeoisie, however, concerns for the preservation of family wealth and advancement of social status made marriage a business of critical importance for many persons other than the bride. The complete surrender of personality required of a woman in marriage was often made without the woman herself having actively made a decision to marry, or to marry the man chosen for her by her parents, who were not bound to consider their daughter's inclinations. Sadly, wrote the English aristocrat Margaret Cavendish, Duchess of Newcastle (1623–1673) "daughters are but branches which by marriage are broken off from the root whence they sprang and grafted onto the stock of another family."

Once married, a woman was largely defined by the interests of the new household. Her dowry wealth was generally given over to her husband to manage (not until modern times were women completely free to manage their own, or their family's, finances), while her behavior and costume were assumed to reflect her husband's social position. Adultery was seen as a woman's crime: a man who had sexual relations with other women outside of marriage committed no wrong, except against the honor of the other woman's husband. A married woman who committed adultery injured her husband so grievously that, in Spain, he was entitled to execute her with impunity and, in France, with slight or no consequence.

Married women had only limited claim to their children, or to their own or their husband's property. Children belonged to their fathers. Only rarely did a married woman leave a household with her children, who were understood to continue her husband's lineage. Wealthy widows were discouraged from marrying again, especially if there were young children who might suffer if a woman's dowry was removed from the household; they were often encouraged to remain in the deceased husband's house, maintaining a chaste condition. Depending on local law, a woman might be—but was not always—entitled to any portion of his property.

Some women protested against the restrictions of marriage. In *Some Reflections on Marriage* (1700), Mary Astell (1666–1731) offered a powerful critique, centered on the need for women to develop their own personalities and faculties prior to becoming a fixture in a household. Women should not rely only on their beauty and adornments—nor should men be satisfied with these, but should seek real companionship with an educated and thoughtful comrade. In all, a woman should consider seriously before she married, since once wed, she was wholly in her husband's power, "and if the matrimonial yoke be grievous, neither law nor custom affords her that redress which a man obtains." Lady Mary Chudleigh (1656–1710) put the matter more succinctly in her poem "To The Ladies":

Wife and Servant are the same,
But only differ in the Name.

The wife's condition might have been more like a prostitute's than a servant's, suggested the writer Daniel Defoe. In *Conjugal Lewdness, or Matrimonial Whoredom* he argued that marriage often amounted to the legally protected sexual exploitation of women.

High rates of child-bearing and high infant mortality were both accepted facts of existence (see Chapter 12). The children of elite families often spent their first years with wet nurses. Sons returned to their mothers only briefly before they again left their parents' homes—perhaps around age fourteen, but possibly as early as eight—to serve an apprenticeship in their destined occupation, to enter a military academy or religious institution, or in other ways to embark on adult life. In another sense, they did not achieve adulthood until their later twenties, when they married themselves (often to a much younger wife, or an older widow), set up their own households, and perhaps succeeded to their fathers' positions.

Despite these bleak realities, the bourgeois families of the early modern era began to reconceptualize childhood. Evidence exists in diaries and letters of a deepened emotional involvement of parents in child-rearing, an increased concern for children's education and welfare. Around the mid-seventeenth century, the severe disciplining of children in school was questioned. Elite mothers increasingly breastfed their own babies; they also dressed them in special clothes (children had previously been dressed just like miniature adults), and supplied them with playthings. Mothers and fathers alike recorded their mourning for children who died, as so many did, by arranging elaborate funerals, commissioning monuments, or writing works describing their grief. In general, family life in the comfortable homes of bourgeois Europeans seems to have become more focused on personal identity and experience. Outside these homes, in the vibrant cities

WITNESSES

Women Protest against Husbands and Predators

A Venetian woman lambasts the tyranny of men (1592): If men usurp our rights, should we not complain and declare that they have wronged us? Or if we are their inferiors in status, but not in worth, this is an abuse that has been introduced into the world and that men have then, over time, gradually translated into law and custom; and it has become so entrenched that they claim . . . that the status they have gained through their bullying is theirs by right. . . . And we would suffer it. . . . if they did not insist on exerting such absolute control over us and in such an arrogant manner, treating us like slaves who cannot take a step without asking their permission or say a word without their jumping down our throats. . . . As fathers, as brothers, as sons or husbands or lovers or whatever other relationship they have to us, they all abuse us, humiliate us, and do all they can to harm and annihilate us.

(Moderata Fonte (Modesta da Pozzo), *The Worth of Women, Wherein is Clearly Revealed their Nobility and their Superiority to Men*, 1592; ed. and trs. V. Cox, 1997)

Artemisia Gentileschi, painter, testifies at the trial of her rapist (1612): Agostino put his head on my breast . . . and said: "Let's walk together a while, because I hate sitting down." . . . After we had walked around two or three times, each time going by the bedroom door, when we were in front of the bedroom door, he pushed me in and locked the door. He then threw me onto the edge of the bed, pushing me with a hand on my breast. . . . Lifting my clothes, which he had a great deal of trouble doing, he placed a hand with a handkerchief at my throat and on my mouth to keep me from screaming. . . . I felt a strong burning and it hurt very much, but because he held my mouth I couldn't cry out. However, I tried to scream as best I could. . . . I scratched his face and pulled his hair and . . . I even removed a piece of flesh. . . . And after he had done his business he got off me. When I saw myself free, I went to the table drawer and took a knife and moved toward Agostino saying: "I'd like to kill you with this knife because you have dishonored me."

(From M. D. Garrard, *Artemisia Gentileschi*, 1989)

of early modern Europe, a new cultural world was also emerging.

Downtown

While some members of the bourgeoisie wished to buy land and noble status, those who remained based in the great European cities created a vital and refined cultural world that imitated, rivaled, and eventually replaced that of the court: the world of "downtown."

Medieval European cities had developed as autonomous commercial centers (see Chapter 11), in which merchant organizations determined the forms of town governments, which wrested political privileges from kings, bishops, and emperors. Each city developed distinctive social and cultural traditions, and different patterns of interaction with the immediate countryside, and with other independent cities.

By the sixteenth century, however, the medieval patterns were changing, in three ways (see also Chapter 16). First, the major urban concentrations shifted from the Mediterranean region to the Atlantic region, where new patterns of urbanization emerged, driven by explosive economic and population growth.

Second, the network of autonomous cities was replaced by networks of integrated regions, in which major cities were the economic focus of a large area that included many medium-sized and small towns. Often these regional supercities were also national capitals, as were London and Paris. As regional centers, these previously isolated centers of commercial endeavor now derived their wealth and resources from far beyond the urban core. They opened themselves up to the countryside beyond, whose goods they purchased and whose needs they supplied.

Third, the pace of urbanization accelerated overall. Not only did the populations of Europe's towns and cities increase, but the proportion of Europeans living in cities rose from under nine percent in 1500 to about twelve percent by 1750 overall (with a still higher proportion in the Mediterranean and northwestern regions). The largest cities in the Middle Ages barely exceeded 100,000 inhabitants; by 1700, the largest broke the barrier of 500,000 and by 1800, approached 1 million. Smaller cities with fewer than 50,000 inhabitants continued to thrive. Constituting three-fourths of all European cities, they were important laboratories of commercial and productive activity and key elements in Europe's unique urbanism.

Increasing in size and in the range of their economic activity, the great European cities lost their walls: they were no longer the exceptional islands they had been in the sea of medieval society. No longer enclosed by gates and walls, the intensity of city life spilled out from busy port and market complexes into the surrounding region and beyond. Reflecting national and continental interests rather than merely local ones, urban planning and architecture adopted new forms. Broad avenues cut through the winding web of medieval streets to provide a stage for royal and religious processions and military parades, for personal communication and commercial traffic. Buildings sprouted up in the imposing Baroque and Neoclassical architectural styles borrowed from aristocratic mansions: official palaces, stock markets, and banks; the townhouses of the nobility and wealthy bourgeoisie. By 1750, the cities were displacing courts, palaces, cathedrals, and monasteries as centers of European civilization.

Against the backdrop of monumental buildings and planned streets, a new urban theater materialized. Medieval cities had been cultural centers, where ritual processions and special events occupied a good part of the annual calendar. Early modern cities engendered different forms of cultural activity. The elites travelled in carriages to visit government officials, business contacts, or personal friends. They promenaded in public gardens and along river embankments. They frequented coffeehouses and teashops, and went shopping on "high" streets lined with speciality shops, stocked with the manufactures of Europe and exotic produce from around the globe.

For the first time, the city also contained theaters in the modern sense. In the Middle Ages, plays based on Bible stories had been enacted in villages, monasteries, and courts, while the Italian Renaissance had seen the revival of Classical drama, and the creation of comedy and tragedy on Classical models. In London from the late 1500s, and in Spain and France in the 1600s, dramatic performances moved into public theaters, where they were enjoyed by audiences mixed in gender and social origin, achieving glorious success. European playwrights of the early modern era included some of the greatest geniuses of the Western tradition: most notably William Shakespeare (1564–1616) in England; Lope de Vega (1562–1635) in Spain; Jean-Baptiste Racine (1639–1699), Pierre Corneille (1606–1684), and Molière in France. Women also wrote for the stage, including the Italian Antonia Pulci (1452–1501) and the English Aphra Behn (1640–1689) (see Chapter 17).

The first operas had been staged for elite audiences in Renaissance Italy. By the 1700s, opera houses stood in most major European cities and played to crowds who came to applaud the brilliant virtuosity of the performers as much as to listen to the music. The

Population Takeoff in Europe

	Approximate European Populations France	Prussia	Russia	Italy	Sweden	England
1600	10,500,000	N/A	10,000,000	12,000,000	1,000,000	4,066,000
1700	21,000,000	1,750,000	14,000,000	13,000,000	1,500,000	5,027,000
1800	29,000,000	9,000,000	30,000,000	19,000,000	2,500,000	8,728,000

Sources: *Based on* Atlas of World Population History *(New York: Facts on File, 1978) and B. R. Mitchell,* British Historical Statistics *(Cambridge: Cambridge University Press, 1988), pp. 7–9, 40–42, 52–54.*

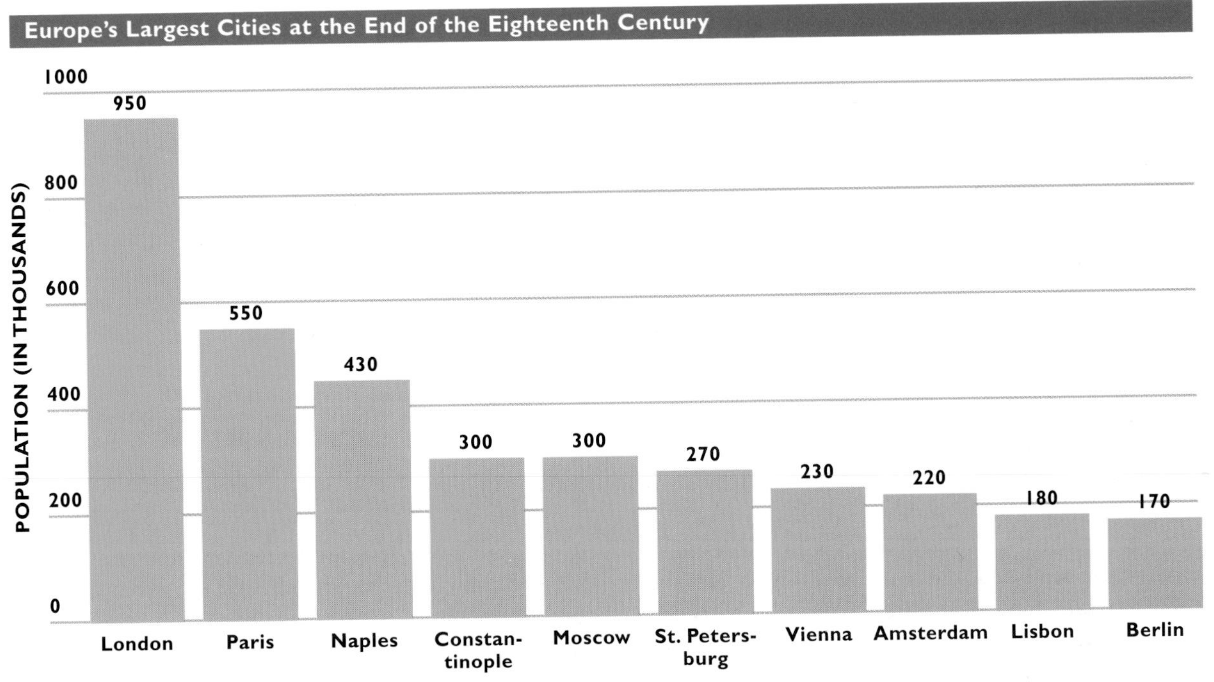

Source: *Based on J. Merriman,* A History of Modern Europe: From the Renaissance to the Age of Napoleon *(New York: W. W. Norton, 1996), p. 385.*

By 1500, Europe began to recover from the catastrophic population losses caused by the Black Death (see Chapter 12). After a slowdown in the rate of growth in the seventeenth century, steady gains were realized after 1700, and by 1800, Europe was densely populated. The first table shows the mounting population of selected European countries in 1600, 1700, and 1800, while the second shows the population attained by some of Europe's most important cities by around 1800.

Classical, tragic themes of the earliest operas were joined by comic themes, often boldly critical of contemporary society, for example in *The Beggar's Opera* by John Gay (1685–1732), which celebrated criminals and prostitutes in a subtle commentary on elite values, or *The Marriage of Figaro* by Wolfgang Amadeus Mozart (1756–1791), based on the play of the French adventurer Pierre-Augustin Caron de Beaumarchais (1732–1799), with its charms concealing a merciless critique of the aristocracy.

While theater developed in part from folk traditions, musical performance evolved from the royal and princely courts, which had provided patronage for composers and musicians. In bourgeois homes, meanwhile, families and friends joined in choral and solo singing, with amateur instrumental accompaniment.

This musical tradition erupted into the life of the city in the seventeenth century with the opening of public opera halls (such as Venice's Fenice), and in the eighteenth century with the creation of the concert hall. The virtuoso skills of composers, musicians, and singers could now be enjoyed by a bourgeois audience that did not reside at court.

The bourgeois outsiders of medieval society were the insiders of the early modern city. City-dwellers imitated the arts of the court to create the urban civilization of the modern Western world, centered not in halls of mirrors but amid the traffic of downtown. The bourgeoisie were not the only residents of the early modern cities, however: they shared their habitat with the poor, who, leaving the countryside, thronged there in search of work.

Workers and Strangers

The ranks of the bourgeois were the elites of the cities that they shared with a multiplicity of people, whose presence made urban life more turbulent and variable than life on the land. Migrants from towns and villages boosted the population levels of early modern cities, which could not be maintained by citizen births alone: migration accounts for much of the urban demographic growth in this period. Some migrants were educated professionals or skilled artisans, who found employment in the city councils, the schools and universities, or guild-regulated shops. But most were unskilled: they packed the streets and filled the rented rooms in cities that provided them with only limited opportunities and no remedies for the harsh realities of the marketplace.

Unskilled men worked as common day-laborers who hauled goods, removed debris, swept chimneys, or groomed horses. Women worked as domestic servants, or as spinners, embroiderers, or seamstresses. Servants were a numerous (and increasingly female) class in all European cities of the early modern period, numbering in the tens of thousands in eighteenth-century London or Paris. Men and women alike were subject to economic cycles that brought high prices and unemployment: just as a migrant from the country could become a city worker, that worker might easily become one of the urban underclass of the desperately poor. After 1500, one of Europe's major problems was what to do with indigents.

WITNESSES

The Urban Poor

A view from the top—sick beggars in Venice must enter the hospital of the *Incurabili* or be banished (1522): Many gentlemen and gentlewomen and others have been moved to take pity on numerous persons sick and sore of the French pox [i.e. syphilis] and other ills. Some of these persons in their bodily weakness languish in the streets and the doorways of churches and public places both at San Marco and at Rialto to beg for a living . . . giving forth a terrible stench and infecting their neighbours and those with whom they live. . . . Now, because the aforesaid charitable persons are making every possible effort to care for these sick people—who are plunged into the deepest destitution and misfortune—in a hospital of theirs at the Spirito Santo . . . , we . . . decree . . . that, if from henceforth any men or women sore of the French pox or other ill are called upon by the agents of the aforesaid hospital to go and enter the place to be nursed and looked after, and yet refuse and will not go, . . . they shall be . . . banished from this our city.

(Decree of the *Provveditori alla Sanità*, February 22, 1522; eds. D. Chambers and B. Pullan, 1992)

A view from the bottom—letter to Mr. James Bailey, J.P., from the poor of Manchester following the violent repression of a food riot in July 1762: This is to asquaint you that We poor of Rosendale Rochdale Oldham Saddleworth Ashton have all mutaly and firmly agreed by Word and Covinent and Oath to Fight and Stand by Each Other as long as Life doth last for We may as well all be hanged as starved to Death and to see ower Children weep for Bread and none to give Them . . . but take This for a shure Maxon, That if You dont put those good Laws in Execution against all Those Canables or Men Slayers That have the Curse of God and all honest Men both by Gods Laws and Mens Laws . . . I know You all have Power to stop such vilonas Proceedings if You please and if You dont amaidatley put a Stopp and let hus feel it the next Saturday We will murder You all that We have down in Ower List and Wee will all bring a Faggot and burn down Your Houses and Wait Houses and make Your Wifes Widdows and Your Children Fatherless for . . . Blood for Blood We Require. Take Care.

(From E. P. Thompson, "The Crime of Anonymity" in D. Hay, et al, *Albion's Fatal Tree*, 1975)

Members of this impoverished underclass were variously called "beggars," "wanderers," "vagabonds," and "paupers." They were a significant presence, constituting about ten to thirty percent of urban population. In Roman Catholic cities especially, charitable institutions offered relief, though only to a very few of the chronically poor, and almsgiving was still practiced. This vulnerable poor population was increasingly unwelcome, however, particularly in the Protestant cities of the north, which often simply expelled indigents. Even Catholic Paris ruled in 1606 that beggars should be whipped, branded, and driven out of town (and in 1749, imprisoned). In clear contrast to the medieval notion that poverty was an opportunity for compassion, poverty was redefined after 1500 as a criminal offense.

In England, poor laws dating from the reign of Elizabeth I (r. 1558–1603) distinguished the "deserving" from the "undeserving" poor. The former could be housed in workhouses (later poorhouses) supported by the local parish. The latter must be set to work, or expelled from the locality—as, frequently, were strangers and foreigners. Such regulations created two strata of poor folk: those immobilized in their parishes, and those adrift on the roads. In London, city officials extended poor relief to those considered "deserving" because of their lack of capacity (able-bodied men were unlikely to qualify) and high moral character. Applying such strictures soothed the tempers of the ordinary folk who paid designated taxes or "poor rents" that supported these enterprises, and who often grumbled that they had to support wastrels as an unwanted burden. The threat of social unrest stilled these complaints. It was better to pay the cost of poor relief than to suffer riot and upheaval.

In France, a workhouse system also supplemented the informal networks of private charity. The *hôpital* ("hospital") continued to house both the hopelessly poor and the hopelessly sick, two groups equally unsupported by home and family. Those able to work labored at menial tasks to pay the cost of their maintenance. Some of the able-bodied poor, willing to work but unable to find employment, were set to road-building and construction tasks organized by publicly funded "workshops." None of these institutions provided sufficient relief to fill the giant well of poverty.

Women and Children Women who had lost the protection of fathers (through abandonment or death) and husbands (through desertion or death) figured disproportionately among the poor. They had less opportunity than men to find well-paid work, and they bore the additional responsibility of caring for children that no one else wanted. In workhouses and poorhouses, they performed the low-level textile work that had traditionally been done by women, while male artisans took on the more highly-skilled jobs of weaving and finishing. Some regions had convent-style asylums where poor women performed low-paid work, perhaps acquired job skills, and engaged in frequent devotions. Despite the variety of these places of refuge, many poor women at the bottom of what one modern historian has called the "hierarchy of hunger" found no support except among the community of those equally adrift, and lived as best they could upon the profits of begging.

Poor mothers, whether married or single, were especially vulnerable to variations in the supply and cost of the food they needed both for themselves and for their children. In line with new economic thinking, towns and cities sometimes withdrew from subsidizing grain, as they had in the Middle Ages, with the result that prices soared to a natural high in times of scarcity. High prices, in turn, provoked riot. In the eighteenth century, women were often in the forefront of those who rioted, their explosive speech and physical unrestraint contrasting with their accustomed condition of controlled subservience.

Poor women often took to prostitution to save themselves from homelessness and destitution. During the Middle Ages, prostitution was generally legal, protected by civic authorities and kings alike as a way of forestalling more serious social problems. From the sixteenth century, that policy shifted: although prostitution was still tolerated and regulated in most urban areas, it was now perceived in both Roman Catholic and Protestant communities as a social evil that threatened the welfare of good citizens. A new category of institutions was created to house women who had been prostitutes, or who might turn to prostitution if not rescued from poverty and the streets. In late Renaissance Italy, asylums for the "badly married" allowed impoverished widows as well as former prostitutes to learn the skills that would enable them to leave the shelter for low-paying jobs outside its walls.

Swift social intervention in the case of prostitution testifies that a social motive was at work beyond the desire to relieve poverty or punish crime. Measures taken to control prostitution attest to a readiness to discipline and monitor sexual behavior. That impulse is also evident in the intensified prosecution of sodomites (the term indiscriminately used for male homosexuals), infanticides, and alleged witches (the latter two groups mostly female). These

WINDOWS ON
Women's Lives

Artemisia Gentileschi,* Judith Slaying Holofernes, *c. 1620

Claudine-Françoise Bouzonnet, after a drawing by Jacques Sella,* Family Evening, *1667

***Attributed to the School of Murillo,* Celestina and her Daughter**

Women's lives in the early modern period revolved around their sexuality—primarily their roles as birthgivers within the family or as prostitutes. In the engraving of a peasant family (top right), shadings of light and dark separate the world of women from the world of men. A harsher reality is indicated by the image of two prostitutes, young and old (or perhaps a prostitute and an aged procuress) looking out from a barred window—a stark reminder of their isolation from the respectable world (above). In a painting by the renowned woman artist Artemisia Gentileschi, a woman revenges herself on a tyrant (top left). The biblical heroine Judith slays Holofernes, an enemy not only of her nation but of the women he victimizes. (above: State Hermitage Museum, St. Petersburg; top left: Uffizi, Florence) trends mark an era also noted for the creation of modern science and Enlightenment rationalism.

Orphaned children formed another significant class of the poor. Orphanages had their roots in the early Christian era, but they were transformed in the eighteenth century by the number of abandoned infants they had to accommodate. Institutionalized in the first few months of life, most orphans were effectively presumed illegitimate, born as a result of rape or prostitution, or simply abandoned. With wet nursing still the only alternative to maternal breastfeeding, and with pediatric medicine still undeveloped, the orphanage system resulted in staggering death rates, in the range of fifty to ninety percent in European capitals. Those who survived the orphanage were placed still young as servants or apprentices.

Other children wandered the city, adrift and alone. In many towns, most beggars were children. Abandoned children swarmed down the roads that led to the cities, ideal recruits for the bands of beggars and thieves and disbanded mercenary soldiers whose gangs often "ruled" a whole neighborhood or district.

Crime and Disease The chronic poverty of so many encouraged crime, and elites suspected virtually all the poor of criminal intent. In cities, it is thought that crime was on a powerful upswing from as early as the seventeenth century. The increased incidence of crime stimulated the use of harsh punishments, such as physical mutilation, public humiliation, deportation overseas, and death. Judicially mutilated men and women could be seen everywhere, and capital punishment for minor property violations became common. Women were punished as harshly as, or more harshly than, men, unless they happened to be pregnant. The gallows alongside the gate reminded new arrivals of the judicial power of the city.

The gallows promised to bring order where society had descended to disorder. Critics horrified by this official use of violence, however, began to speak up against harsh punishment. The moral failing of the criminal, Sir Thomas More (1477–1535) pointed out in *Utopia*, was often a rational response to a harsh economic reality that made people choose between crime and starvation. The poor man stole, and was hanged, while wealthier offenders (often tried in different courts) might escape punishment altogether. A new generation of penologists, or experts on punishment, suggested that the end of justice was the reclamation of the criminal. In 1764, Italian jurist Cesare Beccaria published his influential *Essay on Crimes and Punishments* that heralded the end of torture and capital punishment. The English theoretician Jeremy Bentham later put Beccaria's views to work in his proposal for a model prison, the "Panopticon." Meaning "Total Surveillance," the Panopticon replaced the violence of the gallows with the relentless scrutiny of those committed to the rehabilitation and redemption, rather than the punishment, of criminals.

Early modern experts also sought remedies for disease. But the medicine of university-trained physicians, or surgeons with practical experience of wounds, or folk healers (mostly female) offered few remedies for illness (see also Chapter 17). Unaware of the real causes of infection, surgeons wielded a frightening array of unsanitary knives and scalpels to mend wounds or amputate limbs, or drained blood from patients already weakened by disease.

The main victory in the battle against illness was the end of bubonic plague in western Europe, a victory that owned everything to nature and nothing to health professionals. The plague, which had first arrived in 1347 and wrought unprecedented devastation on European populations (see Chapter 12), continued to return every few years to take new victims as late as the sixteenth and seventeenth centuries. After 1721, the plague had exhausted itself in western Europe (although it remained endemic in eastern Europe into the nineteenth century, and in Africa and Asia into the twentieth). Its last outbreak was in 1720 in the French port of Marseilles. Thereafter, the disease faded out: by a benign historical accident, the black rat, which carried the flea that carried the killer bacillus, lost its ecological niche to a rival species. Meanwhile, prosperity (for some) and better nutrition also made it possible for the population to resist other diseases more successfully. Until just over a century ago, higher caloric consumption was the greatest cause of improved health for most Europeans.

Yet diseases still ravaged unprotected populations. The poorest Europeans, malnourished and badly housed, were the most vulnerable to such killers as typhus, typhoid, scarlet fever, and pneumonia, as well as the smallpox for which, at last, a preventive was found (see Chapter 17). Hospitals, which also housed the elderly and the destitute, were the refuge of the seriously ill whose own families could not assist them. At the margins of city life, the sick became strangers.

Other Outsiders The cities encompassed other outsiders: foreigners, dissenters, and Jews. Cosmopolitan centers such as Venice and Amsterdam had for years accommodated the needs of foreigners (Greeks and Turks, for example) by allowing them to build at their own expense a protected enclave, where they could pursue their own religion and way of life while trading

Urban Riots and Plague

The Fettmilch uprising in Frankfurt: *While drunkenness, crime, and disease oppressed the ordinary citizens, so too did the urban patriciate—an upper crust of the bourgeoisie that monopolized public magistracies. A ferocious urban riot in the city of Frankfurt in 1612–1616 was directed against the patriciate and, as often and tragically occurred, against the city's Jews.* (Historisches Museum, Frankfurt-am-Main)

with the local citizens. Dissenters were those adherents of minority (mostly Protestant) sects who were granted a grudging tolerance in England, and a more generous one in the Dutch Republic. Subject to various restrictions and difficulties, they were at least protected by law, once Europe had weathered its outbreak of religious warfare.

The Jews formed another group of city dwellers whose presence of more than a thousand years among European Christians had won, at best, a reluctant tolerance. They had long since been expelled from some parts of western Europe, most recently (in 1492 and 1497) from Spain and Portugal (see Chapters 12, 14). Still, large communities of Jews lived in the towns of the Holy Roman Empire, northern Italy, and the

Plague ward in a Hamburg hospital: *Pre- and early-industrial cities were notoriously harsh environments. Poverty, squalor, overcrowding, and crime were constant problems. Due to their concentrated populations, cities were also disproportionately at risk for experiencing major outbreaks of infectious disease. This 1746 depiction of a plague ward in a hospital in Hamburg offers few comforts. Note the crude conditions of amputation in the center.* (Germanisches Nationalmuseum, Nürnberg)

Netherlands. They flourished especially in Venice (where they were confined to the ghetto; see Chapter 12), and in Amsterdam, constituting in 1700 four percent of the population. In these regions, they enjoyed considerable freedom, although always subject to social restrictions. Further east, Jewish civic life thrived in the city of Prague in Bohemia. The strongest concentrations of Jewish population were to be found, however, in Poland, Lithuania, and the Balkans. By 1700, Poland alone probably sheltered more than three-fourths of the world's Jews, who constituted over four percent of the whole population.

Jewish communities from 1500 to 1750 benefited from the broadening of European culture stimulated by the Renaissance thirst for Classical learning and the Reformation rupture of Catholic uniformity. As those movements developed in scientific and enlightened directions, Jews continued to enjoy relative autonomy and security, while they were not yet liable, as later, to assimilation. Nevertheless, the horrors of the previous era, marked by anti-Semitic outbursts triggered especially by the Crusades and plague crises, did not wholly disappear. The Jews of Poland were harshly persecuted from 1648 into the 1650s, and blood-libel accusations by both Protestant and Catholic zealots pursued their communities in the Empire and Italy. As the modern age approached, the Jews were still strangers in Christian Europe.

WITNESSES

Peasants' Lives

A German peasant describes his condition (1568):

I am a peasant.
My work is hard and bitter.
I must plow, seed, and harrow,
Then cut, reap, and beat.
I gather wood and make hay and grain.
Rents and taxes break my heart.
I live on plain bread and water,
As the Lord has commanded Adam.

(Jost Amman, "The Peasant"; ed. S. Ozment, 1980)

A Russian peasant exchanges his labor for a loan from a local monastery (1552–1553): Now I, Mosei son of Nifant, and my children, Istoma and Nikifor, have taken from Antonii, cellarer of the Saviour of Priluka a ruble of the monastery's treasury money from St. George's day in the autumn till St. George's day for a year. And for that money we are to till a third [of the arable] of their hamlet, Levashevo, and I am to build a house. But if I do not begin to live at Levashevo on a third, then we are liable to pay 2 rubles according to this obligation. And I am to pay the quit-rent according to the registers. And whichever of us is present, he is liable to the tillage or the money.

(From R. E. F. Smith ed., *The Enserfment of the Russian Peasantry*, 1968)

FIELD AND VILLAGE: THE BOUNDARIES OF PEASANT LIFE

While city-dwellers enjoyed the riches of an urban environment now at the core of Western society, in the country, free peasants and bonded serfs, tenant farmers and sharecroppers, lost out both to the city and to enterprising landowners alike. For most of world history, most people were peasant farmers, and farming remained what it always had been—a stubborn struggle to wrest subsistence from the soil. Plowing, sowing, reaping, tool maintenance, and stock rearing were the enduring framework of peasant life. Changes in that great continuity in the early modern period allowed some Europeans to prosper as never before. Many others lost ground. Change and continuity characterized the rituals of village life, in which the sturdy cultural patterns of traditional Europe were both rehearsed and subverted.

Bread, Beans, and Flocks

The fields of grain—rye, barley, oats, wheat—that stretched across Europe's great plain provided the bread that led to improved health and increased population. Progress in medieval farming techniques lay behind the continent's demographic success: the use of the heavy plow, and the fallowing of one field in a two- or three-field system of rotation (see Chapter 9). After 1600 in the Netherlands and England, entrepreneurial landowners promoted farming techniques that further enhanced the fertility of the land, freeing some of it for the development of cash crops.

Urbanized from an early period, the Netherlands had scarcely enough land to grow the grain necessary for its ample population. In the seventeenth century, after the struggle of the largely Protestant northern provinces to free themselves from the rule of Catholic Spain had been resolved and the Dutch Republic created, Dutch landowners employed agricultural techniques that led to dramatically increased production of high-quality, high-priced agricultural goods. The merchant fleet that hauled grain from eastern Europe to home ports made these innovations possible. Freed from the need to produce wheat for bread, local farmers grew marketable vegetables and raised cows for dairy products. They rotated the sowing of crops in sequences planned so that nutrients lost in one planting would be restored to the soil in the next. In addition, ambitious land-drainage projects increased the amount of arable land that could be devoted to the new kinds of agricultural production. Fat cows and round, ripe cheeses, together with a variety of garden crops (among them the new species imported from the Americas), signified the improved diet and comfortable wealth of the Dutch. These innovations amounted to the first stage of what some historians have called the "Agricultural Revolution."

The English followed the Dutch in agricultural innovation, draining marshland, introducing crop rotation, and planning their agricultural ventures with an eye to the market. In so doing, landowners often displaced peasant cultivators, and installed tenant farmers directly responsible to them. Displaced peasants might become day-laborers or migrants to the cities.

The goal of landowner management was in some cases the increased cultivation of grain and vegetables. Often, though, it was to remove land from cultivation by erecting hedges or fences around common land previously used for grazing by an entire community or medieval-style open fields in the process known as enclosure. This made room for livestock—dairy cows, as in the Netherlands, and more importantly, sheep—which required only one man to oversee a whole herd or flock. English sheep had produced much of the wool woven into cloth in northern Europe throughout the Middle Ages. When an expanding market for wool led landlords to enclose the fields that had once supported numerous peasants, sheep grazed where once men had farmed.

Dutch and English landowners pioneered agricultural methods that would one day benefit farmers everywhere. In both countries, greater agricultural productivity freed land from grain production for the cultivation of high-profit cash crops, dairy products, and raw wool. While the changes had the potential to benefit all in the long run, they pressured some peasant farmers in the short run: many English farmers lost their land to the combined phenomenon of tenant farming and stock-raising. Many eastern European peasants suffered so that their masters might produce the quantities of grain that Dutch merchants paid well to acquire.

Elsewhere the pace of agricultural change was slow and uneven. In eastern Europe, landowners profited from the increased market for grain in the west. They increased their yields by extracting more labor from their serfs, rather than by improving their techniques. In Spain, increased acreage was devoted to sheep-farming organized by the guild of sheeptenders known as the Mesta. In Italy's rich Po river valley, maize (corn) and rice cultivation alongside traditional crops resulted in abundant harvests. Elsewhere, even in populous France, older farming methods remained in use up to the eighteenth century. Peasants living in manorial villages still plowed cooperatively, and grazed their animals on common land. Farmers on thin upland soil still used the wooden plow, and in the extensive forests of Russia and Sweden, slash and burn methods were used to carve out temporary farmlands.

Varieties of Labor

Alongside this great variety in the management of farmlands, a corresponding variety existed in the condition of farmers. In the early modern centuries, differences in farmers' status became more pronounced, ranging from the prosperous English **yeoman** to the Russian serf. The most significant difference was between the condition of the mainly free peasantry of western Europe, and that of the oppressed serfs of eastern Europe. It is in this era that a marked disparity between the economic condition of those two European zones appeared.

In the west, the progress out of serfdom that had begun in the Middle Ages was largely completed. Most farmers were free men or women, legally bound neither to the landowner nor the land. Best off were peasant proprietors, who were freehold owners of a plot sufficient to feed their families and yield a marketable surplus. Even tenant farmers, who paid a landowner for the use of their land, could prosper if their farms were large and fertile. Then came the smallholders and sharecroppers. Smallholders might own just enough land to provide subsistence for their families in good years. In bad years, they borrowed in order to survive, or they starved. Sharecroppers, who owed landowners a share of up to fifty percent of all they produced, lived in a constant state of indebtedness. Even more vulnerable was the condition of day-laborers, who neither owned nor rented land but, continually in search of work, survived from day to day on the wages gained by their labor.

All peasants paid for the land they worked. Some paid "dues" to the landowner, obligations descending from medieval contracts, involving a certain amount of labor or a payment of cash, crops, or livestock. Others paid rent or a percentage share of the produce. Landowners could also collect fees from peasants for the use of the mill to grind grain or the winepress. To

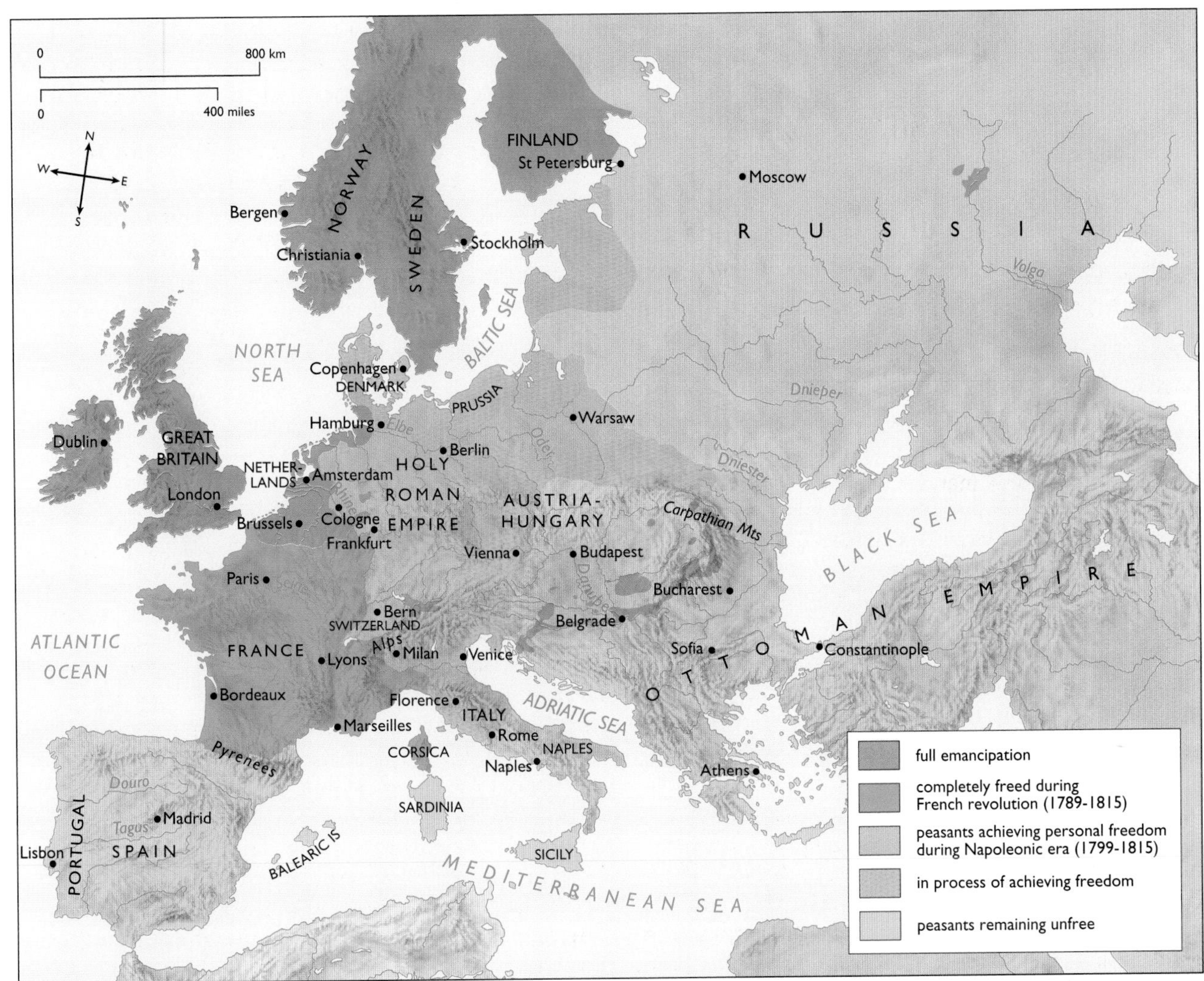

Map 18.1 The Emancipation of the Peasantry up to 1812: *By the end of the eighteenth century, almost all of Europe's peasantry had won their freedom. The exceptions were Russia, Spain and Portugal, and the kingdom of Naples in southern Italy, where serfdom or other forms of unfree labor continued into the nineteenth century. Scandinavia (outside of Denmark) had never known serfdom. In Britain and the Netherlands (including Belgium) the peasants had emerged from serfdom after around 1200. The French Revolution (see Chapter 20) saw the destruction of the remnants of serfdom in France, and encouraged liberation in northern Italy, some of the Austrian lands, and Denmark.*

the king peasants owed taxes on the land, in addition to direct taxes on such commodities as salt, a hated levy that disproportionately burdened the poor. In Catholic regions, the church also took its traditional tenth share or tithe. By the early modern era this was no longer used to support the local priest but rather drained to the big cities or to Rome itself to help fund the great prelates.

In England, farmers were free of the tithe, yeomen could with hard work and good fortune hope to join the gentry, and even tenant farmers could prosper. But the English peasantry suffered greatly from the waves of enclosure, speeded by laws passed by Parliament, that gathered pace in the sixteenth century and continued into the eighteenth. Those who lost their land might work in their homes in the "cottage industries" of textile manufacture (see Chapters 16, 21), or they might seek employment as migrant day-laborers.

The condition of the laborers of eastern Europe, consigned to a "second serfdom" in the early modern era, was worse. In Russia, for example, the tsar granted noble landowners the right to enserf their peasantry in exchange for loyalty and service. Russian nobles measured their wealth not by the extent of their acreage but by the number of "souls"—adult male serfs—who owed them labor.

Peasant Lives

Cultivating and processing flax: *For most peasants, life in early modern Europe continued to revolve around a few basic certainties: the seasonal agricultural cycle, the village, hard labor, and the continual threat of crop shortages or outright famine. In this illustration by Johann Andreas Pfeffel from around 1730, German peasants cultivate flax by hand and a young girl spins it into skeins of finished thread.*

Plight of the peasant: *The seeming stability of rural life masked important, and ultimately revolutionary, changes. This cartoon by Bulloz shows a struggling, elderly French peasant—a "commoner"—bearing the full weight of the other two continental social orders, or "estates," the privileged aristocracy and clergy.*

Polish nobles acquired the same prerogatives without any concessions to the crown, driven by the lure of profits to be gained by exporting grain to western Europe through Baltic ports. Throughout eastern Europe, obligatory labor for the lord was increased to such an extent that peasants were scarcely free to cultivate land for their own use. In Bohemia and Moravia, labor service called the *robot* (meaning "work") left the serfs only one day a week to cultivate their own land. Our modern conception of the mechanical robot descends from these laborers whose spirits were crushed by excessive exploitation. Landowners retained many rights over the peasants, and could demand gifts or prohibit a daughter's marriage. In many regions, nobles exercised judicial powers over serfs, their capacity to exact capital punishment signaled by the gallows standing near the manor house.

Russian landholders attempted to stem the tide of overburdened workers fleeing to places where better conditions prevailed by demanding that their serfs be bound to their land and village. Desperate serfs and other fugitives ran for the "borderlands," the region of Ukraine between old Muscovy, Poland, and the Crimea. Those who remained were virtually slaves, as the landowners might sell not only their land, with attached serfs, but the serfs, bodily, themselves.

Even in oppressed Russian villages, people danced, sang, and celebrated special occasions: the village celebrations of peasants and serfs are the matrix of national traditions inherited by modern states.

Festival and Riot

The village community helped its members weather famine, cold, war, disease, and taxes. Its leaders met regularly to plan planting or harvest, and to address the demands of the landlord, or the misbehavior of the villagers. Together the villagers celebrated joys and experienced sorrow and proclaimed in story and song the clever wiles by which peasants maneuvered and survived. Customs of village carnival and riot, disdained by the grandees of the court and city patricians, gave expression to the energy and talents of those who could neither read nor rule.

The life of the village was a whole world to the peasants. Together they celebrated the festivals of the Christian year, in rituals that were not wholly purged of pre-Christian, pagan practices. Together they feasted at harvest time, and at ceremonies marking births, deaths, baptisms, and weddings. At these events, they engaged in wrestling matches and tugs-of-war, brutal blood sports, and lighthearted entertainments. Self-trained experts played melodies distinctive to the region—"folk" music—on simple string, wind, and percussion instruments, accompanying village singers and dancers drawn from young and old, and men and women.

The young people of the village found wives and husbands in the same community where their parents had found theirs. Groups of adolescent girls paraded together in front of the young men in rituals of courtship. Groups of adolescent boys courted them—but also joined in drunken and violent sprees, creating social and sexual disorder. Village healers or "good" witches could provide potions that aroused love, it was believed, in the opposite sex. Engaged lovers might not wait for marriage before they consummated their understanding.

The village controlled its own members. Most premarital pregnancies resulted in hasty weddings under the guidance of village elders—although some were ended upon consultation of the midwife with herbal concoctions, often dangerous to the mother if not the fetus. In ritual enactments, adolescent gangs mocked those members of the community whose behavior was considered out of bounds—cuckolded husbands, scolding women, men who married women too young or who beat their wives. Also part of the festival celebration was the ritual of role reversal, where women

Pieter Bruegel the Elder, The Peasants' Wedding: *Festive times provided welcome relief from work and were an important part of the peasantry's social and cultural life. Laden with symbolic meanings, at its simplest level this painting by Peter Bruegel the Elder from around 1568 depicts such a scene.* (Kunsthistorisches Museum, Vienna)

dressed like men, beggars like nobles, in a safe but probing critique of social norms.

The festivities of village life were overshadowed by austerity. Peasants dressed in drab tunics and robes of black or gray, often bequests from dead relatives who had also worn them for a whole lifetime. They lived in huts of wood, clay, or rubble, consisting of one or two small rooms shared with animals who needed shelter and provided a source of heat. Unlike the wealthy bourgeoisie or nobles, their homes had no ornament, in fact scarcely any furniture at all: a bench, a table, perhaps a bed, a pot to cook the daily soup that was the main accompaniment of bread. About a pound of bread (of barley, rye, or wheat), if it could be had, was the standard poor person's diet, or porridge or potatoes if grain for bread was scarce, enriched by thin soups of vegetables and occasional eggs.

A famous depiction of a peasant wedding by the Flemish artist Pieter Bruegel (*c.* 1525–1569; see p. 571) shows solid peasants at table, amply supplied with round loaves and cheeses (but, correctly, no meat), boisterous in their celebration of the ample fruits of the earth. But the painting deceives. For the average European peasant's experience was of scarcity rather than abundance.

In the eighteenth century, scarcity was still a problem. In the Middle Ages, local governments often stockpiled grain in the event of crisis, but now it was sold on the open market, to the highest bidder, and its cost pressed ever upward. Periods of scarcity, together with the harshness of landowner exactions, inflamed many to rebel. Peasant unrest—often sparked by crowds gathered for festivals or processions—was ceaseless: the German peasants in 1525; dispossessed Irish Roman Catholics in 1641; the Russian followers of the false tsars Stephen Razin in 1670–1671 and Emilian Pugachev in 1773–1775, convulsed their nations. Amid the pages of a famous genealogy of Venetian noble families may be found periodically the telling comment on the disappearance of a patriarch, "murdered by the peasants."

During the English Civil War, members of two groups put forward radical solutions for social ills. The Levellers and the Diggers proposed the elimination of social distinctions and the assumption of real power by those below the elites. The Leveller leader Henry Denne denied that he wished to turn "the world upside down," yet his proposals for social reform were profoundly unsettling to those who ruled.

Resisting the demands of the landowner, the authority of the church, the tyranny of gender roles, or the rigidity of the whole social hierarchy, villagers had views of their own about their world that were far from those of the educated bourgeoisie or courtly aristocrats. Nevertheless, the ability of the peasant to present his point of view was nullified by the extraordinary refinement of verbal expression possessed by social superiors. His stories would be bound in volumes of folktales, his songs and dances worked into symphonies and operas, but he himself was voiceless.

In the seventeenth and eighteenth centuries, the elites declared war on the popular culture of the villagers. Catholic and Protestant clerics insisted on a "higher" standard of sexual morality than village custom allowed, and oversaw the regular religious instruction of peasant youth. Agents of absolute states called for obedience to the king, the court, and his officials from those who already supported those dignitaries with their tax contributions. Reformers and intellectuals attacked surviving "pagan" and magical beliefs, and brought the standards of urban and courtly refinement to bear on peasant custom. Priests and philosophers, pastors and journalists insisted that peasant culture be modernized, nationalized, and standardized—the peasant, too, should become a gentleman.

Conclusion

THE PRIVILEGED, THE POOR, AND THE MEANING OF THE WEST

In the early modern age, the system of ranked social orders inherited from the Middle Ages became more complex and more dynamic. The gap between the elites and the poor widened as status came to be determined by cultural refinement, in addition to wealth. Being poor became a problem, a reproach, a threat. To escape poverty, to approach nobility, were the aspirations of those in the middle—Europe's would-be gentlemen. An expanding group with limitless ambitions, these would-be gentlemen began their advance, which continues today.

REVIEW QUESTIONS

1. Why did contemporary audiences find Molière's "would-be gentleman" ridiculous? To what extent was the nobility the ruling class in early modern Europe? How did newcomers enter the ranks of the nobility?

2. Why did rulers establish elaborate courts? How did court life influence the high nobility? What roles could noblewomen play at court?

3. What groups made up the early modern bourgeoisie? Why were bourgeois women kept in subordination? How did the concept of childhood change in bourgeois households?

4. How did the medieval pattern of cities change in the sixteenth and seventeenth centuries? How did urban civilization come to rival court culture? Why was migration from the countryside crucial to the growth of cities?

5. How did European societies deal with indigents, poor women, and criminals? Why did so many poor women become prostitutes? To what extent did the position of the Jews improve in early modern Europe?

6. What was the "Agricultural Revolution"? Compare the status of peasants in western and eastern Europe. What role did the village community play in peasant life?

SUGGESTED READINGS

Honorable Pursuits

Asch, Ronald and Adolf M. Birke, eds., *Princes, Patronage and the Nobility: The Court at the Beginning of the Early Modern Age* (London: German Historical Institute; Oxford: Oxford University Press, 1991). Focuses on the role of royal and princely courts as the contact point between rulers and local elites during the early modern era.

Bush, M. L., *The European Nobility* (2 Vols.); Vol. 1: *Noble Privilege* (New York: Holmes & Meier; Cambridge: Cambridge University Press, 1983); Vol. 2: *Rich Noble, Poor Noble* (Manchester: Manchester University Press, 1988). Detailed study of nobilities and their privileges in a variety of time periods and geographical locations.

Kriedte, Peter, *Peasants, Landlords and Merchant Capitalists: Europe and the World Economy, 1500–1800* (Cambridge: Cambridge University Press, 1983). A sophisticated anatomy of social structure and transformation.

Schalk, Ellery, *From Valor to Pedigree: Ideas of Nobility in France in the Sixteenth and Seventeenth Centuries* (Princeton: Princeton University Press, 1986). Argues that the term "noble" connoted virtue, and that the more typical definition—stressing ancestry or breeding—was later added as a defense against an invasion of "new" nobles.

New Ways with New Wealth

Amussen, Susan Dwyer, *An Ordered Society: Gender and Class in Early Modern England* (Oxford–New York: B. Blackwell, 1988). Explores popular notions of rank and gender, stressing the ruling classes' obsession with hierarchy and the role of the family as the basis thereof.

Ariès, Philippe, *Centuries of Childhood: A Social History of Family Life* trans. Robert Baldock (New York: Random House (Vintage), 1962). Classic account of the development of ideas about childhood from the Middle Ages to the early 19th century, centering on France.

De Vries, Jan, *European Urbanization* (Cambridge, MA: Harvard University Press, 1984). In-depth treatment of its subject, which includes much statistical data.

Gottlieb, Beatrice, *The Family in the Western World: From the Black Death to the Industrial Age* (Oxford: Oxford University Press, 1993). A useful survey, including definitions of the family, kinship, marriage, sex, child-rearing, economics, and emotional life.

Hohenberg, Paul M. and Lynn Hollen Lees, *The Making of Urban Europe, 1000–1950*, 2nd ed. (Cambridge, MA: Harvard University Press, 1995). Traces the intersection of urbanization, modernization, and industrialization.

Hufton, Olwen H., *The Poor of Eighteenth-Century France, 1750–1789* (Oxford: Clarendon Press of Oxford University Press, 1974). Surveys the life, conditions, and image of the poor in 18th-century France.

King, Margaret, *Women of the Renaissance* (Chicago: University of Chicago Press, 1991). For the period 1350–1650, examines women in the contexts of the family, the Church, and high culture.

Stone, Lawrence, *The Family, Sex, and Marriage in England, 1500–1800* (New York: Harper & Row, 1977). A monumental work arguing that during this period there occurred a basic shift in human feelings about family, children, the self, and God.

Field and Village

Blum, Jerome, *The End of the Old Order in Rural Europe* (Princeton: Princeton University Press, 1978). The tenacious patterns of peasant society, especially in eastern Europe, and their relation to changing technology, economy, and culture.

Le Roy Ladurie, Emmanuel, *The French Peasantry, 1450–1600* (Berkeley: University of California Press, 1987). Explores the relationship between demographic changes and alterations in patterns of marriage, landholding, rent, and violence.

Munsche, P. B., *Gentlemen and Poachers: The English Game Laws, 1671–1831* (Cambridge: Cambridge University Press, 1981). The English gentry's exclusive privilege to hunt game—and the resentment this caused—serves as a window on rural life in England.

Wolf, Eric R., *Peasants* (Englewood Cliffs, NJ: Prentice-Hall, 1966). Brief introduction to this important social class from Neolithic times to the mid-20th century. Surveys peasantries from all over the world.

INALIENABLE RIGHTS

1600 | 1650 | 1700 | 1750 | 1800 | 1850 | 1900

North America

French and Indian War, 1756–63

War of Independence, 1775–83

American Civil War, 1861–65

Reconstruction Era, 1865–77

- British colony of Jamestown founded, 1607
- First shipment of African slaves arrives in Jamestown, 1619
- British colony of Plymouth founded, 1620
- Coercive Acts, 1774
- First Continental Congress, 1774
- Second Continental Congress, 1776
- Declaration of Independence, 1776
- *Federalist Papers*, 1787
- US Constitution ratified, 1788–89
- Bill of Rights ratified, 1791
- Fugitive Slave Act, 1793
- "Louisiana Purchase," 1803
- War of 1812 against Britain
- Missouri Compromise, 1820
- Monroe Doctrine, 1823
- Mexican War, 1846–48
- Seneca Falls Convention, 1848
- Compromise of 1850
- Dred Scott decision, 1857
- Lincoln elected President, 1860
- Thirteenth Amendment, 1865
- Fourteenth Amendment, 1868
- Fifteenth Amendment, 1870
- Dawes Act, 1887
- Wounded Knee massacre, 1890

Latin America

All Latin American states independent, 1804–28

Juan Manuel de Rosas rules in Argentina, 1829–52

Manuel Belzu rules in Bolivia, 1848–55

Porfirio Díaz rules in Mexico, 1876–1911

- Populaton of Potosí 160,000, 1670
- Toussaint L'Ouverture controls Hispaniola, 1801
- Population of Buenos Aires 250,000, 1869
- Slavery abolished in Cuba, 1886
- Slavery abolished in Brazil, 1888
- Brazilian monarchy ends, 1889

Europe

The Enlightenment, c. 1685–1795

French Revolutionary and Napoleonic Wars, 1792–1815

- French Revolution begins, 1789
- Mary Wollstonecraft's *A Vindication of the Rights of Woman*, 1792
- Congress of Vienna, 1814–15
- Revolutions in France, Belgium, Italy, Poland, 1830–31
- Irish potato famine, 1845–50
- Year of Revolutions, 1848
- Karl Marx and Friedrich Engels' *Communist Manifesto*, 1848
- Charles Darwin's *Origin of Species*, 1859
- John Stuart Mill's *On Liberty*, 1859
- Serfdom abolished in Russia, 1861

Beyond the West

Ming Dynasty, China, 1368–1644

Qing Dynasty, China, 1644–1912

Mughal Empire, India, 1526–1857

Dutch East India Company in East Indies, 1619–1799

British East India Company in India, 1690–1857

- Shaka leads Zulu nation, Africa, 1817
- First Opium War, 1839–42
- US Commodore Perry "opens" Japan, 1853
- Second Opium War, 1856–60
- Sepoy Mutiny, India, 1857
- French gain control of Indochina, 1858
- Meiji Restoration, Japan, 1868

CHAPTER 19

INALIENABLE RIGHTS

Revolution and its Promises in Anglo- and Latin America

1500–1880

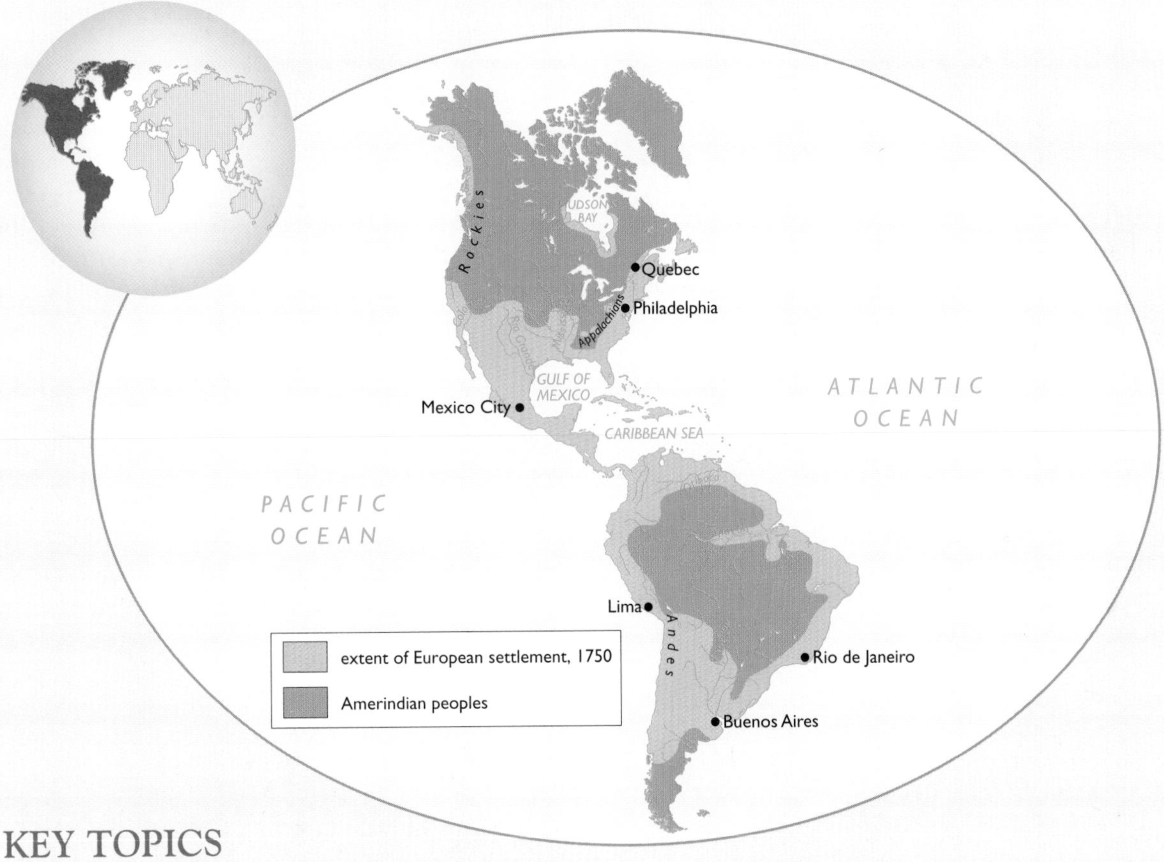

Rockies
HUDSON BAY
Quebec
Philadelphia
Appalachians
GULF OF MEXICO
Mexico City
CARIBBEAN SEA
ATLANTIC OCEAN
PACIFIC OCEAN
Lima
Andes
Rio de Janeiro
Buenos Aires

extent of European settlement, 1750
Amerindian peoples

KEY TOPICS

- **Old and New in the New World:** Settlers create a New World in the Americas north and south, blending elements of European, Amerindian, and African cultures; but it is a new world in which natives and slaves are compelled to labor for the benefit of a new colonial elite.
- **Declarations of Independence:** Inspired by the principles of the Enlightenment and guided by a written Constitution, the Americas give birth to a new nation; the United States soon has many imitators.
- **Fulfilling the Promise:** Their independence achieved, the new nations of the Americas do not extend to all their citizens the promises of freedom and equality inscribed in their constitutions; but by 1900 there is some progress toward that ideal.

Jefferson's Promise *Called upon to declare to the world why North American colonists rebelled against their British masters, Thomas Jefferson (1743–1826) provided a concise statement of the political values of the Enlightenment (see Chapters 15, 17). Ironically a slaveowner himself, he asserted the "self-evident" truth that "all men are created equal," endowed with the "inalienable rights" of "life, liberty, and the pursuit of happiness." Government, said Jefferson, is created by men to protect these rights. When it fails to do so, "it is the right of the people to alter or abolish it," and to institute a new one.*

The United States of America was the first nation in the world to be founded on these Enlightenment principles. Soon the nations of Latin America would also declare their independence. In neither region was the Jeffersonian promise of civic equality fulfilled at first. Yet an ocean away from the European homeland where those ideals were born, some progress was made toward the goal of securing for at least some citizens their inalienable rights.

This chapter explores the career of the nations of the Western Hemisphere during the four centuries after Columbus' first journey, examining the impact of the European legacy upon a world where Europeans, Amerindians, and Africans met, and considering the extent to which the Enlightenment principles Jefferson announced were realized in the Americas.

OLD AND NEW IN THE NEW WORLD

During the colonial period, from 1492 to about 1800 (see Chapter 16), the old and the new converged in different ways in British North America and in Latin America (including those parts of South America, the Caribbean, and Mexico where Spanish, Portuguese, or French, all derived from Latin, are spoken).

In the south, the imprint of European social, religious, and political institutions was heavy; in the north, it was light. In the south, large indigenous Amerindian populations molded colonial culture; in the north, the native presence was slighter. The economy of the southern region depended on plantations, ranches, or mines sustained by impressed Indian or slave labor; the economy of the northern region was more varied. The proportions of old and new in New World civilizations help explain their later development.

Brazil and the Caribbean: Plantation Nations

During the colonial era, Brazil and the Caribbean islands developed plantation economies of a type unknown in Europe, but dominated by European elites. From the outset, Christopher Columbus (1451–1506) began building a New World economy different from the old. The climate was favorable, and the wilderness beckoned with fantasies of countless stores of gold. Columbus established a fortified city, and set six Dominican friars to convert and "civilize" the native Tainos. Within a generation, ships laden with New World treasures sailed regularly to Spain, and returned with tools and other manufactures.

The Caribbean Tobacco was the first cash crop farmed in the Spanish-ruled Caribbean islands, followed by sugar, brought by Dutch merchants by way of Brazil. Having learned to grow sugar in Asia, the Portuguese developed the plantation system, sustained by slave labor, in their Atlantic islands of the Madeiras and São Tomé. Sugar cultivation was imported into Brazil, along with cargoes of slaves. From there, it reached the Caribbean islands.

The Amerindians of the Caribbean—the Tainos, Caribs, and Arawaks—could not supply the huge labor force required to grow, harvest, and mill sugar cane. By around 1600, some ninety percent of the Caribbean natives had vanished. They died from overwork, heartbreak, and disease. African slaves replaced the natives. These provided a labor pool that the armed and well-ordered Europeans managed brutally. Since neither women's labor nor their fertility was deemed valuable, male slaves outnumbered females two to one, which meant that the slave population could not maintain itself through reproduction. New shipments of African captives were constantly required.

The existence of slavery informed every aspect of the new Caribbean culture. African song, dance, and storytelling figured more powerfully than the Christian rituals or European refinements of the elite. A mixture developed of Christian and African customs, particularly in western Hispaniola (modern Haiti), where it became known as **voodoo**.

Soon Dutch, French, and English competitors challenged Spanish dominion of the Caribbean and its coastal rim. With the foothold of Dutch Guiana (later Surinam) on the northern coast of South America, the Dutch continued to play a significant role in Caribbean shipping. The French acquired half of Hispaniola, as well as the islands of Martinique and

Guadeloupe, and the north coastal colony of French Guiana. The British controlled the Bahamas and Jamaica, as well as some islands of the Lesser Antilles, the colony of British Honduras on the mainland of Central America (later Belize), and a British sector of Guiana. The small European landowner class that dominated a much larger slave population relied on its mother countries for defense and supplies.

By 1750, the Caribbean had changed dramatically from the early days of the Spanish conquest. The large population of Africans outnumbered whites and **mulattoes** (persons of mixed African and European parentage) about ten to one. The Amerindian natives had virtually disappeared. The economy was dominated by the production of sugar and the Spanish monopoly had been broken.

Brazil Spain was the principal metropolitan power in the Caribbean, but Portugal dominated Brazil. Early explorers recognized growing near the coast of the new continent a tree used for dyes that Portuguese merchants had previously exported from Asia. Brazil itself was named after this breselwood, or brazilwood. For a generation, the shipping of dyewoods occupied the Portuguese exploiters of the new territory. Later, the Portuguese brought sugar to Brazil, along with the plantation system of sugar farming. On the plantation, slaves tended the sugar plants, cut the canes, and milled the sugar for which Europeans developed an insatiable demand. The plantation farming of sugar, then coffee, became the backbone of the Brazilian economy. As many as 3 to 5 million African slaves were imported to labor on Brazilian plantations from the early 1500s, about one-third to one-half of all slaves imported to the western hemisphere. By 1800, blacks and mulattoes comprised more than half of Brazil's population. The practice of frequent manumission (release from slavery) resulted in a large group of free blacks and mulattoes, who gathered in the cities and intermingled with white elites. The indigenous Amerindians, on the other hand, isolated in the tropical forests of the interior, had little contact with Europeans concentrated on the eastern shore.

The Brazilian economy was more diverse than the Caribbean, which was wholly dependent on plantation crops. In addition to dyewoods, Brazil exported other products from the tropical forest (especially the drugs curare and coca), and mined gold and diamonds. A late-colonial gold rush encouraged the growth of Brazil's southern cities of São Paulo and Rio de Janeiro, which supplanted the original port city of Bahía in importance. Brazilian products amounted to as much as two-thirds of Portugal's exports; as was the case elsewhere, metropolitan prosperity depended heavily on colonial produce.

All three major Brazilian cities also supported small manufacture, whose artisans were often black or mulatto. Blacks and mulattoes also worked in the cities as servants, carters, peddlers, and prostitutes. As one Brazilian observer noted, "it was the black who developed Brazil."

The Portuguese regime in Brazil was similar to that in Spanish South America, although less restrictive. Advised by his overseas Council on New World

HOW MANY?

Death Comes to the New World—Amerindian Mortality in Mexico

1500 20-25

Figures represent millions

1600 1.5

1800 4

The numerous Old World diseases (principally smallpox) that the Spanish inadvertently brought to the Americas nearly annihilated various Amerindian populations, as shown here for Mexico. The Amerindian population recovered somewhat from 1600 to 1800, but remained well below its pre-conquest high.

concerns, the king appointed a viceroy to govern Brazil, who was surrounded by the ceremony and luxury befitting a European monarch. Law courts were headed by royal officials, and a tax commission oversaw the farming of revenues (i.e. the granting to individuals of the lucrative right to collect taxes).

The captains who presided over local regions enjoyed considerable latitude in local administration. They launched a tradition of military leadership in civilian affairs, which saw Brazil push its boundaries westward by the 1700s to the Andes Mountains and south to the Plata River.

Captains were often native Portuguese who later returned to more prominent positions at home, but some were creoles (white Americans descended from European forebears on both sides). Creoles were a social group of critical importance in both Portuguese and Spanish America: from their ranks came the magistrates who headed the councils of local "municipalities," which dealt with land disputes, water supply, or security, in addition to judicial procedures.

The Portuguese system of colonial rule had two main problems. The first was the inevitable tension between creoles and European-born ***peninsulares*** ("peninsulars," or people from the Iberian peninsula), who directed the colony's affairs. While creoles often believed that the peninsulars did not understand the American context, the peninsulars looked down on the creoles. The second problem was that of incompetence, caused by the neglect of duties or corruption. In the eighteenth century, the king's chief minister, the Marquis of Pombal (1699–1777) raised the standard of colonial administration, and reasserted the dominion of the motherland over the creole elite. Recognizing that Portugal's fortunes depended on Brazil's prosperity, he promoted industry and meticulously managed the royal treasury.

The Portuguese crown also closely monitored Brazil's economic life. It held monopolies of important commodities and collected tariffs on nearly all American imports. It permitted only Portuguese ships to carry Brazilian trade, and encouraged only those crops or manufactures that were considered to complement the Portuguese economy. Such restrictions were characteristic of **mercantilism** (see Chapter 16), and weighed heavily on colonial economies.

Nevertheless, some colonial landowners acquired immense wealth from estates as vast as whole provinces of the European homeland. Leading members of the creole elite resented their subordination to peninsular Portuguese and sought higher marks of status. The formation of militias for colonial defense provided an opportunity for such men, whose attainment of high military rank narrowed the social distance between them and peninsular governors.

Portugal also dominated Brazil's cultural and intellectual life, and saw to the firm establishment of Christianity. As elsewhere in Latin America, the conversion of the native Amerindians was a first priority. Unlike the placid Tainos that Columbus first encountered, Brazil's Amerindians resisted both Christianization and Europeanization into the eighteenth century, when decrees from Lisbon still called for natives to wear clothes like the Portuguese.

Brazilians of European descent remained within the cultural world of the motherland, journeying to Europe for study and intellectual discourse. By this route the ideas of the Scientific Revolution and the Enlightenment finally reached Brazil, which by the end of the colonial period still had not a single printing press or university, in contrast to the twenty-three universities in the Spanish zone. The Portuguese crown prohibited the establishment of printing, for fear of its revolutionary potential.

Spanish America: Mine, *Hacienda*, and Village

At its maximum extent, Spanish America stretched from California and Texas in North America to Cape Horn at the remote tip of South America. In this vast realm, as in the Caribbean and Brazil, explorers, conquerors, and settlers created a new economic and social system modeled on European patterns but shaped by local conditions.

Spanish settlements were concentrated in Mexico, called New Spain, and Peru (including also modern Bolivia, Ecuador, Colombia, and Chile), where the Aztec and Inca empires had flourished (see Chapter 16). In the pre-conquest era, the majority of Amerindians lived in this region, with sparser populations inhabiting Brazil, the Caribbean islands, and North America. During the first century of Spanish dominion, disease ravaged the native population, which in places sank to under ten percent of its former strength. While the native population recovered somewhat in the seventeenth century, their numbers remained low into the nineteenth century, well below their pre-conquest levels.

Mexico, for instance, had a population as high as 25 million at the time of the conquest. In the early 1800s, the population numbered no more than 8 million, counting European whites, mulattoes, **mestizos** (of European and Amerindian parentage) and Amerindians—the latter numbering about fifty percent of the whole. In all of Spanish America at that

WITNESSES

Native Laborers in Spanish America

What natives owed two *Encomenderos* who arrived with Hernando Cortés in 1517: [The Amerindians] are assessed each day two chickens and four loads of wood and two loads of maize, and fodder for the horses; and every eighty days twenty petticoats, and twenty shirts, and four loads of blankets of henequen [a plant fiber], and the labor on their plantings of peppers, beans, maize, and wheat, and the carrying of all this to the city, and the completion of the house, and they are not to be charged beyond this. . . .

On April 21, 1553, by agreement, the services of the thirty-two Indians . . . were commuted, so that instead . . . they are to give from now on 192 common gold pesos per year in payments made every eighty days. . . .
(Encomienda Records from Nestalpa, 1547–1553; ed. C. Gibson, 1968)

Miners of Potosí (Bolivia), described by a Spanish missionary (c. 1622): [Once] I went ... into the mine . . . . The ore was very rich black flint, and the excavation so extensive that it held more than 3,000 Indians working away hard with picks and hammers, breaking up that flint ore; and when they have filled their little sacks, the poor fellows, loaded down with ore, climb up ... ladders or rigging, some like masts and others like cables, and so trying and distressing that a man empty-handed can hardly get up them. ... [To support the mine walls, the Indians] keep leaving supports or pillars of the ore itself. ... [Yet] There are men so heartless that for the sake of stealing a little rich ore, they go down out of hours and deprive the innocent Indians of this protection by hollowing into these pillars to steal the rich ore in them, and then a great section is apt to fall in and kill all the Indians, and sometimes the unscrupulous and grasping superintendents themselves....
(From Antonio Vazquez de Espinosa, *Compendium and Description of the West Indies*, 1942)

date, the population numbered just under 17 million. Of this figure less than half was Indian, nearly one-third mestizo, one-fifth white, and a small minority African. Amerindians were the largest group in Mexico and Central America, while Indians and mestizos together constituted a majority elsewhere in Spanish America.

A combination of low population and physical barriers discouraged the settlement of interior regions of South America. Instead Spanish settlers remained in the charted regions of the Mexican plateau and the Pacific coast (eventually extending to the region along the Plata River, consisting of modern Argentina and Paraguay). Here they established an economy based on mining and agriculture, and oriented toward European markets.

The Economy In the early years of the Spanish American settlement, the thirst for gold and silver prevailed. Hernán Cortés (1485–1547), the conqueror of the Aztecs, sent home shiploads of golden trinkets manufactured by native craftsmen, while Francisco Pizarro (c. 1475–1541), the conqueror of the Inca empire, found the "silver mountain" at Potosí (modern Bolivia), one of the richest silver mines ever known. With a population of some 160,000 around 1670, Potosí became the largest city in the New World.

At first, native Amerindian laborers performed the dangerous work of mining, but as their numbers plummeted during the sixteenth century, African slaves were imported. Even so, the number of slaves brought to Spanish America was much lower than in the Caribbean and Brazil, and enforced Indian labor remained central to the mining enterprise.

Further gold and silver strikes were made, and the value of exports peaked in the period c. 1580–1630. Mining experts from Europe introduced the amalgamation process, which used mercury to separate silver from its alloy. At such ports as Havana in Cuba or San Juan in Puerto Rico, consignments of precious metals were loaded onto hefty Spanish ships that sailed in convoy twice a year, guarded by armed men-of-war from attack by Dutch and English privateers.

For nearly two centuries, gold and especially silver were Spanish America's major exports. They enriched neither the native population nor the people of Spain, but trickled through the royal treasury to profit merchants in Amsterdam or London. Later, other minerals, cacao beans and grain, and beef and hides were shipped to European markets. In the eighteenth century, trade increased from a few sailings per year around 1700 to 189 in 1760–1761. The Spanish government's "House of Trade" (*casa de contratación*), headed by the merchants of Seville or Cadiz, operated according to mercantilist principles and designated only a few ports of entry for European manufactures or for American exports.

Spanish America's second major economic activity was farming. Crops were sold locally, supplying villagers, city dwellers, and the large mining communities. European and creole elites sought to own farmland, a source of both wealth and prestige.

The first generation of settlers won ***encomiendas*** from the crown, which were similar to the medieval fief. These grants had been used as a tool of the Reconquest in Spain from the Moors in earlier centuries, and were now brought to the Americas. In exchange for military services, the recipient was granted land and the right to the labor of a certain number of native Indians. In a chronically depopulated region, land without the right to commandeer a workforce valued little. The effect of the encomienda contract was to enserf, if not enslave, the Amerindian workers. For this reason, it was controversial in Spain, where the king had accepted the Church's arguments against the enslavement of native Americans.

In time, the encomienda gave way to the ***hacienda***, a type of large farm, embracing the owner's "great house," family and servants, the workshop and stables, the fields and villages of native Indian farmers. While neither serfs nor slaves, villagers were expected to work on the owner's land, in addition to farming their own plots. Owners provided tools and seeds, or made loans, for all of which repayment was expected. Villagers thus became bound to the proprietor as debt slaves—the **peons**, who soon constituted the majority of native Indians in Spanish America.

The more fortunate peons worked on lands owned by the Roman Catholic Church, which became the largest single landholder in the Americas. The clergy often proved more flexible creditors and sympathetic managers than their secular counterparts. When, in the late eighteenth century, crown-appointed reformers sought to limit church power, everyone suffered.

The Church in Spanish America played a complex role. The Christian clergy were both oppressors, who sought to suppress native culture, and liberators, who guided the people to the best possible life in the framework of the European conquest. They worked for the conversion of the natives, enforcing conformity to European norms, but they were also dispensers

Life on a Hacienda

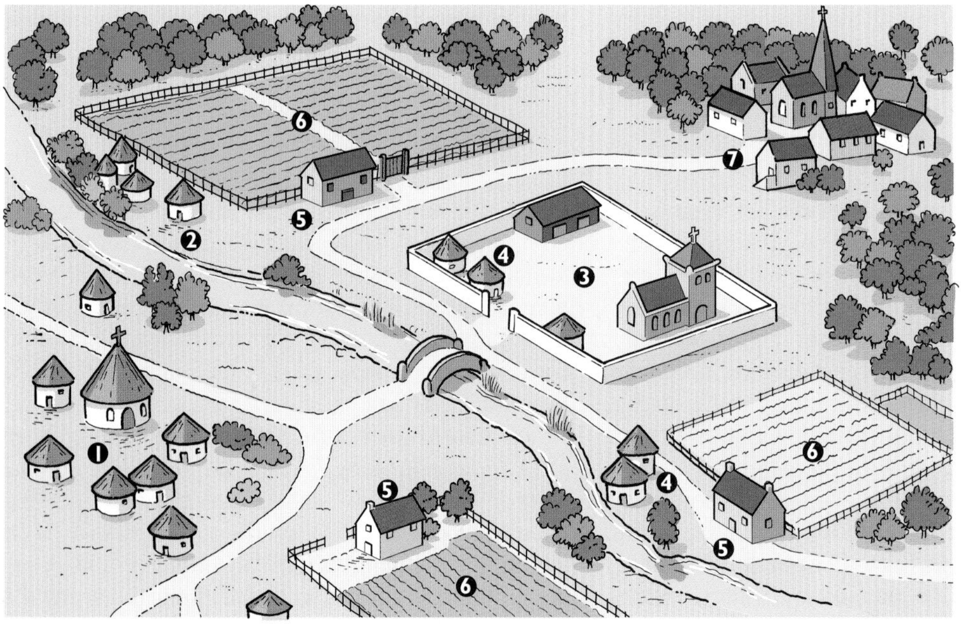

The hacienda was more than a farm. It was a system for the exploitation of the labor of Indian villagers, some resident, some part-time, who were tied to the Spanish owner by contract and debt. A simplified scheme of a typical hacienda is shown here.
Source: *Based on J. Lockhart, S. B. Schwartz,* Early Latin America: A History of Colonial Spanish America and Brazil *(Cambridge: Cambridge University Press, 1983)*

of charity, and the directors of hospitals and schools. They learned the Amerindian languages, and translated oral histories and folktales into Spanish. In the South American universities, they included courses in Indian languages to train new generations of pastors to native populations.

Organized by the very different pursuits of farming for local markets and mining for export, the Spanish American economy at first seems to have defined a two-class society: that of farm and mine owners or managers, and workers. The real situation was more complicated due to the factor of race. Initially, the elite was white, of European descent, while the workers were mostly native Indian. Soon, those racial divisions blurred as a result of miscegenation, or racial intermixture. The shortage of European females encouraged concubinage, and even marriage was legally permitted across race lines as early as 1501. Spanish America was a truly trans-racial society, based on social and sexual contact between Caucasoid, Mongoloid, and Negroid peoples (often identified as the three principal races).

Racial mixing, however, did not yield social equalization. On the contrary, white elites maintained the distinction of their status from those of Amerindians, the majority group that possessed the lowest prestige, and of the intermediate group called ***castas*** (including Africans, mulattoes, and mestizos).

Government Europeans from the homeland, meanwhile, claimed superiority to creoles. Creoles might participate in government at the local level of the "municipality," serve as officers in the militia, or hold high rank in the Church hierarchy. But nearly all the high positions in the government of Spanish America were reserved for peninsulars. These social tensions persisted despite the fact that creoles and peninsulars often intermarried.

The exclusion of creoles from senior government positions mattered, since Spanish America was heavily governed. Two huge viceroyalties were formed in the first generation after the conquest: the Viceroyalty of New Spain, of which Cortés was the first viceroy; and that of Peru. All the affairs of the colonial empire flowed through the viceregal offices. Each viceroyalty was subdivided into regional governments, or ***audiencias***, with only the smaller subdivision of the municipality left to creole governors. Sometimes prone to corruption, the Spanish colonial administration was on the whole efficiently managed.

In the eighteenth century, Spain experienced a change of royal dynasty, when a European war installed Bourbon kings related to the monarchs of France in place of the Habsburg line (see Chapter 15). The Spanish Bourbons brought to colonial administration the tools of government developed under the able ministers of the French king Louis XIV (r. 1643–1715). The viceroyalties were subdivided, with the two new ones of New Granada (1717) and La Plata (1776) being added. A higher standard of efficiency was instituted just at the time, ironically, when both absolute monarchy and the policy of mercantilism were under fire from Enlightenment critics (see Chapters 16, 18).

The creole elites of Spanish America resisted the Bourbon "reforms." Some were critical of the monarchy, many more were critical of mercantilism, and most resented the imposition of peninsular officials upon a society that, they believed, could be better led by themselves. Creole officers grew bold in native militias, while creole leaders centered in Buenos Aires operated large-scale smuggling operations designed to evade prohibitions on imports by sea. Creole elites helped build city centers whose baroque palaces, churches, and other public buildings mimicked European capitals in their elegance and cosmopolitan air. Blind to the possibility of resistance to their regime by native Indian villagers, they were preparing to resist the monarchy and its peninsular minions when the opportunity arose.

At the same time, creole elites supported a Spanish American culture that was deeply attached to Europe. Schools and universities followed European models, while American-born historians, philosophers, and mathematicians kept abreast of European currents in thought. Mexico City and Lima had printing presses already in the 1500s, and by 1800, nearly twenty presses published books for the small confraternity of learned creoles. Entering a convent at age fifteen in preference to marriage, in a career typical of many learned European women, Sor Juana Inés de la Cruz (1651–1695) wrote verse in a classical Castilian indistinguishable from the best produced in Europe.

In Spanish America, creole women continued to pursue the roles that were traditional in European society, where male patriarchs administered property and made decisions. Creole men, however, had few women of European descent available to them—a shortage contributing to the practice of concubinage and the resulting racial mixtures. In licit and illicit relationships, Indian and *casta* women were subject to white males by gender and by race. A European system of gender discrimination was thus reinforced by the American phenomenon of racial discrimination.

In this arena as in many others, Spanish America was a blend of European social hierarchies and cultural outlooks with New World peoples and environments. The two realities met in the person of the creole, who would soon take charge.

The North Atlantic Coast: The Beckoning Wilderness

On the eastern coast of North America, as in Latin America, European newcomers created new societies in the seventeenth and eighteenth centuries that preserved features of the customs and outlook of their homelands. The lands of the future United States of America employed English models of judicial procedure and governance. Religious groups that in Europe had coexisted with difficulty developed side by side in a new environment. In the absence of a hereditary nobility or standing army, and given a nearly limitless expanse of undeveloped territory extending to the west, European settlers sensed possibilities unknown on the far side of the Atlantic. As they pursued their goals, they intruded upon Amerindian natives who were compelled to yield their land to the newcomers; and upon African captives who were compelled to do their labor.

The French, Dutch, and English followed the Portuguese and Spanish to the New World and probed the Atlantic coast of North America. There they found a land thinly settled by Amerindian natives—no Inca or Aztec empires here—lacking conspicuous sources of wealth or any sign of a sea link to the riches of Asia. The first resource that Europeans exploited on the North American continent was a humble one: fish. In the seas of the north Atlantic off modern Newfoundland (claimed by the English) and Nova Scotia (claimed by the French), schools of cod beckoned to merchant shippers. Soon European woodsmen (mostly French) searched the forests for furs, and European farmers (mostly English and Dutch) scratched the new soil to see what it would yield.

Early Settlements The first enduring European settlements north of Spanish Florida were made after 1600. French expeditions reached from Canada to the Mississippi, establishing forts, trading depots, and missions. From Quebec, founded in 1608, French governors administered their American realm as an extension of the homeland. That realm numbered no more than 80,000 citizens in 1756, including fishermen, traders, and hunters clustered around fortified settlements. Valued as suppliers of furs and as wilderness guides, Amerindian natives were neither impressed into labor service, as in Spanish America, nor even displaced, as they were in the British colonies to the south.

In time, the British colonies of North America surpassed the French in population and importance. The first English colonies at Jamestown (1607) and Plymouth (1620) were agricultural ventures with modest aims. They were organized by the Virginia and Plymouth Companies, who provided funds and supplies to start the settlers off in a new land. The settlers too were modest people who sought land to farm and freedom from the economic and cultural restrictions of life in old Europe. These features of the first English settlements were to influence the whole later process of colonial formation.

Other colonies formed around the Chesapeake Bay and in Massachusetts, Rhode Island, Connecticut, and New Hampshire. South of these New England colonies, Dutch companies concentrating on the Hudson waterway founded the province of New Netherland in 1623, the capital of which, New Amsterdam, was seized by the British and renamed New York in 1664. Pennsylvania, New Jersey, and Delaware developed between New York and the Chesapeake region before 1700, absorbing Swedish and Dutch settlements. South of Virginia, the Carolinas were settled in part by migration from the British West Indies, features of whose economy the new colonies displayed. By 1700, all but Georgia (founded in 1732) of the eventual thirteen colonies had been established. They were sparsely populated communities, clinging to the ocean shore and the banks of rivers that emptied into the Atlantic. Several (Massachusetts and Georgia, for example) were assumed to extend from the Atlantic seaboard westward across the continent—from "sea to sea"— long before the nature of that expanse could be known.

Originally organized by joint stock companies or individual proprietors, the colonies built their own institutions of local government, which by 1700 displayed some common features. Most had a governor appointed by a far-away king. The colonists taxed themselves to pay the governor's salary. A legislature decided upon those tax levies and managed other local matters. Colonists meeting minimal property requirements voted for representatives (drawn from the wealthiest stratum of the population). These voters constituted only about forty percent of the adult male population; they excluded all slaves, Amerindians, and women, as well as the poor, the young, and recent immigrants. Experience in self-government over more than 150 years inclined many Anglo-Americans to resist new demands from

African Laborers in a Harsh New World

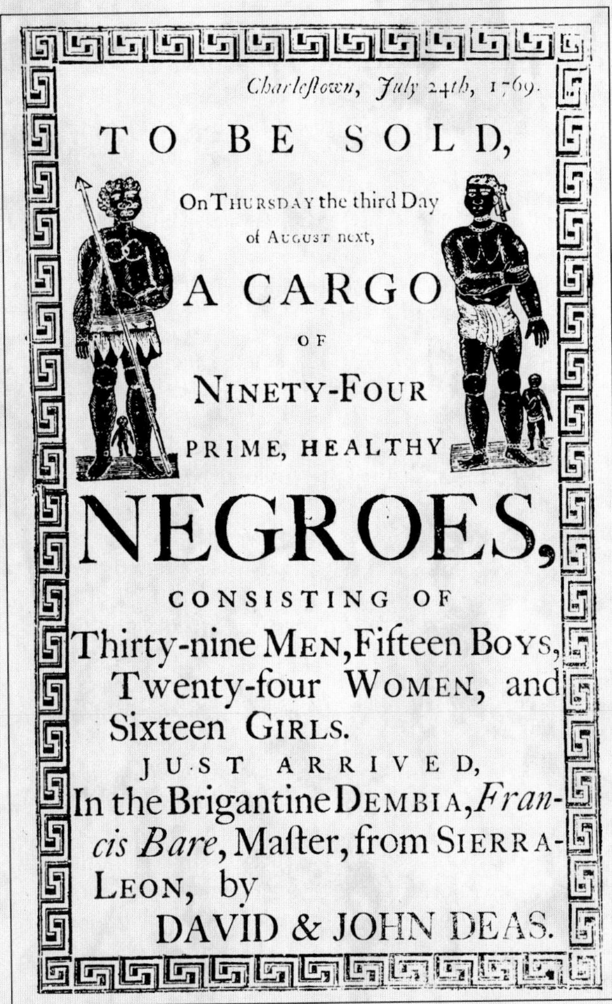

Charlestown, July 24th, 1769.

TO BE SOLD,

On THURSDAY the third Day of AUGUST next,

A CARGO OF NINETY-FOUR PRIME, HEALTHY NEGROES,

CONSISTING OF

Thirty-nine MEN, Fifteen BOYS, Twenty-four WOMEN, and Sixteen GIRLS.

JUST ARRIVED,

In the Brigantine DEMBIA, *Francis Bare*, Master, from SIERRA-LEON, by

DAVID & JOHN DEAS.

Advertisement for sale of slaves, July 24, 1769

After early, unsuccessful attempts to impress Indians into labor service, Europeans in all parts of the Americas began to rely heavily on imported African slaves. A 1769 poster from Charleston advertises the sale of slaves originating in Sierra Leone (above left). The desperation of a slave family on the run in North America is captured in the dramatic image of A Ride for Liberty *by the American painter Eastman Johnson (above right). Such attempts at escape rarely succeeded. In a more prosaic scene, slave women are shown working in the cotton fields, one accompanied by her child (right).* (above right: Brooklyn Museum, New York)

Eastman Johnson*, A Ride for Liberty—The Fugitive Slaves, c. *1862

Slaves picking cotton

Parliament in the decade before the eventual strike for independence.

No European-born nobility held sway in Anglo-American society. Immigrants were often fleeing poverty or repression. The nobility and the wealthier merchants stayed home. Even the governors did not form a cohesive elite, buttressed by ritual and luxury, as they did to the south. Instead, the colonial elite

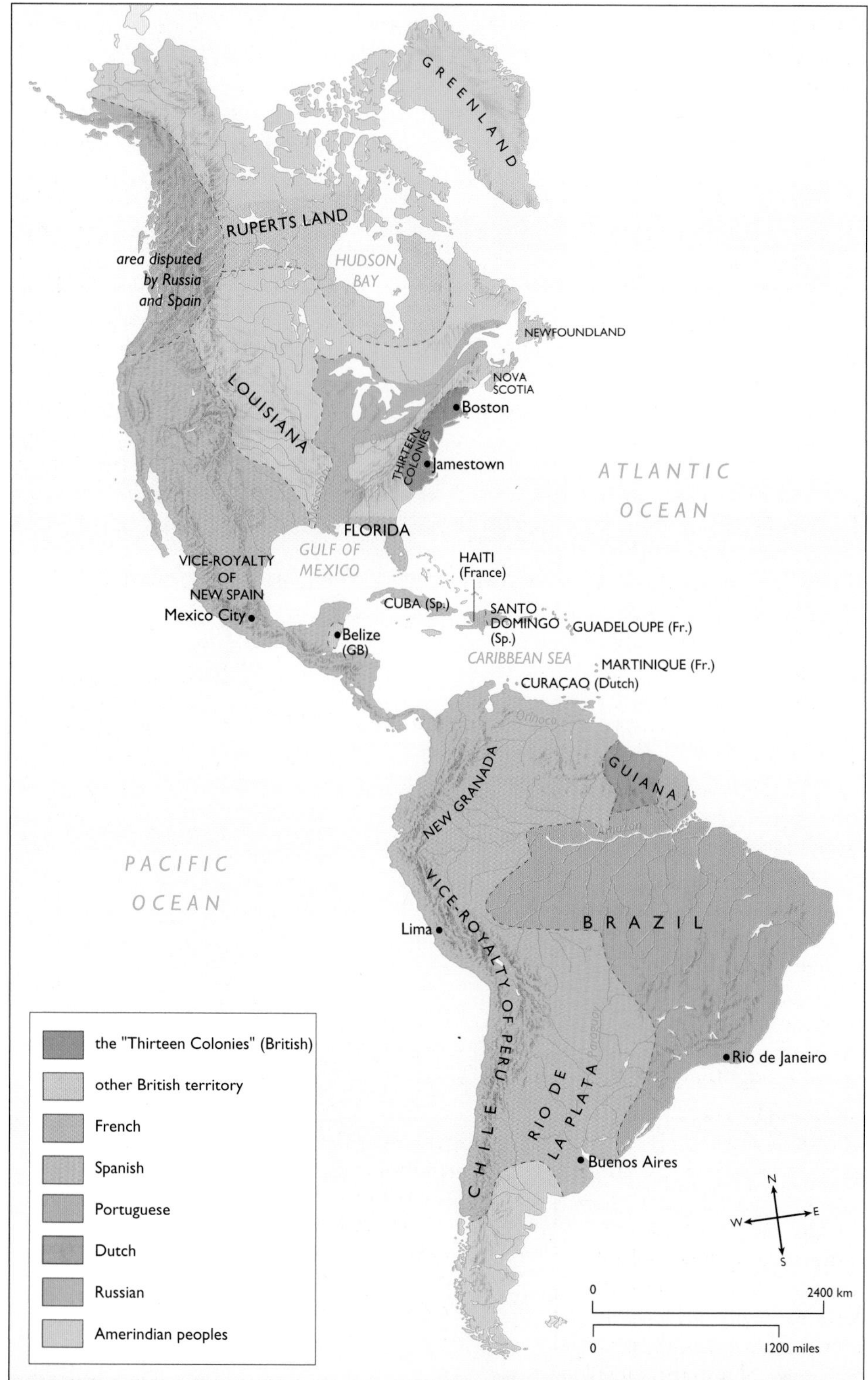

Map 19.1 The European Presence in the Americas on the Eve of Independence (1750): *By 1750, Europeans had staked their claim to most of the territory of the Americas. In the north, France held a vast American empire that dwarfed both Britain's and Spain's, but it was less settled and less developed than either of the latter. After 1763, France's North American territory passed to the British, while it retained control of colonies in the Caribbean and Guiana. With many of their earlier possessions denied them by the British, the Dutch still retained footholds in Guiana (Surinam) and the Caribbean. Britain held thirteen distinct colonies on North America's Atlantic seaboard and several in the Caribbean, while Portugal held the one mammoth colony of Brazil. Spain held the lion's share of South America and the southern and southwestern zones of North America, divided into the viceroyalties of New Spain, Peru, Chile, New Granada, and Rio de la Plata; as well as Caribbean territories, principally Cuba.*

developed from within in a land where upward mobility was possible. Colonial leaders were very different from the hereditary aristocracies who reigned in Europe.

No standing army policed the colonists. To defend against internal rebellion, foreign infringement, or Indian raids, the colonists raised their own militias. Regular army troops were not dispatched to the Americas until war broke out with the French in 1756 (see below). They provided a military education to the colonial militias, who would profit from their lessons a few years later.

At first, the colonial economy relied upon Britain's. Local artisans and merchants fulfilled local needs, although the colonies remained dependent on Britain (as the mother country wished) for manufactures. Mercantile restrictions meant that the colonists were encouraged to produce goods useful to the metropolis, and were required to do all their shipping on British ships. In the early years of colonial development, these restrictions were seen more as benefits than burdens.

The colonists lived in European-style villages, with central church, official buildings, and public spaces. As in Europe, all family members were expected to labor. Men were the main workers outside the house, assisted by the older boys. Women performed domestic chores, spun and wove cloth, tended the vegetable garden and small animals, and trained their daughters in these tasks. The products of their artistry, sold to supplement household income, included textiles, processed foods, soap, candles, and the like.

Families were larger, on the whole, than in the homeland. Once the hardships of the early years were past, families with six or eight surviving children were common. These patterns led to high rates of population growth: in 1700, the British colonies had a population of about 250,000 white Europeans; by 1800, about 5 million people of European descent resided in Britain's former colonies, almost one half of the total population of England. The custom of **primogeniture** that prevailed in Britain (see Chapter 18) was often bypassed, and family property was divided among all children, including girls. Women (especially widows) and children enjoyed a higher status than in British society.

The competition to inherit was eased in the colonies because of the open territory that lay beyond the last fenced plot in the village. Not even natural barriers restricted the opportunities for landownership: in eastern North America, there were no mountain ranges as high as the Andes, no rivers as vast as the Amazon, and no treacherous, disease-ridden jungles. The perceived promise of easy abundance just beyond the next hill or stream shaped the American consciousness and persists to the present day.

Amerindians and Africans That beckoning wilderness was not vacant, of course, but inhabited by some 1 million natives who possessed no concept of private property, considering the land to belong to their tribes and nations. In their first encounters with Amerindian natives, the colonists often established friendly relations. In some cases, settlers negotiated a contract with Indian tribes for the use of their land. The Dutch famously purchased Manhattan island from the Indians of that name, and the Quaker William Penn (1644–1718) bought land as needed from his Indian "Friends." Such peaceful exchanges gave way to conflict. Occasionally, natives displaced from their lands responded by raiding colonial settlements. The colonists replied, fighting small-scale wars along the shores of the James or Connecticut rivers in Virginia and New England. Indian nations leagued together to protect their ancestral territories, sometimes allying with the French against British intruders, or with the British against the French.

The Social Pyramid in Colonial North America, 1775

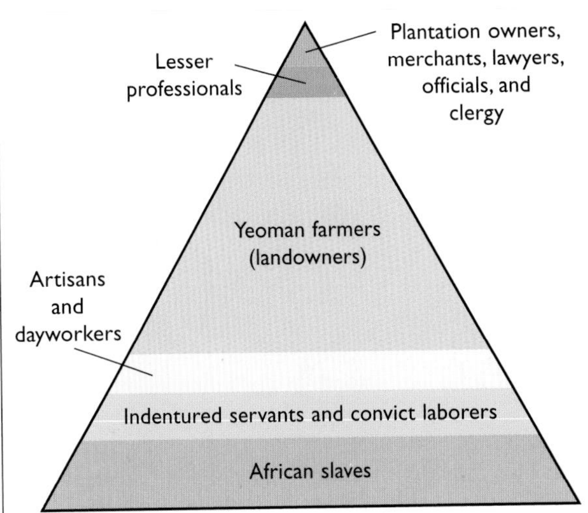

Britain's North American colonies did not avoid the social inequalities of the mother country, but exceeded them. "Merchant princes" and landed gentry sat at the very top of a pyramid that led all the way down to African slaves.

Source: *Based on T. A. Bailey,* The American Pageant: A History of the Republic, Vol. I, *5th ed. (Lexington, MA: D. C. Heath and Co. 1975), p. 70.*

Not all the interactions between Indian natives and European settlers involved violence, however. Religious and intellectual leaders called for the conversion and "civilization" of the Indians, and some were indeed converted in the early decades of settlement. The Protestant missionary effort, however, was a lame thing in contrast to the large-scale mobilization achieved by the Roman Catholic Church in Latin America.

Trade flowed between Europeans and Indians. The former craved hides and furs, and the latter sought guns and other manufactures. European settlers also transmitted their diseases to the natives, who as in Latin America had no natural immunity to smallpox, diphtheria, and other illnesses. Disease caused an absolute decline in the numbers of native populations, so that the demographic balance between the two races shifted: the handful of settlers, who multiplied and prospered, became a majority among a shrinking community of natives. Weakened in numbers, diminished by their need for Western goods, undermined by quasi-legal land grabs and patronizing attempts at conversion, Indian communities were vulnerable as the colonies expanded across a continent they came to see as theirs.

While Indians were not forced to labor on settlers' farms, as in Latin America, African slaves were. The first shipment of slaves arrived in Jamestown on a Dutch ship in 1619, only twelve years after the colony was founded. Thereafter, slaves trickled into British North America, mostly to the southern colonies, where a sub-tropical climate promoted the cultivation of cash crops—first tobacco, then rice and indigo, and finally cotton—in a plantation system similar to that in the Caribbean islands. By 1700, the foundations of a plantation economy had been laid in Virginia and the Carolinas. In the northern colonies, a few African slaves labored as domestic servants, sailors, and artisans.

The slave economy supported a social organization in which African people were assigned the lowest rank. British elites in the West Indies had elaborated this racial perspective, which was adopted by North American planters. Racial prejudices did not prevent racial mixing, however, as slaveholders demanded the sexual cooperation of female slaves and permitted the raising of mixed-race offspring on their plantations.

Racial mixture followed a course different from that in Spanish America, however. In British America, there was little miscegenation of Europeans

New World Cultural Encounters

***John White,* Indian Woman and Child:** *One of the earliest English observers of Amerindians and their culture, colonist John White painted this watercolor (far left) of an Amerindian mother and child—the latter holding a doll dressed in European style—in around 1585.* (British Museum)

***Albert Eckhout,* Mulatto:** *Whereas in the north, European settlers and natives kept their distance, in Spanish America, Africans, Amerindians, and Europeans mixed freely, so that individuals of mixed racial background, such as this mulatto soldier painted in around 1641 (left) were common.* (The National Museum of Denmark)

WITNESSES

Native Removal in Anglo-America

Lewis Cass, Governor of Michigan Territory 1813–1831, discusses the case for Indian Removal (1830): The destiny of the Indians, who inhabit the cultivated portions of the territory of the United States, or . . . their borders, has long been a subject of deep solicitude to the American government and people. . . .

[V]arious plans for their preservation and improvement were. . . pursued. Many of them were carefully taught at our seminaries of education, in the hope that principles of morality and habits of industry would be acquired. . . . Missionary stations were established among various tribes. . . . Unfortunately, they are monuments. . . of unsuccessful and unproductive efforts. What tribe has been civilized by all this expenditure of treasure, and labor, and care?. . .

The cause of this total failure cannot be attributed to the nature of the experiment, or to . . . [those] who have directed it. . . . [T]here seems to be some insurmountable obstacle in the habits or temperament of the Indians. . . .[I]f [the Indians] . . . are anxious to escape . . . [from United States states' laws] ample provision has been made . . . A region is open to them, where they and their descendants can be secured in the enjoyment of every privilege which they may be capable of estimating and enjoying. If they choose to remain where they now are, they will be . . . subject, as our citizens are, to the operation of just and wholesome laws.

(Lewis Cass, *Removal of the Indians*, January 1830; eds. T. Purdue and M. D. Green, 1995)

Andrew Jackson, President 1828–1837, on the need for and progress of Indian removal (1835): The plan of removing the aboriginal people who yet remain within the settled portions of the United States to the country west of the Mississippi River approaches its consummation. . . . All preceding experiments for the improvement of the Indians have failed. It seems now to be an established fact that they cannot live in contact with a civilized community and prosper. . . .

The plan for their removal and reestablishment . . . has been dictated by a spirit of enlarged liberality. [They are to be given ample lands, supplies of clothing and arms, and provisions sufficient for one year after their arrival.] In that time, from the nature of the country and of the products raised by them, they can subsist themselves by agricultural labor, if they choose to resort to that mode of life; if they do not they are upon the skirts of the great prairies, where countless herds of buffalo roam. . . .

[Arrangements have been made to build schools, churches, dwellings for the chiefs, and to provide funds for poor relief, tools, steel, and iron.] And besides these beneficial arrangements, annuities are in all cases paid . . . in all cases sufficiently great, if justly divided and prudently expended, to enable them, in addition to their own exertions, to live comfortably.

(From J. D. Richardson ed., *A Compilation of the Messages and Pages of the Presidents 1787–1897,* 1896–1899)

and Indians. The offspring of European men and slave women, moreover, were considered to be slaves and to be black, regardless of the fairness of their skin.

Slavery developed slowly in the British colonies because of the availability of "indentured servants." These were Europeans, male or female, who had contracted to come to the New World. In return for their passage, they sold their labor for a set number of years—generally four to seven. Unlike the Amerindian peon of Spanish America, or the African slave, the indentured servant might anticipate social opportunity equal to that of any other New World settler when the terms of indenture had been fulfilled.

A New Society The opportunities offered by flourishing British colonies, and by a seemingly limitless wilderness beyond, attracted Europeans other than the English. There came the Scots, Welsh, and Irish from the British Isles, as well as Swedes and Dutch. Even in its first century, although strongly imprinted by its English heritage, the culture of North America was open and pluralistic.

In contrast to European countries, where memories of religious war, and of the demand for conformity, enforced by violence, were still vivid, in British America there was no **established religion**. Some colonies did align themselves with one branch of Christianity, collecting taxes for its support, and inviting dissenters to depart; but they never knew the Inquisition, the demands of an overweening clergy, or the presence of a monolithic Church as chief landowner or creditor. Religion remained a powerful force in British America, but it was not a unitary power.

Nevertheless, in Puritan New England especially, religion ruled sternly, demanding conformity to its understanding of God's will. Puritan austerity gradually waned and during the 1730s and 1740s a tide of religious expression called the Great Awakening swept the colonies. It demanded of worshippers not merely an outward conformity to religious norms but a deep commitment stemming from an experience of transformation, of being "born again" in faith. That religious current has persisted in American life.

Unburdened by an established church, a hereditary nobility, or the excessive control of royal government, the British colonists profited from their freedom. When, after 1763, in the aftermath of the French and Indian War, the British crown imposed a new round of economic demands and mercantile restrictions upon its North American colonists, the latter were unwilling to accept them. The French and Indian War had been the American phase of a worldwide struggle between the two powers of Britain and France, then preeminent in Europe. In its European phase known as the Seven Years' War (1756–1763), Britain struggled to snatch primacy from France and its ally Spain. At the same time, Britain wrested from France the controlling position in the sub-continent of India. In North America, Britain won Canada in the north, and vast unexplored territories to the west which restive colonists were ready to investigate.

The war also brought the British face to face with their own American colonists, whose wealth, military capacity, and incipient claims for cultural and political autonomy became apparent. British citizens shouldered one of the highest tax rates in Europe, and Parliament looked to the colonists to pay a fairer share of the costs of the recent war. Parliament's pursuit of this objective, coupled with its enforcement of mercantilist restraints, was to lead to another war in North America—one the British would lose.

By this time, however, key features of Britain's political and cultural life had been re-rooted on American soil. There they produced new fruit. In British North America, as in Latin America, those who transplanted features of European life into the western hemisphere created exactly what the explorers thought they had stumbled upon: a New World.

DECLARATIONS OF INDEPENDENCE

Within two generations of the Treaty of Paris (1763) that ended the French and Indian War, most of the European New World colonies achieved independence. A North American rebellion against Britain unexpectedly succeeded, and led to the creation of a new nation. Fired by that example and by a favorable tide of events in Europe, the South American colonies rebelled a generation later. The monarchs of France, Spain, Portugal, and Great Britain were made to acknowledge that peoples who were once their subjects were now independent players in the concert of nations.

Atlantic North America: War for Independence

The United States of America was the first nation of the Western world successfully to graduate from colonial status to autonomy. The strength of its own, original institutions enabled the United States to win independence. So did the quality of its leaders, trained in European values and ideas which would find expression in a written constitution that was the legal foundation of the new nation and its many later imitators.

The Roots of Revolution The Treaty of Paris of 1763 granted Britain all the land between the Appalachians and the Mississippi River, as well as Quebec, the core of New France (in addition to Florida, ceded by Spain, France's ally). It also laid the foundations for Britain's defeat in the American War for Independence that broke out twelve years later.

The Proclamation of 1763, as required by the Treaty of Paris, reserved the western territory to the Indian nations settled there, and denied it to angry colonists hopeful of expanding westward. In 1774, Britain further angered the mostly Protestant colonists by extending religious and civil liberties to the Roman Catholic French Canadians. Meanwhile, Parliament had imposed new taxes on the colonists, who believed themselves exempt from taxation, and Parliament powerless to tax them. Parliament for its part needed to repay the heavy costs of fighting the French and Indian War.

Parliament proceeded to levy a series of taxes, culminating in the Stamp Act of 1765, which required the purchase of a license or stamp to read a newspaper or send a letter or execute a legal document. After fierce colonial resistance Parliament repealed the Stamp Act in 1766. At the same time, doggedly, it issued the Declaratory Act, a sullen piece of legislation that affirmed Britain's power to tax its colonies.

In 1767, Parliament imposed the Townshend Duties on imports. The new levies spurred a response from a network of cooperating colonial assemblies, led by Massachusetts. Active resistance in Massachusetts, punctuated by violence, led to military occupation. In 1770, British soldiers fired on unarmed protesters, killing five—the notorious "Boston Massacre."

By 1773, Parliament had removed all duties except a tax on tea, levied as a subsidy to the East India Company then suffering from foreign competition. American consumers protested by the ostentatious non-consumption of tea. The Boston Sons of Liberty, one of the groups of disciplined protesters the colonies had developed since the first resistance of 1765, responded colorfully to the arrival of a shipment in Boston Harbor. On December 16, 1773, dressed up like Indians, they slipped by night onto the anchored ships and threw the tea overboard. Parliament responded with the Coercive Acts of 1774, which ordered Boston Harbor closed until the tea was paid for and established martial law in the city.

The leaders of the colonial revolt against Parliament were members of the affluent merchant and planter classes, whose economic interests had been threatened by parliamentary actions since 1763. Yet it would be too simple to ascribe their opposition to Britain solely to economic self-interest. That would be to exclude the dimension of intellectual culture, at the very moment when, in Europe, its development was high in quality and particularly relevant to the American scene (see Chapter 17).

In America as in Europe, men gathered to discuss the latest ideas and world events in libraries, academies, and clubs. Schools and universities trained Americans on home soil, and literacy was high. American leaders were well-read, both in the Classics and in contemporary discussions of the purpose of government, individual rights, private property, and the social contract. Readers of John Locke (1632–1704) and the Enlightenment *philosophes*, they believed passionately in the quest for individual freedom, the need for toleration, the importance of representation and due process. They extended the Enlightenment analysis of the evils of despotism to the American context, where it no longer made any sense (they believed) for hereditary rulers to govern free men. Enlightenment theory combined with themes of resistance between 1763 and 1776, when the first modern nation declared its abdication from the world's first global empire.

It was not sufficient, however, for lofty minds to form theories; American leaders also had to unite and develop a sense of nationhood. A common purpose is evident in the Committees of Correspondence, established throughout the colonies to spread information about developments in Boston, and in 1774, twelve of

Barry Faulkner, The Declaration of Independence: *Revolution in both North and South America drew heavily on the language, images, and ideals of the European Enlightenment. In this painting from around 1936, Thomas Jefferson presents the Declaration of Independence—a document steeped in Enlightenment ideals—to the Continental Congress. The image of solemn heroes posed against a dramatic natural backdrop is heavily mythologized, rather than strictly historical.* (National Archives Building, Washington, D.C.)

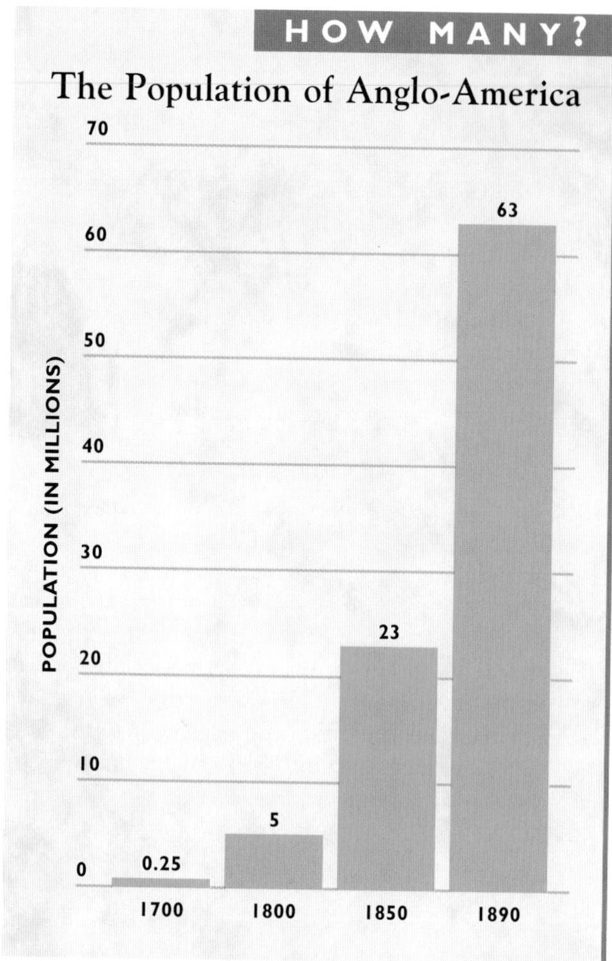

the thirteen colonies (all but Georgia) sent fifty-six representatives to the First Continental Congress. Clearly, colonial leaders had begun to see their enterprise as having national dimensions, distinct from its European roots. Then, in the spring of 1775, a swift series of events carried this movement forward.

Rebellion Fearing a British offensive, Massachusetts militiamen had stockpiled ammunition at the town of Concord outside of Boston. The British dispatched troops to seize it. On April 19, as the redcoated soldiers marched through the village of Lexington, a shot rang out—the famous "shot heard round the world," prefiguring not only the American but subsequent revolutions around the globe. From Concord, where they faced American militiamen, the British returned to Boston harried by the local farmer-soldiers whose guerrilla tactics contrasted memorably with the strict order of the well-drilled redcoats. In Boston itself, martial law reigned.

The battles of Lexington and Concord forced the gentlemen in Congress to make some decisions during the winter of 1775–1776. Did they represent one nation or thirteen colonies? Did what happened in Massachusetts affect the other twelve colonies? If so, should they attempt to heal the break with Britain, or league together to oppose her? An impassioned printer, the recent immigrant Thomas Paine (1737–1809) sharply defined the issues in his pamphlet *Common Sense* (1776). An instant bestseller (some 100,000 copies were circulated), it called on the public to recognize what was already an accomplished fact: the American colonies were a new nation, dedicated to the pursuit of trade and liberation from the tyranny they had left behind in their common European past.

In the spring of 1776, the Second Continental Congress appointed a committee to draft a document declaring independence. The Virginian lawyer and slaveowner Thomas Jefferson, its youngest member, largely composed the text of the Declaration of Independence that, with emendations, the members of Congress signed on July 4. This is the founding moment of the United States as a nation.

Britain dealt brutally with rebels, and those who signed the Declaration of Independence placed their lives at risk. They were supported by some eighty percent of the colonists. The twenty percent who were **Loyalists** stayed in the wings of the British army, or fled to Canada.

The American Revolution, or War for Independence, was fought by badly trained and poorly supplied regular soldiers and militia contingents facing a highly efficient army. Nevertheless, after initial losses and hardships, and aided by a French alliance, the war ended with the surrender of the British general, the 1st Marquis Cornwallis (1738–1805), to George Washington (1732–1799) at Yorktown, Virginia, following a joint American and French blockade. Two years later in 1783 in Paris, diplomats negotiated a peace treaty that recognized the new nation, the United States of America, and granted it land from the Atlantic seaboard to the Mississippi River.

The New Nation What kind of nation was the new United States to be? Would it be modeled on England, with a king and a parliament? Would the thirteen states be self-governing, or would they be subdivisions of one state, relating to each other through the medium of a central, or **federal** government? These issues were hammered out over the next generation.

Under the "Articles of Confederation" the thirteen former colonies each retained autonomy and cooperated in the war effort. In 1787, the Constitutional Convention convened at Philadelphia to consider a new framework for government. The former colonial leaders James Madison, John Jay, and Alexander Hamilton collaborated on the *Federalist Papers*, essays composed to convince the public of the need for a strong centralized, or federal government to guide foreign policy, oversee interstate commerce, adjudicate disputes between states, and fund projects of interest to the whole nation. Despite considerable reluctance, the Constitution was adopted in 1788 after ratification by the necessary minimum of nine states.

The Constitution of the United States adopts principles from two political theorists of the Enlightenment: John Locke and Montesquieu (see Chapter 17). From Locke it takes the principle of rule by an assembly of representatives, whose interests must be respected by any executive power whose own potential for tyrannical rule is thereby curtailed. From Montesquieu it takes the principle of balancing the functions of government (executive, legislative, judicial), so that each checks and balances the others. These principles, committed to writing, have survived without serious challenge and have served as a model for emerging governments around the world.

In 1791, a Bill of Rights containing ten articles was ratified. These became the first ten amendments to the Constitution, guaranteeing freedom of speech, assembly, and the press; the right of citizens to bear arms and thus fight as a militia to defend the nation; the sanctity of the citizen's property and privacy; freedom in judicial matters from the requirement of self-incrimination, and from "cruel and unusual punishment," referring to the use of torture and abusive conditions of imprisonment in contemporary European judicial systems.

The American War of Independence, it has often been noted, was less a revolution than a nationalist revolt. Nothing was "turned over" except the leadership of the country: economy, society, and culture developed after 1783 along the same lines they had pursued prior to 1774. The leaders of the American Revolution nevertheless made two extraordinary conceptual leaps. For the first time in the history of the West, they had envisioned the possibility of a legitimate challenge to established political power by ordinary citizens. And they had created a written instrument of government, again the first in the history of the West, that guaranteed individual rights, guarded against arbitrary power, balanced the different functions of government, and provided a mechanism for its amendment. The government created by these programs was not yet a democracy; but it was a frame within which democracy could, and ultimately did, take form.

Revolution in Haiti and Mexico

The North American precedent of a war for independence soon found imitators in the Latin south. The first of the Latin American revolts occurred in the French Caribbean colony of Saint-Domingue (formerly part of the island of Hispaniola) renamed by the victorious rebels "Haiti." This, too, was a nationalist revolt, which replaced French colonial administrators with a local elite. It was even more a profound revolution, in which slaves rose up against masters, blacks against whites.

The revolution began in 1791, during the French revolution of which Caribbean slaves halfway around the world had heard. They rose up under the leadership of the educated son of African slaves, François Dominique Toussaint L'Ouverture (c. 1748–1803), a slave himself. Leading a half-million slaves and some 25,000 mulattoes against 40,000 whites, by 1801 he had gained control of the whole of Hispaniola. The French, now ruled by Napoleon (1769–1821) (see Chapter 20), captured the insurgent slave. L'Ouverture died in 1803, a prisoner in France. His lieutenants persisted, and in 1804 they declared independence for the western half of the island, which they called Haiti. A state ruled by former slaves, Haiti became the second independent nation in the western hemisphere, the first in Latin America. Slaveowners everywhere trembled.

A struggle for independence in New Spain soon followed. This revolution remained unfinished, however, as more conservative forces seized power in the newly independent country, and creole and peninsular elites struggled for dominance in what later became Mexico. Their quarrel opened an opportunity for the priest Miguel Hidalgo (1753–1811), who in 1810 led an insurgent army of tens of thousands of native Indians against the capital city. He massacred the militia forces sent against him, abolished slavery, declared independence; then, believing his mission fulfilled, he sent his followers home.

Captured and executed by the Spaniards in 1811, Hidalgo was the first leader of the Mexican revolution. The second was José María Morelos (1765–1815), also a priest. Following Hidalgo's lead, he raised an army, called for social equality and the redistribution of land; but in 1815 he, too, was captured and executed. In 1821, Mexico finally gained its independence from Spain. But independence was not accompanied by the social revolution envisioned by the priestly rebels Hidalgo and Morelos. A creole elite (joined by royalist peninsulars) established General Augustín de Iturbide (1783–1824) as emperor.

Changes in the Ethnic Composition of Latin American Populations

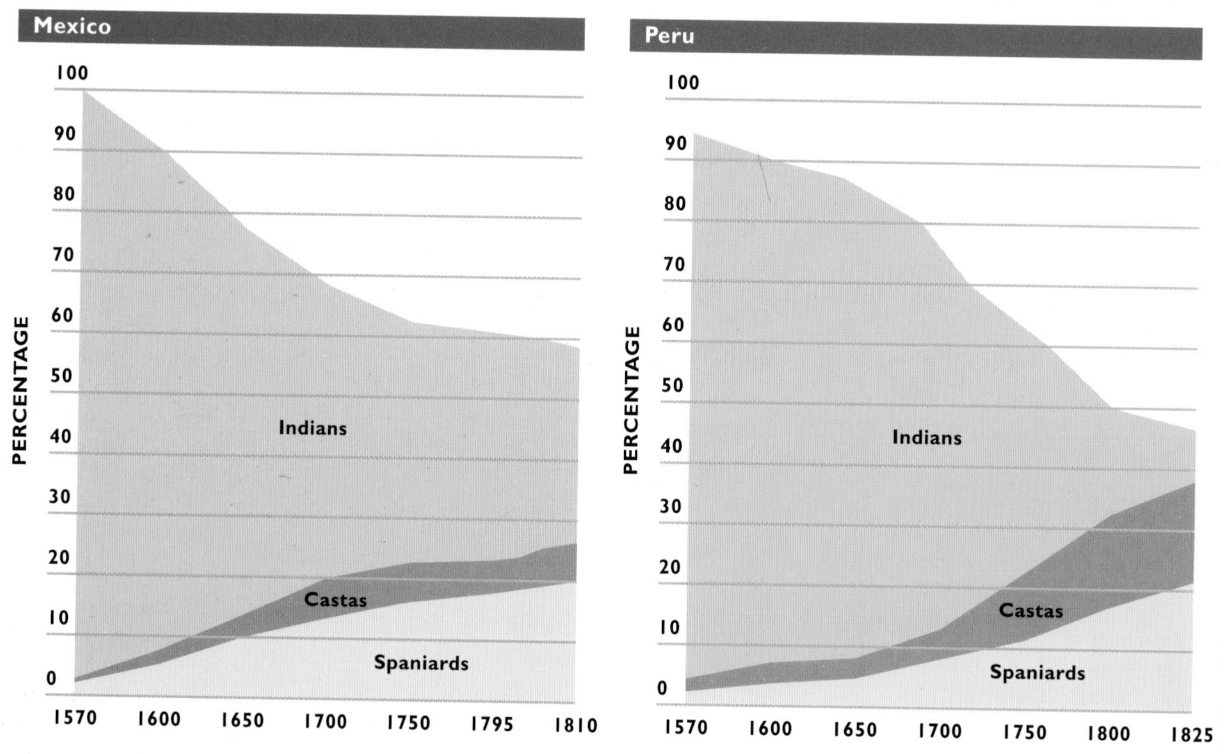

The heavy toll on Indian populations wrought by European diseases, the rise of immigration from the Old World to the New, and miscegenation among Spaniards, Amerindians, and African slaves profoundly altered the ethnic composition of Mexico and Peru during the colonial period. In both cases, the Amerindian component of the population fell markedly while the population of Spanish settlers rose. The population of castas *(an intermediate group including Africans, mulattoes, and mestizos), a consequence of racial diversity and mixing, increased to form about fifteen percent of the Mexican, and thirty percent of the Peruvian population by their respective terminal dates.*

Source: *J. Lockhart, S. B. Schwartz,* Early Latin America: A History of Colonial Spanish America and Brazil *(Cambridge: Cambridge University Press, 1983), pp. 320, 342*

Slavery continued, the Indians won no new land, and Mexico swung from leader to leader for the next few decades.

Transition in Brazil and Paraguay

The violent revolution in Haiti and the unfinished one in Mexico contrast with peaceful transitions from colonial rule to independence in Brazil and Paraguay.

In 1807, as Napoleon blasted through the Iberian peninsula, the prince-regent of Portugal, John VI (r. 1799–1826), fled to take refuge in Brazil, where his presence united and animated the colony. When the king returned to Lisbon in 1821, he left his son and heir Pedro (r. 1822–1831) in Rio de Janeiro to preside over an American court now considered equal to the Portuguese. Creole officials were enthusiastic about the elevation of Brazil, but pressed for greater autonomy. Pedro yielded, declaring Brazil's independence in 1822 and accepting the title of "Constitutional Emperor." The constitution was ratified in 1824 and remained unchallenged until the monarchy fell in 1889. Local support for the constitutional monarchy increased in 1840, when Pedro's American-born son, Pedro II (1831–1889), ascended the throne. Brazil was now a wholly independent and wholly American nation.

Independence also came bloodlessly for Paraguay, accompanied by a profound social revolution. In 1811, while the king of Spain was a captive of Napoleon, a congress of Paraguayans declared their independence both from Spain and from the

Tovar Y Tovar,* Simón Bolívar at the Battle of Carabobo *(detail): *A reference to European developments is made in this 1887 painting of Simón Bolívar. Striking the heroic equestrian pose associated with great leaders, Bolívar (far right) appears as a Latin American Napoleon.* (Capitolio Nacional, Caracas)

viceroyalty of La Plata. They chose a dictator: the lawyer and theologian José Gaspar Rodríguez de Francia (1766–1840), notoriously cruel but admired by historians for his competent administration of a poor and complex nation.

Aided by local creole elites, Francia nationalized the former crown and church lands, which he organized as a series of state ranches, rented for nominal fees to any Indians willing to labor there. Agricultural production increased, easing the poverty of the Indian population and enhancing the country's prosperity. With further improvements in education and manufacture to his credit, the unpleasant Francia emerges alongside the Portuguese monarchs, the former slave L'Ouverture, and the martyred priests Hidalgo and Morelos, as a hero of Latin American independence.

Spanish South America: Victory at Ayacucho

Spanish South America boasted heroes still more celebrated: Simón Bolívar (1783–1830) and his lieutenant Antonio José de Sucre (1795–1830) of Venezuela, Bernardo O'Higgins (c. 1777–1842) of Chile, and José de San Martín (1778–1850) of Argentina. From 1810 to 1826, these creole aristocrats fought Spanish armies and won independence for the regions of New Granada, Peru, and La Plata, from which were carved seven sovereign states of modern South America: Venezuela, Colombia, Ecuador, Peru, Bolivia, Chile, and Argentina.

Argentina swiftly won its independence, then joined the western armies that freed Chile, Peru, and Bolívar's "Great Colombia" (Bolivia, Colombia, Ecuador, and Venezuela). In 1807, British warships sailed into Buenos Aires. The creole militia resisted the attack and took charge of the nation. In 1817, its leader San Martín marched the Argentine army across the Andes to support the Chileans under O'Higgins. In 1820, he pressed on to Peru, the center of Spanish power in America. There, in 1822, he joined Bolívar, whose army had prowled Venezuela and Colombia before heading south into Ecuador, Peru, and Bolivia. The final destruction of Spanish forces was wrought by Antonio de Sucre in 1824 at the battle of Ayacucho, which won independence for the new Latin states, and ensured the dominance of the creole elite.

The victory of these South American heroes was a victory for national autonomy, for Enlightenment values, and for free trade. It did not involve a social revolution, however, such as was dreamed of but abandoned in Mexico, and was secured for former slaves and Indian peons, respectively, in Haiti and Paraguay. The social and economic condition of the majority of the population was not affected by the achievement of independence.

Over the next generation, many of the modern nations of Spanish America emerged as free states, with the exceptions of Cuba, Panama, and Puerto Rico. The British, French, and Dutch retained their Caribbean and Guyanese possessions. As Europe, recovering from the Napoleonic wars (see Chapter 20), considered reviving its interests in the western hemisphere, the United States President issued a stern warning in 1823. The Monroe Doctrine stated that the Americas were not open "for future colonization by any European power," and that the United

WITNESSES

A Different Path for Spanish America

Simón Bolívar's address at Angostura (1819): I must say that it has never for a moment entered my mind to compare the position and character of two states as dissimilar as the English-American [i.e. the United States] and the Spanish-American. Would it not be most difficult to apply to Spain the English system of political, civil, and religious liberty? Hence, it would be even more difficult to adapt to Venezuela the law of North America. Does not [the French *philosophe* Montesquieu] state that laws should be suited to the people for whom they are made ... [and] that they should be in keeping with ... their inclinations, resources, number, commerce, habits, and customs? This is the code we must consult, not the code of Washington!....

Our people are neither European nor North American; rather, they are a mixture of African and the Americans who originated in Europe. ... The greater portion of the native Indians has been annihilated; Spaniards have mixed with Americans and Africans, and Africans with Indians and Spaniards. While we have all been born of the same mother, our fathers, different in origin and in blood, are foreigners, and all differ visibly as to the color of their skin: a dissimilarity which places upon us an obligation of the greatest importance.

Under the Constitution, which interprets the laws of Nature, all citizens of Venezuela enjoy complete political equality. Although equality may not have been the political dogma of Athens, France, or North America, we must consecrate it here in order to correct the disparity that apparently exists. My opinion, Legislators, is that the fundamental basis of our political system hinges directly and exclusively upon the establishment and practice of equality in Venezuela. ... By this step alone, cruel discord has been completely eliminated. How much jealousy, rivalry, and hate have thus been averted!

(From H. A. Bierck and V. Lecuña eds., *Selected Writings of Bolívar*, 1951; trs. L. Bertrand)

States would take any such attempt as "an unfriendly act." Protected by United States policy and, additionally, British interest in maintaining the Americas as a zone of free trade, the Latin American countries were free to pursue their own careers.

FULFILLING THE PROMISE

Both North and South America saw the triumph of liberal principles in the revolutions that occurred during the half-century following 1776. These enacted one of the ideals announced in the United States Declaration of Independence: the right of a people to abolish an abusive government, and institute a new one. They did not attempt to realize the other: the principle that all men are created equal. By 1880, the United States progressed some distance toward securing for all its citizens their "inalienable rights." In Latin America, that principle of liberalism was not yet even on the agenda.

The Reign of the *Caudillo*

From the 1820s through the 1880s, the nations of Latin America took form. Led by educated men descended from the creoles of the colonial era, economy, culture, and society were modernized. At the same time, traditional social patterns persisted, supported by two powerful conservative interests: the Church and the military. Consequently, most people found their condition no better, and perhaps worse, than it had been under colonial rule. To unify societies pulled between the ambitions of the elites and the needs of the masses, the autocratic strongman, or *caudillo*, stepped in. Backed up by the military, the caudillos promoted the construction of new societies while suppressing any signs of disorder.

Trade with the Old World In 1800–1880, the Latin American landowning elite developed its existing agricultural and mining enterprises. Commodities carried from the interior to port cities were transshipped aboard: coffee from Brazil and Central America; beef and hides from Argentina and Uruguay; tin from Bolivia and nitrates from Chile; from the great landed estates, or ***latifundia***, all over Latin America a cornucopia of corn, cacao beans, nuts and bananas, medicinal plants and dyestuffs.

These goods traveled by railroad to waiting steamships, some fitted, after 1876, with refrigerated compartments for the shipment of beef. This new transportation technology had recently been developed in Europe (see Chapter 21), and rapidly found its way to

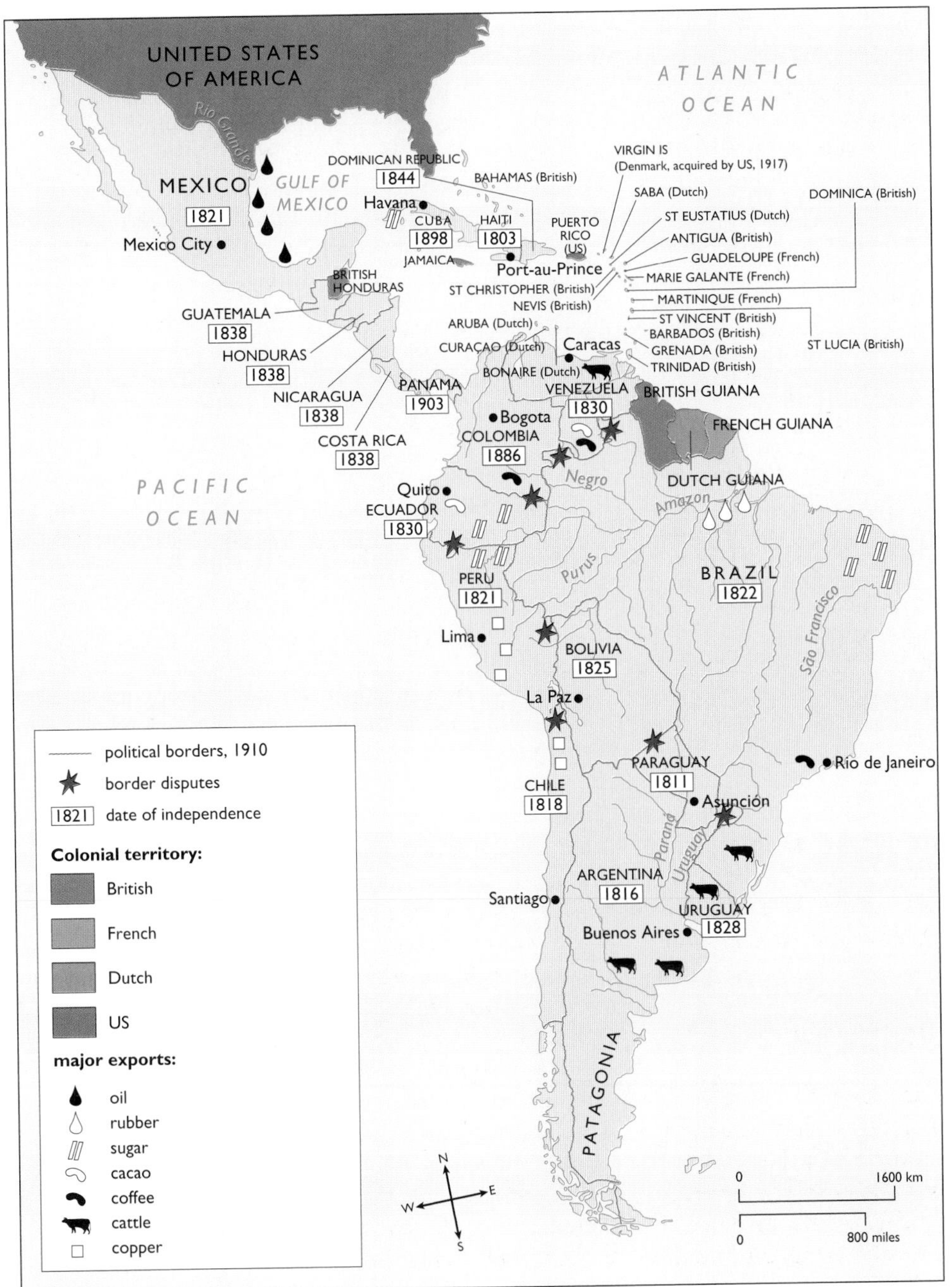

***Map 19.2* Latin America from Independence to 1910:** *From 1804 to 1838, most of Latin America gained independence from European empires. The Spanish, French, Dutch, and British all retained small islands and enclaves, especially in the Caribbean region, but most of these, too, became free by 1910. After achieving independence, the mainland territories fragmented into several states (with only Brazil avoiding fragmentation) to reach an eventual total of twenty autonomous republics for Latin America as a whole.*

assist the western hemisphere as it enlarged its role in the world marketplace. In 1815–1820, as few as two or three ships each year left Chile for England; in 1850, the figure was at least 300. During the same period, the value of exports shipped from Buenos Aires tripled. Boosted by coffee production, Brazil increased its foreign trade six- or sevenfold between 1883 and 1889. Overall, Latin American trade increased forty-three percent between 1870 and 1884, a period in which British trade increased just twenty-seven percent. While foreign trade boomed, local commerce between the regions of Latin America, where overland transport was difficult, lagged.

Trade with Europe caused cities such as Buenos Aires, São Paulo, and Santiago to flourish. By 1869 the population of Buenos Aires rose to 250,000, then increased eightfold; by 1914, one of four Argentinians lived in that port city. In Chile, twenty-seven percent of the population was urban by 1875, forty-three percent by 1900. By 1850, Brazil's Atlantic coast was dotted with prosperous municipalities, with 500 more created between 1890 and 1914.

Some city-dwellers had migrated from the countryside, but many came from the impoverished zones of eastern and southern Europe in search of new opportunities. Those who succeeded joined native elites in striving to make their cities as much like European ones as possible. Adorned with grand boulevards and opera houses, railroad stations, senate buildings, and churches, these imitated the latest trends in European architecture and city planning, aspiring to be as grand as Paris.

Urban elites and landed proprietors purchased the manufactures of industrial Europe, especially Britain. In 1825, half of British exports to the western hemisphere were to Latin America, and half of these to Brazil alone. "Spanish America is free," one British official remarked considering the opportunities there for trade and investment, "and ... she is English." With competition from the fine products of Europe's new factories (see Chapter 21), the wares produced by local artisans sank in value. Latin American manufactures, poorer in quality and prestige, were destined primarily for local markets.

The Latin American economy came to depend on European capital, and financiers set up banks in the expanding cities. They funded the building of roads, ports, and eventually railroads for transporting goods from the interior to the harbors. They also funded the emerging Latin American states, which were often unable to service their debts and suffered bankruptcy.

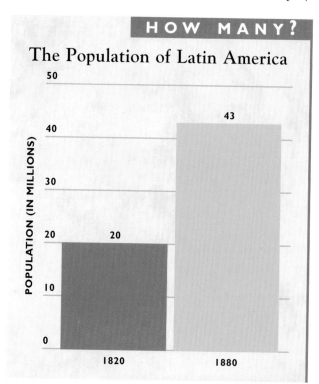

HOW MANY?

The Population of Latin America

Year	Population (in millions)
1820	20
1880	43

Despite wealth accumulated in some social sectors, government and society remained insecure—one consequence of an economy that produced, as was often said, "growth without development."

Divided Societies The beneficiaries of economic growth were the same elite who resisted colonial rule and led their peers to rebellion. They now ruled the fragile nations formed in revolution. Sharing power with them were the leaders of the Church and the army.

As before, the Church's role was complex. On the one hand, it was a major landowner and, before the advent of complex banking, a source of finance capital. On the other, it was attuned to the native Indian population. Nevertheless, while the clergy sometimes supported the villagers against the interests of the great landowners, the Church's role was more often conservative, seeking to defend itself against the encroachment of liberal values.

The military, meanwhile, played a major role in Latin American society—and so it remains to this day. Elegantly uniformed officers represented the self-sufficiency of the new, otherwise illegitimate revolutionary societies of America. Nearly everywhere, they propped up the authority of the president, the king, or the caudillo. Their support was well rewarded. In the first generation of independence, expenditure on the military often took up more than fifty percent of the new nations' budgets. Mexico's military budget between 1821 and 1845 exceeded the total of all government revenues on fourteen occasions.

If colonial social patterns persisted in the Church and the military, the pre-Columbian past endured in the customs of the native Indian majority. Wherever possible, they lived in their ancestral villages, and when displaced to haciendas, mines, or cities they retained their traditional culture, which had survived conquest and revolution alike.

Especially foreign to that culture was any notion of private property. Indians possessed their village lands in common. They cooperated in tasks, rather than compete and stand out beyond their comrades. Despite attempts to integrate the Indians into an economy based on private ownership, their assumption that land existed for communal use remained unshaken. Their village management of land, largely respected in the colonial era, was targeted by the post-revolutionary elites and rulers, whose land grabs enriched those who exported goods to foreign markets.

Nor did the economic prosperity of the post-revolutionary period advance the condition of the slave, before slavery itself was ended. Slaves were a minority in much of Spanish America, but in Brazil, as in the Caribbean, they predominated. Slave rebellions were frequent well into the nineteenth century, and bands of runaway slaves were common in the remote interior.

Persons of mixed race belonged to the group called the *castas*, or "castes," who possessed a social status above that of Indian natives, and who sometimes benefited from economic growth. Those who pursued artisan or merchant careers came to occupy a middling rank. European immigrants—Spanish, Italian, Irish, German, among others—included many skilled laborers or professionals, and could prosper in Latin American society.

Latin American societies were divided between the interests, on the one hand, of the educated elites, assisted by a middling sector of professionals and merchants, buttressed by the Church and army; and, on the other, by those of the masses, Indian, black, and mixed (except in those nations—Chile, Argentina, and Uruguay—whose populations were mostly European). They resembled the societies of Europe in the eighteenth century but were more perilously divided. In Europe the poor were not separated from their rulers by differences of race, culture, and history.

The Latin American economy was linked to the European in a pattern, not easily broken, in which one partner exported resources, the other manufactures. Though the Latin American market was thus subordinated to the European, the owners of the mines, ranches, and *latifundia* reaped handsome profits and had no incentive to alter the arrangement. On the contrary: adopting the views of the French founder of **positivism**, Auguste Comte (1798–1857) (see Chapter 23), they held that an elite of highly trained experts justly led society to greater productivity, harmony, and happiness.

This program of "Order and Progress" would justify much of the social policy of the age, accepted by both "liberals" and "conservatives." Order meant the continuation of existing social patterns, and progress, the growth of profitable foreign trade in a free trade system. Liberals and conservatives were distinguished not by their economic strategies, but by their attitudes toward the Church. Liberals viewed the Church as an obstacle to progress, considered redistributing its property, and terminating its judicial and economic

Native and Elite Caudillos

***Diego Rivera,* A Sunday Afternoon in the Alameda Park:** *Though Amerindians and castas were often marginalized within Latin American society, members of these "lower orders" did occasionally achieve political power. The Zapotec Indian lawyer Benito Juárez, for example, became President of Mexico in 1861 and is depicted at the center of this 1947 mural.*

Porfirio Díaz: *Political power in nineteenth-century Latin American states was generally monopolized by Creole elites and forceful* caudillos*—such as Mexico's Porfirio Díaz (r. 1876–1911), shown here—who ruled primarily for the benefit of wealthy landowners, the church, and military.*

privileges. Conservatives saw the Church as a bulwark of the social order.

The dictatorial leaders who thrived in the first generation after independence would employ at will both liberal and conservative stategies; the strongmen, or caudillos. These autocrats were usually drawn from the social stratum of the elite and nearly always promoted by the military. They well understood the effectiveness of the military in maintaining social order and protecting the interests of "civilization," as they saw it, over "barbarism." At the same time, caudillos of elite origin promoted the economic interests of their class by allowing land takeovers and the manipulation of labor contracts.

Some caudillos, however, often of mixed race, were considered "popular." The popular caudillos pursued land policies that benefited native or mestizo workers. Popular caudillos garnered success as they awakened among the millions of their constituents an appetite for justice. The "throng of aristocrats," one told his followers, takes all wealth and privileges, "leaving you only with misery, disgrace, and work...."

Unlike these populist leaders, most of the caudillos stood for the maintenance of order. Typical is the Mexican caudillo Porfirio Díaz (1830–1915), a mestizo, who rose to the rank of general and battled his way to supremacy. From 1876 to 1910, his autocratic, centralized government promoted economic growth while it protected the traditional interests of landowners, Church, and army—the usual recipe for success in Latin America.

While the old elites retained control, most nations had forged satisfactory constitutions and created representative assemblies which achieved at last the abolition of slavery. Beginning with "free birth" laws early in the century, which held free anyone born on native soil of slave parentage, abolition was attained nearly everywhere by 1880. The last two nations in the western hemisphere to accept abolition were Cuba (1886) and Brazil (1888).

Alone of the Latin American nations, Brazil was ruled by an emperor until the formation of a republic, one year after abolition. Cuba and Puerto Rico were the last of the old colonies to be ruled by Spain. While Haiti and the Dominican Republic were independent, most of the other Caribbean nations were under French, English, Dutch, or Danish rule. These regions did not experience the reign of the caudillo.

By the 1880s, most Latin American nations had developed governments based on limited representation. The majority of the people, Christianized and hispanized though they were, had little role in that government. Jefferson's vision of 1776, resting on the assumption that "all men are created equal," remained alien to Latin America's leaders whose high prosperity demanded that some men—and all women—be left unequal.

HOW MANY?

Unwilling Strangers–Trends in the Trade of African Slaves

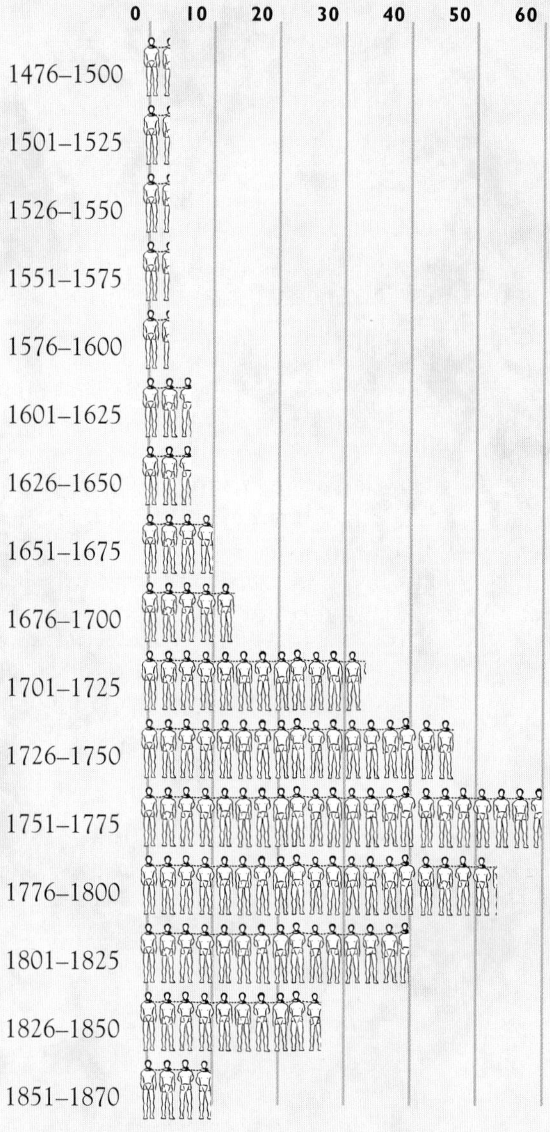

0 10 20 30 40 50 60

1476–1500
1501–1525
1526–1550
1551–1575
1576–1600
1601–1625
1626–1650
1651–1675
1676–1700
1701–1725
1726–1750
1751–1775
1776–1800
1801–1825
1826–1850
1851–1870

Figures represent slaves in thousands

Although the marketing of African slaves by European entrepreneurs began even before 1500, it peaked in the eighteenth century, reaching an apex on the eve of the American revolution.

Source: *H. Spodek,* The World's History *(Upper Saddle River, NJ: Prentice Hall, 1998), p. 451.*

By the People

The citizens of the United States of America were conscious of their nationhood. That consciousness emerged from the shared tragedy of war and the shared creation of a written Constitution with its statement of fundamental, inalienable rights. Over the next three generations, the nation would draw closer to the ideal implied in its founding documents: that all people were equal, and that the government was theirs. By the 1880s, the United States was nearly but was not yet a government "by the people."

The Expansion of a Nation In the interim, the difficult question posed itself: who, and what, was an American? As the nation grew, it absorbed new immigrants and repulsed its own Amerindian natives. It freed its African slaves, and heard the protests of women subordinated to male leadership in the state, church, and family. It expanded territorially from the Atlantic seaboard 3000 miles west to the Pacific shore past the barriers of the Appalachian Mountains, the Mississippi River, the Great Plains, the Rocky Mountains. With each new territory, the definition broadened of who was an "American."

The first frontier lay between the Appalachians and the Mississippi, acquired by the United States in the 1783 settlement of the War for Independence. Pioneers poured into the region and formed the new states of Tennessee, Kentucky, and Ohio. In 1787, the Northwest Ordinance established guidelines for the admission to the Union of states, declared slave-free, to be carved out of the territory bounded by the Ohio and Mississippi Rivers and the Great Lakes.

The remaining additions to the territories of the continental United States occurred in three stages. The first was the Louisiana Territory, an expanse of over 800,000 square miles between the Mississippi and the Rocky Mountains. It was purchased for $15 million from the cash-poor French Emperor Napoleon (see Chapter 20) in 1803, and subsequently charted from 1804 to 1806 by the scholarly officer Meriwether Lewis and his colleague William Clark. In 1819, with the Spanish cession of Florida, the eastern half of the continent south of British Canada belonged to the new United States.

In 1846, the United States made its second large territorial acquisition. This was the Oregon territory, defined by an agreement with Britain establishing the United States–Canadian border at the 49th parallel of latitude. A third set of territories was acquired by war from neighboring Mexico between 1845 and 1853. This territory included much of the future states of Texas (which had previously won its independence), Arizona, New Mexico, Utah, Nevada, and California. A small adjunct to these, including parts of Arizona and New Mexico, was acquired in 1853 as the Gadsden Purchase. (Further additions to United States territory, none contiguous, include Alaska; the Hawaiian islands; Puerto Rico; and scattered Pacific islands; see Chapter 28).

Into the unknown west opened to settlement by purchase, treaty, and war, American settlers moved: pioneers on foot, families in carriages, caravans of covered wagons. The century-long experience of the frontier affected the notion that Americans had of themselves. They had cut loose from the European past and all its restrictive hierarchies and systems of privilege. They were a people engaged in the discovery of the world and themselves.

As the settlers' fortunes rose, those of the native Indian peoples sank. During the first years of colonization, European impact on the Indian way of life was limited. Natives and newcomers sometimes cooperated and sometimes clashed. Until the end of the eighteenth century, however, the natives largely retained their land and their traditional culture.

That situation changed during the first decades of independence. The victors of the War for Independence imposed treaties that forced the east coast Indians to cede their lands and withdraw. With a combined population of about 150,000, these tribes were cooperative and docile. They had long lived in proximity to the settlers; some were Christian converts, and some had acquired literacy. Some of their leaders were the mixed-blood offspring of Indian women and men of European background. Their marginality enabled them to guide their people in negotiations with the new Americans—negotiations they were destined to lose.

In the Northwest Territory opened in 1787, settlers encountered tribes unfamiliar with the habits of white Americans who were more easily deceived into surrendering their land. One American governor purchased much of the future state of Indiana from Miami and Delaware Indians for a mere $10,000. Although the Shawnee chief Tecumseh and his charismatic medicine-man brother resisted such land grabs, Chief Black Hawk (1767–1838) of the Sauk tribe surrendered his people's hunting grounds when, touching the fateful "goose quill," he unknowingly ratified a treaty with the United States government.

Systematic displacement of Indian populations began in the 1820s. Whole peoples were forcibly resettled in strange and less desirable lands, remote from ancestral graves and memories. This new policy affected Indian tribes from Florida, Alabama, and

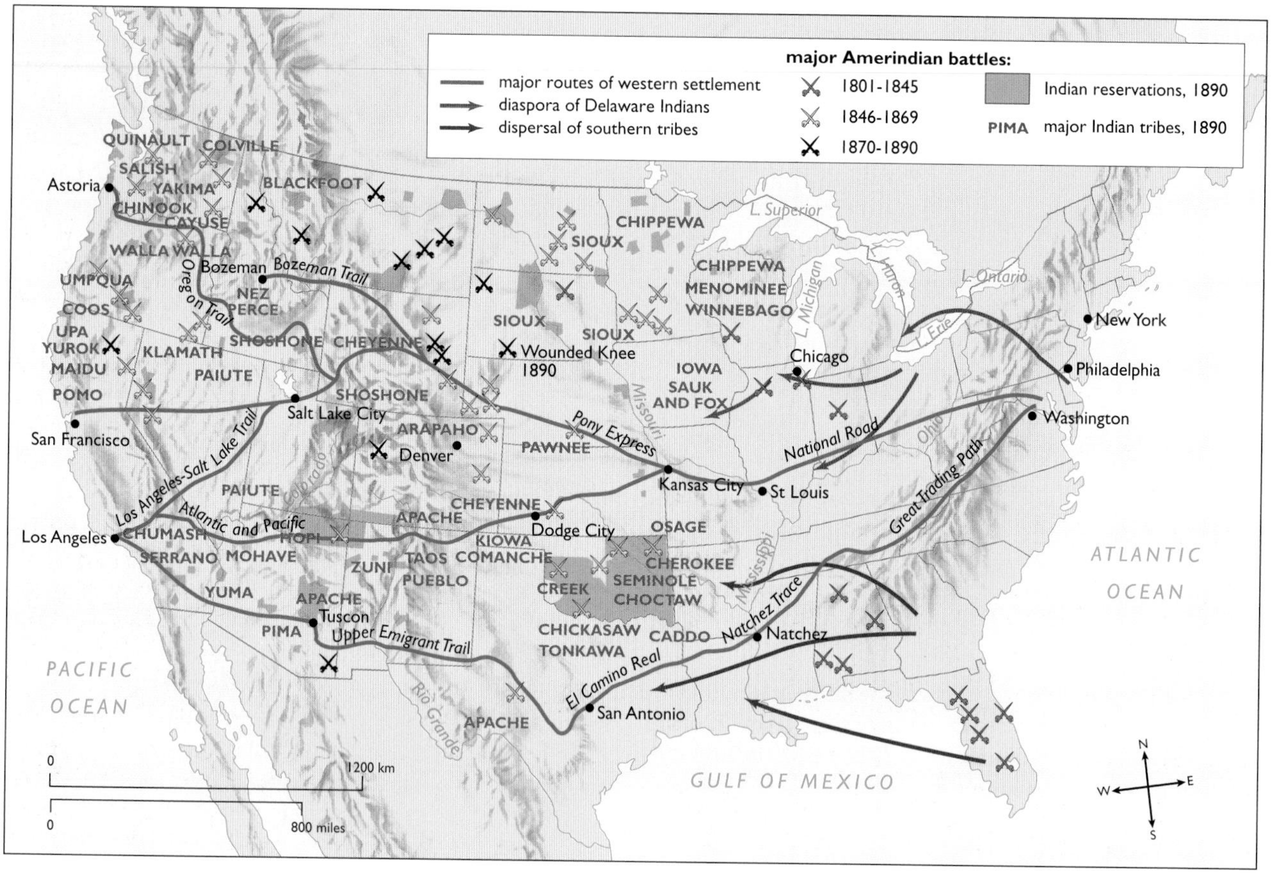

Map 19.3 (above and right) *Manifest Destiny: the Expansion of the United States, Amerindian Relocation, and Consolidation of Canada:* *After winning independence from Britain in 1783, and following its perceived "Manifest Destiny," the United States expanded westward at great speed. By expropriation, war, and purchase, it gained its present dimensions by 1898. Indigenous Amerindians paid a high price for the consolidation of the United States. Numerous battles, forced relocations, and the toll of Old World disease, reduced the pre-settlement population north of the Rio Grande from a peak of about 1 million—speaking 2000 languages—to a few battered and isolated populations languishing on reservations. The removal of Seminole, Creek, Cherokee, Chickasaw, and Choctaw Indians not only placed these groups in unfamiliar territory, but also made them immediate neighbors for the first time. Meanwhile, Canada expanded and consolidated as a dominion of the British Empire, with similar pressure on indigenous peoples (right).*

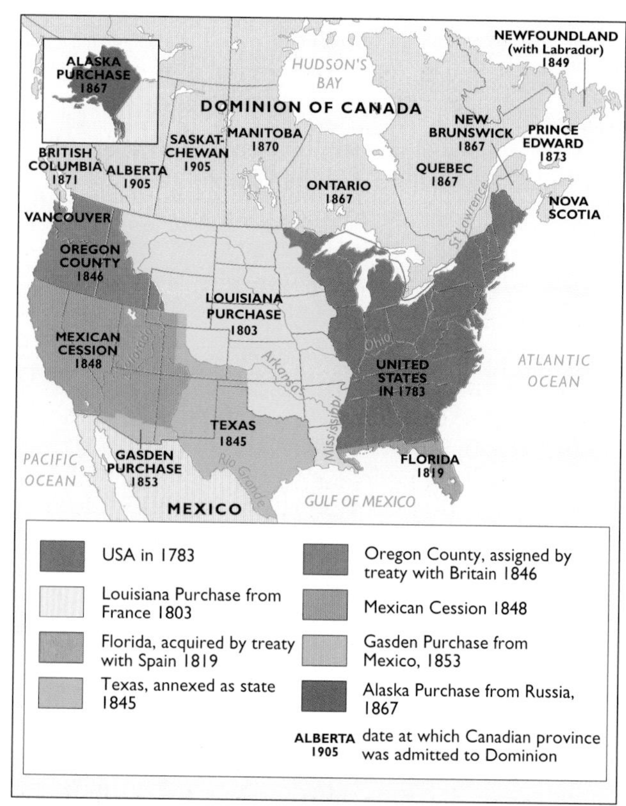

Georgia, and others on the border of Illinois and Iowa. Many were driven west and south to reserved "Indian territory" in modern Oklahoma, an arid region utterly unlike their homelands. The illegal Cherokee forced migration along the Trail of Tears in the winter of 1838–1839, ordered by the Democratic President Andrew Jackson (1767–1845), is one of the

Activists for Feminism and Abolition

Women's rights and abolitionism: *For women, and even more for former slaves, the full and equal inclusion into the American nation, as envisioned in the Declaration of Independence proved an elusive goal throughout the nineteenth century. Shown as partners, Elizabeth Cady Stanton and Susan B. Anthony (left) supported both abolitionist and feminist causes, as did Frederick Douglass (right).* (right: National Portrait Gallery, Washington, D.C.)

saddest chapters in the history of the young United States.

After 1840, the conflict between American whites and native Indians shifted to the region between the Mississippi and the Pacific. While the southwest was home to **pueblo**-dwelling Indians with a long history of interaction with Mexican whites, on the Great Plains there roamed nomadic Indian peoples numbering about 360,000, whose limited contact with European peoples had enabled them to supply themselves with guns and horses. The Plains Indians used these to hunt bison herds, their main economic activity—the bison population of some 30 million could feed, clothe, and equip them indefinitely.

Mobile and aggressive, the Plains Indians resisted the advance of white settlers in a struggle which reached its final phase after 1865. As settlers streamed across the plains, they snapped up Indian land, confronted and killed Indians (who returned violence for violence), and slaughtered the bison. Railroad lines followed them, criss-crossing the Indians' realm in nine interlocking routes (see Chapter 21). Regular army cavalry and infantry, released from duty in the Civil War (see below), moved west to protect American migrants and their homes.

The last battles in this conflict occurred in the final decades of the nineteenth century. In 1881 the Sioux chief Sitting Bull (c. 1831–1890) surrendered his people and his lands to federal troops, by whose fire he was killed in 1890. The Apache leader Geronimo (c. 1829–1909) abandoned his long resistance in 1886. In 1890, at Wounded Knee, South Dakota, federal troops massacred 200 Indian worshipers who had gathered to dance the Ghost Dance, a newly invented ritual of desperation.

In Oregon, the salmon-hunting Nez Percé ("pierced nose," so named by French hunters for their distinctive form of adornment) refused to cooperate with federal officials. They fled to the north; weakened by starvation and exhaustion, just short of the

Canadian border, their gifted leader Chief Joseph (c. 1840–1904) halted and surrendered, defeated by the suffering of his people. "I will fight no more forever," he announced in memorable words that seem to sum up the voice of the Indian peoples of North America.

By 1900, some four centuries after the Spanish conquest, the indigenous peoples of the Americas were no longer in possession of the lands that were the core of their identity. Nearly all the Indian nations under United States dominion had been relocated and dispirited, reduced permanently to a secondary status in the country that was once theirs.

Not all Americans approved of the government's "solution" for the Indian problem. Objections to the policy of Indian resettlement were voiced by Helen Hunt Jackson (1830–1885) in her explosive *A Century of Dishonor* published in 1881; and in 1883, the Women's National Indian Rights Association formed to battle for victims of western expansionism. In 1887, the Dawes Severalty Act attempted to make private farmers of Indians whose tradition of land management was communal. It proposed to make gifts of land in parcels of 160 acres, and to grant full citizenship to all participants. Seeking to impose European social and economic norms on Indian natives, it was a failure.

Slavery and Abolitionism The years of Indian displacement corresponded roughly to those of the rise and fall of African slavery in the United States. Although at the foundation of the republic, most Americans accepted the institution of slavery, many deplored both the slave trade and the exploitation of unfree labor. Implicit in the statement that "all men are created equal" was the seed of **abolitionism**, the theory that slavery was morally wrong and should be abolished.

The Constitution, however, acknowledged and protected the institution of slavery at three critical points. Article I.2 contains the infamous "Three-Fifths Compromise," providing that a slave would count as three-fifths of a person for purposes of representation and taxation. The effect was to guarantee to the southern states, where slavery was concentrated, more representatives in Congress than they would have obtained if slaves were not counted at all. Article I.9 guaranteed that the slave trade would not be impeded by law before 1808 (after which it was indeed ended), while Article IV.2 assured that the United States government would assist those whose slaves had escaped in the recovery of their property. For these provisions, abolitionists viewed the Constitution as flawed. They were further enraged by the Fugitive Slave Law of 1793, which reaffirmed the slaveowners' right to recover escaped slaves.

Ironically, circumstances conspired to boost the growth of American slavery exactly when political developments might suggest it was due to expire. In 1793, the northerner Eli Whitney invented the **cotton gin**, which mechanized the process of removing the small seed pods that grew amid the cotton fibers, making the large-scale production of cotton possible. That capability coincided, by chance, with the moment when British textile mills were converted into factories driven by steam power. The British factories were hungry for raw cotton, and the fertile fields of the American south were ready to provide it. Slavery and cotton thus worked together to dominate the economy, the social relations, and the culture of the south, especially the states from South Carolina to Mississippi, where Africans often outnumbered white Americans. The slave population of the south soared from about 700,000 in 1790 to

Women's activism ridiculed: *Women engaged in revolutionary politics in whatever ways they could, and principally as consumers. Mocking their efforts, this 1775 British cartoon by Philip Dawes depicts a circle of grotesque ladies signing a petition in support of the tea boycott. (Library of Congress)*

WITNESSES

Foundations of Freedom in Anglo-America

Separation from Britain: Thomas Jefferson's Declaration of Independence (1776): We hold these truths to be self-evident, that all men are created equal, that they are endowed by their Creator with certain unalienable Rights, that among these are Life, Liberty and the pursuit of Happiness. That to secure these rights, Governments are instituted among Men, deriving their just powers from the consent of the governed, That whenever any Form of Government becomes destructive of these ends, it is the Right of the People to alter or to abolish it, and to institute new Government, laying its foundation of such principles and organizing its powers in such form, as to them shall seem most likely to effect their Safety and Happiness....

The history of the present King of Great Britain is a history of repeated injuries and usurpations all having in direct object the establishment of an absolute tyranny over these States.... [A list of "injuries and usurpations" follows.]

In every stage of these Oppressions We have Petitioned for Redress in the most humble terns: Our repeated Petitions have been answered only by repeated injury. A Prince, whose character is thus marked by every act which may define a Tyrant, is unfit to be the ruler of a free People....

We, therefore, the Representatives of the United States of America, in General Congress, Assembled, appealing to the Supreme Judge of the World for the rectitude of our intentions, do, in the Name, and by Authority of the good People of the Colonies, solemnly publish and declare, That these United Colonies are, and of Right ought to be Free and Independent States; that they are Absolved from all Allegiance to the British Crown, and that all political connection between them and the State of Great Britain, is and ought to be totally dissolved....

(The Declaration of Independence Made by the Original Thirteen States in Congress at Philadelphia, 1776)

Rights for women (1848): We hold these truths to be self-evident: that all men and women are created equal; that they are endowed by their Creator with certain inalienable rights; that among these are life, liberty, and the pursuit of happiness; that to secure these rights governments are instituted, deriving their just powers from the consent of the governed. Whenever any form of government becomes destructive of these ends, it is the right of those who suffer from it to refuse allegiance to it, and to insist upon the institution of a new government, laying its foundation on such principles, and organizing its power in such form, as to them shall seem most likely to effect their safety and happiness....

The history of mankind is a history of repeated injuries and usurpations on the part of man toward woman, having in direct object the establishment of an absolute tyranny over her. To prove this, let facts be submitted.... [A list of "injuries and usurpations" follows.]

Now, in view of this entire disenfranchisement of one-half the people of the country. . . in view of the unjust laws above mentioned, and because women do feel themselves aggrieved, oppressed, and fraudulently deprived of their most sacred right, we insist that they have immediate admission to all the rights and privileges which belong to them as citizens of the United States.

("Declaration of Sentiments and Resolutions, Seneca Falls, 1848"; eds. E. C. Stanton, S. B. Anthony, M. J. Gage, 1969, pp. 70–73)

The promise renewed: Abraham Lincoln's Gettysburg Address (1863): Four score and seven years ago our fathers brought forth on this continent, a new nation, conceived in Liberty, and dedicated to the proposition that all men are created equal.

Now we are engaged in a great civil war, testing whether that nation or any so conceived and so dedicated, can long endure. We are met on a battle-field of that war. We have come to dedicate a portion of that field, as a final resting place for those who gave their lives that that nation might live. It is altogether fitting and proper that we should do this.

But, in a larger sense, we can not dedicate—we can not consecrate—we can not hallow this ground. The brave men, living and dead, who struggled here, have consecrated it, far above our poor power to add or detract. The world will little note, nor long remember what we say here, but it can never forget what they did here. It is for us the living, rather, to be dedicated here to the unfinished work which they who fought here have thus far so nobly advanced. It is rather for us to be here dedicated to the great task remaining before us—that from these honored dead we take increased devotion to that cause for which they gave the last full measure of devotion—that we here highly resolve that these dead shall not have died in vain—that this nation, under God, shall have a new birth of freedom—and that government of the people, by the people, for the people, shall not perish from the earth.

(From R. P. Basler ed., *The Collected Works of Abraham Lincoln*, vol. 7, 1953)

4 million in 1860. That surge fired the enthusiasm of Northern abolitionists. Other Northerners opposed slavery on economic grounds and opposed its extension into newly opened territories. Some proposed resettling all slaves in Africa.

Slavery drove a wedge between the interests of those states whose economy depended upon slave labor, and those where it did not—between the southern and northern states. Those sectional differences ended in the **secession** of the southern states and the Civil War fought from 1861 to 1865. Even before that confrontation began, attempts had been made to deal with the issues of the abolition, preservation, and extension of slavery.

Twice, congressional leaders offered compromises in an attempt to silence the Sectionalist debates. In 1820–1821, the Missouri compromise provided that unorganized territory north of the 36°30′ parallel should remain free, while slavery could be extended to the south. Missouri would be admitted as a slave state, though north of that latitude, while Maine would be admitted as free.

The Compromise of 1850 reversed the principles of the Missouri Compromise. California was admitted as a free state, but the status of the Utah and New Mexico Territories were to be determined by the decision of the people. Among other provisions, slavery was allowed in Washington D.C., but the slave trade ended, and a stern fugitive-slave law was imposed.

The 1850 Compromise did not settle the slavery issue for long. Four years later, a northern politician proposed the terms of the Kansas-Nebraska Act. It called upon the organization of Kansas and Nebraska as territories, with the slavery issue to be decided upon admission to statehood by the people there resident. Pro-slave and anti-slave activists rushed to Kansas, which became a battleground for the competing interests that soon turned to fraud and violence. "Bleeding Kansas" foreshadowed the horrors to come when, soon, the Civil War began.

The stiff fugitive slave rules of 1850 paved the way for the infamous Dred Scott case, upon which the Supreme Court ruled in 1857. Born a slave, Dred Scott had moved with his master to the Northwest Territory, where he lived for years on free soil. On that basis, he claimed his freedom upon his master's death. The Court ruled against him, and returned him to slavery.

The abolitionists were horrified by the ruling, which seemed to privilege slave-holders. Northerners in general now opposed the extension of slavery, though few favored its abolition where it already existed. That was the position held by Abraham Lincoln (1809–1865), an Illinois lawyer who in 1860 won the nomination for President of a new, northern political party; the Republican.

When Lincoln won the election, the slaveholding states of the lower south (South Carolina, Georgia, Florida, Texas, Mississippi, Louisiana, and Alabama) seceded from the Union, arguing the full sovereignty of each state within the nation. The secessionist states formed the Confederate States of America, loyal to all the principles of the United States polity except those related to slavery.

North Carolina, Virginia, Tennessee, and Arkansas soon joined the Confederacy. Four other slave states—Maryland, Delaware, Kentucky, and Missouri—which formed a border between the slaveholding regions and the north remained within the Union. In Western Virginia opponents of secession formed a new state, staunchly Unionist in allegiance.

Civil War and After In 1861, South Carolina militia men fired on the federal garrison at Fort Sumter in Charleston harbor. Lincoln called a Special Session of Congress to ask for approval of the actions he had taken to counter the southern offensive. He argued against the theory of state sovereignty, calling "States' Rights" a fiction—a "sophistry," or trick of logic. He called on Congress to reaffirm the supremacy of that nation which alone in human history, as he put it, had been called into existence to lighten its citizens' burdens. The Civil War began, the central and most tragic event in the nation's history (see Chapter 20).

It was not the purpose of the Civil War to put an end to American slavery. But that was its result. In 1863, the Emancipation Proclamation made all slaves in rebellious territories "forever free." That partial liberation affected neither northern states nor Confederate territory not under Union control. Yet it freed some half a million slaves by 1865 and struck a blow to the heart of the institution of slavery.

The war over, Congress set out both to reorganize and to punish the south. That mission they pursued until 1877 when "Reconstruction," as the process was called, ended. Former secessionists regained their civil rights. The crowds of reformers and opportunists who had streamed south dwindled, and the programs instituted to help freed men gain land and legal rights ceased. In 1865, all slaves still in bondage were made free by the Thirteenth Amendment to the United States Constitution. In 1868, the Fourteenth Amendment guaranteed freed slaves the rights of citizens. In 1870, the Fifteenth assured them the right to vote.

Legislation could not adequately address the problems left by more than two centuries of slavery. Southern whites took steps to segregate blacks and deny them political rights. Black Codes, which reduced freed men to a condition of virtual serfdom, were barred, but their spirit prevailed and a host of customs and regulations barred African Americans from full civic participation. Black schools and black churches were targets for sporadic, illegal repression, and black leaders were victims of violence. Kept separate, illiterate, vulnerable, and poor, freed slaves did not yet benefit from the guarantee of rights found in the Declaration of Independence, the Bill of Rights, and the post-war amendments.

Yet the promise remained, as President Lincoln restated it in 1863 at the battlefield site of a recent Union victory in Gettysburg, Pennsylvania. In his brief speech honoring the thousands who died, the president linked the moment to the moment of national founding: "Four score and seven years ago," which was to say in 1776, "our fathers brought forth upon this continent ...." He summoned his listeners to a second founding, there on the bloodied Pennsylvania fields, a sacred event. They were to "consecrate" themselves, pledging to fulfill the promise Jefferson once had made to create a government that nurtured the inalienable rights of all: one that was "of the people, by the people, for the people."

When Lincoln summoned Americans to fulfill that promise, slavery was not yet dead. The liberation of former slaves from the habits of discrimination that slavery had ingrained was still to come. Native Indians continued to languish in the bleak reservations built by federal officials. Other groups, moreover, now sought inclusion in the circle of Americans. Poor white males, white immigrant males, and females of all origins claimed their place among those who called themselves "we, the people" of the United States.

In colonial America, as in England, property requirements limited the electorate. In seventeenth-century Massachusetts, just over half of all adult males were eligible to vote; elsewhere the percentage approached twenty percent. After independence, the

WITNESSES

African Bondage in Anglo-America

A colonial slave code (Virginia) aims to discourage runaway slaves: Whereas many times slaves run away and lie hid and lurking in swamps, woods, and other obscure places, killing hogs, and committing other injuries to the inhabitants . . . if the slave does not immediately return, anyone whatsoever may kill or destroy such slaves by such ways and means as he . . . shall think fit. . . . If the slave is apprehended . . . it shall . . . be lawful for the county court, to order such punishment for the said slave, either by dismembering, or in any other way. . . as they in their discretion shall think fit, for the reclaiming any such incorrigible slave, and terrifying others from the like practices. . . .
(From H. Zinn ed., *A People's History of the United States*, 1980)

A former slave who had bought her own freedom in the antebellum South succeeds in buying her daughter's freedom, as recounted by abolitionist Laura S. Haviland (1889): We solicited over seventy dollars for a poor woman by the name of Jackson, from Marseilles, Kentucky, who had bought herself by washing and ironing of nights, after her mistress' work was done. During seven long years she did not allow herself to undress except to change. Her sleep was little naps over the ironing board. Seven years of night work brought the money that procured her freedom. She had a son and daughter nearly grown, and to purchase their freedom she was now bending her day and night energies . . . The master's indebtedness compelled him to sell one of them, and market was found for the girl of sixteen. Nine hundred dollars was offered, and the distressed mother had but four hundred dollars to pay. . . .

In her distress she went from house to house, to plead for a buyer who would advance the five hundred dollars, and take a mortgage on her until she could make it. At length she found a Baptist deacon who purchased her daughter, and she paid him the four hundred dollars. He was to keep her until the mortgage was redeemed by her mother. . . . After working very hard one year, she was able to pay but one hundred and fifty dollars toward the mortgage, when her health began to fail. The deacon told her. . . he could not wait longer than another year, before he would have to sell her.

[Advised by sympathizers, the mother sought the aid of abolitionists in Cincinnati and Oberlin, including the author of the memoir.] A few weeks later the glad mother returned and redeemed the daughter. I saw them together . . . happy in their freedom.
(Laura S. Haviland, *A Woman's Life: Work, Labors, and Experiences*, 1889; ed. G. S. Lerner, 1973)

franchise gradually broadened. By the 1820s all white males had been granted **suffrage**, or the right to vote.

Immigrants, too, of whom some 5 million arrived between 1790 and 1860, sought inclusion in American civil life. Before the Civil War, they were mostly Irish or German, and often Catholics who found a hostile reception in a largely Protestant society. Later in the century, more waves of immigrants arrived from southern and eastern Europe as well as Asia and Latin America. Spurred by the discrimination they met, immigrants gained entry to politics in order to protect their communities as they struggled to succeed in a new world.

Women, like slaves, were denied full participation in American society; all, of whatever rank, were injured by the Jeffersonian statement that "all *men* are created equal." A feminist movement developed alongside abolitionism, leading to the 1848 meeting of women leaders and some male supporters at Seneca Falls, New York. Its outcome was the Declaration of Sentiments, which called for an end to women's subordination to men. Prominent among the grievances were the limits on women's right to hold property or to have custody of their children; their prohibition from higher education or professional careers; their unequal status in the workplace and the unequal pay they received; and the sexual double standard that permitted males to ignore moral norms while requiring women to obey them. The most urgent issue was the right to vote, which some hoped would be achieved for women when it was granted to freed black slaves. Among those supporting the Seneca Falls declaration were male abolitionist leaders, white and black.

After the Civil War, women leaders observed bitterly that while former male slaves now possessed the right to vote (if only in theory), no woman did. This injustice shaped the American women's movement, which now focused almost entirely on suffrage (finally obtained only in 1920). The circle of American citizenship had already expanded, and would continue to do so despite the opposition of those who stood to lose a monopoly on political power.

By the late 1800s, the question "Who is an American?" might be answered as follows: anyone born on American soil or, if born abroad, **naturalized**, or officially accepted as a citizen upon the satisfaction of minimal requirements. A second question still remained: "*What* is an American?" If not of English descent, would he or she speak English? If not of European descent—as the descendants of Africans, Asians, or Amerindians were not—would he or she identify with European culture, the civilization of the West? Though the question remains open, certain facts are clear: the political ideals, and the moral values behind them, that guided the American experiment, were the product of Western thought, the children of Western civilization.

Conclusion

JEFFERSON'S PROMISE, LINCOLN'S PLEDGE, AND THE MEANING OF THE WEST

From independence through the late nineteenth century, the United States proceeded in the direction of the inclusion of all its peoples in the task of government, and the recognition of their inalienable rights—goals that Jefferson promised, and Lincoln pledged. The nations of Latin America, where the task of inclusion was more difficult, did not.

In the north, the majority of the population was of European descent at the time the United States was founded. Amerindians numbered a sparse few hundred thousand, and Africans, slave and free, amounted to perhaps ten percent of the population. The cultural imprint of the European old world was therefore powerful.

In most of Spanish America, in contrast, the Amerindian population was a majority at the time that independence was won, while Africans dominated the Caribbean and Brazil. The elites of European descent who created the economic, political, and social foundations of their nations were a minority, who imposed their language and religion as a standard for all. Yet to this day the traditional cultures of native peoples are not wholly merged with that of the elites. Is Latin America an heir to Western civilization? It seems so. Not all of its people, however, belong to that civilization. Nor will they, or should they, unless they acquire through schooling the cultural values of the West—values responsible both for their domination in the colonial era and, subsequently, their liberation.

REVIEW QUESTIONS

1. What is Latin America? Why did colonial society in Latin America differ from that in North America? Why did the Plantation system dominate the economies of the Caribbean and Brazil?

2. Describe the economy of Spanish America. What role did the Church play in the Spanish colonies? Why did tension develop between the Creole elite and the Spanish government?

3. What were the origins of the British North American colonies? Describe their form of government. How did religion affect colonial society? Why did slavery develop in the southern colonies?

4. Why did the French and Indian War lead to conflict between Britain and its colonies? Why did the United States succeed in winning its independence? How did Enlightenment principles influence the United States Constitution?

5. Why did independence not lead to a social revolution in most of Latin America? What role did the caudillos play in the nineteenth century? Why did Latin American elites retain power after independence?

6. How did the expansion of the United States affect the Amerindians? Describe the rise and fall of African slavery in the United States. To what extent was the United States a "government of the people" at the end of the nineteenth century?

SUGGESTED READINGS

Old and New in the New World

Burkholder, Mark A. and Lyman L. Johnson, *Colonial Latin America*, 2nd ed. (New York: Oxford University Press, 1994). Thorough and up-to-date overview of colonial life and administration.

Cronon, William, *Changes in the Land: Indians, Colonists, and the Ecology of New England* (New York: Hill & Wang, 1983). Environmental historian's approach to the relationship among natives, settlers, and natural environment in the American Northeast.

Crosby, Alfred, *The Columbian Exchange: Biological and Cultural Consequences of 1492* (Westport, CT: Greenwood Pub., 1972). Examines the meeting of old and new worlds in 1492 as a critical moment not only in human, but also in ecological history.

Gutiérrez, Ramon A., *When Jesus Came, the Corn Mothers Went Away: Marriage, Sexuality and Power in New Mexico, 1500–1846* (Stanford: Stanford University Press, 1991). Explores the encounter between missionaries and natives, finding incomprehension on both sides.

Inikori, J. E., and S. L. Engerman, *The Atlantic Slave Trade: Effects on Economies, Societies, and Peoples in Africa, the Americas, and Europe* (Durham, NC: Duke University Press, 1992). Traces the connections and inter-relations of a wide diversity of groups and experiences.

Declarations of Independence

Bailyn, Bernard, *The Ideological Origins of the American Revolution* (Cambridge, MA: Belknap Press of Harvard University Press, 1967). Classic overview, stressing ideas more than social or economic issues.

Draper, Theodore, *A Struggle for Power: The American Revolution* (New York: Time Books, 1996). Sees the Revolution as resulting from a struggle for power rather than as an outgrowth of republican ideology or economic interest.

Higgonet, P., *Sister Republics: Origins of the French and American Revolutions* (Cambridge, MA: Harvard University Press, 1988). Examines the impact of individualism (in contrast to French corporatism) on the development of republicanism in America.

Langley, Lester D., *The Americas in the Age of Revolution, 1750–1850* (New Haven, CT: Yale University Press, 1996). Offers a "comparative history of the revolutionary age," taking in both American continents.

Lynch, John, *The Spanish-American Revolutions 1808–1826* (New York: Norton, 1973). Traces the origins of revolution, showing why these revolutions ultimately led to the creation of authoritarian regimes.

Wood, Gordon, *The Radicalism of the American Revolution* (New York: Knopf, 1992). Argues that insurgent egalitarianism and opportunism released by the revolutionary process resulted in radical transformation.

Fulfilling the Promise

Blackburn, Robin, *The Overthrow of Colonial Slavery, 1776–1848* (London–New York: Verso, 1988). The struggle for African liberation in the Americas, and its connections with capitalism and class struggle.

Burns, E. Bradford, *Latin America: A Concise Interpretive History*, 5th ed. (Englewood Cliffs, NJ: Prentice-Hall, 1990). Traces major themes in Latin American history primarily since independence.

Gaspar, David Barry and Darlene Clark Hine, eds., *More than Chattel: Black Women and Slavery in the Americas* (Bloomington: Indiana University Press, 1996). Essays exploring the intersection of race and gender within the slave systems of North America, Brazil, and the Caribbean.

Kerber, Linda K. and Jane Sherron De Hart, eds., *Women's America: Refocusing the Past*, 3rd ed. (New York: Oxford University Press, 1991). Including both primary sources and excerpts from recent monographs, this collection documents the history of women in the United States, and that of the United States from a feminist perspective.

Kolchin, Peter, *American Slavery: 1619–1877* (New York: Hill & Wang, 1993). A concise introduction explaining how slavery in the United States diverged from Caribbean and South American patterns.

Lynch, John, *Caudillos in Spanish America, 1800–1850* (Oxford: Clarendon Press of Oxford University Press, 1992). Traces the cultural, social, and political origins of the early caudillos, and their place in Latin American history.

REVOLT AND REORGANIZATION IN EUROPE

1750 | 1775 | 1800 | 1825 | 1850 | 1875 | 1900

Revolution and Reorganization

American War of Independence, 1775–83

French Revolution, 1789–94

Napoleonic era, 1799–1815

- Tennis Court Oath, June 21, 1789
- Storming of Bastille, July 14, 1789
- *Declaration of the Rights of Man and the Citizen*, Aug. 27, 1789
- March on Versailles, Oct. 5–6, 1789
- Civil Constitution of the Clergy, July 12, 1790
- Declaration of Pillnitz, Aug. 27, 1791
- September Massacres, Sept. 2–6, 1792
- Louis XVI executed, Jan. 21, 1793
- *Levée en masse*, Aug. 23, 1793
- Festival of Reason, Nov. 10, 1793
- France ends slavery in colonies, 1794
- Olympe de Gouges guillotined, 1794
- "Thermidor": fall of Robespierre, July 28, 1794
- Directory, 1795–99
- Napoleon becomes First Consul, 1799
- Concordat between Napoleon and Catholic Church, 1801
- Napoleon becomes Emperor, 1804
- Civil Code established in France, 1804
- Napoleon victorious at Austerlitz and Trafalgar, 1805
- Napoleon invades Russia, 1812
- Congress of Vienna, 1814–15
- Napoleon defeated at Waterloo, 1815
- Carlsbad Decrees, 1819
- Peterloo Massacre, 1819
- US Monroe Doctrine, 1823
- Decembrist Revolt in Russia, 1825
- Revolutions in France, Belgium, Italy, and Poland, 1830–31
- Greek independence, 1832
- First Reform Act in Britain, 1832
- Year of Revolutions, 1848
- Louis Napoleon restores Empire in France, 1851
- Victor-Emmanuel becomes king of Italy, 1861
- Austro-Prussian War, 1866
- Dual Monarchy of Austria-Hungary established, 1867
- Second Reform Act in Britain, 1867
- Franco-Prussian War, 1870–71
- Italian unification, 1870
- Paris Commune, 1870
- Bismarck made Chancellor, 1871
- German unification, 1871
- Third Reform Act in Britain, 1884

Society and Ideas

The Enlightenment, c. 1685–1795

- Adam Smith's *Wealth of Nations*, 1776
- Edmund Burke's *Reflections on the Revolution in France*, 1790
- Mary Wollstonecraft's *A Vindication of the Rights of Woman*, 1792
- Condorcet's *Progress of the Human Mind*, 1795
- Eugene Delacroix's *Liberty Leading the People*, 1830
- Factory Act in Britain, 1833
- German customs Union, the *Zollverein*, formed, 1834
- Poor Law Amendment Act in Britain, 1834
- Louis Blanc's *The Organization of Work*, 1839
- Potato Famine devastates Ireland, 1845–50
- Emancipation of serfs in Russia, 1861
- Slavery abolished in US, 1865
- Second International, 1889

Beyond the West

Mughal Empire, India, 1526–1857

Qing Dynasty, China, 1644–1912

British East India Company in India, 1690–1857

Dutch East India Company in East Indies, 1619–1799

- Shaka leads Zulu nation, 1817
- First Opium War, 1839–42
- US Commodore Perry "opens" Japan, 1853
- Second Opium War, 1856–60
- Sepoy Mutiny, India, 1857
- French gain control of Indochina, 1858
- Suez canal opens, 1869
- Meiji Restoration, Japan, 1868
- Britain's Queen Victoria becomes Empress of India, 1877
- Congress of Berlin sets off "Scramble for Africa," 1885
- Indian National Congress founded, 1885

CHAPTER 20

Revolt and Reorganization in Europe

From Absolute Monarchy to the Paris Commune

1750–1871

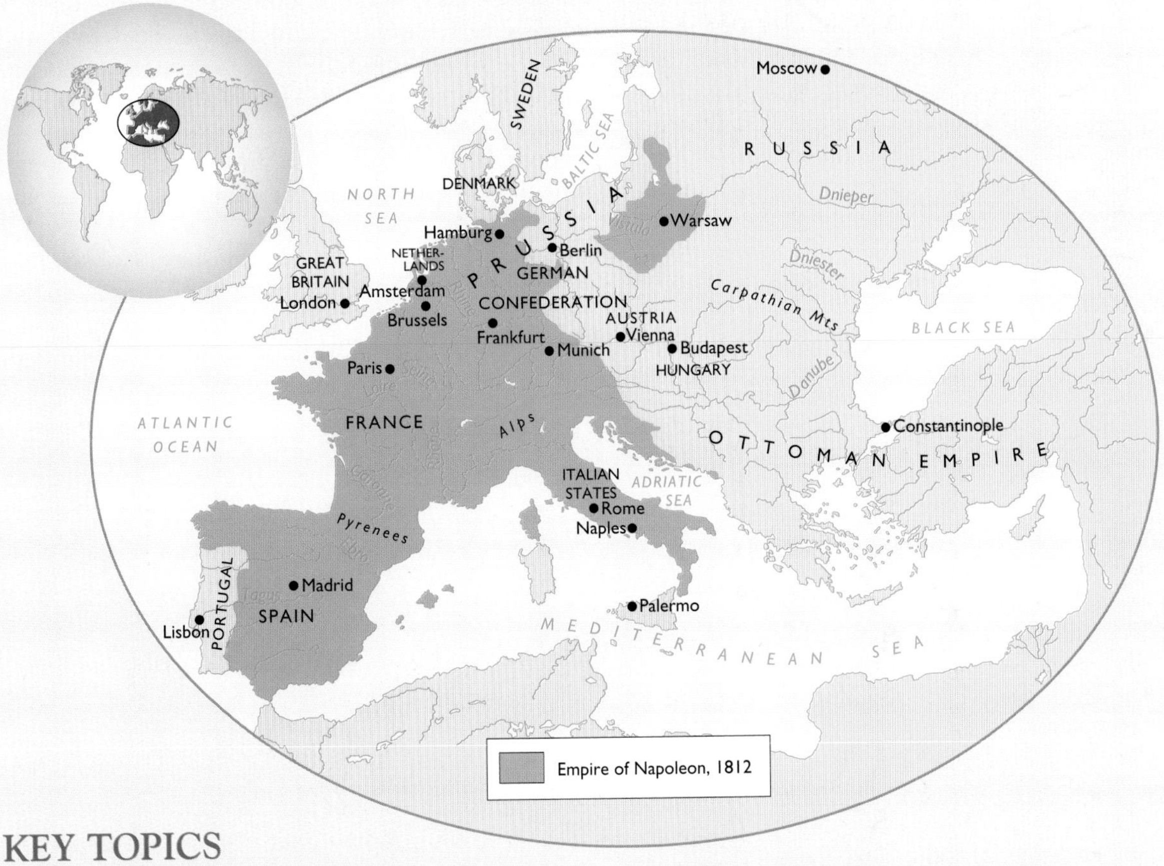

KEY TOPICS

- **Preludes to Revolution:** Nobles, peasants, and intellectuals resist the Old Regime.
- **The Rights of Man:** Liberal leaders declare the rights of men (but not women).
- **The Birth of a Nation:** Peasant protest and urban riot drive the French Revolution onward.
- **The Imperial Adventure:** Seizing power, Napoleon reconfigures Europe and returns France to autocracy.
- **Power to the People:** Victorious over Napoleon, Europe's major nations set out to suppress revolution and the very thought of revolution; but citizens demand autonomy.

Thermidor *On July 26, 1794—in the hot summer month the French revolutionaries had renamed "**Thermidor**"—Maximilien Robespierre (1758–1794) addressed the National Convention for the last time. For two years he had led that body of young radicals in loosing a torrent of change and spilling a torrent of blood. But on this morning, his former colleagues shouted him down. The next day, he was arrested and tried; the following morning, executed by the guillotine. The* ***Terror*** *he had launched with his decrees, and defended with his fiery orations, ended with his death.*

Robespierre was the last leader of the Revolution that destroyed absolute monarchy in France and, with it, the ***Ancien Régime***, or "Old Regime," the society of traditional Europe. In 1870, kings and aristocrats still ruled nearly everywhere, but they trembled as they clung to power, besieged by the twin forces of liberalism and nationalism that sparked the energies of the massed peoples of Europe. "The people" had made their presence felt, and announced their implacable demands.

The French Revolution transformed Europe, leading the way to a new kind of nation, responsible not to kings but to the masses of its people—citizens, no longer subjects.

PRELUDES TO REVOLUTION

Enlightenment critics of the Old Regime had identified its faults: absolute monarchs, foolish laws, unproductive aristocrats, prying churches, and inquisitive censors. Resistance to these phenomena began even before the French Revolution broke out in 1789.

Resistance to Absolutism

The English launched the first successful assault on absolute monarchy in two revolutions that culminated in 1688, establishing the principle that the monarch ruled only by consent of Parliament (see Chapter 15). Later, in British North America, the very concept of monarchy received a powerful rebuke in the War for Independence of 1775–1783 (see Chapter 19). The new United States created a government with balanced executive, judicial, and legislative powers defined by a written constitution. As Thomas Paine (1757–1809) proclaimed in his tract *Common Sense* (1776), in America, "the law is king."

Meanwhile, the Italian republics and the Swiss cantons had long managed without kings, but only on the fringes of the political mainstream. The Dutch Republic (created when the Northern Netherlands had gained independence from Habsburg Spain) was vulnerable to the aspirations of the princes of Orange who sought to make their leadership hereditary. The monarchs of Sweden and Poland were overshadowed by a powerful nobility that resisted the development of centralized monarchies. In Poland, this attitude resulted in the annihilation of the nation by its aggressive neighbors in 1795.

A few "enlightened" monarchs adopted the *philosophes*' advice to promote the welfare of their people (see Chapter 17). In Prussia, Frederick II (r. 1740–1786) reformed the state bureaucracy and promoted industry and commerce. In Austria, Joseph II (r. 1765–1790) freed the serfs, while his successor Leopold II (r. 1790–1792) introduced enlightened principles when he ruled the Italian state of Tuscany (1765–1790). In Russia, Catherine the Great (r. 1762–1796) planned to reform that nation's legal code in line with Enlightenment principles. A patron of education and the arts, Catherine argued that a monarch "possesses all the means for the eradication of all harm and looks on the general good as his own."

Empty coffers: *In this lampoon of the French financial crisis of the years before 1789, entitled "Le Déficit," Louis XVI and his chief finance minister contemplate the crown's empty coffers while a priest and an aristocrat exit with bags full of money.* (British Museum, London)

"Enlightened" monarchs introduced reforms while defending the institution of monarchy itself.

In France, aristocrats resisted the claims of absolute monarchy. In contrast to the era of Louis XIV (r. 1643–1715), when the most important noblemen were summoned to the court at Versailles to dance attendance on the Sun King, their successors claimed greater independence. When in 1787 the young king Louis XVI (r. 1774–1793), desperate for funds, proposed a new tax from which nobles would not be exempt, they refused. Having nowhere else to turn, the king summoned the Estates-General, a medieval assembly which had not met since 1614. This course of action was fateful both for the monarchy and, ultimately, the aristocracy. It provoked the Revolution that swiftly followed.

Peasant Revolts and Free Trade

While landowning elites resisted absolute monarchs, peasants often rebelled against landowners. Peasant revolts were numerous, violent, and unsuccessful in European history, regularly kindled anew by famine or abuse.

The eighteenth century saw a hardening of the landlords' position throughout Europe. In a market economy, where agricultural surpluses could be sold for a profit, landlords pushed to increase the productivity of their lands. They deprived villagers of the rights to graze livestock on common land, or to glean forest products and insisted on the performance of "servile duties" traditionally attached to laborers' plots of soil.

While the *philosophes* denounced these labor services, the strategies of economic theorists (in France, the **physiocrats**) exacerbated the hardships of the poor. The "free trade" policies they advocated (*laissez-faire*, in French, "let it be") interfered with traditional anti-famine practices of grain hoarding by local lords or municipalities. Now, in periods of scarcity, people could obtain grain only by paying a steep price. Those who could not pay starved. Remote from rural farms, the urban poor were especially vulnerable.

Meanwhile, merchants and entrepreneurs opposed the mercantilist practices favored by absolute monarchs (see Chapter 16), such as the tariffs and fees that burdened trade; the granting of monopolies; the obsession with bullion; and the costly competition between nations. To these, the physiocrats again proposed the alternative principle of free trade. Their critique of mercantilist controls was incorporated in the influential *Inquiry into the Nature and Causes of the Wealth of Nations* (1776) by the Scots philosopher Adam Smith.

The War of Ideas

As nobles and kings, landlords and peasants, mercantilist statesmen and entrepreneurs confronted each other, Enlightenment thinkers engaged in a war of ideas against the evils of superstition and intolerance.

Enlightenment critics identified the Church as the sinister agent of superstition. It promoted childish beliefs in its saints and miracles, persecuted dissenters, preached intolerance, and opposed the explorations of philosophy. The clergy in general, and especially the elite order of Jesuits, were seen as defenders of absolute monarchy.

As two alternatives to established religion, intellectuals favored Deism and Freemasonry. The first won favor because it was free of doctrine, positing only a "supreme being," the creator of the universe. The second gained adherents because it claimed authority in a pre-Christian and rationalist tradition based on an ideal of brotherly love. Both of these "religious" movements formed part of a process of **secularization** that had been underway since the Italian Renaissance (see Chapter 13). Thereafter, the spread of literacy and advent of printing promoted a culture in which received dogmas were increasingly open to question. By the mid-eighteenth century, the cheap print media exposed even the poor to critiques of the political status quo. Subversive literature, including pornographic caricatures of such figures as Louis XVI's hated consort Marie-Antoinette (1755–1793), inflamed popular resentment of the monarchy.

Intellectuals, merchants, peasants, and aristocrats all resisted the ways of the Old Regime. Although its vestiges lingered in places until World War I, it was already moribund by May 1789, when there arrived in Versailles—a royal palace twelve miles from Paris—the elected representatives to the Estates-General.

THE RIGHTS OF MAN

This arrival opened the first phase of the French Revolution: a liberal revolution that established the "rights of man and the citizen." Those rights included the civil rights defined in the unwritten English constitution and the written American one. They also included more universal concepts of right derived from ancient philosophy via Thomas Hobbes (1588–1679), John Locke (1632–1704), and the *philosophes*. These rights would be guaranteed under a constitutional monarchy.

A second phase of the Revolution began soon after the first and unfolded simultaneously: the radical revolution. Its effect was to transform the society of the Old Regime, and reinvent the cultural values and religious beliefs of the people. These changes were achieved by the mobilization of masses of people, who gained access to the political process for the first time.

The Work of the National Assembly

The Estates-General (an assembly of representatives from the First, Second, and Third **Estates** consisting respectively of the clergy, nobility, and all commoners) had not met for 175 years. During the winter of 1788–1789, the electorate, comprising all adult male taxpayers, chose its representatives and compiled some 40,000 *cahiers de doléances*, or "notebooks of grievances." The grievances included complaints about judicial incompetence, official misbehavior, the censorship of the press, religious intolerance, abuses by landowners, unjust taxation, and the condition of the roads. They amounted to a critique of the existing political system, and showed considerable agreement across class lines. Seventy-four percent of the participants from the Third Estate, for example, demanded liberty of the press, as did eighty-eight percent of the nobility; forty-two percent of the Third and thirty-five percent of the nobility advocated Free Trade.

One set of complaints concerned the structure of the Estates-General itself. In 1614, it had consisted of the same number of representatives of each of the three estates, which voted as a body, so that the whole assembly produced only three votes. Two estates could thus ally to determine the outcome; the privileged First and Second Estates often dictating to the Third.

In 1788, liberal critics targeted these "forms of 1614" for change. They pointed out that the Third Estate could no longer be considered a single social order of "commoners." Comprising some ninety-eight percent of the French population, it consisted of people from different regions, occupations, and levels of wealth; master craftsmen and unskilled laborers; the highly educated and those who couldn't read. Nearly ten percent of the Third Estate consisted of members of the bourgeoisie, which was itself divided between merchants, public officials, property owners, and professionals. Why should so large and diverse a group receive only one vote of three?

Other issues raised by the summoning of the Estates-General were stated with particular clarity in the pamphlet entitled *What Is the Third Estate?* by Emmanuel Joseph Sieyès (1748–1836), a young priest of bourgeois origin. He concluded that the Third had no need of the First and Second Estates, but constituted a complete nation, whose members performed all the productive work. They, and not idle clerics and aristocrats, were the nation. They should be allotted votes accordingly.

Sieyès modestly requested just two critical changes—changes also requested by other pamphleteers and listed in many of the *cahiers*. The first was that the number of representatives of the Third Estate should equal the total number allotted to the other two; the second was that the votes be counted by head. The effect of these proposals would be that the Third Estate, by acquiring the support of one of the other groups, could achieve a majority and control the assembly.

***Jacques-Louis David,* Oath of the Tennis Court:** *The Revolution proper began with the convocation of the Estates-General in May 1789 and the Third Estate's historic decision to constitute itself a National Assembly. Here in Jacques-Louis David's 1790 painting, members of the Third Estate, barred from the main meeting room, meet at a nearby tennis court and swear never to disband until a Constitution has been established.* (Musée Carnavalet, Paris)

HOW MANY?

Land Ownership by Social Category on the Eve of the French Revolution

	Clergy	Nobility	Bourgeoisie	Peasantry
Land in France owned by each group	6–10%	20–25%	30%	40–45%
Each group as a percentage of the total population	2%	1.5%	8.4%	82–87%

One of the long-term causes of revolution in France was the great inequality in wealth, measured in land ownership. This graph shows that two of the smallest groups in the population–clergy and nobility, or the First and Second Estates–together owned nearly one-third of all land in France.

In the end, only the first of these proposals was approved. On May 5, 1789, when the representatives to the Estates-General arrived in Versailles, the representatives of the Third Estate numbered about 600, double the number for each of the other two estates. But when the elaborate preliminaries were over, they were instructed to vote by order and not by head.

The method of voting was accordingly the first item of business taken up by the Estates-General in debates that lasted several weeks. The king and his advisers, meanwhile, contemplated the possibility of an assembly where the Third Estate possessed a majority. On June 17 the Third Estate announced itself to be the **National Assembly**, a body truly representative of the people of France. The king struck back, and on June 21, the delegates of the Third Estate found their meeting hall barred. They reconvened in an indoor tennis court near by.

There the stakes were raised. The issue was no longer the structure of the Estates-General, nor even the method of voting. The angry representatives swore an oath that they would not disband until they had written a constitution for France. That constitution would secure the rights of man, and the demotion of the king.

From 1789 to 1791 the representatives to the National Assembly composed the legislation that would define a new state. They came from the educated bourgeoisie. They were young. Most were lawyers. They addressed the key matters of landowners' rights, the power and wealth of the Church, and the rights of all citizens. Finally, they debated the place of the monarchy in a new constitution.

The events of summer 1789 drove the agenda of the National Assembly forward. The citizens of Paris seized a royal fortress, and peasant rebellions erupted around the nation (see below). Frightened aristocrats fled from the "Great Fear," as the rural revolt was called, many seeking refuge in friendlier nations where they remained throughout the Revolution. In a tense all-night session on August 4, 1789, the Assembly voted to dismantle the customary rights of landowners, and thus to abolish the system of noble privilege that had prevailed for a millennium.

Later that month, the National Assembly addressed the issue of civil rights. They promulgated on August 27 the "Declaration of the Rights of Man and the Citizen." This spelled out key republican principles and established the framework for a future constitution. A later version of the "Declaration" is part of that nation's constitution today.

Opening with the statement that "ignorance, neglect, or contempt of human rights, are the sole causes" of failed government, the "Declaration" defines those rights in full. It affirms that "men are born, and always continue, free, and equal in respect of their rights," and that the purpose of government is to preserve "the natural and inalienable rights of man." Human liberty is unrestricted, except by the need to allow for the liberty of others. Free speech and freedom of worship are also to be guaranteed, along with civil protections against improper arrest and prosecution. Citizens are accorded the right to consent to taxes levied upon them, and private property is protected.

Article X of the "Declaration" provides for freedom of worship. To achieve that goal, revolutionary leaders needed to rein in the powerful Roman Catholic Church. On November 2, 1789, the Assembly confiscated all church property, amounting to fifteen percent of the land in France. The following month, it issued a new paper currency, backed by the huge value of former church lands, now considered national property.

On February 13, 1790, the Assembly further suppressed convents and monasteries in Paris. On July 12, 1790, it promulgated the Civil Constitution of the Clergy, which dismantled the traditional institution of the Church. All priests (totaling some 40,000) would receive salaries from the new secular state, and freedom of worship was extended to Protestants and Jews. By an addendum of November 27, 1790, priests were required to swear an oath of loyalty to the revolutionary government. Only about one-half complied; many others, in hiding, became a focus for resistance to the Revolution.

On September 3, 1791, the National Assembly approved in final form the constitution it had pledged to formulate. Reluctantly, the king acceded. Allowed to retain his title, and permitted direct authority over foreign policy and the army, Louis XVI surrendered his claim to absolute power.

The Legislative Assembly and National Convention

At this point, the members of the National Assembly surrendered power of their own. Having completed

WITNESSES

The Collapse of the Old Regime

Abbé Sieyès asks: "What is the Third Estate?" (1789): We have three questions to ask:

1st. What is the third estate? Everything.

2nd. What has it been heretofore in the political order? Nothing.

3rd. What does it demand? To become something therein. . . .

What are the essentials of national existence and prosperity? *Private* enterprise and *public* functions. Private enterprise may be divided into four classes: [those engaged in agriculture; those engaged in industry and production; "dealers and merchants"; and the professional and service classes, ranging from scientists to domestic servants]. . . . Such are the labors which sustain society. Who performs them? The third estate.

Public functions. . . . may [also] be classified under four headings: the Sword, the Robe, the Church, and the Administration. . . .[T]he third estate everywhere constitutes nineteen-twentieths of them, except that it is burdened with all that is really arduous, with all the tasks that the privileged order refuses to perform. . . .

Who, then, would dare to say that the third estate has not within itself all that is necessary to constitute a complete nation?

(From J. H. Stewart ed., *A Documentary Survey of the French Revolution*, 1951)

Decrees passed the night of August 4, 1789, in response to the "Great Fear": 1. The National Assembly abolishes the feudal regime entirely, and decrees that both feudal and [other contractual] rights and dues . . . are abolished without indemnity. . . .4. All seigneurial courts of justice are suppressed without any indemnity; nevertheless the officials of such courts shall continue in office until the National Assembly has provided for the establishment of a new judicial organization. 5. Tithes of every kind . . . are abolished subject to the devising of means for providing in some other manner for the expenses of divine worship, . . . and for all establishments, seminaries, schools, colleges, hospitals, communities and others, to the maintenance of which they are now assigned. . . . 9. Pecuniary privileges, personal or real, in matters of taxation are abolished forever. Collection shall be made from all citizens and on all property, in the same manner and in the same form. . . . 11. All citizens may be admitted, without distinction of birth, to all ecclesiastical, civil, and military employments and offices.

(From J. H. Stewart ed., *A Documentary Survey of the French Revolution*, 1951)

The foundations of liberal government are defined in the Declaration of the Rights of Man and the Citizen (1789): The Representatives of the French People, organized in National Assembly, considering that ignorance, forgetfulness, or contempt of the rights of man are the sole cause of public misfortunes and the corruption of governments, have resolved to set forth in a solemn declaration the natural, inalienable, and sacred rights of man, in order that such declaration, continually before all members of the social body, may be a perpetual reminder of their rights and duties. . . . 1. Men are born and remain free and equal in rights; social distinctions may be based only upon general usefulness. 2. The aim of every political association is the preservation of the natural and inalienable rights of man; these rights are liberty, property, security, and resistance to oppression. 3. The source of all sovereignty resides essentially in the nation; no group, no individual may exercise authority not emanating expressly therefrom.

(From J. H. Stewart ed., *A Documentary Survey of the French Revolution*, 1951) their mission, they intended to go home. A decree that none of their number would be eligible to serve in the next assembly (introduced, ironically, by Robespierre), meant that a new body of delegates must be elected to a new institution. The delegates of the Legislative Assembly who took up their one-year term in October were younger and less experienced than the representatives chosen in 1789.

When the Legislative Assembly concluded its term in September 1792, a third assembly convened: the National Convention. Legislators who had served previously were eligible for election, and its delegates included both experienced legislators and younger entrants to the legislative project. It also included persons of different "parties," or sets of political beliefs. Since 1787, political clubs had sprung up all over Paris and in the provinces, numbering 4000 by 1794. Among these were the Girondins (named after the Gironde region in southwest France), and the **Jacobins** (named after their meeting-place in the Dominican church of St. Jacques) led by Maximilien Robespierre. The average age of the delegates to the Convention was a youthful thirty-five, and most were open to radical change.

The more moderate Girondins had considerable influence at first, but they were shouldered aside by the more extreme Jacobins, who emerged as leaders of the Convention and of the Revolution in the fall of 1792. Over the next three years, these revolutionaries attended to the unseating of the king and the radical transformation of society.

Meanwhile, events in Paris had captured the attention of observers from abroad. Among them was the professional revolutionary Tom Paine (1737–1809). Author of rousing pamphlets promoting the cause of American independence, Paine wrote his monumental *Rights of Man* during his stay in France in 1791 and 1792. *The Rights of Man* interpreted the Revolution as a necessary struggle between liberty and tyranny. Paine was arrested by Jacobin leaders in December 1793, and emerged from prison nearly one year later to find the Revolution over.

The English writer Mary Wollstonecraft (1759–1797) celebrated the Revolution in *A Vindication of the Rights of Men*, written in Paris in 1790. When the National Convention voted to exclude women from political life, however, Wollstonecraft responded with *A Vindication of the Rights of Woman* (1792), a revolutionary work of a different sort—the first major work of Western feminism.

Edmund Burke (1729–1797), another Briton riveted by events in France, challenged in his *Reflections on the Revolution in France* (1790) the basic assumption of revolutionary activity: that it is possible to create a new society better than the old. The wisdom of past human communities, Burke argued, had produced leaders, religious values, the rituals of civilized human association. While these had defects, could a single generation concoct new social forms without also planting the seeds of new forms of injustice and cruelty?

Written early in the Revolution, the *Reflections* seems to predict the turmoil that soon followed. The Revolution destroyed much, as Burke feared, and it created a government perhaps no better than that it replaced. Soon the struggle grew violent, spreading into the streets and fields where the poor pushed the Revolution in unanticipated directions.

THE BIRTH OF A NATION

From 1789 through 1794, a second phase of the French Revolution unfolded which sought the transformation of society—a *total* revolution. Its architects were the crowds of people, and their self-appointed agents, who had heretofore occupied no place in the political hierarchy. Their activity marks the entry into history of "the people." It consisted of artisans, peasants, and dayworkers, and women as well as men—all those who had traditionally been excluded from power.

Peasants and Sans-Culottes

Two agents of revolution consisted of two groups: the peasants, including both proprietors and landless laborers from all over France; and the laborers, artisans, and shopkeepers of the cities, primarily of Paris. These were the *sans-culottes*, so called because they wore long trousers rather than the knee-breeches and silk stockings of the elites. Their wives, daughters, and mothers also joined in, at times vigorously. Within the first six months of the Revolution, peasants and *sans-culottes*, both armed and dangerous, burst onto the political stage.

Bastille and Famine In June 1789, disturbing rumors reached Paris of events under way at Versailles. Would the king send an army to subdue the Parisians as he had used armed guards to intimidate the delegates to the Third Estate? On July 14, a crowd of 80,000 rushed to the Bastille, an ancient royal fortress then on the edge of the city. Commanded by an old governor in charge of a small garrison, it interested the crowd because of its ammunition stores. They stormed in, released the prisoners (there were only seven), killed several soldiers and the governor himself, whose severed head they displayed on a spike. The storming of the Bastille remains today the symbol of the French Revolution.

News of the fall of the Bastille reached Versailles along with reports of mass peasant uprisings. Armed bands roamed the countryside, breaking into the landowners' great houses and castles in search of documents specifying labor and monetary dues. These they burned, and often the houses as well. The Great Fear stimulated the National Assembly to abolish all traces of noble landlord privilege, as has been seen, and, in this environment of great urgency, to issue the "Declaration of the Rights of Man."

In Paris, meanwhile, famine held sway. The grain crop had failed in 1785, 1787, and 1788; stores of food had vanished; and the price of bread soared to eighty-eight percent of a worker's daily wage. As often in traditional society, women, whose responsibility it was to feed the children, raged at the food shortage. On October 5, 1789, around 10,000 Parisian women, armed with pikes, knives, clubs, and muskets, marched in a driving rain on the palace of Versailles. Accompanying them was a contingent of 12,000 soldiers commanded by the nobleman the Marquis de Lafayette (1757–1834), who had once fought in support of the American Revolution.

Revolution in the streets: *Parisian citizens stormed the Bastille on July 14, 1789 and provided themselves with gunpowder with which to defend the revolution. In this contemporary illustration by Cholat, ordinary people, male and female, engage in decisive action. Contrast the image on page 612, where male members of a well-dressed elite dedicate themselves to the project of defining a new political order.* (Musée Carnavalet, Paris)

The women burst into the palace and killed some guards. They compelled the king, queen, and their son to return with them to Paris, shouting as they marched that they had gotten "the Baker, the Baker's wife, and the Baker's boy"—their taunts bespeaking their expectations that their royal captive would somehow provide them with bread. The king was thus removed from his zone of power in Versailles to Paris, where the people held sway. The National Assembly followed. Paris was thereafter the home of the Revolution.

Defending the Revolution From 1791 to 1793, the presence of the king, the fervor of the crowd, and the anxieties of other European monarchs were the forces that reshaped the Revolution. While the king still hoped to preserve his authority, the National Assembly attempted to design a constitution, and the people, now "citizens," who milled in the streets and snatched up each morsel of news, demanded famine relief, a responsive government, and the destruction of their enemies.

On June 20–21, 1791, the king fled Paris with his family; caught and arrested, he returned five days later, a prisoner. All this time, noble refugees urged rulers abroad to intervene against the Revolution, who eyed nervously the events unfolding so near their borders. On August 27, 1791, the monarchs of Prussia and Austria issued the Declaration of Pillnitz, announcing their intent to do so. Joining into a coalition several months later, thus provoking a French declaration of war, they invaded in August 1792 to be confronted, and repulsed, by French armies. Here began France's war on the monarchies of Europe that lasted until 1815.

Paris was declared a Commune on August 10, 1792, its citizens collectively dedicated to the defense of the revolutionary cause. Angry mobs stormed the royal Tuileries palace. In September, they invaded the prisons that held suspected enemies of the Revolution, whom they summarily tried and murdered with pikes, clubs, and knives. These September Massacres resulted in the slaughter of more than 1200 prisoners—one-half of those detained. On September 22, the National Convention proclaimed France to be a republic. That day became the first day of the first month of Year I of a new revolutionary calendar.

In December, the king faced trial. "The tree of liberty can only grow if watered by the blood of kings," pleaded one deputy. By a slim majority, the Convention sentenced him to death. On January 21, 1793, he was executed before 20,000 onlookers by the guillotine, newly invented to be both humane and democratic. The executioner displayed the royal head, for the "crowned fools" of Europe to see and reflect upon. By early March, Britain, the Netherlands, Spain, and Sardinia had joined the First Coalition against France. Surrounded and isolated, the French mobilized furiously to defend their Revolution.

On April 6, 1793, the Committee of Public Safety was formed to do whatever was necessary to mobilize the nation. Led at first by Georges-Jacques Danton (1759–1794), it was soon taken over by Maximilien Robespierre, who saw to his rival's execution in April 1794. For a little over a year, Robespierre managed France and the Revolution.

On August 23, 1793, the **Committee of Public Safety** ordered a "mass levy" of troops—a target figure of 300,000 men. Every adult male was eligible, with unmarried or childless men between eighteen and twenty-five to be called up first. Women were to be mobilized, too, "to make tents and clothes, and [to] serve in the hospitals." Even the old men had their assigned task: to "preach the unity of the Republic and hatred of kings." The mass levy was a recipe for total war, calling for the dedication of each citizen to the new **Republic**.

Robespierre's mass levy marks a new departure in warfare. Until now, army officers almost invariably came from the nobility, precisely the class that had fled France in 1789. Now officers would be recruited from the people, and promoted on the basis of merit. The million men (out of a population of 28 million) mobilized in the 1780s were *"enfants de la patrie"* ("children of the fatherland"), in the words of the battle-song "Marseillaise," fighting for France and the Republic. It was in the French revolutionary armies that nationalism was born—an ideology centered on allegiance to the nation, its culture, and people that would figure centrally in Europe's subsequent political history.

The French army mobilized not only against foreign enemies, but also against counter-revolutionaries. A revolt struck in the Vendée region in the west from March to December 1793. Ascribed to "the ignorance, fanaticism and subservience of the country people" or "the criminality and hypocrisy of the priests," it involved 60–100,000 artisans and peasants, encouraged by dissident clergy. Loyalist soldiers of artisan and peasant origin brutally suppressed the uprising. Citizens shot citizens in the Vendée, in massacres that prefigured those of modern times.

The Terror Critics of the Revolution were also targeted for suppression. From June 1793 to July 1794, as many as 300,000 political dissidents were imprisoned, and tens of thousands executed. The victims included persons who were guilty only of having once been privileged—among them the chemist Antoine-Laurent Lavoisier (1743–1794) and the *philosophe* Marie Jean Antoine-Nicholas Caritat, Marquis de Condorcet (1743–1794), author of a rosy *Sketch for a Historical Picture of the Progress of the Human Mind*. Condorcet died on his first night in prison, perhaps by suicide. These two were among a group of some 200 writers, intellectuals, and artists who constituted the French cultural elite in 1789. Nearly half of France's cultural leaders were detained, watched, driven abroad, or executed during the Revolution.

This period of extreme repression is known as the Reign of Terror. Its main author, and last victim, was Robespierre, whose activity foreshadows that of the totalitarian dictators of the twentieth century. In his earlier career he had been an idealistic disciple of Rousseau. And in the National Assembly, where he pressed for democratic reform, his principled stance won him the epithet "the Incorruptible." Assuming leadership of the Jacobins by 1791, he won election that year as a delegate to the National Convention. In 1793, he supported the execution of the king and the purge of the Girondins.

Elected to the Committee of Public Safety in July 1793, Robespierre became its spokesperson. He advocated the emergency measures undertaken to mobilize the nation and destroy political opponents in 1793–1794, initiating the Reign of Terror, the perhaps inevitable consequence of the dictator's creed that Revolution was a "war waged by liberty against its enemies." The purges of the spring of 1794 worried even his supporters. To prevent more devastations, the Convention had Robespierre arrested and tried on July 27, 1794 (9 Thermidor). Along with more than a hundred of his supporters, he died by the guillotine the next day.

Robespierre's call for the suppression of all dissent opened the path to even greater violence. In his brilliant speeches, the confusion between democratic idealism and brutal repression is striking. His important speech of February 5, 1794, for example, argued the need to defend democratic virtue with "terror"—a just and ideal violence. The republic was in peril both externally ("all the despots surround you") and internally ("all the friends of tyranny conspire"). It must "annihilate" both sets of enemies or "perish with its fall." Both virtue and terror are essential in time of revolution: "virtue, without which terror is destructive; terror, without which virtue is impotent." In these startling phrases, Robespierre, demagogue and dictator, manipulates language to link the antitheses of virtue and terror.

The Culture of Revolution

Amid the terror and political transformations of the early 1790s, revolutionary leaders also engineered a cultural revolution that achieved the reshaping of religious and intellectual values, the democratization of society, and the remodeling of the family. It aimed to eradicate all the imprints of custom and tradition on the human spirit, beginning with Christian belief and aristocratic privilege.

By 1790, the Roman Catholic Church had lost its property and its privileges. In 1792, the Convention desanctified the church of Saint Geneviève, patron saint of Paris, and rededicated it as the Panthéon to the celebration of national heroes. On October 5, 1793, in the midst of the Terror, Christianity was abolished in France. In November, the Festival of Reason was organized to proclaim the end of religion and the elevation of the human mind. Averse to atheism, Robespierre offered instead the deist "cult of the Supreme Being," launched with the Festival of the Supreme Being on June 8, 1794. These efforts to eradicate Christianity from French soil and spirit did not succeed. Many people clung to their faith and rituals. They protected the priests who had gone into hiding and detested the Revolution.

Secularization and rationalization came also to the system of weights and measures, which was reorganized on a decimal basis, requiring the creation of new units of measurement. The "meter," for instance, currently the basis of measurements in most Western nations, was defined in 1791 by the French Academy of Sciences as a precise fraction of the quadrant of the Earth's circumference running from the North Pole through Paris to the equator.

The revolutionary spirit also called for the reorganization of the calendar. To replace names derived from classical or Christian concepts, new ones were selected that reflected the natural year—"Germinal," or "budding," for mid-March to mid-April; "Thermidor," or "heat," for mid-July–mid-August; "Brumaire," or "foggy," for mid-October–mid-November. The years were renumbered to recognize revolutionary events. Year I was defined as beginning at the moment of the creation of the Republic (declared on September 22, 1792). This system of numeration, based on secular events, contrasted sharply with earlier calendrical schemes measured from a presumed date of the creation of the world or the irrelevant date, as it seemed to these revolutionaries, of the birth of Jesus.

Revolutionary culture spurred the publication of newspapers and pamphlets. Even ordinary people had access to these digests of the revolutionary events of the day. Among the revolutionary leaders, Jean-Paul Marat (1743–1793) and Jacques-René Hébert (1757–1794) (the first murdered, the second guillotined) were journalists who used the press to forge a national consciousness.

New outlooks also shaped daily behavior, transforming the manners of the Old Regime. The deference formerly shown to persons of high social status was abolished. Where it was previously customary to bow to members of the elites and address them as "*monsieur*" and "*madame*," it was now decreed that all people address each other as "*citoyen*" ("citizen") and "*citoyenne*," using the familiar "*tu*" ("you"), rather than the formal "*vous*." Men of the bourgeoisie adopted the long trousers of the *sans-culottes*, and wealthy women dressed modestly in plain fabrics.

The democratization of society extended to the matter of slavery. In 1791, slavery was abolished within France, and in 1794, abolition was extended to the colonies (see Chapter 19). On the French Caribbean island of Saint-Domingue, the abolition of slavery stimulated an independence movement headed by the black general Toussaint L'Ouverture (1748–1803). Although L'Ouverture was later a victim of Napoleon's attempt to reconquer the colony, the nation of Haiti won its independence.

The family was the scene of a different kind of slavery, according to revolutionaries—the product of patriarchal arrangements for the preservation of

MUST READS

Books and Pamphlets from the French Revolution

Emmanuel Sieyès	*What Is the Third Estate?* (1789)
Edmund Burke	*Reflections on the Revolution in France* (1790)
Olympe de Gouges	*Declaration of the Rights of Woman and the Citizen* (1791)
Tom Paine	*Rights of Man* (1791)
Mary Wollstonecraft	*A Vindication of the Rights of Woman* (1792)

WINDOWS ON

The Radical Revolution

Anonymous, **Execution of King Louis XVI, January 21, 1793**

The Abolition of Slavery Proclaimed to the Convention on 16 Pluviôse, Year II, c. ***1794***

Festival of the Supreme Being

Villeneuve*, Something to Ponder for the Crowned Fools of Europe, *1793

The Revolution entered a second, more radical stage after August 1792. The National Convention abolished the monarchy and proclaimed a Republic. On January 21, 1793, the deposed King Louis XVI went to the guillotine, as depicted in a contemporary painting (top). Supporters of the revolution vaunted the regicide, in a tone that echoed the message of the image shown here (right). The French inscription that accompanied the bloody, severed head of the king challenged the "crowned fools" of Europe to reflect on the fate of those who opposed the revolution.

The radical phase of the Revolution brought huge, if only temporary, social and cultural changes. Among the most positive was the abolition of slavery throughout the French Empire, which was proclaimed to the Convention on February 4, 1794 (left center). With the demotion of Roman Catholicism, Robespierre attempted to create a new kind of religion, fully rational and free of superstition, as he saw it. The engraving here depicts the Festival of the Supreme Being held on June 8, 1794 (left).

(top and left center: Musée Carnavalet, Paris; right and left: Bibliothèque Nationale, Paris)

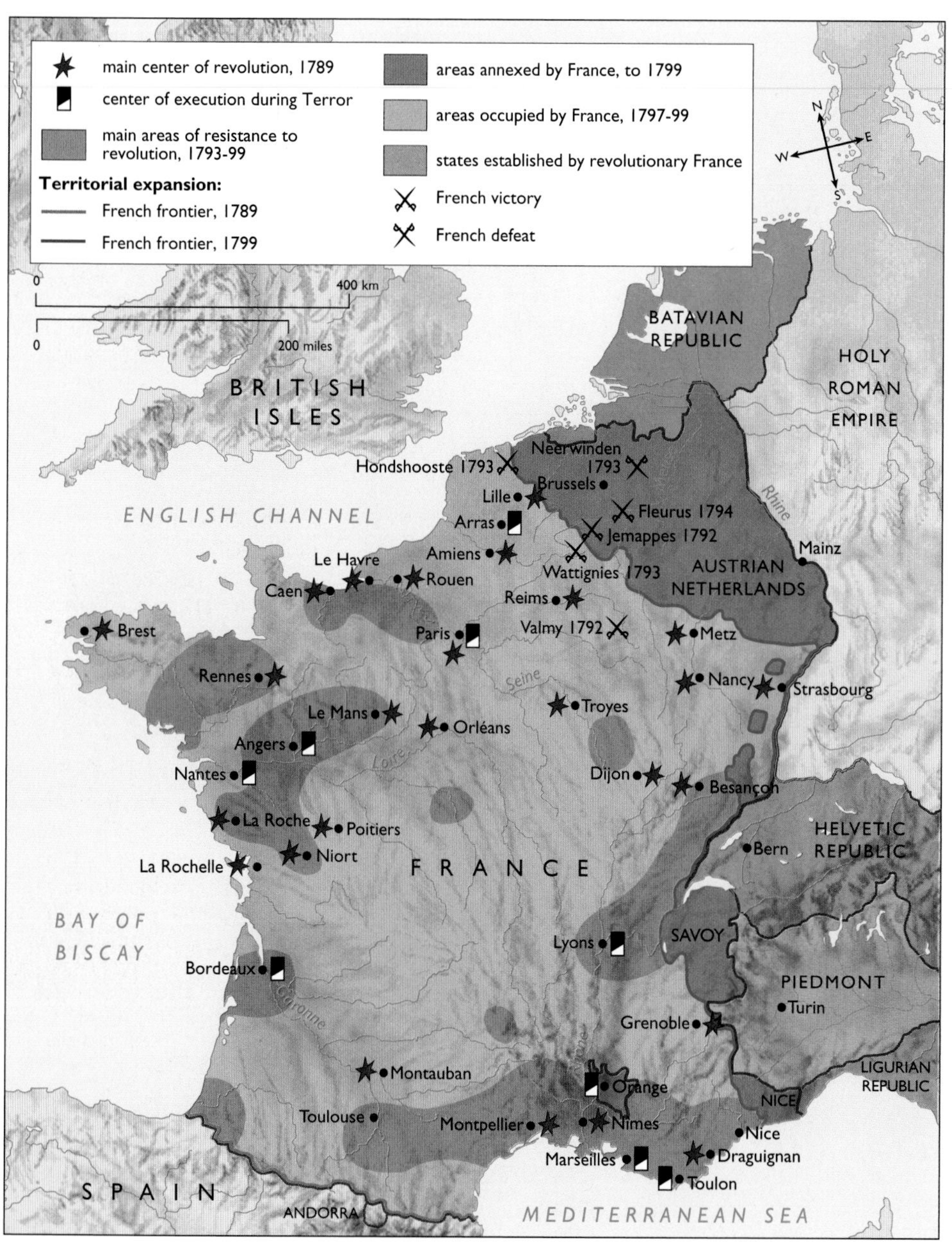

Map 20.1 The Revolution, 1789–1799: *The Revolution involved the whole of France, where entire regions were either loyal to the new government or in opposition. The Terror also affected the entire nation, although repression was centered in the capital. Even before Napoleon's advent, the revolutionary armies won victories against their European opponents. Shown here are main centers of revolutionary activity, executions during the Terror, and early battles.*

property. Fathers controlled their children's marriages and directed inheritances away from daughters so that elder sons could inherit family wealth intact. The Revolution introduced several laws that tore at this patriarchal structure. It legalized divorce, enabling women to exit families (as some 6000 did in Paris alone between 1793 and 1795). It mandated the sharing of inheritance among all heirs, female as well as male, where the deceased had not left a will. It even, briefly, declared equal inheritance rights for illegitimate offspring.

Despite the granting of these unprecedented rights, women did not gain the right to participate in civic life. Olympe de Gouges (1748–1793), a self-educated butcher's daughter, quickly detected the bias of revolutionary legislators. In response to the promulgation of the "Declaration of the Rights of Man" in August 1789, she published in 1791 her "Declaration of the Rights of Woman." Women, she argued, had heretofore suffered a double deprivation of rights, by the state on the one hand, and by their husbands and fathers on the other. Moreover, disturbingly, the male delegates to the National Assembly had not thought to do anything about it.

De Gouges presents these arguments in the Preface to her *Declaration of the Rights of Woman and the*

WITNESSES

Revolution Turns Radical

Olympe de Gouges demands rights for women also (1791): The mothers, daughters, sisters, representatives of the nation, ask to constitute a National Assembly. Considering that ignorance, forgetfulness or contempt of the rights of women are the sole causes of public miseries, and of corruption of governments, they have resolved to set forth in a solemn declaration, the natural, unalterable and sacred rights of woman, so that this declaration, being ever present to all members of the social body, may unceasingly remind them of their rights and their duties . . . Woman, wake up! The alarm bell of reason is making itself heard throughout the universe; recognize your rights. The powerful empire of nature is no longer beset by prejudices, fanaticism, superstition and lies. The torch of truth has dispelled all clouds of stupidity and usurpation. The enslaved man multiplied his forces but has had to resort to yours to break his chains. Once free he became unjust to his female companion. O women! women, when will you stop being blind? What advantages have you received from the revolution? A more profound scorn, a more marked contempt?
(From E. S. Riemer and J. C. Fout eds., *European Women: A Documentary History, 1789–1945*, 1980)

Decree establishing the *Levée en masse*, or mass levy of troops (August 23, 1793): Henceforth, until the enemies have been driven from the territory of the Republic, the French people are in permanent requisition for army service. The young men shall go to battle; the married men shall forge arms and transport provisions; the women shall make tents and clothes, and shall serve in the hospitals; the children shall turn old linen into lint; the old men shall repair to the public places, to stimulate the courage of the warriors and preach the unity of the Republic and hatred of kings. . . . The levy shall be general. Unmarried citizens or childless widowers, from eighteen to twenty-five years, shall go first; they shall meet, without delay, at the chief town of their districts. . . . The battalion organized in each district shall be united under a banner bearing the inscription: *The French people risen against tyrants.*
(From J. H. Stewart ed., *A Documentary Survey of the French Revolution*, 1951)

The Abbé Carrichon describes the execution by guillotine of a group of nobles (1793–1794): At last we reached the fatal spot. . . . The moment was overwhelming. . . . The sacrifice was due to begin. The noisy merriment of the spectators and their ghastly jibes add to the sufferings of the victims. . . . The executioner and his assistants climb on to the scaffold and arrange everything. The former puts on over his other clothes a blood-red overall. He places himself on the left ... while his assistants stand on the other side. . . . When everything is ready . . . [the first victim] goes up the steps with the help of the executioners. The chief headsman takes him by the left arm, the big assistant by the right and the other man by the legs. In a moment they lay him flat on his face and his head is cut off and thrown with his body into a great tumbril, where the bodies swam in blood: and so it goes on. . . . The Maréchale was the third to go up. They had to make an opening in the top of her dress to uncover her neck. Mme d'Ayen was the tenth.
(From G. Pernoud and S. Flaissie eds., *The French Revolution*, 1961)

Citizen. The main text, consisting of seventeen articles, amusingly parodies the "Declaration of the Rights of Man," unveiling its misogynist assumptions. According to de Gouges, women, as much men, are "born free," and in possession of inalienable rights no government may infringe. De Gouges pursues the logical implications of this principle. For example, in matters of criminal law, where women's presumed incapacity had exempted them from prosecution, she insists on their responsibility. Indeed, women have the right "to mount the scaffold," to face the supreme penalty. De Gouges herself was guillotined in 1793, a victim of the Reign of Terror that saw an activist for women's rights, however revolutionary, as an enemy of the Revolution.

The inability of male revolutionaries to undertake the civil liberation of women is not, in 1793, surprising. At that time, women's voices were only faintly heard (see Chapter 17). The demand for political rights was wholly new, as new as the meter and Year I. It could only have arisen in the context of a male revolution against illegitimate authority. Although men did not welcome feminist claims during the French Revolution, the revolutionary environment prompted the articulation of those claims.

The cultural revolution was as profound as the political, and ultimately as irreversible. And so it was that Robespierre fell from power not on July 27, 1794, but during Thermidor of the Year II. The Revolution would soon, once more, change course.

Reaction Sets In: The Directory

Robespierre's opponents took control of the National Convention. By August 1795, a new constitution provided for the creation of a five-man executive committee, the **Directory**, which would preside over an assembly elected by limited suffrage. (The election of 1792 had been, in contrast, by universal manhood suffrage.) It proceeded to limit the freedoms gained by the Revolution, to shed its cultural innovations, to repress dissent, and to prosecute abroad the war whose aim had shifted from self-defense to expansion. Luxury and gaiety returned in the circles of those who had profited from the Revolution, or whose wealth had survived it. Hardship returned to the now-tamed *sans-culottes*—the Revolution had not tamed the monsters of scarcity and inflation. The secret police monitored royalist and popular conspiracies alike. Repression and reaction reigned.

The liberal phase of the Revolution that began in 1789 won for the French the same kinds of rights that Anglo-Americans had achieved in their War for Independence and just-ratified Constitution (see Chapter 19). The radical phase of the Revolution also began in 1789. It was characterized by peremptory decrees, by the abolition of long-established customs, by the imposition of new ones, above all by violence. It was accomplished by the people *en masse*, peasants and the *sans-culottes*, unloosed by legislative assemblies whose modest programs for change escalated rapidly.

Both phases of the Revolution, the liberal and the radical, would be undone as the Directory yielded to Napoleon (1769–1821). Yet both had an afterlife, in France and beyond, in years to come.

THE IMPERIAL ADVENTURE

The Directory lasted for only four years. On one side, it faced resistance from royalists who wished to dismantle the Revolution and recover the Old Regime. On the other, it faced disenfranchised commoners, who still believed the Revolution was theirs. It suffered, too, from its own inefficiency, incompetence, and corruption. Financial problems went unresolved. The demands of the army aggravated the financial crisis.

The war begun in 1792 to defend the nation had become a ceaseless, roaming venture, which broadcast revolutionary ideas as it shuffled political boundaries and won glory for its generals. Outstanding among these was Napoleon Bonaparte, whose career emerged amid the smoke of the dying Revolution. It would not end until he had returned France to autocracy, and transformed Europe.

The Coming of Napoleon

Napoleon Bonaparte would have been a nobody forever in the pre-revolutionary army where only men of high social rank attained the top positions. He came from a minor noble family of Corsica, a newly acquired Mediterranean island, whose native language was closer to Italian than to French. He suffered the humiliations of being poor, short, and foreign in the military academy where he was sent to prepare for the best career open to boys of his background. Yet he displayed his talents early: he won a commission in the artillery in 1785 when still adolescent; and in 1793, at age twenty-four, seized the fortified harbor of Toulon for the Revolution in the face of a British naval assault. In October 1795, he won the gratitude of the Directory when he dispersed royalist dissidents (killing about 100 of them) with, as he is said to have remarked, "a whiff of grapeshot." Rewarded with promotion, he departed for wars abroad where the rippling effects of the Revolution in France began to be felt.

By 1795, the First Coalition that had formed against revolutionary France included Austria, Russia, Britain, the Netherlands, Spain, and Sardinia; Prussia

Le Gros, Napoleon on the Battlefield of Eylau: *A legislator, a critic, an educator, Napoleon was above all a war-maker—a successful one, too, until the last years of his career. In this 1808 painting he is seen with his loyal followers and soldiers on the field of the battle of Eylau in 1807.* (Louvre, Paris)

had withdrawn. During the next four years, the French would oppose the Austrians in Italy and the British wherever they had interests—in the Mediterranean and North Africa, India, and the Caribbean. Napoleon fought both sets of adversaries.

From spring 1796 to late 1797, Napoleon stormed through northern Italy. He transformed his troops into a dauntless force capable of speed and concentrated attack. By the Treaty of Campo Formio (October 17, 1797), Napoleon became master of the region, much of which he reorganized as the Cisalpine and Ligurian Republics, satellites of France. The peace settled, Napoleon returned to France to promote his project to defeat the critical enemy: Britain.

Napoleon's career in Italy already displayed the features that would characterize his later military ventures. He did not merely win battles. He also reshaped states, and did so with a purpose beyond territorial gain. He built more coherent, governable states than those he found in his path. Meanwhile, his extraordinary charisma won him the devotion of his troops and impressed spectators throughout Europe.

He was also, in his way, a revolutionary. Napoleon promoted elements of the revolutionary agenda in the lands where he held authority. For example, he embraced the anti-clericalism of revolutionary **liberalism**, suppressing religious orders throughout northern Italy and converting moldering churches to secular uses. He imposed French law, abolishing serfdom, limiting noble privilege, and protecting the inheritance rights of all children. His soldiers broadcast the ideals of "liberty, equality, and fraternity" that were the hallmark of the liberal revolution. At the same time, their fierce patriotism awakened nationalist sentiments among the peoples they encountered which were the seeds of great political energies in the coming century.

Returning briefly to France, Napoleon set out again in 1798, this time for Egypt. (Here one of his adjutants found the Rosetta Stone, with its key to deciphering ancient Egyptian scripts; see Chapter 1). Nominally controlled by the Ottoman Empire (see Chapter 15) and allied with Britain, Egypt represented to Napoleon a stepping stone to India and the heart of the British Empire. He defeated a Mamluk army at the Battle of the Pyramids; but soon afterward the British Admiral Horatio Nelson (1758–1805) destroyed the French fleet at the battle of the Nile. The French general returned to France, where conspiracy was afoot.

Napoleon found a situation favorable to his ambitions: the government was foundering and France was in disarray. He joined forces with Emmanuel-Joseph Sieyès, author of the inflammatory 1789 tract *What is the Third Estate?* (see above). Now one of the Directors, Sieyès helped plan the events that occurred on 18 Brumaire (by the revolutionary calendar), or November 9, 1799. With a small group of armed supporters, Napoleon marched into the assembly of the two ruling councils and announced that he would take charge. The deputies discussed arresting him, but Napoleon's brother Lucien (1775–1840), president of the lower council, ordered the soldiers to expel those in opposition.

Napoleon had usurped power by a *coup d'état* (sudden seizing of power). He proclaimed a new government of which he would be "First Consul." For the next sixteen years, the story of France is the story of Napoleon.

Napoleon's France

In 1802, Napoleon made himself sole Consul for life and in 1804, Emperor. The people of France approved each of these appointments by plebiscite (vote of the whole nation), and Napoleon procured the blessing of Pope Pius VII (r. 1800–1823) at the coronation ceremony. He placed the crown on his own head and on that of his wife, Josephine de Beauharnais (1763–1814).

As Napoleon's titles accumulated, republican institutions wasted away. After 1799, when he imposed a new constitution, the elected assembly was replaced by an appointed Senate, and a Tribunate (eliminated by 1808), chosen by the Senators from a list of 6000 "notabilities." Those two bodies disposed of legislation proposed by a Council of State, chosen by Napoleon. This apparatus of government was approved by a plebiscite in which all adult males were permitted to vote. A little more than a decade since the promulgation of the first republican constitution, an overwhelming ninety-nine percent of the electorate voted yes to authoritarianism.

Napoleon centralized and bureaucratized the government. In each *département*, or district, an appointed prefect executed his orders. He recruited his magistrates from all social classes, and rewarded efficient service well. To promote commerce, he established the Bank of France in 1800, regularized the system of taxation, abolished most internal customs tolls, and standardized weights and measures. To control the circulation of ideas, he censored the theater and the press, shutting down all but thirteen of seventy-three newspapers, and unleashed the secret police. To underscore his eminence, he created a new nobility from an assortment of former aristocrats,

WITNESSES

Napoleon, According to Himself and to an Enemy

Napoleon anticipates most of the charges that history will make against him, and defends his record (c. 1815): I closed the gulf and cleared the chaos. I purified the Revolution, dignified Nations and established Kings. I excited every kind of emulation, rewarded every kind of merit, and extended the limits of glory! This is at least something! And on what point can I be assailed on which an historian could not defend me? Can it be for my intentions? But even here I can find absolution. Can it be for my despotism? It may be demonstrated that the Dictatorship was absolutely necessary. Will it be said that I restrained liberty? It can be proved that the licentiousness, anarchy, and the greatest irregularities, still haunted the threshold of freedom. Shall I be accused of having been too fond of war? It can be shown that I always received the first attack. Will it be said that I aimed at universal monarchy? It can be proved that this was merely the result of fortuitous circumstances, and that our enemies themselves led me step by step to this determination. Lastly, shall I be blamed for my ambition? This passion I must doubtless be allowed to have possessed, and that in no small degree; but at the same time, my ambition was of the highest and noblest kind that ever, perhaps, existed—that of establishing the empire of reason, the full exercise and complete enjoyment of all the human faculties!

(From Marquis de Las Cases, *Memoirs of the Life, Exile, and Conversations of the Emperor Napoleon*, 1894; ed. J. K. Sowards, 1992)

Literary critic, novelist and *salonière* Madame de Staël (1766–1817) gives her impressions of the dictator (1816): I very quickly saw, in the various occasions I had to meet him during his stay in Paris, that his character could not be defined by the words we ordinarily use; he was neither good, nor fierce, nor gentle, nor cruel, like others we know. Such a being, having no equals, could neither feel nor arouse any sympathy: he was more than a human being or less than one. His appearance, his mind, and his speech were foreign in nature—an added advantage for subjugating the French.

Far from being reassured by seeing Bonaparte more often, I was made increasingly apprehensive. I had a vague feeling that no emotions of the heart could influence him. He considers a human being a fact or a thing, not a fellow man. He does not hate nor does he love. For him, there is nothing but himself; all others are ciphers.

Every time I heard him speak I was struck by his superiority: yet it had no resemblance to that of men educated and cultivated by study or by social intercourse, such as may be found in England or France. But his speech showed a feeling for the situation, like the hunter's for his prey.

(Madame de Staël, *On Politics, Literature and National Character*, 1818; ed. J. K. Sowards, 1992)

loyal magistrates, and army officers, bestowing 3600 titles between 1808 and 1814. The former revolutionary Sieyès, who had engineered his rise to power, he made a count.

Napoleon revised the legal system, creating the massive *Code Napoléon* (Napoleonic Code, or Civil Code), still in force in France today as well as in many other countries. It combined the comprehensive approach of Roman law with Enlightenment and, to some extent, revolutionary principles. To anxious bourgeois survivors of the Revolution, the Civil Code guaranteed the sanctity of private property, while limiting the rights of workers. Within the family, the Code reaffirmed the traditional rights of male householders. A wife could not buy or sell property without her husband's approval, and her income was considered to belong to him and his heirs. Divorce was possible but extremely difficult and, as in centuries past, adultery was considered a more serious violation for a woman than for a man. Napoleon saw the role of women as chiefly consisting in the bearing and rearing of children.

Those children were, like their mothers, subordinated to their father's will. Parents could choose marriage partners for their children, or reject their children's choices. Fathers could even have their children jailed—one of the hated features of the Old Regime. The Code retained, however, the Revolution's bar of primogeniture (the practice by which the eldest son inherited the bulk of family property).

Under Napoleon's guidance, France surpassed almost all other states in providing for the general education of the young. He ordered that each village establish a school for the elementary education of both sexes. A system of secondary schools, or *lycées* (open to boys whose parents could afford the fees but not to girls), was the foundation for an educational system of high quality and, in time, universal access. Napoleon also organized a public university system.

Napoleon's settlement with the Roman Catholic Church was a complex matter. The Revolution had been anti-clerical from the start, yet many Frenchmen and women remained loyal Catholics. By the Concordat of 1801, the compromise negotiated with Pope Pius VII, Napoleon reestablished the Roman Catholic Church in France under terms favorable to its ruler. The Church surrendered its claim to all property confiscated by the Revolution. Clergy must swear allegiance to the state or resign. Priests could pursue their pastoral work unfettered, but were required to read official pronouncements from the pulpit. Freedom of worship was guaranteed, even to Protestants and Jews (together numbering about five percent of the population). All clerical salaries would be paid by the state. Loyal Catholics might return to their churches, but the Catholic Church had forever lost the privileges it enjoyed in pre-revolutionary France.

Napoleon did not restore the monarchy; rather he instituted dictatorship. His intentions were clearly expressed in his actions—in his undoing of the Revolution, his disenfranchisement of the people, his restoration of the patriarchal family, his resurrection of court and nobility, his sweeping reconfiguration of government.

Muscular, small, and brilliant, Napoleon was a tireless worker, "never happier than in the silence of his own study," wrote a modern historian, "surrounded by papers and documents." After an active day, he retired at ten, to awake a few hours later to write letters (80,000 or so in the course of his career) and compose orders much of the night. On this impressive schedule, he accomplished the reorganization of France, and the conquest of Europe.

Napoleon and the *Grande Armée*

If Robespierre, in mobilizing the whole nation, was the first founder of the modern French army, Napoleon was the second—the adored leader of the *Grande Armée* (Great Army), and one of the greatest military commanders in history. Already a hero because of his brilliant Italian campaign of 1796–1797, Napoleon's mature campaigns of 1800–1811 seemed to mark him as invincible. All Europe admired or dreaded him, and it took most of Europe to defeat him.

From 1793 to 1815, France faced a series of three coalitions (the First, 1793–1797; Second, 1798–1802; and Third, 1805–1815), united first against the Revolution, and then against Napoleon. The first coalition derived from the Prussian–Austrian alliance of 1792, and by 1795 also included Britain, Russia, the Netherlands, Spain, and Sardinia. The second had formed by 1798, and included Britain, Austria, and Russia. In 1805, the Third Coalition formed, including the same combatants as the second, with the addition of Prussia in 1806. Prussia and Austria supported Napoleon in 1812, but both joined Russia and Britain and other allied forces against France in 1813, in a last phase of this struggle, a great war to liberate Europe from Napoleon.

To oppose these enemies required constant readiness. From 1798, the institution of an annual draft meant that every young Frenchman faced the prospect of conscription. Over the twenty-three years of warfare, some 2 to 3 million men served in the army. Some resisted conscription, especially in rebellious regions of the south where over fifty percent of those called failed to comply; and some deserted once drafted. For those who fought, and showed courage or talent, the opportunity for promotion was open.

Napoleon's army employed tactics that marked a new stage in the evolution of military force. For the sake of speed, it lived off the land, devastating the fields and seizing the stores of those it "liberated." Unencumbered by supply lines, the French could move swiftly, strike where they were not expected, and wring victory even from superior forces. Assisting them were ample cannon mounted on mobile carts, handled by skilled gunnery crews. The French bombardment exhausted the enemy who then succumbed to a powerful charge. Napoleon grouped combined forces of infantry, cavalry, and artillery into larger corps. Each corps acted as a disciplined entity united by pride in shared experience and common symbols.

Further, Napoleon exploited the possibilities of the infantry column. His opponents generally fought in line formation (even the British, whose excellent guns and peerless discipline allowed them to withstand Napoleonic tactics), maneuvering into close formation for defense. Napoleon sent his soldiers forth in concentrated, marching columns, driven by drumbeat, terrible to behold, and seemingly implacable. The powerful columns sliced through enemy lines, scattering frightened soldiers who became the prey of cavalrymen's sabres and their horses' hooves.

Napoleon's tactic was wasteful of men, as the emperor knew: "A man such as I does not consider the deaths of a million men," he commented. Those

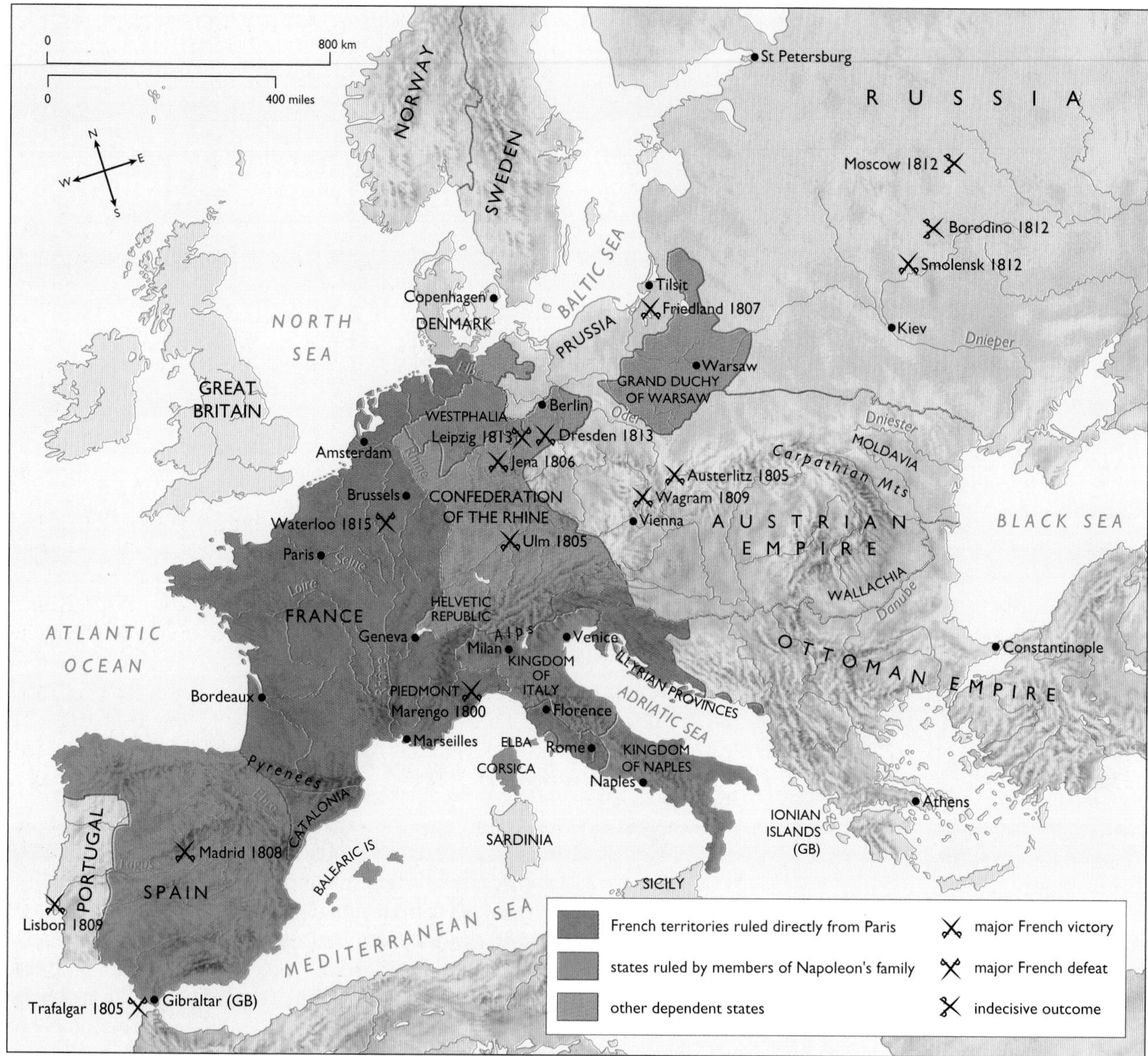

***Map 20.2 Napoleon's Empire and Major Battles, 1799–1815:** Napoleon's empire consisted of a core of areas conquered and annexed to France, others conquered and ruled by members of his family, and a periphery of dependencies (where local governments survived but owed obedience to France).*

in the front ranks were devastated by gunfire, but those in the rear surged past their dead comrades to avenge them. It was France's large population that made Napoleon's tactics possible, while the emperor convinced his followers that their sacrifice was warranted.

In 1800–1815 Napoleon's armies fought in the German lands, Spain, and Russia. They won their greatest victories in the first area, where French armies absorbed the left bank of the Rhine, compensating Prussia, Austria, and some other German states for the loss of their domains. In 1798 Napoleon had imposed a constitution on Switzerland, now dubbed the Helvetic Republic. The region was briefly at peace.

At this juncture, Napoleon attempted the reoccupation of Haiti and the reinstitution of slavery (see Chapter 19). The attempt failed; by 1804, the island was lost. Meanwhile, Napoleon disposed of another colonial possession, the huge Louisiana Territory, sold in 1803 to the United States (see Chapter 19).

In 1805, returning to the German lands, Napoleon decisively defeated Austrian and Russian forces at Ulm and Austerlitz. In 1806 he reorganized the hundreds of German principalities into the more rational Confederation of the Rhine, while overseeing the dissolution of the Holy Roman Empire, accomplished when its Austrian Habsburg emperor (Napoleon's future father-in-law) relinquished that title.

Dismayed by these victories, Prussia joined the Third Coalition, and the next year met and lost to Napoleon's army at Jena. In 1807, Napoleon defeated a Russian army at Friedland, forcing the tsar to agree to the Treaty of Tilsit that made him France's reluctant ally. The three major continental powers had all been sidelined. Only Britain still stood undefeated against France.

The Tide Turns In 1805, Nelson destroyed the French fleet off Cape Trafalgar, near Gibraltar—and with it Napoleon's hopes of invading England. In 1806, Napoleon closed all continental ports to British ships, a strategy he called the Continental System. He aimed to cripple the British economy by denying it European markets for its manufactures and reexported colonial products. But smugglers managed to feed a trickle of British goods to the continent, crucially undermining the Continental System.

Napoleon's will to defeat Britain brought him to the Iberian Peninsula in 1808. Beyond Spain lay Portugal, Britain's ally. A large French force marched toward the capital, Lisbon, triggering the flight of the Portuguese king to his colony of Brazil and the forced abdication of two Spanish kings in favor of Napoleon's brother Joseph Bonaparte (1768–1844). It also precipitated the combined opposition of the powerful Spanish Catholic Church, its nobility, and peasant multitudes, who, returning atrocity for atrocity, fought a guerrilla war against the invaders. The British army, under Arthur Wellesley (1769–1852), later Duke of Wellington, supported native resistance. It trapped more than 400,000 of Napoleon's Great Army on the Iberian Peninsula, and in 1813, drove it out in tatters.

By then, Napoleon's power had been fatally wounded elsewhere. His new alliance with the Austrian Habsburgs (divorcing Josephine, he had married the Habsburg princess Marie-Louise), and his ambitions in the eastern Mediterranean, made Russia his next target. In June 1812, with 450,000 men, he crossed the Polish border into Russia in hope of rapid victory. Instead, a general Russian retreat and scorched earth tactics drew Napoleon deep into the interior, in pursuit. After a costly battle at Borodino seventy miles to the west of Moscow, Napoleon

***Francisco Goya,* The Executions of the Third of May, 1808:** *Napoleon met his first serious setbacks in the Peninsular War in Spain, where French troops committed atrocities that aroused native resistance. Here in Francisco Goya's 1814 painting, a French firing squad executes guerrilla rebels, the chief victim's body extended in the form of the crucified Christ.* (Prado, Madrid)

captured the city in September. The capital had been evacuated and fire broke out the day the French entered. Napoleon was left stranded in hostile territory on the verge of the Russian winter. A 1500-mile retreat followed, deadly both to the emperor's men and to his ambitions. The abject Napoleon returned to Paris in December, ahead of the remnant of his army—130,000 soldiers. The others had died of cold and gunfire, disease and hunger in one of the worst episodes in the history of war.

The emperor's enemies were heartened by the Russian disaster. At Leipzig in October 1813, the "Battle of the Nations" was a resounding victory for the allied armies, which pursued and surrounded Napoleon in Paris in March 1814. In April, he abdicated and attempted suicide. He was exiled to the tiny island of Elba, near Corsica, from which he soon escaped.

Napoleon returned to France in March 1815, marching northward from the Mediterranean coast toward Paris. Troops and generals joined his train, crying, as on the battlefield, *"Vive l'empereur"* ("Long live the Emperor"). The allies were dismayed; though Wellington was not surprised. Napoleon invited the next encounter, which took place at Waterloo on the Belgian plains, where he had marched with 125,000 recruits. He was met by British forces, relieved late in the day by Prussian allies. The French attack was fearsome, but victory went to the allies. "He has ruined us," a wounded French officer lamented, "yet I love him still."

Napoleon was once again imprisoned, and once again exiled, this time under British guard, to St Helena, a remote island in the south Atlantic, from which there could be no escape. Napoleon sickened, lingered, and died six years later. The British feared even his corpse. They released it to the restored French monarch Louis-Philippe (r. 1830–1840) in 1840, who placed it reverently in the Hôpital des Invalides, formerly a military hospital. Thus did a cousin of Louis XVI, victim of the Revolution, honor the Corsican upstart who had carried forward the mission of the Revolution in immeasurably altered form.

The victors of Waterloo, meanwhile, set about eradicating the joint legacies of the Revolution and Napoleon. Their impress on the European consciousness, however, could never be erased. Europe had seen monarchy bloodied and restored; it had beheld liberation and conquest; and it had glimpsed the promise of universal rights, and stirred with a passion for national integrity. Which of these possibilities would bear fruit? "I live only for posterity," Napoleon said. His gift to posterity was a time bomb packed with potentialities both good and evil.

The Conservative Response

To the representatives of the victor nations who met at the Congress of Vienna from 1814, Napoleon was the culmination of all they disliked. He was an illegitimate ruler whose intrusion among European leaders remained a profound threat, even after he himself had met his defeat.

Even more, the French Revolution continued to threaten catastrophe. It had established a liberal agenda of human and civil rights that challenged the authoritarian powers of European monarchs. Though the Revolution itself had foundered, the French army broadcast its message in all the lands it entered, inspiring, it was feared, new revolutions abroad.

Moreover, the French Revolution had triggered a surge of patriotic sentiment, or **nationalism**. To these ideological threats, the diplomats of Vienna adopted a third ideological stance: that of **conservatism** (see Chapter 24).

The pioneering conservative Edmund Burke had cautioned against the destruction of institutions built up over centuries. A harsher conservatism emerged from the Vienna discussions, articulated by the Austrian aristocrat, Prince Clemens von Metternich (1773–1859).

Metternich urged the following goals: to suppress revolutions everywhere; to restore legitimate rulers; to support the nobility and established churches; to limit dissent by controlling the press and unleashing secret police forces. Now monarchy, nobility, and the Church would resume their preeminence and bury the memory of Napoleon.

POWER TO THE PEOPLE

The plans spun at the Congress of Vienna contained rebellious impulses in Europe for fifteen years. Thereafter, they could no longer mute the aspirations of bourgeois liberals, nationalists of all social classes, and workers. Most of the European monarchies that held power in 1815, or were restored to power thereafter, retained their positions into the next century. But the people, seeking to be no longer subjects but citizens, demanded rights and recognition. Their aspirations exploded in 1830, and once again more forcefully in 1848. After 1848, as the European nations continued to take their modern form, many states began to accommodate the demands of their peoples. By 1871, a future without lords and kings could be sighted on the horizon.

Revolution and Counter-Revolution 1815–48

In 1815, the Congress of Vienna restored to power the monarchies disrupted by Napoleon and Revolution, and the religious establishments that had supported them. These set about suppressing liberalism and nationalism in the German and Italian states, in France, and even in Britain. They were unable to stop the revolutions that swept the European colonies in South America and the Caribbean (see Chapter 19), and, ironically, supported a revolution in Greece against the Ottoman Empire. Within their own boundaries, they muzzled dissent by breaking up associations of workers and students, by censoring the press, and by unleashing secret police forces to compel obedience to the regime—all attempts to stave off revolution.

Nationalism and Liberalism in the Habsburg Empire and German Lands Austria, Metternich's homeland, was especially vulnerable to disruption by nationalist movements. Over the previous centuries, Austria had expanded from a mere duchy within the Holy Roman Empire to a kingdom whose Habsburg monarch held the imperial title. During the course of that expansion, Austria had absorbed a large part of central and southeastern Europe. Among its dominions were Bohemia, Moravia, and Hungary; parts of Poland, Russia, and Italy; Transylvania, and the Ottoman Balkans, including parts of Croatia and Serbia. Besides Austrian Germans, its peoples included Italians, Czechs, Slovaks, Magyars, Poles, Romanians, Slovenes, and Croats. They spoke at least twenty different languages, and adhered to Roman Catholicism, Eastern Orthodoxy, Judaism, Islam, and varieties of Protestantism.

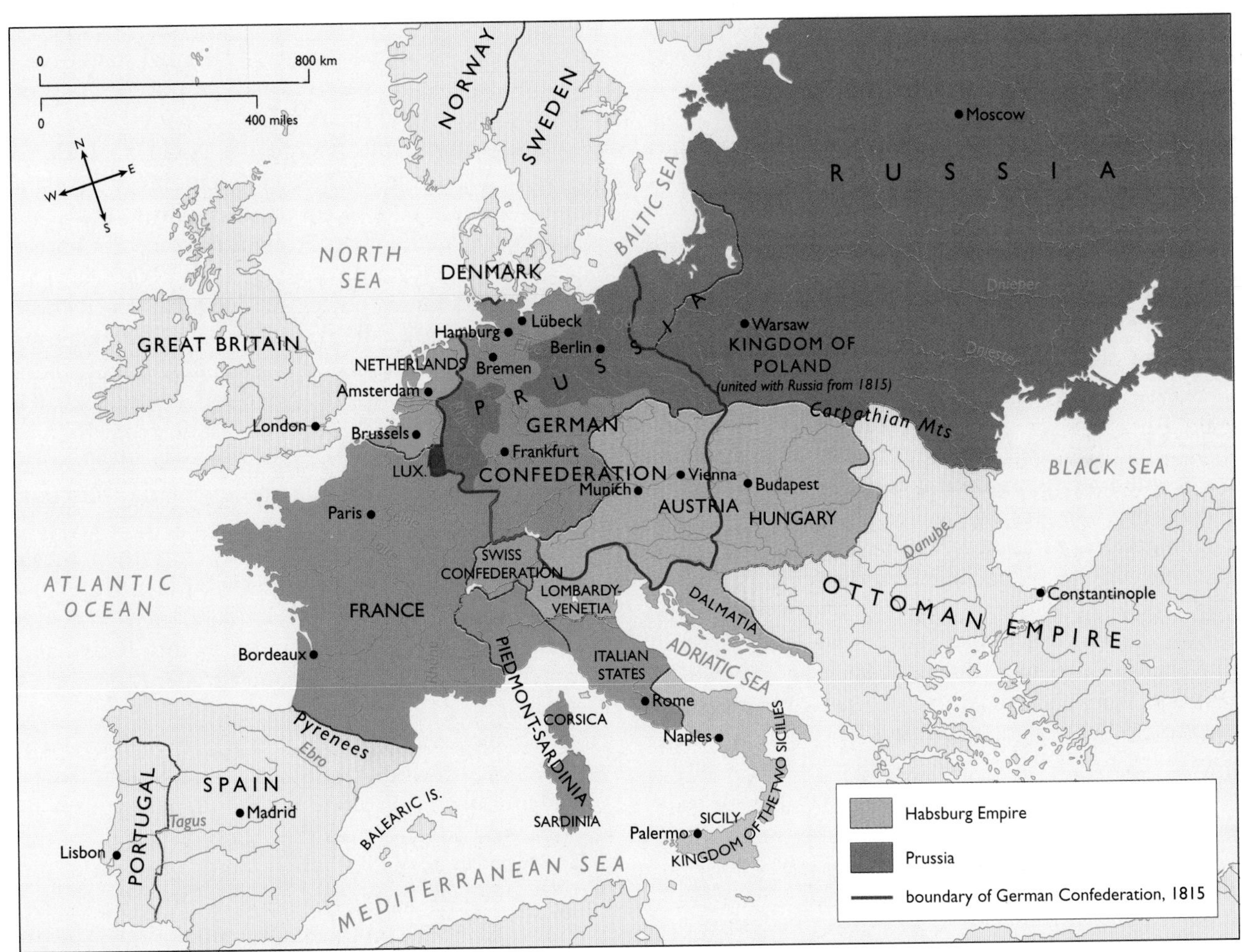

Map 20.3 Europe in 1815 as Established by the Congress of Vienna: *In 1815, the participants of the Congress of Vienna rearranged the map so as to reverse most of Napoleon's adjustments and to achieve the European balance of power that was a main object of their diplomacy.*

The German-speaking Austrian and Czech bourgeoisie shared the outlook of western European liberals. They hoped to limit Habsburg autocracy, to gain rights and secure freedom of the press. Czech liberals were also moved by nationalism, as were the powerful nobles of Hungary and Croatia, These aristocrats could be persuaded to cooperate with the Austrian government, which supported their lordship over a subject peasantry, but still demanded greater independence within the Habsburg regime. Northern Italians sought freedom from Habsburg rule.

In 1831 in Italy, insurrections broke out against Austrian and papal domination, calling for a unified Italian nation. Although those rebellions were suppressed, the ardent patriot Giuseppe Mazzini (1805–1872) took leadership of the nationalist mission. He organized disparate groups of ***carbonari*** ("charcoal-burners") into the liberal–nationalist organization "Young Italy." Organized as a secret society, admission to which involved oaths hedged with threats of retribution, it grew into a major movement that spurred progress toward national unification achieved by 1870.

Nationalist movements inspired by liberal principles flourished in the German cities and principalities. The Congress of Vienna continued the work Napoleon had begun, creating a Confederation of thirty-nine German states, including Prussia and Austria, whose representatives attended a Federal Diet at Frankfurt. Rather than unifying Germany, this reorganization underscored the autonomy of the component states.

German university students and their professors were the spearhead of liberal and nationalist sentiment. The Carlsbad Decrees of 1819, conceived by Metternich and proposed jointly by the rulers of Prussia and Austria to the complaisant Diet of the German Confederation, abolished the student proto-revolutionary clubs, and silenced the press.

Censorship, however, could not choke off news of the 1830 outburst in France (see below), which sparked further rebellions in Belgium, Poland, and elsewhere. At Heidelberg and Frankfurt, university students gathered to call for a united Germany. The "Ten Articles," issued by the Diet of the German Confederation, scripted the suppression of liberal movements throughout the German states, but failed to silence a generation of young men who would become the lawyers, magistrates, and professors of a new nation. Meanwhile, though political unification was postponed, the customs union (*Zollverein*) of 1834, which eliminated internal tariffs and promoted the economic unity of many of the German states, was of great significance for Germany's future.

The Congress of Vienna created a united kingdom of the Netherlands, including both the northern, largely Protestant provinces and the southern Catholic ones formerly under Habsburg rule. The new king William I (r. 1815–1840), of the line of the princes of Orange, consolidated his position in the north. The southern provinces resisted amalgamation, and revolted in 1830 (in the wake of the French revolt of that year). Belgium became an independent nation under a constitutional monarch.

Revolution in Russia, the Iberian Peninsula, and Greece The Russian empire, like the Austrian, had expanded territorially over the previous centuries. It now contained many Asian minorities, of which some groups were Muslim; and in 1831 it had absorbed the kingdom of Poland that Napoleon had briefly reconstituted as the Grand Duchy of Warsaw. These subject territories were not, however, the main source of difficulty for Tsar Alexander I (r. 1801–1825). Rather, it was his nation's social rigidity. The great majority of the Russian people were virtually enslaved serfs, the personal property of the nobility.

Russia's minuscule bourgeoisie could do little to resist the autocratic regime, but a handful of dissident nobles attempted a coup in December 1825, on Alexander's death. Their attempt to place the former tsar's brother on the throne failed, and Nicholas I (r. 1825–1855) claimed power, subdued the "Decembrist Revolt" (as it was called), and executed or exiled its leaders, inaugurating an era of even fiercer repression.

"Serfdom is a powder keg under the state," warned one of the tsar's noble advisers in 1839. From 1826 to 1849, serfs rose up in revolt on nearly 2000 occasions—not always with the success of the fifty-four peasants who in 1835 managed to kill 144 estate owners and twenty-nine stewards before their rebellion, like the others, was suppressed. Meanwhile, dissident intellectuals, mostly noble, fed on the thousands of foreign books smuggled into Russia and pondered nightly by impassioned student ideologues (see Chapter 24).

In Spain and Portugal, whose monarchs were restored by the Congress of Vienna, dissent still simmered and liberal revolutions were suppressed in both countries by 1823. Across the Atlantic, several of the Spanish colonies revolted more on the pattern of the North American revolt of 1775 than the French one of 1789 (see Chapter 19). By the 1820s, independent nations had been created out of the continental Spanish American colonies. European efforts to reverse these changes were halted by the policy declared in 1823 by President James Monroe of the new United States: any intervention by European powers in the affairs of the western hemisphere would be seen as an "unfriendly act."

In Greece, insurrection broke out in 1821 against the Muslim Ottoman regime, which had been in power since the fifteenth century (see Chapters 14, 15). The anti-revolutionary principles of the European states here clashed with anti-Turkish and pro-Christian sentiments. Writers, intellectuals, and young people all over Europe, and especially in England, cheered the Greek revolt on, while their suspicious rulers did nothing to protect the legitimate regime. By 1832, Greece had won its independence from the Ottoman empire.

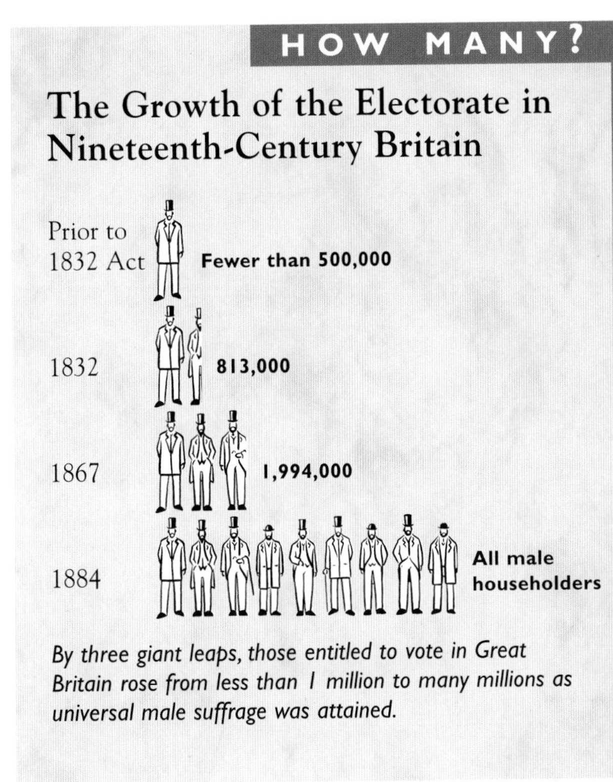

HOW MANY?
The Growth of the Electorate in Nineteenth-Century Britain
Prior to 1832 Act
Fewer than 500,000
1832
813,000
1867
1,994,000
1884
All male householders

By three giant leaps, those entitled to vote in Great Britain rose from less than 1 million to many millions as universal male suffrage was attained.

Pressure for Change in Great Britain Britain, which had already undergone an industrial transformation (see Chapter 21), still shared the difficulties faced by the other principal nations during the post-Napoleonic period. Liberals demanded the broadening of the franchise and other civil rights, while workers sought to better their condition. As protest stirred, old Combination Acts barring the formation of workers' organizations were sternly enforced until eventual repeal in 1824. "Corn Laws" (which protected landowners' profits) taxed grain imports, keeping the price of bread artificially high. The government suppressed mass protests against such restrictive tariffs—as witnessed when soldiers fired on a crowd of 60,000 people gathered on St. Peter's Fields in Manchester, killing eleven in the "Peterloo Massacre" (named after Waterloo) of 1819. Until 1829, Roman Catholics were barred from holding political office in Britain and Ireland. The Roman Catholic population of Ireland, subject to mostly Anglo-Irish Protestant landlords, suffered unremitting discrimination.

Britain proceeded over the next generation, however, without revolution, to open access to government and to nurse the wounds caused by two generations of economic change. The Reform Act of 1832 nearly doubled the franchise. Now the wealthiest one-fifth of adult male citizens could vote for representatives in Parliament—an improvement, but still far short of universal suffrage.

The Poor Law of 1834, despite its still harsh effects, signaled the government's readiness to address the social problem of poverty. In 1846, the repeal of the Corn Laws permitted the importation of cheaper grain, while the Factory Act of 1833 and Mines Act of 1842 did something to improve the conditions faced by the most exploited industrial workers. Workers' attempts to win a People's Charter, or Great Charter, however, were unsuccessful. The Great Charter demanded universal male suffrage, a secret ballot, and electoral reform, among other changes. Its supporters met and marched throughout the 1830s and 1840s, engaging a generation of ordinary people in a participatory democracy. Millions of citizens signed petitions sent to Parliament in 1839 and 1842, but left unheeded. In 1848, stirred by news of continental revolutions, the Chartist movement culminated in a last great, but futile, march.

Even more deeply estranged from British public life were the people of Ireland, saddled by absentee landlords and religious intolerance, unrepresented in Parliament, and unassisted by the government when, in 1845, crisis struck (see Chapter 23).

Irish farmers had taken to growing potatoes (see Chapter 16), which grew easily and provided bountiful nourishment from a small area. In Ireland, where most peasants possessed only the tiniest of plots of soil from which to gain their whole sustenance, the potato took over not merely as the chief, but virtually the sole crop. In 1845, the potato crop failed. A "Great Hunger" seized Ireland, killing millions, leaving others malnourished, and driving hundreds of thousands more to emigrate (mostly to the United States). The longstanding hostility to British domination was to blaze still hotter among those who remembered the years of famine.

France: Laboratory of Revolution In the years after Waterloo, France experienced both counter-revolution and further revolution. In 1815 (as he had briefly in 1814), Louis XVI's brother took the throne as Louis XVIII (r. 1814–1824) (the child Louis XVII had died in prison in 1795). He ruled subject to a constitution, appointing the upper chamber of a two-chamber assembly, while a tiny electorate of 100,000 adult males (in a nation of 30 million) chose the deputies to the lower chamber. The Napoleonic Code continued in force, and Napoleon's Concordat was retained, with modifications that effectively reestablished Roman Catholicism in France.

Upon Louis XVIII's death in 1824, his brother Charles X (1757–1836) succeeded with the support of conservatives and royalists. Determined to reinstate absolutism, Charles restored the privileges of the Roman Catholic Church, imposed stricter censorship, and protected the powerful. In July 1830, he issued the July Ordinances, shrinking the electorate even further to a thin stratum of wealthy men. The response was explosive: liberal bourgeois and angry workers spilled out into the streets of Paris. They threw together makeshift barricades of scrap wood and castoff objects and, in a pattern that would be repeated often in years to come, they faced with their irregular weapons the king's regular troops.

Charles abdicated, and in his place, Louis-Philippe (r. 1830–1848), of a younger branch of the Bourbon dynasty, took the throne without ceremony or pretense to absolutist principles. Unlike Charles X, he did not wear royal robes or a crown, but the same kind of business suit as his banker might have worn. And in his hat he wore the tricolor cockade: a piece of ribbon showing the red, white, and blue of the party of Revolution. This was a "Citizen King" who wished for no further revolution. He ruled

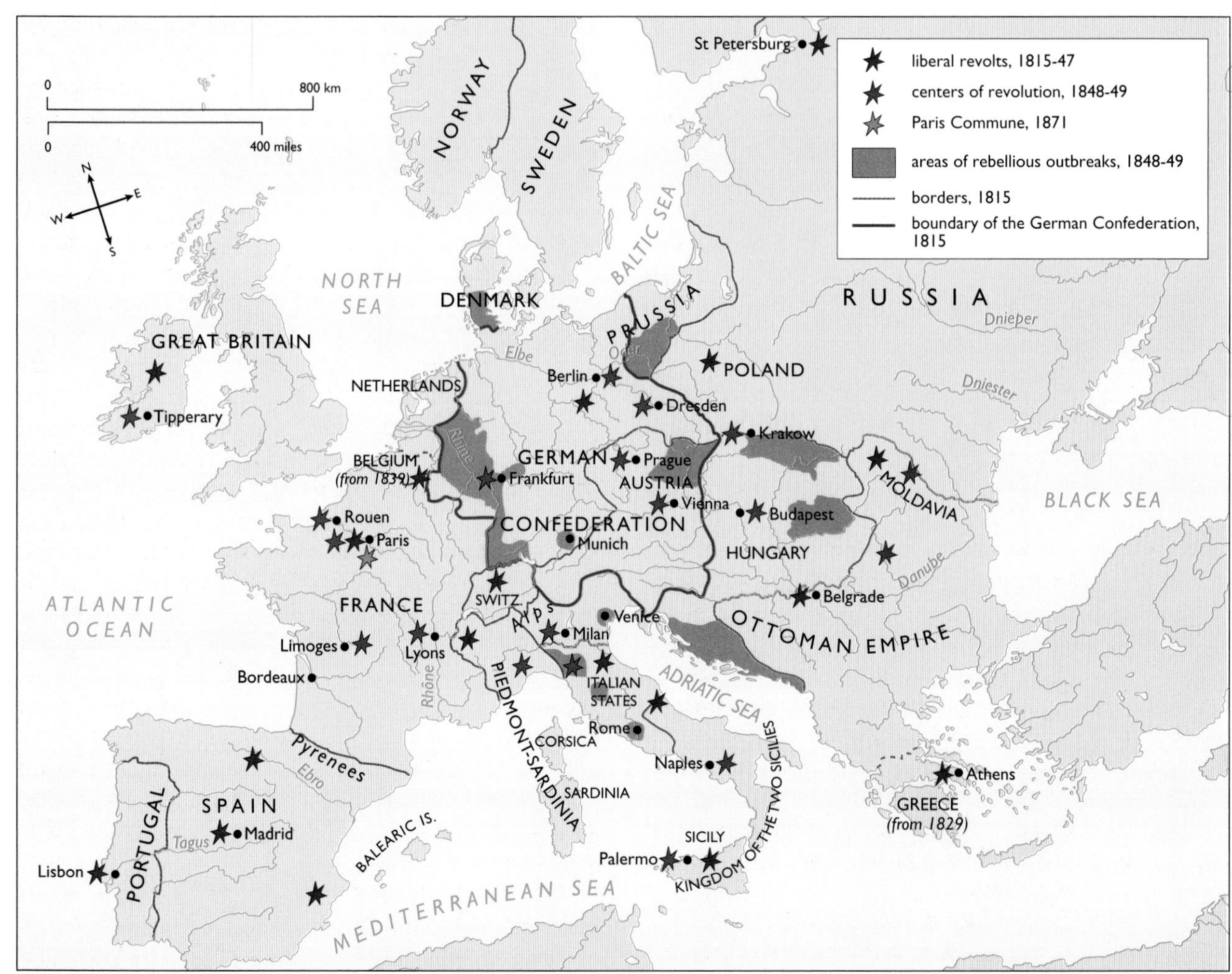

Map 20.4 ***Liberal, Nationalist, and Socialist Uprisings in Europe, 1815–1871:*** *The French Revolution had many offshoots in the form of liberal, nationalist, and socialist uprisings between the Congress of Vienna settlement and 1871.*

subject to a constitution, and the electorate—still small—nearly doubled.

What happened in France in 1830 was precisely what Metternich and his cronies had feared—but their day had passed. No longer could conservatives hope for a true counter-revolution and the return to a chess-board world of nobles, kings, and bishops. Indeed, even as liberals and nationalists clashed with conservative monarchies, they came into conflict with workers voicing their own claim to participation in political life. The arrival of the worker as a political force is viewed first in France.

France had not yet completed its career as a laboratory of social change. Between 1830 and 1848, French popular resistance to monarchical government displayed two main sets of interests. The first comprised the bourgeois businessmen and professionals who, even under the comparatively liberal regime of Louis-Philippe, were excluded from the suffrage. They sought the liberalization of the constitution and economic policy.

The second was the growing stratum of urban workers, their ranks swelled by recent migrants from the countryside, who threatened disruption. They were encouraged by the theories of a new group of radical political thinkers, the socialists (see Chapters 22, 24). Embracing liberal notions of civil rights, socialists held, in addition, that states were responsible for improving the lives of their citizens through public policy and direct subsidies requiring the redistribution of private property. The bourgeois liberals who opposed the authority of kings would also oppose the demands of militant workers that they surrender all, or even a modicum, of their accumulated wealth.

These two revolutionary streams—the bourgeois and the worker, the liberal and the radical—intersected in 1848. Late in February, a mass demonstration turned into revolution when panicky soldiers fired on the crowd, killing forty people. The crowd carried the martyred citizens through the streets, seized public buildings, and erected barricades.

Louis-Philippe abdicated, and the Second French Republic was born. A provisional government formed, which proclaimed universal manhood suffrage and the abolition of slavery in all French colonies—Napoleon had restored the institution, earlier abolished by the 1789 Revolution. It also called for the election of a National Assembly to write a republican constitution.

The February revolution was a bourgeois revolution. It would be followed by a revolt of workers and artisans, just as in 1789 the moderate revolution gave way to a radical one. The economy descended into crisis, while prices and taxes soared. Workers pressed the government to provide work for unemployed laborers in national workshops—a program devised by the socialist Louis Blanc (1811–1882) which the provisional government initially had undertaken, but later revoked. Parisians and provincials enlisted in hundreds of political clubs. These were liberal, radical, and even feminist in orientation, as women insisted not only on civil rights but on rights specific to women—the right to divorce, female suffrage, the equality of women before the law.

In April, eighty-four percent of the electorate (all adult males were eligible to vote) chose a legislature that was strongly conservative and monarchist; socialists and radical republicans won only one in nine seats. On June 23, this new National Assembly announced the abolition of the national workshops. The workers took to the streets, and barricades went up in the workers' sections of Paris.

The three-day insurrection known as the "June Days" was suppressed by the middle-class youth of the National Guard, and the lower-class youth of the Mobile Guard, a special tactical force established by the Assembly to keep order—men as poor as those they faced across the barricades. The bourgeois Guardsmen shot hundreds of workers, and the Mobile Guard swept through the streets killing about 1500 people. Some 12,000 insurgents were arrested, about 8000 of these imprisoned, of whom some 4000 were sent to penal colonies in Algeria and French Guiana to face a scant chance of survival.

By November 1848, the political clubs had dissolved, censorship was reinstituted, women withdrew from view, and the constitution of France's Second Republic was promulgated, calling for presidential elections the following month. On December 10, the victory went to Louis-Napoleon Bonaparte (president 1850–1852; emperor 1852–1870), nephew of the defeated Napoleon. He would be reelected in 1851, with the approval of ninety percent of those voting—and then dissolve the Second Republic he had twice been elected to lead. The following year, by another overwhelming vote, the empire was restored under Napoleon III, as he was called (Napoleon Bonaparte's son, also Napoleon, having died in 1832). Having fought three revolutions and constructed two republics, the French by the vote of a resounding majority knelt once more to autocracy.

The rest of Europe studied Paris in 1848, as it had in 1789 and 1830. The revolt in France set off a series of revolts in other European centers, reaching the Austrian empire, the German and Italian states, Italy, the Netherlands and Belgium, Russia, Spain, and Portugal—a total of over fifty outbreaks. In these

WITNESSES

The People Take Charge

Giuseppe Mazzini on Young Italy and the Italian nation (1831). Young Italy is a brotherhood of Italians who believe in the law of *Progress* and *Duty*, and are convinced that Italy is destined to become one nation. . . . They join this association in the firm intent of consecrating both thought and action to the great aim of reconstituting Italy as one independent sovereign nation of free men and equals. Young Italy is *Republican* and *Unitarian*. Republican . . . because all true sovereignty resides essentially in the nation . . . [and] because both history and the nature of things teach us that elective monarchy tends to general anarchy; and hereditary monarchy tends to general despotism. . . . Young Italy is *Unitarian* because, without unity, there is no true nation.
(From G. B. Kirsch, F. M. Schweitzer, W. Stoiko, G. L. Mahoney eds., *The West in Global Context: from 1500 to the Present*, 1977)

Alexis de Tocqueville, shortly before the Revolution of 1848, foretells its approach: I am told that there is no danger because there are no riots; I am told that, because there is no visible disorder on the surface of society, there is no revolution at hand. Gentlemen, permit me to say that I believe you are deceived. True, there is no actual disorder; but it has entered into men's minds. See what is passing in the breasts of the working classes, who, I grant, are at present quiet. . . . Do you not see that there are gradually forming in their breasts opinions and ideas which are destined not only to upset this or that law, ministry, or even form of government, but society itself, until it totters upon the foundations on which it rests today? Do you not hear them repeating unceasingly that all that is above them is incapable and unworthy of governing them; that the present distribution of goods throughout the world is unjust; that property rests on a foundation which is not an equitable foundation? And do you not realize that when such opinions take root, when they spread in an almost universal manner, when they sink deeply into the masses, they are bound to bring with them sooner or later, I know not when nor how, a most formidable revolution?
(*The Recollections of Alexis de Tocqueville*, ed. A. T. de Mattos, 1896)

An eyewitness reports on women's participation in revolution in Dresden (1849): Many women, who came from all ranks of society, took part in the struggle . . . . Many helped build the barricades, dragging stones and furniture, others supplied the fighters with meals on the streets which they had cooked. Still others took care of the wounded, bandaging their wounds in the rain of bullets on the open street or dragging them into their houses. A maiden whose fiancé . . . had fallen on the first day, defended a barricade for three days with the courage of a lion, shooting down many soldiers before she knew she herself was felled by an enemy bullet.
(From B. S. Anderson and J. P. Zinsser, *A History of Their Own: Women in Europe from Prehistory to the Present*, Vol. 2, 1988)

A British journalist describes the collapse of the Paris Commune (1871): The Versaillist troops collected about the foot of the Rue St. Honoré, were enjoying the fine game of Communist hunting. The Parisians of civil life are caitiffs [scoundrels] to the last drop of their thin, sour, white blood. [Only] yesterday they had cried "Long live the Commune!". . . . To-day they rubbed their hands with livid currish joy to have it in their power to denounce a Communist and reveal his hiding place. Very eager at this work are the dear creatures of women. They know the rat holes into which the poor devils have got, and they guide to them with a fiendish glee. . . . They have found him, the miserable [fellow]! Yes; they drag him out . . . and a guard of six of them hem him round as they march into the Rue St. Honoré. A tall, pale, hatless man, with something not ignoble in his carriage. His lower lip is trembling, but his brow is firm, and the eye of him has got some pride and defiance in it. They yell—the crowd—"Shoot him; shoot him!"—the demon-women most clamorous, of course. . . . He is down; he is up again; he is down again. . . . But it is useless. They are firing into the flaccid carcase [*sic*] now. . . . His brains spurt on my boot and splash in the gutter.
(From R. M. Golden and T. Kuehn eds., *Western Societies: Primary Sources in Social History*, Vol. 2, 1993)

places, bourgeois revolutionaries fought for written constitutions, freedom of the press, judicial equality, and a wider franchise. Nationalists fought for autonomy in the Austrian empire and German and Italian lands. Students, professors, journalists, and workers took part in urban revolts that were violent and brutally suppressed.

While not one of these revolts of 1848 was successful, they changed Europe. Rulers rejected pleas for popular representation or autonomy. At the same time, they took note of the volcanic force that resided in the people, whose pleas could not go unheard forever. If 1789 spelled the beginning of a process that would put an end to the rule of kings, nobles, and bishops, 1848 offered further promise that that objective was in sight.

Toward Accommodation: 1848–1871

After 1848, the nations of Europe struggled to ease the strains that developed in the post-Napoleonic era. The quest for national status met with success in Germany and Italy, with less success elsewhere. The demands of liberals for voting rights and economic freedom were realized impressively in Britain, partially elsewhere, and at least entertained in other places. The attempt by urban and rural workers to gain entry to political life displayed itself powerfully in France, more mildly but more effectively in Britain. Elsewhere these groups were still ignored.

Italian and German Unification From 1848 to 1871, the many component states of the Italian peninsula and of the German-speaking lands (except for Austria) achieved unification in the new nations of Italy and Germany. In both cases, though liberal nationalists had long championed the cause, unification was achieved from above by senior statesmen who were themselves of noble birth. And in both cases, the new nations were monarchies.

The Italian and German cases are distinct. Long before they were reduced to third-rate status and subjected to Austrian, Spanish, and papal domination, the Italian states had been the central region of the Roman Empire (see Chapters 5, 6) and the homeland of the Italian Renaissance (see Chapter 13). After Napoleon swept through the peninsula, Mazzini and Giuseppe Garibaldi (1807–1882) led a broad nationalist movement—the *Risorgimento*, or "Resurgence"—supported actively by bourgeois professionals. Joining these leaders after 1842 was the nobleman Camillo di Cavour (1810–1861), the new prime minister of Piedmont–Sardinia, a prosperous and constitutional monarchy. Cavour schemed, negotiated, and fought to achieve the unification of Italy.

Promising Napoleon III of France the provinces of Nice and Savoy, Cavour won the French emperor's support. A joint Piedmontese and French army pushed the Austrian army out of much of northern Italy in 1859, though Austria retained Venetia. In 1860, several other states voluntarily ceded themselves to Piedmont. Meanwhile Garibaldi, a veteran revolutionary, led an irregular volunteer force of 1000 "Red Shirts" in a daring invasion of Sicily. Joined by some of the men he had "liberated," Garibaldi crossed to the mainland and swept up to Naples, bringing the whole of the south under Piedmontese dominion. The military victory was later confirmed by plebiscites. Before he could reach Rome and challenge Cavour's monarchist state with a republican Italy, Cavour's troops rushed south to join Garibaldi in Naples.

In 1861, Victor Emmanuel II, king of Piedmont–Sardinia, was declared king of Italy. In 1866, as a result of Italy's support of Prussia in the Austro-Prussian war, Venetia was ceded to Italy. In 1870, Italian troops took Rome. With the Roman people assenting, Rome was declared the capital of Italy in 1871. The pope, previously the ruler of the central fifteen percent of the peninsula, retreated to the tiny precinct of the Vatican on the far side of the river Tiber. Political unification had been achieved.

The unification of Germany was achieved by the inspired but often ruthless methods of the Prussian nobleman Otto von Bismarck (1815–1896). He completed a process begun by Napoleon and furthered by the Congress of Vienna, of rationalizing the many German cities and principalities into a coherent whole. But the thirty-nine states of the German Confederation, which included both Prussia and Austria, did not amount to a nation. In the spring of 1848, revolution provided the setting for a first attempt at unification. This forced initial promises of liberalization, followed by the reassertion of central authority. In Frankfurt, more than 800 delegates from many of the German states met to design a constitution for a future nation. Over eighty percent of those delegates had attended universities, and two-thirds were judges, lawyers, professors, teachers, or bureaucrats—a cross-section of the liberal bourgeoisie, though businessmen were scarce.

Their liberalism went only so far. Confining the franchise to propertied men, the Frankfurt Parliament had few supporters. In 1849, nevertheless, it promulgated a constitution of a united German state and offered the Prussian king Frederick William IV (r. 1840–1861) the crown—which he spurned, disdaining the bourgeois republicans who had made the offer, as a "crown from the gutter."

In 1862, a struggle between the new king William I (king of Prussia 1861–1888; German emperor 1871–1888) and the Prussian Parliament resulted in Bismarck's appointment as prime minister. Aiming at any cost to defend the monarchy within Prussia, and Prussia's states in Germany and Europe, he pursued a strategy based on clear-sighted identification of the state's real interests, that would be dubbed *Realpolitik*. Accordingly, he undertook war against Denmark (1864), Austria (1866), and France (1870–1871), to secure Prussian dominance within the German confederation and preeminence in a united Germany.

The war against Denmark won the province of Schleswig for Prussia. The Austro-Prussian war humiliated Austria militarily and resulted in the elimination of the German Confederation (which had included Austria) and the creation of the North German Confederation (which did not). The war against France saw Prussian forces rapidly defeat the French army, then besiege Paris. The peace settlement awarded Prussia the border provinces of Alsace and Lorraine, where many German-speakers lived, and a cash indemnity. On January 18, 1871, in the palace of Versailles, the German Empire was officially proclaimed, with William I as emperor and Bismarck as chancellor. German unification had been achieved.

Reforms in Austria, Britain, and Russia Whereas Italy and Germany had sought unification, the numerous minority populations of the Austrian Empire sought independence or some form of autonomy within the Austrian state. The Habsburg state ignored these aspirations, although it did encourage economic development. Emperor Francis Joseph (r. 1848–1916) addressed dissent by firing his unpopular head of government (who directed the secret police) and experimenting ineffectively with new constitutions that gave greater representation to subject nationalities. Meanwhile, the emperor's reputation plummeted as Austria suffered repeated battlefield losses against Piedmont and Prussia. Reluctantly, he agreed to the Compromise of 1867, creating the Dual Monarchy of Austria-Hungary. He remained king of Hungary, as well as emperor of Austria, but Hungary gained a separate political identity and the right of self-rule. Hungarian resistance to Habsburg rule had been neutralized, although Slav minorities in Hungary and elsewhere remained restless.

It was in Britain that the liberal agenda won its greatest victory, as the expansion of the franchise in 1832 set Britain on the path it would follow for decades. Guiding Britain during this period were two highly capable prime ministers, William Gladstone (1809–1898) for the Liberal party and Benjamin Disraeli (1804–1881) for the Conservative party.

Despite the cautions of wealthy businessmen, aristocrats, and Queen Victoria (r. 1837–1901), a second Reform Bill in 1867 extended the franchise yet again, more than doubling the number of those entitled to vote in 1832. That franchise resulted in a more liberal Parliament, which reformed the army, legalized trade unions, and limited the privileges of the Church of England. In 1884, the franchise was extended once more to include all adult males. The foundations of modern democracy were now solidly laid.

The Russian tsardom did not possess the flexibility of the British government. In 1848, Russian autocracy was still based on a nobility whose loyalty was repaid with concessions over a serf population that—since merchants and middle-class professionals were few—was nearly coterminous with the Russian people.

By 1860, it was clear that serfdom must end. In a rapidly changing world, serfs had become inefficient, as workers, as soldiers, as citizens. Serf labor discouraged innovation—on the part of both landowners, who lived sufficiently on the labor of others, and serfs themselves, who clung to traditional methods of organization. While freed serfs, as a large new class of tax-

WHO'S WHO

In Europe During the Revolutions, 1789–1871

Louis XVI (r. 1774–1793) King of France, and labeled "Louis the Last" by contemptuous revolutionaries; both unintelligent and unlucky, he was condemned on January 19, 1793 and guillotined two days later.

Maximilien Robespierre (1758–1794) inspired orator and determined Jacobin leader, head of the Committee of Public Safety, and engineer of the Reign of Terror that resulted in some 40,000 deaths.

Napoleon Bonaparte (1769–1821) conqueror of much of Europe during the period 1799–1815; trained under the monarchy and progressed rapidly to the rank of general in the French revolutionary army; seized power in 1799 and declared himself Emperor of France in 1804.

Clemens von Metternich (1773–1859) Austrian nobleman and diplomat, key figure at sessions of the Congress of Vienna of 1814–1815, and architect of the repressive strategy and counter-revolutionary principles of many European nations between 1815 and 1848.

Camillo di Cavour (1810–1861) nobleman, diplomat, and prime minister of Piedmont–Sardinia; achieved the unification of Italy under the leadership of his king Victor Emmanuel II.

Otto von Bismarck (1815–1896) Prussian nobleman, prime minister, and chancellor, responsible for the unification of Germany under Prussian rule.

Power to the People

Polish uprising: *Following the Congress of Vienna, the European alliance of conservative Great Powers had to contend with a variety of liberal and nationalist uprisings. In this illustration by J. N. Lewicki entitled "Great Saturday," Polish nationalists seeking independence from Russia establish a provisional government in 1831 following a major revolt. Russian control was soon reestablished.* (National Museum, Cracow)

payers, might be a source of state revenue, escaped and rebellious serfs were a drain on the purse and a threat to order. If Russia was to rate alongside the great powers of the West, it was necessary to emancipate the serfs.

On March 3, 1861, Tsar Alexander II (r. 1855–1881) proclaimed the emancipation of 22 million serfs. The state would recompense landowners for the loss of their land, which would be distributed among the former serfs by the village council of male householders. The former serfs would reimburse the state in forty-nine annual payments, with the village being collectively responsible for the debt. During that time, the serfs were rooted to their village. It would be almost two generations before large sections of the peasant population were truly free. In the meantime, former serfs were no longer counted among the "souls" with which landowners had reckoned their capital, and could no longer be beaten or killed at a nobleman's nod.

Alexander introduced further reforms. In 1864, he created village and regional *zemstvos*, or assemblies. In 1870, he created a similar structure of *dumas*, or councils, for cities. In both cases, the delegates were chosen by local officials and could not operate as representative institutions. Nevertheless, they were the first institutional structures of the kind in Russia, and had potential for further political development. Alexander also instituted courts of justice (necessitated by the handover of judicial powers from landowners to the state) and reformed the army, which now relied on free peasant rather than impressed serf conscripts.

Freeing the serfs did not make Russia a liberal state. The tsarist Third Section police harried "political criminals" (anyone construed as an enemy of the regime) and tried to safeguard Russia from revolutionary ideas that arrived between the covers of foreign books, which were smuggled in by the millions. In contrast to western Europe where liberal intellectuals were also teachers, journalists, or physicians, Russian

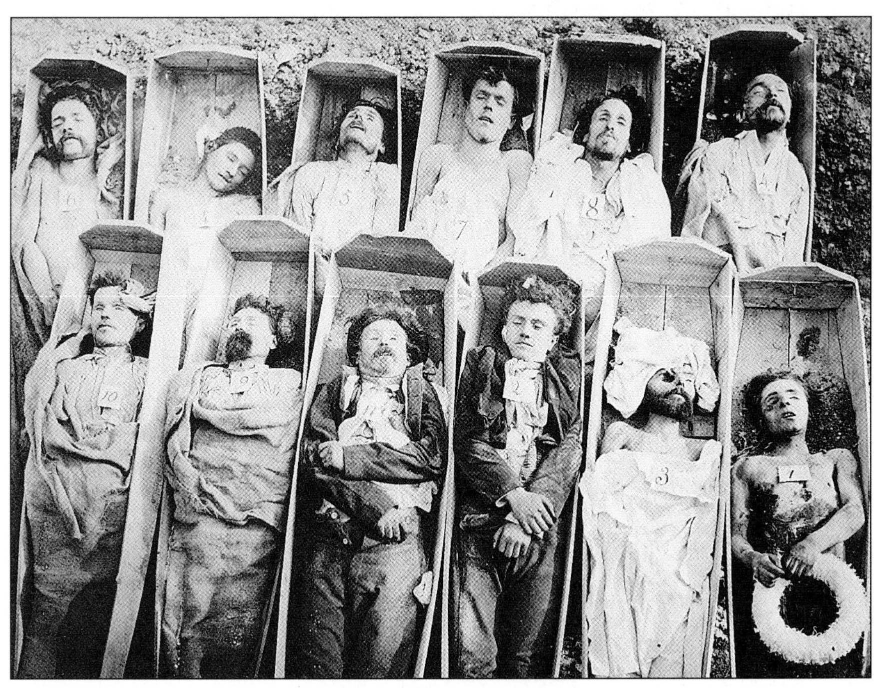

Corpses of the Communards: *French politics continued along a radical path after the Congress of Vienna. The short-lived Paris Commune, an autonomous state created by left-wing intellectuals and urban workers, ended with the massacre of the defenders. Note the corpse of the young woman lined up with those of her companions, a few among the thousands executed by government soldiers and prepared for mass burial.* (Musée Carnavalet, Paris)

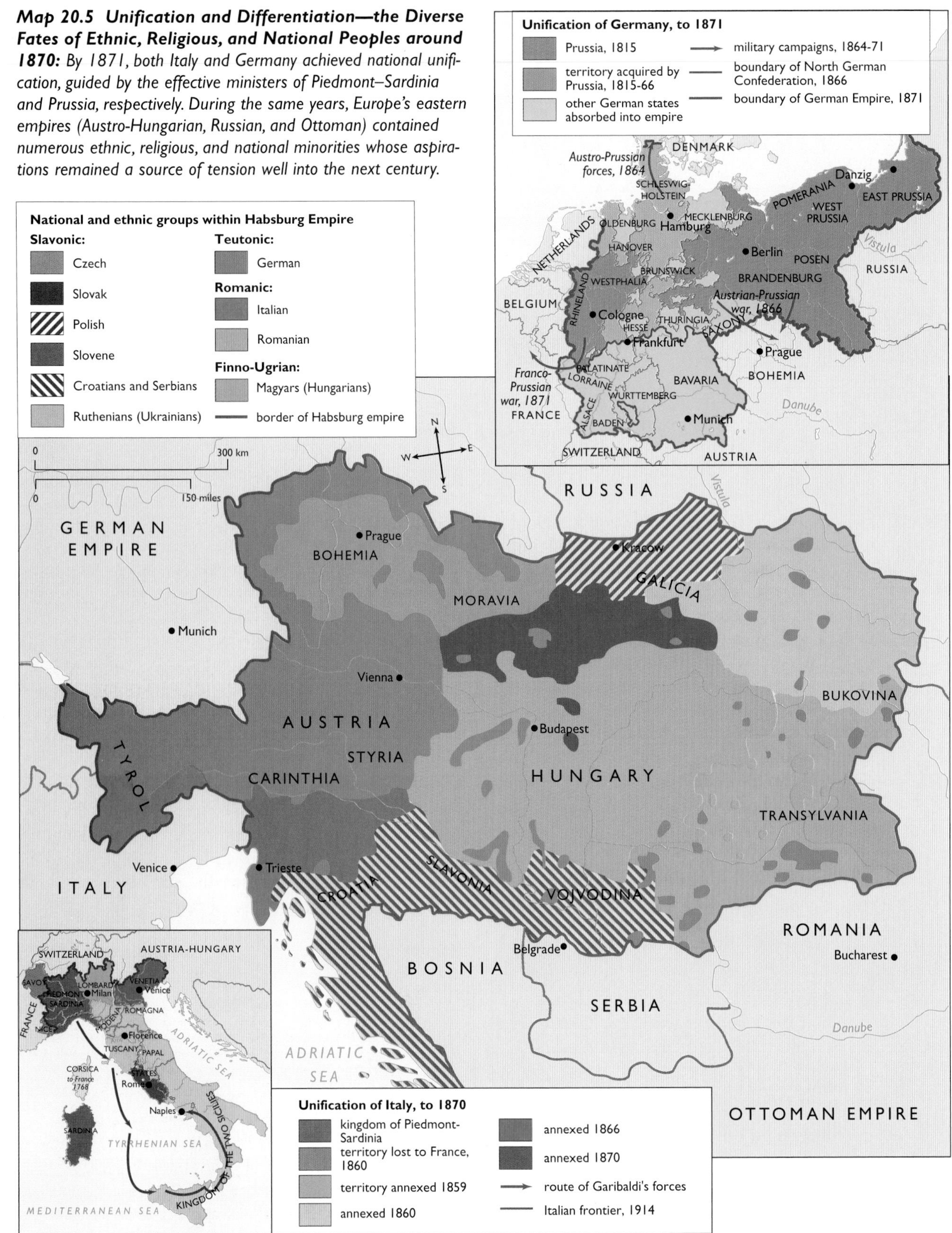

Map 20.5 Unification and Differentiation—the Diverse Fates of Ethnic, Religious, and National Peoples around 1870: *By 1871, both Italy and Germany achieved national unification, guided by the effective ministers of Piedmont–Sardinia and Prussia, respectively. During the same years, Europe's eastern empires (Austro-Hungarian, Russian, and Ottoman) contained numerous ethnic, religious, and national minorities whose aspirations remained a source of tension well into the next century.*

society fostered the development of a permanent group of professional revolutionaries, largely from the nobility, many of whom became martyrs to the cause of social revolution. The benevolent tyrant himself, Alexander II, was also a martyr of sorts, assassinated in 1881 (after earlier attempts) by members of a radical political club.

The Paris Commune Of the major European nations at this time, Russia was the most repressive. France should have been different, but the government in power from 1851 (when the Second Republic was dissolved) to 1870 discouraged the liberalization for which many clamored. Napoleon III presided over an empire where all adult males were eligible to vote (the only nation in Europe that could so boast); where strikes were legal (after 1864); and where the government encouraged commerce, urban renewal, and railroad construction. Yet it was a nation where the wealthy lived to excess; where the press was censored; the Roman Catholic Church was privileged; where political patronage and favoritism reigned. Nowhere in Europe were the bourgeoisie more solid or content (in Britain, they still dwelled in the shadow of aristocracy). And nowhere in Europe were the strivings of workers—not factory workers, who were few (see Chapter 21), rather artisans such as shoemakers and tailors—more fierce or explosive.

In 1870–1871, the workers of Paris resisted Prussian invaders and their own countrymen, briefly creating the world's first socialist state amid the last spasms of the Franco-Prussian War. In September 1870, Prussian armies blazed through northeastern France, and captured and exiled Napoleon III. In Paris, the French proclaimed the Third Republic, established a provisional government, and laid plans to elect a National Assembly that would create a new constitution. The provisional government then withdrew to Tours, as the Prussians besieged Paris, abandoned to its poorest citizens.

Siege brought starvation but did not daunt the progress of political feeling within the city. Revolutionary clubs sprang up abundantly, while women's groups pressed for political and social rights, such as day care for working mothers. Workers' groups declared the "Paris Commune," a stateless society of free producers engaged in what Lenin (1876–1924) was later to call a "festival of the oppressed." In Versailles, powerful men proclaimed the German Empire in January 1871, and settled an armistice in February. In Paris, the war had not ended.

The enemy had changed, however, and the attack that began in Paris in March 1871 was made not by Germans but by Frenchmen, the regular army of the new Third Republic. In May they burst into the city and took Paris from its Communard defenders in the streets and marketplaces, neighborhood by neighborhood. It took a week, and the slaughter was immense. More than 20,000 Parisians were killed, men and women alike, in the bloodiest episode in almost a century of sporadic revolution. Their bodies were bundled into mass graves dug in the lovely parks the Emperor Napoleon had built for the recreation of the citizens.

The dead buried, the political life of France and of Europe resumed. Between 1789 and 1871, the landscape had fundamentally changed. Germany and Italy were nations; the Austro-Hungarian Empire not the overweening power it once was. France was a republic and Britain approached democracy. Russia no longer rested on the shoulders of its serfs, and Spain and Portugal were fading into twilight. Kings, emperors, and aristocrats held onto power in most of Europe, but their reign had been questioned, and marked for extinction. In Europe, as in the Americas, the masses of the people had arrived at the political front and they would not thereafter go home.

Conclusion

REVOLUTION, COUNTER-REVOLUTION, AND THE MEANING OF THE WEST

A medley of political formations characterizes Europe from 1789 to 1871. Monarchy and aristocracy; democracy and socialism; unimaginable brutality and broadminded social legislation; and revolution and counter-revolution cycle before our eyes. But from this kaleidoscopic array one common theme emerges. By the 1880s in the Western world, in the European homeland as on the far side of the Atlantic, key propositions had been put forward for the first time in history: that human society should be ruled by laws not monarchs, and that all the people, and not just a few, should participate in the framing of those laws. The next chapters examine the economic and cultural lives of those peoples who fought to reach the frontier of political power.

REVIEW QUESTIONS

1. How did aristocrats and intellectuals resist absolute monarchy? What role did Enlightenment thinkers play in undermining the Old Regime? Why did they attack the Church?

2. Why did Louis XVI summon the Estates-General in 1789? Why did the French Revolution enter a radical phase after 1789? Who were the sans-culottes?

3. What was the reign of terror? How did foreign opposition affect the course of the Revolution? How did the French Revolution transform the nature of warfare?

4. How did the Revolution change French society? To what extent did Napoleon improve the condition of women? Were the social changes introduced during the Revolution permanent?

5. How did Napoleon gain supreme power in France? To what extent did Napoleon undo the reforms of the Revolution? What were his most lasting achievements for France?

6. How successful was the Congress of Vienna in repressing the principles of the French Revolution? What victories did nationalism and liberalism win between 1815 and 1871? Why can we say that European politics were more liberal in 1871 than they had been in 1789?

SUGGESTED READINGS

Preludes to Revolution

De Tocqueville, Alexis, *The Old Regime and the French Revolution*. Trans. Stuart Gilbert (Garden City, NY: Doubleday, 1955). Timeless analysis by an eminent 19th-century thinker.

Doyle, William, *The Ancien Regime* (Atlantic Highlands, NJ: Humanities Press International, 1986). An ideal introduction.

The Rights of Man and The Birth of a Nation

Chartier, Roger, *The Cultural Origins of the French Revolution* (Durham, NC: Duke University Press, 1991). Sees the cynicism and politicization of the French masses as causing the Revolution.

Doyle, William, *Origins of the French Revolution* (Oxford: Oxford University Press, 2nd ed., 1988). Synthesis of new scholarship.

Hampson, Norman, *The Terror in the French Revolution* (London: Historical Association, 1981). Excellent account of the most bloody and radical stage of the Revolution.

Hufton, Olwen H., *Women and the Limits of Citizenship in the French Revolution* (Toronto–Buffalo: University of Toronto Press, 1992). Essays exploring the ultimate disillusionment of women in the Revolution.

Lefebvre, Georges, *The Coming of the French Revolution, 1789* (Princeton: Princeton University Press, 1947). Its class-based interpretation is now out of favor, but this is still the basic reference point for later scholarship.

Schama, Simon, *Citizens: A Chronicle of the French Revolution* (New York: Knopf, 1989). The Revolution and its import on a grand scale.

Scott, Joan Wallach, *Only Paradoxes to Offer: French Feminists and the Rights of Man* (Cambridge, MA: Harvard University Press, 1996). Critical moments and themes in the history of feminism in France.

The Imperial Adventure

Forrest, Alan, *Conscripts and Deserters: The Army and French Society during the Revolution and Empire* (Oxford: Oxford University Press, 1989). Fascinating study of social origins and social attitudes of revolutionary and Napoleonic foot-soldiers.

Herold, J. Christopher, ed., *The Mind of Napoleon* (New York: New Columbia Press, 1955). Invaluable guide to the man's character.

Schom, Alan, *Napoleon Bonaparte* (New York: HarperCollins, 1997). A recent, comprehensive biography.

Woolf, Stuart J., *Napoleon's Integration of Europe* (London–New York: Routledge, 1991). Critical study of Napoleon's efforts to create a unified European system.

Power to the People: Revolution and Counter-Revolution

Church, Clive H., *Europe in 1830: Revolution and Political Change* (London–Boston: Allen and Unwin, 1983). Focuses on this often under-explored revolutionary year.

Droz, Jacques, *Europe Between Revolutions, 1815–1848* (New York: Harper & Row, 1967). General account of the period 1815–1848.

Greenfield, Liah, *Nationalism: Five Roads to Modernity* (Cambridge, MA: Harvard University Press, 1992). The development of nationalism in four major European states and in the US.

Sperber, Jonathan, *The European Revolutions, 1848–1851* (Cambridge: Cambridge University Press, 1994). Synthesis of recent scholarship.

Power to the People: Toward Accommodation

Edwards, Stuart, *The Paris Commune, 1871* (New York: Quadrangle Books, 1971). Good general narrative.

Hause, Steven C., with Anne R. Kenney, *Women's Suffrage and Social Politics in the French Third Republic* (Princeton: Princeton University Press, 1984). The struggle for women's suffrage in 19th-century France.

Mosse, W. E. *Liberal Europe: The Age of Bourgeois Liberalism, 1848–1875* (New York: Harcourt Brace Jovanovich, 1974). Good overall account of the era, with comparative focus.

Smith, Dennis Mack, *Cavour* (New York: Knopf, 1985). Superior biography of a central figure in Italian unification.

PART SIX

THE WEST BECOMES MODERN

Industrialization, Imperialism, Ideologies (1750–1914)

The arrival of the machine set Western civilization on the path to modernity that was largely completed by 1914. In Britain at first, then in Belgium and France, Germany and the United States, and finally in the rest of Europe and Japan, human beings made machines that produced commodities for use and export in quantities never before conceivable. Machines transformed Western society, where distinctions between rich and poor shifted and deepened. An increasingly bourgeois elite enjoyed a level of comfort previously known only to royalty and aristocracy, while a vast industrial working class experienced the unprecedented hardships of industrial work and urban life.

As European merchants, administrators, and generals ventured abroad to establish colonies and protectorates all over the globe, they recreated far from home the social rifts found in industrial cities. A European elite delighted in luxury as it managed the transmutation of native societies according to Western expectations, and enlisted laborers of many colors and customs to produce cheap goods. Success abroad encouraged Western ideologues to think that people of European descent had gained supremacy over the other peoples of the world because of their inherent racial, or genetic, superiority.

Critics of both social systems, the industrial and the colonial, denounced these injustices. Other thinkers fought to preserve liberal principles, to promote nationalist causes, to advocate rights for women or slaves, or toleration for Catholics, Protestants, or Jews. They spoke and wrote in a rich cultural milieu where, as Classical style gave way to Romantic and Realist movements, the modern repudiation of ancestral norms was already visible. By the end of the nineteenth century, with the death of God proclaimed by the German philosopher Friedrich Nietzsche, the self had lost its coherence, and the ability of the mind to apprehend a certain fixed reality was wholly cast in doubt.

MACHINES IN THE GARDEN

1700	1725	1750	1775	1800	1825	1850	1875	1900	1925

Britain

Britain industrializes, 1750–1850

- Thomas Newcomen's steam pump first used, 1712
- John Kay's flying shuttle, 1733
- James Hargreave's spinning jenny, 1764
- James Watt's steam engine, 1769
- Richard Arkwright's water frame, 1769
- Samuel Crompton's "mule," 1779
- Henry Cort's puddling process, 1783
- Edmund Cartwright's power loom, 1785
- Robert Owen opens factory in Manchester, 1789
- Richard Trevithick's locomotive, 1804
- Henry Bell's steamship *Comet* launched, 1812
- First railroad in England, 1821
- George Stephenson's "Rocket," 1829
- English railroad network almost complete, 1850
- The Great Exhibition at London's Crystal Palace, 1851
- Henry Bessemer's converter, 1856
- British steam engines' total output equals 40,000,000 men/6,000,000 horses, 1870

Western Europe and the US

American and French Revolutions, 1775–94

French Revolutionary and Napoleonic Wars, 1792–1815

Western and central Europe and North America industrialize, 1815–1900

- French introduce steam-driven cart, 1770
- French develop steam boat, 1783
- Eli Whitney's cotton gin, 1793
- Robert Fulton's steamship sails from New York to Albany in 32 hours, 1807
- William Cockerill's iron and steel factory system in Liège, Belgium, employs 2,000 workers, 1812
- First Atlantic crossing by sail-and-steam-powered ship, 1819
- German Customs Union, the *Zollverein*, established, 1834
- First transatlantic steamshipping line opened, 1838
- Transatlantic cable laid, 1866
- First transcontinental railroad in US, 1869
- French lose coal and iron fields in Alsace and Lorraine to Germany, 1871
- Alexander Graham Bell invents telephone, 1876
- Thomas Edison invents lightbulb, 1879

Eastern Europe and Russia

Russia industrializes, 1870–1918

- Steam engine used for cotton manufacture in Russia, 1805
- Henry Cort's puddling process introduced to Russia, 1836
- Railroad line opens from Dresden to Leipzig, 1839
- Moscow and St. Petersburg linked by railroad, 1851
- St. Petersburg has 900 factories, 1914

Beyond the West

Japan industrializes, 1870–1918

- Shaka leads Zulu nation, Africa, 1817
- First Opium War, 1839–42
- Treaty of Nanjing, 1842
- US Commodore Perry "opens" Japan, 1853
- Sepoy Mutiny, India, 1857
- French control Indochina, 1858
- Meiji Restoration, Japan, 1868
- Suez canal opens, 1869
- First railroad opens in China, 1882
- "Scramble for Africa" begins, 1885

CHAPTER 21

MACHINES IN THE GARDEN

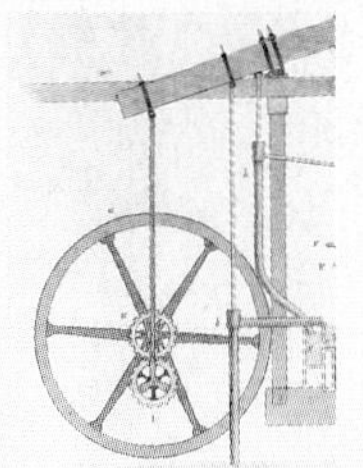

The Industrialization of the West

1750–1914

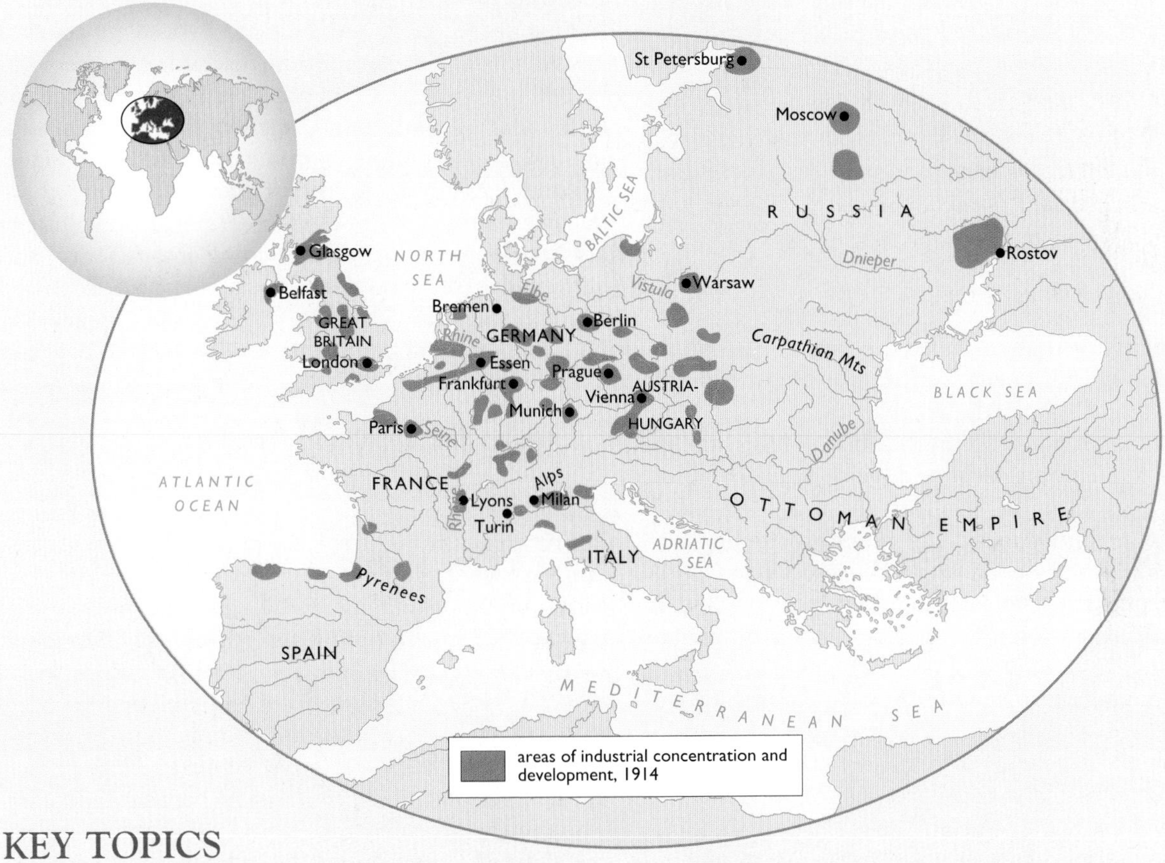

KEY TOPICS

- **Before Industrialization:** The foundations of European industrialization are laid in the Middle Ages and early modern era: an urban grid, the putting-out system, agricultural innovation, military reorganization, and political centralization.
- **Britain Industrializes:** With the building blocks of cotton, water, coal, and iron, Britain leaps ahead, introducing steam-powered factories and transportation systems amid green fields and hills, and creating a modern industrial economy by 1850.
- **Catching Up:** France, Belgium, Germany, and the United States industrialize and modernize, suffering profound dislocations in the process. They are followed by the remaining European nations and Japan, and finally other nations of the world.

Satanic Mills *The English author Charles Dickens (1812–1870) described in his novel* Hard Times *a town he dubbed "Coketown," transformed for the worse by the advent of the steam engine and the factory. "It was a town of machinery and tall chimneys," he wrote, "out of which interminable serpents of smoke trailed themselves for ever and ever, and never got uncoiled." It had a canal turned black, and a river turned purple from the pollutants that issued from the factory where a "steam-engine worked monotonously up and down like the head of an elephant in a state of melancholy madness." Into a peaceful natural world of clear sky and clean water, the machine had introduced poisons and dirt and demonic beasts—smoke serpents and mad elephants. Into the garden of pre-modern Europe the machine had burst with all its attendant maladies, staining the landscape of the pre-industrial paradise with, in the words of the visionary poet William Blake (1757–1827), "dark Satanic mills."*

But the machine that despoiled the "garden," as wordsmiths nostalgically perceived it, of the pre-modern West was not simply destructive in its effects. Its arrival marked a new stage in the ability of the human species to create wealth and gain freedom from scarcity. Beginning in Britain in the late eighteenth century, the transformation of industrial production was accomplished on an astounding scale and with amazing speed, in barely a generation. This process of **industrialization**, often called the "Industrial Revolution," is the most significant change in the history of humankind since hunters and gatherers settled down to farm and live in villages at the end of the Neolithic era thousands of years earlier (see Chapter 1). For many historians and economists, it overshadows the French Revolution (see Chapter 20), or indeed any series of merely political events, in importance for the future of the human race.

This chapter explores the preconditions for industrialization in Britain and in Europe that existed well before 1780. It then describes the many innovations in technology and in the organization of work that together constituted the process of industrialization in Britain, well established by 1850. Finally, it traces the steps by which the industrial tide spread through Europe by around 1870, and thereafter to the rest of the globe where, far from Blake's England, there also sprang up "Satanic mills."

BEFORE INDUSTRIALIZATION

Long before Satanic forces, as Blake perceived them, planted machines in the garden of pre-industrial Europe, the foundations of an industrial economy and society had been laid. They were laid by men and women who could not have conceived of machine power, precision-made parts, or factory systems of production. Societies that had not pursued the European path of economic and social development were not, however, as well-equipped to develop new industrial methods. The features that made Europe the first region in the world to develop modern industry were these. First, from about the twelfth through the fifteenth centuries there developed an urban grid, home to extensive craft production, whose system of employment and distribution reached into the adjacent countryside (see Chapters 11, 12). Urban centers and their rural hinterland together provided a market for goods, stimulating production and exchange. Second, beginning in the sixteenth century, there occurred a rapid series of interconnected revolutionary developments in warfare, commerce, science, and agriculture (see Chapters 15, 16, 17, 18). Together, Europe's medieval social and economic framework, and the early modern advances in technology and knowledge, created the stage for industrialization.

Medieval Foundations: The Urban Grid

After the collapse of Roman power in western Europe during the fifth century C.E., Europe had few towns, and very few large ones. During the next several centuries, urban development ceased, as Europe fell prey to waves of invasion and suffered chronic economic recession. The exchange of goods never ceased, however, and as soon as circumstances permitted, it accelerated. Merchants who had previously journeyed with the goods they had for sale carried either on their own back or on that of a pack animal became sedentary. They settled in communities and the communities of merchants became the nuclei of European towns and cities.

In other civilizations—for example in China or Islam—a few enormous cities served as centers of political, religious, or intellectual life. Europe's cities, in contrast, were small, numerous, and commercial in character. They clustered in certain regions and exchanged goods among themselves, providing centers for both local and more extensive markets. Together, they formed a continuous urban grid that extended north to south from the lowland ports on the North Sea to the north Italian cities, both inland

and coastal, of Tuscany, Lombardy, and the Veneto. Numbering in the hundreds, most had only 2 to 3 thousand inhabitants; substantial towns had 20 to 30 thousand; and the biggest cities at their height reached about 100,000. At first, their residents were almost all artisans or merchants. In time, they also accommodated significant numbers of day workers, servants, migrants, vagrants, priests, and noblemen. But the merchants (who exchanged goods locally, regionally, and long-distance) and artisans (who produced and exchanged goods locally) were the key social groups in European cities, and impressed their character upon them.

By 1300, successful artisans and merchants formed craft guilds, associations of those engaged in the same kind of production or exchange. These self-governing associations established rules for the conduct of the craft or trade, defined procedures for training (apprenticeship) and entrance, and set standards for price and quality. The more important guilds and guildsmen were the city leaders, or "patriciate," who frequently negotiated **charters** with the noble or monarch who had sovereignty over the region. These charters made the towns independent of feudal networks, based on the exchange of land rights and services, and allowed townspeople to rule themselves.

Towns were centers of both trade and production. Merchants organized the import and export of raw materials, essential goods, and luxury commodities, the latter procured from distant locations in eastern Europe, Asia, and Africa. They developed commercial techniques that facilitated the keeping of accounts, the sale of goods, and the exchange of currencies. And they established networks of agents in remote European and non-European **entrepôts** or markets to manage long-distance trade. Those agents kept exquisite commercial records and wrote letters to their home offices describing foreign mercantile practices which their mastery of foreign languages permitted them to understand.

Artisans and merchants together participated in the production of Europe's main manufacture: textiles. Raw wool, especially from Spain and England, was processed in Flemish and Italian workshops, in grades ranging from the utilitarian to the highly refined. Linen and, in time, silk (from raw fiber processed in Italy and France) were also processed in similar ways. Metalwork was Europe's second most important manufacture. Swords and later guns joined bolts of cloth in the bellies of ships that traversed the Mediterranean to foreign markets.

The manufacture of both textile and metal products, though centered in towns, rested on an **infrastructure** that reached out to rural areas. Mining by its nature was a rural enterprise, that needed to be connected with purchasers and metalworkers in the towns. The raw materials for textile production, including not only the fiber itself, but also the materials for washing and dyeing, came from nearby as well as distant regions. Moreover, the country provided many of the textile workers, especially the myriad women who spun cloth on simple spindles or, after about 1300, the hand-operated spinning wheel.

In highly-urbanized Italy, the more advanced processes of textile production—weaving, fulling, dyeing, finishing—were performed in town, often in large workshops. In other less-urbanized areas (including parts of England, France, and central Europe), these processes might be performed in the cottages of workers in an arrangement called the "**putting-out system**" (see Chapter 16). Town and country were linked together, communicating through itinerant merchants or their agents, who distributed materials, collected finished products, and provided payment. These linkages multiplied and strengthened over time, and by the eighteenth century amounted to a "**protoindustrial**" system centered in towns and radiating out into adjacent rural areas.

The main features of Europe's urban grid were all in place, and some were long-established, by 1500. They prepared the way for later industrialization, which harnessed merchant energies and commercial techniques while at the same time rapidly modernizing methods of production.

Early Modern Changes

Soon after 1500, some revolutionary changes began to impact upon the social, economic, and intellectual realms, setting the stage for a later process of rapid industrialization. Historians sometimes refer to a "military," a "commercial," a "scientific," and an "agricultural" revolution. All occurred between 1500 and 1750, and all are preconditions for industrial development after 1780.

Changes in military technology and organization were developed especially by Italian generals and engineers just before 1500 (see Chapter 15). The cannon became more accurate and mobile, while improvements in hand-carried guns and muskets gave infantry an advantage over cavalry and precipitated changes in army organization. The plans of individual fortresses and strategies for national defense adjusted to new realities, guided by military theoreticians. Armies became larger and more expensive to equip and maintain, necessitating (as one among many

WITNESSES

Buying and Selling Before the Industrial Age

Daniel Defoe describes the Yorkshire cloth market (c. 1724): The Market itself is worth describing. . . . The street is a large, broad, fair and well-built Street, beginning . . . at the Bridge, and ascending gently to the North. Early in the Morning, there are Tressels placed in two Rows in the Street, sometimes two Rows on a Side . . .; then there are Boards laid cross those Tressels, so that the Boards lie like long Counters on either Side, from one end of the street to the other. The clothiers come early in the Morning with their Cloth; and as few clothiers bring more than one Piece, the Market being so frequent, they go into the Inns and Publick-Houses with it, and there set it down. At seven a Clock in the Morning . . . the Market Bell rings; . . . without hurry or noise, and not the least disorder, the whole Market is fill'd; all the Boards upon the Tressels are covered with Cloth . . . and behind every Piece of Cloth, the Clothier standing to sell it. As soon as the Bell has done Ringing, the Merchants and Factors, and Buyers of all Sorts, come down . . . . [T]hey reach over to the Clothier and whisper, and in the fewest Words imaginable the Price is stated; one asks, the other bids; and 'tis agree, or not agree, in a Moment. . . . [I]n less than half an Hour you will perceive the Cloths begin to move off, the Clothier taking it up upon his Shoulder to carry it to the Merchant's House; and by half an Hour after eight a Clock the Market Bell rings again; immediately the Buyers disappear, the Cloth is all sold, or if here and there a Piece happens not to be bought, 'tis carried back into the Inn, and, in a quarter of an Hour, there is not a Piece of Cloth to be seen in the Market.
(From D. B. Horn and M. Ransome eds., *English Historical Documents, 1714–1783*, 1957)

The British government moves to protect domestic wool and silk manufactures by banning the use of printed calicoes, imported from India (1721): WHEREAS it is most evident, That the wearing and using of printed, painted, stained and dyed callicoes in apparel, household stuff, furniture, and otherwise, does manifestly tend to the great detriment of the woollen and silk manufactures of this kingdom, and to the excessive increase of the poor, and if not effectually prevented, may be the utter ruin and destruction of the said manufactures, and of many thousands of your Majesty's subjects and their families, whose livelihoods do intirely depend thereupon: for remedy thereof may it please your most excellent Majesty, That it may be enacted . . . by and with the advice and consent of the lords spiritual and temporal, and commons, in the present parliament assembled, . . . That from and after [25 December 1722], it shall not be lawful for any person or persons whatsoever to use or wear in Great Britain, in any garment or apparel whatsoever, any printed, stained or dyed callico, under the penalty of forfeiting to the informer the sum of five pounds of lawful money of Great Britain for every such offense.
(From D. B. Horn and M. Ransome eds., *English Historical Documents, 1714–1783*, 1957)

The economist Friedrich List describes impediments to trade and industry in the German states (1819): Thirty-eight customs boundaries cripple inland commerce, and produce much the same effect as ligatures which prevent the free circulation of the blood. The merchant trading between Hamburg and Austria, or Berlin and Switzerland must traverse ten states, must learn ten customs tariffs, must pay ten successive transit dues. Anyone who is so unfortunate as to live on the boundary line between three or four states spends his days among hostile tax-gatherers and custom house officials; he is a man without a country. . . . Only the remission of the internal customs, and the erection of a general tariff for the whole Federation [of German states], can restore national trade and industry and help the working classes.
(From W. O. Henderson, *The Rise of German Industrial Power, 1834–1914*, 1975)

factors) the centralization of nation states and the creation of new systems of taxation. By 1750, professional soldiers wore regimental uniforms, drilled in formation, fired in lines, and were subject to strict military discipline. Advanced gun technology and more intensive organization, discipline, and planning were related to the later process of industrialization.

Starting just before 1500, the Portuguese, Spanish, Dutch, English, and French—the Atlantic-facing nations of Europe—sent their ships around the globe in search of new commodities and new markets (see Chapter 16). The result was a remaking of the European economy, affecting prices, manufacturing methods, consumer habits, political administration, agricultural organization—just about every aspect of life. All of these were important for later industrialization, but none more important than the network of trade routes that now criss-crossed the globe like a web, and the ever-increasing value of foreign trade—effects sometimes called the "commercial" revolution.

Meanwhile, the revolution in science (see Chapter 17), began with astronomy, physics, and mathematics, later embracing biology, medicine, and chemistry. New paradigms for the structure and workings of the universe encouraged the kind of thinking about complex systems that later informed industrial organization. The use of the experimental method, developed by Galileo Galilei (1564–1642) and other early scientists to test their theories, further encouraged the understanding of material objects and processes, and required scientists, or the artisans they employed, to design new artifacts and make things work. Pumps, thermometers, telescopes, microscopes, and other pieces of special equipment invented to aid experimentation, observation, and measuring, littered the scientist's laboratory. More widely, the idea that specific requirements could be met by the invention of completely new artifacts was to underpin important aspects of the coming industrial era. Accumulating knowledge of the properties of chemicals and gases would similarly prove useful in industrial processes. Just as important as the tinkering inspired by science were the habits of thought that accompanied it: the attention to quantity and number; the zeal to find a simpler, more direct or elegant explanation; the desire to know even more, in the words of one historian (referring to the medieval magician, Dr. Faustus, who sold his soul to the devil in order to obtain unlimited knowledge), the "Faustian spirit of mastery."

Related to these earlier "revolutions" were profound changes in agricultural techniques developed from the seventeenth century in the Netherlands and, soon afterward, in Britain (see Chapter 18). Networks of ditches and dikes for drainage and flood control, and canals for irrigation, required advanced engineering skills and encouraged practical thinking about water supply, transportation, and communication. The elimination of the **fallow**, in some regions, opened new fields for experimental techniques of crop rotation, quickly resulting in enormously increased productivity and fertility. Increased yields meant improved nutrition, at the same time that specialized agricultural management of restricted fields radically changed the pattern of rural labor.

Enclosure of previously open, communal fields, especially in England in the seventeenth and eighteenth centuries, resulted in large-scale dislocations in the life of rural communities. Overall, the main effects of the many initiatives in agriculture during this period were, simultaneously, population growth, the practice of using hired labor, and the availability of large numbers of landless day laborers for agriculture and manufacturing. All were important for the process of industrialization, which required a mobile, flexible labor force, and a mass market for manufactured goods.

By 1750, the impact of revolutionary changes in these different but interconnected areas had been felt, especially in the northwestern region of Europe that had surged ahead of the Mediterranean region both in wealth and creativity. By this date in Britain, the process of industrialization was already, on a small scale, under way.

BRITAIN INDUSTRIALIZES

Beginning soon after 1700, Britain experienced the first stages of industrialization, which accelerated rapidly after about 1780. By 1850, the process of industrialization had peaked. Britain was now the foremost manufacturing and trading nation in the world. The miracle of British industrialization was born from the interconnected histories of basic substances: coal, water, iron, and cotton.

Cotton and Water

Wool, not cotton, had been the lynchpin of medieval manufacture in Europe. The raw fiber came from sheep who grazed abundantly on Europe's relatively cool, well-watered fields. Complex workshop systems evolved to process the raw wool into a range of textiles for local as well as foreign consumption. Around 1700, wool was Britain's major export, amounting to some eighty or ninety percent of the total. Around the same time, however, British consumers, more numerous and more affluent as agricultural conditions improved, developed a taste for cotton cloth.

Bright, washable calicoes (fabrics from Calicut) were produced in India and imported by the British East India Company, which had by that time established virtual sovereignty in the Asian sub-continent. Cotton grew easily in India's hot climate. Indian women spun fine, strong yarn, which they wove into lightweight yet durable fabrics. Imports of these fabrics more than tripled in the last third of the seventeenth century—861,000 pieces for the period 1699–1701, compared to 240,000 pieces for 1663–1669.

British manufacturers, hoping to compete with the desirable new import, acquired raw cotton from American colonies, whose sub-tropical climate proved favorable to the recently transplanted Asian crop. British workers, however, or British techniques,

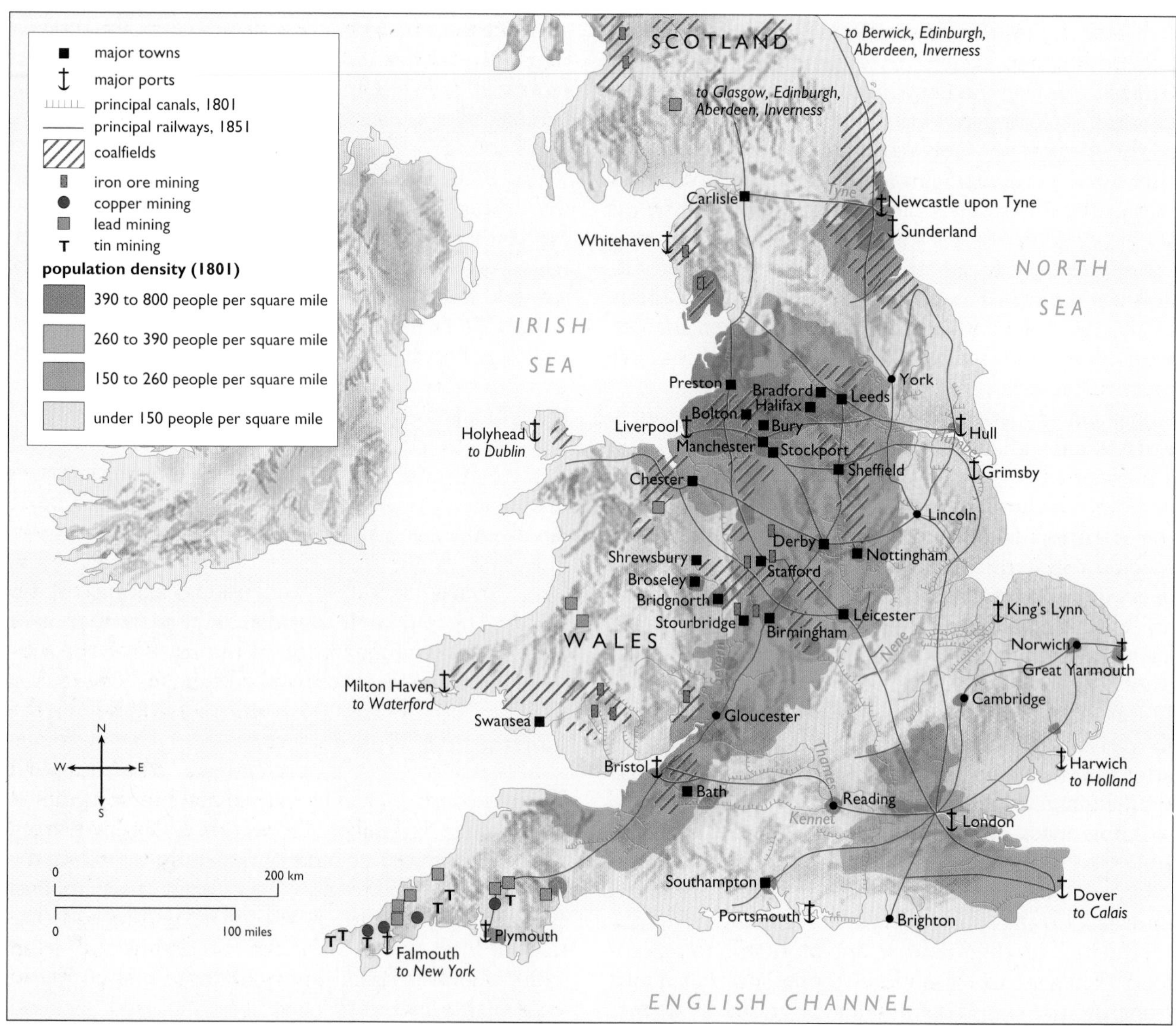

Map 21.1 Great Britain Industrializes, 1750–1850: *From 1750 to 1850, Britain leaped ahead of the rest of Europe and the world in industrial production. Some of the causes for and consequences of that progress are illustrated here: natural resources (coal, iron, copper, lead, tin); natural and artificial waterways; large industrial and commercial centers with large concentrations of human populations; and railroad links.*

could not produce a satisfactory cotton textile. They succeeded in interweaving cotton yarn with linen to make a product called fustian. But consumers wanted unblended cotton.

The Beginnings of Industrialization If there was no way to wean the public from a taste for cotton, could the means be developed to produce cotton cloth in Britain, entrepreneurs asked, so that they might reap the profit at home? The need for a solution to this problem stimulated a series of inventors to develop machinery that shattered traditional norms of textile manufacture once and for all. Those inventions were: the flying shuttle patented by John Kay (1704–1764) in 1733 and widely used from the 1750s; the spinning jenny, introduced in 1764 by James Hargreaves (d. 1778) and patented in 1770; the water frame, which automated the jenny, patented by Richard Arkwright (1732–1792) in 1769; the "mule," developed by Samuel Crompton (1753–1827) in 1779 (he couldn't afford to patent it), combining the jenny and the water frame to produce a fine, strong yarn; and the power loom, patented by Edmund Cartwright (1743–1823) in 1785.

Spinning and weaving are the two major processes of textile manufacture. (Other ancillary processes include washing, combing, fulling, dyeing, etc.) For centuries, weaving had been accomplished on a loom, which permitted the horizontal weft to be laced through the stretched vertical fibers of the warp. Kay's flying shuttle mechanized that process. The laborer had only to pull a cord to push the shuttle, and it wove the yarn horizontally through the warp threads. Not only did this innovation greatly speed the process of weaving (provoking some wrathful handloom weavers to destroy the inventor's model). It also put pressure on spinning.

Spinning was the real bottleneck in textile production. Traditionally, it was performed by women who worked with two rod-like tools, the distaff and spindle. The former held the mass of raw fiber, drawn out by fingers and spun to produce a twisted length of thread. The latter held the finished, weavable yarn yielded by the repeated, tedious process of separating and twisting fiber into thread and winding fine thread into durable yarn.

The innovation of the crank-operated spinning wheel speeded up the spinning process. The spinning-wheel, however, still produced only one thread of yarn at a time; it took between six and ten spinners to produce the yarn for one loom operator. Hargreaves' spinning jenny produced the first major breakthrough in spinning since the earliest days of textile work. It enabled a single laborer to produce several threads at once: six, twelve, twenty-four—the only limit was the force that could be exerted on the cranking mechanism. British laborers could now produce pure cotton yarn comparable to that spun by practiced Indian spinners, in virtually unlimited quantity.

WHO'S WHO

Inventors of the Industrial Age: Textiles

John Kay (1704–1764) the flying shuttle

James Hargreaves (1720?–1778) the spinning jenny

Richard Arkwright (1732–1792) the water frame

Samuel Crompton (1753–1827) the "mule"

Edmund Cartwright (1743–1823) the power loom

Eli Whitney (1765–1825) the cotton gin

As jennies became larger, however, spinning could no longer be done in the workers' cottages. The workers had mostly been women, who won welcome distraction from the tedium of the task by chatting with daughters, kinfolk, and friends engaged in the same work, and by supervising younger children also assigned useful labor. The invention of the jenny disrupted cottage-based spinning. Soon the new machines were being installed in specially constructed manufacturing shops, alongside several others. Workers, still women, walked from their cottages to the shop on a specified schedule. The children they brought with them performed ancillary tasks. A new kind of workplace was taking form.

Soon the jenny was linked by Arkwright's water frame (and later Crompton's mule) to an alternative source of power—the wheel. Water wheels, and more rarely windmills, were the sole forms of machinery known in the Middle Ages that were not driven by either human or animal muscle. Used mostly for grinding grain, their capacity to perform repetitive work had been known for centuries. With the creation of the jenny, and its placement in a workshop rather than a cottage, the opportunity offered by the time-tested wheel became apparent. The workshop was located next to a running stream, which turned a wheel that transmitted power to the moving parts of the jenny. The human laborer was no longer needed to turn the jenny's crank, but only to tend the machine, feed it raw fiber, and replace its bobbins (the machine version of the spindle) on which the strong, uniform yarn was wound. Cotton and water came together, marking an important step toward industrialization.

With the availability of an infinitely expandable supply of cotton yarn, the burden of further development in textile production fell on weaving. The male laborers who had installed a loom in their cottages were now kept busy, and new entrants to the field learned the skill. For a generation more (up to three generations in some regions) the handloom weavers commanded high rates for their work. Their labor services were essential if cloth production was to rise to the level of the availability of raw cotton and processed yarn.

Effects at Home and Abroad But how could weavers keep up with the enormous quantity of yarn spun by the tireless, ever-expandable jennies? Cartwright's power loom presented the solution. With water power driving the flying shuttle, little but supervisory attention was required from the laborer. As power-driven looms slowly took their place alongside

WINDOWS ON

Spinning, Old and New

Cottager spinning wool, 1814

Traditional cottage industries were highly inefficient and unproductive compared with what came later. Compare the home-operated, single-spindle spinning wheel (above) with the multiple-spindle jenny, invented by James Hargreaves (right). Once the concept of multiple, simultaneous spinning of many threads caught hold, the era of mass production was near. It is evidenced in the mass-output "mule" depicted here in this mid-nineteenth-century British factory (below). So fundamental to textile production was the multiplication of spindles, that factory capacity was measured in "spindlage"—not the number of machines, or workers, or even bolts of cloth, but of the spindles on which was wound mechanically produced thread.

James Hargreaves' spinning jenny, c. 1780

Interior of a cotton factory, Lancashire, England, 1835

jennies in the mills, weaving as well as spinning entered the industrial age. The handloom weavers lost their specialist niche in the manufacturing process, and faced demoralizing transformation into ordinary mill workers.

On two other continents, many more people suffered from the mechanization of cotton cloth production in English mills, which still nestled in the country alongside rushing streams. In India, the export trade in cotton cloth declined for a century and by 1830 was dead. For centuries, Indian spindles and looms had provided cottons throughout Asia and the Middle East. But with the advent of industrialization, these regions preferred to import cheap, durable cotton textiles from distant Britain. In India, workers lost employment in the textile sector, and the economy geared downward to export cash crops and resources. That shift amounted to the deindustrialization of India, a prelude to its political defeat (see Chapter 23).

In the British colonies of North America (more than the Caribbean, where sugar cultivation was the economic mainstay), increasing numbers of African slaves were imported to sow, tend, and harvest fields of cotton. The plant had only recently been introduced in the southern Atlantic colonies, where tobacco, indigo, and rice had preceded it as major cash crops. Cotton grew well in the Western Hemisphere, however. Its success encouraged the establishment of more and larger plantations, modeled on those created for the farming of Caribbean sugar and Virginian tobacco. British slave ships were never busier than in the century when cotton became established in the American south. By the late eighteenth century, Africans were a large minority of the residents of the continent, their enslavement encouraged by the yawning British market for raw fiber. And cotton production had not yet peaked.

The American phase of the story of cotton continued uninterrupted throughout the War for Independence (1775–1783). Not long after that conflict was resolved and the United States Constitution ratified, another invention, the creation of an American engineer, joined the new technologies

***Joseph Wright of Derby,* Cotton Mills by Night:** *To the despair of the poets who lamented the implantation of "Satanic mills" in England's green countryside, the factory age arrived. Here the inventor Richard Arkwright's cotton mill is nestled in a traditional landscape in a painting from around 1782.* (Private collection)

that transformed cotton manufacture. In 1793, Eli Whitney (1765–1825) was staying with a friend in Georgia, the manager of a cotton plantation. There he learned that one task above all slowed the process by which the cotton fibers were plucked from the plant, cleaned, and packaged for export. When first picked, the cotton fibers were tangled with seed. Valuable labor time was devoted to plucking and pulling out the seeds.

Familiar with industrial organization in New England mills, Whitney understood the value of this lost time and set out to find a way to reduce it. Within ten days, he had designed a model of the "cotton gin," a simple machine operated by human or horse power that spun the raw cotton, agitating and extracting the seeds. The cotton gin did efficiently what human workers did poorly. From 1793 to 1800, the amount of cotton exported jumped from 18 to 83 million pounds, more than a fourfold increase. In the end, however, the machine meant not less work for African slaves, but more. Speeding up the processing of fiber only encouraged the growing, picking, ginning, baling, and shipping of more cotton in the quest for greater profits. The gin inaugurated the reign of King Cotton in the American south, that did not falter until the Civil War (1861–1865) brought an end to slavery.

Meanwhile, the series of revolutionary technical innovations in cotton cloth manufacture already discussed made Britain the leading world producer of the textile. In due course, the new technology would be adapted for the manufacture of wool, linen, and silk textiles. But first, the cotton mill would undergo a final transformation. The water wheel made way for the steam engine, the end product of another story of successful technological innovation. That story must be told before we return to see the mill reborn as the modern factory.

Coal and Water

The creation of the cotton mill resulted from the marriage of cotton textile production with the water-driven wheel. The steam engine resulted from a different combination of natural resources: coal and water. Coal heated water to produce steam. Steam was used to power the pumps needed to remove water from deep mines where coal (the principal fuel of the era, at least in Britain) lay hidden in the earth. The elegant circularity of these relations is important. It is precisely where these two substances lay in close proximity that the steam engine was developed to provide a solution.

Coal mining accelerated in Britain from the seventeenth to the eighteenth centuries. Charcoal, derived from wood, was the fuel previously used for a major task of traditional manufacture: the smelting of iron. But charcoal was in short supply. Most of Britain's forests had long since been felled to clear fields for cultivation, and to provide fuel and construction materials. Timber for housing and shipbuilding was imported, from Russia and the American colonies. Unlike wood, however, coal was plentiful. In the 1600s, it began to be used for metallurgical and domestic heating purposes. With the increased use of iron in both machines and manufactures, demand for iron rose, and consequently also for coal. Mining boomed.

At first, coal was easily removed from near the surface. As those seams were exhausted, however, miners dug deeper into the earth, until mineshafts and tunnels reached well below the water table, and became liable to flooding. Flooding both weakened the tunnels and made it harder to remove the coal. Workers removed the water in buckets and carts. In places they adapted pumps of the kind used in the ships of the British Navy to keep the water that seeped in from sinking the vessels. Pumping by hand was constant, tiresome work. The need became apparent for a way to power pumps without wasting human effort.

At this juncture, the British inventor Thomas Savery (c. 1650–1715) adapted the design for a steam-powered engine already explored by the French Huguenot immigrant Denis Papin (1647–c. 1712). It utilized simple principles. When water turns to steam, its volume expands 1600 times. The force generated by that expansion can move a piston back and forth in a cylinder, and the piston can drive a pump—or, in later applications, virtually any machinery. The materials needed were also basic, both found nearby in the flooded mine: water and coal. These were the building blocks of the gigantic steam engine that Savery designed. He displayed it to fellow scientists at a meeting of the Royal Society, where Britain's leading experts gathered (see Chapter 17), and to King William III (r. 1689–1702) at one of his country residences, Hampton Court, and patented it in 1698.

Thomas Newcomen (1663–1729) invented an improved engine (first used 1712). For the next half-century, the huge, awkward steam engines created by Savery and Newcomen loomed over the lips of coal mines, and pumped out water from the deep galleries below.

The early steam engines were inefficient, however. After the water was heated, and the resultant steam did its work, it needed to be cooled, and then heated

WINDOWS ON

Power from Steam

Newcomen steam engine, 1717

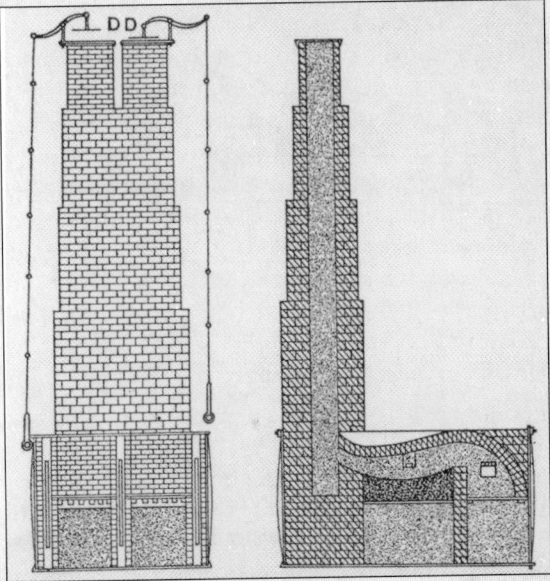

Henry Cort's "puddling furnace," 1784

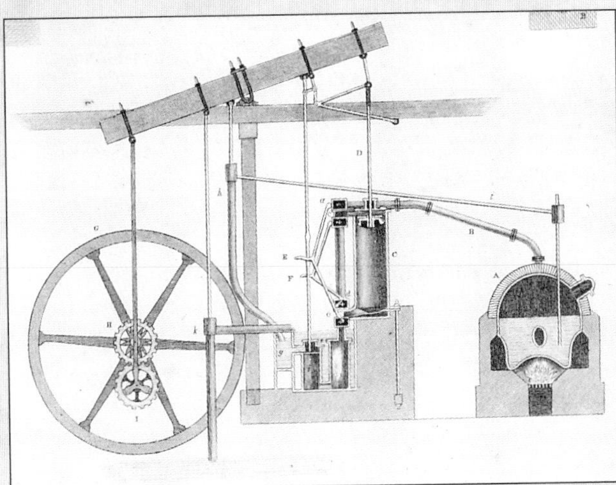

James Watt's design of a rotary engine, 1782

Bessemer converter, 1856

Like the breakthrough of multiple spindlage, the development of the steam engine burst the bounds of previous technology, increasing the power available for work not by a factor of two or ten or even hundreds, but by thousands and tens of thousands. Whereas power historically had been limited by the capacity of muscle, wind, or water, now it was virtually unlimited. The amazing machine that turned ordinary water into limitless power is seen in its early stage of development in Newcomen's 1717 model (top left; note the human figure on the left for scale), and in its later refinement in James Watt's elegant 1782 plan of a rotary engine, capable of turning a shaft for advanced industrial applications (bottom left).

Besides their use in textile manufacture and transportation, steam engines powered the new "iron age" (approximately 1760–1856), speeding up and improving iron and steel production. Henry Cort's "puddling furnace," patented in 1784, removed the impurities introduced into molten iron by the coke used for smelting it (top right). The transition from iron to steel was made possible in large part by the invention of the Bessemer converter in 1856 (bottom right).

again. Both time and fuel were wasted in the process. Having been commissioned to repair a Newcomen engine, the Scottish instrument-maker James Watt (1736–1819) began his search for a solution to these problems. Working over twenty years, he developed an efficient steam engine that burned only half as much fuel as its predecessors. Not only more effective in mining operations, it could also be adapted for other settings—as it would be for textile and iron production and, eventually, transportation.

Watt introduced several improvements to the original steam engines. First, he designed a separate condensing chamber where the water could be cooled and then recirculated. Second, he mounted an air pump to move steam into the chamber. Third, he insulated parts of the engine to prevent energy loss. Watt patented his improved engine in 1769, and in the 1770s, in partnership with the engineer and entrepreneur Matthew Boulton (1728–1809), developed a new engine capable of delivering rotary power, adaptable to many machine uses.

One of the problems Watt faced in developing an efficient engine was the need for precisely measured cylinders. Without them, the steam was not sufficiently contained in the cylinder, so that force was lost and fuel wasted. The solution he found for this problem is yet another illustration of how different technologies cross-fertilized each other in the development of modern industry. Watt employed the skill of gunmakers to craft his cylinders (what is a gun, after all, but a cylinder through which a missile is channeled and exploded?). A precision-made gun barrel insured both accuracy and safety. Its qualities also served well in the operation of the steam engine.

The efficient new steam engine was important in coal mining, where the results were evident: by 1830, Britain was responsible for four-fifths of the world's total coal production. But now the steam engine could also assist with other tasks—virtually any task that presented itself—greatly outpowering human or animal workers. Attention turned to the textile mills, recent innovations themselves, where water power, transmitted from rushing stream to turning wheel, drove the machines that spun yarn and wove cloth. By the 1780s, steam engines were utilized to drive these machines, marking the beginning of the history of the "factory" (derived from "manufactory," a place where things were manufactured). In factories, machines made things; human "hands" (signified by the Latin "*manu*" of "manufacture") worked mainly to tend machines.

After 1785, when Edmund Cartwright patented his power loom, steam-powered textile factories multiplied rapidly. Factories no longer needed to be located near streams. They could be established near to centers where coal was mined or easily delivered, and where bolts of finished cloth were easily transferred to canal barges or ships for export. Often they were near river or ocean ports or, in time, railroad depots. Profits were enormous. The industrialist Robert Owen (1771–1858) opened a factory in Manchester in 1789 for £100 in startup capital. Twenty years later, he paid £84,000 in cash to buy out his partners in the venture.

Outside of mining and textile manufacture, steam engines could be used to grind flour, brew beer, spin potting wheels, or prepare ceramic glazes, refine sugar, or power a printing press—and above all, to produce the parts of other machines. By 1800, 500 engines were at work in British factories, principally in the heavy industries (metals and textiles). By 1870, Britain's steam engines produced as much power as could have been generated by 6 million horses, or 40 million people—more than the entire population of the nation.

While machines for textile manufacture greatly increased Britain's industrial output, and the steam engine raised that output still further, the availability of more and better iron drove it astronomically higher. That effect was achieved when the steam engine was applied to the manufacture of iron.

WHO'S WHO

Inventors of the Industrial Age: Power and Metallurgy

Thomas Savery (c. 1650–1715), **Thomas Newcomen (1663–1729)**, **James Watt (1736–1819)** — the steam engine

Henry Cort (1740–1800) the "puddling" process (iron)

Henry Bessemer (1813–1898) the Bessemer converter (steel)

Iron, Coal, and Steam

From the earliest use of iron (see Chapter 1), the smelting process involved using high heat to melt the metal, release it from its ore, and remove impurities. In pre-modern Europe, first charcoal, and much later coke, distilled from coal, were used as fuels in this

WITNESSES

The Coming of the Machine Age

Edward Baines, a nineteenth-century student of industrialization, describes the great productivity of the machine-powered textile factory (1835): It is by iron fingers, teeth, and wheels, moving with exhaustless energy and devouring speed, that the cotton is opened, cleaned, spread, carded, drawn, roved, spun, wound, warped, dressed, and woven. . . . All are moving at once—the operations chasing each other; and all derive their motion from the mighty engine, which, firmly seated in the lower part of the building, and constantly fed with water and fuel, toils through the day with the strength of perhaps a hundred horses. Men, in the meanwhile, have merely to check its slight and infrequent irregularities—each workman performing, or rather superintending, as much work as could have been done by *two or three hundred men* sixty years ago. . . . When it is remembered that all these inventions have been made within the last seventy years it must be acknowledged that the cotton mill presents the most striking example of the dominion obtained by human science over the powers of nature, of which modern times can boast.

(Edward Baines, *History of the Cotton Manufacture in Great Britain*, 1835; ed. M. J. Daunton, 1995)

The steam engine as a living beast (1834): It is [in] the property which the steam-engine possesses of regulating itself, and providing for all its wants, that the great beauty of the invention consists. It has been said that nothing made by the hand of man approaches so near to animal life. Heat is the principle of its movements; there is in its tubes circulation, like that of the blood in the veins of animals, having valves which open and shut in proper periods; it feeds itself, evacuates such portions of its food as are useless, and draws from its own labours all that is necessary to its own subsistence. . . . The motion of the fluids in the boiler represents the expanding and collapsing of the heart; the fluid that goes to it by one channel is drawn off by another, in part to be returned when condensed by the cold, similar to the operation of veins and arteries. Animals require long and frequent periods of relaxation from fatigue, and any great accumulation of their power is not obtained without great expense and inconvenience. The wind is uncertain; and water, the constancy of which is in few places equal to the wants of the machinist, can seldom be obtained on the spot, where other circumstances require machines to be erected. To relieve us from all these difficulties, the last century has given us the steam engine . . . the noblest machine ever invented by man—the pride of the machinist, the admiration of the philosopher.

(M. A. Alderson, essay, 1834; ed. R. L. Hills, 1993)

process. The availability of the steam engine permitted new innovations in iron manufacture.

Britain's own iron ores were of inferior quality, laced with impurities that injured the resultant metal's strength and malleability. Iron ore was imported from Sweden, Russia, and (after 1776) the United States. Meanwhile, some manufacturers experimented with coke, as opposed to the traditional charcoal, as a fuel for the production of raw or "pig" iron. In 1784, Henry Cort (1740–1800) patented his technique of "puddling," which allowed coke to be used throughout the process of iron manufacture. The pig iron was heated with the coke to form a paste, which was then stirred with iron rods, the agitation allowing the impurities to be burned away. The resultant molten iron was then passed between rollers, which pressed out any remaining impurities. A means had been found to use native ores in the manufacture of top-grade iron.

Innovations in iron manufacture meant a surge in production. In 1750, Britain produced 28,000 tons of pig iron. By 1790, after puddling had been introduced, that figure more than tripled, to 87,000 tons; in 1818, it was 325,000 tons, in 1830, 700,000 tons, and in 1870, 4 million tons. Over 120 years, these staggering figures amount to a sum 142 times the original value—a rate of increase immeasurably beyond what could be achieved by human or animal power alone.

The introduction of the steam engine permitted further advances in metallurgy. The engine could operate bellows to blast hot air into the molten iron—work previously done, less well, by hand. By 1856, Henry Bessemer (1813–1898) further developed a method of using the steam engine to operate both bellows and rollers in the process of iron refining, making the use of expensive, skilled "puddlers" unnecessary, and, by reintroducing carbon to the

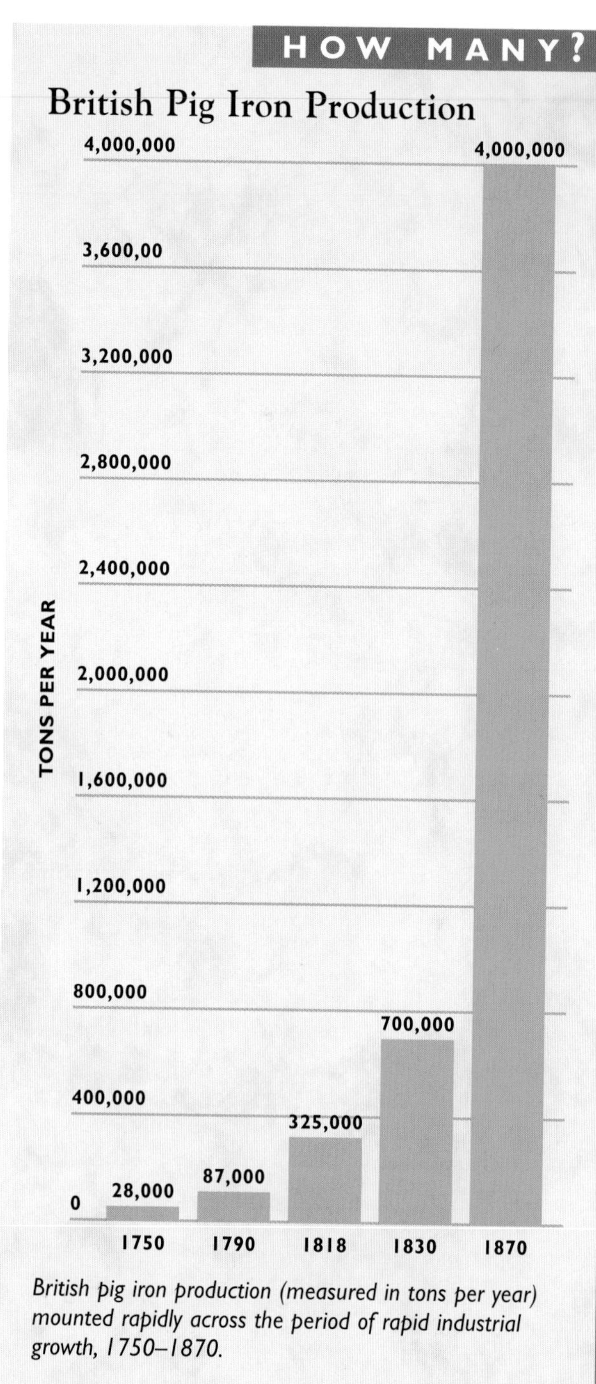

British pig iron production (measured in tons per year) mounted rapidly across the period of rapid industrial growth, 1750–1870.

refined iron, to produce steel—harder and finer than iron. The steam engine operated in one continuous process to produce a high-grade metal capable of serving the needs of a machine age. Almost a luxury metal in the early years of industrialization, steel commanded a price more than ten times that of pig iron. But steel became cheap as production bounded from about a half-million tons worldwide in 1870 to almost thirty times that figure (14,600,000 tons) in 1895.

The iron and steel employed domestically or exported abroad had many uses. In Britain at first, and then elsewhere, these increasingly included the construction of new machines—steam engines to power factories, and the machines that produced goods in the factories. Once again, a circular process is observed: machines made it possible to produce the substance from which to make more machines. Interrelations such as this characterized the building of the industrial era, where each innovation was promptly applied to other purposes.

Railroad and Steamship

Just as the power of the steam engine could be used to drive machines that stood in place, it could also be adapted to machines that moved. The possibilities of using steam to revolutionize transportation presented themselves from the beginning. In 1770, the French had attempted to develop a rudimentary steam-driven cart, followed by a steamboat in 1783. Useful steam-driven vehicles, however, were not developed until the early 1800s, when the necessary components—the steam engine, together with abundant supplies of iron and coal—were assembled.

A "railroad train" is a series of carts or carriages linked together (the train) whose wheels run on a pathway of parallel rails drawn by an engine (the locomotive). The steam engine itself, it has been seen, had origins intimately linked to the coal mine. Similarly, the railroad train was initially developed for mining work, assembling its parts from elements of the mining enterprise. The carts derived from those the miners used to transport coal or mineral-bearing ore from the rock face to the surface (when they did not carry baskets, or push crates). The rails, at first made of timber, were laid to permit the wheels of the carts to roll freely without becoming mired in mud. They were laid in the galleries of the mine or on the road from the mine to a depot by a river or canal, where the heavy mining products were loaded on barges for shipment to market. As early as 1556, a classic Renaissance treatise on metallurgy described the use of rails for just these purposes.

The carts, the rails, and the engine were first put together near the mines. They formed short railroad lines that ran from the mine to a coastal, river, or canal depot transporting coal. In 1804, the engineer Richard Trevithick (1771–1833) developed a locomotive capable of carrying heavy loads on such truncated lines. The first expanded lines date from the 1820s, and in 1821, a rail line extended from Darlington, a mining center, to Stockton, a port; by

Steam Outdoes Men and Beasts

Sheffield, England, in 1879: *One of the industrial boom towns of the nineteenth century, Sheffield specialized in the production of steel and steel implements (such as cutlery and files). This scene displays the prominence of factories and belching smokestacks—and the continuity of traditional life in their midst, evidenced by the presence of countryfolk and their cows.*

1825, this line was offering both freight and passenger services.

The next step in the development of the railroad came with the idea that the railroad could exist apart from the mine. It could link markets and ports, and could transport goods other than mining products. It might carry, for instance, bolts of cotton cloth, or loads of cabbages, to market centers. By 1829, George Stephenson (1781–1848) had successfully developed the locomotive *Rocket* (which could clock a good 36

TREVITHICKS,
PORTABLE STEAM ENGINE.
Catch me who can.
Mechanical Power Subduing
Animal Speed.

Advertisement for Trevithick's engine: *This advertisement for Trevithick's primitive locomotive (developed in 1804, and called here a "portable steam engine") reads "Catch me who can!" and, even more defiantly, "Mechanical Power Subduing Animal Speed." This last concise phrase sums up the heroic achievement of industrialization.*

mph on a normal run—several times the speed of a horse pulling a cart). It operated on a line between the booming factory town of Manchester and the port of Liverpool, serving the Atlantic trade. By 1850, England was crisscrossed with a network of rail lines—an infrastructure that still exists in part 150 years later.

The railroad might be considered the most significant breakthrough in transportation since the days, millennia earlier, of the introduction of the wheel or the sail (see Chapter 1). Previously, in most parts of the world and certainly in Europe, the transportation of heavy materials over long distances was usually accomplished by water—whether on the sea or by river or canal. (Exceptions were the long pack animal trains that traversed the Silk Road in Asia, or the camel caravans across Middle Eastern deserts.) The railroad was faster, safer, and nearly limitless, reaching wherever rails could be laid. Railroad stations, the scenes of myriad comings and goings, became the new foci of industrial civilization. Timetables that clocked those goings and comings were objects of passionate scrutiny, offering the promise of arriving at a specified time at any given destination.

The steamship developed in tandem with the railroad, in due course replacing the sail, as rail replaced the wheeled cart. The American Robert Fulton (1765–1815) developed the prototype of the modern

The Railroad and the Automobile

Claude Monet, Gare Saint-Lazare: *The 1877 work of French Impressionist painter Claude Monet captures the excitement of the railroad, the culminating symbol of triumphant industrialization. The huge Paris railroad station, with its multiple divergent tracks eliciting the wonder of distant lands, receives the mighty engine in its nimbus of gray smoke.* (Musée d'Orsay, Paris)

Karl Benz at the wheel: *The century that opened with the development of the railroad closed with that of the internal combustion engine that powered the modern automobile, first available in the 1880s. Here is Karl Benz, creator of the Benz automobile, steering his new product in 1887.*

steamship from the unsuccessful design created by a French inventor in 1783. In 1807, Fulton's 150-foot *Clermont*, powered by a Boulton and Watt engine, traveled upriver from New York City to Albany in thirty-two hours, averaging a little under five miles per hour. In Britain, Henry Bell (1767–1830) launched his steamship *Comet* in 1812. A steamship first crossed the Atlantic in 1819, powered partly by sail and partly by steam-driven paddlewheels, taking thirty days. The first transatlantic steamship line opened in 1838. By the 1850s, sturdy, reliable steamships fitted with screw propellers (which replaced the paddlewheel) were visiting all the major ports of the globe. The career of the sailing ship, which had opened the Atlantic and Pacific oceans to commerce, would soon close.

Industrialization took place in Britain first because of a number of favorable circumstances. Britain's colonial empire linked it with the cotton workshops of India and the cotton fields of the Americas. Its own land yielded coal and iron in abundance, and its ample waterways and harbors made transportation and communication easy. Its sound banking system, ready capital, landlords that were friendly to profitable innovation, and eager entrepreneurs promoted investment in new ventures. Its government encouraged commerce but did not intervene too much to protect or restrict. Its large supply of unskilled laborers was available to work in the industries developed largely by a pool of talented artisans, who, unlike their continental colleagues, were unhampered by guild restrictions. Beyond these factors, a willingness to experiment and spirit of risk seem to characterize the makers of what some historians call an industrial revolution in Britain.

By 1870, industrialization had transformed Britain. Machine power—"unconquer'd steam" (in the words of Erasmus Darwin, grandfather of naturalist Charles Darwin)—had demonstrated its superiority over animal strength, and machines were planted in the garden of the countryside. Over green fields loomed huge, brash factories (Blake's nightmare), their smokestacks telling the tale of the storming, blasting steam engines within. Sleek, fast trains carried coal and iron, bolts of cloth, and the machines to make them to every corner of the country.

No other state could compete with Britain in output or market share, at home or abroad. In 1851, the "Great Exhibition of the Works of Industry of all Nations" was held in London's Crystal Palace, specially designed for the occasion. In that building whose walls were fabrics of glass and steel, assembled on-site from factory-made components, more than 6 million visitors from around the globe admired 13,000 exhibits of the miracle of British industrialization. After about a century of development, Britain remained unsurpassed in its industrial capacity. By 1870, however, four other nations had set out on the road to industrialization—Belgium, France, Germany, and the United States—two of which would overtake Britain in industrial capacity by 1900. Those other states had begun industrializing early, profiting from Britain's prior experience.

CATCHING UP

How does industrialization spread? Not like dye in water, or like an infection spread through droplets in the air. Each innovation in technology, in manufacture, in distribution had to be introduced on new ground by an individual engineer or merchant or investor. Energetic men (women did not figure noticeably in this process) from other nations visited, observed, and documented industrial processes in Britain. Or sometimes British experts, lured by the promise of bonuses or new opportunities, traveled abroad with a precious cargo of mental capital.

By a succession of such efforts—made covertly, as British law forbade the export of technology and the emigration of experts—other nations developed industrial foundations. By 1870, much of western

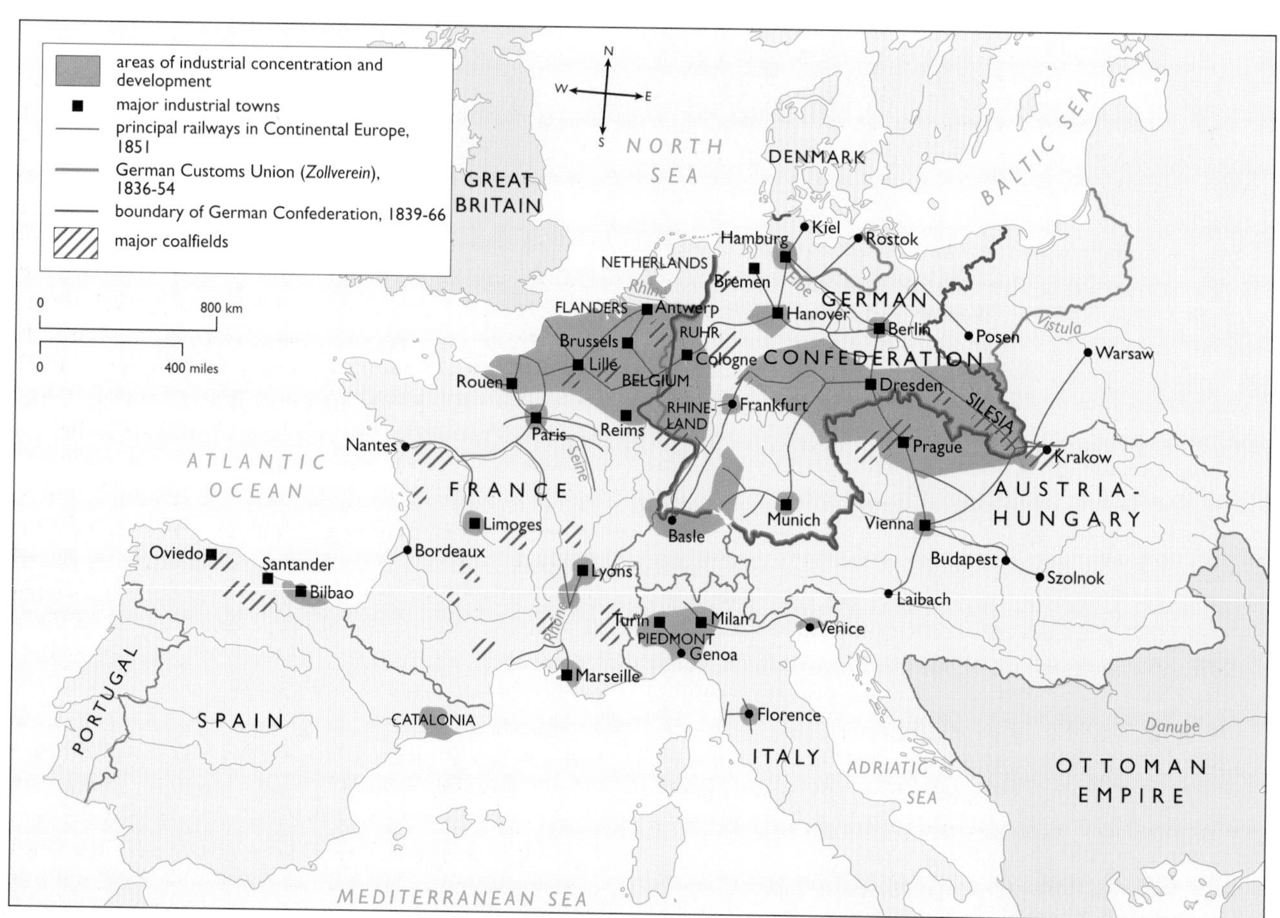

Map 21.2 The Industrialization of Continental Europe, 1815–1860: *As in Great Britain, industrial concentration in continental Europe occurred in the vicinity of mineral deposits and major ports. The flow of goods was encouraged by the elimination of tariffs and customs. The German customs union (the* Zollverein, *1834), which incorporated most of the German states, was one of the most effective of these free trade systems. Note the lower levels of industrial growth and railroad building in southern and eastern Europe.*

Europe and parts of North America were industrialized or had begun the process of industrialization. Between 1870 and 1914, other nations challenged and even surpassed the British lead, while other regions did not begin to industrialize until the twentieth century.

The First Imitators

The first imitators of industrial Britain were its neighbors in northwestern Europe—France, Belgium, and Germany—and its former North American colony, the United States. Beginning soon after the Napoleonic settlement (see Chapter 20), entrepreneurs in these regions began to expand the manufacture of textiles and metals, and to build railroad networks. By 1870, the industrial economies of these nations had developed to a point where they were competing directly with Britain. Germany and the United States proceeded to pass Britain's high-water mark by 1913. This later phase of industrialization, sometimes called the "Second Industrial Revolution," was characterized by the use of chemicals in manufacturing processes, electricity for power and light, and communication technologies.

France and Belgium In the 1700s, France had been a vigorous producer of manufactures, but fell behind its rival Britain during the early industrial era of steam power. Until the late eighteenth century, France and Britain were not only the two main colonial powers, but the two leading manufacturing powers in Europe. Domestic or cottage industry flourished in France as well as Britain, producing textiles for local and foreign markets. France's iron production exceeded Britain's, while its cotton consumption was about the same.

Around 1760, Britain began to pull ahead in industrial capacity—even before the disruption caused after 1789 by the French Revolution. Signs of the quickening of Britain's economic progress are evident in the number of patents granted for new inventions, the volume of foreign trade, the rate of urbanization, and the production of textiles and iron. Though the French government actively intervened to promote the growth of manufactures, private entrepreneurship in Britain proved more effective, while economic blockades of revolutionary France reduced its ability to import raw materials. By 1800, Britain greatly exceeded France in all statistical measures of industrial activity.

Not only did Britain spurt forward at the end of the eighteenth century, but France dropped out of the race after 1789. Until Napoleon's defeat in 1815, France was preoccupied with a political and social transformation that left little opportunity, or wealth, for economic development. At the end of the revolutionary era, French manufacture had fallen below its level in 1789. In the meantime, Britain had enjoyed a near monopoly of foreign trade.

The period that followed, from the restoration of the monarchy through the inauguration of the Third Republic (1815–1871; see Chapter 20), was favorable to the development of an entrepreneurial bourgeoisie. Some of Napoleon's innovations proved helpful—the abolition of guilds, the removal of internal **tariffs**, and the standardization of commercial law. The mechanization of textile manufacture proceeded on the British model—French entrepreneurs often hired skilled British workers, of whom there were 15,000 in France by 1830.

The French state actively intervened in economic matters. Through monarchical, republican, and imperial eras, official policy favored those who invested funds or launched companies, especially family firms. The government built the national railroad system (in place by the 1840s), then leased the component lines for terms of more than one hundred years to private companies. Napoleon III (r. 1850–1870) encouraged banking firms to invest in industrial ventures. Still, French industrialization was slowed by the commitment of so much of the economy to agriculture, and by the scarcity of coal and iron (exacerbated by the loss of Alsace and Lorraine to Germany in 1871, following the Franco-Prussian War). In 1870, France lagged behind Britain, and would soon fall behind Germany and the United States.

The Belgian economy, which resembled that of France in 1789, followed its neighbor's lead and drew profitably on British expertise, in defiance of British law. A major coup was the enlistment of the Cockerill family of expert British manufacturers. William Cockerill (1759–1832) (honored with French citizenship by Napoleon in 1810 for his introduction of textile manufacture to France) built a factory system for the combined production of metals and machines in Liège (modern Belgium, under French domination 1797–1815 and Dutch domination 1815–1830). In 1812, it employed 2000 workers; by the 1830s, it was the largest such plant in the world—reflecting a mission, as one observer thought, "to fill the whole world with machinery." The machines built in Cockerill's factory permitted the rapid development of mining, shipbuilding, and railroad systems. To set up their railroad system, the Belgians hired Britain's first expert, George Stephenson.

The power of electricity: *By the 1870s, electricity was widely used for interior and street illumination and as a new source of power. Here a French factory is lit by electric "candles" in an 1883 illustration by Georges Dary.*

Germany The German nation was only constituted in 1871, at about the time that German industrial activities surged ahead to new highs of production. The earlier stages of German industrialization had been undertaken primarily by Prussia. In the eighteenth century, Frederick the Great of Prussia (1712–1786), whose talents encompassed military management, literature, and music, had also been alert to his small state's economic interests. He outlined his goals neatly: first, to bring money in from abroad; second, to prevent its seeping out to foreign countries. He promoted silk, wool, and cotton manufactures, welcomed French Huguenot and Jewish immigrants whose diligence contributed to economic development wherever they settled, and seized Silesia from neighboring Austria in part to acquire its mineral resources, especially coal. Still, outside of the industrial regions of Saxony and the newly acquired Rhineland (1815), Prussia was primarily an agricultural nation; its prosperous manufactures formed only a small part of its economy.

Napoleon's consolidation of the German states in the early nineteenth century was, ironically, a spur not only to German nationalism but also to economic progress. (His abolition of guilds and serfdom also promoted innovation and labor mobility.) In 1834, a further consolidation for economic purposes only—the *Zollverein*, or "Customs Union"—was voluntarily adopted by nearly all the German states. With the elimination of customs barriers among these still autonomous states, new enterprises, such as modern textile factories, could flourish, and new industries find markets and resources. Among these resources were coal, which from the 1840s began to be mined intensively in the Ruhr, Silesia, and Saar regions, and iron, smelted with coke from the 1850s. Coal production increased steadily in volume (more than doubling in the period 1851–1857 alone), until Germany, having incorporated the valuable provinces of Alsace and Lorraine, became Europe's greatest producer. Bismarck had said that Germany would be unified by "blood and iron" but, a modern economist has

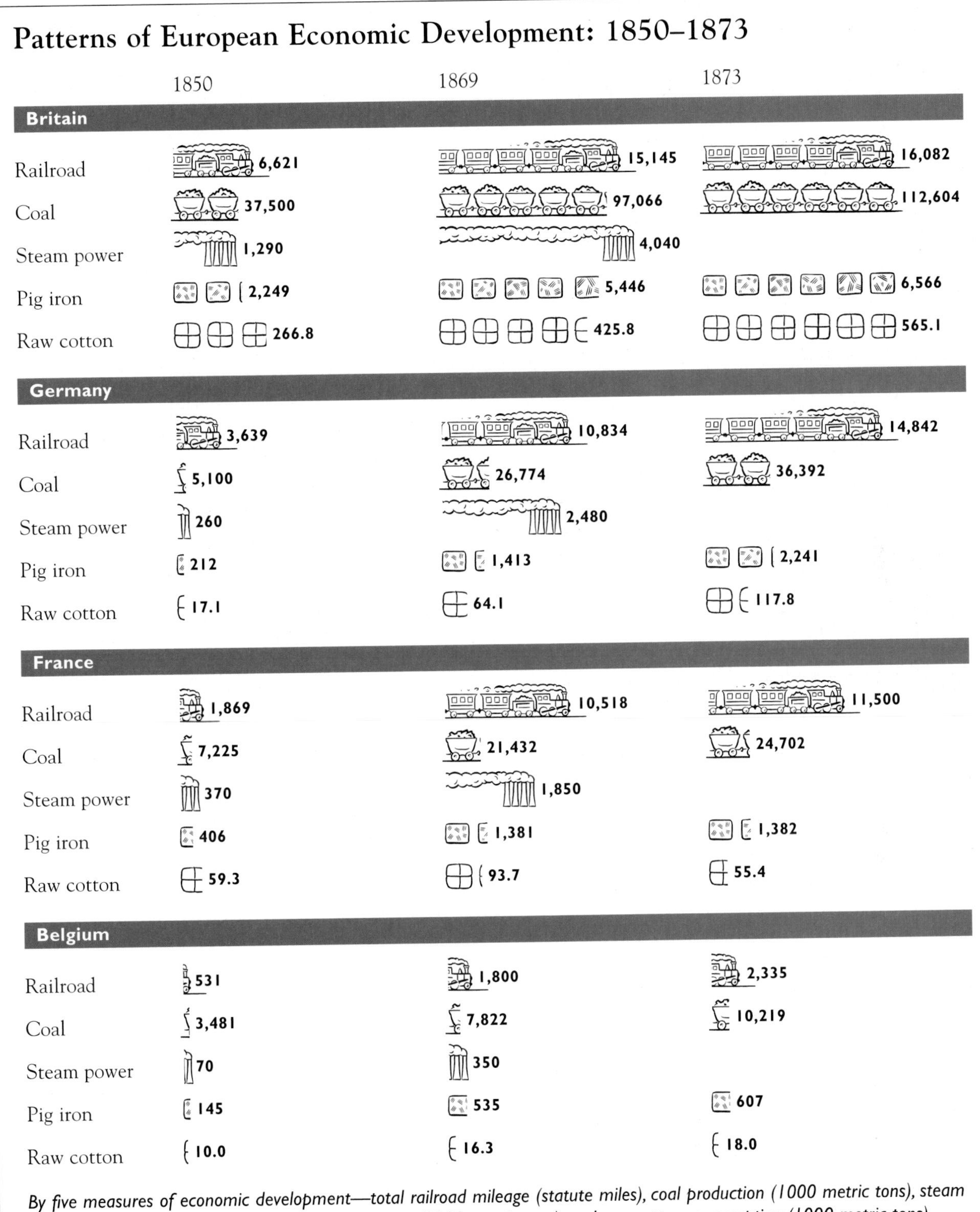

By five measures of economic development—total railroad mileage (statute miles), coal production (1000 metric tons), steam power capacity (1000 horsepower), pig iron output (1000 metric tons), and raw cotton consumption (1000 metric tons)—Britain outpaced her three leading European rivals from 1850 to 1873. The gap narrowed, however, especially between Germany and Britain. Note Germany's sevenfold increase in coal production, compared to Britain's threefold increase, and Germany's sevenfold increase in cotton consumption, compared to Britain's, which slightly more than doubled.

Source: Based on *D. Landes,* The Unbound Prometheus (Cambridge: Cambridge University Press, 1969), *p. 194.*

observed, it could be more truly said to owe its success to "coal and iron."

At the same time, even before the German nation formally came into being, a German rail system developed. By 1839, with the opening of a railway from Dresden to Leipzig, the German states were on their way to the development of a mature railroad system. Construction proceeded in the 1840s, and by 1860 total German rail mileage surpassed that of any other nation of continental Europe. As elsewhere, the creation of a railroad network stimulated industry and the labor market.

At first, German observers faithfully pursued the British model of industrial development. Like the French and the Belgians, they traveled to Britain and came home with new ideas. Alfred Krupp (1812–1887), called the "Cannon King," was the most famous member of a dynasty that controlled one of Germany's largest firms into the mid-twentieth century. Krupp visited Britain in 1838 to learn about metallurgical techniques. He later established the major German steel company that made possible the new nation's rapid development of machines, ships, and weapons later in the century. At the Crystal Palace in 1851, Krupp showed off his own 4300-pound steel block, impressing even the British with the quality and mass of the product, and a gun barrel of brilliant cast steel. By 1862, he had installed a Bessemer converter at the Krupp works in the Ruhr.

Krupp's enormous metalworks were typical of German industrialization after 1871. Germany's industries grew swiftly, rivaling British capacity by 1900. German businesses tended to be on a large scale for several reasons: first, Germany possessed the natural resources that fed heavy industry; second, the state actively subsidized and promoted new enterprises and investment; and third, funding was readily provided by modern credit banks, which especially encouraged exports to foreign markets. Patterns of investment encouraged the formation of **cartels**, in which one or two large firms dominated a whole industrial sector. Only two firms, for instance, controlled ninety percent of the electrical industry, pioneered in Germany. Germany's rapid industrial growth can be measured in its changing share of the world output of manufactured goods: from thirteen percent in 1870 to sixteen percent in 1900, while Britain's slid from thirty-two to eighteen percent.

The United States Like France, Belgium, and Germany, the fledgling United States learned to industrialize from Britain. Like Germany, its industrial economy surged in the last few decades of the nineteenth century during the "Second Industrial Revolution."

From early colonial days, the economy of the United States was tightly linked to Britain's. It had sent timber and tobacco to the motherland, and foodstuffs to her Caribbean colonies, enabling them to pursue the monoculture of sugar. By the middle of the eighteenth century, cotton cultivation in the southern Atlantic colonies grew steadily in volume, accelerating rapidly after the War for Independence. Cotton bound the United States economy to industrial Britain from 1783 until the 1860s, when the Civil War (1861–1865) disrupted the plantation system and put an end to slavery.

In the late eighteenth century, entrepreneurs returning from tours of inspection abroad established the first textile mills in the New England states. In 1793, Samuel Slater (1768–1835) established on the British model the first water-powered textile mill in the United States, in Rhode Island. Only fifteen more mills were built by 1808, but in 1809, eighty-seven additional mills were established. By 1814 in Waltham, Massachusetts, Francis Cabot Lowell (1775–1817) built a weaving factory designed on British models, its looms powered by steam engines. By 1831, the young industrial nation boasted 795 cotton factories, with a capacity of 1.2 million yarn spindles—nearly forty times the capacity of 1809. By the 1840s, sewing machines, invented by Isaac Singer (1811–1875), were busy in factories producing ready-made clothing.

British railroad construction won prompt attention from United States entrepreneurs. Beginning with the Baltimore and Ohio Railroad, local lines were already developed in the 1830s, and by the 1840s there were 3000 miles of interregional rail lines. Private businessmen were the main developers of rail capacity, in contrast to France or Germany where the state dominated the establishment of railroad systems. The distances traversed by rail lines in the United States were huge, since railroads needed to carry manufactured products and migrating peoples from the Atlantic to the Pacific coast, 3000 miles away, and to return with grain and beef. The demand for boxcars and rails was consequently enormous, and stimulated steel and machine production.

Northern railroads supplied Union soldiers all along the battlefront and helped win the Civil War against the South, whose underdeveloped rail network served mostly to carry bales of cotton from farm areas to coastal ports. While the guns still roared, railroad companies began to stretch new lines across the belly of the nation. In 1869, with the war only four years over, rail lines extending from the Midwest and California met at Promontory Point, Utah, amid the peaks of the Rocky Mountains. The completion of the first transcontinental railroad anywhere on the globe was marked by the ceremonial driving of a golden spike, the hammer wielded by California entrepreneur John Leland Stanford (1824–1893). The Atlantic was now linked with the Pacific, from whose coast the West would find another vantagepoint on the East.

Railroad development encouraged other economic projects. It not only boosted machine and metal production, but facilitated the distribution of textiles and other manufactures, and foodstuffs. Another factor in industrial development was the existence of a large mobile labor force, augmented after the 1840s by immigration from Europe (especially refugees from the Irish famine) and, to a lesser extent, Asia. Government support in the form of federal land grants to entrepreneurs venturing westward was helpful, while government interference remained limited. By the 1870s, large corporations such as Andrew Carnegie's (1835–1919) steelworks employed hundreds or even thousands of workers, who shopped in company-run stores and were supervised by a private police force—maintained unapologetically by a man who would become one of the greatest United States philanthropists.

Although the economy of the United States remained heavily agricultural, its agricultural production was increasingly mechanized with the invention of tractors and harvesting machinery, and refrigeration systems for rail cars and steamships. The nation's seemingly limitless natural resources—both mineral and agricultural—and its ambitious, often ruthless entrepreneurs, had by 1914 made the United States the world's leading industrial nation.

The Second Phase By this late date—more than a century after the founding of the first textile mills, or the refinement of the steam engine—industrialization on both sides of the Atlantic had entered a second phase. Joining the heavy industries (metals and textiles) of early industrialization, were newer industries concerned with producing chemicals or providing gas and electrical power. Chemical products (often derived from petroleum) were employed in textile manufacture, agriculture, mining, and construction in the form of dyes, fertilizers, or explosives. From the early 1800s, gas lamps illuminated streets, shops, homes, and factories—"Gas has replaced the sun!" enthused one contemporary.

Electricity soon replaced gas as a source of power. In 1879, the American Thomas Edison (1847–1931) invented the incandescent light bulb, making electricity usable to light homes and public places. By the 1880s, electricity had taken over for the lighting of city streets, department stores, hotels, and public buildings. Gradually, ordinary homes were wired, and

Industrializing farmwork: *As industrialization spread from Britain to the rest of the West and beyond, the United States outdid all other countries in mechanizing basic agricultural processes. McCormick's horsedrawn reaper, patented in 1834, improved productivity by about two-thirds and laid the foundations for numerous further inventions including the combine harvester.*

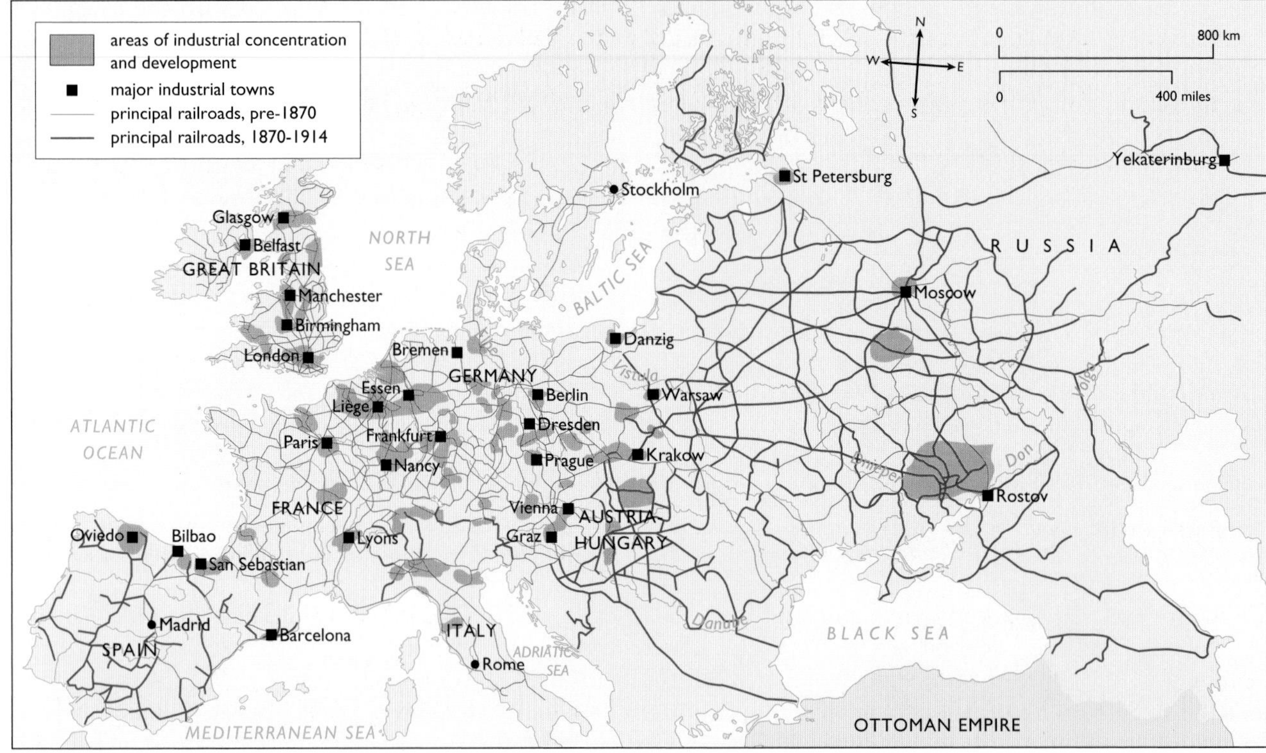

Map 21.3 Industrialized Europe by 1914: *By 1914, areas of industrial concentration in Europe had increased in number and the railroad system was greatly expanded (compare Map 21.2, p. 660).*

housewives felt privileged to have sewing machines, refrigerators, and vacuum cleaners that operated by electrical power. Electricity powered local transportation—the streetcars or "trolley" cars that first opened up suburban housing for workers, who were enabled to live in surroundings pleasanter than the immediate area of their industrial workplace. Bicycles, too, allowed workers to glide swiftly through city streets and in the countryside. By 1885, a workable internal combustion engine was available to power the first generation of automobiles. By 1909, a French observer announced: "It's finished, the tranquility of our streets, and the charm of promenading either on foot or in a carriage. . . . Paris belongs to the machines."

Communications, meanwhile, had developed to meet the needs of entrepreneurs around the globe. First the telegraph (which could communicate even across the Atlantic ocean, thanks to a cable laid in 1866), then the telephone, patented by Alexander Graham Bell (1847–1922) in 1876, conquered the distances that modern economies traversed. From the 1890s, wireless communication was made possible by the work of Guglielmo Marconi (1874–1937), and by the early 1900s radio broadcasts could be received in ordinary households. During those same years, silent motion pictures began to be screened (by 1908, France had more than 1000 movie theaters), and couples could dance in their living rooms to music produced by the gramophone (see Chapter 26).

By 1900, Western civilization had been transformed by industrialization, and could be called modern—for industry, which brought machines into the garden of traditional society, was in itself the creator of modernity.

The Rest of the West and the Asian Vanguard

By 1870, France, Belgium, Germany, and the United States had joined the select circle of industrialized nations. Over the next generation, other European nations entered—the Netherlands and Scandinavia, northern Italy, parts of Spain, Portugal, and Ireland, Poland and the region around Prague (the present-day Czech Republic), following in the footsteps of earlier neighbors. So too did Russia, as well as Canada, Australia, and Japan.

Tsar Peter the Great (r. 1682–1725) had put Russia on the path to industrialization. He traveled

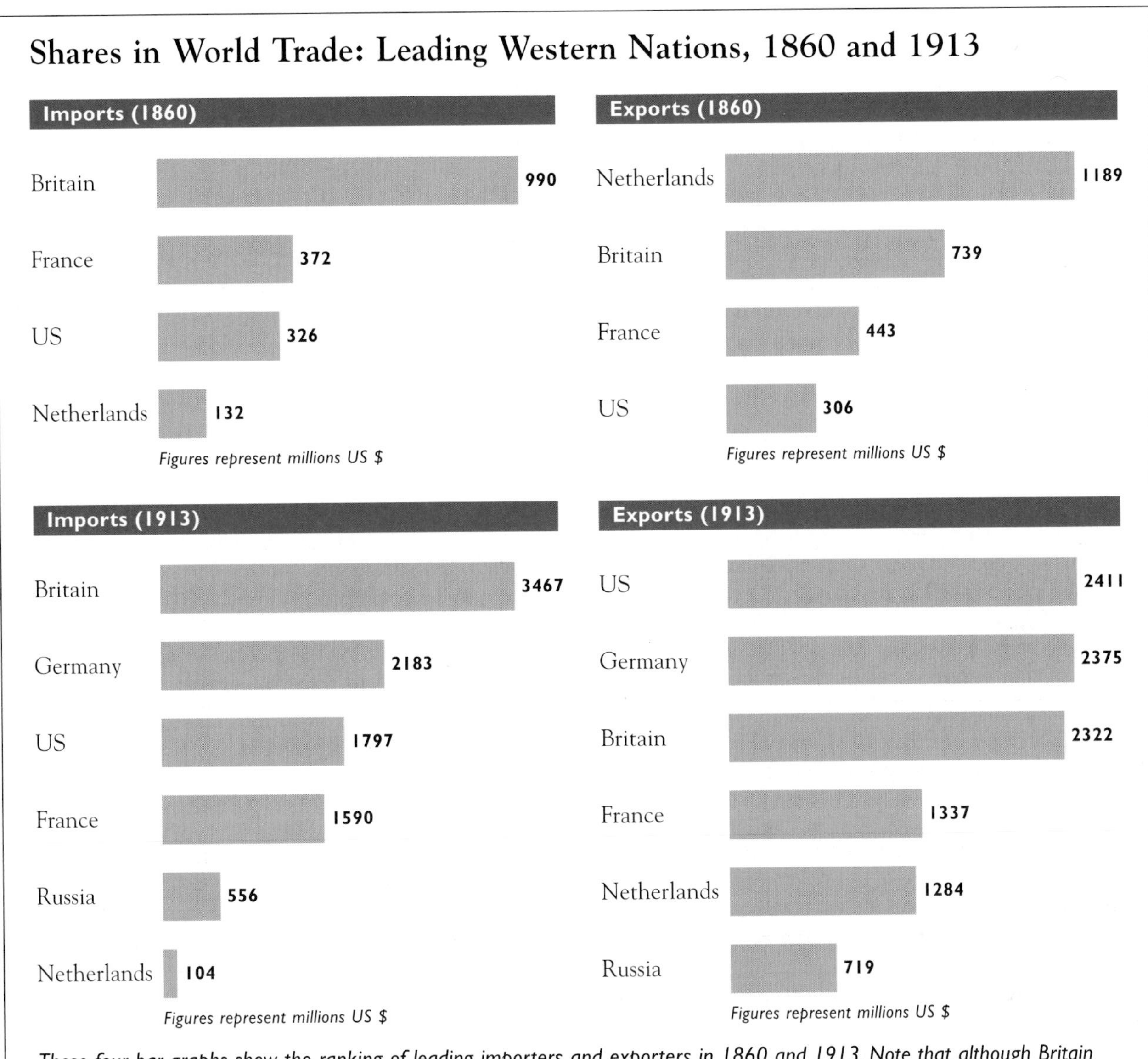

These four bar graphs show the ranking of leading importers and exporters in 1860 and 1913. Note that although Britain retains her lead as importer in 1913, as in 1860, both the United States and Germany are approaching her level in 1913. The Netherlands is the leading exporter in 1860, but has fallen well behind the closely matched frontrunners Britain, Germany, and the United States—with the latter in the lead.

himself to western European nations, studying their military and shipbuilding technology especially. The state supported the production of heavy manufactures, and eighty-six manufacturing enterprises were launched. By the end of the eighteenth century, Russia's iron production was second only to Britain's, and its urban populations had tripled.

These ventures had a limited impact, however, given the vastness of the nation and its entrenched system of agricultural production based on serf labor. In the nineteenth century, Russia industrialized but only slowly, on the model established by Britain in the previous century. In 1805, a steam engine was first used for cotton manufacture. In 1836, Cort's puddling process was introduced for the production of iron. Beginning in 1843, foreign consultants oversaw the importation and installation of updated machinery for textile manufacture, and planned the development of railroad and steamship systems. From 1820, a steamboat regularly plied the river Volga. By 1851, a rail line ran from St. Petersburg to Moscow. The numbers of factories and free (non-serf) laborers multiplied,

WITNESSES

Catching Up in Argentina, Germany, and Russia

Argentinian journalist and diplomat Juan Bautista Alberdi hails the railroad as a tool for unity and prosperity (1852): The railroad offers the means of righting the topsy-turvy order that Spain established in this continent. She placed the heads of our state where the feet should be. For her ends of isolation and monopoly this was a wise system; for our aims of commercial expansion and freedom it is disastrous. We must bring our capitals to the coast, or rather bring the coast into the interior of the continent. The railroad and the electric telegraph, the conquerors of space, work this wonder better than all the potentates on earth. The railroad changes, reforms, and solves the most difficult problems without decrees or mob violence. It will forge the unity of the Argentine Republic better than all our congresses. The congresses may declare it "one and indivisible," but without the railroad to connect its most remote regions it will always remain divided and divisible, despite all the legislative decrees.

(From B. Keen ed., *Latin American Civilization: History and Society, 1492 to the Present*, 4th ed., 1986)

Friedrich List on England's leadership in global industrialization (1841): Far from having been stopped in its progress by England, the world has received from her its strongest impulse. She has served as a model to all nations in her internal and external policy; in her great inventions and grand enterprises of every kind; in the advancement of the useful arts; in the construction of roads, railways and canals; in the discovery and cultivation of lands in a state of nature, particularly in displaying and developing the natural wealth of tropical countries, and in the civilization of tribes, savage or subsiding into barbarism. Who can tell how far behind the world would have been if there had been no England?

(Friedrich List, *The National System of Political Development*, 1941; ed. T. H. von Laue, 1969)

Russian Finance Minister Sergei Witte argues that Russia must industrialize if it is to flourish (1900): The experience of all peoples clearly shows that only the economically independent countries are fully able to assert their political power. . . . At present the political strength of the great powers which are called to fulfill great historical tasks in the world is created not only by the spiritual valor of their peoples but also by their economic organization. Even the military preparedness of a country is determined not only by the perfection of its military machine but by the degree of its industrial development. Russia . . . needs . . . a proper economic foundation for her national policy and her culture. . . . International competition does not wait. If we do not take energetic and decisive measures so that in the course of the next decades our industry will be able to satisfy the need of Russia and of the Asiatic countries which are—or should be—under our influence, then the rapidly growing foreign industries will break through our tariff barriers and establish themselves in our fatherland and in the Asiatic countries mentioned above and drive their roots into the depths of our economy. This may gradually clear the way also for triumphant political penetration by foreign powers. . . . It is possible that the slow growth of our industries will endanger the fulfillment of the great political tasks of the monarchy. Our economic backwardness may lead to political and cultural backwardness as well.

(Sergei Witte, "On the Condition of Our Industry," 1900; ed. T. H. von Laue, 1969)

while serf workers labored in industrial workshops and serf entrepreneurs built and extended them.

But the economic base on which these impressive increases rested was inadequate. The nation was overwhelmingly agricultural (and continued demand for basic commodities—timber, grain, wax—encouraged it to remain so). Moreover, Russia had no tradition of artisan manufacture and only a tiny merchant class—about one-fourth of one percent of the population. The tsars' earnest support and the purchased services of Western experts had slight impact.

A transformation of the Russian economy along modern lines would only begin in the last years of the nineteenth century. By that time, a full generation after the abolition of serfdom, large numbers of laborers released from the land were available. These joined the skilled, mobile workers clustered in those cities large enough to support full-scale industrialization, funded by foreign capital. The exploitation of coal fields near the Black Sea, oil wells near the Caspian Sea, and iron lodes in the Ural Mountains, linked now by railroad to western Russian centers, made Russia competitive with the most advanced nations of the West. Urbanization gathered pace, the urban population rising from under 6 million around 1860 to more than 23 million in 1913. During this period, the population of Moscow increased from 500,000 to more than 1.5 million, and that of St. Petersburg from about 500,000 to 2 million. Despite a slow start, St. Petersburg, boasting 900 factories in 1914, was an industrial center among the largest in Europe.

In the Russian industrialization of the 1890s, Minister of Finance Sergei Witte (1849–1915) labored to promote important enterprises and to lure foreign capital to fund them. Above all, he saw to the construction of an improved railroad system that linked Moscow and St. Petersburg to ocean ports and navigable rivers, and to manufacturing, agricultural, and mining centers. In 1899, under his direction, more than 3000 miles of the Trans-Siberian railway line had been completed. Arching across the whole continent of Asia, it opened Siberia to colonization. When he was dismissed in 1906, Russian industrialization, though still lagging behind the leaders of western Europe, was well under way.

The economies of colonial Latin America—Spanish and Portuguese, Caribbean and continental—were firmly linked, like the English and French ones of North America, to Europe (see Chapters 16, 19). The trade in tobacco, rice, and indigo, timber, fur, and fish in the latter case; silver, gold, and sugar in the former, formed chains across the Atlantic.

The silver and gold extracted from South American mines, mainly with native Amerindian labor, flowed through Spain and Portugal for three centuries, and provided Europe generally with the bullion necessary to trade with the nations of Asia. Sugar from Brazil and the Caribbean islands, raised and harvested mainly by imported African slaves, fed European appetites no longer content with a diet of bread and soup. In all these cases, the pattern is the same: the fruits of the earth, the produce of the mine, or the bounty of the fields were sent to Europe. In return came manufactured goods, especially metal products and textiles, such as the cotton fabric used to clothe plantation slaves, purchased in the Americas primarily by those of European descent. Thus supplied, they spurned the cruder handicrafts produced by native artisans. This trading pattern was distinctly unbalanced to the disadvantage of the dark-skinned laborers of Latin America.

Although the commodities traded changed with time, the same pattern prevailed for a century after the 1820s, the point at which most Latin American nations (all but Cuba and Puerto Rico, and the English and French Caribbean colonies) achieved their independence (see Chapter 19). The exports of silver and gold dwindled, to be replaced by other profitable products of the mines and large landed estates (**latifundias**): nitrates and tin, coffee, beef, and grain, medicinal plants and dyestuffs. The manufactured goods received in return were now machine-made textiles and metals, which competed with, and dispirited native artisans. Sugar exports from the Caribbean continued to flow, as Europeans continued to favor sweet treats and sweeteners for the exotic beverages, coffee and tea, that they had made their own.

In this context, Latin America failed to industrialize. Beginning in the 1850s, railroad lines were built to bring goods from the mines and the *latifundias* to the ports. Trade was directed toward Europe, and not toward the vast interior which remained largely untouched by the rail. Steam engines were employed in updated mines, thanks to foreign investment capital, mostly British. They also powered sugar refineries as early as 1815, requiring slaves to produce more and more raw cane to feed the vigorous new machines. But the failure to acquire the machinery for local manufacture was virtually total. As a consequence, Latin America as a whole lagged well behind the industrialized nations of the world into the twentieth century—despite its vigorous participation in foreign trade, and despite the wealth of a thin stratum of elite consumers, landowners, and entrepreneurs.

A quite different pattern holds for the far-flung British colonies of Australia, New Zealand, and Canada, later independent units of the Commonwealth, from 1931 the political association of former British colonies (see Chapter 28). These regions

WHO'S WHO

Inventors of the Industrial Age: Transportation and Communication

George Stephenson (1781–1848) the locomotive

Robert Fulton (1765–1815) the steamboat

Thomas Edison (1847–1931) the incandescent lightbulb

Alexander Graham Bell (1847–1922) the telephone

Guglielmo Marconi (1874–1937) the radio

Industrialization Beyond the West

Visit of the Mikado (Meiji) to a foundry: *During the late 1800s, Japan and, to a lesser extent, Russia engaged in rapid industrialization, studying, importing, and adapting Western European models. Here the Japanese emperor watches a demonstration of European casting techniques at a foundry in Yokosuka.*

began to claim a stake in world trade (based at first on exports of abundant raw materials, such as foodstuffs, wool, and minerals) and industrial development by the late nineteenth century. As industrial powers, their fuller development, however, belongs to the twentieth century.

Apart from European nations, their colonies, and former colonies, Japan was the sole region to industrialize before the twentieth century. It did so because of the shocking challenge presented to its proud traditional culture by the advent, from the 1850s, of foreign economic intervention backed by the threat of force (see Chapter 23). Until that date, Japan, like China, considered itself economically self-sufficient. Although largely agricultural, it produced fine craft manufactures, and had some familiarity with Western gun technology (the gift of the Dutch merchants who, alone of Europeans, were allowed to deal with the Japanese through the port of Nagasaki).

Once "opened," however, by the arrival of the American Commodore Matthew Perry (1794–1858), the Japanese accomplished within a generation an astounding political and economic revolution. By the 1880s, Japan had established a textile-based industrial economy, which featured steam-driven factories, modern machinery, vigorous steel production, and an effective system of transportation by railroad and steamship. The Japanese economic miracle continued to flower into the next century, enabling it to defeat militarily a European rival—Russia—as early as 1905 (see Chapter 23).

Postponed Industrialization

By 1870, industrialization had reached maturity in several Western nations, and had begun in others, as it had in Japan. Elsewhere in Asia and Africa—in India, China, southeast Asia and Oceania; in Islamic west Asia and North Africa, and in Sub-Saharan Africa—industrialization had to wait until the twentieth century. During the 1800s, these regions exported cheaply-priced resources to the West, and in return purchased expensive manufactured goods, to their economic disadvantage (see Chapter 23).

Prior to the mechanization of British textile manufacture, as has been seen, India had been not only an active participant in Afro-Asian commerce, but also an active center as producer and exporter of cotton cloth. By the 1830s, it had become a consumer of British manufactures, including cotton textiles. In less than two generations, India had been transformed from a productive region to a non-productive one. The continued British presence (until 1947) meant that the Indian economy continued to serve British needs, as market and as provider of resources. The construction of a major railroad network from the 1850s, carrying both freight and passengers, increased mobility and stimulated commerce. But it did not encourage India to develop its own industries. Rather, it facilitated the export of cash crops, including raw cotton, and the penetration of British manufacturers deep into the interior of the vast sub-continent.

Further east, China, like India, had played a central role in the Asian economy for many centuries. China produced prized manufactures, notably silk and porcelain, as well as tea, an expensive agricultural commodity. Her busy merchants carried these exports overland to India and western Asia, and shipped them throughout the South China Sea and western Pacific—to Korea and Japan, southeast Asia and Oceania. Despite China's strong economic position, however, it lagged with regard to the West at a critical juncture.

The Chinese outlook was conservative, resistant to novel products or methods of production. As one seventeenth-century European missionary observed, "they are more fond of the most defective piece of antiquity than of the most perfect of the modern . . .," unlike Europeans, "who are in love with nothing but what is new." The prevailing Chinese philosophy of Confucianism, moreover, which has conditioned Chinese values into the modern age, denigrated merchants and profit-seeking, an attitude that was a disincentive to industrial development. In addition, in the eighteenth century, China had begun to experience a demographic crisis, and the amount of land per capita shrank. At the same time, the reigning Manchu dynasty (1644–1912) began to weaken.

Meanwhile, Western nations sought greater access to Chinese ports, jealously closed to foreigners (see Chapter 23). In 1793 and 1816, the British sent representatives to China seeking more favorable treaty arrangements. Huge quantities of tea, which the British public craved, triggered these overtures. In this period, tea made up about half of British imports from China, which increased nearly eightfold

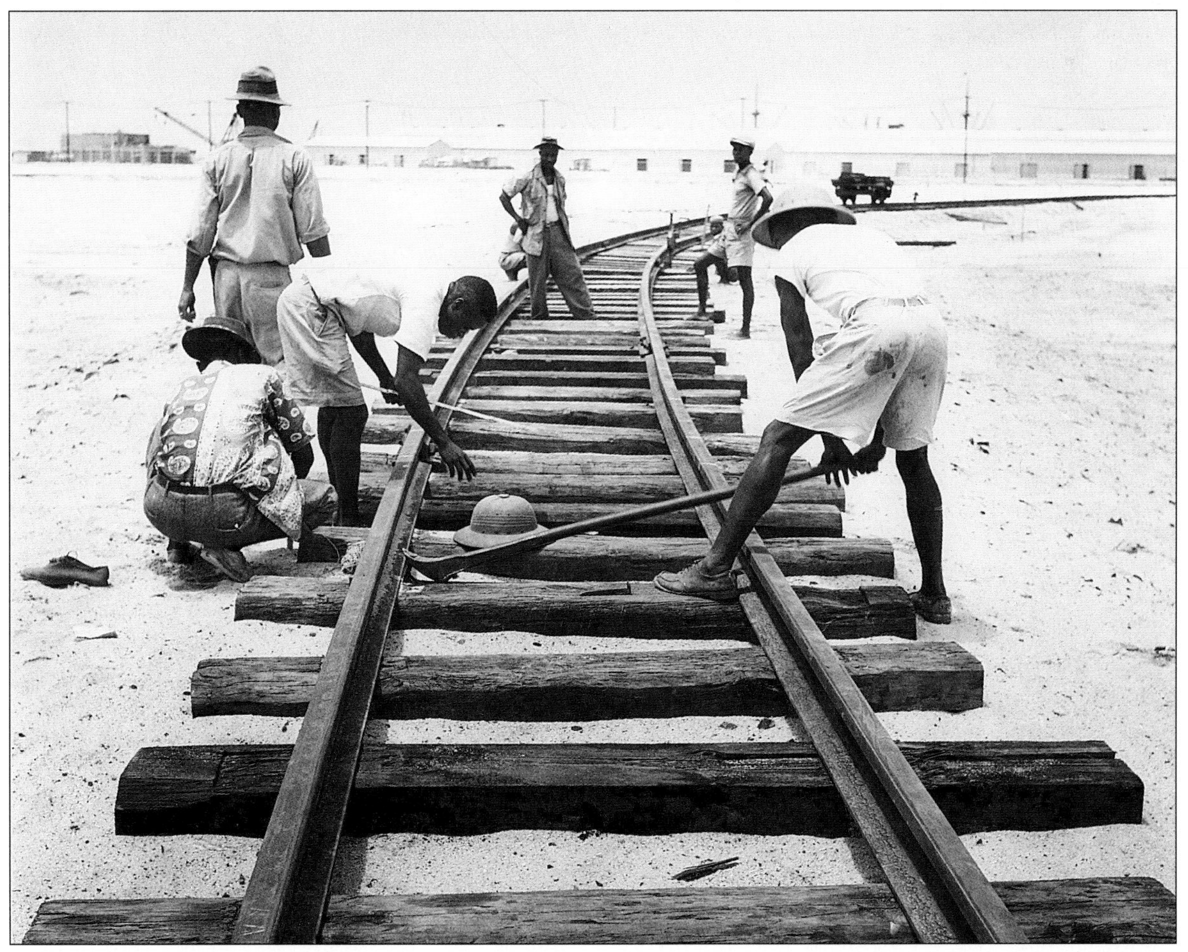

Liberia's first railway: *Industrialization has achieved global proportions in the twentieth century, as suggested by this photograph of Liberian workers building that nation's first railroad in 1950—one hundred years after Britain, the homeland of the steam engine, completed its essential railroad grid.*

between the 1780s and 1815. In exchange for tea, the British offered textiles, lead, and tin—and, covertly and illegally, opium processed from the poppy crop grown in India. Chinese officials were uninterested in the former, and furious about the latter.

In 1837, the imperial official Lin Tse-Hsu (1785–1850) addressed to the British Queen Victoria (r. 1837–1901) a stern letter about the opium trade. Whereas the Chinese exported many goods, all of benefit to humanity, he wrote, the British sent to China, along with benign products, an addictive poison. How could they sanction exposing Chinese people to a dangerous substance not permitted to their own citizens? To stop the traffic in drugs, the Chinese would punish any foreigner found participating in it—the penalty being decapitation. Not long after, the First Opium War (1839–1842) broke out, as British warships shelled several Chinese ports that were defenseless against superior Western weaponry. By the 1842 Treaty of Nanjing, the British gained access to Guangzhou (Canton), Shanghai, and other ports.

Thereafter, several Western nations followed the British in "opening up" China to trade. As in India, the influx of Western manufactures had the effect of retarding China's own industrial development. The first successful railroad, a short line for hauling coal to port, dated only from 1882. No factories for the machine production of textiles were established until the end of the century. The lofty Chinese empire sank rapidly to economic dependence upon contact with the West.

The experience of the Ottoman states of North Africa and western Asia followed a similar trajectory. These regions considered themselves superior to Europe in every regard—in religion, in statecraft, in commerce. In the course of the nineteenth century, however, Western manufactures had their now familiar, and fatal, effects on native economies. Despite attempts, especially in Egypt, to establish factories under the guidance of Western advisers, these regions failed to industrialize. They became exporters of agricultural and mineral commodities, locked into an unfavorable trade relationship with the European nations.

The nations of Sub-Saharan Africa were even less able than India, China, or the Ottoman Empire to withstand the economic dominance of Europe. With the cessation of the slave trade during the nineteenth century, their merchants were starved for cash. Despite a strong commercial tradition, and long experience in the manufacture of iron, Africans, too, became suppliers of raw materials to the industrialized West. That economic subordination, as will be seen, was merely a prelude to an even more complete subordination to those nations.

Conclusion

DESPOILED GARDENS AND THE MEANING OF THE WEST

By 1870, the productivity of the Western world far exceeded any measure imaginable in 1770. More things were made than ever before; exchanged faster; and sent further. The agent of this nearly inconceivable jump in material capacity was the machine operating by non-human, non-animal power—the first important innovation in the human ability to produce since the first human ancestor wielded the first tool.

Henceforth, humankind would share its earthly domain with the machine. For Enlightenment thinkers, the human being was much like a machine—a wholly rational being, a mechanism governed by mind. Julien Offray de la Mettrie (1709–1751), a case in point, argued in his aptly titled *Man the Machine* (1748) that the soul was nothing more than an extension of the body, itself a mechanical system. Now the machine approached the realm of the human. Like their human inventors, machines made things, and machines made machines. The machine commanded its human operator to tend it and feed it. If the human was a machine, could the machine be seen as possessing spirit, as it possessed heat and locomotion? Could the machine do good or evil?

The new machines caused Enlightenment optimism to cloud over, giving way to a darker, indeed Satanic, vision. The machines that invaded and despoiled the gardens of Western civilization promised abundance, but they devastated nature and deformed human lives. The following chapters will consider the impact of the machine on human society in the West and beyond, and on the ideas and images created by those who lived under its sway.

REVIEW QUESTIONS

1. What was the Industrial Revolution? Why was Europe the first region in the world to industrialize? Why did some thinkers call machines "dark Satanic mills"?

2. Why was Britain the first country to industrialize? How did the demand for cotton cloth spur industrialization in Britain? How did the steam engine transform mining and manufacturing?

3. Describe the improvements in iron and steel-making that occurred after 1750. Why were these improvements so important? How did railroads and steamships affect the growth of commerce?

4. What were the next states to industrialize after Britain? What role did the state play in industrialization in France and Germany? What was the Second Industrial Revolution?

5. Why did industrialization escalate in Russia in the late nineteenth century? Why was Latin America so slow to industrialize? Why was Japan the only non-European nation to industrialize before the twentieth century?

6. Why was the United States able to industrialize so rapidly toward the end of the nineteenth century? How did industrialization transform relations between the West and Asia and Africa? Why did China resist industrialization?

SUGGESTED READINGS

General studies

Landes, David S., *The Unbound Prometheus: Technological Change and Industrial Development in Western Europe from 1750 to the Present* (Cambridge: Cambridge University Press, 1969). A comprehensive, wide-ranging, and authoritative account of the technological and economic aspects of the Industrial Revolution.

Landes, David S., *The Wealth and Poverty of Nations: Why Some Are So Rich and Some So Poor* (New York: Wal Mardon, 1998). Thought-provoking study of the global distribution of wealth. Argues that what has made some nations rich and others poor is industrialization and the cultural patterns that tend either to promote or discourage it.

Stearns, Peter N., *The Industrial Revolution in World History* (Boulder, CO: Westview Press, 1993). Examination of the Industrial Revolution from a global perspective. Integrates and compares industrialization in Britain, Europe, the US, Russia, Japan, the Pacific Rim, Latin America, and elsewhere.

Before Industrialization

Laslett, Peter, *The World We Have Lost* (London: Methuen, 1965); *The World We Have Lost: Further Explained*, 3rd ed. (New York: Scribner's, 1983). Both versions of this classic book explore pre-industrial society. Laslett argues that the Industrial Revolution destroyed a world that was far more small-scale, intimate, and humane than the one it created.

Overton, Mark, *Agricultural Revolution in England: The Transformation of the Agrarian Economy 1500–1850* (Cambridge: Cambridge University Press, 1996). General introduction to the changes in farming that helped create Britain's rising wealth and which ultimately facilitated industrialization.

Britain Industrializes

Crafts, Nicholas F. R., *British Economic Growth During the Industrial Revolution* (Oxford: Clarendon Press, 1985). A thought-provoking study. Sees Britain's economic transformation as a long process of growth rather than as a relatively sudden "revolution."

Mathias, Peter, *The First Industrial Nation: An Economic History of Britain, 1700–1914*, 2nd ed. (London–New York: Methuen, 1983). Good general introduction.

Timmins, Geoffrey, *The Last Shift: The Decline of Handloom Weaving in Nineteenth-Century Lancashire* (New York: St. Martins Press, 1993). Nineteenth-century handloom weavers are seen as the exemplar of skilled artisans replaced—and in many cases ruined—by technological advances in the textile industry.

Catching Up

Blackwell, W. L., *The Beginnings of Russian Industrialization, 1800–1860* (Princeton: Princeton University Press, 1968). Older but useful general introduction.

Gerschenkron, Alexander, *Economic Backwardness in Historical Perspective* (Cambridge, MA: Harvard University Press, 1962). Classic account comparing industrialization in several national contexts. Emphasis on the varying sources of investment capital, the consequences thereof.

Henderson, W. O., *The Rise of German Industrial Power, 1834–1914* (California: University of California Press, 1975). Standard economic and political study of German industrialization. Includes discussion of the creation and significance of the *Zollverein*.

Milward, Alan S. and S. B. Saul, *The Development of the Economies of Continental Europe, 1850–1914* (Cambridge, MA: Harvard University Press, 1977). Detailed study of the economic history of European industrialization.

Morris-Suzuki, Tessa, *The Technological Transformation of Japan from the Seventeenth to the Twenty-First Century* (Cambridge: Cambridge University Press, 1994). Good, general economic history of Japan over several centuries. Synthesizes Japanese and Western scholarship.

Trebilcock, Clive, *The Industrialization of the Continental Powers, 1780–1914* (London–New York: Longman, 1981). Focuses primarily on Germany, France, and Russia, but also discusses Italy, Spain, and Austria-Hungary. Excellent critique of earlier historical theories.

LIVES OF THE OTHER HALF

1750 | 1775 | 1800 | 1825 | 1850 | 1875 | 1900 | 1925

Society and Politics

American and French Revolutions, 1775–1794

French Revolutionary and Napoleonic Wars, 1792–1815

- ◆ Revolutions in France, Belgium, Italy, Poland, 1830–31
- ◆ First Reform Act in Britain, 1832
- ◆ Severe cholera epidemics in London and Paris, 1832
- ◆ Poor Law Amendment Act in Britain, 1834
- ◆ Repeal of Corn Laws in Britain, 1846
- ◆ Communist League founded in Britain, 1847
- ◆ Revolutions in Europe, 1848
- ◆ Public Health Act in Britain creates sewage system, 1848
- ◆ First underground (subway) system, London, 1863
- ◆ School mandatory for children up to age of 10 in Britain, 1880
- ◆ British population more than 67% urban, 1880
- ◆ Nearly 75% of Parisian streets with sewers, 1887
- ◆ School fees abolished in Britain, 1891
- ◆ 75% of French population urban, 1900
- ◆ Paris metro (subway) opens, 1900
- ◆ New York subway opens, 1904

Labor and Economy

Britain industrializes, 1750–1850

Western and central Europe and North America industrialize, 1815–1900

Russia and Italy industrialize, 1870–1918

- ◆ Workers' combinations outlawed in France, 1791
- ◆ Workers' combinations outlawed in Britain, 1799–1800
- ◆ Luddites' industrial sabotage, Britain, 1811–12
- ◆ "Peterloo Massacre," Manchester, England, 1819
- ◆ British Combination Acts repealed, 1824
- ◆ National Union of Cotton Spinners in Britain, 1829
- ◆ British Factory Act, 1833
- ◆ Robert Owen's Grand National Consolidated Trades Union, 1834
- ◆ Chartist movement, 1838–48
- ◆ British Mines Act, 1842
- ◆ Anti-industrial riots among linen weavers in Silesia, 1844
- ◆ British Ten Hours Act, 1847
- ◆ Karl Marx and Friedrich Engels' *Communist Manifesto*, 1848
- ◆ National workshops set up in France, 1848
- ◆ Amalgamated Society of Engineers formed in Britain, 1851
- ◆ First International, 1864
- ◆ Combinations legal in France, 1864
- ◆ Second Reform Act in Britain, 1867
- ◆ Paris Commune, 1870
- ◆ Bismarck introduces social welfare for workers in Germany, 1883–89
- ◆ Third Reform Act in Britain, 1884
- ◆ Second International, 1889

Beyond the West

Japan industrializes, 1870–1918

- ◆ Shaka leads Zulu nation, Africa, 1817
- ◆ First Opium War, 1839–42
- ◆ US Commodore Perry "opens" Japan, 1853
- ◆ Mughal Empire in India ends, 1857
- ◆ French gain control of Indochina, 1858
- ◆ Meiji Restoration, Japan, 1868
- ◆ Suez canal opens, 1869
- ◆ "Scramble for Africa" begins, 1885

CHAPTER

22

LIVES OF THE OTHER HALF

Western Society in an Industrial Age

1750–1914

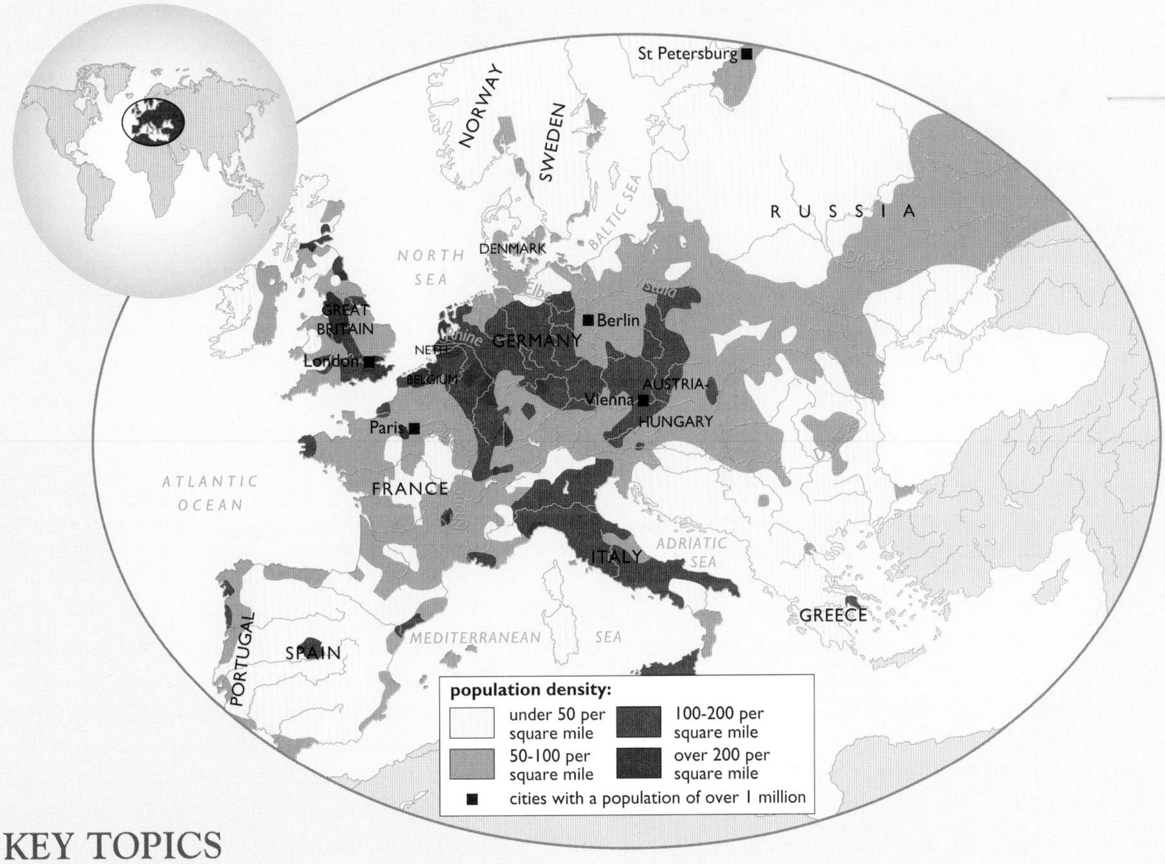

population density:
under 50 per square mile
50-100 per square mile
100-200 per square mile
over 200 per square mile
cities with a population of over 1 million

KEY TOPICS

◆ **Workers and Workplace:** Industrial workers laboring in the mill, mine, and factory under new and harsh conditions learn to unite as a social group and an economic force.

◆ **The Industrial City:** Burgeoning cities develop new structures and infrastructures as migrants arrive to work in factories and workshops, throng cafés and beerhalls, and spill out onto the streets.

◆ **The Two Halves at Home:** The divergent worlds of the townhouse and the tenement reflect the great rift between rich and poor in the industrial city; on the one hand, leisure, luxury, the duties of philanthropy, a culture of conformity, and the pursuit of "culture"; on the other hand, hunger, tedium, violence, dirt, disease, and hopelessness.

Domains of Rich and Poor *In his 1890 book* How The Other Half Lives, *the photojournalist Jacob Riis (1849–1914) revealed to middle-class New Yorkers the lives of the laboring poor and the hopelessly poor trapped in the seamier districts of their city. Only a few steps away from prosperity, he wrote, we encounter poverty. "We stand upon the domain of the tenement. . . . Suppose we look into one?" And so we shall.*

This chapter surveys the lives of rich and poor in nineteenth-century cities transformed by the advent of the machine. It peers into the places where workers labored and the places where they lived. Then it will cross town to visit other neighborhoods, not far away but a world apart, to consider the lives of the rich, whose wealth depended on the labor of those who owned nothing and commanded no one—those of the other half.

In industrial society, the poor were many and various. They were wageworkers who hauled loads and constructed homes, railroad stations, and public buildings; they were skilled **artisans** who tailored men's clothing or made precision tools; they were laundresses, prostitutes, thieves, and the jobless; and they were, most conspicuously, the new social group of **factory** workers, or **proletarians**. All these lived together in the squalid streets of bursting cities, where they contended with filth, disease, and crime.

Across town (or sometimes just around the corner), lived the wealthy, not nearly so numerous, yet still various. Among the rich were the modern descendants of the old nobility, and the heirs of the old bourgeoisie—bankers, merchants, and professionals (including lawyers, physicians, engineers, accountants, and university professors). Preeminent among the bourgeoisie was a new group of factory owners, investors, and entrepreneurs: the capitalists, whose enterprises harnessed the power of machines to generate profits that were reinvested to create even more wealth. The rich lived in a world apart from the poor—a world filled with broad boulevards, grand homes, lavish consumption, and elaborate social ritual.

As the machine transformed the landscape of the Western world, it also transformed society, whose two halves in their separate domains, the rich and the poor, now faced each other in a new setting, across new and daunting barriers.

WORKERS AND WORKPLACE

As industrialization proceeded from the late eighteenth into the early nineteenth century (see Chapter 21), the nature of work changed. Machines established the framework of things, and workers obeyed the command of their clatter and roar. Machines transformed people just as they transformed the workplace, creating in the industrial proletariat a self-conscious working class—organized "labor."

Mine, Mill, and Factory

Workers in the mine pit, water-powered mill, and steam-driven factory experienced labor conditions harsher than those that rural workers knew in their villages, cottages, and fields. Workers of all ages and both sexes labored long days, in poor light and bad air, with little time to eat or rest. They were unprotected from dangerous equipment and subject to the peremptory commands and stern punishments of foremen or owners.

The underground universe of the mine had always been a place of horror for those who probed the earth's recesses for tin and copper, gold and silver, iron and coal. In antiquity, slaves were employed to work the mines—an expendable workforce who could be subjected to heavy loads, noxious gases, and frequent cave-ins and explosions. The same risks attended mining in the early modern era, when heightened demand for iron and coal required deeper pits and more intensive production. These risks were often borne by the most fragile workers. Children, for example, were assigned to haul goods from the deepest mine tunnels because their slight bodies could adapt to the cramped underground spaces. Conditions in the mines only deteriorated as industrialization progressed and demand for their products increased.

Meanwhile, in the mills, rows of large machines wound newspun yarn on multiple spindles. Little was expected of their human operators, who were there to provide fresh raw fiber, realign yarn that had wandered or snapped, and keep up with the relentless pace of the machine. The machines themselves did the work, without artistry perhaps, but also without fatigue.

The relation between the worker and his work—more often her work in the early days of the mill—changed drastically. Previously a woman alone would spin all that was required for her family. Equipped with the simple distaff or spindle, she worked at home, amid childcare and household duties, assisted by unmarried female kin and neighbors. Her husband or some other local artisan would weave the thread into cloth in his cottage or workshop. In the proto-industrial "putting-out" system (see Chapter 16)—also called "domestic" or "cottage industry"—both spinning and weaving were performed on contract for production beyond household needs. The entrepreneur and his agents managed supplies, assigned fees, and collected profits, but left the village environment and the social world of the cottage unaltered.

WITNESSES

The Factory Observed and Resisted

A Luddite group determined to destroy the machines that put them out of work threatens an English manufacturer (1812): Information has just been given in that you are a holder of those detestable shearing Frames, and I was desired by my Men to write to you and give you fair Warning to pull them down. . . . You will take Notice that if they are not taken down by the end of next week, I will detach one of my Lieutenants with at least 300 Men to destroy them and furthermore take Notice that if you give us the Trouble of coming so far we will increase your misfortune by burning your Buildings down to Ashes and if you have Impudence to fire upon any of my Men, they have orders to murder you, & burn all your Housing, you will have the Goodness to your [neighbors] to inform them that the same fate awaits them if their Frames are not speedily taken down.

(From E. P. Thompson ed., *The Making of the English Working Class*, 1964)

Factory rules, distributed to all workers in a Berlin factory (1844): 1. The normal working day begins at all seasons at 6 a.m. precisely and ends, after the usual break of half an hour for breakfast, an hour for dinner, and half an hour for tea, at 7 p.m., and it shall be strictly observed. Five minutes before the beginning of the stated hours of work until their actual commencement, a bell shall ring and indicate that every worker employed in the concern has to proceed to his place of work, in order to start as soon as the bell stops. . . . Workers arriving 2 minutes late shall lose half an hour's wages . . . 7. All conversation with fellow-workers is prohibited. . . . 9. Every worker is responsible for cleaning up his space in the workshop. . . . All tools must always be kept in good condition, and must be cleaned after use. . . . 12. It goes without saying that all overseers and officials of the firm shall be obeyed without question, and shall be treated with due deference. Disobedience will be punished by dismissal. 13. Immediate dismissal shall also be the fate of anyone found drunk in any of the workshops.

(From G. B. Kirsch et al, *The West in Global Context: from 1500 to The Present*, 1997)

Andrew Ure, defender of industrialization, gives high marks to factory conditions for child laborers (1835): I have visited many factories . . . entering the spinning rooms, unexpectedly, and often alone, at different times of the day, and I never saw a single instance of corporal chastisement inflicted on a child, nor indeed did I ever see children in ill-humour. They seemed to be always cheerful and alert, taking pleasure in the light play of their muscles,—enjoying the mobility natural to their age. . . . It was delightful to observe the nimbleness with which they pieced the broken ends, as the mule-carriage began to recede from the fixed roller-beam. . . . The work of these lively elves seemed to resemble a sport. . . . As to exhaustion by the day's work, they evinced no trace of it on emerging from the mill in the evening; for they immediately began to skip about any neighboring playground, and to commence their little amusements with the same alacrity as boys issuing from a school.

(Andrew Ure, *The Philosophy of Manufactures*, 1835; eds. G. B. Kirsch et al, *ibid*, 1997)

Flora Tristan reports on conditions in English factories (1842): Most workers lack clothing, bed, furniture, fuel, wholesome food—even potatoes! They spend from twelve to fourteen hours each day shut up in low-ceilinged rooms where with every breath of foul air they absorb fibres of cotton, wool or flax, or particles of copper, lead or iron. They live suspended between an insufficiency of food and an excess of strong drink; they are all wizened, sickly and emaciated; their bodies are thin and frail, their limbs feeble, their complexions pale, their eyes dead. . . . In English factories . . . you will never hear snatches of song, conversation and laughter. The master does not like his workers to be distracted from their toil for one moment by any reminder they are living human beings; he insists on silence, and a deathly silence reigns. . . . Between master and man there exist [no] . . . bonds of familiarity, courtesy and concern . . . bonds which soften the feelings of hatred and envy that the rich, with their disdain and harshness, their excessive demands and their love of luxury, always rouse in the hearts of the poor.

(*The London Journal of Flora Tristan*, 1842; ed. J. Hawkes, 1982)

With the advent of the mill, the cottage workers—men, women, and children—journeyed from the village to the river's edge. There they worked under the formal direction of an overseer and at the pace set by the machine. Just as, for centuries, many of the textile workers had been women, women were numerous among the employees of the mills. And just as their children had assisted with simpler tasks at home—washing, carrying, sorting—they, too, joined the labor force in the mill. The first generations of industrial workers consisted of all the members of the preindustrial family, as yet unaltered by the requirements of modern industrial processes.

When the mills expanded to become factories—buildings containing many machines—the machine became a tyrant. Huge, belching, raucous steam engines, fed with mountains of coal by laborers' shovels, powered the machines which could be multiplied to the limit of the factory's power capacity. The workforce expanded to meet the demands of the machines. Battalions of workers streamed into the factories at a set hour, announced by the clocks and bells and whistles that governed precious industrial time.

Strict rules enforced by a system of fines and punishments disciplined this large and potentially restive labor force. Workers were required to report to work and depart at certain set hours. They were to avoid surly or aggressive behavior, keep their own workplace clean, and meet a work schedule. Corporal punishment, especially of children, kept the tired or the resistant properly at work, with summary dismissal as a final sanction. These oppressive regulations kept workers in line although noise was deafening and light dim, meals swift and cheerless, and the machinery hazardous. Many workers lost fingers or limbs in the churning machinery, unshielded by any device, unregulated by any law.

Even labor under these conditions, however, was preferable to the alternative—no work at all. Business cycles were volatile during the early expansion of factories. Workers often found themselves unemployed because of overproduction, when warehouses were full, or simply because of seasonal shifts in demand. As industrialization progressed, some craftsmen found their products, and their skills, became obsolete. Such was the fate of the English handloom weavers, who for a few brief decades had made out handsomely by processing into cloth the huge product of mechanized spinning jennies. Between 1805 and 1833 their wages fell by seventy-five percent.

Women and Children Factories employed women and children well into the industrial era, an inheritance from the system of mill or cottage textile production. Owners found women to be useful employees on many counts. Women workers were strong enough to manage most machines, and offered little resistance to the demands of the workplace. They were cheap as well, earning as little as one-half a man's salary. During the early years of industrialization, they made up as much as one-third of the workforce. Yet in Britain, at least, women's factory labor was gradually curtailed. Legislation of the 1830s and 1840s limited their workday (and prohibited their employment in mines). After the mid-nineteenth century, British factory workers were overwhelmingly male. Women's labor did not end, however, but was transformed. In their homes, in the homes of others, and on the streets of the city, for lower pay and with lower status, they performed non-factory work.

The labor of children (technically those under age twenty, but in practice as young as eight or nine) was also essential in the early years of industrialization. One British historian has judged their exploitation "one of the most shameful events" of his nation's history, while a French scholar has termed it not only the exploitation but "martyrdom" of the young. Many children entered the factories alongside their parents, or at their bidding. Owners also procured child workers *en masse* by contracting with local orphanages and poorhouses. Children could be given simple jobs, such as sweeping or loading and switching bobbins of yarn. Their labor, like that of their mothers and older sisters, was cheap—a child earned about one-fourth the wage of an adult male. Like women, they were pliable and obedient to the commands of the foreman. If resistant, they could be physically punished, as children regularly were at home. Such abuse was only one aspect of their exploitation. The long hours of work, the lack of exercise, the absence of instruction and access to the open air, led to permanent physical and mental injury.

Child labor was not officially or generally repudiated in the Western world until the twentieth century. It was, however, gradually restricted, at first in Britain and France. In 1833, the British Factory Act set a maximum of a nine-hour workday for children under thirteen. In 1847, further legislation reduced the workday of women and older children to ten and a half hours. In 1842, the Mines Act prohibited work for women and girls underground, as well as boys under ten. In France, where the state had never before intervened in employers' relations with their workers, a child labor law passed in 1841 banned factory work for children under eight, and limited the workday to eight and twelve hours respectively for

WINDOWS ON

Workers and Workplace

Käthe Kollwitz, drawing from the series* A Weavers' Uprising, *1897

Nothing was more central to the Industrial Revolution than the factory. It was at once the symbol and the engine of change, housing new technologies and machinery, creating a totally new type of workforce, and even transforming the natural environment. Here, a Welsh ironworks is depicted in a painting dated 1788 (right), and workers at the Krupp plant in Essen, Germany, are seen tending to "Fritz," an enormous steam hammer originally invented in Britain (below). The weavers of Lyons, in France, who had formed themselves into a trade association, hoist their pickaxes ominously as they go out on strike (top). (right: Welsh Industrial and Maritime Museum, Cardiff; top: Käthe-Kollwitz Museum, Berlin)

Attributed to George Robertson,* Nant-y-glow Ironworks, *1788

Workers at the Krupp plant, Germany, 1903

children under and over age thirteen. Yet in Britain (as elsewhere), child labor remained an important component of the workforce as late as 1874, when fourteen percent of textile workers were children, and even 1900, when thousands of children under fourteen labored in mines and factories.

Children were not the only martyrs to industrialization. Workers throughout Europe suffered, especially in the early development of the iron and textiles production that made Europe the wealthiest region in the world. In the end, the workers, too, benefited. They began to do so when they learned to join together to form organizations that could extract from a booming economy some fair share of the wealth that they helped generate.

The Birth of Labor

With industrialization, it became possible to produce and sell more goods. It was capitalism that made that potential actual. Capitalism is an economic system resting on the pre-industrial commercial achievements of European merchants, and theorized by Adam Smith in his embrace of market systems of supply and demand and his rejection of the state-managed economics of mercantilism (see Chapters 11, 16). In a capitalist system, entrepreneurs are free to invest their money, or capital, to acquire machines and factories (the astonishing capacity of which had only recently become a reality) and thereby to seek maximal profits with minimal government intervention. Proponents of capitalism argue that the great productivity achieved, and enormous profits gained, ultimately benefit every member of a society through an absolute increase in the amount of wealth, greater economic opportunity, increased availability of consumer products, and higher standards of living.

With industrialization, organized by capitalism, the history of the "working class" begins. Laborers began to think of themselves as a collective entity—as "**labor**" as opposed to "capital," the factory owners and entrepreneurs. They formed collective organizations to provide mutual support and to press for greater concessions from their employers. Eventually, **trade unions** gained the right to bargain collectively with their employers. Sometimes they used the device of the **strike**, withholding their labor in order to compel owners to accede to their demands. Trade unions worked toward two principal goals: to secure both better working conditions and higher living standards for their members. By 1900, industrial workers and their families lived better than they did in 1800.

Early Labor Associations The formation of modern trade unions was a complex process involving several intermediate steps. First, associations of skilled artisans formed to fill the vacuum left by the waning of the medieval guilds (see Chapter 11), which by the late eighteenth century were under pressure, especially in Britain and France, for their resistance to the mechanisms of the **free market**. A system driven by supply and demand, contrary to the ideals of the guild, might threaten product quality (which had been carefully specified) or allow profits to exceed what an older generation considered "just" (i.e. based on the cost of materials and labor rather than on the highest price obtainable in an open market). Guilds fought to retain their influence in many regions, but failed to do so in the wealthier nations. In Britain their power had faded by the late eighteenth century. In France, they fell victim to the Revolution, which tolerated no limitations on urban workers in the archaic name of quality.

Nevertheless, in the absence of any form of state welfare, workers still needed the protections the guilds had provided. The associations that provided services to skilled artisans and their families, called "combinations," aroused alarm in the authorities. The British Combination Acts of 1799–1800 were intended to suppress them, while laws passed during the Revolution (1791) and under Napoleon outlawed them in France. Although these prohibitions were repealed in 1824 and 1864 respectively, workers' combinations continued to be viewed with suspicion.

Skilled artisans often joined with their fellows to resist the mechanization of their trades. In Britain, France, and the German lands, such workers rioted. The English Luddites, textile-workers who rallied under the name of the (probably mythical) leader Ned Ludd, expressed their rage in 1811–1812 by smashing the machines that aimed to replace them. In 1831 and 1834 in the French city of Lyons, where thirty percent of the nation's exports were manufactured, journeymen weavers rose up against workshop owners. During the same decade, the tailors of Paris, finding their incomes plunge as factory production undercut their opportunities, took revenge on the machinery that threatened their economic status. In Prussian Silesia, linen-weavers rioted in 1844, rebels against a factory-type system that threatened to turn high-skilled artisans into mere laborers.

Throughout the nineteenth century, the plight of the skilled artisan remained perilous. Tailors, shoemakers, and cabinetmakers figured among the leaders of revolutionary episodes and organizations—most conspicuously in Paris during the revolutions of 1830,

1848, and 1871 (see Chapter 20). It was precisely their kind of labor that was most threatened by competition from the factories that spewed out cheap goods at low prices.

Such outbreaks of violence fueled government determination to suppress them. At the same time, they prefigured the strikes of a more ordered labor movement that began to emerge around the mid-nineteenth century in Britain. There some groups of highly-skilled workers formed a new type of professional craft association, exemplified by the Amalgamated Society of Engineers, founded in 1851. A national organization supported by members' dues, it offered health benefits and unemployment protection, as well as a platform from which to negotiate for economic and political benefits. Such early trade unions sprang from the craft workshop tradition and not from the "Satanic mills" where unskilled workers

WITNESSES

Workers' Lives

A Yorkshire Chartist recalls his boyhood and youth experiences during the 1820s–1840s: Tom Brown's Schooldays would have had no charm for me, as I had never been to a day school in my life; when very young I had to begin working, and was pulled out of bed between 4 and 5 o'clock . . . in summer time to go . . . take part in milking a number of cows. . . . I went to a card shop [i.e., textile workshop] afterwards, and there had to set 1500 card teeth for a ½d. . . . I have been a woollen weaver, a comber, a navvy on the railway, and a [quarryman] . . . [and so] I claim to know some little of the state of the working classes.
(B. Wilson, *The Struggles of an Old Chartist*, 1887; ed. E. P. Thompson, 1964)

Irish stevedores unload sacks of oats at the Liverpool docks (1830s): These men . . . received the ful sacks as they were lowered by the crane off the hitch on their shoulders and carried them across the road. They pursued their heavy task during the working hours of a summer's day at a uniform, unremitting pace, a trot of at least five miles an hour, the distance from the vessel to the storehouse being full fifty yards . . . At this work a good labourer earned, at 16d. per 100 sacks, ten shillings a day; so that consequently he made seven hundred and fifty trips . . . thus performing a distance of . . . forty-three miles.
(Sir G. Head, *A Home Tour of Great Britain*, 1835; ed. E. P. Thompson, 1964)

Seventeen-year-old Patience Kershaw describes her work in the coal mines to a parliamentary committee of inquiry (1842): My father has been dead about a year; my mother is living and has ten children . . . three lasses go to mill; all the lads are colliers [i.e., coal mine workers]. . . . I never went to day-school; I go to Sunday-school, but I cannot read or write; I go to pit at five o'clock in the morning and come out at five in the evening; I get my breakfast of porridge and milk first; I take my dinner with me, a cake [a plain oatcake], and I eat as I go; I do not stop or rest any time for the purpose; I get nothing else until I get home, and then have potatoes and meat, not every day meat. I [work] in the clothes I have now got on, trousers and ragged jacket . . . sometimes they [the male workers] beat me, if I am not quick enough, with their hands; they strike upon my back; the boys take liberties with me . . . I am the only girl in the pit; there are about 20 boys and 15 men; all the men are naked; I would rather work in the mill than in coal-pit.
(Evidence given before Lord Ashley's Mines Commission, 1842; eds. G. B. Kirsch et al, 1997)

German socialist Luise Zietz (1865–1922) recalls her childhood in the 1870s: We had to pluck apart and oil the raw wool, to run it through the "wolf," which compressed it further, then it had to be put through the carding machine two times. A pair of dogs, who switched off, drove this machine by a large treadwheel, and when one of the large dogs died on us, we ourselves had to get down in the wheel. . . . Spinning was a terrible torture for us children. We crouched hour after hour on the low stool behind the spinning wheel at the horrible monotonous and exhausting work, just spinning, spinning, spinning.
(From B. S. Anderson and J. P. Zinsser, *A History of their Own: Women in Europe from Prehistory to the Present*, Vol. 2, 1988)

A French housekeeping manual describes the female servant's duties (1896): The maid of all work should get up at six, fix her hair, get herself ready, and not come down to the kitchen without being ready to go out to the market. From 6 to 9 o'clock, she has the time to do many things. She will light the furnace and the fires or get the stove going. She will prepare the breakfasts, do the dining room, brush the clothes and clean the shoes. When the masters arise, she will do their rooms, will put water in the water closets, carry up wood or coal, and carry down the excrement. For all these tasks, she will put on oversleeves and a white apron and take care to wash her hands. Then, . . . the dining room is restored to order, the tableware washed and put away, the cooking utensils cleaned.
(From B. S. Anderson and J. P. Zinsser, *ibid*)

still labored without any associations that could offer mutual consolation and assistance.

Skilled workers held high prestige and could command good wages (although these were still only a small fraction—one-third or one-fourth—of the income of a member of the bourgeoisie). Such privileges raised them well above the condition of the semi-skilled and unskilled workers whose numbers ballooned with the expansion of factory production, who earned only two-thirds or one-half as much. It is these new workers (called "proletarians" after the underclass of Roman citizens who were considered to serve the state only by reproducing and peopling the Republic) whose oppressed condition led to the formation of the modern labor movement.

The Proletariat The condition of the proletarians, or proletariat, appeared permanent and inescapable. Not only did these workers labor long hours, in appalling conditions, for barely a subsistence wage, but they could aspire to little better. Moreover, they had no higher aspirations for their children, whom they generally introduced to the same form of employment. In the absence of any encouragement from employers or the state, and in the absence of a system of mass education, few workers expected their children to achieve greater wealth or status than they themselves possessed. It is unlikely that more than an exceptional few even pondered the possibility.

There were an exceptional few, however, who sought to improve their own understanding of the world to assist their advancement. They joined self-help movements, or attended voluntary lectures on science, business, and the arts, that offered a random but still advanced education. While working in his family's cotton mill in Manchester, the German industrialist and later **Communist** Friedrich Engels (1820–1895) was impressed by the popularity of such lectures, commenting in 1844, "I have sometimes come across workers, with their fustian jackets falling apart, who are better informed on geology, astronomy and other matters than many an educated member of the middle classes in Germany."

The workers who found their way to evening lectures on geology were greatly outnumbered by those who sought out taverns for relaxation or who returned to their beds to rest, after sixteen hours of labor. But even this more numerous group began, in the early years of industrialization, to seek each other out for solidarity, the necessary first step in the building of the labor movement. From the 1760s onward, they formed voluntary groups, variously called "friendly" or "mutual aid" or "cooperative" societies.

In the early nineteenth century, when such associations of workers were closely scrutinized by authorities, their objectives were limited. Funded by members' dues, they offered loans, unemployment and death benefits, and assistance to orphans. They established cooperative stores, where goods could be purchased at close to their wholesale cost, enabling working families to stretch their slight wages. By 1803, about 9600 friendly societies in Britain boasted over 700,000 members. By 1851, such organizations had founded 130 cooperative stores. The movement spread to the continent. By the mid-nineteenth century, cooperative banks sprang up in the German lands, with one in nearly every city by century's end. In France several thousand friendly societies enrolled about 800,000 workers by 1870, approximately thirteen percent of the workforce.

Utopia and Reform The originators of **socialism** (see Chapter 24), joined by some sympathetic entrepreneurs, encouraged worker cooperation. Early socialist thinkers envisioned a future society where workers lived in dignity, harvesting the wealth that workshops and factories produced with their labor and sharing equally in those profits. Families would live and work together and children would be educated. The patriarchal strictures that bound traditional families—requiring female chastity and obedience—could be abolished or at least modified. Relationships between men and women could be founded in love, not necessity. Women would enjoy the same sexual freedoms that men had always claimed. The state itself would be altered. Engineers and scientists might take the lead, qualified for the undertaking by competence rather than social origin. They would displace traditional leaders chosen from members of noble or bourgeois elites.

While most such **utopian** societies remained merely theoretical, some visionaries attempted to give them reality. In Britain, the successful self-made industrialist Robert Owen (1771–1858), an artisan's son, devoted much of his career to bettering the condition of the worker. Owen had prospered in cotton manufacture in the last decade of the eighteenth century, turning a £100 investment into a huge fortune (see Chapter 21). In 1800, struck by the miserable living and working conditions of his textile workers, he moved his operation from Manchester, England's greatest boom town, to New Lanark, near Glasgow, Scotland. There he established not merely a factory but an entire community, including housing, cooperative stores, a sewage system, schools for workers' children, and a humane workplace. The whole

WHO'S WHO

Chroniclers and Builders of the Industrial Age

Jeremy Bentham (1748–1832) English political theorist, proponent of "Utilitarianism," and designer of the model prison, the "Panopticon."

Edwin Chadwick (1800–1890) disciple of Jeremy Bentham; promoted the building of systems for the delivery of water and the removal of sewage in his 1842 *Report on the Sanitary Condition of the Labouring Population of Great Britain.*

Robert Owen (1771–1858) self-made English entrepreneur, factory owner, experimentalist in utopian community building, and founder of the Grand National Consolidated Trades Union.

Louis Blanc (1811–1882) French socialist theorist and proponent of "national workshops" that would provide unemployed laborers with work and a decent wage.

Karl Marx (1818–1883) German-born intellectual; author, in collaboration with Friedrich Engels, of the *Communist Manifesto*; creator of modern socialist theory and progenitor of all modern communist systems.

Friedrich Engels (1820–1895) German industrialist and later communist; author of a classic study of life in British Manchester during a period of rapid industrialization.

Georges Haussmann (1809–1891) pioneer urban designer and adviser to French emperor Napoleon III; recreated Paris by razing its old structures to make way for a planned system of streets and monumental buildings.

Josephine Butler (1828–1906) British philanthropist and feminist; battled for the repeal of the Contagious Diseases Act of 1864 (mandating the medical supervision of prostitutes).

Jacob Riis (1849–1914) Danish-born crime reporter turned photojournalist; chronicler of how "the other half" lived in New York City during the industrial age.

experiment, eagerly viewed by European industrial experts and visitors, embodied a new moral code based on cooperation, rather than competition.

In the 1820s, Owen journeyed to North America, to launch new cooperative ventures in an unfinished country where anything might be possible. He established an experimental community of New Harmony in the state of Indiana, where agricultural and industrial workers came together to form a self-sufficient society. It later disintegrated, but by then Owen had moved on to other things.

After his return from the United States, Owen organized a mass workers' movement in 1834: the Grand National Consolidated Trades Union. This was meant to be a single organization that would unite all workers in the country, who would therefore wield the irresistible negotiating weapon of a general strike. Owen's aim was not merely to improve workers' pay and conditions, but also to influence the political process. His initiatives should be seen in the context of the politicization of labor (see below), that progressed as the century aged.

Owen's giant union soon collapsed, as had his perfect communities, and those of other designers of utopias. A new generation of social critics put utopianism aside and focused more concretely on solving immediate problems such as low wages and unemployment. In France, the socialist theorist Louis Blanc (1811–1882) proposed the creation of "national workshops." These would be funded by a benevolent state that guaranteed workers the right to work and a decent wage immune to the pressures of competition. The republican government formed in early 1848 committed huge sums to subsidize such workshops, intended to absorb workers unable to find employment elsewhere. They proved immensely popular, and their dissolution a few months later was one trigger of the workers' revolt and the suppression of the June Days (see Chapter 20).

In June, French workers' concerns turned from economic to political aims. Embittered by the closing of the national workshops, they exploded with antigovernment feeling, setting up street barricades in the time-honored fashion of French revolutionaries. This uprising was suppressed with excessive violence in which 4000 died. That outbreak was a major episode in the political history of workers' movements, but it was not the only one. Throughout industrialized Europe, urbanized, unskilled workers constituted a huge and potentially volatile part of the population. Wherever their demands became assertive, the possibility of political revolution loomed.

Well before the uprisings that took place in France, Germany, and elsewhere in 1848 (see Chapter 20), British workers had joined middle-class reformers to agitate for the Reform Act of 1832 (which broadened the franchise to middle-class men and made electoral reforms) and the Factory Act of 1833 and subsequent workplace legislation. They opposed the Corn Laws, which protected high-cost, local grain against cheaper imports, to the disadvantage of the poor—their opposition peaking in the notorious "Peterloo Massacre" (named for St. Peter's Field, Manchester, and the battle of Waterloo) of 1819 when mounted soldiers charged on a mass meeting. Workers also opposed the 1834 Poor Law Amendment Act, which withdrew support for unemployed able-bodied adults unless they were employed in state-run workhouses.

From 1838 to 1848, a movement to petition Parliament to pass a "People's Charter" harnessed workers' aspirations, which they determined to pursue "Peaceably if we may, forcibly if we must." Drafted by the London Working Men's Association, the Charter contained six points that were sure to alarm lawmakers. In addition to petitioning for electoral reform, these included a call for universal manhood suffrage. Presented to Parliament and rejected in 1839, again in 1842, and a final time in 1848, the Charter represented the heroic attempt of British workers to gain political objectives. Though it failed, those who participated in the Chartist movement had gained valuable practical experience of the political process.

Workers in the industrializing nations of continental Europe learned that same lesson later in the century, as the utopian socialism of its early decades gave way to an urgent, militant socialism in its latter half. Workers leaned to a variety of "**social democratic**" political parties, which proposed to win benefits for their supporters by gaining majorities in representative assemblies. Some joined the Communists, a group of socialists to whom a mission and a program were provided by the German intellectuals Friedrich Engels and Karl Marx (1818–1883) in their *Communist Manifesto* of 1848 (see Chapter 24). Both analytical and inspiring, the brief *Manifesto* is one of the key monuments of modern politics. It marks the moment when the possibility was first voiced of a complete reversal of the social order. Workers should throw off the chains that bind them by abolishing private property, eliminating the capitalist bourgeoisie, and taking control of both the factories and the state. These ideals animated the Communist League established in London in 1847, and subsequently the much larger International Workingmen's Association, or "First International," in 1864, and the "Second International" in 1889.

Even more threatening than the Communists to established elites were the French syndicalists and Russian anarchists. The former urged that workers gain their ends through coordinated, violent strikes against the state. The latter urged the annihilation of the state itself, which they saw as inherently alien to human welfare. In autocratic Russia, and in France where workers' revolts had twice been bloodily suppressed, syndicalism and anarchism won followers. But in Britain and other industrializing nations, trade unions were the primary institutions upon which workers relied in their quest for betterment.

Trade Unions Trade unions can be distinguished from both the "friendly societies" and utopian communities. They are workers' organizations whose main goal is to negotiate with employers for wage and workplace improvements. Trade unions continued to provide the kinds of benefits that mutual aid societies had offered, but they also attempted to deal with the managers and owners of large enterprises in negotiations known as **collective bargaining**. While capitalist entrepreneurs resisted the formation of trade unions, the trade union movement encouraged an orderly approach to workers' rights and pay, in contrast to outbreaks of riot and revolution that had frightened entrepreneurs and stiffened their resolve to yield little to workers.

Where negotiation failed, trade unions wielded the weapon of the strike. In the early years of the labor movement, strikes were often violently suppressed, but by the late nineteenth century, they had matured to become a practical tool in the mission of organized labor to wrest from employers some of the wealth that their members' labors had generated.

The earliest trade unions formed in Britain soon after the repeal of the Combination Laws. Thus the National Union of Cotton Spinners was organized in 1829, the National Association for the Protection of Labor in 1830, and Owen's Grand National Consolidated Trades Union in 1834. But they soon collapsed, and from the later 1830s to 1848, the goals of Chartism took over from unionization. In the mid-century, skilled workers recruited from the artisan classes began to form crafts associations. After 1875, when the tactics of collective bargaining were finally recognized as legal, trade unions expanded in earnest. Their ranks were filled by unskilled and semi-skilled workers persuaded by such examples as the successful strikes of the London dockworkers in 1889, or the London match girls in 1888. By 1900, a century and a half after the beginnings of industrialization, membership in British trade unions had risen to over 2 million workers.

In Germany, too, union membership climbed from the 1860s to about 2 million around 1900, although

WINDOWS ON

Women and Work

Interior of a British cotton mill, 1835

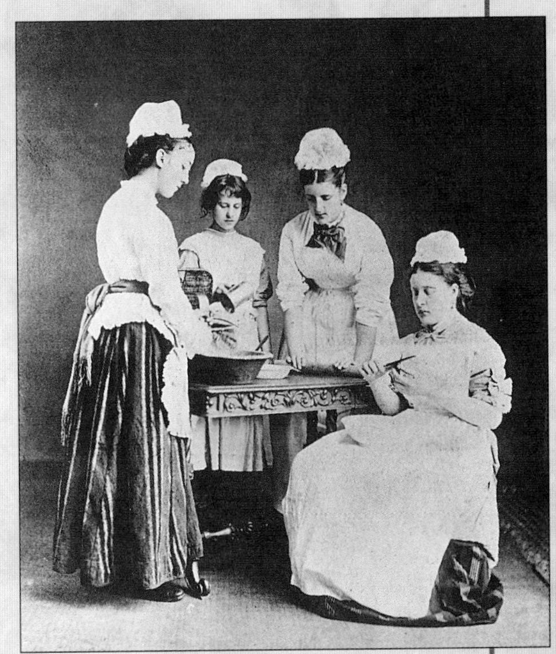

Maidservants in the kitchen, 1860s–1870s (right)

The Industrial Revolution created a variety of working environments for women. For much of the nineteenth century, women, often of a tender age, provided most of the workforce in textile mills. Here women are seen operating power looms in a British cotton factory (above). Not all women laborers worked in factories, however. Many were domestic servants, like the ones working in this kitchen (right). Others were pieceworkers, who, seated close to a small stove, sewed garments to be sold by the "piece" (below left).

Women of higher social standing tended not to work. Instead, they remained at home, where their main functions were to provide beauty, grace, and children. They could also go shopping in one of the new department stores, where they participated in a booming economy as consumers rather than laborers. The ribbons gallery of the great French department store, the Bon Marché *was a vibrant, inviting space for those who had no need to work (below right).*

(below left: Museum of the City of New York)

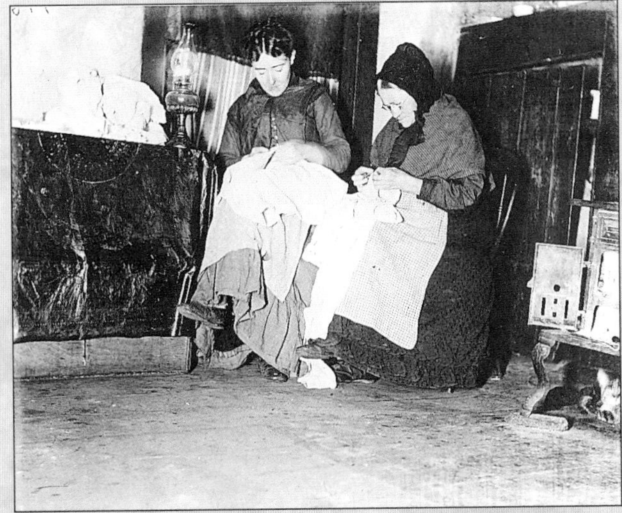

Jacob Riis,* Sewing and Starving in an Elizabeth Street Attic, *c. 1890

Illustration of the* Bon Marché *from* Le Monde Illustré, *c. 1875

the chancellor Otto von Bismarck (1815–1898) had tried to suppress the tactic of the strike. Here union members often supported the Social Democratic party, with a socialist, but not communist agenda, which militantly advocated workers' interests. In France, in the 1860s a nascent trade movement succumbed to the general repression following the 1871 Paris Commune (see Chapter 20). Driven underground, French unions or *syndicats* tended toward the violent solutions of syndicalism.

By the last two decades of the nineteenth century, workers had made considerable progress. Their standard of living had begun to rise. They now had more food and better food to eat than their fathers and grandfathers. Their wages were sufficient to purchase necessities and even to allow a small surplus for entertainment and brief vacations. If they suffered unemployment, or faced a strike, their trade union could assist with funds. They could not entirely put behind them the fear of want, nor had they yet attained the dignity that solid and regular pay afforded, but real gains had been made.

In the 1880s, the newly constituted state of Germany led the way to a new stage in the relations between workers and society. Bismarck instituted government insurance programs that would protect workers in the events of illness and disability, unemployment and old age. After 1900, Britain, France, the United States, and most other Western nations in turn instituted similar measures. Why was Bismarck, of all leaders seemingly the least indulgent to workers' petitions, the one to initiate a modern program of social insurance? He sought to lessen the momentum of social democracy by assuaging the workers with popular programs. Thus appeased, they might ignore calls for militant action against the state.

The modern working class suffered much in the formative stages of industrialization. Yet it achieved much before the end of the nineteenth century. Its members experimented with self-help groups and shopping cooperatives, utopian communes, riot and strike, with political initiatives and with collective bargaining. By 1900, although most still struggled to feed themselves and their families, the workers of the Western world had improved their standard of living beyond that achieved by any laborers of past ages.

THE INDUSTRIAL CITY

Cities had long been centrally important to the development of the European economy (see Chapters 11, 18). In the late eighteenth century, as population spurted as a result of improvements in agriculture, cities swelled prodigiously. Their populations approached and even (in the case of London) exceeded the 1 million mark that separates modern from pre-modern urban centers in the West. These already swollen cities, some of which became industrial centers after 1800, and others of which were major commercial centers, experienced an influx of workers that pushed population levels to several millions—exceeding those of any concentration of human beings previously known to have existed on the face of the globe.

As city populations exploded, urban structures and networks were transformed. The old, jumbled buildings and narrow, winding streets became overcrowded. As overcrowding fostered the spread of disease, the city developed systems of water supply and sewage removal. Streetcars moved people quickly across town, electric lighting made nighttime activities possible, and professional police and fire forces provided security. Neighborhoods developed distinctive personalities. Elegant boulevards designed by urban planners sliced through the districts where the wealthy resided. Narrow streets and alleyways, which the planners left untouched, snaked through the districts of the poor. These were an ideal setting for criminals and prostitutes—"streetwalkers"—who considered them their own. Whether they dwelled on mean streets or ample boulevards, city dwellers were prone to the **alienation** that haunted urban life, where the multiple goings and comings of many meant for some the atomization of humanity and the reduction of the human spirit.

Boom Towns

Already in the early modern era, streams of people flowed from the country to the city where jobs might be found. With the arrival of the factory, the din of the steam engines, the whirr of machinery, beckoned new throngs of migrants. The big cities which had reached nearly 1 million in 1800, reached several million by 1900.

The first nation to industrialize, Britain offers ample evidence of spectacular rates of urban growth. In 1750, Britain had only two cities with populations over 50,000. A century later, there were twenty-nine. The ten largest cities all at least doubled in the first half of the nineteenth century, with those centered in the new manufacturing regions near coalfields and seaports growing fastest. Leeds and Birmingham more than tripled; Manchester, Liverpool, and Glasgow more than quadrupled.

Population of Europe's Largest Cities, 1750–1950

	1750		1850		1950	
Rank	**City**	**Population**	**City**	**Population**	**City**	**Population**
1	London	676,000	London	2,320,000	London	8,860,000
2	Paris	560,000	Paris	1,314,000	Paris	5,900,000
3	Naples	324,000	St. Petersburg	502,000	Moscow	5,100,000
4	Amsterdam	219,000	Berlin	446,000	Ruhr	4,900,000
5	Lisbon	213,000	Vienna	426,000	Berlin	3,707,000
6	Vienna	169,000	Liverpool	422,000	Leningrad	2,700,000
7	Moscow	161,000	Naples	416,000	Manchester	2,382,000
8	Venice	158,000	Manchester	412,000	Birmingham	2,196,000
9	Rome	157,000	Moscow	373,000	Vienna	1,755,000
10	St. Petersburg	138,000	Glasgow	346,000	Rome	1,665,000

European cities grew enormously during the era of incipient and maturing industrialization. Simultaneously, their rank order often shifted. Note in this table the mounting importance of Moscow and the new British industrial centers of Manchester and Birmingham. As they escalated, traditional centers like Vienna and Rome, although growing respectably, fell to a lower place in the ranking of top ten cities. And three giants of early modern commerce—Lisbon, Venice, and Amsterdam—disappeared entirely from the top ten. London and Paris, whose populations exploded, maintained their top-rank positions.
Source: *P. M. Hohenberg and L. H. Lees,* The Making of Urban Europe, 1000–1950 *(Cambridge, MA: Harvard University Press, 1985; 2nd ed., 1995), p. 227.*

Manchester alone, nearly one-third of whose residents were engaged in the mechanized production of cotton cloth, doubled between 1801 and 1831 (from 70,000 to 142,000), then more than doubled again (to 409,000) over the next twenty years. Like "an industrious spider," as a contemporary French observer remarked, from its bustling center Manchester spun a web of roads and railways reaching out to the swelling towns of the region from where it received supplies and workers. Another commentator marveled: "From this foul drain the greatest stream of human industry flows out to fertilize the whole world. From this filthy sewer pure gold flows."

Though it did not increase at the pace of the northern manufacturing centers, the population of London increased from about 1 to 5 million by the end of the nineteenth century, when it was home to more than one-sixth of the nation's people. By 1850, more than fifty percent of Britain's population lived in cities; by 1880, more than two-thirds.

Rates of growth outside of Britain were slower but still substantial. Paris nearly doubled between 1800 and 1850, then doubled again over the next thirty years. By 1900, a majority of France's population lived in cities. Berlin (Germany) and St. Petersburg (Russia) doubled in the first half of the nineteenth century, and St. Petersburg then quadrupled, reaching a population of 2 million by 1914. From an 1800 population figure of 170,000, Berlin reached a total of 1.6 million by 1890. Vienna (Austria) increased about eighty percent, while Budapest (Hungary) more than tripled from 287,000 in 1867 to nearly 1 million in 1914. (Elsewhere in east-central Europe, where industrialization had scarcely started, large cities were few and increased only slowly.) The percentage of people living in cities, and the numbers of Europeans overall, both increased, resulting in a growth of urban populations by 1910 to six times their 1800 level.

These increases were achieved, for the most part, not through a growth in the birthrate but through

Levels of Urbanization in Leading European Nations (with the United States and Japan), 1800, 1850, 1910

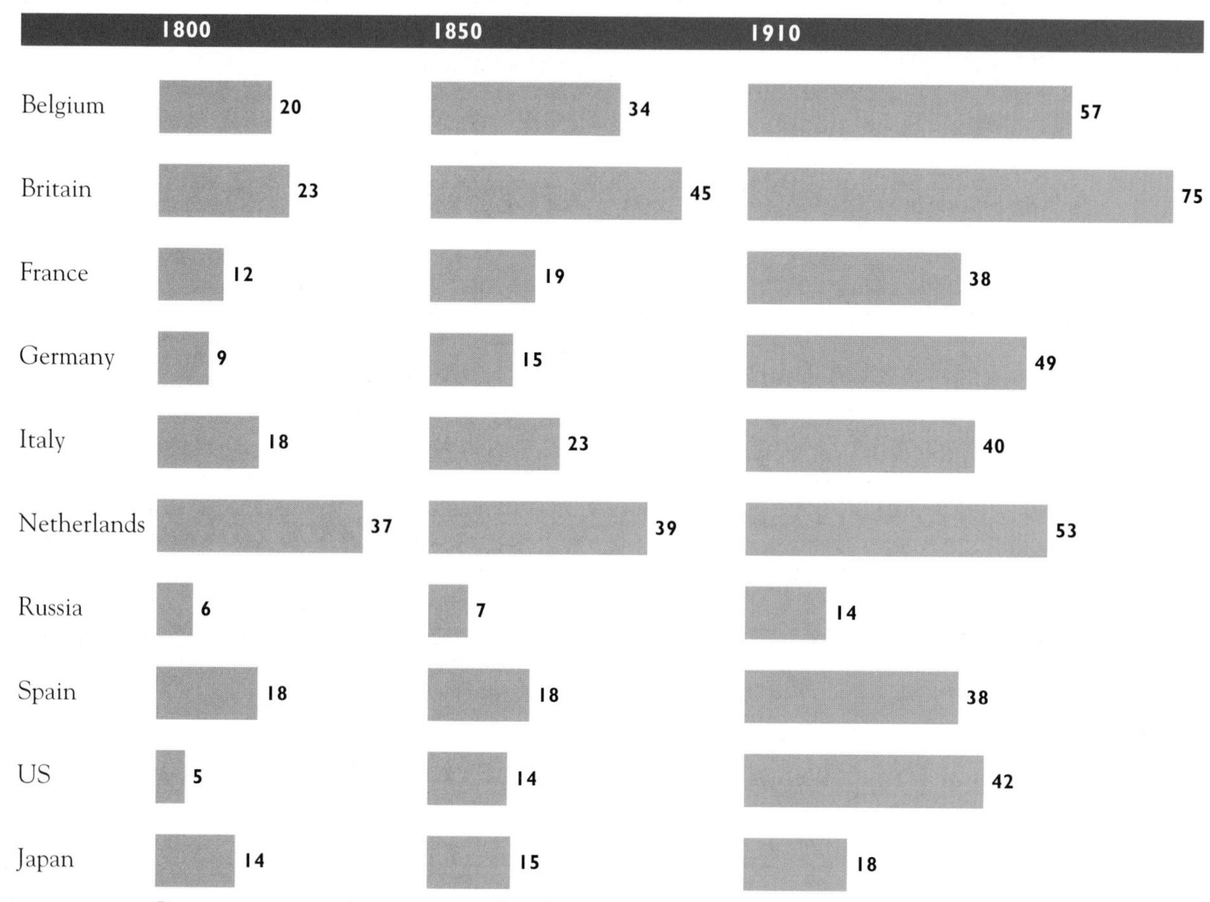

As industrialization developed, more workers moved to cities. This bar graph shows the increasing percentage of urban-dwellers relative to the whole population in ten countries at three junctures in time. Note Britain's rapid and huge urbanization, by which it surpassed the citified Netherlands within the fifty-year span of its peak industrialization (1800–1850). Belgium, too, leapt forward to take second place in 1910, also ahead of the Netherlands. The level of urbanization in Britain, Belgium, and France approximately tripled in 1800–1910. In Germany, it increased more than fivefold, and in the United States, more than eightfold. In contrast, Italy, Spain, Russia, and Japan—even the Netherlands, despite its initial advantage—are slower to increase their levels of urbanization.

Source: *P. Bairoch,* Cities and Economic Development: From the Dawn of History to the Present, *trs. C. Braider (Chicago: University of Chicago Press, 1988), p. 221*

migration to the cities. Only about one-half of those who lived in nineteenth-century London and Paris had been born there. Until the twentieth century, cities did not reproduce themselves. They required constant immigration from the countryside, continuing on a larger scale a pattern that dated from the Middle Ages, when peasants sought employment and refuge in towns.

Urban migrants were of two sorts: those who came but left, and those who came and stayed. The former worked for a period in the city, then returned to country villages. When they did so, they brought with them the outlook of experienced urbanites, contributing to the increasing connectedness of country folk to city things. The second category of migrants came to the cities and stayed, driving down (since most migrants were young) the average age of city dwellers. These migrants often joined the armies of the poor: those who labored in workshops and factories, who hauled and lifted and hammered, who cleaned and cooked in the well-kept houses of professionals, merchants, bureaucrats, and nobles.

For not all jobs in the city were factory jobs. Only in the handful of cities, such as Manchester, that were created during the process of industrialization, did industrial workers constitute a majority of workers. In most cities, there was a greater mix of occupations. In London in 1891, for instance, factory workers comprised about thirty-eight percent of all male, and thirty-three percent of all female workers. But servants also constituted a large group, comprising only seven percent of the more numerous male laboring population, but fifty-four percent of female workers. After factory workers, servants (who were mostly female) were the largest occupational group in European cities. By 1900 in Britain, half of all working women worked as servants.

A notable development was the emergence of the category of "white-collar" workers, as they were later designated because they wore the clean clothes of the respectable middle classes rather than the heavy, durable blue of those who worked with their hands. They were bank tellers, secretaries in utility and insurance companies, draughtsmen and bookkeepers, tax-collectors and food inspectors, sales clerks in the new department stores and teachers in newly-mandated public schools. Their recruitment to government offices was rapid in the last decades of the century, when state bureaucracies in the advanced countries came close to doubling. Most white-collar workers were men, but women also prospered in this sector, especially as teachers, nurses, and sales and office clerks.

Although white-collar workers often aspired to enter the middle classes themselves—and sometimes succeeded—most workers were poor. For them, the **demographic** patterns of urban life were remorseless. The poor were less likely to survive childhood, and more likely to die young than the wealthy in the cities of nineteenth-century Europe. Although birthrates among the poor were high, their infants often died, with infant mortality running at up to fifty percent of all births. Toward the end of the nineteenth century, cities became more healthful and these demographic trends improved. Death rates fell, including infant deaths, and life expectancy increased. Meanwhile, although birthrates fell overall due to the increased practice of birth control, out-of-wedlock births rose—a marked characteristic of the modern era. These patterns meant that by around 1900, the city at last reproduced itself. No longer a killer of people, the city had also become the norm, rather than an exception in the social fabric of life in many European countries.

Structure and Infrastructure

Some of the headiest urban growth of the early years of industrialization involved new cities that suddenly developed—as did Manchester—from mere villages. More often, however, the greatly expanded urban areas of the nineteenth century involved a medieval or even ancient city, whose familiar buildings, streets, and walls were inadequate to house the influx of newcomers. The structures and infrastructures of these established cities became greatly strained as populations grew.

Where were people to live? They crowded into the existing building stock, squeezing in unrelated groups into **tenement** rooms. Or they occupied new, cheap housing hastily constructed on city outskirts. In some cities, wageworkers stayed in the city's poor districts in the dilapidated remnants of its older buildings. They doubled up, sharing rooms and facilities with strangers. This was the case in Paris, for example, where the population increased by twenty-five percent in the period 1817–1827, while housing capacity increased by only ten percent. In other cities, such as Manchester, where there was no ancient building stock into which the poor might flow, entrepreneurs hastily constructed large, cheap, and anonymous buildings on the outskirts of the industrial core. Outside French and German industrial towns straggled rows of company-built, barracks-like houses or high-rise multi-residential buildings.

While poor residents crowded into old buildings, or spilled outward in shapeless, spreading suburbs, the wealthy bourgeoisie and aristocracy also found new housing. They either pushed outward, establishing new neighborhoods beyond the haunts of the poor, or established themselves in elegant enclaves within the city. Among the latter were the areas around the grand boulevards of western Paris. These had been opened up by Baron Georges Haussmann (1809–1891), Napoleon III's adviser and pioneer urban designer, by tearing down the cramped, old housing of workers' districts. (Haussmann's project not only beautified the city, but also helped to control civil unrest by depriving would-be revolutionaries of their defenses and exposing them, when necessary, to gunfire.) Other such areas were the *Ringstrasse* ("ring streets," formed on the pattern of the old walls that had ringed the medieval city) of Vienna, and the

On and Under City Streets

Gustave Caillebotte, Rainy Day: *Slum clearance and the creation of wide boulevards offered easier traffic flow and broad urban vistas, though at the expense of the old neighborhoods. Baron Haussmann's program of urban renewal during the 1850s and 1860s transformed Paris from a crowded medieval town to a spacious modern city, shown here in a work from 1876–1877 by the Impressionist painter Caillebotte.* (Musée Marmottan, Paris)

streets bordering London's fine parks. These new developments were graced by elegant public buildings—modern museums and hospitals, post offices and monuments.

Until the late nineteenth century, the wealthier urbanites traversed the city by carriage, while workers walked. The absence of affordable transport for the poor meant that they had to live within walking distance of their workplace. This situation changed in the last decades of the century. New forms of transportation including trolley car systems powered by electricity, underground railroads, for example in London (1863), Paris (1900), and New York (1904), and bicycles made it possible for working families to move out to choicer and relatively cheaper suburban areas. By the mid-nineteenth century in major cities, gas lamps lighted the streets (replaced by electrical lamps by the end of the century), so that citizens of all classes could stroll abroad with confidence. By that era as well, running water and sewage lines had begun to challenge that great specter of urban life: infectious disease.

Cholera, spread through contaminated food and water supplies, was the great killer of city dwellers. It arrived in the early 1830s and returned periodically throughout the century. It struck London first in 1832, and then again in 1847, when 53,000 died throughout the nation, of whom 14,000 died in London alone. It visited Paris in 1832 and 1849, striking the poor more viciously than the wealthy. The death statistics revealed the outlines of a pitiless social classification, remarked one horrified observer, in itself "a savage denial of the doctrines of equality" that had supposedly been secured by the sacrifices of the Revolution. From 1892 to 1895, again, cholera took the lives of 300,000 Europeans, the great majority (270,000) Russians.

By that time, the work of Louis Pasteur (1822–1895) had uncovered the bacterial origins of disease (see Chapter 24), and the role of water as a vehicle for bacterial transmission was understood. Social reformers began to rank water supply systems as an issue of prime importance. In Britain, Edwin Chadwick (1800–1890), a disciple of the radical thinker Jeremy Bentham (1748–1832; see Chapter 24), urged the building of systems for the delivery of water and the removal of sewage in his 1842 *Report on the Sanitary Condition of the Labouring Population of Great Britain*. Here he argued that the consequences of disease were "greater or less . . . according as there is more or less sufficient drainage of houses, streets, roads, and land, combined with more or less sufficient means of cleansing and removing solid refuse and impurities." According to the guidelines of the Public Health Act passed through Chadwick's advocacy in 1848, Britain built sewage lines, water delivery systems, and reservoirs. After the first cholera epidemic, the French slowly instituted a similar system. By mid-century, only one building in five in Paris received piped water, and sewage systems often served only privileged quarters of the city, leaving workers to use old collective toilets. By 1887, nearly three-quarters of Parisian streets had sewers.

Although cholera was the worst epidemic disease that Europeans faced in the nineteenth century, there were others. Smallpox still killed and destroyed, although vaccination, when used, was effective in controlling it. Venereal disease, whose spread was linked to the prostitution that thrived in cities, was a serious problem. Tuberculosis, which again ravaged the poor and malnourished far more cruelly than the wealthy, was judged responsible for about one-fifth of the deaths in England in 1839. The pollutants that increased mightily with industrialization also contributed to disease and death. These included the dyes and chemicals from shops and factories, as well as the black smoke produced by the coal burned to power the industrial machine.

Above and below ground in Paris: *The mid- and late-nineteenth century saw substantial improvements in urban life. The installation of municipal sewage systems greatly improved public health. This contemporary sketch of the Parisian system shows the complex of drains and sewers below street level that gradually extended throughout the city, eventually bringing clean water and removing waste in poor as well as privileged neighborhoods.*

On the Streets

Crime and Punishment Meanwhile, other dangers roamed the streets. The concentration of wealth that was essential to city life was an invitation to crime, with the anonymity of urban life allowing predator and prey to coexist. Citizens succumbed to paralyzing fears of a hold-up in the solitary darkness, or a surreptitious and deadly assault. "For the past month," noted a French observer to his correspondent in December, 1843, "the sole topic of conversation has been the nightly assaults, hold-ups, daring robberies . . . [The assailants] attack rich and poor alike . . . At one time the advantage of being poor was that at least you were safe; it is so no longer."

Urban police forces were established, and police records reported mounting instances of assaults on the innocent—if only because their record-keeping methods had become more sophisticated, so that every instance was noted. Newspapers daily reported the crimes of the night before, and devoted space and lurid description to the executions of condemned perpetrators.

Criminals who were not executed were incarcerated or deported. Around 1830 in Paris, about 43,000 people (more than eighty percent male) were shut in prisons, or more than one in every thousand adults. Of these, the majority (seventy-one percent) were guilty of crimes against property. Imprisonment was increasingly the preferred form of punishment, following the influential theories of the Enlightenment theorist Cesare Beccaria (1738–1794). His influential *Essay on Crimes and Punishments* (1764) had heralded the end of torture and routine capital punishment, and his views were taken up by Jeremy Bentham in his proposals for a new form of prison, the "Panopticon" (see below). Deportation to the more remote and deadly colonies (in the Caribbean, North Africa, Australia) was also a commonly imposed penalty in France and Britain.

As the numbers of the imprisoned increased, prison reform initiatives sprang up. Christian activists (especially in Britain and the young United States) urged that the aim of incarceration be redefined as the redemption of the convicted, rather than their mere immobilization. The use of solitary confinement, the requirement of strict silence, the assignment of uniforms, and the imposition of compulsory labor came to characterize prison life. In Jeremy Bentham's Panopticon, constant scrutiny by officials would ensure the proper behavior of the inmates. The name, meaning "a place where all can be seen," suggested a kind of psychological control over deviant behavior that, despite the author's humane intentions, heralded devices of modern totalitarian control.

Though crime was reported more regularly, policed more thoroughly, and punished more effectively, it was no more frequent in urban than it had been in rural settings. It became more terrifying, it seems, merely because the numbers of urban residents meant the multiplication of the fear aroused by malefactors.

The nocturnal voyager along the city's streets, in fact, was more likely to encounter a drunkard or a vagrant than a thief. The consumption of distilled alcohol (gin, vodka, whiskey) became widespread in the nineteenth century, competing with the more familiar beverages of beer and wine. Consumption of these latter favorites also soared—workers disbursed a large fraction of their wages on drink consumed before, during, and after work, while the wealthy considered dining incomplete without a trail of fine vintages. Alcoholism became a serious problem, even among women, previously excluded from the convivial settings of tavern and café where heavy drinking took place. The frustrations of industrial employment, or the isolation of urban existence, may have promoted excessive drinking in both sexes. Conversation accompanied social drinking. An abundance of both sometimes stimulated the formation of political attitudes, especially among workers—to such an extent that, in Paris, the café was deemed "the parliament of the people."

A vagrant or beggar was often only an unemployed drifter. Others belonged to gang-like groups, which sought mutual assistance and occasionally veered into criminal activity. Since the early sixteenth century, vagrancy had been eyed suspiciously by city officials, who often refused to distinguish between thieves and itinerant traders such as peddlers. Selling portable, cheap items, peddlers too had a marginal role in the world of shops, factories, and public spaces that made up the modern city.

Prostitution Walking the streets of the city were also the least fortunate of the prostitutes, whose trade reached a new importance in the nineteenth century. The large modern city had tens of thousands of prostitutes (London, for example, as many as 80,000). These ranged from wealthy, pampered **courtesans** who received their clients in well-furnished apartments, to the occupants of a brothel under the command of a madam or pimp. And they also included the stray, impoverished or part-time, often married, sexworker who picked up clients on the street. Some prostitutes were initiated by their own mothers, often poor and desperate, or prostitutes themselves. Some were forcibly recruited by abduction and rape, or turned to the profession when, as unmarried domestic servants discovered to be pregnant, they were cast out of their employers' homes. Some adopted the career freely because it offered higher wages, easier work, and shorter hours than unskilled female wageworkers could otherwise command. Some remained prostitutes for only a brief interlude, before accumulating a dowry and marrying. Others were trapped in the dim underworld where prostitution, crime, and addiction converged.

All prostitutes, however, depended on the demand created by men with the money to purchase their services. These men came from all social classes, and, despite the rigid moral and social codes that governed, at least outwardly, the lives of the wealthier classes, their behavior was tolerated throughout most of Europe. Prostitution was generally considered (with the exception of some reformers) a forgivable and necessary accommodation to the supposed realities of male sexual life.

If prostitution was tolerated, prostitutes themselves were kept under careful surveillance. As potential carriers of venereal disease, they posed a threat to public health. In many states (in France and Russia, for instance), brothels were frequently inspected by police, and prostitutes, who had to be licensed with the authorities, were examined for disease. (Their male associates, however, who were just as likely to be carriers, were spared the official scrutiny directed toward women sexworkers.)

In 1866–1869, the British parliament inaugurated the medical examination of prostitutes in garrison towns and seaports with the Contagious Diseases Acts, which provided for the isolation of those who proved to have the disease. The determined opposition of Josephine Butler (1828–1906), a clergyman's wife and an early campaigner for women's sexual freedom, led to the law's repeal in 1886. Still in Britain as elsewhere, the tendency was to isolate brothels to special "red light" districts where middle-class men would not willingly go.

WITNESSES

Friedrich Engels' Portrait of the Industrial City (1844)

Manchester: The view from the bridge—mercifully concealed from smaller mortals by a parapet as high as a man—is quite characteristic of the entire district. At the bottom the Irk flows, or rather stagnates. It is a narrow, coal-black stinking river full of filth and garbage . . . out of whose depths bubbles of miasmatic gasses constantly rise and give forth a stench that is unbearable even on the bridge forty or fifty feet above the level of the water. . . . Above Ducie Bridge there are tall tannery buildings, and further up are dye-works, bone mills and gasworks. The total entirety of the liquid wastes and solid offscourings of these works finds its way into the River Irk, which receives as well the contents of the adjacent sewers and privies. . . . Below Ducie Bridge, on the left, one looks into piles of rubbish, the refuse, filth and decaying matter of the courts on the steep left bank of the river. Here one house is packed very closely upon another, and because of the steep pitch of the bank a part of every house is visible. All of them are blackened with smoke, crumbling, old, with broken window panes and window frames. The background is formed by old factory buildings, which resemble barracks.—On the right, low-lying bank stands a long row of houses and factories. The second house is a roofless ruin, filled with rubble, and the third stands in such a low situation that the ground floor is uninhabitable and is as a result without windows and doors. The background here is formed by the paupers' cemetery and the stations of the railways to Liverpool and Leeds. Behind these is the workhouse, Manchester's "Poor Law Bastille." It is built on a hill, like a citadel, and from behind its high walls and battlements looks down threateningly upon the working-class quarter that lies below.

London: [T]he inhabitants of London have had to sacrifice the best part of their humanity. . . . The very bustle and tumult of the streets has something repugnant in it, something that human nature feels outraged by. Hundreds of thousands of people from all classes and ranks of society crowd by each other. Are they not all human beings with the same qualities and faculties: Do they not all have the same interest in being happy? Must they not in the end seek their happiness through the same means and methods? Yet they rush past each other as if they had nothing in common, nothing to do with one another. They are in (tacit) agreement on one thing only—that everyone keep to the right of the pavement so as not to interfere with the crowds that stream in the opposite direction. Meanwhile it occurs to no one that others are worth even a glance. The brutal indifference, the unfeeling isolation of each individual person in his private interest becomes the more repulsive and offensive, the more these individuals are packed into a tiny space. We know well enough that this isolation of the individual—this narrow-minded self-seeking—is everywhere the fundamental principle of modern society. But nowhere is it so shamelessly unconcealed . . . as in the tumultuous concourse of the great city. The dissolution of mankind into monads, each of which has a separate purpose, is carried here to its furthest point. It is the world of atoms.

From this it follows that the social war—the war of all against all—has been openly declared. . . . Men here regard each other only as useful objects. Each one exploits the other with the result that the stronger tramples the weaker underfoot, and that the few who are strong, the capitalists, seize everything for themselves, while for the many who are weak, the poor, there remains scarcely a bare existence.

(Friedrich Engels, *The Condition of the Working Class in England*, 1844; ed. S. Marcus, 1974)

The Problem of Poverty The high incidence of prostitution, like that of crime and vagrancy, mirrored the existence of widespread poverty. Urban poverty took on new dimensions in the bloated industrial cities, putting many individuals at risk of incarceration, violence, and abandonment, and inviting new sets of social attitudes and social policy. Before 1800, poverty was the concern of the churches or of small local agencies of government. By 1900, it was seen as a problem to be managed by the national state.

Britain pioneered in creating a national system of poor relief. The Poor Law Amendment Act of 1834 established a series of residential workhouses, to which the unemployed poor could be forcibly removed. These functioned much like prisons. Strict discipline prevailed, work obligations were heavy, and food was plain and meager. Worse still, the workhouse system resulted in the break-up of families. Able-bodied men, who were expected to seek and find employment, were excluded. Women, children, and the old or infirm became the main beneficiaries—or victims—of the workhouse.

The British workhouse system found few imitators in other nations where, by the late nineteenth century, legislation in favor of workers served to moderate the effects of poverty. In Germany, as has been seen, Bismarck instituted a system of benefits that cushioned employed workers and their families from unemployment, disability, ill health, and lack of income in old age. That model would be followed by many modern states. Trade unions, in addition, offered help in the case of unemployment, strike, or the death of a primary wage-earner. Private charities of a traditional sort continued to serve the poor, as did a new set of **philanthropic organizations**, which won the active support especially of some middle- and upper-class women.

Nevertheless, the poor continued to suffer particular disabilities. They were often uneducated or even illiterate. They had higher rates of illegitimacy and infanticide, suicide and mental illness than the rest of the population, less resistance to disease and lower life expectancy. They more often committed crimes, and were more often its victims. They ate less than the affluent, their nutrition deficit evident to the eye—the average laborer was several inches shorter than the average member of the middle class. In this pattern of starvation, that of poor women who were mothers of children—an "autostarvation" for the sake of their offspring—was a constant.

The poor were seen by the wealthy not merely as a class apart, but almost as a separate race, with a distinct culture and society. If the city was the site of the "dissolution of mankind into monads [very small units]," as Friedrich Engels observed—or the place where, uniquely, "the human heart is sick," according to the Romantic poet William Wordsworth (1770–1850)—surely those who were most deprived of selfhood and burdened with sick hearts were the dispossessed poor of the modern city.

THE TWO HALVES AT HOME

Crowding a new generation of industrial workers into the existing frame of urban life had tremendous consequences. The effects could be seen out on the street. The cityscape displayed sharp contrasts between the lives of the rich and those of the "other half." Such contrasts gain deeper reality, however, when the observer turns from the streets to the homes of workers and their employers. A chasm yawned between the tenement and the townhouse, marking the distance between rich and poor.

In the Tenement

However miserable the peasant's hovel (and some were mere piles of mud, or ditches covered with entangled branches), a peasant family normally had a place to live within an established village. The newly urbanized workers of the industrial age had nothing of the sort. They lived in one or two rooms shared with kin or strangers in the aging building stock of established cities, or in hastily-erected tenements in new towns or suburbs destined soon to deteriorate into **slums**.

In those rooms, heated if at all by a fireplace also used for cooking, they ate, slept, and gathered together. There were generally no separate rooms for food-preparation or dining, for bathing or toileting, for sleeping, or for intimate relationships of body or mind. There was neither running water nor artificial light (well after these had become available to the affluent). For the performance of bodily functions, there were outhouses, or an old pot inside, the contents of which were disposed of at intervals from open windows by a centuries-old custom to add to the muck in the streets below.

The peasant household, moreover, possessed a stability the worker's household often lacked. In the countryside, male and female roles were clearly distinguished. While both men and women worked, sometimes side by side in the fields, they had different jobs. Men more often handled heavy tools, especially the plow, while women more often took care of barnyard chickens and other small animals, a cottage garden, housekeeping tasks, and above all the ceaseless labor of cooking and spinning. The worker's household instead was characterized by shifting, uncertain relations between the genders. In the early years of industrialization, men worked in factories alongside their wives and children. As women left the factories, they took up other work, still essential to family fortunes, while children often stayed in the factory. There they labored under dangerous conditions, subject to abusive employers, for the sake of a meager wage donated to support the family as a whole. Male heads of households depended for income on their children and wives. Frequently the householder was himself unemployed—for unemployment was a common, cyclical reality in the early industrial era—while his wife and children worked.

These different relations to work were reflected in personal relationships within workers' families. Women continued to bear responsibility for housework, the burden of which was added to paid labor outside the home. Since it was they who shopped for

WITNESSES

The Two Halves at Home

The urban poor: description of domestic conditions among workers in Lille, France (1832): In their obscure cellars, in their rooms, which one would take for cellars, the air is never renewed, it is infected; the walls are plastered with garbage. . . . If a bed exists, it is a few dirty, greasy planks; it is damp and putrescent straw; it is a coarse cloth whose color and fabric are hidden by a layer of grime; it is a blanket that resembles a sieve. . . . The windows, always closed, are covered by paper and glass, but so black, so smoke-encrusted, that the light is unable to penetrate . . . everywhere are piles of garbage, of ashes, of debris. . . . One is exhausted, in these hovels, by a stale, nauseating, somewhat piquant odor, odor of filth, odor of garbage. . . .

. . . I have seen individuals of both sexes and of very different ages lying together, most of them without nightshirts and repulsively dirty. Father, mother, the aged, children, adults, all pressed, stacked together. I stop. The reader will complete the picture, but I warn him that if he wishes it to be accurate, his imagination must not recoil before any of the disgusting mysteries performed on these impure beds in the midst of obscurity and drunkenness.

(From W. H. Sewell, *Work and Revolution in France: The Language of Labor from the Old Regime to 1848*, 1980)

The wealthy: Flora Tristan describes the life of the bourgeois Englishwoman (1842): It has long been the fashion to extol English liberties, but England is the seat of the most abominable despotism, where laws and prejudices submit women to the most revolting inequality! A woman may inherit only if she has no brothers; she has no civil or political rights and the law subjects her to her husband in every respect. . . .

This is what happens in wealthy families: the children are confined to the third floor with their nurse, maid or governess; the mother asks for them when she wishes to see them . . . [and] she addresses them in a formal manner. As the poor little girl is starved of affection, her capacity for loving is never awakened . . ., while for the father she hardly knows, she has a respect mingled with fear, and for her brother she keeps the consideration and deference she has been obliged to show him from her earliest childhood.

The system followed for the education of young girls seems to me fit to turn the most intelligent child into a blockhead. . . . It is concerned solely to imprint on these young minds the *words* of all the European languages without the slightest thought for the *ideas*. . . .

Young ladies have very few amusements: as family life is formal, arid, and intolerably boring, they plunge headlong into the world of the novel. Unfortunately, these romances revolve around lovers such as England has never known, and their influence gives birth to hopes that can never be fulfilled. . . . [T]he fate of the married woman is very much sadder than that of the spinster; at least the unmarried woman enjoys a certain freedom, she can enter society and travel with her family or with friends, whereas once a woman is married, she cannot stir from the house *without the permission of her husband*. The English husband is like the *lord and master* of feudal times. . . .

The English husband sleeps with his servant, casts her out when she is pregnant or after she has given birth. . . . In England the wife is not the mistress of the household as she would be in France. In fact she is almost a stranger in her own home; the husband holds the money and the keys. . . . [H]e has sole charge of everything.

(*The London Journal of Flora Tristan, 1842*; ed. J. Hawkes, 1982)

necessary supplies, they often controlled family finances. Managing the money that their husbands and children brought home, they sometimes rescued it from the hands of a spouse hoping to spend it at the local tavern.

Workers' wives could find employment as laundresses, daily servants, pieceworkers, and, later in the nineteenth century, laborers in the "**sweated industries**." Piecework entailed sewing items of clothing, such as shirts, embroidering luxury items, or knitting stockings or caps. They might also market these products in the streets, as peddlers. The sweated industries employed a few laborers in workshops, or "sweatshops," outside the factory, generally dedicated to clothing manufacture. In all these cases, the wages they received were lower than those earned by male factory workers, or indeed by men doing work of equal difficulty. Overall, women may have earned about one-half the wages that men did for comparable work and hours.

Lower wages were not the only disability that women in working-class households experienced. They were often left to support whole families when the male head of household was unemployed or, as

Slums and Tenements

Living in poverty: *Early industrial workers' homes reflected the grim reality of their tenants' lives. Many were dirty, dark, overcrowded, and unsanitary. In one of journalist Jacob Riis's now classic photographs of working-class existence in New York City dated c. 1890, an English Coal-Heaver sits at home with his family.* (Museum of the City of New York)

happened quite frequently, when he deserted his family altogether. They were often the victims of physical abuse from desperate and drunken husbands.

Single women workers were freer to move about to seek employment. In Britain, they often worked as domestic servants in the homes of bourgeois or aristocratic families (see below). As servants, they were frequently made pregnant by their masters or their masters' sons—a familiar cause for dismissal and social disgrace. Unmarried women in other job categories also often found themselves pregnant in the industrial city, where the restraints of village life had withered and died. Women who gave birth out of wedlock frequently abandoned their babies to the care of

Occupations of Women Workers in Milan (1881), London (1891), and France (1906)

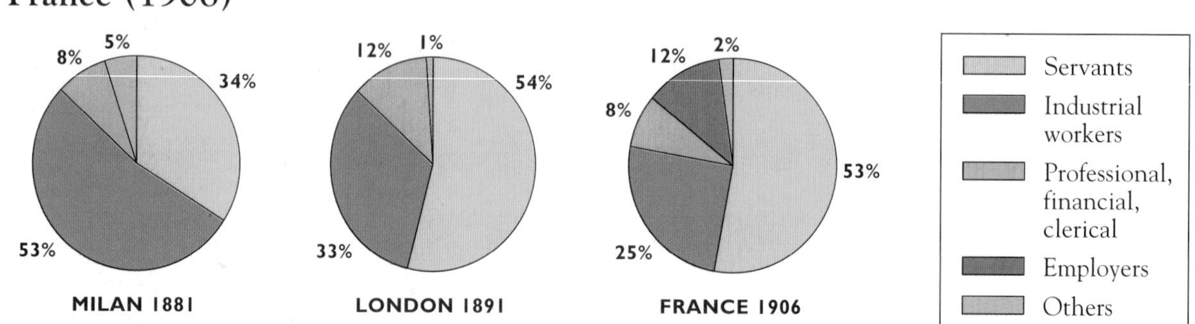

As in the early modern period, a great many of the women who worked found employment as servants. By the end of the nineteenth century, however, large numbers of women were working in factories, and in clerical and administrative positions in offices and stores—even as owners of shops and other enterprises.

Sources: *Based on P. M. Hohenberg and L. H. Lees,* The Making of Urban Europe, 1000–1950 *(Cambridge, MA: Harvard University Press, 1985; 2nd ed., 1995), p. 210, and R. Price,* A Social History of Nineteenth-Century France *(New York: Holmes & Meier, 1987), p. 213* foundling homes or orphanages, now become numerous, and sometimes killed them. Many such women were forced into prostitution.

Whatever their circumstances, the laboring poor shared this characteristic with the incarcerated prisoner or the workhouse resident: they had nowhere to go. They had little expectation that conditions would improve for them, or that their children could aspire to higher positions than those they themselves occupied. Their wages purchased little beyond food and that food was mostly bread. Well over half a workers' wage was spent on food, and, after expenses of housing and clothing, barely ten percent was left—often dispensed on drink and entertainment. After their long workday, male and female workers alike sought recreation in tavern, café, or **music hall**, the social clubs of the poor. If they spent too much of their meager supply of cash on these amusements, pawnbrokers and loansharks were available to lend them more, and bind them even more firmly to a condition of poverty.

By the late nineteenth century, and a little earlier in Britain (where workers' diets and prospects were somewhat better), standards of living for the working poor in northern and western Europe began at last to rise. In Britain, real wages increased by one-third between 1850 and 1875, and by nearly one-half again between 1870 and 1900. Advances in Germany were nearly as great. Improvements in agriculture resulted in lower food costs, at least in these privileged regions, falling to about half of the family budget. More money became available for housing, for clothes (cheap, well-cut ready-mades were now widely available), and for entertainment. Workers' diet became more varied, including grain and even meat, shipped in refrigerated compartments from the Americas and Australia. No longer a luxury, meat consumption among workers rose steadily.

Another step toward the eventual advancement of the working class was the advent of public schooling for its children (see also Chapter 24). By the eighteenth century, elementary schooling had become more widely available for the young children of ordinary folk in such areas as Prussia, Scotland, and parts of Anglo-America. The nineteenth century saw the expansion of mass secular education. From the 1880s, Britain and France instituted mandatory, free public schools for all children; most states of the United States had done so by the end of the nineteenth century. With access to public education in at least these leading nations, all children—the tenement dweller as much as the child of privilege—had an opportunity to gain the skills by which they could strive for greater success.

In the Townhouse

Out in the countryside in pre-modern Europe, the grand manor house or castle of the local landowner dominated the huts or cottages of the peasants. The gulf between rich and poor was equally apparent in the city, which contained both the opulent townhouse or apartment of the bourgeois or nobleman and the worker's rented room. In the industrial era, as the dwellings of the poor became even bleaker in the multi-storied anonymity of the tenement, the homes of the well-off became softer, warmer and more comfortable than ever.

Domestic comfort had only recently become an important consideration for the upper classes as the industrial age opened. Since the fifteenth century, aristocratic homes had developed differentiated private and public spaces, both suitably adorned with fine furniture and tapestries. By the seventeenth and eighteenth centuries, aristocratic homes in country

London slum: *For large numbers of urban workers, city environments—whether at home or at work—were drab, crowded, unhealthy, and dangerous. Slums such as those of London, drawn here by French artist Gustave Doré, were all too common.*

Workhouse and Café

Dinnertime in St. Pancras workhouse: *Significant numbers of poorer urbanites lacked even the most basic housing, and made their homes instead at workhouses or other institutional refuges. Here, women eat in the St. Pancras, London workhouse, in a scene from around 1900.*

and city featured lush furnishings and expensive adornments—and the great luxury of windows. As industrialization proceeded in the nineteenth century, the ever-larger and ever-wealthier bourgeoisie imitated the pacesetting nobility and furnished their townhouses and apartments to suit their enhanced social and economic position.

The number of rooms multiplied, and more things filled those rooms. The homes of the wealthy now possessed parlors and studies, bedrooms and nurseries, and formal dining-rooms. Walls lined with brocaded cloth or richly designed papers were hung with prints and paintings, and adorned with fine wood or plaster moldings. Candelabras hung from the ceiling or were mounted on the wall. Scattered about were fine musical instruments—such as a piano in the parlor—showpiece clocks on pedestals or mantels, and collections of small precious things—crystal, silver, porcelain. Furniture included elegant tables and wardrobes and soft, deep chairs, resting on patterned carpets.

The dusting and cleaning of such large houses stuffed with so many possessions were the constant care of servants, who now served in European cities in veritable armies. Most domestic servants were women who lived in closets and attics, consumed the same kinds of food as their employers' families, and could expect reasonable conditions of life and work despite their meager pay. Even in less wealthy bourgeois households, a single maid-of-all-work might clean the house, tend the fires, and wait at table, among other tasks. Servant labor made the bourgeois style of life possible.

Ladies of Leisure Like their female servants, elite women were also dedicated to the maintenance of the bourgeois or aristocratic household. They were expected to avoid work themselves—exemption from labor was essential to the status of "lady"—but to manage the labor of servants in housekeeping and food preparation tasks. The boundaries between the privileged and those considered "inferior" lay in these delicate social distinctions between the housewife who labored and the one who, having at least one female servant, did not.

Bourgeois and aristocratic women turned their skills and aptitudes instead to other household functions. They exercised their taste in the choice of furnishings and works of art, in the selection of schools and tutors for their children, and in the arts of hospitality—the entertainment of neighbors and business associates with afternoon tea, elaborate dinners (served in multiple courses by servants in formal attire), or for extended visits, all arranged by the genteel exchange of invitations in person or through written notes on luxury stationery. The elite household consumed much—food and drink, furniture and furnishings, the labor of servants—and women were charged with procuring these consumables. They hired servants, dealt with tradesmen, and visited the new department stores (the first of which appeared in Paris soon after 1850)—those palaces of consumerism which, observed the French writer Emile Zola (1840–1902; see Chapter 24), threatened to replace the churches in the hearts of many.

When not shopping or visiting, elite women stayed current by reading sentimental novels or ladies' magazines which had been published since the eighteenth century, filled with articles about fashion, entertaining, and childcare. They employed their leisure with activities that produced little of practical use but much of beauty: embroidery, knitting, and other forms of needlework. One advice book for young ladies explained: "The intention of your being taught needlework, knitting and such like is not on account of the intrinsic values of all you can do with your hands, which is trifling, but to enable you to fill up, in a tolerably agreeable way, some of the many solitary hours you must necessarily pass at home."

Women of the elites were responsible for the households in which they led lives of ease. At the same time, they had little connection with the public world beyond the household—the realm of work, wealth, and power. The distinction between a woman's life close to the household and a man's apart from it was not new to the industrial age, but it was to become even sharper as the "separate spheres" of home and work involved wholly different activities. Work had been wholly removed from the household, which was once itself a zone of productive activity, and it moved to the factory, the bank, the office building. The household now became the site for recuperation from work, a place reserved for the consumption of goods and services. Here women bore the responsibility of equipping their male kin for the distant, different place of work.

The widening gap between home and work among the elites, the spheres of female and male, was expressed in the new fashions of the industrial age. A generation after the French Revolution, driven forward by the rage of the *sans-culottes* (see Chapter 20), bourgeois and aristocratic men abandoned knee-breeches for trousers, a fashion associated with practical, serious work, rather than the frivolities of the court. At the same time, they gave up powdered wigs and perfume, silks (except in the relic of the tie) and velvets, jewelry and high-heeled shoes. They dressed in black or grey, suggesting sober attention to duty,

***Pierre-Auguste Renoir,* Le Moulin de la Galette:** *After dark, the city was full of opportunities. Working-class and middle-class urban-dwellers alike shopped, attended theaters and music halls, strolled in parks, and relaxed in taverns and cafés. In Paris, cafés such as this one—painted by Impressionist artist Pierre-Auguste Renoir in 1876—were popular places to socialize.* (Louvre, Paris)

Bourgeois Lives

Living in luxury: *Far from the slums and the workers' quarters, wealthier families lived in luxurious townhouses or gracious apartment buildings. Such dwellings lined the elegant Ringstrasse in Vienna, shown here in an 1891 engraving by W. Gause.*

with the distinction between the wealthier and the less-wealthy evident not in the style of clothing but only in such details as the cut of the garment and the quality of the fabric. Elite women, however, continued to wear (after an interlude of studied simplicity during the Napoleonic era) the huge skirts, tight and revealing bodices, and brilliant colors of female aristocrats of the previous era. Their elaborate dress proclaimed their leisured status and their feminine mission to bear children—their fertility announced daily to the world by the contrast between full skirt and corseted waist. Indeed, hoops and crinolines made women gigantic, larger than their menfolk but frailer, physically absurd in a way that suggested their continued rootedness to a natural world amid the frantic pandemonium of modern industrial life.

Although women's reproductive mission was thus displayed in their costume, privileged women in the wealthier nations were in fact beginning to bear fewer children—especially in France, where birthrates dropped drastically toward the end of the nineteenth century. Such declining birthrates witness the practice of birth control, especially the traditional but unreliable method of *coitus interruptus*, or male withdrawal. Condoms, though known, were crude, and mostly used with prostitutes, and the other possibilities (herbal remedies and home surgery) were unpleasant, dangerous, and often deadly.

Family Life A declining rate of infant mortality perhaps encouraged people to have fewer children. Economic factors were also important: increased costs associated with childrearing, especially private education, affected the middle classes, while, for working-class families, child labor laws and compulsory education meant that younger children could no longer contribute to family income. Whatever the case, fewer children in the family meant that nonworking mothers could devote more time and care to their children's rearing. They worried over child health and education, seeking the opinion of experts and carefully selecting schools. For the first time in

Western history, women of the elites breastfed their own infants, both to nourish them better, and to surround them with the maternal tenderness that so many infants through the ages had never known.

This trend toward the deepening attachment of middle-class women to their children (aristocratic women generally still consigned theirs to the care of servants) coincided with changes in the medical treatment of childbirth. Male midwives, and then male doctors, took over the business of supervising birth for women of the upper classes (although they did so in women's homes rather than in hospitals, where poor women suffered the dangers of infection and neglect). The development of the forceps in the eighteenth century had helped infants and mothers to survive difficult births. A century later, two other developments assisted the mother. The first was the adoption of the principle of antisepsis (see Chapter 24), by assuring the cleanliness of surgical instruments and environment, which greatly reduced the rate of maternal mortality. The second was the introduction of anesthesia, initially by the use of chloroform—an innovation that Queen Victoria (r. 1837–1901) personally experienced and approved enthusiastically.

The intensifying involvement of better-off women with their young children was one aspect of a general intensification of family feeling. More often than in the past, men and women married partners of their choosing. Encouraged in part by the powerful cultural movement of Romanticism (see Chapter 24), whose message resounded in books, opera, and theater, they sought marriages founded on love. Meanwhile, marital love was valued by the public consensus as it had not been in earlier ages, when duty, obedience, or mutual affection was the expressed ideal. Advice books glorified family life, and manuals on conjugal love encouraged both men and women to seek sexual gratification within marriage for the sake of the harmonious community of mother, father, and children.

In the intense theater of family life, privileged women were the source not only of heightened sentiment, but also of a "higher" morality. It was the women who conveyed moral lessons, and saw to their children's moral as well as intellectual growth. Mothers supervised religious instruction, presiding over family prayers and seeking to instill the values of self-control and self-reliance that had become newly important in industrial society.

Women's association with the moral realm also reached beyond the household. Many engaged in charitable activities that took them across their own thresholds, and out beyond the boundaries of their neighborhood and caste to tend to the needs of those of the other half: orphans, unwed mothers, prostitutes, the sick, the poor. They gathered in clubs and

***Claude Monet,* Garden at Sainte-Adresse:** *Wealthy families had the opportunity to leave their homes and take holidays in the mountains or at the seashore. Middle-class vacationers are seen here in a work dated 1867 by Impressionist painter Claude Monet.* (Metropolitan Museum of Art, New York)

organizations for charitable purposes, where as volunteer treasurers, secretaries, and presidents, they acquired the experience of management they were barred from in the professional world of work.

Despite their vigorous role in philanthropic activities (which also appealed to many men of the affluent classes), and their competence in running large and complex households, women were still expected to defer to men in matters concerning money. In most countries, a woman's dowry was still her husband's to use, if it was not absolutely his property. In some, women could own no property in their own name, and could negotiate loans only with the co-signature of a husband, father, or guardian. In France, where the Revolution had insisted on daughters' equal right to inherit, the Napoleonic Code (see Chapter 20) classed women as legal incompetents along with children, the insane, and criminals.

Nearly everywhere, a woman's adultery was still viewed by the law as a more serious offense than a man's—and in some countries, it was permissible for a husband who caught his wife in the adulterous act to kill her. Divorce, too (where it was obtainable at all), was more easily obtained by a man than a woman, who needed to prove amply and without question her husband's offenses. In the event of divorce or separation, it was fathers who generally held all custodial rights over children—and not their mothers, whose sentimental attachment to them was increasingly part of family life.

These barriers to women's independence would be resisted in the new feminist movement of the later 1800s (see Chapter 24). In the meantime, most propertied families functioned as though these problems did not exist, appearing to enjoy wholeheartedly the many opportunities their comfortable lives offered. Besides receiving visitors at home, and visiting others, men and women of the bourgeoisie and aristocracy attended concerts, the theater, and the opera, where they sat in halls among audiences who were more orderly than in the past, and listened more attentively than had their ancestors—even entertainment was becoming a serious matter in the industrial age, requiring a disciplined and responsible attitude.

They also frequented teashops and cafés, strolled in well-groomed parks, borrowed books from libraries, attended lectures at literary or philosophical societies, and relaxed at their (mostly all-male) clubs. They traveled by the new railroad lines to the beach and to spas, where they bathed in and drank mineral-laden waters thought to be beneficial to their health. Equipped with guides to monuments, museums, and restaurants, they toured the cities of Europe, and, boarding steamships where they slept in luxurious staterooms and enjoyed elaborate dinners, ventured to colonial centers abroad (see Chapter 23).

Far from home, the men and women of the privileged classes enjoyed comforts and refinements unthinkable in the tenements where the other half lived.

Conclusion

THE ONE HALF, THE OTHER HALF, AND THE MEANING OF THE WEST

During the nineteenth century, industrialization recreated the human and urban landscape of the wealthier Western nations. It created new social groups—that of the factory worker who bore the burden of the pain entailed by the reconstruction of the modern economy, and that of the capitalist, for whose profit the worker labored. At the same time, it created a new, previously inconceivable, kind of city—a huge and diverse place, embracing factories and libraries, department stores and brothels, all knit together by sewage and water pipes, gas lines, and electrical cable. Within that city the astoundingly rich coexisted with the desperately poor, and contrasts between wealth and poverty were vivid and shocking. The disparity between rich and poor, long a concern of the Christian churches, would henceforth be taken up by the secular leaders of the Western world—a problem with moral, practical, and political dimensions, threatening both stability and conscience. At the dawn of the twenty-first century, the problem persists still.

Even as rich and poor confronted each other in the capitals of the Western world, the West was vigorously extending its influence in the world beyond the West, as the following chapter will show, confronting a different sort of poverty, and creating a new set of relationships between those who command and those who serve.

REVIEW QUESTIONS

1. What groups of people made up the poor in industrial society? How did machines change the nature of work? How did the factory system affect the social and economic roles of women and children?

2. What is capitalism? What effect did industrialization have on skilled workers? Who were the proletariat?

3. Why did workers join trade unions in the nineteenth century? What was the significance of the *Communist Manifesto*? How had workers' lives improved by 1900?

4. Why did European cities grow so rapidly between 1800 and 1900? Who were the "white-collar" workers? How did industrialization transform the cities and why had they become more healthful by 1900?

5. Why were the lives of the urban poor so different from those of the rich and the middle class? How widespread was crime in nineteenth-century cities? How did urban poverty affect the lives of working women?

6. What roles were elite women expected to play at home and in society? Why did the size of urban families decline in the late nineteenth century? How did smaller families affect attitudes toward children?

SUGGESTED READINGS

Workers and Workplace

Biernacki, Richard, *The Fabrication of Labor: Germany and Britain, 1640–1914* (Berkeley: University of California Press, 1995). Explores national differences in concepts of labor and wages.

Himmelfarb, Gertrude, *The Idea of Poverty: England in the Early Industrial Age* (New York: Knopf, 1984). Surveys of attitudes, ideas, and action regarding poverty and its relief.

Horn, Pamela, *Children's Work and Welfare, 1780–1890* (Cambridge: Cambridge University Press, 1995). Useful introduction to an important and frequently under-examined area of industrial history.

Jones, Gareth Stedman, *Languages of Class: Studies in English Working Class History, 1832–1982* (Cambridge: Cambridge University Press, 1983). Essays on cultural aspects of class formation and identity.

Sewell, William, Jr., *Work and Revolution in France: The Language of Labor from the Old Regime to 1848* (Cambridge: Cambridge University Press, 1980). How French artisan-workers integrated collectivist demands with newer language of freedom and individualism.

Thompson, E. P., *The Making of the English Working Class* (New York: Pantheon, 1964). Landmark study of the struggles of the workers in early industrial England.

The Industrial City

Bairoch, Paul, *Cities and Economic Development: From the Dawn of History to the Present* (Chicago: University of Chicago Press, 1988). Examines urbanization and its significance in world history.

Briggs, Asa, *Victorian Cities* (Berkeley: University of California Press, 1993; orig. 1963). Classic series of portraits of various industrial cities in the English-speaking world.

Hohenberg, Paul M. and Lynn Hollen Lees, *The Making of Urban Europe, 1000–1950*; 2nd ed. (Cambridge, MA: Harvard University Press, 1995). Excellent introduction to the history and significance of the city over a thousand years of European history.

Landers, John, *Death and the Metropolis: Studies in the Demographic History of London, 1670–1830* (Cambridge: Cambridge University Press, 1993). Seeks the cause of London's high mortality rates, focusing on unhealthy environmental conditions and disease.

Papayanis, Nicholas, *Horse-Drawn Cabs and Omnibuses in Paris: The Idea of Circulation and the Business of Public Transit* (Baton Rouge: Louisiana State University Press, 1996). Describes innovations in transit which connected center with suburban housing.

The Two Halves at Home

Corbin, Alain, *The Lure of the Sea: The Discovery of the Seaside in the Western World 1750–1840* (Berkeley: University of California Press, 1994). Traces the significance of the sea-shore as both a physical destination and a cultural artifact.

Fuchs, Rachel G., *Poor and Pregnant in Paris: Strategies for Survival in the Nineteenth Century* (New Brunswick, NJ: Rutgers University Press, 1992). How poverty and abandonment led to bleak outcomes.

Haine, W. Scott, *The World of the Paris Café: Sociability Among the French Working Class, 1789–1914* (Baltimore: The Johns Hopkins University Press, 1996). Identifies the café as the cultural center of French workers' lives in the 19th century.

Miller, Michael B., *The Bon Marché: Bourgeois Culture and the Department Store, 1869–1920* (Princeton, NJ: Princeton University Press, 1981). Explores how the *Bon Marché*, and department stores in general, both reflected and helped shape bourgeois culture.

Ross, Ellen, *Love and Toil: Motherhood in Outcast London, 1870–1918* (Oxford: Oxford University Press, 1993). Examines how mothers struggled to keep working families intact and nurture children.

Thompson, F. M. L., *The Rise of Respectable Society 1830–1900* (Cambridge, MA: Harvard University Press, 1988). Essays on Victorian society, including family, home, and leisure.

Walkowitz, Judith R., *Prostitution and Victorian Society: Women, Class and the State* (Cambridge: Cambridge University Press, 1980). Explores effects of British legislation to control contagious diseases.

THE WESTERN *IMPERIUM*

	1750	1775	1800	1825	1850	1875	1900	1925

Europe

- Seven Years' War, 1756–63
- French Revolutionary and Napoleonic Wars, 1792–1815
- World War I, 1914–18
- ◆ Irish patriot Wolfe Tone rebels against Britain, 1798
- ◆ Roman Catholic Emancipation Act in Britain, 1829
- ◆ Potato famine devastates Ireland, 1845–50
- ◆ Year of Revolutions in Europe, 1848
- ◆ The Great Exhibition at London's Crystal Palace, 1851
- ◆ Serfdom abolished in Russia, 1861
- ◆ Alfred Dreyfus falsely accused of treason, 1894
- ◆ Theodore Herzl's *The Jewish State*, 1896
- ◆ J. A. Hobson's *Imperialism, a Study*, 1902
- ◆ 400 Jews killed in pogrom in Odessa, 1905

The Americas

- Atlantic slave trade, 1500–1888
- American Revolution, 1775–83
- All Latin American states independent, 1804–28
- American Civil War, 1861–65
- ◆ Haiti first independent Latin American nation, 1804
- ◆ Brazilian independence, 1822
- ◆ Canada becomes constitutional monarchy within British Commonwealth, 1867
- ◆ Transcontinental railroad completed in US, 1869
- ◆ Panama Canal opens, 1904
- ◆ Trans-Andean railroad completed, 1910

Africa and the Middle East

- South African War, 1899–1902
- ◆ British take control of Dutch Cape Colony, 1795
- ◆ Shaka leads Zulu nation, 1817
- ◆ France annexes Algeria, 1830
- ◆ Suez canal opens, 1869
- ◆ Britain occupies Egypt, 1882
- ◆ Congress of Berlin sets off "Scramble for Africa," 1885
- ◆ Ethiopia defeats Italy at Battle of Adowa, 1896
- ◆ "Young Turks" topple Ottoman sultan, 1908
- ◆ Italy occupies Libya, 1911
- ◆ Spain and France partition Morocco, 1912

Asia and Oceania

- Qing Dynasty, China, 1644–1912
- British East India Company in India, 1690–1857
- Dutch East India Company in East Indies, 1619–1799
- First Opium War, 1839–42
- Second Opium War, 1856–60
- Trans-Siberian railroad constructed, 1891–1904
- ◆ Britain acquires Australia, 1788
- ◆ Dutch government absorbs Dutch East India Company, 1799
- ◆ British gain "overlordship" of India as Mughal power declines, 1803
- ◆ Treaty of Nanjing, 1842
- ◆ American Commodore Perry "opens" Japan, 1853
- ◆ Sepoy Mutiny in India, 1857
- ◆ French gain control of Indochina, 1858
- ◆ Meiji Restoration in Japan, 1868
- ◆ Indian National Congress founded, 1885
- ◆ Chinese lose Sino-Japanese War, 1895
- ◆ Japan victorious in Russo-Japanese War, 1905
- ◆ Japan annexes Korea, 1910
- ◆ Chinese Republic declared, 1911–12

CHAPTER 23

THE WESTERN IMPERIUM

European Migration, Settlement, and Domination around the Globe

1750–1914

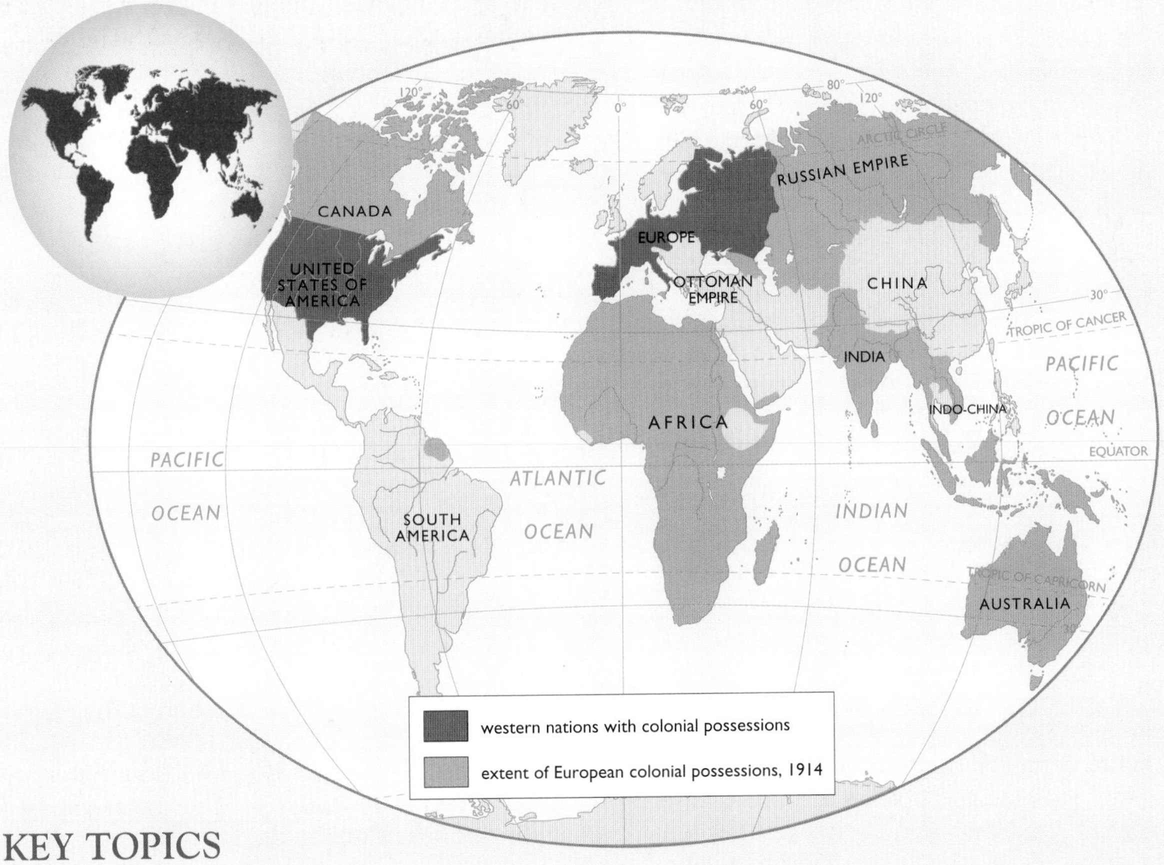

KEY TOPICS

- **Lands of European Settlement:** Europeans transplant the civilization of the West in the Americas, Australasia, and greater Russia.
- **Imperialism in Asia:** European merchant companies gain dominance in India, the Philippines, and East Indies, while China and Japan are forcibly opened to European trade.
- **Imperialism in the Middle East and Africa:** European nations establish protectorates in the Middle East and, in a "scramble for Africa," partition that continent.
- **Dominion Within:** Within Europe itself, the Irish and the Jews are persecuted minorities.
- **Migrants and Money:** European ventures abroad result in an integrated world economic system, where money, goods, and peoples cross boundaries and transform cultures.

The Better Bookshelf *In 1835, in a "Minute on Indian Education" prepared for the British Parliament, the English historian Thomas Babington Macaulay (1800–1859) declared that "a single shelf of a good European library was worth the whole native literature of India and Arabia." Thus he dismissed all of India's lofty literature, whose sacred texts rested on traditions at least as old as those of the Hebrew Bible. In this document Macaulay promotes the cause of education in India, then part of the British Empire. Although generally a humane thinker, he betrays here an attitude characteristic of the Europeans who, by 1914, had gained control of much of the globe. Just as the Romans, who once dominated the ancient Mediterranean world, had dubbed that sea* mare nostrum *("our sea"; see Chapter 5), the forgers of the Western* **imperium** *claimed superiority to all other peoples and considered the planet theirs.*

The Western *imperium* expanded from around 1500, when European ships first set out across the Atlantic and Indian oceans (see Chapter 16). Explorers, conquerors and entrepreneurs established outposts of Western culture and customs in the Americas, Australasia, and elsewhere. European commercial ventures also extended into Asia, the Middle East, and Africa, whose own societies had been developing in distinctive ways since the sixteenth century.

In all these regions, the system of coastal trading depots established by European merchants centuries earlier would be transformed during the nineteenth century into systems of economic or territorial domination, encouraging Western thinkers to develop theories of the racial superiority of peoples of European descent. In consequence, Western imperialism brought about the globalization of the world's economy and culture: a system of interconnected regions across which goods, money, and people freely circulate.

The process of European expansion and domination of remote peoples is here called **imperialism**. The term **colonialism** is reserved for those cases where Europeans established settlements in largely undeveloped lands with no existing state system. In practice, these terms are ambiguous and often interchanged in a usage that reflects political issues and interests. European politicians might refer to their "colonial" policies, even in regions such as India, which was not a "colony"; and those who lived under European domination resisted "colonialism." More recently, the economic policies of the wealthier nations of the world are often referred to as "**neo-colonialism**."

The Western *imperium* gravely burdened the peoples and civilizations it engulfed. Yet the imperialist legacy is not entirely negative. The West also spread abroad principles of human rights and parliamentary democracy, later embraced by non-Western nations as they forged, in time, their own liberation (see Chapter 28). And although the West imposed its own cultural, technological, and economic norms on often unwilling peoples, these have also led to improved health care, expanded educational systems, and agricultural and industrial modernization. The West meanwhile has also learned much from the rest of the world, enriching its own civilization by its experience of other cultures encountered in its global ventures.

LANDS OF EUROPEAN SETTLEMENT: COLONIAL VENTURES

In the lands settled by European migrants, the culture of the West developed new economic, social, and political patterns that would energize and transform the world.

Nowhere were these innovations more profound than in the Americas, the two continents opened to European development by the train of explorers, conquerors, and entrepreneurs that began with Christopher Columbus in 1492 (see Chapters 16, 19). Their positive effects do not excuse nor lessen the pain inflicted over four centuries on the two populations enlisted to serve the interests of European settlers: those of displaced native Amerindians and forcibly imported Africans. Yet the European creators of what they called the New World were not wholly hostile in intent. The mixed legacy of the European settlement includes many of the acknowledged strengths and benefits of modern society.

The Anglo-American Pattern: Economic and Political Innovation

By the late nineteenth century, two Anglo-American societies had emerged in North America—the United States, from 1783 an independent republic, and Canada, from 1867 a constitutional monarchy within the British Empire. In both, a system of law rooted in English precedents promised citizens justice without regard to rank or birth. Both societies had expanded westward from the Atlantic coast, an expansion which came at huge cost to Amerindian populations (see Chapter 19). Both regions were rich in mineral resources and capable of enormous agricultural production. They industrialized rapidly—the United States during the second half of the nineteenth century, Canada during the early twentieth. This process was marked by the construction of railroad lines extending across 3000 miles of mountain, plain, desert, and prairie. The more densely populated United States, especially its northern states, industrialized dramatically: by 1914 it had overtaken its European competitors to become the world's leading producer of steel.

In a cataclysmic struggle, those northern states fought a ferocious war with secessionist southern states whose economy depended on the plantation system of agricultural production, and thus on slave labor (see Chapter 19). As a result of that struggle, the southern states were returned to the Union and slavery was abolished, with pathbreaking legislation promising full citizenship rights, including the suffrage, to former slaves. Those promises were gainsaid by formal and informal systems of segregation that barred those of African heritage from the enjoyment of their presumed civil rights. Women, too, in the United States as in Canada, did not enjoy political emancipation before the end of World War I (see Chapter 26).

Yet by the early twentieth century Anglo-American societies had created vibrant economies and free polities, where opportunities abounded for many of those who sought them. Race, gender, and poverty kept some from reaching for those opportunities. Nevertheless these societies were more nearly free, and the principles upon which they rested embraced the principle of equality more firmly than any others in the world.

The European traditions underlying both Anglo-American civilizations were respected and cultivated. During the colonial era, elementary and secondary education followed patterns established in European schools. In eleven universities founded by the time of the American Revolution, the heritage of European ideas was authoritatively transmitted to later generations. Cultural institutions such as academies and concert halls were also founded, offering cultural opportunities available mostly to elites.

The English language created the cultural unification of North America, and was adopted even by immigrants from non-English speaking European

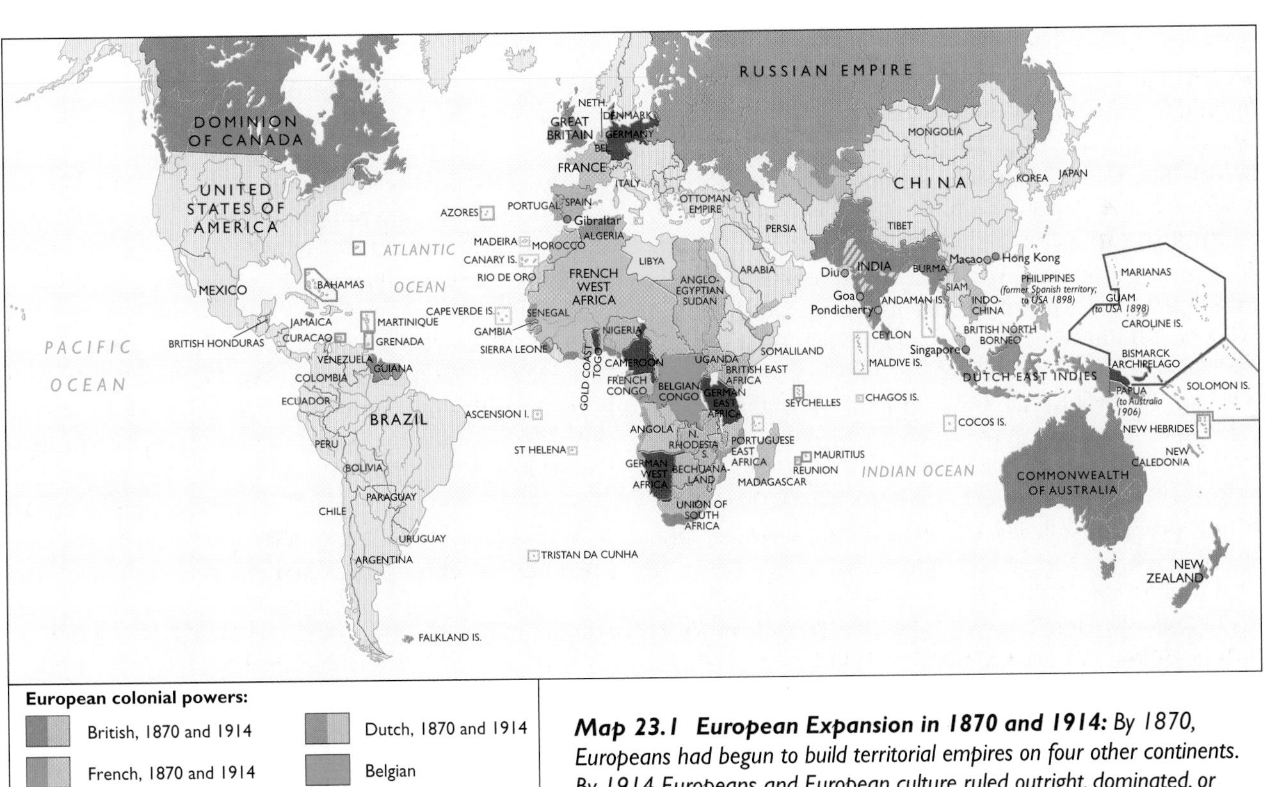

***Map 23.1 European Expansion in 1870 and 1914:** By 1870, Europeans had begun to build territorial empires on four other continents. By 1914 Europeans and European culture ruled outright, dominated, or heavily influenced the vast majority of the world's peoples.*

regions. One significant exception was the Canadian province of Quebec, where the descendants of French settlers taught their children the language and Roman Catholic religion of their forebears. Elsewhere, Anglo-Americans were generally Christians with roots in different denominational traditions, including the Anglican church in Canada, and a variety of Protestant denominations in the United States, where immigration resulted in increasing numbers of Roman Catholics.

In language, religion, educational traditions, and political and social values, Anglo-America remained firmly tied to European patterns into the twentieth century, even as its emerging societies diverged from European models.

The Spanish-American Pattern: Racial Mixture and Persistent Autocracy

A new civilization also took form in the Spanish-speaking regions of the Americas. By 1900, independent nations had emerged from most of the colonies that Spain had ruled for centuries. Cuba was the last to do so (while Puerto Rico was shifted from Spanish to United States rule, along with the Pacific islands of Guam and the Philippines), as a result of the Spanish–American war of 1898.

At that point Spanish-American nations were only beginning to develop democratic institutions such as those established in the Anglo-American north. Most were still ruled by despots and dominated by the military. A few had adopted constitutions that protected civil rights, limited church privileges, and abolished slavery.

The societies of these Spanish-American nations were also markedly different from those of Anglo-America. Centuries of cross-ethnic sexual relations meant that many citizens of Spanish-American nations had mixed Amerindian, African, and European ancestry. Persons of all skin colors were found among the ruling and commercial elites, as well as among the poor. In the country villages, however, where peasants labored for wealthy landowners, the populations were heavily Amerindian.

The Spanish-American economies generally depended on the export of agricultural and mineral produce. They did not undergo the industrialization and consequent modernization that occurred in Europe and Anglo-America. This economic system benefited the owners of mines and land, who relied on the exploitation of impressed Amerindian workers.

As in Anglo-America, the cultural institutions of Spanish America were modeled on European ones. With the explorers and conquerors had come Roman Catholic priests, monks, and missionaries, who saw to the creation of cathedrals, diocesan and parish organization, monasteries and convents, and the Inquisition. Churchmen labored to convert native peoples to Christianity, and where possible to provide them with an elementary education in the Spanish tradition. Male members of the creole elites were schooled much as were their European counterparts, and often finished their education in European cities and universities. European traditions also prevailed in the realm of the arts (where native Amerindian artistic styles influenced the visual arts) and ideas, and Spanish-American capitals resembled the great cities of Europe.

By 1900, Spanish America had not entirely shaken off its colonial past. The economic and political innovations that had transformed Anglo-America failed to take root in its southern neighbors, where industrialization was only partial and where *caudillos* ("strongmen") and landowners or mineowners had replaced the autocratic rule of kings with equally authoritarian systems. The intermixture of peoples greatly invigorated the civilization, but did not result in its democratization.

Much of the rest of Latin America followed the Spanish-American pattern. Exploited mainly for their sugar crop during the colonial era, the French, English and Dutch-speaking societies of the Caribbean and Central America were heavily populated by African slave laborers until abolition was finally achieved in 1886. African religions, speech, and customs strongly influenced the cultures of these regions, although Christian practices and European languages remained dominant.

In Portuguese-speaking Brazil, the plantation economy likewise resulted in a huge presence of Africans, and many Brazilians had some African ancestry. In contrast, the Amerindians of the Amazon, isolated from the mainstream of Brazilian development, resisted both Europeanization and Christianization. Although Brazil's ample mineral and agricultural resources contributed to a vigorous economy, it remained an economy dependent on the export of cash crops and minerals, and had few industrial manufactures to export.

Australasia: Another Anglophone Success

More than 200 years after the Spanish and Portuguese first settled in the Americas, Britain launched a similar undertaking in the south Pacific. Australasia (including Australia, the world's smallest continent, and the nearby islands of New Zealand) had first been sighted by the Dutch. Between 1769 and 1771 it was charted by the British navigator Captain James Cook (1728–1779) in the course of his expeditions to discover a legendary inhabited southern continent (which he determined did not exist).

Australasia resembled North America in that the indigenous peoples had attained only a simple level of technical development. The **Aborigines** (meaning "those there from the beginning"), were expelled from the most desirable lands as mostly British (including Irish) migrants and deported criminals settled after formal possession by Britain in 1788. New Zealand was home to nearly 150,000 Maoris, a relatively advanced native group of Polynesian origin. Here British settlers established a colonial society based on an agreement in 1840 with native peoples (the Treaty of Waitangi), subsequently violated, assuring equal rights. In both regions European settlers developed a prosperous economy based on the exploitation of natural resources and the development of sheep and dairy ranches.

Australia and New Zealand remained British colonies during the nineteenth century, developing culturally as European enclaves of Anglophone culture. Their vigorous cultural institutions resulted in the attainment of high levels of literacy and physical well-being for their European populations, although the New Zealand Maori and Australian aboriginal peoples remained largely excluded from these benefits.

The Russian Empire: Russification Across Five Thousand Miles

By 1500, the Russian state had expanded to become the largest nation in the world. Throwing off Mongol suzerainty (see Chapters 8, 9, 15), native rulers centered at Moscow pressed south and east into Asia, reaching the Caspian Sea with the conquests of Kazan (1552) and Astrakhan (1556) and then beyond the Urals to Siberia. In the seventeenth century, fur traders and explorers crossed Siberia to the Pacific.

In the eighteenth century, Tsars Peter I ("the Great"; r. 1682–1725) and Catherine II ("the Great"; r. 1762–1796) eroded Ottoman claims in the southeast while simultaneously intruding westward into Poland and the Baltic. In the later nineteenth century, recovering from the humiliation of the Crimean War (1853–1856; see Chapter 20), Tsars Alexander II (r. 1855–1881) and Alexander III (r. 1881–1894) advanced in the Caucasus, central Asia, Siberia, and even North America—which latter territories were sold to the United States in 1867. With these gains, Russia established sovereignty across northern Asia and south to a belt of natural mountain, desert, and river borders with Persia, Afghanistan, India (later Pakistan), and China.

By 1914, the Russian empire's vast dimensions were nearly double those of any of the other modern behemoths—the United States, China, India, or Brazil. An expression of its gigantic stature and industrial capacity was the Trans-Siberian railroad. Constructed between 1891 and 1904, it joined lines earlier constructed to arch from the capital of St. Petersburg to Vladivostok, founded in 1860 on the Pacific coast. Russia's further aims in Asia met traumatic defeat during a conflict with newly-vigorous Japan—the Russo-Japanese war of 1904–1905.

Russian expansion in Asia involved the exploitation of ample natural resources and the imposition of European traditions on sparsely-settled peoples of different origins. The European nucleus of Russia was already well-endowed with mineral resources and fine, flat fields. Subsequent additions in the Caucasus, the Urals, and Siberia brought great wealth in the form of natural gas and oil, coal and iron, gold, diamonds, and furs—even though much of the eastern region is too cold for crop cultivation.

Resident in these Asian lands were peoples of nearly a hundred nationalities, ethnicities, or language groups. Many groups resisted Russian domination in an ongoing pattern of tension and rebellion that continues into the twentieth century, creating problems for tsarist, communist, and post-communist rulers. The largely Muslim peoples of south central Asia, dwelling along the route of the ancient Silk Road (see Chapters 5, 6, 8), had old and distinct cultural traditions, and remain unassimilated.

In the Asian zone of the Russian empire, as in Australasia and the Americas, European colonists opened huge regions to economic development and exploitation. One result of that expansion was the displacement, or subjugation, of native peoples. Another was the implantation of European cultures in a distant and distinct context. In all these regions, Old World traditions developed under the stimulus of changed conditions, leading to the creation of new forms of wealth, new social structures, and new political traditions.

OLD WORLD ENCOUNTERS: IMPERIALISM IN ASIA

Europeans did not rest with the establishment of colonies in the remote and sparsely populated regions of the Americas, Australasia, and northern Asia. They also pressed their commercial interests in the crowded Old World zones where established states and advanced civilizations did not welcome intruders from the West, but were compelled to admit them.

Europeans had sought for centuries the luxury goods of Asia (see Chapters 5, 6, 8, 11). Merchants had traveled overland by foot, horse, or camel, or by ship across the Indian Ocean and on to the South China sea, to acquire expensive silks, perfumes, and

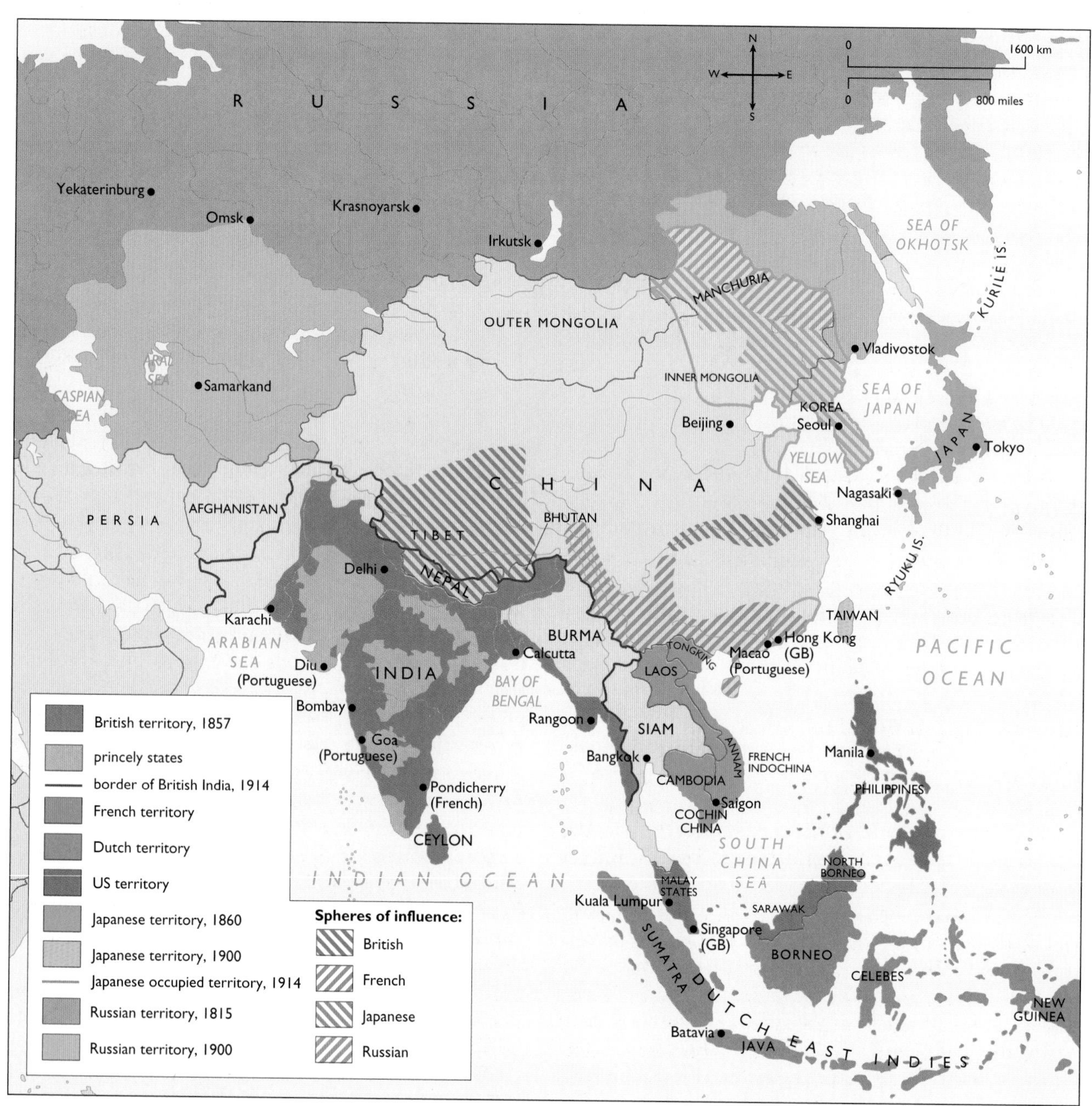

***Map 23.2* Europeans in Asia:** *European territorial expansion in Asia prior to 1914 includes gains made by the British, the French, the Russians, and the Dutch. The British dominated India in 1857 (at the time of the Sepoy Mutiny) and parts of southeast Asia in 1826–1915. To the east of Burma in Indochina, the areas of Vietnam, Laos, and Cambodia long under Chinese influence fell to the French after 1884. Thailand, however (indicated on the map under its old name, Siam), remained independent. The lands of the Dutch East India Company in the East Indies were ceded in 1799 to the Dutch government, which by 1910 controlled most of Indonesia. Though often overlooked as one of the major European colonial powers, Russia greatly expanded its authority in central and east Asia during the nineteenth century, building a contiguous empire with many parallels to the more far-flung holdings of other European powers.*

spices. The quest for spices drove Portuguese navigators to hazard the Atlantic currents, and sent Columbus westward to seek a direct route, as he thought, to Japan (see Chapter 16).

During the sixteenth century, Portuguese, French, Dutch, Spanish, and English merchant depots dotted the coasts of India, the East Indies (the Malay archipelago and Indonesia), and the Philippines, and even remote China and Japan. By the eighteenth century, cotton textiles, porcelains, and tea joined the list of important commodities that the West sought in the East. European entrepreneurs and the states that backed them, responding to increased commercial demand, insisted upon greater access to the economies of the Asian nations and in some cases seized dominion over them. In this process of imperialism, here as elsewhere, European nations exploited the resources of other regions for their own benefit, and imposed upon other peoples European political, economic, and cultural systems.

The Western encounter with Asia is pursued here by examining, first, those regions where systems of trading depots became the basis for the later establishment of direct imperialist rule (the Indian sub-continent, and the island regions of the East Indies and the Philippines). The account then turns to those regions that were relatively isolated (China, Korea, Indochina, and Japan), resistant to penetration, and "opened up" to European trade only by the threat, or the reality, of force.

India: A Sub-continent Subdued

In 1500, various kingdoms, both Muslim and Hindu, flourished in the huge Indian sub-continent. By 1800, it was controlled by the British East India Company; and after 1858, directly ruled by the British government.

Established by Muslim Turkic invaders from central Asia, the Mughal Empire was the first large, centralized state on the Indian sub-continent since the Gupta empire more than one thousand years before (see Chapter 8). Its founder was the occasional poet and memoirist Babur (1483–1530), a remote descendant of the feared conqueror Tamurlane (1336?–1405) who had not so long before ravaged western Asia. Defeating native armies at Panipat in 1526, deep within the Ganges region, Babur united the squabbling Muslim princedoms of northern India into a state further consolidated by his successors.

Notable among these were Babur's grandson Akbar (r. 1556–1605), Akbar's grandson Shahjahan (r. 1627–1656), and Shahjahan's son Aurangzeb (r. 1658–1707). Akbar won the support of Hindu leaders from the Rajput region, thus forging a mixed Hindu–Muslim state efficiently managed by bureaucrats ranked in a hierarchy modeled on that of his army. Encouraging literature and the arts, he presided over a golden age which saw a synthesis, especially in miniature painting, of Persian and native forms.

Shahjahan shared Akbar's artistic tastes. He was renowned as the patron of the Taj Mahal which he had built as a mausoleum (completed in 1643) for his young wife (who had died prematurely in 1629). Symbolizing the paradise in which the royal couple would be reunited, the bejewelled monument is considered one of the world's finest buildings. Aurangzeb oversaw the expansion of the empire to its maximum by 1680, then faced the crises that pointed to its eventual decline. Rajput revolts in the northwest, and the sudden growth of the Marathas, a dynamic Hindu people of western India, undermined the Mughal system.

By that date, English officials of the East India Company had shouldered aside their competitors, Arab, Dutch, Portuguese, and French (see Chapter 16). Soon after 1600, the merchants of the British East India Company arrived, establishing themselves at Bombay on the west coast, and on the east at Madras and Calcutta, where they founded an administrative center in 1690. Meanwhile, the French seized footholds at Pondicherry and Chandernagore (now Chandarnagar) in 1697. The military forces of the French and British merchant communities came into conflict after 1740, just as their national armies faced each other in the War of the Austrian Succession (1740–1748) and the Seven Years' War (1756–1763) (see Chapter 15). In 1757, the British general Robert Clive (1725–1774) defeated a native force supported by the French at Plassey in Bengal. When the Seven Years' War was concluded by the Treaty of Paris of 1763, Britain gained Canada, territories in the Caribbean and Africa, and control of India. The British East India Company was now the chief European power on the Indian sub-continent, and would soon acquire mastery over native states as well.

From 1763 to 1857, this company of profit-seeking merchants gained control of India. Deploying an army of about 100,000 mostly native troops, the governors of the British East India Company absorbed the native princedoms or reduced them to vassal status. As the Company's success mounted, and rumors of corruption surged, the British government intervened to supervise its operations. As a result of the Regulating Act of 1773 and the East India Company

Imperial Pretensions

Prestige and profit: *European nations saw their empires—in Asia and elsewhere—as sources of both prestige and economic benefit. The benefit of prestige is well illustrated by A. E. Harris's illustration of the British King Edward VII as he receives a group of maharajahs and other dignitaries in 1901 (left). That of profit is evident in the 1931 poster below urging British consumers to "buy empire."* (left: Roy Miles Gallery, London)

Act of 1784, Parliament scrutinized the administration of Indian territories. By these steps, an imperial realm took form in the sub-continent.

India was a site of imperialism in action, as British officials exploited India economically, ruled it peremptorily, and often denigrated native culture—although many British officials and visitors admired India's civilization. The region's yield of spices, tea, and cotton textiles was cheaply purchased and sold profitably at home, without modernizing agricultural production in India itself (although British governors did promote the construction of irrigation and drainage systems). The trade in those commodities now left India poor as returns on agricultural commodities diminished. Textile exports also dwindled as the Industrial Revolution (see Chapter 21) transformed British textile production and flooded world markets with cheap cotton cloth. Industrialization made India an importer of manufactured cottons, reversing for the first time in history its favorable balance of trade.

As India sank into the kind of adverse economic relationship with a colonial power that already characterized South America, its people became the target of European attitudes of racial superiority. Indian natives were barred from political decision-making, from military and administrative offices, and from the social circles of the resident British elite.

That elite also often dismissed India's impressive literary and religious heritage (see Chapter 1)—Hindu, Buddhist, Muslim—as alien and inferior. Missionaries converted few of these adherents of ancient faiths to Christianity. (Missionary efforts to improve health services and education did, however, bear fruit.) Certain customs that the British elite found repugnant—such as the caste system, that relegates millions to permanent social disability, or *suttee*, the supposedly voluntary burning of wives on a husband's funeral pyre—are still viewed as contrary to universal moral concepts. Others, such as the Hindu refusal to eat beef, or the Muslim refusal to eat pork, were rejected only because unfamiliar.

1873 FIRST TEA FROM CEYLON
1876 FIRST CANNED SALMON FROM CANADA
BUY EMPIRE EVERY DAY
1929 Ceylon sent out 250,000,000 lbs of tea
1929 Canada sent out 60,000,000 lbs of salmon

Economic exploitation, inflexible rule, and cultural incompatibilities stimulated the mutiny of native soldiers (called **sepoys**) in the Company's Indian army that erupted into war in 1857 and changed the nature of British sovereignty in India. Over the previous century, common soldiers had been

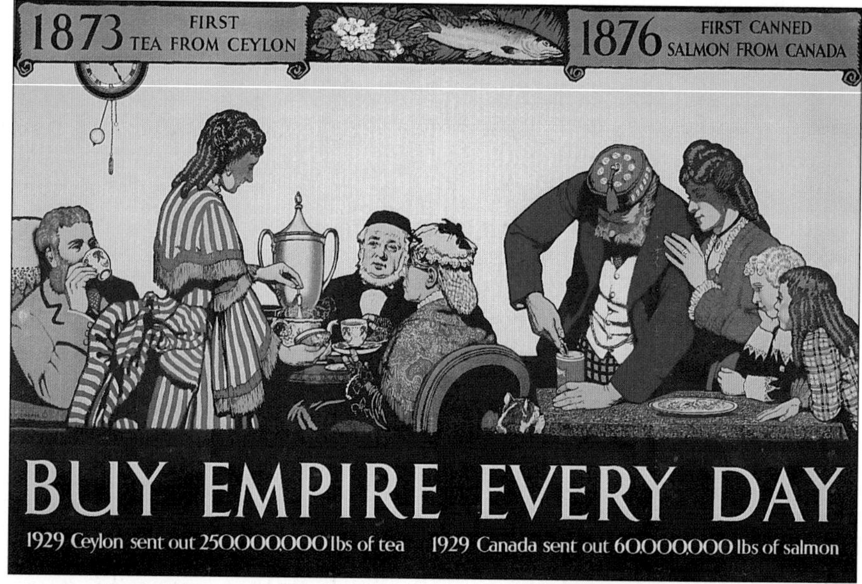

recruited from among Hindu and Muslim natives, and trained to modern European standards. Some native soldiers rose in rebellion in May 1857, provoked perhaps by a perceived religious insult (their cartridges of ammunition, which they needed to break open with their teeth, were rumored to be coated with beef or pork fat, each kind offensive to either Hindu or Muslim troops) as well as deeper grievances.

Over the next fourteen months, sepoy rebels resisted British forces, while atrocities occurred on both sides. In the aftermath, the British Parliament instituted some reforms, including the guarantee of religious toleration, changes in land administration and military procedures, and the admission of Indian natives to some advisory councils and offices. In the India Act of 1858, having disposed of the British East India Company, the British Parliament declared it would henceforth administer India directly. In 1877, India was constituted as a monarchy subordinate to the British crown, and the British Queen Victoria (r. 1837–1901) was crowned empress. Some 1000 British administrators staffed the Indian Civil Service and lower offices, which ruled the sub-continent through the agency of hundreds of thousands of subordinate, native bureaucrats. Indian subjugation was complete, and Indian nationalism was born.

From 1858 to 1917, though the British grip on India was firm, new cultural currents pointed toward eventual emancipation—a promise indeed envisioned by discussions between British and Indian leaders in 1917–1918. Extensive railroad construction facilitated interior trade and communication, and some native entrepreneurs were able to insert themselves in the foreign-dominated commercial system. These developments, together with the effects of the opening of the Suez Canal in 1869 (see below), resulted in a sevenfold increase in India's foreign trade.

For ordinary families, uncontrolled population increase outpaced gains in domestic product. The high-status natives who succeeded in entering the provincial civil service educated their children at schools recently instituted on the European model, or at British boarding schools and universities. This educated native elite was able to criticize British rule in its own terms. Its representatives in the Indian National Congress founded in 1885, the sub-continent's first national political movement, began to press for independence. Between 1907 and 1916, the Congress split into moderate and radical factions. Later on, Muslim–Hindu hostilities further split the Congress, fracturing the religious unity that Babur had tried to construct four centuries earlier. In the years following World War I (1914–1918), the Indian sub-continent nourished the intellectual and political leaders who would one day lead it to independence.

The Philippines and East Indies: Enduring Mercantile Empires

In the Philippines and the East Indies (including modern Malaysia and Indonesia), small European merchant settlements founded in the 1500s led, as in India, to enduring domination by European powers.

The huge tropical archipelago of the East Indies, extending more than 3000 miles west to east and lying on the sea route between India and China, was a magnet for merchant adventurers. It was originally populated around 1000 B.C.E. by migrants from the Asian mainland, and had seen the arrival of earlier traders in two waves: first, Indians around the seventh century C.E., who introduced Buddhism and Hinduism, and second, Arabs from the fourteenth century onward, who introduced Islam.

In contact with the advanced civilizations of the region, island natives developed states of their own. On Sumatra and Java, two native kingdoms emerged, respectively Buddhist (the Sri Vijaya) and Hindu (that of the Majapahits). These kingdoms flourished successfully from the seventh through the fifteenth centuries. Soon thereafter, Islam was established throughout the region, which splintered into separate political units.

The islands later named the Philippines (after King Philip II of Spain) form another tropical archipelago, extending about 1200 miles north to south. They were first populated about 30,000 years ago, and from about 1000 C.E. they had commercial relations with Chinese, Japanese, and Malaysian merchants (carriers of Buddhism), and with Arab merchants (who introduced Islam) from the fifteenth.

The first European to arrive was the Portuguese navigator Ferdinand Magellan (c. 1480–1521; see Chapter 16) who claimed the islands for Spain in 1521. In 1571, merchants established a permanent station at Manila, after which the "Manila galleon" regularly journeyed between New Spain (modern Mexico) and the Philippines. Filipino companies exchanged native commodities for American silver in a commerce protected from foreign interlopers into the 1830s: spices, sugar, and coffee.

Spanish governors and armies, meanwhile, established a regime that endured until 1898. Ruled by a viceroy advised by an appointed royal council, or *audiencia*, it fought off pirates and competitors, and was disturbed by stirrings of rebellion only in its last years. Just as nationalist forces were poised to win

WITNESSES

Britain's Empire in India

Lord Wellesley defends the East India Company (1813): There never was an organ of government, in the history of the world, so administered, as to demand more of estimation than that of the East India Company. There might ... be points of error to correct; but if their Lordships looked at the general state of our Empire in India— ... if they adverted to the state of real solid peace, in which countries were now placed, that had in previous times been so constantly exposed to war and devastation ... they would see that ... the administration ... of the East India Company had been productive of strength, tranquillity and happiness. The situation of the natives had been meliorated and improved—the rights of property, before unknown, had been introduced and confirmed.... A judicial system had been established which, though not perfect, contained with it all the essentials of British justice.

(Lord Wellesley, Speech in the House of Lords, April 9, 1813; *English Historical Documents*, 1959, vol. XI)

Historian and statesman Thomas B. Macaulay urges that the British Parliament establish an English-language educational system in colonial India (1835): We have a fund to be employed as Government shall direct for the intellectual improvement of the people of [India]. The simple question is, what is the most useful way of employing it?

All parties seem to be agreed on one point, that the dialects commonly spoken among the natives of this part of India, contain neither literary nor scientific information, and are, moreover, so poor and rude that, until they are enriched from some other quarter, it will not be easy to translate any valuable work into them. It seems to be admitted on all sides, that the intellectual improvement of those classes of the people who have the means of pursuing higher studies, can at present be effected only by means of some language not vernacular amongst them.... The whole question seems to me to be, which language is the best worth knowing....

I have no knowledge of either Sanscrit or Arabic.—But I have done what I could to form a correct estimate of their value. I have read translations of the most celebrated Arabic and Sanscrit works. I have conversed ... with men distinguished by their proficiency in the Eastern tongues.. .. I have never found one among them who could deny that a single shelf of a good European library was worth the whole native literature of India and Arabia....

How, then, stands the case? We have to educate a people who cannot at present be educated by means of their mother-tongue. We must teach them some foreign language. The claims of our own language it is hardly necessary to recapitulate. It stands preeminent even among the languages of the west.... Whoever knows that language has ready access to all the vast intellectual wealth, which all the wisest nations of the earth have created and hoarded in the course of ninety generations. It may safely be said, that the literature now extant in that language is of far greater value than all the literature which three hundred years ago was extant in all the languages of the world together.... The English tongue is that which would be the most useful to our native subjects.

(Thomas B. Macaulay, "Minute of 2 February 1835 on Indian Education"; ed. G. M. Young, 1957)

The Bombay poet Dalpatram Kavi laments "The Attack of King Industry," which has transferred all wealth into the hands of foreigners (1861):

Fellow countrymen, let us remove all the miseries of our
country,
Do work, for the new kingdom has come, its king is industry.

Our wealth has gone into the hands of foreigners. The
great blunder is yours
For you did not unite yourselves—fellow countrymen.

Consider the time, see for yourselves, all our people
have become poor,
Many men of business have fallen—fellow countrymen.

...

Introduce industry from countries abroad and achieve
mastery of the modern machinery.
Please attend to this plea for the Poet Dalpat—fellow
countrymen.

(Dalpatram Kavi, "The Attack of King Industry"—"Hunnarkhanni Chadayi"; eds. C. Trivedi and H. Spodek, 1998)

independence from their Spanish overlord, Spain lost a decisive naval battle in Manila Bay (1898) to the United States. Within the year the United States had acquired sovereignty over the Philippines, to the dismay of many public figures opposed to such foreign ventures.

Their dismay deepened when Filipino leaders turned to guerrilla warfare, capitulating only in 1901. The United States spent more money, and sacrificed more lives in suppressing the revolt than it had in the Spanish–American War (1898)—a measure of Filipino determination. In 1914, the largely Christian

Filipinos (converted by Spanish missionaries) were English-speaking dependents of the United States.

The East Indies were colonies first of the Portuguese and then of the Dutch. Portuguese interest in the region came when spices were the most valued commodity in the European trading system and the East Indies archipelago was the world's principal source of spices (especially the sub-group of nearly 14,000 islands known as the Moluccas, and formerly as the Spice Islands). In 1511 the Portuguese captured the city-state of Malacca, poised on the Malay straits that were the gateway to the Indies. By 1513, they had reached the Moluccas, and controlled the spice trade.

In the seventeenth century, Portuguese mastery yielded to the merchants, admirals, and governors of the Dutch East India Company. Over the next three centuries they acquired in the East Indies a total dominion comparable to that achieved by the British East India Company in India. Establishing their headquarters at Batavia (present-day Jakarta), founded in 1619 on the island of Java, they seized Malacca from the Portuguese in 1641, then the Moluccas, outposts on the island of Sumatra, and, by stages, the whole of the islands of Java and Bali. In 1910, all of modern Indonesia (except for the Portuguese enclave of East Timor) was in Dutch hands. After 1799, when the Dutch East India Company was dissolved, the Dutch government took direct control.

The Dutch now possessed the world monopoly of the Moluccan spice trade. In the eighteenth century the Dutch also promoted other exports: coffee, for which Europeans developed a passion, along with tea and tobacco. As in Spanish America, an economy based on the processing of agricultural commodities short-circuited any native attempts at modernization or diversification.

Native resistance to Dutch policies exploded in rebellion in Java in 1825–1830 and on all three major islands—Java, Bali, and Sumatra—from the 1880s. At the beginning of the twentieth century, the so-called Ethical Policy provided greater educational and administrative opportunities for talented natives. But in 1914, Dutch imperialism in the region remained repressive and unyielding.

China, Korea, and Indochina: Forced Entry

In India and the East Indies, European merchant depots were the wedges that opened vast regions to direct domination by European nations. That pattern was not repeated on the mainland of east and southeast Asia. Although merchant footholds were established from the 1500s at Malacca, Macao, and Nagasaki (in present-day Malaysia, China, and Japan), these were scant. Before 1800, the advanced societies of the Asian mainland were little affected by European presence in the South China Sea.

After 1800, however, when Asian nations faced European states possessing military and technological superiority, the situation changed. They were unable to withstand the insistent demand for access to sources of wealth as yet untapped by European commerce.

In 1800, China was the oldest and most secure monarchy in the world (see Chapters 2, 8, 16). For centuries, it had imposed its law on neighboring states in Korea, Indochina, and Mongolia—over which states, at times, it exercised sovereignty. China collected tribute from these and even more distant regions. It exported prized commodities and manufactures: silk textiles, porcelain and lacquer goods, tea and other agricultural produce. Its merchants carried on a busy commerce within China and abroad, reaching India, the East Indian archipelago, and parts of Oceania, as well as central Asia and Mediterranean ports via the ancient Silk Road.

Along these routes, China also diffused its high literary and philosophical culture—Buddhist, Taoist, and Confucian. Trained in that Confucian tradition, China's scholars and poets were also its government officials (if they succeeded in passing licensing examinations). They administered the mammoth empire for the most part judiciously and efficiently. Science and technology also flourished in China, the world leader in those endeavors until the seventeenth century. China first gave the world paper, gunpowder, and block printing, among other inventions.

These patterns prevailed over a series of dynasties extending back to the Shang, Zhou, and Qin of the Bronze and Iron Ages; and to the Han, Tang, Song, and Yüan that ruled from the period of ancient Rome to the threshold of the European Renaissance (see Chapters 1, 2, 8, 16). They continued thereafter under the Ming (1368–1644) and Qing, or Manchu rulers (1644–1912). With the latter, who were exhausted, corrupt, and subjected to European overlords, the venerable procession of emperors and dynasties ended.

In 1368, rebel leader Chu Yan-chang established the Ming dynasty after thirty years of popular resistance to Mongol Yüan rule. He and his Ming successors rebuilt the region, which had been devastated by the wars leading to Mongol victory in 1279. The imperial economic policy favored agriculture over

E. Duncan, painting of the steamer Nemesis: *Western warships wreaked havoc on traditional societies that had no weaponry to defend themselves. Here, the steam-powered* Nemesis *destroys Chinese junks at Guangzhou, China in 1843, as the British force the opening of China to Western trade.* (National Maritime Museum, Canada)

commerce. That decision resulted in conservative government in the countryside, exercised by gentry landowners who belonged to the same social stratum as Confucian political officials.

Under Ming rule the economy flourished. Textiles, raw cotton, and grain, the main domestic commodities, traveled to and from the major trading centers in the Yangzi delta (especially Nanjing) and the newly founded (1421) capital at Beijing, which provisioned a large network of frontier garrisons in the north. Population soared from a depressed 60 million at the time of Ming takeover to more than 100 million in the late 1500s. At that time more people lived in China than in all of Europe.

Early successes permitted the Ming to challenge the Mongols, invade Vietnam (in Indochina), and reduce Korea to vassalage. From the late sixteenth century, they withdrew to a defensive posture, as Japanese pirates harried their coasts, boldly entered the Yangzi, and challenged China's preeminence in Korea. Ineffective emperors ceded authority to corrupt eunuchs, who had withstood government reform efforts. From 1627, a rash of rebellions left China vulnerable to incursion once again from the north. In 1644, the Ming fell to a new dynasty which was to be China's last: the Qing.

The Manchu, a non-Chinese people who originated in Manchuria, swept into the Chinese region from the 1620s, established themselves as the Qing dynasty at Beijing in 1644, and consolidated their sovereignty in the resistant south and west by 1680. During the following century, they expanded into Mongolia, central Asia, and Indochina, as the costs of expansion injured an already precarious economy.

By 1800, economic crisis loomed. Virtually all the arable land of China was under cultivation, and had reached the limit of what it could produce. Food supply was further strained by a population rise from about 100 million in 1650 to more than 300 million by 1800 and 420 million by 1850. The hungry peasants rebelled, as did subject states corralled unwillingly into the Manchu Empire.

Meanwhile, the value of opium imported into China by Western merchants had risen to exceed the value of Chinese exports. For the first time, China's trade balance was negative. Trammeled by a fraying bureaucracy, the Qing rulers did little, maintaining Chinese isolation in the face of European demands for free access to Chinese ports.

The self-sufficiency of the Chinese Empire did not permit the notion of free trade with Western states that Asian sages considered "barbarian." That world view collided with the mercantile outlook of Westerners, for whom all credos must yield to the paramount goal of profit. The conflict led to the First Opium War of 1839–1842 resulting in a mandate for the economic opening of China by European merchants and states.

Since 1557, Chinese officials had allowed the Portuguese to maintain a trading station at Macao on the southern coast. British and French merchants later obtained a foothold at nearby Guangzhou (Canton), and the Dutch, briefly, on the island of Taiwan. From these depots, they exported the Chinese tea and luxuries craved by Western elites. Unsatisfied, they sought greater access to Chinese markets. The British, particularly, hoped to gain buyers for cotton textiles from Britain's new mills (see Chapter 21); or opium, in quantities of close to 2000 tons annually, imported from British-held India.

The imperial government rebuffed British pleas for greater access. Opium carried on British ships, in violation of Chinese law, succeeded in corrupting port officials, as well as causing the addiction of millions of natives. Chinese bureaucrats investigated and condemned the trade, and formally protested to Queen Victoria, advising her of the penalty decreed for European peddlers of opium: decapitation. In 1839, responding to Chinese confiscation of opium stores, British warships trained their cannon on several coastal cities. Overwhelmed by Western superiority in weaponry, the Chinese capitulated.

The Treaty of Nanjing (Nanking) of 1842 put an end to the First Opium War and compelled China to open its gates to Western commerce and control. Protected by the new policy of "**extraterritoriality**" (which exempted Westerners from Chinese law), European trading stations operated at Macao, Guangzhou (Canton), Shanghai, and other ports. In addition the British gained control of Hong Kong, an island later (1898) leased to Britain for ninety-nine years. In 1856, the Second Opium War erupted as the Chinese attempted to block European encroachments. A British and French force destroyed the imperial summer palace outside Beijing, and occupied the city. In 1860, China backed down, accepting a treaty that delivered some fifty ports to foreign control, permitted European diplomatic residents in Beijing, allowed Christian missionary activity, and, a final blow, legalized the importation of opium.

The humiliation of China continued for another generation. From 1848 to 1865, the Chinese government spent its energies suppressing the massive Taiping Rebellion, whose leader, a Christian-trained mystic and moralist, offered promise of national regeneration. Between 1862 and 1897, the French seized Vietnam and Laos in Indochina, previously dominated by China. An updated Japanese army

WITNESSES

The European Arrival in East Asia

The futility of traditional resistance: a modern historian describes Chinese efforts to repel British ships during the First Opium War (1842):

[Chinese volunteer] Pei Ch'ing-ch'iao's . . . assignment was to superintend the making of five hundred rocket mortars. The model was an ancient specimen supplied by the aged Commander Tuan Yung'fu, and came from Yünnan. Pei was ashamed, he says, that . . . the best they could produce was a contrivance that looked as though it emanated from the pages of the *Fire-dragon Book*, a seventeenth-century treatise on artillery. These mortars were supposed to be used in setting fire to the sails and rigging of foreign ships, but do not seem ever to have come into action.

Someone suggested that fire-crackers should be tied to the backs of a number of monkeys, who would then be flung on board the English ships. The flames would spread rapidly in every direction and might with luck reach the powder-magazine, in which case the whole ship would blow up. Nineteen monkeys were bought, and . . . were brought in litters to the advanced base. After the failure of the Chinese attack they accompanied the retreating armies. . . .

(From A. Waley ed., *The Opium War Through Chinese Eyes*, 1958)

Ito Hirobumi, chief architect of Japan's modernizing Meiji Constitution of 1889, recounts his efforts to understand and learn from the West (1909): It was in the month of March, 1882, that His Majesty [the Japanese emperor] ordered me to work out a draft of a constitution to be submitted to his approval. No time was to be lost, so I started on . . . an extended journey . . . to make as thorough a study as possible of the actual workings of different systems of constitutional government . . . . I took young men with me, who all belonged to the elite of the rising generation, to assist and to cooperate with me in my studies. I sojourned about a year and a half in Europe, and having gathered all the necessary materials . . . I returned home in September, 1883. Immediately after my return I set to work to draw up the Constitution.

(Ito Hirobumi, *Reminiscences on the Drafting of the New Constitution*, 1909; ed. W. T. de Bary, 1958)

claimed Taiwan and other smaller territories in the Sino-Japanese War of 1894–1895. Russia, meanwhile, crept into the northeast and briefly dominated Manchuria. By 1900, France, Britain, Germany, and Russia had imposed on the Qing government a system of **concessions**, or economic spheres of influence. These effectively partitioned China, weakened by famine and unrest. Progressive officials attempted to modernize and reform the Chinese government, in a program known as "self-strengthening." Their efforts came too late. Western subjugation of a once great, now decadent state was nearly complete.

The expropriations of European merchants, the arrogance of military leaders, the contempt of European officials for an ancient civilization, and the alien promptings of Christian missionaries, stimulated explosive and violent native resistance movements. The most famous of these was the rebellion of the Boxers (1898–1901), as the Europeans called them. Properly named the "Righteous and Harmonious Fists," this was a secret society hostile to all Western political and cultural influence encouraged by the dowager empress Tz'u-Hsi (1835–1908) and her conservative courtiers. The Boxers deplored not only China's political takeover by the West, but the demoralization of the Chinese by foreigners whose technical and military power they recognized but whose intellectual and religious culture they despised.

Although the Boxer rebellion failed, native intellectuals had begun to conceive of national independence—both from the failing Qing dynasts and from European interlopers. A series of uprisings in 1911 dismantled the Qing dynasty. Sun Yat-sen (1866–1925) became president of the resulting republic in 1912, but was pushed aside the next year by the dictator Yüan Shih-k'ai (1859–1916). That new government was forced to surrender some territories to Japan during World War I. In 1914, the great empire that had loomed over east Asia for more than two millennia faced an uncertain future.

The native kingdoms of Indochina, meanwhile, which had for centuries been prey to Chinese incursions, fell to British and French expansionism. By 1885, Britain controlled all of Burma (now called Myanmar). In addition, between 1786 and 1819, she had acquired three strategic city-states on the Malay Peninsula (and a protectorate over the region) that assured access to Chinese ports: Penang, Malacca (by Dutch cession), and Singapore, the latter established as a free port. One of the four European concession powers in China, France took direct control of modern Laos, Vietnam, and Cambodia in a war waged from 1862 to 1897. By 1914, with the exception of Siam (modern Thailand), Indochina was part of the European *imperium*.

Japan: Point, Counterpoint

Alone of the non-Western nations of the globe, Japan successfully resisted Western encroachment, responding to aggression with a disciplined program of self-development that rendered it, by 1914, one of the major world powers. Unlike China, which suffered repeated disruptions between the fifteenth and nineteenth centuries, Japan was politically unified and well-poised to meet the challenge of Western intervention when it came in 1853.

In 1603, after the suppression of more than a century of disorder, the *samurai* Tokugawa Ieyasu (1543–1616) seized the supreme position of *shogun* (the military leader of Japan, appointed by the imperial court which itself wielded no effective power). He initiated a period of stability that lasted two and a half centuries, reining in the competing samurai clan-leaders, or *daimyos*, who had established themselves as independent territorial lords. Rewarding loyal samurai with offices and privileges and suppressing those who resisted, he compelled the Japanese nobility to recognize a strongly centralized government: the *bakufu*, located in Edo (modern Tokyo), a capital distinct from the imperial court of Kyoto.

Tokugawa and his successors established a legal code, a highway system, and a network of fortifications from which to suppress any future challenge to the now-powerful state. Prosperity returned, and the population climbed from about 20 million in 1600 to about 30 million in the eighteenth century.

The Tokugawa shogunate enforced a policy of isolation, shunning the Western adventurers who sought a foothold in Japan. Portuguese traders had arrived in 1542, followed quickly by Jesuit missionaries. The Tokugawa expelled the missionaries in 1614, and Christianity was soon extirpated in a series of persecutions in the 1630s. Even Buddhism was subordinated to Shinto religious institutions (see Chapters 1, 8), which elevated the shogun (the emperor for the moment in eclipse) as a ritual leader. And Confucianism, an import from China, supported the development of a samurai code of conduct appropriate to the new regime. The shogunate discouraged all contact with Western customs and even Western technology. The European guns that Tokugawa forces used to gain sovereignty, quickly imitated by Japanese military technicians, were banned soon after.

The shoguns did, however, allow the Dutch, established in Nagasaki since 1567, to remain in carefully supervised isolation. The Japanese were instructed to have nothing to do with their culture, their religion, or even their method of writing with letters that ran oddly sideways, in contrast to the vertical columns of Asian characters.

Yet the West demanded access, as it had in China. Between 1793 and 1853, several Western ships visited Japan's key ports seeking permission to trade. The last and most famous visitor, in 1853, was the United States Commodore Matthew Perry (1794–1858), who threatened the Japanese with bombardment if they did not cooperate. Japan admitted the foreigners, submitting to the humiliating Harris Treaty of 1858.

Nevertheless, the Japanese managed to avoid Western domination. By 1868, the capitulation had triggered a fantastic series of events. A group of young, determined samurai expelled the shogun and restored the emperor as ruler, removed from obscurity in Kyoto to the capital at Tokyo, and to power. This was the sixteen-year-old Mutsuhito (1852–1912) who, as the descendant of the sun goddess (according to tradition and official doctrine until 1945), was seen as destined to fulfill the divine plan for Japan's governance. The revolutionary event is known as the "Meiji" (the term means "enlightened rule") restoration.

These innovators created a new imperial bureaucracy in which promotion was based on talent, abolished feudalism, and created a conscript army (1873). They sent experts to the major Western capitals to study law codes and parliamentary constitutions, and technicians to study industrial production. They introduced cabinet government, bicameral legislature, and a formal constitution (1885–1889). They set up schools (enrolling ninety percent of all school-age children by 1900) and universities to train future generations to manage a renewed Japan.

Japan and the West

Commodore Perry's "Black Ship": *The threat of imminent attack on Japan was posed by the warship that the American Commodore Perry piloted into Japanese waters in 1853. Such naval force served ultimately to bring both China and Japan into the Western-dominated global economy during the nineteenth century.* (The Mariner's Museum, Virginia)

By 1914, Japan was a modern nation, having swiftly experienced the processes of industrialization and urbanization that had taken centuries in Europe. Using one-third of the revenues gathered from a reformed tax system, the government promoted industry, transportation (a railroad network was rapidly built), and communications. Textile and steel production sped forward in the 1880s and 1890s, boosting Japan's trade balance—the nation was now an exporter of manufactures, an importer of raw materials. Population continued to climb, and by 1914, about one-third of the population lived in cities.

Streamlined, industrialized, and fully competitive with the West, Japan now pursued its own imperialist goals in east Asia. Seizing the adjacent Kuril and Ryukyu Islands in 1875 and 1879, as a result of the Sino-Japanese War of 1894–1895 she further acquired

***Adachi Ginko*, Women of Fashion Sewing:** *Unlike China, which clung to tradition, Japan quickly modernized. Here in an 1887 illustration, fashionable Japanese ladies make garments on modern sewing machines, much as their Western contemporaries would have done.* (Museum of Fine Arts, Boston)

Taiwan and part of Manchuria. In the Russo-Japanese war of 1904–1905, the unanticipated Japanese victory announced that nation's entry to the circle of great world powers. In 1910, Japan annexed Korea and, as a participant in World War I, claimed further Chinese territories in its notorious Twenty-One Demands of 1915 (see Chapter 25).

Japan was the exception among Asian states. Not only did the Japanese resist domination by a foreign power, but they acquired the military and technical skills that gave Europeans their edge in the age of imperialism. By 1914, Japan was an imperialist power, too.

OLD WORLD ENCOUNTERS: IMPERIALISM IN THE MIDDLE EAST AND AFRICA

More easily than in Asia, European powers came to dominate the native peoples of the Middle East and Africa. In the Middle East, a weakening Ottoman Empire gave the principal imperialist nations opportunities to exert economic and political influence. In Africa, the European nations intruded swiftly and decisively in 1880–1900.

The Middle East: The Last Islamic Empire

From ancient times, a series of vigorous empires ruled the Middle East (see Chapters 1, 8). The last of these—that of the Turkish Ottoman dynasty—reached its peak in the sixteenth century, weakened in the seventeenth and eighteenth, and succumbed in the nineteenth to the superior commercial and military power of those western European nations it had once scorned.

From the seventh century, followers of the prophet Muhammad carried the religion of Islam (from the Arabic term for "submission" to God) through the Middle East and North Africa, into Spain, the Balkans, India, and the East Indies. From the eleventh century C.E., the regimes of the Arabic rulers, or caliphs, yielded to new incursions of Asian steppe nomads—Turkish and Mongol polytheists who converted to Islam and ruled in its name.

In 1500, three Islamic dynasties ruled in the Middle East: the Safavids in Persia (modern Iran); the Mamluks in Egypt and Syria (including modern Palestine/Israel, Lebanon, and Jordan); the Ottomans in Asia Minor (Anatolia, now Turkey) and south-east Europe, nearly as far north as modern Hungary (see also Chapters 14, 15, 16). By 1600, the Mamluk lands fell to the Ottomans, who had also absorbed the coastal regions of North Africa and the Black Sea while containing the Safavids to the southeast.

Meanwhile, the Ottoman navy seized most of the strategic island bases in the Mediterranean from Venice, Genoa, and Spain, capturing Euboea (Negroponte) (1470); Lemnos (1479); Rhodes (1522); Cyprus (1573); and Crete (1669). Their rivals stopped Ottoman maritime expansion only in 1571, at the battle of Lepanto off the Peloponnesian coast of Greece. On land, Ottoman armies had advanced by 1529 through Hungary as far as Vienna, where they were narrowly repulsed by a combined force of European armies.

By 1600, however, the Ottoman Empire had already spent its first vigor. Over the next two centuries, the Austrian Habsburgs and the Russian tsars pushed back the Ottoman borders in southeastern Europe. In 1683, combined European armies repelled a second Ottoman attempt to take Vienna, and the Treaties of Karlowitz (1699) and Passarowitz (1718) opened southeastern Europe to Habsburg advance at Ottoman expense. From 1768 to 1783, Russia under Catherine the Great seized the northern shore of the Black Sea, finally acquiring an outlet to warm-water seas. Meanwhile, the British navy patrolled the Mediterranean to protect its trade link to India from pirate raids issuing from Ottoman-held ports.

By 1800, the Ottoman empire was, it was said, the "sick man of Europe"—a phrase repeated gleefully by several European monarchs who hoped to profit from its disease. The following century saw its disintegration. In 1914, the Ottoman Empire retained only one-third of the territory it had ruled in 1800. Moreover, the seeds had been planted for later resistance to Western intervention by Asian and African people previously under Ottoman rule.

In Europe, the dismantlement of Ottoman power began with the successful revolution from 1821–1830, by which Greece won its independence. The Balkan states to the north—Serbia, Montenegro, Albania, Bulgaria, and Romania—had all broken away from Ottoman dominion by 1914. Bosnia–Herzegovina and Bessarabia were wrested away from Ottoman rule and incorporated, respectively, by Austria and Russia.

In Syria, Ottoman officials continued to rule ineffectually (with Lebanon under Christian governors after 1861) as British, French, and Russian interests took hold. The regions further east and south—Iraq and the Arabian Peninsula—came under British influence during the years prior to 1914, while Russian influence prevailed in Iran and in the Caucasian states of Georgia, Armenia, and Azerbaijan.

In North Africa, independent local rulers asserted themselves in Egypt (which dominated Sudan to its south), Libya, Tunisia, and Algeria; Morocco, an independent sultanate, never fell under Ottoman rule. All of these, including Morocco, became subjected to European states as their economies faltered due to the disruption caused by foreign intervention. France annexed Algeria (1830) and Tunisia (1881); Britain dominated Egypt (1882); Spain and France together partitioned Morocco (1912); and Italy occupied Libya (1911). By 1914, European powers had absorbed the whole of North Africa.

Shocked into an awareness of modern warfare and administration by Napoleon's presence in 1798–1801 (see Chapter 20), the Ottoman governors of Egypt detatched the region from the parent state. The Macedonian governor, Muhammad 'Ali (1769–1849) reorganized the tax system, imported Western technology, encouraged factory construction, created public schools, modernized the army, and established his own dynasty—which failed to implement further the changes he had initiated. Under his successors, native entrepreneurs became dependent upon British and French bankers who poured into the European quarters of Alexandria. In 1882, the country went bankrupt. The British occupied this strategic region (extending into the Sudan) to protect its bankers' investments and its merchant navy's access to the Suez Canal.

Under the direction of the French entrepreneur Ferdinand de Lesseps (1805–1894), the Canal had been constructed to solve an ancient problem: how to connect the goods that came to Mediterranean ports from the interiors of Africa and Europe with the Indian Ocean trade routes that led to India, the East Indies, and east Asia? Portuguese explorers had a water route around the southern tip of Africa (see Chapter 16). But that journey was now shortened by the creation of a water link between the Mediterranean and the Red Sea—the Suez Canal—completed in 1869. A British-built rail link from Alexandria to Cairo and the Canal, completed in the 1850s, further facilitated the export of African goods to Asia.

The Middle Eastern regions of the failing Ottoman Empire had already lapsed into economic decline before 1800. Thereafter, they further suffered from the **economic imperialism** of European companies and states. Their traditional crafts and artisanal organizations weakened as these regions became suppliers of primary materials for European factories. Middle Eastern workers produced cotton, most importantly, but also sugar and tobacco for export, in exchange for

WITNESSES

Europe in Africa and the Middle East

Ernest Linant de Fellefonds, a French Catholic missionary, recounts a conversation with Kabaka Mutesa (M'Tesa), the ruler of Buganda, East Africa (1875): In answer to all M'Tesa's questions concerning the earth, the sun, the moon, the stars and the sky and in order to make him understand the movement of the heavenly bodies, I had to make shapes on a board, the heavenly bodies being represented by little glass balls. The lecture took place today. . . .

M'Tesa grasped everything perfectly. . . . [and] was able to inspire . . . in many of his people this quest for understanding, for self-instruction and for knowledge. . . . They are an inquiring, observant, intelligent people with minds longing for the learning of white people whose superiority they recognize . . .

(From D. A. Low, *Mind of Buganda: Documents of the Modern History of an African Kingdom*, 1971)

Jamal al-Din al-Afghani, an Islamic reformer, speaks on science (1882): The Europeans have now put their hands on every part of the world. The English have reached Afghanistan; the French have seized Tunisia. In reality this . . . conquest has not come from the French or the English. Rather it is science that everywhere manifests its greatness and power. . . .

If we study the riches of the world we learn that wealth is the result of commerce, industry, and agriculture. Agriculture is achieved only with agricultural science, botanical chemistry, and geometry. Industry is produced only with physics, chemistry, mechanics, geometry, and mathematics; and commerce is based on agriculture and industry.

Our *ulama* [Islamic theologians] . . . have not understood that science is a noble thing that has no connection with any nation, and is not distinguished by anything but itself. . . .

The father and mother of science is proof. . . . The truth is where there is proof, and those who forbid science and knowledge in the belief that they are safeguarding the Islamic religion are really the enemies of that religion.

(Al-Afghani, *On the Importance of Science*, 1882; ed. M. R. Keddie, 1983, 2nd ed.)

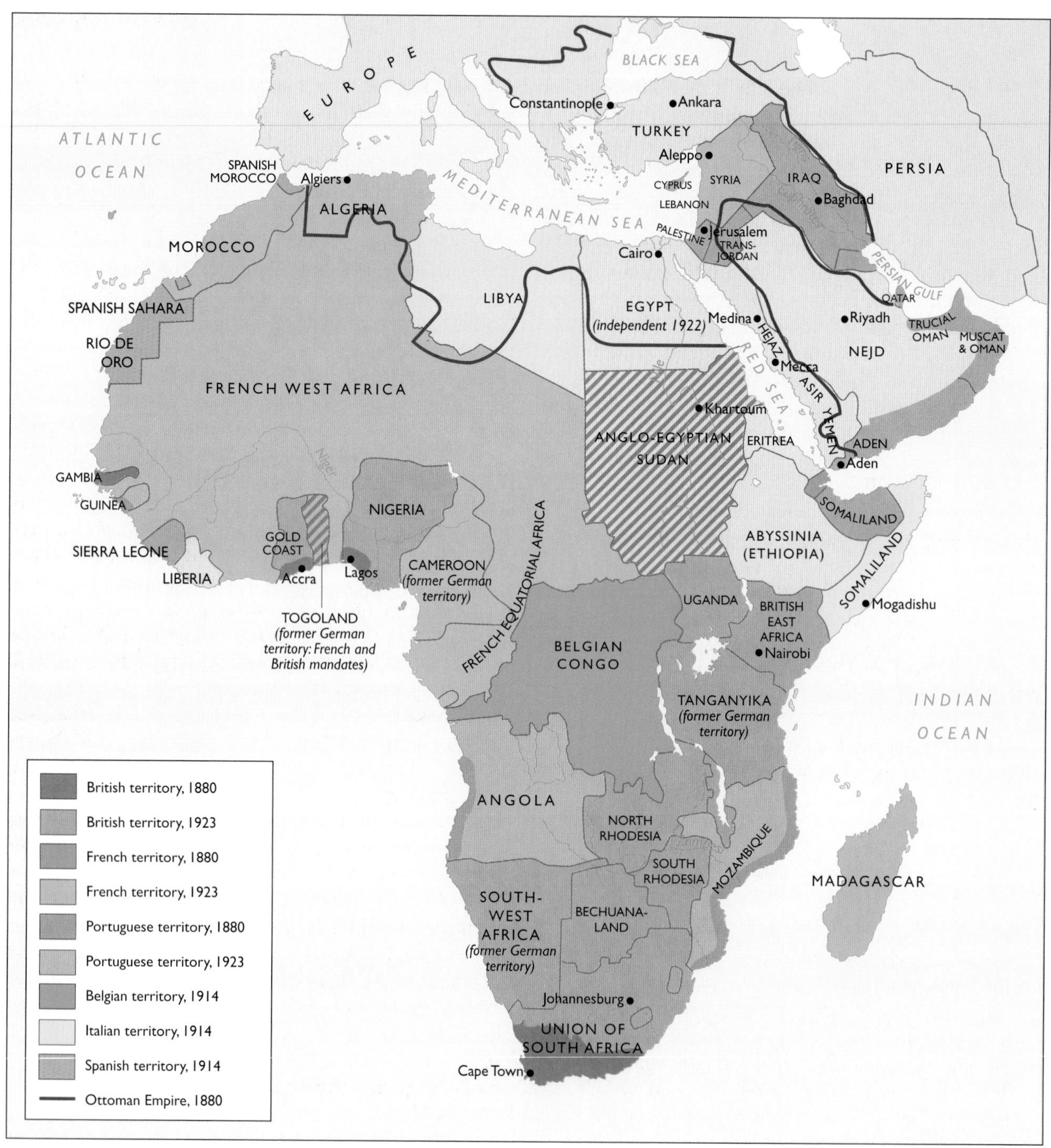

Map 23.3 Europeans in Africa and the Middle East: *As the Ottoman Empire's control of the Middle East and North Africa disintegrated after 1800, European powers rushed in to grab what they could. In the former region, they established protectorates, direct dominion, or zones of influence by the achievement of the post-World War I settlement of 1923. Africa in general, both northern and sub-Saharan, was partitioned by the European powers between 1880 and 1913. The national boundaries of modern African states reflect the interests and are largely the creation of Western imperialists. They bear little relationship to pre-existing African political borders or to African boundaries of ethnicity, language, or tribal community (see Map 23.4 opposite).*

high-priced European manufactures. The resulting balance of trade favored European interests, while it was ruinous to the natives, creating underdevelopment where there had once been prosperity.

European economic domination aroused native resistance under the influence of Islamic leaders called ***ulamâ***, and judges, or ***qâdi*** (see Chapter 8). Islamic rebellions erupted, especially following the

French and British interventions in northern Africa in 1881 and 1882. In Egypt, there was a call for a revival of Islamic traditions, and a new ***jihad***, or religious struggle, against the infidel intruders. An Islamic resistance inspired by the **Mahdi**, the charismatic prophet Muhammad Ahmad (1849–1885), controlled the Sudan from 1881 to 1898, targeting both Egyptians, who had subjugated their nation, and the Europeans who now ruled Egypt.

While popular resistance movements flared, Muslim intellectuals faced a stony reality: adherence to Islam meant clinging to tradition, but independence from European domination could only be achieved by rapid modernization of ideas and institutions. The debate took place in schools and academies, and in the press, itself modeled on the traditions of Western journalism. The cultural elite was divided. Traditionalists chose to look backward to a purer era of Islam. Modernists, such as the teacher and journalist Jamal ad-Din al-Afghani (1838–1897), called for a new orientation of Islam in scientific rationalism, recalling the great age in the ninth through twelfth centuries when Islamic scientists and philosophers were the world's most innovative thinkers (see Chapter 8).

Attempts to modernize through direct political action came in the early twentieth century. Following the 1890 concession to foreign merchants of the tobacco production and export by the **shah** (ruler) of Iran, protest culminated in the revolution of 1906 which established a representative assembly on Western models. The shahs subsequently suppressed the assembly and ruled autocratically until deposed decades later not by a liberal parliament but by an Islamic revolt that established a **theocracy** (see Chapter 28).

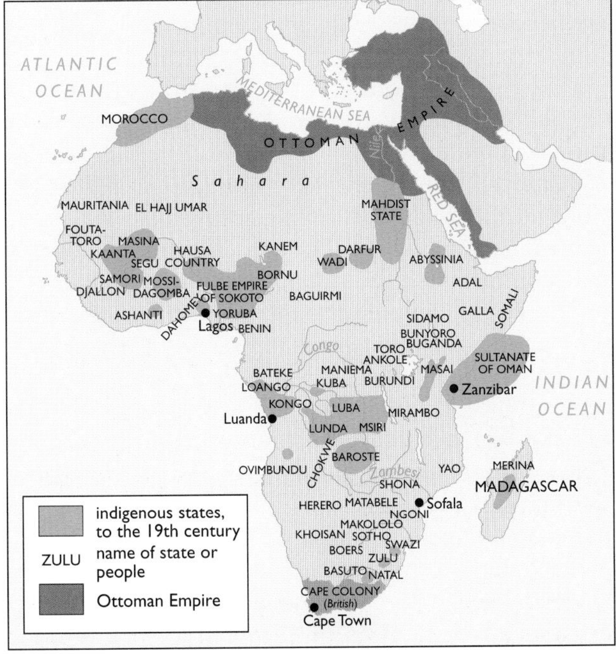

Map 23.4 African States and People Before 1880

Modernization was desperately needed at the core of the Ottoman Empire, in what would in 1921 become the nation of Turkey. Here a succession of corrupt or ineffective sultans and advisers had permitted the empire to weaken. From 1839 to 1876, reformers introduced the policy of Tanzimat, or "reordering," which involved changes in areas of justice, taxation, education, and minority rights. But these did not stop the decline. In 1875, the Ottoman sultan declared that interest would no longer be paid on the public debt; the state was bankrupt. As in Egypt, that economic collapse opened the gates to European bankers. In 1881, a foreign commission undertook to supervise the imperial finances. In 1878, European powers at the Congress of Berlin saw to the further fragmentation of the Ottoman Empire, apportioning Bosnia-Herzegovina to Austria-Hungary, while Britain received Cyprus, and France, Tunisia.

These compounded humiliations at last stimulated a movement of young native intellectuals, or "Young Turks." Their resistance culminated in a 1908 revolution that deposed and replaced the sultan, and eventually replaced his government by one that was more modern but not less brutal. Among the defeated nations in World War I (see Chapter 25), the last of the Islamic empires expired in 1918. Its remnant, Turkey, adopted a Western model of political order, and contended on equal ground with the nations of Europe, while the other nations of the Middle East still lay under the sway of European entrepreneurs and governments.

Sub-Saharan Africa: Divided and Despoiled

By 1914, the economic exploitation of Africa south of the Sahara had resulted in its division. Every corner of the region, except the states of Ethiopia and Liberia had fallen under European sovereignty.

In 1500, the European presence in Africa was minimal (see Chapters 8, 16, 19). The Islamic states and settlements on the northern and eastern coasts were far more important for the internal development of the continent. From the north, Arab traders crossed the Sahara, visiting the rich cities of the Sudan to acquire gold, spices, the exotic products of the jungle, and slaves. These cities were not only commercial nodes stimulated by Arab trade, but also the religious and cultural capitals of Islamized native African states—including Songhay, the successor to Mali and Ghana—that had developed over previous centuries and now extended almost continuously across the grassland region to the south of the desert.

To the east, along the Red Sea and Indian Ocean coasts, stretched a string of Islamic centers that traded with the peoples of the interior. By 1500, Islamic Adal near the Horn of Africa was in stiff competition with Ethiopia just inland. Further south, intense commercial activity had stimulated the development of interior states, notably the rich, fortified center of Zimbabwe, whose exports were sent as far as China.

Other native states flourished in interior regions, created by the iron-using farmers and herders of sub-Saharan Africa, as yet untouched by Christianity or Islam (see Map 23.3 on p. 722). A cluster of small states developed between Lakes Tanganyika and Victoria. Further south, the Bantu states of Luba and Lunda supplied eastern coastal depots, but also the western native state of Kongo, just inland of the Atlantic coast south of the Congo river. North and west of Kongo, stretching west of the Niger delta along the "Gold" and "slave" coasts, native states developed after about 1500 (Benin, Oyo, Asante), stimulated by trade with Songhay and the Hausa states of the western and central Sudan, whose flourishing cities impressed European travelers.

In this western region, as well as around the Cape and, to a lesser extent, on the eastern coast near the mouth of the Zambezi River, European merchants established their trading centers. The process began with the Portuguese just before 1500. The Dutch, British, French, Spanish, Germans and even Danes followed in the seventeenth century. In 1652, the Dutch settled the Cape, and over the next centuries expanded toward the interior. Between 1795 and 1803, Britain occupied the Dutch settlement.

European merchants sought the same commodities from African kings and chieftains as Arab merchants had long done. Following the European settlement of the Americas after 1500, however, one economic activity became preeminent: the trade in slaves (see Chapter 16). Kidnapped, captured, or purchased by native leaders, often from Arab intermediaries, and sold or resold to Europeans, some 10 million black slaves, mostly male, were compelled to sail the Atlantic "middle passage" in wretched conditions prior to further resale and lifelong unpaid labor. Arab merchants also dealt in slaves, transporting them in growing numbers from the east coast to Mediterranean and Indian Ocean ports.

After 1807, Western prohibitions of the slave trade pressured the economies of African states. Slave-trading now shifted south and eastward, where slave-hunters joined elephant hunters in the search for human beings and ivory tusks. Asian and European consumers wanted ivory for luxury objects such as billiard balls and piano keys, and native communities grew wealthy from the trade. A good share of the profit was spent on guns to equip the armies of militaristic native states springing up on the eastern coast to exercise dominion over the interior.

No longer in the market for slaves, nineteenth-century European merchants sought tropical products such as peanuts, palm oil, and rubber which they exchanged for European industrial manufactures—textiles, metals, and guns. There were goods more valuable still to be found. Gold and diamond deposits made the fortunes of many European companies formed to mine them—the source of the great wealth and influence of the British imperialist and entrepreneur Cecil Rhodes (1853–1902)—along with iron, coal, and copper. Entrepreneurs enlisted armies of migrant laborers to work their mines for starvation wages and in horrific conditions.

As knowledge of Africa grew, the extent of the continent's mineral wealth became clear. From the 1790s through the 1870s, the promise of the interior stimulated a series of expeditions (mostly by British explorers, with African guides and servants) to investigate its topography and peoples. (Such expeditions were made possible, in part, by the European discovery of **quinine**, derived from cinchona bark native to the Andes of South America, to control the effects of malaria.) The contribution of late nineteenth-century explorers was to map the major river highways that led to the African interior: the upper Nile, the Zambezi, the Zaire. Their aims were in part scientific, and their expeditions culminated in reports to learned societies; they were also in part religious, in part commercial. The missionary David Livingstone (1813–1873) explored the lakes and rivers of central Africa for more than twenty years, striving to promote the two civilizing forces, as he saw it, of Christianity and commerce. The journalist Henry Morton Stanley (1841–1904), employed variously by United States, British, and Belgian interests, explored the Congo during the 1870s and 1880s to assess the commercial value of its jungle abundance.

Pressing further into the interior, Europeans sparked religious conflict. Christian missionaries established themselves in the vicinity of European settlements, especially in west Africa. They opened schools and hospitals, providing needed services even

German invasion of Tanzania

Europeans and Africans

Europeans had a popular notion of themselves as bearers of civilization, commerce, and culture. Here, a less optimistic portrait of European–African relations—a battle between German and native troops in Tanzania—is drawn by early twentieth-century African artist Maru Bomera (left).

Superior military technology most often resulted in European victories over native fighters. A remarkable exception was Ethiopia's victory over the Italians at the Battle of Adowa in 1896 (center). As a result, Ethiopia, virtually alone among African nations, remained independent.

Most Africans, however, were brought under European domination and integrated into the imperial economies. Here, African workers in Dakar, Senegal carry heavy sacks across gangplanks at the foot of a mound of peanuts awaiting export (bottom).

(left: Tanzania National Museum)

Battle of Adowa, 1896

African workers

as they battled African **animist** and magical beliefs. Soon, native converts began missions of their own, adapting Christianity to local customary belief, song, and dance. Although many Africans resented the imposition of Western religious and cultural values, others were ardent converts themselves and proponents of Christian expansion. The Christian presence also encouraged Islamic jihads, especially in the central and western Sudan, where recently-converted Muslims sought zealously to impose a strict orthodoxy on nominal believers and proselytes. Islamic influences intensified on the eastern coast as the trade in ivory and slaves increased.

In only a few places did European states exercise direct domination over African territory before 1880: the French in Algeria; the Spanish in Guinea; the Portuguese in Angola and Mozambique; and the British at the Cape. The displaced Dutch settlers, called **Boers** (from the Dutch word for farmer), plunged in stages deep into the interior—most famously in the "Great Trek" of 1835–1837—where they founded the Orange Free State and the state of Transvaal, first recognized, then absorbed by the British. In these regions, they came in contact with several African peoples who, in their turn, were driven to migrate to distant lands by the consolidation of the Zulu nation in 1817 under their brilliant chief Shaka (c. 1787–1828). Shaka's Zululand, centrally administered, like his disciplined army of 40,000 conscripts, eventually fell to the British after the founder was murdered by his half-brothers.

From 1880 to about 1900, the major European powers effected the complete partition of Africa. At the 1878 Congress of Berlin, called to forestall conflict among those powers, the principle was established that sovereignty in Africa would be determined by "effective occupation." In the ensuing "scramble for Africa," the main feature of what some historians call a "second" or "New" imperialism, all raced to occupy effectively what they could.

The occupation of the African interior swept inward from the coasts. The British and the French moved south from the Mediterranean coast, establishing colonies in the Sudan (French West Africa and, in condominium, the British–Egyptian Sudan). From the east, the Italians, Portuguese, Germans, and British snatched up the lands they called Eritrea and Somaliland, German and British East Africa (Tanganyika and Kenya), and Mozambique. From the Cape, the British expanded north to the Rhodesias (named after Rhodes) and Bechuanaland. In the Anglo-Boer War (1899–1902), they recaptured the Orange Free State and Transvaal from the Boer or **Afrikaner** settlers (after the dialect they now spoke, composed of Dutch and African elements), who had once been permitted to settle there. Of these units, the British forged the Union of South Africa.

On the west, proceeding north from the Cape, the Germans, Portuguese, and French established German South West Africa, Angola, and French Equatorial Africa, while along the Congo river the Congo Free State fell to Belgium, and specifically to its king Leopold II (r. 1865–1909), who set a new standard for the brutal exploitation of native labor. Further north along the Atlantic coast, the British, Germans, Spanish, and French established, respectively, Nigeria and the Gold Coast; the Cameroons and Togoland; Rio de Oro and Spanish Morocco; French Morocco (as a protectorate, while Islamic sultans continued as nominal rulers) and Senegal. French, Italian, and British-dominated states, part of the Middle Eastern cultural zone, stretched along the Mediterranean. In 1914, nothing of Africa was left to the Africans but Liberia, founded by freed American slaves, and Christian Ethiopia, which repulsed Italian invasion at the Battle of Adowa in 1896.

The partition of Africa accomplished the final partition of the inhabited globe, reorganized as nation states according to European definitions made without regard to native custom or ethnicity. Domination stretched and altered the European consciousness; Europeans dominated everywhere, and they dominated even those, a little different from themselves, who dwelled within their own domains.

DOMINION WITHIN

By 1914, Europeans had spent four centuries establishing their dominion over other peoples of the world in Africa and the Americas, Asia and Oceania. Their imperialism was not restricted to these remote regions. It also affected cultural, religious, or other minorities within their own boundaries. Among those groups whose histories prepared them to be viewed as targets for oppression were the Irish and the Jews.

The Irish: Despised and Persecuted

In the early Middle Ages, after their conversion to Christianity under Saint Patrick (see Chapter 10), the Celtic peoples of Ireland created a splendid civilization that in many ways outshone those of the Anglo-Saxon, Frankish, and Lombard kingdoms. From these regions, capable youths traveled to study in Irish monasteries, the most disciplined and productive in Europe, and home to an unrivaled school of manuscript illuminators. Ireland also sent its missionaries and teachers abroad. Outside of the monasteries, the chiefs of the Irish clans, though they fought each other, supported cultural development and patronized poets who served as historians and theologians as well, the scribes of national memory and conscience.

Struck hard by Viking raids in the eighth and ninth centuries (see Chapter 9), Ireland lost its cultural preeminence. In the twelfth century, the pope placed it under the protection of the king of England, Henry II (r. 1154–1189). English nobles acquired Irish lands and proceeded to exploit the native peasantry. From the twelfth through the sixteenth century, Ireland was a colony of England's.

Ireland's subjugation took a harsher turn when, in the 1530s, King Henry VIII (r. 1509–1547) repudiated the pope and created a new Protestant Church of England, with himself as its head (see Chapter 14). As England's colony, Ireland, too, was supposed to accept the new religious settlement, which made the king supreme head of the Church of Ireland in 1537. As in England, monasteries were dissolved, nonconverting priests dismissed, and the people required to abandon ancient customs. But in Ireland, the people identified the new prayers and rites with their English oppressors. As often elsewhere, the attempt to convert a subjugated nation to the religion of its masters was unsuccessful. Religious difference added to the tension between the Irish and the English, whose domination was now not only political and military, but also cultural.

From 1537 until 1798, the discord was intense. English absentee landlords confiscated Irish lands and peonized the laborers. From the early seventeenth century, the English sent more willing colonists—loyal and Protestant—to settle in the remote north of the island, where their descendants live still. English monarchs and the English Parliament twice sent their armies across the Irish Sea to suppress rebellions and punish the population. The brutal occupation of

Ireland in 1649–1650 by Oliver Cromwell (see Chapter 15), then head of the Parliamentary army, is unforgotten in that nation's history.

The worst period of anti-Catholic repression followed. British authorities shut down Roman Catholic schools, and hounded and slaughtered the priests, often hidden at great risk by peasants and nobles. In 1798, the Irish patriot Wolfe Tone (1763–1798), the Protestant founder of the Society of United Irishmen, received support from French revolutionary forces in launching a rebellion against their common enemy, the British. The rebellion was harshly suppressed, and Tone committed suicide in prison, evading the reprisals that once again ravaged Ireland.

The plan first outlined by the British prime minister William Pitt the Younger (1759–1806) for settling what was delicately called the "Irish problem" involved two key actions. By the first, taken in 1800, Ireland was incorporated into a new political entity, the United Kingdom of Great Britain and Ireland, and ruled directly by the British Parliament to which it would elect 100 members. Irish leaders condemned this coerced unification, and now pressed for "home rule" by their own national assembly.

The second, realized in the Roman Catholic Emancipation Act of 1829, was more conciliatory. For the first time, Roman Catholics were able to take a seat in Parliament. By 1800, Roman Catholics had already regained some economic and political rights denied them since the reign of Henry VIII: the rights to worship freely, and to educate their children, to marry, and to conduct their personal lives according to that faith. Further, they were permitted to hold some public offices, upon the taking of a loyalty oath, and to enter the military forces and the universities. Subsequently, in 1869, the resented Protestant Church of Ireland—to which some one million Irish Protestants adhered—was disestablished.

Some progress had been made in settling the differences between the British and the Irish when, in 1845, the great potato famine began. The Irish peasantry had become dependent upon the potato as a primary, often their sole crop. Introduced from the Americas and established as a field crop by the eighteenth century, it edged out the cultivation of grains that required fallowing if they were not to exhaust the soil (see Chapter 16). Infestation by a fungus specific to the potato resulted in catastrophe. Famine struck,

WITNESSES

Dominion Within: The Jews and the Irish

The German historian Heinrich von Treitschke condemns the "Jews Among Us" (1889): The instinct of the masses has . . . identified a severe danger, a threat to the new life of Germans and one to be taken quite seriously. . . .

Our Eastern border delivers year in, year out, a swarm of young [Jewish] men . . . who are content for now to sell trousers but whose children and grandchildren will run stock exchanges and newspapers. Immigration grows before our eyes, and the question of how we can melt this alien folk element together with our own keeps getting more serious. . . .

The loud agitation of the moment emerges as a brutal, but natural, reaction of German folk feeling against a foreign element which has begun to take up too much space. . . . Let us not deceive ourselves: the movement is deep and strong. . . . Even in the highest-educated circles, among men who would denounce every thought of religious intolerance or national arrogance, the words resound with a single voice: "The Jews are our misfortune!"

(Heinrich von Treitschke, *Ein Wort über unser Judenthum*, 1889; ed. P. Riley, 1998)

Friedrich Engels characterizes the centuries of British rule of Ireland: Characteristic of this country are its ruins. . . . The most ancient are all churches; after 1100, churches and castles; after 1800 the houses of peasants. . . .

The country has been completely ruined by the English wars of conquest from 1100 to 1850. . . [so that the people themselves] feel that they are no longer at home in their own country. . . . The Irishman knows he cannot compete with the Englishman, who comes with means in every respect superior; emigration will go on until the predominantly . . . Celtic character of the population is all to hell. How often have the Irish started to try and achieve something, and every time they have been crushed, politically and industrially! By consistent oppression they have been artificially converted into an utterly demoralized nation and now fulfill the notorious function of supplying England, America, Australia, etc., with prostitutes, casual labourers, pimps, thieves, swindlers, beggars and other rabble.

(*Marx–Engels, Selected Correspondence, 1846–95*, 1934; ed. N. Mansergh, 1965)

and persisted for four years. An estimated 1 million died, and 1 million emigrated, causing the population of Ireland to drop by some twenty-five percent between 1845 and 1850. Over the next decades, 2 million more persons emigrated, leaving a population of about 4 million in 1900, half the pre-famine figure. The devastation was comparable to that wrought by the Black Death of 1348–1349, the greatest demographic catastrophe in European history.

Britain's perceived failure to assist Ireland, coupled with its record of persecution and oppression, convinced many Irish leaders of the necessity of national independence, even as significant progress was being made toward greater autonomy for Ireland within the United Kingdom. Indeed, Parliament voted to permit home rule in 1914. The coincident outbreak of World War I (see Chapter 25), however, prevented its enactment, and Ireland was poised for revolution.

The British who ruled Ireland came to detest the Irish peasantry. Their Roman Catholicism was seen as dangerous, their poverty an affront—even though it was British land policies and taxation that exacerbated Irish poverty. The Anglo-Irish writer Jonathan Swift (1667–1745) had assailed British attitudes in his satirical essay "A Modest Proposal," which outlined a solution to the crisis of poverty and overpopulation: the children of poor parents might be boiled and eaten. Around 1800, as Britain industrialized, Irish immigrants squeezed into urban slums and performed the most despised jobs. Drunkenness, laziness, and criminality were all seen as the attributes of the Irish, the people whom the British had themselves reduced to poverty and desperation.

The Jews: The Intimate Enemy

By 1750, European Jews had already experienced centuries of persecution (see Chapters 12, 14, 18). They suffered mob violence; discrimination, including special dress requirements and exclusion from certain professions; and expulsion, from England and France in the thirteenth and fourteenth centuries, from the German lands in the fourteenth and fifteenth, and finally from the Iberian kingdoms in 1492 and 1497. Pushed into eastern Europe, by the eighteenth century most lived under the rule of Russian, Polish, Prussian, or Austrian monarchs. Here, in village *shtetls* or city ghettos, they labored as tailors, soapmakers, tanners, furriers, and as financiers, raising fortunes for kings, and moneylenders, serving the poor who resented their wealth.

During these years, Jews maintained their religious traditions. The center of every Jewish community was the synagogue: a place for learning, judgment, prayer, and the exercise of charity, supporting a sizeable elite of learned males—students, cantors, scribes, and rabbis—who committed themselves to learn and transmit the traditions of the Jewish people. The primacy of learning, and the respect for tradition, enabled an isolated people to survive and to flourish.

Since the fall of the Temple (see Chapter 7), the tradition of learned and logical commentary in Judaism coexisted with a mystical, more emotional tradition of worship. During the thirteenth century, the former tradition reached its apogee in the work of Maimonides (Moses ben Maimon; 1138–1204). Maimonides presented the foundations of Jewish thought in his scholarly works including the classic *Guide of the Perplexed*, composed in Arabic but circulated in Hebrew and Latin translations. Combining Jewish law and Greek philosophy into one rational system, his work paralleled that of contemporary Islamic and Christian philosophers, who were also building rational theological systems on the foundations of ancient thought (see Chapters 8, 10).

Meanwhile, an alternative, mystical tradition flourished, based on the study of **kabbalah**, a body of orally-transmitted "secret" knowledge—expressed in patterns of ten divine numbers and the twenty-two letters of the Hebrew alphabet—that would allow the worshiper to approach directly to God. Such studies culminated in the Zohar, a thirteenth-century southern French work that presented a mystical interpretation of Old Testament passages and themes.

During the seventeenth and eighteenth centuries, a series of messianic movements erupted, the most famous being that of Shabbetai Zevi (1626–1676). In 1665 in Smyrna (Izmir, modern Turkey), Zevi proclaimed himself to be the long-awaited Messiah. The mystic and scholar Nathan of Gaza (1644–1680) promoted his cult in diaspora communities of the Ottoman Empire and Europe, resulting in mass enthusiasm and the eruption of miraculous events across those regions. In 1666, Zevi journeyed north from Palestine to Smyrna. Denounced and imprisoned, he appeared before the sultan's court and was offered the choice of death or apostasy. Zevi chose the latter, converted to Islam, and snared a good job as the sultan's gatekeeper.

In the next century, **Hasidism** developed in eastern European regions of dense Jewish settlement. This was a modern religious movement growing out of earlier medieval seekings of the "pious" (the *hasid*) for spiritual comfort. The Ukrainian spiritual leader Israel ben Eliezer (c. 1700–1760) devoted himself to serving the needs of ordinary people, who awarded

Colonized Europeans: The Jews and the Irish

Le Petit Journal

Le Petit Journal
CHAQUE JOUR 5 CENTIMES
Le Supplément illustré
CHAQUE SEMAINE 5 CENTIMES

SUPPLÉMENT ILLUSTRÉ
Huit pages : CINQ centimes

ABONNEMENTS
PARIS 1 fr. 2 fr. 2 fr 50
DÉPARTEMENTS 1 fr. 2 fr. 4 fr.
ÉTRANGER 1 50 2 50 5 fr.

Sixième année
DIMANCHE 13 JANVIER 1895
Numéro 217

LE TRAITRE
Dégradation d'Alfred Dreyfus

"The Traitor—The Degradation of Alfred Dreyfus," cover of Le Petit Journal, *January 13, 1895*

Thomas Nast, "The Day We Celebrate," 1867

Like few other events in modern history, the Dreyfus affair focused the attention of educated Europeans on questions of anti-Semitism. In this illustration (above left), Dreyfus, wrongfully convicted of treason, looks on as the French Ecole Militaire strips him of his buttons and braids and breaks his sword.

Jews were more often victims of harsher persecution. Here, victims of a pogrom (anti-Jewish riot) are laid out in the Ukraine in a scene from around the end of World War I (bottom).

The Irish also suffered from discrimination and negative stereotyping. Thomas Nast's satirical cartoon (above) depicts the Irish as drunkards and ruffians.

(bottom: The Jewish Museum, New York).

Pogrom victims in the Ukraine, 1918–1920

him the name Ba'al Shem Tov, or "Master of the Good Name." He and his followers held that the pious man could be a poor man who reached God not through years of study, but through zealous piety. Their celebrations marked by joyous and even ecstatic song and dance, Hasidic communities flourished and spread throughout eastern Europe and, later, the United States.

Meanwhile, the rational strain of Jewish thought also produced new fruit. In seventeenth-century Amsterdam, home to many Sephardic Jews (descended from those expelled from Spain and Portugal), Baruch Spinoza (1632–1677) developed a pantheistic philosophy grounded in Jewish thought but transformed by contemporary gentile philosophy (see Chapter 17). In his *Ethics*, *Treatise on the Correction of the Mind*, and *Theological–Political Treatise*, Spinoza demonstrated the continuities between human and divine, the compatibility of religion with political stability and with free thought, and the historical understanding of scripture. Yet the work of this proponent of philosophical freedom was condemned during his life by the Amsterdam Jewish community.

Spinoza's focus on freedom was characteristic of the mental world of the seventeenth and eighteenth centuries, during which ideas circulated more freely than ever before. In that open atmosphere, many Jews flourished. Some became wealthy serving as financiers for nobles and kings, and had adopted aspects of the dress, the behavior, and the outlook of their employers. Others, like Spinoza, had involved themselves in the intellectual debates of the age. The Enlightenment raised the prospect that Jews, too, might enter mainstream European society, and even attain equal civil rights. In the mid-seventeenth century, Cromwell's regime in England and, in the 1790s, the revolutionary regime in France moved to exclude religion from the public realm, facilitating Jewish **assimilation**.

In the eighteenth century, small circles of privileged Jews within major western European capitals were able to enter the mainstream of culture, such as Moses Mendelssohn (1729–1786), who wrote rational explanations of Judaism in modern languages for the non-Jewish audience. In the following century, Jews and converted Jews were among Europe's leading poets, musicians, and political and scientific theorists—Heinrich Heine (1797–1856), Felix Mendelssohn (1809–1847, Moses' grandson), Karl Marx (1818–1883), and Sigmund Freud (1856–1939; see Chapter 24) are famous examples. Among other eminent Jews who remained fully committed to Judaism as a religion and a community were members of the Rothschild family of international bankers.

Yet discrimination continued and indeed intensified under the conservative monarchs of eastern Europe. Even the cosmopolitan West saw outbreaks of virulent anti-Semitism, as in the case of the French army captain Alfred Dreyfus (1859–1935) who in 1894 was falsely accused of selling sensitive documents to the Germans. Although the case against him was flimsy (he was later proved innocent), high-ranking generals allowed Dreyfus to be publicly degraded and exiled to a penal colony on Devil's Island off the South American coast. An outcry from the French intelligentsia followed, the highlight of which was the detailed rebuttal by novelist Emile Zola (see Chapter 24), headlined "*J'Accuse*" ("I Accuse You") and dramatically displayed in 1898 on the front page of the newspaper *L'Aurore* ("The Dawn"). Dreyfus was eventually released.

In the Russian Empire, an outbreak of **pogroms** shattered the precarious security of the Jewish communities in rural villages and big cities. From 1881 until 1917, with the tsar, bureaucracy, and police failing to intervene in time, anti-Semitic riots caused the murder of many Jews and the destruction of their communities, as in Odessa during four days in 1905, when 400 Jews were murdered. A steady exodus of Russian Jews streamed to western Europe and the Americas.

The pogroms convinced many Jewish intellectuals that there could be no safety for the Jews in Europe. "In countries where we have lived for centuries we are still cried down as strangers," wrote the Hungarian journalist Theodor Herzl (1860–1904). Herzl proposed a solution: the evacuation of European Jews to their ancient homeland of Palestine. His arguments, outlined in his 1896 book *The Jewish State*, constitute the original document of the program of **Zionism**, largely realized after awesome struggles in the following century (see Chapter 28).

The Psychology of Domination

If anti-Semitism is an extreme case of hostility directed against a people because of their cultural distinctiveness, it is far from the only one. During the late nineteenth century, Western intellectuals inscribed in their speeches, letters, treatises, and dispatches to the press the inferiority of other peoples of the world—those of other "races." The use of the term "**race**" in these decades has no scientific basis, but emerged from discussions of the theory of evolution recently proposed by Charles Darwin (1809–1882; see

Chapter 24) and was colored by assumptions of Western superiority reinforced by the experience of imperialist ventures. Racial theory relates differences between peoples to their ancestry, rather than to differences in their culture or history.

Among those contributing to late nineteenth century racial thinking were the French politician Jules Ferry (1832–1893), architect of that nation's system of public education and advocate of colonial expansion, and the British entrepreneur Cecil Rhodes. Rhodes exemplifies that outlook: "I contend that we are the finest race in the world and that the more of the world we inhabit the better it is for the human race." Social Darwinists (see Chapter 24) looked for progress to emerge from the competition between "superior" and "inferior" peoples. The statistician Karl Pearson (1857–1936), an advocate of **eugenics**, urged the systematic "improvement" of populations. It was his "scientific view" that a nation's people should be "substantially recruited from the better stocks," and kept efficient through competition in war with "inferiors," and in commerce with equals. "This is the natural history view of mankind," he wrote, "and I do not think you can in its main features subvert it."

Imbued with such attitudes of racial superiority, many Europeans considered it their duty to introduce Western values to the rest of the world: it was the "white man's burden," the title of a poem by the muse of British imperialism, the Indian-born Rudyard Kipling (1865–1936). Liberty of the press, religious toleration, representative government, impartial justice, were the exports that European elites could bring to Asian and African states.

Christian missionaries believed that they brought sound truths to the peoples of the rest of the world, and many dedicated men and women lost their lives in seeking to accomplish that purpose. In Africa, they won many converts; and though their contempt for native customs aroused resentment, mission schools trained many of the new African nations' future leaders, and mission hospitals provided services not otherwise available. In Asia, loyalty to ancient religious traditions—Hindu, Buddhist, Confucian, Taoist, Islamic—and outright hostility to the missionary effort, resulted in few conversions. Missionaries did not (at least at first) understand, however, that their benevolence implied their assumption of the preeminence of their customs and values—the assumption that their supremacy was due to their inherent superiority.

Writers, politicians, and generals, and even priests, pastors, nurses, and nuns shared in the assumption that Asians and Africans and Amerindians and other indigenous peoples would benefit by acquiring Western culture. Nevertheless, there were those who criticized imperialism and its racist assumptions. The Polish-born English novelist Joseph Conrad (1857–1924) described the corruption of the spirit that came from dominion over others as in his account of Belgian occupation of the Congo in the *Heart of Darkness* (1902). English author George Orwell (1903–1950), Indian-born and employed in

WITNESSES

Europe's "Burden" or Benefit? Contrasting Views of the Purpose and Morality of Imperialism

The poet of imperialism, Rudyard Kipling, proclaims it the "white man's burden" to bring civilization to the natives of other continents, viewed as "sullen" inferiors: "half devil and half child" (1899):

Take up the White Man's burden—
Send forth the best ye breed—
Go bind your sons to exile
To serve your captives' need;
To wait in heavy harness,
On fluttered fold and wild—
Your new-caught, sullen peoples,
Half devil and half-child.

(Rudyard Kipling, *Verse*, 1899)

Lord Lugard identifies profit as the motive for Britain's expansion into Africa (1893): The "Scramble for Africa" by the nations of Europe . . . was due to the growing commercial rivalry, which brought home . . . the vital necessity of securing the only remaining fields for industrial enterprise and expansion. It is well, then, to realize that it is for our *advantage* . . . that we have undertaken responsibilities in East Africa. It is in order to foster the growth of the trade of this country, and to find an outlet for our manufactures and our surplus energy, that our far-seeing statesmen and our commercial men advocate colonial expansion.

(Captain F. D. Lugard, *The Rise of our East African Empire*, vol. I, 1893)

his youth as a colonial policeman in Burma, repudiated imperialism as a crime against others and a poisoner of the European consciousness. Hilaire Belloc (1870–1953), another English anti-imperialist, sardonically identified the source of the European power to enslave others: the machine gun.

> *Whatever happens we have got*
> *The Maxim-gun; and they have not.*

In the United States, opposition arose to United States involvement in crushing the independence movement that broke out in the Philippines after the Spanish–American War (1898). In the Platform of the American Anti-Imperialist League, leading intellectuals, businessmen, and politicians argued that such imperialist aggression violated the fundamental principles of the United States Constitution: in the land of George Washington and Abraham Lincoln, it should not be necessary "to reaffirm that all men, of whatever race or color, are entitled to life, liberty and the pursuit of happiness," they wrote, insisting that "the subjugation of any people is . . . open disloyalty to the distinctive principles of our Government."

The British economist J. A. Hobson (1858–1940), in his *Imperialism, a Study* published in 1902 and later used by the Russian Marxist theorist Vladimir Ilyich Ulyanov, called Lenin (see Chapters 24, 25, 27), identified the greed of capitalist investors as the source of a baneful European expansionism, whose effect was the impoverishment of peoples abroad as well as at home. Racial theories propounded by intellectuals and politicians were only a disguise, he suggested, for mere acquisitiveness: "biology and sociology weave thin convenient theories of a race struggle for the subjugation of the inferior peoples, in order that we . . . may take their lands and live upon their labours."

The spectacle of money and goods, workers and refugees, flowing to and from Europe lends support to the notion that imperialist expansion was essentially economic in motivation.

MIGRANTS AND MONEY

Prodded by entrepreneurs, "opened" by foreign states, menaced by gunfire, warships, and armies, by 1914 the nations of the world had been joined into a single economic system. Steamships journeyed between continents, exchanging copper, rubber, and silk for machine parts and cotton textiles. Telegraph cables linked distant regions, railroads spanned whole continents and blasted through and under mountains, and two great canals in two hemispheres (see below) abolished barriers to trade.

From the industrial centers of Europe money flowed to fund development in China or Chile, Russia or the Sudan. And money flowed back to Europe and the United States, a rich return on their investments. In antiquity and the Middle Ages, trade abroad had been trade in luxuries. The quantities were limited, the value small, producers and consumers few. In the modern age, a global economy involves huge quantities and astonishing sums, and affects everyone.

People moved, too, across the face of the globe, in search of work, safety, or freedom. Their movements changed the distribution of cultures and skin colors on all the inhabited continents, as populations nearly everywhere rose. The world's wealth multiplied, but unevenly, enriching those living in industrialized regions more than those who did not, whose poverty, relatively speaking, deepened.

The Global System: Money and Goods

The trading system across Europe, Africa, and Asia that developed in antiquity expanded after 1500 to include the Americas and the great oceans. It expanded again after 1750 to embrace the whole globe.

By 1900, a pattern was established in which the regions outside of Europe mostly provided raw materials and foodstuffs to the now industrialized giants of the West. China supplied silk, porcelain, and especially tea; India tea, cotton, spices, and jute; southeast Asia spices and coffee, rubber and tin; and Australasia minerals, including gold and copper, and foodstuffs, especially meat and dairy products (carried to remote purchasers by refrigerated ships).

The Middle East grew raw cotton for European factories, and Asian Russia yielded furs and minerals. Africa supplied gold, diamonds, and other minerals, rubber, palm oil, and other tropical produce. In all of Afro-Asia, Japan alone exported manufactured goods in quantity. By 1918, forty percent of all its exports were manufactures, and only fifteen percent of imports. The value of its foreign trade increased about sixty-fold between 1878 and 1918.

Latin America, whose main products at the outset were silver and gold (see Chapter 19), soon also produced sugar, tobacco, and coffee (the Caribbean and Brazil), nitrates and meat (Chile and Argentina), and other minerals and foodstuffs. North America at first supplied the West Indies with grain and fish, and later both Canada and the United States exported foodstuffs round the world. By 1914, the United States

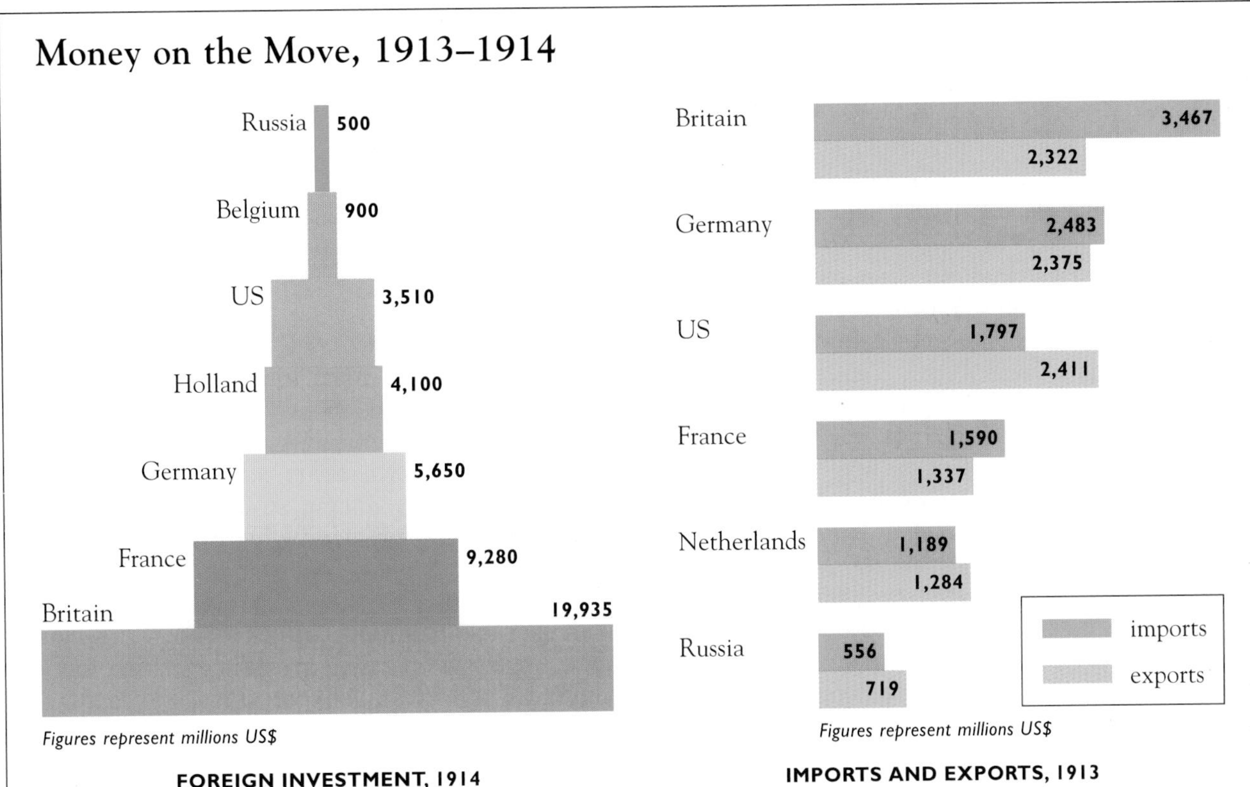

By the eve of World War I, the European nations were moving money and goods all over the globe. The graph on the left shows the relative amount of foreign investment disbursed by each of seven major nations. Note that British investments far exceed those of the nearest competitor, France, and that those of the United States lag behind four European colonial powers. The graph on the right shows the value of imports and exports for each of six nations on the eve of World War I. Note that the leading importers of goods are Britain and Germany, while the United States surpasses the other European traders. In exports, however, the United States is at the head of the class, exporting a greater value of goods than any European nation in absolute terms, and a much greater value relative to imports. Germany, too, has become a strong competitor to Britain. The increasing economic strength of Germany and the United States would be displayed in the political sphere over the next decades (see Chapters 25, 27).
Source: Times Atlas of World History, 4th ed. *(London: Times Books, 1993), pp. 256–257.*

was highly industrialized and a net producer of manufactured goods. Within Europe itself, the eastern regions shipped grain to west, which exported industrial manufactures and skills to the rest of the continent.

This gigantic exchange of commodities and manufactures was accomplished especially by steamship and railroad, two new forms of transportation. In the British merchant marine, steam replaced sailing ships rapidly; elsewhere, steam triumphed only in the last generation before 1914. Large and powerful steamships carried more goods than sailing ships, conquering distances that had once been nearly insuperable.

Railroads were also critical in the world trade network, and their web expanded wherever money, ships, and merchandise traveled. In 1870, more than ninety percent of all the rail mileage in the world was in western Europe and North America, which region also saw the first great transcontinental links—the United States in 1869, Canada in 1885. The next generation saw the trans-Siberian railroad reach Vladivostok (1916) and the trans-Andean line in South America (1910). Later, railroad lines spread across Africa and the Middle East, India, and China. By 1911, one-quarter of world rail mileage lay outside of Europe and North America.

The telegraph and telephone also helped shrink the world. By 1914, telegraph cables connected the Americas, Europe, the Middle East, and Africa; before long, the network extended to east Asia. Two great canals cut across slivers of land in the Mediterranean and Central America to connect on different poles the eastern and western halves of the globe. The Suez Canal (see above), connecting the Mediterranean with the Red Sea, opened in 1869; the Panama Canal, connecting Atlantic and Pacific Oceans, in 1914. The latter was a United States project, which united the two coasts of North America and opened Asia to eastern American ports.

From 1800 to 1914, the total value of world trade more than quintupled and foreign trade as a proportion of all trade increased from three to thirty-three percent. In this vast marketplace, the largest single player was Britain, which in 1860 was responsible for the value of one-quarter of all the world's trade. It was the pivot of international commerce, and the largest banking center. The total value of Britain's investments abroad was only slightly less than the total value of the wealth invested by France, Germany, Belgium, the Netherlands, and the United States together—no other countries approached these in the magnitude of their foreign investments. The British were especially active in South America, the French and British in the Middle East, the British again in India, China, and Australia. In addition, Europeans invested in North America, Russia, the Balkans, and the Ottoman Empire.

The Global System: Peoples and Culture

While money invigorated the economies of emerging nations, so too did the arrivals in new lands of hunted, hungry, and restless peoples from the old regions of the globe. After 1500, the distribution of the peoples of the world shifted: people of different nationalities, religions, and civilizations resettled far from their homelands. Between 1800 and 1914, the most dramatic migrations were of Europeans, especially to the Americas. Asian emigration within Asia and to the Americas was also significant.

About 40 million Europeans resettled in other continents during this period of global reshuffling. After 1845, driven by the Great Famine (see above), about 3 million Irish left, mostly for North American cities. After 1848, traumatized by the failure of political revolution in central Europe, about 5 million Germans resettled in the United States and South America (especially Argentina). Poverty drove 5 million Italians to the United States and South America (especially Argentina) in the later nineteenth century. Between 1881 and 1917, during a surge of pogroms in the Russian Empire, nearly 2 million Jews fled, again, to the Americas.

More than 12 million English, Welsh, and Scots emigrants—constituting the single largest national group—journeyed to the Americas or to even more remote Australia and New Zealand. Lured by cheap land, nearly 2 million Scandinavians came to North America. After 1900, another 2 million Italians settled mostly in the coastal cities of North and South America. More than 1 million French migrants established themselves in Morocco and Algiers in North Africa.

Chinese emigrants settled on the west coast of the United States and in the Caribbean, where they often worked as indentured laborers. Indian emigrants, similarly, became indentured workers in the Caribbean, while, in their settlements in South Africa, they formed a thin merchant stratum between white European bosses and African natives. Both Chinese and Indian entrepreneurs moved into the East Indies, the Chinese also to Indochina, where they formed merchant communities. Until the 1880s, the waning slave trade still operated across the Atlantic to Cuba and Brazil and to Arabian ports.

Within Europe, English factories employed a large population of Irish workers, and Polish peasants found opportunity in the new Ruhr industrial zone of western Germany. About 7 million European Russians resettled in the great expanse of Siberia. In addition, Russian peasants moved seasonally, streaming to St. Petersburg and Moscow to find factory work during the winter months, returning to the countryside come spring to work on the land. In 1900, such peasant workers constituted nearly 1 million, or two-thirds, of St. Petersburg's population. Italian migrant workers journeyed in the same way to do seasonal work in southern France and Germany—and even remote Argentina.

Even as the poor, the frustrated, and the endangered folk of Europe piled on steamers bound for other continents, the population of Europe itself increased—faster than any other region of the world. While the population of the globe nearly doubled (increasing from 900 to 1600 million between 1800 and 1900), the European proportion of the whole increased from about one-fifth to more than one-quarter of this total (about 423 million), and the white proportion to about one-third.

By 1910, the sparsely-inhabited lands that Europeans had settled in the Americas, the southern Pacific, and Asian Russia contained 200 million people, most of European descent—nearly half as many as in the European homelands. From 1800 to 1900, the population of the United States nearly quintupled, while that of Mexico doubled, that of

Brazil quadrupled, and that of Argentina had risen tenfold, from about one-half million to almost 5 million. European domination of the globe was mirrored in a surge in the quantity of Europeans.

That surge correlated to disproportionate wealth, as imperialism shifted the world's balance of wealth and poverty. One thousand years earlier, Europe had been poor; Islamic, Indian, and Chinese civilizations

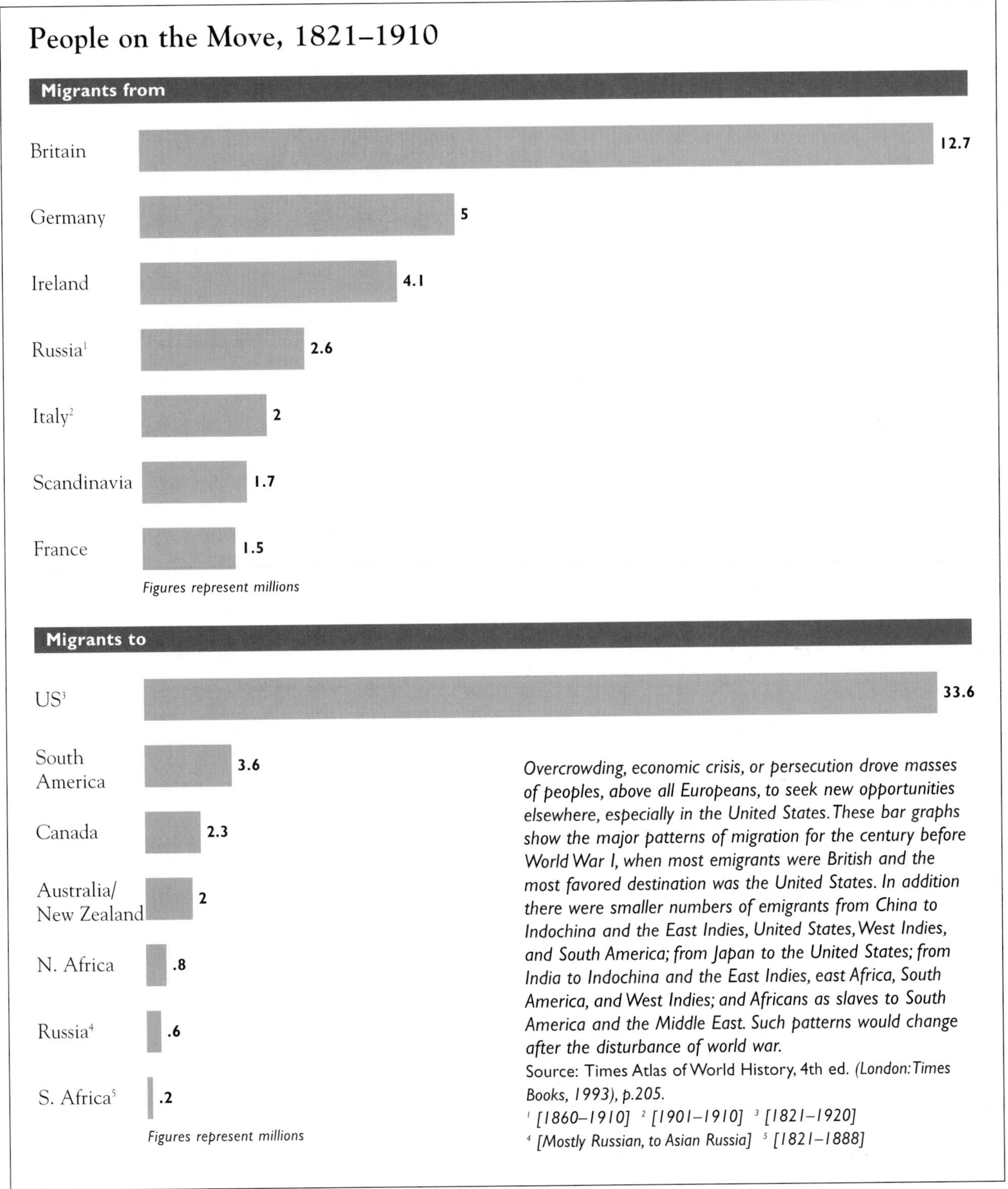

Overcrowding, economic crisis, or persecution drove masses of peoples, above all Europeans, to seek new opportunities elsewhere, especially in the United States. These bar graphs show the major patterns of migration for the century before World War I, when most emigrants were British and the most favored destination was the United States. In addition there were smaller numbers of emigrants from China to Indochina and the East Indies, United States, West Indies, and South America; from Japan to the United States; from India to Indochina and the East Indies, east Africa, South America, and West Indies; and Africans as slaves to South America and the Middle East. Such patterns would change after the disturbance of world war.

Source: Times Atlas of World History, 4th ed. *(London: Times Books, 1993), p.205.*

[1] [1860–1910] [2] [1901–1910] [3] [1821–1920]

[4] [Mostly Russian, to Asian Russia] [5] [1821–1888]

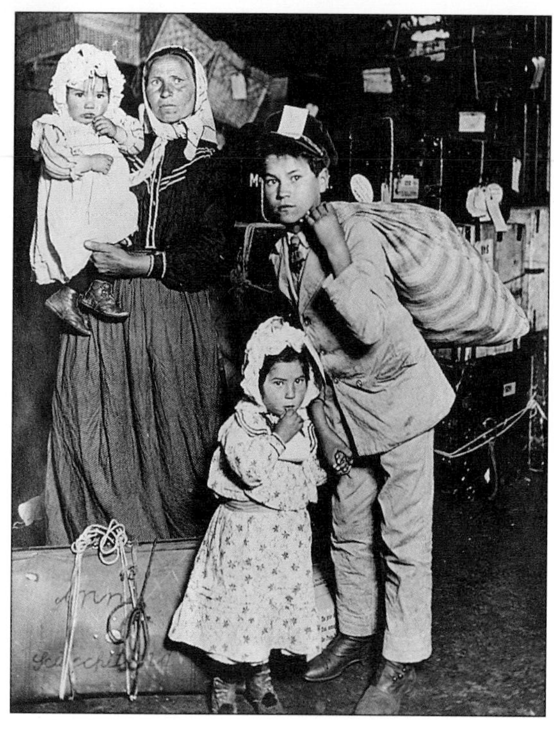

***Immigrants at Ellis Island:** Factors such as increasing globalization, hunger, economic opportunities, and religious and ethnic persecution stimulated huge waves of migration throughout the nineteenth and early twentieth centuries. Here, in a 1905 photograph by Lewis Hine, an Italian family arrives at the port of New York on the far side of the Atlantic.* (Museum of the City of New York)

had been wealthy. In 1914, Europe and its offshoots were wealthy; and so, too, the Japanese. But now the peoples of Africa, the Middle East, and Asia labored to grow, mine, and process those products needed to supply Europe and its children. Wealth had shifted to Europe, and poverty to the other peoples of the Old World, the Americas, and Australasia.

By 1914, nevertheless, nearly all the globe's inhabitants were part of one integrated economic system which held the potential of greater wealth for all. In Europe and in lands of European settlement, previously unsurpassed standards of living had been attained, and were enjoyed by a larger part of the population. Famine had been conquered in western Europe, North America, and Australasia. In time, as the newly-poor regions of the globe struggled free of European domination (see Chapter 27), they would not spurn the wealth of the West, but would struggle to attain such well-being for themselves. If that goal is one day achieved, it would be a fine, if unintended consequence of the Western *imperium*.

Conclusion

THE WESTERN *IMPERIUM* AND THE MEANING OF THE WEST

Between 1500 and 1914, Europe brought most of the world under its control. By 1914, Germany, France, and the Netherlands ruled millions of non-Europeans in Africa, Asia, and the Americas. The sprawling Russian Empire engulfed millions of Asian Muslims. The United States had acquired dominion over the Philippines and Puerto Rico. Britain flew its nation's flag over one-fifth of the surface of the globe, and ruled one-fourth of its inhabitants. Just as the ancient Romans proclaimed the Mediterranean "our sea" (see Chapter 5), Europeans might survey the planet Earth and declare it theirs.

The effect of Europe's expansion was not merely to control, but also to unify. Imperialist ventures integrated the world's peoples, nations, and civilizations. This was not the first attempt to unify the corners of the earth. The Persians, Hellenistic Greeks, Romans, Islamic caliphs, and Mongol khans had understood that challenge (though their empires lacked the racial dimension of later Western rule). The dominion these earlier conquerors won through violence did much to make disparate nations aware of each other, and promote the exchange of important technologies. The European nations also employed violence as they expanded, and brought about integration.

The European *imperium* was more successful than its precursors; it was also undeniably brutal. That brutality was encouraged by assumptions of cultural superiority. Western elites dismissed the customs and ignored the genius of the peoples they encountered—as did the genial historian Macaulay in his characterization of Indian culture with which this chapter opened. Their arrogance and their brutality were neither unprecedented nor unique. A glance back at Roman campaigns of conquest, or Mongol raids that left no creature alive, dispels that notion. Nevertheless, they committed deep injustices that would demand, in time, painful remedies (see Chapter 28). Few concerned themselves with that possibility during an era when Western civilization, as the next chapter will show, seemed unassailable.

REVIEW QUESTIONS

1. How is colonialism different from imperialism? What cultural and economic ties bound the Americas and Australasia to Europe before 1914? Describe the expansion of the Russian Empire by 1914.

2. How was Britain able to gain control of the Indian sub-continent? What currents in Indian life after 1858 were eventually to lead to independence? What were the bases of British rule in India?

3. Why were the advanced societies of the Asian mainland less able to withstand European states after 1800? Why did the Chinese Empire decline in the nineteenth century? Why was Japan able to resist Western imperialism and become a great power?

4. Describe the Ottoman Empire before 1914. Why were the Ottomans unable to resist European encroachment? How did economic imperialism affect the Near Eastern states in the nineteenth century?

5. What was the "scramble for Africa"? What role did religion play in British rule in Ireland? How strong was anti-Semitism in Europe before 1914?

6. What role did racism play in European imperialism? How did the West dominate the world economy before 1914? What benefits did Western rule bring to the rest of the world?

SUGGESTED READINGS

Lands of European Settlement and General Overviews

Baumgart, Winfried, *Imperialism: The Idea and Reality of British and French Colonial Expansion, 1880–1914* (Oxford: Oxford University Press, 1982). First-rate brief introduction and overview.

Darby, P., *Three Faces of Imperialism: British and American Approaches to Asia and Africa, 1870–1970* (New Haven, CT: Yale University Press, 1987). How considerations of "power," "moral responsibility," and "economic interest" shaped foreign affairs.

Etherington, Norman, *Theories of Imperialism: War, Conquest, and Capital* (Totowa, NJ: Barnes & Noble Books, 1984). Suggests that Europeans were fascinated with empire primarily for economic, rather than cultural or political reasons.

Imperialism in Asia

Arnold, David, *Colonizing the Body: State Medicine and Epidemic Disease in Nineteenth-Century India* (Berkeley: University of California Press, 1993). Explores how epidemic disease and ideas about its treatment shaped British conceptions of India and of their role as colonizers.

Waley, Arthur, *The Opium War Through Chinese Eyes* (London: Allen & Unwin, 1958). Compelling account based on Chinese sources.

Imperialism in The Middle East and Africa

Edgerton, Robert B., *Fall of the Asante Empire: the Hundred-Year War for Africa's Gold Coast* (New York: Free Press, 1995). The struggle of a wealthy native African empire that once controlled much of Ghana, but fell to the British and was reorganized as the colony of the Gold Coast.

Lewis, Bernard, W., *The Arabs in History* (6th ed.) (Oxford: Oxford University Press, 1993). Classic account of the history of the Arabs from pre-Islamic days through their marginalization in recent centuries.

Oliver, Roland, *The African Experience: Major Themes in African History from Earliest Times to the Present* (New York: Icon Editions, 1992). Balanced overview by a master scholar.

Pakenham, Thomas, *The Scramble for Africa: 1876–1912* (New York: Random House, 1991). Comprehensive study of this central theme of the imperial era.

Dominion Within

Burns, Michael, *Dreyfus: A Family Affair, 1789–1945* (New York: HarperCollins, 1991). The famous incident of Captain Alfred Dreyfus seen from the vantage point of his heritage and descendants.

Foster Robert, *Modern Ireland, 1600–1972* (London: Allen Lane/Penguin, 1988). Synthesis of recent scholarship in Irish history.

Kinealy, Christine, *The Great Calamity: The Irish Famine, 1845–1852* (Boulder, CO: Roberts Rinehart, 1995). The social, economic, and cultural dimensions of this central event in Irish history.

Steiman, Lionel B., *Paths to Genocide: Anti-Semitism in Western History* (New York: St. Martin's Press, 1998). Investigates the evolution of anti-Semitism in Europe and the West, from the crusading era through the Enlightenment and the 19th-century turn to racism.

Migrants and Money

Baines, Dudley, *Emigration From Europe, 1815–1930* (Basingstoke: Macmillan, 1991). Brief and accessible. Excellent starting point for historical and historiographical investigation.

Bodnar, John E., *The Transplanted: A History of Immigrants in Urban America* (Bloomington: Indiana University Press, 1985). Paints an optimistic picture of immigrant self-reliance, countering some historians' views of immigrants as uprooted or disoriented.

Cohen, Robin, ed., *The Cambridge Survey of World Migration* (Cambridge: Cambridge University Press, 1995). Encyclopedic, authoritative, and indispensable.

STORM, STRESS, AND DOUBT

1775 | 1800 | 1825 | 1850 | 1875 | 1900 | 1925

Politics, Society, and Economy

Congress of Vienna, 1814–15

World War I, 1914–18

- Revolution in France, 1830
- First Reform Act in Britain, 1832
- Factory Act limits child labor in Britain, 1833
- New Poor Law limits welfare benefits in Britain, 1834
- Year of Revolutions in Europe, 1848
- Serfdom abolished in Russia, 1861
- First International, 1864
- Slavery abolished in US, 1865
- Second Reform Act in Britain, 1867
- Education Act in Britain, 1870
- Unification of Italy, 1870
- Unification of Germany, 1871
- French establish compulsory schools, 1879–81
- Women's right to own property assured in Britain, 1882
- Third Reform Act in Britain, 1884
- Second International, 1889
- 94% of conscripts into French army literate, 1901
- Literacy rates in Russia around 43%, 1917

Arts and Ideas

- Thomas Malthus' *Essay on Population*, 1798
- Johann Wolfgang Goethe's *Faust*, 1808–32
- David Ricardo's *Principles of Political Economy and Taxation*, 1817
- Eugene Delacroix' *Liberty Leading the People*, 1830
- August Comte coins term "sociology," 1838
- Louis Blanc's *The Organization of Work*, 1839
- Charlotte Bronte's *Jane Eyre*, 1847
- Karl Marx and Friedrich Engels' *Communist Manifesto*, 1848
- Charles Dickens' *Hard Times*, 1854
- Gustave Flaubert's *Madame Bovary*, 1857
- Charles Darwin's *Origin of Species*, 1859
- Fyodor Dostoevsky's *Notes From Underground*, 1864
- Joseph Lister's first successful use of antisepsis on patient, 1865
- Gregor Mendel publishes work on genetics, 1866
- John Stuart Mill's *On the Subjection of Women*, 1869
- Ernst Renan's *Life of Jesus*, 1869
- Dmitri Mendeleev invents Periodic Table, 1871
- Émile Zola's *Germinal*, 1885
- Emile Durkheim's *Suicide*, 1897
- Marie Curie discovers radium, 1898
- Sigmund Freud's *The Interpretation of Dreams*, 1899
- Albert Einstein's special theory of relativity, 1905
- Eduard Bernstein's *Evolutionary Socialism*, 1909

Beyond the West

Mughal Empire, India, 1526–1857

Qing Dynasty, China, 1644–1912

First Opium War, 1839–42

Second Opium War, 1856–60

- American Commodore Perry "opens" Japan, 1853
- Sepoy Mutiny in India, 1857
- Meiji Restoration in Japan, 1868
- Suez canal opens, 1869
- Indian National Congress founded, 1885
- South African War, 1899–1902
- Boxer Rebellion in China, 1900
- Panama Canal opens, 1904
- Japan wins Russo-Japanese War, 1905
- "Young Turks" topple Ottoman sultan, 1908
- Chinese Republic declared, 1911–12

CHAPTER

24 STORM, STRESS, AND DOUBT

European Culture from Classicism to Modernism

1780–1914

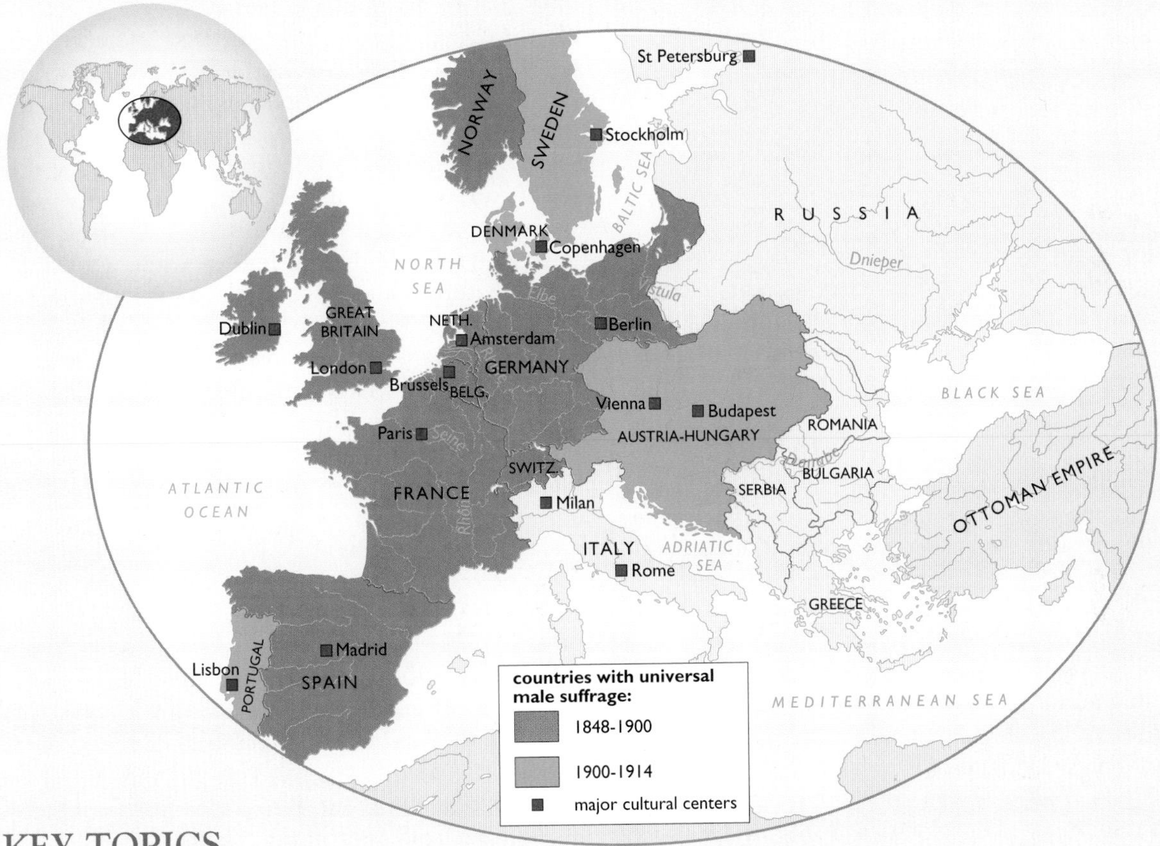

countries with universal male suffrage:

1848-1900

1900-1914

major cultural centers

KEY TOPICS

◆ **From Romanticism to Realism:** The calm elegance of Classicism yields to the styles of Romanticism and Realism in the arts, literature, and thought—suitable complements to the revolutionary era and an age of disenchantment.

◆ **The Sciences and the Schools:** New disciplines in the sciences and social sciences take their place in the universities, as workers and peasants go to school for the first time.

◆ **Ideals and Ideologies:** New ideologies, expressing different interests, compete with liberalism in appealing to the masses of men and women who seek an active place in the political realm.

◆ ***Fin-de-Siècle* and the Advent of the Modern:** As some thinkers proclaim the death of God and an end to the rule of good and evil, others lay the foundations of Modernism in literature, the arts, and thought.

*N**otes from Underground*** *In 1864, the Underground Man—the narrator of* Notes from the Underground *by Russian author Fyodor Dostoevsky (1821–1881)—announced the failure of the Enlightenment and its keynote principle of rationality. Reason, he conceded, "is an excellent thing, there is no disputing that, but reason is only reason and can only satisfy man's rational faculty." The human being will never abandon sensation and impulse for the presumed good that reason supplies. Our life may be worthless, concedes the Underground Man, ". . . yet it is life nevertheless and not simply extracting square roots." Given the choice between feeling and reason, human beings will always choose feeling in the end—even if feeling means suffering: "man will never renounce real suffering, that is, destruction and chaos."*

That terrifying voice erupting from underground is the voice of the "Modern," marked by its repudiation of Enlightenment rationalism, a complex and doubt-tinged worldview that evolved between 1789 and 1914.

FROM ROMANTICISM TO REALISM

That long century saw the accumulation in the Western world of great wealth and great power. Industrialization resulted in the accelerated production of goods that were exchanged around the globe (see Chapter 21). Colonial and imperial ventures resulted in the European domination of much of the rest of the world (see Chapter 23). In response to these changes (see Chapters 20, 21, 22, 23), a succession of styles and outlooks in the arts and ideas reshaped Western consciousness. In the arts, **Classicism** gave way to **Romanticism**, which elevated feeling over reason; and Romanticism to **Realism**, which inspected the contemporary world without sentiment or illusion.

Romanticism and Revolt

Enlightenment rationalism and Classical style, which mirrored its calm certainty, did not long survive the French Revolution (see Chapter 20). The post-revolutionary world invited artists and thinkers to put down their books and seek not to know but to feel.

Art Painted by the French artist Eugène Delacroix (1798–1863), in the midst of the revolution of 1830, *The 28th July: Liberty Leading the People* exemplifies the new spirit of Romanticism, which aimed at capturing the passion and energy of the moment. In Delacroix's *Liberty*, all is in motion. The fierce female figure symbolizing Liberty, with breasts bared, represents the savage mother of a revolutionary generation. With her raised flag she signals the crowd of revolutionaries onward, over the bodies of dead and wounded comrades: a child wielding two revolvers, an artisan in frock coat and top hat, a bravo with saber drawn, each from a different social rank within the masses of "the people." This is a painting that celebrates change, passion, and action.

Other major Romantic artists included, the Englishmen J. M. W. Turner (1775–1851) and John Constable (1776–1837). Spurning the idealized landscapes of Classical style, these artists depicted nature in its primal, disorderly condition, often setting their subjects in wild forests or burgeoning gardens, in storms, or at night. In Constable's landscapes of spreading green fields enveloping a few anonymous figures, nature, though benign, engulfs the human realm. Turner's spraying seas or roaring railroads dissolve into mist, as all that is solid melts into the ambient natural world. Romantic artists might also seek historical and exotic subjects, such as ruined castles or harems drawn from their fantasies about the Middle East.

Music In music as in art, Classical clarity and order gave way to stormy variations and shifts of mood and tempo in a direct appeal to the emotions. The later works of the German composer Ludwig van Beethoven (1770–1827), whose career bridged from Classical to Romantic, are boldly innovative with rich orchestral texture that shocks and stimulates. Writing often for the voice, an apt instrument for the expression of feeling central to the Romantic impulse, the Austrian composer Franz Schubert (1797–1828) crafted contemporary poetry, with its celebration of love and loss, into brilliant art songs.

Opera benefited from the transition to Romantic style. Singing accentuates the meaning of words by mirroring them in music. Opera's sung drama is the ideal medium for grand themes such as love, death, sacrifice, betrayal, and patriotism that Romantic style could portray with rich emotional power. In the operas of the Italian composer Giuseppe Verdi (1813–1901), passion and self-sacrifice are lavishly expressed by orchestra and singers, whether the world of the Italian Renaissance is painted in *Rigoletto*

WINDOWS ON

The Cycle of Styles: Classicism, Romanticism, and Realism

Eugène Delacroix*, Liberty Leading the People, *1830

Western art passed through three broad stages during the first several decades of the nineteenth century. The carefully controlled scenes created by Classicists such as the French Revolutionary-era artists Jacques-Louis David soon gave way to more emotional and romantic images. Eugène Delacroix's Liberty Leading the People *(top)—which emphasizes the passion and action of the 1830 Revolution in France—epitomizes the new movement. Similarly, the English painter J. M. W. Turner challenges Enlightenment notions of the order of nature in his* Shipwreck *(bottom), stressing instead uncontrollable power and majesty.*

By mid-century, however, Realist artists were turning from the heroic to the mundane and creating accurate depictions of the minutiae of ordinary life. Jean-François Millet's The Man with the Hoe *(above right) illustrates this trend.*

Photography, developed in the 1830s by L. J. M. Daguerre, provided a medium well suited for realism. It could capture life more or less in its actuality—as demonstrated here by the portrait of the American politician and orator Daniel Webster (below right)—freeing artists later in the century to pursue more innovative approaches and styles referred to as Modernism.

(top: Louvre, Paris; bottom: British Museum, London; above right: The J. Paul Getty Museum, Los Angeles; below right: Museum of Fine Arts, Boston)

Jean-François Millet*, The Man with the Hoe, *1860–1862

A. S. Southworth and J. J. Hawes*, Daniel Webster, *1851

J. M. W. Turner*, Shipwreck, *1823

(1851) or that of an up-to-date Parisian courtesan in *La Traviata* (1853).

Literature Romanticism infused literature, and especially poetry, the preeminent vehicle for the expression of emotion and the exhibition of intuitions of the self. The work of the English poet William Wordsworth (1770–1850) exemplifies the centrality of nature for Romantic poets. His friend Samuel Taylor Coleridge (1772–1834) depicted the poet as an inspired genius of magical dimensions in his "Kubla Khan":

Beware! Beware!
His flashing eyes, his floating hair!
Weave a circle round him thrice,
And close your eyes with holy dread:
For he on honey-dew hath fed,
And drunk the milk of Paradise.

The centrality of heterosexual love, both marital and adulterous, as a literary theme prompted the participation of women in the cultural world of Romanticism. Women were often the subjects of Romantic literature and opera—betrayed wives, dying lovers, tormented courtesans. But they were also often creators in their own right. The wife of the English poet Percy Bysshe Shelley (1792–1822) was also a writer—Mary Shelley (1797–1851), the daughter of early feminist Mary Wollstonecraft (1759–1797; see Chapter 17). Likewise, the wife of the German poet Wilhelm von Schlegel (1767–1845), whose translation of Shakespeare stirred the Romantic imagination, was Caroline Michaelis (1763–1809), an intellectual in her own right, who left her first husband for the German idealist philosopher Joseph von Schelling (1775–1854). As in the Enlightenment, learned women continued to shine in salons, but were now more likely to be themselves thinkers of stature—as was Rahel Varnhagen von Ense (1771–1833). Born Rahel Levin, a Jew, she converted to Christianity and, as the wife of an aristocrat, hosted an important Berlin salon from the 1790s to the 1820s.

Germaine de Staël (1766–1817), a salonière but much more, was the daughter of Jacques Necker (1732–1804), the Swiss finance minister of the former French king Louis XVI. She married a Swedish diplomat, and, as both hostess and author, surveyed a turbulent period of French history, from Revolution to Empire and Restoration, interrogating the meaning of it all. She wrote novels featuring female heroines in tragic situations, but was even more important as a literary critic and political commentator. Her essay "On the Influence of the Passions on the Happiness of Individuals and of Nations" (1796) was a fundamental work of Romantic theory. After traveling through Germany and observing at first-hand developments in literary, musical, and philosophical circles, she introduced the rest of Europe to some of the pioneers of Romanticism, the creators of the movement known as ***Sturm und Drang*** ("Storm and Stress").

Romanticism had first emerged in the German states. The German language, with its complex consonant combinations and heavy, surging rhythms lends itself to a poetry that represents emotion, especially the linked themes of love and death that were a keynote of the Romantic imagination. Thus Johann Wolfgang von Goethe (1749–1832) expressed the uncontrollable strivings of the human spirit in his verse drama *Faust* (completed 1832), and the overwhelming, indeed deadly power of love in his novel *The Sorrows of Young Werther* (1774). In *Faust*, the legendary late medieval sage and magician, who wished to know the hidden mysteries of the universe, suffers the consequences of his unbridled ambitions: death and damnation. The tormented young Werther, failing in love, commits suicide.

Historical settings evoked a powerful response among Romantic authors, especially among the Germans, whose sense of a common past was based on language, for they had not yet achieved a unified national state. Romantic writers looked upon the medieval past as a treasure store in which could be detected the origins of modern civilization. Rejecting

WHO'S WHO

In the Arts: the First Generation (1789–1914)

Johann Wolfgang von Goethe (1749–1832) Germany's greatest Romantic poet, playwright, and philosopher; author of *Faust* (1808–1832).

Ludwig van Beethoven (1770–1827) German composer whose various works exemplify the transition from Classical to Romantic forms.

William Wordsworth (1770–1850) English Romantic poet; pioneer of Romantic style.

J. M. W. Turner (1775–1851) English Romantic painter best known for his expressive seascapes.

L. J. M. Daguerre (1789–1851) French painter and physicist; invented first practical photographic process.

Enlightenment deism (see Chapter 17), the Romantics reconsidered the legacy of medieval Christianity. An interest in the past also related Romanticism to the nationalist movements of the nineteenth century, especially German, Italian, Polish, Czech, and Hungarian (see Chapter 20). History abounded with national heroes from an epic past, a shared heritage for people who otherwise knew only that they spoke the same language and worshiped in the same faith.

Romanticism also impacted upon philosophy, and found an advocate above all in G. W. Friedrich Hegel (1770–1831). History and feeling both played a central part in his work. Throughout history, the realm of the spirit evolved, which would one day reach its final culmination in the political state of Germany. It was not reason that made that nation great, according to Hegel, but its spirit, or will, or passion.

Realism and Disenchantment

If the powerful emotion in Romantic works rediscovered the passion in a world that the Enlightenment had demystified, Realism accomplished a second time the world's disenchantment.

Realist painters depicted ordinary human beings in everyday settings, eating, working, burying their dead. *The Man with the Hoe* by the French artist Jean-François Millet (1814–1875) exemplifies that approach. The man in the painting is nameless—he is identified by his labor, by his bent back, his rugged tool, and the invincible toughness of the soil. He is a figure of the present moment, whose image bespeaks the condition of the peasant worker, wholly identified with the work he must do.

A new medium, perfectly suited to Realism, was developed in the 1830s by L. J. M. Daguerre (1789–1851)—photography. The camera selected and recorded a segment of reality, as seen by the eye, unmediated—so it was believed—by the adornments or fantasies of the artist. Photography quickly became popular as an inexpensive means of recording the faces of family members, departed loved ones, and scenes of personal or public triumph. Photography shops sprang up in major cities, while expert photographers employed the camera as a witness to contemporary events, for example Jacob Riis (1849–1914; see Chapter 22) in his narrative and photographic account of the poor in New York, *How the Other Half Lives*.

Realist literature found its ideal vehicle in the novel, which created a convincing background of events against which the stories of individuals struggling for survival or self-realization unfolded. The French novelist Honoré de Balzac (1799–1850), for example, drew more than 2000 portraits of contemporary Parisians in the roughly ninety novels that make up the series entitled *The Human Comedy*. His compatriot Gustave Flaubert (1821–1880) looked to the stultifying life of the provinces, where his fictional character, the adulterous Madame Bovary lived. His novel of that title (1857) tells the story of a woman who is compelled by soul-deadening tedium and the absence of an outlet for her fantasies to disrupt moral boundaries and eventually to destroy herself. The novels of Emile Zola (1840–1902) examine the lives of ordinary people—coal miners in his *Germinal* (1885), a prostitute in *Nana* (1880)—as they attempt to survive in a hostile environment. In England, Charles Dickens (1812–1870) depicted in more than fifteen novels the squalor of the lives of the poor, the psychology of industrial capitalists, and the experiences of neglected or abandoned children.

Whereas Romanticism had resisted industrialization and retreated into nostalgia and the celebration of nature, Realism faced it ruthlessly. The ugliness of the physical environment, the deterioration of the laborer's body, the flattening of the spirit, and the endurance of the individual were grim subjects that called for unblinking investigation.

Did Realist writers have a political agenda? In their searing portrayals of poverty and exclusion, they present problems that begged for solutions. In the context of recurrent political revolution on the one hand, and of the mounting force of socialism on the other (see below), it would seem that literary Realism straddles the realms of art and politics. Some Realist authors indeed represented a new type of intellectual—an activist concerned with concrete and pressing issues. Zola's public championship of Alfred Dreyfus (see Chapter 23), a Jewish officer wrongfully convicted on charges of spying in 1894, marks the public birth of this phenomenon.

Novelists also considered the situation of women. Some of these were men, like Zola and Flaubert, but others were women. In the early nineteenth century, the English novelist Jane Austen (1775–1817), focused on love and marriage as the central issues in women's lives and the social world. Mid-century, the sisters Charlotte (1816–1855), Emily (1818–1848), and Anne Brontë (1820–1849), and George Eliot (the masculine pseudonym of Mary Ann Evans; 1819–1880) described the choices women made constrained by family demands and the desire for personal self-expression. In France, George Sand (a masculine pseudonym, again, for Amandine A. L. D. Dudevant;

WITNESSES

Pioneers of Literary Style: Romanticism and Realism

A manifesto of Romanticism—Walt Whitman would rather look at the stars than listen to an expert (c. 1864):

When I heard the learn'd astronomer,
When the proofs, the figures, were ranged in columns
before me,
When I was shown the charts and diagrams,
to add, divide,
and measure them,
When I sitting heard the astronomer where he
lectured
with much applause in the lecture-room,
How soon unaccountable I became tired and sick,
Till rising and gliding out I wander'd off by myself,
In the mystical moist night-air, and from time to time,
Look'd up in perfect silence at the stars.

(Walt Whitman, "When I Heard the Learned Astronomer," c. 1864)

The French intellectual Fernand Desnoyers promotes Realism in literature and art (1855): Realism is the true depiction of objects. . . . We must admit that, without being an apologist for ugliness and evil, realism has the right to represent whatever exists and whatever we see. . . . Now no one is denied the right to like what is false, ridiculous, or faded and to call it the ideal and poetry; but it is permissible to deny that this mythology is our world, in which it is perhaps high time we took a look around.

(Fernand Desnoyers, "Du Réalisme," 1855; ed. G. J. Becker, 1963)

Olive Schreiner, a self-educated woman, writer, and feminist compares Realist and non-Realist styles in literature (1883): Human life may be painted according to two methods. There is the stage method. According to that each character is duly marshalled at first, and ticketed; we know with an immutable certainty that at the right crises each one will reappear and act his part, and, when the curtain falls, all will stand before it bowing. There is a sense of satisfaction in this, and of completeness. But there is another method—the method of the life we all lead. Here nothing can be prophesied. There is a strange coming and going of feet. Men appear, act and re-act upon each other, and pass away. When the crisis comes the man who would fix it does not return. When the curtain falls no one is ready. When the footlights are the brightest they are blown out; and what the name of the play is no one knows. . . . Life may be painted by either method; but the methods are different.

(Olive Schreiner, preface to *The Story of an African Farm*, 2nd ed., 1883; ed. G. J. Becker, 1963)

A *Miner's Life*—an extract from a Realist novel (1885): That started them all off, and each threw in his word, while the fumes of the oil lamp mingled with the reek of fried onions. You worked like a beast of burden at a job that used in the olden days to be a punishment for convicts, more often than not you died in harness, and with all that you could not even have meat on the table at night. Of course you had food of a kind, you did eat, but so little that it was just enough to keep you suffering without dying outright, weighed down by debts and hounded as though you had stolen the bread you ate. . . . The only pleasures in life were to get drunk or get your wife with a baby, and even then the beer made you too fat in the paunch, and when the child grew up he didn't care a bugger about you.

(Emile Zola, *Germinal*, 1885; trs. L. Tancock, 1954)

1804–1876) wore men's clothes and smoked cigars, while she pursued alliances with men of the intellectual elite and wrote novels, letters, and memoirs.

Music, too, took up some of the themes associated with Realism. Composers incorporated in their works melodic motifs from the song and dance of the peasants, or the "folk," evoking an older, pre-industrial and pre-urban Europe. Thus Polish and Hungarian motifs are showcased in the polonaises and mazurkas of Frédéric Chopin (1810–1849) and the *Hungarian Songs* of Johannes Brahms (1833–1897), and later became a central feature of the work of Béla Bartók (1881–1945). Composers of Italian opera focused on contemporary settings and characters from the lower strata of society.

The Realists' immersion in the world linked them to socialism and **feminism** as it distanced them from both the polite salons of Enlightenment Classicism and the impassioned dreaminess of the Romantics. Their role in literature was paralleled in the universities by the work of scientists, social scientists, and scholars.

THE SCIENCES AND THE SCHOOLS

While artists and authors depicted the world about them, intellectuals also studied nature and society with an unfiltered gaze. Their studies led to the development of new professional disciplines which found a place in the teaching programs of modern universities. Meanwhile, the spread of public education at the elementary level allowed talented young people access to professional careers.

The Past as It Really Was

The political and intellectual currents of nineteenth-century Europe are reflected in the writing of history, or **historiography**. In the Enlightenment, the writing of history was considered an art, in which the author's opinions were allowed to color his view of the past. In the nineteenth century, historians saw themselves as the synthesizers of concrete evidence, which, often in the form of original, official documents, bound them to the conclusions that emerged from their analysis. The product of this method, they believed, would be an objective history. It would be, in the famous words of the German historian Leopold von Ranke (1795–1886), a description of the past *wie es eigentlich gewesen ist*, "as it really happened."

Underlying these scholarly endeavours was the principle of **historicism**, according to which a scientific historical method was the proper vehicle for understanding the world. Historians compiled extensive accounts of the development of major institutions, primarily the modern state. Von Ranke himself wrote histories of Germany, France, Italy, and England. Thomas Babington Macaulay (1800–1859) produced a history of England in five volumes; Jules Michelet (1798–1874) one of France in twenty-four volumes; and J.-C.-L. Simonde de Sismondi (1773–1842) one of Italy in sixteen volumes. The creation of these national histories coincided with the crystallization of national identities that took place throughout Europe in the nineteenth century.

Historians also looked beyond the sphere of the state. The nature of the historical Jesus, for instance, intrigued the French historian Ernest Renan (1823–1892), whose *Life of Jesus* (1863) shocked Christian Europe with its realist, anti-Christian stance. The English writer George Grote (1794–1871) explored the history of ancient Greece, at a time when the non-Christian, Classical antecedents of Western civilization intrigued many intellectuals. The Swiss historian Jacob Burckhardt (1818–1897) described the Italian Renaissance as the birthplace of the modern spirit.

In these multiple and massive endeavors, professional historians took possession of the European past which they interpreted in terms that were meaningful for their own age. At the same time, they established the writing of history as an academic discipline on a level with the traditional subjects of theology, medicine, or law in university faculties. Germany led the way in creating a multi-departmental university, in which the new historical discipline found a home. There it was joined by other humanistic pursuits such as Classics, the study of the language and civilization of ancient Greece and Rome, and modern languages and linguistics.

The World as It Came to Be

In establishing history as an evidence-based inquiry, historians were imitating scientists, who tested and proved their theories, or hypotheses, with evidence. Science made important advances during the nineteenth century, especially in the field of biology, with investigations in microbiology and genetics and the theory of evolution fundamentally changing the way human beings understood their place in the cosmos.

Microbiology and Genetics Louis Pasteur (1822–1895) was the culminating figure in a sequence of scientists who located the living organisms that caused many infectious diseases and began to control them. With the aid of the microscope, Dutch, Italian, German, and French scientists had begun to explore a world invisible to the unaided eye, gazing at the tiniest independent animals, or protozoa; the different cells found in the brain, the skin, the blood, or the parts of plants; and bacteria.

Continuing these investigators' earlier work, Pasteur explained the processes of fermentation in yeast, and the souring of milk, both the result of bacterial activity. He developed the process to destroy bacterial contaminants in milk, called after him "**pasteurization**." Disproving the age-old theory of **spontaneous generation,** he demonstrated that the apparent self-generation of **microorganisms** in non-organic media in fact derived from microorganisms introduced by contamination. Subsequently, he identified the bacteria responsible for forms of anthrax and cholera affecting farm stock, and the pathogens that ravaged silkworm populations essential for the textile industry. Finally, he isolated the bacterium responsible for rabies, a disease that terrorized rural populations exposed to infected animals. Pasteur's

WITNESSES

Pioneers of the Intellectual Disciplines: History, Social Science, and Science

The German historicist Leopold von Ranke calls for the critical evaluation of historical sources (1824): One who for the first time confronts the multitudinous monuments of modern history must [feel like one] who confronted a great collection of antiquities in which genuine and spurious, beautiful and repulsive, important and insignificant, from many nations and periods, were heaped together without order.... The material confronted would speak in a thousand voices.... Some of the specimens . . . attempt to derive from the past theorems for the future. Many want to defend or to attack. Not a few are zealous to develop the explanation of occurrences . . . from the basis of subjective conditions and emotions. Then there are some which have only the purpose of passing along what has [actually] happened. . . . The persons participating in the action speak. Original sources, alleged and actual, are present in abundance. Before all the question arises, "Which among many is a source of original knowledge? From which can we be truly instructed?"
(Leopold von Ranke, *Towards a Critique of Modern Historiography*, 1824; ed. A. W. Small, 1924)

Thomas Malthus gauges the implications of unrestrained population increase (1798): I have read some of the speculations on the perfectibility of man and of society with great pleasure. . . . I ardently wish for such happy improvements. But I see great, and to my understanding, unconquerable difficulties in the way to them. [Malthus defines two premises affecting population growth and its outcome.]

> First, That food is necessary to the existence of man.
> Secondly, That the passion between the sexes is necessary and will remain nearly in its present state. . . .

Thus I say that the power of population is indefinitely greater than the power in the earth to produce subsistence for man. Population, when unchecked, increases in a geometrical ratio. Subsistence only increases in an arithmetical ratio. A slight acquaintance with numbers will show the immensity of the first power in comparison of the second. By the law of our nature which makes food necessary to the life of man, the effects of these two unequal powers must be kept equal. This implies a strong and constantly operating check on population from the difficulty of subsistence. This difficulty must fall somewhere and must necessarily be severely felt by a large proportion of mankind. . . .
(Thomas Robert Malthus, *First Essay on Population*, 1798; Royal Economic Society, 1926)

Emile Durkheim insists that sociology is an independent science (c. 1901): A discipline may be called a "science" only if it has a definite field to explore. Science is concerned with things, realities. If it does not have a datum to describe and interpret, it exists in a vacuum.... Before social science [or sociology] could begin to exist, it had first of all to be assigned a definite subject-matter. . . . The subject-matter of social science is social things: that is, laws, customs, religions, etc. [which] are actual things, like all other things in nature; they have their own specific properties, and these call for sciences which can describe and explain them.
(Emile Durkheim, lecture, c. 1901; ed. A. Giddens, 1989)

Darwin outlines how species evolve by natural selection (1859): It has been seen . . . that amongst organic beings in a state of nature there is some individual variability: . . . But how is it that varieties, which I have called incipient species, become ultimately converted into good and distinct species . . . ? All these results . . . follow from the struggle for life. Owing to this struggle, variations, however slight and from whatever cause proceeding, if they be in any degree profitable to the individuals of a species, in their infinitely complex relations to other organic beings and to their physical conditions of life, will tend to the preservation of such individuals, and will generally be inherited by the offspring. The offspring, also, will thus have a better chance of surviving, for, of the many individuals of any species which are periodically born, but a small number can survive. I have called this principle, by which each slight variation, if useful, is preserved, by the term Natural Selection.
(Charles Darwin, *The Origin of Species*, 1896; vol. 1)

development of vaccines to prevent these diseases opened the road to the conquest of infectious disease that would proceed over the next generations. (Before Pasteur, only smallpox could be prevented through vaccination; see Chapter 17.)

The Austrian monk Gregor Johann Mendel (1822–1884) investigated the role of genes in biological reproduction through meticulous observations he made in his monastery garden. Like Pasteur, his work rested on that of early microscopists. Their careful analyses of animal and plant forms had contributed to the work of eighteenth-century **taxonomists**, who grouped and ranked the species of living things. The question of inheritance then presented itself: how did species transmit to their descendants their characteristic features?

Mendel's study of ordinary garden peas led him to the genetic theory of inheritance. The plants were long or short; their seeds were smooth or wrinkled. By carefully arranged cross-pollination of the plants in various permutations, he pointed to the existence of paired genes, of which some were dominant, which determined the characteristics of offspring. His genetic theory countered the prevailing theory, associated with the French scientist Jean-Baptiste Lamarck (1744–1829), that acquired characteristics could be inherited. Although his work was published in 1866, Mendel's obscurity and the disdain of professional scientists meant that it was not circulated until after 1900.

Darwin's Theory of Evolution The work of the English naturalist Charles Darwin (1809–1882) depended, like Mendel's, on systematic observation. In the 1831 voyage of the British ship *Beagle*, in which he traveled as ship's naturalist, Darwin recorded his observations of species from many regions, notably the exotic species that had developed in isolation on the Galápagos islands (an archipelago 600 miles west of the coast of Ecuador). His observations led to questions: why and how did these creatures develop their distinctive characteristics? In response, he constructed the theory of evolution of species, publishing in 1859 his *On the Origin of Species by Means of Natural Selection, or the Preservation of Favoured Races in the Struggle for Life*. The theory of natural selection was an epochal breakthrough, and the springboard for biological investigations ever since.

It postulated that species of living things had constantly to struggle for existence. In the competition to eat and reproduce, individuals possessing certain biological characteristics were more successful than others. To the extent that those more desirable characteristics were inherited by subsequent generations, those descendants would win the struggle to survive, and accomplish the evolution of the species. Less desirable characteristics would result in the failure of individuals and of their offspring to compete successfully. Their biological future was bleak. No divine intervention, no special efforts of an individual to surpass his biological destiny, entered into the process. Nature itself made the decision.

Darwin's theory was the culmination of recent generations of biological and social thought. His understanding of the struggle for survival as a race for food and sexual reproduction within a limited system owed much to Malthus (see below), while his understanding of the great expanses of time over which species had evolved drew on the geological studies of Charles Lyell (1797–1875). His notion of a struggle for existence among competing animals had first been raised by his own grandfather, Erasmus Darwin (1731–1802). Another influence was the work of Alfred Russel Wallace (1823–1913), who had studied the varied species of the Malay Peninsula, and was about to publish his own account of biological evolution that threatened to preempt Darwin's.

The theory of natural selection explained, first, how existing species might have come into being without specific acts of divine creation. Second, it explained how variations in species characteristics might have developed other than by acquisition—that is, by the inherited behavior of individuals. Third, it embraced the animal, the vegetable, and even the human realms, claiming that the human being was firmly embedded in the natural order and subject to processes of change. This controversial point Darwin stated explicitly in his 1871 volume *The Descent of Man, and Selection in Relation to Sex*.

WHO'S WHO

In the Sciences (1789–1914)

Charles Darwin (1809–1882) English naturalist; author of *Origin of Species*; created the theory of evolution by natural selection.

Gregor Mendel (1822–1884) Austrian monk and botanist; established the mathematical principles of the science of genetics.

Louis Pasteur (1822–1895) French biologist and pioneer of bacteriology; developed the concept and process of "pasteurization."

Joseph Lister (1827–1912) English surgeon and medical scientist; established the principles of antisepsis in hospitals.

Marie Curie (1867–1934) Nobel-prize-winning Polish-born French scientist; with her husband Pierre pioneered the study of radioactivity.

Albert Einstein (1879–1955) German physicist; creator of relativity theory and the notion that mass and energy are interconvertible.

Although Darwinian theory had great explanatory power, it also presented difficulties. It posed challenges to religion, to humanism, and to liberalism. If nature selected some species for survival and others for extinction, what became of God? If human beings were simply accidents thrown up by the evolutionary process, where was the dignity of Man? If the fittest species alone survive, what did that imply for the status of persons whose race, nationality, class, or sex varied from the norm that Darwin himself represented—an upper-class Englishman?

Darwinian theory would soon be challenged on all of these points. Religious leaders protested immediately, while Social Darwinism (see below) applied the Darwinian model to the competition between classes, nations, and races, and feminists challenged Darwin's argument that women had reached a level of biological evolution lower than that attained by men.

Other Scientific Advances The physical sciences also made considerable advances, developing Newtonian principles in models of sub-molecular motion, of electricity, magnetism, and light (to explain which a wave theory was developed, coexisting with the Newtonian corpuscular theory). Chemists expanded the list of known elements which were ranked by atomic characteristics in the summary periodic table. The discovery of radium in 1898 by the Polish-born physicist Marie Curie (1867–1934) launched her and her husband Pierre Curie (1859–1906) on the investigation of the phenomenon of radiation (the process by which energy is emitted from a body and absorbed by another). For this work she received Nobel prizes in 1903 (with her husband) and 1911. On her husband's death in 1906, she assumed his university position, becoming the first woman to teach at the Sorbonne in Paris.

Pasteur's work promoted medical research, as physicians identified infectious diseases and devel-

Pioneers of Science

"Man is But a Worm": *In 1859, Charles Darwin published his epoch-making* Origin of Species *establishing the theory that species evolve over time by a process of natural selection. Darwin's theory, and especially its implications for the origins of humans, inspired frequent satire. One example is seen in this cover illustration from* Punch magazine *(December 6, 1881), where a circle of apes, having evolved from a worm, evolve in due course into a smartly dressed Englishman.*

Marie Curie and Pierre Curie: *Nineteenth- and early twentieth-century women increasingly carved out places for themselves at the forefront of intellectual, scientific, and political life. The Polish-born French scientist Marie Curie, seen here in a scene from 1895 relaxing with her husband-collaborator Pierre, pioneered the study of radiation.*

oped preventive vaccines. Of key importance was the development of antisepsis (killing or inhibiting bacteria) earlier in the century. The British surgeon Joseph Lister (1827–1912), having studied with Pasteur, applied the principle of antisepsis to hospital environment. Now surgical patients would be treated in antiseptically clean hospital operating rooms, attended by teams of robed, masked physicians and assistants. From the 1840s, nitrous oxide, ether, or chloroform could achieve general anesthesia or mask the experience of pain. The physicians of the British Queen Victoria (r. 1837–1901) famously employed chloroform during her eighth childbirth in 1852: "the effect was soothing, quieting and delightful beyond measure," she reported.

Sciences of Society

Like history, the scientific disciplines, and medical research, the social sciences found a place in nineteenth-century universities, with the emergenge of political science, economics, sociology, psychology—fields of study that did not exist as such prior to the nineteenth century.

The science of economics had been pioneered by Adam Smith (1723–1790), author of *The Wealth of Nations* (see Chapter 16), who formulated the principles of the market forces of supply and demand and the benefits of the division of labor. Economics crystallized further because of the work of two Englishmen, the businessman David Ricardo (1772–1823), son of Dutch-Jewish immigrants, and the clergyman Thomas Malthus (1766–1834). These theorists and their followers established the theory of capitalism, which was already at work in the real world (see Chapter 21).

What gave a commodity value, Ricardo asked—its intrinsic worth, or something else? If the former, why did prices often exceed the cost of materials? In answer to these questions he developed in his *Principles of Political Economy and Taxation* (1817), the "labor theory of value," later utilized by Karl Marx (see below). The value of an item derived not only from materials, and from the owner's proprietary (overhead) costs, but also from the cost of hiring the labor necessary to produce it.

Since it was in the interest of sellers to keep prices low in order to sell more, they exerted a downward pressure on labor costs. Workers' wages were kept as low as possible—and the lowest possible figure was always and everywhere exactly the same: that sum that would allow the worker to subsist, and no more. Ricardo's explanation accorded well with experience. Workers' wages tended to devolve to subsistence level by what Ricardo called the "iron law of wages."

In his 1798 *Essay on Population*, Malthus explored the mechanisms of population growth and the question of human happiness—why it had not been obtained by the great mass of people. He discovered that irrepressible appetites for food and sex constrained human beings mercilessly, as though by an iron law such as the one Ricardo described. Sexual activity resulted in more births, which led to more mouths to feed, and the eventual exhaustion of the food supply. When food supply could not keep pace with human population growth, that population became vulnerable to disease and starvation (two terrible forces that Malthus called "positive checks" on population), and soon shrank. Human communities that wished to eat needed to restrict their fertility. Malthus advised them to do so through late marriage or abstinence, as historically they had done.

Both Ricardo and Malthus, though amateurs, contributed to social and political thought. Soon such studies would emerge as autonomous professional disciplines. Social theory was the concern of the Frenchman Auguste Comte (1798–1857), the founder of sociology, the term he coined in 1838, the scientific study of human social behavior. Comte was a proponent of **positivism**, the creation of knowledge based on concrete evidence, a method that he thought happily characterized the age in which he lived. Positivism looked carefully at hard facts and aimed at practical ends. The positivist study of the facts of human societies would lead, Comte argued, to sociology, which could then point the way to the creation of optimal human communities.

Later in the century, the French sociologist Emile Durkheim (1858–1917) was less certain that positivism led to well-functioning communities. Rather, cohesiveness derived from the set of moral and religious assumptions that a community collectively shared. When those shared assumptions broke down, misery set in. In *Suicide* (1897), Durkheim ascribed the phenomenon of suicide to the fragmentation of social values.

The English philosopher Herbert Spencer (1820–1903) was less concerned with community than with the individual. Superior individuals, he argued, derived from a superior inheritance—they were, in brief, racially superior. The most competent individuals—whom Spencer identified as those of the Anglo-Saxon race—would in time, and rightly, gain superiority over others. This theory of individual success based on competition and racial aptitude, seeming to mirror Darwin's theory of natural selection, acquired an air of scientific authority. Spencer's "Social Darwinism," however, has been repeatedly rejected by scientists, who note the confusion between Darwin's theory of the biological evolution of *species* and Spencer's notion of the willed competition between individuals *within* a species. Spencer's views were employed to justify European imperial expansion over "races" presumed to be "inferior" (see Chapter 23).

The development of economics and sociology was important for political thinking, even as the liberalism that had displaced theories of monarchical rule was itself fragmented into conservatism and nationalism, socialism, communism, feminism, and anarchism (see below). Political thought, too, found a respectable university niche, as it animated thinkers attempting to define the best polity for human beings—reformers and revolutionaries, whose work will be considered below. First, the system of schooling must be described by which youngsters were prepared to enter into the social mainstream.

WHO'S WHO

In Political, Philosophical, and Social Thought: the First Generation (1789–1914)

Edmund Burke (1729–1797) English statesman and philosopher of Conservatism.

Thomas Malthus (1766–1834) English clergyman, economist, and demographer; his *Essay on Population* (1798) foresaw the dangers of overpopulation.

Jeremy Bentham (1748–1832) English Utilitarian philosopher; argued that the only true standard for good was that which served the "greatest good for the greatest number."

G.W. Friedrich Hegel (1770–1831) German Idealist philosopher and important influence on Marx.

F. M. Charles Fourier (1772–1837) Pioneer "Utopian" Socialist; proposed the creation of workers' communities based on a *phalange*, or communal association, of carefully selected personality types.

Auguste Comte (1798–1857) French Positivist thinker and founder of sociology.

Leopold von Ranke (1795–1886) German historian; promoted the use of official sources as the basis for writing history "as it really happened."

Schooling the Masses

The idea that all children should receive at least an elementary education is a recent one. Prior to the nineteenth century, nearly all elementary education was private. For the elites generally, into the eighteenth century, such education aimed at Latin literacy; and even thereafter, an education in Latin classics was considered essential. In some merchant circles, vernacular literacy was deemed sufficient, and mathematical skills were stressed. In Protestant communities, literacy was linked to Bible reading and basic religious instruction. For girls, along with literacy and perhaps some bookkeeping, needlework skills were essential. Privileged girls would also learn drawing, dancing, and music. Those sent to convent schools additionally received a thorough, often tedious, religious training.

Prior to 1800, however, most children did not go to school. Children of working-class families might be apprenticed to a craftsman, do agricultural work, or labor as servants. Many did not learn to read, write, or perform arithmetic; many did not speak the official national language, but a non-standard dialect—as was the case with over ten percent of children in France as late as 1863.

The public schooling of the masses began in France and Britain in the late nineteenth century. It was schooling guided by a secular state that had begun to broaden its franchise, and looked to equip its citizens to participate in civil life. In France, anti-clerical republicanism called for a completely secular, public education. Its advocates wanted to terminate the clergy's long monopoly of the schools. From 1833 each commune (a local administrative unit) had been required to operate a primary school. Often the teachers were clergy who, though subject to secular standards, continued to teach religious doctrine under the guise of moral instruction. By 1847, nearly 4 million children attended these schools, and by 1875, literacy rates had climbed significantly.

From 1879 to 1881, the Minister of Education (later Premier) Jules Ferry (1832–1893) instituted a program of school reforms. These established free, secular, coeducational, and compulsory public schools in each village, built and maintained by government funds. Centrally-controlled teacher-training schools graduated idealistic school teachers of republican sympathies. By 1901, 83,700 primary schools of all types existed to instruct more than 5 million children (of a national population of 38.9 million) in basic subjects. By the same date an impressive ninety-four percent of army conscripts (a cross-section of the nation's male youth) were literate.

Secondary schools expanded as well, including girls as well as boys. Even so, few students, mostly from wealthy families, went on to secondary school (a fraction of a percent). Even fewer attended university (although attendance had tripled by 1900), the pathway to careers in law, medicine, and the civil service.

In Britain, Church-directed Sunday Schools were established from the late 1780s to provide even the poorest children with basic skills. Hannah More (1745–1833), an early advocate, defined their aim "to train up the lower classes in habits of industry and piety." By 1833, nearly half of the school-age population was enrolled. For many working-class children, Sunday School was their only encounter with formal schooling. The Sunday Schools could not by themselves produce educated workers (whose literacy rates in the early years of industrialization hovered depressingly around five percent for men, and two percent for women). Yet they laid the groundwork for a system of comprehensive, mass education enacted later in the century.

Parliament mandated the operation of public schools by the Education Act of 1870. The Quaker member of Parliament William Foster (1818–1886), among others, had put the case: "On the speedy provision of elementary education depends our industrial prosperity, the safe working of our constitutional system, and our national power." In 1880, Parliament required school attendance for all children up to age ten; in 1899 it extended the requirement through age twelve; in 1891, it eliminated all fees, making elementary schooling absolutely free. An educated citizenry and an educated workforce were now viewed as essential for an advanced nation.

Other European nations followed the lead of France and Britain. In Italy prior to unification, the state of Piedmont in 1847 was the first to establish such a system. After unification, general progress was made, resulting in increasing the literacy rate from 1860 rates of about twenty-five percent for men and ten percent for women to an overall rate of seventy-five percent by 1914. That figure disguises the great division in Italy between the affluent, largely literate northern provinces, and the impoverished, southern ones, where fewer than one-half of all children attended schools.

In Germany after 1870, an affluent, newly unified nation moved swiftly to train its youth. By 1900, less than one percent of the population failed to meet the standard of literacy. In Russia, where serfdom had been abolished only in 1861, the general literacy rate had risen to forty-three percent by 1917, with the countryside still lagging behind the cities, and women behind men. The government attempted to close higher education in Russia to all but the nobility, although some non-nobles did succeed in attending secondary school and university.

Although secondary and higher education remained remote for most Europeans, the elementary education now available to many meant a transformation in the intellectual world. Readers of all classes consumed novels, magazines, and newspapers—the latter evolving from monthlies to weeklies to dailies. As a result, the gap between the culture of the learned and the "popular" culture of workers and peasants, which had opened wide since the age of the Renaissance (see Chapters 13, 17), narrowed considerably. Reading and schooling encouraged national consciousness and culture that complemented the spirit of nationalism and the democratization of politics that characterized the age.

The establishment of public schooling in the wealthier nations of western Europe opened unprecedented possibilities for the children of the poor. Such a child might someday attend university, participate in the creation of new knowledge, and read, view, and listen to the cultural products of artists and intellectuals in what was then the most dynamic center of the world's civilizations.

IDEALS AND IDEOLOGIES

The idea of public education was one fruit of a democratic vision fostered by **liberalism**, the dominant **ideology** of the nineteenth century. (An ideology is a set of ideas linked to a program of social or political action.) Liberalism was, however, only one of several ideologies that flourished in this complex century whose political systems ranged from tsarist autocracy in Russia to republicanism, the product of repeated revolution, in France. Others included conservatism and nationalism, and socialism and its several offshoots (including communism), and feminism.

Liberalism: Freedom and Rights

The ideas fundamental to liberalism originated long before the French Revolution. Deriving from ancient, medieval, and Renaissance traditions, they were crystallized around 1690 by the English philosopher John Locke (see Chapters 15, 17), and further developed by Enlightenment thinkers. Liberalism assumes the rationality of the universe and the human capacity for rational thought. It values individual freedom, including the free possession of private property; the protection of civil rights, including the right to remove an abusive government; and government by a representative assembly with decisions made by majority vote. These principles inspired the American, French, and Latin American revolutions (see Chapter 19).

During the nineteenth century, liberalism reached its zenith. Supporters of constitutional monarchy called upon its principles, as did supporters of free trade. Liberalism encouraged the toleration of minority religions—leading in Britain, for example, to the admission of Catholics, Jews, and Dissenters to political office. In multinational regions, it encouraged the equalization of rights for ethnic minorities. It invited the expansion of the suffrage (the right to vote), first to male property owners, then to all male citizens without regard to property qualifications, and eventually to women. Finally, liberal principles, buttressed by religious arguments, underlay abolitionist arguments for the elimination of slavery and serfdom (see Chapters 16, 19). Nineteenth-century liberalism did not, however, insist on the participation of all citizens in the political process—the fundamental principle of democracy, in which supreme power resides in the whole people, who exercise it either directly or through elected representatives.

Several British thinkers developed liberal theory in the direction of social reform. The formulator of **utilitarianism**, Jeremy Bentham (1748–1832), extended liberal principles to argue that society as a whole, through government mechanisms, should work to secure "the greatest good for the greatest number." Such reasoning reduced liberalism's focus on the individual, and extended existing concepts of government's responsibility to the governed. The teaching of Bentham and his disciples led to the regulation of factory conditions, prison reform, the installation of water supply and sewage systems, and the establishment of mass public education.

The philosopher John Stuart Mill (1806–1873), was the conscience of liberalism. While supporting the activist morality of utilitarianism, he focused again on the fundamental issue of individual freedom. In his essay *On Liberty* (1859), published in the same year as Darwin's epochal *Origin of Species*, he argued for respecting the absolute liberty of the individual,

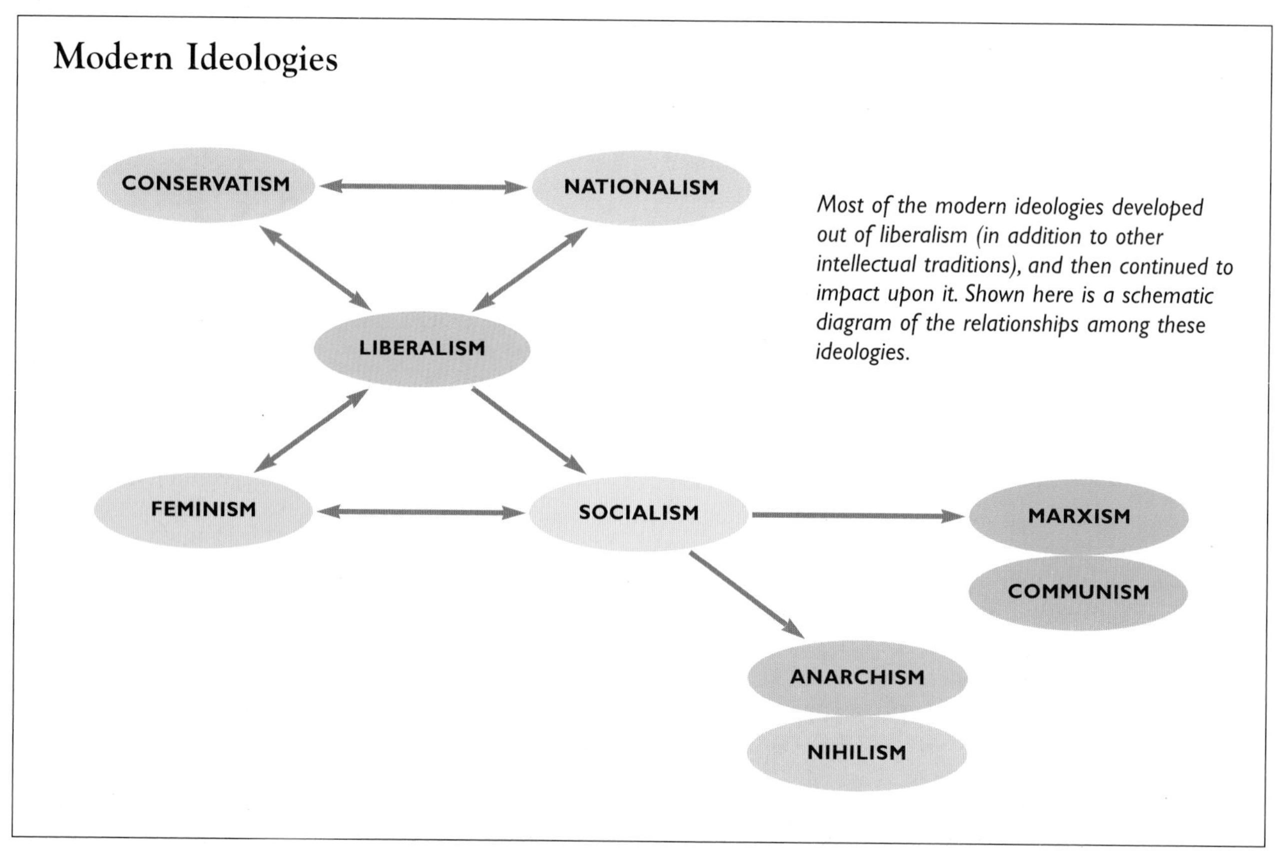

Most of the modern ideologies developed out of liberalism (in addition to other intellectual traditions), and then continued to impact upon it. Shown here is a schematic diagram of the relationships among these ideologies.

despite the pressures of communitarian needs. Free speech, for instance, must remain uninfringed, even if the speaker gives voice to ideas that are dangerous, offensive, or wrong.

Mill further advocated the rights of women, based on the same assumptions of individual freedom, in his *On the Subjection of Women* (1869). Mill's feminism had profited from a twenty-year collaboration with Harriet Taylor (1807–1858), who had previously written in favor of female suffrage, to whom he was married after her first husband's death in 1851.

Conservatism: Valuing Tradition

While liberal thinkers reaffirmed the freedom of the individual, conservatism argued reverence for traditional institutions, obedience to religious and secular authority, and resistance to change. Conservatism as a conscious theoretical position first emerged in Edmund Burke's (1729–1797) critique of the French Revolution, the *Reflections on the Revolution in France* (1790). Burke argued that political institutions evolved slowly and expressed accumulated wisdom of many generations. They might be changed slowly and cautiously; but if destroyed rapidly, they would give way to new institutions that were no better than the old and perhaps far worse.

Those who gathered at the Congress of Vienna (1814–1815) to arrange the post-Napoleonic peace settlement of Europe, still shaken by the Revolution in France, were conservatives who wished to erase the effects of recent change (see Chapter 20). They were determined to restore monarchy in France, and to guarantee its supremacy elsewhere. They vowed to counter all revolutionary activity wherever it occurred—as it soon did in Latin America. They disliked constitutions, they detested the Enlightenment, and they distrusted young university students with their dangerous talk of freedom and equality. They hated the newspapers that abounded, many in the despised languages of ethnic and religious minorities, that promoted disorder and the defiance of established religious and political authority.

How could traditional authority fight such enemies? Prince Clemens von Metternich (1773–1859), the key Austrian official at the Congress of Vienna (see Chapter 20), pointed the way, urging legislation that would impose censorship and halt revolutionary activity. Those aims were achieved for the German states in the Carlsbad Decrees of 1819. In Austria, Prussia, and Russia the secret police (an institution Napoleon had pioneered) hovered over revolutionaries and intellectuals.

Nationalism: A Sacred Purpose

Among those watched by the secret police were advocates of nationalism. Nationalism emerged in the 1790s from the fervor of French armies that fought against overwhelming odds to defend their new revolutionary order (see Chapter 20). It was more than the sentiment of patriotism; it was a love of country that enthused the masses, a sense of sacred purpose and unity.

Nationalism could also be a powerful force among those who aspired to nationhood. The German peoples, conscious of a common language and a common past, had been splintered for centuries into hundreds of states, then reorganized by the Congress of Vienna into thirty-eight (see Chapter 20). Now, many of them yearned to be one. Intellectuals looked to German history for heroes and memories, in order to create a cultural unity that prefigured a hoped-for political unification. When that unification was achieved in 1871, it could draw on a sense of nationhood constructed by poets and philosophers.

Italy's aspirations for nationhood likewise emerged some time before its ultimate unification in 1870 (see Chapter 20). For centuries, the region housed a multiplicity of city-states and despotisms, some ruled by foreigners. These were eventually unified by capable political and military leaders, but also through the efforts of committed idealists and intellectuals who stirred nationalist feeling in the acadamies, the universities, and the daily press, while dodging the Austrian secret police.

Nationalist sentiment was especially strong among those peoples who, though possessing a sense of cultural and historical unity, were subject to another nation. In the Americas, new nations emerged as a result of the nationalist strivings of the British, Spanish, and Portuguese colonists (see Chapter 19). Minority nationalities within the multinational empires of Europe sought a similar autonomy. These included the Poles within Prussia and Russia; the Belgians subject to the Netherlands (until 1830); the Norwegians subject to Sweden (until 1905); the Jews and Muslims of the subject nations of Central Asia within Russia; the Hungarians, Croats, Serbs, Slovaks, Slovenes, and others within the Austrian Empire; and the Bulgarians, Romanians, Albanians, Serbs, and Greeks within the Ottoman Empire. Tensions mounted throughout the century, precipitating the Greek war for independence, several Balkan wars and other nationalist uprisings and terrorist episodes, including the one that precipitated World War I (see Chapter 25).

Nationalist feeling within Europe's dominant nations often coincided with theories of racial supremacy (see Chapter 23) and militarism. These were in turn both related to the imperialist ventures of the European states which reached their height in the generations before 1914. For example, English advocates of the preeminence of the "Anglo-Saxon race"—a version of nationalist thinking—often also advocated the use of military force in defending British interests. Similar statements could be heard in all the major European languages during an era when both nationalist and racial concepts peaked.

Nationalism also had a complex relationship to the kindred ideologies of conservatism and liberalism. In some settings (the Serbs under Ottoman or Austrian rule, for instance), nationalism was conservative, looking toward a lost past of cultural freedom, and finding strength in traditional religious affiliations. In others, as in Italy, nationalism was liberal, seeking to affirm human rights and throw off the yoke of abusive government. Nationalism's ability to sustain very different political agendas would also reveal itself in the twentieth century, when it was linked with Fascism (see Chapter 27), and even, as in the Nazi (National Socialist) program, with socialism.

Socialism, however, was essentially international, or transnational. It looked to a human community that preceded the state, and repudiated the system of private property that had led, according to liberal theory, to the creation of the state (see Chapter 15). For communism, which developed from socialism, national boundaries were also meaningless. The state itself would be obliterated when the workers of the world acquired the reins of power. Feminism, linked

WITNESSES

Idealists and Ideologues (I)

John Stuart Mill defines human liberty as limited only by the possibility of harm to others (1859): The sole end for which mankind are warranted, individually or collectively, in interfering with the liberty of action of any of their number is self protection. . . . The only purpose for which power can be rightfully exercised over any member of a civilized community, against his will, is to prevent harm to others. His own good, either physical or moral, is not a sufficient warrant. He cannot rightfully be compelled to do or forbear because it will be better for him to do so, because it will make him happier, because, in the opinion of others, to do so would be wise or even right. . . . The only part of the conduct of anyone for which he is amenable to society is that which concerns others. In the part which merely concerns himself, his independence is, of right, absolute.
(John Stuart Mill, *On Liberty*, 1859; Norton Critical Edition, 1975)

Edmund Burke warns of chaos to follow when the edifice of government is torn down (1790): The science of government . . . [is] a matter which requires . . . more experience than any person can gain in his whole life. . . . It is [thus] with infinite caution that any man ought to venture upon pulling down an edifice which has answered in any tolerable degree for ages the common purposes of society, or on building it up again, without having models and patterns of approved utility before his eyes. . . . When ancient opinions of life are taken away, the loss cannot possibly be estimated. From that moment we have no compass to govern us; nor can we know distinctly to what port we steer. . . .
(Edmund Burke, *Reflections on the Revolution in France*, 1790)

Two nationalists see nationhood as language, tradition, and culture: *Johann Gottlieb Fichte*: The first, original, and truly natural boundaries of states are beyond doubt their internal boundaries. Those who speak the same language are joined to each other by a multitude of invisible bonds by nature herself, long before any human art begins; they understand each other and have the power of continuing to make themselves understood more and more clearly; they belong together and are by nature one and an inseparable whole. . . . From this internal boundary, which is drawn by the spiritual nature of man himself, the marking of the external boundary by dwelling places results as a consequence. . . .
(Johann Gottlieb Fichte, "Thirteenth Address," 1806; ed. G. A. Kelly, 1968)

Giuseppe Mazzini: [The people of one nation] speak the same language, they bear about them the impress of consanguinity, they kneel beside the same tombs, they glory in the same tradition; . . . Nationality ought . . . to be . . . the assertion of the individuality of a human group called by its geographical position, its traditions, and its language, to fulfill a special function in the European work of civilization.
(Giuseppe Mazzini, "Europe: Its Condition and Prospects," 1852; ed. W. Clark, 1880)

to liberalism as well as socialism, also saw the state primarily as an obstacle to the advancement of women, who even in the most advanced states had historically been denied access to political expression.

Socialism: Sharing the Wealth

Rooted in the French Revolution, and given urgency by industrialization, socialism flowered in the years following Napoleon's defeat. It employed liberal principles of equality and justice to critique the concentration of wealth, and envisioned society as a community of workers capable of exercising political power. It differed from liberalism in its repudiation of the principle that the ownership of private property was an essential human right, and looked to the community or state to provide for the welfare of all.

Socialist principles began to be formulated during the Revolution's second, more violent and creative phase. The notion that the state was immediately responsible to the people at large—not just those in the Convention, but those in the street—was preliminary to socialism. So were the ideas of such revolutionaries as François-Noël Babeuf (1760–1797) (who survived Robespierre to be guillotined by the Directory) who argued that the wealth of the rich should be redistributed to the poor.

A generation later, Henri de Saint-Simon (1760–1825) announced that it was a function of the state to assure a certain minimum of material welfare for its populace. So that it could do so efficiently, the state should be controlled by those endowed with the highest rational and administrative capacities—a consortium of industrialists and scientists. These views he presented in several works, beginning with the audacious *On the Reorganization of European Society* (1814). The positivist philosopher and pioneer sociologist August Comte supported Saint-Simon in this political program, until the latter developed, just prior to his death, a new mystical religion, centered on the relief of the misery of the poor. Compassion for the poor in the Saint-Simonian system linked the medieval religious and the modern socialist traditions.

Saint-Simon's compatriots and contemporaries F. M. Charles Fourier (1772–1837) and Etienne Cabet (1788–1856) further developed a visionary, or "utopian" socialism. Fourier proposed the creation of communities of workers—each group of workers a *phalange* (or phalanx, after the ancient Greek military unit), accommodated in a *phalanstère* (phalanstery)—who would live together, males and emancipated females, in harmony. They would engage in productive work, participate in artistic and musical projects, and enjoy fulfilling lives unfettered by conventional religious or moral restrictions.

Without adopting Fourier's phalanstery system, Cabet also envisioned a harmonious workers' community. His *Voyage to Icaria* (1840) described an imaginary voyage to a workers' paradise organized by principles he called "communist" (the first use of the term). Cabet tried to put his ideas in action, setting off with hundreds of followers in 1848 to plant a communitarian settlement in Nauvoo, Illinois, on the site of one just abandoned by Mormon sectarians bound for Salt Lake City, Utah.

The dreamy socialism of Fourier and Cabet received more urgent and hostile expression in the theoretical work of Pierre-Joseph Proudhon (1809–1865). An opponent of the state (which he thought should be abolished) and of the capitalists who, he believed, were its principal beneficiaries, he envisioned workers' communities based on equity and justice. His 1840 book *What is Property?* posed that central question. Those who accumulate property, according to Proudhon, remove wealth from the common store and deprive the poor of basic necessities. He responded to his own question with an unequivocal reply: all property was theft.

Across the Channel, meanwhile, the attempts of Robert Owen (1771–1858) to build real workers' communities in Britain and the United States (see Chapter 22) contributed to later socialist development. In France again, Louis Blanc (1811–1882) proposed in his 1840 book *The Organization of Work* a system of government-funded national workshops as a remedy for unemployment. These, too, were failures. At the same time, they were precedents for later workers' organizations. More, they announced the principle that government owed its citizens a right as substantial as the rights to free speech or worship: the right to work.

Marxism, Communism, Anarchism: Transfers of Power

After 1848, the utopian visions of the early socialists gave way to pragmatic programs promoted by workers' organizations, or trade unions, and social democratic political parties (see Chapter 22). Many of their leaders were influenced by the form of socialism that came to predominate in the latter half of the century, termed **Marxism** after its exponent Karl Marx (1818–1883).

Marxism combined economic analysis, social criticism, historical description, ethical philosophy, and political theory into an intellectual system of

WITNESSES

Idealists and Ideologues (II)

Karl Marx and Friedrich Engels define history as a series of class struggles (1848): The history of all hitherto existing society is the history of class struggles. Freeman and slave, patrician and plebeian, lord and serf, guild-master and journeyman, in a word, oppressor and oppressed, stood in constant opposition to one another, carried on an uninterrupted, now hidden, now open fight, a fight that each time ended, either in a revolutionary reconstitution of society at large, or in the common ruin of the contending classes. . . . The modern bourgeois society that has sprouted from the ruins of feudal society has not done away with class antagonisms. . . . Society as a whole is more and more splitting up into two great hostile camps, into two great classes directly facing each other—bourgeoisie and proletariat. . . .
(Karl Marx and Friedrich Engels, *The Communist Manifesto*, 1848; ed. S. Moore, 1888)

Pierre-Joseph Proudhon—an anarchist—asks, "What is Government?" (1851): To be GOVERNED is to be kept under surveillance, inspected, spied upon, bossed, law-ridden, regulated, penned in, indoctrinated, preached at, registered, evaluated, appraised, censured, ordered about, by creatures who have neither the right, nor the knowledge, nor the virtue to do so. . . . It is, under the pretense of public benefit and in the name of the general interest, to be . . . extorted, squeezed, hoaxed, robbed; then at the slightest resistance, . . . to be squelched, corrected, vilified, bullied, hounded, tormented, bludgeoned, disarmed, strangled, imprisoned, shot down, judged, condemned, deported, sacrificed, sold, betrayed . . . . That's government, that's its justice, that's its morality! And to think that there are democrats among us who claim that there is some good in government—socialists who support this infamy in the name of Liberty, Equality, and Fraternity—proletarians who proclaim their candidacy for the Presidency of the Republic! Hypocrisy!
(From R. Hoffman ed., *Anarchism*, 1970)

Emmeline Pankhurst, the English feminist and suffragette explains why women are militant (1913): The extensions of the franchise to the men of my country [Britain] have been preceded by very great violence, by something like a revolution, by something like civil war. In 1832 . . . it was after the practice of arson on so large a scale that half the city of Bristol was burned down in a single night . . . that the Reform Bill of 1832 was allowed to pass into law. [This enfranchised middle-class males.] In 1867 . . . rioting went on all over the country, and as the result . . . the Reform Act of 1867 was put upon the statute books. [This enfranchised urban working-class males.] In 1884 . . . rioting was threatened and feared, and so the agricultural laborers got the vote. Meanwhile, during the '80s, women, like men, were asking for the franchise. . . . Meetings of the great corporations, great town councils, and city councils, passed resolutions asking that women should have the vote. More meetings were held, and larger, for Woman Suffrage than were held for votes for men, and yet the women did not get it. Men got the vote because they were and would be violent. The women did not get it because they were constitutional and law abiding . . . .
(Emmeline Pankhurst, speech, October 21, 1913; ed. J. Marcus, 1955)

immense weight and complexity. It first appeared in a pamphlet written on the eve of the volcanic revolutions of 1848, the *Communist Manifesto*, on which Marx collaborated with fellow German intellectual Friedrich Engels (1820–1895). Together they had been founders the previous year of a political party they called the "Communist League." Now, dismissing as mere quackery the visionary socialism of Saint-Simon or Owen, they outlined the fundamentals of a "scientific" socialism.

Surveying a society transformed by industrialization, they distinguished two major social groups, or classes: the bourgeoisie and the **proletariat**. For Marx and Engels, the term "**class**" denoted not merely a group of people, but a group that shared a certain relation to "the means of production," the tools for the creation of wealth. The "bourgeoisie" included those who manufactured on a vast scale in machine-powered factories, conducting business worldwide. It was the bourgeoisie who owned the "means of production"—the machines and factories of an industrial economy—and who used their financial resources (capital) in order to create even more wealth.

The workers whose labor was hired by bourgeois capitalists were themselves powerless and poor. These were the "proletariat," whose wretchedness derived from their position in industrial society as mere "appendages" of the machines that spun, wove, drilled, and rolled the goods that made other people wealthy.

These two social classes identified by Marx and Engels were locked in an epochal battle; indeed it was history's final battle. All of history, the joint authors explained, was a history of "class struggle." Earlier eras had seen the clash of landowners and slaves, of knights and serfs. In each age two primary classes emerged from the broader society to fight a duel, their struggle creating new social conditions that became the foundations of the next historical era. That process had continued to the present moment, when the class struggle was more intense than ever heretofore.

Its greater intensity derived from tangible, measurable conditions. Never before had so many people fallen into one of the two competing social classes. Never before had the wealthy been so powerful and their servants so deprived of power. History approached that moment when all but a few would be of one group—the proletariat—and only a few would oppose them—the bourgeoisie. At that moment, the many would seize power, and appropriate for themselves the means of production. Now wealth would belong to the workers, which is to say, to society as a whole. Socialism would have been achieved, and the resulting society, a workers' paradise, would be wholly classless, or communist.

Karl Marx: *The* Communist Manifesto *by Karl Marx, who is shown here, and collaborator Friedrich Engels was published in 1848 and subsequently translated into every major European language. It reestablished socialism on a firmer, more scientific basis than that provided by previous Utopian theories.*

In this way, communism grew from socialism, its theory systematized by Marx and Engels, who predicted as inevitable the destruction of all private property and the victory of the unified industrial workers of the world. "Workers of the world, unite!," the *Manifesto* closes, "you have nothing to lose but your chains!"

Marx lived for thirty-five years after the publication of the *Manifesto*. During that time, he continued to theorize (making regular use of the British Museum Reading Room in London, where he lived), to write, and to organize, supported financially by Engels. Engels also contributed importantly to communist theory in his *The Conditions of the Working Class in England* (1845) and *The Origin of the Family, Private Property, and the State* (1884). Marx's most important work was the three-volume *Capital*, an exhaustive analysis of the modern industrial economy. He also encouraged the formation of workers' unions and social democratic parties, and in 1864 organized the First International (the common name for the First Working Men's Association), an important step in the movement of communism from the realm of theory to that of action. After Marx's death in 1883, the Second International was formed in 1889.

In the late nineteenth century, Marxist theory developed most vigorously within the German workers' movement, where it branched in several directions. An "orthodox" school of thought, represented by Karl Kautsky (1854–1938) adhered to the original Marxian formulations. A "revisionist" school, represented by Eduard Bernstein (1850–1932), while respectful of the Marxist analysis, urged socialists to respond flexibly to emerging new conditions. These now offered the possibility of an evolution through a series of parliamentary reforms in the direction of communism, rather than the violent revolution that Marx prophesied. Christian Socialists—a seeming paradox, as Marx himself was militantly atheist—urged blending Christian values of compassion and mutual assistance with a Marxist analysis of society.

Socialist parties flourished according to the German pattern in Austria, Belgium, the Netherlands, and the Scandinavian countries. That pattern failed to crystallize in the United States, where Marxian socialism had little appeal in an environment of relative ease and freedom. The broad and flexible principles of the Socialist Labor Party formed

WHO'S WHO

In Political, Philosophical, and Social Thought: the Second Generation (1789–1914)

Giuseppe Mazzini (1805–1872) Italian nationalist and founder of "Young Italy."

John Stuart Mill (1806–1873) English liberal philosopher; author of *On Liberty* (1859).

Mikhail Bakunin (1814–1876) Russian thinker and pioneer of philosophy of Anarchism.

Karl Marx (1818–1883) German philosopher; creator of Scientific Socialism and co-author (with Friedrich Engels) of the *Communist Manifesto*.

Herbert Spencer (1820–1903) English sociologist; best known for developing a theory of "Social Darwinism."

Friedrich Nietzsche (1844–1900) German anti-Christian philosopher who heralded the "Death of God."

Sigmund Freud (1856–1939) German psychologist and founder of psychoanalysis.

Emmeline Pankhurst (1858–1928) English radical feminist and suffragette; founder and leader of the Women's Social and Political Union.

by Eugene Debs (1855–1926) were more popular. In Britain, despite the presence of Marx, Marxist principles did not catch hold as on the continent. In their place, the Fabian Society (founded 1883/84) urged the gradual introduction of socialist values.

In France and Russia, socialist movements and their offshoots inclined toward violence. France's revolutionary past, and the recent bloody suppression of the Paris Commune of 1871 (see Chapter 20) led socialists in that nation to view the Fabian gradualism or Bernstein's revisionism as unimpressive. While Jean Jaurès (1859–1914), the pacifist assassinated on the eve of World War I, worked to build a vigorous socialism through parliamentary means, French **Syndicalists** (the term derived from the French word for trade union, or *syndicat*) planned instead for a violent revolution, to be engineered by workers' associations and precipitated by a general strike.

Anarchists, mostly Russian, advocated an immediate, violent assault on all government authority as the only means of acquiring social and political liberty. The theorist Mikhail Bakunin (1814–1876), having outlined the essential principles of **anarchism**, was expelled from the First International. But anarchism won followers in Spain and Italy, whose undeveloped economies provided fertile soil for extremism. **Nihilists**, specifically Russian, posited the non-meaning of everything, and promoted a violent and terroristic attack on all authority. Not surprisingly, terror ensued (see Chapter 25).

Feminism: Rights for Women

As liberals and socialists posed their different visions of the ideal life, women claimed for themselves a full role in contemporary society. Their movement, called feminism, drew on ideas developed from Renaissance humanism and the Enlightenment. Mary Wollstonecraft's *A Vindication of the Rights of Woman* (1792) had summoned women to construct lives for themselves outside of marriage and regardless of their sexual destiny. In the next century, modern ideologies introduced a new dimension to women's aspirations.

The seventeenth and eighteenth centuries had seen at least some real progress for women. Elite women gained prestige from the occupation of child-rearing, while many also extended their educative and nurturing activities into the wider society, engaging in philanthropic work that was often specifically directed toward women or children. A few engaged in intellectual circles as authors, critics, or patrons. Further down the social scale, some women found employment in theatrical and dance companies—marginal professions viewed by many as not differing much from prostitution, but offering talented women, nevertheless, greater independence and visibility.

The French Revolution saw female activism emerge in social groups outside of the elites. For such women, food crisis riots had been a characteristic form of political participation (see Chapter 20). Now they became revolutionaries: they shouted slogans, stormed prisons, cheered executions, marched on Versailles, and formed a network of revolutionary clubs. Meanwhile, revolutionary leaders passed legislation favorable to women, permitting divorce (which saw a brief boom) and facilitating inheritance of property by women. It appeared briefly as though substantial rights for women might be secured in the flux of revolution.

The Revolution itself, however, put an end to what it began. Never admitting women to the franchise (even as universal male suffrage was briefly instituted), in 1793 it ordered the women's political clubs closed down. In the same year, Olympe de

Gouges, author of the provocative *Declaration of the Rights of Women* (1790) went to the guillotine (see Chapter 20). As the painter Elisabeth Vigée-Lebrun remarked in her memoirs, women had ruled before 1789, but "the Revolution dethroned them."

The Revolution's retreat from the matter of women's rights was seconded by the Directory and reaffirmed in Napoleon's Civil Code of 1804. The Civil Code returned women to the rule of the patriarch. Their property rights and personal freedoms were again sharply restricted, and they were restored to political nullity.

The Struggle for Women's Suffrage From that nullity, liberalism and socialism offered different possibilities of emancipation. Liberalism seemed to promise women the same freedom and rights that it promised men. In Britain and the United States, progress was made toward achieving that goal. John Stuart Mill advocated women's complete civil equality, to be marked by voting rights and the ability to hold political office. In 1867 he proposed a woman's suffrage amendment to the Reform Bill that expanded the male franchise. The amendment's failure prompted the formation the following year of the National Society for Women's Suffrage that would lead a growing movement for voting rights.

Thereafter, mostly middle-class women activists focused on suffrage at the expense of other issues, such as jobs or training. The movement came to a head with the protests of Emmeline Pankhurst (1858–1928), joined by her own daughters and other followers, whose demands for political rights turned militant in the early twentieth century. Imitating tactics employed by agitators for Irish independence, they smashed windows, cut telegraph wires, and vandalized post boxes. "The argument of the broken pane of glass," proclaimed Pankhurst, "is the most valuable argument in modern politics." Their acts of civil disobedience resulted in imprisonment and, when they protested with hunger strikes, painful and demeaning forced feeding.

Progress was also made in areas besides the franchise. By 1865, twenty-nine states of the United States granted married women the right to own and administer property. The British Parliament followed suit in 1882. Before 1900, women's colleges were established at the old English universities (Girton and Newnham at Cambridge; Somerville and Lady Margaret Hall at Oxford), and women gained admittance to the University of London, as they did to some colleges and universities in the United States. The British philanthropist Josephine Butler (1828–1906) defended women's rights by opposing the Contagious Diseases Acts (in force 1864–1886), which instituted the medical regulation of prostitutes. The *Englishwomen's Journal* and other publications kept readers informed of issues important to women.

Emmeline Pankhurst: *Founder of the Women's Franchise League and the Women's Social and Political Union, Emmeline Pankhurst often turned to violence in her fight for women's suffrage.*

The Struggle for Social Equality Feminists also turned to socialism for a more radical analysis of the sources of women's social inequality. Why were women still pressed into subordination to men, principally fathers and husbands? Why were their rights to own and dispose of property, especially if married, still limited? Why did their husbands, not they, have custodial rights to children? Why was divorce largely unavailable in the event of marital breakdown? Why was adultery still seen as a woman's crime? Why should women not enjoy the same sexual liberty that men had always claimed? Why were all women outside the protected zone of the elite—servants and workers—considered the proper sexual prey of elite men?

Just as socialism, and especially Marxism, offered men of the laboring classes the dream of freedom from the domination by whose who monopolized the ownership of property, it offered women of all classes freedom from the domination of the very same men—as heads of propertied households, at once their employers and their male kin.

The early socialists already included the emancipation of women in their visionary plans to reform society. Though the household remained their fundamental unit, Fourier's phalansteries granted women complete economic and sexual freedom. Fourier himself saw the liberation of women as an index of human liberation, announcing that, as a general principle, "social progress and historic changes occur by virtue of the progress of women toward liberty." Saint-Simon and his followers posited women's right to inherit property and to full citizenship status. In 1832, the Saint-Simonian women's newspaper *La Tribune des Femmes* ("The Women's Tribune") argued for the combined struggle for emancipation of women and workers. After Marx's death, his benefactor and collaborator Engels delineated the historical progress of the subjugation of women in *The Origin of the Family, Private Property, and the State* (1884).

The confluence of socialism and feminism, seen especially in France, was most dramatically realized in the revolutions that periodically erupted there throughout the nineteenth century. In 1848, women's political clubs sprang up in Paris, much as they had after 1789. Their concerns were economic and political, but also addressed issues concerning the family and sexuality. In 1870, again, women's intense political activism embraced both the economic and political issues that concerned their male colleagues, and issues of particular interest for women. The suppression of the Commune marked a defeat not only for the working class, but for women as well.

Feminism drew on both liberal and socialist theory in its quest for the further liberation of human sexuality. Medieval restrictions on sexual expression were enforced by the Roman Catholic Church. Even harsher sanctions were introduced in the early modern era, which prosecuted the "crimes" of sodomy, infanticide, and witchcraft (linked to a variety of deviant sexual activities). The seventeenth and eighteenth centuries saw an upsurge of libertinism among the elites, accompanied by the circulation of pornography and obscene political art and writing. By the revolutionary era, the novels of the French nobleman, the Marquis de Sade (1740–1814), described practices, deemed deviant in the extreme, that caused pleasure through the infliction of pain.

During the nineteenth century, despite great reticence about sexual matters, evidence mounts of the increased intensity of romantic courtship and love within marriage; so does that of resistance to restrictions on premarital and homosexual activity, and on women's sexuality within and outside of marriage. During the last decades before 1914, at least among the vanguard urban elite of western Europe, an era of greater sexual freedom began to dawn.

FIN DE SIÈCLE AND THE ADVENT OF THE MODERN

The *fin de siècle* ("end of the century") and the first years of the new century saw a riotous repudiation of traditional restraints on behavior, thought, and expression. The long weekend was cut short by the outbreak of war in 1914 (see Chapter 25). By then, Europe's cultural world had cut loose from its past; its religious and moral systems crumbled. Their place was taken by new understandings of the human mind, new models of the structure of the universe, and new ways of seeing the world, supplied by the scientists, philosophers, writers, and artists who created the Modern.

The Death of God

During the nineteenth century, the religious outlook that had characterized Western civilization since its origins had come under attack on all sides. The eighteenth century saw the growth of evangelical movements that appealed to the poor and lower middle-class—the **Methodists** in England, and the **Pietists** in the German lands, for example. Post-revolutionary conservatism and Romantic nostalgia had promoted Catholic revivals in France and England, an Anglican revival in England, and an invigorated orthodoxy among German Lutherans. But these revivals did not prevent the decline of the churches that marked the late nineteenth century. Church attendance dropped, especially among men. Christianity, especially Roman Catholicism, became a woman's concern. Judaism yielded to secularization as some successful Jews assimilated with a mainstream culture. By 1914, though religion remained the mainstay of the rural poor and of bourgeois homemakers, urban workers, self-confident elites, and cultivated opinion-makers had largely abandoned it.

Profound religious faith did not die out entirely among intellectuals, however. The Danish theologian and philosopher Sören Kierkegaard (1813–1855) powerfully argued for the centrality of religious experience. Tormented by the disintegration of spiritual confidence, seeing no certain or concrete demonstration of God's existence, he nevertheless advocated a radical choice for Christian theism. In England, the sermons and tracts of John Henry Newman (1801–1890) guided a revival of Anglicanism (the "Oxford Movement"). Following his conversion to Catholicism in 1845, Newman led many of his followers back to that faith.

The "death of God"—for thus the philosopher Friedrich Nietzsche (1844–1900) hailed the downfall of the religious outlook—followed from the twin onslaught of science and revolution. By its nature, the scientific outlook disputes the religious. In search of system and certainty, scientists pushed aside the mysterious nebula that necessarily enfolds religious experience. The unavoidable rivalry between science and religion began with the first phases of the Scientific Revolution (see Chapter 17), and troubled the careers of Copernicus, Galileo, and Bruno.

WITNESSES

The *Fin de Siècle* and the Advent of the Modern

Fyodor Dostoevsky's "Underground Man" declares the primacy of the will, personality, and irrational urges (1864): Oh, tell me, who first declared . . . that man only does nasty things because he does not know his own real interests; and that if he were enlightened, if his eyes were opened to his real normal interests, man would at once become good and noble. . . . You see, gentlemen, reason, gentlemen, is an excellent thing, there is no disputing that, but reason is only reason and can only satisfy man's rational faculty, while will is a manifestation of all life, that is, of all human life including reason as well as all impulses. And although our life, in this manifestation of it, is often worthless, yet it is life nevertheless and not simply extracting square roots. . . . But I repeat for the hundredth time, there is one case, one only, when man may purposely, consciously, desire what is injurious to himself, what is stupid. . . . This very stupid thing . . . this caprice of ours, may really be more advantageous for us, gentlemen, than anything else on earth . . . because . . . it preserves for us what is most precious and most important—that is, our personality, our individuality.
(Fyodor Dostoevsky, *Notes From the Underground*, 1864; ed. E. P. Dutton, 1988)

Friedrich Nietzsche repudiates morality and religion (1888):
What is good?—All that heightens the feeling of power, the will to power, power itself in man.
What is bad?—All that proceeds from weakness.
What is happiness?—The feeling that power *increases*—that a resistance is overcome.
Not contentment, but more power; *not* peace at all, but war; *not* virtue, but proficiency (virtue in the Renaissance style, *virtù*, virtue free of moralic acid).
The weak and ill-constituted shall perish: first principle of *our* philanthropy. And one shall help them to do so.
(Friedrich Nietzsche, *Twilight of the Idols/The Anti-Christ*, 1888; ed. R. J. Hollingdale, 1968)

Sigmund Freud on civilization's discontent (1930): Men are not gentle creatures who want to be loved . . . ; they are, on the contrary, creatures among whose instinctual endowments is to be reckoned a powerful share of aggressiveness. As a result, their neighbour is for them not only a potential helper or sexual object, but also someone who tempts them to satisfy their aggressiveness on him, to exploit his capacity for work without compensation, to use him sexually without his consent, to seize his possessions, to humiliate him, to cause him pain, to torture and to kill him. . . . Civilization has to use its utmost efforts in order to set limits to man's aggressive instincts. . . . Hence, therefore, the use of methods intended to incite people into . . . relationships of love, hence the restriction upon sexual life, and hence too the ideal's commandment to love one's neighbour as oneself—a commandment which is really justified by the fact that nothing else runs so strongly counter to the original nature of man. . . .
(Sigmund Freud, *Civilisation and its Discontents*, 1930; ed. J. Strachey, 1961)

The French poet Guillaume Apollinaire discusses the new trends in art (1913): [Modernist] painters, while they still look at nature, no longer imitate it, and carefully avoid any representation of natural scenes which they may have observed. . . . Real resemblance no longer has any importance, since everything is sacrificed by the artist to truth, to the necessities of a higher nature whose existence he assumes, but does not lay bare. The subject has little importance any more. Generally speaking, modern art repudiates most of the techniques of pleasing devised by the great artists of the past. While the goal of painting is today, as always, the pleasure of the eye, the art-lover is henceforth asked to expect delights other than those which looking at natural objects can easily provide.
(Guillaume Apollinaire, *The Cubist Painters: Aesthetic Meditations*, 1913; ed. L. Abel, 1962)

A new phase of that conflict began with Darwin's announcement of his theory of evolution. The theory of evolution ruled out neither the existence of God nor the human experience of worship. But it did refute the notion of a divine creation at one moment and for all time. God's creative activity, if that notion was not abandoned altogether, was confined to an earlier moment in cosmic history than the creation of the biological species. Those evolved continuously over vast reaches of time, without divine intervention, through entirely natural mechanisms. **Darwinism** outraged traditionalists all over the West, and outrages many still. It constituted a revolution in thought; as some would claim, the single most important one of the nineteenth century.

Darwin was not himself an enemy of religion; Marx was. For him, religious institutions were at best instruments of the bourgeoise in their oppression of the proletariat. At worst, they promoted obfuscations that kept the defenseless poor enthralled—religion was, as he succinctly put it, the "opiate of the masses." Aside from some mystical elements in utopian socialism, and the compassionate radicalism of the Christian socialist parties, nineteenth-century socialism and its descendants were unswervingly atheistic.

Contemporary philosophy also dispensed with God. During the Enlightenment, philosopher Immanuel Kant (1724–1804) had both elevated rational criteria of judgment, and shown their compatibility with a secular morality. During the Romantic era, Hegel marked the progress through history of supreme spiritual values. Neither Kant nor Hegel attached their moral or spiritual views explicitly to traditional Christianity. A generation later, Arthur Schopenhauer (1788–1860), influenced by both Romanticism and Indian mysticism, described a universe driven alternatively by "will" or "idea"—by an emotion-laden driving force or by rational thought, severing the two tendencies of Western thought that medieval philosophers had coaxed into a synthesis.

The irrational tendencies of Schopenhauer's philosophy reappeared in extreme form in Nietzsche's. With penetrating insight, Nietzsche lambasted all the shaky preconceptions and prejudices of his day—including, or so it seemed to him, the trite promises of religion. He unwrapped the hypocrisy of moralistic bourgeois shopkeepers, of self-satisfied politicians, of slogan-spouting demagogues, of silken-tongued professors, of Christianity (a "slave religion") and Judaism. Above all these ordinary folk, he elevated the "superman" (*Übermensch*)—an individual of supreme will and daring, who disdained to be bound by any strictures of morality or tradition. Modernism reaches its epitome in Nietzsche, whose trenchant prose disposed of dead ideals and transported Western civilization beyond the rigors of Good and Evil.

New Visions

The new worldview, termed **Modernist**, that emerges in Nietzsche's work was not merely destructive. A new world was emerging, as new visions of reality formed. Among the heralds of a dawning twentieth-century worldview, Sigmund Freud (1856–1939) and Albert Einstein (1879–1955) stand out.

Sigmund Freud A medical doctor specializing in neurology, Freud developed from his clinical work (notably with women suffering from mental illnesses that the nineteenth century diagnosed as "hysteria") the theory of the **unconscious**. This Modernist concept threw overboard the Western understanding of mind—that it was essentially rational. Instead, Freud described forces that operated below the level of consciousness—desires for pleasure, instincts of rage (the realm of the id, Latin for "it")—to modify behavior not quite successfully directed either by the rational, conscious self (the ego, or "I"), or the body of rules and conventions imprinted on the mind in early childhood (the superego, "above the ego").

From Freud's theories developed the modern fields of clinical psychology, psychiatry, and psychotherapy, with wide-ranging consequences for counseling, education, and social work. More, they yielded a more complex understanding of human personality as it functioned in life and in the arts. Modernism here gave birth to the modern human being.

Albert Einstein Einstein reshaped the Western understanding of the universe as Freud did that of the self, rupturing the Newtonian cosmos and describing one more complex, more dynamic, and more fraught with uncertainty. Two major contributions can be noted which profoundly affected general culture as well as the more specialized concerns of physicists.

The first of these is the theory of **relativity**. If the speed of light is constant, and natural laws prevail, then time and motion will be relative to the observer. For the scientist, Einstein's theory explains observed cosmic phenomena. For the lay person, what once appeared to be dependably true had become relative, or mutable. What seems true here is not necessarily true there; what is true now is not necessarily true later; even the ideas of here, there, now, and then are fluid and undefinable.

WHO'S WHO

In the Arts: the Second Generation (1789–1914)

Frédéric Chopin (1810–1849) Polish-born French Romantic pianist and composer.

George Eliot (1819–1880) Pseudonym of Mary Ann Evans; English Realist novelist who developed techniques of psychological analysis used widely in subsequent literature.

Claude Monet (1840–1926) French painter; pioneer and advocate of Impressionism.

Emile Zola (1840–1902) French Realist novelist; his Rougon-Macquart series of twenty "naturalist" novels were presented as "social history."

James Joyce (1882–1941) Irish Modernist novelist; his major works, including *Ulysses* (1922) and *Finnegan's Wake* (1934), are bold experiments in language and method.

Pablo Picasso (1881–1973) Spanish Modernist painter; best known for his development of Cubism.

Igor Stravinsky (1882–1971) Russian Modernist composer; his "The Rites of Spring"—which violated accepted standards of tone and rhythm—outraged its audience when first performed in Paris in 1913.

The second contribution was the principle that the relation between mass and energy could be expressed in an equation; thus they were convertible, and one could be changed into the other. The equation is the famous $e = mc^2$, stating that a quantity of energy (e) can be obtained which is equal to the mass of a particle (m) times the square of the velocity of light (c). For scientists, this principle had many applications. For the world at large, it underlay the development of the most terrible weapon ever known, the atomic bomb, whose explosive force derives from the release of tremendous energy from a small quantity of matter. An idealist and pacifist, Einstein was horrified by the prospect of a bomb, understanding from the first the destructive potential of his apparently innocent equation (see Chapter 29).

Modernism and the Arts In a universe where things were relative and the human mind was not what it seemed, literature and the arts took new directions. Such writers as the Swedish dramatist August Strindberg (1849–1912), the American poet Ezra Pound (1885–1972), and the Irish novelist James Joyce (1882–1941), among others, hammered out forms of expression appropriate to a new age.

In the visual arts, Modernist tendencies appeared as early as the 1860s. From the Renaissance forward, the artist's skill was measured by his or her ability to represent clearly defined subjects—a building, a dramatic scene, or a beautiful woman (see Chapter 13). By the later nineteenth century, the primacy of the object yielded to a different imperative. The modern artist's goal became the depiction of the experience of a fleeting moment, to see with the artist's inner vision. The paraphernalia of daily life were matter to be manipulated by the artist's mind and hand.

The French Impressionists can be considered the first school of modern art, although this term is imprecise. Claude Monet (1840–1926) and Pierre Auguste Renoir (1841–1919), among others, painted domestic scenes, landscapes, and figures with a new intent. They studied the effects of light, which varies at different moments of the day, changing our perception of forms. In 1874, this group of young painters presented an exhibition of their paintings—disdaining the official annual Salon of the French Academy, which had previously refused their work. From the title of Monet's picture *Impression–Sunrise*, they became known as Impressionists. Though attacked by art critics at first, by the 1880s the new style had triumphed; by 1886 it had been superseded.

Where the Impressionists tried to capture visual reality through the sparkling, momentary play of light, younger innovators focused on the turbulent inner world of emotions and the unconscious. The Dutch painter Vincent van Gogh (1853–1890) invested people, landscapes, and simple objects with the intensity of his personal world. His *Potato Eaters* (1885), portraying a family of miners, is a supreme expression of the impoverishment of the human spirit. His depictions of ordinary objects—his shoes, his chair—describe in worn leather and bent wood his own passionate and suffering nature. His *Starry Night* (1889) portrays the modern cosmos, the explosive sky overwhelming the natural landscape, in which human beings must dwell.

In the twentieth century, artists turned from representationalism to paint **abstract** forms. The Russian Vasily Kandinsky (1866–1944) sought to express ideas and evoke emotions by the sheer power of line and color, unmediated by exposition of realistic objects. The Spanish master Pablo Picasso (1881–1973), who explored many stylistic approaches

Claude Monet, Impression–Sunrise, 1872

WINDOWS ON

Fin de Siècle and the Advent of the Modern

Modernism arose as nineteenth-century notions of God, progress, order, and purpose collapsed before the twin onslaught of science (especially Darwinism) and Revolution. While Friedrich Nietzsche and Sigmund Freud helped dismantle the presuppositions of Western society—especially Christianity, traditional morality, and the presumption of human rationality—Impressionist, Post-Impressionist, Expressionist, and abstract styles inaugurated Modernism in the visual arts.

Impressionists such as Claude Monet—here represented by his Impression–Sunrise *(top)—strove to describe their inner worlds rather than recreate the outer world represented by Western artists since the Renaissance. The Impressionists were soon overtaken by other artists and styles, each increasingly non-representational. In the Post-Impressionist* Starry Night *by Vincent Van Gogh (center), the heavens throb and pulse with light and energy, totally overwhelming the frail mortal realm beneath.*

During the twentieth century, artists including the Russian Vasily Kandinsky abandoned representation altogether in favor of purely abstract images (bottom).

(top: Musée Marmottan, Paris; center: Museum of Modern Art, New York; bottom: Städtische Galerie im Lenbachhaus, Munich)

Vincent van Gogh, Starry Night, 1889

Vasily Kandinsky, Study for Composition VII, 1913

in the course of his long career, was a pioneer of **Cubism** around 1907. This style fragmented forms into multiple facets, just as the eye in reality takes in objects from several angles. Like Kandinsky, he was painting a reality that dwelled in his mind alone—not what seemed, but what he knew to exist.

In music, also, where representation had never been a possibility, traditional norms fractured in the later nineteenth century. The operas of Richard Wagner (1818–1883) pushed to an extreme the Romantic understanding of music—that it was to express, and arouse, intense emotion. His overpowering musical compositions accompanied a vision of German history, the German soul, and German destiny informed by both Romanticism and nationalism. In this regard, Wagner is often seen as a forerunner of Nazism (see Chapter 27)—a possibility supported by his well-documented anti-Semitism.

In the early twentieth century, Igor Stravinsky (1882–1971) and Arnold Schoenberg (1874–1951) took up a Modernist attack on traditional musical form that paralleled the rejection of representationalism in the visual arts. Stravinsky's ballet *The Rite of Spring*, performed in Paris in 1913, provoked the audience to outrage with its rhythmic and tonal violations of prevailing standards of composition, as well as its celebration of primal emotions and a pagan worldview. Audience members were horrified as dancers clad in bizarre costumes writhed obscenely, accompanied by music that to them was raucous and chaotic. It was the clarion call of the twentieth century.

Schoenberg's **atonal** music, the first examples of which were performed in 1909, aroused not so much horror as confusion. Listeners did not understand the composer's disavowal of the tonal structures that had been the framework of all previous Western music. The new, abstract structures of Schoenberg's compositions not only did not sound tuneful, but they did not seem to communicate any comprehensible human emotion or idea.

This creative ferment among artists and intellectuals scarcely affected the ordinary worker, or merchant, or leisured aristocrat—even as it transformed the mental universe their descendants would inhabit. To the extent that they could, they spent the last decades before World War I amusing themselves. The music halls and cabarets, theaters and beer halls provided light-hearted song and dance—heavily laden, nevertheless, with messages that overturned the moral values of an earlier era. Outside, and in the daylight, an equivalent disruption of norms was accomplished by the new world of speed. In automobiles and balloons, on motorcycles and bicycles, and especially in airplanes, people of all social classes and both genders soared beyond the confined worldview of their ancestors, who had been limited by the compass of nature to the speed of mammalian limbs.

In 1896, the Olympic Games were held again, for the first time since antiquity (see Chapter 4). But these were Modernist games. The ancient Greeks had competed to win glory and to worship their gods. The races run by modern Europeans were complicated by nationalist resentments and by the convulsive efforts by competitors to go faster and get further. Such were the ingredients, too, of the cataclysm that put a stop to the joyous rebellion of the *fin de siècle* and the experiments of Modernism: the first war to engulf the whole of the globe.

Conclusion

THE ADVENT OF THE MODERN AND THE MEANING OF THE WEST

A giant creativity marks the era of Western culture bounded by the French Revolution and the outbreak of World War I. Artists, authors, and intellectuals leapt from Classical, to Romantic, to realist, to modern abstract styles, and from the mission of depicting a reality that existed in fact to one that existed in the mind of the subject. Scientists discovered radiation and the cell, and introduced the theories of evolution, genetic inheritance, and relativity. Biology, chemistry, and physics, along with history, psychology, sociology, and economics, became modern disciplines housed in university departments. The children of peasants and workers went to school in their millions, as they would soon go to war. Liberals, conservatives, nationalists, socialists, communists, anarchists, and feminists spun the webs of their competing ideologies and contended for followers and for power. By 1914, Western culture was Modern and modern people cast aside the traditions that had both guided and constrained them. In 1914, as the following chapter relates, the elders whose values they rejected led the children of the Western world into the cataclysm of world war.

REVIEW QUESTIONS

1. Why did faith in reason decline after the French Revolution? How did Romanticism differ from Classicism in art, music, and literature? How did Romanticism promote the participation of women in cultural life?

2. Why was photography the perfect Realist medium? What was the goal of Realist novelists and historians? Why did historians try to emulate the practices of scientists?

3. What were the major advances in biology and the physical sciences in the nineteenth century? What challenges did Darwinist theory pose to religion and liberalism? How did the fields of economics and sociology develop in the nineteenth century?

4. How did public elementary education affect European society? Why did nineteenth-century liberalism lead to public reform?

5. Why was nationalism opposed to socialism and communism? What was the theory of Marxist socialism? What were the goals of parliamentary socialism before World War I?

6. What was the connection between feminism and socialism? How did scientists, artists, and intellectuals create the modern? Why were Freud and Einstein the "heralds" of the twentieth century?

SUGGESTED READINGS

From Romanticism to Realism

Becker, George, J., *Master European Realists of the Nineteenth Century* (New York: F. Ungar Publishing Company, 1982). Spotlights Chekhov, Flaubert, Zola, and several others.

Honour, Hugh, *Romanticism* (New York: Harper & Row, 1979). Classic account of the historical, intellectual, and political background of European Romanticism.

The Sciences and the Schools

Brooks, Jeffrey, *When Russia Learned to Read: Literacy and Popular Literature, 1861–1917* (Princeton, NJ: Princeton University Press, 1985). The emergence of literate culture in late Tsarist Russia.

Bynum, W. F., *Science and the Practice of Modern Medicine in the Nineteenth Century* (Cambridge: Cambridge University Press, 1994). Examines the interaction of scientific theory and medical practice.

Desmond, Adrian J. and James Moore, *Darwin* (New York: Viking Penguin, 1991). Perhaps the best biography of this important figure.

Maynes, Mary Jo, *Schooling in Western Europe: A Social History* (Albany: State University of New York Press, 1985). Brief, accessible, and interesting study of education reform, its methods, goals, and results.

Quinn, Susan, *Marie Curie: A Life* (New York: Simon & Schuster, 1995). Comprehensive account of this major scientist, placing her firmly in the context of women's history.

Vitezslav, Orel, *Gregor Mendel: The First Geneticist* (Oxford: Oxford University Press, 1996). Excellent biography, covering most aspects of Mendel's life and work.

Ideals and Ideologies

Himmelfarb, Gertrude, *The De-Moralization of Society: From Victorian Virtues to Modern Values* (New York: Alfred A. Knopf, 1995). Stimulating comparison of Victorian and modern values.

McLellan, David, *Karl Marx: His Life and Thought* (New York: Harper & Row, 1974). One of the best recent biographies.

Rendall, Jane, *The Origins of Modern Feminism in Britain, France and the United States 1780–1860* (New York: Schocken Books, 1984). Comparison of women's status in the US, Britain, and France during the first half of the 19th century.

Semmel, Bernard, *John Stuart Mill and the Pursuit of Virtue* (New Haven, CT: Yale University Press, 1984). Outstanding exploration of Mill's thought, emphasizing his consistent choice of virtue over pleasure.

Stites, Richard, *The Women's Liberation Movement in Russia: Feminism, Nihilism and Bolshevism, 1860–1930* (Princeton, NJ: Princeton University Press, 1978). Traces the emergence in Russia of a feminism intimately tied from the first to radical political movements.

Fin de Siècle and the Advent of the Modern

Butler, Christopher, *Early Modernism: Literature, Music and Painting in Europe, 1900–1916* (Oxford: Oxford University Press, 1994). Synthetic examination of early modernism in painting, literature, and music.

Gilman, Sander L., *Freud, Race and Gender* (Princeton, NJ: Princeton University Press, 1993). Contends that *fin de siècle* medical science, and the work of Freud, was permeated by notions of a racialized Jewish identity.

Karl, Frederick Robert, *Modern and Modernism: The Sovereignty of the Artist, 1885–1925* (New York: Atheneum, 1985). Surveys modernism in the visual arts, literature, and music from Post-Impressionism to Surrealism.

Mainardi, Patricia, *The End of the Salon: Art and the State in the Early Third Republic* (Cambridge: Cambridge University Press, 1993). Focusing on the institutions controlling the exhibition of new art, explains how modern style came to the fore in late 19th-century Paris.

Schorske, Carl E., *Fin de Siècle Vienna: Politics and Culture* (New York: Vintage, 1981; orig. Alfred A. Knopf, 1979). Essays on the culture-transforming influence of the Viennese middle class, covering among others Freud, Klimt, and Herzl.

PART SEVEN

TOWARD A NEW WEST

Post-War, Post-Modern, Post-Industrial (1914–2000)

Three enormous conflicts overshadow the twentieth century and put the whole project of Western civilization in jeopardy: World War I, World War II, and the Cold War.

World War I marked the point at which the West was no longer in the ascendant over the other regions of the world. A wounded civilization limped on to confront the crises of economic collapse, social upheavals, and the advance of totalitarian states.

World War II purchased the defeat of fascism, which had threatened to reverse the Western tradition, at the cost of more than 40 million lives. The victory over fascism, won by an alliance of the democratic United States and Britain and the Communist Soviet Union, was a vindication of the civilization of the West.

The Cold War pitched two of the victors of the prior conflict against each other in an epochal duel between communism and capitalism. The two Superpowers faced each other in a bi-polar system that split the world, armed with weapons that could not be used—for they threatened the annihilation of human life itself. The face-off continued until, in 1989, communism began to self-destruct in Europe and the Soviet Union. Meanwhile, the regions of the earth that, in 1900, had been dominated by Europeans had won their autonomy, and claimed their stake in the world of nations. The transmission of knowledge edged out industrial manufacture in the world economy, as systems of communication and transportation came to unite the most remote regions of the earth.

In 1900, the West was secure in its political, military, and cultural superiority. In 2000, after the shock of three massive conflicts, the West inhabits a global world. It is a post-war, post-modern, and post-industrial West that enters the new millennium. Whether it maintains its identity and rediscovers its mission through a reflection on its traditions and achievements is in the hands of the present generation.

THE MIGHTY ARE FALLEN

1860 | 1870 | 1880 | 1890 | 1900 | 1910 | 1920

Politics and War

- Unification of Italy, 1870
- Franco-Prussian War, 1870–71
- Unification of Germany, 1871
- Congress of Berlin on the "Eastern Question," 1878
- Germany and Austria-Hungary form Dual Alliance, 1879
- Italy, Germany, and Austria-Hungary form Triple Alliance, 1882
- Berlin Conference to partition Africa, 1884–85
- Russia and France ally, 1894
- Britain and Japan ally, 1902
- Lenin's *What Is To Be Done?*, 1902
- Britain and France form *Entente Cordiale*, 1904
- Russo-Japanese War, 1904–5
- Revolution in Russia, 1905
- Britain launches first Dreadnought battleship, 1906
- Austria-Hungary annexes Bosnia-Herzegovina, 1908
- Archduke Franz Ferdinand of Austria-Hungary assassinated, June 1914
- Germany invades Belgium, Aug 1914
- Britain declares war on Germany; Battle of Tannenberg, Aug 1914
- Battles of the Marne and Masurian Lakes, Sept 1914
- Battle of Gallipoli, Apr 1915
- Germans sink *Lusitania*, May 1915
- Execution of nurse Cavell, Oct 1915
- Battle of Verdun, Feb 1916
- February Revolution in Russia, March 1917
- Lenin's "April Theses," Apr 1917
- Russian general Kornilov fails to overturn Provisional Government, Sept 1917
- October (Bolshevik) Revolution, Nov 1917
- Woodrow Wilson's "Fourteen Points," Jan 1918
- Treaty of Brest-Litovsk, March 1918
- Second Battle of the Marne, July 1918
- Armistice signed ending war, Nov 1918
- Treaty of Versailles, 1919

Society and Ideas

- Serfdom abolished in Russia, 1861
- First International, 1864
- Slavery abolished in US, 1865
- British Parliament makes school mandatory for children up to 10, 1880
- Bismarck creates social welfare system for workers in Germany, 1883–89
- Combustion engine developed, 1885
- Second International, 1889
- 400 Jews killed in pogrom in Odessa, 1905
- St. Petersburg has 900 factories, 2 million population, 1914

Beyond the West

Qing Dynasty, China, 1644–1912

Atlantic slave trade, 1500–1888

- Meiji Restoration in Japan, 1868
- Suez canal opens, 1869
- Congress of Berlin divides Ottoman empire, 1878
- "Scramble for Africa" begins, 1885
- Indian National Congress founded, 1885
- Chinese lose Sino-Japanese War, 1894–95
- South African War, 1899–1902
- Boxer Rebellion in China, 1900
- Panama Canal opens, 1904
- Japan wins Russo-Japanese War, 1905
- "Young Turks" topple Ottoman sultan, 1908
- Republic declared in China, 1911–12

CHAPTER 25

The Mighty are Fallen

The Trauma of World War I

1914–1920

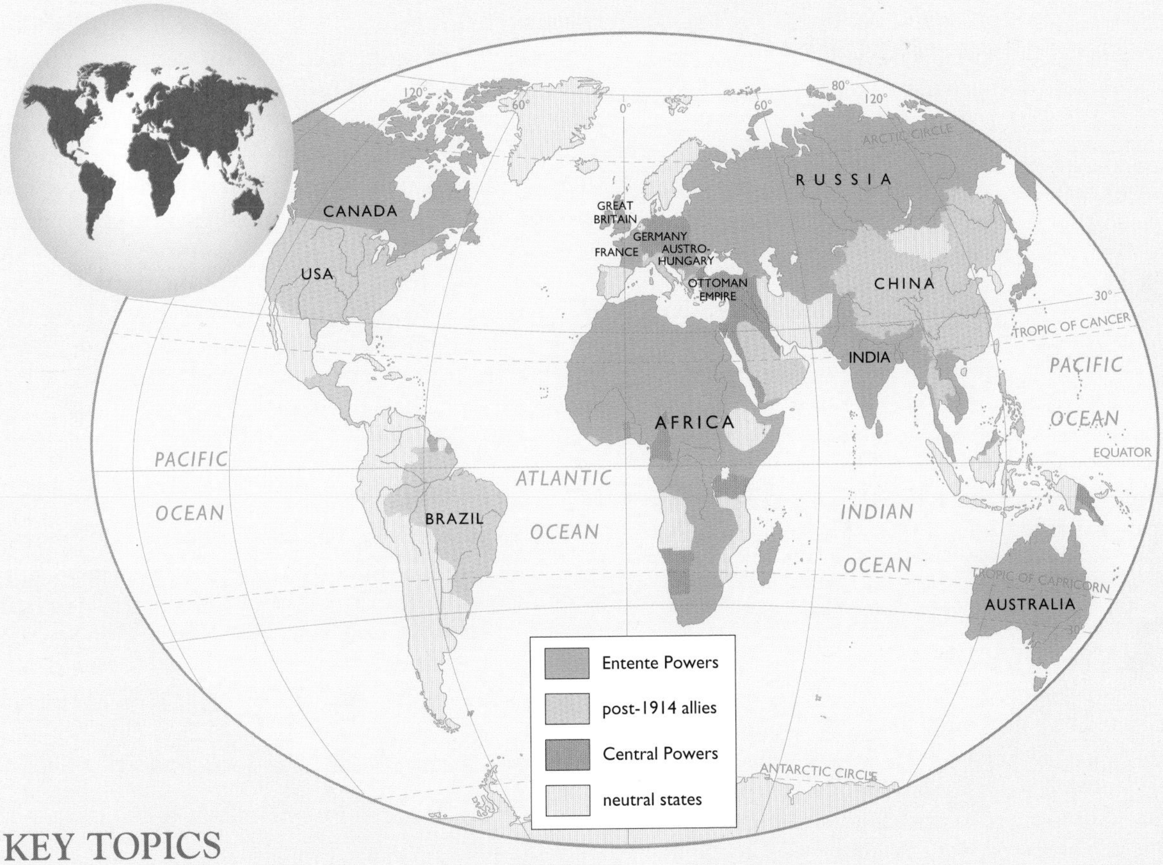

KEY TOPICS

- **Pathways to War:** The states of Europe avoid major conflicts between 1815 and 1914, until an assassin's bullet on the continent's southeastern rim sends a generation of young men off to war.
- **In the Midst of Battle:** On the western front, stalemate and carnage; on the eastern, slaughter; at sea, the stealthy assault of submarines; at home, factories, shops, and services manned by women; in Russia, revolution; repercussions around the world.
- **In Search of Peace:** Like the revolutionary Lenin, the visionary Wilson yearns for peace; but his peace plans become the blueprint for more war to come.

The Generation of 1914 *In August 1914, European leaders sent a generation to war. In companies, brigades, and regiments, young men marched off to the cheers of parents, teachers, and kings, their minds set on honor and glory. They found slaughter, filth, vermin, starvation, and disease. More than 65 million fought. More than 21 million were wounded by bullets, bombs, and poison gas, or mentally ravaged by the horrors concocted by the most advanced civilization on the globe. More than 8 million died—"the unreturning army that was youth," wrote the English poet Siegfried Sassoon (1886–1967), one of the startling poets this war called forth. And, snarled the American poet Ezra Pound (1885–1972), for what purpose?*

> *For an old bitch gone in the teeth,*
> *For a botched civilization.*

When the smoke finally cleared, the mighty too had fallen—emperors, politicians, and generals were dead, and with them the complacency of an age irretrievably gone. The remnant of the generation of 1914 stumbled on into the rest of the twentieth century without a guide and stalked by despair.

This chapter traces the origins, course, and settlement of the war that brought down the generation of 1914 and its elders, and radically altered the history of the West.

PATHWAYS TO WAR

Many paths led to global conflagration, the first major European conflict since the Napoleonic wars. During the "long century" between the post-Napoleonic settlement at Vienna in 1815 and the first hostilities of 1914, diplomats secured the cooperation of contending nations and resolved potential conflicts. Their efforts were largely successful; except for colonial ventures and brief outbreaks of limited war, Europe was at peace. Even so, as the old century turned, hidden threats to peace, at home and in faraway continents, asserted themselves. Beneath the calm surface, seeds of conflict had already sprouted.

Congresses, Alliances, and Conflicts

During the nineteenth century, European leaders resolved most disputes by diplomatic agreement, sometimes in congresses involving the representatives of several nations. The Congress of Vienna provided the model for these diplomatic summits. Later congresses held at Berlin in 1878 and 1884–1885 dealt with some important issues—the European balance of power and the regulation of colonial acquisitions (see Chapter 23)—but failed to resolve others.

Despite such efforts, some disputes broke out in wars. The Crimean War (1853–1856) pitted French, Piedmontese (Italian), British, and Turkish armies against Russia, whose ambitions in the Black Sea region under Ottoman rule threatened British commercial and naval interests. Napoleon III of France (r. 1850–1873) supported Britain, while Camillo di Cavour (1810–1861), premier of Piedmont-Sardinia supported France in exchange for services in Italy. These allied western European powers intervened to prop up the Ottomans, delivering Russia to a decisive defeat. The Russians retired to digest the meaning of their failure, which would soon stimulate political reforms and an accelerated program of industrialization.

Three years later, Napoleon III allied with Cavour again, reluctantly, this time against Austria in the Austro-Sardinian war of 1859. The two allies defeated the Habsburg army, and obtained Austrian withdrawal from the northern Italian province of Lombardy (although it retained Venetia), an important step toward the eventual unification of Italy in 1870 (see Chapter 20).

Before 1866, the Austrian Empire outweighed Prussia in political importance; but Prussia seized the advantage in the Austro-Prussian war of that year. In a conflict lasting only seven weeks, it humiliated

HOW MANY?

Great Power Battle Deaths in European Wars, 1803–1918

Napoleonic Wars (1803–1815)	1,869,000
Crimean War (1853–1856)	217,000
Franco-Prussian War (1870–1871)	180,000
World War I (1914–1918)	7,734,300

Source: *C. Tilly,* Coercion, Capital and European States, AD 990–1990 *(Cambridge, MA: Basil Blackwell, 1990), pp. 165–166.*

Austria, weakening its influence within the German Confederation. The next step followed shortly: German unification under Prussian auspices.

The Franco-Prussian war of 1870–1871 accomplished the political humiliation of France. It was fought over the same strip of territory for which Charlemagne's grandsons contended in the ninth century, and resulted in the annexation by Prussia of part of it—the rich provinces of Alsace and Lorraine. It also precipitated the collapse of the Second Empire, the departure of Emperor Napoleon III, and the inauguration of the French Third Republic.

While Europeans confined themselves to a few wars on their own territory, abroad they battled freely as they saw fit (see Chapter 23). In Asia, Britain suppressed rebellion in India and waged war on China, while Russia struggled with (and lost to) Japan. In Africa, the European colonial powers battled native armies, nearly always overcoming their huge numbers with a maximum of firepower and a minimum of casualties—on the European sides. In Indochina and North Africa, the competing colonial interests of European nations caused friction, but these difficulties generally fell short of military confrontation.

The swift, brisk wars of the nineteenth century were not greatly dangerous. Yet they may have encouraged complacency about the frightening possibilities of sustained warfare between industrialized nations. Diplomats labored to ward off potential conflicts, nevertheless, by constructing complex (and secret) defensive alliances. These proliferated toward the end of the century.

Two general patterns of alliance can be discerned, one succeeding the other, with Russian **Pan-Slavism** serving as the hinge. Pan-Slavism was a nationalistic movement seeking to promote the common interests of all ethnic Slavs, including those under Austro-Hungarian control. Until the 1880s, Austria and Prussia (later Germany) were allied with Russia, while France and Britain remained aloof. From the 1880s, however, Russian Pan-Slav policies antagonized the central European empires, with Russia eventually finding support from France and Britain. The latter two nations had traditionally been enemies; now political shifts united their interests on the eve of world war.

The earlier of the two alliance systems began with the Holy Alliance of Austria, Prussia (later Germany), and Russia, a product of the counter-revolutionary agenda of the Congress of Vienna, which aimed to reassert the authority of monarch and church. In this agreement, the three rulers of central and eastern Europe sought to promote the interests of their churches, and to gain enhanced reputation from their role as protectors of religion. The three-party alliance was revived at the instance of German Chancellor Otto von Bismarck (1815–1898) in the Three Emperors' League of 1873 (renewed in 1881), even after Austria-Hungary had joined the other combatants in punishing Russia in the Crimea.

The second alliance system emerged in the aftermath of the Crimean War. Russia's earlier solidarity with the two central European emperors had been shaken in the Crimea and destroyed by the Congress of Berlin of 1878. After 1890, Russia sought the support of the two remaining Great Powers—France and Britain. Long-standing cultural ties united France and Russia, recently strengthened by infusions of French capital to fund Russia's railroads and burgeoning industries. By 1894, the two nations had forged a joint defensive alliance.

Insular Britain, sheltered by navy power, refused initially to join any of the alliance systems that entwined the European nations in a web of mutual assurance and fear. Her natural sympathies were with Germany, and she had long been hostile to France. Rapid German naval buildup in the late 1890s soon eroded those sympathies. By 1904, Britain's diplomats inclined to France, with whom they signed the Entente Cordiale ("cordial agreement").

Britain did not as yet turn to Russia, with whom it competed for influence in Persia (modern Iran) and Afghanistan. Moreover, after 1902, Britain supported Japan, the world's newest industrialized power, which was soon to defeat Russia in the Russo-Japanese War of 1904–1905 (see Chapter 23). By 1907, nevertheless, deciding that Russia was less of a threat than Germany, and seeking friends where they could be had, Britain settled its differences with its rival in the Middle East. The Entente Cordiale, enlarged by the participation of Russia, was now the Triple Entente. In response, Germany and Austria-Hungary formed the Dual Alliance of 1879, which Italy joined (but would desert during wartime) to make the Triple Alliance in 1882. The powers of the Triple Entente and Triple Alliance faced each other, tense with mutual fears, in the last years before 1914.

The furious signing of treaties of alliance, accelerating as the new century turned, testified to mounting political tensions. These radiated from several troublespots. All would figure in the conflict of world war.

Hot Spots

In the decades before the outbreak of World War I, the map of the globe was dotted with "hot spots," or danger zones where long resentment and counterposed interests provided fertile ground for conflict.

French and German interests collided in the area west of the Rhine. French leaders and patriots saw the German seizure of the provinces of Alsace and Lorraine following the Franco–Prussian War as a tragic and unforgivable provocation.

Germany also faced a rival to the east. Here Russia, long dependent on western European technology and experts, was beginning to modernize and industrialize. A formidable military power, it had lost face, nevertheless, by its defeats in the Crimea and by the Japanese, and was troubled by revolution in 1905. Russia still looked strong, however, and with its Polish and Ukrainian territories loomed dangerously close to Germany's eastern border.

Russia also posed a threat to Austria-Hungary (a "dual monarchy" after 1867; see Chapter 20) and to the whole of Europe as a result of its policies in the Balkans. As Ottoman power in the region waned after 1699 (see Chapters 15, 20), the peoples of the Balkans sought to gain national autonomy, while Austria-Hungary sought to extend its sphere of influence southward into the peninsula. After the Berlin conference of 1878, Austria-Hungary effectively ruled Herzegovina and Bosnia, which they annexed in 1908. Finding that their Ottoman masters had been replaced by Austrian ones, Serb nationalists vowed resistance.

The Slavic-speaking Balkan peoples who lived under Austro-Hungarian rule were ethnically related but culturally diverse. They included Roman Catholic Croats and Slovenes with allegiances to Rome and western Europe; Muslims converted under Ottoman rule; and Eastern Orthodox Serbs who had resisted Ottoman overlordship and had paid heavily for that resistance. The different interests of these diverse groups made for tension and instability.

Outside of the Austro-Hungarian zone, Orthodox Serbs, Bulgars, and Romanians (the latter speaking a Romance language), had won freedom from Ottoman overlordship and formed autonomous states in 1878. As a result of the two short Balkan Wars of 1912–1913, the Turks lost control of the region, except for a belt around Constantinople (modern Istanbul). In addition, the boundaries of the Balkan

WITNESSES

The Onset of War

On the eve of war, nationalist and militarist sentiments abounded, as expressed in these words of the German theorist Heinrich von Treitschke (1915): When the State exclaims: My very existence is at stake! Then social self-seeking must disappear and all party hatred be silent. The individual must forget his own *ego* and feel himself a member of the whole, he must recognize how negligible is his life compared with the good of the whole. Therein lies the greatness of war that the little man completely vanishes before the great thought of the State.

(Heinrich von Treitschke, *Die Politik*, 1915; eds. M. Perry et al, 1995)

On the eve of Britain's declaration of war British Foreign Secretary Sir Edward Grey explains to the House of Commons why war must be fought and what war might bring (August 4, 1914): We have great and vital interests in the independence ... of Belgium. If Belgium is compelled to submit to allow her neutrality to be violated, of course the situation is clear.... [I]f her [Belgium's] independence goes, the independence of Holland will follow. I ask the House from the point of view of British interests, to consider what may be at stake. If France is beaten ... [and] becomes subordinate to the will and power of one greater than herself ... and if Belgium fell under the same dominating influence, and then Holland, and then Denmark.... We are going to suffer, I am afraid, terribly in this war whether we are in it or whether we stand aside....

(*Hansard's Parliamentary Debates*, 5th Series, vol. 65, 1809–1827)

In London as war is declared, Bertrand Russell, British philosopher and mathematician, is troubled by the bloodthirstiness of the populace (August 15, 1914): Although I did not foresee anything like the full disaster of the war, I foresaw a great deal more than most people did. The prospect filled me with horror, but what filled me with even more horror was the fact that the anticipation of carnage was delightful to something like ninety per cent of the population.... I had supposed that most people liked money better than almost anything else, but I discovered that they like destruction even better.

(Bertrand Russell, Letter to London's *Nation*, August 15, 1914; eds. M. Perry et al, 1995)

nations were redefined to the disadvantage of Bulgaria and the advantage of Serbia, while Albania and Montenegro gained national autonomy. Thereafter Serbia supported Slav resistance to Austrian rule in Bosnia and Herzegovina. So did that other, much larger Orthodox and Slavic nation—the Russian Empire, protector of Pan-Slavic nationalist aspirations. In the Balkans, nationalism was a disruptive force that drove the world to war.

As Russia supported Pan-Slav objectives in the Balkans, it sought to wrest from the decaying Ottoman sultans their strategic post at Constantinople. Constantinople was one of the world's major ports, strategically positioned at the entrance to the Black Sea from the Mediterranean. It had particular interest for Russia, whose only warm-water ports lay in the Black Sea, and whose free access through the Dardanelles strait commanded by Constantinople's fortresses was essential for international trade. While Russia had designs on Constantinople, the other European powers, propping up the empty Ottoman suit, worked industriously to keep the city Turkish.

Weakening Ottoman influence prompted European maneuvers at the extremities of the Ottoman Empire as in southeast Europe. In North Africa, European nations now sought to acquire footholds through military or economic means (see Chapter 23). To the west, Spain and France held protectorates in Morocco. In 1905 and 1911, Germany challenged French authority in Morocco with shows of support for Moroccan autonomy. The two crises these moves precipitated drove France and Britain into alliance. In 1911, the Italians invaded Libya in the center of the north African littoral, while Egypt, where British and French financial interests had long competed, was occupied by British troops from 1882, becoming a protectorate in 1914. In the Middle East, Britain and Russia competed for influence in Persia, Iraq, and Afghanistan.

Far to the east, Japan had acquired the Chinese island of Formosa (Taiwan) in the Sino-Japanese war of 1894–1895. Ten years later, in the Russo-Japanese war, it obtained footholds on the Asian continent, in South Manchuria and Kwantung, as well as the southern half of the island of Sakhalin (Karafuto). In 1910, Japan annexed Korea, and in 1914, when war broke out in Europe, declaring support for the Entente powers, swiftly seized German protectorates in China: Manchuria, Shandong, and Fujian, as well as several Pacific islands. The Chinese simply acquiesced to the territorial claims Japan announced in the Twenty-One Demands, lands Japan was allowed to retain by the 1919 treaties of Paris (see below). Chinese popular outrage at these losses triggered the student-led May Fourth Movement, a focal point in the later revolutionary politics of that nation (see Chapter 28).

In Europe, meanwhile, political tensions would soon erupt into war. On June 26, 1914, in the Bosnian capital of Sarajevo, a nineteen-year-old terrorist of the secret "Black Hand" society shot the Archduke Franz Ferdinand (1863–1914), fifty-year-old sportsman and heir to the Austrian throne, and his wife. The assassination gave Austrian diplomats an opportunity to put pressure on Serbia. Encouraged by Germany, Austria issued an ultimatum; Serbia prevaricated, and Austria declared war, provoking Russian mobilization. These rapid exchanges in late July

Arrest of an assassin: *Nationalism, imperialist squabbles, and a division of Europe into two hostile alliances served as the tinder for war. The fatal spark was supplied by the assassination of the Archduke Franz Ferdinand and his wife in Sarajevo, June 28, 1914—the same day this photograph was taken of the arrest of the adolescent Serbian terrorist Gavrilo Princip (second from right).*

triggered the activation in early August of the European system of alliances for mutual defense. The Serbian assassination and the Austrian ultimatum together cut the cord. For the next four years, the nations of Europe were at war.

Men and Boys at War

With the onset of war, old and young prepared to fight. Elderly diplomats and generals, their experience shaped by memories of such conflicts as the Crimean War and colonial campaigns where Europeans easily outgunned native forces, planned to mobilize a generation of young men.

Even the battle plans of the generals were, on the whole, old. Although Europe's military elite had fought few battles during the nineteenth century, they had constructed many battle plans. German planning was especially intense, both because of the traditional militarism of the old Prussian **Junker** generals, and because of Germany's understandable fear of encirclement. Planted in Europe's center, with neither mountains nor seas as buffers, Germans knew that in any war they might have to face an enemy on two fronts, both west and east.

Addressing this difficulty, Alfred von Schlieffen (1833–1913), veteran of the Franco-Prussian war and former chief of the German General Staff, devised by 1905 the most important of Europe's battle plans. Upon his death at age eighty, in 1913, never having had the opportunity to use it, he bestowed the "Schlieffen plan" upon Field Marshal Helmuth von Moltke (1848–1916), himself a man of advanced age. Von Moltke understood it to be his duty to follow the Schlieffen plan faithfully. The grand design that would determine the destinies of Europe's youth was already a decade old.

Other nations had their battle plans, too. The French Plan XVII urged an offensive posture—"always the offensive!" French generals bellowed—by striking into Alsace and Lorraine and then, from that vantagepoint west of the Rhine, boldly on to Berlin. The British trusted in their new Dreadnought battleships—so named after the first hefty Dreadnought launched in 1906, imposingly armed with heavy-caliber guns—and their traditional naval strength. To support their ally, they would dispatch a small expeditionary force to France. The Austrians had plans, too, but deferred to leadership from Berlin. The Russian army had plans to modernize its weaponry and its communications, goals not yet achieved when war erupted. Its generals sent millions of young peasants off to the front, desperately undersupplied.

In another, subtler way, old men held the fortunes of young men on the eve of world war. In schools and homes, the old taught the young the unhealthy message that their duty to their nation surpassed all other duties, that honor surpassed all other values, and that greatness displayed itself above all on the battlefield. The pseudo-scientific theories that circulated among late nineteenth-century intellectuals (see Chapters 23, 24) taught that some "races" were superior to others, and that the conflicts of nations, like the competition between species, were part of an epochal natural struggle in which the "fittest" would survive. Cultural habits reinforced these beliefs and encouraged an escalating militarism. In the time-honored tradition, boys from elite families played sports as a preparation for war. As though the violent defeat of an adversary could be an elegant game, they strove to fence, hunt, and shoot as gentlemen should, impeccably dressed and in style.

When orders for mobilization went up on walls and were broadcast in the newspapers, a generation of young men lined up for battle, democrats, socialists, and former pacifists together. In Britain, they volunteered. Elsewhere, they were drafted. They went in high spirits, cheered on by their mothers, unaware of the horrors they were to face. The war would be over "before the leaves fall," said the pundits in August; before Christmas, at the very latest. The young men left home trusting the words of their elders, and the war plans that lay ready in the desk drawers of aging generals born in an older Europe. Wrote Rudyard Kipling (1865–1936):

> *If any question why we died,*
> *Tell them, because our fathers lied.*

The generation of 1914 marched as children to the front. Only half returned whole. When they did return, they too were old, grayed by the memory of slaughter.

IN THE MIDST OF BATTLE

Fronts formed immediately where invaders met defenders and no one blinked, but both sides held their ground. Germany faced France and Britain at the western front, parallel lines of fortified trenches stretching from Switzerland to the English Channel. Germany faced Russia on the eastern front, among ravaged villages, swamps, and forests. On the seas, around the world, merchant ships laden with military hardware and foodstuffs bound for Allied ports ran a gauntlet of German **U-boats** (*Unterseeboote*, or submarines), while British battleships choked off the

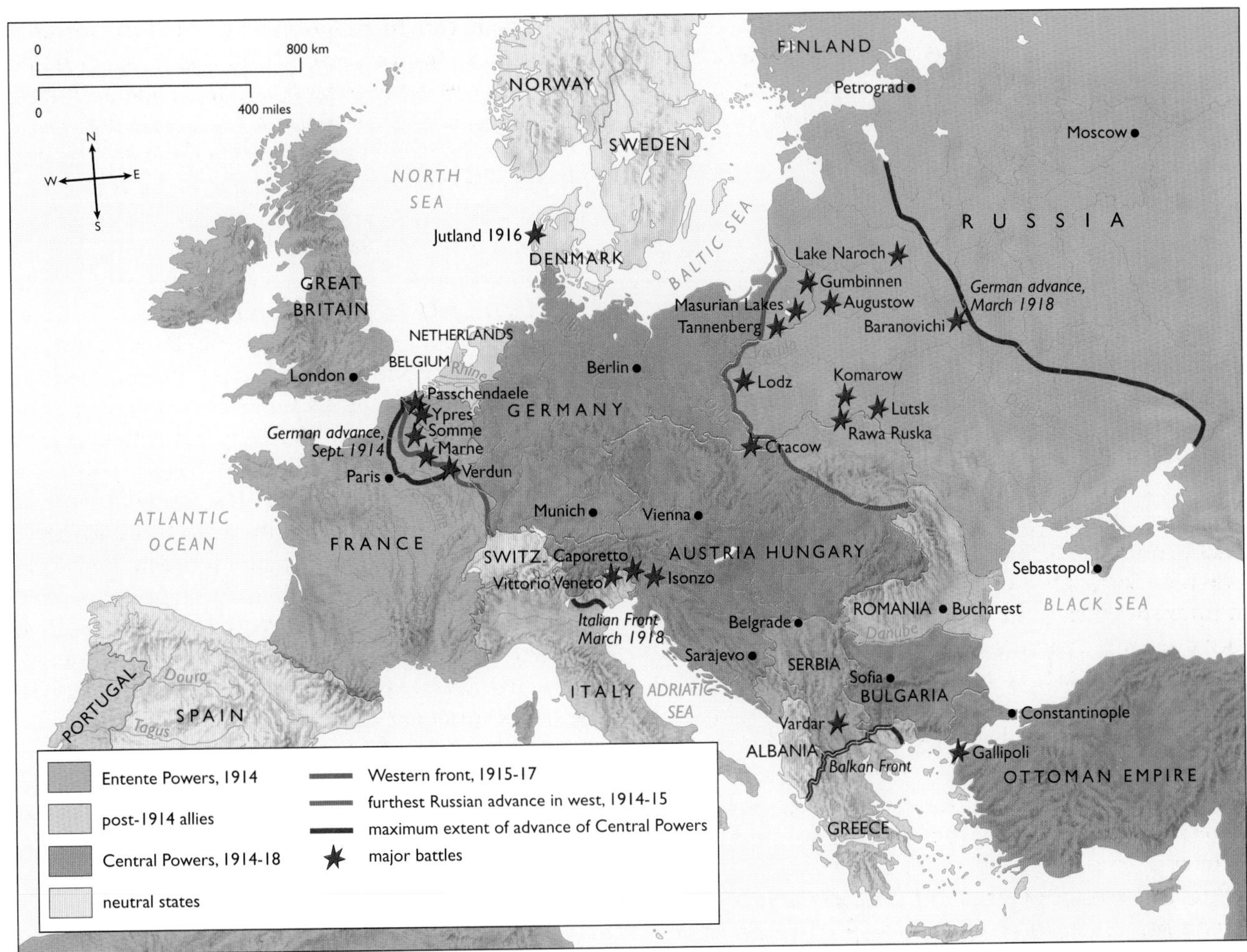

Map 25.1 Europe—A Two-Front War: *After the German army smashed through Belgium and pushed toward the French capital of Paris, war on the western front settled into a stalemate and was fought largely from trenches. Despite staggering loss of life on both sides, little movement was made in either direction. The eastern front was a different matter. While also a very deadly affair, war was fought here on the move, with trenches the exception rather than the rule. The Italians, however, were locked in futile combat with the Austrians during 1915 to 1917, fighting eleven battles at the river Isonzo with negligible result.*

flow of such goods to German ports. At home, women were employed in munitions factories, making the numberless bullets and bombs needed at the fronts, and hoarded food to feed their children. In Russia, soldiers without food to eat or bullets to defend themselves left the military front for the one back home—the struggle for peace, bread, and land.

Stalemate in the West

The Schlieffen plan called for a rapid, disabling blow at France, making possible the concentration of forces on the east to deal with Russia, regarded as the major threat. Although France could be reached from Germany by crossing the Rhine and pounding through Alsace and Lorraine, that was not the route Schlieffen prescribed. Instead, he had proposed a giant encirclement of Paris from the north. German forces would cut through Belgium, violating that nation's neutrality, in a vast arc around Paris, edging so close to the coast that, as Schlieffen envisioned it, a soldier on the powerful right flank might "brush the Channel with his sleeve." Having taken Paris, they would swoop eastward to pounce on the French forces who, as it was rightly predicted, would have foolishly charged to Alsace-Lorraine, leaving the heart of their homeland undefended.

It was only a minor obstacle for the German general staff that Belgium was a neutral nation. At its inception in 1830, the combined nations of Europe had pledged themselves to protect Belgium's neutrality. As Belgium's rulers began to suspect German

Atrocities in Belgium

Belgian refugees: *The German Schlieffen Plan called for a swift strike against France through Belgium and, to the horror of a watching world, the violation of Belgian neutrality. Here, Belgian refugees in Noeux-les-Mines flee from the advancing Germans.*

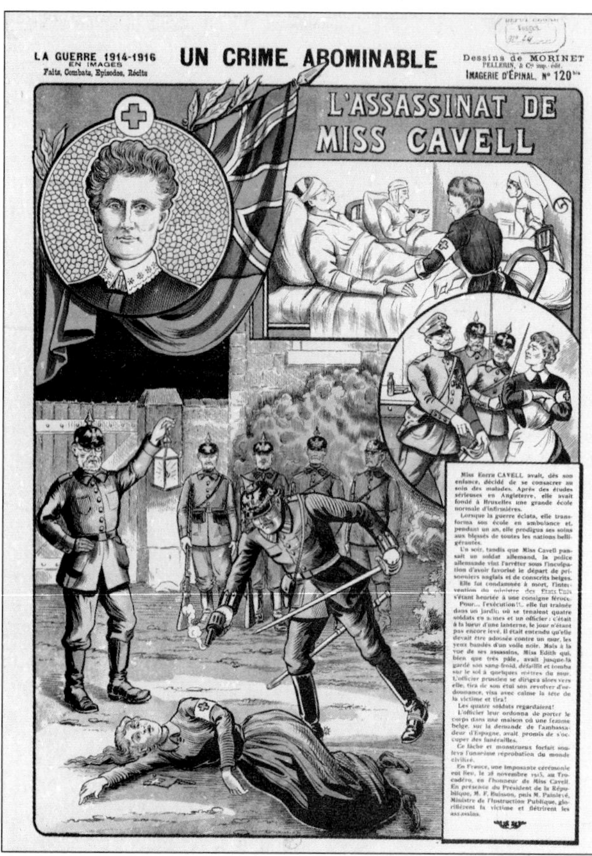

Execution of British nurse Edith Cavell: *This French poster calls upon that nation's citizens to remember the martyrdom of British nurse Edith Cavell, executed in Brussels on October 12, 1915—"an abominable crime." Note the German officer holding a pistol over the dead woman's body—a scene that aroused horror in an era when women were held properly to be exempt from the first-hand sufferings of war.*

designs, they attempted to convince their incredulous allies of the impending crisis. The Germans were already on the move.

The First Moves The great fortifications at Liège, guarding the road to Brussels, were considered the best in Europe. The city was ringed by ramparts, and defended by a garrison; a circle of satellite fortresses surrounded it. It seemed, and should have been, impregnable. But the Belgian army had not yet moved up to defend it. And the Germans came with new long-range guns of an unprecedented destructive capacity. On August 16, 1914, the city surrendered, barely two weeks after the war began. The German invasion thrust on past the Belgian town of Namur, across the river Meuse and into the Ardennes forest.

The German advance through Belgium seemed to display a unique and novel brutality. The resisters who harassed the German advance provoked furious reprisals: the execution of hostages, including women and children, the burning of homes, the slaughter of livestock. At the university town of Louvain, angered by snipers, the German command ordered the citizens to be massacred and the city burned. The library was destroyed, a library that had guarded for centuries one of the finest collections in Europe.

The horrors of the German assault on Belgium were exaggerated further in the propaganda reports that circulated in Britain and France and beyond. Press reports, cartoons, and posters told of brutalized infants, and raped and murdered women, including the British nurse Edith Cavell (1865–1915) who was charged with assisting prisoners and refugees and executed in 1915. Propaganda aroused war fever among the allied nations of western Europe.

For by now, they had formally become military allies. For years, the French pressed the British to agree to a defensive treaty; for years, Britain evaded making that commitment. At last, the British recognized the threat to France, and thus to the Channel, and to themselves. How many men must they send the French as a sign of their support? Just one, responded the French, and we shall be sure that he gets killed—for one British soldier dead by a German bayonet would seal the alliance in the popular mind.

Joining Up

French troops: *The announcement of hostilities was met with general euphoria across Europe. Here, French soldiers depart for war in buoyant mood. In Britain, where there was no system of conscription (until 1916), enthusiastic volunteers crowded into recruiting offices.*

In the end, the British sent an expeditionary force across the Channel, while the French sent troops toward Alsace and Lorraine. The French did not yet comprehend the nature of the war they must fight. Their troops were brightly uniformed, with perky red hats; the Germans marched in a battlefront gray suited to modern warfare. The plan was to attack—"the offensive! Always the offensive!" shouted the French generals, who trusted in the *élan* (a quality of dash or verve) that they believed all Frenchmen to possess. Indeed, they had taken the offensive in Alsace and Lorraine, thus diverting their main strength from the spot where the real enemy vanguard struck—in the Ardennes, where outnumbered French defenders fought German invaders blindly in the forest, with disheartening casualties.

Meanwhile, the British were slow to arrive, slow to fight, and slower still than the French to understand the strength and determination of their opponents. At last, the British Expeditionary Force took its place alongside the French at Mons (Belgium), facing the right of the German offensive front. By August 24, this combined Allied force was in retreat, permitting the Germans to begin their arc toward Paris.

The German forces that set out on that arc were weaker than they should have been—weaker than old Schlieffen had wished, whose dying injunction was "only keep the right wing strong." Von Moltke had detached some troops to resist the French advance in Alsace-Lorraine, and he permitted one of his best generals to leave the western front and begin operations in the east. As a result, the German right wing did not, as intended, sweep west of Paris to encircle it, but slipped down to the east of the capital.

Informed of the German position, the general in charge of the Paris garrison acted promptly. Requisitioning whatever vehicles could be found—including famously the city's taxis—he sent soldiers from the garrison out to join with regular French forces and meet the Germans. Just thirty-five miles from Paris, on the river Marne, these French forces won on September 5–8 one of the most important Allied victories of the war. They stopped the German

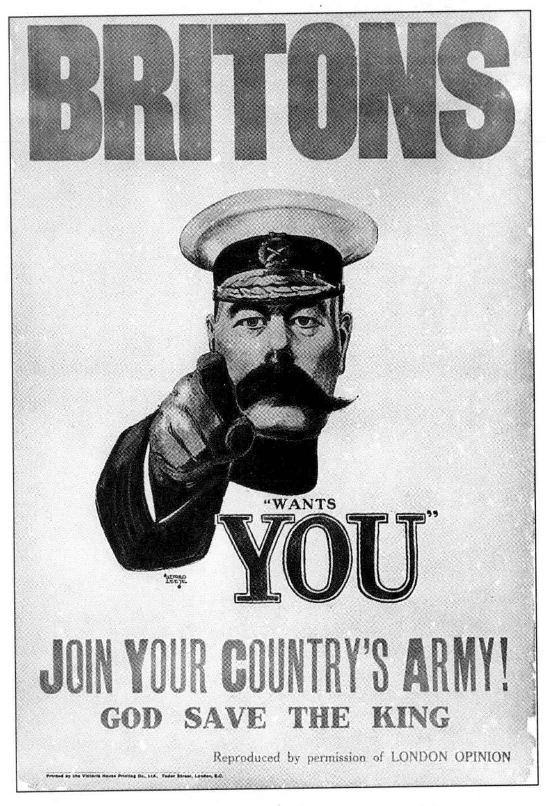

British recruitment: *In a classic recruitment poster from 1914, secretary of war Lord Horatio Kitchener points at the viewer, summoning all Britons to join up and fight for king and country.*

Russian soldiers in trenches

WINDOWS ON

At the Front

Optimism about the war quickly evaporated as reality sank in. In trenches, men who withstood cold, hunger, filth, and rodents faced the onslaught of the enemy, demonstrated here by Russian soldiers who stand guard as the injured are brought in on stretchers (left). In the photograph below, French soldiers wear gas masks in preparation for a German attack with the latest in offensive weapons.

French soldiers in gas masks

advance, denied them Paris, and forced them to retreat. Pushed back forty miles to the river Aisne, the Germans dug a trench, a fortification quickly available wherever there were soldiers with spades.

Digging In Before winter settled in 1914, the line of German trenches stretched from the Aisne north to the Channel, and south past the western face of Alsace to the Swiss border. Opposite those 466 miles of German fortifications stretched a parallel line of trenches dug with French and British spades. From 1914 until 1918, that line scarcely moved, though brave men on both sides hurled themselves repeatedly across the "no-man's land" that lay between the two lines of trenches. In 1915, French offensives in the north gained no ground. In February 1916, the Germans struck mightily at the border fortress of Verdun, killing so many French soldiers that their proclaimed goal to "bleed France white" seemed fulfilled. Yet in this protracted battle that engaged 2 million men, the "victors" suffered casualties nearly as high (350,000) as the French "losers" (400,000).

In July 1916, the British countered with a huge offensive along an eighteen-mile front on the river Somme. Here preliminary bombardment by the British guns ripped up the ground, slowing their own

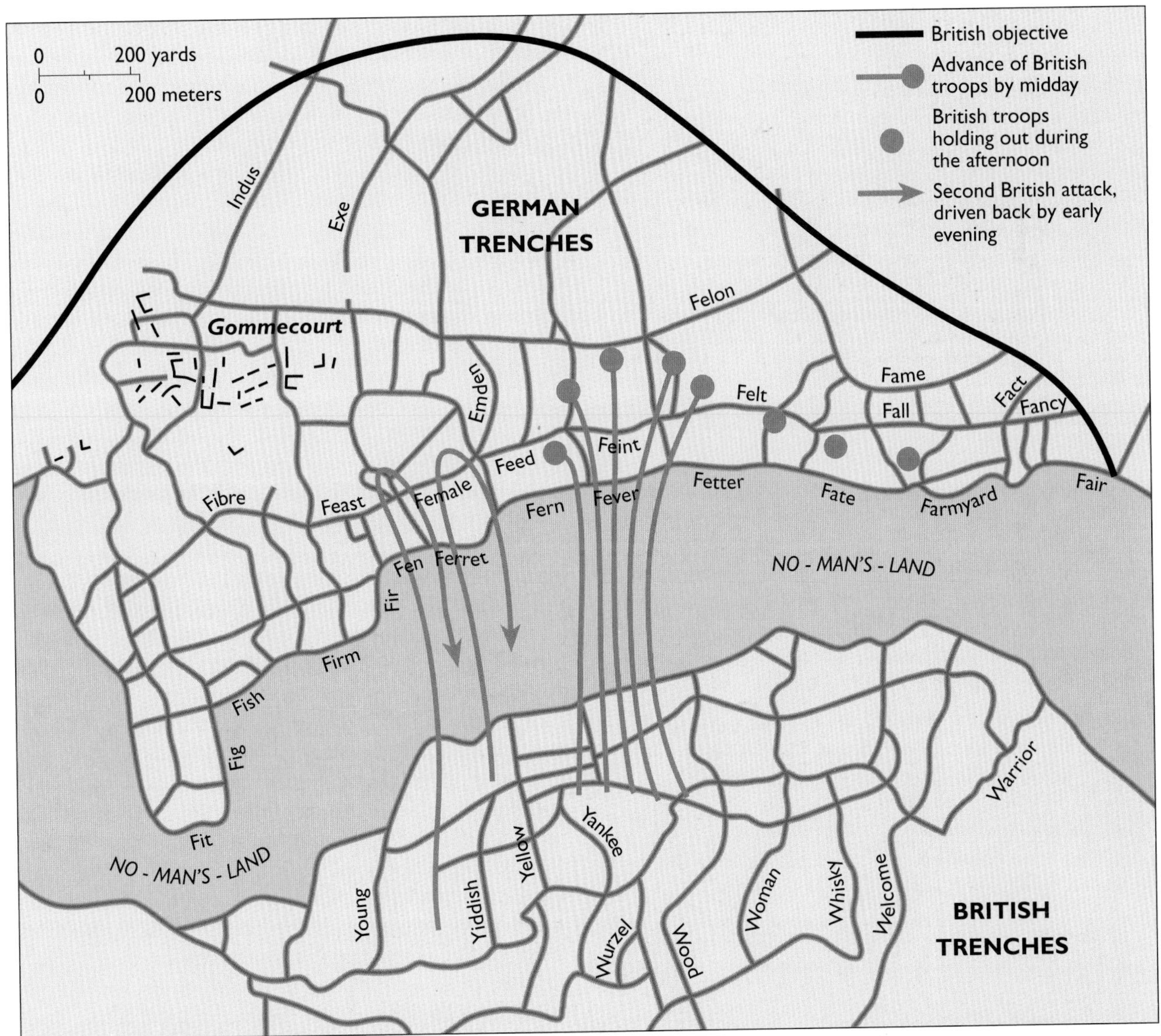

***German and British trenches at the Somme:** This diagram shows the alignment of trenches (named by the soldiers as shown) on the first day of the battle of the Somme (July 1, 1916), when the British charged the German trenches penetrating only 200 yards. On the section of the front shown here, measuring 1000 yards in length, 1000 British soldiers lay dead by the end of the day.*

WITNESSES

At the Front (I)

English soldier and poet Wilfred Owen describes a German gas attack (1915):

Gas! GAS! Quick, boys! – An ecstasy of fumbling,
Fitting the clumsy helmets just in time;
But someone still was yelling out and stumbling,
And flound'ring like a man in fire or lime . . .
Dim, through the misty panes and thick green light,
As under a green sea, I saw him drowning.

In all my dreams, before my helpless sight,
He plunges at me, guttering, choking, drowning.

If in some smothering dreams you too could pace
Behind the wagon that we flung him in,
And watch the white eyes writhing in his face,
His hanging face, like a devil's sick of sin;
If you could hear, at every jolt, the blood
Come gargling from the froth-corrupted lungs,
Obscene as cancer, bitter as the cud
Of vile, incurable sores on innocent tongues,
My friend, you would not tell with such high zest,
To children ardent for some desperate glory
The old lie: *Dulce et decorum est*
*Pro patria mori**.
[*"Pleasing and right it is to die for one's country."]

(Wilfred Owen, "Dulce et Decorum est . . .," 1915; ed. S. Sassoon, 1920)

English poet and soldier Siegfried Sassoon lashes out at those who stayed home and sent young men off to die:

. . . You smug-faced crowds with kindling eye
Who cheer when soldier lads march by,
Sneak home and pray you'll never know
The hell where youth and laughter go.

(S. Sassoon, "Suicide in the Trenches"; ed. M. Gilbert, 1970)

Song sung by the British troops who took their positions on July 1, 1916 for the battle of the Somme, in which thousands were slaughtered:

We beat them on the Marne,
We beat them on the Aisne,
    We gave them hell
    At Neuve Chapelle
And here we are again!

(From M. Gilbert, *The First World War: A Complete History*, 1994)

men's assault across a stretch of no-man's land while fully exposed to German machine guns. Those British soldiers who did reach the German line were trapped and shot down on the barbed wire, too thick for their wirecutters. In the first day of battle alone, over fifty percent of the British force of 110,000 were casualties; nearly twenty percent died.

By the end of the Somme offensive, the tally sheet of casualties was again nearly even: 620,000 British and French to 650,000 Germans. The next year, the news was worse. In 1917, half the French army mutinied when, after another failed offensive, yet another was ordered. Launching a third offensive from the same Belgian town of Ypres that had seen terrible slaughter in 1914 and 1915, the British hurled themselves suicidally at the Germans at Passchendaele (Belgium)—and gained four miles. The German generals who resisted them began, for the first time, to despair of winning.

From 1914 to 1918, there was stalemate on the western front, where millions of corpses lay buried, some in the trenches they had defended. The trenches, as deep as men were tall, sheltered soldiers on an open field and fortified their position. Trench warfare was not new: it had been used by Napoleon's soldiers, and by both Northern and Southern forces in the American Civil War. But the trench was the hallmark of the western front, where men battled for a few more yards of ground beyond the enemy's entrenched position. If those few yards were taken, a new trench was dug, perhaps to be surrendered to the enemy when he counter-attacked.

In all, some 25,000 miles of trench scarred the elongated front, dug in parallel networked systems between a few yards and a mile apart. The most advanced German position, achieved early in the war, yielded to an Allied advance only when fresh American divisions arrived late in 1917. In the final campaigns of 1918, the now superior Entente forces pushed the Germans back to the Belgian border.

British, French, and German soldiers ate, slept, and passed time in the trenches—aware that, in safe positions to the rear, their generals dined well and plotted out the battle with sets of colored pins. Conditions were repellent: mud and excrement, rats and lice (no one escaped the lice, thus all the soldiers were "lousy"—the original meaning of that term), tedium, and fear. Ordered to attack, they climbed out of the trenches and went "over the top" across "no-man's land," in the face of enemy fire. That mad charge of wholly exposed men against an enemy's fortified position, repeated again and again over four years, explains the resulting slaughter.

If the trench defined the war's western front, it was not its only military characteristic. Machine guns firing 600 rounds a minute were concentrated in nests that could annihilate repeated waves of charging infantry. Developed by American inventors Richard Gatling (1818–1903) and Hiram Maxim (1840–1916), these guns were employed successfully in colonial wars to wreak rapid devastation on native armies without firearms. They caused high losses in Europe as well. "Three men and a machine gun can stop a battalion of heroes," observed a French general of the battle at Verdun.

Barbed wire, used on American ranches to control herds of cattle, helped defend the lines of trenches. Enemy soldiers had to stop and cut wire before they could continue their charge. As they worked, howitzers lobbed shells at them from distant, unseen positions. Explosive grenades, known as early as the fifteenth century, had become varied in shape, range, and deadliness. Poison gas, a recent invention first used by the Germans in 1915 but quickly imitated, disabled the enemy who could then be overcome, or evaded, by masked troops—or such was the intention; in fact the flow of gas could not be controlled and often disabled the users. The British developed tanks, heavily armored vehicles that crawled on caterpillar treads over trenches, wire, and ground churned up by bombardment. Both sides used airplanes for reconnaissance; the Germans were the first to set machine guns to shoot in rhythm with the rotation of the propeller.

WITNESSES

At the Front (II)

Czech draftee Jaroslav Hasek remembers his commanding officer, with no fondness (c. 1914): Apparently by way of encouraging the rank and file . . . [the commanding officer] asked where the young recruit came from, how old he was, and whether he had a watch. The young recruit . . . said he hadn't got one, whereupon the aged general gave a fatuous smile . . . and said, "That's fine, that's fine," whereupon he honored a young corporal, who was standing near, by asking him whether his wife was well.

"Beg to report, sir," bawled the corporal, "I'm not married."

Whereupon the general, with a patronizing smile, repeated, "That's fine, that's fine."

Then the general, lapsing still further [into] senile infantility, asked Captain Sagner to show him how his troops numbered off in twos from the right, and after a while, he heard them yelling, "One-two, one-two, one-two."

The aged general was very fond of this. At home he had two orderlies, and he used to line them up in front of him and make them number off: "One-two, one-two."

Austria had lots of generals like this.

(Jaroslav Hasek, *The Good Soldier Schweik*, c. 1914; ed. P. Selver, 1963)

A German soldier writes home from the trenches (1915): Our regiment has been transferred to this dangerous spot, Souchez. No end of blood has already flowed. . . . A week ago the 142nd attacked and took four trenches from the French. It is to hold these trenches that we have been brought here. . . . This letter has been interrupted no end of times. Shells began to pitch close to us—great English 12-inch ones. . . . One . . . struck the next house and buried four men, who were got out . . . horribly mutilated. I saw them and it was ghastly!

Everybody must now be prepared for death in some form or other. . . . [T]he newspapers have probably given you a different impression. They tell only of our gains and say nothing of the blood that has been shed, of the cries of agony that never cease. The newspaper doesn't give any description either of *how* the "heroes" are laid to rest. . . . [U]p here . . . one throws the bodies out of the trench and lets them lie there, or scatters dirt over the remains of those which have been torn to pieces by shells.

(Alfons Ankenbrand in A. F. Wedd, ed., *German Students' War Letters*, 1929)

Slaughter and horror are far from the mind of English poet Jessie Pope as she celebrates the women who will "keep their end up" until the khaki-uniformed soldiers come home (1916):

There's the girl who clips your ticket for the train,
And the girl who speeds the lift from floor to floor,
There's the girl who does a milk-round in the rain,
And the girl who calls for orders at your door.
Strong, sensible, and fit,
They're out to show their grit,
And tackle jobs with energy and knack.
No longer caged and penned up,
They're going to keep their end up
Till the khaki soldier boys come marching back.

(Jessie Pope, "War Girls," 1916; ed. C. W. Reilly, 1981)

The Midst of Battle

Otto Dix*, Wounded (Fall 1916, Bapaume) *plate 6 from* The War *etchings: *In Otto Dix's etching from 1924, a fallen soldier is outraged and anguished by his pain, which twists his face into a hideous mask.* (The Museum of Modern Art, New York)

***Paul Nash*, We are Making a New World:** *Paul Nash's painting from 1918 of the battlefield near Ypres (Belgium), sardonically entitled* We Are Making a New World, *describes with grotesquely exaggerated forms the devastation wrought by constant and massive bombardment.* (Imperial War Museum, London)

Zeppelin airships dropped bombs on enemy cities. As the instruments of death multiplied, the numbers of the dead mounted.

The Eastern Steamroller

The eastern front was another scene of carnage. Here Austrian and German infantry faced the immense army of the Russian Empire, one of the world's four most populous nations. The rest of Europe regarded Russia as an enormous military steamroller that could burst out of the east and unstoppably roll westward. In reality, the Russian soldiers, mostly peasants, set out to war with too little food, and too few boots and bullets. And the Russian officers, all nobles, were a mixed lot of the heroic, the undisciplined, and the treacherous. Within a few months of the start of warfare in the east, the steamroller had paused, and Russia was in peril. By 1917, its prospects were desperate.

In the summer of 1914 in Petrograd (formerly St. Petersburg, renamed that year), Russian officers gallantly welcomed the war. Spurred by Pan-Slavic enthusiasm, and French persuasion, they marched promptly to battle. Too promptly; for the Russians were unprepared. Their supply lines were unready (and hampered in any case by their rail lines, constructed to a different gauge than those in western Europe) and their supplies were inadequate.

Even in the first month of the war, those deficiencies already mattered. The Russian army's first strike had been successful—they won the battle of Gumbinnen over a small German army on August 20—and their swift penetration of the German **salient** in eastern Prussia alarmed von Moltke. Contrary to Schlieffen's principles, the German commander detached from the western campaign one of his most competent younger generals (not yet fifty), Erich Ludendorff (1865–1937), prominent in the capture of Liège, and sent him along with Paul von Hindenburg (1847–1934), aged sixty-seven, an elderly hero plucked out of retirement, to block the forward thrust of the Russian steamroller.

The Russian generals made it easy for the Germans. Not only did they send hungry men and starved horses to the front lines, but they broadcast to each other uncoded messages detailing their positions that the German radio corps happily intercepted. The Germans delivered the uncoordinated Russian armies a crushing defeat at the Battle of Tannenberg (August 26–31). The war had barely begun, and Russia's failed Prussian offensive cost around 250,000 casualties—a fraction of the bloodletting still to come that would leave nearly 2 million of Russia's 12 million soldiers dead.

The following January (1915), Germany's Austrian allies attacked a Russian army in the Carpathian Mountains on the Hungarian border. A winter war at those elevated altitudes brought new miseries—both guns and fingers froze. In the spring, the Germans arrived to do the job their allies could not, driving the Russians 100 miles back from the front. Having secured east Prussia on the north of the front, and taken the Carpathians on the eastern front, and taken the Carpathians on the south, the victorious Germans pushed through the center of Poland beyond Warsaw to Brest-Litovsk. By the end of 1915, a new front ran from the Baltic to the Black Sea, leaving much of Russia's richest territory under German command.

The butchery continued. On the Russian side, generals and commanders were disgraced and replaced, while trainloads of fresh conscripts arrived at the front to freeze, starve, and bleed. On the German side, Hindenburg and Ludendorff were relentless. In 1916, the energetic Russian general Aleksey Alekseyevich Brusilov (1853–1926) launched a serious offensive on the south of the front into Austrian Galicia and German-occupied Poland. In 1917, as the Germans pushed back in an offensive that, by 1918, brought them deep into the interior, Russian soldiers mutinied. In Petrograd, revolution was afoot. In March 1917, the Petrograd workers' Soviet (or council) issued Army Order No. 1. Those in the ranks, it stated, need no longer obey their commanders, but should form committees and take power into their own hands. Soldiers streamed home from the front, disgusted with war and ready to throw their lot in with the revolution (see below).

The Russian military disaster was complicated by the nature of the army. The British and French armies (the German and Austrian less so) were effectively popular, or citizen armies, whereas the Russian army reflected a more traditional society. The officers were nobles and the soldiers peasants. They shared an allegiance to the tsar and a profound religious tradition. But history divided them. The peasants had always obeyed, whether on the land or at the front, and the nobles commanded. The slaughter at the front, combined with starvation and disease, awakened in peasant conscripts the thought that perhaps they would obey no longer.

South of the Russian positions on the eastern front, Austro-Hungarian forces (with German assistance or, often, direction) battled in the Balkans and in Italy. Bulgaria and the Ottoman Empire had leagued with the Central Powers. Between these nations and the Austrian border lay Romania and Serbia, which joined the Entente, as did Greece, tempted by promises of key chunks of Ottoman territory at the war's end. By 1916, overcoming stiff resistance from Slav Serbs and Romanians, the Central Powers controlled the whole Balkan Peninsula north of Greece.

Further west lay Italy, which had secretly negotiated a favorable treaty with Britain and France which detached them from their prior allegiance to the Central Powers. Italian armies battled to regain the *terra irredenta* ("unredeemed land") arching north along the Adriatic toward Trieste which, their leaders held, was rightfully Italian. Eleven times they faced an Austro-German force at the Isonzo river from June 1915 to May 1917, where more than 500,000 Italians were wounded or killed while edging only a little closer to the Adriatic. Even that progress was reversed, when they were pushed back seventy-five miles from Caporetto to regroup only twenty miles from Venice; from there, in 1918, they plunged on to win, at last, a victory at Vittorio Veneto. With the eventual peace settlement, Italy recovered her *terra irredenta*, at the cost of hundreds of thousands of irredeemable lives.

At Sea and Abroad

Prior to World War I, the British navy was the most powerful in the world, and the British trusted it to shield their nation from European conflicts. But over the previous two decades, the Germans had begun to construct a naval force that rivaled Britain's, equipped with battleships that were modern and almost unsinkable. Alarmed, the British responded by developing the Dreadnought, launched in 1906, the fiercest battleship ever constructed, equipped with ten heavy guns of unprecedented 12-inch size.

Over the next years, German and British shipyards raced to build more ships on its pattern. At the same time, the Germans developed a fleet of more than 100 submarines (an American innovation) or U-boats. Capable of slipping secretly in and out of ports, their torpedoes threatened the enemy's mighty Dreadnoughts and the merchant carriers of its suppliers.

The big ships had few opportunities to meet each other in battle. They did so in only one significant open battle, at Jutland, off Denmark, in the North Sea on May 31, 1916. The British lost more ships and more men, but the Germans fled; the battle had no clear result. More serious than such encounters was the war of attrition in northern seas. In the North and Baltic seas, British ships blocked supplies—foodstuffs as well as military goods—from reaching German ports. British ships also brought European armies to fight the allies of the Central Powers in the Middle East, and to dismantle Germany's colonial empire, while distant Japan, an Allied power, seized German protectorates in the Chinese provinces of Shandong and Manchuria.

The blockade choked Germany and Austria-Hungary, whose citizens were near starvation by 1917. The Germans in return aimed to stop the flow of goods to British and Allied ports, targeting especially the richly-laden ships of the neutral United States (as that nation sought to retain its neutrality while continuing to reap profits from its Atlantic trade with European powers on both sides). In these attempts, the submarine was their best and only tool.

On May 7, 1915, a German U-boat sank the British liner *Lusitania* in the Irish Sea, as a result of which 1200 persons died (including 128 United States citizens). It was found to contain (although the United States denied it) American-produced ammunition bound for Allied use, encouraging Germany to view the United States as a potential enemy. In 1916, when more Americans were wounded in the sinking of the French ship *Sussex*, President Woodrow Wilson (1856–1924) protested vigorously, eliciting a pledge from the Germans to renounce such tactics. In January 1917, regardless, Germany declared a policy of unrestricted submarine warfare against Allied shipping, and acted upon it. Until a convoy system was instituted in May of that year, one-fourth of all British ships that left port were sunk, as were one-fourth of all those seeking to make port.

Germany's U-boat tactics misfired. Now Britain was able to convince the United States that the Germans displayed a perfidy that could not be ignored with safety. Isolationist, pacifist, and even pro-German sentiments eventually yielded to such arguments. On April 6, 1917, the United States Congress declared war, sending the first United States forces (of an eventual total of about 4 million mobilized) to Europe the following summer.

Meanwhile, the war had expanded to other theaters. All the French and most British leaders thought it should be fought and won on the western front. Some British strategists, however, argued for pursuing hostile objectives further from home. They would thus weaken their opponents on the European fronts, and at the same time secure some fine colonial territories abroad.

Their first objective was the Ottoman Empire, now under a military despotism headed by the Young Turks (see Chapter 23). The Ottoman navy attacked Russia's Black Sea ports in October 1914 and closed the Dardanelles straits in November, blocking Russia's access to the Mediterranean. A British strike at the Dardanelles would support their ally, and at the same time serve to protect British interests in the Mediterranean. In 1915, the British sent thirteen battleships and more than 400,000 men (mostly colonial troops from Australia and New Zealand) to take the straits. The infantry landed at Gallipoli, fought and lost horribly to Turkish defenders, and were forced to evacuate late in 1915 and early in 1916, after suffering casualties of fifty percent.

Assisted by the forces of rebellious Arabs from the Hejaz (the coastal region of the Arabian Peninsula), the British also fought Turkish armies in Palestine and Mesopotamia, eventually capturing Damascus and

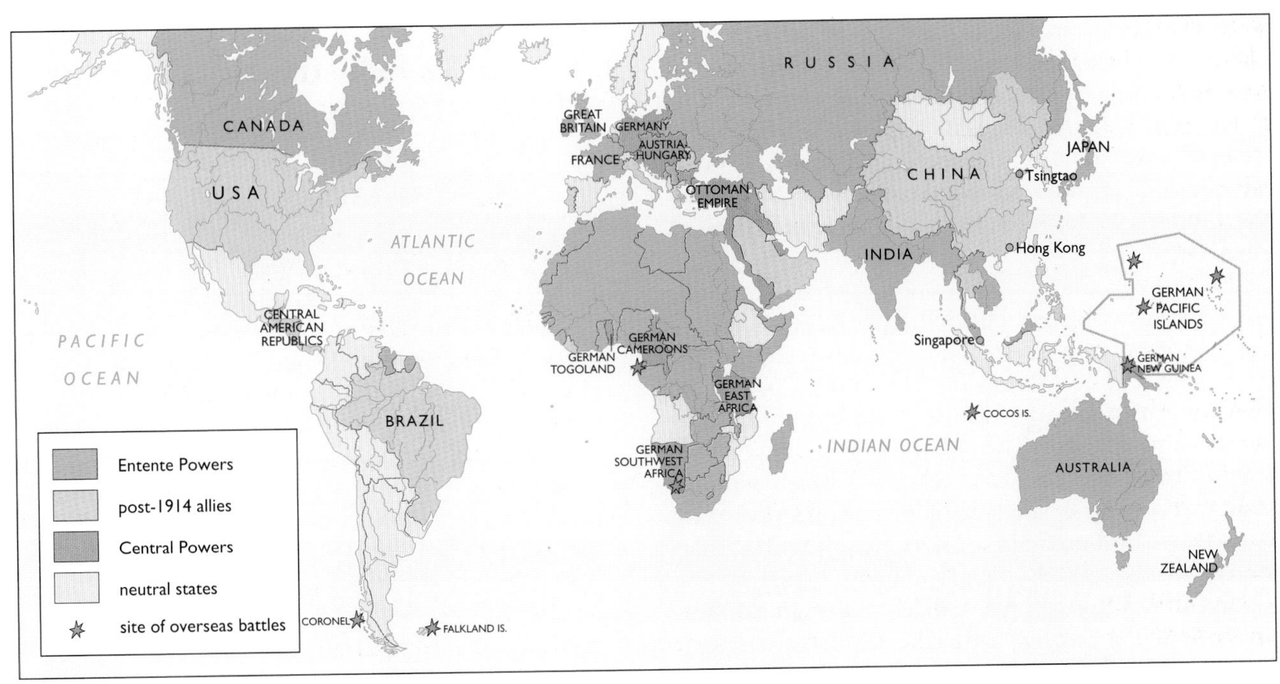

***Map 25.2* A World at War:** *The truly global nature of World War I can be seen here. Note the site of battles in Germany's various African colonial holdings.*

Baghdad. From the Mediterranean, the war spilled over to Africa and east Asia, where Germany's colonies and protectorates fell to Britain (assisted by South African soldiers in Africa) or allied Japan (in China).

In still another way, the wider world contributed to the war centered in Europe. From all parts of the globe, the colonies supplied pack animals and automobiles, tools and blankets, guns and bullets. Colonial soldiers—from Senegal and South Africa, India, Australia, New Zealand, Canada, India, and Morocco, fought alongside Europeans. More than 2 million were casualties.

At Home

As the European conflict spread around the globe, important changes were occurring at home. The tremendous demand for military supplies sent women into the factories. Capital, too, was put to work, as bankers, speculators, and smugglers aided the army in prosecuting the war. These changes were meant to last for the duration. Their effects were far greater and longer.

War meant an accelerated demand for virtually everything that factories produced—textiles for uniforms, blankets, and bandages in addition to normal civilian use; metals, machines, and tools; weapons and ammunition; packaged and canned food and, for the blockaded Central Powers, food substitutes. War production required the service of bankers, who floated loans for the new factories and the purchase of supplies, and reaped their interest on the huge sales of factory products. As huge quantities of goods needed to be distributed within each country and abroad, more investment was required to fund packaging and transportation. On an unprecedented scale, money circulated to sustain the war effort.

Stepped-up war production meant the mass employment of millions of women, many of whom had never before been wage-earners. Women stood in

HOW MANY?

British Munitions Production 1915–1917

Bullets	1,820,000,000
Artillery shells	42,000,000
Grenades	19,000,000
Rifles	956,000
Machine guns	30,300
Heavy guns	4,600
Trench mortars	3,152

assembly lines to make guns and shells, drove trucks, collected tickets, and read gas meters. Jobs that once were filled only by the poor, male or female, were now often held by middle-class women, whose social awareness expanded with their new experience. Many later became involved in social movements to remedy the conditions of work and home life for the laboring class.

Exposure to the world of work triggered changes in women's behavior and outlook. For the first time in the history of the West, women's skirts rose above their ankles. The fashion for voluminous petticoats and crinolines of not so long ago disappeared, along with stifling corsets, to be replaced by flowing clothes that followed the lines of the body. Women publicly took up smoking and drinking, stayed out late unescorted, and walked briskly and alone through the streets of the city. It was a modern woman who emerged from the war years, independent in outlook, and often of necessity, with the death of so many young men, self-supporting.

While many women worked in factories, others supported the war effort by working as nurses. Once the province of the religious orders, nursing had recently become a modern, secular profession—a transformation largely due to the pioneering work of one determined upper-class British woman, Florence Nightingale (1820–1910), who had volunteered to serve in a hospital in Scutari (in Turkey) during the Crimean War. As in other pre-modern wars, disease was as much a killer as gunfire: thousands died from infected wounds, cholera, and dysentery. Nightingale introduced standards for sanitation, acquired funding for proper equipment and medications, and trained other women to attend properly to the needs of the ill and wounded. Her example would be followed in the American Civil War by Clara Barton (1821–1912); and during World War I by the courageous, mostly privileged women who staffed the field hospitals erected immediately adjacent to the killing fields and cared for the dying, wounded, and diseased men sent back from the front lines.

Among other features of life on the home front was the demoralization which followed upon the news of the mounting dead, when nearly every family lost a son, a father, a cousin, or a friend. The stresses of wartime encouraged behaviors that would have been condemned before 1914—heavy drinking and high rates of out-of-wedlock births. Food and other shortages meant rationing, price controls, and standing in line. Speculators profited from the shortages, and many became rich acquiring and selling such commodities as oil or rubber.

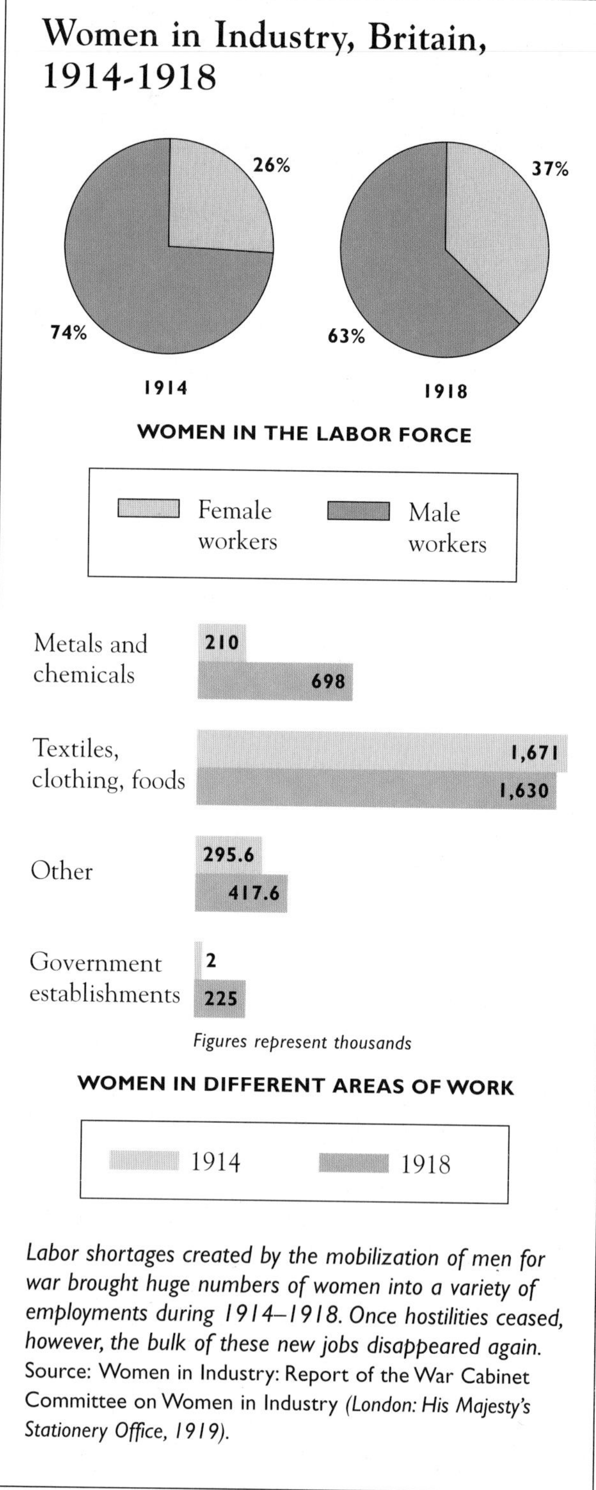

Labor shortages created by the mobilization of men for war brought huge numbers of women into a variety of employments during 1914–1918. Once hostilities ceased, however, the bulk of these new jobs disappeared again. Source: Women in Industry: Report of the War Cabinet Committee on Women in Industry *(London: His Majesty's Stationery Office, 1919).*

The mass mobilization required for world war had to be supported by the will of the whole nation—as the French revolutionary wars had been by drafted soldiers and commoner officers. Armies relied on conscripts (and in Britain, at the start, on volunteers),

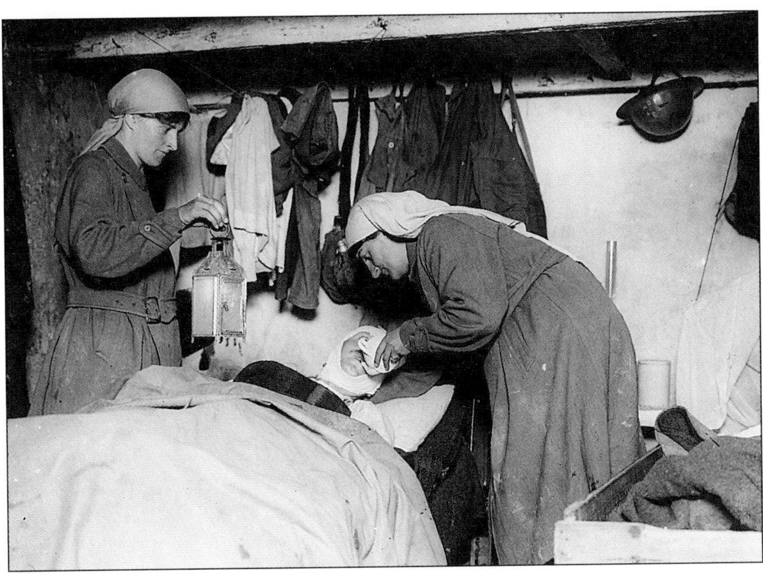

Women as Nurses, Workers, and Mourners

Nurses on the front line: *Women played a variety of critical roles in the war. Here two nurses are seen tending a wounded Belgian soldier in a scene from 1917.*

who could only be activated if their families stood behind the effort. Those families, safely at home, faced privations, too—especially in central Europe, where the peoples of the blockaded nations were starving by 1917. It was essential that the public of the combatant nations receive the right information—not always true information—circulated to the public in newspapers, through posters, and in broadcast speeches. Information, often sliding into propaganda, was a necessity on the home front. It was supplied by newswriters and war correspondents, whose new profession dated from the Crimean War.

Not all the news during the war years came from the battlefront. Much was going on at home. In Britain, the Liberal candidate David Lloyd George (1863–1945) became Prime Minister in a coalition government in 1916. Elsewhere, social democratic parties and labor organizations protested the war, at least at the outset—for many socialists believed, erroneously, that workers united to overthrow the capitalist order would never fire on each other. In Germany, the women pacifists and socialists Clara Zetkin (1857–1933) and Rosa Luxemburg (1870–1919) were imprisoned for their opposition to the war. Dutch socialists summoned an international peace conference. The French suffered a soldiers' mutiny, but German presence on their soil ultimately restored solidarity. Food

Women in a munitions factory: *By working in traditionally "male" environments—the factory, for example, amid an ocean of freshly minted artillery shells—women helped to undermine entrenched stereotypes of gender and place.*

Käthe Kollwitz, Die Eltern (The Parents): *As mothers, women mourned the millions of their sons, an unprecedented toll, who died terrifying deaths far from home. One such mother was the German artist Käthe Kollwitz, who tried to salve her grief after the conflict by producing a sculpture of the two stricken parents at their son's grave, forever weeping stone tears in his memory.*

shortages in Germany (caused by the British naval blockade) resulted in food riots in 1916, and the deaths of about 750,000 citizens by war's end. Domestic tensions, meanwhile, reached serious levels in Russia, which had already sacrificed millions of men to the butchery of the eastern front, when the soldiers made it known they would go on no longer.

Russia Turns Back

In Russia, as further west, the factories roared furiously to produce armaments and supplies for the soldiers at the front. Russian industrialization had progressed rapidly in the generation before 1914 (see Chapter 21), and millions of workers—fully one-third of them women—crowded into the poorer districts of Moscow and Petrograd. However, as famine struck an already restive peasantry, production quotas drove the workers, and wounded or renegade soldiers returned from the front with tales of starvation and mayhem, the conditions for revolution crystallized. By the end of the single thunderous year of 1917, tsarist monarchy had yielded to a communist dictatorship.

Military Expenditures of the Great Powers, 1890 and 1914

	Year	Total Defense Expenditure ($ millions)	Cost per Capita Home Population
Japan	1890	24	0.6
	1914	96	1.75
Germany	1890	144	2.95
	1914	554	8.52
British Empire	1890	157	4.03
	1914	384	8.53
France	1890	186	4.87
	1914	287	7.33
Russia	1890	145	1.32
	1914	442	2.58
US	1890	67	1.06
	1914	314	3.20

The massive mobilization of people and resources in World War I meant a reorientation of economies and huge financial burdens on the citizenry. As this table shows, the increase in military costs per capita in wartime (1914 figure) ranged from about 150 percent (France) to about 300 percent (Japan and US) of their cost in peacetime (1890 figure).

Source: W. S. Morton, Japan: Its History and Culture, 3rd ed. (New York: McGraw Hill, 1994), p. 182.

The 1905 Revolution These things might have happened otherwise if the tsar had responded differently to the upheaval of 1905. But Tsar Nicholas II (r. 1894–1918) learned to rule from his predecessor, Alexander III (r. 1881–1894), who had pursued a dual policy of the repression of political enemies and the Russification of ethnic minorities—policies resulting in a succession of riots and pogroms (see Chapter 23) and the exile or execution of radical intellectuals.

Succeeding to the monarchy in 1894, Nicholas was determined to uphold the tsarist system of terror and repression. Backed up by the army, the secret police, obsequious ministers, the fanatically nationalist Black Hundreds, and an imperious, apparently hysterical wife—the German-born Alexandra (1872–1918), granddaughter of Britain's Queen Victoria—he met the demands for reform posed in 1905 uncomprehendingly and inflexibly.

In 1905, with Russian military failure in the war with Japan as somber backdrop, the demands of liberal nobles and bourgeois for a national parliament on the western European model coincided with the petitions of workers for political reform. In January, a group of the 100,000 factory workers then on strike in St. Petersburg presented to the tsar at his Winter Palace their petition for better working conditions and the right to unionize. The police ordered the workers to disperse; they refused. The police fired, killing about 100 people, including women and children. This "Bloody Sunday" massacre triggered strikes and rebellions throughout Russia.

Advised by his reform-minded chief minister, Sergei Witte (1849–1915), who urged concessions to the progressive agenda, Nicholas issued his October Manifesto. It called for the formation of a national representative assembly, or **Duma**, to be chosen by universal male suffrage. In addition, it permitted the formation of local and municipal councils, and allowed freedom of the press. Further unrest in December, however, and the return of the army from Asia, encouraged the tsar to take back many of his concessions. He ordered workers' leaders arrested and minority uprisings suppressed, while unleashed forces of repression engaged in renewed anti-Semitic pogroms (see Chapter 23).

Nevertheless, the Duma met the following April (1906). Its largely liberal representatives (the more radical Social Democratic and Social Revolutionary delegates refused to participate) pressed for agrarian and political reform. To limit these reformist moves, the tsar created an upper assembly, of whom half the members were obedient appointees. When the Duma protested, it was dissolved. A second, more conservative Duma was elected. It, too, was dissolved. A third Duma elected in 1907 continued to press ineffectively for reform. Meanwhile, the reformist Witte had been dismissed and replaced by the more conservative chief minister Peter Stolypin (1862–1911).

In 1911, Stolypin himself was assassinated, having marked himself as too liberal by introducing reforms that allowed enterprising peasants (called *kulaks*) to establish their own farms. Nicholas retreated further into his circle of conservative supporters, who urged an ongoing campaign of repression and Russification and maintained a stubborn ignorance of the great storm that was brewing. Liberals and progressives chafed, while socialists of various shades of opinion discussed revolution.

Factions and Visionaries Between 1905 and 1917, Russian political parties were active and multifarious. They shared a determined opposition to tsarist autocracy (the latter supported by the high clergy and conservative nobles, along with officials whose loyalty had been purchased with privileges); otherwise they disagreed.

They were arrayed in three main groups. The first included the progressive nobles and bourgeois, professionals and liberal intellectuals, of whom the foremost were the Kadets (Constitutional Democrats), who aimed to establish a constitutional monarchy on European models. The second consisted of the several socialist parties intent on land reform (addressing the still unresolved condition of the eighty-five percent of Russia's population composed of former serfs), of which the best known were the Social Revolutionaries. The third group was that of the Marxist parties, who advanced the revolutionary potential of industrial workers (the proletariat; see Chapters 22, 24). These included the pacifist Internationalists, and the Marxian Social Democrats, themselves split into **Bolshevik** (meaning "majority," as this faction once held a majority at the 1903 party congress) and **Menshevik** (meaning "minority") factions. Other revolutionary groups also proliferated, including those of the anarchists (see Chapter 24). The different parties produced their own newspapers to interpret political events for their readership. These were produced irregularly and distributed secretly, evading the censors.

Russian politics were further complicated by the fact that most of the revolutionary leaders were not in Russia. By 1900, the Okhrana, the tsarist secret police, had tracked most of them and seen them banished to Siberia. After their release, they often sought refuge in London, Brussels, or Zurich. From these cities, they published articles of political analysis for the party press or telegraphed instructions to colleagues in St. Petersburg, and met with leaders of like-minded European parties at international congresses. Supported by party funds, parental largesse, or their own labor, they lived this existence of political exile for decades on end.

Such was the career pattern of Vladimir Ilyich Ulyanov (1870–1924), who adopted the revolutionary pseudonym "Lenin," the leader of the Bolshevik faction of Marxian social democrats. Radicalized by the execution in 1887 of his older brother, charged under Alexander III with participating in an assassination plot, Lenin committed himself to the career of professional revolutionary.

Arrested and exiled in 1895, Lenin departed in 1900 for Switzerland. A brilliant theorist as well as an active conspirator, Lenin produced analyses of capitalism and imperialism, and blueprints for revolution that adapted Marx to the peculiar circumstances of the Russian Empire. The essential points were outlined in his *What Is To Be Done?* (1902). Revolution could be achieved in Russia, and a proletarian state created, but not by the workers alone. A disciplined **cadre**, or core group of committed and educated leaders, would lead the rank and file of workers, who would join with the peasantry (for Lenin, an unformed and unreliable group) to dethrone autocracy and create a revolutionary society.

Another exile who became a prominent leader of the Bolshevik revolt was Lev (Leon) Davidovich Bronstein (1879–1940), who adopted the pseudonym "Trotsky." In 1917, when news of mounting crisis arrived, he was living in the United States. Returning immediately to Petrograd, he joined with the Menshevik faction and became active as a leader of the Petrograd **Soviet**, an informal association of workers' councils. The Mensheviks hoped to work through such councils so as to be ready to act once bourgeois liberals had formed a constitutional government. As the events of 1917 unfolded, however, Trotsky joined with Lenin and the Bolsheviks.

Precipitating the Crisis The revolutionary year 1917 was preceded by the crisis of leadership of 1916, itself provoked by the experience of war. The tsar himself decided to go to the front to rally the troops, and left at the helm of the Russian Empire his obsequious ministers, his haughty wife, and her intimate friend and counselor, the drunken, unstable but charismatic fanatic Grigorii Rasputin (1872–1916). Having won over the tsarina by convincing her that he alone could save her hemophiliac son, the heir to the throne, Rasputin exerted his influence in political affairs. Never has a state managed by such incompetents faced opponents of such exceptional intelligence and resolve.

In December 1916, a group of noble conspirators poisoned, shot, bludgeoned, and finally drowned Rasputin, who died at last beneath the ice of the Neva River. Now Russia was wholly without leadership. The pitiless winter descended, news from the front was bad, factory workers went on strike, and food shortages peaked. In March 1917, the women of Petrograd took to the streets—how often in the past women had rioted for bread! But rarely with such effect.

The women's protest turned into revolution—the "February" revolution by the old Russian calendar then in use. Workers joined the women, while mobs seized public buildings, and armed themselves with

WITNESSES

Revolution in Russia

Lenin defines the need for a Vanguard Party to lead the workers (1902): We have said that *there could not have been* Social-Democratic [revolutionary] consciousness among the workers. It would have to be brought to them from without. The history of all countries shows that the working class, exclusively of its own effort, is able to develop only trade-union consciousness. . . .

I assert . . . that no revolutionary movement can endure without a stable organization of leaders maintaining continuity . . . that such an organization must consist chiefly of people professionally engaged in revolutionary activity. . . . [who] will centralize all the secret aspects of the work—the drawing up of leaflets, the working out of approximate plans; and the appointing of bodies of leaders for each urban district, for each factory district, and for each educational institution. . . .
(V. I. Lenin, *Collected Works*, vol. 5, 1973)

Nadezhda Krupskaya, Lenin's wife and secretary, describes their return to Russia (1917): The masses of Petrograd—workers, soldiers and sailors—came to welcome their leader. . . . We were in the midst of a surging sea of people.

No one who has not lived through the revolution can have any idea of its solemn grandeur. Red banners, a guard of honor of Kronstadt sailors, searchlights from the Peter and Paul fortress . . ., armoured cars, files of working men and women guarding the road. . . .

When Ilyich stepped out on to the platform, a captain came up to him, stood at attention and reported. Taken by surprise, Ilyich returned the salute. A guard of honor was lined up on the platform, and Ilyich was led past it. . . . Then we were seated in motor-cars, while Ilyich was placed on an armoured car . . . "Long live the socialist world revolution!" Ilyich shouted into the vast crowd swarming around us.

Ilyich already felt the beginning of that revolution in every fibre of his being.
(Nadezhda Konstantinovna Krupskaya, *Lenin*; ed. B. Isaacs, 1960)

Upon his return to Russia following the collapse of the Tsarist regime, Lenin proclaims his revolutionary strategy in the April Theses (1917):

2. The specific feature of the present situation in Russia is that the country is *passing* from the first stage of the revolution—which . . . placed power in the hands of the bourgeoisie—to its *second* stage, which must place power in the hands of the proletariat and the poorest sections of the peasants. . . .

   This peculiar situation demands of us an ability to adapt ourselves to the special conditions of Party work among unprecedentedly large masses of proletarians who have just awakened to political life.
3. No support for the Provisional Government. . . .
4. . . . The masses must be made to see that the Soviets of Workers' Deputies are the *only possible* form of revolutionary government, . . . therefore our task is . . . to present a patient, systematic, and persistent explanation of the errors of [the Provisional Government's] . . . tactics, an explanation especially adapted to the practical needs of the masses.

(Lenin's April Theses, proclaimed 1917)

guns from the arsenal. Factory workers formed themselves into militias of self-appointed "Red Guards," and, prodded by Menshevik organizers, created the Petrograd Soviet of Workers' and Soldiers' Deputies. On March 12, Duma leaders created a Provisional Government to maintain order. Three days later, Tsar Nicholas abdicated, the last Romanov ruler of Russia, and the first emperor to lose his throne as a result of World War I.

Heading the Provisional Government was a committee of directors including both Kadets and socialists. Its aim was to restore order at home, manage food distribution, prosecute the war, introduce reforms, and arrange for the election of a constituent assembly that would, at long last, write a constitution. The moderate social democrat Alexander Kerensky (1881–1970), who emerged as its leader (and would die in exile in New York City fifty-three years later, one of the longest-lived of the generation of 1917), might have succeeded in meeting those goals had not the Petrograd Soviet formed other goals of its own.

In April 1917, Lenin returned from Switzerland. He had journeyed most of the overland distance in a sealed railroad car supplied by the German government, Russia's enemy, which recognized the profit to be gained from planting in Petrograd a Bolshevik agitator. The British politician Winston Churchill later described the transhipment of Lenin as a form of biological warfare—the transmission of a "plague bacillus" to destroy the enemy.

Safely arrived, Lenin joined the leaders of the Petrograd Soviet, which now had some 3000 members. By summer, his Bolsheviks controlled it. With their simple sociology (there were only two classes, the exploited proletariat and the exploiting bourgeoisie, and one must choose to serve one or the other) and their irresistible promises—"Land, Bread, Peace"—the Bolsheviks soon won influence in the workers' soviets of Moscow and other major cities. Taking the initiative, the Petrograd Soviet issued Army Order No. 1 (see above), an invitation to soldiers to disobey their officers with impunity. During the spring and summer of 1917, Russian soldiers "voted with their feet" (in Lenin's pungent phrase). They arrived in Petrograd from the front just in time to join the revolution.

Whereas Kerensky's Provisional Government wanted to win the war and secure a democratic constitution, the Bolsheviks wanted to end the war and seize power. The two sets of aims competed, much as the crowds of frock-coated officials in the Winter Palace jostled against the crowds of workers and soldiers in the street. In July, the moderate forces gained the upper hand; soon, though, the Bolsheviks rebounded and gained control. In September, the reactionary general Lavr Kornilov (1870–1918) attempted a coup, which Kerensky suppressed. Thereafter, enemies of the revolution were branded "Kornilovites," whether or not they had joined in the attempt at military putsch.

***Lenin addressing troops:** Hard hit by the war, the Russian people abandoned it in 1917, led by the Bolshevik revolutionary Vladimir Ilyich Lenin. He is shown here in Moscow's Red Square addressing Russian troops who had escaped the battlefields of World War I but now fought a civil war against the enemies of the new order.*

In October, as Kerensky's supporters awaited the formation of a constituent assembly, and as Lenin's supporters awaited the arrival of the delegates to the All-Russian Congress of Soviets, Lenin saw a moment of opportunity and grabbed it. As the delegates of the soviets arrived, but before they had the opportunity to oppose Lenin's move, supported by squads of workers, soldiers (from the Petrograd garrison), and sailors (from the nearby naval base at Kronstadt) the Bolsheviks stormed the Winter Palace. Kerensky was expelled, and all power passed, as Lenin had wished, from the Provisional Government to the soviets. That event of November 6, 1917 marks the onset of the Bolshevik Revolution. By the old Russian calendar, the date was October 24; hence the event is known as the "October Revolution."

In Petrograd, the Bolsheviks seized the post office and telephone exchanges, government offices and ministries, the railroads, banks, and newspaper offices. In Moscow, they seized the Kremlin, the sacred center of the Russian state. Former Menshevik Leon Trotsky, head of the Military Revolutionary Committee that had coordinated the insurrection, organized the Red

Army, and Felix Dzerzhinsky (1877–1926) the secret police, or Cheka.

The further course of the Bolshevik Revolution is a story to be told elsewhere (see Chapter 27). For the moment, its significance is that it resulted in Russia's withdrawal from the war. With the title People's Commissar for Foreign Affairs, Trotsky conducted the delicate negotiations with the Germans. An armistice was reached in December 1917. There remained the terms of the peace. When Trotsky rejected the German demands, they responded instantly by smashing into Ukraine, the Crimea, and Georgia to the east, and north to the Gulf of Finland, barely 150 miles from Petrograd. Checked, desperate, on March 3, 1918 Trotsky signed at Brest-Litovsk in Belarus a peace treaty that left Russia mutilated. Russia sacrificed Poland, Moldova, Bessarabia, Ukraine, Georgia, the Baltic states, Finland—nearly one-fourth of the Russia the tsars had built, nearly one-third of its farmland, more than half of its industries, nearly all of its coal mines, cotton, and oil. The Bolsheviks who had wished to leave the war at any price paid a tremendous price; yet Lenin believed the losses unimportant, since they were bound to revert to Russia in the imminent world-wide communist revolution. Meanwhile, they were free to secure their revolution, and the Germans were free to return to the anguish of the western front.

Lenin the revolutionary was also a visionary. Seeing a new world ahead, he sacrificed all else—his own youth and livelihood, the lives of millions, the traditions of a nation—to make that vision real. Nearly halfway around the globe, a more prosperous nation with its own unique traditions had as its leader another visionary—the American president Woodrow Wilson (1856–1924)—for whom democracy and peace were imperatives that loomed as large as did revolution for Lenin. These two visionaries from the peripheries of the Western world foreshadowed its future more accurately than any of the leaders of the core nations of Europe, older now, after four years of war, exhausted, and transformed.

IN SEARCH OF PEACE

Woodrow Wilson was elected president in 1916 in part because he opposed American involvement in the war then raging in Europe—"He Kept Us Out of War" was his campaign slogan. The following year, he brought the United States into the war. As a fresh American army arrived in 1917 and, in 1918, swept German forces back through Belgium and across the Rhine, Wilson announced his blueprint for the future. Viewing this war as the "war to end all wars," he insisted that the settlement must provide for long-term goals: the establishment of democracy and the securing of a permanent peace.

In the event, the visionary Wilson did not succeed in realizing his plan. The peace settlement was achieved by deal-making and manipulations that left the work of building the future undone, and the defeated nations hungry for vengeance.

In Search of Peace

Woodrow Wilson's vision of the post-war order—the principles of justice and self-determination guide his "Fourteen Points" (1918): We [the US] entered this war because violations of right had occurred which touched us to the quick and made the life of our own people impossible unless they were corrected and the world secured once for all against their recurrence. What we demand in this war, therefore, . . . is that the world be made fit and safe to live in; . . . The program of the world's peace, therefore, is our program; and that program, the only possible program, as we see it, is this:

I. Open covenants of peace, openly arrived at, after which there shall be no private international understandings of any kind but diplomacy shall proceed always frankly and in the public view.

II. Absolute freedom of navigation upon the seas, outside territorial waters. . . .

III. The removal . . . of all economic barriers and the establishment of an equality of trade conditions among all the nations consenting to the peace. . . .

IV. [International arms reductions]. . . .

V. A free, open-minded, and absolutely impartial adjustment of all colonial claims, based upon a strict observance of the principle that . . . the interests of the populations concerned must have equal weight with the equitable claims of the government whose title is to be determined.

VI. The evacuation of all Russian territory. . . .

VII. Belgium . . . must be evacuated and restored. . . .

VIII. All French territory should be freed . . . and the wrong done to France by Prussia in 1871 in the matter of Alsace-Lorraine . . . should be righted. . . .

IX. A readjustment of the frontiers of Italy should be effected along clearly recognizable lines of nationality.

X. The peoples of Austria-Hungary [including various Slavs] . . . should be accorded the freest opportunity of autonomous development.

Peace Plans

On January 8, 1918, in an address to both houses of the United States Congress, President Wilson outlined his "Fourteen Points." Underlying them were three fundamental principles. First, war must and could be avoided in the future if the nations in concert obeyed certain guidelines, above all the accomplishment of "open covenants of peace, openly arrived at." Second, national status should rest on ethnic self-determination—if a people considered themselves a unity, their living together "along historically established lines of allegiance and nationality" should be assured. Third (the substance of the crucial Fourteenth Point), an international body should be created, the League of Nations, to negotiate conflicts between nations before war erupted: "A general association of nations must be formed under

WITNESSES

XI. Rumania, Serbia, and Montenegro should be evacuated; occupied territories restored; Serbia accorded free and secure access to the sea; and the relations of the several Balkan states . . . determined . . . along historically established lines of allegiance and nationality; . . . .
XII. The Turkish portions of the present Ottoman Empire should be assured a secure sovereignty, but the other nationalities which are now under Turkish rule should be assured . . . an absolutely unmolested opportunity of autonomous development. . . .
XIII. An independent Polish state should be erected. . . .
XIV. A general association of nations must be formed under specific covenants for the purpose of affording mutual guarantees of political independence and territorial integrity to great and small states alike.
(*Congressional Record*, vol. 56, 1918, pt. 1)

From the Treaty of Versailles—guidelines for the containment and punishment of Germany as the instigator of war (1919):
Article 42. Germany is forbidden to maintain or construct any fortifications either on the left bank of the Rhine or on the right bank to the west of a [specified] line . . .
Article 45. . . . Germany cedes to France . . . the coal mines situated in the Saar Basin. . . .
Article 51. The territories [of Alsace and Lorraine] . . . are restored to French sovereignty. . . .
Article 80. Germany acknowledges and will respect strictly the independence of Austria. . . .
Article 81. Germany . . . recognizes the complete independence of the Czecho-Slovak State. . . .
Article 84. German nationals habitually resident in . . . the Czecho-Slovak State will obtain Czecho-Slovak nationality *ipso facto* and lose their German nationality. . . .
Article 87. Germany . . . recognizes the complete independence of Poland. . . .
Article 116. Germany acknowledges . . . the independence of all the territories which were part of the former Russian Empire on August 1, 1914.
Article 119. Germany renounces . . . all her . . . overseas possessions. . . .
Article 159. The German military forces shall be demobilized and reduced. . . .
Article 198. The armed forces of Germany must not include any military or naval air forces. . . .
Article 231. The Allied and Associated Governments affirm and Germany accepts the responsibility of Germany and her allies for causing all the loss and damage to which the Allied and Associated Governments and their nationals have been subjected as a consequence of the war imposed upon them by the aggression of Germany and her allies.
Article 232. . . . Germany undertakes that she will make compensation for all damage done to the civilian population of the Allied and Associated Powers and to their property . . . as [elsewhere] defined. . . .
(*Peace Treaty With Germany*, 66th Congress, 1st Session, Senate Document 49, 1919)

Sigmund Freud on the legacy of the war—not peace but disillusionment (1915): Then the war in which we had refused to believe broke out, and it brought—disillusionment. Not only is it more bloody and more destructive than any war of other days, because of the enormously increased perfection of weapons of attack and defence; it is at least as cruel, as embittered, as implacable as any that has preceded it. . . . It tramples in blind fury on all that comes in its way, as though there were to be no future and no peace among men after it is over. It cuts all the common bonds between the contending peoples, and threatens to leave a legacy of embitterment that will make any renewal of those bonds impossible for a long time to come.
(Sigmund Freud, "Thoughts for the Times on War and Death," 1915 in *Collected Works*, vol. 4; authorized trs.)

specific covenants for the purpose of affording mutual guarantees of political independence and territorial integrity to great and small states alike."

Wilson's proposal also advocated free trade and freedom of the seas; a general disarmament "to the lowest point consistent with domestic safety"; the restoration of just boundaries and the protection of neutrality; an equitable settlement of colonial claims; and the relinquishing to Russia (then in the midst of civil war), in the spirit of self-determination, of its own destiny: "The treatment accorded Russia by her sister nations in the months to come will be the acid test of their good will, of their comprehension of her needs as distinguished from their own interests, and of their intelligent and unselfish sympathy."

Although Wilson's Fourteen Points may have been overly hopeful, he was the only world leader to grasp one essential desideratum: the avoidance of war in an age when war's destructive power could no longer be endured by humankind. To reach that end, he urged the embracing of democratic procedures under universal standards of justice.

The idealist Wilson was not alone in envisioning peace in 1918. On both sides of the conflict, people clamored for peace. In Britain, France, Italy, and Belgium they called for compensation and revenge. In Russia, sentiments for peace merged with the tide of revolution. Elsewhere in eastern Europe they were the platform of increasingly popular parties whose speakers called for peace without delay, without annexations of territory, without indemnities—a truce without winners or losers.

In Germany and Austria-Hungary, centrist socialists and republicans managed two revolutions during the last days of the war. These forced the expulsion of the Hohenzollern and Habsburg emperors, whose dynasties had reigned so long. The German revolution, sparked by naval mutinies and followed by general strikes, achieved the abdication of the emperor and the establishment of a democratic republic on November 9, 1918. The Austrians had already withdrawn from the war six days before. The flight of the last Habsburg, Charles (r. 1916–1918), who had succeeded Franz Joseph (r. 1848–1916) in 1918, meant the dismemberment of that multiethnic empire. Austria declared itself a republic, releasing Hungary to pursue its own path.

These revolutions enabled new governments to sue for peace. But the transition from empire to republic in central Europe did not proceed without turmoil. As in Russia, a variety of political parties struggled to gain leadership. Whereas the Bolsheviks were victorious in Russia, moderate socialists held on to power in Germany and Austria. In Germany, centrist leaders weathered naval mutinies, a Bavarian socialist secessionist movement, and street rioting in Berlin. In that city, they faced the radical "Spartacist" faction of the Socialist Party (named after the slave who had led a revolt in ancient Rome; see Chapter 5). It was led by the brilliant theorists Karl Liebknecht (1871–1919) and Rosa Luxemburg, who guided the formation of workers' and soldiers' militias, modeled on those that had gained power in Petrograd in 1917. Fearful of a second Bolshevik revolution, the new German government unleashed the army to quell the uprising. Army agents were to murder Liebknecht and Luxemburg on January 15, 1919, just as the representatives of the victorious nations gathered at Versailles to decide on the terms of peace. The Spartacist socialists subsequently became the German Communist Party.

Meanwhile, the war reached closure on the military fronts. In a last, desperate offensive in March 1918, the Germans advanced westward with more than 1 million men, intending to finish what they had started in the fall of 1914. In June, some 300,000 still fresh United States troops responded with irresistible force, pushing the German armies back to Belgium, the Rhine, and beyond. In Germany, only the emperor and his generals still spoke of victory—and now the generals began to urge an armistice.

In October 1918, the German premier Prince Max von Baden (1867–1929) approached Wilson, expressing interest in the Fourteen Points and the promise of "peace without victory." But Wilson's patience had been tried by the loss of American lives. He left von Baden to deal with the British and the French, made pitiless by the experience of the slaughter on the western front. With these the Central Powers signed an armistice on November 11, 1918. Champagne flowed in London, Paris, and New York. The war was

HOW MANY?

What Germany Lost

100%	of her pre-war colonies
80%	of her pre-war fleet
48%	of all iron production
16%	of all coal production
13%	of her 1914 territory
12%	of her population

over, but peace would not easily follow. As the combatants had bloodied each other in battle, the victors now set out, with paper and pen, to bloody the losers at the conference called to set the terms of surrender.

Settlement at Paris

Attending the peace conference in Paris were the prime ministers of France, Britain, and Italy, and the president of the United States: respectively, Georges Clemenceau (1841–1929; known as "the tiger"), David Lloyd George, Vittorio Orlando (1860–1952), and Woodrow Wilson. In addition to these "Big Four," there were delegates from twenty-three other nations and four British dominions. No delegates represented the defeated powers; none were welcome from Russia, which had bled for the Allied cause but had exited the struggle early. The delegates wrangled, and the Big Four retired behind closed doors to work out the future of Europe. Clemenceau and Lloyd George looked for revenge and reparations; Orlando wanted land; and Wilson conceded much while fixing his sights on a future League of Nations.

The Peace of Paris resulted in a series of separate treaties with the defeated powers, each named after the Parisian suburb in which it was signed during 1919–1920. Of these the Treaty of Versailles, which settled affairs with Germany, overshadowed the others. In discussions held from January to June, these points emerged. First, Germany must be forced to admit its guilt as the aggressor and instigator of the terrible conflict. Second, it must repay the Allies the cost of war. Third, it must be demilitarized to the extent that it could cause no new conflict. Fourth, the defeated nations must surrender territory in Europe and possessions around the globe to the victor nations, who demanded a reward for their wartime sacrifice.

Germany, indeed, was humbled and stripped bare. Article 231 of the Treaty of Versailles signed on June 28, 1919—the famous "war guilt" clause—stated that Germany accepted full responsibility for all losses and damages suffered by the Allies "as a consequence of the war imposed upon them by the aggression of Germany and her allies." Germany was ordered to pay a **reparation** of 132 billion gold marks (about $33 billion) over a period of years, a sum arrived at by rough calculation of the cost of war to the victor nations—a penalty of unimaginable dimension, little of which was ever paid. Their army was reduced to 100,000 volunteers, their airforce was eliminated, and their navy limited to six warships and no submarines. Even their merchant and fishing fleets were limited, and their shipyards assigned to supply the victor nations with new vessels at no cost. The Rhineland (the rich western sector) would be occupied by the French army until such date as the reparations were paid, and the coal-rich Saar region administered by an international committee until 1935, when a plebiscite would determine whether it became French or German. (The citizens of the Saar eventually chose German citizenship.) Kipling applauded the harsh settlement:

These were our Children who died for our Lands.
They were dear in our sight . . .
The Price of our Loss shall be paid to our Hands . . .
That is our Right.

Germany also accepted territorial concessions. The provinces of Alsace and Lorraine were returned to France; other German territory was ceded to Denmark, Belgium, and Poland, the latter reconstituted nation thus gaining "a corridor" to the Baltic Sea (except for the "free" city of Danzig, now Gdánsk) which divided East Prussia from the rest of

War's imprint on children's bodies: *In addition to Germany, Austria was devastated and the old Austro-Hungarian empire dismantled. Here in a picture from* The Illustrated London News *(January 4, 1919) emaciated children, brought by their mothers wrapped in newspaper to the doctor's clinic in Vienna, are examined for signs of the influenza that swept Europe in the aftermath of the war.*

the German homeland. German colonies in Africa and Asia were transferred to the Allied powers.

Austria, the remnant of the Austro-Hungarian Empire whose Balkan policies had triggered the war, gave up so much territory that its final dimensions were smaller than the medieval duchy of Austria the Habsburgs had ruled for centuries. From the lands it lost, whole new nations were constituted, their boundaries drawn (as much as possible) according to the Wilsonian principle of ethnic self-determination. Hungary became an independent republic. Czechoslovakia and Yugoslavia united, respectively, the Czechs and Slovaks and the southern Slavic Croatians, Slovenes, and Serbs. Romania doubled its territory. The south Tyrol (in the Alps) and parts of the Adriatic coast were conceded to Italy, which reclaimed thereby much of its *terra irredenta* but not enough to satisfy the Italian nationalists, who denounced this as a "mutilated peace."

A corridor of states was created of what was once western Russia—for, although the Brest-Litovsk treaty became invalid with the defeat of Germany, Russia had still surrendered its destiny to the victorious powers. From its borderlands were formed the independent states of Poland, Lithuania, Latvia, Estonia, and Finland; while Bessarabia was ceded to Romania. Bulgaria gave up territory to Romania, Greece, and Yugoslavia.

The former Ottoman Empire, soon to be reconstituted as the modern nation of Turkey, was assigned to yield to Greece and Italy much of its European land, as well as key positions in Asia Minor and the island of Rhodes. These demands the Turks resisted, driving out the Greek forces that had rapidly moved into Asia Minor, and forcing the Europeans to accept a few Aegean islands in compensation. Leading the resistance was the young general Mustafa Kemal (1881–1938), who from 1923 until his death became Turkey's dictator (see Chapter 28).

The new state of Turkey was a truncated rump of the former Ottoman Empire. Although still a major power in the Middle East, on the European side of the straits (which were now open to all nations) it contained only the area around Constantinople (now Istanbul). Its North African and Middle Eastern territories were all lost. The belt from Morocco to Afghanistan became a patchwork of British, French, Spanish, and Italian colonies, protectorates, and "mandates." A mandate was the commission to administer a region (such as those of the former Ottoman Empire and former German colonies) under the auspices of the League of Nations, the institution Wilson had envisioned and which had a brief life between 1919 and 1939. It was the most hopeful, if flawed, outcome of the Paris conference.

The League of Nations was formed in 1919 to secure peace among nations so that the world, as Wilson had wished, would be made "safe for democracy." On its executive committee were British, French, Italian, and Japanese delegates. As at Versailles, delegates from the former Central Powers and communist Russia (now the Union of Soviet Socialist Republics, or USSR) were not represented. Neither was the United States. President Wilson had returned home from Paris to find his own nation in the grip of an isolationist mood. Republicans had a majority in the Senate (Wilson was a Democrat), while Irish, Italian, and German minority constituents all reported to their representatives their dissatisfactions with the peace settlement. In November 1919, the proposal that the United States join the League of Nations failed, and Wilson's spirits crumbled. Without American leadership, the League did not have the necessary strength to fulfill its mission.

It certainly could not overcome the bitter feelings left by the peace treaties that the victor nations presented their former enemies: Versailles, with Germany, June 28, 1919; Saint-Germain, with Austria, September 10, 1919; Neuilly, with Bulgaria, November 27, 1919; Trianon, with Hungary, June 4, 1920; Sèvres, with Ottoman Turkey, August 10, 1920. No sooner issued, the treaties were challenged by the defeated nations. The next war was already in the making, as the French Marshal Ferdinand Foch (1851–1929) understood when he said of the Versailles agreement, "This isn't a peace, it's a twenty-year truce!" It lasted not quite twenty years.

Outcomes

In his 1865 Second Inaugural Address, President Abraham Lincoln reflected on the bitter experience of the American Civil War (see Chapter 19). It was longer and more cruel than anyone had anticipated. But its achievements were also monumental—the reestablishment of the American democracy, and the abolition of slavery. Had Lincoln spoken fifty-four years later of the record left by World War I, he would have noted a slaughter far greater, but an outcome less hopeful. Its main effect was to increase, as the humanist Desiderius Erasmus (1469–1536) said of wars long before, the "empire of the dead."

The chief outcome of World War I was the fall of the mighty—the rulers of four empires (German, Austro-Hungarian, Russian, and Ottoman); the values of European civilization that had reached its

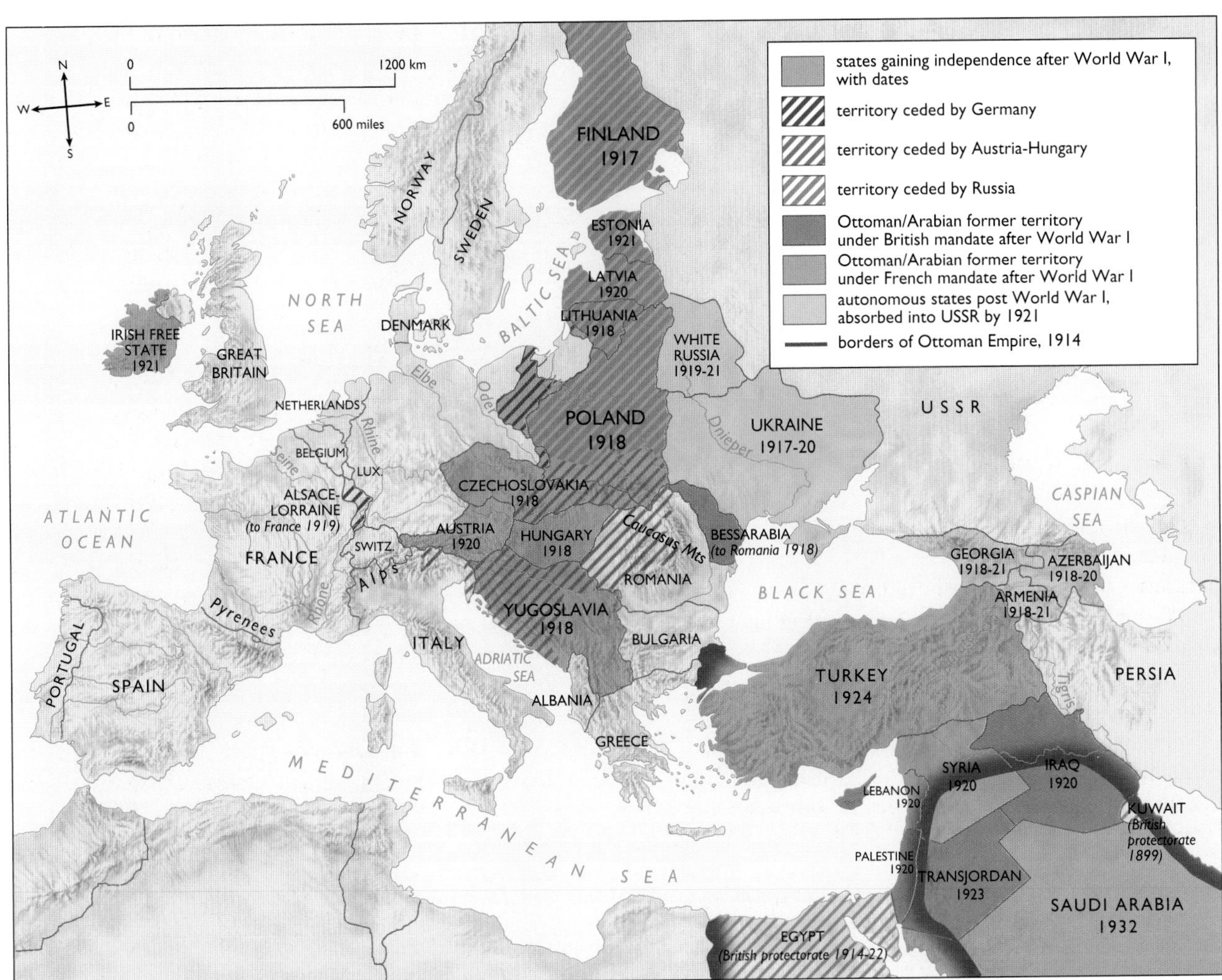

Map 25.3 Redrawing the Boundaries: *Post-war Europe looked very different from its pre-war incarnation. Hoping to resolve the varied nationalist tensions blamed for provoking the conflict in the first place, negotiators broke up large multinational empires and created (or recreated) a swath of countries along supposed lines of "national self-determination." The settlement also destroyed, or weakened, numerous European empires. The Ottoman Empire, long considered the "Sick Man of Europe," was one of the chief casualties. Germany was compelled to yield her colonies to the protection of victor nations. They were greedy to assume their new "mandates" but too exhausted to manage them effectively (see also Map 23.3 on p. 722).*

zenith in the century just ended; and an entire generation of young men. "How are the mighty fallen/ and the weapons of war perished!" (2 Samuel 1:25).

The first of these effects this chapter has already traced. The second will be described in Chapter 26. The third left a Europe populous with orphans, black-garbed widows, and mutilated men, who lived to visit the fresh-dug graves that crowded immense new cemeteries. Casualty rates in the armies of Germany, France, and Russia reached, respectively, sixty-three, seventy-one, and seventy-six percent; in Britain, never invaded, and Italy, only peripherally engaged, the rates were thirty-four and thirty-nine percent. The United States, a late entrant, mobilized about 4 million men, and suffered only eight percent casualties. The Austro-Hungarian Empire suffered the highest rate of casualties, fighting simultaneously on two fronts, in cold, and amid mountains. Of the 7.8 million men mobilized, seven million—almost ninety percent—were killed or wounded.

Overall, some 8.5 million combatants died (not counting those dead of disease and other war-related causes)—thirteen percent of the 65 million mobilized. The French, German, Austrian, and Romanian dead were sixteen, sixteen, fifteen percent and a staggering forty-five percent of combatants respectively. The French dead, more than 1.3 million men of 8.4 million sent to war, were a number equivalent to one-

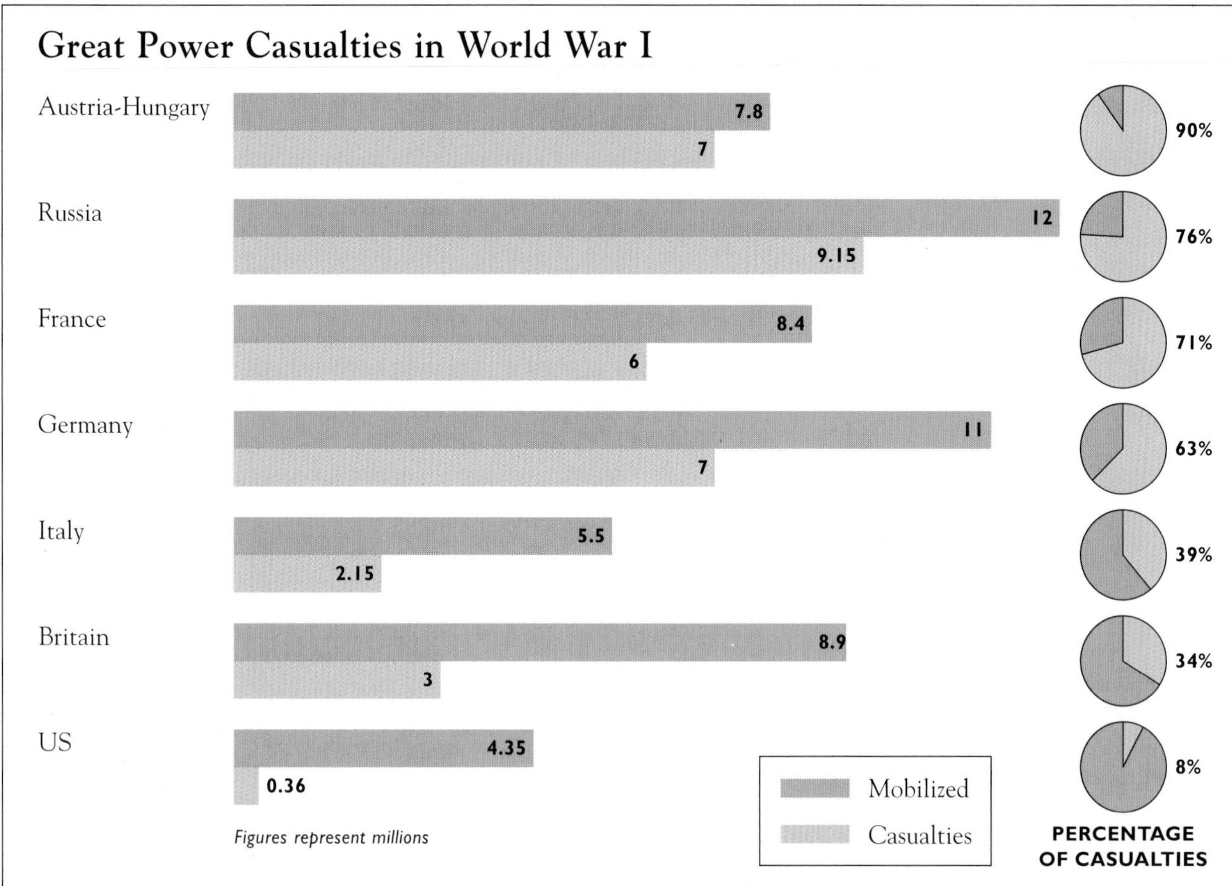

As this graph of World War I casualty rates (including dead and wounded) for seven nations shows, Austria suffered catastrophic losses, followed by its opponents Russia (which had the largest commitment of soldiers), and France. The United States, a latecomer to the conflict, committed few soldiers and suffered only slight losses.
Source: *J. L. Stokesbury,* A Short History of World War I *(New York: Quill, 1981), p. 310.*

half of all those who, in 1914, were between eighteen and thirty-two years of age—one-half a generation.

Thirty million more were to die in the aftermath of war—the victims of the worst ever influenza epidemic. Probably borne to Europe by United States soldiers in the spring of 1918, the disease raged among the undernourished survivors of total war and their colonial brethren of every continent. The horrors of the battlefront nourished the still greater cataclysms that hostile Nature could wreak.

Conclusion

GLOBAL WAR AND THE MEANING OF THE WEST

World War I marked the point at which the West ceased to be in the ascendant over the other civilizations of the world. Its political influence had peaked and its cultural confidence was shattered—it seemed a "botched civilization," as Pound had written. Over the next three generations, though pressed by economic collapse (Chapter 26), the loss of empire (Chapter 28), the hell of totalitarianism (Chapter 27), and the joint terrors of genocide and the atomic bomb (Chapters 27, 29), the West would nevertheless endure.

REVIEW QUESTIONS

1. Why was there no general war in Europe in 1815–1914? How did the limited wars of the nineteenth century affect attitudes toward war? Why had two rival alliance systems been formed in Europe by 1914?

2. What role did rivalries outside Europe play in raising tensions among the Great Powers in the decades before World War I? What role did Pan-Slavism play in the road to war? Why did Austria declare war on Serbia in July 1914?

3. Why was there so much support for war in 1914? How did European leaders envisage the war? How did the war affect women in European society?

4. Why did the Schlieffen plan fail? Why could neither side win a quick victory on the Western Front? How did modern technology affect war? Why were the Germans more successful in the east than in the west?

5. Why did the United States enter the war? Why were the Bolsheviks able to get control of Russia? What territories did Russia lose?

6. How did the ideals expressed in Wilson's 14 Points compare to the terms of the Treaty of Versailles? Why was the Versailles Treaty not a lasting foundation for peace in Europe? What were the major political and territorial changes that the war brought about in Europe, the Near East, and Asia?

SUGGESTED READINGS

Pathways to War

Berghahn, V. R., *Germany and the Approach of War in 1914*, 2nd ed. (New York: St. Martin's Press, 1993). Written from a German point of view, a useful balance to more Anglocentric war studies.

Joll, James, *The Origins of the First World War*, 2nd ed. (London–New York: Longman, 1992). Argues that alliances and decisions made long before 1914 drove Europe almost irresistably to the brink, reducing freedom of action in the final, fateful days before hostilities began.

Langdon, John W., *July 1914: The Long Debate, 1918–1990* (New York: St. Martin's Press, 1991) Discusses six key questions concerning the outbreak of World War I, including the culpability of Germany, Serbian complicity in the assassination of Archduke Franz Ferdinand, and British diplomacy on the eve of war.

Stevenson, David, *Armaments and the Coming of War: Europe 1904–1914* (Oxford: Clarendon Press of Oxford University Press, 1996). Explores the military technologies of each of the major European powers during the late 19th and early 20th centuries.

In the Midst of Battle

Cecil, Hugh, *The Flower of Battle: How Britain Wrote the Great War* (South Royalton, VT: Steerforth Press, 1996). Looks at the war through the eyes and literary writings of twelve British and Irish participants.

Gilbert, Martin, *The First World War: A Complete History* (New York: H. Holt, 1994). Scholarly and detailed account of the war.

Macdonald, Lyn, *1915: Death of Innocence* (New York: Henry Holt, 1994). Portrait of the generation most impacted by war.

Offner, Avner, *The First World War: An Agrarian Interpretation* (Oxford: Clarendon Press of Oxford, University Press, 1989). Highlights the vital role played in the war by available food supplies.

Winter, Jay, *Sites of Memory, Sites of Mourning: The Great War in European Cultural History* (Cambridge: Cambridge University Press, 1995). The trauma of the war lingered long after the peace treaties were signed, marked by the cemeteries and monuments that sprang up as "sites of mourning" over the face of Europe. Fascinating study of the impacts of events on consciousness.

Woollacott, Angela, *On Her Their Lives Depend: Munitions Workers in the Great War*, (Berkeley: University of California Press, 1994). Explores the lives, conditions, and consequences of women's work in munitions factories in Britain during the war.

The Russian Revolution

Clements, Barbara Evans, *Bolshevik Women* (Cambridge: Cambridge University Press, 1997). Studies from the women who made the Russian Revolution, the pre-revolutionary generation of agitators to the death of the last female Bolshevik in the post-Stalinist era.

Fitzpatrick, Sheila, *The Russian Revolution*, 2nd ed. (Oxford: Oxford University Press, 1994). Assesses the revolutionary achievement from 1917 to the early 1930s, challenging notions of the Bolsheviks as merely totalitarian dictators.

Pipes, Richard, *The Russian Revolution* (New York: Knopf, 1990). Exhaustive and controversial account of the Revolution by one of its most outstanding and outspoken recent critics.

Wolfe, Bertram, *Three Who Made a Revolution* (New York: Dial Press, 1948; 4th rev. ed., New York: Dell, 1978). Classic study of Lenin, Trotsky, and Stalin.

In Search of Peace

Ascher, Abraham, *The Revolution of 1905*, 2 Vols, (Stanford, CA: Stanford University Press, 1988–92). Authoritative account of the 1905 Revolution, evaluated on its own terms rather than as a prelude to 1917.

Keynes, John M., *The Economic Consequences of the Peace* (New York: Harcourt, Brace & Howe, 1920). Negative assessment of the Versailles settlement by an eminent economist who experienced the event.

Schwabe, Klaus, *Woodrow Wilson, Revolutionary Germany, and Peacemaking, 1918–1919: Missionary Diplomacy and the Realities of Power* (Chapel Hill, NC: University of North Carolina Press, 1985). Woodrow Wilson's role in the post-war peace process.

THE TRIUMPH OF UNCERTAINTY

1900 | 1910 | 1920 | 1930 | 1940 | 1950

Politics and War

World War I and the Russian Revolution, 1914–21

World War II, 1939–45

- Mussolini's fascists march on Rome, 1922
- Adolf Hitler achieves power in Germany, 1933
- Italy invades Ethiopia, 1935
- Germany rearms, 1936

Society, Economy, and Ideas

- Max Planck's concepts of quantum mechanics, 1900
- Ellen Key's *The Century of the Child*, 1900
- First films play in "nickleodeons," 1900s
- American Federation of Labor (AFL) represents nearly one-third of US skilled workers, 1901
- Albert Einstein announces principle of Relativity, 1905
- National Insurance Act in Britain, 1911
- Marcel Proust's *Remembrance of Things Past*, 1913–27
- D. W. Griffith's *The Birth of a Nation*, 1915
- Margaret Sanger establishes birth control clinic in New York, 1916
- Alexandra Kollontai forms *Zhenotdel* (Women's Department) in Soviet Russia, 1919
- New Economic Policy (NEP) in Russia, 1921–28
- Luigi Pirandello's *Six Characters in Search of an Author*, 1921
- James Joyce's *Ulysses*, 1922
- T. S. Eliot's "The Waste Land," 1922
- Hyperinflation destroys German currency's value, 1923
- Dawes Plan reschedules German reparations payments, 1924
- Sergei Eisenstein's *The Battleship Potemkin*, 1925
- Virginia Woolf's *Mrs Dalloway*, 1925
- Franz Kafka's *The Trial*, 1925
- Quantum theory established, 1926
- John Maynard Keynes' *The End of Laissez–Faire*, 1926
- Werner Heisenberg formulates "uncertainty principle," 1927
- Bertolt Brecht's *Threepenny Opera*, 1928
- Sergei Eisenstein's *October*, 1928
- Joseph Stalin launches First Five year Plan in Russia, 1928
- US stockmarket crash and start of Depression, 1929
- Hawley-Smoot Tariff, 1930
- Austria's Creditanstalt bank fails, 1931
- 13 million Americans (30% of workforce) unemployed, 1932
- Franklin Delano Roosevelt establishes New Deal, 1933
- "Popular Front" alliances of Communists and Socialists, 1935
- Leni Riefenstahl's *Triumph of the Will*, 1935
- "Popular Front" left–liberal government under Léon Blum in France, 1936
- Jean Renoir's *La Grande Illusion*, 1937
- Sergei Eisenstein's *Alexander Nevsky*, 1938
- Jean-Paul Sartre's *Being and Nothingness*, 1943

Beyond the West

Korean War, 1950–53

- Amritsar Massacre, India, 1919
- British Commonwealth of Nations created, 1931
- Japan invades China, 1937
- Independence and partition of India, 1947
- UN partitions Palestine, Israel declares independence, 1947
- Communist victory in China, 1949

CHAPTER 26

THE TRIUMPH OF UNCERTAINTY

Cultural Innovation, Social Disruption, and Economic Collapse

1915–1945

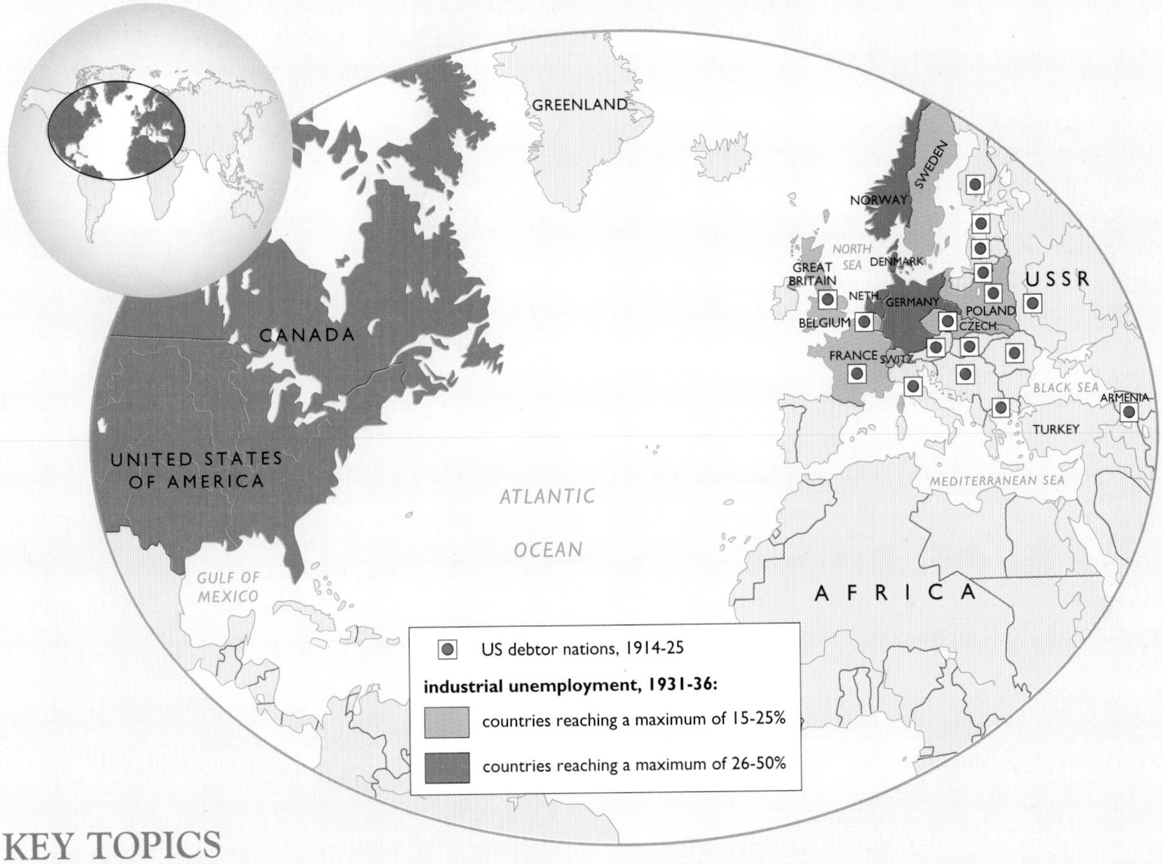

KEY TOPICS

- **Uncertainty in the Arts and in Thought:** The wounded generation that survives World War I amuses itself with the illusions of cinema and the subversive sounds of jazz, while it ignores as much as possible reports that the cosmos is uncertain, indeterminate, and unknowable.
- **Uncertain Boundaries:** New Women go to work in short skirts and with short hair; neither thinking nor acting like their mothers; the family shrinks, losing numbers and purpose, while the state takes on the nurturant functions that family and Church had provided.
- **Economic Uncertainty:** The post-war economic boom crashes, bringing bankruptcy and the dole, except where dictators rule; the shamed and doubt-ridden people of the West are vulnerable to their blandishments.

The Roll of Dice *In 1930, the young physicist Werner Heisenberg (1901–1976) explained his "principle of indeterminacy" to a scientific gathering that included the giant of the scientific world Albert Einstein (1879–1955), creator of the theory of relativity (see Chapter 24). Since the behavior of subatomic particles could not be precisely known, Heisenberg reasoned, it should be described in terms of statistical probability. Einstein found the notion of a merely probable universe intolerable; a moral world, he insisted, depended on a rational universe. "God," he barked, "does not roll dice."*

But Heisenberg's indeterminacy more accurately describes the realities in the Western world in the years after World War I (1914–1918) than does Einstein's vision of order. To most artists and intellectuals—for whom God had long since died (see Chapter 24)—the old certainties had vanished and the future was shadowy. Gender roles and social institutions were also in flux, as women sought personal freedom and citizenship, and as the traditional family lost many of its functions to social workers and state agencies. Western economies boomed and crashed, leaving millions without the savings that had promised security in old age, and millions more without work or without food. This catastrophe struck barely ten years after the close of a war that had left an unprecedented number mutilated and dead (see Chapter 25).

In this age of unknowns, the human condition was fragile. The mood of doubt and the tendency to irrationalism that had characterized the pre-war West mounted to a chronic condition of uncertainty. During the twenty years between the conclusion of the Paris peace treaties and the declarations that opened World War II, uncertainty triumphed in the arts and in thought, in social roles and institutions, and in economic life. Its shadow was not dispelled before the century ended.

UNCERTAINTY IN THE ARTS AND IN THOUGHT

The assault on rationalism that began with Romanticism around 1800 peaked in the early twentieth century. Pessimism prevailed about the nature of reality, the integrity of the self, the limits of language. The visual arts abandoned linear narrative and realistic representation. Scientists and philosophers, despairing of certain knowledge, found ways to describe their uncertainty or abandoned the search for absolute truths altogether. Literature looked inward, or focused on the perils of the human condition adrift in a world that was meaningless or menacing.

Montage: the Disrupted Narrative

Building on **avant-garde** developments in the last years of the nineteenth century, the pioneering artists of the twentieth no longer sought to represent objective reality. Whatever they painted, played, performed, or screened was not intended to imitate what existed in the world, but to present a creative reinvention of that reality. This Modernist project involved the abandonment of earlier artistic norms as new orthodoxies emerged in a rapidfire procession.

THE ILLUSTRATED LONDON NEWS

No. 3798.—VOL CXL. SATURDAY, FEBRUARY 3, 1912. SIXPENCE.

Moving Pictures

King George V and Queen Mary: *The new medium of film allowed two privileged spectators—the British monarchs King George V and Queen Mary, as drawn on the cover of* The Illustrated London News *(February 3, 1912)—to view themselves in a motion picture that recorded a scene from the era of imperialism destined soon to close. This was the Durbar, the occasion for the ritual expression of loyalty to the Crown of native Indian dignitaries.*

Moving Pictures Of the technical innovations, none was more novel than film. Its precursor the photograph had evolved from the 1830s to capture an image of objects in front of a camera—a great man, his family, a battlefield. Fifty years later, film was invented as a sequence of photographs, each viewed very rapidly in turn as the celluloid medium—the film—was drawn before the eye of the beholder. The effect was a moving picture created from the series of separate images. The art form popularly known as "the movies," "flicks," or "films" was more formally called **cinema**, short for "cinematograph" (from the Greek words for "motion" and for "drawing"), a picture engendered by motion.

The moving picture, however, existed nowhere on the film; It existed only in the mind of the viewer, whose brain supplied the continuity between separate still images. Whereas the photograph was the quintessential form of "Realist" art, claiming to reproduce perfectly the real object, film was essentially a modern medium, representing something that conceivably might exist but in fact did not.

In the 1900s and 1910s, fascinated viewers devoured early films in shopfront theaters called "nickelodeons" (because it cost a nickel, or five cents, to view) or peered into machines called "kinetoscopes" (from the Greek words for "motion" and "view"). An alternative to the live entertainment of the music hall or theater was provided by the soundless train rides, battles, robberies, or slapstick routines that formed the staple subjects of films. Studios sprang up as entrepreneurs sought to satisfy the public's appetite for the sixteen-minute-long films (the playing time of the celluloid strip that could be stored on one reel), of which hundreds, then thousands were produced each year. Mass entertainment had been born.

A motley cohort of artists turned film into the characteristic art form of the twentieth century. They were themselves actors, directors, or producers, with prior experience in provincial repertory, music hall, and circus. These were not intellectuals, but pragmatists willing to work fast and risk everything to exploit the moving image for expression and for profit.

Among the first great cinematographers were the American D. W. Griffith (1875–1948) and the Russian Sergei Eisenstein (1898–1948), who boldly appropriated the technology of film to create a new kind of narrative form. Griffith was a Kentucky-born sentimentalist who longed for the patrician South of the United States before the Civil War—a culture based on slavery. His most famous film, *The Birth of a Nation* (1915), was an American epic exploring the soul of the nation by retelling its history. It culminates with a scene repellent to modern audiences of the Ku Klux Klan (a secret society pledged to enforce the subordination of African Americans newly released from slavery) riding out on its nightmarish mission, and defeating the quintessential enemy—the African American soldiers of a United States Army force.

To arrive at his grandiose and unfortunate vision, Griffith introduced many innovations to the business of film-making. Films extended beyond their one-reel, sixteen-minute format to several reels, and two or three hours. And the photographic sequences were edited, so that the viewer saw an assemblage of images that did not necessarily occur in the same place or in sequence—a structural change that added a further element of unreality to the unreality that was already

D. W. Griffith, Birth of a Nation: *Pioneer film-maker D. W. Griffith portrays in 1915 the birth of a nation with novel techniques and old hatreds. Here in the wake of the Civil War, members of the Ku Klux Klan (a racist paramilitary group active in the American south after Reconstruction and into the first decades of the twentieth century) "build" the new United States, as Griffith sees it, through terror.*

inherent in the medium. Griffith juxtaposed scenes that were to be understood as simultaneous in real time—robbers approaching, for instance, while the inhabitants of a house dread their arrival. Drama and suspense created by these juxtapositions enhanced the experience of viewing.

Eisenstein, making films under Communist rule from 1924 until his death in 1948, was an even more sophisticated manipulator of cinematic images. Eisenstein disrupted natural sequences, extracting images as his eye and his concept required to produce specific psychological effects in the viewer. This method of composition, based on disruption or discontinuity, is called ***montage*** (a French word referring to the ordering of images). The director rearranges reality to create a cinematic narrative that is abstract and idea-driven.

Using juxtapositions and interpolations in a pattern whose structure was rooted in the theory of **Marxian dialectic**, Eisenstein constructed sweeping, epic retellings of revolutionary events. His *Battleship Potemkin* (1925) retells an incident of the 1905 Revolution in Russia. Without sound or artificial lighting, or trained actors in major roles, by juxtaposing images of a sailors' rebellion, a popular demonstration, and the repressive violence of a military guard, he communicates the essentials of the revolutionary message: the innocence of the masses of the people, and the evil of those who hold power over them.

The work of Griffith, Eisenstein, and other early film-makers—German, French, Italian, and Swedish as well as American and Russian—paved the way for the mature cinema of the 1920s and 1930s (by which time it had acquired synchronous sound). Many films aimed merely to entertain: grandiose historical epics, westerns, and gangster movies. Others presented social critiques, as did the comic films of Charlie Chaplin (1889–1977). The English-born son of two circus performers, Chaplin was grounded in the high comic tradition and used the persona of the clown in many of his films (which he directed, and in which he often acted) to reveal the absurdities of modern times.

Less comic but equally profound, Jean Renoir (1894–1979), the son of the Impressionist painter Pierre-Auguste Renoir, explored the meaning of World War I in his *La Grande Illusion* ("The Great Illusion") of 1937. Not a wartime adventure story, but an analysis of the disintegration of the traditional European world during World War I, Renoir's film juxtaposes a German and a French aristocrat, and these in turn with a worker and a Jew. Although the French gentleman is the German's prisoner, both are equally the social superiors of the other two—who nevertheless represent the vigorous world of the future, and who alone will survive the reality and the illusion of war.

Whereas some films offered a critique of contemporary society, others were created to celebrate the prevailing political regime. These were the propaganda films of the Communists and the German National Socialists, or Nazis, who recognized the capacity of the new medium to lend grandeur and conviction to their enterprise. In the Soviet Union, Lenin had recognized the importance of film (he called it the most important art form of the century), and his successor Joseph Stalin (1879–1953; see Chapters 25, 27) enlisted it to advance the interests of the new communist state. Film-making was placed under the supervision of an office of *agitprop*—the term abbreviating words meaning "agitation," denoting the arousal of revolutionary enthusiasm, and **propaganda**, meaning the diffusion of concepts favorable to the regime. Eisenstein, who had passionately hymned the Revolution in such films as *The Battleship Potemkin* and *October* (or *Ten Days that Shook the World*) (1928), was muzzled under Stalin by the artistic policy of **Socialist Realism**. Only as World War II approached (see Chapter 27) did his originality reappear in *Alexander Nevsky* (1938). Recalling a medieval confrontation between heroic defenders of Russian Muscovy and the faceless, heartless ranks of Germanic invaders defeated in battle on a frozen lake, the film symbolized the imminent struggle with a modern enemy.

Similarly, the Nazi German leader Adolf Hitler (1889–1945) supported the creation of those films that advanced the Nazi agenda (see Chapter 27). He commissioned Leni Riefenstahl (1902–), Germany's first major woman director, to create the documentary film *Triumph of the Will* (1935), whose chilling message of German supremacy and romanticized aggression caused it to be banned in Britain, Canada, and the United States. Using unusual camera angles to maximize the awesome impression of Nazi leaders, and to announce the capacity for disciplined violence of massed Nazi troops, Riefenstahl advanced Hitler's project to install the third, final, and eternal Reich, or empire (the first was the medieval, Holy Roman Empire; the second lasted from 1871 to 1918).

Far from Russia and Germany during these interwar years, the film industry installed itself in Hollywood, part of Los Angeles, California, a new city where the weather was almost always good. Promiscuity and gangsterism flourished in this root-

René Magritte,* The Betrayal of Images, *1928

Uncertainty, Now and To Come

Like the performing arts, the visual arts reflected twentieth-century currents in thought and feeling. This painting by René Magritte (above) gives expression to the uncertainties of the age. A familiar object is labeled with a description that says it is not what it is: "Ceci n'est pas une pipe" *("This is not a pipe").*

More confidently, Futurist artists looked ahead to new human triumphs over nature and history. In 1914, Antonio Sant'Elia imagined the city of the future—not very distant from our own cities today, but immensely different from those of Europe on the verge of World War I, where many buildings, streets, and squares were still defined by the architectural norms of previous centuries. (above: Los Angeles County Museum of Art; below: Paride Accetti Collection, Milan).

less society of instant celebrities, awash (especially during the years of Prohibition, 1920–1933, when alcohol was officially banned) in a flood of alcohol, nicotine, and drugs. Hollywood became the capital of mass communications. It would communicate to vast audiences the reconstructions of reality assembled in a montage from photographic fragments—an unreal representation of a concrete reality.

Other Visual Arts Film may have been—and may still be—the most important medium of the visual arts in this century, as Lenin had said; but its career paralleled that of the others. In painting and sculpture, various schools of abstract art ("abstract" in that they considered themselves free from the "concreteness" of the represented object) flourished in the major artistic centers, especially Paris: Cubism, Expressionism, Surrealism, and others (see Chapter 24). Novel and original, the artistic works produced shared a more or less marked tendency to distort, segment, displace, superimpose, or otherwise violate the recognizable objects of the real environment.

In architecture, despite its inherent "concreteness," innovations also abounded. Architects rejected the traditional vocabulary of building—the arches, columns, and

***Antonio Sant'Elia,* Electric Center**

domes, the grand entrances and decorated windows informed by Classical, Gothic, Renaissance, and Baroque forms. Instead, they designed the buildings needed by a modern age—factories, office blocks, railroad stations—that were expressive of their function, stripped of decoration, employing conspicuously the building materials of the modern age: concrete, glass, and steel.

The Jazz Age Unlike painting and sculpture, seen only in museums, architecture reached the eyes of multitudes. Like film, it was a medium of mass communication. In the same way, while some forms of music remained esoteric in the interwar years, a new form of music—**jazz**—became truly popular. Heard in bars and restaurants, on phonographs or radios, it gave its name to the era. The Jazz Age marked a new musical genre, and a new kind of audience.

The new vocabulary of jazz distinguished it from the classical repertoire, naive folk song, and music hall ditties. North American in origin but quickly appreciated in Europe, jazz was a kind of musical montage derived from the experience of African Americans, based on the sounds invented during centuries of plantation slavery. A fusion of African harmony, melody, and rhythm with Western styles, these sounds were heard in work songs and lamentations, in field shouts and Christian spirituals, and later woven into the new forms of jazz—**blues**, ragtime, Dixieland, swing, bop, and successive styles.

Jazz diverged sharply from the classical tradition both in sound and culture. In contrast to the symphony orchestra, jazz was played by bands (playing such instruments as trumpet, trombone, and tuba, saxophone and clarinet, bass, banjo, and guitar, drums, and piano). It was improvisational: the lead performer invented and varied both melody and rhythm at will backed up by a band that spontaneously responded to the soloist's cues. Its rhythms were therefore freer than those heard in the concert hall, and its melodies featured non-standard repetitions, dissonances, improvisations, and the characteristic flattened thirds and sevenths of the chord that established the tonality of sadness supplied by the experience of slavery. The blues, generally vocal, highlighted that sadness in songs about poverty, abandonment, and despair.

Jazz came from the other side of town—from the slums, ghettos, and working-class districts alongside the railroad tracks and the docks. Most of its performers were black, although white bands and orchestras adopted the style and popularized it among audiences outside the South. At first, jazz was widely denounced by respectable people as music that celebrated sex and had wild jungle rhythms. Many of its performers, and many listeners, like the Hollywood stars and starlets, led a fast life that came to characterize the era: the 1920s are often called the "jazz age." Jazz was nevertheless a sophisticated musical form—popular in every sense—created by ordinary people, and from the experience of their unique past, and addressed directly to audiences of ordinary, untrained listeners; yet it was able to rival in expressive capacity and in audience appeal the classical forms of the high musical tradition.

At the same time that jazz challenged classical sound, the new compositions of classically-trained composers, now experimenting with atonality, were rapidly disenchanting concert audiences (see Chapter 24). As the new symphonies and operas became less

Louis Armstrong's jazz combo: *Just as film pieced together real images into a constructed new reality, modern dance and popular music utilized bits of classical art forms to construct patterns of movement and sound expressive of a modern age. Depicted here is Louis Armstrong (seated left), leader of the Hot Five combo that flourished in the 1920s, and the figure who brought the new sound of jazz from New Orleans in the American south to affluent urban audiences.*

comprehensible even to educated listeners, these demanded to hear the works of the older classical and Romantic repertory. Requiring a familiarity with a historical musical tradition, the concert hall became increasingly remote from contemporary experience—something to be enjoyed by well-to-do consumers of a specialized cultural product. Dance suffered a similar rupture: classical ballet was remote from the experience of most people, for whom dance meant the dances performed in music hall and cabaret, or by the audience of jazz bands, who became participants in the process of expressive improvisation. In the United States, modern dance freed itself from the rituals of ballet, formulated in royal courts, to incorporate some elements of folk dance movement, and convey emotion more expressively. In Europe, ballet continued to win popular attention in Russia, opera in Italy. Elsewhere, however, the repertoire of the Jazz Age dominated, as it did in the cabarets of Europe whose song and dance, jaded successors to the lighthearted fare of turn-of-the-century music halls, mocked society and its guardians.

The jazz idiom, and its message of a world where the disinherited and irreverent reigned was dramatized in the blazingly original plays of the German author Bertolt Brecht (1898–1956). Brecht's angry Marxism, seen in his savage critique of capitalists as exploiters of the poor, shocked his audience. So did his unblinking honesty which uncovered moral failings in the oppressed as well as the oppressor, and his break with the custom of theatrical illusion. Brechtian theater used some of the devices of cinematic montage. Narrative continuities were disrupted so as to arouse emotions—outrage, disgust, hostility—in the viewer. *Die Dreigroschenoper* (*The Threepenny Opera*, 1928), based on an eighteenth-century play about London's criminal underworld, *The Beggar's Opera* (1728), combines Brecht's drama with the jazz score of composer Kurt Weill (1900–1950) to yield a theatrical achievement—midway between the century's two world wars and on the eve of global economic crisis—that is the epitome of the Modern.

In challenging conventional morality, Brecht had allies in Britain and across the Atlantic. Irish-born playwright George Bernard Shaw (1856–1950) assaulted Victorian assumptions about class, religion, and sex in his plays, while American Eugene O'Neill (1888–1953) explored in his dramas the tragic hypocrisy of family relationships. Neither Shaw nor O'Neill, however, stabbed so viciously as Brecht at the comfortable assumptions of contemporary society.

Brecht's acid cynicism was more nearly matched by the humorous but black pessimism of the Italian author Luigi Pirandello (1867–1936). Pirandello's dramas are disturbing not because, like Brecht's, they violated moral and theatrical conventions, but because they invaded the boundary between reality and illusion and left viewers confused and doubt-ridden. Perhaps no play more accurately mirrors the uncertainty of the twentieth-century Western outlook than Pirandello's *Six Characters in Search of an Author* (1921), describing that world as a vacuum whose Creator has ceased to exist. Contemporary scientists and philosophers had similar doubts about a universe without author, purpose, or compassion.

WHO'S WHO

Writers and Artists in an Age of Uncertainty

Luigi Pirandello (1867–1936) Italian novelist and playwright; his *Six Characters in Search of an Author* (1921) developed the technique of "theater within the theater."

D. W. Griffith (1875–1948) American pioneer motion-picture director; his *The Birth of a Nation* (1915) has been hailed for its innovative technique and condemned for its racist message.

Eugene O'Neill (1888-1953) Leading American dramatist; major works include *Long Day's Journey into Night* (produced posthumously in 1956) and *The Iceman Cometh* (1946).

Charlie Chaplin (1889–1977) British-born American actor and film director; his "lovable tramp" character earned him critical and popular acclaim; major films include *Modern Times* (1935) and *The Great Dictator* (1940).

Jean Renoir (1894–1979) French-born film director; son of the Impressionist painter Pierre-Auguste Renoir; his films—including *Madame Bovary* (1934) and *Grand Illusion* (1937)—are known for their dramatic realism.

Bertolt Brecht (1898–1956) German playwright and poet; author of *Threepenny Opera* (1928); pioneered the use of theater as a vehicle for leftist political criticism.

Sergei Eisenstein (1898–1948) Russian film director and Soviet propagandist; his *Battleship Potemkin* (1925), *October* (1928), and *Alexander Nevsky* (1938) combined major historical themes with ground-breaking cinematography.

Indeterminacy: the Limits of Knowledge and Action

In the nineteenth century, the biological sciences had flourished; the early twentieth century, in contrast, was the age of new discoveries in physics. These dismantled the Newtonian cosmos, which had affirmed the rationality, consistency, and predictability of all universal actions—a paradigm that had for two hundred years governed the thinking of experts and public alike. The cosmos that took its place was changing, bent, and uncertain.

The Anxieties of Science The principle of relativity announced by Albert Einstein in 1905 (see Chapter 24) shattered Newtonian certainties. In Newton's universe, definable laws acted uniformly on objects that behaved predictably and consistently. Into this ordered world, Einstein introduced the element of uncertainty. Time and space were relative to the observer. What was true in one set of conditions was not true in another. Instead of inspiring faith in a Creator, the new condition of the universe aroused anxiety.

That anxiety increased with the investigation of the **atom** by the scientists Neils Bohr (1885–1962), Max Planck (1858–1947), and Werner Heisenberg. Previously, the atom had been understood as the smallest particle, irreducible and changeless, of any substance. That notion had originated with the ancient Greek philosopher Democritus (see Chapter 4), but it rapidly disintegrated after 1895, when the discovery of X-rays and the investigation of radiation by the Curies (see Chapter 24) inaugurated a new scientific venture: the investigation of subatomic particles.

Within the atom, scientists discovered an inconceivably small universe anchored by a nucleus about which other particles whirled (the electrons); and within the nucleus, further particles (protons and neutrons). Over the next generation, they attempted to align the model of the motion of subatomic particles with that of planetary bodies in the solar system. They learned that the particles' electrical nature—they were positive (the protons), negative (the electrons), or neutral (the neutrons)—caused them to repel or attract each other and hold the system in balance. They learned that the disruption of the nucleus resulted in the release of enormous stored energy—the fundamental principle behind the atomic bomb (see Chapter 27).

Planck proposed that the energy emitted by atomic particles did not flow smoothly but jumped in discontinuous spurts, or quanta (hence "**quantum** theory"). And yet the wave theory of light, or electricity, could not be entirely abandoned for a particle theory, if all phenomena were to be explained. Scientists concluded that both wave and particle theories, though seemingly contradictory, were correct, and that the two coexisted logically though absurdly—the theory of "complementarity."

Werner Heisenberg's 1927 formulation of the awesome "principle of indeterminacy" or "uncertainty," pointed out the limits of knowledge. Heisenberg demonstrated that it was impossible to know certainly both the position and the velocity of a subatomic particle. The more precise knowledge of one attribute became, the less precise knowledge of the other was rendered. Since certainty was impossible, the investigator should describe each by a range of statistical possibility. In a universe that was indeterminate, or uncertain, the scientist could never attain more than probable knowledge. It was this surrender to a permanent condition of uncertainty that Einstein—refused to accept. One day, he preferred to hope, the

WHO'S WHO

Scientists and Philosophers in an Age of Uncertainty

Albert Einstein (1879–1955) German-born Jewish physicist; developed special and general theories of relativity, and the notion that mass and energy are interconvertible as expressed by the equation "$e = mc^2$."

Werner Heisenberg (1901–1970) German physicist and philosopher; his Uncertainty Principle (1927) proposes that it is impossible accurately and simultaneously to measure the position and velocity of a particle.

Bertrand Russell (1872–1970) Nobel-Prize winning English philosopher and mathematician; ardent advocate of pacifism and nuclear disarmament.

Ludwig Wittgenstein (1889–1951) Austrian-born English philosopher, his *Tractatus Logico-Philosophicus* (1922) treated the nature and limits of language.

Jean-Paul Sartre (1905–1980) French novelist and existential philosopher; argued that the essential meaninglessness of existence presented humans with an opportunity for total freedom.

WITNESSES

The World Becomes Uncertain

French writer and thinker Paul Valéry discusses the cultural and psychological effects of World War I (1922): We are a very unfortunate generation, whose lot has been to see the moment of our passage through life coincide with the arrival of great and terrifying events, the echo of which will resound through all our lives. . . . You know how greatly the general economic situation has been disturbed, and the polity of states, and the very life of the individual; you are familiar with the universal discomfort, hesitation, apprehension. *But among all these injured things is the Mind.* The Mind has indeed been cruelly wounded; its complaint is heard in the hearts of intellectual man; it passes a mournful judgment on itself. It doubts itself profoundly.
(Paul Valéry, speech, 1922; ed. M. Cowley, 1954)

Albert Einstein's Theory of Relativity described by a peer (Lincoln Barnett) (1954): It [Einstein's Theory of Relativity] explains why all observers in all systems everywhere, regardless of their state of motion, will always find that light strikes their instruments and departs from their instruments at precisely the same velocity. For as their own velocity approaches that of light, their clocks slow down, their yardsticks contract, and all their measurements are reduced to the values obtained by a relatively stationary observer. . . . From this it follows that nothing can move faster than light, no matter what forces are applied.
(Lincoln Barnett, *The Universe and Dr. Einstein*, 1954)

Werner Heisenberg explains how war inspired his scientific thought (1952): When I left school in 1920 in order to attend the University of Munich, the position of our youth as citizens was very similar to what it is today. Our defeat in the first world war [*sic*] had produced a deep mistrust of all the ideals which had been used during the war and which had lost us that war. They seemed hollow now and we wanted to find out for ourselves what was of value in this world and what was not: we did not want to rely on our parents or our teachers. Apart from many other values we re-discovered science in this process.
(Werner Heisenberg, *Philosophical Problems of Nuclear Science*, 1952; ed. F. C. Hayes, 1966)

Painter Vasily Kandinsky learns that the artist's goal should be to express feeling and not represent objects, whose very existence science has called into doubt (1913): Previously I had only known realistic art . . . and suddenly for the first time I saw a *painting*. That it was a haystack [by impressionist Claude Monet] the catalogue informed me. I could not recognize it. This nonrecognition was painful to me. I considered that the painter had no right to paint indistinctly. I dully felt that the object of the painting was missing. And I noticed with astonishment and confusion that the picture not only draws you but impresses itself indelibly on your memory. . . . All this was unclear to me, and I could not draw the simple conclusions of this experience. But what was entirely clear to me—was the unsuspected power of the palette, which had up to now been hidden from me. . . . And unconsciously the object was discredited as an indispensable element of a painting. . . .
(Vasily Kandinsky, "Reminiscences," 1913; ed. R. Herbert, 1964)

rationality of the universe, and thus its moral center, would be reaffirmed.

Philosophical and Religious Responses Philosophers studied the new science. In such an uncertain universe, some decided, philosophers should restrict themselves to discussing only what was indisputably true and knowable—only those logical deductions that were impenetrable to criticism, only those statements that were about things that were clearly "the case." Philosophy should cease to speculate about unseen or unknowable things, which should be left to spiritualists, novelists, and quacks.

These assumptions characterize the school of **logical positivism**, also called logical or scientific empiricism. Derived from the work on scientific logic of the British thinkers Bertrand Russell (1872–1970) and Alfred North Whitehead (1861–1947), and the investigations into the imprecision of language presented by George E. Moore (1873–1958), it was developed immediately following World War I by a group of mathematicians and philosophers known as the Vienna School. This circle published the writings of the Austrian Ludwig Wittgenstein (1889–1951), who had been Russell's student at Cambridge. Wittgenstein's *Tractatus Logico-Philosophicus* (1921) spelled out the philosopher's duty to clarify ideas, not to theorize about the unknown. Wittgenstein's understanding of the relations between language, the mind, and reality subsequently took root in Britain (where he taught from 1929 until his death) and the United States, where they are loosely described as the "analytic school."

Continental theorists who found Anglo-American logical positivism unsatisfying, offered different responses to the challenge of indeterminacy. **Existentialists** argued that, though the universe was admittedly unreliable and incoherent, and even the personal self was a great mystery, the actions taken by the conscious mind in themselves created a reality that, though dangerous, was genuine. Existentialism never formed a clearly demarcated school. Only the French thinker Jean-Paul Sartre (1905–1980) explicitly identified himself as an "existentialist." He expounded his view of the non-existence of God or meaning outside the unfettered, committed, acting self in novels and plays, as well as in his principal philosophical work *Being and Nothingness* (1943).

In the world presented by scientists and philosophers, either God did not exist or, if he existed, he did not control anarchic and obscure realities. Many turned from this psychological despair once again to religion and mysticism. Some embraced **spiritualism**, attempting to contact the spirits of the dead through professional mediums and special rituals. Others rediscovered the benefits of religious faith. Among Roman Catholics, interest in the miraculous swelled, and thousands sought healing and relief at shrines such as those at Lourdes (France) and Fátima (Portugal)—the latter founded as recently as 1917. In the United States, Protestant **fundamentalism** flourished in response to the destructive critique that Modernism made of religious principles and of the Bible.

Although most intellectuals remained aloof from orthodox religion, important exceptions included the French philosopher, paleontologist, and Jesuit priest Pierre Teilhard de Chardin (1881–1955). His views about cosmic evolution blended scientific theories of evolution with Christian humanist and cosmological views. Also French, the Jewish-born philosopher Simone Weil (1909–1943) turned to a mystical Roman Catholic Christianity in her quest for a greater closeness between humanity and God. In Germany a series of Protestant thinkers, much influenced by existentialism, such as Dietrich Bonhoeffer (1906–1945), adhered to fundamental Christian principles while restating biblical concepts in the light of the modern critique of religious faith. The Austrian Jewish theologian Martin Buber (1878–1965), influenced by both existentialism and Hasidic pietism (see Chapter 23), described in his influential *I and Thou* (1923) the intimate relationship attainable between God and worshiper.

By the twentieth century, the official pronouncements of Europe's largest church, the Roman Catholic, had become more open to modernization than when, in 1870, Pope Pius IX (r. 1846–1878) defined the doctrine of "papal infallibility." Pius' successor Leo XIII (r. 1878–1903) encouraged both a deep spirituality and social reform. His encyclical, or pronouncement, *Rerum novarum* ("Of New Things") in 1891 spoke against revolution and socialist utopianism, but in favor of equity in worker–employer relations, and the need for a just and adequate wage. Subsequent popes continued to speak for social justice within Europe, and for the easing of poverty and the need for peace throughout the world.

Nevertheless, the Church represented moral views now widely perceived as rigid and outdated. They seemed absurd to the progressive writers who flourished in the interwar years. Works of fiction such as *Ulysses* (1922) by the Irish novelist James Joyce (1882–1941) or the seven-volume *Remembrance of Things Past* (1913–1927) by the French writer Marcel Proust (1871–1922) ruptured at once the narrative continuities and moral certainties of nineteenth-century literature. The symbolic, sometimes surreal, stories and novels of the Czech Jew Franz Kafka (1883–1924) centered on threatened, anxiety-ridden individuals who reveal the terrifying truths behind bourgeois appearances. The hero of Kafka's *The Trial* (1925) experiences the annihilation of his identity when, faced with a tribunal governed by no discernible rules, he is accused of a crime he cannot remember committing.

While Kafka pointed to the menace implied in the modern world, the American-born expatriate poet T. S. Eliot (1888–1965) saw modernity as not so much menacing as empty, a meaningless vacuum, sliding toward destruction. His poem "The Hollow Men" (1925) sums up the feelings of a generation, shortly after World War I:

> *This is the way the world ends*
> *This is the way the world ends*
> *This is the way the world ends*
> *Not with a bang but a whimper.*

Here Eliot doubts not merely the prospect of human survival but more, its significance. In the great uncertainty of the age, the harshest uncertainty was this: whether human life had any value at all.

UNCERTAIN BOUNDARIES: THE NEW WOMEN, THE SHRINKING FAMILY, THE NURTURANT STATE

Just as intellectual pessimism and artistic sabotage assailed old truths and disrupted old forms, familiar notions of the role of women, the function of the family, and the mission of the state dissolved in the face of new social realities. Over the next generation, a "new woman" emerged. Economically independent, sexually liberated, she was in appearance and behavior everything her mother was not. The dismantling of the traditional family that had begun with industrialization (see Chapter 22) proceeded apace as the family's social, economic, and cultural functions dwindled. At the same time, the state assumed duties of nurturing and protection that had once been provided (if at all) by the family or religious institutions.

The New Woman

During World War I, women quite suddenly acquired unprecedented freedom along with exceptional responsibilities (see Chapter 25). Their fathers, sons, and brothers were at war, and the conflict generated an insatiable need for guns, bullets, uniforms, and bandages. To supply these, and to sustain the civilians in whose name the slaughter was undertaken, factories must produce overtime, buses run, schools and hospitals function, foodstuffs reach shops and pantries. With millions of men called away from their work to fight, millions of women poured into the workforce. Their successful performance of essential tasks brought them prestige, wages, and aspirations for a new future.

At war's end, men returned to the factories and women, for the most part, to their homes. Governments and employers pushed women out of their wartime occupations. The jobs were needed for the returning men. Married women were deemed to be dependents of their husbands, whose labors earned a "family wage." Resuming the traditional roles forgotten for the duration of the emergency, they nurtured the children whose numbers would partly compensate for wartime fatalities.

Women in Politics Women returned home often with ballot in hand. In appreciation of their wartime contributions, and in response to sustained pressure from the **suffragist** movement, many nations awarded women the right to vote (see Chart 26.1).

From one point of view, the granting of female suffrage marked the culmination of women's long-

The Extension of the Franchise to Women through 1947

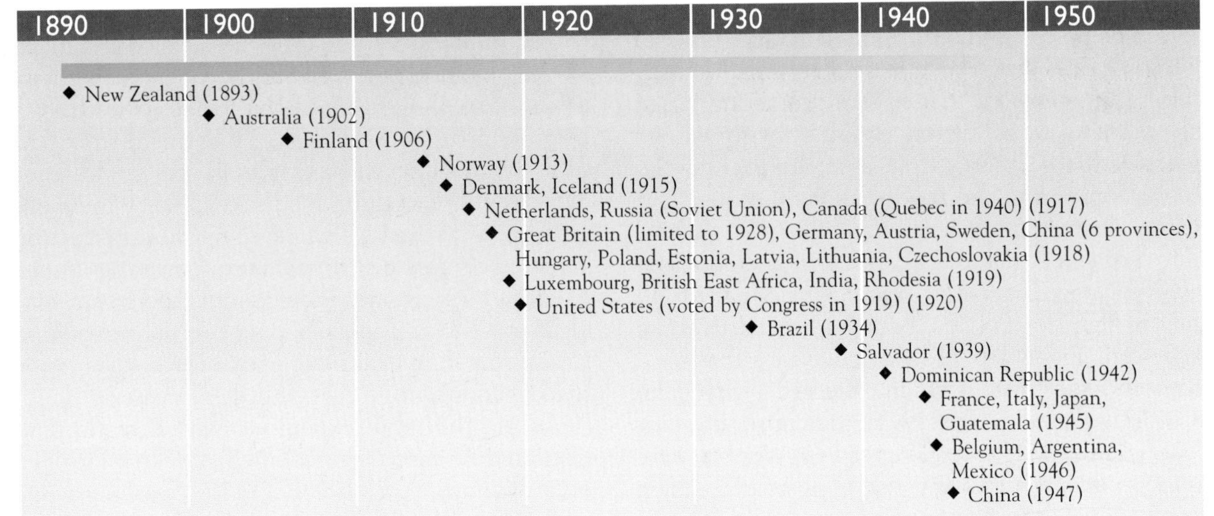

Many nations recognized the crucial role women played in the economy of World War I by extending the franchise to women during the conflict or shortly thereafter. New Zealand, Australia, Finland, and Norway had already done so before the war. Others did so only at the end of World War II.

expressed aspirations. From another, it was an insufficient response to the intractable problem of women's unequal condition, rooted in their enduring experience of subordination to patriarchal families and societies. The first view was that of most bourgeois feminists, whose outlook was shaped by the prevailing liberalism of the governing classes (see Chapter 24). Liberal theorists had argued for women's right to be "active" citizens, a status marked by the right to vote. Bourgeois women had embraced that goal. By 1900, bourgeois feminism had narrowed almost entirely to the suffragist agenda.

Many women of the laboring classes, in contrast, had aligned themselves with socialism and the social democratic parties that attracted large worker memberships during the late 1800s (see Chapters 22, 24). The socialist agenda for women was generally more ambitious than the liberal. It often included the right to divorce, to maternal custody of children, to property and contract, and to sexual freedom. In many social democratic parties, women met separately, created their own hierarchies, and had a significant role in the creation of policy. For socialist women, the granting of the right to vote in a political system they found inadequate offered little when compared to their great ambitions for the elevation of the female condition.

German socialism was especially friendly to women's issues. Its early theoretician August Bebel (1840–1913) had written *Woman and Socialism* (1883), calling for women's civil, economic, and sexual rights, and dismissing as nonsense the notion that women were by nature limited to the tasks of childrearing and housekeeping. Later Karl Kautsky (1854–1938) predicted that by working alongside of men, women would gain equality with them: "[Woman] will be [man's] free companion, emancipated not only from the servitude of the house, but also from that of capitalism." On the eve of World War I, Clara Zetkin (1857–1933) criticized the suffragist movement as short-sighted, and called on women to fight for full economic and social freedom from both men and capitalism at once.

Russian socialism (which merged with the Bolshevik movement after 1917), was more militant than its counterparts (see Chapter 27). Women were prominent in the numerous socialist parties active before World War I, as organizers, propagandists, agitators, and even assassins. Most notably, Alexandra Kollontai (1872–1952), an aristocratic Bolshevik advocate of free love, encouraged the factory women of St. Petersburg to embrace simultaneous feminist and socialist missions. Some revolutionaries opposed Kollontai's approach, which they felt distracted everyone from the essential point, the class struggle. Kollontai survived the 1917 Revolution, however, to become a key figure in the new Communist government, whose leader Lenin (see Chapters 25, 27) detested women's subordination within the family and considered household drudgery to be "barbarously unproductive, petty, nerve-wracking, stultifying and crushing." As a leader of the Communist Party's Zhenotdel, or Women's Department (in existence 1919–1930), she was able to define feminist goals—female literacy and education, economic equality, freedom from housework and childcare, and sexual freedom—as part of that body's agenda.

The Bachelorette Few women, however, were socialist activists of the caliber of Zetkin or Kollontai. The spur to more substantial change in women's lives came neither from socialism nor liberalism, but from the cultural explosions of the Jazz Age. Women's behavior—at least that of a vanguard of young, risk-taking women—reframed the issue of women's rights and women's place.

A New Woman emerged in the post-war years. She was a pleasure-seeking androgyne—a "*garçonne*" as the type was popularized in a daring 1922 French best-seller of that name, a "girl-boy" or "bachelorette." Her lean contours—a contrast to the bustled, corseted figure of her mother's generation—declared that her first function was not reproduction. She cut, or "bobbed," her hair, and applied lipstick, eyeshadow, rouge, and nail polish (previously regarded as the adornments of prostitutes). She wore slim skirts whose hemlines rose a shocking ten inches above her ankles, revealing more of the female body than had been seen (at least in fashionable dress) since antiquity. She was sexually liberated, and could use the devices and procedures made available by the medical profession to limit birth through **contraception** or **abortion**. Pressured by advertising and the advice of columnists in women's magazines, she might smoke cigarettes, drink cocktails, dance to the new sound of the jazz band, live alone or with a lover, have her own bank account, drive cars, and fly airplanes.

While the more expensive new recreations were restricted to rich young women, the attitudes of the New Woman were also adopted by working women. Such women might work in a shop, an office, or a profession. Certain professions enrolled large numbers of women, perhaps because of women's continued interest in gender-related matters. Teaching, nursing, and the new profession of social work were especially recognized as women's callings, where women could

WITNESSES

Rethinking Women's Roles and Possibilities

Charlotte Perkins Gilman criticizes women's economic dependence on men (1898): [M]en produce and distribute wealth; and women receive it at their hands. As men hunt, fish, keep cattle or raise corn, so do women eat game, fish, beef, or corn. . . . The economic status of the human race in any nation, at any time, is governed mainly by the activities of the male. . . . Although not producers of wealth, women [do, however] serve in the final processes of preparation and distribution. [Thus] their labor in the household has a genuine economic value. . . . The labor of women in the house, certainly, enables men to produce more wealth than they otherwise could; and in this way women are economic factors in society. But so are horses. The labor of horses enables men to produce more wealth than they otherwise could. The horse is an economic factor in society. But the horse is not economically independent, nor is the woman. . . .
(Charlotte Perkins Gilman, *Women and Economics*, 1898; ed. M. Schneir, 1972)

The end of women's work and the traditional family? Alexandra Kollontai describes life and work under Soviet communism (c. 1920): The individual household is dying. It is giving way . . . to collective housekeeping. Instead of the working woman cleaning her flat, the communist society can arrange for men and women whose job is to go round in the morning cleaning rooms. . . . Instead of the working woman having to struggle with the cooking . . . communist society will organise public restaurants and communal kitchens. . . . The working woman will not have to slave over the washtub any longer, or ruin her eyes darning her stockings and mending her linen. . . .

[T]he workers' state will [even] come to replace the family; society will gradually take upon itself all the tasks that before the [Bolshevik] revolution fell to the individual parents. . . . We already have homes for very small babies, creches, kindergartens, children's colonies and homes, hospitals and health resorts for sick children, restaurants, free lunches at school and free distribution of text books, warm clothing and shoes to school children. All this goes to show that the responsibility for the child is passing from the family to the collective. . . .
(From A. Holt ed., *Selected Writings of Alexandra Kollontai*, 1977)

Russian anarchist and United States immigrant Emma Goldman celebrates free love and free women (1910): Free love? As if love is anything but free! . . . Yes, love is free; it can dwell in no other atmosphere. In freedom it gives itself unreservedly, abundantly, completely. . . . Love needs no protection; it is its own protection. So long as love begets life no child is deserted, or hungry, or famished for the want of affection. I know this to be true. I know women who became mothers in freedom by the men they loved. Few children in wedlock enjoy the care, the protection, the devotion free motherhood is capable of bestowing. . . .
(Emma Goldman, "Marriage and Love," 1910; ed. M. Schneir, 1972)

perform at the professional level the kinds of work seen as appropriate for women who, in the family framework, taught the young and cared for the sick and elderly. "She who cared only for her own flesh and blood," enthused the American economic theorist and feminist Charlotte Perkins Gilman (1860–1935), "is now active in all wide good works around the world."

The new field of social work emerged only after World War I in response to urban poverty in working-class and immigrant communities. Social workers aimed to assist individuals and families to improve their prospects by adapting to their communities and availing themselves of neighborhood resources. In the past, assistance of this sort had been provided by large family networks, or by religious institutions with long traditions of subventions to children, the poor, the elderly, the abandoned, the chronically ill, and socially-marginalized women—prostitutes, out-of-wedlock mothers, and widows. But family networks had often broken down among the urban poor and immigrant communities, and religious institutions had lost prestige and were insufficiently funded. Their place was taken by social workers.

Especially privileged and talented women sought careers as physicians, studying at those few European universities that from the 1890s opened their medical programs to women (or, in the United States, at the Women's Medical College of Philadelphia, established in 1851; the first medical program in the world available to female candidates). Women physicians inclined to those specializations which, like teaching and nursing, were extensions of activities traditional for females—pediatrics, gynecology, and obstetrics.

Although many working women of the post-war years pursued careers in teaching, nursing, medicine, and social work, most were office-workers, telephone operators, or shop-clerks. (Together with many male workers, they constituted the **white-collar** labor force, in contrast to blue-collar industrial workers.) Of these, many were young single women, who would cease work upon marriage and take up family responsibilities. But increasingly, they were married women who worked to supplement family income, or single women who chose not to marry (an increasingly large category).

Charlotte Perkins Gilman, editor of the journal *Forerunner* and author of *Women and Economics* (1898), encouraged the trend for mature women to seek lifelong careers. Only financial independence, she argued, could give women genuine independence and dignity. Women who demonstrated their intellectual capacity and effectiveness in the workplace refuted the notions of nineteenth-century theorists (Darwin foremost among them; see Chapter 24) who held that women were biologically inferior to men. Men had reached a more advanced evolutionary stage, Darwin contended, than had women, children, or the pre-state peoples of the globe whom he termed "savages" (one instance of the linking of presuppositions about race or ethnicity with those about gender). Like proto-feminist thinkers from the Renaissance forward, Gilman rejoined that men and women shared a common, human nature. Women could as well as men, she argued, acquire the necessary expertise to work in the business and professional world.

Women's Choices

Margaret Sanger: *The early twentieth century brought new possibilities for women. Fundamental to women's liberation (and often, survival) was contraception, which freed the poorest women from a deeper descent into poverty, and middle-class women from unwanted domestic responsibilities. Here Margaret Sanger, pioneer of the birth control movement in the United States, makes an appeal to a senate committee for legislation on birth control in a scene from the 1930s.*

Optional Motherhood In order to do so, women might need to shed the burdens of housework, and postpone (or abjure) motherhood, or limit the number of births. Modern medicine made birth-control options available to women as never before in history: the use of the diaphragm that permitted safe, effective birth control without any requirement of abstinence; and safe surgical abortion by trained experts in antiseptic conditions. These breakthroughs provided release from the cycle of childbirth and lactation that had previously determined the lives of most women. They are, some experts suggest, the preconditions of women's liberation.

Some methods of birth control had been known for centuries (*coitus interruptus*, or male withdrawal before ejaculation, is described in the Bible and was regularly used throughout the European Middle Ages). But modern birth-control procedures had a short history. Underground information circulated during the 1800s about condoms, douches, and diaphragms. In 1882, Aletta Jacobs (1854–1929) established the first modern birth control clinic in Amsterdam. Over the next generation, Dutch clinics trained socialist and sexual radical advocates from Britain and the United States. One of these, Margaret Sanger (1879–1966) founded a clinic in Brooklyn, New York in 1916—so that every woman might "control her own body"—and was imprisoned for thirty days for doing so. At first socialist in outlook (she urged working women not to propagate children who would slave in capitalist factories and die in capitalist wars), she broadened her message after World War I to invite all women to the sexual freedom that existed with the availability of birth control.

The Great Procession: *On the home front, liberation meant women's ability to control her reproduction. On the political front, it meant suffrage—the right to vote. In the Great Procession on June 18, 1910, members and supporters of the Women's Social and Political Union organized by British feminist Emmeline Pankhurst march for women's suffrage. Note that the women still wear the long skirts that had been the fashion for centuries but which would soon rise during World War I, a costume change marking a radical shift in the public role of women.*

The birth control movement also flourished in Britain and northern Europe (though not in the Roman Catholic countries to the south). In 1921, a clinic was established in London by Marie Stopes (1880–1958), author of two widely-read books that advocated planned births. These pioneering establishments operated in a hostile environment, where religious stricture and national law condemned or forbade the distribution of birth-control information and devices. Sweden was an exception: here, from the 1930s, the state both permitted and subsidized the use of birth control.

The availability of birth control marks a watershed in the history of women's quest for equality and autonomy. The ability to control their bodies had the potential to free women more profoundly than the acquisition of civil or political rights. So momentous a social change aroused objections from different quarters. Many religious leaders protested contraception on moral grounds. The Roman Catholic Church forbade it, holding that the creation of new life fell under God's authority, and not that of the woman who might bear the child. Many political leaders, mostly male, also opposed birth limitation. They adhered to a traditional model of the family in which women remained subordinate members, with special responsibility for childrearing and housework.

Abortion aroused even greater alarm than contraception. It was condemned by most religious groups (the Roman Catholic Church forbade it under any circumstances in 1869), and was generally illegal. Nevertheless, women desiring abortions could generally obtain them. Poor women often fell victim to untrained or unscrupulous practitioners, who cheated them, seriously injured, or even killed them. Wealthy, well-informed women, in contrast, could achieve perfectly safe abortions clandestinely in properly-equipped clinics or hospitals.

However restricted, the capacity women acquired to control their reproductive lives enfranchised them as powerfully as did the right to vote. This capacity has enabled modern women to act as full and equal citizens of their nations and their world.

The Shrinking Family and the Nurturant State

The liberation of women was one of several circumstances that has led to the diminished importance of the parent-headed household in modern Western societies. The twentieth-century family has been a shrinking family—shrinking in size, shrinking in functions, shrinking in prestige, and shrinking in its capacity to socialize its children. As the family unit became less influential, the state was summoned to nurture its citizens and provide physical and emotional support to unprotected individuals or families in crisis.

Declining Birthrates in France and Britain, 1801–1951

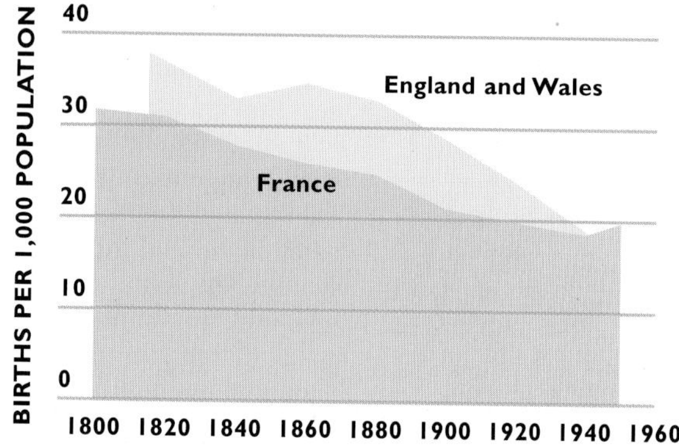

England and Wales   France

During the nineteenth and into the mid-twentieth century, birthrates declined in the most affluent Western nations. The main reason for this was that as mortality declined and the demand for consumer and cultural goods increased, families adopted strategies for the preservation of household resources.
Source: *B. Mitchell,* European Historical Statistics, 1750–1970 *(Columbia University Press, 1975).*

New Patterns of Family Life The average western European family had been shrinking since the nineteenth century. The utilization on a large scale of some method of birth control meant lower fertility. As improvements in nutrition and medicine enhanced survival rates for infants and children, families deliberately limited the number of children born. Parents were therefore less burdened by dependents who required care and expense. Family limitation seemed to be in the interests of both children and parents.

Among the elites, smaller families meant that children became the objects of intense concern. Their health, schooling, and well-being preoccupied parents, who lavished wealth on vacations, tutors, and amusements. Those privileged youngsters, in turn, could expect to inherit a larger share of family wealth than had their predecessors. Among the poor, smaller families meant a greater chance at survival. Scarce resources insufficient to nurture five or six children might adequately feed two, and permit better-nourished parents to withstand disease and live longer. Poor women eagerly sought the services of birth-control professionals, when these became available, not so much for the selfish indulgence in unregulated sexuality (as critics charged), but so as to protect children already born from the competition of those not yet conceived.

In Soviet Russia, women were promised that they did not need to forego marriage or pleasure or children; the state would feed, nurture, and school their offspring. The early radicalism of the Bolshevik outlook of the 1920s on sex quickly waned, however, partly because the resources to set up the new forms of housing were simply not available. The promise of elaborate social support for women was in any case

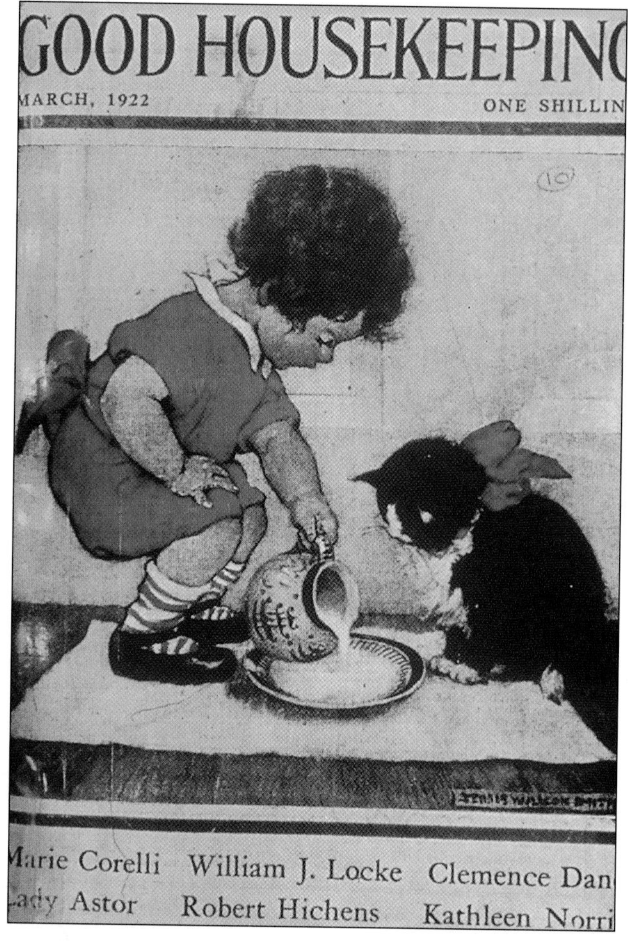

***Good housekeeping:** While some women sought greater personal freedom and public responsibility, others cultivated the joys of home and family. In doing so, they were guided by a new generation of publications targeting women as homemakers and consumers. Shown here is one such magazine,* Good Housekeeping *(March 1922), which beckons to women readers with promises of domestic comfort and pleasure embedded in soft and alluring forms—a clean, cheerful child; a soft, beribboned kitten; and the gentle act of feeding, the central mission of the home.*

lost after 1930 when, under Stalin (see Chapter 27), the Women's Department was abolished, marriage laws were stiffened, abortion outlawed, and women told both to work and to clean, shop, and care for their children, somehow, at home.

Although the Soviet state urged its young families to reproduce freely, most European societies experienced the opposite phenomenon of family limitation. The decline in birthrates continued. By 1900 in France, they had fallen nearly twenty-five percent since 1810. From highs of about thirty-five births annually per thousand population in France and Britain in the early 1800s, birthrates slipped below twenty by the interwar period. As women tended to marry earlier and have fewer children, they found they were still in the prime of life when they no longer had major responsibilities for the welfare of their families. These trends freed women to take on other tasks.

Families were also shrinking in the range of functions they performed, and in the prestige that they enjoyed. In the twentieth century, the functions performed by a family were very different from those of the noble clans that had organized social relations in ancient Greece and Rome and during the European Middle Ages. These families had waged war, apprehended and punished criminals, settled disputes, and appeased gods or saints. In the modern age, families (or their male heads) no longer took responsibility for war, justice, and religion, but had delegated these to national armies, to legal professionals, and to the clergy. There was little left for families to do. Their remaining functions were primarily social (they participated in community affairs) and cultural (they transmitted values and knowledge to their children).

The diminution of family functions meant that the performance of those that remained was the focus for heightened attention. Concerns with the feeding and rearing of children became obsessive. Manuals compiled by "experts" told mothers what to do, implicitly doubting whether mother would be able to measure up to the task. The ability of the family to perform its cultural mission was disrupted, moreover, by the emergence of the youth peer group as a culturally influential section of society. While families tried to instill traditional values, young people looked to each other for standards of behavior that would define them as a group apart. Popular music, reshaped now by jazz, especially marked the world of the youth peer group, which distanced the family further from the social formation of its children.

Changes in the way families functioned meant that many families lost control over their children, or might be unable to feed and nurture an obstinate or rebellious child. The economic failures of the 1930s exacerbated these tendencies. Fathers might not be able to provide sustenance for their young, who in turn left the family home to fend for themselves.

The readjustment of such families, if they were poor, became the business of social workers. They attempted to teach, counsel, comfort, and heal the wounds caused by poverty, delinquency, and dysfunction. In her mission to the poor immigrants of Chicago, as an instance, the American Jane Addams (1860–1935) established Hull House in 1889, the prototype of the "settlement house," a community center that served as the site for the distribution of middle-class largesse. Providing classes in English and gymnastics, and opportunities for socialization as well as social services, it was an enormous success, drawing more than 1000 participants each week. By the 1920s, privately and publicly funded social work endeavors of this sort had outpaced those of religious organizations in attending to the needs of poor and troubled families.

As Western families diminished in size and in functions, many looked back nostalgically to the imagined warmth of traditional families. But many celebrated the freedom that could be enjoyed as the power waned of the father and head of household to dominate his wife and children. Those who hailed this new freedom were unconcerned when national states began to assume some of the functions the family had relinquished.

New Roles for the State The growth of the nurturant, or "motherly" state—a state committed to the care of its citizens and not merely to their defense or moral discipline—was a phenomenon that marked the twentieth-century West. Earlier political theorists had proposed that the state might restrain the sinfulness of its members; or that it might act without regard to good and evil as a purely secular and autonomous entity; or that it must not intrude upon its citizens' private lives (see Chapter 15). In the nineteenth century, there developed the notion that the state was responsible for the welfare of its citizens, and especially the weakest among them: the very young and very old, the disabled and the impoverished.

The modern state began to intervene in family life with the social welfare legislation of the late nineteenth century (see Chapter 22). In the 1880s in Germany, the chancellor Otto von Bismarck instituted programs that protected workers against loss of income due to disability, unemployment, or old age.

Britain and France followed in the early 1900s. The experience of World War I stimulated further legislation in favor of the poor, of workers, and of families. So many millions had fought and suffered. The state, it was felt, must ease their financial pain and, however feebly, attempt to remedy their personal losses.

To this period may be traced the beginnings in the Western democracies of the modern **welfare state**. In addition to providing social insurance plans protecting workers against unemployment, disability, and old age, the state taxed its citizens—who were willing to bear the cost—to provide maternity leave, food subsidies, childcare centers and kindergartens, counseling, job training, and medical services, variously according to the customs and expectations of each society. The working-class population (lured away by such mechanisms from the bait of revolution) came to look to the state for support in the moments of crisis that had once been alleviated only by family or the Church.

Some theorists, while supporting state intervention in family life, resisted the trend toward a diminished maternal role in the socialization of children. The books of the Swedish writer Ellen Key (1849–1926) entitled *The Century of the Child* (1900) and *The Renaissance of Motherhood* (1914), both widely translated, elevated the role of the biological mother in childrearing at the same time that they called for the state to provide financial support for families and welfare guarantees for mothers without partners.

Proponents of **natalism**, especially in the fascist nations of Italy, Spain, and Germany, also stressed the mother's role and her need for state support. Their objectives were more complex than Key's. They sought to reaffirm the subordination of women within the family while encouraging the rapid birthing of new citizens (and new soldiers) for societies devastated by war fatalities. Birth control and abortion were accordingly banned. "The use of contraceptives means a violation of nature," announced German leader Adolf Hitler, "a degradation of womanhood, motherhood, and love."

In fascist societies, support of mothers was not part of a broader intervention in support of women, but was narrowly directed to bolstering the state's own aims. The Western nations under liberal or socialist governments also celebrated motherhood, awarding medals to mothers of multiple legitimate offspring and placing Mother's Day on the annual calendar. In these societies, support for mothers was balanced by support for other categories of the needy, including those who were outside of marital families.

For a variety of reasons, most Western nations took on nurturant functions in the decades after World War I. The reinvention of the state as the family of last resort was confirmed in the 1930s, at the nadir of worldwide economic catastrophe. How it did so will be observed in due course. First, it must be shown how that catastrophe came to be.

ECONOMIC UNCERTAINTY: FROM PROSPERITY TO THE BREADLINE

In the 1920s, the economies of Western nations and their allies, colonies, and trading partners around the globe struggled to recover from the dual trauma of world war and the Communist revolution (see Chapters 25, 27). Within a few years, prosperity, it seemed, had returned. That prosperity was illusory. The nations of the West and the world followed the United States into a tenacious depression triggered by unrestrained speculation and a stock market crash. Efforts to tame the Great Depression failed until, ten years later, as another war began, military production defeated the monster of depression and put an end to the era of economic uncertainty.

Happy Days

After the war and the revolution, the shocked, grieving, and hungry peoples of the Western world longed to return to normalcy. The United States led them all as it rapidly recovered from a wartime economy and attained unprecedented prosperity. These were happy days for a young nation that had recently taken the lead in economic production and political affairs.

Boomtime in the United States By the outbreak of World War I, the United States was world leader in industrial production and foreign trade. In the ten years following the Versailles settlement, United States production spurted forward. Its exports supplied half the manufactures produced in the world, as well as seventy percent of the oil and forty percent of the coal.

One of the secrets of that great productivity was the efficiency of American factories and their workforce. The assembly line, developed by entrepreneur Henry Ford (1863–1947) to speed up the manufacture of his automobiles, maximized the productivity of industrial labor. So too did the methods of industrial organization advocated by Frederick Winslow Taylor (1856–1915). Closely observing workers' behavior in his famous time–motion studies, he showed how

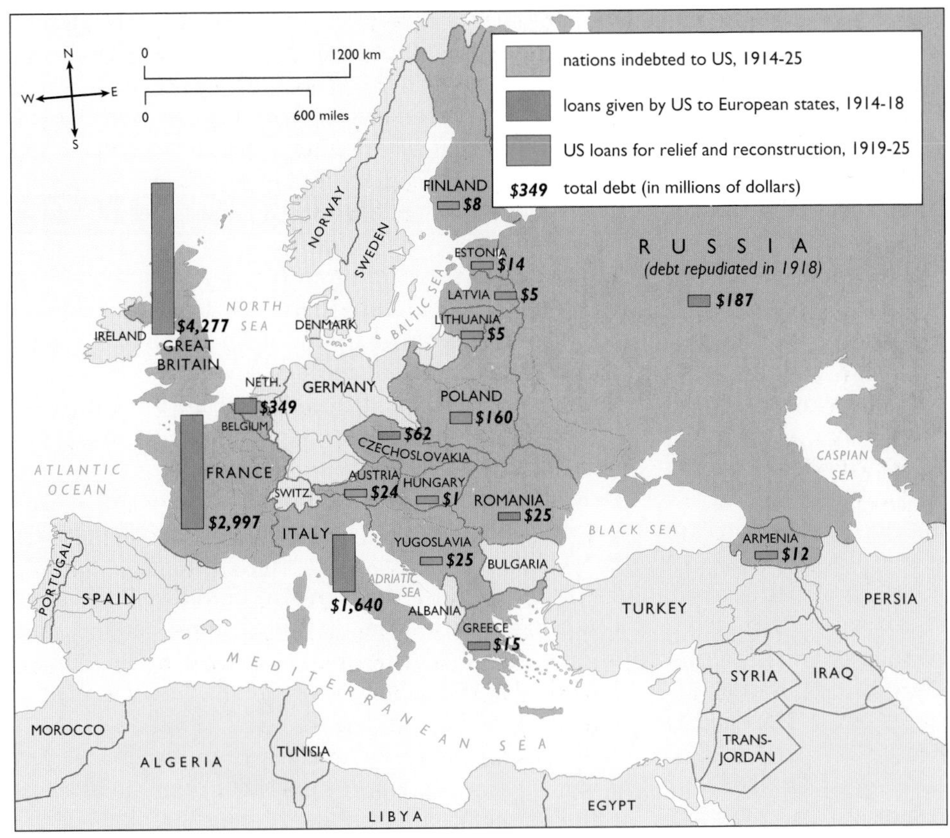

Map 26.1 European Debts to the United States, 1914–1925—War Loans and Loans for Relief and Reconstruction: *Europe's economic landscape was transformed by four years of war. Victors in battle, the Allied nations found themselves hugely in debt to the United States for war loans and other assistance. Of these nations, only Finland ever paid its debt in full. The Soviets repudiated their war debt, refusing to acknowledge tsarist obligations. Other nations had their debts canceled by the United States, or simply neglected to pay them. The vectors of capital transfer between Europe and North America are evidence of Europe's surrender of global economic leadership to the United States in the twentieth century.*

reorganization of space, tools, and procedures could lead to greater productivity.

The workers who accepted these regimens were organized in trade unions, which crystallized into two main groups representing skilled and unskilled workers respectively. The former of these, the American Federation of Labor (AFL), at its origin in 1886 a gathering of twenty-five unions of skilled laborers, had grown by 1901 to represent nearly one-third of all skilled workers. The latter, the Congress of Industrial Organizations, emerged only in 1935 in opposition to the AFL's exclusionary policies.

Labor unions resisted employers who demanded too much work, for too little pay, under unsafe conditions. A series of strikes and riots, violently suppressed, marked the formative years of the American labor movement: the Great Railroad Strike of 1877; the Haymarket Square Riot (between labor unionists and police) of 1886; the 1892 steelworkers' strike against the mill in Homestead, Pennsylvania; the 1894 strike of railroad Pullman workers. A new series of strikes erupted in the 1930s. By that era, the unions had retreated from militant demonstration and even political activity, and elevated "bread-and-butter" issues—salaries and benefits. The trade unionists pressed for a minimum wage, and restricted child labor. The number of laboring children aged from ten to fifteen dropped by 1930 to a third of its 1910 high, before it was at last made illegal in 1938.

United States trade unions avoided socialism. Some workers were intrigued by international socialism and supported the presidential ambitions of Eugene V. Debs (1855–1926), but most did not support the Bolshevik takeover in Russia in 1917. American workers remained within established political frameworks, voting for Democratic and Republican presidents, as did their employers.

As in Europe, many wage-earners were not industrial workers. Agricultural workers, mostly non-unionized, were already suffering from an agricultural depression which had set in during the 1920s. White collar workers—salesmen and women, managers, clerks, and secretaries, as well as professionals such as accountants and engineers, teachers and professors, nurses, lawyers, and physicians, often better paid than industrial workers—were generally not unionized.

In the prosperous 1920s, American consumers eagerly purchased the goods produced by American factories—phonographs, telephones, vacuum cleaners, sewing machines, and, especially, automobiles. Spending for consumption, for leisure, for the home, they fueled a rapidly growing economy.

The companies producing these goods were traded on the stock market, or required investment loans. These needs were handled by the brokers and bankers, many of them based in Wall Street, New York City, the home of the world's busiest exchanges.

The stock exchanges were closely linked with American banks, which purchased stocks, and made loans to domestic and foreign companies and governments. American bankers had by now displaced the British as the main players in an international money system. It was largely American money that had financed World War I, sending about $10 billion to some twenty nations. As those loans were repaid, others were issued. Gold flooded into the United States as a result of debt repayment, reaching unprecedented levels.

In 1900, the international currency system was anchored by the British pound sterling, itself tied to a gold standard—pounds were literally as good as gold. After World War I, the American dollar, also linked to gold, displaced the pound as the principal international currency. The gold standard supported the global trading system by ensuring convertibility among currencies. It was, however, inflexible. The supply of currency was limited to the value of gold the nation possessed. The government could not print more money to stimulate the economy. Without sufficient money to purchase goods and services, production could drop, and deflation follow.

As the world's greatest manufacturer and banker, the United States was central to the global trading system. So long as goods and money flowed smoothly out from the United States and back again, that commercial system was healthy. If the behavior of American investors or producers changed, the system was jeopardized. During the 1920s, trade barriers and the distractions of the stock market began to interfere with international commercial rhythms.

Many historians fault American foreign trade policy during the 1920s. It encouraged the export of manufactures and agricultural produce, and insisted that markets abroad should be kept open for all comers. But stiff tariffs limited imports of products that might compete with American merchandise. From its origins, the United States had inclined toward protectionism (while Britain in contrast adhered to free trade for the period from 1846 to World War I). Duties on the value of most imported manufactures amounted to thirty-five percent in 1816, forty percent by 1832, forty to fifty percent in 1875, and forty-four percent in 1913. These tariff walls were erected, proponents argued, to protect the "infant industries" of a newly industrializing nation and, later, to protect the wages of American workers from foreign competition. Employing the same logic, Congress enacted the Hawley-Smoot Tariff in 1930—raising the tariff rate on imports to the unprecedented high of about forty-eight percent. Foreign producers could not sell their goods in an American market which had made them artificially expensive; without those sales, they were unable to repay their debts to American bankers.

The investment mania that swept over Wall Street in the late 1920s further disrupted the free flow of global trade. Money that might otherwise have been sent abroad poured into American stocks and funds. From 1928 to 1929, the amount of capital sent abroad dropped sharply—loans to Germany, for instance, shrank from $277 to $29.5 million. Quick, dramatic returns appealed more to investors than the slow growth of distant enterprises. The richest people in the United States, the most powerful nation in the world, knew happy days were with them and did not consider that what went up fast might descend catastrophically.

HOW MANY?

The Decrease in World Trade, 1929-1932

1929

35% DECREASE IN VOLUME

60% DECREASE IN VALUE

Source: *P. Bairoch,* Economics and World History: Myths and Paradoxes *(Chicago: University of Chicago Press, 1993), p. 9.*

Post-war Europe As Americans rejoiced in their prosperity, Europe inched forward. Rebuilding commenced, and standards of living improved. By 1925,

WINDOWS ON

Highs and Lows

Issuing of the "Rentenmark," November 15, 1923

A first surge of prosperity following World War I preceded a decade of economic turmoil. Above, German officials are ready to dispose of chests of bills which have lost much of their value in an era of devastating inflation. The hyperinflation that struck Germany in the early 1920s was a premonition of the depression and deflation that struck worldwide after the crash of the New York stock market in 1929. On the eve of that crash, the Wall Street brokers in the image shown here (right) happily read the news on slender lengths of ticker tape of their ever-mounting profits. Those highs would soon give way to cataclysmic lows, and the worst depression of the modern era. Depression followed the stock market crash, bringing unemployment to millions of workers around the globe. Ten years later, the Depression still lingered. Below, protestors against unemployment in April 1939 are stopped by police as they attempt to deliver a giant "postcard" to British prime minister Neville Chamberlain.

Wall Street, October 1929

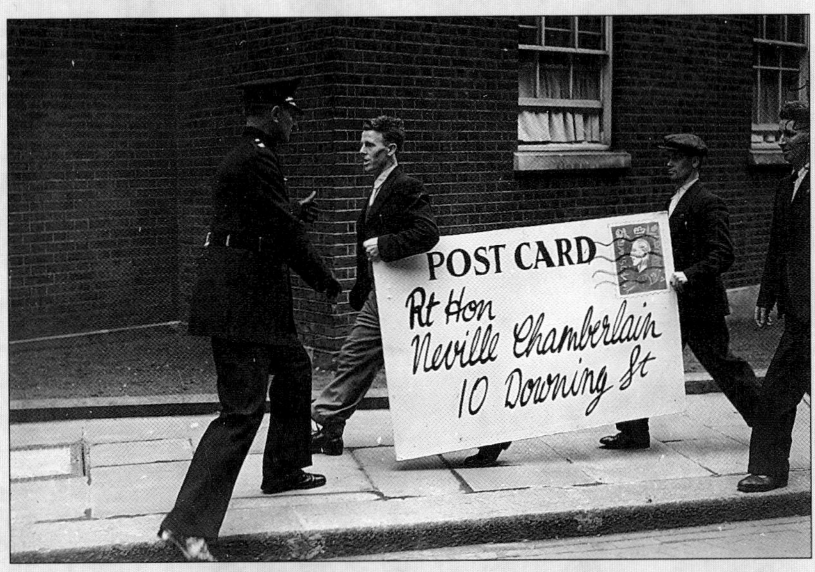

A postcard for Neville Chamberlain, April 13, 1939

for the first time the production of food and raw materials surpassed their 1913 high.

Britain and France were strained by the need to assume the costs of new social programs. War debts burdened them. Productivity lagged. To protect manufactures, both nations imposed tariffs. In doing so, Britain broke with the free trade tradition in place since 1846. In the hope of bolstering British currency, in addition, the government returned in 1925 to the gold standard abandoned during the war (as did some forty nations in all); then repudiated it finally in 1931.

Both British and French governments also faced well-organized demands for higher wages and benefits from industrial workers. In Britain, the election of 1924 led to a Labour government (whose constituents were mostly union members) with Liberal support. Nevertheless, conservative interests continued to direct the economy. In 1931, a "National Government" (a coalition of Labour, Liberal, and Conservative ministers) took over, but failed to exercise effective leadership.

In France, socialist and communist parties competed, failing to capture a majority. Following the 1934 turnabout in policy announced by the Comintern (the Soviet organization monitoring extra-Soviet communist parties), communists, socialists, and other groups joined in a Popular Front against the menace of Fascism (see Chapter 27). In 1936, a left-liberal government was elected with a strong fifty-seven percent of the vote. One of the Popular Front governments linking left and central political parties, it was led by the Jewish socialist Léon Blum (1872–1950), who attempted to steer a course between the agendas of Left and Right. Although it liberalized the workplace, and established annual vacations and a forty-hour workweek, the Popular Front could not reverse an economic downturn, as productivity slipped and investment lagged.

Lackluster economic performance was the general pattern in western Europe, as in France and Britain. Everywhere, communist parties were springing up, branching off from social democratic parties, as communists and socialists competed for the loyalty of trade unionists.

In central Europe, the defeated nations of World War I faced disheartening economic problems. Germany, above all, was saddled with the burden of reparations—calculated so as to recompense the victor nations for the total expense of the war. These were not amounts that a demoralized and starving nation was willing to pay. To do so would have required a double sacrifice: a voluntary decrease in consumption of goods, and an increase in taxes. That two-pronged strategy was unacceptable. Instead, Germany defaulted through 1922. The next year French and Belgian forces occupied the coalfields of the buffer Ruhr region, intending to seize the value of the debt in the form of coal. Only the intervention of the United States and Britain in 1924 prevented a meltdown to violence (as the local population resisted) and chaos. By the terms of the Dawes Plan, a more acceptable payment plan was established. The United States would make loans to Germany according to a complex schedule, enabling Germany in turn to repay the French.

In the end, Germany never paid the reparations owed. Yet the reparations crisis had wreaked terrible damage upon the German economy. To raise funds to pay the Ruhr laborers while they resisted French occupation, the German government printed paper currency at will. By November 15, 1923, the Deutschmark had fallen to twelve-billionths of its 1922 (July) value (from 493.2 to 4,200,000,000,000 marks per dollar). Viewed differently, it fell to a flabbergasting one-trillionth of its value of 4.2 marks per dollar in 1914 (July). This single fact bespeaks an economic trauma whose effects on the history of Germany and the world would be played out tragically over the next twenty-two years (see Chapter 27).

With cheap—indeed worthless—marks, the government paid the Ruhr workers. But in 1923 devaluation caused hyperinflation that terrified the German people. The sturdy, prudent middle class found that their lifesavings had been made worthless by unbridled inflation. Those on fixed incomes became paupers, while workers had to be paid several times per day with bills of rapidly declining worth—and to carry their wages home in a suitcase or wheelbarrow.

Those scarred by hyperinflation would not forget the crisis. Yet Germany revived later in the decade, and the young entrepreneurs and managers who benefited most from that boom reveled in a new, though limited, prosperity.

To stimulate production in the Soviet Union, in 1921 the Communist leader Lenin, loosened briefly the economic controls imposed after 1917 (see Chapter 27). Under Lenin's New Economic Policy (NEP), retail trade and light industry were returned to private ownership and peasants were allowed to cultivate their own land. By 1929, with Lenin dead (in 1924) and Stalin in power, that policy was reversed. A series of Five-Year Plans set production goals for state-controlled industry that boosted the Soviet Union to the forefront of the developed nations.

The Scandinavian nations of Denmark, Finland, Norway, and Sweden found a "middle way" between the imposition of state controls in the Soviet Union and the free-market principles of the western European nations. Here the government promised benefits to every citizen from cradle to grave, paying for them with heavy taxation. Some major industries were nationalized, but many others were permitted to flourish in free-market competition. Economic experimentation yielded both industrial growth and improved living conditions. The Scandinavian system posed a reasonable alternative to the hectic buying and selling and uncertainty of outcomes that characterized the United States economy at this period.

In 1929, on the far side of the Atlantic, speculation in stocks, the spawning of holding companies, and the multiplication of unsecured loans marked an economy that might, at any point, go haywire. Speculation soared in the period from 1923 to 1929, years that saw the quadrupling of the volume of shares traded. Investors believed the market would never go down. They borrowed in order to buy, the only collateral being the value of the shares purchased. Such an unprecedented "bull market" led to catastrophe as stocks became desperately overvalued, and finance capital outstripped the capacity of consumers to buy. On October 24, 1929, "Black Thursday," disaster struck. That day, on which nearly 13 million shares were sold, and losses mounted to 3 billion dollars, marks the beginning of the Great Crash. Another plunge came five days later. Stock prices plummeted from an index of 216 to 145 by the end of November, and over the next three years pursued an unsteady descent to bottom out at 34—from $87 billion at their peak to $18 billion at their low. The financial giants of Wall Street trembled, shocked by their own losses and uncertain about what was to come. What came was a broadening of economic crisis into every corner of the United States, Europe, and the world.

On the Dole

The collapse in stock values in October 1929 set off a chain of events culminating in a profound, stubborn depression—the Great Depression. Banks had been involved in the speculative excess of 1928–1929. Pressed by their losses, they called in the

WITNESSES

Living Through the Great Depression

United States president Calvin Coolidge speaks to Congress on the state of the American economy on the eve of the Crash and Great Depression (1928): No Congress of the United States ever assembled, on surveying the state of the Union, has met with a more pleasing prospect than that which appears at the present time. . . . The great wealth created by our enterprise and industry, and saved by our economy, has had the widest distribution among our own people, and has gone out in a steady stream to serve the charity and the business of the world. . . . The country can regard the present with satisfaction and anticipate the future with optimism.

(President Calvin Coolidge, Message to Congress, December 4, 1928; ed. E. Hobsbawm, 1996)

The American economy—the general condition of the unemployed multitudes (1932): You are a carpenter. Your last cent is gone. They have cut off the gas. . . . You can't get a job now for love or money. What do you do? . . . [Y]ou go to the cop. He pulls out his directory and sends you to one of the listed charitable societies. . . . You draw the Episcopal Family Relief Society. The Relief Society clears your name through the central agency to see that you are not receiving help elsewhere. . . . Eventually it will allot you $2 to $8 a week, depending on the locality and the funds available. If its funds are exhausted it asks you to wait.

(From *Fortune* magazine, September 1932; ed. J. A. Garraty, 1986)

African American leader Malcolm X recalls the Depression's effects on poor blacks in Michigan (1934): By 1934, we really began to suffer. This was about the worst depression year, and no one we knew had enough to eat or live on. Some old family friends visited us now and then. At first they brought food. Though it was charity, my mother took it. . . . In Lansing, there was a bakery where, for a nickel, a couple of us children would buy a tall flour sack of day-old bread and cookies, and then walk the two miles back out into the country to our house. . . . But there were times when there wasn't even a nickel and we would be so hungry we were dizzy. My mother would boil a big pot of dandelion greens and we would eat that.

(From J. A. Garraty ed., *The Great Depression*, 1986)

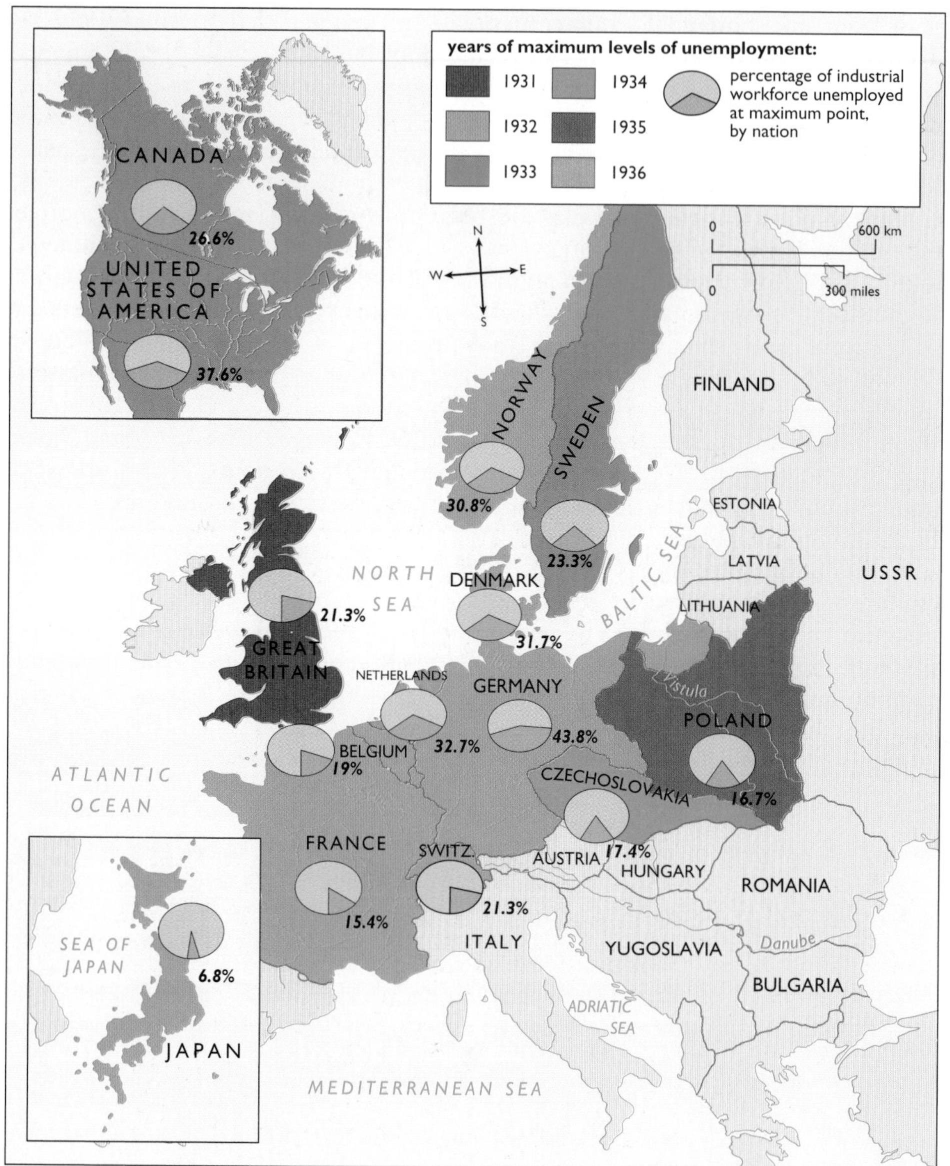

Map 26.2 Maximum Unemployment Rates for Industrial Workers, 1930–1938: *The Great Depression hit different regions at different times and with varying intensity. Shown here are the year and approximate rate of maximum unemployment during the period 1930–1938 for fourteen nations. The Soviet Union, in the midst of its Five Year Plans, remained insulated from the unemployment that the Great Depression brought other nations. Japan, engaged in industrial expansion, suffered less than most. The maxima for Germany and the United States exceeded all others. The great disruption unemployment caused in these nations was expressed in divergent social and political responses: for Germany, the rise of Fascism (see Chapter 27), and for the United States, the launching of the New Deal.*

monumental loans they had issued to fund the investment frenzy. Their debtors could not pay. Banks fell, precipitating the failure of thousands of others, and cheating depositors of their savings. Those deposits were uninsured (insurance of small bank deposits was instituted only in 1933). Lifesavings were lost. Public confidence plummeted.

The banking crisis combined with larger economic trends to create monumental hardship. Production fell twenty percent from 1929 to 1930; by 1932, it stood at one-half its 1929 level. Wages fell, and workers were laid off. The number of unemployed rose to more than 13 million by 1932—almost thirty percent of the workforce in the United States. Since workers were also consumers, spending slowed, especially on big-ticket items whose high rate of sales was an index of prosperity—housing and automobiles. Even necessities were expensive, and consumers bought on credit, accumulating unmanageable debt.

The emergency deepened. Warehouses packed full with merchandise canceled their factory orders. The unemployed could not pay their rent. Homeless, they moved out into the streets, building shanties for their families of scrap lumber and debris. Shanty towns grew up outside the cities which a few years earlier had beckoned to newcomers with the promise of work and good fortune. Called "Hoovervilles" after Herbert Hoover, president from 1929–1933 when the Depression settled on the nation, they were visible monuments to the plight of the dispossessed.

The Shame of Need, the Dignity of Work

New York during the Depression: *Unemployment forced millions of men and women into a poverty and degradation symbolized by, above all, the breadline. Scenes such as this one in New York were repeated in cities and towns around the world.*

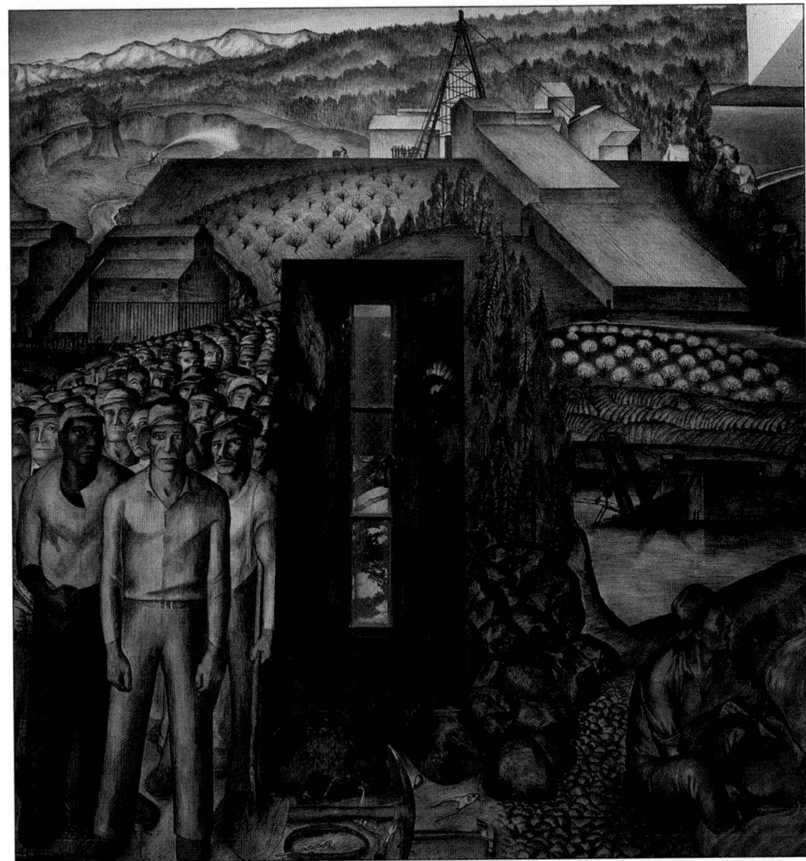

John Langley Howard, California Industrial Scenes: *The workers' faces painted in their honor by Paul Langley Howard in a mural series from around 1934 show great ethnic and racial variety but a single mood of determination, tinged by sadness* (Coit Tower, San Francisco).

The central symbol of the Depression, however, was not the shanty town. It was the breadline, or the "dole," the food handout that signaled the degradation suffered by the millions who could no longer feed themselves. Relief organizations opened soup kitchens and distributed food. Every day, lines of hungry adults and children reached outside and snaked around corners, as the hopeless and dishonored waited to eat from the giving hands of strangers.

Effects in Europe The stock market crash rocketed around the globe. American investment overseas dropped drastically from 1929 to 1933, then virtually ceased for the rest of the decade. While the flow of dollars abroad dried up, American bankers called in their loans from foreign borrowers (mostly European). The flow of gold and coin to the United States swelled, while European stores were depleted, and they still groaned under the burden of war debt. At a conference in Lausanne, Switzerland, in 1932, an attempt was made to unloose the knot of debt obligations. France agreed to end reparations with a final transfer from Germany—which Germany never made. France defaulted, in turn, on its debt to the United States, which continued to insist, even as the demand paralyzed European economies, that all war debts be honored.

European banks failed if they could not respond to American calls for funds. In 1931, the Austrian giant Creditanstalt, drained by withdrawals of foreign funds, closed its doors. That move set off financial panic in Europe as depositors rushed to their banks to withdraw their endangered funds. In Britain, they withdrew gold, depleting the supply. Humiliated, Britain was forced finally to repudiate the gold standard that had anchored the pound. Now the pound inflated heavily, losing twenty-eight percent of its value in 1931.

Britain and her trading partners (including members of the newly-founded Commonwealth of Nations) fled gold, but the United States maintained the gold standard (aside from a brief interlude, and subsequent devaluation of the dollar), along with France, Belgium, the Netherlands, and Switzerland. These nations formed a separate trading bloc, distinct from the British. In addition to these two, a third bloc developed in central Europe, led by Germany. The barriers between these three isolated, exclusionary trading blocs were bolstered by forbiddingly high tariffs, installed to discourage foreign imports and protect domestic manufactures. The free and integrated trading network of the West in its boom years had vanished.

The remedies adopted for economic crisis only yielded more crisis. Currency inflation, economists reasoned, might help. With a cheaper currency, prices would decline and people could buy more goods. Protective tariffs would force them to purchase domestic manufactures, and sustain employment. These were illusions. Instead, trade declined, and production and employment levels sickened and fell. At the depths of the Depression in the early 1930s, unemployment in the developed nations may have reached as high as 30 million—around one-fourth to one-fifth of the workforce, and in Germany as much as two-fifths (about 6 million workers)—with many others forced into part-time work.

The effects of stock market collapse, bank failure, production slowdown, and mass unemployment were felt round the globe. Many of the colonized nations of Asia, Africa, and Latin America were primary producers of agricultural commodities. Their fortunes had soared during World War I, when Europe needed their products. After the war, Europeans relied less on the importation of primary products. As the market became glutted with certain commodities, agricultural prices fell worldwide. The producers of wheat, sugar, rice, coffee, and other staples could not rapidly adjust to a changed marketplace. (India, an exception, took advantage of Britain's crisis to develop its own steel and textile industries.) The laborers deprived of the profits on their goods could not purchase the exports of the industrialized nations. Agricultural surplus and weakened sales exacerbated the international depression, as world trade sank by 1933 to nearly one-third of its 1929 level.

The Soviet Union and Germany The Great Depression never came to the Soviet Union. It struck Germany hard, but was defeated. Between 1929 and 1938, these two nations ruled by totalitarian governments (see Chapter 27) had annual growth rates per capita of 4.3 percent and 4.2 percent respectively—the highest in the Western world, or indeed anywhere in the world except Japan (where the figure was 5 percent). By the 1930s, the Soviet Union had experienced a brief return to capitalism under Lenin's NEP (New Economic Plan) and was suffering the forcible creation of a fully industrialized and fully socialized economy under the terms of Stalin's First Five Year Plan (see Chapter 27). Workers and peasants labored to meet Stalin's high quotas for agricultural and industrial production. While agricultural output remained weak, industry boomed, constantly fed by massive capital reinvestment allocated by the central government. Although the Soviet people suffered grievously from Stalin's policies, they were isolated from the depression that gripped western Europe.

Similarly, Germany benefited from the policies of the Nazi leader Adolf Hitler. Of the Western nations, Germany was hardest hit by depression. It had suffered a staggering unemployment rate and a catastrophic thirty-nine percent drop in production. That misery was Hitler's opportunity; he seized power in 1933 and brought the Depression to an end. His Four Year Plan launched in 1936 (financed by deficit spending on the **Keynesian** model also adopted in the United States by Roosevelt) aimed at economic self-sufficiency and a rapid increase in industrial production—especially military production. Commercial agreements made with Poland, Hungary, and Romania in central and eastern Europe assured Germany a supply of agricultural products and raw materials for industrial use. Meanwhile, German industrial scientists developed synthetic substitutes for exotic resources (cotton, wool, rubber) to bypass the need for foreign imports. The total control that Hitler exercised over economic life allowed him to mobilize people, commodities, and money to enhance industrial growth and assure military readiness.

Searching for Remedies Elsewhere the Depression persisted. People looked to their governments to take some action. Governments remained committed to deflation and steep tariffs. Workers defeated by hardship lined up for the dole.

HOW MANY?

Rise and Fall of Annual Growth Rate in the United States, Japan, and the Soviet Union Before and After 1929

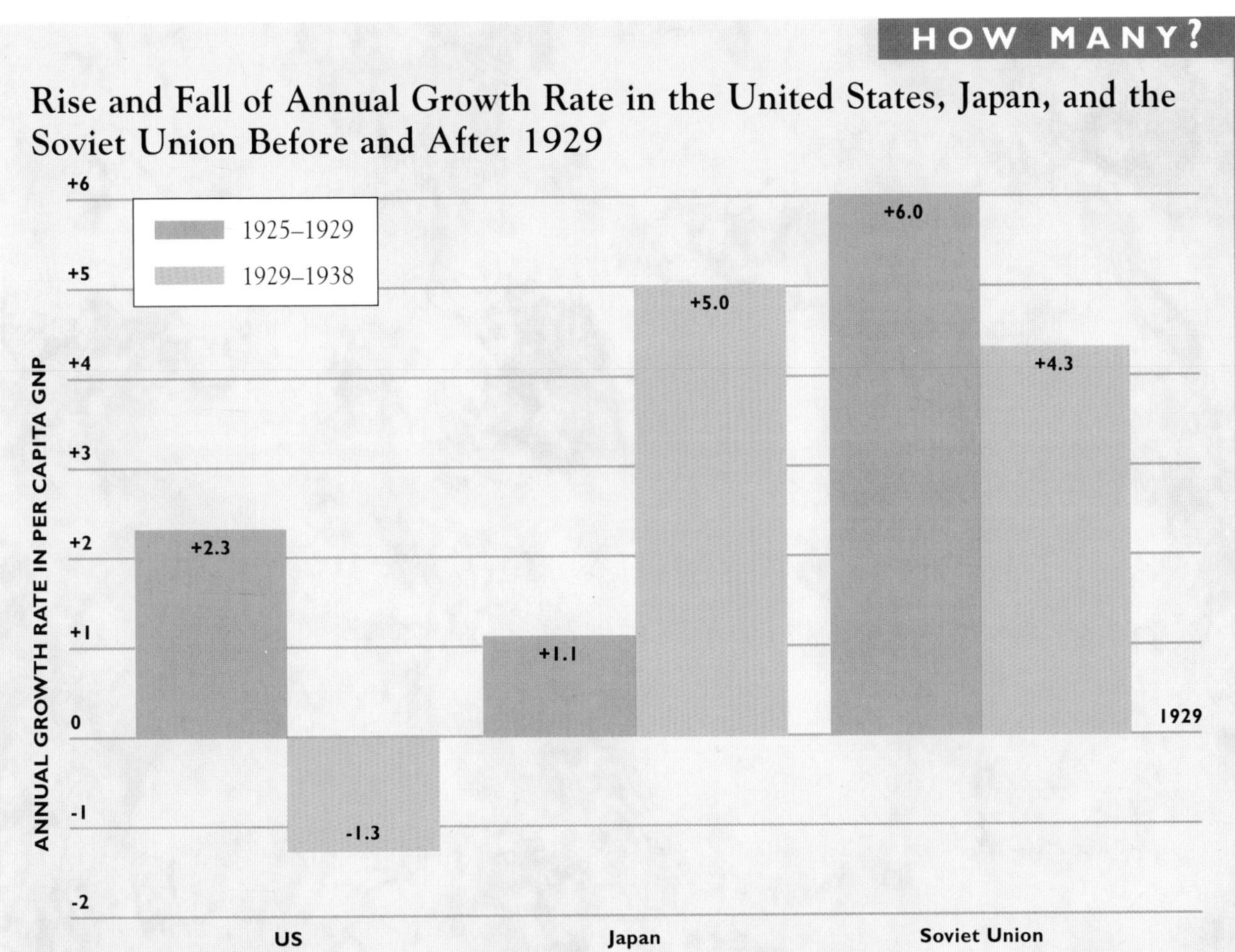

The Great Depression played havoc with national rates of production and world trade (see Box on p. 820). Here the hard-hit United States suffers a steep decline in its annual growth rate, while the Soviet Union, turning from its NEP (New Economic Policy) developed under Lenin to the Five Year Plans developed under Stalin, suffers a more modest loss. Japan, arming itself for expansion in its Asian hinterland, experiences rapid growth.

Source: *P. Bairoch,* Economics and World History: Myths and Paradoxes *(Chicago: University of Chicago Press, 1993), p. 8.*

In the United States, the election of Franklin Delano Roosevelt as president (1933–1945), brought fresh hope and the **New Deal**, which brought some relief and new aspirations. With an expression of compassion that had not been heard in American political life since perhaps Abraham Lincoln, Roosevelt defined the cause of the economic emergency, named the guilty parties, and announced the cure in his inaugural address as president. The cause was greed; the guilty parties were the rich speculators; and the cure was the largesse to be provided by the government for the "one-third of the nation" that was, as Roosevelt put it in his second inaugural address, "ill-housed, ill-clad, ill-nourished."

The first task was to organize cash relief. The Federal Emergency Relief Administration, created in 1933, handed out millions of dollars to states and private agencies to help relieve hunger and homelessness. Two years later, the Social Security Act established for the first time in the United States the principle that those who could not work—children, the elderly, the disabled—should receive state benefits. It created a new social contract between government and people, superseding the system of private charity and self-help that had prevailed in the past.

In addition to these first steps toward establishing a modern welfare state—a state that assumes the obligation to sustain its citizens from cradle to grave—the New Deal set up programs to put the unemployed to work in public works projects and to sustain artists and writers by assigning them historical and cultural projects with a government salary. As a further measure to protect workers' interests, the New Deal created the National Labor Relations Act in 1935 that supervised unions and protected their right to engage in collective bargaining. To prevent future economic catastrophes, it passed legislation in 1933 and 1934 that insured bank deposits and supervised the stock exchanges.

All of these programs were expensive. Indeed, the New Deal sought to accomplish its goals by going into debt, with the government borrowing to support its programs. That tactic represented an abandonment of conventional views of government spending that dictated a balanced budget, especially during crisis periods. Instead, the New Deal embraced the novel economic theories of the British economist John Maynard Keynes (1883–1946), author of the 1926 work *The End of Laissez-Faire*. Keynes urged the state to engage in "counter-cyclical" activity: when times were hard, it should spend; when prosperity returned, it should raise taxes to enhance revenues and conserve wealth. The free market could not be relied upon to reequilibrate economic systems, which required the deliberate intervention of state spending stimuli and restraints. Keynes's theory seemed to offer a compromise position between capitalism, with its program of unrestrained profit-seeking, and socialism, with its tendency to deaden individual initiative. The New Deal set out to spend its way to recovery, imbuing American liberalism with a new, pro-government ethos. As promised in Roosevelt's campaign song, "happy days" would come again, brought by a newly activist state.

Conclusion

UNCERTAIN LIVES AND THE MEANING OF THE WEST

Roosevelt's Depression remedies may have alleviated some of the pain caused by economic collapse. But they did not reverse the economic trend. In 1938, unemployment was nearly as high as at the low point of Depression. World trade had stagnated, restricted by narrowly nationalistic economic policies. Only renewed military production was sufficient to stimulate the economy. By 1939, as European leaders rearmed their nations in preparation for another war, the factories hummed again, producing bullets, guns, and profits. The people of the Western world were able to go off the dole only because they were once again sent off to the front.

The economic volatility of the postwar years, and especially the Great Depression, had brought not only hardship but also anxiety to the people of the West and of the world. The era of the Modern had arrived—and then it crashed. Who, if anyone, was at fault? What, if anything, could be done? When would normalcy return? Amid the uncertainties born of economic crisis, many looked for strong leaders, who gave clear answers, and promised that certainty would rise from despair. Those leaders came, promising the certainty that only totalitarian regimes can give a demoralized and disoriented populace; but with them came tragedy.

REVIEW QUESTIONS

1. How did the outlook of Western artists and intellectuals change after World War I? Why did Heisenberg's indeterminacy theory describe this outlook better than Einstein's theory of order? Why did the art of the 1920s and 1930s abandon the attempt to depict objective reality?

2. To what extent can cinema be called "the first form of mass entertainment"? How did the Soviet Union and Nazi Germany use the cinema to advance their political aims?

3. What made jazz and the works of dramatists like Bertolt Brecht "modern"? What was Existentialism?

4. How did World War I affect the position of women in Western societies? How did birth control help to liberate women? Why did bourgeois and working-class women have different political and social goals?

5. What services did the welfare state offer to its citizens after World War I? How did increased state intervention affect the attitude toward families and motherhood in the Fascist nations?

6. To what extent was Europe able to return to normalcy in the 1920s? Why did the stock market crash in 1929 cause the Great Depression? How did the European countries and the United States cope with the Depression?

SUGGESTED READINGS

Uncertainty in the Arts and in Thought

Bradbury, Malcolm and James MacFarlane, eds., *Modernism, 1890–1930*, 2nd ed. (New York: Penguin, 1991). Essays on Modernism in literature, art, poetry, drama, with its national variations.

Brian, Denis, *Einstein: A Life* (New York: J. Wiley, 1996). Comprehensive and up-to-date biography of this monumental figure.

Gamow, George, *Thirty Years That Shook Physics: The Story of Quantum Theory* (Garden City, NY: Doubleday Anchor, 1966). Accessible introduction to quantum physics.

Hughes, H. Stuart, *Consciousness and Society: The Reorientation of European Social Thought, 1890–1930*, rev. ed. (New York: Vintage, 1977; orig. 1958). Classic and essential general survey of the changing culture and philosophy of the period.

Sklar, Robert, *Film: An International History of the Medium* (New York: Prentice Hall–H. N. Abrams, 1993). Surveys the development of cinema from its earliest days to the recent past, with an emphasis on the interaction of cinema, society, and technology.

Uncertain Boundaries: The New Women, the Shrinking Family, the Nurturant State

Bock, Gisela and Pat Thane, eds., *Maternity and Gender Policies: Women and the Rise of European Welfare States, 1880s–1950s* (London–New York: Routledge, 1991). Sets the rise of maternalist and pronatalist policies in Europe into the continent's national and political contexts.

Boris, Eileen, *Home to Work: Motherhood and the Politics of Industrial Homework in the United States* (Cambridge: Cambridge University Press, 1994). Interesting account of the variety of hurdles and challenges faced since about 1870 by women who work at home.

Copely, Antony, *Sexual Moralities in France, 1780–1980: New Ideas on the Family, Divorce and Homosexuality: An Essay on Moral Change* (London–New York: Routledge, 1989). Traces the confrontation between libertarian and "Victorian" values in the two centuries following the French Revolution.

Dwork, Deborah, *War is Good for Babies and Other Young Children: A Study of Child Welfare in England* (London: Tavistock, 1987). The role of wars as catalysts for action on improving the education and welfare of children.

Lee, W. Robert and Eve Rosenhaft, eds., *The State and Social Change in Germany, 1880–1980* (Oxford: Berg, 1990). Collection of essays exploring the roles of state and society in creating and developing the first modern welfare system.

Pedersen, Susan, *Family, Dependence, and the Origins of the Welfare State: 1914–1945* (Cambridge: Cambridge University Press, 1993). Comparative study of the movements pushing for family allowances in France and Britain during the first half of the 20th century.

Stites, Richard, *The Women's Liberation Movement in Russia: Feminism, Nihilism and Bolshevism, 1860–1930*, 2nd ed. (Princeton, NJ: Princeton University Press, 1991). Examines the historical development of the "woman question" in Russia during the 19th and early 20th centuries.

Economic Uncertainty

Eichengreen, Barry, *Golden Fetters: The Gold Standard and the Great Depression, 1919–1939* (Oxford: Oxford University Press, 1992). Focuses on policy decisions regarding the gold standard as key to the onset and nature of the Depression.

Garraty, John A., *The Great Depression: An Inquiry into the Causes, Course, and Consequences of the Worldwide Depression of the Nineteen-Thirties, as seen by Contemporaries and in the Light of History* (San Diego: Harcourt Brace Jovanovich, 1986). Valuable account of the Depression, attributing its severity to the fact that the world was (and is) integrated economically, but divided politically into nation-states.

Kanigel, Robert, *The One Best Way: Frederick Winslow Taylor and the Enigma of Efficiency* (New York: Viking, 1997). Taylor pioneered time and motion studies and their application to work, helping create the 20th-century workplace.

Weber, Eugen, *The Hollow Years: France in the 1930s* (New York: W. W. Norton, 1994). Informative study of Depression-era France treating in detail the arts, culture, and ordinary life.

STATES IN CONFLICT

1910 | 1920 | 1930 | 1940 | 1950

Fascism, Communism, and Prelude to War

World War I and the Russian Revolution, 1914–21

New Economic Policy in Soviet Union, 1921–28

Spanish Civil War, 1936–39

World War II, 1939–45

- Treaty of Versailles humiliates Germany, 1919
- New Economic Policy (NEP) launched, 1921
- Mussolini's Black Shirts "March on Rome," 1922
- Hitler's "Beer Hall Putsch" in Munich, 1923
- Locarno Treaty, 1925
- Stalin's First Five Year Plan, 1928
- Lateran Treaty between Mussolini and papacy, 1929
- Japanese invade Manchuria, 1931
- Hitler assumes German chancellorship, Jan 1933
- "Night of the Long Knives," 1934
- Brutal purges terrorize Soviet society, 1934–39
- "Popular Front" alliances of Communists and Socialists, 1935
- Nuremburg racial laws passed in Germany, 1935
- Rome-Berlin Axis, 1936
- "German Art" and "Degenerate Art" exhibitions, 1937
- Guernica bombed, 1937
- Japan invades China, 1937
- *Kristallnacht* pogrom in Germany, 1938
- Germany annexes Austria, 1938
- Munich Conference, 1938
- Germany annexes Czechoslovakia, 1939
- "Pact of Steel", 1939
- Nazi-Soviet Non-Aggression Pact, 1939
- Trotsky murdered, 1940

World War II

- Germans invade Poland, Sept 1, 1939
- Germans enter Paris, June 14, 1940
- Germany invades Soviet Union, June 22, 1941
- Japanese attack Pearl Harbor, Dec 7, 1941
- Nazi "Final Solution" begins, 1942
- Germans surrender at Stalingrad, Jan 31, 1943
- Allies land in Sicily, July 10, 1943
- D-Day, June 6, 1944
- VE Day, May 8, 1945
- Allies push Japanese from open Pacific, May 1945
- Potsdam Conference, 1945
- Hiroshima and Nagasaki bombed, Aug 6, 9, 1945
- Japan surrenders, Aug 14, 1945
- Nuremberg Trials begin, Nov 20, 1945

Society, Economy, and Ideas

- Ludwig Wittgenstein's *Tractatus Logico-Philosophicus*, 1921
- James Joyce's *Ulysses*, 1922
- Sergei Eisenstein's *The Battleship Potemkin*, 1925
- Max Eastman's *Since Lenin Died*, 1925
- Adolf Hitler's *Mein Kampf*, 1925
- John Maynard Keynes' *The End of Laissez-Faire*, 1926
- Great Depression begins, 1929
- Leni Riefenstahl's *Triumph of the Will*, 1935
- Sidney and Beatrice Webb's *Soviet Communism: A New Civilisation?*, 1935
- Sergei Eisenstein's *Alexander Nevsky*, 1938
- Anton Ciliga's *The Russian Enigma*, 1940
- Arthur Koestler's *Darkness at Noon*, 1940
- Jean-Paul Sartre's *Being and Nothingness*, 1943
- George Orwell's *Animal Farm*, 1945
- George Orwell's *1984*, 1949

Beyond the West

Korean War, 1950–53

- Amritsar Massacre, India, 1919
- Independence and partition of India, 1947
- UN partitions Palestine; declaration of state of Israel, 1947
- Communist victory in China, 1949

CHAPTER

27

STATES IN CONFLICT

Communism, Fascism, Democracy, and the Crisis of World War II

1917–1945

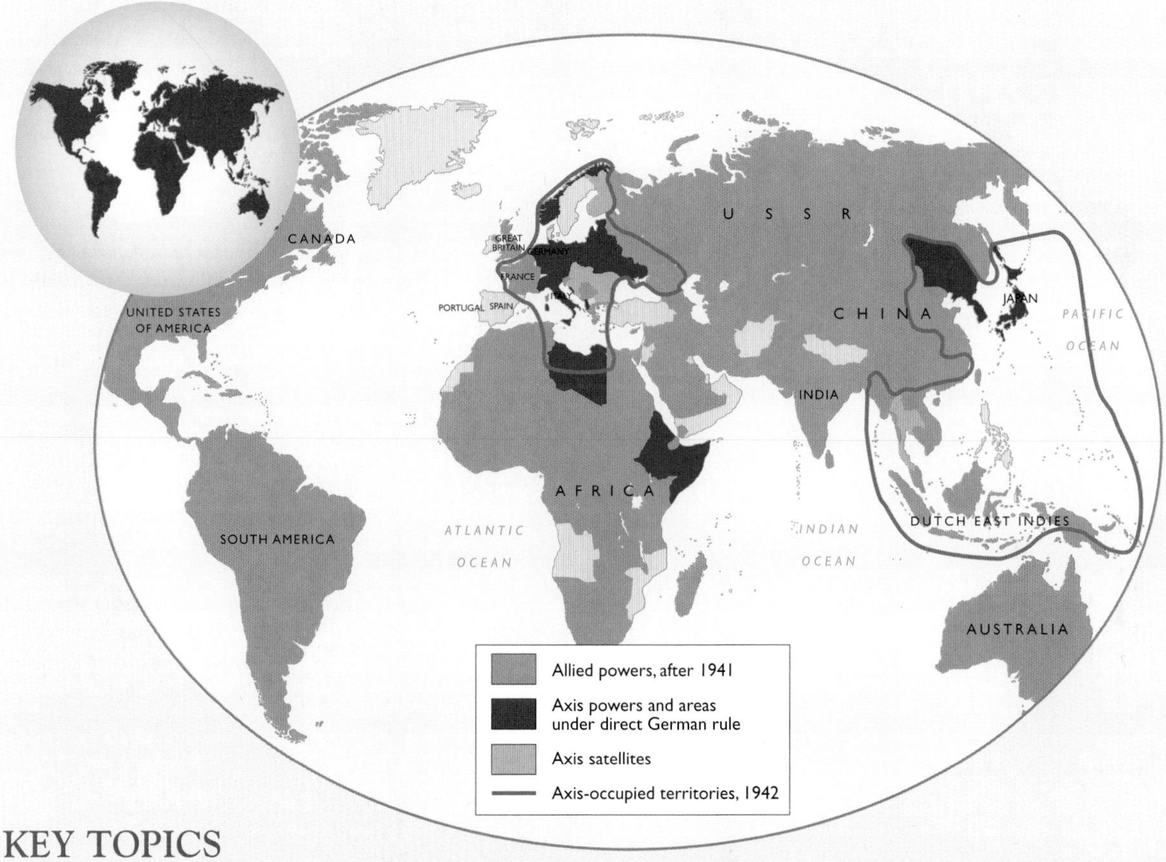

CANADA
UNITED STATES OF AMERICA
SOUTH AMERICA
GREAT BRITAIN
GERMANY
FRANCE
PORTUGAL
SPAIN
ITALY
U S S R
CHINA
JAPAN
INDIA
AFRICA
DUTCH EAST INDIES
AUSTRALIA
ATLANTIC OCEAN
INDIAN OCEAN
PACIFIC OCEAN

Allied powers, after 1941
Axis powers and areas under direct German rule
Axis satellites
Axis-occupied territories, 1942

KEY TOPICS

- **Bolsheviks and Communists:** In the Soviet Union, Lenin rewrites Marx, Stalin transforms the economy, and citizens have new access to jobs and opportunities—all at the price of totalitarian rule, the censorship of the arts and thought, police surveillance, and terror.
- **The Faces of Fascism:** Many nations incline to fascism or quasi-fascist ideologies that combine nationalism and militarism with the cult of the "leader" and, in German Nazism, with virulent and lethal anti-Semitism.
- **The Second World War:** As fascist leaders rearm and plan war, the democracies seek peace, and wake up to find, by 1942, the Axis powers dominant in Europe and Asia; by 1945, victory is obtained in both theaters of war, but only after unprecedented slaughter and the terrible evil of "final solutions."

The Omnipotent State *"Everything within the state, nothing outside the state, nothing against the state!" With this summons, the Italian fascist leader Benito Mussolini (1883–1945) convinced the Italian people, in the uncertain years after World War I, to embrace the certainty offered by totalitarianism. The German Nazi leader Adolf Hitler (1889–1945) voiced a similar ideal:* "Ein Reich, ein Volk, ein Führer!" *("one state, one people, one leader").*

These are the formulas of **totalitarianism**, a term often used to characterize those regimes that demand the complete surrender of the human will to the demands of the omnipotent state. No state has ever succeeded in exercising such control over its citizens. But through persuasion, propaganda, and terror, some have attempted to do so. Totalitarian regimes (along with kindred despotisms or monarchies, often termed **authoritarian**) repudiate liberal principles of individual rights, freedom of conscience and expression, and access to political power.

During the 1920s and 1930s, totalitarian governments came to power in many European nations: notably **fascism** in Italy and Germany (where it was known as Nazism); and communism in the Soviet

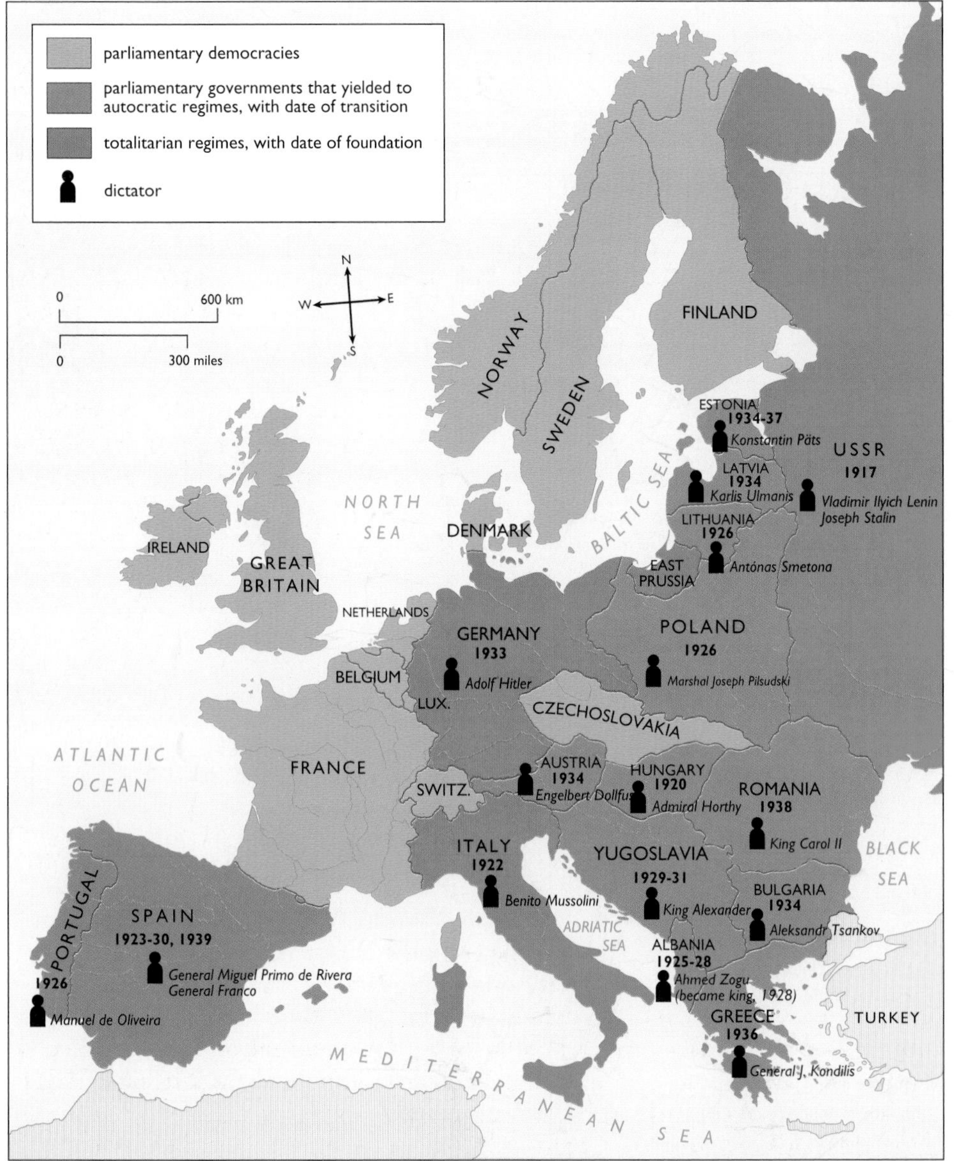

Map 27.1 Democratic, Authoritarian, and Totalitarian Government, 1919–1937: *Between the two great wars, most of Europe (and in Asia, Japan) drifted to authoritarian or totalitarian rule. Totalitarian governments—governments that attempted to direct all aspects of the lives of their citizens while repressing individual freedoms—prevailed in the Soviet Union (communism, from 1917), Germany (Nazism, from 1933), and Italy (fascism, from 1922). Other European nations fell for some period of years to authoritarianism—systems whose rulers came to power outside democratic procedures and governed without representative assemblies or through the manipulation of docile parliaments. Democracies survived on the north and northwestern fringes of Europe and in Czechoslovakia—areas that had long parliamentary traditions, or had not suffered territorial loss as a result of World War I, or had advanced industrial bases.*

Union (1917–1991, consisting of Russia and many of the lands of the former Russian Empire). In 1939, the aggressions of one of these states—Germany—provoked World War II. It ended in 1945 with the defeat of Nazi Germany, fascist Italy, and imperial Japan by the alliance of Britain and the United States, both democracies, and the communist Soviet Union.

Allied triumph was overshadowed by the matchless tragedies of the conflict. Of these one was mass **genocide**, directed against the Jews of Europe, the direct consequence of Nazi racial theory. The second was the explosion in two Japanese cities, in August 1945, of atomic bombs, with their consequences of mass death, mutilation, and disease, and the threat of universal destruction.

This catastrophic war brought an end, however, to the interwar era of uncertainty (see Chapter 26). Certainty returned as the nature of Nazism became clear: it was an evil that could not be tolerated. Reluctantly at first but decisively at last, its opponents massed to defeat it.

MUST READS

Key Books by Key Leaders

Vladimir Ilyich Lenin	*What Is To Be Done?* (1902)
Adolf Hitler	*Mein Kampf (My Struggle)* (1925)
Winston Churchill	*The Speeches of Winston Churchill* (1941–1945)

BOLSHEVIKS AND COMMUNISTS

In Russia, the Bolsheviks who seized power in 1917 in the name of desperate masses (see Chapter 25) established a totalitarian state that employed modern tools of regulation, propaganda, and terror in order to compel the obedience of its peasants, workers, and intellectuals.

A generation of brilliant leaders accomplished the transformation of Russia from autocracy to the communist dictatorship called the Soviet Union (properly the USSR, the Union of Soviet Socialist Republics). Foremost among them were Vladimir Ilyich Lenin (1870–1924) and Joseph Vissarionovich Dzhugashvili (1879–1953), known as Stalin ("man of steel").

Lenin had reconstructed Marxian socialism (see Chapter 24) to suit Russian circumstances, as he perceived them. Stalin derived from Lenin a model for the forcible imposition of socialism. He also learned—from Lenin but also from Mussolini and Hitler—strategies for seizing and maintaining power. By 1939, when war once again engulfed Europe, Russian communism had reached maturity.

Lenin: Rewriting Marx

By 1917, Lenin had reconstructed the theories of Marxian socialism to suit Russian realities: a semi-industrialized country with a minuscule bourgeoisie, a nascent proletariat, and a vast peasantry. In 1917, his version of Marxism (henceforth Marxist-Leninism) became the political orthodoxy of the new communist state.

In his 1902 book *What Is To Be Done?* (see Chapter 25), Lenin announced the key points in his rewriting of Marx. An elite of trained intellectuals was necessary, he argued, to instruct and lead the proletariat. **Trade union** organizations were immature. Russian industrialization had been laggard. Many of the workers were not truly urbanized proletarians but peasants who labored for a season in the factory, then returned to the fields. They needed, Lenin believed, to be guided by a cadre of intellectuals who would serve as permanent, professional revolutionaries. Lenin's Marxism was thus modified not only by the condition of Russian workers, but also by the Russian tradition of a radical, elite intelligentsia (see Chapter 24).

When the revolution began in the spring of 1917 (see Chapter 25), Lenin expounded his principles in simple terms to mass audiences. At a ripe moment, the Bolsheviks acted, swiftly and almost unopposed, storming the Winter Palace and ousting the provisional government. The Bolsheviks were only a faction of a faction, which in a nation of about 170 million had recruited perhaps 200,000 followers; now Bolshevism would shape the future of Russia. That nation was soon to learn that the dictatorship of the proletariat was, in the end, but another, and brutal, dictatorship.

War Communism and the New Economic Policy

It required three years of struggle to consolidate power, during which the Bolsheviks waged war against rival political factions, tsarist counterrevolutionaries, and foreign detachments. Even as Trotsky negotiated the Brest-Litovsk settlement (see Chapter 25), he built up the Red Army to safeguard the state Lenin had snatched in the October Revolution.

Establishing the Communist State The Red Army faced a formidable task. In all directions, rival, or "White" organizations formed to oppose it. In the south, it faced troops of the general Lavr Georgyevich Kornilov (1870–1918; see Chapter 25) and his successors, joined at first by the Don Cossacks. In the Caucasus region, the Red Army needed to recover Georgia, Armenia, and Azerbaijan, which had declared their independence in 1918. In the east, they faced a conservative counter-government established at Omsk in Siberia, as well as an autonomous republic of social revolutionaries at Kuybyshev (now Samara). To the southwest, they aimed to recover Ukraine. In the north, Allied forces had occupied Murmansk and Archangel, ostensibly to protect Allied stores of war material. By 1920, the White opposition had been suppressed, rebellious nationalities brought to heel, and the foreigners dispersed. Russia was devastated. Between 10 and 30 million, mostly civilians, were dead.

Wartime atrocities, committed by both sides, were followed by the terror unleashed by the hated Cheka, a political police force organized in 1917 by the Bolshevik Felix Edmundovich Dzerzhinsky (1877–1926) to secure the new regime. The Cheka annihilated thousands of suspected enemies of the people, its persecutions mounting to 118 in the single month of February 1921. Modeled on its tsarist predecessor, the detested Okhrana, the Cheka surpassed that organization in the numbers of those executed, in the use of torture, and in the conditions of exile (now to forced labor camps) to which "politicals" (political prisoners) were subjected. The heritage of the Cheka endured in successor secret police organizations including: the GPU (State Political Administration), from 1922 (or OGPU, the word "united" added at the start, after 1923); the NKVD (People's Commissariat of Internal Affairs) from 1934; and the KGB (Committee of State Security) from 1953.

There remained the problem of disciplining not merely people, but thoughts. Censorship began promptly after the 1917 October Revolution with the closing of the "counterrevolutionary" press. By the summer of 1918, all independent dailies, weeklies, and monthlies had been suppressed. In 1920, suspect books were targeted. All but two copies each (these to be kept apart in "special reserve") of the works of ninety-four suspect authors—including Plato, Descartes, and Tolstoy—were removed from library shelves and destroyed. The instruction for this action proceeded from Nadezhda Krupskaya (1869–1939), member of the **commissariat** on education, Lenin's wife and loyal companion during the years of exile.

Krupskaya also supported the campaign for the "liquidation of illiteracy" launched in 1919 for all citizens between eight and fifty. In 1917, the Russian masses were largely (fifty-seven percent) illiterate. On farms and in workplaces, adults labored to learn to read. Some progress had been made by 1926, when just over half—fifty-one percent—of Russians had attained literacy.

The need to communicate socialist theory to an uninstructed population gave impetus to film, theater, and art, which were charged to "agitate" audiences to revolutionary zeal. Krupskaya promoted the director Sergei Eisenstein (1898–1948), whose pioneering films presented historical and sociological concepts through purely visual means (see Chapter 26). Theatrical performances celebrated heroic peasants and derided counterrevolutionaries. Posters presented bold images of ideal types—workers, peasants, soldiers—selflessly laboring for the creation of a new society.

Economic Measures To establish the socialist foundations of the new Soviet state, stern measures were also required in the economic sphere. Lenin had promised land to his peasant supporters and saw to the redistribution of landowners' property. Much farmland, however, was ravaged by the battles of the Civil War; while peasants, compelled to surrender their grain stores, had reduced their sown acreage. The consequence was a great famine in 1921, resulting in 5 million deaths. As people died in the streets where packs of starving, abandoned children roamed, the new government sought and received international aid to ameliorate the crisis.

Even as famine struck the countryside, Lenin requisitioned grain for the cities—workers would eat at the expense of the peasants. The workers, meanwhile, had been organized into self-governing soviets, which were responsible for meeting the production quotas set by a supreme council that regulated the industrial economy. They labored hard, at low wages and under unsafe conditions, compelled to forego consumer goods—housing, food, and clothing—to support maximum reinvestment in manufacturing enterprises.

People resisted the heavy economic burdens imposed by what was called "War Communism." Moscow and Petrograd shriveled, and industrial production plummeted. In 1921, Lenin adopted the more moderate approach announced in his NEP (New Economic Policy). It permitted small entrepreneurs to operate freely and peasants to acquire their own farms and livestock. This strategy encouraged a stratum of landowning peasants, called ***kulaks***, and won popular support for communism at a crucial moment.

WITNESSES

Bolsheviks and Communists: Forging Communist Society

Among the other harsh measures that constituted "War Communism," a decree on food procurement orders the extraction of grain supplies from peasant proprietors (May 13, 1918): DECREE OF THE ALL-RUSSIAN CENTRAL EXECUTIVE COMMITTEE . . . While the consuming provinces are starving, great stocks of cereals, including the 1916 harvest and the 1917 harvest which has not yet been threshed, lie, as habitually, in the producing provinces. These stocks are in the hands of rural *kulaks* [better-off peasants] and wealthy people, in the hands of the rural bourgeoisie. . . . [T]his rural bourgeoisie remains deaf and unresponsive in the face of the moanings of starving workers and poor peasants; it refuses to dispatch cereals to the state station points . . . while at the same time it sells for its own benefit . . . at fabulous prices to speculators and bagmen. The obstinacy of the greedy *kulaks* and wealthy peasants must be brought to an end. . . . The reply to the violence of grain holders upon the rural poor must be violence upon the bourgeoisie.

Not a single *pud* [unit of weight] of grain must remain in the hands of the grain holders, except the quantity needed for sowing and subsistence of the household until the next harvest.

(From R. A. Wade, ed., *Documents of Soviet History, vol. 1: The Triumph of Bolshevism, 1917–1919*, 1995)

In a speech to the Managers of Socialist Industry, Stalin urges ceaseless efforts to industrialize for the sake of the fatherland (1931): To slacken the tempo would mean falling behind. And those who fall behind get beaten. But we do not want to be beaten. No, we refuse to be beaten! One feature of the history of old Russia was the continual beatings she suffered for falling behind, for her backwardness. She was beaten by the Mongol Khans. She was beaten by the Turkish beys. She was beaten by the Swedish feudal lords. She was beaten by the Polish and Lithuanian gentry. She was beaten by the British and French capitalists. She was beaten by the Japanese barons. All beat her—for military backwardness, for cultural backwardness, for political backwardness, for industrial backwardness, for agricultural backwardness. . . .

We are fifty or a hundred years behind the advanced countries. We must make good this distance in ten years. Either we do it, or they crush us.

(J. V. Stalin, speech to Managers of Socialist Industry, 1931)

Writer V. Zazubrin celebrates the coming industrialization of the Soviet Union as a necessary step in the creation of socialist society (1926): Let the fragile green breast of Siberia be dressed in the cement armor of cities, armed with the stone muzzles of factory chimneys, and girded with iron belts of railroads. Let the *taiga* [Russian forest] be burned and felled, let the steppes be trampled. Let this be, and so it will be inevitably. Only in cement and iron can the fraternal union of all peoples, the iron brotherhood of all mankind be forged.

(V. Zazubrin, speech to the 1st Congress of Siberian Writers, 1926; ed. B. Komarov, 1980)

The Communist government system also took form during these years. Immediately following the October Revolution (see Chapter 25), Bolshevik leadership had been affirmed by the National Congress of soviets then meeting in Petrograd (although only after the Mensheviks and Socialist Revolutionaries walked out). Lenin took the chairmanship of the newly constituted Council of People's Commissars, or "ministers" (and so served until his death), in which Trotsky served as foreign commissar, and Stalin as commissar of nationalities. This new government council and the Politburo (short for political bureau) or policy committee of the Bolshevik party, soon relocated to Moscow.

In January 1918, the newly elected Constituent Assembly convened for the first time. But the Bolsheviks had not obtained a majority of its delegates, and so immediately disbanded the assembly—the last chance Russia had for a democratic, constitutional, and representative government. Instead, by the principle of "democratic centralism," the hierarchy of local and regional soviets sent recommendations upward, ultimately to the Communist central committee, which made a final decision—the "party line," binding upon all.

The Comintern Lenin hoped to stimulate new communist revolutions abroad, reminding his followers "that the interests of socialism, the interests of world socialism, are superior to national interests, to the interests of the state." In 1919, he launched the Third, or Communist, International, the "Comintern," which was to consist of foreign delegations under strict Soviet leadership. Its task was to subject all foreign communist parties to the discipline of Soviet communism and so to promote world revolution.

By 1920, the Comintern's "Twenty-One Conditions" for parties seeking affiliation outlined the essentials of "true" communism. The Comintern regularly communicated to foreign communist parties the Soviet "line," or policy on international and domestic matters. From 1928, it instructed them not to compromise with liberal or socialist parties—a bold stand, since social democrats alone outnumbered foreign communist party members more than fifteen to one. In 1935, in a sudden policy reversal, the Comintern directed otherwise. It now encouraged communists abroad to join with center and left parties in Popular Front coalitions aimed at combating fascism.

By that time, under Lenin's successor Stalin, the hope for spontaneous, world-wide communist revolution had been set aside. From 1928, Stalin had proposed a different goal for which to strive: "socialism in one country." Lenin had wished to establish world-wide socialism; instead, Stalin established a national communist state, under one-party rule, disciplined by the threat of violence, and governed by the *nomenklatura* (those who held positions, or "names"), the obedient servitors of the Politburo. Stalin then turned to transform the stubborn Russian economy according to socialist principles.

Stalin: Gravedigger of the Revolution?

To do so, he enlisted the labor and the lives of the peasants, the workers, and his own revolutionary comrades. He compelled the peasantry to work on collective farms, dispossessing the one rural class that had shown enterprise and leadership—the now vilified kulaks. He subjected industrial workers to harsh conditions dictated by rigid production quotas, while denying them consumer goods. He bullied and silenced his Bolshevik comrades, veterans of the 1917 takeover and the harsh Civil War, as well as millions of party functionaries, military officers, and citizens. Shocked by his despotism, Leon Trotsky called him the "gravedigger" of the Revolution. Perhaps; but at the same time, Stalin was, with Lenin, the builder of Soviet communism.

Stalin had always been different from the other leading Old Bolsheviks. A native of Georgia (in the Caucasus, and then part of the Russian empire) and the son of a shoemaker, Stalin became a Bolshevik in 1903. But he was not an intellectual, and did not join in the esoteric debates enjoyed before 1917 of fine points of Marxian theory.

Stalin was an effective manager who by the early 1920s had demonstrated his ability to execute instructions ruthlessly. This quality Lenin appreciated until, at the edge of death, he learned that it was accompanied by self-serving ambition. In declining health, having suffered from several strokes, and communicating only through written memoranda, Lenin dictated a "political testament" during his last weeks urging Stalin's removal from his post as general secretary of the party. But Stalin had already asserted himself. The testament was ignored, and then suppressed (it was not publicized until after Stalin's death in 1956). At his lowest moment, Trotsky was given the task of denying to Western skeptics that such a document existed. Thus he rescued a man he saw as an enemy—the "gravedigger of the Revolution."

In 1924, Lenin's embalmed body was laid to rest in a mausoleum in Red Square, Moscow's civic center, to be venerated as a deity in the public religion of communism. Now Stalin began in earnest to maneuver for power, "exposing" each of his colleagues in turn as extremists or deviationists. By 1930, he had expelled them all from the Politburo, and surrounded himself with lackeys. By 1940, every one of the six men with whom he shared power in 1924 had been killed. Trotsky, the last, was tracked by Stalin's agents to Mexico, and murdered by a Spanish NKVD agent with a mountaineer's ice pick.

As Stalin rose, debate ceased. All decisions proceeded from him, as once from the tsars. Even the information presented to him, in time, was filtered so as not to disagree with the dictator's presuppositions.

By 1930, Stalin had edged out all his rivals in the central committee. He now proceeded to target new groups of supposed opponents, extremists, and "enemies of the people," who were paraded in "show trials" put on for the attention of the Soviet people and the watching world. There were trials of engineers, of industrial managers, of party leaders and officials. Disoriented or impassive after torture and threats, strangely compliant defendants confessed to crimes against the state before being sent to the labor camps or to death. In the course of trial, some of the accused went insane, committed suicide, or mysteriously died.

After the murder in 1934 of the Old Bolshevik Sergei Mironovich Kirov (1888–1934), who had spoken critically of Stalin's despotism in party meetings, the killing mounted to a frenzy. The murder was probably ordered by Stalin (who subsequently disposed of all the principals in the plot, including the assassin and his NKVD directors). But at the time, Stalin mourned Kirov's loss, and proceeded to "investigate" the murder.

Between 1934 and 1939 hundreds of inner-circle Communists were arrested, tried, and executed. Those killed included 98 of 139, or seventy percent, of Central Committee members; and 1,108, or fifty-six percent of the 1966 representatives to the 1934 XVIIth party congress held in 1934. Thousands, perhaps millions, of other public officials, artists, intellectuals, and ordinary people were also victims. According to Roy Medvedev (1925–), a dissident survivor of the Soviet regime, the total arrested during 1934–1939 mounted to around 3 to 5 million, with hundreds of thousands shot. At the peak of the purge, over 200 executions were recorded per day in the Lubyanka, the NKVD central prison; "not streams, these were rivers of blood."

A purge of military officers in 1937–1938 complemented the purge of party officials. By 1939, Stalin had eliminated half of the Red Army officer corps—more than 40,000, of whom 400 were of the rank of colonel and above, including three of the five marshals, thirteen of the fifteen army commanders, nine out of ten army generals, and six out of seven admirals. When the German army attacked the Soviet Union in 1941, two-thirds of its generals were novices.

Those arrested in the purges were imprisoned, tortured, sent to labor camps, or shot. Of these destinies, the labor camp or **gulag** is the special emblem of the Stalinist era (although its history begins under Lenin, with sixty-five in existence by 1922). Supervised by special government agencies, the labor-camp system went well beyond the penal regimes of the tsarist era. Prisoners worked at heavy tasks, for extraordinarily long work days under extreme conditions, especially of cold, as gulags were mostly in the Arctic. They were housed in barracks without heat or furnishings, denied adequate food (rations were deliberately withheld to present an incentive to productivity) and subjected to physical and psychological abuse. The labor of these prisoners dug canals, mined gold, and felled forests, contributing significantly if horribly to the nation's economic success.

Few survived. The camp served the combined purpose of work and extermination. Frequent shipments of fresh prisoners (criminals and politicals) restocked the labor gangs when their predecessors had died of hunger, exhaustion, or brutality. In just a few years, the special killing squads of the Nazi security force (the SS, or *Schutzsstaffel*)—these were the executioners, on the fronts or in the death camps, of Jews, Poles, and others—would show they had learned much from the Stalinist gulag.

HOW MANY?

Stalin's Deathlist

Costs of collectivization, 1928–1933
People: about 10 million dead (the nation suffered a net loss in total population of 20 million from 1917–1934)
Livestock: 1 million head of cattle, pigs, sheep, and goats destroyed

Arrested, 1937–1938 5 million, of whom 1 million were executed

In jail, 1938 1 million

In gulags, 1935–1937: 6 million
1938: 7 million

Survival rate of purge-era prisoners: about 10%
Purged by 1939 of those active in 1934: Central Committee members: 98 of 139 (70%)
Representatives to the XVIIth Party Congress (1934): 1,108 of 1,966 (56%)

Socialism in One Country

Among the political prisoners transported to the gulag were millions of kulaks. These small rural proprietors Stalin declared to be a peasant aristocracy that he would "liquidate as a class", as part of his program to attain "socialism in one country."

Small peasant proprietors were a relatively new social group. In the wake of the 1861 emancipation of the serfs, a handful of peasants had been able to establish themselves on small farms. With the Bolshevik confiscation of large estates in 1918, more were able to do so. The policies of War Communism bore heavily on this peasant elite, whose stores of grain were requisitioned for use by the Red Army and industrial workers. Under the NEP instituted in 1921, however, determined kulaks again increased their landholdings.

Even so, the peasant elite that existed in 1928 when Stalin launched his policy of **collectivization** was hardly a class of oppressors, as was charged. Kulaks (a term of abuse, signifying tight-fisted greed) typically owned seventy to eighty acres of land and two or three draught animals, and often hired their neighboring smaller peasants or day laborers to assist with farm tasks. Far from wealthy, kulaks more closely resembled a struggling middle class.

It was this social group that the collectivization campaign destroyed. Stalin's agents in the countryside demanded stated amounts of grain from each region. The grain was needed to feed the cities and industrial

WITNESSES

Communist Totalitarianism: Repression and Terror

The Kronstadt sailors, participants in the 1917 October Revolution, denounce the communist dictatorship (March 1921): With the October Revolution the working class had hoped to achieve its emancipation. But there resulted an even greater enslavement of human personality. . . . [But now there is resistance.] Here and there the land is lit up by the fires of rebellion in a struggle against oppression and violence. . . . The Generals of Communism see clearly that it is the people who had risen, the people who have become convinced that the Communists have betrayed the ideas of Socialism. . . . [L]ife under the Communist dictatorship is more terrible than death. . . . [The Kronstadt rebellion was quickly crushed by Red troops.]
(Alexander Berkman, "The Kronstadt Rebellion," 1922)

An episode from the unpublished novel of M. N. Averbakh, member of a special brigade charged to liquidate the kulaks (1930): The door opened. The brigade burst into the house. The . . . officer in charge of the operation was in front, brandishing a revolver.

"Hands up!"

Morgunov was barely able, in the gloom, to make out the frail figure of the class enemy. He was wearing white drawers and a dark undershirt, and was barefoot. . . . The eyes, wide with terror, glanced from place to place. . . . He kept blinking and crossing himself, shifting from one foot to the other, . . . and suddenly be began to sob. . . . His wife, not a young woman, jumped down from the high sleeping bench and began to wail at the top of her voice. The children began crying. A calf lying beside the stove, apparently not in very good health, began to bawl.

Morgunov looked around, aghast. He saw that the hut contained nothing but the one room and the big Russian stove. In the front corner . . . were two simple wooden benches and a crude table made of planks. No chest of drawers, no beds, no chairs. . . .

The class enemy!
(From R. Medvedev, *Let History Judge: The Origins and Consequences of Stalinism*, rev. ed., ed. G. Shriver, 1989)

Writer Nadezhda Mandelstam, whose husband, the poet Osip Mandelstam, died a prisoner in 1938, recalls the Stalinist terror: Anybody who breathes the air of terror is doomed, even if nominally he manages to save his life. Everybody is a victim—not only those who die, but also the killers, ideologists, accomplices and sycophants who close their eyes or wash their hands. . . .

The principles and aims of mass terror have nothing in common with ordinary police work or with security. The only purpose of terror is intimidation. To plunge the whole country into a state of chronic fear, the number of victims must be raised to astronomical levels, and on every floor of every building there must always be several apartments from which the tenants have suddenly been taken away. The remaining inhabitants will be model citizens for the rest of their lives.
(Nadezhda Mandelstam, *Hope against Hope: A Memoir*, ed. M. Hayward, 1970)

Before his execution by Stalin's political police, Nikola Bukharin dictates to his wife a letter to a future generation of party leaders, to vindicate himself and testify to the terror (1938): I am leaving life. . . . I feel my helplessness before a hellish machine, which . . . has acquired gigantic power, fabricates organized slander, acts boldly and confidently. . . .

Storm clouds have risen over the party. My one head, guilty of nothing, will drag down thousands of guiltless heads. . . . I have been in the party since I was eighteen, and the purpose of my life has always been to fight for the interests of the working class, for the victory of socialism. . . .

I appeal to all party members! In these days, perhaps the last of my life, I am confident that sooner or later the filter of history will inevitably sweep the filth from my head. I was never a traitor; without hesitation I would have given my life for Lenin's, I loved Kirov, started nothing against Stalin. . . . Know, comrades, that on the banner, which you will be carrying in the victorious march to communism, is also my drop of blood.
(From R. Medvedev, *ibid*)

centers, where the proletariat labored to modernize a still-backward economy. The quotas were set so high that peasants were left with insufficient stores for themselves; at one point, the amount of grain requisitioned amounted to more than the total harvested.

The peasants resisted these demands. Sometimes they protested violently; sometimes they refused to grow the crops that they would not be allowed to enjoy. Inflamed, Stalin responded with a drive to remove the entire peasantry to collective farms, to be governed by soviets and supervised by official ideologues, or commissars. At the same time, he would boost grain yields (as he believed) by eliminating the kulaks who, he thought, clung to an outmoded, privatist model of rural production.

From 1928 to 1933, Communist officials confiscated kulak farms, seized grain stores, invaded cottages, and sent the occupants away homeless and penniless—if they did not shoot them outright or deport them to the gulag. Millions starved to death, in their devastated villages or in the camps. Millions snatched their revenge in advance, burning their own farms and killing their livestock. In the winter of 1932–1933, this disruption of agriculture triggered famine. Peasants throughout Russia suffered through this artificially induced scarcity which followed by only a few years the war-induced famine of 1921. The cost of collectivizing the countryside mounted to about 10 million deaths.

As Stalinist policies enforced socialism in the agricultural sphere, the industrial workforce also experienced the rigors imposed by a rapidly transforming economy. The workers, too, suffered shortages, and were harried by unrealistic production goals set by central economic planners. By their labors, nevertheless, Soviet Russia became a major world producer of steel, weapons, and machines. And a whole new elite of trained managers and engineers gained an autonomy their parents had never known.

The massive industrialization of the Soviet economy accomplished between 1928 and 1939 was guided by successive Five Year Plans. The first was

The war on the class enemy: "liquidate the kulaks": *Stalin's plan to build "socialism in one country" required the collectivization of agricultural production—which in turn required the elimination of small peasant proprietors (the kulaks). In this 1930 photograph, Russian villagers, well-prompted by Soviet advisers, march with a banner asking to "liquidate the kulaks as a class."*

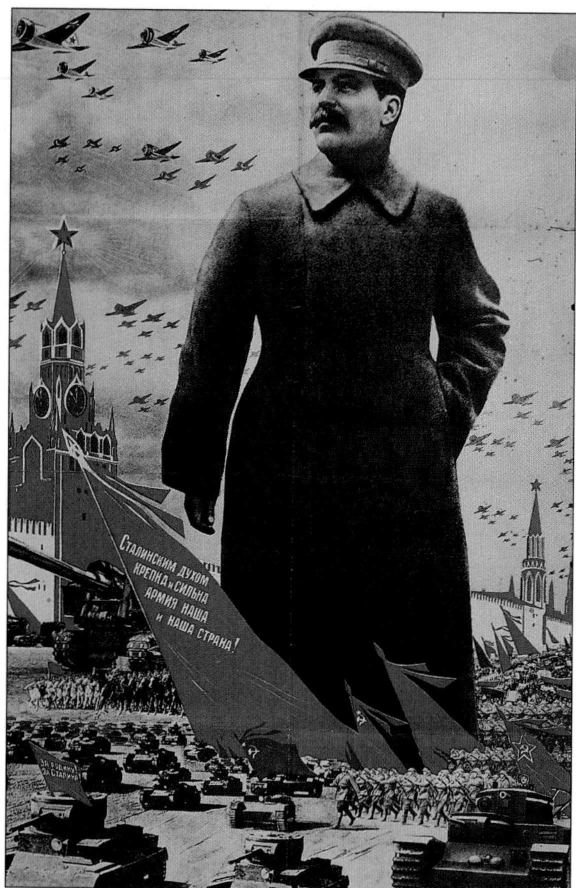

Stalin—father of his country: *This 1939 poster of Stalin as exultant master of an armed and ready Soviet Union expresses the nation's state on the eve of World War II—not a peaceful and democratic society but a militarist and despotic one. The words on the large unfurled banner exalt the leader: "Our army and our country are strengthened with the spirit of Stalin."*

approved in 1929, the second in 1933, the third in 1938, this last cut short by the outbreak of World War II. Each plan set production quotas to spur growth, especially in the heavy industries (metals, machines, and textiles). Although statistics were often falsified to give the illusion of success, the plans did lead to a dramatic expansion of Soviet infrastructure and industrial capacity.

The Five Year Plans accomplished nearly as much as they had ambitiously proposed. By 1938, the Soviet Union outdid Britain, and nearly equaled Germany, as a producer of pig-iron and steel. Agricultural production, too, eventually improved. But there had been deficits: rapid modernization required workers to endure low living standards, peasants to starve to feed the workers, and the most energetic stratum of the peasantry—the kulaks—to be sacrificed in order to achieve socialism in one country.

Socialist Realism, Soviet Realities

Social and cultural changes reshaped the lives of urbanized workers during the two interwar decades. Communism called for a transformation of the family and the repression of religion, the arts, and thought.

The Soviet Family Dismantling the family meant the liberation of women from male authority (see Chapter 26). The first steps in this direction were taken as early as 1918, when a new Family Code declared women's equality, erased the distinction between legitimate and illegitimate births, removed marriage from religious to civil jurisdiction, and permitted divorce. Two years later, a further decree made abortion legal if performed by a physician. Married or unmarried, women were to participate fully in society—their labor was required to build the socialist economy. Women were also active in the Communist Party, and worked as teachers and bureaucrats to build the new society that Lenin envisioned.

Many of these measures were revoked under Stalin, however, whose Family Code of 1936 made abortion illegal and divorce difficult, restored the category of illegitimacy, criminalized homosexuality, and sought to rehabilitate the family.

The nurture and instruction of children was a responsibility the Soviet state took seriously. It undertook to rear and educate all of its young. Neighborhood and factory nurseries cared for infants from birth onward. Well-run elementary schools trained the offspring of parents of whom many were themselves illiterate. In an egalitarian setting, these schools prepared children for the technical requirements of a modern society, at the upper levels training engineers, research scientists, teachers, and officers. At the same time, schools and Komsomol (youth organization) units instilled communist values into their young charges—some of whom won favor, during the purges, for denouncing their parents.

The Manipulation of Culture Those born in the early years of the Communist regime had been raised as ardent supporters of the Soviet state. That state had replaced tsardom, aristocracy, and Church with a system that guaranteed social services to all and the opportunity for advancement to high position on the basis of merit.

As adults were retrained to participate in Soviet society, they were weaned from the Church that had for centuries been the mainstay of Russian culture. Official decrees desacralized churches, intimidated priests, and banned the performance of sacraments (restrictions briefly eased in 1941 when it was necessary to reaffirm traditional culture to support the "Great Patriotic War").

Communist censors understood the power of cultural expression in forming the minds of citizens. Writers, film-makers, and artists were gathered into unions that controlled the ideological content of books, plays, films, and paintings. Holding relatively high status in Soviet society, writers and artists largely followed the party line in matters of taste and style.

So too did historians, linguists, psychologists, musicians, and even biologists, whose works were required to endorse the Soviet regime. Psychologists, for example, avoided Freudian psychoanalytic theories, as the notion of an unruly unconscious self countered Soviet understanding of the fully conscious and ideologically committed citizen. Biologists could not explore the field of genetics, as the notion of inherited characteristics countered the Soviet assumption of a wholly malleable human nature.

By the 1930s, the bureaucratic control of the arts and ideas resulted in a serious loss of vitality. As the French author (formerly a communist sympathizer) André Gide (1869–1951) predicted, where there is no liberty, "art loses its meaning and its value . . . as . . . the assent of the greatest number . . . goes to the qualities the public is best able to recognize, that is to say conformity." In the visual arts, the officially sanctioned style of Socialist Realism prevailed, which celebrated the heroism of Soviet workers in a blandly academic manner. Film-making languished until, on the eve of World War II, Eisenstein produced his prophetic *Alexander Nevsky* (see Chapter 26).

The specter of the gulag kept many intellectuals in line. The novelist Maxim Gorky (1868–1936), an ardent participant in the debates of 1917, remained in favor as the leading intellectual of the new state that he never really endorsed. The poet Boris Pasternak (1890–1960), whose silence throughout the 1930s betrayed his hatred for the regime, was for the moment tolerated. The adventurous productions of the Old Bolshevik playwright Vsevolod Meyerhold (1874–1940?), however, invited repression in the end; he was arrested, tortured, and probably executed. The poet Osip Mandelstam (1891–1938?), who had criticized Stalin, was exiled, and died *en route* to the gulag. The poet Anna Akhmatova (pseudonym of Anna Andreyevna Gorenko; 1889–1966)—whose two husbands were executed by Lenin and Stalin, whose son was exiled to the gulag, and who was herself twice denounced for the "bourgeois decadence" of her now widely-acclaimed work—outlived the dictator.

Under Stalin, words were dangerous. For decades, some of the most important Soviet works of literature and thought were "published" only in manuscript and typescript, and circulated secretly (known as samizdat, "self-published"). Such was the case with the writings of Aleksandr Isayevich Solzhenitsyn (1918–), which at last escaped the censors to inform the peoples of the outside world about terror and the gulag in the world's first communist state.

Views from Abroad Until the circulation abroad of Solzhenitsyn's *One Day in the Life of Ivan Denisovich* (1962) and *The Gulag Archipelago* (1973), exposing the Soviet labor camp system, ignorance about conditions in the Soviet Union was persistent. Idealistic sympathizers abroad, such as the British Fabian socialists Sidney and Beatrice Webb (see Chapter 24), described the factories and labor camps with honeyed intonations in their *Soviet Communism: A New Civilisation?* (1935). The Dublin-born playwright George Bernard Shaw (1856–1950) approved of Stalin, who combined, he thought, the qualities of field marshal and pope. The novelist H. G. Wells (1866–1946) found him "candid, fair and honest," and the American industrialist Armand Hammer (1898–1990) commended his resourcefulness. These and other observers, including thousands of communist party workers around the world, ignored rumors and even hard evidence of the purges, the mass slaughter, and the bridling of free thought.

Some early followers did become disillusioned. The American writer Max Eastman (1883–1969), an enthusiastic supporter at first, soon renounced Bolshevism after visiting the Soviet Union in 1922. His *Since Lenin Died* (1925) unveiled the corrupt power plays of the 1920s. (It was to Eastman that an abject Trotsky denied the existence of Lenin's "testament" repudiating Stalin.) The English writer George Orwell (pseudonym of Eric Arthur Blair, 1903–1950),

MUST READS

Opponents of Totalitarianism

Arthur Koestler	*Darkness at Noon* (1940)
Anne Frank	*The Diary of Anne Frank* (1947)
George Orwell	*1984* (1949)
Alexander Solzhenitsyn	*The Gulag Archipelago* (1973)

a socialist who had previously critiqued the hypocrisies of imperialism and absurdities of war, assailed communism for dehumanizing the individual in his epochal works *Animal Farm* (1945) and *Nineteen Eighty-Four* (1949).

The Yugoslav communist Anton Ciliga (1898–1992) exposed the failures of Soviet society (where he lived from 1926 to 1936) in *The Russian Enigma* (1940). Arthur Koestler (1905–1983), a Hungarian-born former Communist who was disillusioned by the 1930s purges, explored the phantom confessions of Stalin's victims in the classic *Darkness at Noon* (1940). Since the late 1980s, which brought the disintegration of the Soviet regime and the opening of the archives, scholars have been able to document the atrocities committed by a totalitarian state in the name of "the people."

Derived from the humane traditions of democratic socialism and liberalism, communism took a different turn in 1917, as Lenin and Stalin redefined its purposes. By the early 1920s, communism in the Soviet Union had crystallized as a totalitarian system sustained by terror and deception. The people it meant to serve benefited in many ways from its programs of economic modernization and mass education. But they suffered from the brutality of a state that elevated itself above the people's own will.

THE FACES OF FASCISM

In the decade after 1917, as Russian communism turned despotic, other European nations embraced different forms of fascism. Exalting a new type of charismatic leader—a *duce*, *Führer*, or *caudillo* (as these were named in Italian, German, and Spanish)—they chose nationalism, militarism, and corporatism over individual rights and freedom.

Why did so many Europeans abandon liberalism?—to the extent that, in 1938 when Hitler dismembered it, there remained but one democracy, Czechoslovakia, among all the nations of central or eastern Europe? The nations of Europe were unable to adjust to the outcomes of World War I. In some cases, their leaders were seen as having accepted too easily the grievous burdens of the Paris peace settlements. Or they could not manage the hammer blows in rapid succession, as in Germany, of inflation and economic depression. Or the people trusted too much the dynamic new leaders from the streets, who openly embraced violence, youth, and unreason as antidotes to the ineptitudes of the politicians. For reasons such as these, support for fascist movements surged through Europe during the 1920s.

Fascism: an Ideology for the Twentieth Century

Fascism is a modern ideology, a child of the twentieth century. Unlike socialism or conservatism, rooted in a liberal past, it is the antithesis of liberalism. Fading toward monarchism or military despotism at one pole, toward anarchy at the other, but never toward democracy, the apparently inchoate phenomenon of fascism can be identified by some key features.

First, fascism is ultra-nationalistic—in contrast to the internationalism (or **cosmopolitanism**) of communism. It exhorts individuals to subordinate themselves to the whole "people." In the same anti-individualistic vein, fascism is **corporatist**, promoting identification with multi-class groups—industry-based councils or youth groups—which in turn support the nationalist agenda. Summoning individuals to identify themselves with nation rather than class, it is anti-socialist and anti-communist.

Second, fascism celebrates irrationalism, in contrast to communism's appeal to "scientific" theory. The elaborate symbols and images it devises appeal to myth rather than history, looking to memories of past greatness, and to premodern, even prehistoric episodes of heroic conquest. Fascism thrives on propaganda—the opposite of reasoned discourse—and specifically the propagation of pithy lies, slogans laden with hatred, resentment, or regret. Esteeming frenzy over reason, the will over the intellect, it prefers youth to age, and recruits its first followers among the discontented young.

Third, fascism promotes war and detests pacifism—in contrast, again, to Soviet communism, which came to power amid war's devastation promising "peace, land, bread." It exalts the qualities that accompany wartime heroism: courage, sacrifice, great efforts of will. "War alone brings all human energies to their highest state of tension," said Mussolini, "and stamps with the seal of nobility the nations which have to face it." Where war cannot be had, fascism admires bellicosity nonetheless, if only in the form of terror.

Fourth, fascism advocates masculinism, and abhors any feminization of culture or politics. It upholds traditional gender roles in society—in contrast to communism which, in theory, denies gender inequality; or to liberalism, which must, in theory, recognize the rights of individuals irrespective of gender. Its vitalism and militarism are masculine ideals. It rejects pacifism and socialism as effeminate. Fascists are men. Women serve the fascist cause by tending to household needs and by bearing children, future mothers and soldiers.

Fifth, fascism is modernist—more so than communism, whose grand theoretical structures are rooted in nineteenth-century and even earlier streams of thought. The only one of the major Western ideologies to emerge in the twentieth century, fascism embraces novelty, especially new technologies and styles. Embracing **futurism**, it concocts visions of a mythicized future. It tends, consequently, to revolution, to the annihilation of existing structures and the fabrication of new ones: here, fascism does resemble communism, which also rejoices in the revolutionary meltdown of inherited institutions.

Finally, fascism is autocratic—at odds with communist theory, which promises power to a triumphant proletariat. It elevates an individual with charismatic qualities, who claims to represent the will of the people. To its *duce* or *Führer* it demonstrates allegiance in mass celebrations that turn the mere individual into a faceless servitor of his "leader" as of his state. It is by nature, therefore, anti-democratic (for democracy would give each person political power) and anti-liberal (for liberalism grants to each inalienable rights).

Although fascism cannot coexist with communism ("the Left"), to which it is opposed in essence, it could and did make alliances with conservatism ("the Right"). Conservatism, which enlisted monarchists and militarists, honored the institutions and traditions that communism would dismantle. Accordingly fascists and conservatives could accede to a nationalist, anti-communist, anti-pacifist program that excluded female activism and promoted a strong leader.

Europe's two principal fascist states arose in Italy and Germany. At the same time, Spain and Portugal, Hungary and Poland, Yugoslavia and Romania, and distant Japan among others had conservative governments with fascist components. By 1937, with the exception of the Soviet Union and the democracies of northwestern Europe (France, Britain, the Netherlands, Belgium, Switzerland,

Mussolini in Genoa, 1938

The Duce and the Führer

Both Mussolini and Hitler were masters of self-presentation, staging spectacular processions and rallies that evoked high emotion and memories of past grandeur while they maximized the figure of the leader. Here, a triumphal Roman arch forms the backdrop to Mussolini's public address in Genoa, underpinning the self-proclaimed magnificence of the duce (above). In the second image (right), Hitler and high Nazi officials mount a flight of stairs flanked by thousands of Nazi soldiers, whose standards bear the regime's symbol of the swastika.

Hitler at a Nazi rally, 1934

and the four Scandinavian nations), and Czechoslovakia, the sole democracy in central Europe, fascist or authoritarian governments ruled everywhere in Europe.

Mussolini and His Imitators

In Italy, the least of the Great Power victors of World War I, fascism first took form in the hands of Benito Mussolini, the least of the century's great dictators. A product of resentment, confusion, and force, Italian fascism was important as a model for other authoritarian regimes.

Though a victor nation that gained territory as a result of the 1919 Paris treaties, Italy was disappointed with her reward for the sacrifices made by her soldiers in the icy battlefields at the Isonzo River (see Chapter 25). Austria surrendered the Alto Adige (Italian Tyrol), the Triestino (Trieste and its environs), and Istria. But the newly-formed state of Yugoslavia incorporated regions for which Italy felt it had bargained and bled.

Italians were also troubled by unrest in the streets and weakness in the parliament. Industrialized relatively late, the Italian economy had been strained by wartime demands. Striking workers, often prodded by communist recruiters, poured into the streets. There they tangled with self-appointed black-shirted gangs of thugs and demobilized soldiers, the *fasci di combattimento* (combat "bundles," or squads) that abounded after 1918. These *fascisti* ("fascists") detested communists and socialists, and suppressed their opponents by cudgeling, kidnapping, torture (castor oil, which they forced their victims to swallow in quantity, was a fascist trademark), and murder.

The Italian government—a constitutional monarchy dating only from the nation's unification in 1870—was dismayed by the disorder and looked for a leader who could contain it. King Victor Emmanuel III chose the easiest, most dangerous solution. He invited Benito Mussolini, leader of the black-shirted fascist gangs, and since 1921 a member of parliament for the new National Fascist party, to form a coalition government. Mussolini took a berth on the overnight train to Rome (this was his "March on Rome") to take up his appointment. By 1924, he personally dominated the government, having first dispatched by assassination his rival, the socialist leader Giacomo Matteotti (1885–1924), and destroyed those who protested the act.

The man who acquired power so swiftly had been born poor. Like his proletarian father, a blacksmith, he was a committed socialist. From 1912, Mussolini edited the newspaper of the Italian socialist party *Avanti!* ("Forward"). He advocated worker activism and international pacifism until 1914, when, in an about-face, he joined those agitating for war. He fought, attaining (as did Hitler) the unexalted rank of corporal. After the war, he developed the political ideology of fascism, promoting it through violence and propaganda.

Once in power, Mussolini pursued a disparate agenda focused only in its ardent nationalism. He supported the large corporations by disabling trade unionism (while pretending to give workers a voice through corporation-based associations). In the Lateran Treaty of 1929, he forged an agreement with the papacy, which had lost the papal states in 1870. The pope was granted official recognition of his sovereignty over an autonomous Vatican state, and the Roman Catholic Church was permitted to resume its role in education; in exchange, the state recognized the validity of Catholic marriage, which meant that there could be no divorce. In return for these concessions, the pope agreed to recognize the authority both of the Italian state and of Mussolini himself, who became the first leader of a unified Italy to be recognized by the Church.

In the arts, Mussolini promoted futurism, and cultural activities that magnified state interests. He centralized the bureaucracy and, famously, made the railroads run on time. He enforced the continued subordinate status of women, launching a natalist program, which encouraged women to reproduce prolifically in the interests of increasing national population (see Chapter 26). "Go back home," he told fascist party delegates in 1927, "and tell the women I need births, many births." He spoke to large, enthusiastic crowds gathered in vast cathedrals and arenas, monuments of past greatness, about Italy's ancient glory—Rome, he reminded them, had once ruled the Mediterranean world.

To recover that glory, Mussolini, too, must become a conqueror. He waited patiently to attain that status. In 1925, he took part with Britain, France, Belgium, and Germany in the agreement at Locarno (Switzerland) that guaranteed the maintenance of Germany's western (but not eastern) frontiers. In 1935, he joined once again with Britain and France in the agreement of Stresa (Italy), reaffirming the then allies' interest in preventing German aggrandizement. Later that year (on October 2, 1935), however, he struck at Ethiopia, which Italy had tried and failed to conquer in 1896 (see Chapter 23). The League of Nations punished Mussolini with weak economic sanctions; they did not, importantly, limit his access to oil, without which Mussolini could not maintain his army.

In 1939, Mussolini struck at Albania, across the Adriatic Sea. In the meantime, both Mussolini and Hitler had been sustaining a rebel Nationalist army in Spain as it battled the democratically elected Republican government (for the Spanish Civil War, see below). Mussolini sent divisions of "volunteers," fully equipped with aircraft and tanks, in support of the forces led by the Nationalist General Francisco Franco (1892–1975). Between Stresa in 1935 and the Albanian invasion in 1939, Italy edged gradually toward alliance with Germany. In 1936, Mussolini and Hitler reached an agreement described as the Rome–Berlin Axis. In 1937, Italy joined Japan and Germany's Anti-Comintern Pact.

Other European nations followed the pattern of Mussolini's fascism, without necessarily adopting all of its ideological features. In the decade 1929–1939, they included Greece and the Balkan nations of Bulgaria and Yugoslavia; Hungary, Poland, and Austria; the Baltic states of Lithuania, Latvia, and Estonia; and Spain and Portugal. Here dictators with a nationalist agenda ruled in league with kings and military elites, sometimes, as in Italy, with the support of the Roman Catholic Church. Fascist movements surfaced even in democratic Britain (led by Sir Oswald Mosley, 1896–1980) and France.

WITNESSES

Fascism and Nazism: the Flight from Reason

Benito Mussolini defines the principles of Italian fascism (1932): Fascism . . . repudiates the doctrine of Pacifism. . . . War alone brings up to its highest tension all human energy and puts the stamp of nobility upon the peoples who have the courage to meet it. . . .

Such a conception of life makes Fascism the complete opposite of . . . so-called scientific and Marxian Socialism, the materialist conception of history. . . .

Fascism combats the whole complex system of democratic ideology, and repudiates it. . . . Fascism denies that the majority, by the simple fact that it is a majority, can direct human society; . . . and it affirms the immutable, beneficial, and fruitful inequality of mankind. . . .

The foundation of Fascism is the conception of the State, ... Fascism conceives of the State as an absolute, in comparison with which all individuals or groups are relative. . . . The Fascist state is itself conscious, and has itself a will and a personality. . . .
(Benito Mussolini with Giovanni Gentile, "The Political and Social Doctrine of Fascism," *Enciclopedia Italiana*, 1932)

Adolf Hitler on Aryans, Jews, and *Lebensraum* (1925): What we see before us of human culture today . . . is almost exclusively the creative product of the Aryan. . . . If one were to divide mankind into three groups: culture-founders, culture-bearers, and culture-destroyers, then as representative of the first kind, only the Aryan would come in question. It is from him that the foundation and the walls of all human creations originate. . . .

The Jew forms the strongest contrast to the Aryan. . . . The Jewish people, with all its apparent intellectual qualities, is nevertheless without any true culture, especially without a culture of its own. . . . He is and remains the typical parasite, a sponger who, like a harmful bacillus, spreads out more and more if only a favorable medium invites him to do so. . . .

[W]e National Socialists must cling un-flinchingly to our foreign-policy aims, that is to guarantee the German nation the soil and territory to which it is entitled on this earth. . . . We take up at the halting place of six hundred years ago. We terminate the endless German drive to the south and west of Europe, and direct our gaze towards the lands in the east . . . and proceed to the territorial policy of the future.
(Adolf Hitler, *Mein Kampf*, 1925; trs. R. Mannheim, 1943, 1971)

Lilo Linke observes Hitler as a girl in Germany (1935): For an hour and a half Hitler spoke, every few minutes interrupted by fanatic acclamations. . . . He thrust his chin forward. His voice, hammering the phrases with an obsessed energy, became husky and shrill and began to squeak more and more frequently. His whole face was covered with sweat. . . .

The audience was breathlessly under his spell. This man expressed their thoughts, their feelings, their hopes; a new prophet had arisen . . . and had the power to lead them into the promised land if they were only prepared to follow him. . . .

A single question as to reason or proof or possibility would have shattered the whole argument, but nobody asked it—the majority because they had begun to think with their blood, which condemns all logic. . . .
(Lilo Linke, *Restless Days*, 1935, 1963)

Imperial Japan, Imperialist Ventures

Authoritarian government also took root in Japan, a country whose ancient imperial traditions and recent rapid modernization predisposed it toward despotism. Dominated by a military elite with expansionist plans and equipped with the latest technology, while Europe floundered, Japan was extending its power purposefully in east Asia.

In 1915 Japan imposed its Twenty-One Demands on China, claiming key footholds in Chinese territory and, in effect, made all China a Japanese dependency (see Chapter 25). Although Japan retained many of these claims in 1919, it was later forced to relinquish them. In 1921–1922, the Washington Conference, including Britain, France, Japan, and the United States, agreed to respect the independence and sovereignty of China. Japan agreed to restore the former German holding of Shandong to China, and to remove its troops from Siberia. It seemed that Japanese expansion had been contained.

The economic depression that gripped the Western world (see Chapter 26) also affected overpopulated Japan. Its poor peasants (its recent wealth was largely urban-based) could not afford to purchase Japanese products, and its industries relied on foreign markets. When the world demand for Japanese manufactures, especially silks, collapsed in the Depression, economic crisis in Japan followed. As in the West, crisis provided the cue for a militarist element to subvert the regular institutions of governance. A group of generals took over from the parliamentary regime that was reestablished after World War I. They now dealt directly with the emperor, believed to be the descendent of deities, who continued to inspire the sacrificial devotion of the Japanese people. They argued that Japan must expand on the mainland so that its people could eat. They were also concerned by the gathering strength of the Soviet Union to their north, and, to their west, by the concentration of power in the hands of the Chinese Nationalists under Chiang Kai-shek (Jiang Jieshi).

Upon the death in 1925 of revolutionary leader Sun Yat-sen (1866–1925; see Chapters 23, 28), Chiang took over the Nationalist, or Guomindang forces his predecessor had assembled. In 1926–1927, with communist allies from whom he soon separated, Chiang drove north from Guangzhou on the South China Sea to the interior industrial center at Wuhan. His forces then wheeled eastward along the lower Yangzi River to prosperous Nanjing and the East China Sea port of Shanghai. By 1928, Chiang controlled a core of the eastern provinces from his capital at Nanjing. This regime he steadily expanded to the south and west, contending with local warlords, some his former allies. The rival communist factions withdrew into the countryside and began the recruitment of peasant supporters that would be the basis of their ultimate victory in 1949 (see Chapter 28).

Meanwhile, beginning in 1931, Japan began to tear at northeastern China, a region wedged between Soviet and Guomindang strongholds. Japanese forces invaded Manchuria in 1931, which they organized in 1932 as the puppet state of Manchukuo (under the last emperor of China, who had abdicated in 1912, a member of the last imperial dynasty, the Qing, or Manchu). Japan paid little attention to the mild rebuke issued by the League of Nations in 1933 and withdrew from that body. Manchukuo, rich in resources and laced with railroad lines, sustained the Japanese economy. The military resumed its advance, controlling much of northern China by 1935. In 1937, Japan would seize the major Chinese cities of Beijing, Tientsin, Shanghai, Hangchow, and Nanjing—subjecting the last, the capital, to pillage and massacre, resulting in between 200,000 and 300,000 Chinese civilian deaths. Taking Tsintao and Guangzhou the following year, and the province of Hainan in February 1939, Japan controlled China's eastern provinces and most important ports. Like Europe at this date, Asia faced the prospect of domination by a mighty power that aimed to take from its neighbors what land and wealth it desired.

For by this point, Adolf Hitler and his Nazi party had achieved dominion in Germany, and had set out to dominate Europe, and the world.

Nazism: the German Form of Fascism

In Germany, fascism developed the distinctive form of Nazism, a product of Germany's particular history and Hitler's unique personality. The events of World War I, and the Versailles treaty imposed at its conclusion, had left Germany abject and defeated. By the late 1930s, Hitler led a prosperous, armed, and nazified Germany prepared to take the next step toward war and mastery.

The Roots of Nazism Germany's military defeat in World War I had profound political consequences at home. Although the German generals had informed the government from the summer of 1918 that the war was unwinnable (see Chapter 25), the armistice of November 11 of that year was actually arranged by the centrist provisional government that had replaced that of Emperor Wilhelm II (r. 1888–1918) only days earlier. Upon those Weimar politicians (named for the university town where the Constitutional Assembly of the new republic met) fell the duty of negotiating the Versailles peace treaty—a treaty that, its opponents felt, crippled and dishonored Germany. The generals who had failed to win the war presented themselves as having suffered a dastardly "stab in the back," when defeatist civilian leaders had signed the Armistice. The path was open to the rehabilitation of the military at the expense of parliamentary democracy.

The Versailles settlement stripped Germany of important territorial possessions. The industrial Saar district in the Ruhr region was placed (until a plebiscite in 1935) under international administration, the Rhineland was occupied and demilitarized, with Alsace and Lorraine, west of the Rhine, returned to France. The German army and navy were sharply cut back to the size of a police force barely capable of self-defense. Germany was effectively disarmed.

Moreover, the notorious "war guilt" clause in Article 231 of the Versailles treaty declared Germany responsible "for causing all the loss and damage" suffered by the Allies in a war "imposed upon them by the aggression of Germany and her allies." Crippled and starved by the conflict, Germany was to pay punitive "reparations." These provisions resulted in an ominous sense of national humiliation and deep resentment. Furthermore, the expense was unbearable. In an attempt to meet its costs, the government printed paper currency, leading to the ruinous hyperinflation of the 1920s (see Chapter 26).

In sum, the Versailles treaty amounted to a guarantee of renewed conflict. The Germans felt themselves dishonored, and plundered by the victor nations of World War I. Soon they would welcome a war of retaliation. But that war would be driven by other forces as well, including that of an explosive nationalism, fueled by popular racial theory.

Germany had only recently become a nation (see Chapter 20). It had developed an intense sense of nationhood from the experiences leading to unification in 1871: the Prussian resistance to Napoleon, the events of 1848, and Bismarck's construction of Prussian leadership (see Chapter 20). National pride was further bolstered by the cultural unity of the German-speaking domains.

The cohesion of German culture could be traced to the work of the reformer Martin Luther (1483–1546), who first distinguished national German interests from those of the cosmopolitan papacy. Since then, German-speakers had been among the leading figures of the scientific revolution and Enlightenment, and the Classical and Romantic movements in the arts (see Chapters 17, 24). In the nineteenth century, the German universities were the most advanced in Europe, training students in Classical and modern disciplines.

But German nationalism, as it emerged in the nineteenth century, also had deeper, troubling, dimensions. It was characterized by expansionist fantasies built on medieval precedents, and colored by racial theories. From the Middle Ages came the legacy of the "*Drang nach Osten*," or "drive to the east," the movement of German-speaking peoples to open new territories in eastern Europe and to Christianize pagan Slavs. There lingered a sense of German entitlement to eastern lands, and of superiority over their peoples, who had indeed often been pressed into dependency in the Middle Ages.

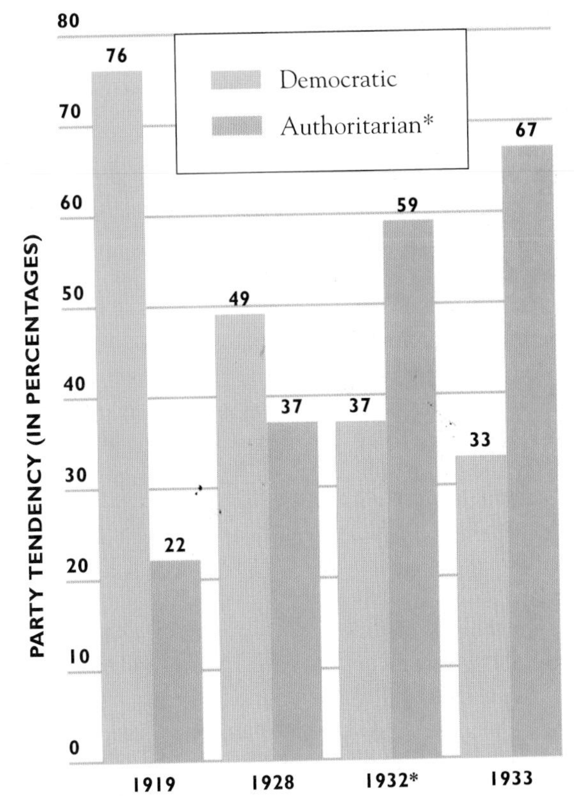

* *including Nazis*
Source: *Based on B. Porter,* War and the Rise of the State: The Military Foundations of Modern Politics *(New York: Free Press, 1994).*

German attitudes toward the Slavic peoples also had ideological origins. Imperialist ventures and Darwinian theory encouraged the development of racial theories in the late nineteenth century (see Chapter 24). German academics constructed the notion of a superior Aryan race (related to ancient Indo-Aryan speakers of languages ancestral to those of modern Europe; see Chapters 1, 2). As Aryans, Germans were superior to Slavs, Jews, gypsies, and others, with a special place in the hierarchy of races.

The Rise of Hitler These notions of German racial superiority, national destiny, the superiority of military to parliamentary rule, and the humiliations of the Versailles settlement, were the ingredients of the ideology of Nazism formulated by Adolf Hitler in his sprawling and incoherent *Mein Kampf* ("My Struggle," 1925). To these Hitler added a strident anti-Bolshevism and an economic justification for territorial expansion—the principle of Germany's need for (and hence entitlement to) *Lebensraum* ("living space").

Born in Austria–Hungary, the son of a government functionary and a doting mother, Adolf Hitler gave no evidence in his youth of the power he would someday wield. With ambitions of becoming an artist, he gravitated to the political and cultural capital of Vienna. Living on the margins in those pre-war years, when philosophies stormed about, he picked up small jobs, slept in flophouses, and imbibed the prevailing currents of thought (see Chapter 24): a mix of anti-Semitism, race theory, Nietzscheanism, socialism, and nationalism.

Hitler moved to Germany and joined the German army in Munich in 1914. He fought with distinction, achieving the rank of corporal and winning the Iron Cross. When an exhausted German government signed the armistice, Hitler, like his superiors, felt that he had been stabbed in the back.

With the war over, Hitler returned to Munich and became a political agent. In the confused, crisis-ridden 1920s, that meant recruiting like-minded comrades in beer halls and fostering squads of thugs who roamed the streets in search of enemies to maul. It also meant nursing the grievances the past had delivered: against Jews, against communists (among them, Jews), against rich speculators (among them, Jews), against the enemies of Germany, and politicians. As an informer in the pay of army intelligence, he infiltrated one of the fringe political parties—the NSDAP, or National-sozialistische deutsche Arbeiterpartei ("National-socialist German Workers' Party"), or Nazi for short—Hitler found a home.

Hitler was now a beer-hall orator, and commanded an armed gang of brown-shirted "stormtroopers," the later SA (*Sturmabteilungen*). In 1923, he led the Munich Nazis in a **putsch**, an attempted government takeover. Thrown in prison with a five-year sentence, he was released after a little more than six months. During that interlude, he wrote *Mein Kampf*. In contrast to the works of Lenin, characterized by their concision and logic, *Mein Kampf* impresses by the virulence of its ideas, the randomness of their expression, and the consistency of its maxims with the Nazi project Hitler later brought to culmination.

By the late 1920s, Nazis were as strong a presence as their chief political opponents, the communists, and began to win seats in the *Reichstag*, or parliament. When the Depression struck in 1929, Nazis and communists courted its victims. The communists both recruited a following from among the industrial workers. The Nazis appealed to the lower and middle bourgeoisie, white-collar workers, small business proprietors, bureaucrats—who were at once economically threatened and fearful of Bolshevism.

By 1930, the Nazis gained a real foothold in the Reichstag, winning 107 seats (of a total of 556) to the communists' 77; in July 1932, 196 seats. Meanwhile, the government floundered, as center-left leaders and ineffective chancellors came and went; the presidency remained in the hands of the elderly World War I veteran Paul von Hindenburg (1847–1934; see Chapter 25), now nearly ninety. With conservative support, Hitler became chancellor on January 30, 1933, and formed a cabinet dominated by Nazis. It was to be the Weimar republic's last government. Twenty months later, after Hindenburg's death on August 2, 1934, the chancellorship and the presidency were merged. Hitler had reached the highest office in the German government by strictly legal means. He would now consolidate his power by force.

Hitler in Power On February 27, 1933, a fire broke out in the Reichstag building. Nazi arsonists were probably responsible, but blame was assigned to Hitler's communist opponents. The emergency gave Hitler the opportunity to suspend civil liberties and grab control. On March 23, 1933, the Enabling Act granted Hitler dictatorial powers. On August 19, 1934, a plebiscite approved the delegation of all executive power to Hitler as Führer, or "leader." Now Hitler moved to enact the nightmarish fantasies outlined so vividly—for any who had a mind to consult them—in *Mein Kampf*. "No human being has ever declared or recorded what he wanted more often than I," Hitler reminded an unseeing world.

Hitler's first goal was to climb out of the Depression (see Chapter 26). Two-fifths of German workers were without jobs, while production and foreign trade had dropped to disastrous lows. Hitler's solution for this crisis was threefold. First, he aimed at self-sufficiency, or **autarky**. With the institution of his Four Year Plan (October 19, 1936), the whole southeastern region of Europe was to trade almost exclusively with Germany. Second, Hitler encouraged barter exchange with other countries as an alternative to wealth-draining foreign trade, and had the chemical industries develop synthetic or "**ersatz**" equivalents of consumer staples and industrial supplies. Third, Hitler let loose the war machine. With factories producing guns, ammunition, and equipment, German workers found jobs, and a new appreciation for their Führer.

His economic program did not distract Hitler from the task of reshaping social patterns. He encouraged groups of all sorts in a policy of *Gleichschaltung* (enforced conformity). Youth groups, choral groups, and sports clubs all offered opportunities for Nazi indoctrination and discouraged individualism. Christian organizations were a problem. Hitler did not like them; but many Germans did, and they were at least a force for social order. In 1933, Hitler made his peace with the Roman Catholics—and could not have been pleased to learn in 1937 that a papal encyclical denouncing Nazi racial policies had been read aloud in the churches. In 1933 he reorganized the mainstream Protestant churches into the nazified German Evangelical Church. More than sixty percent of German Protestants accepted the Nazi leader. Critics of Nazism formed a counter-church, the remnant of which resisted or fled.

Nazism promoted the sense of belonging to the *Volk*, or the people ("folk"), and history, legend, and song reinforced that sentiment. In art and in film, Hitler liked to see heroic images of the German people which defied the uncertainties of the twentieth-century world. In 1937, the Nazis mounted two art exhibitions: "German Art" paraded paintings of Aryan-type heroes, while "Degenerate Art" displayed the kind of images—Surrealist, Dadaist, Expressionist, Modernist, many by Jewish artists—that Hitler condemned.

In intellectual life, the Nazis required conformity, and burned books of which they disapproved. Some thinkers, such as the novelist Thomas Mann (1875–1955), refused to cooperate and lived in exile. Others, including the philosopher Martin Heidegger (1889–1976), gave the raised-arm Nazi salute on request and supported the regime.

Hubert Lanzinger, Hitler as Knight: *Like Russian artists who adopted the style of "Soviet Realism" to give expression to communist ideology, German artists celebrated Nazi themes. In this painting by Hubert Lanzinger from around 1936, Hitler is portrayed as a knight in armor, bearing a swastika standard, in a pose that echoes the medieval image of the Teutonic Order of Knights who conquered and converted the Slavic peoples of eastern Europe.*

Hitler directed women to resume their traditional roles. Central to Nazi ideology was the restriction of women to the realm of home and family—to *Kinder, Kirche, Küche* (children, church, kitchen). A Nazi "Women's Union," headed by the ideologue Gertrud Scholtz-Klink (1902–), supervised the political indoctrination of German women. In Nazi theory, the greatest service women could perform for the state was the bearing and rearing of Aryan children. The birthrate rose over forty percent between 1933 and 1939.

The Anti-Semitic Tide For none of Nazism's programs to promote fellowship and *völkisch* memory included Jews and other non-Aryans. Hitler's "racial laws" of 1935 were part of the process that became progressively uglier until it reached monstrous dimensions in the "Final Solution." This new era of persecution began with a call to boycott Jewish businesses. Jews were expelled from their positions in universities and the civil service. In time, they were denied citizenship; their properties were confiscated; they were forced to wear the yellow Star of David on their clothing. Slogans circulated: "The Jew is the cause and the beneficiary of our misery"; "The Jew is the plastic demon of the decline of mankind"; "The Jew is our greatest misfortune."

If it was still possible in 1933 for Jews to hope for a change of policy, over the next few years they should have abandoned all hope. Now stormtroopers beat up Jews on the street, destroyed Jewish places of business, and broke into Jewish houses to rob and rape. When Hitler seized Austria, Nazi agents burst into the Vienna residence of the founder of psychoanalysis, Sigmund Freud (see Chapter 24), a Jew. Mrs Freud, having watched the thugs tear apart her home, put some coins on the table and invited the brown-shirted gentlemen to take those as well. Freud himself was spirited out of the country to London. Less privileged Jews were left to face the full Nazi fury signaled by the horror of Kristallnacht ("Crystal Night," the night of broken glass, November 9–10, 1938). On order, SS Hitler Youth squads gutted 7,500 Jewish places of business and destroyed 177 synagogues. Ninety-one Jews were killed, hundreds more injured, and hardly anyone protested.

Nazism also targeted other groups for exclusion and extinction. The communist members of the Reichstag were arrested in 1933, and along with those swept up from the streets and factories, sent to detention camps and prisons. Gypsies, homosexuals, the disabled and permanently ill were all marked for persecution. Influenced by the theories of eugenics then in vogue, which discouraged the propagation of those seen as "unfit," Hitler's race theory dictated that the lives only of healthy Aryans were valuable—those likely to reproduce. The others served no purpose, and should be eliminated. Scientists and physicians cooperated; even non-Nazis made no effective protest against orders to neglect or kill these unfortunates. They instituted a full-scale "euthanasia" program, which some scholars have seen as a pilot program for the wholesale killing of Jews undertaken in 1942.

Hitler's economic and social projects were publicized by speeches, radio announcements, and press features that broadcast Nazi propaganda. With their simple rhetoric and bald misrepresentation of truth, these effectively shaped popular attitudes. The aim was not to educate the elite, but to win instant recognition from the ignorant. "The larger the mass of men to be reached," Hitler advised in *Mein Kampf*, "the lower its purely intellectual level will have to be set." In view of the "primitive simplicity" of the mind of the mass of the people, Hitler argued, the true leader must use a "big lie" to win their trust. Deception on a grand scale was necessary if the German people were to accept Hitler's views about Jews, communists, the Aryan Master Race, and *Lebensraum*.

Even those unconvinced by Nazi propaganda were impressed by the ruthless brutality with which Nazism could act. In a preemptive stroke on June 30, 1934, Hitler used his private army, the SS, to purge the brown-shirted SA that had raised him to power—about 2 million strong, the scum of the streets, career criminals, habitual killers. In the "Night of the Long Knives," about eighty SA leaders were killed. By this massacre, Hitler detached himself from his early supporters and aligned himself with the interests of the industrial and military elite. In 1938, a more discreet purge of army officers followed, many of them from the old aristocracy.

At this juncture, Hitler needed to rid himself of upper-level officers whose patrician upbringing might have intruded a tradition of civility and even moral principles. For he was embarked on a program that required the violation of Germany's agreements with most of the nations of Europe. The German form of fascism had reached its maturity. Now Nazism would lead the world into war.

THE SECOND WORLD WAR: FASCISM DEFEATED

Having seized power in Germany, Hitler rearmed and allied with the Axis powers of Italy and Japan. The principal European democracies stood by, their inaction and incomprehension facilitating the arms buildup and first hostilities.

Fascism advanced to a high tide in 1942. Over the next three years, it was beaten back to a total defeat by the Allied powers—at first Britain alone, then Britain with two latecomer participants from the peripheries of the West, the Soviet Union and the United States.

In 1945, an era of Western history came to a close with the explosion of two atomic bombs in Japan and the liberation of the Nazi concentration camps, which had annihilated the targeted victims of Hitler's Final Solution.

The Dictatorships: Rearmament and Realignment

From 1933, Hitler rearmed Germany and allied with Italy and Japan. By 1936, all three Axis powers had undertaken expansionist projects in Europe, Africa, and Asia.

Map 27.2 Expansion and Aggression West and East, 1930–1939: *Between 1930 and 1939, the three nations that would become the Axis aggressors in World War II began programs of expansion in their separate spheres. Japan's expansion in east Asia and the Pacific had begun as early as 1895, advanced in 1905 as a result of the Russo-Japanese war, and culminated in the 1930s, with a push into Manchuria and northern and eastern China (and subsequently into Indochina, the Philippines, and other Pacific islands). Italy added to its existing African sphere of influence in Libya, Eritrea, and part of Somaliland by invading Ethiopia in 1935, and seized Albania in 1939, on the eve of war. Germany steadily followed up its first aggression of 1936—the remilitarization of the Rhineland—with annexations of Austria and the Sudetenland (Czechoslovakia) in 1938, and the rest of Czechoslovakia, the Baltic port of Memel, and Poland in 1939. The last aggression triggered the outbreak of war.*

In 1925, Britain, France, Belgium, Italy, and Germany met at Locarno in Switzerland to put a close to the issues that the Versailles peace had left unresolved. Those discussions brought voluntary recognition by Germany of its borders in the west (though not the east), left the matter of unpaid reparations in genteel silence, and welcomed Germany back into the community of European nations. In 1927, Germany gained admission to the League of Nations. It joined the ongoing series of disarmament conferences that many hoped would assure the goal United States president Wilson had enunciated, that the

Great War would prove to be the war to end all wars. Amid the prosperity of the late 1920s, such hopes flourished.

International cooperation would not survive Hitler's advent to power. On July 15, 1933, Hitler joined with Britain, France, and Italy in signing the Four-Power Pact that affirmed adherence to the principles of the Locarno Treaty, the League covenant, and the Versailles treaty. But by the fall of that year, he began to repudiate all those principles and more. On October 14, 1933, Germany withdrew from disarmament discussions, and from the League of Nations itself. In 1934, the Soviet Union took Germany's place in the League of Nations.

Hitler rearmed. Army officers maximized the potential of the minimal forces allowed to Germany by the Versailles settlement, grooming an officer cadre and covertly sending pilots to train under Red Army instructors in the Soviet Union. On March 7, 1936, Hitler tested his military strength by reoccupying the Rhineland with a mere 22,000 troops (the Rhineland, German territory west of the Rhine, had been demilitarized by the terms of Versailles and evacuated by the French only in 1930). On March 16, he repudiated the disarmament clauses of the Versailles treaty. Hitler had sent a clear message to the European powers: he intended to take what he wished by force. They were surprisingly slow to grasp this message.

The remilitarization of the Rhineland challenged the authority of the Treaty of Versailles. In April, Hitler's former Locarno partners, Britain, France, and Italy, met at Stresa in Italy to consider a possible response. France, meanwhile, signed a treaty of mutual assistance with the Soviet Union and explored treaties with Czechoslovakia, Yugoslavia, and Romania (the "Little Entente" from 1920). These diplomatic moves proved valueless. Hitler had negotiated an agreement (June 18, 1936) with the British, who sought to placate this alarming Führer, permitting Germany to build its navy up to thirty-five percent of British strength. The British government sought to use German strength as a bulwark against communism. The Soviet Union was seen as a greater threat than Germany, and there was considerable sympathy for Hitler at the highest levels of the administration. Thus was Hitler rewarded for invading the Rhineland and flouting international law.

In the fall of 1936, Hitler pursued alliances with Italy and Japan, who would become his partners in the coming war. On October 3, 1935, Mussolini had invaded Ethiopia. His democratic colleagues responded weakly; the League of Nations (before which the beleaguered emperor Haile Selassie, 1891–1975, had pleaded Ethiopia's cause), imposed toothless sanctions on Italy. Irritated, Mussolini secured the Ethiopian capital of Addis Ababa on May 5, 1936, and approached Hitler. The two agreed on an alliance, which Mussolini proclaimed on October 25, 1936 as the Rome–Berlin axis. A few weeks later (November 25), Germany and Japan joined in the Anti-Comintern Pact against the Soviet Union. Italy joined a year later.

The Axis powers were now ready to expand. The Germans would recover what was justly theirs—its "unredeemed" lands that the last war had denied them, the lands of the Slavs, and racial and territorial dominance in Europe. The Italians would gain an overseas empire and the glory of the Roman Empire. Japan would seize dominion in eastern Asia so as to provide resources for its people and its factories, and achieve its supposed imperial destiny.

The Democracies: Frailty and Confusion

By the end of 1937, the Axis league had crystallized. Yet the Western democracies still misread the clear signal that catastrophe loomed. Were they misled? Were they inept? Were they so paralyzed by memories of the last war that they could not confront, when it was still possible to do so, those who would launch the next? These are difficult questions. Noting the following two factors may assist in finding answers.

First, the diplomacy of the principal democracies was aimed at maintaining the status quo achieved by the 1919 Paris treaties. The goal of their opponents, in contrast, was to subvert it. From 1919 through 1936, the League of Nations worked to achieve the "collective security" of Europe. In the 1920s, it sought to ease tensions in the Rhineland, and encouraged the settlement of the issues of reparations, war debt, and disarmament. In 1932, the League's Lytton Commission denounced the Japanese invasion of Manchuria as an "act of aggression." In 1935, when Italy invaded Ethiopia, the League imposed sanctions—but they were insufficient.

In each case, the League sought to diminish tensions, but nations set upon expansion reneged on international agreements. By 1936, the League had become ineffective. The nations that had depended upon it found themselves without a defender.

Second, political discussion in the free countries was marked by confusion and ideological fragmentation. In the Axis nations, in contrast, there was clarity of thought and unity of purpose. The major democracies cycled through coalition governments in

Communism and Fascism: Right or Left?

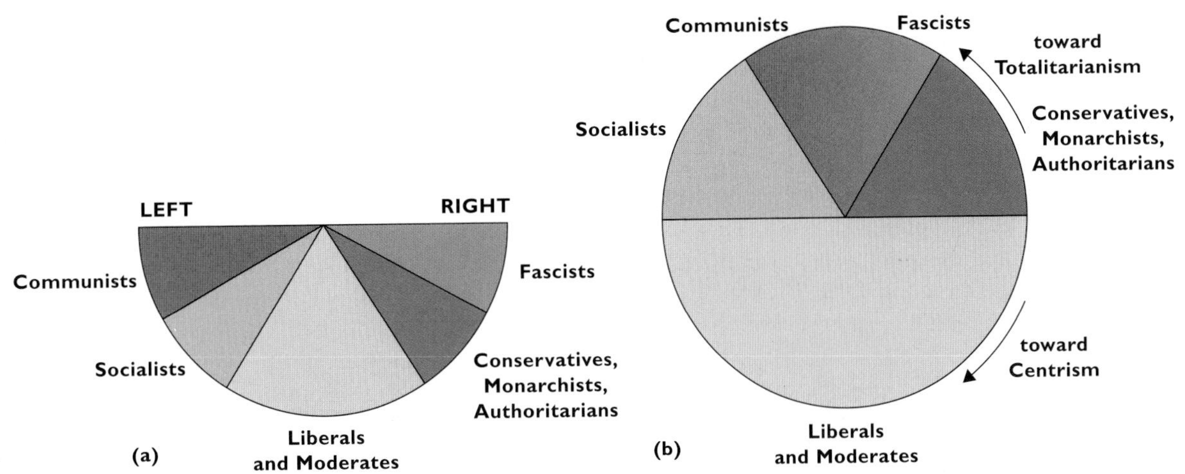

How are the phenomena of communism and fascism to be understood in relation to the more familiar spectrum of conservative and liberal political ideologies? A graphic representation can help, using the once again familiar categories of "left" for liberalism and socialism and their extremes, and "right" for conservatism and its extremes. For many scholars, communism, with its connection to democratic socialism, itself an outgrowth of liberalism, should lodge on the "left" of such a spectrum. Fascism, accordingly, with its links to conservative and authoritarian views, should lodge on the "right." These relationships are shown schematically in (a). Other scholars view communism and fascism as phenomena more closely related than that scheme implies, sharing such features as manipulation of mass sentiments through propaganda and indoctrination, futurism or modernism, anti-parliamentarianism, anti-liberalism, atheism, and inclination to violence. As totalitarian movements, then, they approach each other. This relationship is seen in (b).

Source: *Based on H.R. Kedward,* Fascism in Western Europe: 1900-1945 *(Glasgow: Blackie and Son Ltd., 1971), pp. 240–241.*

the 1920s and 1930s; with the Popular Front coalitions of the 1930s, ideological variety reached a maximum, while the ineffectiveness of political leaders across the spectrum inspired little respect for any of the ideological alternatives represented.

Nor were those alternatives clearly distinguished. Apart from communists, there were on the left both democratic and anti-democratic socialists. Opposing them were conservatives and fascists. Fascism, however, in its appeals to group solidarity, and its repudiation of individualism, could tend toward socialism, in which it had its origins—Mussolini had been a socialist; Nazism had originally embraced a working-class activism. Conservatives were so fearful of communism that they failed to see the more serious imminent threat of fascism. Liberal democrats, meanwhile, might be tempted by socialist, fascist, or communist alternatives, believing these to be the defenders of the working class, or the nation, or (as in the United States) of marginalized groups such as blacks and Jews.

Communism and fascism, finally, though viewed as opposites—both because of communist theory (which equated fascism with capitalism and imperialism) and fascist proximity to conservative aristocratic and clerical interests—had, ironically, strong resemblances. Both fascist states and the communist Soviet Union were ruled by dictators, repressed dissent, broadcast propaganda, and employed random terror to maintain control. Liberal democrats and democratic socialists occupied a weak center between wings that were not distinctly "right" or "left" on the political spectrum, but equally totalitarian.

In this stew of political alternatives, a well-meaning European could not easily make a rational choice. Neither could whole nations. They were rescued from perplexity by the advent of crisis: a preliminary crisis in Spain, followed by the graver one in central Europe.

The Spanish Civil War: Rehearsal for World War

From 1936 to 1939, civil war raged in Spain, on the periphery of continental politics. An elected center-left government faced a military revolt that eventually resulted in the creation of an authoritarian regime. While the European democracies stayed aloof, totalitarian powers both communist and fascist sent soldiers and supplies. Their intervention in the Spanish Civil War was a prologue to World War II.

The civil war was in origin a traditional conflict between liberalism on one side, and monarchy and entrenched elites on the other. Spain's era of greatness was long gone by 1898, when it lost the last of its major colonies (see Chapter 23). King Alfonso XIII (r. 1902–1931) ruled weakly thereafter as a constitutional monarch, bolstered by the Roman Catholic clergy and military leaders. Amid labor unrest and separatist revolts, Alfonso turned to the right and supported as prime minister José Antonio Primo de Rivera (1870–1930). In 1923, Primo de Rivera suspended the constitution, censored the press, and clamped down on the universities. When the Depression came in 1929, these tactics were unsustainable.

In 1931, leftist Republican parties triumphed in municipal and national elections, forcing Alfonso to leave Spain. The new constituent assembly was dominated by socialists, communists, anarchists, and syndicalists. This body drafted a liberal constitution granting universal suffrage, basic freedoms, separation of Church and state, secular control of mass education, and the nationalization of church property. The disestablishment of the Roman Catholic Church was one platform on which nearly all agreed.

In 1933, new elections produced a rightist government which promptly undid earlier reforms. In 1936, the pendulum swung again; new elections yielded a left-center majority and a Popular Front government, alarming the wealthy, the clergy, and the military. On July 17, 1936, army officers in Spanish Morocco, North Africa, launched a revolt against the government. Ferried back to Spain in Italian ships, under the leadership of the general Francisco Franco, the Nationalists, as they were called, took control of the Spanish central region, which supported the rising. The Loyalists held the capital at Madrid, the Basque Country, and the developed eastern seaboard, including Catalonia with its cosmopolitan capital at Barcelona.

By all rights, the legitimate, elected government should have won this struggle against a handful of insurgent generals. That it did not has to do with the behavior of the onlooker European nations. The ever-cautious democracies, fearful of war, would not intervene, even to provide the Spanish government with weapons and supplies. The dictatorships, however, intervened vigorously. Mussolini's Italy sent guns, tanks, planes, and men. Hitler unleashed his airforce, or Luftwaffe, including the elite Condor Legion, which practiced in Spain the tactics it would use in the larger conflict to come. Stalin's Soviet Union fed the Loyalists supplies and armaments, for which it required payment in full, and in gold. These were delivered along with the usual political commissars, urging allegiance to the party line.

Loyalist volunteers arrived in Spain as well—the International Brigades, about 40,000 volunteers from Europe and the United States, democrats, socialists, communists, and workers eager to fight for a new order. Thus strengthened, the Loyalists fought desperately against Franco and his supporters (including the Roman Catholic Church, of whom they murdered more than 1000 priests and nearly 300 nuns).

The efficient Franco—a soldier rather than a fascist, but in league with fascism none the less—made steady progress. His German allies pursued their experiments. Their blanket bombing on April 26, 1937 of the Basque town of Guernica was a tragedy not only for the Basques, but for the whole world, now introduced to a new tactic—the deliberate bombing of unwarned civilians. Its cruelty is conveyed in the coldly eloquent monochrome of Picasso's painting *Guernica*.

By the end of 1938, Franco's forces seized Catalonia; by spring 1939, Valencia and the capital of Madrid. The Loyalists and their international volunteers fled, or were captured, tortured, and murdered. Fascism was on the march.

Still the democracies did not act, and would not do so until they were forced to go to war once again, war total and world-wide.

First Hostilities

In 1938, Hitler moved on two fronts, the opening sallies of the next world war. He took over two neighboring regions: the state of Austria and the Sudetenland region of Czechoslovakia. In justification, he could cite the Wilsonian principle of self-determination (see Chapter 25): the ethnic Germans of Austria (the majority of Austrians) and Czechoslovakia (a majority in the Sudetenland) rightly wished to be part of Germany rather than exist as a minority, subject people. In March 1938, he accomplished the *Anschluss*, or annexation, of Austria—a kindred nation already under its own fascist dictator, with a strong native Nazi party and compliant populace to support Hitler's arrival.

Hitler's ingestion of Austria was scarcely noted by European onlookers. They were more disturbed when later the same year he annexed the Czech Sudetenland, which had a German majority and was dominated by a Nazi party. Poland joined in to pick up the district of Czechoslovakia with a strong presence of ethnic Poles.

Alarmed, the British prime minister Neville Chamberlain (1869–1940) met with Hitler three times in 1938, pursuing a policy of **appeasement**. Britain and France were determined to avoid war at all costs. Their citizens had not yet recovered from the slaughter of the previous war (see Chapter 25). Moreover, they hoped that a pacified Germany would serve as a bulwark against communism. In the culminating journey to Munich, Chamberlain obtained (along with French and Italian representatives) a commitment, signed September 29, 1938, that in return for permission to occupy the Sudetenland, Germany would make no further territorial demands.

On that promise the appeasers rested their hopes. Returning to Britain, Chamberlain waved the piece of paper and exulted that it meant "peace in our time." In fact, it meant peace for eleven months. For the following spring, Hitler returned to Czechoslovakia. He engrossed what remained of the western part (the provinces of Bohemia and Moravia) on March 16, 1939, and organized the eastern sector as the puppet state of Slovakia. Czechoslovakia was no more. In exchange for a brief and specious peace, the Western democracies had delivered Czechoslovakia—and soon the Slavs, the Jews, and virtually all of Europe—to the Nazis.

False Promises

"Peace in our Time": *The tragedy of Guernica and the Spanish Civil War gave way in 1938–1939 to the dark comedy of appeasement and realignment. On September 30, 1938, British prime minister Neville Chamberlain promised that the Munich agreement just negotiated with Hitler would bring "peace in our time." Here he reads its terms. War began within a year.*

A meeting of dictators: *Stalin and his advisers may also have been deceived by Hitler when they agreed to a pact in the summer of 1939. The absurdity of this Nazi–Communist marriage was generally noted, as in this cartoon from London's* Evening Standard *on September 20, 1939. On a corpse-littered battlefield the two armed dictators greet each other: "The scum of the earth, I believe," says Hitler cordially; "The bloody assassin of the workers, I presume?" says Stalin.*

Hitler's actions caused even Chamberlain's confidence to crumble, and stirred his British and French colleagues to confront Germany's aggressions. Poland would likely be his next target; on March 31, Britain certified to Poland that, if Germany invaded, it would declare war. In the meantime, stifling their distrust of communism, Britain and France would seek an alliance with Stalin's Soviet Union. A diplomatic party set out in August 1939.

But the Germans got there first. On August 23, 1939, Hitler's representatives signed with Stalin a Non-Aggression Pact, assuring mutual neutrality if either party was attacked; and some Polish and Baltic territories for the Soviets in the event that war did ensue. The Germans, who detested the Soviets both as Slavs and as Bolsheviks, had bought freedom for their invasion of Poland. The Soviets detested the fascists no more than the democrats, whose war they did not wish to fight. The Comintern was alerted. Communist officials around the world dictated the new party line to their surprised followers: they had fought fascism in Spain, but now they must support Nazism. Consternation also struck Western diplomats, who had hoped to play Germany against the Soviets, or the Soviets against Germany—and now awoke to find that their playthings were arrayed against them.

Meanwhile, Hitler seized the Baltic port of Memel; Italy seized Albania on April 7, and on May 22 formed a ten-year military alliance with Germany—the "Pact of Steel." On September 1, 1939, Hitler let loose **Blitzkrieg** ("lightning war," war as stupendous as a bolt of lightning) on Poland. (On that same day he ordered, his racial theories always in the forefront of his mind, the execution of some 70,000 mentally ill patients in German hospitals.) On September 3, Britain and France declared war on Germany.

WITNESSES

Fighting the Second World War

On the eve of war, Hitler muses on its future (1939): Since the autumn of 1938 . . . I decided to go with Stalin. After all there are only three great statesmen in the world, Stalin, I and Mussolini. Mussolini is the weakest. . . . So in a few weeks hence I shall stretch out my hand to Stalin at the common German–Russian frontier and with him undertake to re-distribute the world.

Our strength lies in our quickness and in our brutality; Genghis Khan has sent millions of women and children into death knowingly and with a light heart. History sees in him only the great founder of States. As to what the weak Western European civilisation asserts about me, that is of no account. I have given the command and I shall shoot everyone who utters one word of criticism. . . . Who after all is today speaking about the destruction of the Armenians?

(Speech by Adolf Hitler, as recorded by a witness; from E. L. Woodward and R. Butler, eds., *Documents on British Foreign Policy, 1919–1939*, 1954)

Japanese nationalist writer Tokutomi Iichirō comments on the Japanese Imperial Declaration of War (1941): In Nippon [Japan] resides a destiny to become the Light of Greater East Asia and to become ultimately the Light of the World. However, in order to become [the former] . . . we must have three qualifications. The first . . . is strength. . . . [W]e must expel Anglo-Saxon influence from East Asia with our strength. . . .

The second qualification is benevolence. Nippon must develop the various resources of East Asia and distribute them fairly to all the races within the Greater East Asian Co-Prosperity Sphere. . . .

The third qualification is virtue. . . . It was the favorite policy of the Anglo-Saxons to make the various races of East Asia compete and fight each other and make them mutually small and powerless. We must, therefore, console them, bring peace and friendship among them, and make them all live in peace with a boundlessly embracing virtue.

(From R. Tsunoda et al, *Sources of the Japanese Tradition*, 1958)

In speeches to the British Parliament, Churchill rallies the nation that would soon oppose Nazism alone (1940): *May 13, 1940*: . . . I have nothing to offer but blood and toil and tears and sweat. We have before all of us an ordeal of the most grievous kind. We have before us many, many long months of struggle and of suffering. If you ask what is our policy I will say it is to wage war . . . war by air, land and sea, war with all our might and with all the strength that God can give us, and to wage war against a monstrous tyranny never surpassed in the dark and lamentable catalogue of human crime. That is our policy. If you ask us, "What is your aim"? I can answer in one word—victory. . . victory however long and hard the road may be.

June 4, 1940 [after describing the evacuation of British forces from Dunkirk, on the far side of the Channel coast]:

We shall fight in France, we shall fight on the seas and oceans; we shall fight with growing confidence and growing strength in the air. We shall defend our island whatever the cost may be. We shall fight on the beaches, we shall fight on the landing grounds, in the fields, in the streets, and in the hills. We shall never surrender. . . .

(Winston Churchill, speeches to British Parliament, 1940)

From Appeasement to Victory

Appeasement failed utterly, less than one year after Chamberlain announced he had won "peace in our time." The world was at war again in a conflict that was to involve Europe, east and southeast Asia, North Africa, and the Middle East—with combatants recruited, additionally, from the United States and the British dominions. World War I had been fought with trenches, barbed wire, and nerve gas. World War II would be fought with airplanes, aircraft carriers, and amphibious landings; codebreakers, spies, and radar; resistance cells, suicide missions, and covert operations; tanks and bombs, conventional and atomic. Never had so much wealth been channeled to produce so many machines that killed; never had so many human lives been valued so little.

In the European theater of the war, the German offensive pressed forward to 1942 when it received its first setbacks in the Soviet Union and Africa. Thereafter the tide turned in favor of the Allies, who concluded the European war with a giant encirclement of Germany.

The Nazi Invasion of Poland and Western Europe By the end of September 1939, the German invasion of Poland was virtually complete. Now the invaders subjected that country to a savage occupation, killing in all about 3 million Poles. As an inferior race, according to Nazi ideology, the Slavic Poles were to be reduced to a docile, illiterate serfdom. Poles were barred from schools, denied privileges and position, subjected to arbitrary violence, or deported. Their leaders and intellectuals were slaughtered, and the large Jewish population ghettoized. Eastern Europe learned quickly the nature of Nazi conquest as it swept beyond Poland and into the Balkans.

Nazi occupation seemed gentler, at first, when it came to the western nations of Norway and Denmark, the Netherlands, and Belgium, nations Hitler gathered up in the first six months of 1940. On June 14, 1940, the Germans entered Paris, having breached the supposedly impregnable fortifications of the "Maginot Line." The French swiftly capitulated, while the government, headed by Marshal Philippe Pétain, an aging hero of the previous war, entered into collaboration with the Nazi victors. He would run a puppet French state from the southern resort town of Vichy, while Germans held the north and west. From France, Hitler determined to take Britain.

The Air War: Germany vs. Britain From June 1940, when its Expeditionary Force escaped the continent from the northern French port of Dunkirk in fishing boats and yachts, until June 1941, when the Soviet Union joined the conflict, the British faced the Nazi behemoth alone. It was, as Sir Winston Churchill, prime minister from May 10, 1940, both the poet and the chief strategist of the conflict, intoned, "their finest hour." Britain had a small army, a still vital navy, and a trained, eager airforce—fortunately, for the Channel, which had previously sheltered the island from invasion, could now be easily bridged by air. In what came to be known as the Battle of Britain, Royal Air Force (RAF) pilots, aided by the recent invention of radar, narrowly staved off invasion by the numerically superior Luftwaffe. Never, said Churchill, had so few done so much for so many.

The Luftwaffe commenced the bombing of British military targets in July 1940; soon it bombed cities as well, including Birmingham, Manchester, Liverpool, and Southampton. Above all, London was a target—its children preventively evacuated since 1939, and its citizens taking nightly refuge in subway stations. The "blitz" of London peaked in September but continued through spring 1941. London's great cathedral of St. Paul's survived amid the surrounding wreckage. In the industrial Midlands region, the lovely cathedral of Coventry was destroyed. Later in the war, strategic bombing by the Allies was to destroy great swathes of the German cities of Hamburg, Cologne, and Dresden, whose churches were reduced to scarred debris, and whose "unavoidable" civilian casualties included the elderly and infirm, women and children.

Although the British fought mostly in the air, they had other, secret weapons. These included a squad of cryptologists (Polish exiles broke the German cipher early in the war) who intercepted tens of thousands of German messages per month, and the best intelligence operation in Europe, which kept the Germans ignorant or deceived about their opponents' actions.

At sea, meanwhile, the Germans initially had the advantage as their U-boats preyed on shipping along the western approaches to Britain. After 1941, they moved out to the mid-Atlantic (safe from British aerial patrol). After the United States entered the war late in 1942, they found new targets further west and in the Caribbean. Eventually, long-range planes equipped with radar were able to track the U-boats, and settle the "battle of the Atlantic."

The Germans in the East and in North Africa By 1941, Hitler was planning a new venture for the spring: the invasion of his ally, the Soviet Union. On June 22, German armies launched a three-pronged assault on the Russian heartland. In the north, they targeted Leningrad; from the center, the capital, Moscow; to the south, the Crimean ports and lower river Don. The Germans dubbed this undertaking "Operation Barbarossa" in remembrance of the medieval German emperor Frederick I Barbarossa.

Until this moment, the Russians had observed their agreement with Germany. Two weeks after the Germans invaded Poland from the west, according to prior agreement, the Red Army did so from the east. One consequence of that invasion was the massacre in 1941, by Stalin's order, of 4443 Polish officers, in Katyn forest, near Smolensk. In 1944, Stalin shifted the blame for this massacre to the Nazis. Recent investigations assign it unequivocally to the Soviets—who were surely responsible also for 10,000 more Polish officers missing since the Soviet occupation. The incident is one relic of the brief period of Nazi–Soviet cooperation. In 1939–1940, Soviet forces allied with Germany also invaded the Baltic states, Finland, and Romania.

In June 1941, German forces smashed through the thin crust of Soviet defenses on the western frontier, taking Stalin thoroughly by surprise. The Red Army was not ready; it was in any case ill-trained. Stalin's Five Year Plans, however, had brought to a maximum the Soviet Union's capacity to produce armaments (it had nearly twice as many tanks at the front as the German attackers). And of people, it had an abundance. Communists around the globe celebrated Soviet strength—instructed now, after their abrupt about-face in 1939, to turn about once again.

In 1941 and 1942, the Germans advanced, tearing through Ukraine and the Crimea to the river Don, the Caucasus mountains, and almost to the Caspian Sea. But Soviet forces denied them Moscow, and the citizens and soldiers holding Leningrad—where a siege of almost 900 terrible days cost over 1 million lives—saved that city as well. In August 1942, German forces reached the industrial center of Stalingrad, on the river Volga, gateway to the Caucasus oilfields. They struggled for months with the city's defenders, commanded by General Georgi Konstantinovich Zhukov (1896–1974), in the streets, face to face, from house to house.

As winter arrived, the battle hardened. Soviet armies encircled the Germans, who froze and starved, and were soon to die as newly minted tanks emerged from the Stalingrad factories, already blasting destruction from their turrets. On January 31, 1943, the remnant of 91,000 German soldiers surrendered to the Soviet army. German military morale never recovered from the humiliating defeat at Stalingrad.

The following summer, the Germans met the Soviets at Kursk. Here 9000 tanks came to grips, tough German Panzers ("panthers") against even heavier Soviet tanks, which won the battle. From Kursk, the Red Army surged westward, its sights on Berlin. The Soviets had borne the brunt of the German war and sacrificed an estimated 20 to 28 million soldiers and civilians, dwarfing casualty rates for Britain or the United States, or even Germany. For the Soviets, this had not been simply a struggle between communism and fascism, or communism and imperialism. It had been a war for Mother Russia, the Great Patriotic War.

The year 1943 was pivotal in other theaters too. In North Africa, German forces under General Erwin G. Rommel (1891–1944) had arrived early in 1941 to blast through to Egypt and the Middle East. But at El Alamein in Egypt in October 1942, British general Bernard Montgomery (1887–1976) bested Rommel, the mastermind of tank warfare, with his own tactics. (Montgomery had profited from reading the book Rommel wrote on the subject.) Soon thereafter, United States forces landed in northwest Africa under General Dwight D. Eisenhower (1890–1969) to complete the German rout by the winter of 1943.

The War in Asia In east Asia also, 1942 was a turning point. In 1941, the Japanese had launched a campaign to control all the lands and islands of the western Pacific and southeast Asia. These were to form an outer zone of the Japanese Empire, complementary to the inner zone of home islands and Korean and Chinese possessions in a unified system called the Greater East Asia Co-Prosperity Sphere. Only the United States had a Pacific force capable of challenging them. To neutralize that potential enemy, the Japanese attacked first, and without warning, the United States naval base at Pearl Harbor in the Hawaiian islands, on December 7, 1941.

Until then, the United States had maintained an official neutrality, while supplying the Allies with armaments at first on a "cash and carry" basis, and after March 11, 1941 under the Lend-Lease program, on the promise of future payment. But the Pearl Harbor attack prompted an immediate response. The next day, Congress declared war on Japan; soon after, Germany declared war on the United States. American factories soared into full production, and by spring 1942, troops were pouring into Britain, Africa, and Asia while a fleet strong enough to patrol two oceans gathered in the south Pacific. After Pearl Harbor the vigilant Churchill, the lone fighter, then wary ally of the Soviets, relaxed.

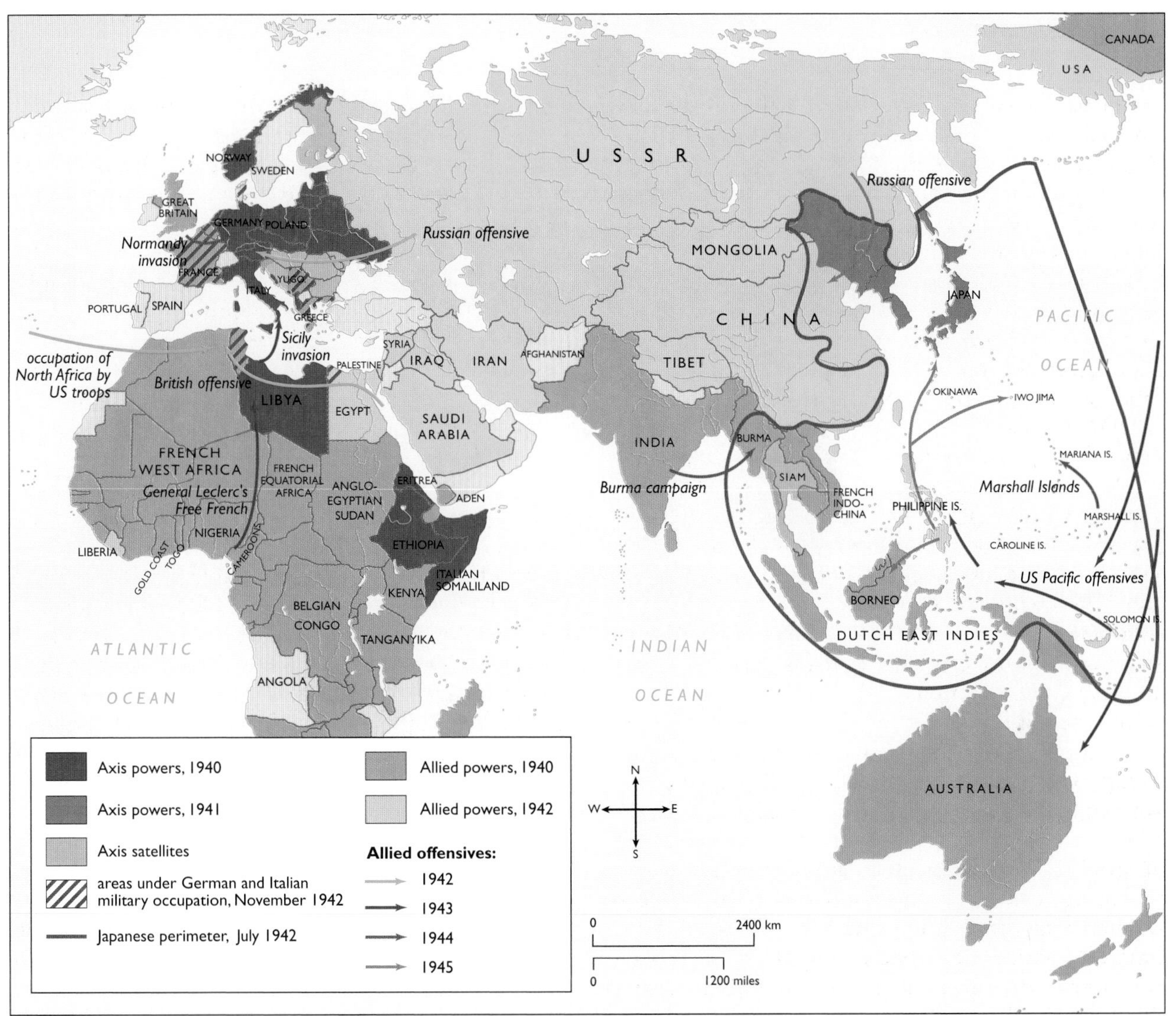

Map 27.3 Axis Advance and Allied Victory—World War II, 1939–1945: *The early years of the war saw the Axis powers expand in both the European and Asian zones almost to the point of total control. After 1943 turning points—the Russian victory at Stalingrad, the Allied invasion of Sicily and southern Italy—Axis-dominated Europe was put on the defensive. The June 1944 liberation of Rome and invasion of Normandy spelled the end of the Nazi empire, with final surrender in May 1945 following the Soviet sweep across eastern Europe and into Berlin. Meanwhile, the Allied war with Japan in the Pacific was effectively won by May 1945, although Japanese surrender followed only the epochal use of force—the release of two atom bombs—in August 1945.*

From September 1941 to early 1942, the Japanese roared through Asia, defeating native and colonial defenders, deporting survivors to concentration camps where many were tortured and starved. When the first United States ships arrived to join Allied defenders (British, Dutch, New Zealand, and Australian) in spring 1942, Japan controlled mainland and islands to a vast perimeter. Its dominions included much of eastern China, parts of Indochina and the East Indies, and many islands, including the Philippines, seized immediately after Pearl Harbor and the evacuation of United States general Douglas MacArthur (1880–1964).

After some initial defeats, and victories at Midway and Guadalcanal, United States forces drove the Japanese out of the Pacific islands over the next two years. Japanese defenders (whose casualties exceeded those of the Allies ten to one) dug into foxholes, hid in caves, rushed in desperate, futile charges. As their code of honor dictated, encircled garrisons stood to the death, and both combatants and civilians often chose suicide over capture. The last defenders were suicide bombers, who blew themselves up with the enemy ships they attacked—the *kamikaze*, named after the seemingly miraculous wind that in 1281 had saved Japan from a Mongol invasion.

Starvation, Siege, and Sack

Leningrad and Shanghai: *Among the many images of the brutality of war, this one from Leningrad (left) in 1942 (where starvation and terror endured during a siege of almost 900 days) and another from Shanghai (right) in 1937 (where Japanese forces bombed and sacked the city) are particularly poignant. In the first, parents pull a sled laden with the body of their dead child down Leningrad's Nevsky Prospect. In the second, an infant sits amid the wreckage of a railroad station.*

By May 1945, the Allies had swept the Japanese from the open Pacific. The Japanese airforce and navy were largely destroyed. Japan's home islands, gripped by hunger, suffered steady United States bombardment from island bases. The British launched land attacks from India, and the Chinese fought where they could. Yet, cornered, the Japanese resisted.

Victory in Europe The drive to free Europe began in earnest in 1943. In July of that year, Allied troops recently victorious in the North Africa campaign crossed the Mediterranean to land in Sicily and, on September 3, to the Italian mainland. Germany's ally, and a belligerent since June 1940, Italy surrendered; the Italian people welcomed the Allied soldiers as liberators. The now hated Mussolini was dismissed by the (still reigning) king Victor Emmanuel III, then arrested and imprisoned. He was subsequently rescued by the Germans, but finally shot, with his Jewish mistress, on April 28, 1945, after a hasty court-martial by **partisans** (unofficial **resistance** forces).

The final liberation of Italy from tenacious German forces took many months. By June 5, 1944, the Allies had fought their way to Rome, but the Germans still held the north. Venice, the last major city to fall, was taken only nine days before the German surrender on VE Day ("Victory in Europe"). In the Tuscan hills and the Po Valley, resistance forces linked up with the Allies and aided the liberation.

For there had been resistance groups in all the nations of occupied Europe. Active in many were communists receiving orders from Moscow; elsewhere nationalists who were instructed by governments-in-exile based in Britain; elsewhere Jews whose best choice was to fight Nazism wherever they could. The most effective were the Yugoslav partisans (divided between communist and monarchist units) who had fled to the mountains upon the German invasion of 1941, and there famously tied up twenty German divisions with their guerrilla tactics. Among the most daring perhaps were the German army officers whose attempt to assassinate Hitler on July 20, 1944, had it succeeded, might have saved the world millions of fatalities; but they were caught and savagely executed. The most ill-fated were the Poles of Warsaw, who perished on the brink of liberation in 1945, abandoned to Nazi fury by Stalin as he stalled outside the city. The French resistance groups pulled together at the end when on June 6, 1944, D-Day, Allied forces crossed the Channel to land on the Normandy coast, under the supreme command of United States general Eisenhower. In league with them were the forces of General Charles de Gaulle (1890–1970), who had escaped ahead of the Nazi takeover in 1940 and, from exile in Britain, organized the "Free French."

From Normandy, the Allied armies pushed eastward to meet the Soviets in Germany in April 1945. They moved swiftly, for the Soviets were storming westward, pushing the Germans out of Russia and

Ukraine. By 1944, they had replaced the Germans as occupiers in Yugoslavia and Hungary, and, in 1945, Czechoslovakia and Poland. By April 30, 1945, the Soviets entered Berlin, and subdued it by May 2. On May 8, VE Day, with the surrender of German forces, the European war ended.

It was a dreadful liberation, accomplished with looting, terror, and the rape of tens of thousands, perhaps hundreds of thousands of women aged from ten to eighty in Germany alone. German prisoners could expect little mercy from Soviet avengers of their more than 20 million dead. But these cruelties could not equal what the Soviet troops found in the Nazi concentration camps they liberated—mass graves, machines of torture and death, a remnant of starved survivors—the evidence of unutterable evil, a secret and hideous **genocidal** war against the Jews.

FINAL SOLUTIONS

For the Jews, Hitler's chief advisers devised a "Final Solution," launched in spring 1942. From the start, Jews had been rounded up in the conquered nations. Some were shot, like the 100,000 at Babi Yar near Kiev in Ukraine, between 1941 and 1943. A total of some 500,000 Jews would be killed in the Soviet Union before the German retreat. Some were ghettoized, like the 60,000 Jews of Warsaw who revolted in 1943 and were massacred, by April 20, to the last woman and child. Others were transported to concentration camps—along with resisters, communists, gypsies, homosexuals, Russian and Polish prisoners, and others. There they were tormented, starved, and worked to death. Many died from the privations of the camps, the brutality of the guards, and the

Map 27.4 Final Solutions, 1941–1945: *Hitler's Third Reich launched its "Final Solution" to the "Jewish question" in January 1942—the project to eliminate the Jews of Europe and their ancient culture, which continued until the Nazi defeat in 1945. One million Jews had already died, but now the killing became systematic: ghetto raids, massacres, deportations and death marches and, above all, the death camp, the machine designed especially for the destruction of human beings. The main map here shows the locations of the principal death camps, while the pie graphs document the extent of the destruction. The two atomic bombs that destroyed the Japanese cities of Hiroshima and Nagasaki on August 6 and 9, 1945, shown in the inset map, took fewer victims (see chart on p. 866), but aroused matchless terror. This previously inconceivable weapon had the potential to annihilate not merely thousands or millions but the entire human race.*

WINDOWS ON

The Holocaust

Vicious anti-Semitism, culminating in the Final Solution (the attempt to exterminate all European Jewry) earned Nazism its special recognition as uniquely evil. Here, respectably dressed and unsuspecting Dutch Jews carry their belongings with them as they are about to board the train that will take them to concentration camps and, for most of them, their deaths (top left). Their clothes bear the yellow star they were required to display by Nazi regulations. Nazi soldiers supervised the massacre of Jews (top right), and the rounding-up and deportation of Jews to the Warsaw ghetto (bottom right). This last photograph was presented in evidence at the Nuremberg trial of those accused of war crimes. The Allied forces that liberated the Nazi death camps, such as the Belsen camp (bottom left), found a few starved survivors amid heaps of corpses and bones. The remains of some 9 million people were located, about 6 million of them Jews.

Jews before their deportation, Amsterdam, 1943

Belsen death camp, 1945

Kovno pogrom, Lithuania, July 27, 1941

Jews removed to Warsaw ghetto, April 1943

grotesque "scientific" experiments performed on these dehumanized subjects. The Final Solution was devised to ensure that they would all die. Its aim was to achieve the extermination of the Jews as a people—an aim it very nearly achieved. It was the consummate expression of Nazi ideology, rooted in racism and terror.

The Germans established more than twenty concentration camps on German and Polish territory to warehouse their victims and extract what labor they could from them before they succumbed to starvation and disease. Of these, a few were designated as death camps—in German literally "places of annihilation"—whose purpose was the extermination of human beings: among them Auschwitz (which also served as a labor camp), Belsen, Chelmno, Majdanek, Sobibor, and Treblinka. The Nazi extermination camps were unique. The Japanese, too, built concentration camps, and mistreated their prisoners of war—more than one-quarter of the Allied soldiers held captive died. But they did not use the camps for genocidal ends as the Nazis did.

Nazi managers invented a method of mass extermination: the gas chamber. SS guards packed hundreds, even thousands of prisoners at a time into the sealed rooms of specially designed crematoria. They then introduced a precise quantity of Zyklon-B gas (crystallized prussic acid, normally used as a pesticide). Death followed in just a few minutes—between three and fifteen, reported a camp commander to the Nuremberg Tribunal for war crimes. Squads of Jewish slave laborers then ripped out gold teeth, and searched the bodies for gold, jewelry, and gems; then burned or buried them. In a few hours, all trace of the slaughter was removed—bones, blood, ashes, all vanished. At Auschwitz, the most efficient of the death camps, this pitiless system killed as many as 9000 people per day, and a total of perhaps 2.5 million during its years of operation.

Why did no one intervene to stop the slaughter? Much of it happened in secret. But enough was known. By 1942, the Allied governments knew that Jews were being killed on a large scale, but authorized no rescue missions. On the other hand, the occupied Danes managed brilliantly to ship most of their Jewish population to safety in neutral Sweden; and many individuals, at dire risk to themselves, from moral or religious motives, saved individual Jews.

The Nazis kept careful records of their extermination program. The death camps killed about 9 million people, of whom nearly 6 million were Jews (of these, more than 1 million were children, the first to be sent to die). Over the last half-century, some of the survivors have told their stories, and Jewish organizations have reconstructed the unforgettable part of the past now called the **Holocaust** (a Greek word meaning a sacrifice offered for burning, or a "sacred offering") or Shoah (a Hebrew word meaning "destruction"). Now schoolchildren and museum-goers learn, so that the events may never be repeated, of the unique evil rationally planned and deliberately executed by a presumably civilized people.

The deed did not go wholly unpunished. After the war, from November 1945 through October 1946, an international tribunal convened at Nuremberg in Germany to investigate the war crimes of Nazi leaders. Twelve were sentenced to death, others to long sentences; three were acquitted. A separate tribunal began early in 1946 to consider the crimes of twenty-five Japanese civil and military leaders, all of whom were found guilty, and of these seven executed. Of other collaborators tried in their own nations' tribunals, the eighty-nine-year old French general

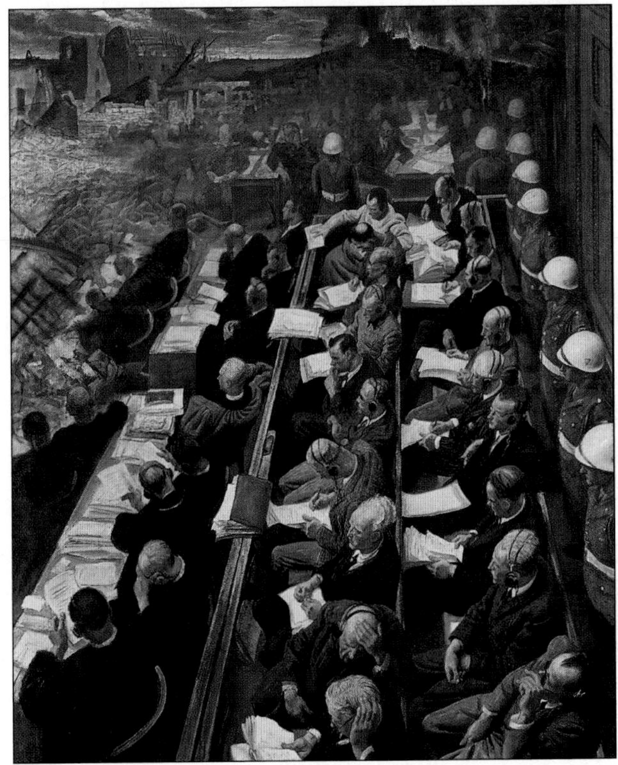

Dame Laura Knight*, The Nuremberg Trial, *1946:
German and Japanese leaders who had committed what were felt to be crimes against peace and humanity were tried in 1945–1946. Most were found guilty. This allegorical painting of the Nuremberg Tribunal shows accused Nazi leaders (seated in the last two rows) listening to the evidence against them, in a space encompassed by scenes of the suffering they had caused. (Imperial War Museum, London)

WITNESSES

Final Solutions

German engineer Hermann Graebe testifies at Nuremberg about a Nazi massacre of Jews in the Ukraine (1942): The people who had got off the trucks . . . had to undress upon the orders of an SS man, who carried a riding or dog whip. They had to put down their clothes in fixed places, sorted according to shoes, top clothing and underclothing. . . .

Without screaming or weeping, these people undressed, . . . kissed each other, said farewells. . . . I watched a family of about eight persons. . . . An old woman with snow-white hair was holding the one-year-old child in her arms and singing it and tickling it. . . . The couple were looking on with tears in their eyes. The father was holding the hand of a boy about ten years old and speaking to him softly. . . .

At that moment the SS man at the pit shouted something to his comrade. The latter counted off about twenty persons and instructed them to go behind the earth mound. . . . I walked around the mound and found myself confronted by a tremendous grave. . . . [T]he pit was already two-thirds full. I estimated that it already contained about 1,000 people. . . . The people, completely naked, went down some steps . . . to the place to which the SS man directed them. . . . Then I heard a series of shots.
(USGPO, *Nazi Conspiracy and Aggression* 1946; document PS 2992)

Concentration camp commander Rudolf Hoess testifies at Nuremberg (April 5, 1946): I was ordered to establish extermination facilities at Auschwitz in June 1941. . . . The Camp Commander at Treblinka told me that he had liquidated 80,000 in the course of one-half year. . . . He used monoxide gas and I did not think that his methods were very efficient. So when I set up the extermination building at Auschwitz, I used Cyclon B, which was a crystallized prussic acid which we dropped into the death chamber from a small opening. It took from 3 to 15 minutes to kill the people in the death chamber. . . . We knew when the people were dead because their screaming stopped. . . . After the bodies were removed our special commandos took off the rings and extracted the gold from the teeth of the corpses. . . . Another improvement we made over Treblinka was that we built our gas chambers to accommodate 2,000 people at one time, whereas at Treblinka their 10 gas chambers only accommodated 200 people each.
(USGPO, *Nazi Conspiracy and Aggression*, 1947; document PS 3868)

Survivor, author, and Noble Peace laureate Elie Wiesel reflects on the past (1987): In those days and nights, humanity was distorted and twisted in this city, the capital of a nation proud of its distant history, but struggling with its recent memories.

Everything human and divine was perverted then. The law itself became immoral. . . . It became legal and praiseworthy to . . . destroy human beings—sons and daughters of an ancient people—whose very existence was considered a crime. . . .

Still, not all Germans alive then were guilty. . . . Only the guilty were guilty.

Children of killers are not killers but children. I have neither the desire nor the authority to judge today's generation for the unspeakable crimes committed by the generation of Hitler.

But we may—and we must—hold it responsible, not for the past, but for the way it remembers the past. . . . Memory is the keyword. . . . [S]alvation, like redemption, can be found only in memory.
(Elie Wiesel, *The Kingdom of Memory*, 1990)

President Truman recalls the dropping of the atomic bomb (1945): On August 6 . . . came the historic news that shook the world. I was eating lunch . . . when Captain Frank Graham, White House Map Room watch officer, handed me the following message:

TO THE PRESIDENT
FROM THE SECRETARY OF WAR

Big bomb dropped on Hiroshima August 5 at 7:15 PM Washington time. First reports indicate complete success. . . .

I was greatly moved. I . . . said to the group of sailors around me, "This is the greatest thing in history. It's time for us to get home."
(*Memoirs by Harry S. Truman, I: Year of Decisions*, 1955)

English journalist Wilfred Burchett reports from Hiroshima (September 5, 1945): In Hiroshima, thirty days after the first atom bomb destroyed the city and shook the world, people are still dying, mysteriously and horribly, people who were uninjured in the cataclysm—from an unknown something which I can only describe as the atomic plague. Hiroshima does not look like a bombed city. It looks as if a monster steamroller had passed over it and squashed it out of existence. I write these facts as dispassionately as I can in the hope that they will act as a warning to the world.
(From P. Knightley, *The First Casualty: From the Crimea to Vietnam: The War Correspondent as Hero, Propagandist and Myth Maker*, 1975)

Pétain and the Nazi-appointed Norwegian president Vidkun Quisling (1887–1945), whose name has come to mean "traitor," were sentenced to death. (Pétain's life was spared at de Gaulle's request.) Hitler himself escaped. He had committed suicide in his Berlin bunker, to evade Soviet capture, on the night of April 28–29, 1945—the day after Mussolini's execution, and two weeks after president Roosevelt's peaceful death.

The discovery of the slaughter of the Jews began with the Soviet liberations of 1944–1945. Not long after its terrors began to be known, another horror was in preparation: the atomic bomb.

The lifelong pacifist Albert Einstein (1879–1955), who had foreseen the horror of the bomb (see Chapters 24, 26), wrote President Roosevelt in 1939, explaining how the power of nuclear fission could be harnessed to create a weapon of unprecedented force. Late in 1941, the "Manhattan Project" began for the development of that lethal device. A team of British, Canadian, and United States scientists labored over the next years to achieve its implementation. (Soviet, German, and Japanese scientists were also at work on the same project, but were well behind.) Roosevelt, Churchill, and their military strategists approved of the enterprise. It would be the weapon of weapons, the war-winner without equal, a tool that must be made and, if necessary, used.

On July 16, 1945, a test explosion showed the bomb was ready. At the Potsdam conference outside Berlin (July 17–August 2), the Soviet Union, United States, and Britain issued an ultimatum: Japan must surrender unconditionally. When Japan declined to do this, President Harry S. Truman (who had succeeded to the presidency on Roosevelt's death in April), ordered United States planes to drop on two Japanese cities the most powerful weapon ever made.

The bombs destroyed the cities in an instant, their destruction signaled by the mushroom-shaped cloud that immediately formed above the ruins. On August 6, the explosion of "Little Boy" (the bomb's name; the B-29 bomber was named Enola Gay, after the pilot's mother) immediately killed 78,000 of Hiroshima's 300,000 people—vaporized, burned, crushed. Many more were injured. The remainder lived to suffer mutilation and the horrible consequence of radiation. At Nagasaki, on August 9, "Fat Boy" killed more tens of thousands.

The deadly bombs brought a prompt result. Japanese leaders had already been discussing surrender

Hiroshima bombed: *The Holocaust is often likened to the devastation caused by the atomic bombs dropped by United States planes on the Japanese cities of Hiroshima and Nagasaki. The obliteration of whole cities, the sudden or prolonged deaths of hundreds of thousands, and the introduction of a new category of weapon, one that would have the capacity to cause almost unlimited destruction, certainly exceed the limits of what had been known or imaginable in previous human conflict. This photograph shows what remains of the flourishing city of Hiroshima after its bombing on August 6, 1945.*

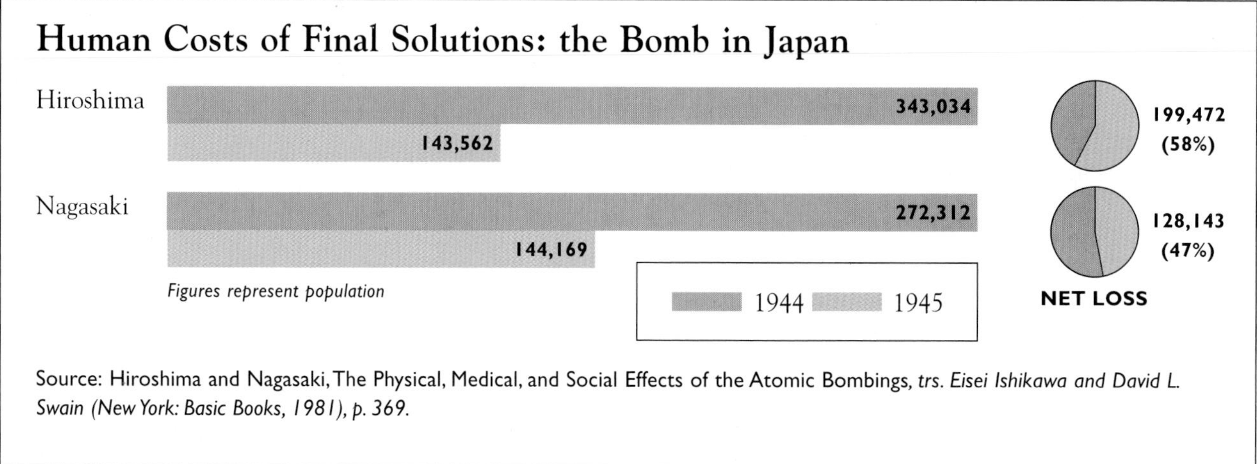

Source: Hiroshima and Nagasaki, The Physical, Medical, and Social Effects of the Atomic Bombings, *trs. Eisei Ishikawa and David L. Swain (New York: Basic Books, 1981), p. 369.*

before the bombing of Hiroshima. On August 10, the Japanese government communicated to the Allied command Japan's surrender, which Allied Supreme Commander General MacArthur accepted on September 2 on board the battleship *Missouri.*

No war tribunals gathered to judge the scientists and politicians who unleashed the power of the atomic bomb on the human race. They believed the use of the weapon was justified. Indeed, their arguments are powerful. An Allied invasion of Japan would almost certainly have cost more Japanese (and American) lives; but then the option to drop the bombs over relatively uninhabited areas, as a powerful warning, was not chosen. All arguments diminish next to the sheer magnitude of the destruction caused by that terrible weapon, and the threat of annihilation it posed and poses to all subsequent human generations (see Chapter 29).

Conclusion

THE DEFEAT OF FASCISM AND THE MEANING OF THE WEST

Nazism sprang from a combination of the worst of the Western traditions—irrationalism, extreme nationalism, racism. It failed because of the best of them—the traditions of liberty and justice that had evolved over centuries and had been inscribed in the constitutions of the Western democracies. The struggle of committed democrats against all forms of fascism, joined by Russian communist defenders of their ideals and their soil, spelled its destruction in 1945.

The cost of the war was enormous. Combatant and civilian deaths came to an estimated total of 46 million. The Soviet Union alone suffered 11 million military, and between 10 and 20 million civilian deaths, a tremendous toll from a population of about 190 million. Germany suffered over 4 million deaths, civilian and military; the Chinese perhaps 15 million; the Japanese nearly 2 million (and scarcely any wounded—the Japanese preferred death); the Jewish dead came to nearly 6 million, the Polish 3 million. Most lightly touched, the British, the French, the Italians, and the Americans together suffered a little over 1 million combat deaths; among the occupied French, an additional 350,000 civilians died.

The slaughter purchased the defeat of fascism. Yet it did not spell the end of totalitarianism in the West, where fascism in Spain and Portugal, and communism in the Soviet Union, endured until 1974–1975 and 1991 (see Chapter 29). In the postwar decades, new non-Western nations often inclined toward authoritarian or communist governments (see Chapter 28).

The future would also be burdened by memories: the destruction of cities and the willful deaths of non-combatants; the Holocaust; the atomic bomb. These savageries would haunt future generations. For many, the West had been discredited. Certainly the old world-system was dead. Another world was about to emerge, in which the meaning of the West and its vaunted traditions would be subject to question.

REVIEW QUESTIONS

1. How did Lenin adapt Marxist theory to fit conditions in Russia? Why were the Bolsheviks able to seize and retain power in Russia? What steps did Lenin take to impose communism within Russia?

2. How did Stalin gain control of the Communist Party? What did he hope to gain from the purges? How were the purges related to the collectivization of agriculture and the drive to industrialize Russia?

3. Why did so many Europeans find fascism attractive? How did it differ from communism? How did Mussolini seize and hold power in Italy? Which other European nations set up fascist regimes in the 1930s?

4. Why did the Weimar Republic fail? How did Hitler achieve supreme power in Germany by 1934? What role did racism play in his program for Germany and Europe? What did Hitler, Stalin, and Mussolini believe the role of women to be?

5. What were Hitler's goals in Europe? Why did Britain and France fail to stop Hitler in the 1930s? Why did Japan become an aggressor state after World War I? Why did Stalin reach an agreement with Hitler in 1939?

6. What were the decisive battles that led to the defeat of the Axis in World War II? Why was the war more brutal than previous wars? What was the Final Solution, and how did the Nazis put it into effect?

SUGGESTED READINGS

Bolsheviks and Communists *(see also Chapter 25)*

Conquest, Robert, *The Great Terror: A Reassessment*, rev. ed. (Oxford: Oxford University Press, 1990). Revised and updated edition of this compelling account of Stalin's purges during the 1930s.

Gleason, Abbott, *Totalitarianism: the Inner History of the Cold War* (Oxford: Oxford University Press, 1995). Deals with the concept of "totalitarianism" in Anglo-American, Russian, French, German, Spanish (including Latin American), and Italian sources.

Malia, Martin, *The Soviet Tragedy: A History of Russian Socialism, 1917–1991* (New York: Free Press, 1994). Argues that Stalinism was inevitable given Leninist principles.

Medvedev, Roy, *Let History Judge: The Origins and Consequences of Stalinism*, rev. ed., trs. George Shriver (New York: Columbia University Press, 1989). An impassioned account by a professional historian, dissenter, and survivor of the Soviet regime.

Service, Robert, *A History of Twentieth-Century Russia* (Cambridge, MA: Harvard University Press, 1998). Authoritative, balanced, and scholarly history of the Soviet Union.

Siegelbaum, Lewis, *Soviet State and Society Between Revolutions, 1918–1929* (Cambridge: Cambridge University Press, 1992). Focuses on social, rather than political, currents in early Soviet history.

The Faces of Fascism

Bullock, Alan, *Hitler and Stalin: Parallel Lives* (New York: Knopf, 1992). Juxtaposes Hitler and Stalin at parallel stages of their careers.

De Grazia, Victoria, *How Fascism Ruled Women: Italy, 1922–1945* (Berkeley: University of California Press, 1992). Explores fascist Italy's efforts to enroll women in the political nation while demanding that they function essentially as producers of children.

Koonz, Claudia, *Mothers in the Fatherland: Women, the Family and Nazi Politics* (New York: St. Martin's Press, 1987). Compelling exploration of the relationship between German women and Nazism.

Laqueur, Walter, *Fascism: Past, Present, Future* (Oxford: Oxford University Press, 1995). Treats fascism as an ideology of enduring appeal to those who feel left behind by modernization and change.

Payne, Stanley, *A History of Fascism, 1914–1945* (Madison: University of Wisconsin Press, 1995). Scholarly and definitive study.

The Second World War: Fascism Defeated

Bartov, Omer, *Murder in Our Midst: The Holocaust, Industrial Killing, and Representation* (Oxford: Oxford University Press, 1996). Stimulating essays on the Holocaust. The term "Industrial Killing" refers to murder that is impersonal and efficiently organized by the state.

Dawidowicz, Lucy, *The War Against the Jews* (New York: Holt, Rinehart & Winston, 1975). Classic general account of the Holocaust.

Duus, Peter, R. H. Myers, and M. R. Peattie, eds., *The Japanese Wartime Empire, 1931–1945* (Princeton, NJ: Princeton University Press, 1996). Essays on Japanese imperial practices in northeast and southeast Asia.

Fogelman, Eva, *Conscience and Courage: Rescuers of Jews During the Holocaust* (New York: Anchor Books, 1994). Restores one's faith in the existence of human goodness during the darkest of times.

Goldhagen, Daniel Jonah, *Hitler's Willing Executioners: Ordinary Germans and the Holocaust* (New York: Knopf, 1996). Controversial book that focuses on the complicity of ordinary Germans in the Nazis' efforts to annihilate European Jewry.

Hicks, George, *The Comfort Women: Japan's Brutal Regime of Enforced Prostitution in the Second World War* (New York: W. W. Norton, 1995). Useful treatment of one of Japan's most notorious wartime activities.

Weinberg, Gerhard L., *A World at Arms: A Global History of World War II* (Cambridge: Cambridge University Press, 1994). Immense and scholarly. Weaves the Pacific and European conflicts together as interconnected parts of a single, titanic struggle.

Weitz, Margaret Collins, *Sisters in the Resistance: How Women fought to Free France, 1940–1945* (New York: J. Wiley, 1995). Examines the role of women and the limits and meaning of "resistance".

THE END OF IMPERIALISM

1880 | 1900 | 1920 | 1940 | 1960 | 1980 | 2000

The Western World

World War I and the Russian Revolution, 1914–21

World War II, 1939–45

- "Easter Rising," Ireland, 1916
- Great Depression begins, 1929
- Commonwealth of Nations created, 1931
- Ireland ("Eire") independent, 1937
- UN Universal Declaration of Human Rights, 1948
- Cuban Missile Crisis, 1961
- Civil Rights Act, 1964
- NOW (National Organization for Women) created, 1966
- Martin Luther King shot, 1968
- Helsinki Accords, 1975
- Soviet Union dissolved, 1991
- European Union created, 1994

Middle East and North Africa

- Balfour Declaration, 1917
- Ottoman Empire ends, 1919
- Atatürk president of Turkey, 1922
- Iraq independent from Britain, 1932
- Egyptian independence ends, 1937
- UN partitions Palestine, 1947
- Israel declares statehood, 1947
- Nasser nationalizes Suez Canal, 1956
- Algeria independent from France, 1962
- Six-Day War, Israel, 1967
- Oil crisis, 1973–74
- Iranian Revolution, 1978
- Palestinian "Intifada," 1987
- Gulf War, 1991

Africa

South African War, 1899–1902

Many African nations gain independence, 1960–68

- National party takes control, 1948
- Bantu Education Act, 1953
- Ghana independent, 1957
- Sharpeville massacre, 1960
- Nelson Mandela freed, 1990
- Mandela elected president of South Africa, 1994

India, Pakistan, and Bangladesh

- Indian National Congress Party founded, 1885
- Amritsar Massacre, India, 1919
- Gandhi's resistance campaign begins, 1919
- Independence and partition of India, 1947
- Gandhi assassinated, 1948
- Indira Gandhi prime minister of India, 1966
- Bangladesh established, 1971

East and Southeast Asia

Korean War, 1950–53

US military involvement in Vietnam, 1954–73

- Japanese annex Korea, 1910
- Chinese Revolution, 1911–12
- Japan invades China, 1937
- Nagasaki and Hiroshima bombed, 1945
- Vietnam declares independence, 1945
- French leave Indochina, 1954
- China's "Great Leap Forward," 1958–60
- Cultural Revolution begins in China, 1966
- Marcos regime overthrown, Philippines, 1986
- Tiananmen Square protests suppressed, 1989
- Hong Kong returns to Chinese control, 1997
- Indonesia's Suharto ousted, 1998

Latin America

- Spanish–American War, 1898
- Mexican Revolution, 1911
- FDR's "Good Neighbor" policy, 1933
- Organization of American States formed, 1948
- Castro seizes power in Cuba, 1959
- Bay of Pigs fiasco, 1961
- Chile's Salvador Allende overthrown, 1973
- Sandinistas take charge in Nicaragua, 1979
- Democratic elections in Argentina, Brazil, Mexico, Nicaragua, and Paraguay, 1980s

CHAPTER 28

The End of Imperialism

Decolonization and Statebuilding around the Globe

1914–1990s

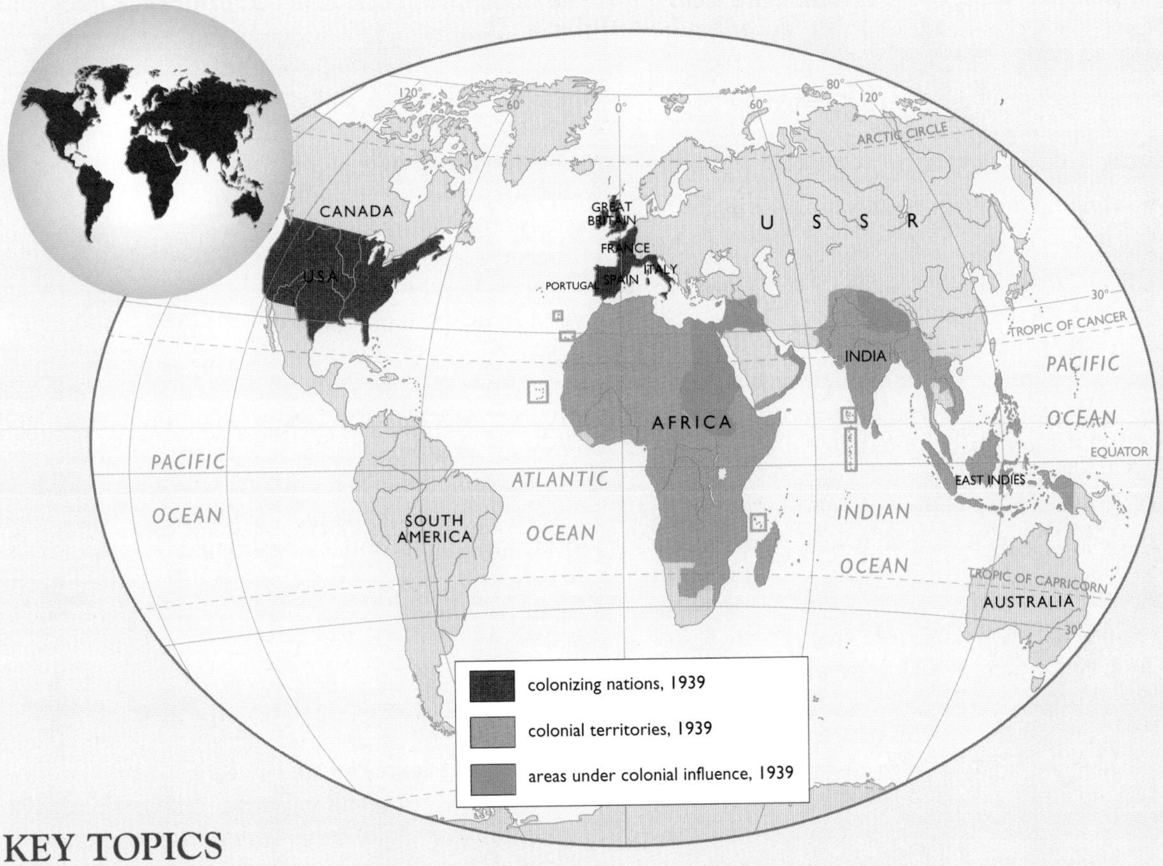

colonizing nations, 1939

colonial territories, 1939

areas under colonial influence, 1939

KEY TOPICS

- **Fading Empires:** Anti-colonial resistance begins even before 1914, then flares up after World War I, and leads after World War II to a thirty-year process of decolonization; at the end, the European empires are no more.
- **New World Orders:** In Asia, Africa, and the Middle East, new states take form, shaped for better and for worse by their colonial experience, and representing a spectrum of political types—democratic, monarchical, socialist, and communist, but most often autocratic.
- **The Last Imperialist:** A latecomer to imperialism, the United States acquires colonies in Asia and protectorates in Latin America, and intervenes as Cold War policeman in distant conflicts; at home the color line dividing the United States' own people is at last acknowledged.

Sunset and Sunrise At his trial in 1964 for conspiracy against the government of South Africa, and on the eve of his imprisonment that would last twenty-six years, Nelson Mandela (1918–) spoke eloquently of his hopes for his people. All Africans should receive a living wage, have access to work and housing, be free to move about, and enjoy full civil rights, "because without them our disabilities will be permanent." Then he reaffirmed his commitment to democracy: "During my lifetime . . . I have fought against white domination, and I have fought against black domination. I have cherished the ideal of a democratic and free society . . . It is an ideal which I hope to live for and to achieve. But if needs be, it is an ideal for which I am prepared to die." Thirty years later, in 1994, Mandela was elected by universal suffrage the president of a democratic Republic of South Africa. He invited the black majority and white minority to join in shaping the nation's future.

Mandela's triumph marks the passing of the age of imperialism—its sunset. The Union of South Africa was a relic of British and Dutch colonialism, the last area of the continent to be dominated by people of European descent. Now it would be African.

Mandela's words also mark the opening of a new age—a sunrise. The new Republic of South Africa would be a democracy with universal suffrage. With the fading of imperialism new nations were born, which had suffered tragically from the experience of colonial rule, but which would yet embrace the best ideals of the Western world.

From 1919, when the several treaties of Paris concluded World War I, until 1997, when the British colony of Hong Kong reverted to China, the imperialist ventures of Western nations in Asia, Africa, and the Americas faded and died. Sometimes the end of imperialism came peacefully, sometimes violently. The new nations that emerged struggled with its legacy—the distortions of native societies, economies, and cultures caused by the imposition of foreign rule. Some moved easily into the new world order; some have still not broken out of the impasse in which the colonial experience had left them. But the maps of the last decade of the twentieth century, in contrast to those of the first, display on every inhabited continent the free nations of a world that has outlived and surpassed imperialism.

FADING EMPIRES: ANTI-COLONIALISM AND DECOLONIZATION

By the outbreak of World War I, the principal European powers had devoured nearly all of the Old World (see Chapter 23). Exceptions were China, where the European presence was nevertheless strong, Siam (now Thailand), Iran, Japan and its colonies in Asia; and Liberia and Ethiopia in Africa. Then the tide of empire-building turned. A first wave of colonial resistance to imperial claims swept through the Old World in response to World War I.

Even before 1914, European encroachment in Asia and Africa had not gone unchallenged. The British, Dutch, and French met fierce resistance, for example, to their dominion in the Sudan, Indonesia, and Indochina. So did the United States in its takeover of the Philippines. In India, as cultural elites pressed for independence, British rulers faced sporadic terrorist incidents. In North Africa and the Middle East, Islamic and nationalist movements threatened European suzerainty, as did revolts of Ashanti, Tutsi, Hutu, Hottentot, Herero, Zulu, and other native groups in sub-Saharan Africa.

Aroused colonial elites came to see the Europeans' political power as unwarranted, their exploitation of native economies unjust, and their imperialist and often racist outlooks intolerable. European armies and bureaucracies held the colonies in line, but their ascendancy was everywhere vulnerable. Following World War II, a second and unstoppable wave of resistance, a great quake of **decolonization**, resulted in the dismantlement of the remaining major European empires.

The Sun Sets on the British Empire

In 1919, the British Empire ringed the world, so that it could be said that "the sun never sets on the British Empire." British colonies and **dominions** dotted the maps of Africa, Asia, Australasia, and the Americas. Over the next half-century, this empire fragmented. Some former colonies with populations largely of British origin became members of a **Commonwealth** of equal and autonomous states. Colonies in Asia and Africa, in contrast (together with European Ireland), bid for and achieved independence. Of these the most important, the "jewel in the crown," was India.

Independence in India In India, a British elite of a few thousand military officers, civil servants, missionaries, and teachers ruled a nation of 300 million

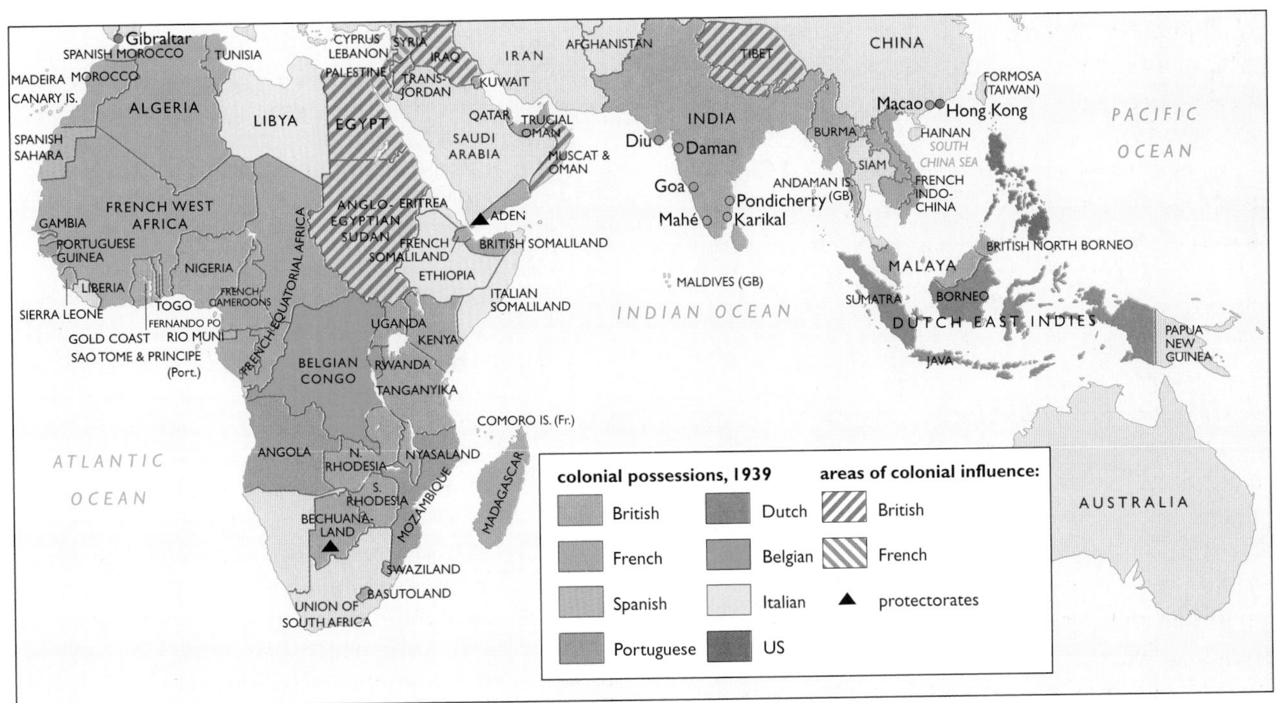

***Map 28.1* Colonial Possessions in Africa and Asia, 1939:** *In 1939, despite the shocks and realignments of World War I, much of Asia and Africa still lay under the domination of a European power. Native nationalist movements arose especially in colonized Asia and the Middle East, stimulated in some cases by the Japanese (who would soon occupy southeast Asia and the East Indies), the Chinese nationalist Guomindang, Soviet-dominated Comintern, or by Nazi Germany or Fascist Italy.*

people, subdivided by political, regional, caste, and religious affiliations (see Chapter 23). The persistent poverty of the population aroused the concern of foreign administrators, but had positive uses. The British were the beneficiaries of an unequal economic strategy, whereby India exported agricultural commodities and raw resources, and purchased British manufactures in exchange. Poverty had other causes as well, including early marriage and high fertility, which led to insupportably high rates of population increase. The more India grew, the more it ate.

From 1919 to 1947, India struggled toward independence. India's support of Britain in World War I—she supplied more than 1 million troops to serve with Allied forces—made Indian soldiers and political leaders more aware of their nation's place in the world system. After the war, British repression of popular political aspirations triggered outrage, as at Amritsar (April 13, 1919), when British troops fired on a peaceable assembly of unarmed civilians, killing 400 and injuring others. Nationalist leaders such as Subhas Bose (1897–1945) and Jawaharlal Nehru (1889–1964) called for independence, while Mohandas Gandhi (1889–1948) aroused popular support for his agenda of nonviolent resistance to British domination.

Born a Hindu in India, trained as a barrister in London, Gandhi moved to South Africa in 1893 where he worked as an attorney. Shocked by the harsh discrimination suffered there by Indians, he led a protest movement. From that experience he developed the strategy of nonviolent resistance against colonial rule, or *satyagraha*. It rested on an amalgamation of Hindu and Christian values and Western political philosophy. By suffering violence and causing none in return, his followers exposed to the world their oppressors' injustice and their own righteousness.

Back in India in 1915, Gandhi instructed his followers in nonviolent resistance. Beginning in 1920, in response to British concessions he spurned as inadequate, Gandhi pursued his resistance campaign of protest marches and demonstrations. Although these assemblies sometimes broke down into rioting, in all, they had the effect that he intended: a worldwide awakening to the injustice of continued British colonialism in India.

Gandhi's opposition to foreign rule included a critique of colonialist economies. He urged Indians to boycott British manufactures, and to reestablish native industrial production. Modeling the sacrificial behavior he expected of others, he labored constantly

Independence for India

Gandhi and Nehru: *Mahatma Gandhi (on the right, in traditional garb), the prophet and builder of Indian national independence, confers with Jawaharlal Nehru, president of the India National Congress and first elected president of that nation on July 6, 1946.*

at cotton-spinning. Gandhi also wanted to purify (but not end) the caste system that was so central a feature of Indian (specifically Hindu) society, and called for the abolition of the status of "untouchability."

Gandhi's leadership was crucial during the inter-war years, his great moral authority signaled by the title given him of "Mahatma," or "great soul." But such leaders as Bose and Nehru, whose approach was both more secular and more militant, also found supporters. Growing opposition convinced the British that they would have to yield. In 1942 they promised to grant independence as soon as the war was over. Nationalist leaders repulsed the offer, demanding immediate independence and launching a "Quit India" movement. In 1942, the British imprisoned these opposition leaders, and suppressed the strikes and riots that erupted in protest. Bose fled India and raised an Indian National Army in Singapore with the assistance of Britain's enemy Japan.

After the war, Britain did quit India. While diplomats worked out the terms of independence with Indian leaders, the tension between Muslims and

WITNESSES

Asia: Independence for India and Vietnam

Mohandas Gandhi weighs what freedom means for the starving (1926): A starving man thinks first of satisfying his hunger. . . . He will sell his liberty and all for the sake of getting a morsel of food. . . . Such is the position of millions of the people of India. For them, liberty, God, and such words are merely letters . . . without the slightest meaning. . . . They will extend a welcome to any person who comes to them with a morsel of food. And if we want to give these people a sense of freedom we shall have to provide them with work which they can easily do in their desolate homes and which would give them at least the barest living. This can only be done by the spinning wheel. And when they have become self-reliant and are able to support themselves, we are in a position to talk to them about freedom. . . .

(M. K. Gandhi, "Young India," in *The Collected Works of Mahatma Gandhi*, Vol. 30, 1968)

The Vietnamese Declaration of Independence repeats the American and French Founding Declarations, and asks for the same rights (1945): "All men are created equal. They are endowed by their Creator with certain inalienable rights; among these are life, liberty and the pursuit of happiness."

This immortal statement was made in the Declaration of Independence of the United States of America in 1776. . . .

[After a recitation of French and other violations of Vietnamese autonomy.] For these reasons, we . . . solemnly declare to the world that Vietnam has the right to be a free and independent country—and in fact is so already. The entire Vietnamese people are determined to mobilize all their physical and mental strength, to sacrifice their lives and property in order to safeguard their independence and liberty.

(Ho Chi Minh, "Declaration of Independence of the Democratic Republic of Vietnam," 1945)

Refugees from Pakistan: *Hindus from Pakistan flee across the border to Amritsar, India on October 16, 1947 as part of the mass migrations that accompanied the establishment of the separate nations of India (mainly Hindu) and Pakistan (mainly Muslim).*

Hindus within India remained an issue. Massive conflicts causing more than 200,000 deaths resulted in the partition of India and the creation of a new state (Muslim Pakistan, with territory on the Punjab in the northwest and eastern Bengal in the northeast), the wrenching dislocation of some 10 million people, and the slaughter of 1 million. India became an overwhelmingly Hindu state with a Muslim minority.

Although Gandhi himself had hoped to avoid religious conflict, strife between religious groups persisted. Ironically, he was a victim of it. Angered by Gandhi's policy of tolerance, a Hindu assassin shot and killed him in January 1948, only months after he had seen the last British soldiers depart and India and Pakistan declared independent in August 1947.

The Indian experience spelled the end of British dominion in Asia. Independence followed for Ceylon (now Sri Lanka) and Burma (now Myanmar) in 1948, and Malaya in 1957 (in 1963 merged with Singapore and other entities, it was reconstituted as Malaysia). In 1997, according to the terms of their ninety-nine-year lease, the British surrendered Hong Kong, their last Asian possession, to China.

The Middle East and Africa In the Middle East and North Africa, Britain retained control during the interwar years. Her most significant possession was Egypt, where the Suez Canal was the lifeline of her international commerce. Spurred by a 1919 revolt, Britain granted Egypt independence by stages between 1922 and 1936, while maintaining a garrison zone around the Canal. At the same time, Egypt and Britain jointly administered Sudan; Sudan subsequently became independent in 1956.

Britain also gained control of Palestine and Iraq as **mandates** under the 1919 Paris settlement (and had considerable influence in independent Iran). Iraq gained independence in stages between 1921 and 1932, though Britain maintained military bases there. Iran (Islamic but not Arab) acquired in 1925 a new monarch, or *shah*, friendly to the British (and United States)—Reza Khan (1878–1944), a military officer who seized the ancient Persian throne, installing by force the Páhlevi dynasty that would rule until 1979. In Palestine, however, the British unhappily remained, as an influx of Jewish Zionist settlers from Europe competed with indigenous Palestinian Arabs.

In 1946, Britain gave independence to the state of Jordan, and attempted to suppress the bloody struggles of Palestinians and Jewish settlers. On November 29, 1947, the United Nations (successor organization to the League of Nations; see Chapter 29), recommended the partition of Palestine, with the assignment of one part to the Jews. On May 14, 1948, Britain withdrew, and Israel declared herself an independent Jewish state. The Jews began to hope that their historic longing for this land might at last be satisfied, and resolved to fight for Israel's survival. The move was a guarantee of future anguish, however, as some 600,000 Palestinians fled Israel and Arab neighbor states resisted what they perceived as Israel's alien presence (see below). Britain further withdrew from the region, when, in 1967, her Arab **protectorates** on the Persian Gulf and Arabian Sea became the independent states of South Yemen in 1967, and Bahrain, Oman, Qatar, and the United Arab Emirates in 1971.

After World War II, an exhausted Britain also released its colonies in sub-Saharan Africa. In west

Africa, the Gold Coast (formed from the native Ashanti, or Asante, nation, plus neighboring Togo) gained independence as Ghana in 1957—the first African nation to do so outside of South Africa. Nigeria, Sierra Leone, and Gambia followed in 1960, 1961, and 1965. In east Africa, the British colonies of Uganda, Kenya, and Tanganyika won independence in 1961 to 1963; so did the protectorates of British Somaliland (1960) and Zanzibar (1963), while Tanganyika later merged with adjacent Zanzibar to form Tanzania in 1964.

In the southeast, Northern Rhodesia and Nyasaland became independent as Zambia and Malawi in 1964, Botswana (formerly Bechuanaland) in 1966, and the tiny Lesotho (formerly Basutoland) and Swaziland in 1966 and 1968. Southern Rhodesia broke from Britain in 1965, its European planter elite clinging to policies of racial division similar to those of South Africa. After bitter guerrilla struggle against an unyielding white regime, its black African majority finally won black enfranchisement and in 1980 the state was renamed Zimbabwe. South Africa, formerly under British rule, had been since 1910 a dominion within the British Empire. It would follow its own unique course (see below). But adjacent Namibia, illegally occupied by South Africa since 1914, became independent in 1990.

The Commonwealth and Ireland The creation of the Commonwealth of Nations in 1931 permitted some former colonies, though independent, to continue to enjoy privileged economic relations with Britian. Canada, Australia, and New Zealand, lands largely populated by those of European descent, were Commonwealth members and supported the motherland vigorously during World War II. Other former British colonies that have joined the Commonwealth include India and several African and Caribbean states.

Ireland alone remained an intractable problem for post-imperial Britain (see Chapter 23). The British government finally approved Home Rule for Ireland in 1914; but the bill was suspended when World War I broke out, and was never subsequently enacted. Ireland was uninterested in the war that now occupied Britain's attention—except for Protestant northern Ireland, or Ulster. The Irish nationalists, meanwhile, had formed political parties—the Home Rule party and, after 1902, Sinn Fein ("We Ourselves")—and events moved rapidly toward the secession of southern Ireland from Britain. The British suppressed a rebellion that broke out on Easter Monday, 1916, and executed its leaders. Repression garnered a mass following for Sinn Fein, whose candidates won seats in Parliament in 1918 but refused to take them up, declaring themselves an independent Irish parliament. Outlawed, they went underground, warring against the detested Black and Tans, the special troops Britain dispatched to tame the rebellion.

The war over, saner heads sought a peaceful settlement. In 1920, a bill partitioned Ireland into two self-governing areas within the United Kingdom, Northern Ireland and Southern Ireland. In 1921, the Irish Free State in the south was declared a dominion within the British Empire, and in 1937, the British relinquished sovereignty altogether. After nearly eight centuries of British rule, Ireland was free. But it was not united, and not at peace: the internal struggle between British and Irish, Catholic and Protestant, would continue sporadically through the end of the century (see Chapter 29).

Reluctant Disengagement: the End of European Empires

In contrast to the British, the Dutch and French were determined to win back their colonies at the end of World War II. Portugal, Belgium, and Spain retained their African dominions as well. A defeated nation, Italy lost hers, which temporarily were granted as mandates to other states before being freed. In time, all yielded to the current of decolonization.

By 1900, the Dutch Empire had largely shrunk to its lucrative core of East Indian possessions (see Chapter 23). Frequent nationalist uprisings persisted despite the Dutch government's concessions. In the 1930s the Japanese swept the East Indies into the "Greater East Asia Co-Prosperity Sphere" and drove out its Dutch rulers. After the war, nationalists under Sukarno (1901–1970) took power.

The Dutch soon returned and attempted to reestablish their dominion. In 1949 they agreed to a Dutch–Indonesian union, an alliance Sukarno cast off in 1954. In 1957, when the Dutch refused to surrender Netherlands New Guinea to the new Indonesia, he ordered a billion dollars in Dutch assets seized and severed diplomatic relations. In 1963, Indonesia forcibly acquired that last Dutch colonial enclave. The Dutch, meanwhile, granted Suriname (in South America) a parliament in 1954, and full independence in 1975.

The French masters of Indochina had also been displaced by the Japanese during World War II. Before the end of the conflict, the French proposed granting their colonies self-governing status within the French Union. Cambodia and Laos agreed, but Vietnamese

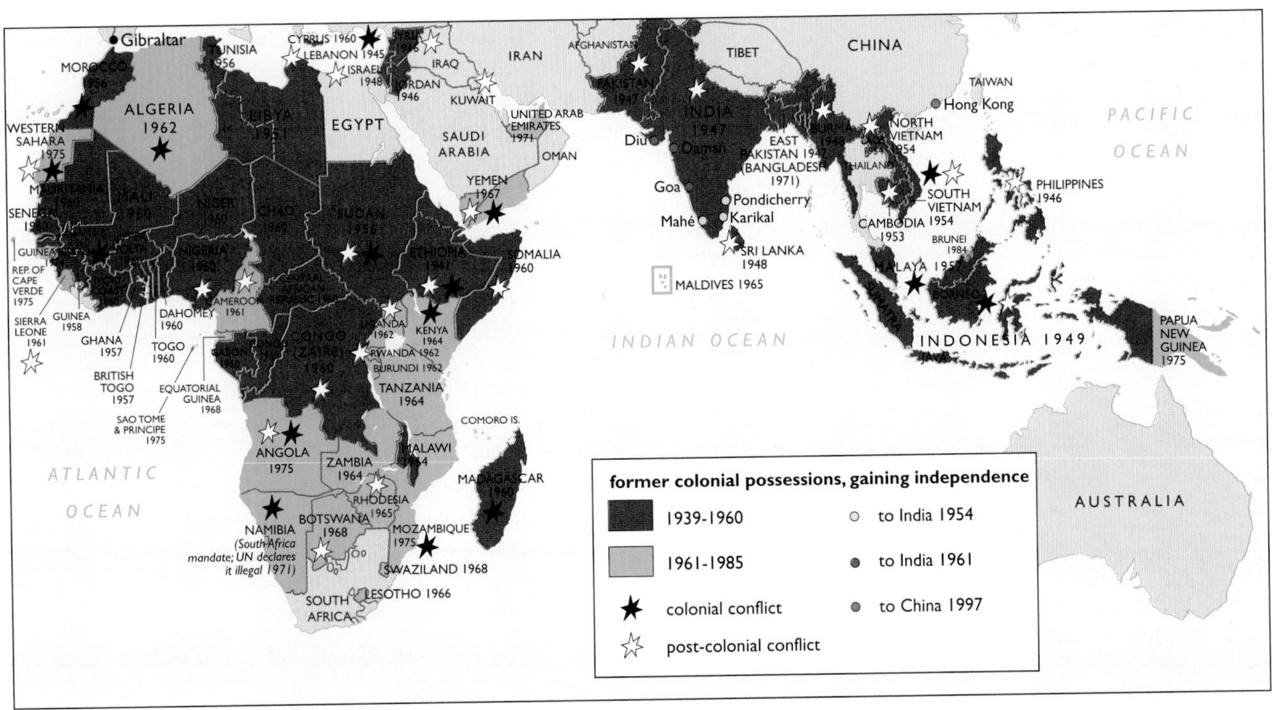

Map 28.2 Independence Gained in Africa and Asia Since 1939: *The tired victors of World War II could not maintain their empires. The British and the French, the greatest imperialist powers, were the first to relinquish direct domination of Asian and African colonies. The last were Belgium, Spain, and Portugal. Decolonization was largely completed around the world by 1975.*

nationalists under the leadership of Ho Chi Minh did not. In 1945 Vietnam declared independence, and war broke out between French and nationalist forces. In 1954, badly beaten at the climactic battle of Dien Bien Phu, the French withdrew. The 1954 settlement signed at Geneva granted Vietnam independence. But it also partitioned the country, with the north left in Ho Chih Minh's control, and the south scheduled to determine its own future in a 1956 election. That settlement never went into effect (see below).

In the Middle East, the war-weary French could not maintain authority in their mandates of Syria and Lebanon against spirited opposition from the league of Arab states. Persuaded by the British, the French yielded. Both nations attained independence in 1945.

In 1956, the French surrendered their North African protectorates of Tunisia and Morocco, held since 1881 and 1912 respectively, to native rulers. But Algeria, which the French had ruled since 1830, was seen by many to be an extension of France. Here many European French had settled (constituting ten percent of the population) and created a colonial civilization, much like the Spanish settlers of the Americas. But nationalist and Islamist groups demanded that they leave and revolts broke out in 1954 after the French defeat in Indochina. The subsequent conflict, marked by mutual atrocities, resulted in the deaths of some 250,000 Algerians (of a population of 9 million) and nearly tore France apart as opinion at home polarized. In 1958, a revolt of the French army brought World War II hero Charles de Gaulle (1890–1970) back from retirement. He was elected president, his supporters believed, in order to maintain "*Algérie française*," a French Algeria. Too good a strategist to battle in vain, de Gaulle returned Algeria to the Algerians in 1962.

The Algerian experience served as a model to avoid south of the Sahara. The French possessions of west and equatorial Africa (modern Guinea, Senegal, the Ivory Coast, Cameroon, Mali, Togo, Niger, Benin, Burkina Faso, Chad, Gabon, Mauritania, the Congo Republic, and the Central African Republic) gained their freedom with relative ease. Beginning in 1956, the French offered these colonies limited self-government within the French Union, an offer accepted by several. All had gained full independence by 1960 (but the east African colonies of the Comoros and Djibouti not until 1975 and 1977).

Portugal, the first of the European powers to win African and Asian footholds, was determined not to surrender colonies it had held so long and profitably. Nationalist movements in their colonies of

WITNESSES

Africa: the Debate over Algeria

Jacques Soustelle, Governor-General of the French colony of Algeria, says France will never relinquish Algeria (1955): France is at home here, or rather, Algeria and all her inhabitants form an integral part of France, one and indivisible. All must know, here and elsewhere, that France will not leave Algeria any more than she will leave Provence and Brittany. Whatever happens, the destiny of Algeria is French.
(From K. Nkrumah, *I Speak of Freedom*, 1961)

Psychiatrist Frantz Fanon welcomes a new and autonomous Algeria (1959): On the Algerian soil a new society has come to birth. The men and women of Algeria today resemble neither those of 1930 nor those of 1954, nor yet those of 1957. The old Algeria is dead. All the innocent blood that has flowed on to the national soil [as a result of war with France] has produced a new humanity.
(Frantz Fanon, *A Dying Colonialism*, 1971)

Mozambique, Angola, and Guinea-Bissau, however, overwhelmed the military and economic capacity of Portuguese hard-liners. In 1974, military officers who recognized the impending failure of Portugal's colonial policy ousted the dictator Marcelo Caetano (1906–1980). With his fall came independence for Portugal's African colonies, as well as the island territories of Cape Verde and São Tomé and Principe. Portugal's neighbor Spain, having surrendered its section of Morocco, retained only a few African enclaves; nearly all were independent by 1968.

Belgium's African empire consisted of the great central Congo region and adjacent Rwanda and Burundi. Notorious exploiters of the people and resources of the Congo, the Belgians had failed to train a native managerial elite and the Congolese opposition was unprepared for political administration when the Belgians suddenly withdrew. The new nation achieved independence in 1960 as the state of Zaire (now the Democratic Republic of Congo), under Patrice Lumumba (1925–1961) as prime minister. It was to be a troubled transition. Rival leaders representing ethnic minorities opposed Lumumba's nationalist strategy. They assassinated Lumumba and seized power. Rwanda and Burundi gained their independence in 1962.

In addition to their colonies in Asia, Africa, the Middle East, and the Americas, the European powers surrendered small islands in the Pacific, Atlantic, and Mediterranean. So passed the era of European imperialism. The new states that formed after independence repudiated that heritage. They found it was not easy to create better governments than those their masters had imposed upon them.

NEW WORLD ORDERS: STATEBUILDING IN AFRICA, THE MIDDLE EAST, AND ASIA

As the imperial powers exited, the stage was left to the premiers, presidents, and parliaments of the new nations of Asia and Africa. Newcomer states sought to form stable governments, stimulate economies, adopt new technologies, and provide for the health and education of their people, while still saddled with the legacies of imperial rule. Some met these goals readily; many others struggled or failed. In 1990, more nations lived under their own freely chosen leaders than ever before, and had begun the task of achieving security and prosperity for their peoples.

Statebuilding in Africa: from Village to Nation

Between 1945 and 1975, some forty independent states took form in Africa. They experienced great disruption in their passage from subordinate colonies to modern democratic nations—even when the former colonial authority was supportive. Three barriers above all stood in the way of an easy transition from village to nation.

The Legacy of Colonialism First, the national identities of the new states were inherently frail. Prior to the imperial scramble for Africa, the continent was governed by a variety of African kingdoms and pre-state, networked village communities. The European nations that partitioned Africa by 1914 created colonial territories whose boundaries were superimposed on traditional political divisions. When the European powers released their colonies, African nationalist leaders could not recover the political identities of pre-conquest times. But neither could they make the artificial new boundaries natural. Sometimes those borders divided ethnic or tribal groups, or encompassed two or more rival groups. Loyalty to the new nations was strained by ethnic tensions, linguistic divisions, and tribal memories. Pan-African congresses provided an important setting for the discussion of future projects, but did not lead to plans for political organizations larger than the colonial units.

Second, although colonialism had modernized the African economies, it had done so to benefit the metropolitan power rather than the colonized Africans. Once independence was won, the African nations found it difficult to reorient their economies in line with the broader needs of their peoples.

Colonized Africa had a cash crop economy. Peanuts, palm oil, coffee, cotton, and tobacco crops found foreign buyers. But the exclusive devotion of vast tracts of the best land to these profitable exports meant that less land was devoted to subsistence crops. The population was left vulnerable to food shortages, a situation exacerbated, as often in the 1970s and 1980s, by periodic drought. In addition, when the prices of export crops dipped, the whole economy staggered. From 1970 to 1990, food production declined, while the population grew unabatedly.

What was true of cash crops was also true of minerals. Their exploitation led to great wealth, but also to difficulties. Copper, gold, and diamonds were valuable exports, but these, too, were subject to commodity price fluctuation. Moreover, mineowners recruited large labor forces (generally all male) from the villages to work in the mines. With the men far from home, many women had to tend the fields alone. Not only did those women assume burdens of isolation and increased responsibility, but productivity often suffered, and the risk of famine increased.

New nationalist leaders found it difficult to shed the established model of the commodity economy—especially as it enriched an emerging urban elite of merchants, professionals, and bureaucrats. Turning to foreign capital to fund new enterprises led to increased dependence on Western economies. Some leaders sought the solution of nationalizing some enterprises, or redistributing agricultural lands.

A third barrier to the establishment of modern democracy was cultural. Colonial administration had trained a small vanguard of Africans in European schools and universities. This elite was minuscule amid a vast sea of people untutored in political ideas. In the 1960s, at the peak of decolonization, scarcely three percent of the population had received a secondary education, and barely ten percent were literate. Religious allegiances—Muslim, Christian, polytheist, and **animist**—overlapped tribal and state boundaries, and did not serve to unify at the national level. Africa's divided, inexperienced, and ill-educated peoples were vulnerable to manipulation by propaganda and to control by dictators.

With these deficits, early efforts to establish democratic states understandably foundered. Nearly all the new African nations succumbed to authoritarian rulers who led one-party states that suppressed dissent. Their aims were not always malevolent: some pursued sound plans for economic development and human welfare. But even well-meaning dictators were tempted by wealth and power. Unchallenged by a democratic opposition, they became corrupt and inefficient. Often, these dictators were artificially sustained by Western nations or corporations which continued to seek profits in post-colonial era.

Cocoa Prices Fall in Ghana, 1954–1965

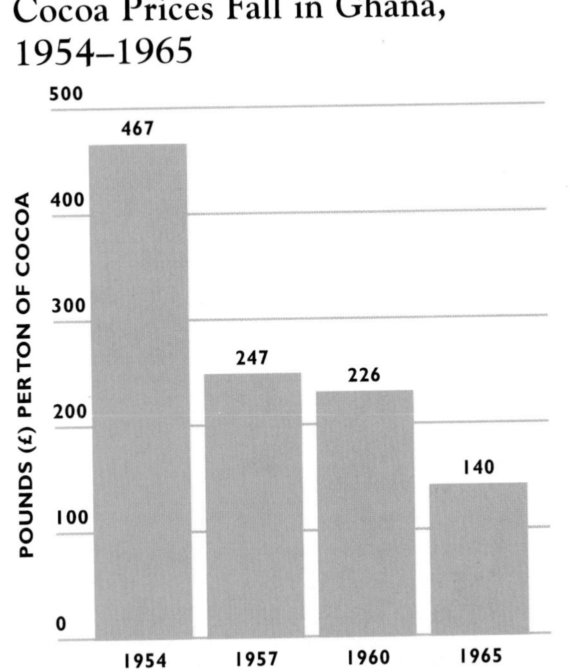

Like many newly independent nations in Africa and Asia, Ghana was a commodity exporter. It suffered gravely when the price of cocoa, which accounted for the bulk of its foreign exchange, fell sharply during the 1950s and 1960s.

Source: *A. A. Mazrui and M. Tidy,* Nationalism and New States in Africa *(Nairobi: Heinemann, 1984), p. 62.*

When corruption and inefficiency became intolerable, a military **coup** might oust a dictator and install the rule of generals—trained managers, but occasionally brutal ones, with little patience for claims of civil rights. Military governments might recivilianize the nation, once reform measures had been taken. But if the civilian governments failed again, military rule returned. During the 1950s and 1960s, military coups were frequent; during the 1970s and 1980s, they outpaced any other form of political change in Africa.

Several major African states experienced this rocky progression from hopeful independence to authoritarianism to military rule. Ghana, the former

Independence Days

Nigeria and South Africa: *Independence came to most nations of Africa in the decades following World War II as colonial powers withdrew. Here, Nigerian dancers in traditional costume prepare to celebrate independence from Britain in 1960 (left). As most African nations gained their independence, they began the process of state-building under their own leaders. South Africa, in contrast, had been under the control of white Europeans whose increasingly racist policies excluded African natives from power, education, and high-paid employment. The opposition leader Nelson Mandela, imprisoned from 1964 and released after twenty-six years, is shown here in 1990 with his wife Winnie (below). In 1994, he became president in South Africa's first post-apartheid elections.*

British Gold Coast colony, was governed by the idealistic pan-Africanist Kwame Nkrumah (1909–1972), a former teacher who studied in the United States and Britain. From 1948, he rallied urban elites and commercial farmers to the cause of "Self-Government Now." Arrested, imprisoned, and released, he emerged in 1951 as key leader of the semi-autonomous state. Upon full independence in 1957, he became prime minister; in 1960, president. In that role, Nkrumah turned to authoritarianism and one-party rule. Having nearly bankrupted the nation with grandiose but often disastrous development projects, he was ousted by a military coup in 1966.

Patrice Lumumba, author, thinker, and nationalist leader, led an independent Zaire after the Belgian exodus in 1960. But leaders of tribal factions resisted Lumumba's nationalist message, and one rich province seceded. In 1965, after Lumumba's assassination in 1961, a military coup put general Joseph (later Sese Seko) Mobutu (1930–1997) in power, in which position he remained propped up by the United States for thirty-two years.

These patterns reappeared in other settings. The brutal despot Idi Amin (1925–) held control of Uganda from 1971 until 1979; by then, he had caused the deaths of some 200,000 Ugandans, immigrants, and members of minority ethnicities. Nigeria, riven by tribal conflict, rocked between the corrupt authoritarianism of civilian and military governments.

In these states, authoritarian rule descended into disorder and violence. In those nations where a large white settler caste had established itself in the pre-independence era, the potential for violence was even greater. In Kenya, African nationalists waged a guerrilla war for years before the settler elite yielded to native rule. In Southern Rhodesia, white settlers cut ties with Britain in 1965, before Britain could grant independence to the territory as a free African state in which blacks could vote. Rhodesian prime minister Ian Smith (1919–) fought guerrilla movements from 1973 until 1980, when Robert Mugabe (1924–), Marxist leader of one of the revolutionary parties, became head of the country now named Zimbabwe.

The Struggle against Apartheid The largest group of white settlers lived in the Union of South Africa, from 1910 an independent state, and the one fully industrialized nation in Africa. Here, as of the 1970s, those of European descent numbered 4 million, "coloreds" 2 million (including Asians and those of mixed identity), and black Africans some 20 million—yet a white ruling caste controlled every aspect of the economy and the government. In 1948, white voters installed the National Party, dominated by the Afrikaner descendants of the original Dutch settlers. Against their policies stood the African National Congress, founded in 1912. From the 1960s, the ANC organized resistance to National Party principles, publishing its own Freedom Charter in 1955.

The National Party's goal was to forestall black independence. The 1950 Population Registration Act and Group Areas Act assured the permanent economic disability of black South Africans. The first established classification by race. The second assigned those of the African classifications to live in "Bantustans," or tribal "homelands," constituting a mere fourteen percent of the land. By the Bantu Education Act of 1953, they were barred from excellent mission schools and compelled to attend government-run schools that enforced racial hierarchies and taught only rudimentary subjects. As workers, they received lower wages than whites for similar work.

Other laws established the social norms of **apartheid** ("separateness"), mimicking the segregation laws of the southern states of the United States (see below). Such laws barred blacks from white-designated public facilities, banned interracial marriage, and required blacks always to carry an identity card documenting their inferior status. The efforts of African nationalist leaders to resist apartheid resulted in their arrest, but also in the worldwide condemnation of the government of South Africa. More powerfully, the killing of unarmed demonstrators at Sharpeville in 1960 (leaving at least 67 dead, 180 wounded) and Soweto in 1976 (where police fired on a crowd of 15,000, killing 575, including 134 children) aroused world opinion against South Africa. The Anglican archbishop Desmond Tutu (1931–), winner of the 1984 Nobel Peace Prize, carried the story of racial injustice around the globe.

World opinion strengthened by economic sanctions forced President Pieter W. Botha (1916–) to resign in 1989. His successor Frederik Willem de Klerk (1936–) searched for a compromise between black aspirations and Afrikaner obduracy. De Klerk lifted the ban on the African National Congress in

WITNESSES

Africa: Post-Colonial Quandaries

Kwame Nkrumah on the need to forget the past and press forward to African unity (1961): For centuries, Europeans dominated the African continent. The white man arrogated to himself the right to rule and to be obeyed by the non-white; his mission, he claimed, was to "civilise" Africa. Under this cloak, the Europeans robbed the continent of vast riches and inflicted unimaginable sufferings on the African people.

All this makes a sad story, but now we must be prepared to bury the past with its unpleasant memories and look to the future. . . . It is clear that we must find an African solution to our problems, and this can only be found in African unity. Divided, we are weak; united, Africa could become one of the greatest forces for good in the world.

(Kwame Nkrumah, *I Speak of Freedom: A Statement of African Ideology*, 1961)

L. S. Senghor, first president of Senegal, on the importance of retaining the French language in post-colonial Africa (c. 1963): It is a fact that French has made it possible for us to communicate to our brothers and to the world that unheard message which only we could write. It has allowed us to bring to Universal Civilization a contribution without which the civilization of the twentieth century would not have been universal.

(L. P. Senghor, "Negritude and the Concept of Universal Civilization," 1963; eds. A. A. Mazrui and M. Tidy, 1984)

Caught between two worlds, Mozambican hero E. C. Mondlane speaks out on national independence and superpower alignment (1967): What are we supposed to do if, apart from the Africans only the Communists will train and arm us? It apparently was all right for the West to arm itself with the Communists against the Fascists [in World War II] but, when we are denied Western aid [extended instead to the Portuguese, the former colonial rulers of Mozambique], we are expected to do without Communist aid as well. We need the support of China and Russia because they are sympathetic to us and have no connection with the Portuguese.

(Interview with E. C. Mondlane in *The Observer* (UK), January 29, 1967; eds. A. A. Mazrui and M. Tidy, 1984)

1990 and released its leader Nelson Mandela after twenty-six years of imprisonment. The two leaders worked together for a multiracial and democratic society, calling for elections based on universal suffrage. Held in 1994, after forty-six years of rule by the National Party, that election made Mandela president, De Klerk one of two deputy presidents. An African pledged to win justice for both Africans and Afrikaners led South Africa for the first time.

Varying Models of Independence In other states, where independence was attained only after guerrilla struggle—as in the former Portuguese colonies of Guinea-Bissau, Angola, and Mozambique, or the former French colony of Algeria—socialism appealed to the embittered nationalist victors. In addition, by the 1970s, the animosities between the United States and the Soviet Union generated by the Cold War (see Chapter 29) intruded upon African politics, as each antagonist funded and supplied friendly guerrilla forces and client states.

In Angola in 1975–1976, Soviet arms and some 45,000 troops from Cuba, then a Soviet client state, aided one guerrilla group against another supported by the United States. The Soviet protégés won, and a Marxist government was formed. In Algeria, upon the final departure of the French in 1962, a socialist government took over foreign interests and nationalized industries. In Libya, army colonel Muammar el-Qaddafi (1942–) toppled a pro-Western monarchy in 1969, nationalized foreign petroleum assets, removed United States and British military bases, and accepted Soviet aid and arms. In 1974, a self-proclaimed Marxist–Leninist regime took over in Ethiopia by overthrowing the last emperor Haile Selassie (r. 1930–1974). Ethiopia soon went to war with neighboring Somalia (pieced together in 1960 from former British and Italian Somalilands), also a Soviet client since 1974. For a while, the Soviet Union supplied both sides with arms and military experts. But on the whole, few African nations gravitated to the Soviet sphere of influence.

Among the conscientious African leaders who guided the continent into a modern age of political responsibility were the intellectuals Léopold Senghor (1906–) of Senegal, Patrice Lumumba of Zaire, and

WITNESSES

Africa: the Debate over South Africa

Nelson Mandela speaks in his own defense at his trial at the Pretoria Supreme Court, Rivonia (1964): Africans want to be paid a living wage... to live where they obtain work... to be part of the general population, and not confined to living in their own ghettoes.... Africans want to be allowed out after eleven o'clock at night and not to be confined to their rooms like little children.... Africans want a just share in the whole of South Africa; they want security and a stake in society.

Above all, we want equal political rights, because without them our disabilities will be permanent. I know this sounds revolutionary to the whites in this country, because the majority of voters will be Africans. This makes the white man fear democracy....

During my lifetime I have dedicated myself to this struggle of the African people. I have fought against white domination and I have fought against black domination. I have cherished the ideal of democratic and free society in which all persons live together in harmony and with equal opportunities. It is an ideal which I hope to live for and to achieve. But if needs be, it is an ideal for which I am prepared to die.

(Nelson Mandela, *The Struggle is My Life*, 1990, 3rd ed.)

Archbishop Desmond Tutu implores the United Nations Security Council to help black South Africans gain their freedom (1984): White South Africans are not demons; they are ordinary human beings, scared human beings, many of them; who would not be, if they were outnumbered five to one? Through this lofty body, I wish to appeal to my white fellow South Africans to share in building a new society, for blacks are not intent on driving whites into the sea but on claiming only their rightful place in the sun in the land of their birth.

We deplore all forms of violence, the violence of an oppressive and unjust society and the violence of those seeking to overthrow that society, for we believe that violence is not the answer to the crisis of our land.

We dream of a new society that will be truly nonracial, truly democratic, in which people count because they are created in the image of God....

I say we will be free, and we ask you: Help us, that this freedom comes for all of us in South Africa, black and white, ... that it comes soon.

(Desmond Tutu, statement to the UN Security Council, October 23, 1984)

Jomo Kenyatta (c. 1893–1978) of Kenya. Senghor wrote several volumes of poetry; Lumumba wrote a study of his compatriots in *Congo: My Country* (1962); and Kenyatta wrote about the native traditions of his people in *Facing Mount Kenya* (1938) and *Suffering without Bitterness* (1968).

The socialist leaders Julius Nyerere (1922–) of Tanzania and Robert Mugabe (1924–) of Zimbabwe hoped to build African states on African principles, while serving citizens' welfare needs according to Western political theory. Nyerere's controversial concept of *ujamaa* (familyhood), a politics based on village-centered popular rule, foundered in economic crisis, however. And Mugabe's achievements—building bridges to the economically important white minority of Zimbabwe, and seeking improved relations with South Africa—must be balanced against the defects of his increasingly repressive regime.

Under Nelson Mandela's leadership, notably, the African National Congress did not incline to Marxist socialism. Mandela staunchly adhered to democratic principles, displaying qualities for which, in 1993, he was recognized by the award of the Nobel Peace Prize.

Mandela's 1994 election as president of South Africa with two-thirds of the popular vote was a triumph for democracy. But South Africa was not alone in the early 1990s. After decades of post-colonial experimentation and readjustment, and with the development of an indigenous educated and professional elite, many African states are moving in the direction of parliamentary procedures, multi-party elections, and economic privatization.

Statebuilding in the Middle East: Israel, Oil, and Islam

World War I accomplished the dismemberment of the last great Islamic empire in the Middle East—that of the Ottomans. Over the next decades, its component territories became independent states. After World War II, the inherent tension between Islamic traditions and modernization sharpened (see Chapter 23). The politics of oil, a sub-soil treasure concentrated in the Arabian Peninsula, further destabilized the region. So too did the presence of Israel, created by European Zionists as a refuge for the Jewish people. These factors have made the Middle East a major trouble spot of the later twentieth century.

Turkey The Ottoman Empire entered the twentieth century moribund. In 1914, it ruled only one-third of the lands it had held in 1800. Allied with the Central Powers in World War I, the Empire disintegrated at war's end. By the 1920 Treaty of Sèvres, it lost its North African, Middle Eastern, and European territories, along with some Aegean islands (confirmed as Italian possessions), leaving only Anatolia (in Asia Minor) as a homeland. Even in Anatolia, a valuable commercial strip near Smyrna was assigned to Greece, a reward for loyalty to the victors' cause.

As Greek and Italian forces rushed to claim their prizes, Mustafa Kemal (1881–1938) led a swift counter-strike. An army commander during the recent war, Kemal was one of the Young Turks who had unseated the sultan in 1908. From 1919 to 1923, he recaptured Asia Minor and expelled the Greek occupiers. He won title not only to the whole of Anatolia, but also to a limited zone around Constantinople, now renamed Istanbul, on the European side of the Hellespont. The empire had been lost, but Turkey was born.

Made president in 1922 and henceforth known as Atatürk ("father of the Turks"), Kemal recast Turkey as a modern, secular state. He established compulsory public schools, for girls as well as boys, and by 1932 cut the illiteracy rate in half from its 1914 level. He established a civil law system (replacing traditional Muslim courts), discouraged Islamic customs, donned Western dress, made marriage a civil function, and transcribed the Turkish language in the West's Roman alphabet. He permitted elections (by universal suffrage) within a one-party system to a representative assembly whose decisions he consulted. By his death in 1938, Atatürk had transformed Turkey, which has since been democratized by later constitutions (in 1961 and 1982).

Egypt While Atatürk reshaped Turkey, the Arab regions of the former Ottoman Empire gained new contours. The most successful of these was Egypt, technically independent since 1936 but retaining a "preferential alliance" with Britain which ensured the latter continued control of the Suez and port of Alexandria and certain military privileges. In 1952, a military coup forced out the reigning king and, in 1956, obtained the independence of Sudan. In 1956, Egyptian president Gamal Abdel Nasser (1918–1970) seized and nationalized the Canal, the conduit through which passed two-thirds of the oil used by western Europe. Nasser's provocative strike nearly precipitated a military confrontation with Britain and her allies (who were restrained by the United States).

Nasser proceeded to nationalize banks and industries, dispossess the great landowners, redistribute lands to the peasants, and promote higher education.

Funded by the Soviet Union, he built the Aswan High Dam (completed 1970). Aswan controlled the Nile floods that had for centuries irrigated the land and made Egypt the granary of the Mediterranean. A great project that he likened in scale to the pyramid building of ancient pharaohs, it was intended to boost peasant productivity and generate electric power.

Nasser also galvanized the states of the Middle East, forging an international alliance for a pan-Arab, Islamic "socialism" that would be independent of both the West and communism. His successors have failed to resolve Egypt's economic problems, and face growing opposition from **Islamist** parties, which seek to unify Muslims and revitalize the religion and culture of Islam.

The Middle East In the Middle East, Britain and France relinquished their post-World War I mandates and protectorates after World War II. Newly independent, these states confronted the tasks of creating a modern economy, transportation system, and institutions of health and education. Their accomplishment was complicated by the presence in the Middle East of the state of Israel, an abundance of oil, and increasing Islamic militancy.

A memo of November 2, 1917 by British minister Arthur Balfour (1848–1930) first approved the concept of a "national home for the Jewish people"—vague words that promised no support and gave no idea of how it would come into being. By 1917, Jewish immigrants had already founded a handful of settlements in Palestinian territory still under Ottoman rule (joining the approximately 68,000 Jews, mostly in Jerusalem, who had lived in Palestine for four centuries). From 1917 to 1948, at first tens and then hundreds of thousands of immigrants poured into Palestine, as Jewish settlers increased their share of the population from about one-tenth to a half.

The first settlers were committed Zionists (see Chapter 23) followed by refugees from Nazism. In time, these were joined by immigrants from other Middle Eastern states who had lived under Ottoman rule as a tolerated minority. With the financial assistance of Jews around the world, these pioneers installed irrigation systems and reclaimed once barren lands. When the new nation of Israel declared its independence in 1948, it was more highly urbanized, better educated, better fed, and better armed than the surrounding Arab states.

Conflict was inevitable between the new state of Israel and its neighbors. Wars broke out in 1948, 1956, 1967, 1973, and 1982. In 1948, following the Israeli proclamation of independence on May 14, Arab forces from a league of neighboring states invaded the new nation. Highly motivated and better organized, the Israelis repulsed them. The territorial settlement based on the ceasefire lines gave them even more territory than had the United Nations' 1947 partition. Many Palestinian natives fled Israel; in time, about half became refugees in neighboring Arab lands, while around 1 million still remain within Israel, as a significant minority in that nation whose population is currently about 5.5 million.

Responding to border raids or threats of imminent invasion, Israel attacked Egypt in 1956, and its Arab neighbor states in 1967. At the close of the 1967 Six-Day War, Israel occupied lands south and west to the Suez Canal (the Sinai Peninsula) and east to the Jordan River (the region of the "West Bank," including the Old City of Jerusalem) as well as the Gaza Strip along the Mediterranean and the Golan Heights in Syria. Defying a United Nations injunction, Israel refused to leave until the Arab states agreed to negotiate; the Arabs refused to do so.

In 1973, after a six-year standoff, Egypt and Syria counterattacked. At the ceasefire they obtained a partial Israeli withdrawal from its 1967 high tide. In 1982, Israel invaded Lebanon to destroy the PLO headquarters that had relocated there. (The PLO, or Palestine Liberation Organization, was the official advocate of statehood for the uprooted Palestinians.) During these years, the United States provided Israel, and the Soviet Union its Arab opponents with arms, such activity serving to increase the volatility of the region's politics.

The problem remained that Israel occupied lands from which millions of now stateless Palestinians had been displaced. Over the next decades, some progress has been made toward resolving this intractable issue, which pits the moral right of the Jewish people to the homeland promised them against the moral right of Palestinian natives to the land which had long been theirs. In 1977, Egyptian president Anwar Sadat (1918–1981) bravely journeyed to Jerusalem to attempt to negotiate a settlement. That action culminated in the Camp David peace negotiations, hosted in 1978 by United States president Jimmy Carter (1924–). The resulting treaty between Egypt and Israel of March 26, 1979 obtained the complete Israeli withdrawal from the Sinai. Egypt became the only Arab state to have made peace with Israel.

In 1981, Sadat was assassinated, the penalty for his peacemaking role. Fundamentalist groups, both Israeli and Arab, sprang up to resist the forces for peace. (Fundamentalists adhere strictly to the tenets of their religion and resist secular values and institutions;

both Islamic and Jewish militancy may be linked to fundamentalist concerns.) In 1993, Israeli prime minister Yitzhak Rabin (1922–1995) and PLO chairman Yasir Arafat (1929–) signed a peace accord, following negotiations brokered by the United States and Norway. It allowed for Palestinian self-rule in the Gaza Strip and in the city of Jericho in the occupied West Bank, and called for a settlement by the end of a five-year transitional period. Further details within the same treaty framework were settled in 1995. These arrangements rankled nationalists on both sides.

Recent years have seen a heightening of Arab resistance and Israeli nationalism. In 1987, young Palestinians in the Israeli-occupied territories of the West Bank and Gaza Strip launched the uprising called the *Intifada* ("shaking")—an informal campaign of stonethrowing, strikes, and demonstrations. In addition, Islamist groups (notably the Hamas and the Islamic Jihad) have launched random terrorist attacks, including suicide bombings, on Israeli civilians. These have inspired ferocious Israeli determination to resist. Assassinated in 1995, Rabin was replaced by Benjamin Netanyahu (1949–), of the conservative Likud Party, a figure reluctant to compromise with Palestinian groups. In 1999, the election of the moderate Ehud Barak (1942–) gives hope of a new settlement.

Israeli soldiers, Jerusalem: *Tension between Jewish settlers in Palestine and the native Arabs of the region has led to war in 1948, 1956, 1967, 1973, and 1982—indeed, there has been no peace, since Palestinian resistance to the Israeli presence still continues. Here, on June 1, 1967, Jewish soldiers in the Israeli sector of Jerusalem eye the Jordanian section, which Israel would occupy, placing the whole of Jerusalem in Jewish hands for the first time since antiquity.*

HOW MANY?

Palestinians Resident in the Middle East

Country	Resident Palestinians
Jordan	700,000
West Bank	675,000
Israel	350,000
Gaza	375,000
Lebanon	275,000
Syria	175,000
Egypt	25,000
Iraq	10,000
Persian Gulf countries	170,000
TOTAL	2,755,000

Estimated figures, March 1973

The destiny of 2.75 million stateless Palestinian Arabs, more than half of whom live as refugees in countries outside of Israel, is one of the greatest sources of tension in any region of the world.

Source: *D. A. Schmidt,* Armageddon in the Middle East *(New York: New York Times, 1974), p. 148.*

Oil and Fundamentalism Meanwhile, Israel's Arab neighbors had grown wealthy. Oil had become the chief fuel of the twentieth century, and sixty percent of the world's oil lay under the sands of the Arabian peninsula (with other rich deposits in the United States and Canada, Mexico, Venezuela, Nigeria, Indonesia, Russia, and Kazakhstan). Since World War II, as the West and Japan became increasingly dependent on oil, the oil-producing Arab states reasserted control of their reserves. Suddenly wealthy, their economy is sustained by the export of a single precious commodity.

In Africa and Latin America, commodity-based economies suffered with fluctuations in world markets. To control that volatility, in 1961 the Arab states united (with other oil-rich nations) as the Organization of Petroleum Exporting Countries

WITNESSES

New Orders in the Middle East: Israel, the Palestine Liberation Organization, and Revolutionary Iran

Declaration of the establishment of the State of Israel (1948): The land of Israel was the birthplace of the Jewish people. Here their spiritual, religious, and political identity was shaped. Here they first attained statehood, created cultural values of national and universal significance, and gave to the world the eternal Book of Books. . . .

On the 29th of November, 1947, the United Nations General Assembly passed a resolution calling for the establishment of a Jewish state in the land of Israel. . . . This recognition by the United Nations of the right of the Jewish people to establish their state is irrevocable. This right is the natural right of the Jewish people to be masters of their own fate, like all other nations, in their own sovereign state.

(From J. N. Moore, ed., *The Arab–Israeli Conflict: Readings and Documents*, 1977)

The goals of the Palestine Liberation Organization, founded to represent the interests of the Palestinians made stateless by the creation of Israel (1968):

#8: The Palestinian people is at the stage of national struggle for the liberation of its homeland. . . .

#9: Armed struggle is the only way of liberating Palestine. . . .

#26: The Palestine Liberation Organization . . . is responsible for the struggle of the Palestinian Arab people to regain, liberate and return to their homeland and to exercise the right of self-determination in that homeland.

(From Zuhair Diab, ed., *International Documents on Palestine*, document no. 360, 1971)

Iranian revolutionary leader, the Ayatollah Ruhollah Khomeini, defines the nature of the victory won (1980): God Almighty has willed—and all thanks are due Him—that this noble nation be delivered from the oppression and crimes inflicted on it by a tyrannical government and from the domination of the oppressive powers, especially America, the global plunderer. . . . It is our duty to stand firm against the superpowers, as we are indeed able to do, on condition that the intellectuals stop following and imitating either the West or the East, and adhere instead to the straight path of Islam and the nation. . . . Beloved youths, it is in you that I place my hopes. With the Qur'an in one hand and a gun in the other, defend your dignity and honor so well that your adversaries will be unable even to think of conspiring against you. . . . Know well that the world today belongs to the oppressed and sooner or later they will triumph. They will inherit the earth and build the government of God.

(Ayatollah Ruhollah Khomeini, "New Year's Message, 1980"; ed. M. Algar, 1981)

(OPEC), with the aim of preventing outsiders from dictating the value of their principal resource by collectively setting oil prices. Between 1973 and 1975, they quadrupled the cost of a barrel of oil, triggering hardship in the oil-consuming West.

The wealth derived from oil profits has flowed to a variety of projects: construction, health, education, wages—and the personal enrichment of elites and rulers. By the late 1990s, though they eluded the worst dangers of a free marketplace, the Arab states had not succeeded in using the profits from oil to diversify their economies or to establish industrialization.

In nearby Iran, under the autocratic rule of the shahs, modernization and secularization proceeded rapidly at the expense of the exploited and zealously religious masses. By the 1970s, religious leaders denounced the Western moral values that pervaded urbanized and industrialized society. They identified the West as the enemy of traditional Islamic culture—which in Iran was **Shi'ite**, as opposed to the Sunni form of Islam practiced in most of the region—and particularly the United States, a supporter of the shah and a major source of foreign capital and ideas.

The tension between Islamism and modernization erupted in 1979 in a coup that took the West by surprise. The elderly ayatollah (the title of a senior Shi'ite expert in Islamic law) Ruhollah Khomeini (1902–1989) ousted the brutal and corrupt regime of shah Muhammad Reza Pahlevi (1941–1979). Khomeini proceeded to reverse the course of Iranian development, leading a revolution which in November 1979 seized the United States embassy and held sixty-nine officials and workers hostage, most of them for fifteen months. Further, he dissolved the hated SAVAK (the foreign-bankrolled secret police); confiscated United States properties and expelled United States military personnel; restructured schools

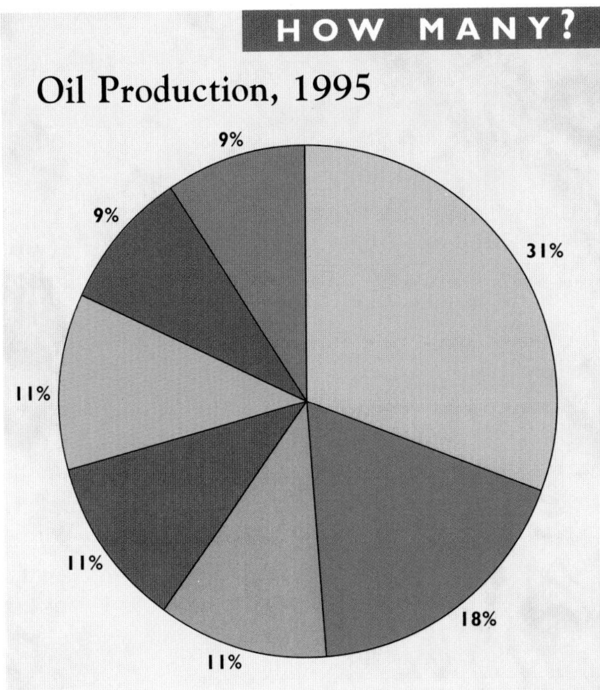

	Barrels Per Day
Middle East	19,102
North America	10,982
Far East & Oceania	7,047
Eastern Europe & former USSR	7,020
Africa	6,935
Western Europe	5,878
Central & South America	5,482
TOTAL	62,446

In 1995, world production of crude oil (still the most important source of fuel) reached 62,446 barrels per day. The chart above shows each region's share of global output, with the Middle East producing 19,102 barrels per day, or thirty-one percent of the total, compared to forty-one percent in 1929. In recent decades, Central and South America, western Europe, Africa, and the Far East and Oceania have significantly increased their share of world production.

Source: New York Times 1998 Almanac, *p. 504.*

and universities, and restored Islamic law. His agents policed morals, censored newspapers and broadcast media, and banned alcohol. Women once again wore the veil in a wholesale repudiation of the cultural values of the West—the homeland of the "Great Satan," the United States. After the death of Khomeini in 1989, deeply mourned by the Iranian people, his regime stayed the course, with recent elections and student resistance pointing toward a more moderate regime in the future.

Meanwhile, Islamic fundamentalism has proved to be a powerful force throughout North Africa and the Middle East, and has been aimed not only at Western interests but also native, secular states. Islamist forces have supported terrorism in Egypt and Algeria, while in 1996 Taliban fundamentalists swept into Afghanistan (previously a state within the Soviet sphere of influence) and transformed political culture and private life.

Not religion but nationalism and opportunism were the motives for the invasion by Iraqi leader Saddam Hussein (1938–) of adjoining Kuwait in 1990. His action provoked air attacks and ground invasion by the United States and allies (the Middle Eastern nations of Syria, Egypt, Saudi Arabia, and some smaller Gulf states as well as Western powers and Japan) in the second Gulf War. A swift victory for the Western forces in a fully televised conflict momentarily stymied Saddam's bid for territorial expansion and Arab leadership. The dictator contented himself with the brutal suppression of Shi'ite Muslim and Kurdish revolts at home.

By the end of the 1990s, the Middle East remains one of the world's most volatile regions. With the exception of Israel, its states are all dictatorships—military, princely, theocratic, oligarchic. Unifying forces include Islamic culture and pan-Arab nationalism—and the common hatred of Israel. But several factors destabilize the region: rivalries among even the Arab nations; the resurgence of Islamic fundamentalism; the abundance of oil, essential to power the industries of the West and Japan; the stockpile of sophisticated weapons supplied during the Cold War era by both superpowers and their allies; the presence of aggrieved minorities (Christian, Druze Muslims, Armenian, Kurd); and competing Israeli and Palestinian aspirations.

Statebuilding in Asia: Democracy, Communism, and Capitalism

The new post-colonial nations of Asia represent a variety of political forms. Some states (such as

The Ayatollah Khomeini: *In 1970, the exiled Ayatollah Ruhollah Khomeini returned from exile in Paris to the Iranian capital of Tehran, where street demonstrators had finally ousted the hated United States-backed dictator Muhammad Reza Pahlavi. Here the seventy-seven-year-old religious leader is greeted enthusiastically by the supporters who would shortly boost him to power.*

Pakistan and Indonesia) are reminiscent of those African nations that turned to autocracy when their colonial rulers left. But the major states of India and China offer contrasting models of democracy and communism, and the powerhouse micro-states of the Pacific Rim, resembling Japan more closely than India or China, are showcases of capitalism.

India and Pakistan India has maintained its democratic institutions, with a brief interruption, from independence in 1947 until the present day. Its first head was the nationalist leader Jawaharlal Nehru (1889–1964), an associate of Gandhi's who ruled for seventeen years. Attempting to remain nonaligned (independent of either of the two Cold War superpowers), he imitated features of both kinds of states in his administration of India—and unfortunately slid, like many of his fellow dictators, toward cronyism, distributing key posts to family members and friends. In 1966, after a two-year interim, Nehru's daughter Indira Gandhi (1917–1984) became prime minister. By 1975, her economic policies (the nationalization of banks and control of private enterprise) aroused opposition, and she was charged with corruption. She responded by suspending the constitution and ruling personally. In elections in 1977, Gandhi and her party were repudiated and democratic institutions restored. She was reelected in 1980, but was assassinated during 1984 riots between Sikhs and Hindus by Sikh members of her own security guard. Gandhi's son Rajiv (1944–1991) succeeded her as prime minister and retained the ministry until 1989. He too was assassinated, in 1991.

India's democracy remained intact through the Nehru–Gandhi years. The security of India's political institutions, however, continues to be menaced by enduring social and cultural problems. These include religious and ethnic conflicts (Hindu–Muslim violence flared up again in 1992); resentment against elites, who dominate government and cultural life; and a runaway rate of population growth that threatens prosperity even as productivity grows in both agricultural and industrial domains.

Neighboring Pakistan, often ruled by military dictators since 1958, has not enjoyed India's democratic experience. East Pakistan, now Bangladesh, broke away in 1971 to form an independent state—one of the world's poorest. It too has been subject to authoritarian government and one-party rule.

Indonesia The great archipelago of Indonesia also fell under authoritarian rule after winning liberation from the Dutch. Its president Sukarno, an architect of Indonesian independence, was still in power in the 1960s as that state slid into the orbit of communist China. In 1965, a United States-backed military coup under General Suharto (1921–) seized power (retaining Sukarno as figurehead until 1967), expelling communist officials and massacring their followers, along with about 750,000 ethnic Chinese. Suharto established an authoritarian regime, joining SEATO (the Southeast Asia Treaty Organization), a regional defense organization with close ties to the United States. He promoted economic modernization and attracted foreign investment, especially Japanese, while he suppressed dissent and restored Islamic law and customs. In 1998, mired in corruption and failed policies, Suharto was deposed by a mass movement led by university students demanding free elections and a democratic constitution.

China In China, the revolution of 1911–1912 brought freedom from emperors and the intrusion of Western powers (see Chapter 23). From 1912 to 1927, the armies of the Nationalist or Guomindang Party, eventually trained and bankrolled by the Soviets, gradually won control of much of eastern and southern China (see Chapter 27). Their commander Chiang Kai-shek (Jiang Jieshi, 1887–1975) fought against local warlords. Meanwhile, Communist leaders (the Chinese Communist Party was founded in 1921) built up their power-base among the peasants in the countryside, whose cooperation they won with land redistributions.

In 1927, Chiang expelled or murdered the communists in the Guomindang, who fled to the interior regions of south China. In 1934, he attacked their stronghold at Jiangxi. Some 100,000 people, including thirty-five women, fled to the north in the heroic "Long March" (more than 6000 miles) of 368 days. Harried by Guomindang pursuers, barely one-tenth survived to establish a secure base at Yan'an in Shaanxi Province. Led by the charismatic Mao Zedong (1893–1976), their forces of some 1 million men cooperated cautiously with Chiang's armies of 3 million when the Japanese invaded in 1937.

The Japanese occupation of the industrial zones of eastern China deprived Chiang of his supporters among the wealthy commercial elites. Following the Japanese surrender in 1945, he resumed his struggle with the communists in a weakened condition. In 1948, with United States air and naval assistance, Chiang rashly attacked strong enemy positions in the north. Communist troops smashed and rolled past him, armed by the Soviets. They swept southward and fanned out over the whole of China. Chiang and his followers escaped to the island of Taiwan, removed by the peace settlement from Japanese domination. Chiang declared himself head of the Chinese state in exile. In 1949, Mao became the leader of the new, Communist People's Republic of China. With fewer than 3 million Communist supporters, he had conquered a nation of 600 million people. After a century of fragmentation (see Chapter 23), China was united under one leader.

From 1949 until his death in 1976, Mao Zedong consolidated the Communist regime and transformed Chinese economy, society, and culture. Fittingly for a nation where peasants constituted eighty percent of the population, Mao's revised Marxist–Leninist principles made agricultural production a priority. Peasant collectives seized great estates, without compensation to the owners—who were "tried" and often executed by peasant tribunals. Productivity mounted during the 1950s. To boost it further, Mao launched the Great Leap Forward in 1958, whose goal was the complete collectivization of agriculture. The countryside was organized into large communes whose leaders directed the peasants' life and work. The experiment failed, undermined by floods, drought, and peasant resistance.

Some 10 million peasants died in the resulting famine. After 1961, the peasants returned to their smaller village collectives and generated modest gains in productivity, which gave them a living standard higher than in recent memory. Production in excess of the government-set quota was theirs to sell in local markets. Enhanced agricultural production promoted industrialization. Heavy industries (metals and machinery) in urban centers were developed first, followed by more diversified factories in rural areas, offering employment alternatives for peasant workers. Organized as government-run enterprises, these industries invited foreign investment and trade.

Mao also undertook a profound reorientation of the traditions of ancient Chinese society and culture. He had the prerevolutionary intellectual and political elites arrested, "reeducated," or silenced. The press was censored, and religious groups, including numerous Christian missions, disbanded. Government officials supervised each village and household, seeking to break down traditions of family loyalty and social deference in favor of revolutionary and collective behavior. The advanced skills needed in a modern society, along with Maoist principles, were taught in schools that all children, male and female, were required to attend. Individuals selected for higher training or leadership positions were identified by party officials and notified of their destinies. Party members themselves—a mere one percent of this presumably egalitarian society—submitted to programs of indoctrination that denigrated prerevolutionary assumptions and values.

In 1966, detecting an ebb of revolutionary energy especially among party leaders, Mao launched the Great Proletarian Cultural Revolution. Its aim was to achieve "permanent revolution"—a state of constant criticism, by the yardstick of Maoist doctrine, of all in authority. In schools and factories, young people formed into revolutionary squads (the "Red Guards") to spread propaganda and denounce those lagging in communist exuberance—targeting senior officials and members of their own families. Thousands of intellectuals and party functionaries were deported to the countryside for "reeducation" as manual laborers. Others were persecuted, imprisoned, tortured, or murdered. Mao's wife Jiang Qing (1914–1991) participated in the hunt, naming "counterrevolutionary" intellectuals. As the purges of the Cultural Revolution subsided, the stunned survivors waited, and the world watched, to see who might succeed the titanic Mao at his death in 1976.

Communism in China

Victors and victims: *Mao Zedong forged a unique form of communism in China based on peasant village organization and Marxist–Leninist principles. The poster shown here depicts youthful followers—with numberless others in the background—ardently studying the "Little Red Book" that contained the founder's philosophy. The poster gives an idealized vision of Mao's Communist regime, however. Maoism also entailed the harsh suppression of landowners and "rich peasants" who were identified as oppressing the other peasants. In the photograph below, a landowner is denounced and sentenced by a peasant tribunal.*

That event brought Mao's now elderly companions of revolutionary days to power, foremost among them Deng Xiaoping (1904–1997). Survivors and in some cases victims of the Cultural Revolution, their first act was to oust from power Mao's widow and her three colleagues (publicly reviled as the "Gang of Four"). Deng proceeded to liberalize economic policy, permitting material incentives, a return to family-centered farming and factory-based (rather than centralized) decision-making. He encouraged foreign investment and trade, and promoted the scientific and technical training arrested by the anti-intellectualism of the Cultural Revolution. Resulting gains in productivity positioned China in the 1990s to participate actively in the modern system of global commerce. The price of this progress has been the continued curtailment of individual rights, backed up by censorship and repression of dissent. Especially controversial was the government's attempt to reverse rates of population growth by limiting family size to one child, with compulsory abortion for late pregnancies.

The children of the victims of the Cultural Revolution, who have no memory of the 1949 triumph, form a new generation. Many resist the regime of aging Communists who replaced Mao in 1976. In 1989, on the seventieth anniversary of the angry May Fourth Movement (see Chapter 25), university students led a massive demonstration in Tiananmen Square, the great central space of the capital of Beijing. The debates and demonstrations went on for weeks, televised worldwide, calling for an end to censorship and for free elections. Dissidents raised in the square a replica of the Statue of Liberty—a monument bestowed upon the United States by the French in 1886 to commemorate common republican traditions. Rechristened the "Goddess of Democracy," this icon made their provocative and dangerous message clear.

Repression was the inevitable response. The People's Liberation Army was dispatched to silence the dissidents. Tanks rolled into Tiananmen Square on June 4, 1989, crushing protestors who did not disperse, firing on unarmed demonstrators, killing about 1300, and arresting thousands more. Student leaders

WITNESSES

Asia: Permanent Revolution in China

Mao Zedong explains the goals of the communist revolution (1949): "You are dictatorial." . . . [T]hat is just what we are. . . . [We must] deprive the reactionaries of the right to speak and let the people alone have that right.

"Who are the people?" At the present stage in China, they are the working class, the peasantry, the urban petty bourgeoisie and the national bourgeoisie. These classes, led by the working class and the Communist party, unite to form their own state and elect their own government: they enforce their dictatorship over the running dogs of imperialism—the landlord class and bureaucrat-bourgeoisie. . . .

"Why must things be done this way?" . . . If things were not done this way, the revolution would fail, the people would suffer, the country would be conquered.

(Mao Zedong, speech, "In Commemoration of the 28th Anniversary of the Communist Party of China," June 30, 1949)

The Central Committee of the Chinese Communist party on the aims of the Great Proletarian Cultural Revolution (1966): The Great Proletarian Cultural Revolution now unfolding is a great revolution that . . . constitutes a new stage in the development of the socialist revolution in our country. . . . The proletariat must . . . meet head-on every challenge of the bourgeoisie in the ideological field and use the new ideas, culture, customs and habits of the proletariat to change the mental outlook of the whole of society. At present, our objective is to struggle against and overthrow those persons in authority who are taking the capitalist road . . . and all other exploiting classes and to transform education, literature and art and all other parts of the superstructure not in correspondence with the socialist economic base, so as to facilitate the consolidation and development of the socialist system.

(From J. Robinson, *The Cultural Revolution in China*, 1969)

were rounded up and jailed without trial; some died from their injuries, some were executed. Witnesses to the repression told the story worldwide by telephone and fax machine; little was told through official channels. Since 1989, the government has released some of the jailed and tortured dissidents, but others are still held as political prisoners, even as China seeks admission to the club of modern nations who observe the rights of their citizens.

Japan and the Pacific Rim Defeated in war, Japan sprang quickly to the first rank in the global marketplace. With Japan occupied by Allied forces from 1945, under the command of United States general Douglas MacArthur (1880–1964), the revered emperor was permitted to remain, but as a figurehead, and only after he had publicly renounced the notion of his divinity. A new constitution emphasized that sovereignty lay with the people and parliament, founded an independent judiciary, and guaranteed civil rights for women as for men. Elementary and secondary education was made compulsory, labor unions made legal, landholding and corporate structures reshaped. The armed forces were disbanded (while the United States was permitted to maintain military bases on Japanese soil). In 1951, a peace treaty was signed and accepted by Japan and the Allies (except for the Soviet Union and China). National sovereignty was restored.

As a democratic, constitutional monarchy, Japan flourished. Its industries, banks, and commercial enterprises resumed their characteristic dynamism. Especially in the areas of electronics and automobile manufacture, Japan's products competed with the finest produced elsewhere, as enormous investment in research and development led to sophisticated technological products. By 1985, Japan was the world's second industrial power, after the United States. Wages were comparable to those in the affluent nations of the West. Until the slowdown that set in with the collapse of the Tokyo stock market in 1989, followed by a banking crisis in the late 1990s, Japan seemed to be on the way to claim first place.

Along with Japan, four other "Pacific Rim" states (so called because of their positioning on the east and southeast Asian coasts facing the Pacific) have emerged as economic powerhouses, albeit under authoritarian rule. Their activity, together with Japan's and China's, has nearly doubled East Asia's share of world production in the last generation, raising the region to parity with the West. From north to south, the first of these is South Korea. After recovering from the trauma of the Korean War in which one-tenth of its people died, it has flourished as a producer of electronic and automotive goods. The second is Taiwan, which has become a major commercial player under the Chinese Nationalist government established in 1949. The third is Hong Kong,

Tiananmen Square, 1989: *More than twenty years after the Cultural Revolution, student-led demonstrations in Beijing's main Tiananmen Square protested against the repressive government that had succeeded Mao's regime. When on June 5, 1989, the government sent armed soldiers and tanks into the Square to end the protest, one lone and anonymous figure planted himself before the approaching column to prevent their advance. The famous photograph has captured a unique moment of modern heroism.*

British-owned from 1898 to 1997 and now reintegrated with China, an island-state that is a center of international finance capital. The fourth is Singapore, fully independent in 1965, another financial capital and exporter of labor-intensive manufactures. Especially in the latter two of these "Four Dragons" (or "Four Tigers") of the Pacific Rim, as they are called, forming a highly concentrated zone of economic endeavor, free enterprise reigns amid the ghosts of empires.

THE LAST IMPERIALIST: THE UNITED STATES ABROAD AND AT HOME

A latecomer to imperialism, the United States was among the last of the Western powers to renounce its dominion over other nations and peoples (see Chapter 19). After the war for independence from Britain (1776–1783), the new United States began a century of expansion across the North American continent, according to the self-defined privilege of **Manifest Destiny**. In that process of nation building, in the view of some observers, it acted as an imperialist power. It expropriated lands from native inhabitants, and annexed other territory from the independent nation of Mexico.

In the twentieth century, certainly, in Latin America, the Philippines, in Vietnam, and even its homeland, the United States has exercised dominion over unconsenting others. In recent years, like its European peers, the United States has repudiated empire and its ambitions.

Good Neighbors: the United States in Latin America

The United States has played a contradictory role in Latin America (a region comprising Mexico and the nations of the Caribbean and South America whose people speak Spanish, Portuguese, or French, all derived from Latin). On the one hand, it has pretended to be a "good neighbor," the role urged by President Franklin Delano Roosevelt (1882–1945) in 1933. On the other hand, it has often intervened in the lives of the Latin American nations—to maintain order, to exclude other interests, to control the course of political events (even by invasion and occupation), to promote the economic interests of its entrepreneurs and investors, acting less like a "good neighbor" than the bully with a "big stick" envisioned by President Theodore Roosevelt (1858–1919).

Until 1898, the United States appeared to be a good, or at least an indifferent, neighbor toward the nations south of its borders. The Monroe Doctrine announced in 1823 declared the integrity of the Americas, warning that the United States would deem hostile any European attempt to recolonize the

Western Hemisphere (see Chapters 19, 23). Except for the episode of the Mexican War, it remained detached over the next decades, engaged in its own expansion and traumatic Civil War (see Chapters 19, 23). After 1898, however, the United States frequently intervened in the political and economic life of the region.

The Spanish–American War of 1898 marked the shift in United States' strategy from indifference to intervention. Throughout the nineteenth century, the British had been the principal foreign presence in the region. British investors funded Latin America's mines and railroads, its manufactures flooded the region's markets, and its navy protected British interests. After 1898, the United States replaced Britain as the region's main foreign investor, developer, exploiter, and master. It made the Caribbean its private lake, and the rest of the region its backyard.

After the 1898 war, Cuba and Puerto Rico, the last two Spanish colonies in the hemisphere, passed to the United States. Puerto Rico was ceded to the United States and, since 1953, has been a "commonwealth" under United States sovereignty. Cuba gained its independence as of 1898 under a constitution drafted according to United States guidelines. In 1901 the "Platt Amendment" gave the United States the right to intervene in Cuban affairs in order to maintain order, and to keep a military force stationed at Cuba's Guantánamo Bay. The new state of Cuba was seen as a protectorate of the United States.

The terms of the Platt Amendment predicted future United States policy toward its Latin American neighbors. The point was reiterated in what is called the "Roosevelt Corollary to the Monroe Doctrine." In 1904 President Theodore Roosevelt defined circumstances under which the United States might intervene in the internal affairs of a Latin American nation: evidence of "chronic wrongdoing," or an "impotence" that threatened civilized norms. Such wrongdoing and ineffectiveness, as defined by the United States, prompted that nation's takeover of Haiti and the Dominican Republic, making protectorates of those Caribbean states.

Panama also became a protectorate. In 1903, the United States encouraged Panama to break away from Colombia. When Panama became established as an independent nation, the United States secured from it on favorable terms (a rental of $250,000 per year, plus a $10 million one-time payment) the land needed to construct a canal across the fifty-mile waist of the isthmus. It obtained a perpetual lease to the ten-mile wide Canal Zone, over which it would exercise sovereign rights. The canal would be a major boon for United States and world shipping, which could span half the globe—from the Asian Pacific, to California, to Caribbean ports, to the European Atlantic ports—without the detour around South America's distant Cape Horn. It was the counterpart of the Suez Canal, built in Egypt by 1869 to link Mediterranean trade by way of the Red Sea with the Persian Gulf and Indian Ocean, avoiding the African Cape of Good Hope (see Chapter 23). Together, the two canals linked the oceans of the world.

When the Canal reached completion in 1914, the economic position of the United States in Latin America had strengthened. Between 1898 and 1914, United States investments in Latin America quintupled. Between 1914 and 1929, they tripled again, while British and other European interests receded. By 1929, almost forty percent of the region's imports came from the United States, which in turn absorbed almost thirty-three percent of its exports. United States businessmen funded copper factories in Chile, oil ventures in Mexico and Venezuela, tin mines in Bolivia, and two-thirds of Cuba's sugar production. Some companies—such as Boston's United Fruit, which built itself a "banana republic" in Central America—had huge territorial holdings.

Mexico The stake that its investors had in Mexico prompted the United States to intervene when revolution broke out in 1910. The Mexican revolution was more than a revolt against the autocratic rule of Porfirio Díaz (1830–1915; see Chapter 19). It was also a broad protest of peasants and workers (mostly Indian and mestizo) against an oppressive social hierarchy topped by a landowner elite and foreign business interests.

Strongman Díaz had welcomed United States capital, and American citizens held Mexican land, mineral resources, and public utilities. Aiming to protect those interests and avoid disruption so close to its borders, the United States supported Mexican leaders it considered "moderate" and opposed those with revolutionary intentions—such as the peasant leader, Emiliano Zapata (1879–1913), and the colorful Francisco "Pancho" Villa (1877–1923), who headed a coalition of rebellious peasants, workers, and cowboys. In 1913, the United States President Woodrow Wilson (1856–1924) permitted arms shipments to the counterrevolutionaries. In 1914, with the unjustified arrest of United States sailors as a pretext, the United States navy occupied the port of Veracruz. In 1916, when Pancho Villa led a raid into New Mexico, Wilson dispatched General John J. Pershing (1860–1948) to capture him (which he failed to do).

WITNESSES

The Americas: a United States Protectorship in Cuba and the Mexican Nationalization of the Oil Industry

The Platt Amendment: United States conditions for the independence of Cuba (1902): I. . . . [T]he government of Cuba shall never enter into any treaty or other compact with any foreign power or powers which will impair or tend to impair the independence of Cuba. . . .
III. . . . [T]he Government of Cuba consents that the United States may exercise the right to intervene for the preservation of Cuban independence, [and for] the maintenance of a government adequate for the protection of life, property, and individual liberty. . . .
VII. . . . [T]o enable the United States to maintain the independence of Cuba, and to protect the people thereof, as well as for its own defense, the government of Cuba will sell or lease to the United States lands necessary for coaling or naval stations at certain specified points to be agreed upon with the President of the United States.

(From C. I. Bevans, ed., *Treaties and Other International Agreements of the United States of America, 1776–1949*, vol. 8, 1971)

Lazlo Cardenas, president of Mexico 1934–1940, defends the nationalization of the oil industry (1938): It has been repeated *ad nauseam* that the oil industry has brought additional capital for the development and progress of the country. This assertion is an exaggeration. For many years, . . . the oil companies have enjoyed great privileges for development and expansion . . .; it is these factors of special privilege, together with the prodigious productivity of the oil deposits granted them by the Nation often against public will and law, that represent almost the total amount of this so-called capital.

Potential wealth of the Nation; miserably underpaid native labor; tax exemptions; economic privileges; governmental tolerance—these are the factors of the boom of the Mexican oil industry.

Let us now examine the social contributions of the companies. In how many of the villages bordering on the oil fields is there a hospital, or school or social center, or a sanitary water supply, or an athletic field . . .?

Who is not aware of the irritating discrimination governing construction of the company camps? Comfort for the foreign personnel; misery, drabness, and insalubrity for the Mexicans. Refrigeration and protection against tropical insects for the former; indifference and neglect, medical service and supplies always grudgingly provided, for the latter; lower wages and harder, more exhausting labor for our people. . . .

(From B. Keane, ed., *Readings in Latin American Civilization, 1942–Present*, 1967)

These inglorious interventions altered nothing. Mexico formed a new government, whose 1917 constitution gravely threatened the interests of native and foreign elites. It seized estates and distributed land to the peasants; established collective organizations and a favorable labor code for workers; introduced limited suffrage (men could vote only for the official party's candidate, and women not until 1954); limited the role of the Roman Catholic Church; and confiscated without compensation all sub-soil rights, including those of United States investors. Neither wholly revolutionary nor truly democratic, the new Mexican government achieved stability and promoted the general welfare, instituting public education, public health programs, and irrigation projects.

The Mexican revolution might have prompted a chain of revolutions in Latin America, as some feared. The Great Depression of the 1930s, which plunged the whole region into desperation (see Chapter 26), also threatened to do so. Dependent on the export of a few commodities, the Latin American economy suffered when demand sank. The elites found themselves without cash, while laborers and peasants grew restive as unemployment and hunger struck. Yet discontent did not lead to revolution. The region's strongmen, or *caudillos*, would not let it do so.

The Rule of *Caudillos* The enduring patterns of Latin American society—the intertwined elite of landowners, military officers, and churchmen—created the *caudillo* (see Chapter 19). The Latin American commodity economy called him into action. The wealth it generated was locked up for the consumption of the rich, and neither flowed to the poor nor stimulated more complex economic enterprises. This system yielded depressingly what some experts have termed "growth without development." It magnified social inequities and necessitated caudillo despots to keep order. From the 1930s through the 1970s, most nations of Latin America have experienced the rule of such bosses. Three may serve as examples: Argentina, Chile, and Brazil.

In Argentina, during the 1930s, dominated by landowning and military elites, the middle and working classes supported the rise to power of the army colonel Juan Perón (1895–1974), elected president in 1946. Backed by his dynamic and beautiful wife, Eva Duarte (1919–1952; "Evita," to her admirers), Perón redistributed wealth, promoted industrialization, and nationalized industries, measures that stimulated uncontrolled inflation and strained national finances. After 1949 the economy worsened, and Perón fled in the face of a military coup in 1955. For the next three decades, Argentina alternated between military and civilian strongmen (among them Perón and his second wife, who returned from 1973 to 1976). The vicious regime in power from 1976 to 1983 murdered more than 10,000 people, and imprisoned, tortured, and "disappeared" many more. The mothers of "missing" adult children, swept up in deadly raids by the military in charge, paraded regularly in the capital city of Buenos Aires to bear witness to their brutality. Since 1983, civilian, democratic governments have taken hold and spurred economic development.

In Brazil, a military coup elevated caudillo Getúlio Vargas (1883–1954), who ruled from 1930 to 1945, and again from 1951 to 1954. Vargas dismissed parliament and canceled elections, while he instituted censorship and a secret police force and encouraged rapid economic modernization. As leftist and liberal movements gained ground in the early 1960s, the military seized power in 1964 in a coup backed by the United States. Protests from the moderate middle class and the social revolutionary left were ruthlessly suppressed. Nevertheless, huge foreign investment spurred an economic miracle, in which industrial exports—rather than coffee and such commodities—generated real wealth for some Brazilians, without alleviating the poverty of others.

Brazil remained under military control from 1964 to 1985. Since then, democratically elected leaders have attempted to restore the free market, while confronting the problems of high inflation and debt. The exploitation of the Amazon River region, resulting in environmental degradation of global consequence, has raised concern, and prompted Brazil to host a United Nations conference on the environment in 1992. During its rocky postwar career, Brazil has industrialized and urbanized, its prosperity threatened still by the great poverty of the masses and rapid population growth.

In Chile, the working and middle classes forged coalition governments from the 1930s through the 1960s. In 1970, a moderate socialist government was elected with reformer Salvador Allende Gossens (1908–1973) as head. Allende's reforms included redistribution of land and the nationalization of banks and industries, especially copper-mining, in which United States entrepreneurs were heavily involved. But these measures triggered uncontrolled inflation and angered the middle classes.

In 1973, supported by the CIA (Central Intelligence Agency) of the United States, a military junta seized control, leaving Allende dead and his government finished. The new regime arrested 13,000 people immediately and, over the next seventeen years, killed some 2000. Under the repressive but modernizing regime of Augusto Pinochet (1915–), which lasted from 1973 until 1989, major industries were restored to the private sector, labor controlled, welfare services reduced, inflation lowered, exports increased, and the economy diversified. In 1989, free elections were reinstated.

The United States often supported the dictators and generals who protected the business interests of its nationals. Yet since the 1930s, it has moved away from the direct exploitation of the Latin American states. Franklin Delano Roosevelt announced the nation's benign intention to respect the rights of other nations in his "Good Neighbor" policy of 1933. In 1948, it helped form the Organization of American States to promote hemisphere solidarity against the threat of communist activity abroad. Postwar presidents Truman, Eisenhower, Kennedy, Johnson, and Nixon supported development in Latin America, as well as programs to bolster its military and police.

Response to Communism In the 1950s and 1960s, the Cold War duel with the Soviet Union (see Chapter 29) added a new dimension to United States involvement in Latin America. Alert to the possibility of communist intervention in what it considered its own backyard, the United States assisted even corrupt and repressive anti-communist governments (see Chapter 29). **Counter-insurgency**—a crusade against leftist revolutionary activity—became a primary objective of United States foreign policy. The United States sent military advisers, and trained and equipped native armies and police forces.

Occasionally United States forces intervened to direct the outcome of Latin American conflicts. In 1954, the United States sent troops to Guatemala to oust a left-leaning, reformist government. In 1979, it intervened in Nicaragua to prop up the conservative regime of Anastasio Somoza (1925–1980). The hostility aroused by this intervention boosted popular support for the Marxist regime of the Sandinistas who then took power. (The Sandinistas were named after the revolutionary hero Cesar Augusto Sandino, murdered in 1934.) Into the 1980s, through covert channels and without congressional approval, United States funds supported the Contra ("opponents") rebels against the Sandinista government. (In 1990, the Nicaraguan people themselves voted the Sandinistas out of power, electing a centrist government under Violeta Chamorro, b. 1929.) As recently as 1983, 1989, and 1993, United States troops intervened in the nations of Grenada, Panama, and Haiti.

Since 1960, the Latin American nation of greatest concern for United States policymakers has been Cuba, just ninety miles offshore of Florida. The United States managed the Cuban government during the early years of its nominal independence. In 1933, the strongman Fulgencio Batista (1901–1973) took over the government with United States support. For nearly thirty years, backed by the elites and the military, he ran a corrupt administration deeply implicated with organized crime interests, which neglected and betrayed the island's impoverished people.

In 1959, the revolutionary Fidel Castro (1927–) headed guerrilla forces that ousted Batista and his supporters; Cuba's wealthy and professional elites fled. Castro installed a socialist regime that redistributed land, nationalized industries, and established health services and universal education for the people Batista had despised. The local Communist party embraced Castro's government, while the Soviet Union supplied Cuba with arms and loans, and purchased its sugar. Tiny Cuba became a major center of world communism.

The displacement of a tame dictatorship by a Communist state in its own Caribbean lake alarmed United States officials. Cautious diplomacy broke down in 1961. The United States had backed an unsuccessful invasion by Cuban exiles at the Bay of Pigs. In response, the Soviets planted nuclear missiles on the island, which could easily reach the United States. In the tensest moment of his brief presidency, John F. Kennedy (1917–1963) "did not blink," as an adviser put it. His refusal to be intimidated forced the Soviets to back down. The United States agreed to plan no further invasions of Cuba.

The crisis past, relations between Cuba and the United States remained volatile, exacerbated by the activism of Cuban exiles now resident in the United States. By the 1990s, with the collapse of Soviet communism (see Chapter 29), together with the aging of the charismatic Castro, those relations eased greatly.

Even in the early 1960s, at the zenith of the Cuban challenge, communism did not spread, as many had feared, to other Latin American nations. The containment of communism was due in part to United States-sponsored repression; communism also failed because Latin American leaders made earnest efforts to reorient the economy so as to benefit the masses as well as the elites. They built new industries, adopted modern technologies, sought a broader spectrum of foreign investment, and diversified production. They accomplished the long-needed breakthrough, escaping the region's narrow dependence on a few export commodities. In addition, without taking the path of Cuban communism, they nationalized some economic functions, and instituted health and welfare programs.

By the 1980s, caudillism began to yield to democracy. A free electorate chose governments in Argentina, Brazil, Mexico, Nicaragua, and Paraguay. Traces of older social hierarchies, concentrations of land ownership in elite circles, militarism, ethnic tensions, and abusive labor relationships persist in the region. But these appear to be yielding gradually to democratization and economic modernization. Whether Latin America's economic development can keep pace with its unrestrained population growth remains an open question.

The nationalist revolutions of the early 1800s promised an end to colonialism. That goal may at last have been accomplished at the close of the twentieth century. With the transfer of the Canal Zone to the nation of Panama in 1978 and the emancipation of a few Caribbean islands and mainland enclaves still in French, British, or Dutch hands, Latin America has crystallized as a region of largely independent, self-governing states. The United States, the last imperialist in the region, by its economic, political, and military interventions sometimes promoted, sometimes impeded, but in the end supports that achievement—as a good neighbor might.

The Domino Game: the United States in Asia

The United States might view the Caribbean as its lake, and the Americas as the paired continents of its hemisphere. But Asia was far away. Although the United States sought commercial access it had initially no large ambitions in that region. Yet the ideological struggles of the Cold War era defined Asia as a testing ground. The states of Asia were like dominoes, in the simile conceived in 1954 by United States president Dwight D. Eisenhower (1890–1969). If one

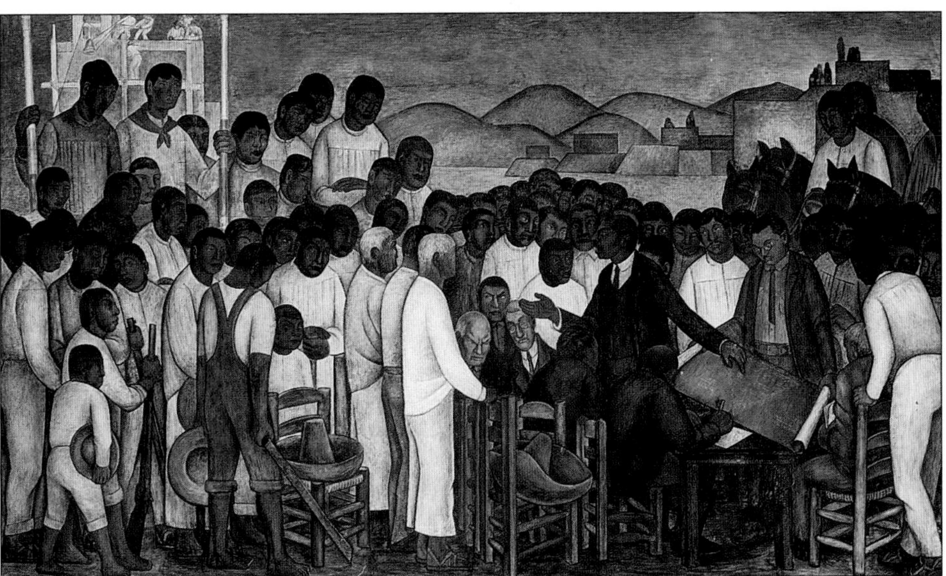

Righting Wrongs in Latin America

***Diego Rivera,* Dividing the Land:** *By 1900, 400 years of colonial exploitation left a legacy of poverty for the Latin American descendants of the natives, slaves, and European immigrants. The Mexican revolution that began in 1910 achieved some equalization of economic opportunity for that nation's citizens. In this fresco by Mexican artist Diego Rivera, government officials redistribute to peasants lands seized from wealthy owners.* (Universidad Autonoma Chapingo, Mexico)

Castro's triumph: *In Cuba in 1959, the guerrilla forces of Fidel Castro drove out the corrupt government that had mortgaged the welfare of the people to American sugar companies. This photograph shows a triumphant Castro embracing one of his supporters as he sweeps through Cuba to take power.*

fell to the alien destiny of communism, all would fall. To avert that outcome, the United States entered, and lost, the domino game.

The United States looked to Asia beginning in the 1850s, as it raced to share in the wealth that international commerce brought the old imperialists of Europe. Its goal, expressed in the "open door" policy enunciated in 1899, was commercial access to China, Japan, and other rich markets (see Chapter 23). Commercial activity, however, led to territorial acquisitions. To support its fleet in an age of steam power, the United States needed fueling stations and naval bases. It began to gather up Pacific islands. From 1851, the United States had a protectorate over Hawaii, acquiring the rights for a naval base at Pearl Harbor by 1887 and annexing the whole area in 1898. It also obtained rights to Midway (1867), Wake Island (1898), and American Samoa (1899). In 1898, it acquired the island of Guam and the archipelago of the Philippines.

The Philippines The Philippines, held by the United States from 1898 to 1946, was the United States' first major non-continental territorial acquisition. The United States had claimed it with difficulty, overcoming ardent native resistance and opposition at home. During the 1930s, it negotiated with Filipino leaders a schedule for independence. In 1941, the Japanese invaded, causing the evacuation of the United States naval garrison and abandoning the inhabitants to a harsh occupation.

In 1946, the Philippines became independent according to schedule (although United States military bases remained until 1992). A landowning elite continued to exploit impoverished peasantry as parliamentary government gave way to increasingly despotic rule after 1965, with the election of Ferdinand Marcos (1917–1989). Marcos' regime became more and more corrupt and violent. Conservative elites supported his suppression of

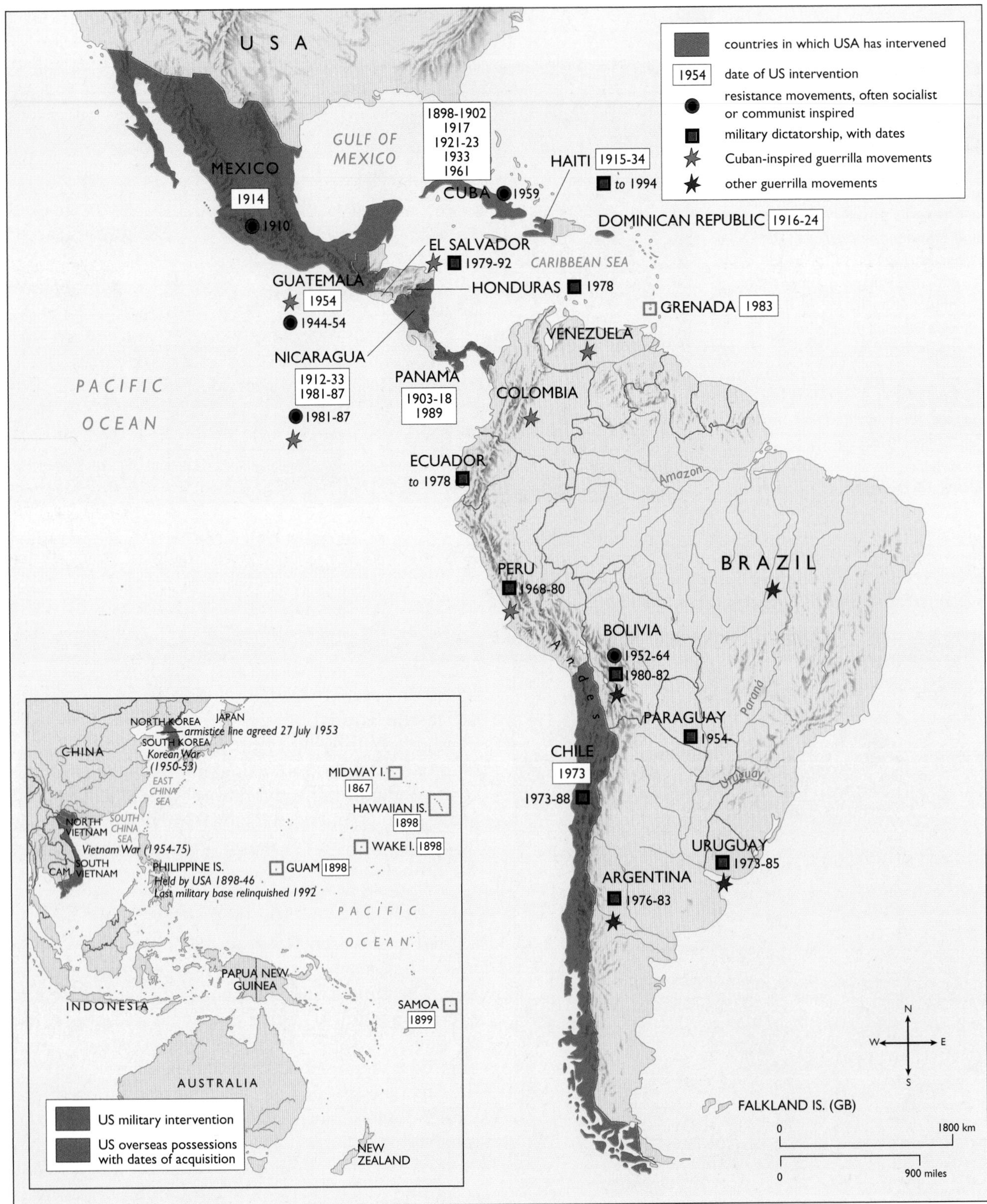

Map 28.3 United States Intervention in Latin America and Asia: *The imperialist ventures of the United States beyond the borders of North America began in 1898, with a series of interventions in Latin America. During the same period, as a result of their own internal development or, in some cases, provoked by the United States presence, the nations of Latin America seesawed between governments of the right and left, and many guerrilla movements took form in resistance to established powers. These complex political changes are indicated in simplified form above. In the Pacific, meanwhile, the United States acquired several possessions between 1867 and 1899, and intervened militarily in Korea (1950–1953) and Vietnam (1954–1975), as shown in the inset map.*

communist and Islamic opposition even as, in 1983, 1 million Filipinos defiantly marched in the funeral procession of his assassinated opponent Benigno Aquino. In 1986, Benigno's widow, Corazon Aquino (1933–), successfully challenged Marcos' reelection, which had been marred by irregularities. Marcos and his hated wife Imelda fled the country whose unsteady economic condition wad due in part to their depredations. Many social and economic problems remain unresolved, but the Philippines have attained democratic government under Aquino and her successors.

Korea The postwar involvement of the United States in Korea and Vietnam developed in response to the perceived threat of communism, which had expanded into eastern Europe and Asia (see Chapter 29). Policymakers feared that communism threatened Africa and the Americas as well.

The partition of Korea at the thirty-eighth parallel of latitude at the end of World War II had positioned two hostile regimes face to face: the communist People's Republic of Korea in the north; and the Republic of Korea in the south. The Korean War broke out suddenly in 1950 when 100,000 northern troops invaded the south and seized the capital Seoul. The North Korean leader, trained and installed by the Soviets, had likely acted at Stalin's prompting. The United States, with a large occupation force based in Japan (see above), saw the invasion as an act of communist aggression that, if not contained, could spread throughout east Asia. It called upon other nations of the recently-constituted United Nations (see Chapter 29) to join in the defense of South Korea. Although a joint effort, the commander-in-chief was the American Douglas MacArthur, and most of the troops came from the United States.

The United Nations forces repulsed the North Korean advance and moved northward toward the Chinese border. About 200,000 Chinese troops swept in from adjacent Manchuria, repelled MacArthur's forces, and, early in 1951, took Seoul a second time. MacArthur freed Seoul and proposed extending the war to China, his aggressive approach leading to his dismissal by President Truman. Peace talks began in the summer of 1951, concluding only in 1953. A new boundary was drawn between south and north, with a demilitarized zone at the crucial border.

Although the United States had not fought alone in Korea, the war was in many ways an American war, not least because United States forces suffered 34,000 fatalities. In addition, the United States had instigated the military response to what might have remained a civil war, setting a precedent for intervention in the internal affairs of other Asian nations. And the United States had declared its determination to battle communist advance in Asia.

Vietnam The Korean war prefigured the Vietnam war, a conflict that occupied American attention for an entire generation. Part of the peninsula of Indochina, Vietnam had often suffered invasion—by the Chinese for centuries, and more recently by the French, who had seized almost all of Indochina by 1897 (see Chapters 8, 23). The French occupation triggered a nationalist movement, led by Ho Chi Minh (1890–1969) after World War I. In 1919, appealing to the principle of self-determination, Ho attempted and failed to persuade the drafters of the Paris treaties to free Vietnam as it had freed the subject nationalities of Europe (see Chapter 25). When they did not, he turned to communism, whose Comintern (see Chapter 27) offered friendly support to anti-colonial movements. In Moscow, Ho learned how to organize an insurgent struggle. In 1930, he formed the Indochinese Communist Party.

When the Japanese took over Indochina from the Vichy French during World War II, Ho formed the multi-party League for the Independence of Vietnam—the Viet Minh. In the meantime, nationalist fighters in Vietnam waged guerrilla war against the Japanese. Repatriated at war's end, Ho promulgated the Vietnamese Declaration of Independence, echoing principles drawn from the American Declaration and other classic sources of Western political thought. That document proclaimed the establishment of the Democratic Republic of Vietnam, with its capital at Hanoi.

Independence was not so easily won, however. Even as the Japanese evacuated, the British occupation forces yielded Vietnam to the French, who returned to reclaim their colonial rights. Vietnamese nationalists now fought the French in a prolonged struggle that ended only in 1954, with the obliteration of a French garrison at Dien Bien Phu, and the humiliation of that nation. Despite the sacrifice of tens of thousands of lives, the French had failed to quell the resistance of a people intent on independence, skilled in guerrilla tactics, and supported by the Chinese and the Soviets.

At first, the United States was also inclined to support Vietnamese independence. It reversed that policy and supported the French instead when the Korean War broke out in 1950. By 1954, the United States was paying seventy-eight percent of the costs of French operations in Vietnam. When the French pulled out, the United States went in.

The United States had no historic mission in Vietnam. What drove it to become involved in suppressing the Vietnamese struggle for independence? Why did a nation that had itself originated in a war for independence muster its resources to suppress another engaged in the same attempt?

The critical factor was the presence of communism. The Soviet Union's aims were patently expansionist. In 1949, moreover, a communist government had established itself in China, on Vietnam's border. In 1950, a communist-inspired invasion of South Korea had dragged the United States into war. In 1954, president Eisenhower proposed his domino theory. Vietnam appeared to be the last bulwark against a communist Asia. The line must be drawn in Vietnam.

The 1954 Geneva Accords did not create an independent Vietnam, although Ho Chi Minh had badly beaten the French. It partitioned the nation at the seventeenth parallel of latitude, giving Ho the north, now communist. The last of the Accords, the Final Declaration, provided for elections throughout the country, north and south, in 1956. Without interference, the likely outcome in 1956 would have been a united Vietnam, under communist leadership. To forestall this event, the United States refused to sign the Final Declaration and assisted Ngo Dinh Diem (1901–1963) in his bid for power in the south.

Diem's actions triggered what came to be known as the Vietnam War. A French-educated Roman Catholic in a nation with a Buddhist majority, the corrupt autocrat Diem suppressed both political and religious opposition. He refused to hold the elections mandated by the Geneva settlement. That decision meant war. Ho Chi Minh's army mobilized. In 1960, thousands of pro-communist nationalists joined in the National Liberation Front to oppose Diem's autocratic government from within South Vietnam. They formed a guerrilla army supplied and guided from the north. These insurgents Diem contemptuously called the "Viet Cong" (Vietnamese communists). The combined activity of the North Vietnamese regular soldiers with the southern Viet Cong, invisible within the southern population, frustrated all attempts to snatch the south from Ho's communist north.

Diem was a disappointment. Disgusted by his corruption, inefficiency, and intolerance—he ordered the destruction of Buddhist temples, among other atrocities—the United States withdrew support in 1963. That action encouraged a group of generals to assassinate Diem and seize power. A stream of generals ruled in turn in the south. The regime remained throughout an unsavory ally for the United States, difficult to defend to the public at home, and incapable of managing the war effort unassisted.

From 1954 to 1968, under presidents Eisenhower, Kennedy, and Johnson, the United States escalated its involvement in Vietnam. In 1954, 275 Americans were advising the South Vietnamese army. By 1960, that figure had more than doubled to 685; by the end of 1961, it had risen to 2600; and by the time of President Kennedy's assassination in 1963, to 16,500. Meanwhile, the United States sent military aid rising to hundreds of millions of dollars annually. In 1965, the United States launched bombing raids in North Vietnam, and, for the first time, sent ground troops to the south—and the die was cast. By the end of 1965, there were 184,000 American soldiers in Vietnam; by 1966, 385,000; by early 1969, some 542,000. Now the United States was not merely an adviser to what it saw as the better side in a civil war. It was a combatant in an alien struggle on the other side of the globe.

As the numbers of ground forces mounted, Americans at home grew restive, then critical, then angry (see Chapter 29). A "credibility gap" grew wider as officials reported gains—measured in the gruesome daily "body count" of dead enemies, many of them civilian—while the Viet Cong and North Vietnamese regulars grew more numerous and more determined. Their stunning Tet offensive of 1968, launched on a sacred Vietnamese holiday, showed that resistance was still powerful and exposed the failure of United States officials to comprehend the depth of nationalist determination.

After 1968, the United States sought to find an exit from the Vietnam quagmire. President Johnson (1908–1973) signaled his awareness of the failure of his policies in Vietnam by withdrawing from the 1968 election. The new president Richard M. Nixon (1913–1994) promised to secure "peace with honor." By a policy of "Vietnamization," he gradually withdrew United States troops (only 25,000 remained at end 1972) and transferred military responsibilities to regular South Vietnamese forces. To cover the withdrawal, he intensified bombing in the north and in the contiguous states of Laos and Cambodia, thereby drawn into the maelstrom of the war. In 1973, Nixon accomplished the final withdrawal of United States troops—withdrawal, without honor or victory.

That withdrawal had the effect of abandoning the South Vietnamese to sure defeat. The 1973 settlement did not bring peace. By 1975, the North Vietnamese army had taken the southern capital of Saigon, and established dominion over a united Vietnam—an outcome for which Ho Chi Minh struggled for half a century before he died in 1969, just

Give Peace a Chance

America in Vietnam: *American involvement in Vietnam dragged on fruitlessly, leading the superpower to employ tactics that discredited the aggressor without damaging the defender. In this famous photograph from June 8, 1972 (right) that aroused horror worldwide (though the attack was accidental), young children flee from an American napalm bombing. An American serviceman showed his disillusionment with the Vietnam war by painting a peace symbol, flanked by the words "love" and "peace," on the surface of a helicopter landing pad, to be viewed by approaching aircraft (below right).*

short of its fulfillment. Drawn into the conflict, Laos and Cambodia also fell to native communist movements, of which the Cambodian Khmer Rouge undertook an unprecidently vicious campaign against its own citizenry (see Chapter 29). Twenty years after the French withdrawal, a generation after the close of World War II, after nearly 58,000 American deaths and millions of Vietnamese deaths, after the rupture of confidence at home and the generation of implacable hostility abroad, Indochina (except for Thailand and Myanmar) was communist.

After Vietnam, the United States redefined its policy in Asia. Henceforth, it would seek commercial agreements, support friendly states, and promote a human rights agenda in the region. The domino game was over. The last imperialist limped home.

The Color Line: Conflict at Home

At home, the citizens and leaders of the United States faced the moral and social problems left by an earlier imperialist era. In pursuit of their Manifest Destiny, the European descendants of the first settlers, and the European immigrants who came in waves to join them, grabbed the land that stretched between the Atlantic and Pacific coasts. They seized it from peoples—Amerindian natives and Hispanic settlers of what had been Mexican territory—who became dispossessed of land and heritage alike. At the same time, the descendants of former slaves whose labor had sustained the economy of the old south remained still, as the twentieth century opened, unintegrated into society and barred from the means of progress.

A Visible Difference Forgotten amid abundance, these groups shared one visible feature—their skin was ruddy, brown, or black. The exclusion of people of color from wealth and power in the world's wealthiest and most powerful nation became the foremost social issue of the century. Democratic principles and habits of compassion alike faltered when they approached the color line.

By 1900, the Amerindian tribes of the United States had all been deprived of their lands and freedom (see Chapter 19). Some had been moved to territories set aside for the purpose; others resisted, and were forcibly driven into those **reservations**. They were wrested from the environment and the economy that had shaped their religion, language, and customs, and that were essential to their self-definition. In alien settings, they languished. Even

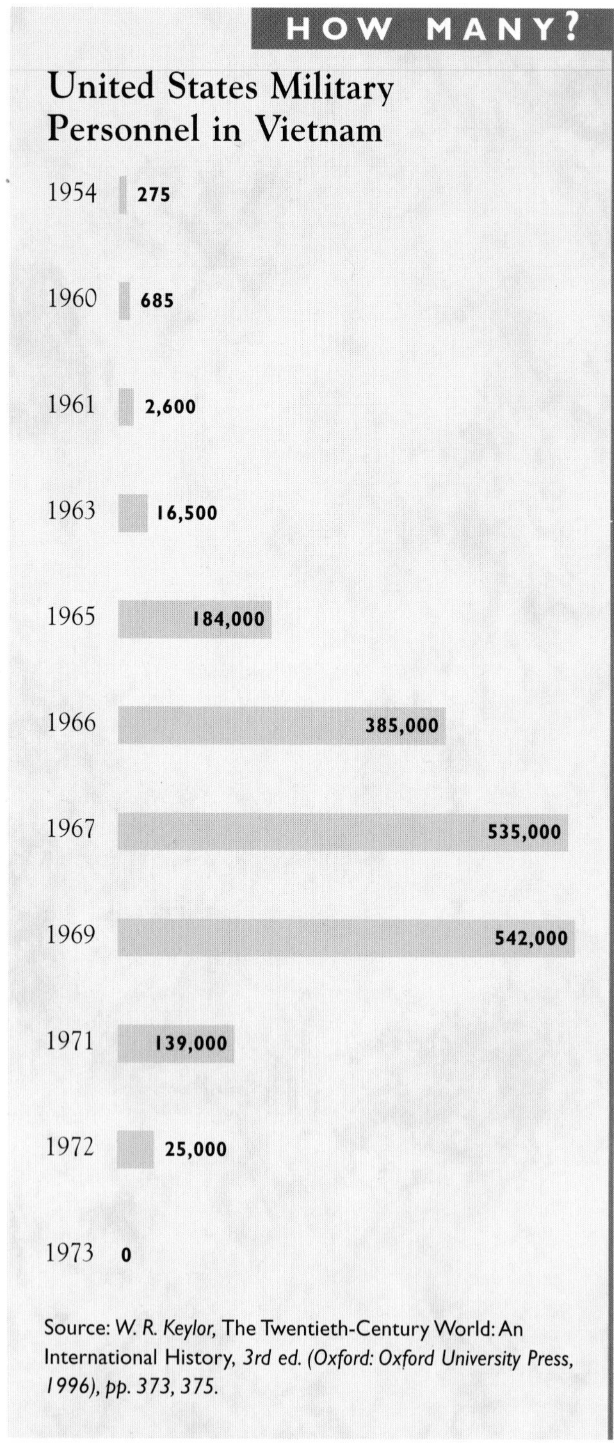

Source: *W. R. Keylor,* The Twentieth-Century World: An International History, *3rd ed. (Oxford: Oxford University Press, 1996), pp. 373, 375.*

when government programs offered opportunities for social and economic advancement, few individuals or tribes took advantage of them.

In the southwestern region of the United States, settlers wrested land from ranchers and planters of Mexican descent. Landless Mexican workers became subjects of the Anglophone United States. These were followed by waves of Mexican immigrants, for whom low-paid work in the United States offered a better opportunity than their homeland. Although some Mexicans assimilated into United States society, most remained a caste apart. Living in self-defined communities, or *barrios*, where they could practice their own religion and customs, they were isolated from most opportunities for education and progress. In systems of public education, their children tended to perform poorly, as poverty and cultural difference interfered with learning. The prejudice exhibited by bureaucrats, officials, and employers further disadvantaged Hispanic citizens and immigrants.

Most isolated of all the groups on the far side of the color line were those of African descent who carried as burdens not only their blackness but the terrible legacy of slavery (see Chapter 19). For two generations after the end of the Civil War, most continued to live in the south among the descendants of their former masters. The white population cooperated in the exclusion of blacks from the vote, from schooling, from housing, from economic opportunity. The Black Codes, laws passed by many states in the post-Civil War era, gave way to "Jim Crow" laws that limited the access of African Americans to housing, transportation, schooling, recreation, a lengthy list of possible avenues to advancement or happiness.

The condition of African Americans worsened as the twentieth century opened. The Supreme Court decision in the case of Plessy v. Ferguson (1896), introducing the principle of "separate but equal," permitted the relegation of African Americans to separate institutions—schools, houses, public facilities—as long as those institutions were "equal" (which they were not). Blacks attended different schools, ate in different restaurants, drank from different water fountains, and sat in different sections of public buses.

Southern society prevented any deviation from these norms by a strategy of terror. The Ku Klux Klan, formed soon after the Civil War and reconstituted in 1915, was a loose network of secret societies that championed the white man's vision of the south. Disguised in fear-inspiring white robes and hoods, Klansmen terrorized blacks and their white supporters, leaving behind them as a sign of their implacable hostility a burning wooden cross. Klansmen often joined in lynchings, the execution by hanging (generally without trial) of those deemed guilty of crimes or hated without reason. In the 1880s, these had mounted to a high of over one hundred per year. They subsided, then returned, tripling in the key Depression year 1932–1933.

Despite terror, hatred, and discrimination, African Americans built their own neighborhoods and communities in the homeland they had never chosen. Christianized under slavery, they formed their own black churches (mostly Baptist and Methodist) headed by black pastors, who became the acknowledged leaders of African American communities. With the impediments to legal marriage and property ownership that slavery imposed now gone, they formed strong families and worked to secure land and housing, although they were more often forced into tenancy and sharecropping.

Voices of Protest African American leaders had different visions of how best to promote their people. Scholars often note the classic opposition between two late nineteenth-century figures: Booker T. Washington (1856–1915), a freed slave; and William E. B. du Bois (1868–1963), the mixed descendent of Africans and Europeans, raised and educated in the north. Rising from the mine pits where he worked as a child immediately after emancipation, Washington became an educator, a reformer, and a public advocate on behalf of all African Americans and through his own efforts and intelligence. He urged upon his own community the values of hard work, especially in industrial tasks that would earn laborers respect and decent wages. He was cautiously non-revolutionary in his rhetoric, seeking to persuade white listeners of the diligence and benevolence of blacks rather than to frighten them with unsettling demands.

Du Bois took a different approach. A brilliant theorist and writer, he received a doctoral degree from Harvard (1895) and subsequently taught at Atlanta University in Georgia. Despite his mainstream credentials, Du Bois was no academic onlooker. He criticized Washington for kowtowing to white audiences and underestimating black competency. Calling on the "talented tenth" of black leaders to organize for political action, he formed the Niagara Movement in 1905, which in 1909, inspired the foundation of the National Association for the Advancement of Colored People (the NAACP), still a major force in the advocacy of equal rights for blacks. In 1961, concluding that American society would never truly welcome its black citizens, Du Bois joined the Communist Party, and moved to Ghana, in Africa, where he died in 1963. In such works as *The Souls of Black Folk* (1903) Du Bois argued for the radical emancipation of African Americans from deep-seated attitudes that he considered profoundly racist. In that work he diagnosed what he saw as the incapacity of white Americans to cross or erase the "color line," which he believed to be the defining issue of the twentieth century.

The color line grew bolder in the 1920s and 1930s when blacks emigrated in large numbers from the south to northern cities. As opportunities for unskilled workers shrank in the south (and most blacks were unskilled because segregation patterns barred them from high-quality schooling and training), they hoped to work in northern factories, on the railroads, and in the streets. Transplanted, they found that the north was also segregated. Denied access to the better schools and neighborhoods, they formed their own neighborhoods and church-centered communities. In isolated neighborhoods called ghettoes, African Americans led a life apart from other Americans—separate but not equal.

It was to these African Americans that Marcus Garvey (1887–1940) spoke most passionately. A Jamaica-born activist, Garvey lived in the United States from 1916 to 1927. Pointing to the long record of European mistreatment of non-Europeans, Garvey promoted rebellion and secession. He urged blacks "back to Africa," to build that continent from which their ancestors had been ripped centuries before. Convicted in 1925 of mail fraud in the management of his Black Star steamship line (founded to carry his followers back to Africa), Garvey was deported from the United States in 1927.

Among those who heard the voices of African American leaders calling for a new pride in the face of white dominance were the artists, performers, and writers of the Harlem Renaissance. The lights blazed nightly on New York City's Lenox Avenue and 135th Street where well-dressed blacks and radically chic whites visited clubs and theaters and conversed heatedly on the streets. Soon the voices were silenced by the Depression, which hurt black Americans even more than whites. Now movement leaders gathered into organizations such as the NAACP. The 1930s saw the political consciousness of the larger African American community broaden, as though in preparation for the vital struggles ahead.

The Harlem Renaissance was in full swing and the Great Depression had not yet stalled black progress when the greatest of African American leaders, Martin Luther King, Jr. (1929–1968), was born. A minister and a minister's son, the recipient of a doctoral degree in theology, King was a worthy successor to Washington and du Bois. He combined Washington's understanding of the need to strive for advancement within a predominantly white society, with du Bois' deeper critique of that society's unremitting hostility to black success.

The Civil Rights Movement King began by protesting unjust barriers—the segregation of public transportation and public education. He became the prophet of the Civil Rights movement, which grew from resistance to bus segregation by a lone black woman, Rosa Parks (1913–), in 1955, to the high tide of 1964, when the Civil Rights Act was signed into law, barring discrimination by color in public facilities or in employment. More than any other single figure, he achieved widespread acknowledgment of the right—if not yet the reality—of black Americans to live, learn, and work as freely as their white counterparts. It may have been his great success that prompted an assassin to shoot King in 1968, when he was not yet forty and at the zenith of his career.

Du Bois' NAACP had prepared the way during the 1930s and 1940s for the drive against segregation that King led in the 1950s. Its team of lawyers brought cases that exposed segregationist practices. Chief counsel of the NAACP legal team from 1940 to 1961 was attorney Thurgood Marshall (1908–1993), appointed in 1967 the first African American justice of the Supreme Court. In 1954, the NAACP won a landmark judgment that effectively overturned Plessy v. Ferguson. In Brown v. Board of Education of Topeka, the Supreme Court ordered that "separate" schools were by nature unequal and discriminatory against black citizens. The next year, it ordered the twenty-one states that had segregated school systems to desegregate "with all deliberate speed." That mammoth victory opened the floodgates of reform.

In 1955, King led the boycott of the bus system of Montgomery, Alabama, that had been triggered by the arrest of Rosa Parks. In 1956, the Supreme Court vindicated that protest, declaring the segregation

WITNESSES

The Americas: Racial Equality and Racial Separatism in the United States

Martin Luther King, Jr.: a letter from Birmingham Jail (1963): My Dear Fellow Clergymen:

... I think I should indicate why I am here in Birmingham.... I am in Birmingham because injustice is here....

You deplore the demonstrations taking place in Birmingham.... It is unfortunate that demonstrations are taking place ... but it is even more unfortunate that the city's white power structure left the Negro community with no alternative.

We [Black Americans] have been waiting for more than 340 years for our constitutional and God-given rights. The nations of Asia and Africa are moving with jetlike speed toward gaining political independence, but we still creep at horse-and-buggy pace toward gaining a cup of coffee at a lunch counter.

(Martin Luther King, letter from Birmingham Jail, April 16, 1963; eds. A. P. Blaustein and R. L. Zangrando, 1968)

Marcus Garvey, leader and founder of the Universal Negro Improvement Association, stresses the need for racial purity and separateness (1925): ... [T]he other Negro movements in America ... sought to teach the Negro to aspire to social equality with the whites, meaning thereby the right to intermarry and fraternize in every social way. This has been the source of much trouble.... The organization of the Universal Negro Improvement Association on the other hand believes in and teaches the pride and purity of race. We believe that the white race should uphold its racial pride and perpetuate itself and that the black race should do likewise. We believe that there is room enough in the world for the various race groups to grow and develop by themselves without seeking to destroy the Creator's plan by the constant introduction of mongrel types.

(From A. Jacques-Garvey, ed., *Philosophy and Opinions of Marcus Garvey*, 1925; eds. A. P. Blaustein and R. L. Zangrando, 1968)

The US Supreme Court decision in the case Brown v. Board of Education of Topeka, overturning the "separate but equal" principle established by Plessy v. Ferguson (1896), orders school integration "with all deliberate speed" (1954): Today, education is perhaps the most important function of state and local governments. Compulsory school attendance laws and the great expenditures for education both demonstrate our recognition of the importance of education to our democratic society.... In these days, it is doubtful that any child may reasonably be expected to succeed in life if he is denied the opportunity of an education. Such an opportunity ... is a right which must be made available to all on equal terms.

We come then to the question presented: Does segregation of children in the public schools solely on the basis of race, even though the physical facilities and other "tangible" factors may be equal, deprive the children of the minority group of equal educational opportunities? We believe that it does.

(Brown v. Board of Education of Topeka, 347 US 483–496, 1954)

WINDOWS ON

Civil Rights for African Americans

As much as any colonized people abroad, Americans of African descent faced a long struggle for civil rights and guarantee of social and economic justice. Largely through the efforts of Martin Luther King, Jr.—shown here in August 1963 outside the White House (left)—a landmark Civil Rights Act was signed in 1964. Other battles remained. The fiercely committed Malcolm X is seen here summoning his followers to action (below right). He holds aloft a newspaper with the headline "Our Freedom Can't Wait!" The unfinished nature of the quest for equality is vividly illustrated in another photograph (below left), where striking Memphis (Tennessee) sanitation workers, most African American, wearing placards saying "I am a man," parade in front of a row of National Guardsmen with rifles ready and bayonets affixed.

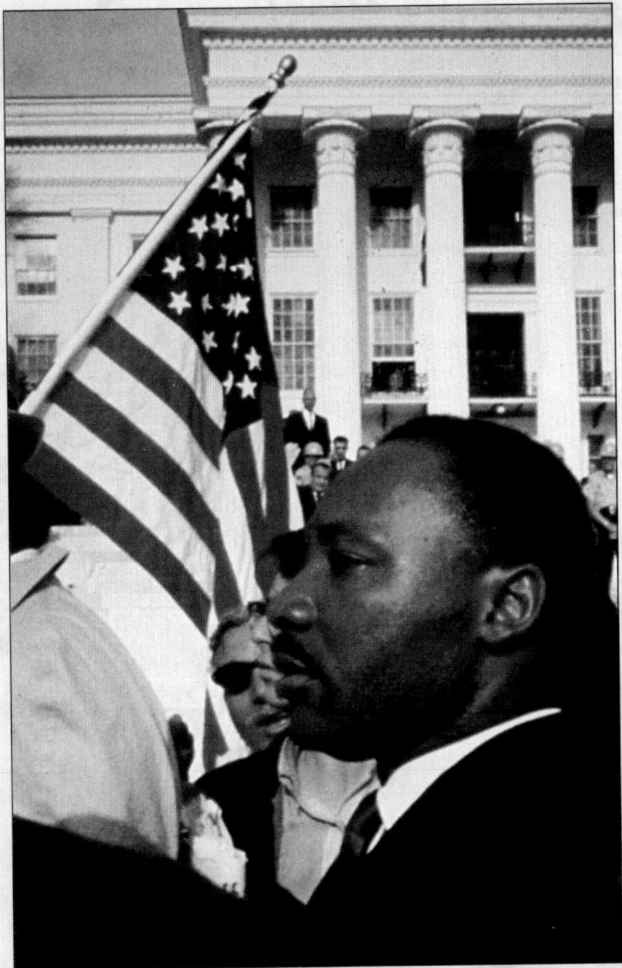

Martin Luther King, Jr., August 1963

Memphis sanitation workers' strike, March 1968

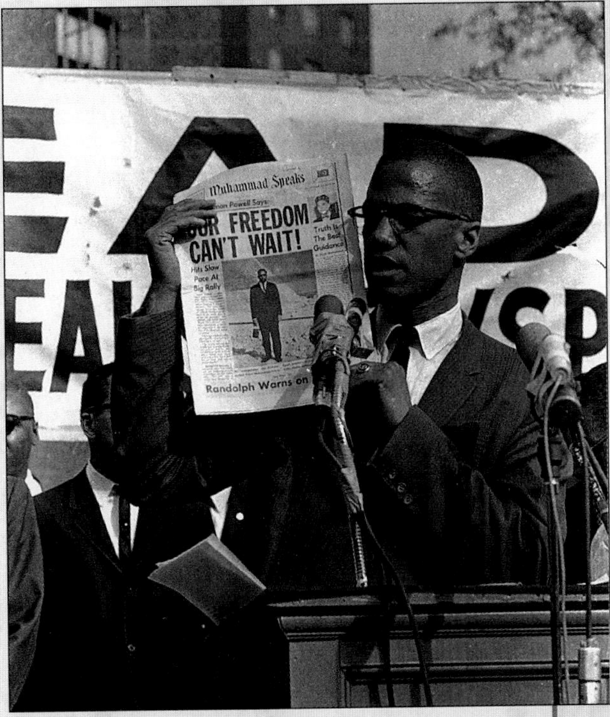

Malcolm X, New York, 1963

unconstitutional. The next year, with other leaders King worked to secure the enrollment of nine black students in the main white high school in Little Rock, Arkansas. A reluctant President Eisenhower sent federal troops to handle the crisis, which was resolved only in 1959.

These victories won, King and other civil rights leaders broadened their agenda. Through the SCLC (Southern Christian Leadership Conference), King urged a program of nonviolent resistance, based in part on the methods of Mohandas Gandhi. With the organizations CORE (Congress of Racial Equality) and SNCC (Student Nonviolent Coordinating Committee), activists confronted discrimination through nonviolent resistance. A dynamic coalition of young black southern activists, supported by northern white university students, won battles of conscience in lunch counters, waiting rooms, and polling booths across the south.

These resisters found violence turned against them, as segregationists with policemen and firemen fought against peaceful demonstrators. The rising tide of conflict compelled President John F. Kennedy to introduce a strong proposal for civil rights legislation. When King and 250,000 people came to Washington in August 1963, to proclaim their goal of racial justice, it was already in the works. By summer 1964, the Civil Rights bill was law—although Kennedy did not live to see its passage. The Voting Rights Act, passed the following year, added guarantees of access to the polls.

But these legislative victories seemed almost too late as the volume of protest and threshold of violence rose. In the later 1960s, the militant Black Power movement rejected nonviolence and targeted the underlying racism that denied African Americans, even when accorded legal protections, their rights and their dignity. Riots broke out sporadically in urban centers from 1965 to 1967. The Black Muslim movement advocated black separatism. The courageous and conscientious leader Malcolm X (1925–1965), a survivor of ghetto and prison cell, encouraged blacks to ceaseless struggle against white oppression, later accepting the possibility of racial integration. His former Black Muslim colleagues gunned him down in 1965. A lone gunman shot Martin Luther King in 1968.

In the end, the multiple movements for racial justice profoundly transformed the American consciousness. In 1964, activist Ella Baker (d. 1986) had proclaimed that seekers of freedom could not rest "until the killing of black mothers' sons becomes as important to the rest of the country as the killing of white mothers' sons." In time, it did. By the time of Malcolm X's death in 1965, by King's death in 1968, and certainly by Baker's death in 1986, most Americans had recognized the injustice of the tragic long night of exclusion, segregation, and prejudice. Government agencies officially repudiated those attitudes; in schools and houses of worship, they were assailed. A new liberal consensus had been established. Yet the full social and civil equality of African Americans was not yet a reality nor has it since been achieved. The color line still threads its way through the fabric of American life, the unlovely inheritance of slavery and the West's imperial ventures.

Conclusion

THE SHADOWS OF IMPERIALISM AND THE MEANING OF THE WEST

For 500 years, the most powerful Western nations imposed their will on the other regions of the globe. That age is over, but its shadows hover still. The exploitation of wealth that belonged to others, the coercive reshaping of societies and culture that had different roots and purposes, the demeaning of whole peoples—these actions performed by thousands of Westerners and approved by many millions have left deep wounds and great bitterness.

But though it imposed its will in ways now regretted, the reign of the West has not been without benefit for the other peoples of the world. Its industrial might, its political institutions, its cultural forms, even its religious values now have willing imitators around the globe, who can borrow from the West at will as they develop their own free and independent nations—just as dissident Chinese students, in Tiananmen Square in Beijing in 1989, erected a replica of the Statue of Liberty that stands in New York Harbor, and onlookers throughout the world beheld its message.

REVIEW QUESTIONS

1. Why did World War I weaken European rule? How did Ghandi advance the struggle for Indian independence? Why did Pakistan separate from India in 1947?

2. Which European powers fought to retain their African colonies? Why was Algeria so important to France? Why did so many African states suffer military coups?

3. What were the barriers facing nation-building in post-colonial Africa? Describe the system of apartheid in South Africa. How was apartheid brought to an end?

4. How did Atatürk create modern Turkey? Describe Arab–Israeli relations between 1948 and the 1990s. Why did the Arab states find it hard to accept Israel? Why does Islamism oppose Western influences?

5. How did Asian states seek to modernize their economies after World War II? Why has Japan become a democracy, but not China? Why did the United States become involved in the Vietnam War?

6. To what extent was the United States the last imperialist power? How has the United States intervened in Latin America since 1898? How does United States aggression abroad relate to racist attitudes at home? How did legal segregation end in the United States?

SUGGESTED READINGS

Fading Empires: Anti-Colonialism and Decolonization

Bairoch, Paul, *Economics and World History: Myths and Paradoxes* (Chicago: University of Chicago Press, 1993). Stimulating and important book that challenges notions of the centrality of imperialism to the economic and industrial development of Europe.

Fromkin, David, *A Peace to End All Peace: The Fall of the Ottoman Empire and the Creation of the Modern Middle East* (New York: H. Holt, 1989). Survey of a critical period in the history of the Middle East.

Goody, Jack, *The East in the West* (Cambridge: Cambridge University Press, 1996). Somewhat controversial. Argues that common cultural inheritance unites Europe and Asia; only with the rise of industrialism does Europe pursue a unique path.

Hargreaves, J. D., *Decolonization in Africa* (London–New York: Longman, 1988). Excellent survey, attending to Portuguese, Belgian, and Italian, as well as British and French empires.

Holland, Roy F., *European Decolonization, 1918–1991: An Introductory Survey* (New York: St. Martin's Press, 1985). Depicts a gritty reality of power-hungry elites, false promises, and disunited masses.

Judd, Denis, *Empire: The British Imperial Experience from 1765 to the Present* (New York: Basic Books, 1996). Emphasizes the tragedies, failures, and ultimately the decline of the British Empire.

Keay, John, *Empire's End: A History of the Far East from High Colonialism to Hong Kong* (New York: Scribner's, 1997). Covers the last 500 years, including the decline of foreign rule since the 1930s.

New World Orders: Statebuilding in Africa, the Middle East, and Asia

Gerges, Fawaz A., *The Superpowers and the Middle East: Regional and International Politics, 1955–1967* (Boulder, CO: Westview Press, 1994). Surveys this key geo-political relationship during the High Cold War.

Irokawa, Daikichi, *The Age of Hirohito: The Making of Modern Japan* (New York: Free Press, 1995). Critical assessment of Japanese history during the 62 years' reign of the Emperor Hirohito, who died in 1989.

Jones, Eric, Lionel Frost, and Colin White, *Coming Full Circle: An Economic History of the Pacific Rim* (Boulder, CO: Westview Press, 1993). China was the world's economic center up to about 1400; according to the authors, it will resume this position in the coming century.

Mazrui, Ali A. and Michael Tidy, *Nationalism and New States in Africa* (Nairobi: Heinemann, 1984). Highlights both the common problems faced by African nations and the variety of experiences in dealing with them.

Meredith, Martin, *Nelson Mandela: A Biography* (New York: St. Martin's Press, 1998). Solid biography of this key figure of the late 20th century.

Nanda, B. R., *Jawaharlal Nehru: Rebel and Statesman* (New Delhi–New York: Oxford University Press, 1995). Critical reassessment of the role and significance of India's first prime minister.

Said, Edward, *The Politics of Dispossession: The Struggle for Palestinian Self-Determination, 1969–1994* (New York: Pantheon, 1994). Essays on the history and culture of the Palestinian people.

The Last Imperialist: The United States Abroad and at Home

Cottam, M. L., *Images and Intervention: U.S. Policies in Latin America* (Pittsburgh: University of Pittsburgh Press, 1994). Explores connections between the image of Latin America held by the US and the latter's tendency to conduct foreign policy in Central and South America by means of military intervention and covert operations.

Karnow, Stanley, *Vietnam: A History*, rev. ed. (New York: Penguin, 1991). A coherent account of the long Vietnam conflict.

Lischer, Richard, *The Preacher King: Martin Luther King, Jr. and the Word that Moved America* (Oxford: Oxford University Press, 1995). Focuses on the role played in King's thought by African-Baptist influences.

BACK FROM ARMAGEDDON

1940 | 1950 | 1960 | 1970 | 1980 | 1990 | 2000

The Cold War and Global Politics

Korean War, 1950–53

Vietnam War, 1964–73

- Hiroshima and Nagasaki bombed, 1945
- United Nations founded, 1945
- Churchill's "Iron Curtain" speech, 1946
- Marshall Plan announced, 1947
- Truman Doctrine announced, 1947
- Berlin blockade and airlift, 1948
- UN Universal Declaration of Human Rights, 1948
- NATO formed, 1949
- China becomes Communist state. 1949
- Soviet Union explodes atomic bomb, 1949
- First hydrogen bomb, US, 1952
- Soviet Union has hydrogen bomb, 1953
- Ethel and Julius Rosenberg executed, 1953
- Warsaw Pact formed, 1955
- Sukarno hosts Bandung, Indonesia, conference, 1955
- Nikita Khrushchev denounces Stalin, 1956
- Hungarian uprising, 1956
- Suez Crisis, 1956
- Soviet Union launches *Sputnik I*, 1957
- United States sends *Explorer I* into orbit, 1958
- Berlin Wall erected, 1961
- Chinese–Soviet split, 1961
- Cuban Missile Crisis, 1961
- Nuclear test ban agreement, 1963
- Six-Day War, Israel, 1967
- Nuclear Non-Proliferation Treaty, 1968
- Prague Spring suppressed, Czechoslovakia, 1968
- *Apollo 11*, lunar landing, 1969
- Oil crisis, 1973–74
- Helsinki Accords, 1975
- Soviets invade Afghanistan, 1979
- Solidarity movement, Poland, 1980
- Marshall Tito dies, Yugoslavia, 1980
- Gorbachev launches *Perestroika* and *Glasnost*, 1985
- Chernobyl nuclear disaster, Ukraine, 1986
- Communism collapses in Eastern Europe, 1989
- Tiananmen Square protests suppressed, 1989
- UN Convention on the Rights of the Child, 1989
- START I treaty signed, 1991
- Yeltsin elected president of Russian Republic, 1991
- Anti-Gorbachev coup, Soviet Union, 1991
- Soviet Union dissolved, 1991
- Gulf War, 1991
- START II treaty signed, 1993
- Hutus massacre 500,000–800,000 Tutsis, Rwanda, 1994
- Bosnian Serbs massacre thousands in Srebenica, Bosnia-Herzegovina, 1995
- Dayton (Ohio) Peace Agreement, 1995
- Russian economic crisis threatens reform, 1998
- India and Pakistan carry out nuclear tests, 1998
- NATO bombs Serbia, 1999

Culture, Society, and Economy

- ENIAC computer developed, 1946
- Albert Camus's *The Plague*, 1947
- Simone de Beauvoir's *The Second Sex*, 1949
- European Economic Community (Common Market) formed, 1957
- Federico Fellini's *La dolce vita*, 1960
- NOW (National Organization for Women) formed, 1966
- Beatles' "All You Need is Love" broadcast worldwide, 1967
- Stanley Kubrick's *2001: A Space Odyssey*, 1968
- Woodstock Festival, 1969
- First Earth Day celebration in US, 1970
- Alexander Solzhenitsyn's *The Gulag Archipelago*, 1973
- UN General Assembly establishes World Commission on Environment and Development, 1983
- Spain and Portugal join the Common Market, 1986
- "Earth Summit" meets, Brazil, 1992
- European Union created, 1994
- Kyoto Protocol commits industrial nations to reductions in greenhouse gas emissions, 1997
- Debut of the euro, 1999

CHAPTER 29

BACK FROM ARMAGEDDON

From the Bomb to the Internet

1945–1990

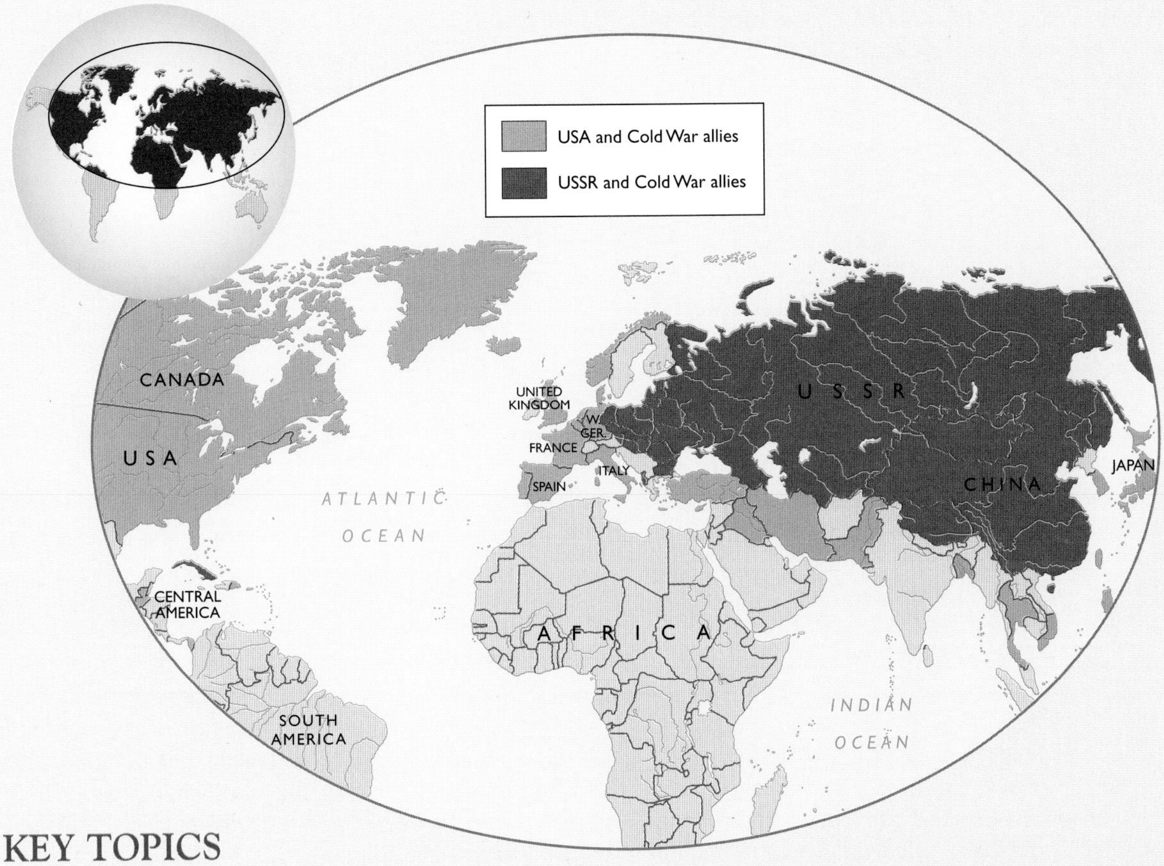

KEY TOPICS

- **Apocalypse Now?:** With the fearful power of the atom unloosed, and with much of Europe under Soviet rule, people of the non-Communist West wonder whether the Apocalypse is about to arrive. Yet it is deferred when, in 1989, the Communist regime begins to unravel and the states of the former Soviet bloc turn to democracy and free markets.

- **All You Need is Love:** In the vanguard United States, the first generation born to face the prospect of nuclear annihilation ignores the Cold War, protests against involvement in Vietnam, and invents a culture based on unhampered self-expression. The Sixties movement spurs sexual revolution and environmentalism, while religious and nationalist forces resurge and provoke small but deadly conflicts around the globe.

Reprieve from MAD: 1989 *On December 29, 1989, dissident playwright Václav Havel (1936–) became the first president of liberated Czechoslovakia as it set out on the path from dictatorship to democracy. "Your government, my people, has been returned to you," he proclaimed in his New Year's address a few days later.*

Havel's ascendancy in a bloodless or "velvet" revolution marked the release of his nation from the Soviet-controlled communist regimes that had held sway since 1945. In 1989, Poland, Hungary, Bulgaria, East Germany (the German Democratic Republic), and Romania also threw off their former rulers, even as, in distant China, student democrats in Beijing's Tiananmen Square confronted the communist state (see Chapter 28). The events of 1989 preceded the dissolution in 1991 of the Soviet Union itself.

With its collapse, the terror eased that had gripped the nations of the West and of the world. From 1945 to 1989, two superpowers, the United States and the Soviet Union, were locked in a condition of ideological stalemate and political confrontation known as the Cold War. For nearly fifty years, the prospect of Armageddon loomed—the great final battle of the nations of the world. That threat faded with the end of the Cold War, while internationalist movements to heal the Earth's ills flourished, rooted in the era of the 1960s when youthful activists proposed a worldwide agenda of human welfare and environmental concern.

APOCALPYSE NOW?

The last scene of World War II was the first scene of the age that followed. The atomic destruction of Hiroshima and Nagasaki in 1945 (see Chapter 27) struck a new kind of fear. "The life expectancy of the human species . . . [has] dwindled immeasurably," the *Washington Post* dismally announced. With the Soviet occupation of eastern Europe, the nations of the Western world divided into two hostile blocs both equipped with nuclear weapons—a communist East and a largely democratic West. For nearly fifty years, people wondered: would Apocalypse (a universal destruction prophesied in the Bible) come now? Or soon? Or could it be forestalled?

Postwar Polarization

From 1945 until 1953, the Soviet Union established its power in eastern Europe while the United States led an alliance of western European nations against further Soviet advance, pledging "massive retaliation" against any aggression.

Europe Divided By late 1945, the Soviet Union had already secured much of Europe. For two years after its 1943 victories at Stalingrad and Kursk (see Chapter 27), the Red Army swept German armies out of Russia and back to Berlin, where the enemy surrendered on May 8, 1945. The Soviet flag flew in Berlin and throughout the lands the Soviets now occupied.

Soviet territorial claims, rooted in older Russian ambitions, were sanctioned by wartime agreements between the Allies. The "Big Three"—United States president Franklin Delano Roosevelt (1882–1945), British prime minister Winston Churchill (1874–1965), and the Soviet leader Joseph Stalin (1879–1953)—convened twice during the war: at Teheran (Iran) in November and December 1943, and at Yalta in the Crimea in February 1945. (In addition, Churchill met with Stalin in October 1944 in Moscow.) A final meeting of the victors took place in Potsdam (Germany) in July 1945, where President Harry S. Truman (1887–1972) replaced Roosevelt, who had recently died; and Clement Attlee (1883–1967) replaced Churchill, defeated in British elections. These meetings yielded agreements that transferred to Soviet control a corridor of states from the Baltic to the Balkans—the European nations created in 1919 from the borderlands of fallen empires, promised by Hitler to Stalin in 1939.

This outcome was not what Roosevelt and Churchill had planned in the Atlantic Charter of August 1941. That charter stated that neither the United States nor Britain sought territorial aggrandizement, and called for the restoration of sovereign rights to nations that had been deprived of them, and the repudiation of the use of force to advance national interests—principles subsequently adopted by the twenty-six signatories of the January 1942 Declaration of the nascent United Nations. Those principles were ignored, however, as the Soviet Union, seeking to defend its borders and conscious of its extraordinary sacrifices in the battle against Nazism, took control of half of Europe. Now a communist megalith faced the nations to the west.

Between 1945 and 1949, Soviet-backed communist governments took over in East Germany, in Poland, Czechoslovakia, Hungary, Romania, Bulgaria, and Albania; Yugoslavia, alone, led by resistance hero Marshall Tito (Josip Broz, 1892–1980) broke with Moscow. In 1940, the Soviets had already annexed the Baltic states of Estonia, Lithuania, and Latvia;

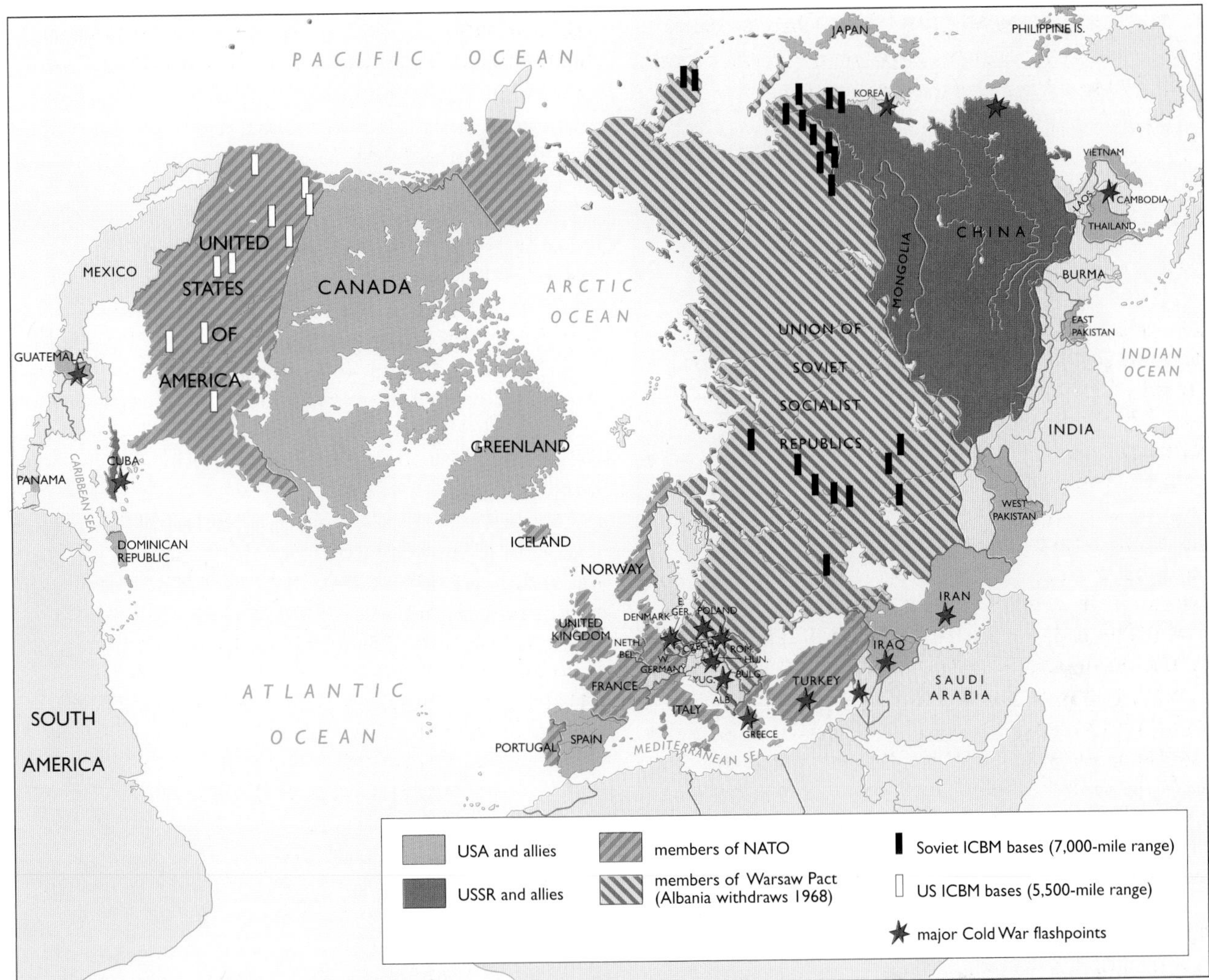

Map 29.1 The Two Superpowers in a Bipolar World, 1955: *By 1955, Europe was divided between those states loyal to the Soviet Union (the members of the Warsaw Pact) and those aligned with the United States (members of NATO). Although many nations beyond Europe remained non-aligned, others also joined in alliances with one or another of the superpowers. The faceoff between the superpowers created, in effect, a "bipolar" world—oriented toward not one pole but two. Both contenders were armed sufficiently to destroy human life on earth.*

now they acquired parts of Finland, Romania, and Czechoslovakia. The citizens of these regions who had suffered Nazi brutality now lived under regimes answerable to the Soviet Union, a totalitarian state that imposed a command economy, agrarian collectives, press censorship, and one-party rule.

Western Europeans observed these developments with alarm. Having survived the Nazi threat, they now confronted a Soviet one. Their economies were in tatters, and their military capacity exhausted; Germany and Austria were wholly disarmed. They looked to the United States to guarantee their security. Would the United States renounce its former isolationism, and return to defend western Europe? In 1945, the answer was not yet clear. But the means were at hand with the terrible power of the atomic bomb.

European Recovery Meanwhile, the task of rebuilding Europe began. Nazi officials and collaborators were purged, and the destruction caused by bombs addressed. Cities were in ruins; some seventy to ninety percent of Germany's urban fabric had been destroyed, as had railroads and bridges, communications systems, and factories. Urban populations needed food and, for those driven to take shelter in warehouses or cellars, new housing. Millions of refugees awaited **repatriation**—Germans who had

Weapons and Warriors

The Big Three: *The leaders of the major combatant nations—Churchill, Roosevelt, and Stalin (the so-called "Big Three")—met at Yalta in the Crimea in February 1945 to discuss Allied military strategy and the end of the war. At least as decisive—both in bringing the war in the Far East to a close and establishing post-War power relationships—was the atomic bomb.*

fled the advancing Red Army, forced laborers detained in Germany, former prisoners of war. Twelve million "displaced persons" were taken under the wing of Allied administrators. German and Soviet prisoners of war unlucky enough to be released in the Red Army zone were shipped back to the Soviet Union; and then on to execution or the oblivion of the gulag.

In western Europe, parliamentary governments were restored and currencies stabilized—often at rates that caused the value of prewar bank accounts to plummet. British, French, and American armies settled down in western Germany and Austria. In the rest of Germany and eastern Europe, the Red Army dug in its heels.

Europe was vulnerable, analysts argued, its impoverished nations prone to communist takeover through open elections or covert design. Where the struggle against fascism had previously united the free world, now many saw communism as a primary global threat. American assistance would be needed for Europe's recuperation, not least as a counter-measure to communist influence. Proposed by Secretary of State George C. Marshall (1880–1959) in 1947, the Marshall Plan (or "European Recovery Program") offered economic aid to any European nation—whatever its political commitments—upon the presentation of a reasonable proposal for its use. Prodded by their masters, the nations of the Soviet zone declined to participate; but the nations of western Europe responded enthusiastically, including the Germans whom Allied leaders had so recently labeled "beasts" and "barbarians."

Funneling United States wealth—$13.2 billion between 1948 and 1952—to the treasuries of non-communist Europe, the Marshall Plan became in effect an economic corollary of the political strategy announced in the Truman Doctrine (see below).

The mushroom-shaped cloud: *Hearing in 1939 that the Nazis had begun efforts to develop the world's first nuclear weapons, the United States strove successfully to beat them to the punch. By 1945 the United States had three bombs: one was tested at Alamagordo, New Mexico in July 1945, and the other two were dropped on Japanese cities in early August 1945. A later test of a similar device in the Nevada desert in 1946 is shown above.*

Early Cold War Activity Crises in the eastern Mediterranean seemed to demand such a policy. In Turkey in 1946, the Soviet Union positioned itself to seize control of the Dardanelles, the straits connecting the Mediterranean and Black Seas for which the Russian tsars had long hungered. In response, President Truman deployed a naval force in the eastern Mediterranean. In Greece, meanwhile, communist opponents of the ruling monarchy were supplied by the new Balkan dictatorships. In 1947, the British Foreign Office informed the State Department that Britain could no longer afford to prop up its embattled ally. The United States assumed that task; communist opposition had failed by 1949.

These circumstances led Truman to define an aggressive international role for the United States. In March 1947, he announced that it "must be the policy of the United States to support free peoples who are resisting attempted subjugation by armed minorities or by outside pressures." This pledge to all nations confronted with the threat of communist takeover was the core of the "Truman Doctrine."

The Truman Doctrine, which energized foreign policy for more than two decades and culminated in the imbroglio of Vietnam (see Chapter 28), announced the strategy of "containment," outlined in 1947 by the State Department representative in Moscow, George F. Kennan (1904–). Kennan viewed Soviet power as opportunistic and aggressive. The United States, he said, must offer an "unalterable counterforce" wherever the Soviets "show signs of encroaching upon the interests of a peaceful and stable world."

Another early Cold War confrontation took place in the German capital of Berlin. In 1945, Britain, France, the United States, and the Soviet Union had occupied separate zones of Germany, as well as four separate sectors of Berlin—an awkward arrangement because the city was located 100 miles deep in the Soviet zone. By spring 1948, the division of Germany by four powers became a rupture between two: the consortium, on the one hand, of the British, French, and Americans in the west (who would organize the region as the Federal Republic of Germany the following year); and on the other, the Soviets in the east (who would respond by creating the German Democratic Republic).

In June 1948, wishing to isolate Berlin from the western zones of Germany (a policy to which the West Berlin municipal government refused to acquiesce), the Soviet Union shut down access to the city by road, rail, or waterway. For nearly a year the western powers organized an unprecedented airlift, supplying the besieged citizens with food and fuel. By May 1949, the Soviets dropped the blockade, having failed to detach Berlin from its ties to the West.

WITNESSES

The Prospects of Nuclear War: Two Reflections

Novelist William Faulkner speaks of the bomb during his Nobel Prize acceptance speech (1949): Our tragedy is a general an universal fear. . . . There are no longer any problems of the spirit. There is only the question: when will I be blown up? . . .

I decline to accept the end of man. It is easy enough to say that man is immortal simply because he will endure; that when the last ding-dong of doom has clanged and faded from the last worthless rock hanging tideless in the last red and dying evening, that even then there will still be one more sound: that of his puny inexhaustible voice, still talking. I refuse to accept this. I believe that man will not merely endure; he will prevail. He is immortal, not because he alone among creatures has an inexhaustible voice, but because he has a soul, a spirit capable of compassion and sacrifice and endurance.

(From Nobel Foundation, *Les Prix Nobel en 1950*, 1951)

Songwriter Sting considers the likelihood of war (1985):

How can I save my little boy
from Oppenheimer's deadly toy?
There is no monopoly on common sense
on either side of the political fence.
We share the same biology,
regardless of ideology.
Believe me when I say to you,
I hope the Russians love their children too.

[Sting's reference is to J. Robert Oppenheimer (1904–1967), one of the leading physicists on the atomic bomb project.]

("Russians," words and music by Sting, 1985)

Cold War Skies: Hope and Fear

The Berlin Airlift: *Angered by United States, British, and French plans to merge their zones of occupation in Germany, the Soviets attempted in 1948–1949 to blockade West Berlin—buried deep within the Soviet zone of occupation—and thus to cut it off from western Germany. The United States and Britain responded with the highly successful Berlin Airlift, making in all some 200,000 flights to drop off food and supplies to the besieged citizens, like those seen here.*

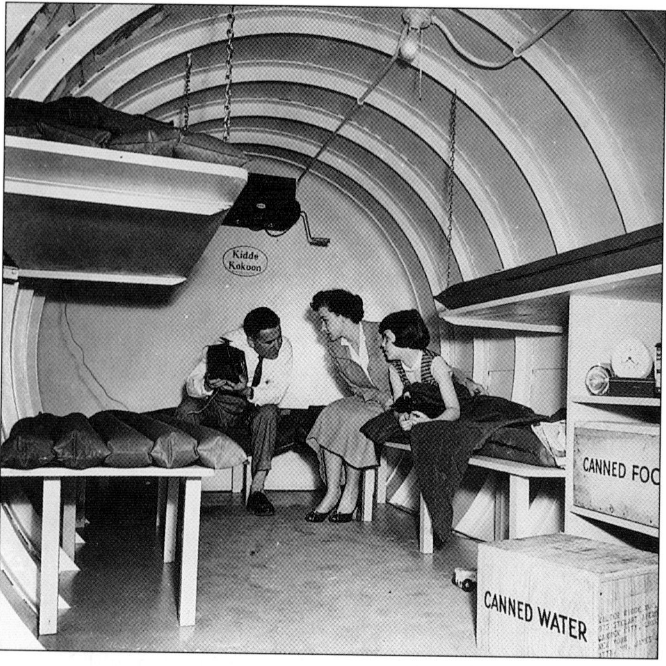

Fallout: *If western Berliners looked to the skies for assistance, many Americans, fearing a Soviet nuclear missile attack, sought the doubtful security of home-made basement fallout shelters during the early Cold War years.*

By the time of the Berlin crisis, the Western world had crystallized into two zones. The "free" and the "unfree" zones were separated by an "iron curtain" (in Churchill's phrase) constituted by the tanks and barbed wire that marked the borders between Soviet and non-Soviet states, and by the ideological gulf between them. As a response to the threat of aggression from the East, the United States, advised by Secretary of State Dean Acheson (1893–1971), guided the creation in 1949 of a multinational military alliance: the North Atlantic Treaty Organization (NATO).

The North Atlantic Treaty provided for mutual aid in case of attack against any of its members (originally twelve), with each nation later providing military units in proportion to its resources. It served not only a military purpose, but also provided a pattern for other cooperative projects. Just as the Marshall Plan had advanced the notion of economic cooperation, NATO nurtured the germs of political unity among the western European states. By 1951, several nations were cooperating in a European Coal and Steel Community, which led to the establishment of the European Economic Community [EEC], or Common Market, in 1957 (now the European Union).

In 1949, the achievement of NATO was to provide a "shield," and the nuclear-armed United States an atomic "sword" that could protect the continent from attack, delivering massive retaliation—"instantly, by means and at places of our own choosing," in the words of United States Secretary of State John Foster Dulles (1888–1959)—against any aggressor. This was not war, but it was like war, as both contenders (equally heirs to Western civilization) eyed each other warily.

Cold War Confrontations

In 1949, the year of NATO's creation, the Soviet Union demonstrated its nuclear capacity by exploding an atomic bomb. By 1952, the United States had developed the hydrogen bomb, 750 times more powerful than the one that destroyed Hiroshima. By 1953, the Soviets had one too. Now both superpowers were armed with weapons capable of annihilating the other—its cities, its people, its air and soil.

The citizens of the world took what comfort they could in the principle of "Mutual Assured Destruction," or MAD—an apt anagram, for the world seemed to have become mad. With each superpower having the capability to annihilate the other, the reasoning went, neither would start a conflict; yet the possibility remained that one would. From 1948 into the 1960s, the tension between the two superpowers was at a zenith. It relaxed somewhat from the late 1960s into the 1970s, then mounted again during the 1980s.

In the early 1950s, both superpowers built up their arsenals. This "arms race" continued throughout the decades of the Cold War until the world had accumulated a total of some 50,000 nuclear weapons. Each contender had long-range bombers and radar detection systems to stop them. They had "intercontinental ballistic missiles" (ICBMs, developed in 1957) that could reach the enemy from a remote position of safety. They had intermediate-range ballistic missiles (IRBMs) that could be launched at an enemy from a nearby country. They had submarine-launched ballistic missiles (SLBMs), and anti-ballistic missiles that tried to find and stop incoming missiles (ABMs). Billions of dollars were dedicated each year to the goal of mutual assured destruction.

Each superpower mustered allies who might enhance its security. Already the chief figure in NATO, the United States promoted the organization of its non-European allies into regional organizations. These included, in Asia, the Central Treaty Organization (CENTO) and Southeast Asia Treaty Organization (SEATO); and in the Americas, the Organization of American States (OAS). In 1955, the Soviets established the Warsaw Treaty organization (or Warsaw Pact) with its east European allies, to defend the communist states from the West. In addition, it could rely on the support of the other major communist nations of the world—North Korea (from 1945), China (until 1960), Cuba (after 1960), and Vietnam (after 1976).

As the race for arms and allies spiraled upward, so too did technological competition in other strategically related areas—in space and in **cybernetics**. In October 1957, the Soviet Union sent up a first satellite, *Sputnik I*, to orbit the Earth. In January 1958, the United States responded to the challenge, sending *Explorer 1* into orbit. In April 1961, the Soviets again surpassed the Americans, launching a manned spacecraft. In July 1969, the United States upstaged the Soviets with the launching of Apollo 11, the first space mission to culminate in a lunar landing. From a lunar module detached from the spacecraft, astronaut Neil A. Armstrong (b. 1930) and his colleagues emerged and took "a giant step for mankind" on the moon's surface, watched on television by one-quarter of the people on earth. Thereafter, both superpowers maintained programs of space exploration, gathering information through satellites, probes, and space stations.

MEANWHILE

The Space Race

1957	Soviet Union successfully launches world's first space satellite, *Sputnik I*
1958	US sends *Explorer I* into orbit
1961	Soviets successfully launch world's first manned spacecraft
1962	John Glenn becomes first US astronaut to complete an orbit of the earth
1963	Valentina Tereshkova of the Soviet Union becomes first female in space, orbiting earth forty-eight times
1967	US and USSR both suffer the loss of astronauts in tragic accidents
1969	US launches *Apollo 11*, the first space mission to culminate in a lunar landing
1971	Soviets launch Salyut Space Station
1973	US launches Skylab Space Station; destroyed in 1979
1984	European Space Agency begins launch program from facility in French Guiana
1986	Soviets launch Mir Space Station
1998	First stage of International Space Station launched; completion scheduled for 2002

War stimulated the development of systems for the electronic storage and manipulation of data. The first computers were designed to help decipher intercepted messages during World War II. Such were Britain's pioneering Colossus, which could manipulate 5000 characters per second, or the massive ENIAC (Electronic Numerical Integrator and Computer) developed at the University of Pennsylvania in 1946.

Thereafter, the United States led the world in the development of computer technology in the new field of cybernetics. The ENIAC weighed fifty tons, had 18,000 vacuum tubes, and could store the equivalent of just twenty words in memory. In the late 1990s, computers based on the silicon chip (about ¼ inch across) could store in memory the equivalent of more than 50 million words. This powerful chip has given its name to "Silicon Valley" (a region of northern California), a site of intense technological innovation. In 1968, the film *2001: A Space Odyssey*, directed by Stanley Kubrick (1928–1999) marked the arrival of the cybernetic space age in popular consciousness. It starred the supercomputer "Hal."

The buildup of arms and strategic technology made nuclear war seem likely. People sought to protect themselves as best they could. In civil defense programs citizens, including schoolchildren, practiced taking shelter, at a signal, from falling bombs—an absurd response to a weapon that could incinerate hundreds of thousands in an instant and kill any survivors with invisible radioactive fallout. Some United States families constructed "fallout shelters" in their basements or back yards, equipped with food and water supplies for long-term hibernation. Mass circulation magazines offered guidance on planning a well-stocked shelter.

The battle for which these Cold Warriors prepared was a contest not merely between nations, but between two ideas, almost two religions. To many, communism seemed an absolute evil; liberal democracy and capitalism, absolute goods. Thus the military and political bifurcation of the Western world was paralleled by an ideological bifurcation, especially in the United States where an extreme, and unique, anti-communism took hold. In Europe outside of Spain and Portugal (where a lingering fascism silenced communist opposition), communist parties and adherents were accepted and active within a parliamentary setting.

From 1948, a committee of the United States House of Representatives known as the House Un-American Activities Committee (HUAC) investigated people associated in any way with the Communist party. Its improper tactics—pressuring witnesses to implicate others, and presuming guilt by association with suspect persons or organizations—were challenged at the time and subsequently condemned. Among HUAC's targets was Alger Hiss (1904–1996), a highly placed former State Department official, convicted of perjury in 1950. He had perjured himself, it was charged, by denying his guilt in spying for the Soviets; a charge of espionage could not be pursued because the statute of limitations had expired. Although many defended Hiss's innocence, recent revelations from materials previously barred to public examination appear to confirm his guilt.

HUAC's activities prepared the way for the emergence of Wisconsin senator Joseph McCarthy (1908–1957), the leader of a furious crusade against presumed communists. McCarthy chaired Senate committee hearings from 1953 to 1954, in which hysterical and unsubstantiated accusations ruined many careers and lives. Eventually, both his Senate colleagues (who censured him) and the public at large denounced McCarthy's "witchhunt" (so called because of its resemblance to the witch persecutions of earlier centuries).

Although McCarthy was repudiated, anti-communist feeling was widespread. Many states made a "loyalty oath" a condition for the employment of government personnel and teachers. In this tense climate, a couple convicted of betraying atomic secrets to the Soviets were executed in 1953: Ethel Rosenberg (1915–1953) and her husband Julius (1918–1953), considered wholly innocent by numerous supporters. As in the case of Hiss, recently-released evidence appears to confirm the complicity of these Cold War martyrs, although their punishment was exceptional: they were the first civilians in United States history executed for espionage.

MEANWHILE

The Coming of the Computer Age

1623 German scientist Wilhelm Schickard invents an adding machine

1642 French mathematician Blaise Pascal builds a machine that adds and subtracts

1804 French inventor Joseph-Marie Jacquard creates a "loom", an early computer using punch cards to execute weaving patterns

1823 British mathematician Charles Babbage designs 20-decimal capacity mechanical calculator

1936 British mathematician Alan Turing invents a programmable "universal machine," precursor of digital computer

1946 ENIAC (Electronic Numerical Integrator and Calculator), the world's first successful digital computer built at the University of Pennsylvania

1947 Bell Labs physicists invent the transistor, greatly increasing computer efficiency and reducing size

1974 Altair 8800, first personal computer developed

1996 IBM's Deep Blue supercomputer wins its first chess match against Russian chess-master Gary Kasparov

The Cold War on the Global Stage

The Cold War Outside Europe The duel between the Soviet Union and the United States was fought in various settings around the world. In Latin America, the United States supported governments that took an anti-communist stance (see Chapter 28), including authoritarian regimes with unsavory reputations. It funded "counter-insurgency" programs to train military units in guerrilla tactics to be used against communist movements and states. Its CIA (Central Intelligence Agency) pursued the destabilization of pro-communist regimes, as in the coup that destroyed the elected government of Chilean socialist leader Salvador Allende Gossens (1908–1973) and in attempts to assassinate the Cuban communist leader Fidel Castro (b. 1927). In Cuba, an abortive invasion by an expatriate force (supported by the United States) and the Soviet installation on the island, in response, of missiles capable of carrying nuclear warheads triggered the most dangerous United States–Soviet confrontation of the era. The Cuban missile crisis of 1961 brought the two superpowers to the edge of nuclear war. A show of firmness by the United States persuaded the Soviets to dismantle their missile bases in exchange for an American promise not to invade Cuba again.

Although the emerging states of Africa were intent on their own internal problems (see Chapter 28), the Cold War contest between the United States and the Soviet Union inevitably intruded. From 1969, the Soviets supported strongman Colonel

WITNESSES

The Origins of the Cold War

Winston Churchill, wartime British prime minister, notes the signs of Cold War (1946): From Stettin in the Baltic to Trieste in the Adriatic, an iron curtain has descended across the Continent. Behind that line lie all the capitals of ancient states of central and eastern Europe. Warsaw, Berlin, Prague, Vienna, Budapest, Belgrade, Bucharest and Sofia, all these famous cities . . . lie in the Soviet sphere and all are subject in one form or another . . . to a very high and increasing measure of control from Moscow. The Communist parties . . . have been raised to preeminence and power far beyond their numbers and are seeking everywhere to obtain totalitarian control. . . . This is certainly not the liberated Europe we fought to build up. Nor is it one which contains the essentials of permanent peace.
(From *New York Times*, March 4, 1946)

United States president Truman outlines the "Truman Doctrine" (March 12, 1947): At the present moment in world history nearly every nation must choose between alternative ways of life. The choice is too often not a free one. One way of life is based upon the will of the majority, and is distinguished by free institutions, representative government, free elections, guaranties of individual liberty, freedom of speech and religion, and freedom from political oppression. The second way of life is based upon the will of a minority forcibly imposed upon the majority. It relies upon terror and oppression, a controlled press and radio, fixed elections, and the suppression of personal freedoms.

I believe that it must be the policy of the United States to support free peoples who are resisting attempted subjugation by armed minorities or by outside pressures. . . .
(US Congress, Congressional Record, 80th Congress, 1st session, 1947)

Soviet official Andrei Zhdanov interprets United States "aid" as imperialism (1947): With a view to consolidating America's monopoly position in the markets gained as a result of the disappearance of her two biggest competitors, Germany and Japan [due to their defeat in the war], and the weakening of her capitalist partners, Great Britain and France [a result of the toll of winning the war], the new course of the United States' policy envisages a broad program of military, economic and political measures, designed to establish United States political and economic domination in all countries marked out for American expansion, to reduce these countries to the status of satellites of the United States and to set up regimes within them which would eliminate all obstacles on the part of labor and democratic movement to the exploitation of these countries by American capital. The United States is now endeavoring to extend this new line of policy not only to its enemies in the war and to neutral countries, but in an increasing degree to its wartime allies [also].
(Andrei Zhdanov, address to conference, September 22–23, 1947; ed. Kirsch et al., 1997)

Muammar al-Qaddafi (b. 1942) in Libya. In 1974, it formed a pact with Somalia, providing weapons and military advice in exchange for naval and air footholds. In 1977, the Somalians cast off the Soviet alliance (and invited United States support) as it invaded neighboring Ethiopia, itself a Soviet client. The following year, Ethiopia defeated Somalia and compensated the Soviets with access to naval facilities. In 1975–1976, the Soviets sent weapons and some 19,000 Cuban troops to Angola to aid one group of insurgents against another supported by the United States. By the late 1970s, hundreds of Soviet advisers and more than 40,000 Cuban troops were deployed in a dozen African countries. The United States countered, enhancing its authority in Africa through programs providing economic advice and assistance. By the 1980s, the Soviets found it increasingly difficult to fund its African agenda. The Western bloc became the preeminent foreign influence on the continent.

In the Middle East, the United States backed Israel, while the Soviets embraced the cause of the dispossessed Palestinians, and supported the Arab states, especially Egypt (until its settlement with Israel in 1979), Syria, and Iraq (see Chapter 28). In east Asia a great communist state was formed in 1949, when Mao Zedong (1893–1976) led his triumphant forces into Beijing (see Chapter 28). Against this massive communist presence, the United States leagued with Japan, now a loyal ally after the period of postwar occupation. Another ally was the government of Taiwan (Formosa), established in 1949 by Chiang Kai-shek (Jiang Jieshi; 1887–1975) and the nationalist army that had taken refuge from the communist forces that had overrun the mainland. Elsewhere in Asia, two major wars in Korea and Vietnam pitted revolutionary communist states against authoritarian, pro-Western ones backed by the United States (see Chapter 28). In Korea, a communist state retained power in the north. After United States disengagement, Vietnam was finally unified as a communist state.

India and Indonesia avoided identification with either Cold War position in a policy of "non-alignment," which aimed to advance the interests of the developing nations of what was now called the **Third World** by trading with both superpowers but declining participation in Cold War struggles. Indonesian leader Sukarno (1901–1970), an advocate of non-alignment, hosted an historic meeting of Asian and African leaders at Bandung in 1955. In the Middle East, Egyptian leader Colonel Gamal Abdel Nasser (1918–1970) also led a bloc of non-aligned Arab nations.

De-Stalinization and Repression in the East While Soviet and United States interests collided abroad, at home the United States presidents from 1952 to 1973 pursued resolutely anti-Communist policies. They faced a shifting Soviet policy as the regime of Joseph Stalin yielded to that of Nikita Khrushchev (1894–1971), and, in due course, Leonid Brezhnev (1906–1982).

After Stalin died in 1953, Khrushchev battled his way to preeminence by 1955. On February 25, 1956, he surprised the Twentieth Congress of the Communist Party with a denunciation of "the crimes of Stalin." Even in Moscow some began to hope that the purges were over, that censorship of the press and the arts would lighten, and that the horror of the gulag would cease.

De-Stalinization in Moscow meant a brief moment of relaxation of Soviet control in eastern Europe, where leaders took the initiative in reaching for greater autonomy. In Poland in 1956, the election as first secretary of Władisław Gomułka (1905–1982), a "national" communist thought to be independent of Moscow, went forward despite a frown from Khrushchev. The same year, a popular revolt in Hungary under the liberalizing prime minister Imre Nagy (1896–1958) threatened the Soviet-backed regime. When Hungary announced its withdrawal from the Warsaw Pact, Soviet forces invaded and crushed the revolution. The victors installed leaders loyal to Moscow, executing Nagy and 2000 supporters. Some 200,000 Hungarians fled to the West.

The suppression of the Hungarian revolt silenced eastern Europe. Five years later, the Soviet Union again made clear its intention to limit dissent. Deep inside the German Democratic Republic, Berlin was the weakest point in the Iron Curtain. Refugees streamed from the eastern Soviet zone to west Berlin—more than 3 million people, including skilled workers and professionals. In August 1961, East Germany closed this gap by constructing the Berlin Wall, a structure of barbed wire and concrete dividing the city. The flow of refugees ceased, while all of Germany could observe in the microcosm of Berlin the great barrier that separated East and West.

In 1968, after Khrushchev had been pushed aside and the bureaucrat Brezhnev had emerged as Soviet leader, resistance to Soviet rule recurred in Czechoslovakia under reformer Alexander Dubček (1921–1992). His promise of "socialism with a human face" aroused widespread support, including that of student activists. A Soviet-led Warsaw Pact army of some 175,000 troops invaded (in its only coordinated effort), the largest mobilization of ground forces on

Stalin is Dead, Europe Lives

Repression and revolution: *Upon becoming the Czechoslovak Communist party secretary in January 1968 Alexander Dubček led his country's efforts to implement pro-democratic reforms and abolish censorship. Warsaw Pact tanks brutally repressed this "Prague Spring" later the same year. Here, Czech patriots vent their anger on a Russian tank (right). Anti-communist protest and reform—all across the Eastern Bloc—met virtually no such opposition in 1989, however. In the photograph below, the Berlin Wall is hacked down by ordinary German citizens.*

the European continent since World War II. It swiftly suppressed the "Prague Spring" that had seemed so hopeful.

Once again, force muzzled protest in eastern Europe. Only after an interlude of more than ten years did there arise another movement of resistance to communist rule, this time in Poland. Here in 1980 the workers in the Lenin Shipyard in Gdánsk (German Danzig), led by electrician and anti-government activist Lech Walesa (b. 1943), formed an independent labor union. It served as the nucleus for a federation of unions, Solidarity, which constituted a democratizing political movement that won 10 million adherents and finally celebrated the collapse of the communist government in 1989.

Talking About Disarmament By the time of Walesa's resistance, relations between the United States and the Soviet Union had experienced a period of easing tension, or ***détente***. The notion of "peaceful coexistence" between the superpowers had been aired as early as the 1950s. In 1954 and 1955, the Soviets had called in the United Nations General Assembly for limitations on conventional and nuclear weapons. In 1959, aware of the strain that the arms race put on the Soviet economy, Khrushchev advocated total disarmament within four years. To secure such disarmament, however, the United States insisted on on-site inspections; and these the Soviet Union refused to allow.

After the Cuban showdown of 1961, both superpowers sought to restrict the testing of nuclear weapons and to prevent their proliferation. In 1963, the United States, the Soviet Union, and Britain agreed not to conduct nuclear tests in the atmosphere or in the sea. In 1967, with France, they agreed not to permit the introduction of nuclear weapons into the Earth's orbit or on the moon. The same year, most

Latin American states agreed to keep their region nuclear-free.

In 1968, the three signatories of the 1963 partial test ban and fifty-nine other states signed a Nuclear Non-Proliferation Treaty (NNT, extended indefinitely in 1995), by which the participants pledged not to supply non-nuclear powers with nuclear weapons or the technology required to produce them. By 1970, additional countries had signed (the non-nuclear powers further agreeing not to acquire such weapons). It was eventually signed by most of the countries in the world, including France and China (but excluding South Africa, India, Pakistan, and Israel). In addition, Iran, Iraq, Libya, and North Korea, who had signed the treaty, were thought to be in violation. Compliance with NNT was to be enforced by an international inspection team under the aegis of the UN International Atomic Energy Administration. This mechanism meant that the non-nuclear nations would be policed, while the nuclear superpowers remained free to develop more weapons—and they did.

Further agreements were necessary to limit all arms development, as well as to prevent the further proliferation of nuclear arms. In seven sessions between 1969 and 1972 held in Helsinki (Finland) and Vienna (Austria), United States and Soviet officials participated in SALT (Strategic Arms Limitation Talks). SALT I limited each superpower to fixed quantities of certain kinds of missiles (while others remained unregulated) over a five-year term to expire in 1977. President Jimmy Carter (1924–) signed a SALT II treaty with Brezhnev in 1979, while President Ronald Reagan (1911–) participated in Intermediate-Range Nuclear Forces (INF) talks beginning in 1981 and START (Strategic Arms Reduction Talks) from 1982.

Despite promising first steps, détente stalled from 1975 to 1985, as both superpowers stockpiled new missiles and bombs. Warsaw Pact armaments in Europe rose to several times more than those available to NATO, though they were generally less powerful, while the United States developed a neutron bomb, or Enhanced Radiation Weapon, that killed with radiation rather than explosive force. In 1979, Islamist rebels threatened the Soviet client state of Afghanistan, provoking a Soviet invasion. Resuming the policy of military containment, President Reagan stirred his listeners to the task of defeating once and for all the "evil empire," as he provocatively termed the Soviet Union in 1983. Still unreconciled, East faced West with distrust and fear.

WITNESSES

As the Cold War Ages: Two United States Presidents Discuss the Soviet Threat

We are not afraid: Jimmy Carter, University of Notre Dame, Commencement Address (May 22, 1977): Being confident of our own future, we are now free of that inordinate fear of Communism which once led us to embrace any dictator who joined us in our fear. For too many years we have been willing to adopt the flawed principles and tactics of our adversaries, sometimes abandoning our values for theirs. We fought fire with fire, never thinking that fire is better fought with water. This approach failed, with Vietnam the best example of its intellectual and moral poverty. But through failure we have found our way back to our own principles and values, and we have regained our lost confidence.

(From *New York Times*, May 23, 1977)

No compromise with an evil empire: Ronald Reagan (March 14, 1983): [The Soviet leadership has . . .] openly and publicly declared that the only morality they recognize is that which will further their cause, which is world revolution. . . . I think the refusal of many influential people to accept this elementary fact of Soviet doctrine illustrates an historical reluctance to see totalitarian powers for what they are. . . . I urge you to beware the temptation of pride—the temptation blithely to declare yourselves above it all and label both sides equally at fault, to ignore the facts of history and the aggressive impulses of an evil empire. . . .

I believe that communism is another sad, bizarre chapter in human history whose last pages even now are being written. I believe this because the source of our strength in the quest for human freedom is not material but spiritual, and, because it knows no limitation, it must terrify and ultimately triumph over those who would enslave their fellow man.

(Ronald Reagan, *Weekly Compilation of Presidential Documents*, March 14, 1983)

Armageddon Deferred: 1985–1991

In 1985, four decades from its inception, the Cold War lingered on. Then the Soviet bloc disintegrated, surprisingly and suddenly, without bombs and without tanks. In 1991, it ceased to be. With its collapse, the fear of imminent nuclear catastrophe abated.

By 1985, it was clear that the Soviet economy did not work. Consumer goods, and especially housing, were in insufficient supply. The ample produce of distant farms was poorly distributed. The eastern European satellites, the annexed Baltic states, and the Soviet republics of Central Asia all sought greater independence. Experts in the Soviet bureaucracy wanted a freer hand to implement reforms, and even the long-muzzled Russian Orthodox Church raised its voice. The United States was winning the arms race. Change was imminent.

In 1985, Mikhail Gorbachev (1931–), the first Soviet leader to possess university training, launched the twin campaigns of ***glasnost*** ("openness") and ***perestroika*** ("restructuring"). By inviting the open discussion of political and economic realities, and then the cautious restructuring of public policy, Gorbachev hoped to save the world's first communist society from disintegration. Instead, open discussion turned to bitter criticism. It appeared that modest repairs could not rescue Soviet society from its path toward self-destruction. The breakdown of the Soviet system was foreshadowed in the disaster that occurred in Chernobyl (Ukraine) in 1986. There a partial meltdown at a badly managed nuclear power plant killed many swiftly, and contaminated vast areas with radioactivity.

A loyal communist but resolute reformer, Gorbachev followed where *glasnost* and *perestroika* led

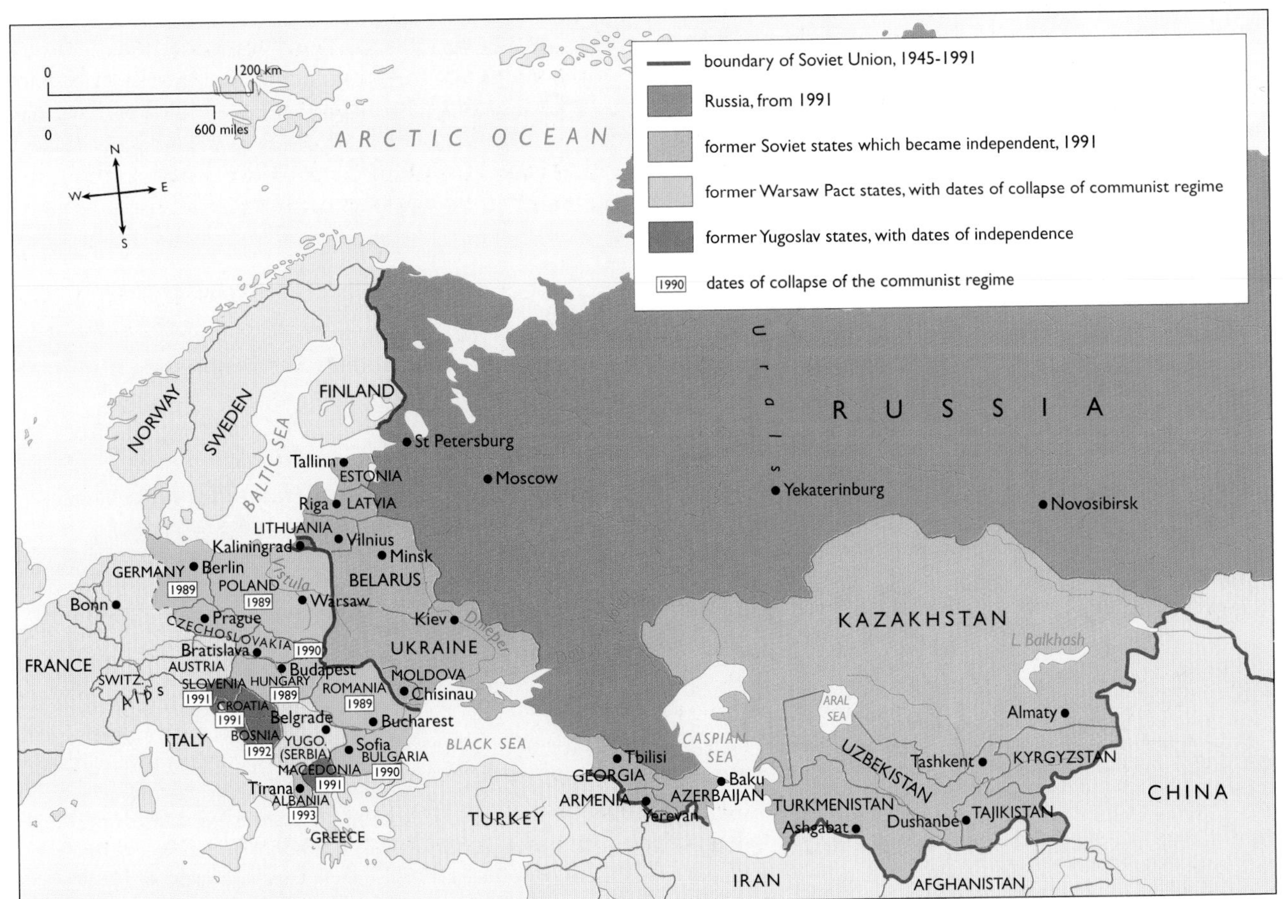

Map 29.2 Collapse of the Soviet Bloc, 1989–1991: *Soviet leader Mikhail Gorbachev's policy of glasnost permitted the largely peaceable but rapid dissolution of the Soviet Union beginning in 1989. The nations of eastern Europe promptly declared their independence and undertook programs of economic and political liberalization. In the Caucasus region and Central Asia, nationalist tensions accompanied the disaggregation of the former empire. By 1991, the USSR disappeared as a state and Russia reappeared on the map for the first time since the Russian Revolution (1917–1921).*

until, by 1989, the communist *imperium* fragmented. The Soviet Union relinquished its military commitments abroad, leaving the communist states of Cuba, North Korea, and Vietnam to fend for themselves (while China had since 1980 been moving in the direction of capitalism). Soviet troops came home from Afghanistan, abandoning the struggle against Islamist rebels who, in 1992, seized power.

Under Gorbachev's leadership, the Soviet Union ceased to monitor eastern Europe, where in a single year revolutions in all six satellite nations rejected pro-Soviet communist governments. In Poland, a newly legalized Solidarity party negotiated reforms that led to free elections and the establishment of a free market economy. In Hungary, a government committee declared independence from Communist party control, rehabilitated the leaders of the 1956 revolution and threw open the border with Austria.

In Czechoslovakia, Václav Havel (1936–) was elected President, while the parliament chose as its speaker the architect of the 1968 Prague Spring, Alexander Dubček. In East Germany, reformers forced the Soviet loyalist leader to resign, flung open the borders, and permitted the jubilant citizens to batter down the Berlin Wall with crowbars, pickaxes, and bare hands—"Stalin is dead; Europe lives!" someone scrawled on the Wall just before its demolition. Massive protests sent the communist strongman of Romania, Nicolae Ceauseşcu (1918–1989) into flight. But he was caught, convicted hastily of "genocide," and shot on Christmas day, the grisly image of his corpse displayed on television screens worldwide to an astonished public. In 1990, the two halves of the German nation reunited, and in 1991 the Baltic states declared their independence along with the former Soviet republics of Belarus, Moldova, Ukraine, Armenia, Georgia, Azerbaijan, Kazakhstan, Kyrgyzstan, and Uzbekistan.

Meanwhile, Gorbachev was negotiating an end to the arms race. Discussions begun with Reagan in Reykyavik (Iceland) in 1986 culminated in 1991 in a treaty signed by Reagan's successor, George Bush (1924–) and Gorbachev: the START I treaty, which achieved a twenty-five percent reduction in the nuclear forces of the Soviet Union and fifteen percent in those of the United States. In the meantime, both nations agreed to the CFE (Conventional Forces in Europe) treaty of 1990, which required a balance of conventional forces attained by the elimination of much of the Soviet arsenal of tanks, aircraft, and artillery.

In Moscow, the economy continued to decline. Gorbachev encouraged greater efficiency in state-run enterprises, and permitted some free-market reforms. But he would not abandon the command economy, which would have caused massive unemployment and monetary stress while, pro-capitalist advisers argued, it opened the road to economic renewal. And he continued to court communist advisers who opposed the turn to a free-market system.

Thus Gorbachev was caught between old-line communists and democratizing reformers. Prominent

A Changing of the Guard

Havel's triumph: *In many cases the collapse of Communism in Eastern Europe and the Soviet Union made outsiders insiders and vice-versa more or less overnight. Here, Czech dissident and renowned playwright Václav Havel—who under the Communists had spent time as a political prisoner—speaks as the newly elected president of Czechoslovakia in 1989.*

Djerzhinsky's fall: *Statues of key Soviet statesmen lie sidelined in a Russian park (including founder of the dreaded secret police Felix Djerzhinsky, who lies face down). Political transformation in the former Soviet Union may be less real than imagined however, since in several republics large numbers of high-ranking Communists, including Russian president Boris Yeltsin, retained power essentially by assuming non-communist political identities. Moreover, communism may show renewed vigor in Russia and elsewhere, as free-market reforms and economic growth fail.*

among the latter was Boris Yeltsin (1931–) elected president of the Russian Republic in 1991. When in August that year a group of military and secret police chiefs imprisoned Gorbachev and attempted to restore the old regime, Yeltsin opposed them, bravely announcing his defiance from atop a tank outside Moscow's parliament building. Together Yeltsin and the reinstated but debilitated Gorbachev watched as the constituent republics of the USSR declared their independence. Together they accepted the dissolution of the Soviet Union, and the end of the seventy-four-year Marxist-Leninist-Stalinist experiment.

With the disintegration of the Soviet Union, anti-communist sentiment swept the region. In parks and city centers, citizens tore down statues of Lenin and Felix Dzerzhinsky, head of the Bolshevik secret police. Worshipers returned to Russian churches, and former communists saw to the baptism of their children. The borders were opened. Jews in large numbers fled the endemic anti-Semitism of their homeland and emigrated to Israel and the United States. Islamic fundamentalism stirred in the newly independent republics of central Asia, supported by Afghan insurgents across the border, and the governments of Iran and Pakistan. Ethnic loyalties surged after the long Soviet interim among the variegate peoples of the Caucasus.

On December 25, 1991, having no nation over which to preside, Gorbachev resigned, Nobel Peace Prize (1990) in hand, to tour the lecture circuit and write his memoirs. Yeltsin managed the remnants of the dissolved Soviet Union, twelve of its fifteen now-independent states joined in the voluntary federation of the Commonwealth of Independent States (CIS). Its technological and military assets, including its stores of nuclear weapons, were reallocated to the member states. The nuclear arsenal of the former Soviet Union had been located in four of the republics—Ukraine, Belarus, Kazakhstan, and Russia itself—all of which cooperated with the commissions established to oversee arms limitation. In 1993, Yeltsin and Bush signed the START II treaty, which obtained the reduction of strategic weapons by twenty-five percent on both sides. In 1994, the United States airlifted from Kazakhstan, with Russia's permission, enough strategic enriched uranium to make twenty-four atomic bombs, lest it fall into the hands of renegade nations or illicit dealers.

In Russia, free-market speculators and corrupt bureaucrats reaped profits from the nation's reorganization. Protests against Yeltsin mounted as the currency collapsed, state employees went unpaid, and living conditions deteriorated. In 1993, communist opponents barricaded themselves in the parliament building, while their supporters fought outside. The military police quelled the revolt, firing on the parliament complex and killing more than 100 people. Yeltsin survived to face a nationalist opponent later that year, and a reelection race against a communist challenger in 1996. Amid domestic crises, while suppressing a revolt in the Caucasian region of Chechnya, Yeltsin endured, health failing, as the economy—beset by corruption, gangsterism, scarcity, and inflation, fueled by the uncontrolled printing of new rubles—went into freefall in 1998.

The dissolution of the Soviet Union meant the dissolution of the Warsaw Pact. In 1999, the Czech Republic (Czechoslovakia had divided in 1993 into

WITNESSES

The Breakdown of Communism and the End of the Cold War

Soviet premier Nikita Khrushchev denounces Stalin three years after the dictator's death (1956): The negative characteristics of Stalin . . . transformed themselves during the last years into a grave abuse of power by Stalin, which caused untold harm to our Party. . . . Stalin acted . . . by imposing his concepts and demanding absolute submission to his opinion. Whoever opposed . . . was doomed to removal from the leading collective and to subsequent moral and physical annihilation. . . .

Stalin originated the concept "enemy of the people." This term . . . made possible the usage of the most cruel repression, violating all norms of revolutionary legality against any one who in any way disagreed with Stalin. . . . In . . . actuality, the only proof of guilt used . . . was the "confession" of the accused himself; and, as subsequent probing proved, "confessions" were acquired through physical pressures [ie, torture] against the accused.

(Nikita Khrushchev, US Congress, 85th Congress, 1st session, 1957)

Soviet premier Mikhail Gorbachev on the background and need for *perestroika* (restructuring) (1987): The Soviet Union is a young state without analogues in history or in the modern world. Over the past seven decades . . . our country has traveled a path equal to centuries. . . . Huge productive forces, a powerful intellectual potential, a highly advanced culture, a unique community of over one hundred nations and nationalities, and firm social protection for 280 million people on a territory forming one-sixth of the Earth—such are our great and indisputable achievements and Soviet people are justly proud of them. . . .

At some stage—this became particularly clear in the latter half of the seventies—something happened that was at first sight inexplicable. The country began to lose momentum. . . . Difficulties began to accumulate and deteriorate, and unresolved problems to multiply. . . . We first discovered a slowing economic growth. In the last fifteen years the national income growth rates had declined by more than half . . . As time went on, material resources became harder to get and more expensive. . . .

(Mikhail Gorbachev, *Perestroika: New Thinking for Our Country and the World*, 1987)

Czech president Václav Havel speaks of the past and present at a New Year's address shortly after the overthrow of communism in his country (1990): For 40 years you have heard on this day from the mouths of my predecessors . . . the same thing: how our country is flourishing, how many more millions of tons of steel we have produced, how we are all happy, how we believe in our Government and what beautiful prospects are opening ahead of us. I assume you have not named me to this office so that I, too, should lie to you. Our country is not flourishing. . . . The state, which calls itself a state of workers, is humiliating and exploiting them instead. . . . [In education] we rank 72nd in the world. We have spoiled our land, rivers and forests . . . and we have, today, the worst environment in the whole of Europe. . . . The worst of it is that we live [also] in a spoiled moral environment. We have become morally ill because we are used to saying one thing and thinking another. We have learned not to believe in anything, not to care about each other, to worry only about ourselves. . . .

(From *New York Times*, "Havel's Vision—Excerpts from Speech by the Czech President", January 2, 1990)

The economic historian Robert Heilbroner on the future prospects for Socialism (1990): I am not very sanguine about the prospect that socialism will continue as an important form of economic organization now that Communism is finished. . . . [T]he collapse of the planned economies has forced us to rethink the meaning of socialism. As a semireligious vision of a transformed humanity, it has been dealt devastating blows in the twentieth century. As a blueprint for a rationally planned society, it is in tatters.

(Robert Heilbroner, "After Communism" in *The New Yorker*, September 10, 1990)

Joel Barr, American-born Soviet spy and defector to the Soviet Union (1950), explains why he renounced communism (1998): I believe that now history will show that the Russian Revolution was a tremendous mistake. . . . It was a step backward. The real revolution for mankind that will go down for many, many years was the American Revolution.

(From *New York Times*, August 16, 1998)

the Czech Republic and Slovakia), Poland, and Hungary were admitted to NATO. Russia itself, the chief member of the "evil empire" NATO had been born to combat, received associate status.

In 1999, as a new century and a new millennium approached, the nations of the world had begun to hope that the deadly logic of "mutual assured destruction" would not end in a final struggle between East and West, communism and capitalism, good and evil. The world had escaped the test of Armageddon, and the Apocalypse, for the moment, had been postponed.

ALL YOU NEED IS LOVE

It was a different world, though, from the one envisioned at Yalta by the victors of World War II. The generation born in the shadow of the bomb—the product of a postwar demographic bubble, bulging in numbers, unique in self-absorption—transformed the world. This "baby boom" cohort, the first ever threatened from birth by global annihilation, reached adolescence during the 1960s when, especially in the United States, they erupted in protest against the Cold War and its makers. Summoned to fight during the unpopular Vietnam War, they retorted "Hell no! We won't go!"; then impudently commanded their elders to "Make love, not war!" "All you need is love," the popular rock music group called the Beatles proclaimed in 1967, in a live performance broadcast worldwide via satellite to some 400 million listeners.

During the next decades, the Sixties generation and its imitators sought to bind up the world's wounds. The needs of others for food, security, and dignity engaged a generation traumatized by Cold War brinkmanship. The Earth itself languished, ravaged by the deadly machines that powered the mindless quest for wealth and power. It, too, cried for love, not war.

Rolling Stones

The Power of Protest The Sixties generation, like "rolling stones" (featured in a song by Bob Dylan, b. Robert Zimmerman, 1941) that had shed the moss of the past, set out to transform the politics, society, and culture of the West. They protested the bomb, joining pacifists of an older generation such as philosopher Bertrand Russell and physicist Albert Einstein (see Chapter 26), and reading Erich Maria Remarque's *All Quiet on the Western Front* (1929) about the futilities of the first World War, or Joseph Heller's *Catch-22* (1961) about the absurdities of the second.

From protesting the bomb, young activists joined with the civil rights movement, seeking to end discrimination against those of African descent (see Chapter 28). Student leaders who had experienced the thrill of mass mobilization and commitment to a cause were determined to defy the conformist culture of their parents with a new militancy.

In 1964, students at the Berkeley campus of the University of California protested against college officials who had interfered, as they saw it, with their right to form political organizations. This Berkeley Free Speech movement, in which the university itself came to symbolize all the repressive forces of society, prefigured the movements soon to emerge to protest United States involvement in the Vietnam War (see Chapter 28).

That war, billed by the "establishment" as a campaign against communism, was identified by the young as one more chapter in the tedious tale of the strong bullying the weak. By 1967, when large numbers of young men were being drafted to serve in Vietnam, anti-war protests flared on college campuses that housed one-third of the cohort born between 1945 and 1949. At teach-ins, faculty mentors explained to a younger generation raised on television and rock 'n' roll where Indochina was, and why Vietnamese independence mattered. At rallies, hundreds or thousands gathered at a chosen moment to witness their opposition to the war. Sometimes protest turned violent, as some participants taunted the security forces sent to keep order, or disrupted traffic, or broke windows.

To student observers, the spectacle of a superpower unleashing its vast arsenal against impoverished Vietnamese peasants in order to deny them the independence they ardently sought was both horrible and absurd. A "credibility gap" yawned wide as televised announcements of specious victories, and exaggerated reports of the number of the slaughtered made politicized students enduringly skeptical of government. "Hey, hey, LBJ, how many kids have you killed today?" they taunted the president in one ditty from the angry repertoire of student protest.

The anti-war frenzy climbed from 1968 to 1972. In 1968, following the debacle of the Tet Offensive, the dispirited President Lyndon B. Johnson (1908–1973) announced that he would not seek another term in office. Later that year, the despair of many Americans intensified with the assassination of two respected leaders: Martin Luther King, Jr. (see Chapter 28), champion of civil rights; and presidential candidate Robert F. Kennedy (1925–1968), younger brother of the charismatic President John F. Kennedy

(1917–1963), the victim of another assassin in 1963. Violence seemed to be winning.

Meanwhile, the American model of youth protest had impressed Europe. In Paris in May 1968, students protested against government cuts in funding for social spending and universities. Provoked by police intimidation of the Parisian Left Bank community of intellectuals and artists, students set up barricades in the streets and harassed the forces sent to maintain order. Many citizens supported the students; industrial workers struck in sympathy. By early June, however, the deft maneuvering of president Charles de Gaulle (1890–1970) brought the revolt to a quick close. The Parisian example of student resistance to government inspired student revolts in Britain, Italy, and, with greater consequence, in Czechoslovakia.

In the United States in 1969, the new president Richard Nixon (1913–1994) implemented "Vietnamization" (see Chapter 28), a dual strategy of escalated bombing and troop reduction leading to an eventual withdrawal of all United States forces in 1973. In 1970, at Kent State University (in Kent, Ohio), National Guardsmen shot at rock-throwing students—their contemporaries—killing four. It seemed as though the nation had reached a nadir of depravity; it devoured its own children, whose one crime was to hate war. Public opposition to the war surged. The Nixon administration quieted the protest by ending the draft, making the United States military a volunteer force. Those who "would not go" did not have to.

The youth of "the movement"—an affluent and largely white minority—won their battle against their elders. Poor white, black, or brown young men from inner cities and rural towns had no choice but to go. They fought a vicious war without popular support and returned to a nation embarrassed by their presence. They did not figure in the perceptions of the youth who forged the counter-culture of the Sixties founded on the right of each individual to unlimited self-expression. Nor did the "silent majority" of citizens, young and old, who were untouched or dismayed by student radicalism.

A Changing Culture The American youth rebellion, led by a privileged few, had wide-reaching social and cultural impact. During the 1950s, the men and women who had endured the Depression and defeated Nazism pursued their careers, bought houses and cars, populated the suburbs, and settled down to enjoy unprecedented economic prosperity. In the 1960s, their children—or at least a rebellious vanguard—spurned those careers, those neighborhoods, that complacency. In their dress, their tastes, and their sexual mores, they cast aside norms that had so recently triumphed with a stunning wartime victory, and replaced them with provocative new ones.

Costume and style tell the story of cultural transformation. Spurning their fathers' gray-flannel suits and their mothers' crinolined dresses, they dressed in stark black, or in exotic peasant frocks, or, most often, in blue jeans, the dark denim uniform of the working class. Movement pacesetters might favor bizarre hats, or accessories with a military theme (camouflage, knapsacks, boots), or non-precious jewelry crafted by the indigenes of the Americas, Africa, or Asia. They spurned steak and potatoes for international menus (Mexican, Chinese, Indian, Vietnamese), or chose a vegetarian regimen. Where older adults sipped cocktails, the student rebels of the Sixties took up drugs.

The psychoactive drugs adopted by the young induced mental conditions that mocked conventional standards of decorum, rationality, and responsibility. They included marijuana preeminently (a substance that produced mild effects comparable to those produced by moderate alcohol consumption), but also "hard drugs" such as LSD (lysergic acid diethylamide), heroin, and cocaine.

Drug use for vanguard rebels had a range of purposes. Drugs might create states of heightened sensitivity. Drug use allowed the avoidance of social responsibility, inviting the initiate to "turn on and drop out." It helped the young create an alternative culture, a moral universe distinct from that of the adults who wielded power and authority.

The Sixties produced a musical style of its own of superb quality and genuinely revolutionary effect—"rock," or "hard rock," evolved from the "rock 'n' roll" of the previous decade. The drug culture shaped rock music in several ways. Listeners and performers alike often used drugs, while song lyrics often celebrated drug use. The lack of restraint induced by drug use may have spurred the innovations of rock artists. The relations between the drug culture and rock are important; yet rock is much more than the musical accompaniment to the aimless leisure of the drug-consuming young.

Rock emerged from the American musical genres of the 1950s. "Pop," or popular music, featured easy melodies sung by polished performers—mainly white—for mainstream record companies. "Country and western" was a nostalgic regional style—also mainly white—that affirmed the customs of the old south and looked back to frontier days. "Rhythm and blues," or "blues," informed by jazz performance, communicated the depths of the African American experience (see Chapter 26). Spurned by most whites, it was the cultivated taste of an affluent few. Then in 1955, the southern white performer Elvis Presley (1935–1977) emerged to sing, gyrate, and sway a new kind of music, a compelling and shocking amalgam of black rhythms and sound.

By the 1960s, the generation formed by the experience of the Cold War had accepted Presley's musical challenge. Rock was not just a blend of musical motifs; it was social criticism. Adopting the simple, direct style of folk music traditions, such singers as Joan Baez (1941–) and Bob Dylan assailed the hypocrisy of mainstream culture. Meanwhile the British group the Beatles, which shot to stardom in 1962, developed Presley's style in a new mix of youth themes and counter-cultural challenges. Young people thronged to rock concerts and danced to the music of the Beatles and their disciples—as did the 450,000 who assembled in 1969, the apogee of rock, at the Woodstock Music Festival in New York State's gracious Catskill Mountains.

Rock's radical challenge to contemporary values was echoed in the cinema of the Sixties. In its visual reconstruction of reality, film had an inherently critical function (see Chapter 26), making it the ideal medium by which to convey the Sixties mood of rebellion. The anti-establishment heroes of *Bonnie and Clyde* (Arthur Penn, director; 1967), shockingly mutilated in the protracted montage of their death at the hands of police pursuers, and of *The Wild Bunch* (Sam Peckinpah, director; 1969), which opens and ends with brutal and senseless massacres, were emblems of the Sixties spirit.

European film had different concerns, elegantly communicated to select audiences while the larger public, fleeing such serious themes, sought primarily to be entertained. In France, Italy, and Sweden filmmakers meditated on the trauma of war and explored the deeper dimensions of the self. The films of Italian directors Federico Fellini (1920–1993) and Michelangelo Antonioni (1912–), notably *La dolce vita* ("The Good Life," 1960) and *L'avventura* ("The Adventure," 1959), evoke brilliantly the contradictions of postwar lives, while the Swedish director Ingmar Bergman (1918–) experimented with visual allegory to probe human emotion, as in *The Seventh Seal* (1956). The French directors of the *nouvelle vague* ("New Wave") that arrived in the 1950s celebrated human self-determination and freedom, as did *Les Quatre cents coups* ("The 400 Blows") by François Truffaut (1932–1984) and *À bout de souffle* ("Breathless") by Jean-Luc Godard (1930–), both released in 1959.

During the 1950s, the themes of human struggle against barbarism and death, a pensive reflection on the first half of a terrible century, found expression in a new generation of novelists, such as the French-Algerian Albert Camus (1913–1960), author of *The Plague* (1947). On the stage, the "theater of the absurd" is exemplified by the work of the Irish playwright Samuel Beckett (1906–1989), whose 1953 *Waiting for Godot* took up the theme of the dramatic exploration of meaning launched in the 1920s by Pirandello and Brecht (see Chapter 26). In the same way, the existentialism of Heidegger and Sartre (see Chapter 26), rooted in the 1930s and 1940s, found a new audience in the postwar era.

From the 1960s, the humanistic themes of the first flush of postwar culture shaded toward disillusionment. Many authors looked to Third World nations for models of political and cultural engagement, while others turned to revising or "deconstructing" established norms of thought and feeling. For instance, the French historian and philosopher Michel Foucault (1926–1984) exposed in his *Madness and Civilization* (1961) the repressive operation of common social practices.

On the other side of the Iron Curtain, where thought was governed by censors, cultural life was quite different (see Chapter 27). There novelists, poets, physicists, and historians covertly circulated in *samizdat* ("self-publication," by hand-delivered manuscript) their vision of a society distorted by communist repression. Boris Pasternak (1890–1960), an author who had experienced the 1917 revolution and its Stalinist aftermath, eluded the censors by

WITNESSES

Culture and Politics in the 1960s

Bob Dylan, The Times They are a-Changin' (1964):

Come mothers and fathers
Throughout the land
And don't criticize
What you can't understand
Your sons and your daughters
Are beyond your command
Your old road
Is rapidly agin'
Please get out of the new one
If you can't lend your hand
For the times they are a-changin'.
(Bob Dylan, *Lyrics, 1962–1985*, 1985)

Years of Protest

Flower power: *Fears of Communist expansion in Southeast Asia led the United States into a demoralizing and increasingly unpopular war in Vietnam, which aroused a whole generation to protest. In this photograph anti-war demonstrators in Washington, D.C. oppose guns with flowers.*

publishing in Italy his *Doctor Zhivago* (1957), a novel breathing disillusionment with the whole Bolshevik experiment. *The Gulag Archipelago* by Alexander Solzhenitsyn (1918–), printed in Paris in 1973 after long *samizdat* currency, appalled the world with the story of Soviet forced-labor camps. The powerful voices of such dissidents as the physicist Andrei Sakharov (1921–1989) and historian Roy Medvedev (1925–) also circulated in secret.

Captivated by the popular culture that radiated from the United States, the commodified product of its protest movement, most Europeans were as indifferent to these trends in literature and thought as they were to art cinema. Rock music and movies, radio and television, the casual dress of anti-establishment youth, above all the uniform of blue jeans and T-shirts—these were the prizes consumers sought. Beyond the Iron Curtain, such treasures circulated in the underground, or "black" market.

To protest, drugs, music, film, and costume the youth movement added another ingredient: sexual revolution. In this most intimate sphere of human behavior, the young again defied the values of their elders. Courtship rituals, female chastity, monogamy, even fidelity in non-marital relationships—all these were questioned and rejected. Where the fear of unwanted pregnancy had once deterred women from the path of sexual radicalism, the new pharmacological discovery—the birth control "pill"—made it feasible. The custom of "swinging" gained popularity among some, which invited promiscuous and multiple sexual encounters, including adulterous, homosexual, and interracial relations.

The sexual radicalism of the Sixties accomplished a profound social revolution. In all previous civilizations, male elites had seen to the sexual regulation of their families.

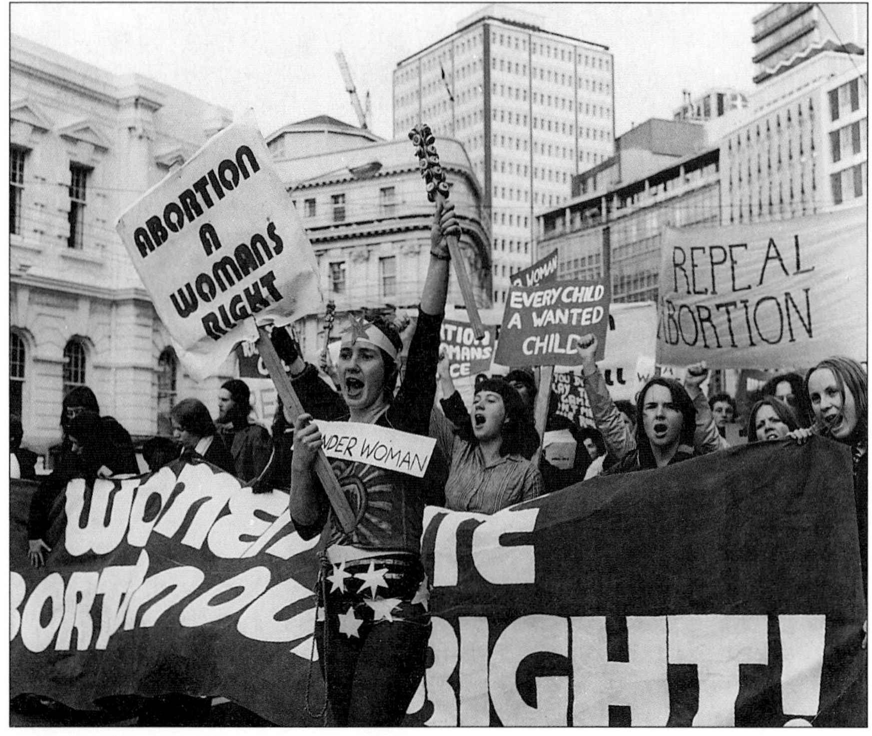

Pro-choice: *The Sixties gave rise to the sexual revolution, encouraging a new wave of feminist activism in support of abortion rights. Here, a star-spangled "Wonder Woman" leads an angry pro-choice rally in New Zealand, 1977, demanding a woman's right to bear only "wanted" children.*

Now a vanguard group, harvesting the product of the socialist and feminist movements of the past two centuries, rejected all sexual regulation, with enduring effects on culture and society. "Your sons and your daughters are beyond your command . . .," Dylan hissed at the elders, "for the times they are a-changin'."

Women of Worth

The sexual revolution born of the Sixties movement in the United States allowed women to reject conventional restraints. It also encouraged the forging of a new feminism that sought freedoms for women of all social classes and of all nations, races, and religions. Now all women everywhere were deemed to be, in the biblical phrase, "women of worth."

The Demand for Equality The new feminism of the 1960s was the culmination of earlier feminist ideals, restated vigorously in two important books. In 1949, the writer Simone de Beauvoir's (1908–1986) brilliant manifesto, *The Second Sex*, made a postwar generation of women aware of the social denigration of women. In 1963, the American Betty Friedan's (1921–) *The Feminine Mystique* identified the cultural forces that denied women power and responsibility. The mirage of "femininity" controlled women's lives, Friedan argued. It confined their thoughts to their housecleaning and their hairdos, and their days to shopping and self-doubt. In 1966, Friedan co-founded the National Organization of Women (NOW), the foremost institutional embodiment of the new feminism.

Women activists called for female autonomy in virtually every aspect of contemporary life. In the political sphere, women leaders pushed beyond the demand for suffrage, the key issue of earlier feminism (see Chapters 24, 26), to seek greater access to power. In many nations, women candidates were elected to political office, some reaching the highest political positions, as did Golda Meir (1898–1978) in Israel, Indira Gandhi (1917–1984) in India, and Margaret Thatcher (1925–) in Britain (1979–1990). Recently, women have gained the highest political positions in Iceland, Ireland, Norway, Portugal, and Poland in Europe; and in Argentina, Bangladesh, Dominica, Nicaragua, Pakistan, Sri Lanka, and Turkey elsewhere. In Europe, they have claimed twenty-five percent of the seats in the European Parliament; the percentage of women worldwide serving as national parliamentarians, in contrast, has changed little since 1975, remaining well under ten percent.

In the workplace as in politics, women's demands heightened. Although women made up an increasing proportion of the workforce in the postwar decades—they are now about one-half of all workers in the United States, about one-third in western Europe—they received lower wages than male workers. The demand for "equal pay for equal work" has brought about in some nations the narrowing, but not the elimination, of the "wage gap."

Expanded training opportunities gained women entrance to previously closed trades and professions. They now work in construction and trucking, as police and postal officials, in the armed forces, and as attorneys and judges, medical doctors and university professors. Professionalization of those careers that women traditionally had entered, such as teaching and nursing, has enhanced their status and salaries. Increasingly, women have reached executive levels of modern corporations where (although an invisible "glass ceiling" retards their entry to the highest positions or levels of compensation) they enjoy great authority and high salaries.

Western women increasingly insist on the right to work unimpeded by verbal or physical intimidation from male co-workers seeking sexual relations or expressing hostility to females. Activists have engaged employers and government in the crusade against "sexual harassment."

Risks to women outside of the workplace have also concerned female activists, where women are victims of rape, including marital rape, and domestic violence—the latter the leading cause, after war, of harm and death to women worldwide. In many countries, feminists have brought these violations into public consciousness, and have had them legally defined as crimes. Liberalized divorce laws in most Western nations enable women to escape abusive marriages.

The Politics of Reproduction Women's rights must include, feminists insist, the liberty to make choices about their bodies. Thus the drive undertaken by early-century feminists (see Chapter 26) to make contraception available to all women has culminated in the "pro-choice" movement of the century's last decades, whose activists have sought to make contraception safe, cheap, and available.

These goals put feminists at odds with the guardians of traditional society, mostly male. That conflict became especially sharp over the issue of abortion. In many countries, clinical abortion was and has remained illegal; in others, the right of abortion has broad acceptance. The development since 1988 of an effective oral abortifacient (RU 486) promises a greater ease of access to abortion than heretofore. In the United States, a struggle between advocates for the right to abort (the "pro-choice" faction) and those opposed (the "pro-life" faction) has been a prominent feature of contemporary life.

Paradoxically, the demands of contemporary feminism for women's complete liberation contradicts the **maternalist** goals advocated by earlier feminist leaders (see Chapter 26). These contended that women's most powerful role was in the family. Recent emphasis on women's reproductive rights, however, points away from maternalism, insisting that women be free to have few or no children; and to make those choices independently of their fathers, or the men whose offspring they carry. Advocates of traditional family generally oppose both these assumptions, as well as abortion and other mechanisms—easy divorce, certain tax measures—they perceive as undermining the stability of the family.

The feminist position dictates that unmarried women should be as free as married women to choose to bear children, and would wholly eliminate the distinction between "legitimate" and "illegitimate" birth. The stigma associated with illegitimacy has largely faded in the developed nations, along with the economic sanctions and legal disabilities that "bastard" children so born once suffered. Furthermore, some feminist theorists argue that women who give birth outside of a marital family are entitled to government support for the raising of their children. Why, they ask, should some women be deprived of the right to raise future citizens merely because of their economic or social position, when modern democratic societies no longer bar access to educational or employment opportunities on those grounds?

The birthing of children, some feminists have argued, has been excessively medicalized. Whereas women in earlier societies (or outside of the West) often gave birth with the assistance of a female midwife, modernization has placed the process of birth in the hospital, frequently under the care of a male physician. Feminism has encouraged a revival of midwifery, and argued for a woman's right to safe and successful childbirth outside of the hospital environment. Where modern medicine may intervene too much with childbirth, however, it has not done enough for other aspects of women's health. Resources have been directed disproportionately to

WITNESSES

Women and the Post-War World: Manifestos, Achievements, Promises

The Redstockings Manifesto by a New York organization of feminists (1969): Women are an oppressed class. Our oppression is total, affecting every facet of our lives. We are exploited as sex objects, breeders, domestic servants, and cheap labor . . . whose only purpose is to enhance men's lives. . . . Our prescribed behavior is enforced by the threat of physical violence. Because we have lived so intimately with our oppressors, in isolation from each other, we have been kept from seeing our personal suffering as a political condition. . . . In reality, every such relationship is a *class* relationship, and the conflicts between individual men and women are political conflicts that can only be solved collectively.
(Circulated in typescript, July 7, 1969)

A new order for Chinese women: China's marriage law, passed by the Communists (1949): Article 1. The arbitrary and compulsory feudal marriage system, which is based on the superiority of man over woman and which ignores the children's interests, shall be abolished. The new democratic marriage system, which is based on free choice of partners, on monogamy, on equal rights for both sexes, and on protection of the lawful interests of women and children, shall be put into effect. . . .
Article 7. Husband and wife are companions living together and shall enjoy equal status in the home.
(*The Marriage Law of the People's Republic of China*, 1959)

Women and the family in Revolutionary Iran: from the Constitution of the Islamic Republic of Iran (1979): The family unit is the foundation of society and the main institution for the growth and advancement of mankind. . . . It is the principal duty of the Islamic government to regard women as the unifying factor of the family unit and its position. They are a factor in bringing the family out of the service of propagating consumerism and exploitation and renewing the vital and valuable duty of motherhood in raising educated human beings. . . . As a result motherhood is accepted as a most profound responsibility in the Muslim viewpoint and will, therefore, be accorded the highest value and generosity.
(T. Y. Ismael, *Iraq and Iran: Roots of Conflict*, 1982)

diseases suffered by men (prostate cancer), or to the male experience of diseases women also suffer (heart disease and stroke), and too little to diseases of women (breast cancer, osteoporosis).

Although feminists agree on most of these issues, they tend to disagree on two others: prostitution and pornography. Some feminists argue that prostitution degrades women. Others respond that women must be free to seek income from the use of their bodies, just as athletes or performers are. Similarly, some feminists see pornography as essentially antifemale, an extension of male acts of violence to representations of masculine power. Others see pornography as a form of expression that must be as free as all other forms of expression, and fear that imposing limits on pornography would open the way to reimposing restrictions on sexual expression so painfully and recently lifted.

Women Outside the West The feminist activists of the Western world have gained widespread support for women's freedoms. These are not equally recognized in other parts of the world. In communist and formerly communist states—the Soviet Union and its satellites, China, North Korea, Vietnam, and Cuba—women, in theory, possessed the same political and economic rights as men, and full freedom of reproductive choice. Yet women faced the dangers of sexual harassment, rape, and domestic abuse in communist societies as they did in the West. Despite official formulations, they have had a disproportionate responsibility for household tasks—housework, childrearing, care of the elderly. Although abortion has been freely available, gynecological and contraceptive services have been restricted.

In China, women's reproductive freedom has recently been constrained by state policy decreeing that no couple should have more than one child. Abortion has been imposed even when not desired, in as late as the ninth month of pregnancy. Yet these restrictions should be seen in the light of the great progress towards women's equality made under communism. In traditional China, patriarchal authority was absolute; women's bodies bore its impress, as the traditional practice of the binding of feet from infancy produced the effect of disproportionately tiny feet in adult women.

Women, ironically, have suffered from the collapse of communism in the Soviet Union and eastern Europe, even as civil liberties have been restored. Communist governments had (in theory) guaranteed access to childcare, maternity benefits, and abortion, and had instituted quotas assuring women's representation in national assemblies. With their fall, women resumed burdens they thought they had lost, and have borne disproportionately the hardships of economic and cultural dislocation. In Poland, for example, the reinvigorated Roman Catholic Church has reaffirmed its uncompromising stand against birth control and abortion. In the central Asian republics of the former Soviet Union, where Islamic customs are being restored, many women are obliged to return to traditional and familial roles.

Women of Islamic societies outside the communist realm also face special obstacles to their liberation. Islam is at once a faith and a way of life, and its law is both religious and civil (see Chapter 8). Its precepts with regard to women have not been secularized, as have been those of Western society. Women are understood to be under the protection of male kin at all times. In the more conservative Islamic societies, they are expected to be veiled in public, and may be barred from public life or even from such occupations as driving a car or going to university.

Non-Islamic Asian women also suffer disadvantages unknown in the West. In Japan, although some women obtain entry to elite universities and positions in a bustling corporate culture, traditional family norms keep many at home or, if in the workplace, in subordinate positions. In India, also, enduring social customs continue to disadvantage many women. Although the custom of *suttee*—where a widow went alive to the funeral pyre of her husband—has virtually disappeared, daughters are still valued less than their brothers in many Indian families. Often they are fed less, sold into prostitution (there are some 300,000 child prostitutes, mostly girls), or married to strangers for the advantage of other family members (and even murdered by their husbands if dowry demands are not met). The great poverty of peasant villagers exacerbates these problems. Women of the elite social strata, in contrast, are more likely to obtain secondary and university education, and to hold important public positions.

In Latin America, poverty also continues to disadvantage women, although maternal mortality rates are lower than in Africa, the Middle East, and southern Asia. A strong Catholic tradition has meant the limited availability of abortion, although contraception is generally available.

Perhaps the condition of women is nowhere more dismal than in Africa, where older social customs, including polygamy and slavery, disenfranchise many, and where exceptional poverty afflicts nearly all. Migrant labor patterns take men out of villages, and leave women behind to manage agricultural work and raise their children alone. Epidemic disease, including measles, tuberculosis, and AIDS (acquired immune deficiency syndrome; see below), has imposed upon women additional burdens of nursing and the trauma of child death. Most seriously, the rate of the heterosexual transmission of AIDS is higher in Africa than anywhere else in the world, resulting in the disproportionate infection of women. Of 3.8 million women worldwide who are infected with AIDS, 3.36 million, or eighty-eight percent, live in sub-Saharan Africa. Moreover, more women than men are carrying the HIV virus that promises the future development of the disease, implying that women will soon exceed men among the African victims of AIDS.

In a band of states cutting across Africa from Guinea in the west to Egypt, Ethiopia, and Somalia in the east, many women undergo at puberty the controversial surgical procedure of clitorectomy—also referred to as "female circumcision" or "genital mutilation". (In clitorectomy, the clitoris and all or part of the labia minora are excised; in the rarer practice of infibulation, part of the labia majora is excised as well, and most of the vaginal opening is stitched closed.) This operation is often performed by midwives without medical training and without anesthesia, in the absence of sterilized implements or a sanitary environment. It is estimated that 130 million women in the world today have undergone some form of genital cutting.

The consequence of clitorectomy performed by traditional methods is often infection and sometimes death. In addition, the surgery results in the diminution of sensation in sexual contacts. That desensitization is at once the reason for clitorectomy, intended to promote the chastity of young brides; but also one reason for the opposition to it that has mounted in recent years. For feminists, clitorectomy is an assault on women's freedom and dignity. For members of those societies where the practice is common, it is a venerable tradition. The women concerned are themselves divided. Some have left their homelands in order to save themselves or their daughters from the experience. Others are proud to observe the customs of their people.

In a world still sharply divided into wealthier and poorer regions, women have different agendas. In the Western world (including Australia, New Zealand, and Japan), women are seeking equity in the workplace and in politics, reproductive rights, support in childcare and household responsibilities, and suitable medical attention. Elsewhere, women of the elites may share some of the concerns of their counterparts in the Western world. But most are poor, and suffer

Map 29.3 (above and right) Women of the World, 1990s: *By the 1990s, the condition of women in the developed world (the West plus Japan) had improved greatly, while women in the rest of the world still suffered grave hardships. Some of the indices of women's welfare are indicated here: violence, literacy, and the female deficit. The female deficit is that number indicating "missing women": the shortfall in the number of women who should be alive given the number of men. Their absence can be explained by several factors, including differential levels of nutrition and selective feticide or infanticide.*

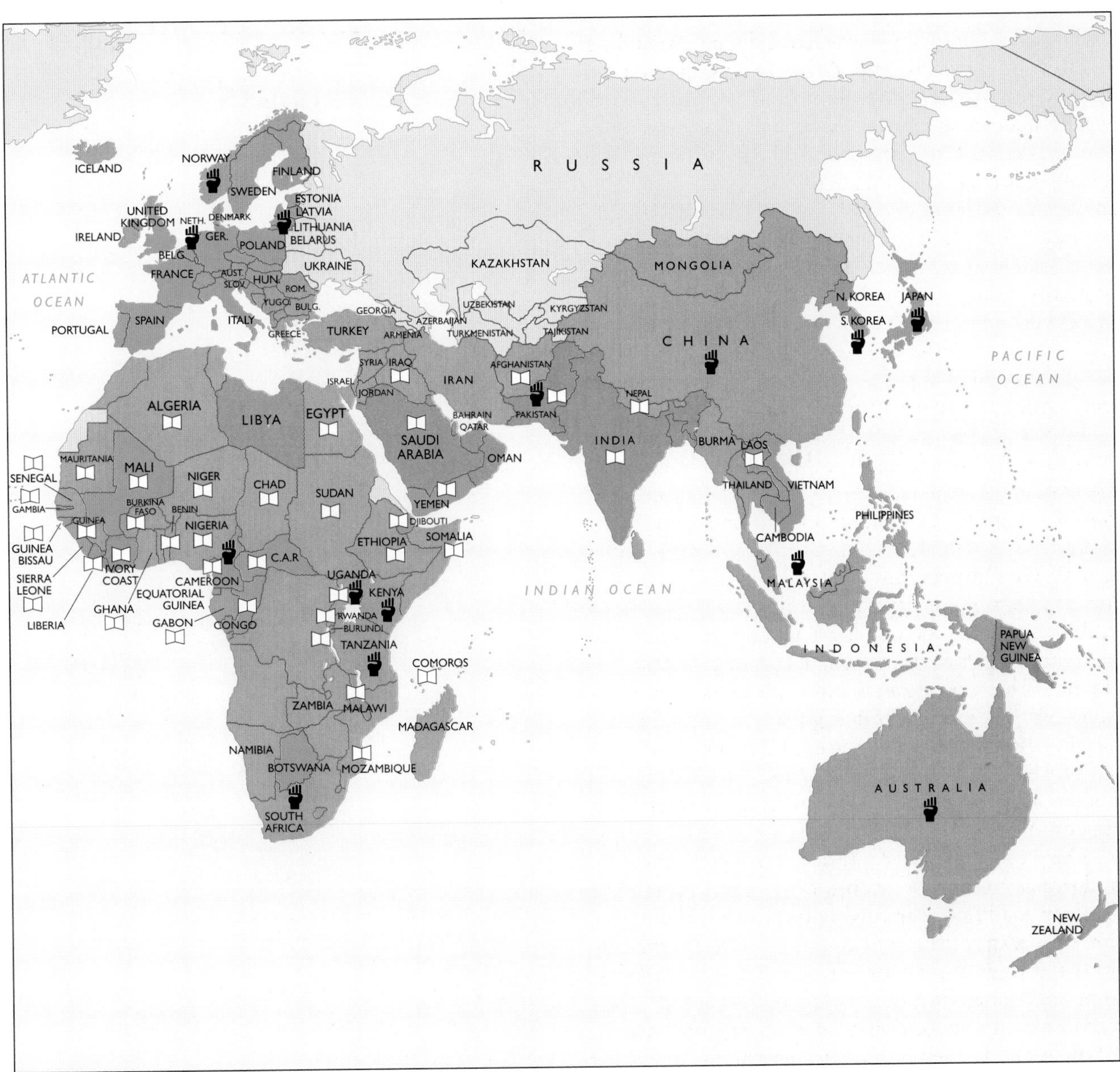

the greater likelihood that they will be undernourished, poorly educated, and exposed to epidemic disease; or sold into prostitution or slavery, or compelled to enter into unwanted or degrading marital relationships.

Perhaps the single greatest indication of poor women's disadvantage in the developing world is their disappearance—for in several of these regions, women are missing in large numbers. Under normal circumstances, 95 girls are born for every 100 boys, and a similar sex ratio should be expected in the adult population. But there are ten percent fewer women than there should be in India, Burma, Pakistan in Asia; in Saudi Arabia, Kuwait, the United Arab Emirates, and Oman in the Middle East; and Libya in North Africa. In addition, several more nations have deficits of five percent, including China (where the deficit amounts to a monumental 20 million women), and several more with deficits up to that level. Almost all of the nations with such deficits are in the developing world (while many of the Western nations, in contrast, have a surplus of women). These aberrations result in a cumulative deficit of some 120 million women worldwide.

This disparity between the quantity of female and male life is an index of discrimination against women. More than men, women are denied nutrition, medical care, shelter, education, and other benefits. They are

Women, Poverty, and War

Zairian Tutsi refugees, 1996

Around the world, women's experience of poverty and war is sharpened because of their role as childbearers. At right, an Indian woman, desperate to conceive a male child, sits in 1993 with her unwanted two-year old daughter, whom she admits having "wanted to kill". She has, she says, already murdered a previous daughter. Genocidal war in Rwanda and Burundi between its Hutu and Tutsi peoples spilled over the border into Zaire and made refugees of thousands, including this Tutsi mother and child in the foreground of the photograph above. In Yugoslavia, a bewildering mix of ethnic, religious, and historical animosities engendered violent campaigns of "ethnic cleansing" and, in response, the NATO bombing of Serbia, perceived as the chief aggressor. In the photograph below an Albanian mother weeps for her son, killed in Kosovo in October 1998, by an explosive left by Serbian military police.

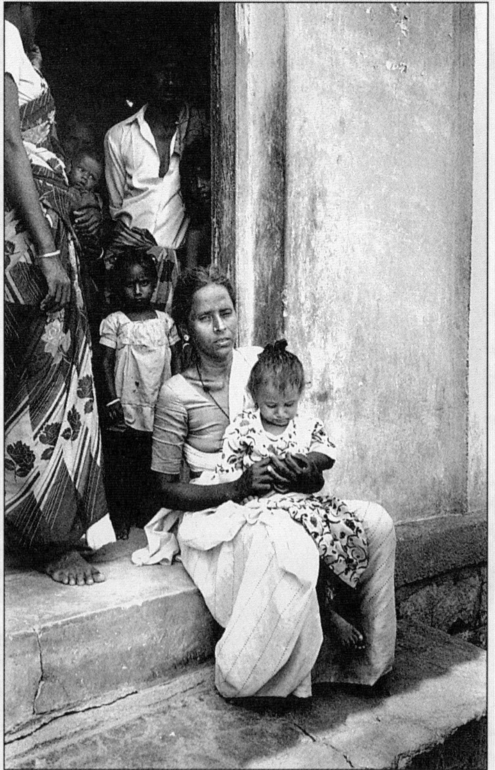

Indian mother and daughter, 1993

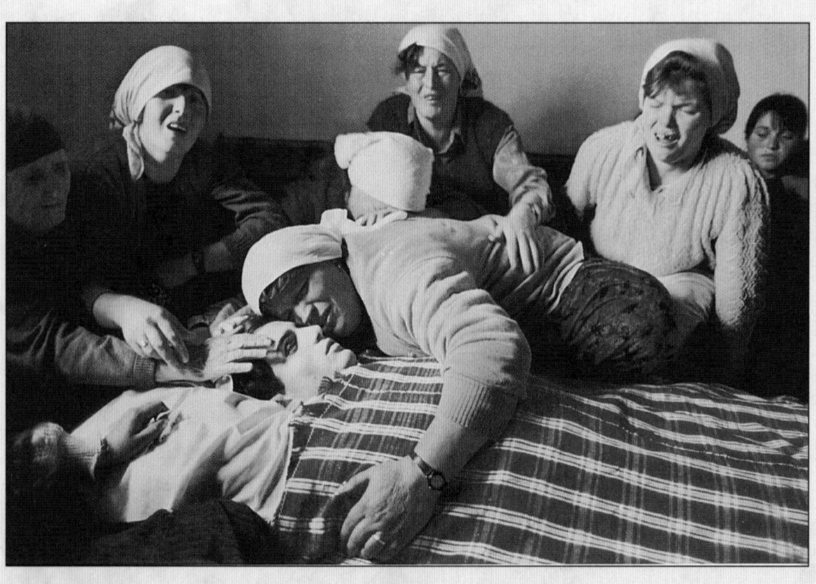

Albanian mother in mourning, 1998

forced into servitude and prostitution, conditions often resulting in premature death. They are killed in childhood, or aborted prenatally, more often than male siblings. Whereas in affluent nations, abortion is a woman's choice, in poorer nations it is more often used to deny female life.

Abortion in general is more widely used in the emerging nations than in the wealthy nations of the world. Although twenty percent of pregnancies worldwide end in abortion, most abortions are performed outside of western Europe and North America. Ironically, the procedure is generally legal and medical facilities are advanced in those regions where abortions are less frequently performed. In regions with the highest rates of abortion, the procedure is more often illegal and improperly performed. Women in developing nations are 300 times more likely than their wealthier peers of the West and the North to experience complications (including death) as a consequence of abortion.

In the world's poorer regions, additionally, women are more likely to be pressed into prostitution and less likely to be educated. Especially in Asia, burdensome daughters are sold into sex slavery, and women without male protection seek income from prostitution. "Sex tourism," a custom where prosperous men from North America, western Europe, Saudi Arabia, and Australia seek recreational sex in certain cooperating markets in India, Indochina, Indonesia, and Brazil, has heightened the demand for child prostitutes.

Furthermore, women in Africa, the Middle East, and Asia show higher rates of illiteracy than men. Among the worst cases are Algeria and Zambia, where, respectively, eighty percent and seventy-four percent of adult women are illiterate, compared to thirty-eight and twenty-nine percent of adult men. These figures may be contrasted with those for most European nations and Japan, where fewer than one percent of women (but two percent in the United States) have failed to achieve literacy.

The disabilities suffered by those who are both female and poor have become the particular concerns of an international movement to uplift the condition of women around the globe. United Nations world conferences on women, attended by increasing numbers of women, met in Mexico in 1975, in Copenhagen in 1980, in Nairobi in 1985, and in Beijing in 1995. The last attracted an attendance of 30,000 women, and official delegates from 185 governments. Most nations of the world have signed the UN Convention on the Elimination of all Forms of Discrimination against Women. The recognition of the worth of women is now an international project.

Love your Mother

Out on the American road in the 1980s, bumper stickers displayed a picture of the Earth, and beneath it the injunction: "Love your Mother." As family ties weakened and religious fervor waned, a devotion to the planet and the welfare of its peoples flourished among the activist young of the Western world.

Population, Disease, and Famine In an arithmetic to which the world was first alerted by Thomas Malthus (see Chapter 24), the welfare of human communities depends on the relation between two quantities: the size of the population and the resources available to sustain life. Where population exceeds resources, disaster results.

Statisticians note with alarm recent population trends. More than 5.8 billion people live on the earth today. That 1996 figure is more than twice the 1950 figure of 2.5 billion; more than three times the 1900 figure of 1.6 billion; more than thirty times the 170 million in the heyday of the Roman Empire. Not only has population soared since 1750, but the rate of increase is itself increasing. Some regions are growing at annual rates of two or three percent, portending the doubling of the population, respectively, in thirty-four or twenty-three years. Some experts fear a "population bomb," population magnitudes that will threaten the welfare of all.

Population pressures vary regionally. In the developed world, population has slowed since a peak rate of growth after 1750. Birth rates declined, witnessing the practices of contraception and family planning. At present, these nations are experiencing a growth

HOW MANY?

World Population Figures, 10,000 B.C.E.–2025 C.E.

Year	Population
10,000 B.C.E.	4 million
1 C.E.	170 million
1900	1,625 million
1950	2,500 million
1996	5,800 million
2025 (projected)	8,250 million

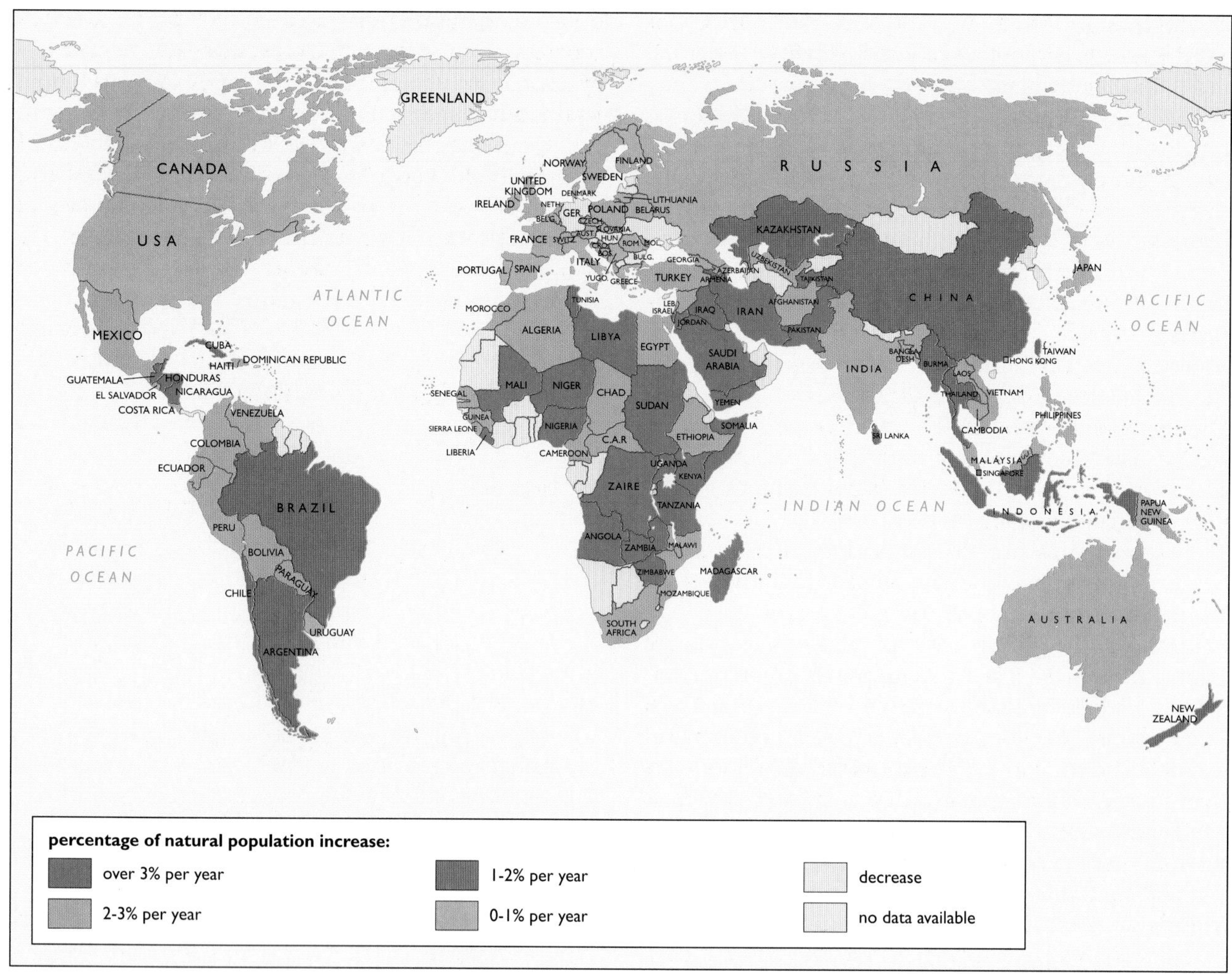

Map 29.4 Rates of Population Growth, 1993: *Reaching a total of 5.5 billion in 1993, the world's population is unevenly distributed, as are rates of growth. In the lead for share of world population are China, with 21.4 percent, and India, with 16.3 percent. These nations are also growing at rapid rates of respectively one and two percent annually (with the effect that their populations will double in thirty-four and sixty-seven years respectively). They are not, however, among the most rapidly growing nations, with rates of growth at an annual three percent. Those nations are concentrated in Africa and the Middle East, and include Nigeria, Sudan, Iran, and Pakistan. In contrast, the nations of the Western world, and Japan, are either increasing at rates lower than one percent annually or actually decreasing.*

Source: *M. Kidron and R. Segal,* The State of the World Atlas, *rev. 5th ed., (London: Penguin Reference, 1995) pp. 28–29.*

rate under one percent. Some are actually decreasing in population, as new childbirths fail to match deaths.

In the developing world (most of Asia, Africa, and Latin America), population growth rates are much higher. These regions contain eighty percent of world population, and account for ninety percent of all births. Here modernization has permitted populations to increase far beyond traditional levels; but it has not progressed sufficiently to feed and nurture the resulting multitudes.

The most populous regions of the world experience deficits in the quality of life visible in lowered life expectancy, harsh conditions, and poor medical care. Whereas life expectancy is greater than seventy-five years in the world's wealthier nations, it sinks to less than sixty-five in India, Indonesia, Egypt, and Peru, among others; to less than fifty-five in most of Africa; to less than forty-five in a few desperate states, including Afghanistan and Uganda. High rates of child mortality correlate to decreased longevity. Among the nations with lowest life expectancy figures, as many as one in five of children under five years old die. That twenty percent rate of child mortality contrasts to a rate of one percent or less in the developed nations of the world. In 1993 in Great Britain and Germany, seven infants died per 1000 births; in Afghanistan, 163.

Harsh conditions—poverty, war, hopelessness—impel people to migrate to places of greater opportunity. Migrants from India and China, for example, have moved to the Middle East and South Africa; to Canada, the United States, and the Caribbean; to Great Britain, Australia, and other Asian nations. In 1960, the United States housed 200,000 Asian immigrants; by 1998, 10 million. Sometimes whole communities of a particular national or ethnic group will migrate, in what is called a **diaspora**, or "scattering." The immigrants' new skills, as well as native customs and languages, serve to enrich the host nations where they settle, even as they often become the targets of ethnic or racial discrimination.

Overpopulation not only strains resources, but also encourages disease. The unprecedented advance of medical science in the twentieth century made it possible to prevent most childhood diseases; to cure many known bacterial infections; to repair broken limbs; to control bleeding; and to relieve pain to an extraordinary degree. By World War II, medical researchers had learned to cure (with antibiotics) or prevent (by immunization, sanitation, and pest control) most fatal epidemic diseases: among them, malaria, smallpox (now eradicated), syphilis, tuberculosis, typhoid, and yellow fever. The vaccination of children lowered the death toll caused by diphtheria, pertussis (whooping cough), and, more recently, measles. The control of influenza, which took 15 million lives in a pandemic at the end of World War I (see Chapter 25), is improving, but is frustrated by the mutability of the viral agent. More recently, progress has been made in the treatment of cancer; with early detection, many malignancies no longer kill.

Medical success in confronting the diseases of the past has not yet been equaled in the case of the deadliest plague of recent times: AIDS, developed by those infected with HIV (or human immunodeficiency virus). The disease originated in Africa, perhaps as a mutation of a dormant, endemic disease of a species of chimpanzee, and spread suddenly to the Americas around 1980. Since then, it has reached Asia, Europe, Australia, and New Zealand. By 1996, more than 6 million people had died of AIDS worldwide, 1.5 million in that one year alone. More than 8 million have developed AIDS to date, and more than 29 million have been infected with HIV—figures predictive of millions more deaths in years to come.

An HIV-infected person may not develop the disease itself for several years. In the wealthier nations, drug combinations are used to delay the disease's progress or, in some cases, prevent death. That therapy is not available to most people in the developing world, where both HIV infection and the number of AIDS cases are soaring. About sixty-three percent of those with HIV or AIDS worldwide live in Africa, already stressed by overpopulation and low levels of technical development. In the tiny nations of Rwanda and Burundi, twenty percent of pregnant

HOW MANY?

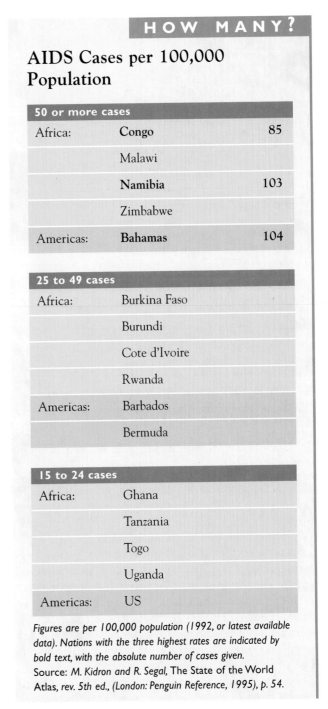

AIDS Cases per 100,000 Population

50 or more cases		
Africa:	**Congo**	85
	Malawi	
	Namibia	103
	Zimbabwe	
Americas:	**Bahamas**	104
25 to 49 cases		
Africa:	Burkina Faso	
	Burundi	
	Cote d'Ivoire	
	Rwanda	
Americas:	Barbados	
	Bermuda	
15 to 24 cases		
Africa:	Ghana	
	Tanzania	
	Togo	
	Uganda	
Americas:	US	

Figures are per 100,000 population (1992, or latest available data). Nations with the three highest rates are indicated by bold text, with the absolute number of cases given.
Source: *M. Kidron and R. Segal,* The State of the World Atlas, *rev. 5th ed., (London: Penguin Reference, 1995), p. 54.*

women (who transmit the disease to their offspring in twenty-five to thirty-five percent of cases) test positive for the disease.

Unlucky Africa suffers other epidemics at the same time—principally measles and tuberculosis, resurgent wherever poverty and insanitary conditions give it leave, and newly virulent due to the development of drug-resistant strains of the bacillus.

Physicians cannot solve malnutrition, the principal cause of human misery, which still afflicts more than one in ten people worldwide. The conquest of malnutrition in the Western world and Japan is virtually complete. Not only is food produced in sufficient quantity in these regions, but it is generally made available even to the poorest citizens through government programs or private charity. Individuals still suffer hunger amid affluence; but their cases are unusual and often involve collateral problems such as mental illness and extreme isolation.

The poorer regions of the world are by definition those that fail to nourish their inhabitants. In 1992, daily caloric intake averaged 1883 in Peru; 1707 in Haiti; 1505 in Somalia (in contrast to 3671 in the United States; 3504 in Italy; and a magnificent 3778 in Ireland, previously devastated by the Great Famine of 1845). Low productivity remains the principal cause of hunger. In these poorer regions, a natural disaster—drought, flood, extreme cold—brings famine. It is in the regions where the margin of survival is narrowest that distribution mechanisms are poorest. Central governments or international agencies may be unable to deliver needed food and fuel supplies.

Another kind of famine is caused not by natural disaster but by human decision-makers. Artificial famine seems all the more cruel because it is not merely preventable, but entirely willful. Warfare among private armies under fourteen different local strongmen led to mass hunger in Somalia, where over 300,000 starved in 1991–1992 as gunmen raided food shipments supplied by international agencies. In Sudan, the policies of strongman ruler Lt. Gen. Omar Ahmed al-Bashir who seized power in a 1989 coup have triggered a great famine, while his violations of human rights have led to the suspension of international aid efforts. These are small tragedies, however, next to those caused by collectivization of agriculture in the Soviet Union in the 1920s and in China in the 1950s, which each caused the deaths by starvation of some 10 million citizens (see Chapters 27, 28).

The Thread of Ecological Disaster Environmentalists are among the experts involved in the struggle against starvation, disease, and overpopulation. Environmentalism is a relatively new phenomenon, triggered by the brooding shadow of the atomic bomb. The possibility of the annihilation of humankind and the ruination of the planet moved a generation to arouse concern for the preservation of the earth which sustains us all.

In 1962, the publication *Silent Spring* by Rachel Carson (1907–1964) introduced a shocked audience to ecology, the beautiful (when undisturbed) interrelationships of plants, animals, and humans and to their natural environment. That wonderful equilibrium was jeopardized, Carson argued, by the use of toxic substances in materials used to promote agricultural productivity—chemicals that killed pests, fungi, and weeds. These agents entered and were retained by the soil, the water, and the air. They entered the tissues of plants and animals and, when ingested by humans, into our own bodies, where they caused

WITNESSES

Love Your Mother: The Environmentalist Movement

Under Secretary of the Interior John C. Whitaker on the emergence of the modern environmental movement (1969): As Americans traveled in their automobiles, . . . they saw garish road signs, fields of junked automobiles, choked and dying streams, overgrazed and eroded hills and valleys, and roadsides lined with endless miles of beer cans, pop bottles, and the tin foil from candy wrappers and cigarette packages. They could no longer move a few hundred miles West: the frontiers were gone.

(From B. Kline, *First Along the River: A Brief History of the US Environmental Movement*, 1997)

Journalist Ross Gelbspan announces that global warming is here (1997): The recent weather record has been marked by more intense rainfalls and severe snowstorms; stronger hurricanes; unseasonal and prolonged droughts, resulting in crop failures and devastating forest fires from Texas to Mongolia; killer heat waves from India to Chicago; and record flooding from Yemen to Nepal. . . . Environmentalists have been warning us about global warming for years. What is news is that global warming is no longer merely a future possibility. The heat is on. Now. Its early impacts, in the form of more extreme and unstable climate, are being felt even as I write.

(Ross Gelbspan, *The Heat is On: The High Stakes Battle over Earth's Threatened Climate*, 1997)

disease. The protection of the environment became a pressing issue, especially for the young—whose perception was that their elders had irresponsibly plundered the natural world.

The environmentalist movement boomed as public education about endangered biological species and the benefits of recycling reshaped public consciousness. The first Earth Day celebration in 1970 (now celebrated annually in some 140 nations on April 22) defined the areas of concern. Earth Day was followed by the United Nations Conference on the Human Environment, held in Stockholm (Sweden) in 1972, which resulted in the establishment of the United Nations Environment Program. In 1983, the General Assembly further established the World Commission on Environment and Development. In 1992, the United Nations Conference on Environment and Development (the "Earth Summit") met in Rio de Janeiro, attended by delegates from more than 178 countries. From the 1970s, "Green" parties joined the spectrum of political groups that contended for seats in European parliaments. The movement to protect the environment, in a brief generation, had leapt to the forefront of the international agenda.

Heating the Globe? Annual Emissions of Carbon Dioxide, 1997

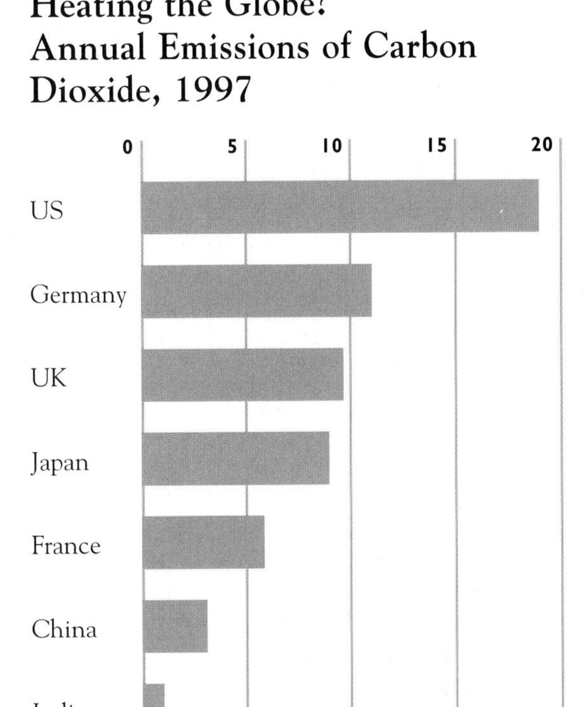

Figures represent Tons per Head

The United States' current world lead in the production of carbon dioxide is projected to slim substantially in the near future as developing economies in highly populous states such as India and China begin to produce increased levels of this and other "greenhouse gases." The result will likely be much higher global emissions.
Source: Understanding Global Issues, *ed. R. Buckley (Cheltenham, UK: Understanding Global Issues Limited, 1997), issue 11, p. 13.*

Among the many issues environmentalists raised were those of pollution, the depletion of the stratospheric ozone layer, global warming, and the endangerment of living species and habitats. Pollution accompanied industrialization. But Europe and the West generally, pioneers of industrialization, had cleaned up its environment to some extent. The major polluters were now in the newly industrializing nations of eastern Europe, India, and China. Yet the developed nations still polluted the air with chemical substances, spraying "acid rain" on humans, animals, and soil. They polluted the seas with waste from factories and naval vessels, imperiling whole categories of marine life. They built nuclear plants to generate power, which sometimes malfunctioned, releasing lethal radiation into the atmosphere.

Pollutants of a certain type, especially chlorofluorocarbons, have resulted in the thinning of the ozone layer, the protective gaseous zone of the earth's atmosphere that blocks the harmful effects of the sun's radiation. When released into the air, chlorofluorocarbons, used in aerosol sprays and in refrigeration and air-conditioning systems, cause the degradation of the ozone layer.

The emission of carbon dioxide and other gases, an accompaniment of industrial processes, is a cause, environmentalists argue, of the tendency toward "global warming" (a phenomenon some experts question). The air thickened by gaseous emissions traps the sun's heat close to the surface of the earth. Temperatures rise as a result; as they have been rising throughout the century.

Living things have suffered from the poisons that modern life broadcasts into air, soil, and water. Environmentalists created lists of "endangered species" and launched campaigns to save those injured by commercial ventures—whales poisoned by oil leaks from tankers, seals cruelly hunted, dolphins trapped in nets. As species are endangered, so natural habitats are jeopardized by the encroachments of modern society. Wetlands and rainforests around the world are shrinking—25 million acres of trees are lost each year—and with them the capacity for vegetable and marine life to replenish the earth and atmosphere.

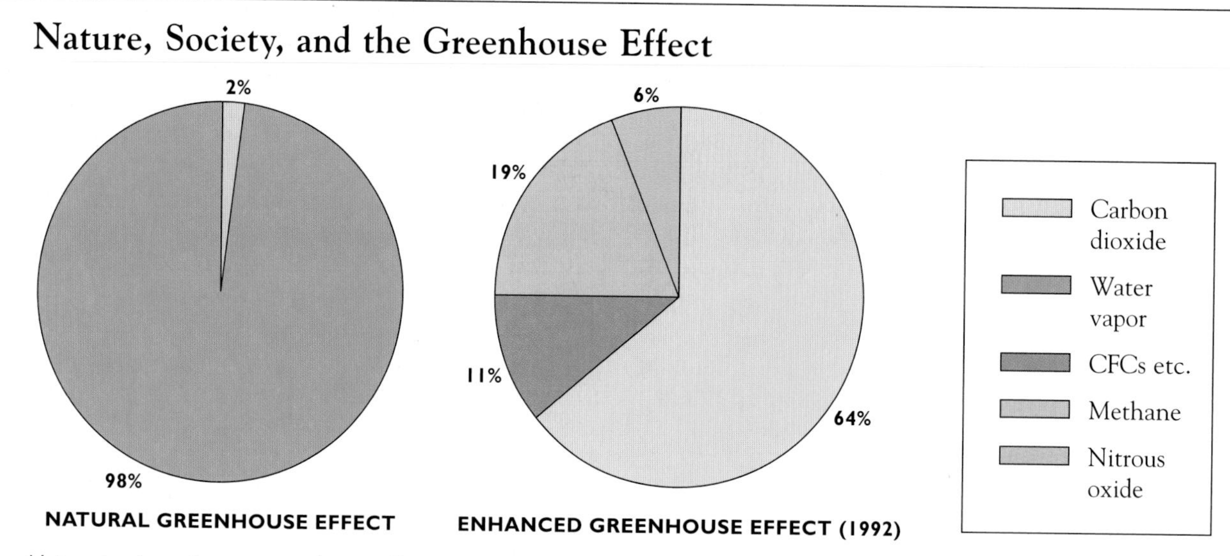

Nature produces its own greenhouse effect, trapping the sun's heat largely via water vapor. Without this natural warming effect, the earth would be too cold to support life. Human activities, particularly the burning of fossil fuels, add a relatively small degree of warming (an "enhanced" greenhouse effect equal to about two percent of the total). Many climate scientists around the world agree that this extra increment has already begun tangibly to alter the world's climate, though the consequences of this trend—and what action should be taken—are still debated issues.

Source: Understanding Global Issues, *ed. R. Buckley (Cheltenham, UK: Understanding Global Issues Limited, 1997), issue 5, p. 6.*

Non-Governmental Organizations Just as an array of international organizations promote environmentalist agendas, others support a variety of humanitarian causes. These "non-governmental organizations" (NGOs), many of them private or Church-related, some sponsored by the United Nations, have guided the movements for human health, welfare, and development. Constituting a new category of cooperative human effort—sometimes called "the third sector"—funded largely by grants from philanthropic foundations (notably the Ford or Rockefeller Foundations, both United States agencies) or private donations, they have become the primary agents of human welfare in a world that has turned from empire and values pluralism.

Senior among these NGOs is the International Red Cross, founded in 1864 (and since 1986 renamed the International Movement of the Red Cross and Red Crescent, to include Islamic national members), and honored with Nobel Peace Prizes in 1917, 1944, and 1963. The Red Cross serves the needs of the wounded and displaced in wartime, and brings food, clothing, medical care, and expert advisors to victims of natural disasters. Especially devoted to the medical needs of impoverished peoples or communities in crisis has been the French organization Médecins sans Frontières ("Doctors without Boundaries"), while CARE tends to the needs of children worldwide. Amnesty International has pursued the cause of identifying prisoners of conscience (those imprisoned for no crime but criticism of government policies) and organizing international support for their release.

In addition, many agencies and programs of the United Nations are devoted to the control and prevention of disease (the World Health Organization, or WHO); the increase and distribution of food supplies (the Food and Agriculture Organization, or FAO); the welfare of children (the United Nations International Children's Emergency Fund, or UNICEF); the facilitation of world trade (the World Trade Organization, or WTO); and the promotion of knowledge (the United Nations Educational, Scientific, and Cultural Organization, or UNESCO). Informing the work of its agencies is the general mission of the United Nations: "to save succeeding generations from the scourge of war," as its Charter reads; and to "reaffirm faith in fundamental human rights, in the dignity and worth of the human person, in the equal rights of men and women and of nations large and small."

Successor to the failed League of Nations, the United Nations was established in 1945, when representatives of fifty nations approved its charter. Consisting of a fifteen-member Security Council and

WHO'S WHO

Selected Nobel Peace Prize Winners Since World War II

1953 George C. Marshall, originator of Marshall Plan (US)

1964 Martin Luther King, Jr., civil rights leader (US)

1975 Andrei Sakharov (USSR), physicist, human rights campaigner

1978 Anwar el-Sadat, president of Egypt, and Menachem Begin, prime minister of Israel, for negotiation of peace accord

1983 Lech Walesa (Poland), Solidarity leader

1984 Desmond M. Tutu (South Africa), Bishop of Johannesburg, anti-apartheid leader

1990 Mikhail Gorbachev (USSR), initiator of Soviet reform and dissolution

1994 Yitzhak Rabin and Shimon Peres, prime minister and foreign minister of Israel, and Yasir Arafat, chairman of PLO, for negotiation of peace pact

a General Assembly, in which all member nations were to participate equally, the United Nations aimed to represent the concerted will of the nations of the globe in seeking peaceful resolution of conflicts and in promoting human welfare. By 1960, about fifty additional nations were admitted to membership, many of them newly independent states of Asia and Africa. By the late 1990s, the roster exceeded 180.

The United Nations has found multilateral solutions for several political confrontations in the postwar era, intervening in the Arab-Israeli crisis of 1947–1948, the Korean War in 1950, the Suez crisis in 1956, and the Congo crisis of 1960. Recently, it has coordinated international humanitarian and military "peace" forces, in the spirit of the 1992 "Agenda for Peace" outlined by Boutros Boutros-Ghali (1922–) of Egypt, UN Secretary-General 1992–1996. The World Court, the judicial organ of the United Nations, adjudicates disputes about territorial rights, sovereignty and nationality, immigration and asylum.

In December 1948, the United Nations adopted the Universal Declaration of Human Rights as a standard to which the nations of the world must be held. Among its principles were those contained in foundational documents of the liberal tradition such as the American Declaration of Independence and the French Declaration of the Rights of Man and the Citizen. To these were added guarantees of equality without distinctions of "race, color, sex, language, religion, political or other opinion, national or social origin, property, birth or other status"; assurances of the enduring right to national citizenship, and the right to flee or return to one's own nation; the legitimation of government by the will of the people, expressed in free and fair elections; the prohibition of both slavery and torture. The UN Declaration notably includes provisions about private matters, likely to be affected by local belief and custom, as marriage (which must rest on the consent of both man and woman) and childrearing (children must receive education that would expand their life chances, and training in respect for human rights and freedom).

The UN Declaration of Human Rights was adopted unanimously (the Soviet bloc nations, along with South Africa and Saudi Arabia, abstaining). A less ambitious, but still pathbreaking agreement was reached at Helsinki (Finland) in 1975. The United States, Canada, and all the countries of Europe, except Albania (including the Soviet Union and its satellites)—signed the Helsinki Accords, pledging their acceptance of human rights standards in validation of the principles of the UN document of 1948. Meanwhile, in November 1989, the United Nations issued a Convention on the Rights of the Child, a corollary to its universal Declaration of Human Rights.

By the time the Cold War ended, consensus had been reached among the world's major powers on the preeminent values of peace and human dignity. But far from the centers of wealth and technological advance, competition for power produced new paradigms of war—small battles but tragic battles, and

MEANWHILE

The United Nations: Key Moments

1945 Foundation of the United Nations

1948 United Nations Universal Declaration of Human Rights

1975 Helsinki Accords

1989 United Nations Convention on the Rights of the Child

WITNESSES

The Age of Human Rights

UN Universal Declaration of Human Rights (1948):
Article 1. All human beings are born free and equal in dignity and rights. . . .
Article 2. Everyone is entitled to all the rights and freedoms set forth in this Declaration, without distinction of any kind, such as race, colour, sex, language, religion, political or other opinion, national or social origin, property, birth or other status. . . .
Article 3. Everyone has the right to life, liberty and security of person. . . .
(From *United Nations Publication* No. 63.1.13, 1963)

UN Convention on the Prevention and Punishment of the Crime of Genocide (1948):
Article 1. The Contracting Parties confirm that genocide whether in time of peace or in time of war, is a crime under international law which they undertake to prevent and to punish.
Article 2. . . . [G]enocide means any of the following acts committed with intent to destroy, in whole or in part, a national, ethnical, racial or religious group, such as: (a) Killing members of the group; (b) Causing serious bodily or mental harm to members of the group; (c) Deliberately inflicting on the group conditions of life calculated to bring about its physical destruction in whole or in part; (d) Imposing measures intended to prevent births within the group; (e) Forcibly transferring children of the group to another group.
(From *Yearbook of the United Nations*, 1950)

UN Convention on the Rights of the Child (1989):
Principle 2. The child shall enjoy special protection, and shall be given opportunities and facilities, by law and by other means, to enable him to develop physically, mentally, morally, spiritually and socially in a healthy and normal manner and in conditions of freedom and dignity. . . .
Principle 4. The child shall enjoy the benefits of social security. He shall be entitled to grow and develop in health; to this end, special care and protection shall be provided both to him and to his mother, including adequate pre-natal and post-natal care. The child shall have the right to adequate nutrition, housing, recreation and medical services. . . .
Principal 6. The child . . . needs love and understanding. He shall, wherever possible, grow up in the care and under the responsibility of his parents, and, in any case, in an atmosphere of affection and of moral and material security; a child of tender years shall not, save in exceptional circumstances, be separated from his mother. . . .
Principle 7. The child is entitled to receive education, which shall be free and compulsory, at least in the elementary stages. . . .
(From UN High Commissioner for Human Rights, 1997)

many hope the last battles, in the long history of human conflict.

Last Battles

"All you need is love," the Beatles sang; but vicious local hatreds persist. As the old powers of the northern hemisphere withdrew from nuclear stalemate, military activity concentrated in the regions of the Third World, encompassing the world's poorest regions located mostly in the southern hemisphere. The militarization of new players on the geopolitical ballfield set the stage for outbursts of violence of exceptional cruelty and, though of small compass, of great importance. In the nuclear era, even an obscure and diminutive conflict arouses the specter of planetary doom.

Even as the superpowers disarmed, other states of the world acquired massive military capacity. China and India stockpiled powerful weapons, as did the less stable states of Israel, Pakistan, Libya, North Korea, and Iraq. India refused to sign the Nuclear Non-Proliferation treaty until its requirements were universal and non-discriminatory—that is, until all nations agreed, and until those states possessing nuclear capacity destroyed their own weapons. (On May 11, 1998, she demonstrated her independence by exploding nuclear devices about seventy miles from the Pakistani border.) Also refusing to sign were India's neighbor Pakistan, South Africa, and Israel.

Even without nuclear weapons, the militarized states of the developing world were dangerous. Some developed biological and chemical weapons (although international agreements prohibit their use), which are cheap, easily acquired, and difficult to monitor. Currently at least twelve nations are thought to have biological weapons. Iraq is known to have chemical weapons (banned by international agreements in 1925 and 1993), which it used against neighboring Iran in the 1980s.

War and Terrorism Conventional arms, however, are the main material of war sought by the new dictatorships of developing nations. These were acquired free from one or the other of the superpowers during the Cold War, or purchased on a growing open market. Armies as well as armaments are available for purchase, as mercenary bands, recruited from the veterans of military conflicts elsewhere in the world, take service under military strongmen who "buy war" in order to gain or keep power. Some states spend twice as much on the military as on health; others a mammoth ten times as much (Nigeria and Angola in Africa, for example, Iraq and Kuwait in the Middle East, and Pakistan and North and South Korea in Asia).

Thus armed, strongman follows strongman in a series of coups and comebacks, increasing the sum of violence. Between 1900 and 1990, 237 wars had been fought worldwide, compared to 205 in the previous century, or 68 in the eighteenth. Even relative to an increased population, the twentieth is the most violent century in human history. In the eighteenth century, wars caused about five deaths per 1000 people; in the nineteenth century, six; in the twentieth, forty-six.

When the military gain power—and some forty percent of the world's states today are controlled by military men—not only is there more violence, but there are violations of the standards of human rights established by the United Nations in 1948. Torture—revived early in the century by the Cheka, the Nazis, and French overseas forces—is inflicted on prisoners around the world; citizens are raped, brutalized, and "disappeared"; political opponents are murdered; and the press, radio, television, and the Internet are muzzled.

The most lawless of the world's states harbor terrorist groups committed to political, religious, or nationalist causes. The prolonged standoff in the Middle East between Israel and the neighboring Arab states has been a prime site for terror. Sporadic assaults on Israeli soldiers, and suicide bombings in Israeli cities by Palestinian terrorists are recalled with horror by Israel's sympathizers. Supporters of the Palestinian cause recall the massacre of twenty-nine Arabs at prayer in a mosque in Hebron in January 1997 by an Israeli zealot.

Outside of the Israeli theater, the bombing of an American plane over Lockerbie, Scotland in December 1988 (by terrorists protected by Libya) aroused general outrage, as did that of the World Trade Center in New York City in 1993, masterminded by an Islamist cleric. So have the attacks of Italy's Red Brigades, responsible for the 1978 murder of premier Aldo Moro, and repeated strikes by members of the Irish Republican Army, Basque separatists in Spain, and Kurdish rebels in Turkey. Islamic fundamentalism has powered terrorist activity in Islamic North Africa and the Middle East in a crusade against modernizing secular states seen as corrupt and decadent.

It was ideology, however, not religion, that in Cambodia from 1975–1978 sparked one of the most ghastly recent episodes of violence. As various factions competed to take control of that nation in the wake of American withdrawal from Indochina, the communist Khmer Rouge ("Red Cambodia") faction under leader Pol Pot (c. 1925–1998) instigated a campaign of terror. In a drive to restructure agrarian production, the Khmer Rouge relocated nearly half the population—some 3.5 out of 7.3 million people—creating famine and disease. The protesters, including virtually all the educated elites, were destroyed in the notorious "killing fields," of which news leaked to a horrified world. Recent investigation has provided evidence of torture and slaughter in the heaped skeletal remains of those butchered by the Khmer Rouge—more than 1 million people, nearly one in seven of the citizens of that unlucky nation.

Genocide at the End of the Twentieth Century With the memory of the Nazi attempt to exterminate the Jews still vivid, the postwar world has also experienced recent episodes of **genocide**. Defined by the 1948 UN Convention on the Prevention and Punishment of the Crime of Genocide as "acts committed with intent to destroy, in whole or in part, a national, ethnical, racial, or religious group," modern genocide began in the first years of the twentieth century with the Turkish persecution of their Armenian minority. More recently, genocidal warfare has overwhelmed the neighboring African states of Rwanda and Burundi.

For centuries, the Tutsi tribespeople of Rwanda and Burundi had dominated a Hutu majority (about eighty percent of the population), in a pattern encouraged by Belgian administrators after 1918. Upon the achievement of independence in 1962, the Hutus were granted political rights. Yet persistent tensions erupted violently in 1965, 1969, 1972, and 1988, mounting to full civil war in 1994. As a Tutsi army drove Hutu forces to the frontier, fleeing Hutus massacred hundreds of thousands of Tutsi men,

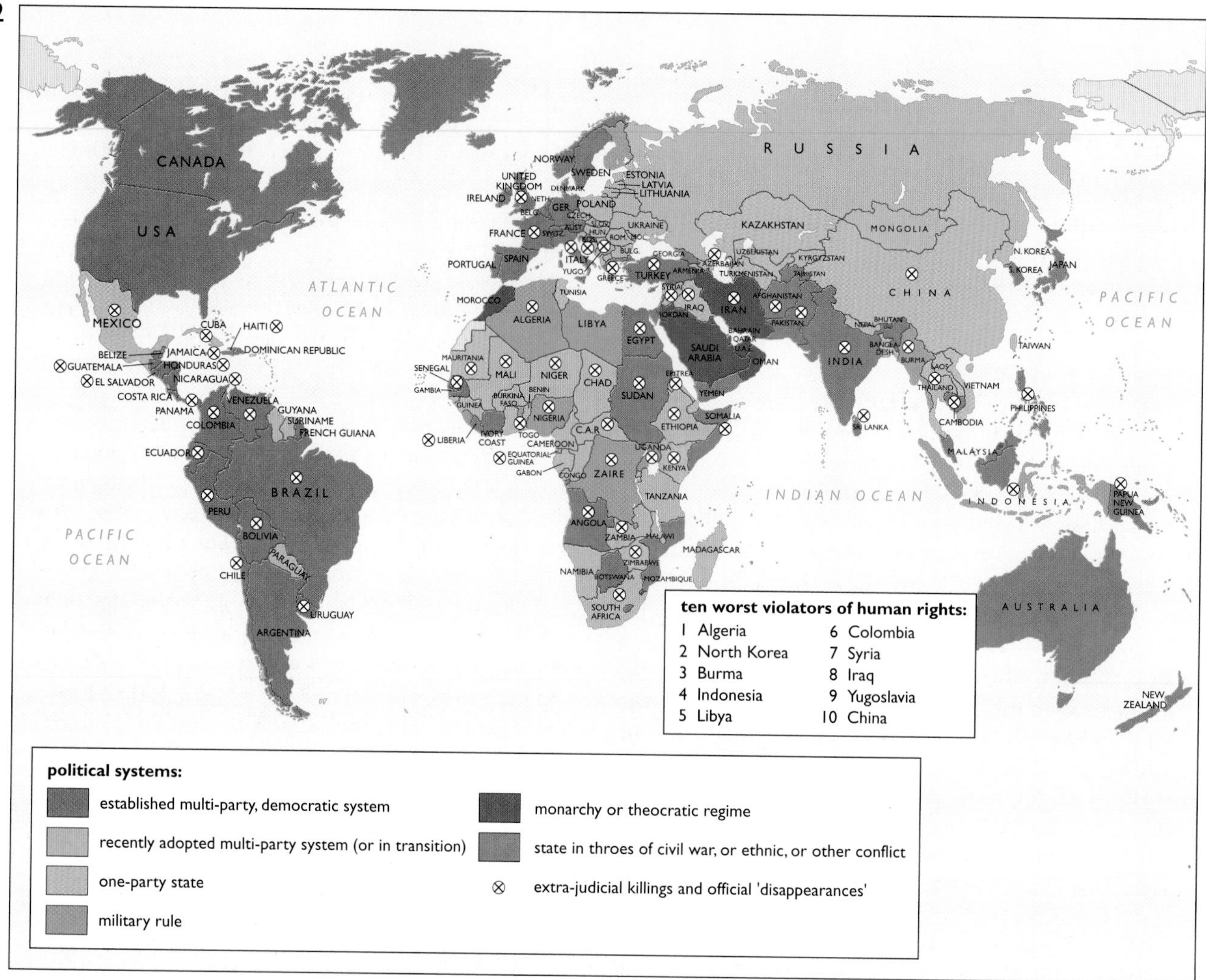

Map 29.5 Repression around the World, 1990s: *Many of the world's nations are now parliamentary democracies, the political system toward which many others still aspire. Others possess different forms of government: one-party systems, despotisms, monarchies, theocracies—or anarchy. International agencies report continued incidence of officially managed extra-judicial killing and other human rights violations in many of the world's nations, most in the developing world. Of 194 nations ranked in the "Human Rights Index" constructed by the British newspaper,* The Observer *(June 28, 1998), the worst ten violators are shown here. Violations considered in constructing ranked place included: extrajudicial killings, use of torture, disappearances, use of the death penalty, denial of free speech, denial of political rights, existence of political prisoners, denial of free movement, denial of child rights, denial of religious freedom, denial of fair trial, denial of minority rights, and denial of women's rights. The UN Human Development Index was used as a multiplier to determine final place rank, to adjust for the impact of wealth and poverty on the ability of a nation to control violations.*

women, and children—at least 500,000, and perhaps as many as 800,000, out of a population of 7.5 million. Three million Hutus (including many of the killers) took refuge in Zaire and Tanzania, where, corralled in refugee camps, they suffered from starvation and disease. Many returned to Rwanda, where ethnic violence continues and resolution is not in sight.

In the Balkans, on Europe's southeastern frontier, enduring hatreds have flared up between Orthodox Christian Serbs, Roman Catholic Croatians, and Muslim Bosnians, all southern Slavs speaking the same tongue (although using different alphabets). For thirty-five years, the independent communist leader Marshall Tito (Josip Broz) had kept these mutually hostile groups together in a union of "all Slavs," or "Yugoslavia." When Tito died in 1980, the union was shaken. It disintegrated with the collapse of communism in 1989.

Yugoslavia dissolved into six federated republics—Croatia, Slovenia, Bosnia-Herzogovina, Montenegro, Macedonia, Serbia. The two "autonomous regions" of Vojvodina and Kosovo lay within Serbia, the most

WITNESSES

. . . Yet the Killing Goes On

Entries from writer Zlatko Dizdarevič's Sarajevo war journal:
1993: From the very beginning of the present war . . . one has heard this theory: "It's an outbreak of sheer madness, ... It is a war which everyone fights everyone else, and you can't make sense out of it." . . . This is not the case. . . . The simple fact is that a conglomerate of fanatical nationalists, political careerists, and malcontents—for the most part, people who never felt comfortable with law, order, and democracy—realized they could launch violent aggression without fear of reprisal from the outside world, since that outside world's "priorities" would keep it from intervening. They were not mistaken.

. . . and 1992: It has been an exceptionally calm day: only six dead and ten wounded. From the bullet-riddled window of my office, I watched some guys cut down one of the five big trees in front of our building. I remember when their foliage hid the view of the hills north of Sarajevo. For some reason, I believed those five giants might be spared, even though nothing and no one is spared here anymore. . . . Their end strikes me as tragic, almost more so than death by mortar shell, which, you'd say, takes a "real" life. Maybe that's because life has become so cheap in this unfortunate city, while trees can represent a little hope for us. It is hard to pin down, but they seemed to prove that things were still more or less normal, although I think you'd have a hard time trying to explain to anyone that people killing each other for no apparent reason is normal.
(Zlatko Dizdarević, *Sarajevo: A War Journal*; ed. A. Hollo, 1994)

The Hutu Genocide of Tutsis in Rwanda (1994): Local media . . . play an essential role . . . broadcast[ing] unceasing messages of hate, such as "the grave is only half full. Who will help us fill it". . . . On 6 April 1994 the plane carrying President Habyarimana [of Rwanda] and President Cyprien of Burundi was shot down. . . . [This] acted as the fuse for the eruption of violence which led to the greatest tragedy in the history of the country. . . . [Hutu] militia leaders divided up the territory under their control so that one man was allocated for every ten households in order to systematically search for Tutsis. . . . In this way every Tutsi family could be denounced by somebody who knew the members personally: pupils were killed by their teachers, shop owners by their customers, neighbor killed neighbor. . . . Churches where Tutsis sought sanctuary were . . . the scenes of some of the worst massacres: 2,800 people in Kibungo, 6,000 in Cyahinda, 4,000 in Kibeho, to give just a few examples . . .
Radio . . . encouraged the violence with statements such as that made at the end of April 1994: "By 5 May, the country must be completely cleansed of Tutsis. . . . The children must be killed too."
The genocide spread rapidly to cover the whole country. . . . By the end of April, it was estimated that 100,000 people had been killed. . . . The killings were . . . meticulously well organized. However, the means used to accomplish them were primitive in the extreme: for example, the use of machetes and *unfunis* (wooden clubs studded with metal spikes).
(From Alain Destexhe, *Ruanda and Genocide in the Twentieth Century*, ed. A. Marschner, 1995)

populous region, which maintained the army of the former Yugoslav state. Slovenia and Croatia withdrew from the federation in 1991, and many of the Serb minority joined the Serbian army to prevent their secession.

Meanwhile, Bosnia-Herzegovina also sought to secede from the Serbian-led federation. Its Orthodox Serb minority (about thirty-three percent of a population that was also forty-four percent Muslim Slav and seventeen percent Catholic Croatian) resisted the March 1992 plebiscite in which a majority voted for independence. Bosnian Serbs, including many Yugoslav army veterans, constituted themselves the "Serbian Republic of Bosnia-Herzegovina" and besieged the capital of Sarajevo. Over the next three years, backed by Serbia under Slobodan Milosevic (1941–) and the regular Yugoslav army, they starved and bombed the city. In a campaign of "ethnic cleansing"—the horrifying term born of this last European conflict—Serb forces persecuted, expelled, bullied, raped, and killed Bosnian Muslims. Atrocities were committed by all contenders; but the massacres by Serbs of thousands in Srebenica in 1995 especially outraged international observers.

The constituent nations of the European Union, NATO, and the United Nations (employing the United States air force to enforce its decreed "no-fly zone") all attempted to halt the carnage in the

Balkans. By the American-sponsored Dayton (Ohio) Peace Agreement of November 1995, the republic was divided into Serbian and Muslim-Croat entities, to be ruled by a single parliament, elected under the eye of United Nations peacekeeping troops. New Serb atrocities in 1999 against the Albanian Muslims of Kosovo have led to further warfare with a truce achieved in June of that year.

Among the provisions of the Dayton accord was that war criminals on both sides would be identified and prosecuted. Massacre, torture, and military rape, all considered illegal by international conventions (rape since 1996), were prominent features of the "ethnic cleansing" of Bosnia-Herzogovina, as they were of most recent wars. The determination to bring to justice those who violate the limits of permissible military violence is another aspect of the gathering world consensus on issues of human dignity and freedom.

Militarism, torture, terror, fanaticism, genocide—these overshadow the last decades of the twentieth century, even as the powerful nations of the developed world, the Cold War behind them, have settled down to the business of building a prosperous global village based on technological innovation.

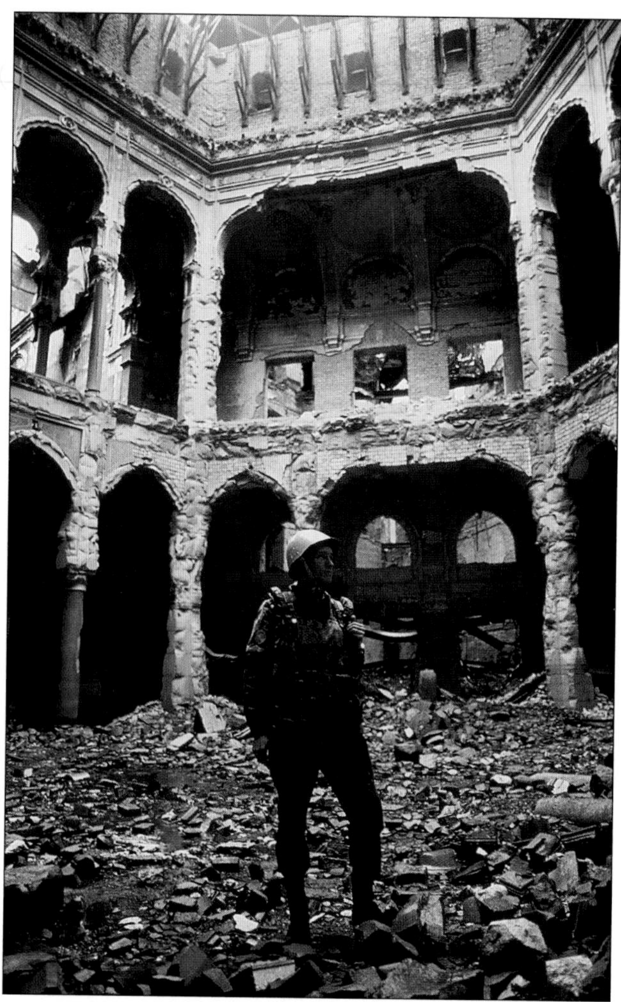

From civilization to barbarism: *Heavy and protracted fighting in the Bosnian capital Sarajevo (in the former Yugoslavia) reduced much of that city, a center of European culture, to rubble. Here, a UN peace-keeper surveys the city's wrecked library in February 1994.*

Conclusion

RETREAT FROM ARMAGEDDON AND THE MEANING OF THE WEST

For more than fifty years after the bombing of Hiroshima signaled the end of World War II, the peoples of the Western world lived in fear. Their world was split between a communist "East" and a "free West," both armed with weapons of mass destruction and locked in mutual hatred. After 1989, with the disintegration of Soviet communism, deadlock eased.

Meanwhile, a younger generation, led by a prosperous and willful vanguard of American students, turned from the Cold War to promote personal liberation, sexual revolution, and global activism. They have learned that the world is divided not so much between the chimeras of "East" and "West," as between North and South, the zones of the developed and developing nations. Disturbingly, that region most burdened by poverty, disease, and overpopulation, also suffers disproportionately from injustice, terror, and war.

Among the questions that emerge from the second half of the twentieth century are these: will a renewed West, freed from the prospect of Armageddon, reassert its commitment to the finest values of the Western tradition? And will it—or can it, or should it—lead the way in the building of a humane and prosperous global civilization?

REVIEW QUESTIONS

1. What was the Cold War? How did post-war Europe become divided into two rival power blocs? What was the Truman Doctrine?

2. What was the principle of "Mutually Assured Destruction"? How did anti-Communist influence United States domestic policy in the 1940s and 1950s? How did the United States–Soviet enmity play out in the Middle East, Asia, and Africa?

3. How did de-Stalinization affect Soviet rule in Eastern Europe? How successful was detente before 1985? Why did the Soviet Union collapse in 1985–1991?

4. What were the roots of youth protests during the 1960s and 1970s? What roles did the drug culture and rock music play in youth culture? To what extent did the Sixties generation change society in the West?

5. What was the sexual revolution? How did it influence the feminist movement? To what extent has women's place in Western society changed since the 1960s? Have similar changes occurred outside the West?

6. Why has the earth's population increased so rapidly? What are the effects of overpopulation? How successful has the UN been in resolving environmental and political problems?

SUGGESTED READINGS

Apocalypse Now?

Boyer, Paul, *By the Bomb's Early Light: American Thought and Culture at the Dawn of the Atomic Age* (Chapel Hill, NC: University of North Carolina Press, 1994). Compelling exploration of the cultural and psychological impact of the bomb on Americans.

Brands, H. W., *The Devil We Knew: Americans and the Cold War* (Oxford: Oxford University Press, 1993). Suggests communism might have collapsed even sooner in the absence of the Cold War.

Daniels, Robert V., *Soviet Communism from Reform to Collapse* (Lexington, MA: D. C. Heath, 1995). Studies efforts to reform the USSR during the 1980s, asking why reform was seen as necessary; why reform failed; and why the USSR collapsed so quickly.

Dunbabin, J. P. D., *International Relations Since 1945: A History in Two Volumes; 1: The Cold War: The Great Powers and Their Allies; 2: The Post-Imperial Age: The Great Powers and the Wider World* (New York–London: Longman, 1994). Readable survey of the post-war world.

Fursenko, Aleksandr, and Timothy Naftali, *One Hell of a Gamble: Khrushchev, Castro, and Kennedy, 1958–1964* (New York: W. W. Norton, 1997). Gripping account of relations among Cuba, the USSR, and the US from the Cuban missile crisis to Khrushchev's fall.

Gorbachev, Mikhail, *Memoirs* (New York: Doubleday, 1996). Lengthy, lively account of late Soviet affairs and the collapse of communism by a key historical actor.

Pei, Minxin, *From Reform to Revolution: The Demise of Communism in China and the Soviet Union* (Cambridge, MA: Harvard University Press, 1994). Considers why efforts to reform communism in China and the USSR escalated in both cases to bring about revolutionary changes.

All You Need is Love

Anderson, Terry H., *The Movement and the Sixties: Protest in America from Greensboro to Wounded Knee* (Oxford: Oxford University Press, 1995). Seeks to answer why so many Americans became interested and actively involved in protest during this time.

Berman, Paul, *A Tale of Two Utopias: The Political Journey of the Generation of 1968* (New York: W.W. Norton, 1996). Links the American movements of the 1960s and the movements that brought down communism in Eastern Europe during 1989.

Buckley, Mary, ed., *Post-Soviet Women: From the Baltic to Central Asia* (Cambridge: Cambridge University Press, 1997). Essays on domestic conditions, the role of female politicians, women's economic status, national identity, and peace movements.

Dizdarevic, Zlatko, *Sarajevo: A War Journal*, trs. Ammiel Alcalay (New York: Fromm International, 1993). Describes life and death in the capital of Bosnia-Herzogovina, sharply criticizing US and international approaches to the tragedy still unfolding in the former Yugoslavia.

Einhorn, Barbara, *Cinderella Goes to Market: Citizenship, Gender and Women's Movements in East Central Europe* (London: Verso, 1993). Argues that women have been disproportionately affected by the termination of state benefits, rising unemployment, etc.

Kaltefleiter, Werner, and Robert L. Pfaltzgraff, eds., *The Peace Movements in Europe and the United States* (New York: St. Martin's Press, 1985). Post-War peace movements on both sides of the Atlantic.

Nelson, Barbara J. and Najma Chowdhury, eds., *Women and Politics Worldwide* (New Haven, CT: Yale University Press, 1994). Vast essay collection, surveying women's experience in 44 countries around the world.

Rothman, Hal K., *The Greening of a Nation? Environmentalism in the United States Since 1945* (Harcourt Brace College Pub., 1998). Surveys the major issues and achievements of the past half-century.

Rowbotham, Sheila, *A Century of Women: The History of Women in Britain and the United States* (London: Penguin, 1997). Assesses women's economic and political progress during the 20th century.

Worster, Donald, *Nature's Economy: A History of Ecological Ideas* (Cambridge: Cambridge University Press, 1985). Surveys major themes and historical development of the science of ecology.

CHAPTER 30

EPILOGUE

The Last Decade: Where We've Been and What May Be

THE 1990S

__The Westward Journey__ The Greek hero Ulysses (the Odysseus of Homer's Odyssey) returned home after twenty years of wandering after the fall of Troy. Then, as imagined in a poem by the English poet Alfred, Lord Tennyson (1809–1892), he set out yet again. Although grizzled and old, he aimed to sail beyond the limits of the Mediterranean world to discover what lay beyond the western horizon,

For always roaming with a hungry heart
. . . strong in will
To strive, to seek, to find, and not to yield.

Ulysses' journey brings to mind the condition of Western civilization as we leave the troubled twentieth century and enter the next millennium. The West is one of the world's youngest civilizations; but it is aging. Will it fade? Or will it continue the journey westward, a "gray spirit yearning in desire," like Ulysses, venturing "to sail beyond the sunset"?

To follow knowledge like a sinking star
Beyond the utmost bound of human thought.

The breakup of the Russian communist empire which began in 1989 (see Chapter 29) dramatically changed the world's political landscape. So momentous is the change that it can be said that the twentieth century has already ended—in the same way that, in a sense, it began only in 1914 with the outbreak of World War I. What comes next, now that the "short twentieth century" (1914–1989) is over? What is the future of the West, bearer of both burdens and benefits to the nations of the world? Historians cannot answer questions about the future; they must approach even the present with hesitation, and can offer only hypotheses about the past. But they can spot some trends. The world, and the West, appear to be moving toward *reconciliation*, *unification*, and cultural and economic *globalization*. These themes will be considered as this final chapter explores the future of the West.

Will there still be a distinctively Western world and a Western civilization when the forces of global

Astride the Prime Meridian: *These schoolchildren harbor no doubts about the meaning of the West. The West lies on one side of the line of longitude that runs through Greenwich, England, from pole to pole; on the other side is the East.*

unity have played themselves out? Will it shrink to "a small and inconsequential peninsula at the extremity of the Eurasian land mass," as one commentator suggests? Or will our civilization, though it has experienced much, set out again on a journey westward, "to strive, to seek, to find, and not to yield?"

RECONCILIATION

On January 22, 1998, Pope John Paul II (1920–) journeyed to Cuba, and met the head of that state, Fidel Castro (1927–). Their greeting, as each aged and masterful figure bent toward the other, was broadcast around the world; for this was an odd coming-together, as though each principal reluctantly conceded the other had some message of value to convey. The Polish-born Pope led a Church that communist rulers had sought to suppress in his homeland. Without appeal to Marxist theory, he urged the wealthy of the world to feed and respect the poor. The Cuban was the triumphant guerrilla leader who, nearly forty years before, had ousted a notoriously corrupt despot (see Chapter 28). An atheist who valued material above spiritual welfare, Castro was not predisposed to welcome this foreign pope. Yet they met, the one thereby acknowledging Castro's leadership of Cuba, the other the Church's right to offer pastoral care to a land which, four decades after its revolutionary inception, still had many Roman Catholics who desired it. The meeting between Castro and the Pope is emblematic of the reconciliations of the 1990s.

In July of the same year, another reconciliation took place in the former Soviet Union, which, bereft of churches, had as its principal holy object a "mummy in a mausoleum" (in the words of a recent historian)—the embalmed body of Lenin (see Chapter 29). Declared an enemy of the people and assassinated in 1918, the last tsar, Nicholas II (1868–1918), was rehabilitated and given official burial. In attendance was the President, former communist Boris Yeltsin (1931–), who apologized for the "monstrous crime" of eighty years ago. He bowed to honor the man who represented the tsarist autocracy the Bolsheviks had fought to tear down. In a similar moment, the former Soviet premier Mikhail Gorbachev (1931–), the communist whose innovations had led to the dismantling of the communist state, had his infant grandson baptized in the Orthodox faith that his predecessors had suppressed. In these moments of reconciliation, Russian leaders reached back across more than seventy years to reestablish a connection with the pre-revolutionary traditions of their motherland.

WITNESSES

1990

The sociological problem today—Daniel Bell: What is taking place now . . . is not the victory of capitalism per se; it is the defeat of central planning and totalitarian state controls and the upsurge of democracy. Since 1975, we have seen country after country . . . asserting a desire for free and democratic institutions . . . .

The list is impressive, and almost no section of earth has been immune: Portugal, Greece, and Spain; Uruguay, Argentina, Chile; the Philippines and Cambodia; Poland, Hungary, the Soviet Union, and, for a brief shining moment, China [referring to the democracy movement of spring 1989], where the Statue . . . of Liberty . . . stood as the symbol of the desire for freedom. A century and a half later, one can say that a specter is haunting communism, the specter of democracy . . . .

The issue is not capitalism versus socialism, but the ability of democratic regimes to manage their economies so as to provide for growth, protect their environments, safeguard the welfare of the disadvantaged, and help other struggling countries to feed their people and find some viable path of development. . . .

(Daniel Bell "On the Fate of Communism," *Dissent*, Spring 1990)

In the southern hemisphere, another awesome reconciliation had taken place in 1990 in South Africa when Frederik Willem de Klerk (1937–) released the African National Congress leader Nelson Mandela (1918–) from prison (see Chapter 28), where he had lingered for twenty-seven years. After decades of apartheid, free elections took place in 1994. Together, old and new citizens chose a government where majority blacks, disenfranchised since 1926, promised to protect the security of the now-toothless white minority population. The possibility that the pattern of exclusion and violence might end and blacks and whites share equally in the nation's future could not have been anticipated only a few years earlier.

Ten years after the Tiananmen Square massacre of June 1989 (see Chapter 28), the Chinese government released one of the dissidents it had arrested at the time. Others remain in prison, and others are silenced, while the Chinese government, officially communist, has permitted the introduction of a free market economy. Many Chinese citizens now give

WITNESSES

1991

The short twentieth century—John Lukacs: The 20th century is now over, and there are two extraordinary matters about this.

First, this was a short century. It lasted 75 years, from 1914 to 1989. Its two principal events were the two world wars. . . . The Russian Revolution, the atom bomb, the end of the colonial empires, the establishment of the Communist states, the emergence of the two superpowers, the division of Europe and of Germany—all of these were the consequences of the two world wars, in the shadow of which we were living, until now. . . .

We know that the 20th century is over . . . mainly because the confrontation of the two superpowers, the outcome of the Second World War, has died down. . . .

In 1991, we live in a very different world. . . . The very texture of history is changing before our very eyes.

(John Lukacs, "The Short Century—It's Over," *The New York Times*, February 17, 1991)

their energies not to political dissent, but to the building of commercial enterprises—efforts which may result, if by a different route, in the greater liberalization of Chinese society.

Elsewhere, the perpetrators of state-sponsored violence are being called to answer for their actions. Former leader Pol Pot (1925/28–) of Cambodia, responsible for the deaths of about 2 million of his fellow citizens from forced labor, starvation, torture, or execution, was fortunate to die peacefully of a heart attack in 1998 for crimes against humanity and escape being tried. Augusto Pinochet (1915–), former President of Chile, in England for medical care in 1998, was charged with violations of human rights committed in Chile after his 1973 rise to power. A Spanish government attorney had applied to extradite him to question him about the torture, killing, and "disappearance" of Spanish nationals. Although Pinochet responded that, as a former head of state, he was immune to all such charges, in 1999 an English court voted to permit his extradition to Spain—but only on a series of lesser charges committed after 1988, when the United Kingdom ratified the Convention Against Torture. Yet the principle was established that a head of state is not to be held free of responsibility for crimes committed by the state under his direction.

Likewise, the Serbian president of Yugoslavia Slobodan Milosevic (1941–) was indicted in May 1999, by the United Nations International Criminal Tribunal for the former Yugoslavia in the Hague, Netherlands, for war crimes committed in the 1998–1999 conflict in Kosovo—including rape (first defined as a war crime in international law in 1998), massacre, arson, and torture. NATO forces had intervened in this conflict following an international outcry at the wholesale violation of human rights by the Milosevic regime.

The humanitarian agenda that accompanied this military intervention can be contrasted with the strategy of terrorist organizations, many protected by rogue states (see Chapter 29). One such group ordered the bombing of the United States embassies in Kenya and Tanzania in August 1998, in which many workers, including native Africans, were killed or injured. Only a few months earlier, however, in

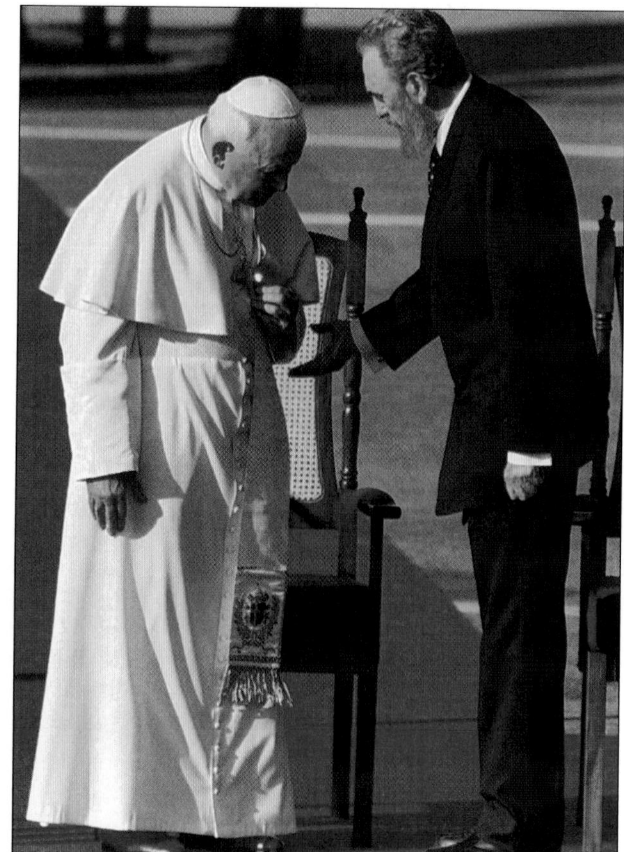

The Pope meets Castro: *The ending of the Cold War has brought into increasing contact societies and individuals long separated by mutual hostility and fear. Here, Pope John Paul II, the head of the Roman Catholic Church, meets Cuban leader Fidel Castro. Cuba is one of the last remaining communist states and is an officially atheist state.*

April 1998, a settlement reached between the Irish Republic and the United Kingdom at last promised resolution of a decades-long conflict marked by terrorist attacks (see Chapters 23, 28). Even here, reconciliation may yet come.

UNIFICATION

As peoples and principles once in conflict have found reconciliation in the 1990s, regions of the Western world appear to be reaching a new unity. From the exhausted, shattered European states that emerged out of World War II in 1945, an increasingly united Europe formed.

In 1945, Europe was divided. A gulf of experience separated the victors from the vanquished, those whose cities had been bombed and populations ravaged from those who had survived without injury. A new barrier of suspicion emerged between the nations of eastern Europe, which became satellites of the mammoth Soviet Union, and the nations of western Europe which aligned themselves with the giant across the ocean, the United States (see Chapter 29).

The free nations of western Europe set out to shape their futures through the parliamentary process. Britain elected a Labour government in 1945, then shifted back and forth between Labour and Conservative over the next fifty years. In 1949, the West Germans elected a Christian Democratic leader of impeccable credentials. Since he stepped down in 1963, Christian Democrats, Social Democrats, and Green parties have led the government.

Postwar Italy and France chose the Christian Democratic (or center-right) road despite the considerable presence of the Communist party. Italy remained under Christian Democrat coalition governments until 1983, when a Socialist coalition took power. Shifting from the leftwing government installed in 1945, France changed course in 1958 with the election of Charles de Gaulle (1890–1970) and, in 1959, the institution of the Fifth Republic. Since De Gaulle's resignation in 1969, first conservative and then, from 1981, socialist and centrist leaders have taken charge.

As postwar governments developed clear direction, two trans-national alliances took form: the Common Market, formed in 1957, and NATO, formed in 1949 (see Chapter 29). The first allowed for

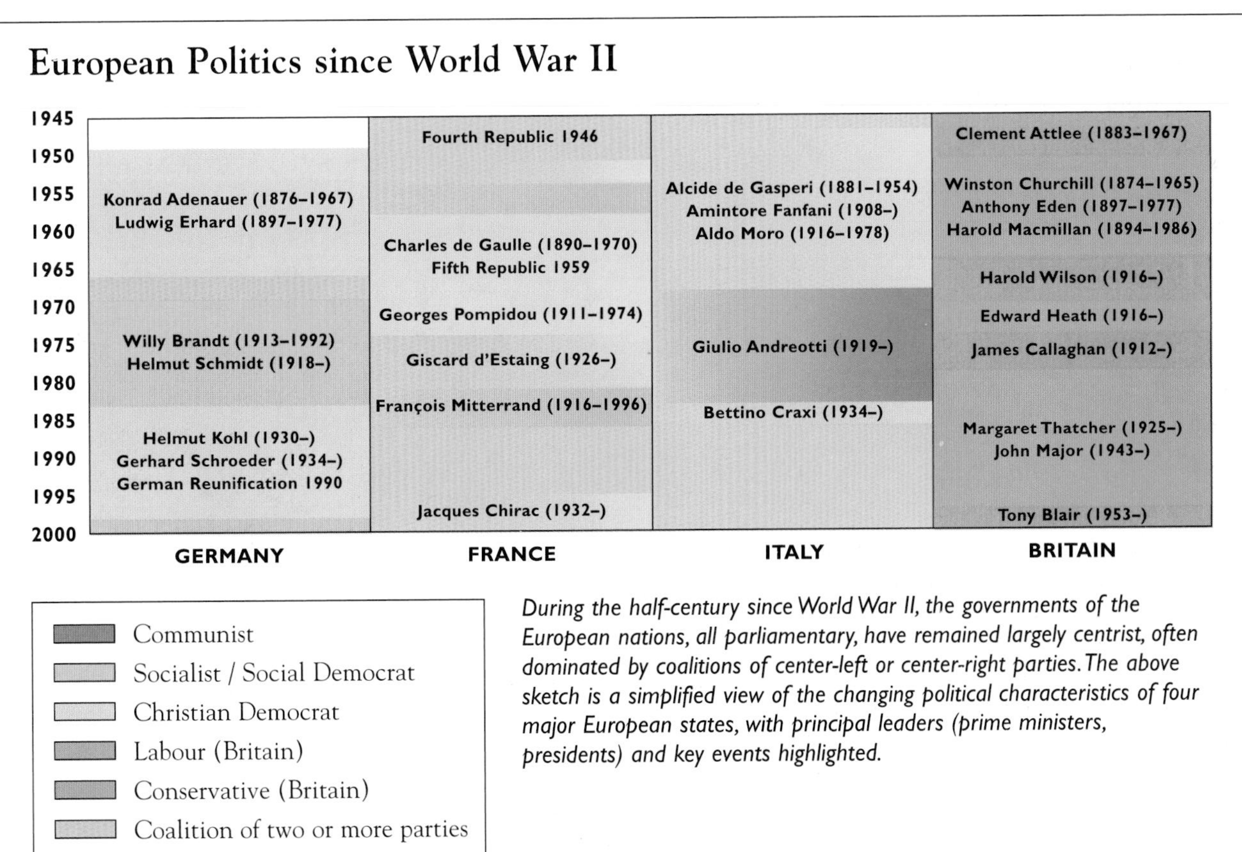

During the half-century since World War II, the governments of the European nations, all parliamentary, have remained largely centrist, often dominated by coalitions of center-left or center-right parties. The above sketch is a simplified view of the changing political characteristics of four major European states, with principal leaders (prime ministers, presidents) and key events highlighted.

the free flow of goods across the borders of member nations. The latter, led by the United States, sought to defend its members against possible aggression from the Soviet Union and its clients (which in 1955 organized the Warsaw Pact of allied eastern European states under its leadership).

Since its founding, the Common Market has expanded to include more states and new forms of cooperation. It was replaced in 1967 by the European Community and in 1993 became the European Union (EU). As of 1999 a partnership of fifteen states, the EU is centered in Brussels (Belgium), with a written constitution and its own parliament (which meets in Brussels or Strasbourg, France). It aims to establish a common foreign policy for its members, and looks to their eventual political and economic integration.

Eleven of the fifteen members of the European Union (all but the United Kingdom, Denmark, Greece, and Sweden) joined in Economic and Monetary Union (EMU). The EMU exercises strict discipline over member states in matters such as national indebtedness and monetary policy. On December 31, 1998, one member proclaiming "the dawn of a new era in the integration of Europe," the EMU introduced its new currency, the "euro." The euro is expected to become in time the principal unit of exchange in Europe—or "Euroland," a vast new entity with 292 million inhabitants and a twenty-five percent share of the world's economic output (nearly equal to the United States' share of twenty-eight percent).

By 1999, on the eve of the new millennium, Europe was well on its way to continental unification—unification at the levels of economic, political, and cultural cooperation. It recalls the Europe of 999, a millennium before, which was building the cultural unity of *Christianitas*, or Christendom, based on a common faith, language, and intellectual traditions (see Chapter 10).

In the western hemisphere, meanwhile, some steps were taken toward inter-regional cooperation. Moved by Cold War anxieties, from the 1950s through the 1980s, the United States had imposed its will on its Latin American neighbors, boosting authoritarian regimes or launching military interventions. By the 1990s, as the Cold War receded into memory, and leading Latin American states developed stable and powerful economies, it became more possible for these nations to cooperate with the wealthier nations to the north. They also benefited from NAFTA (North American Free Trade Agreement), put in practice in 1994, which facilitated trade between Canada, the United States, and Mexico. The possibility that some Latin American economies will "dollarize," or convert their currencies (already linked to the dollar) to United States dollars, points to greater regional economic unity in the future.

WITNESSES

1992

The future hegemony of Western culture—Francis Fukuyama: As mankind approaches the end of the millennium, the twin crises of authoritarianism and socialist central planning have left only one competitor standing in the ring as an ideology of potentially universal validity: liberal democracy, the doctrine of individual freedom and popular sovereignty. Two hundred years after they first animated the French and American revolutions, the principles of liberty and equality have proven not just durable but resurgent. . . .

What is emerging victorious . . . is . . . the liberal *idea.* That is to say, for a very large part of the world, there is now no ideology with pretensions to challenge liberal democracy, and no universal principle of legitimacy other than the sovereignty of the people. . . .

It is true that Islam constitutes a systematic and coherent ideology, just like liberalism and communism, with its own code of morality and doctrine of political and social justice. The appeal of Islam is potentially universal. . . .

[Nevertheless,] it remains the case that this religion has virtually no appeal outside those areas that were culturally Islamic to begin with. The days of Islam's cultural conquests, it would seem, are over: it can win back lapsed adherents, but has no resonance with young people in Berlin, Tokyo, or Moscow. And while nearly a billion people are culturally Islamic—a fifth of the world's population—they cannot challenge liberal democracy on its own territory on the level of ideas. . . . Indeed, . . . [p]art of the reason for the current, fundamentalist revival is the strength of the perceived threat from liberal, Western values to traditional Islamic societies.

(Francis Fukuyama, *The End of History and the Last Man*, 1992)

GLOBALIZATION

The increasing unity of the Western blocs, both European and American, is part of a larger process of growing economic and cultural interconnectedness in the world called globalization. In economic terms, globalization means that the separate markets of the world—local, regional, and continental—are now one. Not only do commodities purchased in the Western world, such as coffee, bananas, and oil, come from other continents, but clothing, carpets, and automobiles, among other goods, are likely to have been manufactured in Asia, Africa, or South America. Business is international, carried on by itinerant entrepreneurs and speeded by technologies of transportation, communication, and computerization.

In the global economy, the processes of industrialization and urbanization that began in Europe before 1800 have become the model for regions remote from that source (see Chapter 23). Progress has been irregular and incomplete. The "developed" world, including the industrialized nations of the West, with Japan and the Asian "dragons" or "tigers" (see Chapter 28), is far wealthier than the "developing" world, including 125 of the world's 170 countries, mostly in Asia, Africa, and Latin America. Nevertheless, increases in levels of wealth, and improvements in health and welfare, have been made worldwide.

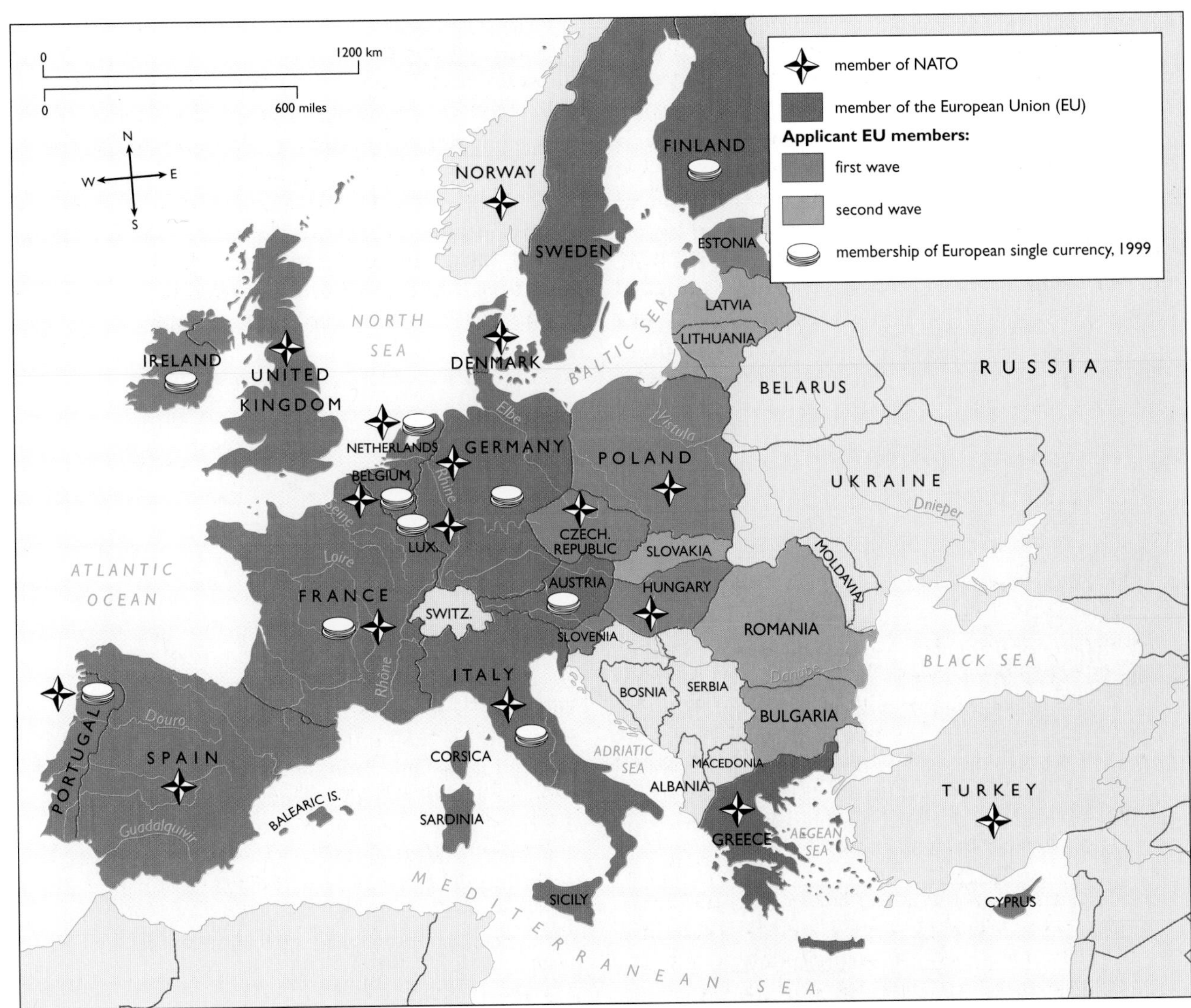

Map 30.1 Europe: the Continent, the Union, the Alliance: *Europe is not only a continent and a set of nations. It also has a unity created by economic alliances, culminating in the European Union and the eleven nations adopting a unitary currency, and the political alliance of NATO (which also includes the non-European states of the United States and Canada).*

The coming of the Euro: *Since the end of World War II, European nations have increasingly committed themselves to integration and cooperation. The introduction of a single currency, adopted by many, though not all members of the European Union on January 1, 1999, marks a critical step toward the ultimate creation of a "United States of Europe," comparable in some ways to the United States of America.*

As manufacturing tasks have shifted to the "developing" zones of the world, the most highly developed have assumed the task of producing information and services rather than things. Rapid progress in cybernetics (see Chapter 29), has transformed the way business, government, and cultural institutions operate. The design of hardware and software systems require highly trained experts; even to operate these systems requires workers skilled beyond the level of the manual laborers who were once the core of the "working class." Those needs place huge demands on the educational systems of societies that aspire to excel in the enterprise of managing information.

Improved technologies have also built rapid transportation and communication networks that facilitate globalization. A dense network of air routes links once-remote entrepots, while greater efficiency has resulted in lower prices. Within highly-developed regions, high-speed trains are convenient and accessible. The Channel tunnel, or "Chunnel," opened in 1994, at last provides a non-stop connection between Paris and London, two main poles of European cul-

WITNESSES

1993

The power of technology vs. the power of population in the century to come—Paul Kennedy: . . . [T]he greatest test for human society as it confronts the twenty-first century is how to use "the power of technology" to meet the demands thrown up by "the power of population"; that is, how to find effective global solutions in order to free the poorer three-quarters of humankind from the growing Malthusian trap of malnutrition, starvation, resource depletion, unrest, enforced migration, and armed conflict. . . .

The technology explosion is taking place overwhelmingly in economically advanced societies, many of which possess slow-growing or even declining populations. However, the demographic boom is occurring in countries with limited technological resources, very few scientists and skilled workers, inadequate investment in research and development, and few or no successful corporations; in many cases, their governing elites have no interest in technology, and cultural and ideological prejudices are ... tilted against change. . . .

. . . [S]imply because we do not know the future, it is impossible to say with certainty whether global trends will lead to terrible disasters or be diverted by astonishing advances in human adaption. What is clear is that as the Cold War fades away, we face not a "new world order" but a troubled and fractured planet, whose problems deserve the serious attention of politicians and publics alike. . . .

(Paul Kennedy, *Preparing for the Twenty-First Century*, 1993) ture. Even as these networks for high-speed movement link the world's capitals, trunk roads and rail lines slowly multiply in the isolated interiors of the developing world.

Communications technologies are able to link even these parts of the world not yet well-served by transportation systems. By means of telephones, cellular phones, fax machines, the radio, and above all the Internet, vocal or digitalized information can be delivered almost instantaneously to governments, institutions, and individuals worldwide. In Africa, the radio has facilitated long distance communications where there were previously almost none. In China in 1989, fax machines distributed information about the Tiananmen Square demonstration and repression. In the Balkan conflict of 1999, both Serbs and Kosovars communicated with outsiders by e-mail, or "electronic mail." E-mail also connects entrepreneurs and intellectuals in New York, Moscow, or Milan, who conclude sales or arrange conferences with their counterparts in Germany, India, or Colombia.

Technology further brings the promise of taming the great distances of the universe. Space programs begun in the context of the Cold War arms buildup have since evolved into a cooperative effort to study the nature of the universe, and to gauge the ways that

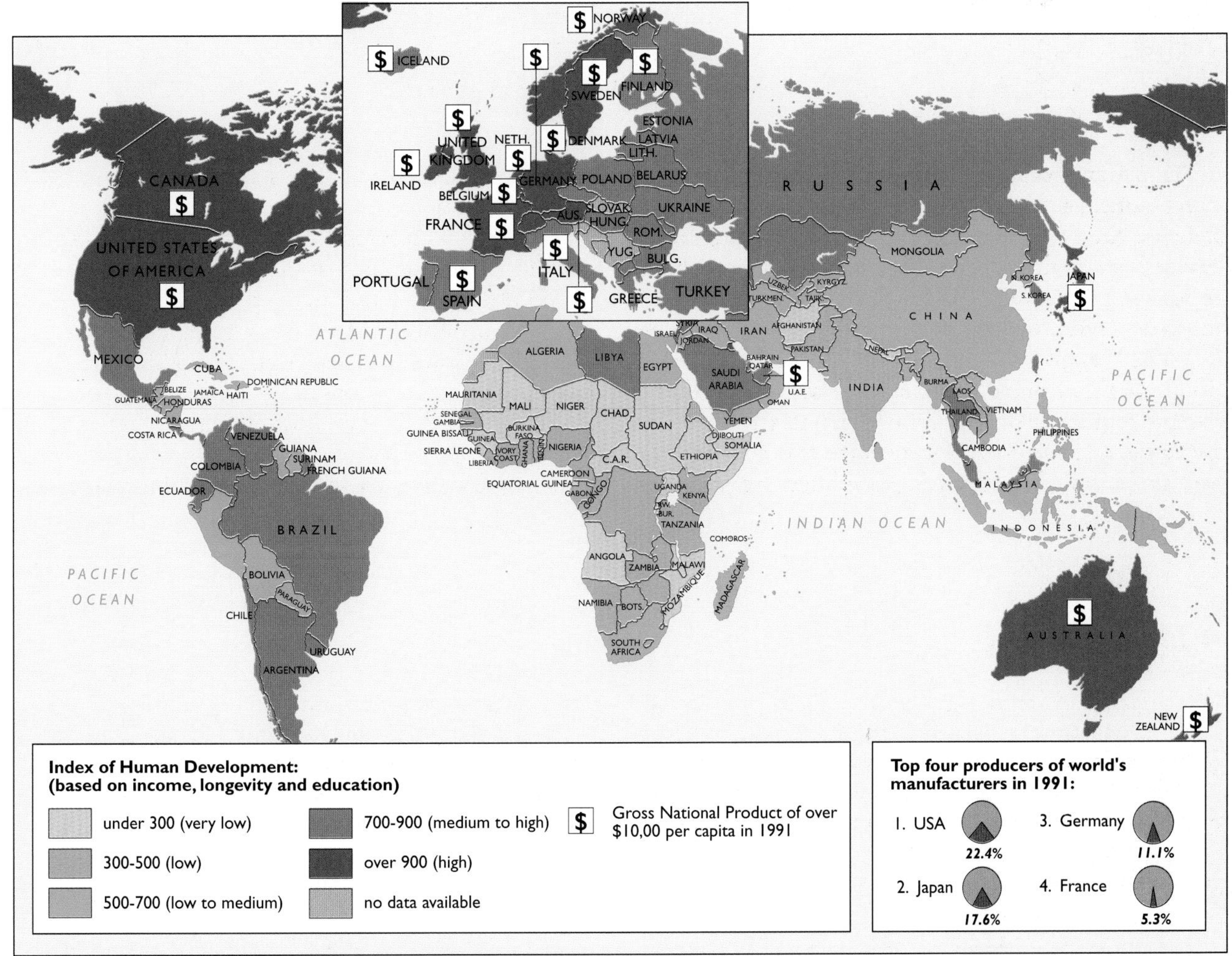

Map 30.2 The Wealth of Nations: Developed and Developing Nations of the World: *As the twenty-first century opens, the world appears to be divided between the wealthier nations, mostly Western, and poorer ones, mostly outside the West. With the exception of Japan, all the nations where the Gross National Product per capita in 1991 exceeded $10,000 were Western. Four nations—the United States, France, Germany, and Japan—produce over half of the value of the world's manufactured goods. Money is not, however, the only index of wealth. The map shown here indicates relative levels of human welfare as indicated by the Human Development Index, a measure based on the three components of longevity, education, and income. Much of Asia and the Middle East, and all of Africa, rank below the highest levels.*

human or animal life can survive in the alien environments of space. The Russian Mir space station, launched in 1986, was finally dismantled in 1999 after a series of mishaps. Before its termination, the seven-story, 35-ton International Space Station with linked Russian and American modules was launched into orbit late in 1998. It is designed to accommodate an international team that will pursue Mir's goals in seeking knowledge about space.

While the Internet annihilates distance and space missions conquer it, perhaps nothing so unifies peoples of the world as their participation in a common culture—a mass culture of television shows and rock music, of youth fashion, sport, and film. Although these trends first appeared in the free, exuberant 1920s, they developed their present form during youth-led countercultural transformations of the Sixties (see Chapter 29). In the 1990s, mass cultural style continued to be dominated by United States youth, whose pursuits of "sex, drugs, and rock and roll" now engage imitators on every continent.

When in 1997 the youthful Diana, Princess of Wales (1961–1997), died in a speeding car in Paris, her popular heroization marked the point at which the values of mass culture triumphed over those of tradition. It was her association with mass culture that powered her elevation above the other members of the British royal family which she had entered by marriage to Prince Charles (1948–), the heir apparent. By birth an aristocrat, she modeled a connectedness to the passions and tastes of ordinary people that the state figureheads seemed to lack, exhibited in her ties to entertainment celebrities, her championing of popular causes, her choices in fashion and leisure activities. Millions of people thronged to her London funeral to hail her as the "People's Princess."

International Space Station: *With the end of the Cold War, the "space-race" between the United States and USSR has increasingly given way to cooperative efforts to explore, and perhaps ultimately to colonize space. The International Space Station—the cargo bay of which is shown here with the module Unity (upper center)—is both the physical centerpiece and key symbol of this new era. It will be built and operated by several nations.*

WITNESSES

1994

The place of the West in world history—an undervalued achievement? Bernard Lewis: [Though Europeans expanded and transformed the ages-old institution of slavery], it was Europe and its daughters . . . that first decided to set the slaves free—at home, then in the colonies, finally in all the world. Western technology made slavery unnecessary; Western ideas made it intolerable. There have been many slaveries; there was only one abolition. . . .

Why . . . did the peoples of Europe embark on [a] . . . vast expansion and, by conquest, conversion, and colonization, attempt to create a Eurocentric world[?] Was it . . . because of some deep-seated, perhaps hereditary vice—some profound moral flaw?

. . . In setting out to conquer, subjugate, and despoil other peoples, the Europeans were merely . . . conforming to the common practice of mankind. . . . The interesting questions are not why they tried, but why they succeeded—and then why, having succeeded, they repented of their success as a sin. The success was unique in modern times; the repentance, in all of recorded history. . . .

Imperialism, *sexism*, and *racism* are words of Western coinage—not because the West invented these evils, which are, alas, universal, but because the West recognized and named and condemned them as evils and struggled mightily, and not entirely in vain, to weaken their hold and to help their victims. If . . . Western culture does indeed "go" imperialism, sexism, and racism will not go with it. More likely casualties will be the freedom to denounce them and the effort to end them.

(Bernard Lewis, "Eurocentrism Revisited, 1994" excerpted from *Commentary*, December 1994)

In Diana's brief career can be seen the "postmodernization" of the British royal family. "Postmodernism" characterizes much of the style of the late twentieth century in the arts and thought. It differs from modernism in rejecting traditional norms by actually incorporating historical elements as "quotations" within decorative fantasies that defy frameworks of logic, chronology, or decorum. Blurring the older distinctions between high culture and mass culture, postmodernism accommodates a globalized world where all the authoritative ideas and institutions of a previous age are placed in question.

Postmodernism has encouraged such movements as gay and lesbian activism, environmentalism, and a commitment to multiculturalism. These movements share an opposition to values once central to Western civilization: respectively, the family defined as a necessarily heterosexual and patriarchal institution; the habit of forceful expansion without regard to the devastations of peoples, other biological species, or natural habitats; and the elevation of certain nations or civilizations above others. Many observers hope that multiculturalism, especially, will promote tolerance and cooperation, and contribute to the life expectancy of the human species.

In a globalized culture where personal identities shift and coalesce, new, or "new-age" religions have won followers worldwide, luring adherents from the failing faiths of their childhood. Some of the new cults have had bizarre or destructive outcomes, for

WITNESSES

1996

The decline of the West and the de-Westernization of the United States—Samuel P. Huntington: The West is overwhelmingly dominant now and will remain number one in terms of power and influence well into the twenty-first century. Gradual, inexorable, and fundamental changes, however, are also occurring . . . and the power of the West relative to that of other civilizations will continue to decline. . . . These shifts . . . are leading and will lead to the revival and increased cultural assertiveness of non-Western societies and to their increasing rejection of Western culture.

The decline of the West is a slow process. The rise of Western power took four hundred years. Its recession could take as long [and will] . . . not proceed in a straight line. . . .

At the peak of its territorial expansion in 1920, the West directly ruled about 25.5 million square miles or close to half the earth's earth. By 1993 this territorial control had been cut in half to about 12.7 million square miles. The West was back to its original European core plus its spacious settler-populated lands in North America, Australia, and New Zealand. The territory of independent Islamic societies, in contrast, rose from 1.8 million square miles in 1920 to over 11 million square miles in 1993. [Similarly, Westerners' share of world population has declined from about 30 percent in 1900 to about 13 percent in 1993.] The Western share of the global economic product . . . has clearly been declining since World War II.

Historically American national identity has been defined culturally by the heritage of Western civilization and politically by the principles of the American Creed on which Americans overwhelmingly agree: liberty, democracy, individualism, equality before the law, constitutionalism, private property. In the late twentieth century both components of American identity have come under concentrated and sustained onslaught from a small but influential number of intellectuals and publicists. In the name of multiculturalism they have attacked the identification of the United States with Western civilization, denied the existence of a common American culture, and promoted racial, ethnic, and other subnational cultural identities and groupings. . . .

The American multiculturalists . . . reject their country's cultural heritage . . . [proposing] to create a country of many civilizations, which is to say a country not belonging to any civilization and lacking a cultural core. History shows that no country so constituted can long endure as a coherent society. A multicivilizational United States will not be the United States; it will be the United Nations. . . .

Rejection of the Creed and of Western civilization means the end of the United States of America as we have known it. It also means effectively the end of Western civilization. If the United States is de-Westernized, the West is reduced to Europe and a few lightly populated overseas European settler countries. Without the United States the West becomes a minuscule and declining part of the world's population on a small and inconsequential peninsula at the extremity of the Eurasian land mass.

(Samuel P. Huntington, *The Clash of Civilizations and the Remaking of World Order*, 1996)

***Princess Diana's funeral:** Many individuals have enjoyed—or suffered—the popularity of Britain's Princess Diana. In life, she was both the glamour-queen of Britain's otherwise relatively staid royal family and a tireless campaigner for various causes and charities. In death, she became "the people's princess"—a national heroine of almost mythical proportions.*

WITNESSES

1996

Europe's role for the twenty-first century—Václav Havel: Humanity is entering an era of multipolar and multicultural civilization. Europe is no longer the conductor of the global orchestra, but this does not mean it has nothing more to say to the world. A new task now presents itself, and with it a new meaning to Europe's very existence.

That task will no longer be to spread—violently or non-violently—its own religion, its own civilization, its own inventions, or its own power. Nor will it be to preach the rule of law, democracy, human rights, or justice to the rest of the world.

If Europe wishes, it can do something more modest yet more beneficial. It can become a model for how different peoples can work together in peace without sacrificing any of their identity; it can demonstrate that it is possible to treat our planet considerately, with future generations in mind; it can demonstrate that it is possible to live together in peace . . . . Moreover, Europe has one final possibility, if it so desires: it can reclaim its finest spiritual and intellectual traditions . . . and join forces with [other civilizations] in a search for the common moral minimum necessary to guide us all so that we may live side by side on one planet and confront jointly whatever threatens our lives together.
(*New York Review of Books*, June 20, 1996)

example, the mass suicides of the Heaven's Gate community in San Diego County, California, in March 1997, or the murder or suicide of forty-eight Canadian solar worshipers in Quebec and Switzerland in October 1994. Less sensationally, sun worshipers attempt to gather each year on the summer solstice at Stonehenge on England's Salisbury Plain, a 4000-year-old megalith, and originally intended for that purpose; and some feminists have revived benign witchcraft and the cults of ancient mother goddesses.

Yet new religions have not replaced the traditional religions, securely rooted as they are in historical experience. Buddhism and Hinduism in China, Japan, Indochina, Tibet, and India are powerful forces for cohesion. Islam retains the loyalty of more than a billion Muslims living in a broad band stretching from Africa to Indonesia, and has recently inspired political movements resistant to Western and mass cultural values (see Chapter 28). Judaism, which does not proselytize, struggles to hold onto its people in the affluent nations of the West, while it flourishes in its homeland of Israel.

Christianity has largely shed its militancy, and observance is lax in many circles. Yet Protestant evangelical and fundamentalist groups are thriving in the United States and actively pursuing missions abroad. The Roman Catholic Church supports outreach programs in Africa, Asia, and Latin America, and recent popes—notably John XXIII (1881–1963) and John Paul II (1920–)—have delineated social and moral issues of universal concern. Overall, Christianity—the predominant religious expression of the Western world—continues to number more adherents (nearly 2 billion) than any other religion worldwide. Some observers expect that traditional religions will continue to draw followers for whom the entertainments of mass culture provide insufficient meaning, or who, after the seventy-year communist experiment, are disenchanted with atheism.

Even traditionalists, however, now inhabit a globalized world where the narrow boundaries of the past—of village, nation, denomination, language—are dissolving. The world is not yet one, and conflicts and hatreds disrupt it. But it is a linked system, in which no one part stands alone, and every thought or deed has potentially worldwide impact.

THE END OF THE WEST?

In a global world, of what importance is the West? Have its historical failings disqualified it for leadership, or do they require it to abandon its claims for greatness? Has it lost its identity? Does it have a future? Or does the arrival of the postmodern era mean the end of the West? Has the last decade been the West's last decade? Or will it, or should it, pursue the goal "to strive and not to yield" into the next millennium?

Western civilization, I will close by arguing, is not only a phenomenon that has existed in the past, but one that is likely to endure in the future. In the twentieth century, two terrible wars brought about by the ambitions of the nations of the West threatened to destroy that civilization. But recovery has occurred, and the principles of human rights and parliamentary democracy have been vindicated. Indeed, they are imitated worldwide. Most of the nations of the developing world seek to establish civil societies on the model of those that exist in the Western world, where they have their origin and history, resting on the core values of Western civilization.

Western civilization has evolved those core values over more than a thousand years. They include: (1) the principle of human dignity: that all human beings are equal in worth, that they possess rights which cannot be taken away, and that to the greatest possible degree they are free; (2) the ideal of justice: that no person should be unfairly privileged above another; (3) the value of democracy: that the power to shape the future of a community belongs to its people as a whole and not to arbitrarily selected leaders; (4) the method of rationalism, which assumes that all phenomena (even those pertaining to God, essence, or spirit) may be subject to the critical scrutiny of the human mind; (5) the inclination to progress, to work toward goals to be achieved in the future; (6) the habit of self-examination, which encourages human beings to examine themselves seriously and often to test whether they have fulfilled their promise and their responsibilities.

The last of these—the habit of self-examination—has yielded an abundant harvest of criticisms. Over the last centuries, the nations of the West claimed authority over other regions of the world, drained them of wealth, and subjugated their peoples. They created and defended the Atlantic system of slavery, and more than a century after its abolition, have not yet admitted the descendants of slaves into full participation in the societies which they were compelled to enter. In the name of Christianity, those nations have waged wars against other nations and peoples, compelled conformity through terror and torture, and excluded dissenters, if they did not actively persecute them, from political and social life. In the service of its ideologies, most notoriously Nazism, Western civilization has spawned episodes of genocide. Characterized by patriarchal family structures, Western societies have injured the women and children whose destinies have been determined by the

WITNESSES

1997

The global market and the coming storm—William Greider: Imagine a wondrous new machine . . . a machine that reaps as it destroys. It is huge and mobile ... but no one is at the wheel. . . . It is sustained by its own forward motion, guided mainly by its own appetites. And it is accelerating. . . .

The machine is . . . modern capitalism driven by the imperatives of global industrial revolution. The metaphor is imperfect, but it offers a simplified way to visualize what is dauntingly complex and abstract and impossible diffuse—the drama of a free-running economic system that is reordering the world. . . .

. . . [T]he symptoms of upheaval can be found most anywhere, since people in distant places are now connected by powerful strands of the same marketplace. The convergence has no fixed center, no reliable boundaries or settled outcomes. . . . The earth's diverse societies are being rearranged and united in complicated ways by global capitalism. The idea evokes benumbed resignation among many. The complexity of it overwhelms. The enormity makes people feel small and helpless.

(William Greider, *One World, Ready or Not: The Manic Logic of Global Capitalism*, 1997)

status concerns of authoritative males. Western expansionism has led to the unrestrained industrialization of regions of the world, resulting in environmental degradation and human misery.

All of these charges are, to some extent, true. It is also true, however, that other civilizations and societies have been brutal and aggressive, characterized by patriarchalism and sustained by slavery. Moreover, the Western world alone has repudiated those behaviors that, by its own moral standards, it has come to condemn. The West has rejected intolerance, terror, torture, and tyranny; it has invited women and the descendants of former slaves and subordinates to join in civic life; it has recognized the need to protect the natural environment and to support the health and education of all its citizens. These stances, as much as the troubled legacy of past failings, are the true harvest of the Western experience.

WITNESSES

1998

The futures of rich and poor—David S. Landes: The old division of the world into two power blocs, East and West, has subsided. Now the big challenge and threat is the gap in wealth and health that separates rich and poor. These are often styled North and South, because the division is geographic; but a more accurate signifier would be the West and the Rest, because the division is also historic. Here is the greatest single problem and danger facing the world in the Third Millennium. . . .

How big is the gap between rich and poor and what is happening to it? . . . [T]he difference in income per head between the richest industrial nation, say Switzerland, and the poorest nonindustrial country, Mozambique, is about 400 to 1. Two hundred and fifty years ago, this gap between richest and poorest was perhaps 5 to 1, and the difference between Europe and, say, East or South Asia (China or India) was around 1.5 or 2 to 1.

. . . [O]ur task (the rich countries), in our own interest as well as theirs, is to help the poor become healthier and wealthier. If we do not, they will seek to take what they cannot make; and if they cannot earn by exporting commodities, they will export people. In short, wealth is an irresistible magnet; and poverty is a potentially raging contaminant: it cannot be segregated, and our peace and prosperity depend in the long run on the well-being of others. (David S. Landes, *The Wealth and Poverty of Nations: why Some are so Rich and Some So Poor*, 1998)

Has the West lost its way at the end of a long road, when the worst of its past is censured, and the best of its ideals now shared by other nations? Where is the West in a global world? What is the West when so many of non-Western ancestry now live in Western societies? In the past, the delineation between the West and the rest of the world seemed clear, at least to Westerners: the West represented freedom vs. tyranny, or Christianity vs. paganism, or civilization vs. barbarism, or sovereignty vs. subordination.

In the eighteenth century, at the Royal Observatory at Greenwich, England, astronomers resolved the thorny problem of longitude with the aid of newly refined chronometers. Their system was anchored by the time current in Greenwich, at a point which, as an international conference in 1884 established, would define the Prime Meridian. The Prime Meridian is that line of longitude that divides East and West, and serves as a universal standard of space and time. It runs from pole to pole through Greenwich, thus conceived to be the preeminent point on Earth. Its creation was an act of both scientific imagination and astounding arrogance, a reminder of the ease with which the West could once partition the globe. Then there was no ambiguity about the question: "where, and what, is the West?"

Nor should there be now. The West is not so clearly a place as it once was. It is not simply the western part of Europe, or the western hemisphere; parts of the West (Australasia, for instance) are not in the "west" in any geographical sense at all. The West is its civilization, its cultural heritage, and the moral and intellectual values that heritage has nurtured. A consideration of the map of the world shows that the West is everywhere—not only in the core area of Europe where its civilization was first developed, but in the regions of European settlement, and ultimately in every part of the inhabited world to which Western influence has extended (see Preface).

Language and religion especially, two key features of culture, point to the worldwide diffusion of Western civilization. European languages are spoken around the world by many peoples not of Western descent. Serving as the languages of international trade, transportation, communication, and tourism, English and French especially have a vast influence in Africa and Asia. And Christianity has adherents everywhere, attracting new converts in nations far from the continent where it developed its modern form.

And so the West, while it is no longer anywhere in particular, is in another sense everywhere. As a civilization, a cultural tradition, a set of moral and intellectual values, it exists wherever there are people who study its past and value its attainments, and seek to extend its future—people like you, the students who read this book. The future of the West lies with those who may choose to take up the mission that Ulysses embraced when he resolved to sail westward, roaming ever with a hungry heart.

Construction of the Millennium Dome: *As the site of the Prime Meridian (0 degrees longitude—the baseline for time-zones around the world), Greenwich in London, England, is a logical place to construct a huge monument to the millennium.*

WITNESSES

1999

The end of the nation-state and the coming of global society—Václav Havel: There is every indication that the glory of the nation-state as the culmination of every national community's history, and its highest earthly value—the only one, in fact, in the name of which it is permissible to kill, or for which people have been expected to die—has already passed its peak.

It would seem that the enlightened efforts of generations of democrats, the terrible experience of two world wars . . . and the evolution of civilization have finally brought humanity to the recognition that human beings are more important than the state.

In this new world, people—regardless of borders—are connected in millions of different ways: through trade, finance, property, and information. Such relationships bring with them a wide variety of values and cultural models that have a universal validity. It is a world, moreover, in which a threat to some has an immediate impact on everyone, in which . . . our individual destinies are merging into a single destiny, in which all of us . . . must begin to bear responsibility for everything that occurs. In such a world, the idol of state sovereignty must inevitably dissolve. . . .

The practical responsibilities of the state—its legal powers—can only devolve in two directions, downward or upward: downward, to the nongovernmental organizations and structures of civil society; or upward, to regional, transnational, and global organizations. . . .

If modern democratic states are usually defined by qualities such as their respect for human rights and liberties, the equality their citizens enjoy, and the existence of a civil society, then the condition toward which humanity will, and in the interests of its own survival must, move will probably be characterized by a universal or global respect for human rights, by universal civic equality and the rule of law, and by a global civic society.

(*New York Review of Books*, June 10, 1999; trs. P. Wilson)

Conclusion

THE PAST, THE FUTURE, AND THE MEANING OF THE WEST

Near the site of the Royal Observatory at Greenwich, the pivot of the Prime Meridian, the British government have erected a huge monument: the Millennium Dome. It recalls earlier monuments, both real and literary—the Globe Theatre, where Shakespeare produced his plays, bringing to life the idea that all the world is a stage, and the stage a microcosm of the whole of the world; the City of the Sun, envisioned by the Italian philosopher Tommaso Campanella (1568–1639), a utopia where people live in peace and harmony; the domed Pantheon in Rome, dedicated by the emperor Hadrian (r. 117–138) to all the gods of the universe. As we exit a barbarous century which has cast doubt upon the achievements of the West, the Dome may represent the promise of a new millennium when Western civilization may be recognized not as the "botched" project decried by the poet Ezra Pound (1885–1972; see Chapter 25) but as a repository of wisdom and reflection that will flourish still on a continuing journey "beyond the utmost bound of human thought" and bear great benefits to the peoples of the West and of the world.

SUGGESTED READINGS

Diamond, Jared, *Guns, Germs and Steel: the Fates of Human Societies* (New York: W.W. Norton, 1997). Traces the success of some human societies to geographic, environmental, and economic accident.

Evans, Gareth, *Cooperating for Peace: The Global Agenda for the 1990s and Beyond* (London: Allen and Unwin, 1994). Written by a foreign minister of Australia. Explores the abilities and role of the UN as an international peacekeeper. Argues too little emphasis has been accorded so far to pre-emptive diplomacy as a means of peaceful conflict resolution.

Fukuyama, Francis, *The End of History and the Last Man* (New York: Free Press, 1992). Controversial. Written immediately after the end of the Cold War. Argues that history is a teleological (i.e. goal-oriented) process that has effectively now come to an end with the triumph of free markets and liberal democracy across the world. Humankind's future—at least in terms of basic economic and political systems—will be much like the present, says Fukuyama.

Greider, William, *One World, Ready or Not: the Manic Logic of Global Capitalism* (New York: Simon & Schuster, 1996). Where some see in the apparent global triumph of free-market capitalism nothing but good, Greider sees little but disaster: falling living standards, global economic disorder, stock market bubbles, and so on. More not less government is needed—and quickly, he argues.

Heilbroner, Robert, *Visions of the Future: The Distant Past, Yesterday, Today, Tomorrow* (New York: Oxford University Press, 1995). Capitalism has become supreme all across the globe, and is currently embarked on an unprecedented project of capital accumulation. Heilbroner, one of America's most important and readable economic historians, ponders the meaning and ramifications of these developments.

Huntington, Samuel P, *The Clash of Civilizations and the Remaking of World Order* (New York: Simon & Schuster, 1996). Views the coming century in relatively somber tones. Huntington foresees increasingly vigorous opposition among non-Western countries to the global hegemony of free-markets, democracy, and Western culture in general.

Kennedy, Paul, *Preparing for the Twenty-First Century* (New York: Random House, 1993). Stressing demographic pressures in the developing countries, foreshadows possible catastrophe if the wealthier nations do not take prior action.

Kindleberger, Charles, *World Economic Primacy: 1500–1990* (Oxford: Oxford University Press, 1998). Economic-historical study of economic primacy—what it is, which powers have wielded it and why, and so on. Covers great economic powers from Venice to the US, Britain to Japan. Kindleberger is generally pessimistic about America's future as a great economic power.

Landes, David S, *The Wealth and Poverty of Nations: Why Some Are So Rich and Some So Poor* (New York: Norton, 1998). Thought-provoking study of the global distribution of wealth. Landes argues that what has made some nations rich and left others poor is their success in industrializing their economies.

Mazlish, Bruce, *The Fourth Discontinuity: The Co-Evolution of Humans and Machines* (New Haven: Yale University Press, 1993). Thought-provoking exploration of the developing relationship between humans and machines, argued from a Marxist perspective. Though Mazlish is concerned ultimately with the present and future, his study assumes a broad historical perspective dating back to antiquity and pre-history.

Mazower, Mark, *Dark Continent: Europe's Twentieth Century* (New York: Knopf, 1998). A pessimistic retrospective, emphasizing fascism's claim on the populace at large and its very near success.

Sowell, Thomas, *Conquests and Cultures* (New York: Basic Books, 1998). Third of three volumes discussing the transfer of culture and its role in the creation of the modern world. Earlier volumes focus on race and migration; here Sowell concentrates on physical conquest as a means of effecting cultural transfer, and in particular on the reasons for the great success of European culture around the world.

White, Donald W., *The American Century: The Rise and Decline of the United States as a World Power* (New Haven: Yale University Press, 1997). Examines America's idea of itself as a nation with a world role. Focuses particularly on the 1940s as both the origin and apotheosis this "social myth."

GLOSSARY

abolitionism: Designation for the movements in the United States and western Europe opposing the Atlantic slave trade and slavery.

Aborigines: The indigenous (native) or earliest-arrived peoples in any given area, especially the original Australian population.

abortion: The termination of pregnancy, spontaneous or contrived (through surgery or drugs), by the removal of embryo or fetus from the uterus.

absolute monarchy: Political system in which the powers of the monarch were theoretically "absolute," that is, not limited by any law or constitution. Absolute monarchs were limited in practice by the claims of the nobility, clergy, and tradition.

absolutism: A political system or project that concentrates power in the hands of the monarch, who becomes absolute monarch.

abstract art: Any of the various artistic styles or movements whose created images are non-representational, bearing little reference to actually-existing objects.

Afrikaner: White resident of South Africa, typically of Dutch or Huguenot (French Protestant) descent, speaking the Afrikaans language (a variant of Dutch). *See also* **Boer.**

alchemy/alchemist: Ancient mystical tradition involving the search for knowledge to transform base metals into gold.

alienation: From Marxist theory, the supposed disconnection of industrial workers from the product of their labor and from their human needs, as a result of the conditions of wage labor under capitalism. *See also* **proletarian**.

ambassador: The highest-ranking diplomatic representative of one country to another, usually accorded the privilege of guaranteed personal security, or "diplomatic immunity."

Amerindians: Aboriginal peoples of the Western Hemisphere, American Indians. Preferred to "Indian" (used to refer to the peoples of the Indian subcontinent) and "Native American" (an anti-immigrant American political party, called "the Know-Nothings").

anarchism: In political philosophy, the rejection of all government and law as the only means of acquiring social and political liberty.

Ancien Régime: Literally, "Old Regime," the term used to describe the traditional European system of legal, social, and political hierarchy which the French Revolution set out to destroy.

animism/animist: The belief that spirits or divinities dwell inside objects and living things, influencing or determining life and events in the natural world.

anti-Semitism: The discrimination against, prejudice, or hostility toward Jews.

apartheid: Literally, "apartness," in twentieth-century South Africa, the policy of segregating the black majority and white minority and granting to the latter the vast preponderant political and economic power.

appeasement: Policy of non-confrontation pursued by Britain toward Hitler's Germany in the 1930s, or any similar policy in general.

apprenticeship: Training in a craft or profession in which the master profits from the labor of the apprentice, and the apprentice receives training.

aristocracy: A government or society in which power is vested in hereditary nobility which claims to be best qualified to rule.

arquebus: A portable, long-barrelled gun, fired by a wheel-lock or match-lock, dating from the fifteenth century.

artisan: A skilled maker of things. Before the development of techniques of mass manufacture, artisans produced earthenware, tools, jewelry, etc. During the Industrial Revolution artisanal labor gave way to factory labor. *See also* **proletarian**.

Aryan: Formerly a term that referred to the assumed racial category composed of people of Indo-European "blood." The notion of an Aryan race was created by nineteenth-century race theorists and adopted by Adolf Hitler. "Aryan" is now used to designate the Indo-Iranian language group and the group of Indo-Aryan speakers who invaded the Indian subcontinent c. 1500 B.C.E.

assimilation: The cultural, ethnic, linguistic, or other absorption of one or more peoples by another, dominant, group.

astrolabe: The most important instrument used by early astronomers and navigators to measure the altitudes of celestial bodies. The altitude of the North Star yields the latitude, and that of the sun and stars yields the time. In the eighteenth century, the astrolabe was superseded by the sextant.

astrology: Pseudo-scientific study of the putative influence occasioned on individuals and societies by the planets. During the Scientific Revolution, the pursuit of astrology helped establish astronomy as a proper science.

atom: Smallest component of an element possessing all the chemical characteristics of that element, consisting of a nucleus and one or more electrons.

atonality: In music, rejection of traditional harmonic elements including the diatonic scale and an obvious tonal center.

***audiencias*:** Governmental institutions or courts in colonial Spanish America designed to administer Spanish royal justice, including the protection of Amerindian rights.

autarky: Economic self-sufficiency. In Hitler's Germany, policy aimed at achieving political goals by establishing regional self-sufficiency.

authoritarianism/authoritarian: An anti-liberal governmental system wherein power resides in a single leader or narrow elite not responsible to the broader population, but which lacks the hallmarks of specifically fascist or other totalitarian regimes. *See also* **fascism, totalitarianism**.

avant-garde: Literally, "fore-guard," or vanguard; in the arts, collective term for pioneers of innovative and unconventional styles.

bastion: A projecting work in a castle wall or other fortification which allows the defenders to fire along the face of the wall.

bayonet: A short sword attached to the muzzle of a rifle. First used in the seventeenth century as an infantry weapon for close combat, eliminating the need for a corps of pikemen.

Bible: The sacred writings of Judaism and Christianity, known to Christians as the Bible, consisting of two parts. The first, called the Old Testament by Christians, stands alone for Jews as the Hebrew Bible. The second, called the New Testament, includes accounts of Jesus's life attributed to four of Jesus's disciples—Matthew, Mark, Luke, and John—known as Gospels (meaning "good news") or collectively as the Gospel.

Blitzkrieg: Literally, "lightning war," the tactic used by Nazi forces during World War II in which an invasion commences with aerial bombardment, followed by armored tank (or Panzer) divisions, then other motorized divisions and infantry.

blues: A musical form, generally vocal and expressing sadness or despair, characterized by the use of repeated "blues" tones.

Boer: Derived from Dutch word for "farmer," a white South African speaking Afrikaans, a Dutch dialect. *See also* **Afrikaner.**

Bolshevik: Literally, "majority persons," Lenin's faction of the Russian Social Democratic Party responsible for the Russian Revolution of 1917, the establishment of communism in Russia, and the creation of the Soviet Union.

bourgeoisie: Literally, "townspersons," including, in particular, artisans, merchants, lawyers, doctors, bankers and, in the nineteenth century, factory-owners and industrial entrepreneurs. *See also* **class, proletarian**.

bourse: *See* **stock exchange**.

brahman: A priest or member of the priestly caste in Hinduism.

bullion: Uncoined gold and silver, molded into bars or ingots.

burgher: In medieval Europe, a citizen of a town (*burg, borough, bourg*). Burghers included the enterprising merchants, bankers, and long-distance traders ("the bourgeoisie").

cadre: A core group within a larger political association or movement by whose activity the larger movement is organized, established, and expanded.

canton: In Switzerland, an independent unit of local government; the Swiss Confederation is divided into twenty-three cantons.

capitalism: An economic system organized around the profit motive and competition, in which enterprises are privately owned and produce goods for a market guided by the forces of supply and demand.

caravel: A type of sailing ship, first developed in Portugal, equipped with square and lateen sails or entirely lateen rigged.

carbonari: In Italy, members of secret societies of liberals and nationalists opposed to the conservative order established at the Congress of Vienna in 1814–1815.

cartels: Voluntary associations of private corporations or individuals, aimed at achieving market dominance in a given sector or industry through violation of free-trade and competitive principles.

cartography: The research and drawing of maps. Begun in ancient times, cartography expanded during Europe's age of exploration from the late fifteenth century, and became more accurate during the Scientific Revolution and Enlightenment.

castas: In Latin American history, intermediate social groups of mixed African, European, and Amerindian ancestry. *See also* **mulatto, mestizo.**

caste: A system of rigid hereditary social stratification, characterized by disparities of wealth and poverty, inherited occupations, and strict rules governing social contact.

charter: Any written instrument establishing basic legal principles among the signing parties.

Christendom: The part of the world in which Christianity predominates; the collective body of Christian believers.

cinema: Short for "cinematograph" (deriving from the Greek words for motion and for drawing), a picture engendered by motion, used popularly as the form of entertainment also called "film" and "the movies"; also the theater where such films are shown.

citizen: In ancient Greece, a free male inhabitant of a *polis*. In modern times, applied to any legal member of the state.

civility: The set of manners and attitudes developed in European princely and royal courts from the late Middle Ages.

civilization: A condition of society characterized by high cultural achievement and complex social development. A society is a civilization if it has (1) class stratification; (2) political and religious hierarchies; (3) a complex division of labor; (4) an economic system that creates agricultural surpluses; and (5) the skills to create architecture, tools, and weaponry.

class: A social or economic group. In Marxist thought, specifically those individuals sharing a common relationship to the dominant means of production, such as the possessors (bourgeoisie, landlords, etc) or non-possessors (the proletariat, serfs).

Classicism/Classical: In the arts, the aesthetics and ideals of ancient Greece and Rome or later forms referring back to these.

clergy: A group ordained to perform religious functions. In Catholicism, the clergy is a hierarchical body headed by the pope.

collective bargaining: Process whereby workers negotiate collectively with their employer(s) or management via elected representatives. *See also* **strike, trade unions.**

collectivization: Under Stalin in the Soviet Union, the forced creation of a system of agricultural organization in which land was held in common under central control.

colonialism: The political, economic, or cultural expansion of national groups at the expense of others, and especially the process by which European nations came to dominate indigenous peoples in the Americas, northern Asia, and Australasia.

colony: an area or people beyond the borders of a state over which that state exercises control.

commissariat: In the Soviet Union, name given to government departments until 1946, such as the People's Commissariat for Education.

Committee of Public Safety: During the radical phase of the French Revolution, executive body composed of nine men wielding total power as France faced counter-revolution and war with much of Europe. Under the leadership of Robespierre, it raised massive conscript armies and initiated the Terror. *See also* **Jacobins, Terror.**

common law: A system of law developed after the Norman Conquest of England (1066), and still partly in use in most English-speaking countries. Unlike civil law (descended from the codified laws of the Roman Empire and from Napoleonic France), common law is not embodied in a text or code. Judges draw instead upon precedents set by earlier court decisions.

Commonwealth: Grouping of individual persons or of autonomous states into a consensual political community. The British Commonwealth, established in 1931, unites various former British colonies in a loose association paying varying levels of allegiance to the British Crown and sharing certain cultural and economic ties.

communism: Socio-political system envisioned by Karl Marx and enacted in the twentieth century in Russia, China, and other countries.

compass: A device that indicates direction on the earth's surface; the principal instrument of navigation.

concessions: Grants of land or of the right to engage in economic activities made to a second party by a government or other ruling body.

conquistadors: Military adventurers who led the Spanish exploration and conquest of America during the sixteenth century.

conservatism: Ideology, developed best by Edmund Burke, hostile to rapid change and esteeming traditional institutions, concepts, and strategies. Conservative principles underlay the order created by the Congress of Vienna in 1814–1815 following the defeat of Napoleon.

constitutional government: Government that rules according to an established body of basic laws, usually but not always written down, and whose power is thus limited.

contraception: The prevention of pregnancy by any of a variety of sexual techniques, mechanical devices, or drugs.

corporatism/corporatist: A hallmark of fascist states, corporatism describes a society based on cross-class grouping, especially the combining of the workers, administrators, and owners of a given enterprise into a single organization. It asserts the primacy of the "national community" and rejects the need for class-based organizations such as unions.

cosmopolis: A culturally prestigious city whose population is composed of peoples from many parts of the world; an urban center of high sophistication.

cosmopolitanism: Belief in or advocacy of an international rather than national community, such as by Marxists, world religions, and so on.

cotton gin: Machine invented in 1793 in the United States by Eli Whitney to remove seeds mechanically from cotton fibers.

counter-insurgency: During the Cold War, term describing the United States' crusade against leftist revolutionary activities around the globe. In this context the United States sent experts to advise anti-communist rulers, equipped native armies and police forces, and set up programs to train foreign soldiers in modern military techniques.

coup d'état: The sudden, violent overthrow of a government by a small group.

courtesan: A kept woman or a prostitute, often highly skilled and capable of circulating among high-status patrons, typically associated with a royal court or clientele deriving from wealthy and powerful elites.

courtier: A person in attendance at a court, and who seeks the ruler's favor.

creole: A fully-formed language that develops from a pidgin language. Most creoles have vocabularies derived from major European languages; some exist only in spoken form. The word also refers to combinations of European and non-European cultures, especially cooking and music, and to people of mixed racial heritage. See *also* **mestizo.**

cubism: Art form pioneered immediately prior to World War I by Georges Braque and Pablo Picasso using fragmented images designed to show several sides of an object at the same time. *See also* **Modernism.**

culture: Learned behavior acquired by individuals as members of a particular group, in contrast to genetically endowed behavior. Each culture has different styles governing behavior and thought. "Culture" includes politics, the arts, philosophy, and so on.

curtain wall: The plain wall of a castle or other fortified place, connecting two towers.

cybernetics: From the Greek for "steersman," the science that studies control and communication systems in entities of any type—including social and business organizations, living organisms, machines, computers, the human brain, and so on.

Darwinism: Pertaining to the theory of Charles Darwin, who argued that organic forms, including humans, are the product of evolution by natural selection taking place over long periods of time.

decolonization: Process ending the control enjoyed by a metropolitan power over its colony, with the latter becoming fully independent. Decolonization of Europe's empires occurred during the post-World War II era. *See also* **metropolis.**

deduction: In logic, the process of inferring specific cases from a general axiom or principle. *See also* **induction, empiricism.**

deism: The belief that God created the universe as a perfect mechanism running according to mechanical laws discoverable through the use of reason rather than revelation.

democracy: Term from the Greek words for "people" and "power." A form of government in which citizens monitor the state directly or through elected representatives, as opposed to oligarchy or monarchy, where the state is controlled by a small minority or individual.

demographic: Pertaining to the study of the structure and dynamics of human populations, including their distribution and movement by category (such as age, gender, ethnicity, occupation, nationality, and so on).

détente: Foreign policy designed to ease tensions with a rival state or bloc.

dhow: A type of sailing vessel with lateen sails.

dialectics: Logical argumentation according to the method of Aristotle and his followers. In modern times, the opposition or reconciliation of conflicting ideas or forces (as for Hegel and Marx).

diaspora: The dispersal of members of a particular ethnic, religious, or cultural group beyond their traditional boundaries or home state, or the condition of living so dispersed.

diplomacy: Conducting negotiations to resolve differences, regulate commerce, make alliances, etc. *See also* **ambassador**.

Directory: French revolutionary government from October 1795 to November 1799, comprising a bicameral legislature and five-man executive.

dominion: Term describing the status, up to 1939, of the following members of the British Commonwealth: Australia, Canada, Eire, Newfoundland, New Zealand, and South Africa. Dominions were regarded as "autonomous communities" sharing equal status and close ties to the British Crown. *See also* **Commonwealth**.

dowry: The property a bride brings to her marriage. It correlates with the wealth or status of the bridegroom.

Duma: From the Russian verb "to think" or "to reflect," the name of the Russian parliament, created for the first time as a consequence of the Revolution of 1905.

dynasty: A succession of monarchs of the same line of descent; a group or family that maintains power for a long period of time.

$E = mc^2$: Energy = Mass multipled by the square of the speed of light; Einstein's revolutionary equation showing that mass and energy are interconvertible and making possible the subsequent development of atomic bombs and atomic power.

economic imperialism: Economic—as opposed to political or military—hegemony of one state or culture over another, such as the dominance of foreign business interests within a developing country.

elite: A small group of persons who control major institutions, exercise military and/or political power, possess superior wealth, or enjoy elevated status and prestige.

empiricism: The use of observation and experiment to gain knowledge about the world.

enclosure: In early modern Europe, process whereby common fields or separate holdings were consolidated into larger agricultural units.

***encomienda*:** In colonial Spanish America, a grant made to an individual by the Spanish Crown of a certain number of Amerindians from whom he could exact tribute in gold, labor, or kind.

Enlightenment: Intellectual movement stressing the improvement of human society through the application of reason.

entrepôts: Ports, trading bases, warehouses, or other places into which goods and commodities are gathered prior to further distribution to sellers and consumers.

entrepreneur: A person who organizes and assumes the risks of a business.

epidemic: A contagious disease that periodically or episodically afflicts many people within a population, community, or region. Severe epidemics have killed large numbers of people, most notoriously the Black Death of fourteenth-century Europe.

ersatz: Hitler encouraged the chemical industries to develop synthetic or "ersatz" equivalents of normally traded goods.

established religion: Any religion sanctioned as the official religion of a given state, such as the Catholic faith in pre-Revolutionary France or the Anglican Church in England.

Estate: In early modern Europe, one of three social orders (clergy, nobility, commoners). The Estates-General was an assembly of representatives of the three "Estates."

eugenics: Field of study or actual practice aimed at controlling human racial development, usually by means of selective breeding. Eugenics assumed probably its most extreme form in the hands of the Nazis, who strove for "Aryan purity" in and beyond Germany.

existentialism/existentialist: Philosophical outlook positing the individual as the basic object of existence, and proposing the non-existence of any absolute values, truths, or meaning. Their absence was construed not as causes for despair but as opportunities for individuals to realize personal autonomy and freedom.

experiment: Procedure designed to test a specific principle or hypothesis by subjecting it to a carefully defined and repeatable test.

extraterritoriality: The condition of being subject to the laws of one's own country rather than those of the country within which one currently lives.

factory: Especially in connection with the Industrial Revolution, an establishment equipped for the application of labor and machinery to the purpose of market-oriented mass production of goods.

fallow: A portion of cultivated land deliberately allowed to lie idle during a growing season.

famine: A shortage of food sufficient to cause widespread privation and a rise in mortality. Famine may be caused by natural events; by war; by political decisions; or by agricultural practices that cause soil erosion.

fascism/fascist: Form of political organization marked by anti-communism, anti-liberalism, governmental suppression of individual rights, militarism, the exaltation of a "national community," and rule of a charismatic leader.

federal: Relating to the central authority governing a federation of individual states, such as the federal government of the United States in relation to individual states.

feminism: Ideology founded in the perception of the unjust social subordination of women, which has had and continues to develop a variety of forms, including women's property and voting rights, abortion rights, or recognition of women's unique capacity to nurture children.

fluyt: A "flyboat;" in early modern Europe, a small, highly efficient vessel invented by the Dutch for inexpensive, utilitarian hauling.

folk: The people as a whole; those who bear and transmit the cultural values of a people.

free market: A market-place where goods and services may be freely exchanged at prices, in quantities, and on terms dictated only by factors of supply and demand, and where there is no regulation of such exchange by any government or other body.

fundamentalism/fundamentalist: In matters of religion or other ideology, an extreme conservative, and often one who is willing to attack any perceived deviation from a given orthodoxy.

futurism: Iconoclastic movement in art during the early twentieth century glorifying machinery, energy, and movement, and notably embraced by the Italian fascist movement under Mussolini.

galley: A warship driven by oars in battle and with sails for cruising. It was the standard European battle vessel until the late sixteenth century, when the sail-powered, more heavily armed, galleon replaced it.

genocide: Deliberate and systematic murder or attempted murder of an entire ethnic, racial, religious, or cultural group.

ghetto: From the sixteenth century, any defined area within a European city beyond which Jews were not legally entitled to live. More recently, any urban enclave whose inhabitants are isolated economically, politically, socially, or from the mainstream population.

glasnost*:** In Russian, "openness" or "publicity," the policy promoted in the 1980s by Soviet leader Mikhail Gorbachev in which the government's control of access to and exchange of information was to be slackened in order to stimulate debate and promote reform. *See also* ***perestroika.

guerrilla: Derived from the Spanish resistance to Napoleon, literally a "little war," referring to the sometimes quite fierce struggle waged by non-regular soldiers, often in support of revolution or native resistance against imperialism. Also used as a personal noun, referring to the guerrilla warrior.

gulag: Acronym of the Russian for "state camp," referring to the notorious network of Soviet prison camps where millions of Russians were forced to labor under extremely harsh conditions, especially during the Stalinist purges of the 1930s.

Habsburg: Princely family, of German origin, prominent from the eleventh century until 1918 and whose members have been sovereigns of the Holy Roman Empire, Spain, and Austria.

***hacienda*:** In colonial Spanish America, a large landed estate, often employing vast numbers of poor, heavily indebted agricultural laborers. *See also* **peons**.

Hasid/Hasidism: Member of the Jewish sect founded by Israel Baal Shem-Tov in Poland during the eighteenth century, and which emphasizes religious mysticism, zeal, and fervent prayer.

hegemony: The domination of one institution, sector, or state over others.

heterodoxy: Deviation from orthodoxy.

hierarchy: A series of persons, graded or ranked in order of authority.

historicism: The idea that any proper examination of history must take the period or subject under consideration absolutely in its own context while avoiding any prejudices or values connected to the historian him or herself or the historian's own time.

historiography: The writing of history, or any of its techniques and theories; the body of historical writing on any given subject.

Holocaust: Literally (from the Greek), "whole burning," or "burnt offering," term describing the Nazis' massacre of Jews during World War II. The notion of the Holocaust specifically as a "burnt offering" reflects the belief of some Jews that their people's suffering was a righteous punishment inflicted by God for the Jews' collective sins, especially assimilation. Uncapitalized, the term may describe any mass murder.

honor: Form or measure of respect given (or withheld from) a person by his peers, especially among elite social groups. In early modern society, honor was often won in military combat or by duelling with an enemy or rival, by cleverness in speech, by the achievement of high office in government or the church, or by membership in prestigious organizations.

hospital: Generally church-related and funded by bequests, the medieval hospital accommodated not only the sick but also abandoned children, "fallen" or deserted women, and the elderly. From the seventeenth century, it increasingly specialized in the treatment of the ill.

house: Stately home with which a particular noble family or "line" was associated and from which its name derived.

humanism: An intellectual movement that emerged in Italy in the late 1300s and spread throughout Europe, centered around the revival of interest in ancient Greek and Roman literature, philosophy, and history.

humors: From ancient Greek medicine, the four elemental body fluids (blood, phlegm, black bile, yellow bile), the imbalance of which was treated by purging or blood-letting.

hypothesis: Proposition, usually intended provisionally. In science, hypotheses are either supported or falsified by experimental and other data. *See also* **experiment**.

ideology: The body of essential ideas, assumptions, and goals underlying a given movement or organization, such as Marxist ideology, capitalist ideology, and so on. *See also* **Marxism, capitalism**.

imperialism: The process by which a state creates, expands, or defends its political or economic dominance over others, as in the domination by Europe of much of the rest of the world during the nineteenth and early twentieth centuries. *See also* **colonialism**.

***imperium*:** Originally the supreme command in war, granted at Rome to consuls and other magistrates; later, authority over a region or empire.

indentured servant: In colonial North America, a European immigrant who worked without wages for a contracted period in exchange for the price of passage to the colonies and clothing, board, and lodging while in service.

Indo-European: An extensive language family, derived from a common ancestor, Proto-Indo-European. The surviving languages include Hindi, Persian, Russian, Polish, Armenian, Albanian, Greek, Italian, French, Spanish, Portuguese, German, English, Dutch, and the Scandinavian languages.

induction: In logic, the process of inferring general rules or axioms from specific cases, such as Newton's assertion of the law of gravitation based on numerous specific examples of motion. *See also* **deduction**.

industrialization/Industrial Revolution: Process of technological, economic, and social transformation involving production for a mass market by means of heavy machinery and human labor deployed in factories. In the nineteenth century, industrializing nations experienced rapid economic growth, and the crystallization of two economic classes, the workers (proletariat) and industrialists (industrial bourgeoisie).

infantry: Armed foot soldiers, as distinct from cavalry, air, or sea forces.

infrastructure: The total of basic structures and services underlying an economy, including roads, railroads, bridges, electric grids, telephone cables, and power plants.

***intendant*:** In early modern France, the absolute monarchy's key regional administrator, regarded by French monarchs as more reliable than hereditary officials.

Islamist: Promotion of the civilization of Islam, whether by religious fundamentalists or secular activists; pertaining to any person or movement attempting to import Islamic religion, law, or values into political life.

Jacobins: During the French Revolution, a political group of radical egalitarians who, under Robespierre, orchestrated the Terror. The name derives from the church of Saint-Jacques, associated with a Dominican convent, in Paris. *See also* **Terror**.

jazz: Broad category of musical forms employing heavy improvization, complex harmonies and melodies, and in many cases unorthodox time signatures, pioneered at the turn of the twentieth century by African Americans.

***jihad*:** In Islam, a holy war or struggle understood to constitute a sacred duty.

joint-stock company: A partnership similar to a corporation that has transferable shares sold at a stock exchange. It is managed by a board of directors elected by the partners (shareholders) who are personally liable for the company's debts. The joint-stock company was instrumental in the expansion of mercantile capitalism and European colonialism. *See also* **stock exchange**.

Junker: Especially in eastern Prussia, Germany, the class of aristocratic landholders, militaristic and authoritarian in disposition, from which many German officers were drawn.

Kabbalah: Esoteric and mystical philosophical tradition within Judaism purporting to grant its initiates access to profound spiritual truths and knowledge of the future.

Keynesian: Pertaining to the ideas of the British economist Sir John Maynard Keynes, particularly his notion that free-market economies cannot always be relied on to self-correct, and must sometimes be actively managed by the central government. *See also* **New Deal**.

***kulak*:** In Russia and the Soviet Union, derogatory Russian term for a wealthy peasant. Literally "fists," kulaks were targeted by the communists for general destruction as a class during the late 1920s and early 1930s.

labor: An economic group whose members perform the basic functions of an economy. Key factors in the creation of industrial societies have included the harnessing of labor to specific productive purposes by an entrepreneurial class, the magnification of labor's productive powers by the application of increasingly powerful technologies, and the more efficient organization of labor in factories. *See also* **proletarian, factory**.

***latifundia*:** In Roman times, a great landed estate, usually worked on by slaves. In Latin America, used to describe large ranches.

legitimacy: The claim of a right to power, based on hereditary succession, electoral rules, or natural law.

liberalism: From the Enlightenment on, an ideology stressing individual liberty. In the economic sphere, liberalism, as championed by Adam Smith, demands that the state adopt a "hands-off" policy, allowing individuals to pursue economic self-interest within a free market. In the political sphere, liberalism requires equal right to participate in the political process, and equal protection by the law, of all citizens.

line: The series of familial connections linking a noble to the ancestral founder of his family's noble status.

logical positivism: General term for the philosophies associated with the Vienna Circle, and which emphasize the verifiability of propositions, utility of empiricism, and logical analysis of language. *See also* **empiricism, positivism**.

Loyalists: Individuals or groups who remained faithful to the English Crown. The term is used primarily in the American Revolutionary context, in relation to the struggle between Crown and Parliament in Britain during the seventeenth century.

Mahdi: In Islam, title given to a leader combining temporal and spiritual authority who is expected to usher in a period of global righteousness.

mandate: In a system prevailing from 1919 to 1946, the grant of permission by the League of Nations to a member state to govern the affairs of a specific territory formerly under Ottoman Turkish or German control.

Manifest Destiny: Term proclaiming a belief that the westward expansion of the United States to the Pacific coast is both inevitable and divinely sanctioned. In some cases the term was also adopted by advocates of the annexation of Carribean and Pacific islands.

Marxian dialectic: From Marxist theory, the mechanism whereby historical change occurs, which Marx conceived as involving the opposition of a given basic socio-economic form—or "thesis"—with its opposite—or "antithesis." The tensions between these are supposedly ultimately resolved in their "synthesis"—or merging. The synthesis then constitutes a new "thesis," allowing the process to begin over again, and so on. The overall mechanism is likened to a conversation, thus the term "dialectic."

Marxism: Referring to or connected with the economic and political philosophy of Karl Marx. Marx, along with Friedrich Engels, believed that history was a "determined" (or inevitable) process involving struggle between opposing economic classes, and periodic revolution leading ultimately to a classless, communist society. *See also* **class**.

materialism: A philosophical theory, first developed in ancient Greece, that physical matter is the only reality. In modern usage, also a cultural style in which the goal is the satisfaction of physical desire and comfort.

maternalist: Pertaining to the belief that women's most powerful role is in the family. Maternalist thinking stresses that the mother who nurtures and instructs her children is the true creator of human society.

Menshevik: Literally, "minority persons," the faction of Russian Social Democrats who in 1903 opposed Lenin's plans for a tightly-knit party organization comprising only professional revolutionaries, preferring a less rigid association of socialists.

mercantilism: An economic system developed in the early modern era to increase the monetary wealth of a nation by regulating the entire national economy.

mercenary: A professional soldier who fights for pay in the army of a foreign country.

meridian: A great circle passing through both poles and any single point on earth. The meridian that passes through Greenwich, England, has been denoted the "prime," or first meridian.

mestizo: A term of social classification used in Spanish America for persons of mixed Amerindian and white ancestry.

Methodism/Methodists: The branch of evangelical Christianity developed in the eighteenth century by the Englishman John Wesley and which appealed in particular to lower and lower-middle class audiences. *See also* **Pietism**.

metropolis/metropolitan: Literally "mother city," in colonial affairs the metropolitan power was the ruling and the colonial the subject state.

microorganisms: Generic term for any microscopic plants or animals, an understanding of the existence and actions of which—particularly bacteria—was a major scientific achievement during the nineteenth century. *See also* **pasteurization**.

missionary: The missionary movement was the Christian effort to convert peoples. The first great missionary to the Gentiles, Paul, helped to spread Christianity in the Mediterranean world. The voyages of discovery in the fifteenth and sixteenth centuries began a surge of Roman Catholic missionary activity. Renewed missionary activity took place as part of nineteenth-century imperialism.

Modernism/Modernist: In art and culture, term for the many non-traditional styles and outlooks embraced by the avant-garde from the late nineteenth to the late twentieth century. *See also* **avant-garde**.

monarchy: Rule by a single individual, usually with life tenure and descended from a line of monarchs.

monotheism: Belief in a single God (as in Judaism, Christianity, and Islam). By contrast, polytheism is the belief that many gods exist and pantheism is the belief that God is suffused throughout the universe. Some religions are non-theistic (Confucianism, Buddhism), but permit belief in gods or spirits.

***montage*:** In the arts, the technique of combining images from various sources into a single image or series of images.

mosque: The Islamic place of public worship (from the Arabic *masjid*, "a place to prostrate one's self [in front of God]"), always oriented toward Mecca, the holy city of Islam. A mosque must have a place for ritual washing, a place from which a leader (*imam*) can start the prayer, and a minaret, a tower from which Muslims are called to prayer.

mulattoes: In the Americas, the mixed offspring of white and black parentage.

music hall: In British history, from the 1830s to around 1900, the most popular arena for mass entertainment. Often beginning as modest adjuncts to pubs, they later included large purpose-built structures, and featured song, dance, comedy, and other entertainments.

musket: A large-caliber, smooth-bore firearm aimed and fired from the shoulder, which first appeared in Spain in the mid-1500s.

natalism: In post-World War I Europe, the promotion of motherhood as a boon to the state. In fascist societies, the encouragement or requirement of women to reproduce frequently in order to increase the national population, and thus war-readiness.

National Assembly: During the French Revolution, the revolutionary representative assembly of the entire nation largely comprising members of the Third Estate. Constituted on June 17, 1789, the National Assembly was reorganized as the National Convention, and later as the Legislative Assembly. *See also* **Estate**.

nationalism: A sense of community among individuals conceived as possessing similar "national" characteristics—history, religion, ethnicity, language, and so on—coupled with an ardent desire to manifest the community as an autonomous political nation.

naturalized: The condition of having gained citizenship through a legal process rather than by birth. Specific requirements for naturalization vary from nation to nation.

neo-colonialism: International relationship characterized by one nation's dominance (usually economic) over another, but which lacks the formal, political, or legal hallmarks of outright colonialism. *See also* **colonialism, economic imperialism**.

New Deal: The peacetime domestic program established during the 1930s by United States president Franklin D. Roosevelt to combat the Great Depression and provide work, assistance, and security to average Americans. Influenced by Keynesian economic ideas the New Deal established many new federal government programs and agencies including the Federal Deposit Insurance Corporation (FDIC), the Civilian Conservation Corps (CCC), the Work Projects Administration (WPA), and Social Security. *See also* **Keynesian**.

nihilism/nihilist: In philosophy, the rejection of all established norms, laws, and institutions as meaningless, and of the possibility that absolute truths can ever be established.

novel: A literary form developed during the eighteenth century, a novel is a lengthy fictional narrative written in prose style.

oligarchy: A form of government in which a minority holds power. Military dictatorships are often oligarchic, as are the political machines that sometimes run city governments in democracies.

Pan-Slavism: Nationalistic ideology or movement stressing the unity and interests of various Slavic peoples, such as Russians, Ukrainians, and Serbs. Pan-Slavism originated in the 1830s as Slavic Balkan nations struggled for independence from Ottoman Turkish and Austrian control.

***parlement*:** In early modern France, a regional supreme court of criminal and civil law. The revolutionary National Assembly of 1789 abolished the *parlements*.

parliamentary government: System of government in which power resides primarily in a legislative body or parliament.

partisan: Member of an unofficial resistance force, such as the French or Italian resistance; the zealous supporter of any given cause.

pasteurization: The process for destroying bacterial contaminants, developed by French nineteenth-century chemist Louis Pasteur.

patriarchy: Social organization marked by the supremacy of the father, the legal dependence of wives and children, and the reckoning of and inheritance from the male line.

patricians: The hereditary aristocratic class of ancient Rome. In early modern cities, a hereditary elite of bourgeois office-holders, *rentiers*, and high-status merchants.

patrilineal: The tracing of ancestry and kinship through the male line. Female offspring are valued insofar as they help preserve the male line, mainly through marriage.

patrimony: The accumulation of familial wealth which can be inherited; originally the wealth that flows through the male line of descent.

patronage: The conferring of jobs, favors, and commissions by a powerful patron to a client in order to promote the patron's interests.

***peninsulares*:** Literally, "from the [Iberian] peninsula," residents of Latin America born in and loyal to Spain, and who dominated Spanish colonial offices up to the early nineteenth century.

peons: Poor agricultural laborers, typically indebted to their employers and thus essentially unable to contract as free workers or seek other employment. Peonage was a common form of labor in Latin America with roots extending back to the Conquest.

perestroika*:** In Russian, "restructuring," Soviet leader Mikhail Gorbachev's policy introduced in tandem with *glasnost* in 1985. *Perestroika* involved efforts to improve the economy and made modest concessions to private enterprise and property. *See also* ***glasnost.

peso: In the early modern era, a widely circulated coin minted from gold mined in Spanish America (also known as a "piece of eight," because it was worth eight *reales*).

philanthropic organization: Any one of the legally defined entities existing to collect, manage, and distribute private wealth to public causes including education, medical care, housing, and so on. Philanthropy literally means "love of humankind."

philosophy: The oldest form of systematic scholarly inquiry (from Greek *philosophos*, "lover of wisdom"). Today "philosophy" means: (1) the study of the principles underlying knowledge, being, and reality; (2) a particular system of philosophical doctrine; (3) the critical study of philosophical doctrines; (4) the study of the principles of a particular branch of knowledge; (5) a system of principles for guidance in everyday life.

physiocracy: Eighteenth-century school of thought, usually considered the scientific approach to economics in contrast to the mercantilist orthodoxies of the day. Physiocrats advocated a laissez-faire economy, and argued that land should be considered the basis of wealth and thus taxation. *See also* **mercantilism**.

Pietism/Pietists: Movement within the Lutheran church in Germany, dating from the 1600s, and which emphasized personal piety over ritual, formality, and orthodoxy.

pike: A weapon consisting of a long wooden shaft with a pointed steel head used by foot soldiers until superseded by the bayonet.

plantation system: Cultivating crops on extensive lands worked by slave labor, developed in the sixteenth century by the Portuguese settlers for sugar cultivation on São Tomé and elsewhere, and later adopted by other European colonizers.

pogrom: From the Russian word for "thunder," a riot or violent attack directed against a minority group, especially Jews, or their property.

portolan: From the thirteenth century on, charts that gave sailing distances in miles and bearings in straight lines. Lacking parallels and meridians, they could not be used on the open oceans.

positivism: Philosophical system developed by Auguste Comte in which the search for final causes and metaphysical knowledge is abandoned in favor of attaining certain or "positive" knowledge of physical matters by scientific methods of inquiry.

Prime Meridian: *See* **meridian**.

primogeniture: The preference given to the eldest son and his descendants in the inheritance of property or position practiced in early modern Europe to maintain estates intact.

proletarian/proletariat: In ancient Rome, the poorest citizens, literally "bearer of children": the proletarian's only service to the state was to reproduce and provide new generations of citizens. In industrial society the term is used to describe the industrial working class which lives by selling its labor for wages to the bourgeoisie.

propaganda: Information disseminated to excite or intensify specific emotions and actions rather than specifically to educate or promote value-free, rational discourse. Propaganda often promotes half-truths or outright lies.

protectionism: The establishment of tariffs and other barriers to trade in order to protect domestic or local producers.

protectorate: Status or designation in international relations establishing the dominion of one state over another. The actual degree of control involved may vary.

protoindustrial: Literally, "first-" or "early-industrial," term applicable to the economic organization of areas of early modern Europe or to the early stages of industrialization itself, and based largely on the putting-out system. *See also* **putting-out system**.

Ptolemaic: Referring to Ptolemy, the second-century Greek astronomer and geographer, whose *Almagest* remained the authoritative explanation of the structure of the heavens until displaced by the Copernican system during the Scientific Revolution.

pueblo: A built structure of stone or adobe used for dwelling and defense by Amerindian groups of the American Southwest.

putsch: Literally, "thrust," any secretly plotted, suddenly carried-out attempt to overthrow a government, such as the Beer Hall Putsch in Germany during 1923.

putting-out system: Especially in early modern western Europe, a largely informal arrangement linking merchant-employers with laborers and craftspersons. Within this system, an entrepreneur purchased basic materials which would then be "put out" to local residents who would return finished products made at home on their own equipment. Also called "cottage" or "domestic" industry.

***qâdi*:** In Islam, a judge whose decisions are based on religious law.

quadrant: An instrument used by astronomers and navigators from medieval times to measure the altitude of the sun or a star and for surveying. The quadrant is a flat plate in the shape of a quarter circle marked with a degree scale along the curved side; two sights are attached to one of the radial sides and a plumb bob hangs from the apex.

quantum, pl. **quanta:** A quantity of energy, the smallest that can be absorbed or emitted as electromagnetic radiation.

quinine: Obtained from the bark of the Andean cinchona tree, a crystalline alkaloid used to treat malaria.

Qur'an: Also called Koran, the holy scripture of the Islamic faith, believed to have been written down as dictated by the angel Gabriel to the Prophet Muhammad. The Qur'an contains the fundamentals also of Islamic law, politics, and culture.

race: Term to designate any group of individuals apparently related by descent, physical characteristics, or geographical location, about whom supposedly valid generalizations can be made.

***raison d'état*:** French for "reason of state," the justification given when the political interests of a nation-state override any moral principles governing the state's actions.

rationalism: The belief or doctrine that reason alone should dictate opinions and actions.

***real*:** In the early modern era, a small Spanish or Spanish-American silver coin, worth one-eighth of a peso.

Realism: In literature and the arts, the representation of objects as they really are or appear to be.

relativity: In physics, Einstein's 1905 theory that physical measurements are not absolute but vary depending on the relative position and motion of the observer and observed.

reparation: Money payments exacted by a victorious power from those it has defeated and reckoned as compensation to the former for the costs of war.

repatriation: The act or policy of returning immigrants, refugees, or other persons or groups considered foreign by legal, ethnic, religious, or other status to their home state. Repatriation can be forced or voluntary.

republic: Literally, "a thing of the public," a state or polity based on the notion that sovereignty resides with the people and which delegates the powers and responsibilities of rule to elected representatives.

reservation: Parcel of public land designated for the use of an Amerindian tribe.

resistance (forces): During World War II, any of the various underground groups in Nazi-held Europe engaged in sabotage, intelligence, publishing, or other anti-Nazi activities.

Romanticism: Philosophical and artistic movement of the late eighteenth to mid-nineteenth century, rejecting the Enlightenment's exaltation of reason and stressing emotions and the imagination. As well as in painting, poetry, and literature, Romantic sentiments found expression in various nationalist platforms, such as Mazzini's Young Italy. *See also* **nationalism**.

salient: In military terminology, the outward-projecting part of a troop formation.

salon: Especially in eighteenth-century France, a gathering of philosophers, writers, artists, and prominent members of society (or the room in which this usually occured) for the purpose of intellectual conversation or readings.

samurai: In medieval and early modern Japan, a class of warriors (from the Japanese *saburu*, "service"). The samurai were originally rural landowners who served as military retainers. Later they became military aristocrats and then military rulers.

Scientific Revolution: The period and process of the creation of modern science, especially astronomy and physics, usually dated from the publication of Copernicus's *On the Revolutions of the Celestial Spheres* (1543) to that of Newton's *Mathematical Principles of Natural Philosophy* (1687), and which established classical physics.

secession: Official withdrawal from a state or other political entity, such as the withdrawal of several southern states from the United States during 1860–1861, which served as the cause of the American Civil War.

sect: A dissenting religious body or political faction, often regarded as heretical or blasphemous by the larger body of believers.

secularization: The process by which politics, economics, society, and culture are detached from religious influences or control; characteristic of Western civilization over the last two centuries and some contemporary Islamic societies.

Separatists: Seventeenth-century Puritans who separated from the Church of England and settled in North America to obtain freedom to practice their form of worship.

sepoy: Literally, "horseman," any Indian soldier, particularly an infantryman, in the service of the British or other European colonial army.

serf: Especially in feudal Europe, a peasant bound by customary law to a given estate and thus to a landlord, and whose unfree status is inherited by his offspring.

sextant: An optical instrument used in navigation to measure the angles of celestial bodies above the horizon from the observer's position.

shah: In Persia (modern Iran), the king or sovereign.

Shi'ite: One who practices Shi'ism, the smaller of the two main branches of Islam, and the dominant religious group in Persia (modern Iran). Shi'ites separated from Sunnism in the seventh century C.E. when, insisting that only descendants of Muhammad's son-in-law Ali could qualify, they rejected the fourth caliph accepted by the majority.

Shintoism: The indigenous religious tradition of Japan, based on the worship of gods, nature spirits, and ancestors. After the eighth century C.E., Shintoism coexisted and blended with Buddhism and Confucianism.

shuttle: In weaving, a device or object used for passing the thread of the woof between the threads of the warp.

Sikh: Member of a breakaway Hindu sect rejecting the caste system, Hindu mysticism and magic, idolatry, and pilgrimages. Sikhs have been at the forefront of Hindu opposition to Muslim domination.

skepticism: In philosophy, belief in the impossibility of obtaining certain knowledge.

slavery: A social practice in which a person is owned by and commanded to labor for the benefit of a master.

slum: Residential area, usually urban, characterized by a variety of social ills including the poverty of its residents, overcrowding, poor sanitation, and other unsafe or unpleasant conditions.

snuff: A preparation of dried, pulverized tobacco to be inhaled through the nostrils, chewed, or placed against the gums.

social democracy: From the late nineteenth century in Europe and America, a philosophy and movement seeking the establishment of socialism not by revolution but by peaceful, evolutionary measures carried out within the existing non-socialist legal and political framework.

socialism: From the early nineteenth century on, any economic system or general philosophy emphasizing collective or state ownership of most forms of property, especially the means of production, and providing for the equitable and artificial rather than free-market distribution of wealth. *See also* **Marxism**.

Socialist Realism: In the Soviet Union, realistic art form glorifying proletarian values and serving as pro-communist and pro-government propaganda. Socialist Realism was established as the Soviet Union's official and only acceptable type of artistic expression during the 1930s.

Soviets: "Councils" of worker, soldier, and peasant deputies (chosen and controlled by the central authorities) who functioned as the primary governmental unit from the national to local levels from the Revolution of 1917 to the collapse of the Soviet Union.

specie: Money in the form of coinage.

species: A biological classification designating a type of organism or population of animals potentially capable of interbreeding.

spiritualism: The belief that the physical world is permeated by a deeper, ultimate reality defined as soul or spirit; popularly, the belief that the spirits of the dead can be accessed by the living with the assistance of an adept, or medium.

spontaneous generation: In biology, the theory that microorganisms come into existence by themselves and from nothing. This belief was widespread until disproved by Louis Pasteur in the nineteenth century.

stock exchange/stock market: A place where brokers and dealers in stocks and bonds transact business together. Stock exchanges facilitated the financing of business and government activity.

stratification: The division of society into separate groups, based on wealth, prestige, and/or ancestry.

strike: In industrial societies, a collective work stoppage initiated by workers, often via their unions, as a protest or weapon against their employer or general conditions of work. By causing economic pain to their employer, striking workers have typically sought to gain specified ends such as increased pay, safety improvements, or other benefits. *See also* **collective bargaining, trade unions**.

***Sturm und Drang*:** Literally, "storm and stress," in literature, term describing the emotional turmoil that characterized not only German Romanticism, but Romanticism generally and the intellectual culture of Europe for at least the first half-century following the French Revolution. *See also* **Romanticism**.

suffrage: The right to vote officials into public office or to vote on specific legislation. In general, suffrage has increased during the late modern period to include wider groups of previously unenfranchized individuals.

suffragist: Pertaining to the struggle for suffrage, that is, the right of an individual or group to vote for political representatives, or an advocate of such rights.

***sunna*:** Literally, "way" or "path," the body of traditional Islamic law believed to derive directly from the words and actions of Muhammad.

Sunnite: A follower of the Sunni branch of Islam to which most Muslims belong. Sunnites claim to follow strictly the *sunna* (practices) of the Prophet Muhammad, as defined and elaborated by the religious authorities (*'ulama*).

sweated industries/sweatshops: Industries marked by especially oppressive and exploitative conditions including lack of basic safety standards, excessive hours of work, denial of legal rights, low pay, and curtailment of personal liberty.

Syndicalism/Syndicalists: A form of unionism prominent in France, which aims at federated union control of the means of production and of society, to be obtained through general strike, sabotage, and terrorism. *See also* **trade unions**.

tariff: Tax levied on goods traded across regional or national borders. The removal or reduction of tariffs during much of the nineteenth century facilitated increased economic and industrial growth.

taxonomy: Especially in biology, the science of organizing and classifying living organisms according to certain salient traits.

tenement: Literally, "that which is held by tenure," the designation for houses or other buildings leased as apartment dwellings, especially in poorer industrial towns and cities, to a number of separate tenants.

Terror, The: During the radical phase of the French Revolution, period of extreme, bloody, and summary revolutionary justice—from September 5, 1793 to July 27, 1794. The Terror, orchestrated by Robespierre and the Committee of Public Safety, resulted in the guillotining of tens of thousands of real and imagined enemies of the Revolution. *See also* **Committee of Public Safety**.

terrorism: The use of isolated, typically random acts of violence, often carried out against collateral or symbolic targets—such as national embassies and airlines—and intended primarily to instill fear and anxiety in a perceived enemy population.

theocracy: Governmental system in which civil law—as well as religious law—is understood as deriving from divine rather than secular sources, and in which ecclesiastical authorities may therefore play the role of legislature, executive, and judiciary.

Thermidor/Thermidorean Reaction: During the French Revolution, name given to the revolt on the ninth day of Thermidor (the "hot" month)—July 27, 1794 by the conventional calendar—leading to the downfall and execution of Robespierre and the cessation of the Terror. *See also* **Terror**.

Third World: Designation accorded in Western parlance to the "developing world" as a whole. The term originated in the context of the Cold War, when the notion was popular that the planet consisted of three "worlds"—the West (or First World), the Communist powers (or Second World), and the Third World of mostly non-aligned and poor states, most of whom had recently gained—or were in the process of gaining—independence from European empires.

totalitarianism: Governmental system and political culture which controls or attempts to control all aspects of life and suppress all forms of dissent. Nazi Germany and Stalinist Russia remain the classic examples of such a system.

trade unions: Workers' combinations dating from the industrial era. Unlike medieval guilds, unions do not regulate entry to trades, set prices, or establish quality standards but instead represent the interests of the workers in negotiation with employers. *See also* **collective bargaining, strike, Syndicalism**.

U-boat: Abbreviation of "Unterseeboot," German submarine, especially of the type first used in World War I, which inflicted heavy damage on Allied shipping.

***'ulama*:** Teachers of Islamic law.

unconscious: In Freudian psychoanalysis, the aspect of the human mind from which derive instinctual ideas and impulses of which the conscious thinking mind is not directly aware. Freudian psychoanalytical theory describes complex interactions among three parts of the human psyche: the instinctual unconscious, or "id"; the conscious self, or "ego"; and the edifice of internalized social and cultural norms, or "superego."

United Kingdom: Officially the United Kingdom of Great Britain and Northern Ireland, comprising the countries of England, Scotland, Wales, and Northern Ireland, organized as a single political entity. The union of England with Wales took place in 1536; of these with Scotland in 1701; and with Ireland in 1801. The division of Ireland in 1922 left only Northern Ireland within the United Kingdom.

utilitarianism: Ethical system developed by the English theorist Jeremy Bentham in which right is perceived as that which brings greatest happiness to the greatest number of persons.

utopia/utopian: Literally "no place," from the work of that name by sixteenth-century English theorist Thomas More, describing an ideal society. In recent times, often used pejoratively of goals considered unrealistic or unattainable in the real world. The word is often applied to pre-Marxist socialisms, to distinguish them from the more "scientific socialism" pioneered by Marx and Engels.

voodoo: A hybrid religious-folkloric system widely practiced in Haiti, combining elements of Roman Catholicism (introduced by French colonialists) and African mysticism (introduced by slave populations from Dahomey—now Benin—in Africa).

welfare state: General term for the collection of laws, programs, and guarantees securing individuals' rights to a basic level of economic security, such as pensions, unemployment benefits, sick pay, and so on.

white-collar: White-collar clerical or professional employees who do not perform manual labor (as do blue-collar workers).

yeoman: In British history, a farmer cultivating his own land.

Zionism: The movement or belief founded in 1896 by Theodore Herzl claiming Palestine as the rightful homeland of the Jews.

INDEX

Bold page numbers refer to picture captions, and to maps